Contents

◀◀ Tomb of Sidi Abdel Aziz, Marrakesh Medina ◀ Erg Chebbi dunes, Merzouga

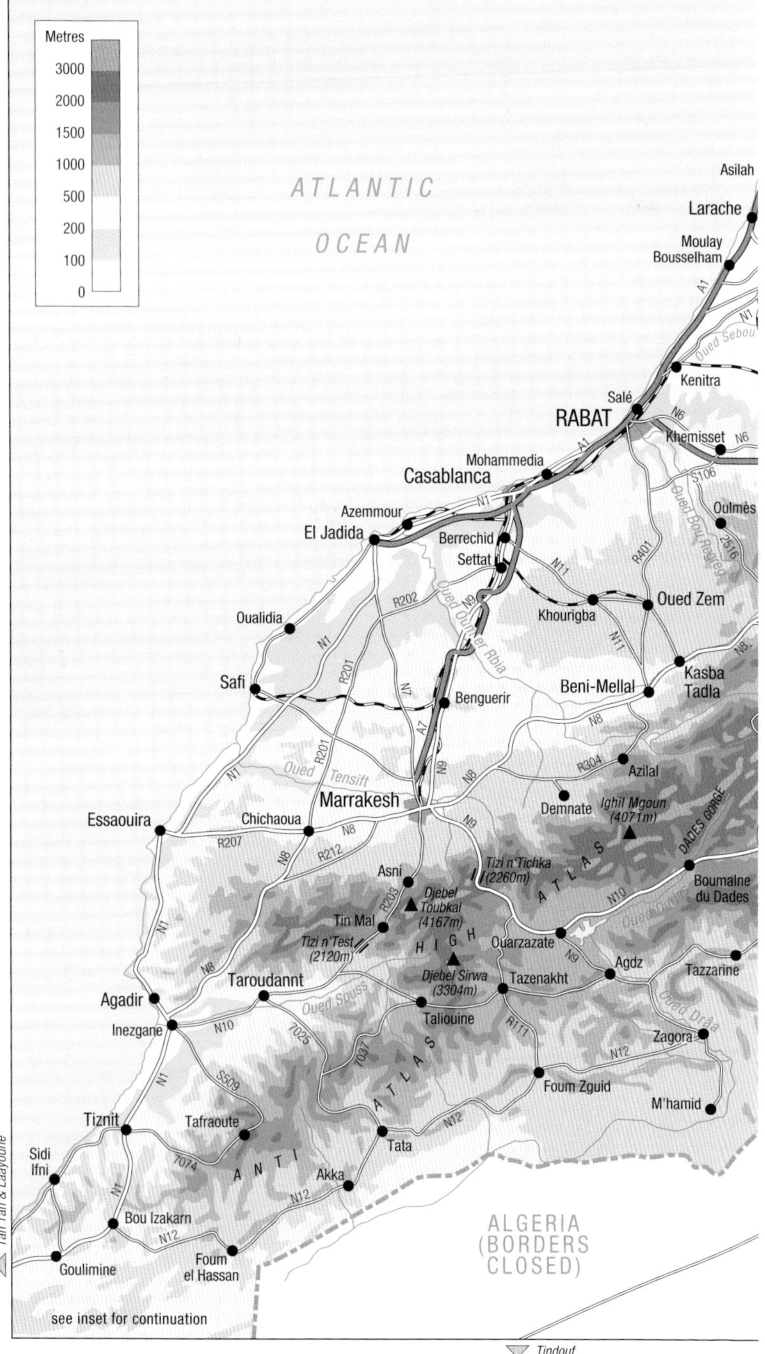
Metres
3000
2000
1500
1000
500
200
100
0
ATLANTIC
OCEAN
Asilah
Larache
Moulay
Bousselham
Kenitra
Salé
RABAT
Khemisset
Mohammedia
Casablanca
Azemmour
El Jadida
Berrechid
Settat
Oulmès
Oued Zem
Khourigba
Oualidia
Safi
Benguerir
Beni-Mellal
Kasba
Tadla
Azilal
Demnate
Marrakesh
Essaouira
Chichaoua
Ighil Mgoun
(4071m)
Tizi n'Tichka
(2260m)
Asni
Djebel
Toubkal
(4167m)
Tin Mal
Tizi n'Test
(2120m)
HIGH
ATLAS
DADES GORGE
Boumalne
du Dades
Ouarzazate
Agdz
Tazzarine
Djebel Sirwa
(3304m)
Tazenakht
Taroudannt
Agadir
Inezgane
Taliouine
Zagora
Foum Zguid
M'hamid
Tiznit
Tafraoute
Tata
ANTI
ATLAS
Sidi
Ifni
Akka
Bou Izakarn
Goulimine
Foum
el Hassan
ALGERIA
(BORDERS
CLOSED)
Oued Sebou
Oued Bou Regreg
Oued Oum er Rbia
Oued Tensift
Oued Souss
Oued Dadès
Oued Drâa
Tan Tan & Laayoune
Tindouf
see inset for continuation

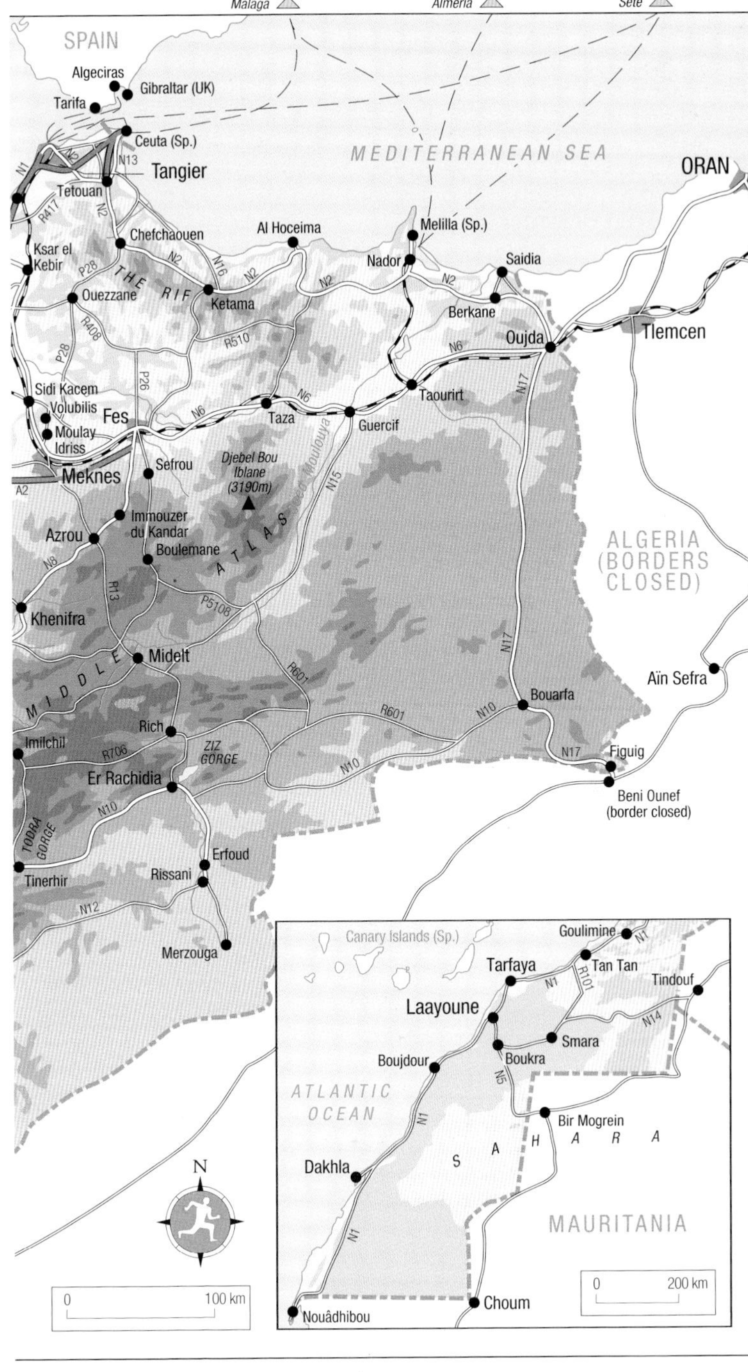
Málaga
Almería
Sète
SPAIN
Algeciras
Gibraltar (UK)
Tarifa
Ceuta (Sp.)
MEDITERRANEAN SEA
ORAN
Tangier
Tetouan
Chefchaouen
Al Hoceima
Melilla (Sp.)
Nador
Saidia
Ksar el Kebir
THE RIF
Ouezzane
Ketama
Berkane
Oujda
Tlemcen
Algiers
Sidi Kacem
Volubilis
Fes
Moulay Idriss
Taza
Guercif
Taourirt
Meknes
Sefrou
Djebel Bou Iblane (3190m)
Oued Moulouya
Immouzer du Kandar
Azrou
Boulemane
ATLAS
ALGERIA (BORDERS CLOSED)
Khenifra
Midelt
MIDDLE
Aïn Sefra
Bouarfa
Rich
Imilchil
ZIZ GORGE
Er Rachidia
Figuig
Beni Ounef (border closed)
TODRA GORGE
Tinerhir
Erfoud
Rissani
Merzouga
N1
N2
N5
N6
N8
N10
N12
N13
N15
N16
N17
R417
P28
R408
R510
P26
A2
R13
P5108
R601
R706
Canary Islands (Sp.)
Goulimine
Tan Tan
Tarfaya
Tindouf
Laayoune
Smara
Boukra
Boujdour
N14
R101
ATLANTIC OCEAN
Bir Mogrein
SAHARA
Dakhla
MAURITANIA
Choum
Nouâdhibou
0 100 km
0 200 km
N

Introduction to Morocco

For Westerners, Morocco holds an immediate and enduring fascination. Though just an hour's ride on the ferry from Spain, it seems at once very far from Europe, with a culture – Islamic and deeply traditional – that is almost wholly unfamiliar. Throughout the country, despite the years of French and Spanish colonial rule and the presence of modern and cosmopolitan cities like Rabat and Casablanca, a more distant past constantly makes its presence felt. Fes, perhaps the most beautiful of all Arab cities, maintains a life still rooted in medieval times, when a Moroccan empire stretched from Senegal to northern Spain, while in the mountains of the Atlas and the Rif, it's still possible to draw up tribal maps of the Berber population. As a backdrop to all this, the country's physical make-up is also extraordinary: from a Mediterranean coast, through four mountain ranges, to the empty sand and scrub of the Sahara.

All of which makes Morocco an intense and rewarding experience, and a country that is ideally suited to independent (or, for activities, small-group) travel. If you have time enough, you can cover a whole range of experiences – hike in the Atlas, drive through the southern oases, relax at the laid-back Atlantic resorts like Asilah or Essaouira, and lose yourself wandering the old streets of Fes or Marrakesh. It can be hard at times to come to terms

▶ Blue-painted door, Chefchaouen

with the privilege of your position as a tourist in a country with severe poverty, and there is, too, occasional hassle from unofficial guides. But Morocco is essentially a safe and politically stable country to visit: the death in 1999 of King Hassan II, the Arab world's longest-serving leader, was followed by an easy transition to his son, Mohammed VI. And your enduring impressions are likely to be overwhelmingly positive, shaped by encounters with Morocco's powerful tradition of hospitality, generosity and openness. This is a country people return to again and again.

Fact file

- Morocco's area of 446,550 square kilometres (722,550 sq km including the Western Sahara) makes it slightly smaller than France or Spain, slightly larger than California. The population of just over 34 million compares with just eight million at independence in 1956.
- Nearly 99 percent of Moroccans are Muslim, with tiny minorities of Christians and Jews. The literacy rate is 52.3 percent (65.7 percent for men, 39.6 percent for women).
- The main languages are Arabic, Berber (Tarfit, Tamazight and Tashelhaït) and French. English is increasingly spoken by young people, especially in tourist areas.
- Morocco gained independence from French and Spanish rule on March 2, 1956. The head of state is King Mohammed VI, who succeeded his father Hassan II on July 30, 1999. The government is chosen from an elected legislature and is currently a coalition of four political parties under prime minister Abbas el Fassi of Morocco's oldest political group, the Istiqlal (Independence) Party. The main opposition is the moderate Islamist PJD (Party of Justice and Development). All legal political parties operate within a political consensus, and are not allowed, for example, to oppose the monarchy.
- Morocco's principal legal exports are clothing, fish (notably sardines), phosphates, fruit and vegetables. Cannabis, though illegal, is also an important export. Morocco's main trading partners are France and Spain.

Arabs and Berbers

The Berbers were Morocco's original inhabitants. The Arabs arrived at the end of the seventh century, after sweeping across North Africa and the Middle East in the name of their new revolutionary ideology, Islam. Eventually, nearly all the Berbers converted to the new religion and were immediately accepted as fellow Muslims by the Arabs. When Muslim armies invaded the Iberian peninsula from Morocco, the bulk of the troops were Berbers, and the two ethnic groups pretty much assimilated. Today, most Moroccans can claim both Arab and Berber ancestors, though a few (especially Shereefs, who trace their ancestry back to the Prophet Mohammed, and have the title "Moulay") claim to be "pure" Arabs. But in the Rif and Atlas mountains, and in the Souss Valley, groups of pure Berbers remain, and retain their ancient languages (Tarfit, spoken by about 1.5m people in the Rif; Tamazight, spoken by over 3m people in the Atlas; and Tashelhaït, spoken by 3–4m people in the Souss Valley region). Recently, there has been a resurgence in Berber pride (often symbolized by the Berber letter ⵣ). TV programmes are now broadcast in Berber languages, and they are even taught in schools, but the country's majority language remains Arabic.

Where to go

Geographically, the country divides into four basic zones: the **coast**, Mediterranean and Atlantic; the great cities of the **plains**; the **Rif** and **Atlas** mountains; and the oases and desert of the pre- and fully fledged **Sahara**. With two or three weeks – even two or three months – you can't expect to cover all of this, though it's easy enough (and highly recommended) to take in something of each aspect.

You are unlikely to miss the **mountains**, in any case. The three ranges of the Atlas, with the Rif a kind of extension in the north, cut right across the interior – physical and historical barriers, and inhabited for the most part by the indigenous Moroccan **Berbers**. Contrary to general preconceptions, it is the Berbers who make up most of the population (only around ten percent of Moroccans are "pure" Arabs) although most people speak Arabic as their first language and would claim mixed ancestry.

▲ Djemaa el Fna, Marrakesh

A more recent distinction derives from Morocco's colonial occupation, when it was divided into **Spanish** and **French** zones – the former contained Tetouan and the Rif, the Mediterranean and the northern Atlantic coasts, Sidi Ifni, the Tarfaya Strip and the Western Sahara; the latter comprised the plains and the main cities (Fes, Marrakesh, Casablanca and Rabat), as well as the Atlas. It was the French, who ruled their "protectorate" more closely, who had the most lasting effect on Moroccan culture, Europeanizing the cities to a strong degree and firmly imposing their language, which is spoken today by all educated Moroccans (after Moroccan Arabic or one of the three local

Tajines

Like paella or casserole, the word tajine strictly refers to a vessel rather than to the food cooked in it. A tajine is a heavy ceramic plate covered with a conical lid of the same material. The prettiest tajines, decorated in all sorts of colours and designs, come from Safi (see p.325), but the best tajines for actual use are plain reddish-brown in colour, and come from Salé (see p.294). The food in a tajine is arranged with the meat in the middle and the vegetables piled up around it. Then the lid is put on, and the tajine is left to cook slowly over a low light, or better still, over a charcoal stove (*kanoun*), usually one made specifically for the tajine and sold with it. The classic tajines combine meat with fruit and spices. Chicken is traditionally cooked in a tajine with green olives and lemons preserved in brine. Lamb or beef are often cooked with prunes and almonds. When eating a tajine, you start on the outside with the vegetables, and work your way to the meat at the heart of the dish, scooping up the food with bread.

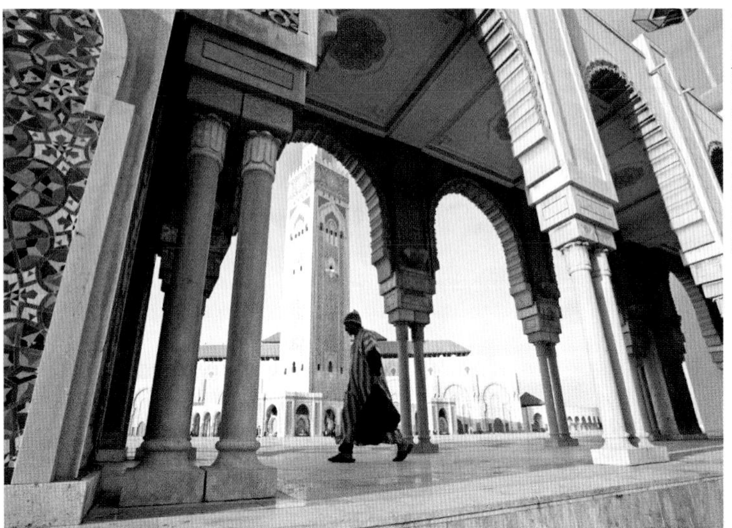

▲ Mosquée Hassan II, Casablanca

Berber languages). Use of Spanish is dwindling fast, and very few young people today can speak it.

Broadly speaking, **the coast** is best enjoyed in the north at **Tangier**, beautiful and still shaped by its old "international" port status, **Asilah** and **Larache**, and in the south at **El Jadida**, at **Essaouira**, perhaps the most easy-going resort, or at remote **Sidi Ifni**. **Agadir**, the main package tour resort, is less worthwhile – but a functional enough base for exploration.

Inland, where the real interest of Morocco lies, the outstanding cities are **Fes** and **Marrakesh**. The great imperial capitals of the country's various dynasties, they are almost unique in the Arab world for the chance they offer to witness some city life which, in patterns and appearance, remains in large part medieval. For monuments, Fes is the highlight, though Marrakesh, the "beginning of the south", is for most visitors the more enjoyable and exciting.

Travel in the **south** – roughly beyond a line drawn between Casablanca and Meknes – is, on the whole, easier and more relaxing than in the sometimes frenetic north. This is certainly true of the **mountain ranges**, where the **Rif** can feel disturbingly anarchic, while the southerly **Atlas ranges** (Middle, High and Anti) are beautiful and accessible.

Hiking in the **High Atlas**, especially around North Africa's highest peak, **Djebel Toubkal**, is in fact something of a growth industry. Even if you are no more than a casual walker, it's worth considering, with summer treks possible at all levels of experience and altitude. And, despite inroads made by commercialization, it remains essentially "undiscovered" – like the Alps must have been in the nineteenth century.

Equally exploratory in mood are the great **southern routes** beyond – and across – the Atlas, amid the **oases** of the pre-Sahara. Major routes here can be travelled by bus, minor ones by rented car or local taxi, the really remote ones by four-wheel-drive vehicles or by getting lifts on local *camions* (lorries), sharing space with the market produce and livestock.

▲ *Le Bougainviller* café, Marrakesh

The oases, around **Tinerhir**, **Zagora** and **Erfoud**, or (for the committed) **Tata** or **Figuig**, are classic images of the Arab world, vast palmeries stretching into desert horizons. Equally memorable is the architecture that they share with the Atlas – bizarre and fabulous *pisé* (mud) **kasbahs** and **ksour**, with Gothic-looking turrets and multi-patterned walls.

Further south, you can follow a route through the **Western Sahara** all the way down to Dakhla, just 22km short of the Tropic of Cancer, where the weather is scorching even in midwinter.

Hammams

"Hammam" means bath or bathroom, but in particular a traditional bathhouse, or "Turkish bath". Actually the North African steam bath dates back to Roman times, and the principle of a hammam is the same as that of a Roman bath. There is a hot room where you gather around you all the buckets of hot and cold water that you need, clean a space for yourself on the floor, and then lie down on it and sweat out all the dirt. Then you, or a friend, or the hammam attendant, scrub your skin with a rough glove called a *kissa*, or with a loofah. For men and women alike, the hammam is a place to socialize, and for female travellers, it's a great place to meet Moroccan women. For men, the big time to visit the hammam is before Friday prayers. When you've sweated it all out and rubbed it all off, you emerge glowing and also very relaxed. Ideally, you then rest in the changing room a while before heading for home (women) or a café (men) to enjoy a nice cup of mint tea.

When to go

As far as the **climate** goes, it is better to visit the south – or at least the desert routes – outside **midsummer**, when for most of the day it's far too hot for casual exploration, especially if you're dependent on public transport. But July and August, the hottest months, can be wonderful on the coast, while in the mountains there are no set rules.

Spring, which comes late by European standards (around April to May), is perhaps the best overall time, with a summer climate in the south and in the mountains, as well as on the Mediterranean and Atlantic coasts. **Winter** can be perfect by day in the south, though desert nights can get very cold – a major consideration if you're staying in the cheaper hotels,

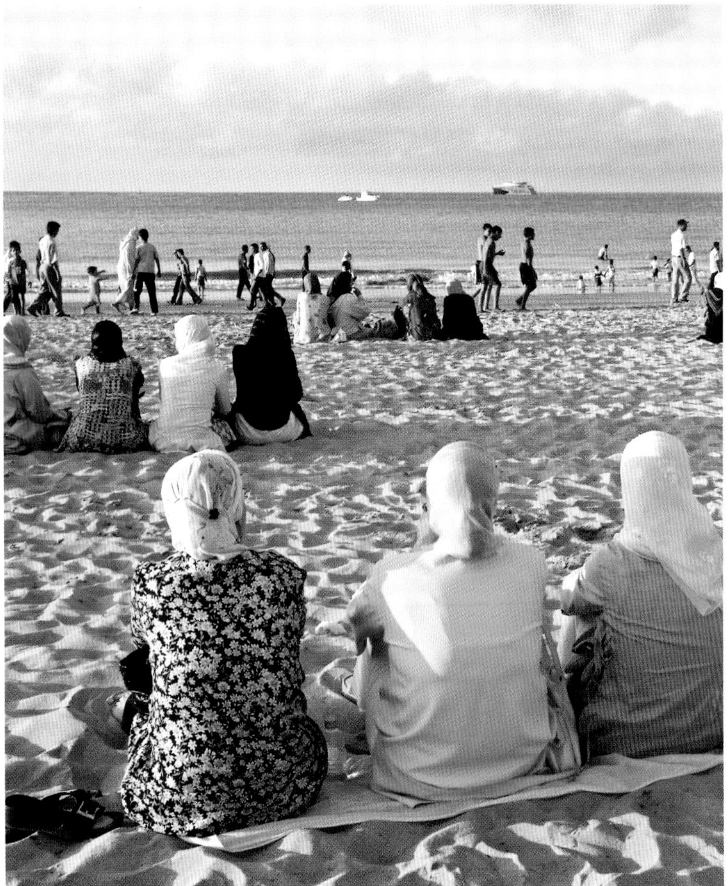

◄ Beach life, Tangier

which rarely have heating. If you're planning to **hike in the mountains**, it's best to keep to the months from April to October unless you have some experience of snow conditions.

Weather conditions apart, the **Islamic religious calendar** and its related festivals will have the most seasonal effect on your travel. The most important factor is **Ramadan**, the month of daytime fasting; this can be a problem for transport, and especially hiking, though the festive evenings do much to compensate. See p.51 for details of its timing, as well as that of other festivals.

▲ Goats climbing argan trees, north of Agadir

Morocco's climate

	Jan	Apr	July	Oct
Agadir				
Daily max/min (°C)	21/7	24/13	27/18	26/15
No. of days rain	6	3	0	3
Casablanca				
Daily max/min (°C)	17/7	21/11	26/18	24/14
No. of days rain	8	7	6	6
Dakhla				
Daily max/min (°C)	26/12	27/14	27/18	30/16
No. of days rain	0	0	0	1
Er Rachidia				
Daily max/min (°C)	17/1	25/8	38/20	27/12
No. of days rain	2	1	1	3
Fes				
Daily max/min (°C)	16/4	23/9	36/18	25/13
No. of days rain	8	9	1	7
Marrakesh				
Daily max/min (°C)	18/4	26/11	38/19	28/14
No. of days rain	7	6	1	4
Tangier				
Daily max/min (°C)	16/8	18/11	27/18	22/15
No. of days rain	10	8	0	8

things not to miss

It's not possible to see everything that Morocco has to offer in one trip – and we don't suggest you try. What follows is a selective and subjective taste of the country's highlights, in no particular order: outstanding natural features, spectacular cities, history, culture and beautiful architecture. They're arranged in five colour-coded categories to help you find the very best things to see, do and experience. All entries have a page reference to take you straight into the Guide, where you can find out more.

01 Djemaa el Fna, Marrakesh Page **353** • Musicians, acrobats and storytellers converge each night on the city's great square.

02 **Birdwatching** Page **585** • Morocco offers much to birdwatchers, from storks nesting on minarets to desert bustards.

03 **Volubilis** Page **196** • Volubilis was the chief city of Roman Morocco, and is today a beautiful, extensive ruin.

04 **Tea** Page **48** • "Whisky Maroccain", they call mint tea – the accompaniment to any discussion or transaction.

05 Atlas passes Pages **403** & **409** • The stunning Tizi n'Test pass and the higher Tizi n'Tichka lead over the Atlas mountains providing breathtaking views.

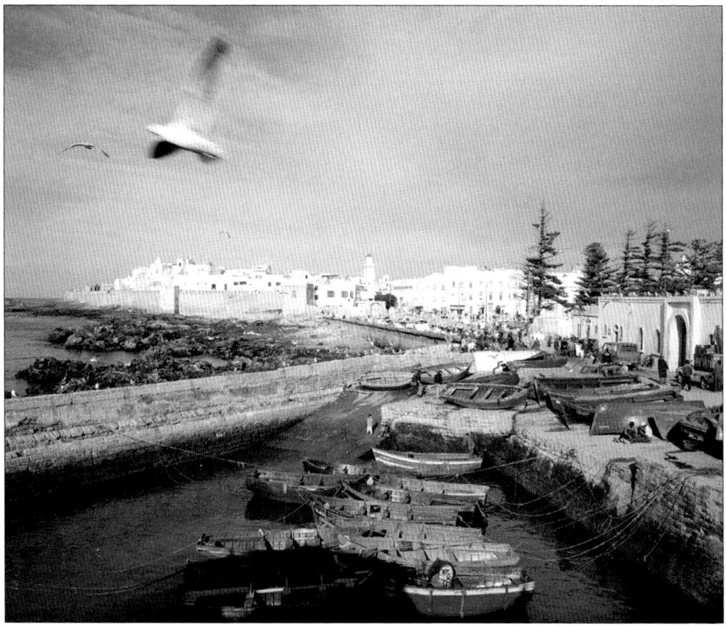

06 Essaouira Page **326** • Relax by the Atlantic at Morocco's most popular resort, home to a growing windsurfing scene.

07 Todra Gorge Page **456** • Take a walk in the majestic Todra Gorge, with its three hundred-metre canyon walls.

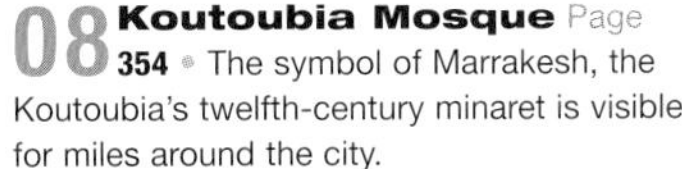

08 Koutoubia Mosque Page **354** • The symbol of Marrakesh, the Koutoubia's twelfth-century minaret is visible for miles around the city.

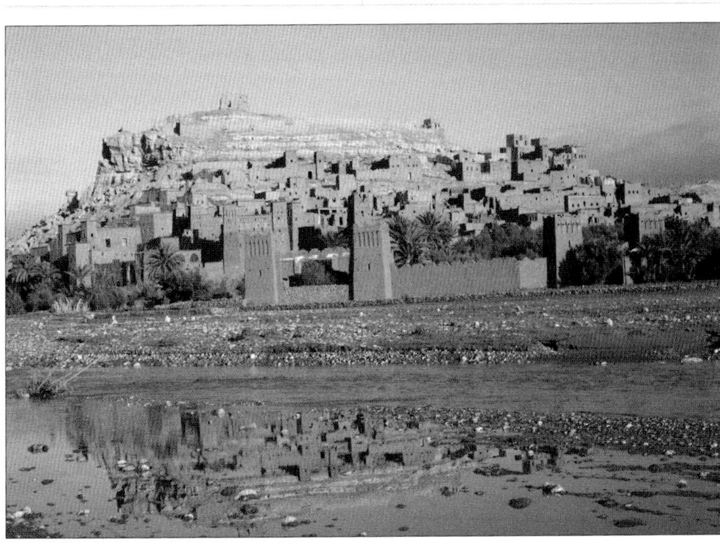

09 Route of the Kasbahs Page **428** • Morocco's southern oases are dotted with mud-built kasbahs, like these at Aït Benhaddou.

10 Crafts see ***Crafts and souvenirs*** colour section • From carpets and leatherwork to pottery, Morocco's craft tradition is extraordinarily vibrant, and entirely on show in its souks.

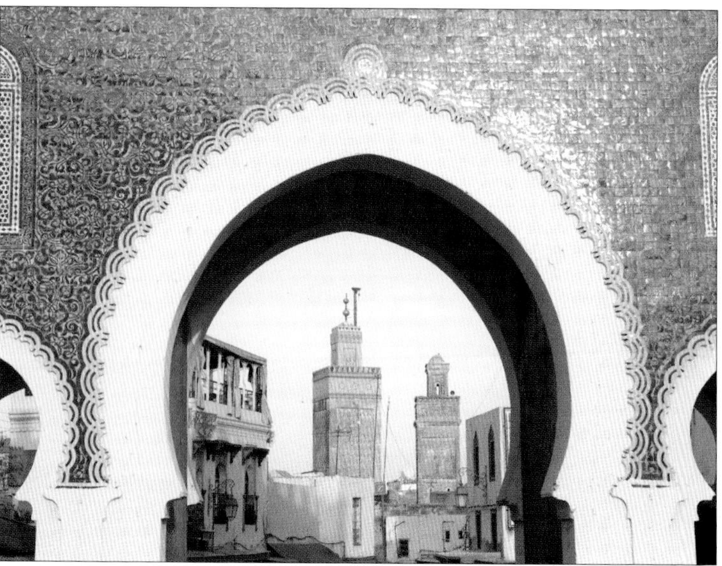

11 Fes Page **202** • The most complete medieval city in the Arab world, Fes's labyrinthine streets hide away monuments and medersas (Islamic colleges), such as the Bou Inania Medersa.

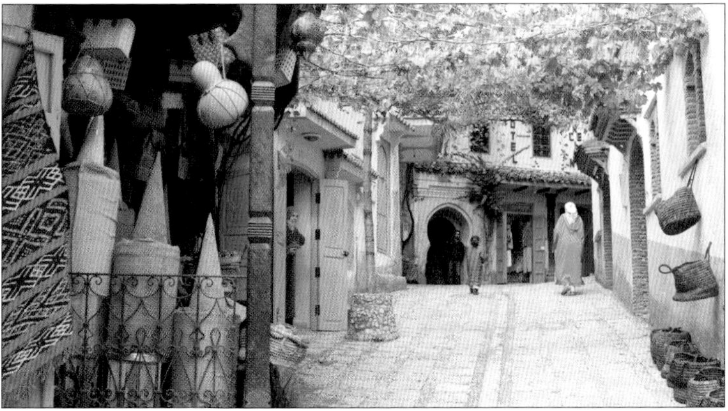

12 **Chefchaouen** Page 131 • Simply the most beautiful small town in Morocco, with its blue-washed walls.

13 **Sidi Ifni** Page 531 • This old Spanish colonial town retains a seductive array of Art Deco buildings.

14 **Prehistoric carvings** Page 390 • The Atlas and indeed the Sahara were rich in wild animals, as depicted in countless rock carvings.

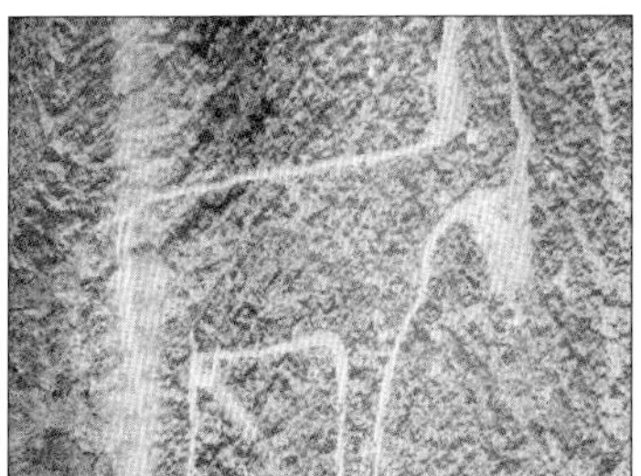

15 **Majorelle Garden, Marrakesh** Page 370 • A lovely, mature botanical garden, maintained by Yves Saint Laurent.

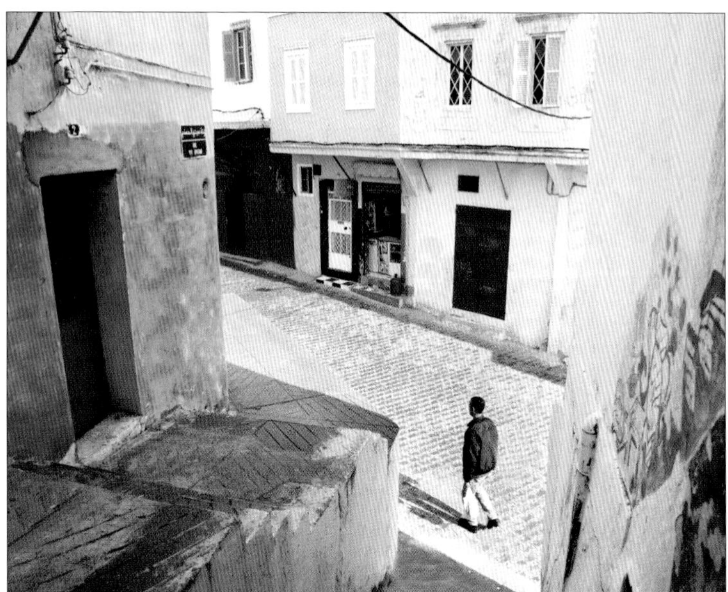

16 **Tangier** Page **82** • The old "International Port", sometime home of Bowles and Burroughs, has a seedy charm of its own.

17 **Skiing at Oukaïmeden** Page **390** • Not many skiers can list North Africa – but this is a reliable, low-key resort.

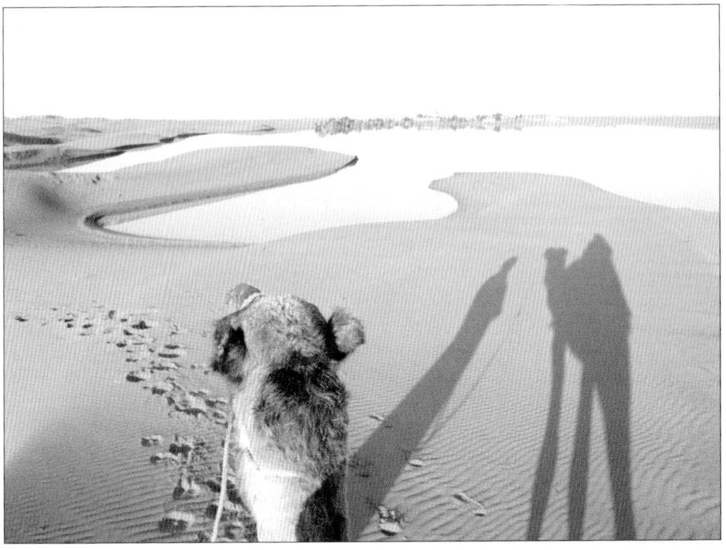

18 **Camel trekking** Page 433 • Try at least a day's camel trek from Zagora, though, according to the local signs it takes 52 days to reach Timbuktu.

19 **Imilchil Wedding Festival** Page 461 • Catch a Moroccan festival if you can – particularly in the Atlas.

20 **Tin Mal Mosque** Page 407 • This great Almohad building, built in 1153–54, stands isolated in an Atlas river valley.

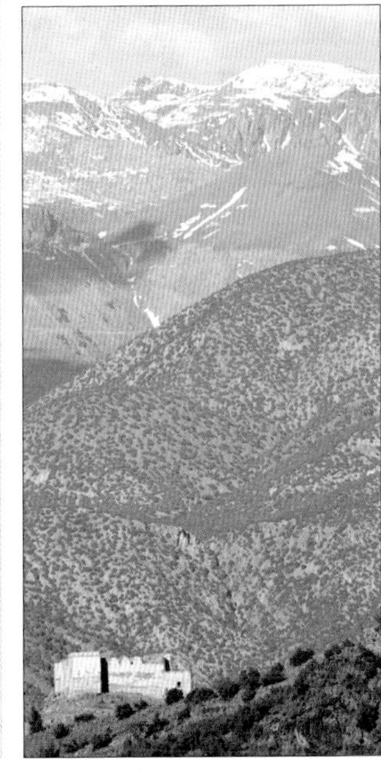

21 Trekking in the Atlas Page **396** • The Atlas mountains offer fantastic trekking opportunities, from day walks to long expeditions.

22 Casablanca Page **298** • Casa's colonial architecture, such as the cathedral, incorporates traditional Moroccan designs into French Art Deco, creating a style known as Mauresque.

23 Riads Page **44** • Stay a few nights in a riad hotel – a renovated old mansion centred on a patio.

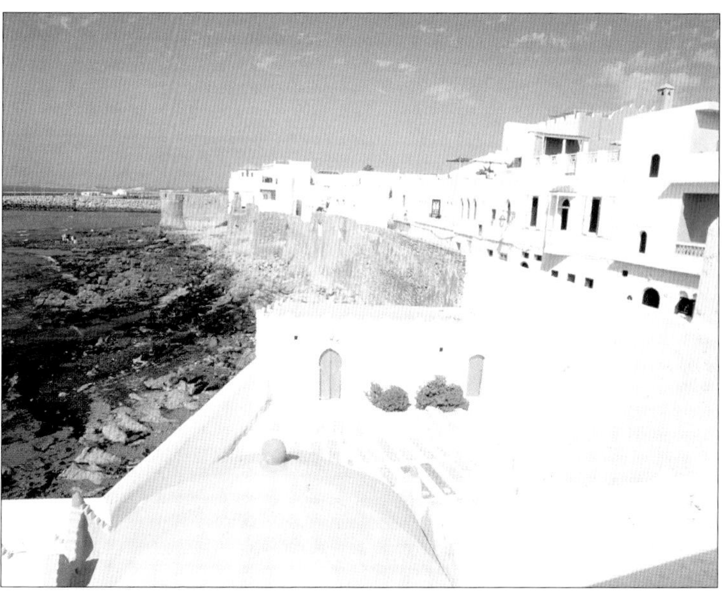

24 Asilah Page **107** • This relaxed northern seaside town hosts an international festival in August, celebrated in music, art and murals.

25 Kasbah Glaoui, Telouet Page **410** • An evocative relic of the time when the Glaoui clan ruled over the Atlas and Marrakesh.

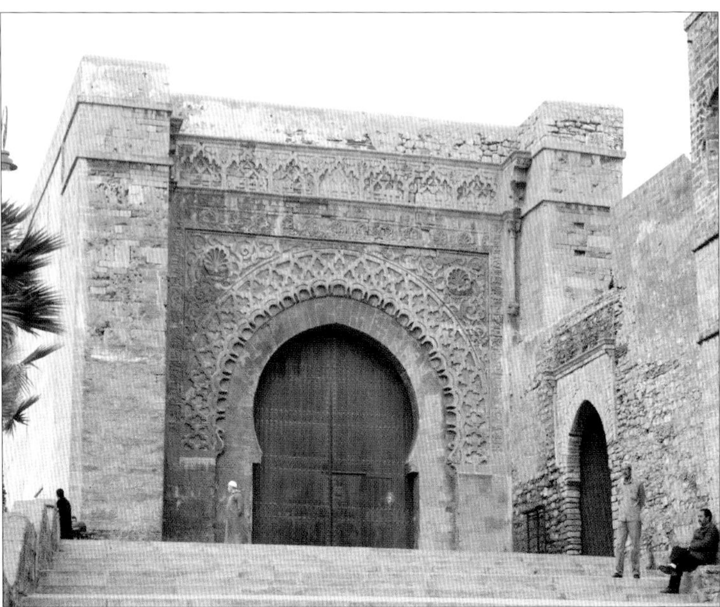

26 **Bab Oudaïa, Rabat** Page **382** • The most beautiful gate of the medieval Moorish world.

27 **Cascades d'Ouzoud** Page **263** • The most dramatic of the country's waterfalls, with overhanging cafés, and pools to plunge into.

28 **Barbary apes** Page **590** • Troupes of apes populate the cedar forests of the Middle Atlas.

Basics

Basics

Getting there

The simplest way to get to Morocco is, of course, to fly. Alternatively, you could fly to France, Spain or Gibraltar and pick up a ferry there; or, from Britain or Ireland, you could go all the way by land and sea.

Fares usually depend on **season**, the highest being at Christmas and the New Year, and at the peak of summer in July and August, when seats can also be scarce. Flying at weekends may cost more than flying midweek.

You can often cut costs by going through an **online or discount flight agent**. The cheapest tickets will be subject to restrictions such as fixed dates, and some may require advance purchase. Price ranges quoted on pp.27–29 include tax and assume midweek travel.

Charter flights may be cheaper than scheduled flights, but departure dates are fixed and withdrawal penalties are high, and it may be cheaper to pick up a **package deal** including accommodation.

When choosing an airline, be aware that if your **baggage goes astray** in transit, you cannot have it delivered to your hotel in Morocco, but will have to go back to the airport to pick it up in person when it does arrive. If arriving on an indirect flight, tight connections make baggage loss more likely.

Flights from the UK and Ireland

Royal Air Maroc (**RAM**) run **direct scheduled flights** daily from London Heathrow to Casablanca and then on to Marrakesh, which is also served by RAM's no-frills subsidiary, Atlas Blue, and by EasyJet, both from London Gatwick, and by Ryanair from Luton. Atlas Blue also fly from Heathrow and Gatwick to Tangier, and from Gatwick to Fes, and ThomsonFly serve Marrakesh and Agadir from Gatwick and Manchester. Flights typically take around three and a half hours.

In addition to these, there are **charter flights** (run by tour operators such as First Choice, Sunway and Thomas Cook) from Gatwick, Birmingham, Manchester, Dublin, and occasionally other British and Irish airports, to Agadir and sometimes Marrakesh, but these do not necessarily fly all year, and they are not especially cheaper than scheduled services; they may also limit you to a two-week stay.

Otherwise, you can get an **indirect flight** to Morocco from most British or Irish airports via London or a European city such as Paris or Amsterdam. Connecting flights from Casablanca reach most other Moroccan airports. The Spanish enclave of Melilla is served by Iberia via Madrid.

A return flight from London to Casablanca with RAM will **cost** £230–1200, depending on the specific flights you choose. Fares on flights with the no-frills airlines depend on demand, and can vary from as little as £90 up to £760 for the round trip (the earlier you book, the lower the price will be). A charter flight from Ireland will cost around €440–640 return, while an indirect scheduled flight will set you back €400–580 depending on the time of year and the popularity of the flight.

It is also possible, and often a lot cheaper, to take a **flight to Jerez, or to Málaga or Gibraltar**, where you can either get a ferry directly across the Straits, or take a bus to Algeciras for more frequent ferries from there (see p.30). Airlines such as EasyJet and

Rough Guides online

Find everything you need to plan your next trip at ⓦwww.roughguides.com. Read in-depth information on destinations worldwide, make use of our unique trip-planner, book transport and accommodation, check out other travellers' recommendations and share your own experiences.

Six steps to a better kind of travel

At Rough Guides we are passionately committed to travel. We feel strongly that only through travelling do we truly come to understand the world we live in and the people we share it with – plus tourism has brought a great deal of **benefit** to developing economies around the world over the last few decades. But the extraordinary growth in tourism has also damaged some places irreparably, and of course **climate change** is exacerbated by most forms of transport, especially flying. This means that now more than ever it's important to **travel thoughtfully** and **responsibly**, with respect for the cultures you're visiting – not only to derive the most benefit from your trip but also to preserve the best bits of the planet for everyone to enjoy. At Rough Guides we feel there are six main areas in which you can make a difference:

- Consider what you're contributing to the **local economy**, and how much the services you use do the same, whether it's through employing local workers and guides or sourcing locally grown produce and local services.
- Consider the **environment** on holiday as well as at home. Water is scarce in many developing destinations, and the biodiversity of local flora and fauna can be adversely affected by tourism. Try to patronize businesses that take account of this.
- Travel with a purpose, not just to tick off experiences. Consider **spending longer** in a place, and getting to know it and its people.
- Give thought to how often you **fly**. Try to avoid short hops by air and more harmful night flights.
- Consider **alternatives to flying**, travelling instead by bus, train, boat and even by bike or on foot where possible.
- Make your trips "**climate neutral**" via a reputable carbon offset scheme. All Rough Guide flights are offset, and every year we donate money to a variety of charities devoted to combating the effects of climate change.

Ryanair run low-cost flights to Málaga from several British and Irish airports. From Gibraltar you'd have to walk across the border to La Linea for the bus; from Málaga airport, it's usually easier to change buses at Marbella than in Málaga itself. A pricier but more exciting alternative is Inaer's helicopter service from Málaga airport to Ceuta (ⓣ+34/952 048 700, ⓦwww.grupoinaer.com), six times daily weekdays, twice on Saturdays and Sundays, costing €134.

Flights from the US and Canada

Royal Air Maroc (**RAM**) run non-stop flights to Casablanca from New York and Montreal (flight time 7hr). The alternative is to take an **indirect flight** with a European carrier, changing planes at their European hub. Those serving Morocco include Air France (to Casablanca and Rabat), Iberia (to Casablanca, Marrakesh, Tangier and the Spanish enclave of Melilla), or Alitalia or Lufthansa (both to Casablanca only). Another possibility is to take a connecting flight to New York or Montreal and continue from there on RAM (Delta codeshare the New York flight, so they should be able to sell you a through ticket without much trouble), or to buy a through ticket via Europe with an airline such as Air Canada, American, Continental, Delta or United in conjunction with a European carrier.

From New York, you can expect to pay (including tax) US$1200 in high season, or $990 in low season, for a fixed-date direct flight with RAM. From Montreal, the fare will be Can$1610/1200 in high/low season. You may be able to save a little on these fares by buying your ticket from an online or discount travel agent such as those listed on p.32, though this may involve taking an indirect flight. Getting to Morocco from the West Coast will obviously cost more:

expect to pay upwards of US$1260/925 to Casablanca from LA in high/low season, or Can$1870/1340 from Vancouver.

Flights from Australia, New Zealand and South Africa

There are no direct flights from Australia, New Zealand or South Africa to Morocco. **From Australasia**, you will need to change planes in Europe or the Middle East. Emirates or Etihad via the UAE are often the most convenient airlines, and offer a decent choice of Australian and New Zealand airports to depart from, but you can also fly with a European airline such as Lufthansa or Air France, or buy a through ticket with Qantas or Air New Zealand in conjunction with their partners in Europe, which has the advantage of offering a wider choice of departure airports.

For the cheapest through ticket, you can expect to **pay** Aus$1475–1830 from Australia (different agents offer the cheapest prices at different times of the year; there is no specific high or low season), or NZ$3260/2910 in high/low season (July/Nov) from New Zealand.

Flying **from South Africa**, you could fly with an operator such as Emirates via Dubai, Qatar Airways via Qatar, Egyptair via Cairo, or Air France via Paris. The most direct route, however, is to fly SAA to Dakar, changing there onto a Royal Air Maroc flight to Casablanca (Air Senegal International operate a code-share with the respective airlines on both sectors of this route). Expect to **pay** upwards of R7100 from Johannesburg to Casablanca year-round.

By rail from the UK and Ireland

London to Morocco by train and ferry via Paris, Madrid and Algeciras, takes a good two days at full pelt, and will usually cost rather more than a flight. The journey from London to Algeciras costs upwards of £180; details can be found on the Man in Seat 61 website at Ⓦwww.seat61.com/Morocco.htm. Tickets for the London to Paris stage are available on line from Eurostar (Ⓦwww.eurostar.com), for Paris–Madrid from Elipsos (Ⓦwww.elipsos.com) or from Rail Europe (Ⓦwww.raileurope.co.uk), and for Madrid to Algeciras from the Spanish railway RENFE (Ⓦwww.renfe.es); be aware that seat reservation is compulsory, and if you do not buy your ticket in advance, your connecting train may be fully booked when you arrive in Paris or Madrid, in which case you will not be allowed to get a ticket.

By bus from the UK and Ireland

There are bus services to Morocco with Eurolines from London's Victoria Coach Station (from £133 one-way to Tangier), changing vehicles in Paris and travelling via the Algeciras–Tangier ferry. It is a gruelling 36-and-a-half-hour journey to Algeciras, including a three-and-a-half-hour wait between buses in Paris. Connections from elsewhere in Britain and Ireland can involve long layovers in London en route.

By car from the UK and Ireland

Driving to Morocco, allow a minimum of four days from London or southern England, five days from Scotland or Ireland. The most direct **route** is: London–Channel Tunnel–Calais–Paris–Tours–Bordeaux–Bayonne–San Sebastián (Donostia)–Madrid–Granada–Málaga–Algeciras. French and Spanish motorways charge hefty tolls, but routes which avoid them are much slower. From Scotland, it's possible to avoid the drive through England by taking a ferry from Rosyth to Zeebrugge with Direct Ferries (Ⓦwww.directferries.co.uk). From Ireland, you can cut out Britain by taking a ferry to France with Brittany Ferries (Ⓦwww.brittanyferries.co.uk) or Irish Ferries (Ⓦwww.irishferries.com). From England, you can cut out the French section of the route by taking a direct ferry to northern Spain with Brittany Ferries (Ⓦwww.brittany-ferries.co.uk) or P&O (Ⓦwww.poferries.com). Otherwise, you can cut out Spain by taking a ferry to Morocco from Sète in France.

Entering Morocco by ferry

Leaving Europe for Morocco proper (not Ceuta or Melilla), you have to go through passport control before boarding the ferry. Once on board, you have to obtain a **disembarkation form** from the purser's

Ferry routes and agents

Fares quoted below (mainly in euros, €1 being roughly 90p or US$1.47) are the cheapest adult passenger fares (steerage if available, shared cabin if not), the lowest car fares (usually for a vehicle up to 2.5m long), and lowest motorcycle fares (usually up to 250cc, but 125cc on Comanav), with seasonal variations shown. Children (up to 12 years) normally pay half fare. Most lines offer discounts (usually 20 percent) to holders of youth and student cards, some to senior citizens too. Buquebus and EuroFerrys do not normally charge for bicycles, but Trasmediterranea, Nautas, FRS and Comanav may charge, though this is inconsistently applied and you can usually avoid it if you take your bike apart, pack it up and carry it on as baggage. Certain firms (Comanav for example) may refuse to take women over six months pregnant. All departures are subject to **weather conditions**. For detailed schedules and prices, contact the operators, or **Southern Ferries**, 30 Churton St, London SW1V 2LP ⓣ0844/815 7785, ⓦwww.southernferries.co.uk, the UK agents for Trasmediterranea, Comanav amd SNCM. Most passenger tickets can be bought at boat stations on departure, but for vehicles, especially at times of high demand, and for departures out of Sète, it is best to book in advance – for vehicles on ferries out of Sète, make that *well* in advance. Also note that the routes listed below (especially those out of Tarifa, Gibraltar, Almería, Sète and Genoa) are subject to change and should always be checked before departure.

Algeciras

Tickets can be bought in Algeciras from any travel agent (there are dozens along the seafront and on the approach roads to the town) or at the boat station. Prices are standard. Boats regularly depart thirty minutes to an hour late, and the next to leave may not necessarily be the first to arrive, since fast ferries frequently overtake slow boats on the crossing.

Algeciras–Ceuta catamaran Trasmediterranea, Nautas, FRS and EuroFerrys. 26 crossings daily (35min). Passenger €33, car €85, motorbike €31, bicycle free.

Algeciras–Tangier ferry Jointly operated by the Spanish companies Trasmediterranea, EuroFerrys, FRS and Lineas Maritimas Europeas, and the Moroccan companies Comanav, Limadet, IMTC and Comarit. Up to 24 crossings daily in summer, depending on demand; 11–12 daily in winter (2hr 30min). Passenger €40, car €110, motorbike or bicycle €40.50.

Algeciras–Tangier fast ferry Trasmediterranea and Nautas. 7 daily (1hr). Passenger €33.50, car €108.55, motorbike €48, bicycle €42.85.

Tarifa

Tarifa–Tangier catamaran FRS (free bus from Algeciras). 8 daily (45min). Passenger €37, car €93, motorbike €31, bicycle €15.

Gibraltar

Gibraltar–Tangier catamaran FRS. 1 weekly (1hr 30min). Passenger £32, car £83, motorbike £30, bicycle £26.

Málaga

Málaga–Melilla ferry
Trasmediterranea. 1 daily (7hr). Passenger €32, car €161, motorbike €54, bicycle €46.

Almería

Almería–Melilla ferry Trasmediterranea. 6 weekly (7hr). Passenger €32, car €161, motorbike €54, bicycle €46.

Almería–Nador ferry Comarit. 1 daily (7hr). Passenger €44, car €182, motorbike €63, bicycle free.

Almería–Nador ferry Ferrimaroc. 6 weekly (7hr). Passenger €48, car €201 motorbike €76, bicycle free.

Almería–Nador ferry Trasmediterranea. 1 daily (7hr). Passenger €48.50, car €188, motorbike or bicycle €70.

Almería–Nador ferry Comanav. 1 daily in summer only (6hr). Passenger €47, car €188, motorbike €75, bicycle free.

Barcelona

Barcelona–Tangier ferry GNV. Weekly (24hr). Passenger €88–96, car €106–235, motorbike €13–101.50.

Sète

Booking well in advance is essential for Sète ferries.

Sète–Tangier ferry Comarit. Every 4–5 days (34hr). Passenger €57, car or motorbike €233–373, bicycle free.

Sète–Tangier ferry Comanav. Every 2–4 days (36hr). Passenger €161, car or motorbike €228

Genoa

Genoa–Tangier ferry Comanav. Every 4–5 days (48hr). Passenger €224, car or motorbike €142.

Genoa–Tangier ferry GNV. Weekly via Barcelona (48hr). Passenger €140–269, car €140–385, motorbike €55–190.

Ferry operators

Comanav (Compagnie Marocaine de Navigation) 7 Bd de la Résistance, Casablanca ⓣ0522 303012; c/o Transbull, Paseo de la Conferencia 13, 2nd floor, Algeciras ⓣ956 57 04 20; c/o SNCM, 4 Quai d'Alger, Sète ⓣ04/6746 6800; c/o SNCM, 3 Tagliamento, Milan ⓣ02/5523 1592; 43 Av Abdou el Alâa el Maari, Tangier ⓣ0539 940488; c/o Transbull, Muelle de Rivera, Almería ⓣ950 28 11 43; Entrée du Port, Beni Enzar (Nador port) ⓣ0536 608628; c/o Southern Ferries (see opposite) in London. *Algeciras, Sète and Genoa to Tangier; Almería to Nador (summer only).*

Comarit ⓦwww.comarit.com; 3 Av Virgen del Carmen, first floor, Algeciras ⓣ956 66 84 62; Estación Maritima, Almería ⓣ950 62 03 03; Résidence Hasnae, Av Mohammed VI, Tangier ⓣ0539 320032; Port Beni Ansar, Nador ⓣ0536 348383. *Algeciras and Sète to Tangier; Almería to Nador.*

EuroFerrys ⓦwww.euroferrys.com; Av Virgen del Carmen 1, 5th floor, Algeciras ⓣ956 65 23 24; Avda Muelle Cañonero Dato, Ceuta ⓣ956 50 70 70; Port, Tangier ⓣ0539 948199. *Algeciras to Tangier and Ceuta.*

Ferrimaroc ⓦwww.ferrimaroc.com; BP 96, Beni Enzar (Nador port) ⓣ0536 348100; Muelle de Ribera, Almería ⓣ950 27 48 00. *Almería to Nador.*

FRS (Ferrys Rápidos del Sur) ⓦwww.frs.es; Estación Maritima, Tarifa ⓣ956 68 18 30; Paseo Maritimo, Algeciras ⓣ956 62 74 45; c/o Turner & Co, 65–67 Irish Town, Gibraltar ⓣ+350/78305; Rue Farabi, Tangier ⓣ0539 942612. *Tarifa, Gibraltar and (in summer only) Algeciras to Tangier; Algeciras to Ceuta.*

GNV (Grandi Navi Veloci) ⓦwww.gnv.it; 17 Via Fieschi, Genoa ⓣ010/209 4591; Estación Marítima, Muelle San Beltrán, Barcelona ⓣ902 454 645; c/o Viamare, Suite 3, 447 Kenton Rd, Harrow, Middlesex (outer London) HA3 0XY, ⓣ020/8206 3420, ⓔferries@viamare.com. *Genoa via Barcelona to Tangier.*

IMTC (International Maritime Transport Corporation) ⓦwww.imtc.co.ma; 50 Av Pasteur, Casablanca ⓣ0522 437620; Port, Tangier ⓣ0539 370983; c/o Vapores Suardiaz, 15 Av Virgen del Carmen, ninth floor, left, Algeciras ⓣ956 66 23 00. *Algeciras to Tangier.*

Limadet (Lignes Maritimes du Détroit) 3 Rue Ibn Rochd, Tangier ⓣ0539 933633; Recinto del Puerto, Algeciras ⓣ956 66 96 13. *Algeciras to Tangier.*

Lineas Maritimas Europeas ⓦwww.lineasme.com; 3 Av Virgen del Carmen, first floor, Algeciras ⓣ956 668 308; c/o Comarit (see opposite) in Tangier. *Algeciras to Tangier.*

Nautas ⓦwww.nautasferry.com; Estación Maritima, Locales F-4 & F-23, Algeciras ⓣ956 58 95 30; Estación Maritima, Ceuta ⓣ856 20 51 90; Port, Tangier ⓣ0539 934463. *Algeciras to Tangier and Ceuta.*

Trasmediterranea ⓦwww.trasmediterranea.es, all telephone enquiries in Spain ⓣ902 45 46 45; Recinto del Puerto, Algeciras; Estación Maritima, Recinto del Puerto, Local E-1, Málaga; Estación Maritima, Almería; Avda Muelle Cañonero Dato, Ceuta; General Marina 1, Melilla; c/o Southern Ferries (see opposite) in London. *Algeciras to Ceuta and Tangier; Málaga to Melilla; Almería to Melilla and Nador.*

office, fill it in, and submit it with your passport for stamping to a **Moroccan immigration** official on the boat. Announcements to this effect are not always made in English, but if you don't have a stamp, you'll have to wait until everyone else has cleared frontier and customs controls before being attended to. When disembarking, show your newly acquired stamp to a Moroccan policeman at the exit.

Returning from Morocco to Spain, you need to collect an embarkation form and departure card and have these stamped by the port police prior to boarding your ferry.

Vehicle red tape

Taking a vehicle to Morocco you must take out **Green Card Insurance**; some insurance companies don't cover Morocco, so you may need to shop around; it speeds things up if the reference to Morocco is prominent and in French.

Entering Morocco, you will need to present the card, along with your vehicle registration document – which must be in your name or accompanied by a letter from the registered owner. Trailer caravans, as well as the vehicle itself, need **temporary importation documents**, which are obtainable at the frontier (or on the ferry, if not travelling to Ceuta or Melilla) for no charge. For information on driving in Morocco, see pp.37–40. For legal requirements, see box, p.38.

Entering Morocco through the Spanish enclaves of Ceuta or Melilla (the most economic crossings for vehicles), try to avoid arriving at the weekend. If there are any problems, you may well be sent back to Ceuta or Melilla to wait until the Monday to sort them out.

Airlines, agents and operators

Airlines

Air Canada ⓦwww.aircanada.com.
Air France ⓦwww.airfrance.com.
Air New Zealand ⓦwww.airnz.com.au, ⓦwww.airnz.co.nz.
Air Senegal International ⓦwww.air-senegal-international.com.
Alitalia ⓦwww.alitalia.com.
American Airlines ⓦwww.aa.com.
Continental ⓦwww.continental.com.
Delta ⓦwww.delta.com.
EasyJet ⓦwww.easyjet.com.
EgyptAir ⓦwww.egyptair.com.
Emirates ⓦwww.emirates.com.
Etihad ⓦwww.etihadairways.com.
Iberia ⓦwww.iberia.com.
Lufthansa ⓦwww.lufthansa.com.
Qantas ⓦwww.qantas.com.
Qatar Airways ⓦwww.qatarairways.com.
Royal Air Maroc ⓦwww.royalairmaroc.com.
Ryanair ⓦwww.ryanair.com.
ThomsonFly ⓦwww.thomsonfly.com.

Charter flights

First Choice ⓦwww.firstchoice.co.uk. Gatwick, Birmingham and Manchester to Agadir.
Sunway Travel ⓦwww.sunway.ie. Dublin to Agadir.
Thomas Cook ⓦwww.thomascook.com. Gatwick and Manchester to Agadir.

Discount agents

North South Travel UK ⓣ01245/608 291, ⓦwww.northsouthtravel.co.uk. Friendly, competitive travel agency, offering discounted fares worldwide. Profits are used to support projects in the developing world, especially the promotion of sustainable tourism.
Trailfinders UK ⓣ0845/058 5858, Ireland ⓣ01/677 7888, Australia ⓣ1300/780 212; ⓦwww.trailfinders.com. One of the best-informed and most efficient agents for independent travellers.
Travel CUTS Canada ⓣ1-866/246-9762, US ⓣ1-800/592-2887; ⓦwww.travelcuts.com. Canadian youth and student travel firm.
STA Travel UK ⓣ020/7361 6162, US ⓣ1-800/781-4040, Australia ⓣ13/4782, NZ ⓣ0800/474 400, South Africa ⓣ0861/781 781; ⓦwww.statravel.com. Specialists in independent travel (especially student and under-26); also student IDs and travel insurance.
USIT Republic of Ireland ⓣ01/602 1906, Northern Ireland ⓣ028/9032 7111, ⓦwww.usit.ie. Ireland's main student and youth travel specialists.

Morocco specialist tour operators

Best of Morocco UK ⓣ0845/026 4585, ⓦwww.morocco-travel.com. Hotels, riads, and upmarket "designer" trekking, culinary tours, birwatching and other specialist options.
Blue Men of Morocco ⓣ+34/952 467 562, ⓦwww.bluemenofmorocco.com. Málaga-based firm run by a Moroccan–American couple, offering

Andalusía/Morocco combination packages as well as tours of Morocco.

Surf Maroc UK ⓣ01794/322 709, ⓦwww.surfmaroc.co.uk. Surfing holidays based at Taghazout, including lessons for beginners and more advanced surfers.

Naturally Morocco Ltd UK ⓣ0845/345 7195 or 01239/710 814, ⓦwww.naturallymorocco.co.uk. Ecologically oriented tours of Morocco, with vegetarian or vegan food if desired and a variety of special services available, including Arabic and Berber language tuition and even Moroccan cookery lessons.

Bus contacts

Eurolines UK ⓣ0871/781 8181, ⓦwww.nationalexpress.com/eurolines, Ireland ⓣ01/836 6111, ⓦwww.eurolines.ie.

Getting around

Moroccan public transport is, on the whole, pretty good, with a rail network linking the main towns of the north, the coast and Marrakesh, and plenty of buses and collective taxis. Renting a car can open up routes that are time-consuming or difficult on local transport.

By air

Royal Air Maroc (RAM; ⓣ0890 000800, ⓦwww.royalairmaroc.com) operates **domestic flights** from its Casablanca hub to major cities nationwide, and **Regional Air Lines** (ⓣ0802 000082, ⓦwww.regionalmaroc.com) serve destinations in the far south and Western Sahara. Between any other two points, you will usually have to change planes at Casablanca, unless both points are stops on a single Casa-bound flight (Dakhla to Laayoune, for example). In general, flying is not really worthwhile except for long-distance routes such as to Laayoune or Dakhla in the Western Sahara, when they can save you a lot of time. A one-way ticket from Casablanca to Laayoune, for example, would set you back 550dh (£46/$66) and take two and a half hours (plus journey time to the airport, check-in time and delays), compared to nineteen hours by bus. Casa to Dakhla – 2724dh (£221/$325) one-way on RAM, but with reduced-fare round-trip tickets at 1499dh (£122/$179) if you buy them far enough in advance to nab one of the limited number available – would take you two hours and ten minutes each way by air compared to 28 hours by bus.

Information on Morocco's airports, including daily departure lists for some of them, can be found on the website of the Office National des Aéroports at ⓦwww.onda.org.ma. You should always confirm flights 72 hours before departure. Student and under-26 youth **discounts** of 25 percent are available on RAM domestic flights, but only if the ticket is bought in advance from one of its offices.

By rail

Trains cover a limited network of routes, but for travel between the major cities they are easily the best option, comfortable and fairly fast, but sometimes subject to delays.

The **map** on pp.4–5 shows all the passenger train routes in the country, and services are summarized in the "Travel Details" at the end of each chapter. There are two main passenger lines: from Tangier in the north down to Marrakesh, and from Oujda in the northeast, also to Marrakesh, joining with the Tangier line at Sidi Kacem. Branch lines serve El Jadida, Safi, Oued Zem and Casablanca airport. A new line is due to open from Nador to Taourirt, and there are plans to extend the railway south to Agadir, and on to Laayoune in the

Western Sahara. Schedules change very little from year to year, but it's wise to check times in advance at stations. **Timetables** are displayed at major train stations, and any station ticket office will print you off a mini-timetable of services between any two stations. You can also check schedules (*horaires*) and fares (*tarifs*) on the ONCF website at Ⓦwww.oncf.ma, though you cannot buy tickets online.

There are two **classes** of tickets – first and second. **Costs** for a second-class ticket are slightly more than what you'd pay for buses; on certain "express" services ("express" refers to the level of comfort rather than the speed), they are around thirty percent higher. In addition, there are **couchettes** (160dh extra) available on the Tangier–Marrakesh and Casablanca–Oujda night trains – worth the money for both the comfort and the security, as couchette passengers are in their own locked carriage with a guard. Most **stations** are located reasonably close to the modern city centres. They do not have **left-luggage** facilities.

By bus

Bus travel is generally only marginally cheaper than taking a shared grand taxi, and around 30 percent slower, but also safer and more comfortable, though on some older buses leg room is limited, and for anyone approaching six feet or more in height, long journeys can be rather an endurance test. Many long-distance buses run **at night** when they are both quicker and cooler. Most are fitted with reading lights but they are invariably turned off, so you will not be able to read on buses after dark. Also note that the rate of accidents involving night buses is quite high, especially on busy routes, and most of all on the N8 between Marrakesh and Agadir.

Travelling during the day, especially in summer, it pays to sit on the side away from **the sun**. Travelling from north to south, this means sitting on the right in the morning, on the left in the afternoon, vice versa if going the other way. Travelling from east to west, sit on the right, or on the left if going from west to east. In fact, Moroccan passengers often pull down the blinds and shut the windows, which can block out the scenery and make the journey rather claustrophobic. Note too, especially on rural services, that some passengers may be unused to road travel, resulting in travel sickness and vomiting.

Distance chart (kilometres by road)

	Ag	Al H	Casa	Dakh	Er Rach	Ess	Fes	Figuig
Agadir	–	1037	511	1208	773	173	756	1151
Al Hoceima	1037	–	570	2245	637	940	281	773
Casablanca	511	570	–	1719	557	351	289	935
Dakhla	1208	2245	1719	–	1981	1381	1964	2359
Er Rachidia	773	637	557	1981	–	676	350	378
Essaouira	173	940	351	1381	676	–	640	1054
Fes	756	281	289	1964	350	640	–	706
Figuig	1151	773	935	2359	378	1054	706	–
Laayoune	694	1731	1205	514	1467	867	1450	1845
Marrakesh	273	764	238	1481	500	176	483	878
Meknes	740	341	229	1948	328	580	60	706
Nador	1063	280	596	2271	554	947	307	525
Oujda	1076	397	609	2284	564	960	320	386
Ouarzazate	375	927	442	1483	296	380	646	674
Rabat	602	479	91	1810	466	442	198	1199
Tangier	880	323	341	2088	595	692	303	1457
Tetouan	873	273	362	2081	595	713	276	1478

CTM and private lines

Buses run by CTM (the national company Ⓦwww.ctm.ma) are faster and more reliable than private services, with numbered seats and fixed departure schedules. CTM services usually have reading lights, though you may have to ask the driver to turn those on. Some of the **larger private company** buses, such as SATAS (which operates widely in the south) and Trans Ghazala (which runs in the north) are of a similar standard, but many other private companies are tiny outfits, with a single bus which leaves only when the driver considers it sufficiently full. On the other hand, such private buses are much more likely to stop for you if you flag them down on the open road, whereas CTM services will only pick up and set down at official stops.

Bus terminals

Most towns have a main **bus station** (*gare routière*), often on the edge of town. CTM buses usually leave from the company's office, which may be quite a way from the main bus station, though in several places CTM and the private companies share a single terminal, and in some cases the CTM bus will call at the main bus station when departing a city, though not when arriving.

Bus stations usually have a number of ticket windows, one for each of the companies operating out of it. There is occasionally a departures board, but it may be out of date and in Arabic only, so you should always check departure times at the appropriate window. Bus conductors or ticket sellers may be calling out destinations in the bus station in any case, or may greet you as you come in by asking where you want to go. On the more popular trips (and especially with CTM services, which are often just once a day in the south), it is worth trying to buy **tickets in advance**; this may not always be possible on smaller private-line services, but it's worth enquiring about.

You can sometimes experience problems getting tickets at **small towns** along major routes, where buses can arrive and leave already full. It's sometimes possible to get round this by taking a local bus or a grand taxi for the next section of the trip (until the bus you want empties a little), or by waiting for a bus that actually starts from the town you're in. Overall, the best policy is to arrive at a bus station early in the day (ideally 5.30–6am).

Laay	Mar	Mek	Nad	Ouj	Ouarz	Rab	Tan	Tet
694	273	740	1063	1076	375	602	880	873
1731	764	341	280	397	927	479	323	273
1205	238	229	596	609	442	91	341	362
514	1481	1948	2271	2284	1483	1810	2088	2081
1467	500	328	554	564	296	466	595	595
867	176	580	947	960	380	442	692	713
1450	483	60	307	320	646	198	303	276
1845	878	706	525	386	674	1199	1457	1478
–	967	1434	1757	1770	1069	1296	1574	1567
967	–	467	790	803	204	321	579	600
1434	467	–	363	380	652	138	267	267
1757	790	363	–	139	840	501	597	547
1770	803	380	139	–	850	518	714	664
1069	204	652	840	850	–	528	783	804
1296	321	138	501	518	528	–	250	271
1574	579	267	597	714	783	250	–	58
1567	600	267	547	664	804	271	58	–

Fares

For **comparison**, between Casablanca and Marrakesh, a train will take three hours and cost 84dh in second class, 125dh in first. A CTM bus will cost 80dh and take three hours, while an ordinary bus will cost 50dh and take around four hours. A shared grand taxi will cost 120dh and take two and a half hours (though on most routes in fact the difference between the grand taxi and ordinary bus fare is less). For the forty-minute plane journey, you would pay 1774dh for a full-fare economy-class ticket, but a limited number (available only if booked far enough in advance) of promotional-fare round-trip tickets are sold for 500dh.

On private-line buses, you generally pay for your **baggage** to be loaded into the hold (or onto the roof). The standard fee is 5dh, but this may be foregone on short hops. Note that you only pay to have your baggage loaded, not to have it unloaded on arrival, whatever anybody may say. On CTM, SATAS and Supratours buses your luggage is weighed and you are issued with a receipt for the baggage charge (usually about 10dh, depending on weight and distance – allow time for this procedure). On arrival, porters with wheeled box-carts (*chariots*) may offer their services, but always agree a price before engaging one.

Supratours buses

An additional service, on certain major routes, is the **Supratours express buses** run by the train company, **ONCF**. These are fast and very comfortable, and run from Nador, from Tetouan, and from Essaouira, Agadir and the Western Sahara to connect with rail services from Oujda, Tangier and Marrakesh. Timetables and fares for Supratours buses can be found along with those for trains on the ONCF website (Ⓦwww.oncf.ma). Supratours services compare, in both time and cost, with CTM buses. They do not use the main bus stations, but depart from outside their own town-centre offices (detailed in the text). Through tickets to and from connecting rail stations are available (Nador through to Fes, for example), and travellers with rail tickets for connecting services have priority. It's best to book tickets in advance if possible.

By grand taxi

Shared **grands taxis** are one of the best features of Moroccan transport. They operate on a wide variety of routes, are much quicker than buses (usually quicker than trains, too), and fares vary from slightly more than the bus to around twice as much.

The taxis are usually big Peugeot or Mercedes cars carrying six passengers (Peugeots are less common but have a slightly less cramped seating arrangement). Most business is along specific routes, and the most popular routes have more or less continuous departures throughout the day. You just show up at the terminal (locations are detailed in the guide) and ask for a place to a specific destination. The best time to arrive is early morning (7–9am), when a lot of people are travelling and taxis fill up quickly; lunchtime, on the other hand, is a bad time to turn up, as fewer people will be travelling, and the taxi will take longer to fill up. As soon as six (or, if you're willing to pay extra, four or five) people are assembled, the taxi sets off. Make sure, when asking about grands taxis, that it is clear you only want a place (*une place* in French, *plassa* in Arabic, or hold up one finger) in a shared taxi (*taxi collectif*), as drivers often "presume" that a tourist will want to charter the whole taxi (see opposite), which means paying for all six places. Women travelling alone may wish to pay for two places and get the front seat to themselves rather than be squashed up against male passengers.

Picking up a grand taxi on the road is more problematic, as they will only stop if they have a place free (if a passenger has already alighted). To hail a taxi on the open road, hold up one, two or more fingers to indicate how many places you need.

Fares for set routes are fixed, and drivers do not usually try to overcharge tourists for a place (though occasionally they try to charge for baggage, which usually travels free of charge). If you think that you are being

Police checkpoints

There are police checkpoints on roads throughout the country. European cars, or rental cars, are usually waved through. Buses (other than CTM services) are more likely to be stopped, but usually only briefly. Sometimes the police may ask to check your passport or (if driving) license, often only because they want to relieve their boredom with a chat. Nonetheless, you should always have your **passport** with you if travelling between towns – even on day-trips.

Checkpoints in the **Western Sahara** are more thorough, and for foreigners they can involve a considerable amount of form-filling and delay. For further details, and suggestions on how to save time at these checks, see box, p.548.

In the **Rif mountains**, especially around Ketama, police may stop vehicles to search for cannabis. Buses are usually delayed more than grands taxis at such checkpoints, and passengers may be searched individually. There are also sometimes lengthy checks for duty-free contraband on buses from Nador to Fes.

overcharged, ask the other passengers, or check the price with your hotel before leaving. Occasionally, five passengers may agree to split the cost of the last place to hasten departure, or one passenger may agree to pay for two places. You pay the full fare for the journey even if travelling only part of the way.

If you want to take a **non-standard route**, or an excursion, or just to have the taxi to yourself, it is possible to charter a whole grand taxi (*une course* in French, *corsa* in Arabic). In theory this should be exactly six times the price of a place in a shared taxi if the route has a set fare, but you'll often have to bargain hard to get that. Hotels can sometimes be useful in helping to charter grands taxis.

Some people consider grands taxis **dangerous**. It is certainly true that they are prone to practices such as speeding, and overtaking on blind curves or the brows of hills, and that they have more than their fair share of accidents. Drivers may work all day and into the night, and it seems a large number of accidents involve them falling asleep at the wheel while driving at night, so you may wish to avoid using them for night-time journeys, especially on busy roads (the N8 between Marrakesh and Agadir is the worst). Note also that with the seating arrangements, it is not usually possible to wear a seat belt, though if you pay for two places, you can get the front seat to yourself and put the belt on.

Trucks and hitching

In the countryside, where buses may be sporadic or even nonexistent, it is standard practice for **vans** and **lorries** (*camions*), **pick-up trucks** (*camionettes*) and **transit-vans** (*transits*) to carry and charge passengers. You may be asked to pay a little more than the locals, and you may be expected to bargain over the price – but it's straightforward enough.

In parts of the **Atlas**, local people run more or less scheduled truck or transit services, generally to coincide with the pattern of local souks. If you plan on traversing any of the more ambitious Atlas *pistes*, you'll probably be dependent on these vehicles, unless you walk.

Hitching

Hitchhiking is not big in Morocco, but you may resort to it on routes where transport is scarce. Fellow tourists may pick you up, and Moroccans may carry you for free, but usually you pay, around the same as a bus or grand taxi fare. This is especially the case in country areas, where local rides can operate in much the same way as truck taxis (see above). As a rule, however, hitching is not really safe, and it is definitely not advisable for women travelling alone. We have heard of (Moroccan) hitchhikers being robbed on the N12 Tata–Bou Izakarn road, and it probably happens elsewhere too.

By car

There are few real problems driving in Morocco, but **accident rates** are high, largely because motorists routinely ignore traffic regulations and drive aggressively and

Driving requirements

The **minimum age** for driving in Morocco is 21 years. EU, North American and Australasian **driving licences** are recognized and valid in Morocco, though an **International Driving Licence**, with its French translations (available from the AA or equivalent motoring organizations) is a worthwhile investment, especially if your domestic licence does not have a photograph on it (Moroccan police will find that strange). You must **carry your driving licence and passport** at all times.

You **drive on the right**.

dangerously (most people pay *baksheesh* for their licence). The N8 between Marrakesh and Agadir is a particular accident blackspot. Do not expect other drivers to indicate or observe lane discipline, beware when coming up to blind curves or hills where vehicles coming in the other direction may be trying to overtake without full view of the road ahead, treat all pedestrians with the suspicion that they will cross in front of you, and all cyclists with the idea that they may well swerve into the middle of the road. All this makes driving a particularly hair-raising experience in towns, and even experienced drivers may find city driving quite stressful. The difficulty of finding places in cities due to lack of street signs adds to the problem. Be particularly wary about driving **after dark**, as it is legal to drive up to 20km per hr without lights, which allows all cyclists and mopeds to wander at will; donkeys, goats and sheep do not carry lights, either.

However, with those caveats in mind, daytime and certainly long-distance driving can be as good as anywhere. Good road surfaces, long straight roads, and little traffic between inhabited areas allow for high average speeds. The usual **speed limit** outside towns is 40km per hr (25mph) in built-up areas, 100km per hr (62mph) or ordinary roads, 120km per hr (75mph) on motorways. There are on-the-spot fines for speeding, and oncoming motorists flashing their headlights at you may well be warning you to slow down for a police check ahead (radar speed traps are common). The French rule of giving priority to traffic from the right is observed at roundabouts and junctions – meaning that cars coming onto a roundabout have priority over those already on it.

By law, drivers and passengers are required to wear **seatbelts**. Almost no one does, but if you follow suit and are stopped by the police, you may have a small fine (possibly unofficial) extracted. Given Morocco's high road-accident rate, it is foolhardy not to wear a seat belt anyway.

Piste and off-piste driving

On the *pistes* (rough, unpaved tracks in the mountains or desert), there are special problems. Here you do need a good deal of driving and mechanical confidence – and if you don't feel your car is up to it, don't drive on these routes. Obviously, a 4WD vehicle is best suited to the *pistes*, but most *pistes* are passable, with care, in an ordinary small car, though it's worth asking local advice first. On mountain roads, beware of gravel, which can be a real danger on the frequent hairpin bends, and, in spring, flash floods caused by melting snow. The six-volume series, *Pistes du Maroc* (Gandini), are invaluable guides for anyone planning on driving *pistes*; they are available in major Moroccan bookshops or on line (Ⓦwww.extrem-sud.com/guides.php). Roaming Yak (Ⓦwww.roamingyak.org) have invaluable information about ten desert *piste* routes on their website, and produce an accompanying DVD.

Driving a 4x4 can be an exciting way of exploring the mountains and desert, off tarmac, or even off *piste*. Some companies lay on vehicles, driver and mess tent, organize food and cooking and will go wherever requested. For economical and practical reasons groups should number five or eleven, so you'll probably find yourself exploring with strangers. UK-based AMIS (see p.54) specializes in this field.

Car rental

Car rental is expensive, from around 3500dh (£300/$420) per week or 500dh (£40/$60) a day (there's usually a three-day minimum) for a basic car with unlimited mileage and insurance cover. You will be expected to leave a large deposit, and fuel prices are high too (see opposite). Having a car pays obvious dividends if you are pushed for time, especially in the **south**, where buses and taxis may be sparse, but chartering a grand taxi and agreeing a daily rate will not cost that much more.

Many visitors rent a car in Casablanca, Marrakesh or Agadir, but it may work out cheaper to **arrange car rental in advance** through the travel agent who arranges your flight. With international firms such as Hertz, Budget, Europcar, National and Avis, you can book from home by phone or on line. Local **car rental firms** are listed in city "Listings" sections in the guide (especially on p.290, pp.312–313 & p.380). Deals to go for are unlimited mileage and daily/weekly rates; paying by the kilometre invariably works out more expensive. Local firms have the advantage that the price is more likely to be negotiable, though the condition of the vehicle should be well checked. Many hotels can arrange car rental at reasonable rates. If you can't or don't want to drive yourself, car rental companies can often arrange a **driver** for around 300dh (£25/$36) a day.

Before making a booking, check whether you can pick the car up in one city and return it to another, and also whether you pay extra for using a credit card. Before setting out, make sure the car comes with spare tyre, tool kit and full documentation – including insurance cover, which is compulsory issue with all rentals. It's a good idea to get full insurance to avoid charges for bumps and scratches. Most car rental agreements prohibit use of the car on unsurfaced roads, and you will be liable for any damage sustained if you do drive off-tarmac.

Equipment

Whether you rent a car or drive your own, always make sure you're carrying a **spare tyre** in good condition (plus a jack and tools). Flat tyres occur very frequently, even on fairly major roads, and you can often be in for a long wait until someone drives along with a possible replacement. Carrying an **emergency windscreen** is also useful, especially if driving your own car for a long period of time. There are lots of loose stones on the hard shoulders of single-lane roads and they can fly all over the place. If you're not mechanically minded, be sure to bring a car **maintenance manual** – a useful item, too, for anyone planning to rent a vehicle.

Fuel and breakdowns

Filling stations can be few and far between in rural areas: always fill your tank to the limit. Unleaded fuel is available at larger stations, but it's always worth filling up when you have the chance as supplies can be sporadic. Fuel prices are generally lower than in Western Europe, at 11.40dh (95p/$1.35) a litre for leaded petrol (*super*) or unleaded (*sans plomb* or *bidoun rasas*), and 7.37dh (62p/88¢) for diesel (*gasoil, pronounced "gazwaal"*). In the Saharan provinces (basically the Western Sahara), fuel is subsidized, and costs about a third less, but unleaded petrol is available there only in Laayoune and at one station in Dakhla. Fuel is duty-free in the Spanish enclaves of Ceuta and Melilla, and around 25 percent cheaper than it is on the Spanish mainland, and a little less than it is in Morocco proper, at around €0.78 (72p/$1.15) for unleaded or diesel (*gasóleo*).

Moroccan mechanics are usually excellent at coping with breakdowns and all medium-sized towns have garages (most with an extensive range of spare parts for most French cars, and usually for Fiats too). However, if you break down miles from anywhere you'll probably end up paying a fortune to get a lorry to tow you back.

If you are driving your own vehicle, there is also the problem of having to re-export any car that you bring into the country (even a wreck). You can't just write off a car: you'll have to take it out of Morocco with you.

Vehicle insurance

Insurance must by law be sold along with all rental agreements. Driving your own vehicle, you should obtain Green Card cover from your insurers. If you don't have it on arrival, you can buy it from Assurance Frontière for 950dh (£77/$113) a month for a car or campervan, at Tangier port (ⓣ0539 949092), Nador port, or the land frontiers at Ceuta and Melilla; to renew it, the main AF office is at 59 Bd Bordeaux, Casablanca (ⓣ0522 484156 or 7).

Parking

Parking in almost any town, you will find a *gardien de voitures*, usually licensed by local authorities to look after cars, and claiming a couple of dirhams by way of parking fees. Alternatively, most of the larger hotels in the Ville Nouvelle quarters of cities have parking spaces (and occasionally garaging). It's always worth paying for a *gardien* or parking in a garage, as new or well-looked-after cars attract a certain level of vandalism. Red and white striped kerbs mean no parking is allowed.

By motorbike

Motorcyclists find Morocco has all the major attractions sought by the enthusiast. If you have never taken a bike abroad before and want to go to Morocco, seriously consider going with a group. H-C Travel in the UK (ⓦwww.hctravel.com), Moto Adventures in Andorra (ⓦwww.motoaventures.com) and Wilderness Wheels in Ouarzazate (ⓦwww.wildernesswheels.com) offer off-road and trailbiking packages. For those on their own, the following are some practical tips to help organize a trip. Our comments on driving (pp.38–39) also apply to motorcyclists.

Renting a motorbike

There is a fair bit of bureaucracy involved in taking a motorbike to Morocco. One way of getting around the hassles is to **rent a motorbike** there (see p.379, p.427 & p.495).

If you take your own motorbike, you will need **special insurance**. Most companies, especially those based outside Europe, will not cover motorcycling as part of a holiday overseas, particularly when off-road riding is contemplated or inevitable (as it often is in Morocco). You'll have to shop around and remember to take the policy with you, together with your bike registration certificate, biker's licence and International Driving Permit. Even large insurance companies don't give clear answers about "**Green Cards**" for motorcycling in Morocco and do not understand that you may encounter up to a dozen police checks a day.

When **entering Morocco**, try to arrive as early in the day as possible. If you are a lone traveller and speak neither Arabic nor French, you may be left queuing until those without queries have been dealt with. If the office then closes, you may have to return the next morning. In these circumstances, it might be worth investing in a tout who, for a fee, will take your papers to a friendly officer. It's also worth picking up a couple of (free) extra immigration forms for the return journey.

What to take and when to go

Don't take a model of bike likely to be unfamiliar in Morocco. It's worth taking cables and levers, inner tubes, puncture repair kit, tyre levers, pump, fuses, plugs, chain, washable air filter, cable ties, good tape and a tool kit. For riding off-road, take knobbly tyres and rim locks, brush guards, metal number plate and bashplate. In winter, take tough fabric outer clothing. In summer, carry lighter-weight clothing, wool pullovers and waterproofs. Drying out leathers takes a long time. In the south, the heat in summer can be overwhelming, making travelling a far from enjoyable experience.

Cycling

Cycling – and particularly **mountain biking** – is becoming an increasingly popular pursuit for Western travellers to Morocco. The country's regular roads are well maintained and by European standards very quiet, while the extensive network of **pistes** – dirt tracks – makes for exciting mountain-bike terrain, leading you into areas otherwise accessible only to trekkers or four-wheel drive expeditions.

Regular roads are generally surfaced (*goudronné* or *revêtue*) but narrow, and you will often have to get off the tarmac to make way for traffic. Beware also of open land-drains close to the roadsides, and loose gravel on the bends.

Cycling on **pistes**, mountain bikes come into their own with their "tractor" tyres and wide, stabilizing handlebars. There are few *pistes* that could be recommended on a regular tourer. By contrast, some intrepid mountain bikers cover footpaths in the High Atlas, though for the less than super-fit this is extremely heavy going. Better, on the whole, to stick to established *pistes* – many of which are covered by local trucks, which you can pay for a ride if your legs (or your bike) give out.

Getting your bike to Morocco

Most **airlines** – even charters – carry bikes free of charge, so long as they don't push your baggage allowance over the weight limit. When buying a ticket, register your intention of taking your bike and check out the airline's conditions. They will generally require you to invert the handlebars, remove the pedals, and deflate the tyres; some provide or sell a cardboard **box** to enclose the bike, as protection for other passengers' luggage as much as for the bike; you are, however, unlikely to be offered a box for the return journey. A useful alternative, offering little protection but at least ensuring nothing gets lost, is to customize an industrial nylon sack, adding a drawstring at the neck.

If you plan to cross over **by ferry to Morocco**, things couldn't be simpler. You ride on with the motor vehicles (thus avoiding the long queues of foot passengers) and the bike is secure during the voyage. At time of writing, bicycles travel for free on Trasmediterranea ferries from Algeciras to Ceuta and Málaga or Almería to Melilla but not on Comanav services from Sète to Tangier or Nador. On Algeciras–Tangier ferries, you in theory pay the same rate as for a motorbike, but in practice they often allow bicycles on for free, though this cannot be guaranteed.

Bicycles and local transport

Cycling around Morocco, you can make use of local transport to supplement your own wheels. **Buses** will generally carry bikes on the roof. CTM usually charges around 10dh per bike – make sure you get a ticket. On other lines it's very much up to you to negotiate with the driver and/or baggage porter (who will probably expect at least 5dh). If you're riding and exhausted, you can usually flag down private-line buses (but not usually CTM services) on the road.

Some **grands taxis** also agree to carry bikes, if they have space on a rack. You may have to pay for this, but of course you can haggle. In mountain or desert areas, you can have your bike carried with you on **truck or transit services** (see p.37). Prices for this are negotiable, but should not exceed your own passenger fare.

Bikes are carried on **trains** for a modest handling fee, though it's not really worth the hassle. They have to be registered in advance as baggage and won't necessarily travel on the same train as you (though they will usually turn up within a day).

Accommodation

Accommodation doesn't present any special problems. The cheaper **hotels** will almost always let you keep your bike in your room – and others will find a disused basement or office for storage. It's almost essential to do this, as much to deter unwelcome tampering as theft, especially if you have a curiosity-inviting mountain bike. At **campsites**, there's usually a *gardien* on hand to keep an eye on your bike, or stow it away in his chalet.

Routes

Rewarding areas for biking include:
Tizi n'Test (High Atlas): Asni to Ijoukak, and an excursion to Tin Mal.
Asni to Setti Fatma (High Atlas: Ourika Valley) and beyond if you have a mountain bike.
Northern and Western Middle Atlas (well-watered side).
Djebel Sarhro and Djebel Bani: a choice of good east–west Anti-Atlas routes.

In summer it wouldn't be a good idea to go much beyond the Atlas, though given cooler winter temperatures, rewarding long routes exist in the **southern oasis routes**, such as Ouarzazate to Zagora or Ouarzazate to Tinerhir, and the desert routes down to Er Rachidia, Erfoud and Rissani.

See box, p.405 for more on mountain biking in the High Atlas.

Repairs

Most towns have **repair shops** in their Medina quarters, used to servicing local bikes and mopeds. They may not have spare parts for your make of bike, but can usually sort out some kind of temporary solution. It is worth bringing with you **spare spokes** (and tool), plus **brake blocks** and **cable**, as the mountain descents can take it out on a bike. **Tyres** and **tubes** can generally be found for tourers, though if you have anything fancy, best bring at least one spare, too.

Obviously, before setting out, you should make sure that your brakes are in good order, renew bearings, etc, and ensure that you have decent quality (and condition) tyres.

Problems and rewards

All over Morocco, and particularly in rural areas, there are stray, wild and semi-cared-for **dogs**. A cyclist pedalling past with feet and wheels spinning seems to send at least half of them into a frenzied state. Normally, cycling in an equally frenzied state is the best defence, but on steep ascents and off-road this isn't always possible. In these situations, keep the bike between you and the dog, and use your pump or a shower from your water bottle as defence. If you do get bitten, a rabies inoculation is advisable.

Another factor to be prepared for is your susceptibility to the unwanted attentions of local people. Small **children** will often stand in the road to hinder your progress, or even chase after you in gangs and throw stones. Your attitude is important: be friendly, smile, and maintain strong eye contact. On no account attempt to mete out your own discipline: small children always have big brothers.

The heat and the long stretches of dead straight road across arid, featureless plains – the main routes to (or beyond) the mountain ranges – can all too easily drain your energy. Additionally, public **water** is very rare – there are few roadside watering places, and towns and villages can be a long way apart.

Despite all this, cycling in Morocco can be an extremely rewarding experience; as one of our correspondents put it: "I felt an extra intimacy with the country by staying close to it, rather than viewing it from car or bus windows. And I experienced unrivalled generosity, from cups of tea offered by policemen at roadside checkpoints to a full-blown breakfast banquet from a farming family whose dog had savaged my leg. People went out of their way to give me advice, food, drink and lifts, and not once did I feel seriously threatened. Lastly, the exhilaration I felt on some of the mountain descents, above all the Tizi n'Test in the High Atlas, will remain with me forever. I was not an experienced cycle tourer when I arrived in Morocco, but the grandeur of the scenery helped carry me over the passes."

City transport

You'll spend most time exploring Moroccan cities on foot. The alleys of the old Medina quarters, where the sights and souks are, will rarely accommodate more than a donkey. In the newer quarters, you may want to make use of city taxis and occasionally a bus. In the new city quarters, you should be aware that pedestrian crossings don't count for very much, except perhaps at junctions "controlled" by traffic lights. And even then, bikes and mopeds pay scant attention to traffic lights showing red.

Petits taxis, usually Fiats or Simcas, carry up to three passengers and (unlike grands taxis) can only operate within city limits. All petits taxis should have meters, and you should insist that they use them. Failing that, you will need to bargain for a price – either before you get in (wise to start off with) or by simply presenting the regular fare when you get out. If you are a lone passenger, your taxi driver may pick up one or two additional passengers en route, each of whom will pay the full fare for their journey, as of course will you. This is standard practice.

Don't be afraid to argue with the driver if you feel you're being unreasonably overcharged. During the daytime, you should pay what is on the meter. After 8pm, standard fares rise by fifty percent. Tips are not expected, but of course always appreciated. Taxis from airports run at fixed rates, which may be on display at the airport taxi rank.

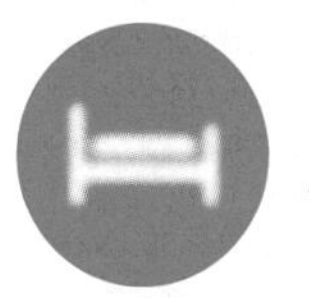

Accommodation

Hotels in Morocco are cheap, good value, and usually pretty easy to find. There can be a shortage of places in the major cities and resorts (Tangier, Fes, Marrakesh and Agadir) in August, and in Rabat or Casablanca when there's a big conference on. Other times, you should be able to pick from a wide range.

In winter, one thing worth checking for in a hotel is **heating** – nights can get cold, even in the south (and especially in the desert), and since bedding is not always adequate, a hotel with heating can be a boon. It's always, in any case, a good idea to ask to see your room before you check in.

Unclassified hotels

Unclassified (*non-classé*) hotels, (price codes ❶ and ❷), are often in the older parts of cities – the walled Medinas – and are almost always the cheapest accommodation options. They have the additional advantage of being at the heart of things: where you'll want to spend most of your time, and where all the sights and markets are concentrated. The disadvantages are that the Medinas can at first appear daunting – with their mazes of narrow lanes and blind alleys – and that the hotels themselves can be, at worst, dirty flea traps with tiny, windowless cells and half-washed sheets. At their best, if well-kept, they're fine, in

Accommodation price codes

Our hotel price codes are based on the rate for the cheapest double room in high season (usually June– Sept), for bed only, without breakfast (unless specified in the text as BB), and including local taxes.

For places that offer **dorm beds**, rates per person are given in dirhams.

- ❶ 99dh or under (under £8/ $13/€9)
- ❷ 100–199dh (£8-16/ $13-26/ €9-18)
- ❸ 200–349dh (£16-28/$26-46/€18-30)
- ❹ 350–499dh (£28-40/$46-65/€30-44)
- ❺ 500–699dh (£40-56/$65-92/€44-61)
- ❻ 700–999dh (£56-80/$92-131/€61-88)
- ❼ 1000–1499dh (£80-120/$131-196/€88-132)
- ❽ 1500–2499dh (£120-199/$196-327/€132-219)
- ❾ 2500dh or over (£199/$327/€219 or over)

traditional buildings with whitewashed rooms round a central patio.

One other minus point for unclassified Medina hotels is that they sometimes have a problem with **water**. Most of the Medinas remain substantially unmodernized, and some cheap hotels are without hot water, with squat toilets that can be pretty disgusting. On the plus side, there is usually a hammam (Turkish bath – see box opposite) nearby.

Classified hotels

Classified (*classé*) hotels are most likely to be found in a town's **Ville Nouvelle** – the "new" or administrative quarter. They are allowed, regardless of **star-rating**, to set their own prices – and to vary them according to season and demand. Prices should be on display at reception.

For Western-style standards of comfort, you need to look, on the whole, at **four-star hotels** (usually price codes ❺ to ❼). But even here, you are advised to check what's on offer. The plumbing, heating and lighting are sometimes unreliable; restaurants are often closed and swimming pools empty. Hotels in this price category are particularly likely to offer discounted and promotional rates off-season, and will almost always be cheaper if booked through a travel agent on line or abroad than at the "rack rates" offered to travellers who just turn up. One safe but boring option at this level is the *Ibis Moussafir* chain (Ⓦwww.ibishotel.com), whose hotels are almost always next to train stations, rather characterless and almost all identical, but comfortable, efficient and good value.

Hotels accorded the **five-star-luxury rating**, (invariably price code ❽ or ❾) can be very stylish, often in a historic conversion (most famously the *Hôtel la Mamounia* in Marrakesh and the *Palais Jamaï* in Fes) or in a modern building with a splendid pool and all the international creature comforts, but Moroccan five-star hotels are more like four-stars elsewhere, service is frequently amateurish by Western standards, and staff ill-trained and unprofessional; this is especially the case in establishments that cater mainly for tour groups.

In the Spanish enclaves of **Ceuta and Melilla**, accommodation at the lower end of the spectrum costs about twice as much as it does in Morocco proper, with a double room in the cheapest *pensiones* at around €30–35. At the top end of the scale, prices tend to be much the same as they are in Morocco, with four-star hotels charging around €90–125.

Riads

Morocco's trendiest accommodation option is in a **riad** or **maison d'hôte**. Strictly speaking, a riad is a house built around a patio garden – in fact, the word *riad* correctly refers to the garden rather than the house – while *maison d'hôte* is French for "guest house". The two terms are both used, to some extent interchangeably, for a residential house done up to rent out to tourists, but a riad is generally more stylish and expensive, while a *maison d'hôte* is likely to be less chic and more homely. In a riad, it is often possible to rent the whole house.

The riad craze started in Marrakesh, and quickly spread to Fes and Essaouira. Since then it has gone nationwide and almost every town with tourists now has riads too. Even the Atlas mountains and the southern oases are dotted with them, and there appears to be no shortage of takers.

Most riads are eighteenth- or nineteenth-century **Medina town-houses** which have been bought and refurbished by Europeans or prosperous Moroccans (often Moroccans who have been living in Europe). Some of them are very stylishly done out, most have roof terraces, some have plunge pools or jacuzzis, pretty much all offer en-suite rooms, and breakfast is usually included in the room price. The best riads have a landlord or landlady who is constantly in attendance and stamps their personality on the place,

However, the sudden popularity of riads has attracted a fair few amateur property developers, some of whom invest minimum money in the hope of maximum returns. Before you take a riad therefore, even more than with a hotel, it is always best to give it a preliminary once-over. Riads may be more expensive than hotels with a similar level of comfort, but at the top of the market, they can be a lot classier than a run-of-the-mill five-star hotel.

Hammams

The absence of hot showers in some of the cheapest Medina hotels is not such a disaster. Throughout all the Medina quarters, you'll find local **hammams**. A hammam is a Turkish-style steam bath, with a succession of rooms from cool to hot, and endless supplies of hot and cold water, which you fetch in buckets. The usual procedure is to find a piece of floor space in the hot room, surround it with as many buckets of water as you feel you need, and lie in the heat to sweat out the dirt from your pores before scrubbing it off. A plastic bowl is useful for scooping the water from the buckets to wash with. You can also order a massage, in which you will be allowed to sweat, pulled about a bit to relax your muscles, and then rigorously scrubbed with a rough flannel glove (*kiis*). Alternatively, buy a *kiis* and do it yourself. For many Moroccan women, who would not drink in a café or bar, the hammam is a social gathering place, in which tourists are made very welcome too. Indeed, hammams turn out to be a highlight for many women travellers, and an excellent way to make contact with Moroccan women.

Several hammams are detailed in the text, but the best way of finding one is always to ask at the hotel where you're staying. You will often, in fact, need to be led to a hammam, since they are usually unmarked and can be hard to find. In some towns, you find a separate hammam for women and men; at others the same establishment offers different hours for each sex – usually mornings and evenings for men, afternoons (typically noon to 6pm) for women.

For both sexes, there's more modesty than you might perhaps expect: it's customary for men (always) and women (generally, though bare breasts are acceptable) to bathe in swimming costume (or underwear), and to undress facing the wall. Women may be also surprised to find their Moroccan counterparts completely shaven and may (in good humour) be offered this service; there's no embarrassment in declining.

As part of the Islamic tradition of cleanliness and ablutions, hammams sometimes have a religious element, and non-Muslims may not be welcome (or allowed in) to those built alongside mosques, particularly on Thursday evenings, before the main weekly service on Friday. On the whole, though, there are no restrictions against *Nisara* ("Nazarenes", or Christians).

Finally, don't forget to bring soap and shampoo (though these are sometimes sold at hammams), and a towel (these are sometimes rented, but can be a bit dubious). Moroccans often bring a plastic mat to sit on, too, as the floors can get a bit clogged. Mats can be bought easily enough in any town. Most Moroccans use a pasty, olive oil-based soap (*sabon bildi*), sold by weight in Medina shops. On sale at the same shops, you'll find *kiis* flannel gloves, a fine mud (*ghasoul*), used by some instead of shampoo, pumice stones (*hazra*) for removing dead skin, and alum (*chebba*), used as an antiperspirant and to stop shaving cuts from bleeding.

Hostels

Morocco has thirteen *Auberges de Jeunesse* run by its YHA, the *Fédération Royale Marocaine des Auberges de Jeunesse* (Ⓣ0522 470952, Ⓔfrmaj1@menara.ma). Most are clean and reasonably well run, and charges vary from 30dh (£2.50/$3.60) to 70dh (£5.85/$8.35) per person per night in a dorm; most have private rooms too. Hostelling International (HI) membership cards are not required but you may have to pay a little extra if you do not have one. The hostels are located at Asni (High Atlas), Azrou (Middle Atlas), Casablanca, Chefchaouen, Fes, Goulmima, Laayoune (Western Sahara), Marrakesh, Meknes, Ouarzazate, Rabat, Rissani, and Tinerhir. Most are reviewed in the relevant sections of the guide; the one in Casablanca recommends booking in advance. Further information on Moroccan youth hostels can be found on the Hostelling International website at Ⓦwww.hihostels.com or in the *International Youth Hostels Guide* (£9.99), often available in public libraries.

Refuges and gîtes d'étape

In the Djebel Toubkal area of the High Atlas mountains, the Club Alpin Français (CAF; 50 Bd Sidi Abderrahmane, Beauséjour, Casablanca ⓣ0522 987519, ⓦwww.ffcam.fr) maintain five huts, or refuges (at Imlil, Oukaïmeden, Tachdirt, Tazaghart and Toubkal) equipped for mountaineers and trekkers. These provide bunks or bedshelves for sleeping at 50–120dh (£4–£9.75/$6–14.30) per person, with discounts for members of CAF or its affiliates. Some refuges can provide meals and/or cooking facilities.

Also in trekking areas, a number of locals offer rooms in their houses: such places are known as **gîtes d'étape**. Current charges are around 80–120dh per person per night, with meals for around 60–75dh.

Camping

Campsites are to be found at intervals along most of the developed Moroccan coast and in most towns or cities of any size. They vary in price and facilities, with cheap sites charging around 10dh (85p/$1.20) per person, plus a similar amount for a tent or a car, and 15–20dh for a caravan or campervan; cheap sites often have quite basic washing and toilet facilities, and usually charge 7–10dh for a hot shower. More upmarket places may offer better facilities and even swimming pools, and cost about twice as much, sometimes more. Comprehensive, and often highly critical reviews of Morocco's campsites, in French, can be found in Jacques Gandini's *Campings du Maroc et de Mauritanie: Guide Critique* (Broché, France), which is available at better Moroccan bookshops, such as Marrakesh's Librairie Chatr (see p.379), and sometimes at campsite shops.

Campsites don't tend to provide much security, and you should never leave valuables unattended. Camping outside official sites, this obviously applies even more, and if you want to do this, it's wise to ask at a house if you can pitch your tent alongside – you'll usually get a hospitable response. If you're trekking in the Atlas, it is often possible to pay someone to act as a *gardien* for your tent. In the south especially, and particularly in the winter, campsites are not much used by backpackers with tents, but rather by retired Europeans in campervans seeking the sun.

If travelling in a campervan, you can often park up somewhere with a *gardien*, who will keep an eye on things for a small tip (usually 20dh per night). Failing that, you may be able to park outside a police station (*commissariat*). In the north of the country, at Larache, Kenitra and Malabata (near Tangier), there are *Aires de Repose*, which are rest areas for tourist coaches, with toilets, showers, a restaurant and *gardien*. There's no fee for parking your camper here or using the facilities, but it is usual to pay a contribution of around 20dh to the *gardien* if you stay overnight.

Food and drink

Basic Moroccan meals may begin with a thick, very filling soup – most often the spicy, bean and pasta *harira*. Alternatively, you might start with a salad (often very finely chopped), or have this as a side dish with your main course, typically a plateful of kebabs – either *brochettes* (small pieces of lamb on a skewer) or *kefta*, (minced lamb). A few hole-in-the wall places specialize in soup, which they sell by the bowlful all day long – such places are usually indicated by a pile of soup bowls at the front. As well as *harira*, and especially for breakfast, some places sell a thick pea soup called *bisara*, topped with olive oil.

Alternatively, you could go for a **tajine**, essentially a stew, steam-cooked slowly in an earthenware dish with a conical earthenware lid. Like "casserole", the term "tajine" actually refers to the dish and lid rather than the food. Classic tajines include lamb/mutton with prunes and almonds, or chicken with olives and lemon. Less often, you may get a fish or vegetable tajine, or a tajine of meatballs topped with eggs.

Kebabs or a tajine usually cost little more than 30dh (£2.50/$3.60) at one of the hole-in-the-wall places in the Medina, with their two or three tables. You are not expected to bargain for cooked food, but prices can be lower in such places if you enquire how much things cost before you start eating. There is often no menu – or just a board written in Arabic only.

If you're looking for **breakfast or a snack**, you can buy a half-**baguette** – plus butter and jam, cheese or eggs, if you want – from many bread or grocery stores, and take it into a café to order a coffee. Many cafés, even those which serve no other food, may offer a breakfast of bread, butter and jam (which is also what you'll get in most hotels), or maybe an omelette. Some places also offer soup, such as *harira*, with bread, and others have stalls outside selling by weight traditional griddle breads such as *harsha* (quite heavy with a gritty crust), *melaoui* or *msimmen* (sprinkled with oil, rolled out thin, folded over and rolled out again several times, like an Indian *paratha*) and *baghira* (full of holes like a very thin English crumpet). If that is not sufficient, supplementary foods you could buy include dates or olives, yoghurt, or soft white cheese (*ejben*).

Restaurant meals

More expensive dishes, available in some of the Medina cafés as well as in the dearer restaurants, include **fish**, particularly on the coast, and **chicken** (*poulet*), either spit-roasted (*rôti*) or in a tajine with lemon and olives (*poulet aux olives et citron*). You will sometimes find **pastilla**, too, a succulent pigeon or chicken pie, prepared with filo pastry dusted with sugar and cinnamon; it is a particular speciality of Fes.

And, of course, there's **couscous**, the most famous Moroccan dish, Berber in origin and based on a huge bowl of steamed semolina piled high with vegetables and mutton, chicken, or occasionally fish. Restaurant couscous can be disappointing as there is no real tradition of going out to eat in Morocco, and this is a dish that's traditionally prepared at home, especially on Friday or for a special occasion.

At festivals, which are always good for interesting food, and at the most expensive tourist restaurants, you may also come across **mechoui** – roast lamb, which may even take the form of a whole sheep roasted on a spit. In Marrakesh particularly, another speciality is **tanjia**, which is jugged beef or lamb, cooked very slowly in the embers of a hammam furnace.

Dessert may consist of a pastry, or a crème caramel, or possibly yoghurt, which is often – even in cheap places – the restaurant's own. Otherwise you may get fruit, either an orange, or perhaps a fruit salad.

Restaurants are typically open noon to 3pm for lunch, and 7 to 11pm for dinner, though cheaper places may be open in the morning and between times too. In the text we have indicated what kind of **price range** a restaurant falls into. At restaurants described as "cheap", a typical meal (starter, main course and dessert) will cost less than 100dh (£8.50/$12). At places described as "moderate", you can expect to pay 100–160dh (£8.50–13.50/$12–19), while anywhere likely to cost over 160dh (£13.50/$19) is described as "expensive". Places that don't display prices are likely to overcharge you unless you check the price before ordering.

Eating Moroccan style

Eating in local cafés, or if **invited to a home**, you may find yourself using your hands rather than a knife and fork. Muslims eat only with the **right hand** (the left is used for the toilet), and you should do likewise. Hold the bread between the fingers and use your thumb as a scoop; it's often easier to discard the soft centre of the bread and to use the crust only – as you will see many Moroccans do. Eating from a **communal plate** at someone's home, it is polite to take only what is immediately in front of you, unless specifically offered a piece of meat by the host.

Vegetarian eating

Vegetarianism is met with little comprehension in most of Morocco, though restaurants in some places are becoming aware that tourists may be vegetarian, and many places do now offer a meat-free tajine or couscous. In Marrakesh there is even a vegetarian restaurant (see p.374), and pizzas are usually available in large towns. Otherwise, aside from omelettes and sandwiches, menus don't present very obvious choices. *Bisara* (pea soup), a common breakfast dish, should be meat-free, but *harira* (bean soup) may or may not be made with meat stock, while most foods are cooked in animal fats. It is possible to say "I'm a vegetarian" (*ana nabaati* in Arabic, or *je suis vegetarien/vegetarienne* in French), but you may not be understood; to reinforce the point, you could perhaps add *la akulu lehoum* (*wala hout*) in Arabic, or *je ne mange aucune sorte de viande* (*ni poisson*), both of which mean "I don't eat any kind of meat (or fish)".

If you are a very strict vegetarian or vegan, it may be worth bringing some basic provisions (such as yeast extract, peanut butter and veggie stock cubes) and a small Camping Gaz stove and pan – canisters are cheap and readily available, and in some cheap hotels, guests may cook in their rooms.

The most difficult situations are those in which you are invited to eat at someone's house. You may find people give you meat when you have specifically asked for vegetables because they don't understand that you object to eating meat, and you may decide that it's more important not to offend someone showing you kindness than to be strict about your abstinence. Picking out vegetables from a meat tajine won't offend your hosts, but declining the dish altogether may end up with the mother/sister/wife in the kitchen getting the flak. One possible way to avoid offence when invited to a home (or to explain your needs in a restaurant) is to say that vegetarianism is part of your religion (this is normal in Hinduism and Buddhism for example), a concept that most Moroccans should have no problems with.

Fruit

Morocco is surprisingly rich in seasonal **fruits**. In addition to the various kinds of **dates** – sold all year but at their best fresh from the October harvests – there are grapes, melons, strawberries, peaches and figs, all advisably washed before eaten. Or for a real thirst-quencher (and a good cure for a bad stomach), you can have quantities of **prickly pear**, cactus fruit, peeled for you in the street for a couple of dirhams in season.

Tea, coffee and soft drinks

The national drink is **mint tea** (*atay deeyal naanaa* in Arabic, *thé à la menthe* in French, "Whisky Marocain" as locals boast), Chinese gunpowder green tea flavoured with sprigs of mint (*naanaa* in Arabic: the gift of Allah) and sweetened with a large amount of sugar, often from a sugar loaf (you can ask for it with little or no sugar – *shweeya soukar* or *ble soukar*). In winter, Moroccans often add wormwood (*chiba* in Arabic, *absinthe* in French) to their tea "to keep out the cold". You can also get black tea (*atai ahmar* in Arabic, *thé rouge* in French, literally meaning "red tea") – inevitably made with the ubiquitous Lipton's tea bags, a brand fondly believed by Moroccans to be typically English. **The main herbal infusion is** verbena (*verveine or louiza*).

Also common at cafés and street stalls are a range of wonderful fresh-squeezed **juices**: orange juice (*jus d'orange* in French, *'asir burtuqal* in Arabic – if you don't want sugar in it, remember to say so), almond milk (*jus d'amande* or *'asir louze*), banana "juice", meaning milk-shake (*jus des bananes* or *'asir mooz*) and apple milk-shake (*jus de pomme* or *'asir tufah*). Also common is *'asir panaché*, a mixed fruit milkshake often featuring raisins. *Leben* – soured milk – is tastier than it sounds, and does wonders for an upset stomach.

Mineral water is usually referred to by brand name, ubiquitously the still Sidi Harazem or Sidi Ali (some people claim to be able to tell one from the other), or the naturally sparkling Oulmès. The Coca-Cola company markets filtered, processed non-mineral water in bottles under the brand name *Ciel*.

Coffee (*café*) is best in French-style cafés – either *noir* (black), *cassé* (with a drop of milk), or *au lait* (with a lot of milk). Instant coffee is known, like teabag tea, after its brand – in this case Nescafé.

Lastly, do not take risks with **milk**: buy it fresh and drink it fresh. If it smells remotely off, don't touch it.

Wine and beer

As an Islamic nation, Morocco gives **drinking alcohol** a low profile, and it is not generally possible to buy alcohol in city Medinas. Ordinary **bars** are very much **all-male preserves**, in which women may feel uneasy (bartenders may occasionally be female, but female Moroccan customers are likely to be on the game), but upmarket bars – especially in Marrakesh or Casablanca or in tourist hotels – are usually fine. On the drinks front, Moroccan **wines** can be palatable enough, if a little heavy for drinking without a meal. The best to be found is the pinkish red *Clairet de Meknès*, made purposefully light in French claret style. *Beauvallon* is another good one, but usually reserved for export. Other varieties worth trying include the strong red *Cabernet*, and *Ksar*, *Guerrouane* and *Siraoua*, which are also red, the rosé *Gris de Boulaoune* and the dry white *Spécial Coquillages*.

Those Moroccans who drink in bars tend to stick to **beer**, usually the local *Stork* or *Flag*. *Flag* from Fes is held by many to be superior to the version brewed in Casablanca (the label will tell you which it is). The most popular foreign brand is *Heineken*, which is made under licence in Morocco.

The media

British dailies and the *International Herald Tribune* are available at some newsstands in city centres and tourist resorts. Failing that, you can always log onto the website of your favourite newspaper from home.

Newspapers and magazines

The **Moroccan press** has a range of papers in French and Arabic, but news coverage, especially of international news, is weak. Of the **French-language** papers, the most accessible is the pro-government daily, *Le Matin* (Ⓦwww.lematin.ma). Others include *L'Opinion* (Istiqlal party; Ⓦwww.lopinion.ma), *Maroc Soir* (independent evening daily), *L'Economiste*, (independent; Ⓦwww.leconomiste.com), and *Al Bayane* (communist; Ⓦwww.albayane.ma). Periodicals include *Maroc-Hebdo* (Ⓦwww.maroc-hebdo.press.ma), *La Vie Eco* (Ⓦwww.lavieeco.com), and the Time/Newsweek-style news magazine *Tel-Quel* (Ⓦwww.telquel-online.com). Among **Arabic** daily newspapers, *El Alam* backs the Istiqlal party, and *El Ittihad el Ichtiraki* supports the nominally socialist USFP party.

In addition to these, Morocco has a number of football magazines, women's magazines and other publications in French, as well as the excellent Francophone African news magazine, *Jeune Afrique* (Ⓦwww.jeuneafrique.com). Also worth a peruse is the English-language online magazine *Tingis* (Ⓦwww.tingismagazine.com), billed as "an American-Moroccan magazine of ideas and culture".

Radio

The **BBC** have cut World Service short-wave broadcasts to North Africa, but with a deft twiddle of the dial you may be able to pick up short-wave broadcasts for West Africa, or MW broadcasts to Europe; programme listings can be found online at Ⓦwww.bbc.co.uk/worldservice. You can also pick up **Voice of America** during the day on 15,580 KHz, at night on 909 or 1530 KHz – see

Ⓦwww.voa.gov for full frequency and programme listings.

Television

Most of the pricier hotels receive **satellite TV** – CNN, the French TV5, and occasionally UK Sky channels. In the north of the country you can also get Spanish TV stations and, in Tangier, English-language **Gibraltar** TV. The independent Qatari news channel Al Jazeera is a major source of news for people in Morocco (many cafés show it), and you may even be able to get it in English if you have access to cable or satellite, but it is unfortunately not obtainable on terrestrial TV.

Morocco's own two TV channels broadcast in Arabic, but include some French programmes – plus news bulletins in Arabic, French, Spanish and, more recently, Berber.

Festivals

Morocco abounds in holidays and festivals, both national and local, and coming across one can be the most enjoyable experience of travel in the country – with the chance to witness music and dance, as well as special regional foods and market souks. Perhaps surprisingly, this includes Ramadan, when practising Muslims, including most Moroccans, fast from sunrise to sunset for a month, but when nights are good times to hear music and share in hospitality.

Ramadan

Ramadan, the ninth month of the Islamic calendar, commemorates the first revelation of the Koran to Muhammad. Most people observe the fast; indeed Moroccans are forbidden by law from publicly disrespecting it, and a few people are jailed for this each year.

The fast involves abstention from food, drink, smoking and sex during daylight throughout the month. Most local cafés and restaurants close during the day, and many close up altogether and take a month's holiday. Smokers in particular get edgy towards the month's end, and it is in some respects an unsatisfactory time to travel: efficiency drops, drivers fall asleep at the wheel (hence airline pilots are excused fasting), and guides and muleteers are unwilling to go off on treks, and when the fast ends at sunset, almost regardless of what they are doing, everybody stops to eat. The month-long closure of so many eating places can also make life difficult if you are dependent on restaurants.

But there is compensation in witnessing and becoming absorbed into the pattern of the fast. At sunset, signalled by the sounding of a siren, by the lighting of lamps on minarets, and in some places by a cannon shot, an amazing calm and sense of wellbeing fall on the streets. The fast is traditionally broken with a bowl of *harira* and some dates, a combination provided by many cafés and restaurants exactly at sunset. You will also see almsgiving (*zakat*) extended to offering *harira* to the poor and homeless.

After breaking their fast, everyone – in the cities at least – gets down to a night of celebration and **entertainment**. This takes different forms. If you can spend some time in Marrakesh during the month, you'll find the Djemaa el Fna square at its most active, with troupes of musicians, dancers and acrobats coming into the city for the occasion. In Rabat and Fes, there seem to be continuous promenades, with cafés and stalls staying open until 3am. Urban cafés provide venues for live music and singing, too, and in the southern towns and Berber villages you will often come across the ritualized *ahouaches* and *haidus* – circular, trance-like dances often involving whole communities.

Ramadan and Islamic holidays

Islamic religious holidays are calculated on the **lunar calendar**, so their dates rotate throughout the seasons (as does Ramadan's), losing about eleven days a year against the Western (Gregorian) calendar. Exact dates in the lunar calendar are impossible to predict – they are set by the Islamic authorities in Fes – but approximate dates for the next few years are:

	2010	2011	2012	2013	2014	2015
Aïd el Kebir	16 Nov	6 Nov	26 Oct	15 Oct	5 Oct	24 Sept
Moharem	7 Dec	27 Nov	15 Nov	5 Nov	15 Oct	25 Oct
Mouloud	26 Feb	16 Feb	5 Feb	24 Jan	14 Jan	3 Jan
1st Ramadan	11 Aug	1 Aug	20 July	9 July	29 June	18 June
Aïd es Seghir	10 Sept	30 Aug	19 Aug	8 Aug	29 July	18 July

Fêtes nationales

Secular *fêtes nationales* are tied to Western calendar dates:

January 1	New Year's Day
January 11	Anniversary of Istiqlal Manifesto (see p.576)
May 1	Labour Day
July 30	Feast of the Throne
August 14	Allegiance Day
August 20	King and People's Revolution Day
August 21	King's Birthday and Youth Day
November 6	Anniversary of the Green March (see p.579)
November 18	Independence Day

Aïd el Kebir and Aïd es Seghir are marked by a two-day **public holiday**, announced or ratified by the king on TV and radio the preceding day. On these, and on the secular *fêtes nationales* listed above, all banks, post offices and most shops are closed; transport is reduced, too, but never stops completely. The largest secular holiday is the **Feast of the Throne**, a colourful affair, celebrated throughout Morocco, with fireworks, parades and music over two to three days.

If you are a **non-Muslim** outsider you are not expected to observe Ramadan, but you should be sensitive about breaking the fast (particularly smoking) in public. In fact, the best way to experience Ramadan – and to benefit from its naturally purifying rhythms – is to enter into it. You may lack the faith to go without an occasional glass of water, and you'll probably have breakfast later than sunrise (it's often wise to buy supplies the night before), but it is worth an attempt.

Other Islamic holidays

Ramadan ends with the feast of **Aïd es Seghir** or **Aïd el Fitr**, a climax to the month's night-time festivities. Even more important is **Aïd el Kebir**, which celebrates the willingness of Abraham to obey God by sacrificing his son (Isaac in the Old Testament, but believed by Muslims to be his older son Ishmael). Aïd el Kebir is followed, about two months later, by **Moharem**, the Muslim new year.

Both *aïds* are traditional family gatherings. At Aïd el Kebir every household that can afford it will slaughter a sheep. You see them tethered everywhere, often on rooftops, for weeks prior to the event; after the feast, their skins can be seen being cured on the streets. On both *aïd* days, shops and restaurants close and buses don't run; on the following day, all transport is packed, as people return to the cities from their family homes.

The fourth main religious holiday is the **Mouloud**, the Prophet's birthday. This is widely observed, with a large number of moussems timed to take place in the weeks around it, and two particularly important moussems at Meknès (see p.192) and Salé (see p.294). There is also a music festival, **Ashorou**, which is held thirty days after Aïd el Kebir, when people gather to play whatever traditional instrument they feel capable of wielding, and the streets are full of music.

Moussems and ammougars

Moussems – or ammougars – held in honour of saints or *marabouts*, are local and predominantly rural affairs, and form the main religious and social celebrations of the year for most Moroccans, along with Aïd es Seghir and Aïd el Kebir.

Some of the smaller moussems amount to no more than a market day with religious overtones; others are essentially harvest festivals, celebrating a pause in agricultural labour after a crop has been successfully brought in, but a number have developed into substantial occasions – akin to Spanish fiestas – and a few have acquired national significance. If you are lucky enough to be here for one of the major events, you'll get the chance to witness Moroccan popular culture at its richest, with horseriding, music, singing and dancing, and of course eating and drinking.

There are enormous numbers of moussems. An idea of quite how many can be gathered from the frequency with which, travelling about the countryside, you see *koubbas* – the square, white-domed buildings covering a saint's tomb. Each of these is a potential focal point of a moussem, and any one region or town may have twenty to thirty separate annual moussems. Establishing when they take place, however, can be difficult for outsiders; most local people find out by word of mouth at the weekly souks. The most important annual moussems are listed in the box opposite, though some are also held around religious occasions such as **Mouloud** (see p.51), which change date each year according to the lunar calendar.

The **accommodation** situation will depend on whether the moussem is in the town or countryside. In the country, the simplest solution is to take a tent and camp – there is no real objection to anyone camping wherever they please during a moussem. In small towns there may be hotels – and locals will rent out rooms in their houses. **Food** is never a problem, with dozens of traders setting up stalls, though it is perhaps best to stick to the grills, as stalls may not have access to running water for cleaning.

Aims and functions

The ostensible aim of the moussem is religious: to obtain blessing, or *baraka*, from the saint and/or to thank God for the harvest. But the social and cultural dimensions are equally important. Moussems provide an opportunity for country people to escape the monotony of their hard working lives in several days of festivities. They may provide the year's single opportunity for friends or families from different villages to meet. Harvest and farming problems are discussed, as well as family matters – marriage in particular – as people get the chance to sing, dance, eat and pray together.

Music and singing are always major components of a moussem and locals will often bring tape recorders to provide sounds for the rest of the year. Sufi brotherhoods have a big presence, and each bring their own distinct style of music, dancing and dress.

Moussems also operate as **fairs**, or markets, attracting people from a much wider area than the souk and giving a welcome injection of cash into the local economy, with traders and entertainers doing good business, and householders renting out rooms.

At the **spiritual level**, people seek to improve their standing with God through prayer, as well as the less orthodox channels of popular belief. Central to this is *baraka*, good fortune, which can be obtained by intercession of the saint. Financial contributions are made and these are used to buy a gift, or *hedia*, usually a large carpet, which is then taken in procession to the saint's tomb; it is deposited there for the local *shereefian* families, the descendants of the saint, to dispose of as they wish. Country people may seek to obtain *baraka* by attaching a garment or tissue to the saint's tomb and leaving it overnight to take home after the festival.

The procession taking the gift to the tomb is the high point of the more **religious** moussems, such as that of **Moulay Idriss in Fes**, where an enormous carpet is carried above the heads of the Sufi **brotherhoods**, each playing its own hypnotic music. Spectators and participants, giving themselves up to the music, may go into a trance. If you witness such events, it is best

Moussem calendar

February	**Tafraoute** Moussem to celebrate the almond harvest.
March	**Beni Mellal** Cotton harvest moussem.
May	**Moulay Bousselham** Moussem of Sidi Ahmed Ben Mansour.
	Berkane Harvest moussem for clementines.
	El Kelâa des Mgouna Rose festival to celebrate the new crop.
June	**Goulimine** Traditionally a camel traders' fair, elements of which remain.
	Tan Tan Moussem of Sidi Mohammed Ma el Ainin. Large-scale religious and commercial moussem. Saharan "Guedra" dance may be performed.
July	**Tetouan** Moussem of Moulay Abdessalem. A very religious, traditional occasion with a big turnout of local tribesmen. Impressive location on a flat mountain top south of the town.
	Sefrou Festival to celebrate the cherry harvest.
	Al Hoceima Festival to celebrate the bounty of the sea.
August	**Setti Fatma** Large and popular moussem in the Ourika valley, southeast of Marrakesh.
	Sefrou Moussem of Sidi Lahcen el Youssi, a seventeenth-century saint.
	El Jadida Moussem of Moulay Abdallah. Located about 9km west of the city at a village named after the saint. Features displays of horseriding, or fantasias.
	Tiznit Moussem of Sidi Ahmed ou Moussa. Primarily religious.
	Immouzer du Kandar Harvest moussem for apples and pears.
	Immouzer des Ida Outanane Week-long honey moussem.
September	**Chefchaouen** Moussem of Sidi Allal al Hadh. Located in the hills out of town.
	Moulay Idriss Zerhoun Moussem of Moulay Idriss. The largest religious moussem, but visitable only for the day as a non-Muslim. Impressive display by brotherhoods, and a highly charged procession of gifts to the saint's tomb. Also a large fantasia above town.
	Imilchil Marriage moussem. Set in the heart of the Atlas mountains, this is the most celebrated Berber moussem – traditionally the occasion of all marriages in the region, though today also a tourist event. In fact there now seem to be two moussems, with one laid on specifically for package tours from Marrakesh and Agadir; the real event is held in the last week in September or the first in October.
	Fes Moussem of Moulay Idriss II. The largest of the moussems held inside a major city, and involving a long procession to the saint's tomb. The Medina is packed out, however, and you will have a better view if you stand at Dar Batha or Place Boujeloud before the procession enters the Medina proper.
November	**Erfoud** Three-day date-harvest festival.
December	**Rafsaï** Olive harvest moussem.

to keep a low profile so as not to interfere with people trying to attain a trance-like state, and certainly don't take photographs.

Release through trance probably has a therapeutic aspect, and indeed some moussems are specifically concerned with **cures** of physical and psychiatric disorders. The saint's tomb is usually located near a freshwater spring, and the cure can simply be bathing in and drinking the water. Those suffering from physical ailments may also be treated at the moussem with herbal remedies, or by recitation of verses from the Koran. Koranic verses may also be written and placed in tiny receptacles fastened near the affected parts.

Sports and outdoor activities

Morocco offers magnificent trekking opportunities, impressive golf facilities, a couple of ski resorts (plus some adventurous off-piste skiing) and excellent fishing. The national sporting obsession is football; enthusiasts can join in any number of beach kick-about games, or watch local league and cup matches.

Trekking

Trekking is amongst the very best things Morocco has to offer. The High Atlas is one of the most rewarding mountain ranges in the world, and one of the least spoilt. A number of **long-distance Atlas routes** can be followed – even a "Grand Traverse" of the full range, but most people stick to **shorter treks** in the **Djebel Toubkal** area (see p.391; best in spring or autumn; conditions can be treacherous in winter). Other promising areas include the **Djebel Sirwa** (see p.510) **Western High Atlas** (see p.413) or in winter the **Djebel Sarhro** (see p.447) and **Tafraoute** region of the Anti-Atlas (see p.525). The **Middle Atlas** has much attractive walking too, in such places as **Tazzeka** (Taza; see p.168), the **Djebel Bou Iblane** range (see p.241) and around **Azrou** (see p.248).

For general **trekking practicalities**, see pp.396–397. For information about trekking **maps**, see p.71. A good source of trekking information is AMIS (Atlas Mountain Interactive Services; UK ⓣ01592/873 546), a small agency and consultancy run by Hamish Brown, author of the High Atlas chapter in this book.

Skiing

Morocco doesn't immediately spring to mind as a skiing destination, but the High Atlas mountains are reliably snow-covered from late January to early April, with good skiing at **Oukaïmeden** (see p.390), and even the Middle Atlas occasionally has enough snow for skiing, with a ski resort at **Mischliffen**. A third prospective ski centre at **Djebel Bou Iblane** in the eastern Middle Atlas (see p.241) is largely abandoned.

Off-piste skiing is popular in the High Atlas, particularly in the **Toubkal massif**, where the Toubkal Refuge (see p.398) is often full of groups. Most off-*piste* activity is ski mountaineering, but skinny skis (*langlauf*) are good in the Middle Atlas if there is snow, in which case the Azilal–Bou Goumez–Ighil Mgoun area is possible. **Snowboarding** is also gaining in popularity at Moroccan resorts. For further information on skiing and mountaineering, contact the Fédération Royale Marocaine du Ski et du Montagnisme (FRMSM; ⓣ0522 474979, ⓔfrmsn@hotmail.com).

Riding

The established base for **riding holidays** is *Résidence de la Roseraie* at **Ouirgane** on the Tizi n'Test road (see p.403), which runs trekking tours into the **High Atlas** (bring your own helmet). Another stable offering horseriding is REHA near Agadir (see p.499). UK-based travel firm Equitours (ⓦwww.equitour.co.uk) offers horseriding packages, and Best of Morocco (see p.32) is among operators offering stays and packages at *La Roseraie*, as well as **camel treks**.

Fishing

Morocco has an immense Atlantic (and small Mediterranean) **coastline**, with opportunities to arrange boat trips at Safi, Essaouira, Moulay Bousselham (near Asilah), Boujdour, Dakhla and elsewhere.

Inland, the **Middle Atlas** shelters beautiful **lakes** and **rivers**, many of them well stocked with trout. Good bases include **Azrou** (near the Aghmas lakes), **Ifrane** (near Zerrrouka), **Khenifra** (the Oum er Rbia River) and **Ouirgane** (the Nfis River). Pike are also to be found in some Middle Atlas lakes (such as Aguelmame Azizgza, near Khenifra), and a few of the huge artificial **barrages**, like **Bin el Ouidaine** (near Beni Mellal), are said to contain enormous bass.

Animal welfare

Animals – and especially pack animals – have a tough life in Morocco. The **Society for the Protection of Animals Abroad** (SPANA; ⓦwww.spana.org), works throughout North Africa to improve conditions for working donkeys and horses, replacing painful, old-style bits, employing local vets and technicians and running animal clinics. There are SPANA centres in Tangier, Rabat, Casablanca, Marrakesh (see p.381), Khémisset, Khenifra, Midelt, Had Ouled Frej (near El Jadida) and Chémaia (near Marrakesh); they also manage the birdwatching reserve at Sidi Bourhaba. All of these can be contacted or visited if you are interested or are concerned about animals you come across. The best initial contact address in Morocco is SPANA's administrative office in Temara (ⓣ0537 747209), 14km south of Rabat. The Society has a British office at 14 John St, London, WC1N 2EB ⓣ020/7831 3999, which can provide details of the Moroccan centres listed above.

For all fishing in the country, you need to take your own **equipment**. For coarse or fly fishing you need a **permit** from the Administration des Eaux et Fôrets at: 11 Rue Moulay Abdelaziz, Rabat ⓣ0537 762694; 25 Bd Roudani, Casablanca ⓣ0522 271598; or any regional office. For trout fishing, you are limited to the hours between 6am and noon; the season starts on March 31.

Water sports and swimming

Agadir has **sailing**, **yachting**, **windsurfing** and **diving**. Taghazoute, just to its north, has become something of a **surfing** village, with board rental and board repair shops and some great surfing sites (see p.500). There are lesser surfing centres at Sidi Ifni, Mirhleft, Kenitra, Bouznika Plage (between Rabat and Casablanca), El Jadida, Safi, and even Rabat. With your own transport, you could scout out remote places all the way down the coast. When they're working, all breaks can be busy in peak season (Oct–Feb), when deep lows come barrelling east across the mid-Atlantic. Wetsuit-wise, a good 3mm will cover winter months (although a thermal rash vest keeps things snug in Jan) and it's also worth bringing booties, unless you enjoy digging urchin spines out of your feet.

For **windsurfing**, the prime destination is **Essaouira**, which draws devotees year round. Online **weather information** for surfers and windsurfers can be found at ⓦwww.windguru.com/int.

The Atlantic can be very exposed, with crashing waves, and surfers, windsurfers and **swimmers** alike should beware of strong undertows. Inland, most towns of any size have a municipal **swimming pool**, but women especially should note that they tend to be the preserve of teenage boys. In the south, you'll be dependent on campsite pools or on those at the luxury hotels (which often allow outsiders to swim, either for a fee or if you buy drinks or a meal).

The High and Middle Atlas have also become a popular destination for **white-water rafting** and **kayaking** enthusiasts. One holiday firm specializing in these sports is Water by Nature (ⓦwww.waterbynature.com).

Golf

The British opened a golf course in Tangier as far back as 1917. Today the country has an international-level course at **Rabat** (see p.291), and eighteen-hole courses at **Mohammedia** (see p.296), **Marrakesh** (see p.380), **Tangier** (see p.103), **El Jadida** (see p.316); and nine-hole courses at **Agadir** (see p.496), **Ben Slimane** (Royal Golf, Av des FAR, BP 83, Ben Slimane ⓣ0522 271785), **Cabo Negro** (see p.103), **Casablanca** (see p.313), **Fes** (see p.236) and **Meknes** (see p.195. Further information on courses can be found online at ⓦwww.golftoday.co.uk/clubhouse/coursedir/world/morocco. Several tour operators (including Best of Morocco; see p.32) offer Moroccan golfing holidays.

Football (soccer)

Football is important in Morocco and the country is a growing force. The national side has made the World Cup finals on four occasions, and was the first African team to reach the finals (in 1970), and the first to progress beyond the group stage (in 1986). Morocco has won the African Nations Cup only once (in 1976), but reached the final in 2004. Moroccan teams have been very successful in African club competitions in the past, though the last Moroccan side to win the African Champions League was Raja Casablanca, back in 1999. More recently, FAR Rabat won the Confederation Cup (equivalent to Europe's UEFA Cup) in 2005, and Raja won its predecessor, the CAF Cup in 2003.

Moroccan clubs compete in an annual **league** and the (knockout) **Throne Cup**. For a long time there was just one full-time professional team, **FAR** (the army), but the 1990s saw the introduction of sponsorship and a number of semi-professional sides, the best of which are **Wydad** (WAC) and **Raja**, the two big Casablanca teams, plus **MAS** from Fes and **Hassania** from Agadir. The result is a fairly high standard of skill in the Moroccan league, but unfortunately Moroccan clubs are unable to afford the money commanded by top players in Europe, with the result that the best Moroccan players end up in European clubs.

Other sports

Morocco has two **marathons**: the Marrakesh Marathon (see p.380) and the even more gruelling Marathon des Sables (see p.437).

Most four-star and five-star hotels (especially in Agadir and Marrakesh) have **tennis** courts, though equipment, if available, is not often up to much, so you're advised to bring your own racket and balls.

Paragliding is increasingly popular in the south of Morocco, around Tafraoute and Mirhleft in particular, where there are thermals even during winter. Paragliding, hang-gliding and paramotoring trips, with instructors, are offered by Welsh Airsports (Ⓦwww.welshairsports.com) and Paraglide Morocco (Ⓦwww.paraglidemorocco.com).

Also popular in the south is **rock-climbing**, particularly in the region around Tafraoute, and at Todra Gorge, where Rock & Sun (Ⓦwww.rockandsun.com) offer package tours for experienced climbers. Claude Davies's comprehensive *Climbing in the Moroccan Anti-Atlas: Tafroute and Jebel El Kest* (Cicerone Press, UK) has marked-up photos and detailed descriptions of Anti-Atlas ascents.

Culture and etiquette

Moroccans are extremely hospitable and very tolerant. Though most people are religious, they are generally easy-going, and most young Moroccan women don't wear a veil, though they may well wear a headscarf. Nonetheless, you should try not to affront the religious beliefs especially of older, more conservative people by, for example, wearing skimpy clothes, kissing and cuddling in public, or eating or smoking in the street during Ramadan.

Clothes are particularly important: many Moroccans, especially in rural areas, may well be offended by clothes that do not fully cover parts of the body considered "private", including both legs and shoulders, especially for women. It is true that in cities Moroccan women wear short-sleeved tops and knee-length skirts (and may suffer more harassment as a result), and men may wear sleeveless T-shirts and above-the-knee shorts. However, the Muslim idea of "modest dress" (such as would be acceptable in a mosque for example) requires women to be covered from wrist to ankle, and men from over the shoulder to below the knee. In rural areas at least, it is a good idea to follow these codes, and definitely a bad idea for women to wear shorts or skirts above the knee, or for members of either sex to wear sleeveless T-shirts or very short shorts. Even ordinary T-shirts may be regarded as underwear, particularly in rural mountain areas. The best guide is to note how Moroccans dress locally.

When **invited to a home**, you normally take your shoes off before entering the reception rooms – follow your host's lead. It is customary to take a gift: sweet pastries or tea and sugar are always acceptable, and you might even take meat (by arrangement – a chicken from the countryside for example, still alive of course) to a poorer home.

Tipping

You're expected to **tip** – among others – waiters in cafés (1dh per person) and restaurants (5dh or so); museum and monument curators (3dh); *gardiens de voitures* (4–5dh; see p.40); petrol pump attendants (2–3dh); and porters who load your baggage onto buses (5dh). Taxi drivers do not expect a tip, but always appreciate one.

Mosques

Without a doubt, one of the major disappointments of travelling in Morocco if you are not Muslim is not being allowed into its mosques. The only exceptions are the partially restored Almohad structure of Tin Mal in the High Atlas (see p.407), the similarly disused Great Mosque at Smara in the Western Sahara (see p.547), the courtyard of the sanctuary-mosque of Moulay Ismail in Meknes (see p.188) and the Mosquée Hassan II in Casablanca (see p.308). Elsewhere, if you are not a believer, you'll have to be content with an occasional glimpse through open doors, and even in this you should be sensitive: people don't seem to mind tourists peering into the Kairaouine Mosque in Fes (the country's most important religious building), but in the country you should never approach a shrine too closely.

This rule applies equally to the numerous whitewashed **koubbas** – the tombs of *marabouts*, or local saints (usually domed: *koubba* actually means "dome") – and the "monastic" **zaouias** of the various Sufi brotherhoods. It is a good idea, too, to avoid walking through **graveyards**, as these also are regarded as sacred places.

Sex and gender issues

There is no doubt that, for women especially, travelling in Morocco is a very different experience from travelling in a Western country. One of the reasons for this is that the separate roles of the sexes are much more defined than they are in the West, and sexual mores much stricter. In villages and small towns, and even in the Medinas of large cities, many women still wear the veil and the street is strictly the man's domain. Most Moroccan men still expect to marry a virgin, and most women would never smoke a cigarette or drink in a bar, the general presumption being that only prostitutes do such things.

It should be said, however, that such ideas are gradually disappearing among the urban youth, and you will nowadays find some Moroccan women drinking in the more sophisticated bars, and even more often in cafés, until quite recently an all-male preserve. In the Villes Nouvelles of large cities, and especially in the Casa–Rabat–El Jadida area and in Marrakesh, you'll see most women without a veil or even a headscarf. You'll also see young people of both sexes hanging out together, though you can be sure that opportunities for pre-marital sex are kept to a minimum. Even in traditional Moroccan societies, mountain Berber women, who do most of the hard work, play a much more open role in society, and rarely use a veil.

Sexual harassment

Different women seem to have vastly different experiences of **sexual harassment** in Morocco. Some travellers find it persistent and bothersome, while others have little or no trouble with it at all. Many women compare Morocco favourably with Spain and other parts of southern Europe, but there is no doubt that, in general, harassment of tourists here is more persistent than it is in northern Europe or the English-speaking world.

Harassment will usually consist of men simply trying to chat you up or even asking directly for sex, and it can be constant and sometimes intimidating. In part this is to do with Moroccan men's misunderstanding of Western culture and sexual attitudes, and the fact that some think they can get away with taking liberties with tourists that no Moroccan woman would tolerate.

The obvious **strategies** for getting rid of unwanted attention are the same ones that you would use at home: appear confident and assured and you will avoid a lot of trouble. Making it clear that you have the same standards as your Moroccan counterparts will usually deter all but the most insistent of men. No Moroccan woman would tolerate being groped in the street for example, though they may often have to put up with cat-calls and unwanted comments. Traditionally, Moroccan women are coy and aloof, and uninhibited friendliness – especially any kind of physical contact between sexes – may be seen as a come-on, so being polite but formal when talking to men will diminish the chances of misinterpretation. The negative side to this approach is that it can also make it harder for you to get to know people, but after you've been in the country for a while, you will probably develop a feel for the sort of men with whom this tactic is necessary. It is also wise not to **smoke** in public, as some men still seem to think this indicates that you are available for sex.

How you **dress** is another thing that may reduce harassment. Wearing "modest" clothes (long sleeves, long skirts, baggy rather than tight clothes) will give an impression of respectability. Wearing a headscarf to cover your hair and ears will give this impression even more. One reader told us she felt a headscarf was "the single most important item of dress", adding that you can pull it over your face as a veil if unwanted male attention makes you feel uncomfortable. Indeed, Western liberals often forget that the purpose of wearing a veil is to protect women rather than to oppress them. However, you will notice that many Moroccan women totally ignore the traditional dress code, and do not suffer excessive harassment as a result. As for immodestly dressed women being taken for prostitutes, the fact is that actual sex workers in Morocco are often veiled from head to foot, as much to disguise their identities as anything else.

Other strategies to steer clear of trouble include avoiding eye contact, mentioning a husband who is nearby, and, if travelling with a boyfriend or just with a male friend, giving the impression that he is your husband. You should also avoid physical contact with Moroccan men, even in a manner that would not be considered sexual at home, since it could easily be misunderstood. If a Moroccan man touches *you*, on the other hand, he has definitely crossed the line, and you should not be afraid to **make a scene**. Shouting "*Shooma!*" ("Shame on you!") is likely to result in bystanders intervening on your behalf, and a very uncomfortable situation for your assailant.

It is often said that women are second-class citizens in Islamic countries, though educated Muslim women are usually keen to point out that this is a misinterpretation of Islam. While sex equality has a long way to go in Morocco, in some ways, at least in theory, the sexes are not as unequal as they seem. Men traditionally rule in the street, which is their domain, the woman's being the home. One result is that Moroccan women will receive their friends at home rather than meet them in, say, a café (although this is slowly changing) and this can make it difficult for you to get to know Moroccan women. One place where you *can* meet up with them is the hammam (see p.45). It may also be that if you are travelling with a man, Moroccan men will address him rather than you – but this is in fact out of respect for you, not disrespect, and you will not be ignored if you join in the conversation. In any case, however interpreted, Islam most certainly does not condone sexual harassment, and nor do any respectable Moroccans. Being aware of that fact will make it seem a lot less threatening.

Gay attitudes

As a result of sexual segregation, **male homosexuality** is relatively common in Morocco, although attitudes towards it are a little schizophrenic. Few Moroccans will declare themselves gay – which has connotations of femininity and weakness; the idea of being a passive partner is virtually taboo, while a dominant partner may well not consider himself to be indulging in a homosexual act. Private realities, however, are rather different from public show (on which subject, note that Moroccan men of all ages often walk hand-in-hand in public – a habit that has nothing to do with homosexuality and is simply a sign of friendship).

Gay sex between men is **illegal** under Moroccan law. Article 489 of the Moroccan penal code prohibits any "shameless or unnatural act" with a person of the same sex and allows for imprisonment of six months to three years, plus a fine. There are also various provisions in the penal code for more serious offences, with correspondingly higher penalties in cases involving, for example, corruption of minors.

A certain amount of information on the male gay scene in Morocco (gay bars, meeting places and cruising spots) can be found in the annual *Spartacus Gay Guide*, available at bookshops at home. Tangier's days as a gay resort are long gone but a tourist-oriented gay scene does seem to be emerging, very discreetly, in Marrakesh (see p.380), and to a lesser extent Agadir, though pressure from religious fundamentalists makes it difficult for the authorities to ease up, even if they wanted to, and arrests of tourists for having gay sex are not unknown.

There is no public perception of **lesbianism** in Morocco, and as a Western visitor, your chances of making contact with any Moroccan lesbians are very small indeed. Moroccan women are under extreme pressure to marry and bear children, and anyone resisting such pressure is likely to have a very hard time of it.

One website which posts up-to-date information on gay rights in Morocco is Behind the Mask at Ⓦwww.mask.org.za. There is also an information exchange for gay and lesbian Moroccans at Ⓦgaymorocco.tripod.com, but it is probably best to avoid accessing this site within Morocco.

Shopping

Souks (markets) are a major feature of Moroccan life, and among the country's greatest attractions. They are to be found everywhere: every town has a souk area, large cities like Fes and Marrakesh have labyrinths of individual souks (each filling a street or square and devoted to one particular craft), and in the countryside there are hundreds of weekly souks, on a different day in each village of the region.

When buying souvenirs in Morocco, it's worth considering how you are going to get them home, and you shouldn't take too literally the claims of shopkeepers about their goods, especially if they tell you that something is "very old" – *trafika* (phoney merchandise) abounds, and there are all sorts of imitation fossils and antiques about.

Souk days

Some villages are named after **their market days**, so it's easy to see when they're held.

The souk days are:

Souk el Had – Sunday (literally, "first market")
Souk el Tnine – Monday market
Souk el Tleta – Tuesday market
Souk el Arba – Wednesday market
Souk el Khamees – Thursday market
Souk es Sebt – Saturday market

There are very few village markets on **Friday** (el Djemaa – the "assembly", when the main prayers are held in the mosques), and even in the cities, souks are largely closed on Friday mornings and very subdued for the rest of the day.

Village souks usually begin on the afternoon preceding the souk day, as people travel from across the region; those who live nearer set out early in the morning of the souk day, but the souk itself is often over by noon and people disperse in the afternoon. You should therefore arrange to arrive by mid-morning at the latest.

Craft traditions

Moroccan **craft** traditions are very much alive, but finding pieces of real quality is not that easy. For a good price, it's always worth getting as close to the source of the goods as possible, and steering clear of tourist centres. **Fes** and **Marrakesh** have a large range but high prices. **Tangier** and **Agadir**, with no workshops of their own, are generally poor bets. A good way to get an idea of standards and quality is to visit **craft museums**: there are good ones in Fes, Meknes, Tangier, Rabat and Marrakesh.

For more on crafts and shopping see the *Crafts and Souvenirs* colour section.

Foodstuffs

Some Moroccan **food products** would be hard to find at home, and make excellent and inexpensive gifts or souvenirs (assuming your country's customs allow their importation). Locally produced **olive oil** can be excellent, with a distinctive strong flavour, and in the Souss Valley there's delicious sweet **argan oil** too (see p.498). Olives themselves come in numerous varieties, and there are also almonds, walnuts and spices available, notably **saffron** from Taliouine, and the spice mix known as Ras el Hanout. A jar of lemons preserved in brine is useful if you want to try your hand at making a tajine back home.

Hypermarkets run by the French firms Macro and Marjane are located on major approach roads at the edge of most big cities, offering a wide choice of Moroccan and imported foods and other goods at discount prices.

Bargaining

Whatever you buy, other than groceries, you will be expected to **bargain**. There are no hard and fast rules – it is really a question of paying what something is worth to you – but there are a few general points to keep in mind.

First, don't worry about **initial prices**. These are simply a device to test your limits. Don't think that you need to pay a specific fraction of the first asking price: some sellers start near their lowest price, while others will make a deal for as little as a tenth of the initial price.

Second, have in mind a figure that you want to pay, and a maximum above which you will not go. If your maximum and the shopkeeper's minimum don't meet, then you don't have a deal, but it's no problem.

Third, **don't ever let a figure pass your lips** that you aren't prepared to pay – nor start bargaining for something you have absolutely no intention of buying – there's no better way to create bad feelings.

Fourth, **take your time**. If the deal is a serious one (for a rug, say), you'll probably want to sit down over tea with the vendor, and for two cups you'll talk about anything but the rug and the price. If negotiations do not seem to be going well, it often helps to have a friend on hand who seems – and may well be – less interested in the purchase than you and can assist in extricating you from a particularly hard sell.

Fifth, remember that even if you're **paying more than local people**, it doesn't necessarily mean you're being "ripped off". As a Westerner, your earning power is well above that of most Moroccans and it's rather mean to force traders down to their lowest possible price just for the sake of it.

The final and most golden rule of all is never to go shopping with a **guide** or a hustler. Any shop that a guide steers you into will pay them a commission, added to your bill of course, while hustlers often pick up tourists with the specific aim of leading you to places that (even if you've agreed to go in "just to look") will subject you to a lengthy high-pressure hard-sell.

An approximate idea of what you should be paying for handicrafts can be gained from checking the **fixed prices** in the state- or cooperative-run Ensembles Artisanals, which are slightly higher than could be bargained for elsewhere.

Travelling with children

Travelling with small children, you may well find that people will frequently come up to admire them, to compliment you on them and to caress them, which may be uncomfortable for shyer offspring. In Moroccan families, children stay up late until they fall asleep and are spoiled rotten by older family members. The streets are pretty safe and even quite small children walk to school unaccompanied or play in the street unsupervised.

As a parent however, you will encounter one or two difficulties. For example, you won't find baby changing rooms in airports, hotels or restaurants, and will have to be discreet if breastfeeding – find a quiet corner and shield infant and breast from view with a light cloth over your shoulder. Beach resort and package tour hotels may have facilities such as playgrounds, children's pools and a babysitting service, but mid-range city hotels are far less likely to cater for children, though many allow children to share their parents' room for free.

You may want to try a holiday with Club Med (Ⓦwww.clubmed.com), whose purpose-built holiday resorts at Agadir and Marrakesh feature kids' club, entertainment and sports facilities on site. Attractions that should appeal to small people include Magic Park in Salé (see p.290), Oasiria in Marrakesh (see p.381), and the tourist train in Agadir (see p.491).

Disposable nappies (diapers) are available at larger supermarkets, and sometimes city pharmacies, at prices similar to what you pay at home, but off the beaten track, you may need to stock up, or take washables. You may also want to take along some dried baby food; any café can supply hot water. Wet wipes are also very handy, if only for wiping small hands before eating when you aren't too sure where they've been.

On buses and grands taxis, children small enough to share your seat will usually travel free, but older kids pay the full adult fare. On trains, travel is free for under-fours, and half price for four- to eleven-year-olds.

Among hazards that you'll need to bear in mind are traffic and stray animals. Dogs can be fierce in Morocco, and can also carry rabies, and there are a lot of feral cats and dogs about. Children (especially young ones) are also more susceptible than adults to heatstroke and dehydration, and should always wear a sunhat, and have high-factor sunscreen applied to exposed skin. If swimming at a beach resort, they should do so in a t-shirt, certainly for the first few days. The other thing that children are very susceptible to is an upset tummy. Bear in mind that antidiarrhoeal drugs should generally not be given to young children; read the literature provided with the medication or consult a doctor for guidance on child dosages. For more tips, see *The Rough Guide to Travel with Babies & Young Children*.

Children on parents' passports

If travelling as a family, note that **children travelling on their parents' passports** must have their photographs affixed to the passport. If this is not done, it is possible that you will be refused entry to Morocco. This is not just a piece of paper bureaucracy: families are sometimes refused entry for failing to comply.

Travel essentials

Costs

Costs for food, accommodation and travel in Morocco are low by European or North American standards. If you stay in the cheaper hotels (or camp out), eat local food, and share expenses and rooms with another person, £150/$200 each a week would be enough to survive on. On £300/$400 each you could live pretty well, while with £700–1000/$1000–1500 a week between two people you would be approaching luxury.

Accommodation costs range from £10/$15 a night – sometimes even less – for a double room in a basic hotel to as much as £250/$350 a night in a top luxury hotel or riad. The price of a **meal** reflects a similar span, ranging from £3/$4 to around £10/$15 a meal. **Alcohol** is really the only thing that compares unfavourably with Western prices: a bottle of cheap Moroccan wine costs £3.50/$4.50, a can of local beer about £1/$1.50 in the shops, £2.50/$3.50 in a normal bar, or £4/$6 in hotel bars and discos.

Inevitably, **resorts** and larger **cities** (Rabat and Casablanca especially) are more expensive than small towns with few tourists, but in **remote parts** of the country (including trekking regions in the High Atlas), where goods have to be brought in from some distance, prices for provisions can be high.

Beyond accommodation and food, your major outlay will be for **transport** – expensive if you're renting a car (prices start at around £300/$420 a week plus petrol), but very reasonable if you use the local trains, buses and shared taxis (see box, p.36 for sample fares).

Youth/student ID cards can save you a small amount of money, entitling you to cheaper entry at some museums and other sights, and a small discount on some ferry tickets and domestic airfares. They're not worth going out of your way to get, but if you have one you may as well bring it along.

In the Spanish enclaves of Ceuta and Melilla, prices for most things are the same as they are in mainland Spain (except that there is no duty on alcohol, tobacco and electronic goods), and around twice as expensive as in Morocco proper.

Hidden costs

You'll probably end up buying a few **souvenirs**. Rugs, carpets, leather, woodwork, pottery and jewellery are all outstanding – and few travellers leave without something.

Harder to come to terms with is the fact that you'll be confronting real **poverty**. As a tourist, you're not going to solve any problems, but with a labourer's wages at little more than 5dh (30p/60¢) an hour, an unemployment rate of nearly twenty percent in urban areas, and nearly one in five people living below the poverty line, even small **tips** can make a lot of difference to people. For Moroccans, giving alms to **beggars** is natural, and a requirement of Islam, especially since there is no social security here, so for tourists, rich by definition, local poverty demands at least some response. Do not, however, dispense money indiscriminately to **children**, which encourages pestering and promotes a dependence on begging.

Crime and personal safety

Keep your luggage and money secure. Morocco does not have a high crime rate, but it is obviously unwise to carry large sums of cash or valuables on your person – especially in Casablanca and Tangier, and to a lesser extent Fes and Marrakesh. Mugging as such is pretty rare – those who fall victim to theft usually have things taken by stealth, or are subject to some kind of scam (see pp.64–65 for more on these). Be especially vigilant at transport stations (new arrivals are favourite targets, and just before departure is a favourite time to strike) and in crowd situations where pickpockets may operate.

Hotels, generally, are secure and useful for depositing money before setting out to explore; larger ones will keep valuables at reception and some will have safes. **Campsites** are considerably less secure, and many campers advise using a **money belt** – to be worn even while sleeping. If you do decide on a money belt (and many people spend time quite happily without), leather or cotton materials are preferable to nylon, which can irritate in the heat.

If you are **driving**, it almost goes without saying, you should not leave anything you cannot afford to lose visible or accessible in your car.

The police

There are two main types of Moroccan **police**: the *Gendarmerie* (who wear grey uniforms and man the checkpoints on main roads, at junctions and the entry to towns), and the *Police* (*Sûreté*), who wear navy blue uniforms or plain clothes. Either may demand to see your passport (and/or driving papers). It is obligatory to carry official ID (in practice a passport), though you should not have any problems if you leave yours in a hotel safe while wandering around town, especially if you carry a photocopy of the important pages. You are unlikely to have any contact with the green-uniformed *Force Auxiliaire*, a back-up force who wear berets and look more like the army.

The *gendarmes* have jurisdiction outside built-up areas, the **police**, within towns. Both are usually polite and helpful to visitors. There is now a *Brigade Touristique* in cities such as Marrakesh and Fes, specifically set up to protect tourists, though there have been reports that the *Brigade Touristique* in Fes will turn a blind eye to the activities of pickpockets, who pay them off for the favour.

If you do need to **report a theft**, try to take along a fluent French- or Arabic-speaker if your own French and Arabic are not too hot. You may only be given a scrap of paper with an official stamp to show your insurance company, who then have to apply themselves to a particular police station for a report (in Arabic). If you cannot prove that a theft has taken place, the police may decline to make any report, especially if the theft is of money only. They will always give you a report, however, if you have lost any official document (passport, driving licence, etc).

The police emergency number is ⓣ19.

Kif and hashish

The smoking of **kif** (marijuana) and hashish (cannabis resin) has long been a regular pastime of Moroccans and tourists alike, but it is nonetheless illegal, and large fines (plus prison sentences for substantial amounts) do get levied for possession. If you are arrested for cannabis, the police may expect to be paid off, and this should be done as quickly as possible while the minimum number of officers are involved (but offer it discreetly, and never refer to it as a bribe or even a *cadeau*). Consulates are notoriously unsympathetic to drug offenders, but they can help with technical problems and find you legal representation.

Obviously, the best way to avoid trouble is to keep well clear – above all, of the *kif*-growing region of **Ketama** in the Rif mountains – and always reply to hustlers by saying you don't smoke. If you are going to indulge, be very careful who you buy it from (definitely do not buy it from touts or hustlers), and above all **do not try to take any out** of the country, even to Spain (where attitudes to possession are relaxed but there's nearly always a prison sentence for importing). Searches at Algeciras and Málaga can be very thorough, with sniffer dogs, which also operate at Moroccan ports and airports, and you'll get sometimes as many as four checks if travelling through Ceuta or Melilla.

For more on *kif* traditions and the hash industry in the Rif, see box, p.146.

Electricity

The supply is 220v 50Hz. Sockets have two round pins, as in Europe. You should be able to find adaptors in Morocco that will take North American plugs (but North American appliances may need a transformer, unless multi-voltage). Adaptors for British and Australasian plugs will need to be brought from home.

Guides, hustlers, conmen and kids

Armed with this book, you shouldn't need a guide, but some people like to hire one to negotiate the Medinas of larger cities. **Official guides**, identified by a large, brass "sheriff's badge", can be engaged through tourist offices or large hotels. They charge a fixed rate of around 150–180dh for half a day, twice that for a full day, plus sustenance. The rate is for the guide's time, and can be shared by a group (though you'd then be expected to give a good tip).

Young Moroccans may also offer their services as **unofficial guides**, which is illegal, and subject to occasional police clampdowns. Be very careful in making use of unofficial guides. Some are indeed genuine, usually unemployed youths hoping to make a few dirhams by showing tourists around, and they should be cheaper than official guides, less formal, and offer a more street-level view, and perhaps show you things that official guides would not – indeed, many tourists end up making lasting friendships with people who've approached them as unofficial guides – but some will be aiming only to get you into shops or hotels which pay them commission, or they may be confidence tricksters. If you do decide to hire an unofficial guide, be sure to **fix the rate** in advance (make it clear that you know the official rates), as well as the **itinerary** (so that it does not include shops, for example – this also applies to official guides). Also be aware that young Moroccans seen accompanying a tourist as a guide can be arrested and imprisoned. In practice this is rarely enforced but **friendships**, especially in tourist cities like Tangier, Agadir, Fes or Marrakesh, should always be discreet. On the whole, once invited to a home, and having met a family, you are unlikely to encounter problems, and your hosts will deal effectively with any enquiries from curious local policemen.

In general, never agree to a guide showing you to a **hotel**, and never go **shopping** with a guide, official or otherwise, as they will only take you to places which pay them a commission, meaning a higher bill for you – often as much as 50 percent higher. Hotels that pay commission to guides for bringing tourists to them are also likely to be dubious in other ways. On the other hand, letting someone guide you to a **café** or **restaurant** won't increase the price of a meal (although waiters will generally make a small tip to the guide).

Conmen and scams

Hustlers and conmen have been largely cleaned off the streets, and those who remain are less persistent, but tourists are the obvious target for them. However, it's important not to treat every Moroccan who approaches you as a hustler – many (though not usually in tourist hot spots) are just trying to be friendly. However, forewarned is forearmed, so a few notes on the **most common scams** follow:

- Most hustlers (and guides, official or not) hope to earn money by steering you, sometimes with the most amazing deviousness, into shops that will pay them a commission, most commonly carpet shops where you will be subjected to hours

Entry requirements

If you hold a full passport from the UK, Ireland, the US, Canada, Australia, New Zealand or any EU country, you require no visa to enter Morocco as a tourist for up to ninety days. However, your passport must be valid for at least six months beyond your date of entry, and always double check your visa requirements before departure as the situation can change. South African citizens are among those who need a visa; applications should be made to the Moroccan embassy or consulate in your country of residence (South Africans should be able to get one in London, but it may be harder in places like Algeciras, Dakar or Nouakchott), with three passport photos, and a form that you can download at Ⓦwww.maec.gov.ma/fr/consulaires/visa.pdf.

Entry formalities are fairly straightforward, though you will have to fill in a form stating personal details, purpose of visit and your of hard-sell. Never be afraid to walk away from such as situation, even if (as is quite likely) you are then subjected to abuse, and never buy anything from a shop that you are taken to by a guide or hustler.

- If a hustler guides you into the Medina till you have no idea where you are, and then demands a large fee to take you back out, don't be afraid to appeal to people in the street, and if you feel genuinely threatened or harassed, threaten or indeed go to the police: hustlers tend to vanish fast at the prospect of police involvement.
- Hustlers may attach themselves to you using the excuse of a letter ("Could you help translate or write one?"), or by pretending to be someone you have met but forgotten – so if someone you don't remember says, "Hey, remember me?" it's probably a hustler trying to practise some scam on you. Another trick is to tell you that a site that you are on your way to visit is closed and that they can show you something else instead, or they may tell you that there is a Berber market taking place and this is the only day of the week to see it. If you ignore these people or turn them down, they may accuse you of being paranoid, angry or racist – and such an accusation is a sure sign that you were right.
- Con merchants, working alone or in couples, may befriend tourists, and then, after a day or two, tell some sad tale about needing money to get a passport or for a sick relative, or some such.
- On trains, especially at Tangier, hustlers sometimes pose as porters or railway staff, demanding an extortionate fee for carrying baggage or payment of supplements. Genuine rail staff wear beige overalls and have ID cards, which, if suspicious, you should ask to see.
- Drivers should beware of hitchhiking hustlers, who spend all day hitching between a pair of towns and can get highly obnoxious in their demands for money when you approach one or other destination. Alternatively, they may wish to thank you for the lift by taking you home for a cup of tea – except that "home" turns out to be a carpet shop, where you are then subjected to hours of hard-sell. A variation on this is the fake breakdown, where people on the road flag down passing tourists and ask them to take a note to a "mechanic", who turns out to be a carpet salesman. This one is particularly common on the N9 between Marrakesh, Ouarzazate and Zagora, and the N10 between Ouarzazate and Tinerhir.

Dealing with children

In the countryside especially, children may demand a dirham, *un cadeau* (present) or *un stylo* (a pen/pencil). Working out your own strategy is all part of the game, but be sure to keep good humour: smile and laugh, or kids can make your life hell. Faced with **begging from children**, we recommend not obliging, as this ties them to a begging mentality, and encourages them to harass other visitors.

profession. In the past, Moroccan authorities have shown an occasional reluctance to allow in those who categorize themselves as "journalist"; an alternative profession on the form might be wise.

Items such as **electronic equipment and video cameras** may occasionally be entered on your passport. If you lose them during your visit, they will be assumed "sold" when you come to leave and (unless you have police documentation of theft) you will have to pay 100 percent duty. All goods entered on your passport should be "cleared" when leaving to prevent problems on future trips. Vehicles need a Green Card (see p.32).

It is in theory obligatory in Morocco to carry official ID at all times. In practice, a photocopy of the important pages of your passport will do, so long as the real thing is in your hotel in the same town. When travelling between towns, you should always have your passport on you.

Duty-free allowances

You can bring in, without charge: one litre of spirits, or two litres of wine; 200 cigarettes, 25 cigars or 250g of tobacco; 150ml of perfume or 250ml of eau de toilette; jewellery; a camera and a laptop for personal use; gifts worth up to 2000dh (£165/$240).

Prohibited goods include arms and ammunition (except for hunting), controlled drugs, and "books, printed matter, audio and video cassettes and any immoral items liable to cause a breach of the peace".

Visa extensions

To **extend your stay** in Morocco you should – officially – apply to the Bureau des Étrangers in the nearest main town for a residence permit (see below). This is, however, a very complicated procedure and it is usually possible to get round the bureaucracy by simply leaving the country for a brief time when your three months are up. If you decide to do this – and it is not foolproof – it is best to make a trip of at least a few days outside Morocco. Spain is the obvious choice and some people just go to Ceuta; the more cautious re-enter the country at a different post. If you are unlucky, you may be turned back and asked to get a **re-entry visa**. These can be obtained from any Moroccan consulate abroad (see opposite).

Extending a stay officially involves opening a bank account in Morocco (a couple of days' procedure in itself) and obtaining an *Attestation de Résidence* from your hotel, campsite or landlord. You will need a minimum of 20,000dh (£1640/$2415) in your account.

Then you need to go to the **Bureau des Étrangers** in the central police station of a large town at least fifteen days before your time is up, equipped with: your passport and a photocopy of its main pages; four passport photos; two copies of the *Attestation de Résidence*; and two copies of your bank statement (*Compte de Banque*). If the police are not too busy they'll give you a form to fill out in duplicate and, some weeks later, you should receive a plastic-coated permit with your photo laminated in.

Foreign embassies and consulates in Morocco

Foreign embassies and consulates in Morocco are detailed in the "Listings" sections for Rabat (see pp.290–291), Casablanca (see p.313), Tangier (see p.103), Marrakesh (see p.380), Agadir (see p.496) and Oujda (see p.172). Foreign representation in Morocco is detailed on the Moroccan Foreign Ministry's website at Ⓦwww.maec.gov.ma (click on "Diplomatic & Consular Corps Accredited in Morocco" under "Diplomatic Network" in the English-language section of the site).

Ireland has honorary consuls in Casablanca (see p.313) and Agadir (see p.496), but no embassy (the nearest is in Lisbon, Ⓣ00-351-1/396 9440). New Zealanders are covered by their embassy in Madrid (Ⓣ00-34/91 523 0226), but can use UK consular facilities in Morocco. Australians are covered by their embassy in Paris (Ⓣ00-33-1/4059 3300), but can use Canadian consular facilities in Morocco.

Moroccan embassies and consulates abroad

A complete up-to-date list of Moroccan diplomatic missions around the world can be found on the Moroccan Foreign Ministry's website at Ⓦwww.maec.gov.ma (click on "Moroccan Embassies & Consulates abroad" under "Diplomatic Network" in the English-language section of the site).

Algeria 12 Rue Branly, al-Mouradia, 12070 Algiers Ⓣ021/697094, Ⓔambmaroc-alg@maec.gov.ma; 26 Av Cheikh Larbi Tebessi, 31000 Oran Ⓣ041/411627, Ⓔconsulatmaroc.oran@assila.net; 5 Av De l'ANP, Sidi Bel Abbes Ⓣ048/543470, Ecgsba@live.fr.

Australia 17 Terrigal Crescent, O'Malley, Canberra, ACT 2606 Ⓣ02/6290 0755, Ⓔsifmacan@bigpond.com.

Canada 38 Range Rd, Suite 1510, Ottawa, ON K1N 8J4 Ⓣ1-613/236-7391, Ⓔsifamaot@bellnet.ca; 2192, Boulevard Lévesque Ouest, Montreal, PQ H3H 1R6 Ⓣ1-514/288-8750, Ⓦwww.consulatdumaroc.ca.

Ireland (Chargé d'Affaires) 39 Raglan Rd, Ballsbridge, Dublin 4 Ⓣ01/660 9449, Ⓔsifamdub@indigo.ie.

Mauritania Av Général de Gaulle, Tevragh Zeina 634, BP621, Nouakchott ⓣ525 1411, ⓔsifmanktt@gmail.com; Av Maritime, Nouadhibou ⓣ574 5084, ⓔconsu.ndh@maec.gov.ma; formalities for entering Morocco (by car, for example) can only be completed in Nouakchott, not Nouadhibou.
Spain c/Leizarán 31, 28002 Madrid ⓣ91 210 9300, ⓦwww.embajada-marruecos.es; c/Teniente Maroto 2, first floor, 11201 Algeciras ⓣ95 666 1803, ⓔcg.algesiras@hotmail.com; Palmera Bldg, Suite 178, 3rd floor, Av del Mediterraneo (corner Sierra Alhamilla), 04004 Almería ⓣ95 020 6179, ⓔcgalmeria@hotmail.com; also in Seville, Barcelona, Tarragona, Valencia, Bilbao, Burgos and Las Palmas (see ⓦwww.embajada-marruecos.es, "Consulados" under "Guia Consular", for details).
South Africa 799 Schoeman St (corner Farenden), Arcadia, Pretoria 001 ⓣ012/343 0230, ⓔsifmapre@mwebbiz.co.za.
UK Diamond House, 97–99 Praed St, London W2 1NT ⓣ020/7724 0719, ⓦwww.moroccanembassylondon.org.uk.
USA 1601 21st St NW, Washington DC 20009 ⓣ1-202/462-7979, ⓦdcusa.themoroccanembassy.com; 10 E 40th St, 24th Floor, New York, NY 10016 ⓣ1-212/758-2625, ⓦwww.moroccanconsulate.com.

Health

For minor health complaints, a visit to a **pharmacy** is likely to be sufficient. Moroccan pharmacists are well trained and dispense a wide range of drugs, including many available only on prescription in the West. If pharmacists feel you need a full diagnosis, they can recommend a doctor – sometimes working on the premises. Addresses of English- and French-speaking doctors can also be obtained from consulates and large hotels.

If you need **hospital treatment**, contact your consulate at once and follow its advice. If you are near a major city, reasonable treatment may be available locally. State hospitals are usually OK for minor injuries, but for anything serious, a private clinic is generally preferable. Depending on your condition, repatriation may be the best course of action.

The latest advice on health in Morocco can be found on the US government's travel health website at ⓦwww.cdc.gov/travel (click on "Destinations" under "Travelers' Health Topics", then scroll down and click on "Morocco").

Inoculations

No **inoculations** are required but you should always be up to date with polio and tetanus. Those intending to stay a long time in the country, especially if working with animals or in the healthcare field, are also advised to consider vaccinations against typhoid, TB, hepatitis A and B, diphtheria and rabies, though these are not worth your while if just going on holiday.

A very low level of malaria does exist in the form of occasional cases between May and October in the region to the north of Beni Mellal and Khenifra, between Chefchaouen and Larache, and in the province of Taza, but local strains are not life-threatening and malaria pills are not normally considered necessary unless you actually fall ill with it (in which case they are easy enough to get at any pharmacy). More importantly, avoid bites; use mosquito repellent on all exposed areas of skin, especially feet, and especially around dusk. Repellents containing DEET are usually recommended for adults.

Water and health hazards

Tap water in most of Morocco is generally safe to drink, though in the far south and Western Sahara it's best to stick to bottled mineral water.

A more serious problem in the south is that many of the **river valleys and oases** are infected with **bilharzia**, also known as **schistosomiasis**, caused by a tiny fluke worm that lives part of its life cycle in a freshwater snail, and the other part in the blood and internal organs of a human or other mammal which bathes in or drinks the water. The snails only live in stagnant water, but the flukes may be swept downstream. Staying clear of slow-flowing rivers and oasis water is the best way to avoid it. If infected while bathing, you'll probably get a slightly itchy rash an hour or two later where the flukes have entered the skin. Later symptoms may take several months to appear, and are typified by abdominal pains, and blood in faeces or even urine. If you suspect that you might have it, seek medical help. Bilharzia is easily cured, but can cause permanent intestinal damage if untreated. Care should be taken, too, in drinking water from **mountain streams**. In areas where there is livestock upstream **giardiasis** may be prevalent and is a common cause of travellers' diarrhoea. Other symptoms include nausea, weight loss and fatigue which usually last no more than two weeks and settle without treatment. If they continue for longer, then a course of **metronidazole** (Flagyl) generally leads to effective eradication, but always finish the course, even after symptoms have gone, and even though this antibiotic will probably make you feel nauseous and precludes consumption of alcohol. Using iodine water purification tablets, or boiling any drinking or cooking water (remember that you'll have to boil it for longer at high altitudes, where the boiling point is lower) is the simplest way to avoid putting yourself at risk from either of these illnesses.

Diarrhoea

At some stage in your Moroccan travels, it is likely that you will get **diarrhoea**. As a first stage of treatment it's best simply to adapt your diet. Plain boiled rice is your safest bet, while yoghurt is an effective stomach settler and prickly pears (widely available in summer) are good too, as are bananas, but other fruit is best avoided, along with greasy food, dairy products, (except yoghurt), caffeine and alcohol. It's important if you have diarrhoea to replace the body fluids and salts lost through dehydration (this is especially the case with children) and dissolving **oral rehydration salts** (*sels de réhydratation orale* in French) in water will help. These are available at any pharmacy, but if you can't get any, then a teaspoon of salt plus eight of sugar per litre of water makes a reasonable substitute. Water (at least two litres per adult daily) should be drunk constantly throughout the day, rather than all in one go.

If symptoms persist for several days – especially if you get painful cramps, or if blood or mucus appear in your stools – you could have something more serious (see p.67 & above) and should seek medical advice.

Other hazards

There are few natural hazards in northern Morocco, where wildlife is not very different from that of Mediterranean Europe. If you venture into the Sahara however, be aware of the very real dangers of a bite from a **snake**, **palm rat** or **scorpion**. Several of the Saharan snakes are deadly, as is the palm rat. Bites should be treated as medical emergencies.

Certain scorpions (see below) are very dangerous; their sting can be fatal if not treated. Avoid going barefoot or in flip-flops (thongs) in the bush, or turning over stones. In the desert, shake out your shoes before putting them on in the morning. Most snakes are non-venomous, and few are life-threatening, but one or two species can be dangerous, most notably the horned viper. All scorpions sting, which can be extremely painful, especially if you are allergic, but again, not many are life-threatening. If you do get bitten by a snake or stung by a scorpion, don't panic – even in the case of life-threatening species, actual fatalities are rare, and you should be in no danger if treated in a reasonable time. Sucking out the poison only works in movies, and tourniquets are dangerous and ill-advised. The important thing is to relax, try not to move the affected part of your body, and seek medical help as quickly as possible. Try to remember what the creature looked like, and if it's possible to kill or catch it without danger, then do so, so that you can show it to doctors or paramedics. Most scorpion-sting fatalities are caused by one species, the fat-tailed scorpion (*Androctonus australis*), 4–10cm long and pale yellow with a darker tail tip, which is typically found under stones and in cracks and crevices. Other dangerous species are the death stalker, (*Leiurus quinquestriatus*), the blacktip scorpion (*Buthus occitanus*), the black fat-tailed scorpion (*Androctonus bicolor*), and two other fat-tailed scorpions (the thin-clawed *Androctonus Mauretanicu* and the *Androctonus amoreuxi*). Photographs of all of these, plus much information and sound advice can be found on the Scorpion Venom website at Ⓦweb.singnet.com.sg/~chuaeecc/venom/venom.htm.

Never underestimate Morocco's **heat**, especially in the south. A hat – preferably light in both weight and colour – is an essential precaution and, especially if you have very fair skin, you should also take a sunblock cream with a very high screening factor, as the sun really is higher (and therefore stronger) in Morocco than in northern latitudes. Resulting problems include **dehydration** – make sure that you're drinking enough (irregular urination such as only once a day is a danger sign) – and **heatstroke**, which is potentially fatal. Signs of heatstroke are a very high body temperature without a feeling of fever, but accompanied by headaches, nausea and/or disorientation. Lowering body temperature, with a tepid shower or bath, for example, is the first step in treatment, after which medical help should be sought.

Contraceptives and tampons

Poor quality and rather unreliable condoms (*préservatifs*) can be bought in most pharmacies, and so can the pill (officially by prescription, but this isn't essential).

Tampons can be bought at general stores, not pharmacies, in most Moroccan cities. Don't expect to find them in country or mountain areas.

Insurance

It's frankly reckless to travel without insurance cover. Home insurance policies occasionally cover your possessions when overseas, and some private medical schemes include cover when abroad. Bank and credit cards often have certain levels of medical or other insurance included and you may automatically get travel insurance if you use a major credit card to pay for your trip. Otherwise, you should contact a specialist travel insurance company, or consider the travel insurance deal we offer (see below). A typical travel insurance policy usually provides cover for the loss of baggage, tickets and – up to a certain limit – cash or cheques, as well as cancellation or curtailment of your journey. Most of them exclude so-called dangerous sports unless an extra premium is paid: in Morocco this could include mountaineering, skiing, water rafting or paragliding. Read the small print and benefits tables of prospective policies carefully; coverage can vary wildly for roughly similar premiums. Many policies can be chopped and changed to exclude coverage you don't need. For medical coverage, check whether benefits will be paid as treatment proceeds or only after returning home, and whether there is a 24-hour medical emergency number. When securing baggage cover, make sure that the per-article limit – typically under £500/$1000 – will cover your most valuable possession. If you need to make a claim, you should keep receipts for medicines and medical treatment, and in the event you have anything stolen, you must obtain an official statement from the police (called a *papier de déclaration*).

Internet

Cybercafés are widespread and usually charge around 5dh per hour, though some places charge double that, and hotels with internet services often charge even more; conversely, some places in small towns in the south charge as little as 3dh per hour.

Laundry

In the larger towns, laundries will take in clothes and wash them overnight, but you'll usually find it easier to ask at hotels – even in

Rough Guides travel insurance

Rough Guides has teamed up with WorldNomads.com to offer great **travel insurance** deals. Policies are available to residents of over 150 countries, with cover for a wide range of **adventure sports**, 24-hour emergency assistance, high levels of medical and evacuation cover and a stream of **travel safety information**. Roughguides.com users can take advantage of their policies online 24/7, from anywhere in the world – even if you're already travelling. And since plans often change when you're on the road, you can extend your policy and even claim online. Roughguides.com users who buy travel insurance with WorldNomads.com can also leave a positive footprint and donate to a community development project. For more information go to ⓦ**www.roughguides.com/shop**.

cheap hotels without an official laundry service, the cleaning lady will almost certainly be glad to make a few extra dirhams by taking in a bit of washing.

Left luggage

You can deposit baggage at most train stations, but it will have to be locked or padlocked (unlockable rucksacks will not be accepted); if you are catching a late train, make sure that the office will be open on your return. There are similar facilities at the main bus stations, CTM offices and ferry stations (Tangier, Ceuta, Melilla). Where no left luggage facilities are available, café proprietors may agree to look after baggage for you, sometimes for a small fee, more often for free in out-of-the-way places.

Living in Morocco

Your best chance of paid work in Morocco is **teaching English**. The schools listed here will require reasonable spoken French and an EFL qualification, and usually do their recruiting at home, but they sometimes advertise jobs on line, and they may be able to direct you to smaller schools in Casablanca, Rabat and other Moroccan towns.

It is also possible to **volunteer** for a **work camp**. Most are open to anyone over eighteen. You pay travel costs but generally receive free accommodation (take a sleeping bag) and meals.

English schools

American Language Center 1 Pl de la Fraternité, Casablanca ⓣ0522 277765, ⓦcasablanca.aca.org.ma. Also in Agadir, Fes, Kenitra, Marrakesh, Meknes, Mohammedia, Rabat, Tangier and Tetouan – for contact details see ⓦmarrakesh.aca.org.ma (in the English-language section of the site click on "contacts and links" then "Contacts for American Language Centers of Morocco").

British Council 36 Rue de Tanger, Rabat ⓣ0537 218130; 87 Bd, Nador, Polo, Casablanca ⓣ0522 529360 ⓦwww.britishcouncil.org/morocco.

The American School 1 bis Rue el Amir Abdelkader, Agdal, Rabat ⓣ0537 671476, ⓦwww.ras.edu.ac.ma; Route de la Mecque, Lotissement Ougoug, Quartier Californie, Casablanca ⓣ0522 214115, ⓦwww.cas.ac.ma; BP 6195, Route de Ouarzazate, Marrakesh ⓣ0524 329860, ⓦwww.asm.ma; 49 Rue Christophe Colombe, Tangier ⓣ0539 939827 or 8, ⓦwww.ast.ma.

Work camps

Amis des Chantiers Internationaux de Meknès (ACIM) BP 8, 50001 Meknes ⓣ0535 511829, ⓔacim_b@hotmail.com. Projects generally involve agricultural or construction work around Meknes – three weeks in July and August, accommodation and food provided.

Association Chantiers de Jeunesse (ACJ) BP 171, CCP 4469 H, 11000 Salé ⓣ0537 855350, ⓔacj.org.maroc@hotmail.com.

Chantiers des Jeunes Volontaires (CJV) BP 558, Batha, 30200 Fes ⓣ0535 700258, ⓔcjv1962@yahoo.fr.

Chantiers Jeunesse Maroc (CJM) BP 1351, 10001 Rabat ⓣ0537 722140 ⓔcjm@mtds.com.

Chantiers Sociaux Marocains (CSM) BP 456, 10001 Rabat ⓣ0537 297184, ⓔcsm@planete.co.ma.

Experiment in International Living ⓦwww.experimentinternational.org; US ⓣ1-800/345 2929, Canada c/o Friends Student Exchange ⓣ604/886-3783; UK ⓣ01684/562 57; Ireland ⓣ021/455 1535; Australia c/o Global Cultural Exchange Australia ⓣ08/8132 0188; New Zealand ⓣ06/323 8700; South Africa c/o SASTS ⓣ021/418 3794. Voluntary work placements with Moroccan NGOs, preceded by a four-week intensive language course in Rabat.

SCI/IVS ⓦwww.sciint.org; US ⓣ1-434/336 3545, ⓦwww.sci-ivs.org; Canada ⓣ1-613/737 6777, ⓦwww.nocona.ca; Great Britain ⓣ0131/243 2745 ⓦivsgb.org; Ireland (Republic and North) ⓣ01/855 1011, ⓦwww.vsi.ie; Australia ⓣ02/9699 1129, ⓦwww.ivp.org.au. Recruits workcamp volunteers.

Volunteers for Peace 1034 Tiffany Rd, Belmont, VT 05730–0202; ⓣ1-802/259-2759, ⓦwww.vfp.org. Recruits volunteers for projects detailed on the website.

Mail

Letters between Morocco and Western Europe generally take around a week to ten days, around two weeks for North America or Australasia. There are postboxes at every post office (*La Poste*) and on the wayside; they seem to get emptied fairly efficiently, even in out-of-the-way places.

Stamps can sometimes be bought alongside postcards, or from some *tabacs* as well as at the PTT, where there is often a dedicated counter (labelled *timbres*), and where stamps may also be sold in the phone section, if there is one. At major post offices, there is a separate window for **parcels**, where the officials will want to examine the goods you are sending. Always take them unwrapped; there is usually someone to supply wrapping paper, string and tape.

Post office hours are typically Monday to Friday, 8am to 4.30pm. Main post offices open Monday to Friday 8am to 6pm, Saturday 8am to noon for stamps, money changing and money transfer, but the same hours as small offices for parcels and poste restante. During Ramadan, offices open Monday to Friday 9am to 3.30pm, larger ones also Saturday 9am to noon.

Poste restante

Receiving letters **poste restante** (general delivery) can be a bit of a lottery, as Moroccan post office workers don't always file letters under the name you might expect. Ask for all your initials to be checked (including *M* for Mr or Ms, etc) and, if you're half-expecting anything, suggest other letters as well. To pick up your mail you need your passport. To have mail sent to you, it should be addressed (preferably with your surname underlined) to Poste Restante at the central post office of any major city.

Maps

The **maps of Moroccan towns** in this book should be sufficient for most needs, though commercial plans of greater Rabat or Casablanca may be useful if you need to visit the suburbs, and detailed maps of the Medinas in Marrakesh and Fes may help to navigate tortuous Medina alleyways.

Reasonable **road maps** are sometimes available at ONMT tourist offices, and these are adequate if you are not driving or going far off the beaten track. Should you wish to buy one, we recommend our own Rough Guide Map on a scale of 1:1,000,000, which shows roads, contours and geographical features clearly, and is printed on waterproof, tear-proof plastic. Among the alternatives, a good choice is GeoCenter's 1:800,000 map, with the Western Sahara on a 1:2,500,000 inset. Also good is Michelin's Morocco map (#959), on a scale of 1:1,000,000 with 1:600,000 insets of the Casa–Rabat area, the Fes–Meknes–Rif area, the Marrakesh area and the Middle Atlas, though much of the Western Sahara is only on a 1:4,000,000 inset. Maps (or guidebooks) which do not show the Western Sahara as part of Morocco are banned and liable to confiscation.

Trekking maps

Topographical maps used by trekkers, climbers, skiers, etc (1:50,000 and 1:100,000) are very difficult to find in Morocco. You have to go in person to the *Division de la Cartographie*, Avenue Hassan II, Km4, Rabat ⓣ0537 295034 (near the *gare routière* bus station, ask for *Residence Oum Kaltoum*), show your passport, and submit an order which *may* then be available for collection two working days later – if the request is approved, which is far from certain. The only exceptions are the maps of Toubkal (both scales) which will be served over the counter. These are also sporadically available at the *Hôtel Ali*, Marrakesh, or in Imlil, the trailhead for treks in the area. However, if you are planning to go trekking, it is best to try and get maps through a **specialist map outlet** before you leave home. Look for 1:100,000 (and if you're lucky 1:50,000) maps of the Atlas and other mountain areas. In Britain, Stanfords (ⓦwww.stanfords.co.uk) does a good pack of four maps covering the Djebel Toubkal area.

AMIS (see p.54) produces brief **map-guides** to the Asni-Toubkal, Western High Atlas (Taroudant) and Sirwa (Taliouine), Anti-Atlas (Tafraoute), Aklim (Igherm) and Djebel Bou Iblane/Bou Naceur (Middle Atlas) areas, written by our High Atlas contributor, Hamish Brown, and useful complements to the coverage in this guide. AMIS do mail order worldwide, and are definitely the best place to try for Moroccan maps that are unobtainable elsewhere.

More **detailed trekking guidebooks** are also available in both English and French. The most useful are Michael Peyron's *Grand Atlas Traverse* (West Col, UK; 2 vols), Robin Collomb's *Atlas Mountains* (West Col, UK), Richard Knight's *Trekking in the Moroccan Atlas* (Trailblazer Publications, UK) and Karl Smith's *Atlas Mountains: A Walker's Guide* (Cicerone Press, UK). Also available from West Col, in English, is a map guide to the Mgoun Massif at 1:100,000, which is useful for a wide region, second only to Toubkal in popularity. For climbing, a modern reproduction of the 1942 Dresch–Lépiney *Le Massif du Toubkal*, available at some bookshops, is useful. The best place to find these in Morocco is Marrakesh's Librairie Chatr (see p.379). Guidebooks are also on sale at the *CAF Refuge* at Oukaïmeden. One useful publication available in Morocco is *Randonées Pedestre dans le Massif du Mgoun*, which has routes shown on a 1:100,000 scale.

Money

Though the easiest way to carry your money is in the form of plastic, it is a good idea to also carry at least a couple of days' survival money in cash, and maybe some travellers' cheques as an emergency back-up.

Morocco's basic unit of **currency** is the **dirham** (dh). The dirham is not quoted on international money markets, a rate being set instead by the Moroccan government. The present rates are approximately **12.50dh to £1**, **8dh to US$1**, **11.50dh to €1**. As with all currencies there are fluctuations, but the dirham has roughly held its own against Western currencies over the last few years. A dirham is divided into 100 **centimes**, and you may find prices written or expressed in centimes rather than dirhams. Confusingly, centimes may also be referred to as **francs** or, in former Spanish zones of the country, as **pesetas**. You may also hear prices quoted in **rials**, or *reales*. In most parts of the country a dirham is considered to be twenty rials, though in Tangier and the Rif there are just two rials to the dirham. Coins of 10, 20 and 50 centimes, and 1, 5 and 10 dirhams are in circulation, along with notes of 20, 50, 100 and 200 dirhams.

In Algeciras, you can buy dirhams at poor rates from travel agents opposite the port entrance, and at slightly better rates from those inside the ferry terminal. You can also buy dirhams at similar rates from agents near the ferry terminals in Ceuta and Melilla. In Gibraltar, moneychangers will usually give you a very slightly better rate than in Morocco itself. When you're nearing the end of your stay, it's best to get down to as little Moroccan money as possible. You can change back dirhams at the airport on departure (you can't use them in duty-free shops), but you may be asked to produce bank exchange receipts – and you can change back only fifty percent of sums detailed on these. You'll probably be offered re-exchange into euros only. You can also change dirhams (at bad rates) into euros in Ceuta, Melilla and Algeciras, and into sterling in Gibraltar. It is illegal to import or export more than 1000dh.

Banks and exchange

English pounds and US and Canadian dollars can all be changed at banks, large hotels and some travel agents and tourist shops, but by far the mostly widely accepted foreign currency is the **euro**, which many people will accept in lieu of dirhams, currently at the (bad) rate of €1 to 10dh. Gibraltarian banknotes are accepted for exchange at a very slightly lower rate than English ones, but Scottish and Northern Irish notes are not negotiable in Morocco, and nor are Australian and New Zealand dollars, South African rand, Algerian dinars or Mauritanian ouguiya, though you should be able to change CFAs. Moroccan bank clerks may balk at changing banknotes with numbers scrawled on them by their counterparts abroad, so change any such notes for clean ones before leaving home.

BMCE tends to be the best bank for money changing. Usually at banks, you fill in forms at one desk, then join a second queue for the cashier, and you'll usually need to show your passport as proof of identity. Standard **banking hours** for most of the year are Monday to Friday 8.15am to 3.45pm. During Ramadan (see p.50), banks typically open 9.30am to 2pm. BMCE and Attijariwafa Bank sometimes have a separate bureau de change open longer hours and at weekends and there are now private foreign exchange bureaux in most major cities and tourist destinations, which open longer hours, often on Sundays too, change money with no fuss or bureaucracy, and don't usually charge commission. Many post offices will also change cash, and large hotels may change money out of banking hours, though their rates may not be good.

There is a **small currency black market** but you are not recommended to use it: changing money on the street is illegal and subject to all the usual scams, and the rate is not particularly preferential.

Plastic

Credit and debit cards on the Visa, Mastercard, Cirrus and Plus networks can be used to withdraw cash from **ATMs** at many banks, but not the ones outside post offices. Otherwise, banks may advance cash against Visa or Mastercard. By using ATMs, you get trade exchange rates, which are better than those charged by banks for changing cash, but your card issuer may add a transaction fee, sometimes hefty.

You can pay directly with plastic (usually with Mastercard, Visa or American Express, though the latter cannot be used in ATMs) in upmarket hotels, restaurants and tourist shops. There is a daily limit on ATM cash withdrawals, usually 3000dh.

Traveller's cheques

Traveller's cheques are as secure as plastic but nothing like as convenient. Some banks won't change them, and staff often find spurious reasons not to do so: they may demand to see the original receipt for the cheques, though of course you are not supposed to carry that and the cheques together (if you do show it, don't let the bank keep it), or even other, non-existent documentation that you will certainly not have. In the event that your cheques are lost or stolen, the issuing company will expect you to report the theft to them and to local police immediately. Most companies claim to replace lost or stolen cheques within 24 hours, though they may drag their feet if they suspect fraud. Visa and American Express offer pre-paid cards that you can load up with credit before you leave home and use in ATMs like a debit card – effectively traveller's cheques in plastic form.

American Express and wiring money

American Express is represented by S'Tours 4 Rue Turgot Racine, Casablanca ⓣ0522 361304, but these are only agents; they can issue Amex traveller's cheques, but they cannot receive mail or wired money, nor cash personal cheques.

For wiring money, **Western Union** is represented at every post office. Money-Gram's local agent will usually be a branch of Crédit du Maroc.

Opening hours

Opening hours follow a reasonably consistent pattern: banks (Mon–Fri 8.15am–3.45pm); museums (daily except Tues 9am–noon & 3–6pm) offices (Mon–Thurs 8.30am–noon & 2.30–6.30pm; Fri 8.30–11.30am & 3–6.30pm); Ville Nouvelle shops (Mon–Sat 8.30am–noon & 2–6.30pm); Medina shops (Sat–Thurs 9am–6pm, Fri 9am–1pm). These hours will vary during Ramadan, when banks, for example, open 9.30am to 2pm, and everything will close before nightfall, when those observing the fast – which is to say, nearly everybody – has to stop and eat.

Phones

The easiest way to call within Morocco or abroad is to use a public phone booth (*cabine*), which takes a **phone card** (*télécarte*) issued by Maroc Télécom. The cards are available from some newsagents and *tabacs*, and from post offices, and come in denominations of 5dh, 10dh, 20dh, 50dh and 100dh. Cardphones are widespread, and you can usually find a number of them by a town's main post office if nowhere else. Unfortunately, they are not very well maintained, and often don't work. Not infrequently, they dock a unit from your card and fail to connect you, but they are still the best and most convenient way to make calls.

An alternative is to use a **téléboutique**, common everywhere. Some use coins – 5dh and 10dh coins are best for foreign calls (you'll probably need at least 20dh) – others give you a card and charge you for the units used. International calls from a hotel are pricey and may be charged in three-minute increments, so that if you go one second over, you're charged for the next period.

Mobile phones can be used from most places (Morocco now has about 90 percent coverage). If using your own SIM card from home, calls are expensive, and you pay to receive as well as make them, and you can't top up in Morocco, so bring enough credit with you. Depending on how long you are spending in Morocco, it may be worth signing up with Maroc Telecom or Meditel, using their SIM card and a Moroccan number for your handset.

Instead of a dialling tone, Moroccan phones have a voice telling you in French and Arabic to dial the number. When calling a Moroccan number, the **ringing tone** consists of one-and-a-half-second bursts of tone, separated by a three-and-a-half-second silence. The **engaged tone** is a series of short tones (pip-pip-pip-pip), as in most other parts of the world. A short series of very rapid pips may also indicate that your call is being connected.

Phone numbers

Maroc Telecom seems to change all its numbers every couple of years. Moroccan numbers are now ten-digit, and all ten digits must be dialled, even locally. All mobile numbers now begin with 06, all ordinary landline numbers with 05. If you have an older number, here's how to convert it:

The Spanish enclaves of **Ceuta and Melilla** have nine-digit numbers, incorporating the former area codes (956 for Ceuta, 952 for Melilla), which must now be dialled even locally. To call from mainland Spain, you will only need to dial the nine-digit number. Calling Ceuta or Melilla from abroad, or from Morocco proper, dial the international access code (00 from Morocco), then 34, then the whole nine-digit number. To call Morocco from Ceuta or Melilla, dial 00-212, then the last nine digits of the number, omitting the initial zero.

Emergency numbers

Fire ⓣ15
Police (in towns) ⓣ19
Gendarmes (police force with jurisdiction outside towns) ⓣ177

International calls

To **call Morocco from abroad**, you dial the international access code (00 from Britain, Ireland, Spain, the Netherlands and New Zealand; 0011 from Australia; 011 from the USA and most of Canada), then the country code (212), then the last nine digits of the number, omitting the initial zero. To **call Ceuta or Melilla**, dial the international access code, then 34, then all nine digits of the number, beginning with 956 for Ceuta, 952 for Melilla.

For an **international call** from Morocco, Ceuta or Melilla, dial **00**, followed by the **country code** (1 for North America, 44 for the UK, etc), the area code (omitting the initial zero which prefixes area codes in most countries outside North America) and the subscriber number.

There is a twenty percent discount on international call rates from midnight to 8am weekdays, and all day at weekends. To reverse call charges, a good policy is to phone someone briefly and get them to ring you back, as collect (reverse charge) calls are hard to arrange.

Photography

Photography needs to be undertaken with care. If you are obviously taking a

Converting phone numbers

	pre-2002	2002	2006	since 2009
Casablanca region	ⓣ02/xxxxxx	ⓣ022 xxxxxx	ⓣ022 xxxxxx	ⓣ0522 xxxxxx
El Jadida region	ⓣ03/xxxxxx	ⓣ023 xxxxxx	ⓣ023 xxxxxx	ⓣ0523 xxxxxx
Marrakesh region	ⓣ04/xxxxxx	ⓣ044 xxxxxx	ⓣ024 xxxxxx	ⓣ0524 xxxxxx
Fes/Meknes region	ⓣ05/xxxxxx	ⓣ055 xxxxxx	ⓣ035 xxxxxx	ⓣ0535 xxxxxx
Oujda region	ⓣ06/xxxxxx	ⓣ056 xxxxxx	ⓣ036 xxxxxx	ⓣ0536 xxxxxx
Rabat region	ⓣ07/xxxxxx	ⓣ037 xxxxxx	ⓣ037 xxxxxx	ⓣ0537 xxxxxx
Agadir region	ⓣ08/xxxxxx	ⓣ048 xxxxxx	ⓣ028 xxxxxx	ⓣ0528 xxxxxx
Tangier region	ⓣ09/xxxxxx	ⓣ039 xxxxxx	ⓣ039 xxxxxx	ⓣ0539 xxxxxx
old mobiles	ⓣ01/xxxxxx	ⓣ061 xxxxxx	ⓣ061 xxxxxx	ⓣ0661 xxxxxx
newer mobiles			ⓣ0xx xxxxxx	ⓣ06xx xxxxxx

International dialling codes

	From Morocco, Ceuta or Melilla	To Morocco	To Ceuta or Melilla
UK	ⓣ00 44	ⓣ00 212	ⓣ00 34
Ireland	ⓣ00 353	ⓣ00 212	ⓣ00 34
US and Canada	ⓣ001	ⓣ011 212	ⓣ011 34
Australia	ⓣ00 61	ⓣ0011 212	ⓣ0011 34
New Zealand	ⓣ00 64	ⓣ00 212	ⓣ00 34
South Africa	ⓣ00 27	ⓣ09 212	ⓣ09 34

photograph of someone, ask their permission – especially in the more remote, rural regions where you can cause genuine offence. In Marrakesh's Djemaa el Fna, taking even quite general shots of the scene may cause somebody in the shot to demand money from you, sometimes quite aggressively. Also note that it is illegal to take photographs of anything considered strategic, such as an airport or a police station, so be careful where you point your camera – if in doubt, ask. On a more positive front, taking a photograph of someone you've struck up a friendship with and sending it on to them, or exchanging photographs, is often greatly appreciated.

Time

Morocco is on Greenwich Mean Time, with daylight saving (GMT+1) from the beginning of June to the end of September – a rather shorter period than the British Isles, North America or Europe. Ceuta and Melilla keep Spanish time, which is GMT+1 in winter and GMT+2 in summer. The difference should be borne in mind if you're coming from Morocco to catch ferries out of Ceuta or Melilla, or trains out of Algeciras, especally when Spain is on summer time but Morocco isn't, as there's then a two-hour time difference.

Tourist information

Morocco's national tourist board, the **Office National Marocain de Tourisme** (ONMT; ⓦwww.visitmorocco.com) maintains general information offices in several Western capitals, where you can pick up pamphlets on the main Moroccan cities and resorts, and a few items on cultural themes.

In Morocco itself, you'll find an **ONMT** office (*delegation de tourisme*) or a locally run office called a **Syndicat d'Initiative** bureau in all towns of any size or interest – often both (addresses detailed in the Guide). They can of course answer queries, though the *delegation*'s main function is promoting tourism and gathering statistics. Both offices should also be able to put you in touch with an officially recognized guide.

In addition, there is quite a bit of information available online, and plenty of books on Morocco (see pp.603–610). The Maghreb Society, based in the UK at the Maghreb Bookshop, 45 Burton St, London WC1H 9AL ⓣ020/7388 1840, ⓦwww.maghrebreview.com, publishes the *Maghreb Review*, the most important English-language journal on the Maghrebian countries, and members get a discount on books sold at the bookshop.

ONMT offices abroad

Canada Pl Montréal Trust, 1800 Rue McGill College, Suite 2450, Montreal, PQ H3A 3J6 ⓣ1-514/842-8111, ⓔonmt@qc.aira.com.
Spain c/Ventura Rodriguez 24, first floor, left, 28008 Madrid ⓣ91 542 7431, ⓔinformacion@turismomarruecos.com.
UK 205 Regent St, London W1B 4HB ⓣ020/7437 0073, ⓔmnto@morocco-tourism.org.uk.
USA 104 W 40th St, Suite 1820, New York, NY 10018 ⓣ1-212/221 1583.

Travel advice

Australian Department of Foreign Affairs ⓦwww.smartraveller.gov.au.
British Foreign & Commonwealth Office ⓦwww.fco.gov.uk.
Canadian Department of Foreign Affairs ⓦwww.voyage.gc.ca.
US State Department ⓦwww.travel.state.gov.

Travellers with disabilities

Facilities for people with disabilities are little developed in Morocco, and, although families are usually very supportive, many disabled Moroccans are reduced to begging. Despite this, able-bodied Moroccans are, in general, far more used to mixing with disabled people than their Western counterparts, and are much more likely to offer help without embarrassment if you need it.

Blindness is more common than in the West, and sighted Moroccans are generally used to helping blind and visually impaired people find their way around and get on and off public transport at the right stop.

There is little in the way of wheelchair access to most premises. In the street, the Ville Nouvelle districts are generally easier to negotiate than the often crowded Medinas, but don't expect kerb ramps at road crossings or other such concessions to wheelchair users. Medina areas in cities like Rabat and even Marrakesh should not be too hard to negotiate at quiet times of day, but in Fes and Tangier, where the streets are steep and interspersed with steps, you would need at least one helper and a well-planned route to get around.

Bus and train **travel** will be difficult because of the steps that have to be negotiated, but grands taxis are a more feasible mode of transport if you can stake a claim on the front seat (maybe paying for two places to get the whole of it) – if you don't have a helper travelling with you, and you require assistance, the driver or other passengers will almost certainly be happy to help you get in and out.

Accommodation at the lower end of the market is unlikely to be very accessible. Cheap city hotels tend to have small doorways and steep, narrow staircases, and often no elevator, though many will have ground-floor rooms. Beach hotels are more able to cater for visitors with mobility difficulties. Some package hotels, especially in Agadir, make an attempt to cater for wheelchair-users, with ramps, for example, but no accessible toilets. It is at the very top end of the market, however, that real changes are being made: new five-star hotels usually have a couple of rooms specifically adapted for wheelchairs. Obviously this needs to be booked well in advance, and it also confines you to very expensive places, but it is at least a start.

You'll probably find a **package tour** much easier than fully independent travel, but contact any tour operator to check they can meet your exact needs before making a booking. It's also important to ensure you are covered by any **insurance** policy you take out.

Hotels with rooms specially adapted for wheelchair users include the *Mövenpick* in Tangier (see p.90), the *Transatlantique* in Meknes (see p.184), the *Palais Jamaï* in Fes (see p.209), the *Sheraton* and *Hyatt Regency* in Casablanca (see p.303 & p.304), the *Sofitel* in Essaouira (see p.333), and the *Atlas Medina*, *Ryad Mogador Menara* and *Sofitel* among other Hivernage hotels in Marrakesh (see p.352). *Auberge Camping Toubkal* in Talioune (see p.509) also has a room adapted for wheelchair users. Other hotels, such as the *Hilton* in Rabat (see p.279) and the *Agadir Beach Club* and *Royal Atlas* in Agadir (see p.490), claim to be accessible, and to cater for wheelchair users, but do not have specially adapted rooms. Obviously, you should always call ahead to check whether any particular hotel can meet your specific needs.

Guide

Guide

Tangier, Tetouan and the northwest

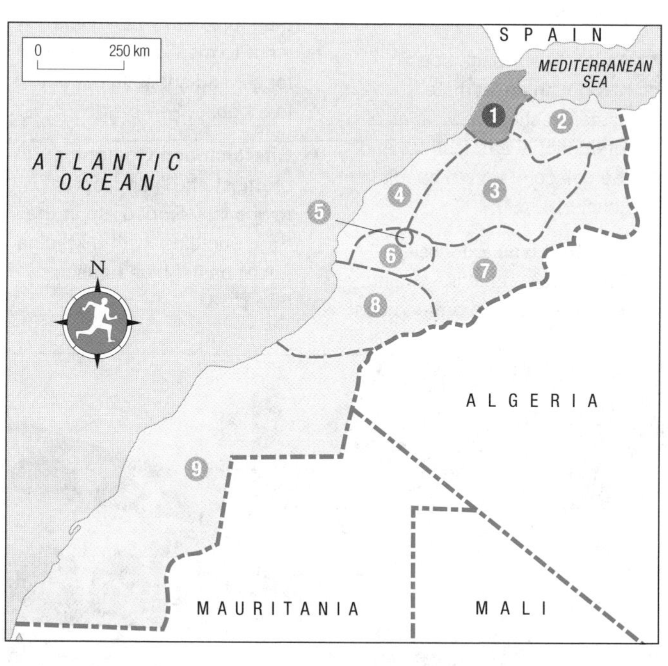

CHAPTER 1

Highlights

✱ **Tangier's Petit Socco** A tiny square home to the favourite café haunts of Burroughs and Bowles, a great place to sip tea and observe the daily drama of Medina life. See p.95

✱ **The Caves of Hercules** Look out to sea from this grotto in the cliffs, through a cave window shaped like Africa. See p.106

✱ **Asilah** A laid-back beach resort with an intimate pastel-washed Medina, an international arts festival, and the palace of an old bandit chief. See p.107

✱ **Ancient Lixus** Extensive Roman ruins in a fine setting, which you'll have pretty much to yourself to explore. See p.114

✱ **Moulay Bousselham** Wander the expansive windswept Atlantic beach and take a boat ride out to the nearby lagoon, home to diverse birdlife and pink flamingos. See p.116

✱ **Ceuta** A Spanish enclave with a couple of forts and no less than three army museums – not to mention good beer, tapas, and shops full of duty-free booze. See p.118

✱ **Chefchaouen** One of the prettiest and friendliest towns in Morocco, up in the Rif mountains, with a Medina full of pastel blue houses. See p.131

▲ Chefchaouen

1

Tangier, Tetouan and the northwest

The northwest can be an intense introduction to Morocco, encompassing the two Moroccan cities – Tangier and Tetouan – that are most notorious as blackspots for hustlers and unofficial guides preying on first-time visitors. **Tangier**, hybridized and slightly seedy from its long European contact, has a culture distinct from any other Moroccan city and an age-old role as the meeting point of Europe and Africa. With new renovation works underway throughout the city and foreign investors gradually returning to the area, spurred on by the completion of the new goods-only Tanger Mediterranée port, the continuing effort to reclaim some of Tangier's former cosmopolitan image is becoming more and more evident.

Heading south from Tangier along the **Atlantic coast** towards Rabat, the best places to get acclimatized are the seaside resorts of Asilah and Larache. **Asilah** is a relaxed and low-key town, well known for its **International Arts Festival**. **Larache** is similarly attractive, with its coastal cafés and proximity to the ancient Carthaginian-Roman site of **Lixus**. A more distinctively Moroccan resort is **Moulay Bousselham**, south of Larache, with its windswept Atlantic beach and abundance of birdlife.

The Spanish enclave of **Ceuta** is a slightly frustrating port of entry though a pleasant change of pace when crossing from Morocco. In the shadow of the wild Rif mountains, Tetouan feels more Moroccan than Tangier – its Medina a glorious labyrinth, its sprawling beaches popular with both locals and visitors. South of Tetouan is the mountain town of **Chefchaouen** – a small-scale and enjoyably laid-back place to come to terms with being in Morocco.

Northern Morocco has an especially quirky **colonial history**, having been divided into three separate zones. Tetouan was the administrative capital of the **Spanish zone**; the **French zone** began at Souk el Arba du Rharb, the edge of rich agricultural plains sprawling southward; while **Tangier** experienced **International Rule** under a group of foreign legations. The Spanish enclave of Ceuta (see p.118) is, along with Melilla (see p.154), a peculiar legacy of this colonial past.

Subsequently, although French is the official second **language** (after Arabic) throughout Morocco, older people in much of the northwest are equally, or more, fluent in **Spanish** – a basic knowledge of which can prove extremely useful.

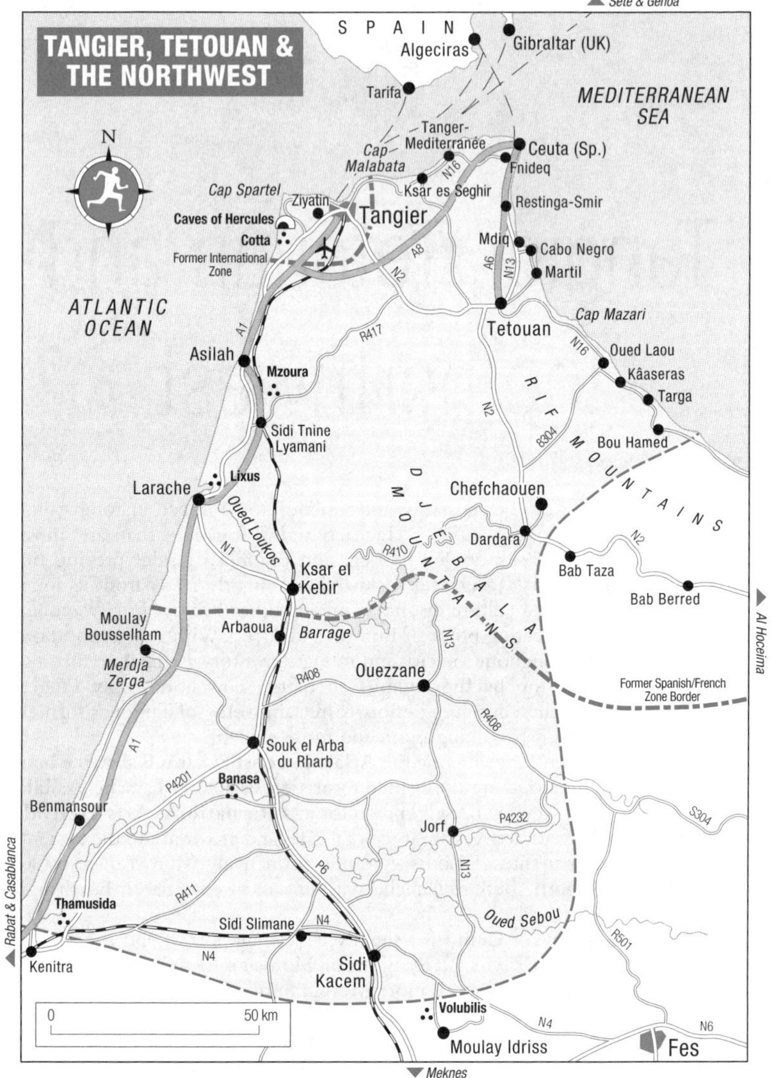

Tangier (Tanja, Tanger) and around

For the first half of the twentieth century **TANGIER** was an international city with its own laws and administration, plus an eclectic community of exiles, expatriates and refugees. It was home, at various times, to Spanish and Central European refugees, Moroccan nationalists and – drawn by loose tax laws and free-port status – to over seventy banks and four thousand companies, many of them dealing in currency transactions forbidden in their own countries. Writers were also attracted to the city. **Paul Bowles**, the American novelist who knew Tangier in the 1930s and called it his "dream city", settled here after 1945.

Tangier's hustlers

Faux guides ("false guides") are petty crooks who attach themselves to new-in-town tourists, usually claiming to be "guiding" you and therefore due payment, or just steering you into hotels or shops where they receive a commission (added to your bill, naturally). At one time, Tangier's *faux guides* were particularly heavy. Nowadays they have largely been cleaned out of town thanks to a nationwide police crackdown,

Generally speaking, *faux guides* now limit their activities to encouraging you to visit the shops that employ them – though if they can hustle you into a hotel that will pay them commission, they will do that too. Most will also try to sell you *kif* (cannabis).

Faux guides have a number of approaches you will soon learn to recognize: a favourite is trying to guess your nationality, or asking "Are you lost?" or "What are you looking for?" If you ignore them or turn down their advances, they will typically accuse you of being angry or "paranoid". The best way to get rid of them is to ignore them completely, or explain politely (while never slackening your pace) that you are all right and don't need any help. As a last resort – and it should not come to this – you can dive into a café or even threaten to go to the police if necessary (the *Brigade Touristique* are based in the former Gare de Ville train station by the port, and there is also a police post in the kasbah). Bear in mind that local residents, as well as the law, are on your side.

William Burroughs, in whose books Tangier appears as "Interzone", spent most of the 1950s here, and most of the Beats – Jack Kerouac, Allen Ginsberg, Brion Gysin and the rest – passed through. Tangier was also the world's first and most famous **gay resort** favoured by the likes of Tennessee Williams, Joe Orton and Kenneth Williams. The ghosts of these times have left a slight air of decay about the city, still tangible in the older hotels and bars. Despite the subtle hints of past excess and glamour, the city's days of hedonism are undoubtedly over.

Rooted in an enduring eccentricity, Tangier's charm is nonetheless undeniable. Until recently, the city's tourism future didn't look too rosy, having, over the years, gained a reputation as somewhere to avoid due to continuing reports of a large population of hustlers and unsavory characters known to prey on foreign arrivals. King Mohammed VI, however, has provided much of the impetus for Tangier to re-invent itself under a flurry of renovation and building projects. Tangier's passenger port, Tanger-Ville, is central to this economic future; there's a constant stream of ferries arriving (nearly around the clock during the August holidays), an influx which has prompted the construction of a new coastal highway that connects Tangier to Casablanca and, ultimately, Marrakesh. Despite all efforts to resurrect Tangier, progress is slow and the city has retained a unique atmosphere very much defined by its sometimes turbulent history.

The **Bay of Tangier** curves around to a pair of capes: Spartel to the west, with the picturesque Caves of Hercules; and Malabata to the east, which has the better beaches. Either makes a pleasant detour or afternoon's trip from Tangier.

Some history

Tingis is Amazigh (Berber) for a marsh, betraying the site's Berber origins, though it was colonized around the seventh century BC by the **Phoenicians**, a seafaring people from what is now Lebanon. In 42 AD, the **Romans** made Tingis the capital of their newly created province of Mauretania Tingitania (roughly the north of modern Morocco). In 429AD, with the collapse of the Roman Empire's western half, Tangier was taken by the Vandals, after which point things become a bit hazy. It seems to have been regained a century or

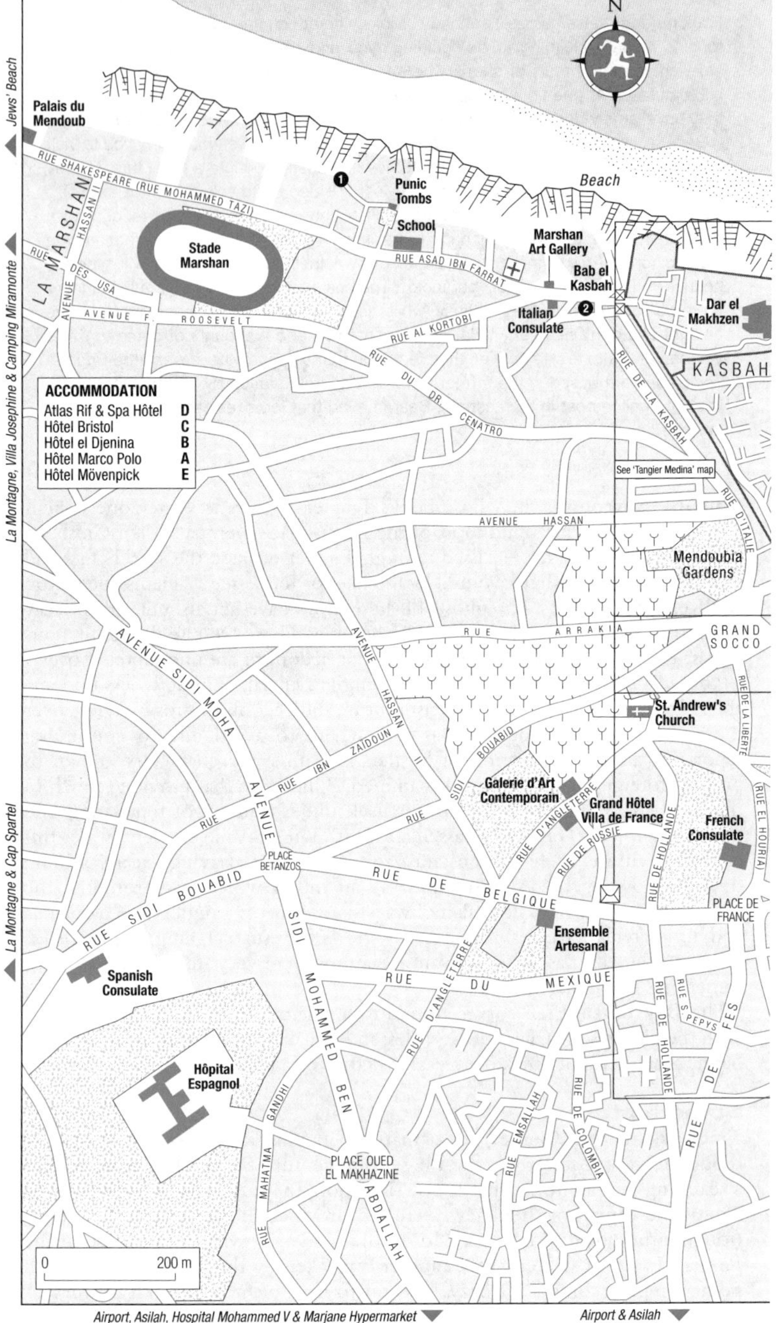
ACCOMMODATION
Atlas Rif & Spa Hôtel D
Hôtel Bristol C
Hôtel el Djenina B
Hôtel Marco Polo A
Hôtel Mövenpick E
Jews' Beach
La Montagne, Villa Josephine & Camping Miramonte
La Montagne & Cap Spartel
Airport, Asilah, Hospital Mohammed V & Marjane Hypermarket
Airport & Asilah
N
Palais du Mendoub
Punic Tombs
School
Beach
Stade Marshan
LA MARSHAN
RUE SHAKESPEARE (RUE MOHAMMED TAZI)
HASSAN II
RUE DES USA
AVENUE F. ROOSEVELT
RUE ASAD IBN FARRAT
Marshan Art Gallery
Bab el Kasbah
Italian Consulate
Dar el Makhzen
KASBAH
RUE AL KORTOBI
RUE DU DR. CENATRO
RUE DE LA KASBAH
See 'Tangier Medina' map
RUE D'ITALIE
AVENUE HASSAN
Mendoubia Gardens
RUE ARRAKIA
GRAND SOCCO
AVENUE SIDI MOHA
AVENUE HASSAN II
St. Andrew's Church
RUE DE LA LIBERTE
RUE IBN ZAIDOUN
SIDI BOUABID
Galerie d'Art Contemporain
Grand Hôtel Villa de France
French Consulate
RUE EL HOURIA
RUE D'ANGLETERRE
RUE DE RUSSIE
RUE DE HOLLANDE
AVENUE
RUE
PLACE BETANZOS
RUE SIDI BOUABID
RUE DE BELGIQUE
PLACE DE FRANCE
Ensemble Artesanal
Spanish Consulate
SIDI MOHAMMED BEN ABDALLAH
RUE D'ANGLETERRE
RUE DU MEXIQUE
RUE S. PEPYS
RUE DE HOLLANDE
RUE DE FES
Hôpital Espagnol
RUE MAHATMA GANDHI
RUE EMSALLAH
RUE DE COLOMBIA
PLACE OUED EL MAKHAZINE
0 200 m

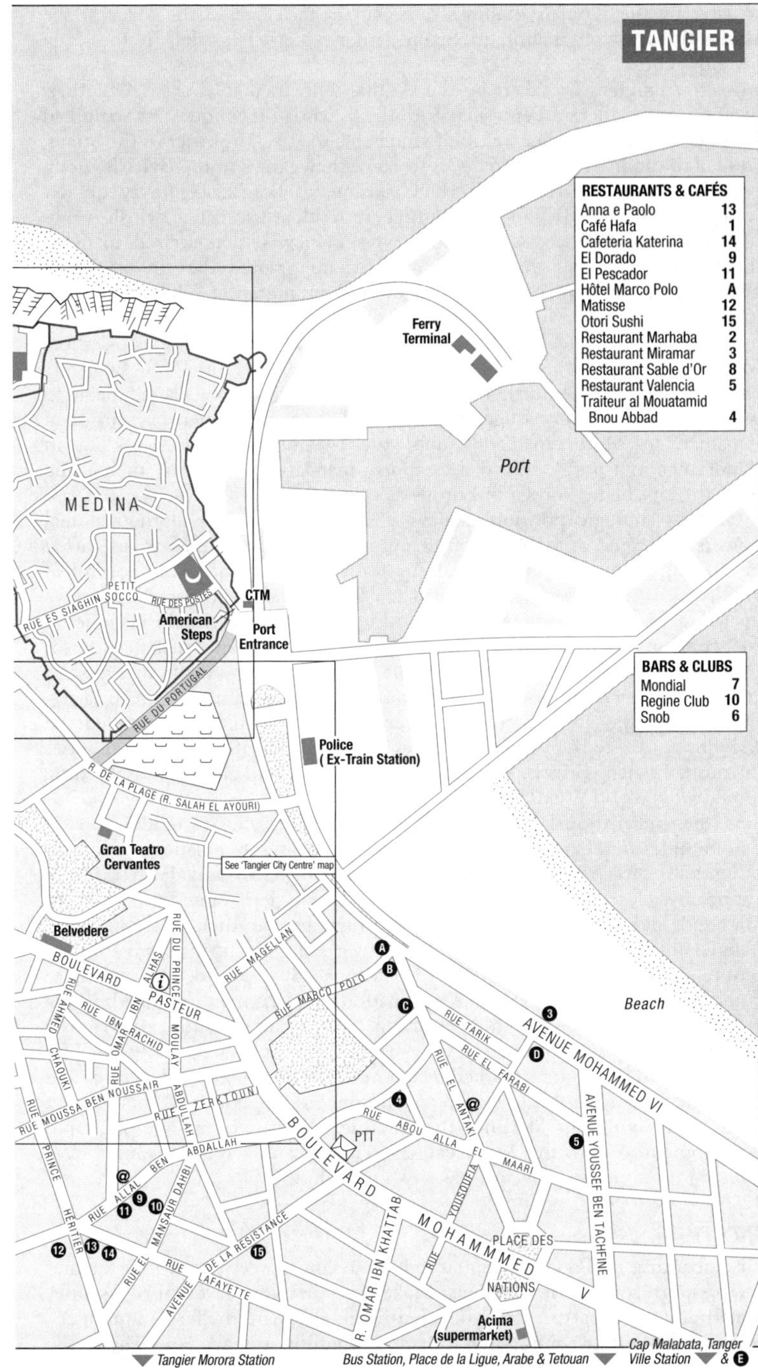
TANGIER
RESTAURANTS & CAFÉS
Anna e Paolo 13
Café Hafa 1
Cafeteria Katerina 14
El Dorado 9
El Pescador 11
Hôtel Marco Polo A
Matisse 12
Otori Sushi 15
Restaurant Marhaba 2
Restaurant Miramar 3
Restaurant Sable d'Or 8
Restaurant Valencia 5
Traiteur al Mouatamid Bnou Abbad 4
BARS & CLUBS
Mondial 7
Regine Club 10
Snob 6
Ferry Terminal
Port
MEDINA
PETIT SOCCO
RUE ES SIAGHIN
RUE DES POSTES
CTM
American Steps
Port Entrance
RUE DU PORTUGAL
Police (Ex-Train Station)
R. DE LA PLAGE (R. SALAH EL AYOURI)
Gran Teatro Cervantes
See 'Tangier City Centre' map
Belvedere
BOULEVARD PASTEUR
RUE DU PRINCE MOULAY ABDULLAH
RUE MAGELLAN
RUE MARCO POLO
RUE AHMED CHAOUKI
RUE IBN RACHID
RUE OMAR IBN ALHAS
RUE MOUSSA BEN NOUSSAIR
RUE ZERKTOUNI
RUE TARIK
RUE EL FARABI
RUE EL ANTAKI
AVENUE MOHAMMED VI
Beach
RUE ABOU ALLA EL MAARI
AVENUE YOUSSEF BEN TACHFINE
BOULEVARD MOHAMMED V
PTT
RUE PRINCE HERITIER
RUE ALLAL BEN ABDALLAH
RUE EL MANSOUR DAHBI
RUE YOUSSOUFIA
R. OMAR IBN KHATTAB
AVENUE DE LA RESISTANCE
RUE LAFAYETTE
PLACE DES NATIONS
Acima (supermarket)
6, 7, 8 & Tangier Morora
Tangier Morora Station
Bus Station, Place de la Ligue, Arabe & Tetouan
Cap Malabata, Tanger Ville Station & E

so later by the Roman Empire's resurgent eastern half in the form of the **Byzantines**, before falling to Spain's rulers, the **Visigoths**, in the early seventh century.

In 707, Tangier was taken by the **Arabs**, who used it as a base for their invasion of the Iberian Peninsula. With the Christian reconquest of Spain and Portugal however, Tangier was itself vulnerable to attack from across the Straits, and fell to the **Portuguese** in 1471. In 1661, they gave it to the **British** (along with Bombay) as part of Princess Catherine of Braganza's dowry on her wedding to Charles II. Tangier's Portuguese residents, accusing British troops of looting and rape, abandoned the town, but new settlers arrived, many of them Jewish refugees from Spain, and Britain granted the city a charter guaranteeing freedom of religion, trade and immigration. The British also introduced tea, now Morocco's national drink. Under virtually constant siege however, they found Tangier an expensive and unrewarding possession. **Moulay Ismail** laid siege to the city in 1678, and in 1680, England's parliament refused any further funding to defend it. Four years later, unable to withstand the siege any longer, the British abandoned Tangier. The city then remained in Moroccan hands until the twentieth century, growing in importance as a port – one of its exports, mandarins, even took their name from the city, being known in Europe as **tangerines**.

Tangier's strategic position made it a coveted prize for all the colonial powers at the end of the nineteenth century. European representatives started insinuating themselves into the administration of the city, taking control of vital parts of the infrastructure, and when France and Spain decided to carve up Morocco between them, Britain insisted that Tangier should become an **International Zone**, with all Western powers having an equal measure of control. This was agreed as early as 1905, and finalized by treaty in 1923. An area of 380 square kilometres, with some 150,000 inhabitants, the International Zone was administered by a representative of the Sultan called the Mendoub, "assisted" by representatives of the Zone's foreign communities (Spanish, French, British, Portuguese, Dutch, Belgian, Italian and Swedish, joined after World War II by the Americans).

At the International Zone's peak in the early 1950s, Tangier's foreign communities numbered 60,000 – then nearly half the population. As for the other half, pro-independence demonstrations in 1952 and 1953 made it abundantly clear that most Tanjawis (natives of Tangier) wanted to be part of a united, independent Morocco. When they gained their wish in 1956, Tangier lost its special status, and almost overnight, the finance and banking businesses shifted their operations to Spain and Switzerland. The expatriate communities dwindled too as the new national government imposed bureaucratic controls and instituted a "clean-up" of the city. Brothels – previously numbering almost a hundred – were banned, and in the early 1960s "**The Great Scandal**" erupted, sparked by a number of paedophile convictions and escalating into a wholesale closure of the once outrageous gay bars. After a period of significant decline, the last decade has been one of rapid development as both the Moroccan government and foreign investors have directed more interest towards the city and its future.

Arrival

Disembarking by **ferry** at Tangier can be a slow process, with long queues for passport control and customs. Make sure that you have your **passport stamped** (and departure card collected) while on board the ferry; announcements to this effect are not always made in English, so make your way to the purser's office during the journey. If you miss out on this, you'll be left until last by the officials in Tangier.

Outside the main terminal building are offices for the various ferry companies and branches of most of the local banks (some with ATM); most sell dirhams at regular rates but they don't always accept travellers' cheques. There is also an Assurance Frontière office in case you need to sort vehicle insurance, and a **consigne** (left luggage) just outside the port entrance, round the corner from the CTM office and about 20m up Rue du Portugal towards the Medina steps. Expect to pay about 10dh per piece.

Unofficial guides – or **hustlers** – can be incredibly persistent around the port entrance, telling you some fairly amazing tales: the hotels are full, the Medina is dangerous, the trains and buses are on strike. Don't take too much of this at face value, and don't feel in any way duty-bound to employ anyone's services – you don't need a guide in Tangier. From the port, it's a relatively short walk into the centre or a short ride by petit taxi (which should be around 10dh on the meter); you may need to insist that it's used.

Tangier's **airport**, Ibn Batouta International, is 15km outside the city. Taxis line up outside the terminal and should charge 120dh for up to six passengers (get a group together before leaving the terminal building). The only other option is to walk 2km to the main road, where you can pick up bus #9, which goes to Rue de Fes in town. The newly built terminal has a few **banks** which are usually open to meet incoming flights; one of them will cash travellers' cheques and they have ATMs. There is also a **post office**, British Airways and Royal Air Maroc desks as well as desks for most of the international **car rental** firms.

Trains arrive and depart from, **Tanger Ville**, 3km from the port, and around 15dh from the centre by petit taxi. The station is served by bus #16, which will get you as far as the bus station (see below), but does not run into the city centre. Tanger Ville is very handy for hotels at the eastern end of the beach and is a short taxi ride from the city centre which is 3km away. The penultimate stop, suburban **Tanger Morora**, is 4km from the city centre. The #13 bus heads directly into town from here. **Bus services** from most towns generally arrive at **Tangier Gare Routière**, south of the Ville Nouvelle. **CTM** has buses from Rabat, Casablanca, Fes, Marrakesh and the other major cities, some of which continue on from the *gare routière* to the port entrance. It's about a fifteen-minute walk into town from the *gare routière*, or around 10dh by petit taxi.

Orientation and information

After the initial confusion of an unfamiliar Arab city, Tangier is surprisingly easy to find your way around. As with all the larger Moroccan cities, it's made up of two parts: the **Medina**, the original Moroccan town, and the **Ville Nouvelle**, built by its several European colonizers. Inside the Medina, a classic web of alleyways and stepped passages, is the old citadel or **kasbah**, with the former Sultanate's palace at its centre.

Together with the **beach** and the seafront **Avenue Mohammed VI** the easiest reference points are the city's three main squares – the Grand Socco, Petit Socco and Place de France. **Place de France** is a conventional, French-looking square at the heart of the Ville Nouvelle, flanked by kerbside cafés and a **terrace-belvedere** looking out over the Straits to Spain with the small port of Tarifa usually visible almost directly opposite. From here, **Boulevard Pasteur** (the main city street) leads off past the helpful ONMT Délégation de Tourisme at no. 29 where official guides can be enlisted (Mon–Fri 8.30am–4.30pm; ⓣ0539 948050), towards the main PTT (post office)on Boulevard Mohammed V.

Street name confusions

Spanish and French colonial names are still in use alongside their Arabicized successors. In addition, both *Rue* and *Calle* are sometimes replaced by *Zankat*, and *Avenue* and *Boulevard* by *Charih*. Local maps tend to use the new Arabic versions, though not all of the street signs have been changed. In the text and maps of this guide, we have used new names only when firmly established. Among the main street-name changes, note:

Main squares
Place de France – Place de Faro
Grand Socco – Place du 9 Avril 1947
Petit Socco – Place Souk Dakhil

Medina
Rue des Chrétiens – Rue des Almouahidines
Rue de la Marine – Rue Djemaa Kebir
Rue des Postes – Rue Mokhtar Ahardane

Beach
Avenue d'Espagne – Avenue Mohammed VI
Avenues des FAR – Avenue Mohammed VI

North from Place de France, **Rue de la Liberté** runs to the **Grand Socco**, a popular open space in front of the Medina. The north side of the square opens onto the Medina's principal street, **Rue es Siaghin**, which culminates in the **Petit Socco**, a tiny square of old cafés and cheap hotels.

City transport

Grands taxis (large cream/beige Mercedes) are permitted to carry up to six passengers. The price for a ride should be fixed in advance – 15–20dh per person is standard for any trip within the city, including tip.

Small blue/green **petits taxis** (which carry just three passengers) can be flagged down around the town. Most of these are metered – a typical rate for a city trip is 10dh per person – make sure the driver starts his meter from zero. On the streets you can **hail a taxi**, whether it has passengers or not; if it is going in your direction it will generally take you. If you join a taxi with passengers, you pay the full fare, as if it were empty. **After 8pm** both grand and petit taxi rates increase by fifty percent.

City buses are not much good to tourists. The most useful route is #2, which runs from St Andrew's Church in the Grand Socco to Ziyatin and on to the village of Jabila, not far from the Caves of Hercules. At weekends in summer, it runs to the caves themselves; other times, you can get a grand taxi from Ziyatin. Route #9 goes from Rue de Fes along the Rabat road to the airport turn-off, some 2km from the airport itself. Route #16 connects the train station and the bus station, and runs on to Cape Malabata, but does not serve the city centre.

Accommodation

Tangier has dozens of **hotels and pensions**, and finding a room is rarely much of a problem. The city does, however, get crowded during July and August, when many Moroccan families holiday here, or spend a few days en route to and from Europe. Cheaper hotels and *pensions* hike up their prices at this time of year, and you'll often get a better deal at one of the mid-range hotels. As always, there is a choice between the **Medina** or **Ville Nouvelle**, the latter offering greater comforts.

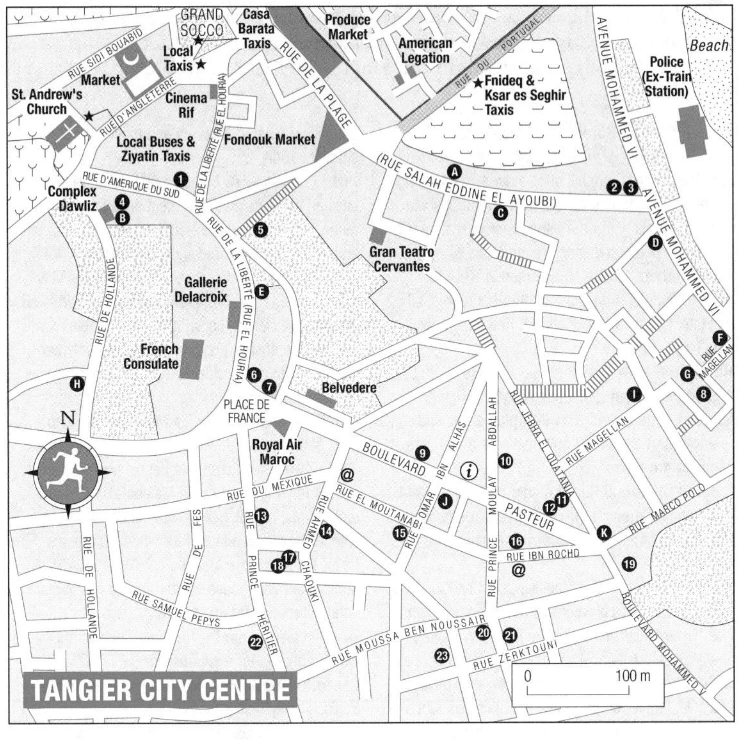

ACCOMMODATION		RESTAURANTS & CAFÉS				BARS & CLUBS	
Hôtel Biarritz	F	Café Metropole	9	Restaurant Hassi		Atlas Bar	22
Hôtel Dawliz	B	Café de Paris	6	Baida	2	Borsalino	20
Hôtel de Paris	J	Casa España	11	Restaurant le Coeur		Caid's Bar	E
Hôtel el Minzah	E	Dolcy's	12	de Tanger	7	Carrousel Bar	17
Hôtel el Muniria	I	El Korsan	E	Restaurant Number One	19	Dean's Bar	1
Hôtel Exclesior	G	L'Marsa	D	Restaurant Pagode	18	Morocco Palace	10
Hôtel L'Marsa	D	Le Mangana	4	Restaurant Populaire		Radio Club	20
Pension Atou	A	Rahmouni	21	Saveur Mediterannée	5	Scott's	15
Pension Hollande	H	Relais de Paris	4	Restaurant San Remo	14	Tanger Inn	8
Pension Miami	C	Restaurant Africa	3	Rubis Grill	16	The Pub	23
Rembrandt Hôtel	K	Restaurant Agadir	13				

The closest campsite to Tangier is the intermittently open *Camping Miramonte*, also known as *Camping Marshan* (☎0539 937133). Another option is *Camping Ashakar* (☎0674 719419), 16km from town above the Caves of Hercules (see p.106).

Seafront hotels

All the places below are along or just off the seafront **Avenue Mohammed VI**. Several hotels are on Rue Magellan, which is easy to miss: it zigzags up from the seafront alongside the *Hôtel Biarritz* towards Boulevard Pasteur in the Ville Nouvelle. A number of others are on Rue de la Plage, which runs uphill from the port to the Grand Socco and is lined with small *pensions*.

All those listed below are within walking distance of the port except for *Hôtel Mövenpick* which is on the outskirts and requires a taxi to get to.

All these hotels are marked on the Tangier City Centre map on p.89, except where stated.

Atlas Rif & Spa Hôtel 152 Av Mohammed VI; ⓣ0539 349300, ⓦwww.hotelsatlas.com. A luxury four-star where Churchill once stayed, overlooking the beach and the best-value pick of the upscale seafront hotels with refurbished rooms, restaurant, swimming pool, fitness centre, and bar. ❼

Hôtel Biarritz 104 Av Mohammed VI ⓣ0539 932473. An old hotel with comfortable rooms, all en suite, and a fair bit of charm. Reductions for long stays. ❸

Hôtel Bristol 14 Rue el Antaki ⓣ0539 942914. A good bet, 100m uphill from the beach, with large en-suite rooms with TVs, plus a bar and restaurant. A 1950s lift still operates and saves climbing the stairs. ❸

Hôtel el Djenina 8 Rue el Antaki ⓣ0539 942244, ⓔeldjenina@menara.ma. Though the rooms are a little on the small side, it's immaculate and an excellent choice. ❹

Hôtel el Muniria 1 Rue Magellan ⓣ0539 935337 or 0510 047227. This is where William Burroughs wrote *The Naked Lunch* (in room 9, no longer available), and Jack Kerouac and Allen Ginsberg stayed here too when they came to visit him. Nowadays it's a clean and quiet family-run *pension* – the main remnant of its Beat history being the adjoining *Tanger Inn* bar (see p.101). En-suite showers, but hot water mornings and evenings only. ❸

Hôtel Exclesior 17 Rue Magellan, straight up from *Hôtel Biarritz* ⓣ0534 436987. This 23-roomed hotel has seen better days but is good value for the price. Large, airy rooms, some with small balconies and views. Shared showers and toilets. Hot showers 10dh. ❷

Hôtel l'Marsa 92 Av Mohammed VI ⓣ0539 932339. Located above its own pavement restaurant with a range of rooms available, some of them with balcony and ocean views. Shared showers and toilets. ❷

Hôtel Marco Polo Corner of Av Mohammed VI & Rue el Antaki ⓣ0539 941124. Recently refurbished and very efficiently run, with 33 comfortable rooms in a new extension, popular restaurant, lively bar (both open to non-residents), fitness centre, and hammam. ❹

Hôtel Mövenpick Route de Malabata; off map, p.85 ⓣ0539 329300, ⓦwww.moevenpick-hotels.com. One of Tangier's most deluxe hotels, 3km east of town on the road to Malabata, with three restaurants, a pool, health club, sauna and casino, with some rooms adapted for wheelchair users. ❽

Hôtel Nabil 11 Rue Magellan ⓣ0539 375407. A refurbished warehouse converted into a first-class hotel. All rooms are en suite, and there are stunning views from the front top-floor rooms. Parking garage for residents. ❸

Pension Atou 45 Rue de la Plage (no phone). Basic, slightly musty rooms with no showers (there are public ones just down the street), but very cheap, especially for singles. ❶

Pension Miami 126 Rue de la Plage ⓣ0539 932900. Beautifully tiled old Spanish town-house said to be over a hundred years old. Pleasant rooms, and bathrooms on each corridor. If full try *Pension Madrid* next door. ❷

Central Ville Nouvelle hotels

Most of these recommendations are within a few blocks of Place de France/ Place de Faro and the central Boulevard Pasteur; coming up from the port, if you've got much luggage, a taxi can be useful as it's a steep climb. All these hotels are marked on the Tangier City Centre map on p.89, except where stated.

Hôtel Dawliz Complex Dawliz, 42 Rue de Hollande ⓣ0539 333377, ⓦwww.ledawliz.com. Facing the once elegant but now ruined *Grand Hôtel Villa de France*, this four-star establishment has a pool and all mod cons (satellite TV, a/c, heating and so on). Breakfast included. ❻

Hôtel de Paris 42 Bd Pasteur ⓣ0539 931877, ⓕ0539 938126. Central hotel with spacious and spotless rooms, good breakfasts, a few Art Deco touches in the public areas, some interesting old photos in the lobby and very helpful staff. Breakfast included. ❹

Hôtel el Minzah 85 Rue el Houria (Rue de la Liberté) ⓣ0539 333444, ⓦwww.elminzah.com. Built in 1931, this remains Tangier's most prestigious hotel, with a wonderful garden, a pool overlooking the sea and town, elegant (if pricey) bar, and a new wellness centre with hammam. Past guests have included Cecil Beaton, Jean Genet and Mick Jagger, and tradition has it that it was from here that World War II Allied agents spied on their German counterparts at the *Hôtel Rif*. ❽

Pension Hollande 139 Rue de Hollande ⓣ0539 937838. Behind the French Consulate, this large, airy house, shaded by trees, offers simple, but good-value rooms and free off-road parking. ❷

Rembrandt Hôtel Corner of blvds Pasteur and Mohammed V ⓣ0539 333314, ⓦwww.hotel-rembrandt.com. A reasonably stylish hotel with bar and pool, but starting to show its age. ❻

Medina hotels

In the Medina you have a choice between basic *pensions* and pricey upscale riads. To reach the Medina from the port, either walk up Rue du Portugal to the Grand Socco, or go up the steps behind the port entrance, round to the Grand Mosque and the junction of Rue des Postes/Rue Dar el Baroud. All these places are marked on the Tangier Medina map on p.94.

Dar Nour 20 Rue Gourna, in the kasbah, off Rue Sidi Ahmed Boukouja ⓣ0662 112724, ⓦwww.darnour.com. Tangier's first guesthouse is now run by a French trio who have created ten individually styled suites in what was once five small houses. Sweeping views from the terrace of the Medina and Straits can be enjoyed over a sumptuous breakfast (included). ❻

Hôtel Continental 36 Rue Dar el Baroud, easily reached from the Petit Socco ⓣ0539 931024, ⓔhcontinental@iam.net.ma. By far the best hotel in the Medina, the Continental was founded in 1865, with Queen Victoria's son Alfred its first official guest, and other notables have included Degas and Churchill. Today, the hotel has a somewhat ragged feel and, despite renovations, is showing its age. However, nothing can detract from the unrivalled view of the port from its terrace – captured in Bertolucci's film of Paul Bowles' novel *The Sheltering Sky*. ❺

Hôtel du Grand Socco (aka *Hôtel Taïef*) Grand Socco, entrance round the back on Rue Imam Layti. The oldest hotel in Tangier. It's seen better days, but the large rooms are reasonable value if shared, and the café has a great vista over the Grand Socco. No showers, but public ones less than 50m away. ❷

Hôtel Mamora 19 Rue des Postes ⓣ0539 934105. Centrally located in the heart of the Medina, with clean, pleasant rooms, all with showers – though there's only hot water in the mornings. ❸

Hôtel Olid 12 Rue des Postes ⓣ0539 931310. Tatty, ramshackle and eccentrically decorated, but still reasonable value for money. Some rooms are en suite. Hot showers 10dh. ❷

La Tangerina 19 Riad Sultan, in the kasbah ⓣ0539 947731, ⓦwww.latangerina.com. Pared, down Mediterranean elegance, stylishly composed interiors, an ambiance of simple luxury and an outstanding terrace overlooking the Straits have quickly established this well-run guesthouse as one of Tangiers' best. ❻

Pension Fuentes 9 Petit Socco, at the heart of the Medina ⓣ0539 934669. One of the first hotels in Tangier and still a friendly and atmospheric dive. The café below can be noisy. ❷

Pension Palace 2 Rue des Postes ⓣ0539 936128. A touch of past splendours – balconies and a central court with fountain – led Bertolucci to shoot part of *The Sheltering Sky* here. Many rooms have a rugged charm and there are a few with en suites. ❷

Riad Tanja 2 Rue Amar Alilech, turn off Rue de Portugal near the American Legation ⓣ0539 333538, ⓕ0539 333054. Less than two years old and already known for exemplary service and a warm, understated character. Five rooms decorated with zellij tiling, all en suite and some with their own sitting room complete with satellite TV. Parking available near the American Steps. Breakfast included. ❻–❼

The beach and Ville Nouvelle

Tangier's interest and attraction lies in the city as a whole: its café life, beach, and the tumbling streets of the Medina. The handful of "monuments", with the notable exception of the Dar el Makhzen palace, are best viewed as adding direction to your wanderings, rather than as unmissable sights.

The town beach

During the day at least, the beach is a pleasant place to escape the city streets. It is easier, safer and some say compulsory to change in a cabin, so when you arrive at the beach you might like to attach yourself to one of the **beach bars**, most of which offer showers and deck chairs, as well as food and drink. With bars and restaurants opening and closing sporadically the favourites change each year. *The Sun Beach*, where Tennessee Williams wrote a first draft of *Cat on a Hot Tin Roof*, is the exception and still manages to tick away all year with a regular flow of clientele. *Mondial* and *Miramar* are two of the better recent additions, and *Miami*, with its gardens to laze around in, is one of the most pleasant.

By day, don't leave anything on the beach unattended. By night, limit your exploration to the beach bars as the beach itself, although floodlit, can still be unsafe and you may become a target.

The Grand Socco and Place de France

The **Grand Socco** is the obvious place to start a ramble around the town. Its name, like so many in Tangier, is a French–Spanish hybrid, proclaiming its origins as the main market square. The markets have long gone, but the square remains a meeting place and its cafés are good points to absorb the city's life. The Grand Socco's official but little-used name, **Place du 9 Avril 1947**, commemorates the visit of Sultan Mohammed V to the city on that date – an occasion when, for the first time and at some personal risk, he identified himself with the struggle for Moroccan independence.

A memorial to this event (in Arabic) is to be found amid the **Mendoubia gardens**, flanking the square, which enclose the former offices of the Mendoub – the Sultan's representative during the international years and a spectacular banyan tree, said to be over 800 years old.

Also of interest is the little **Fondouk Market**, which is to be found by following **Rue de la Liberté** from the Grand Socco towards Place de France, then turning left down a series of steps, before the *El Minzah* hotel. The stalls here offer everything from pottery to spectacle repairs, from fruit and vegetables to bric-a-brac and plain old junk.

Over in the **Place de France**, the cafés are the main attraction – and at their best in the late afternoon and early evening, when an interesting mix of local and expatriate regulars turn out to watch and be watched. The seats to choose are outside the *Café Paris*, a legendary rendezvous throughout the years of the International Zone. During World War II, this was notorious as a centre of deal making and intrigue between agents from Britain, America, Germany, Italy and Japan. Later the emphasis shifted to Morocco's own politics: the first nationalist paper, *La Voix du Maroc*, surfaced at the café, and the nationalist leader Allal el Fassi, exiled in Tangier from the French-occupied zone, set up his Istiqlal party headquarters nearby.

St Andrew's Church and the Galerie d'Art Contemporain

Just south of the Grand Socco, on Rue d'Angleterre, is the nineteenth-century Anglican **Church of St Andrew**, one of the city's odder sights in its fusion of Moorish decoration, English country churchyard and flapping Scottish flag – the cross of St Andrew, to whom the church is dedicated (though, being an English church, they sometimes fly the cross of St George instead). The regular congregation has fallen considerably but the church is still used for Sunday morning services (8.30am & 11am), when the numbers are swollen by worshippers from West African countries, particularly Nigeria, en route (hopefully) to a better life in Europe.

In the strangely serene graveyard, among the laments of early deaths from malaria, you come upon the tomb of **Walter Harris** (see p.601), the most brilliant of the chroniclers of "Old Morocco" in the closing decades of the nineteenth century and the beginning of the twentieth. Also buried here is

Dean of *Dean's Bar* ("Missed by all and sundry"), a former London cocaine dealer (real name Don Kimfull) who left Britain after being implicated in a scandal surrounding the death by overdose of a young actress in 1919 – he tended bar in Germany, France and the *El Minzah* hotel before opening his own bar in 1937, and worked as a spy for British intelligence in Tangier during World War II. Other graves reveal epitaphs to **Caid Sir Harry Maclean**, the Scottish military adviser to Sultan Moulay Abd el Aziz at the turn of the twentieth century; and to a number of Allied aircrew who died over the Straits in the last days of World War II. Inside the church another Briton, **Emily Keane**, is commemorated. A contemporary of Harris, she lived a very different life, marrying in 1877 the Shereef of Ouezzane – at the time one of the most holy towns of the country (see p.137).

A little further along Rue d'Angleterre is a large white-walled villa, formerly the British Consulate and now the recently refurbished and well-funded **Galerie d'Art Contemporain Mohamed Drissi** (Tues–Sun 9am–5:30pm; free) devoted to contemporary Moroccan and European artists with new exhibitions every month. Nearby, only just visible over a high wall, the now sadly derelict remains of the **Grand Hôtel Villa de France** belie its place in art history: the French painters Eugène Delacroix and Henri Matisse both stayed here, and Matisse painted one of his best works through the window of his room.

The American Legation and Gran Teatro Cervantes

If you follow Rue de la Plage out of the Grand Socco, then turn left down towards the port on the Rue du Portugal, you come to a small gate in the Medina wall on the left; climb the steps to the gate and, just through it, is the **American Legation** (Mon–Thurs 10am–1pm & 3–5pm, Fri 10am–noon & 3–5pm, other times by appointment; free; ⓣ0539 935317, ⓦwww.legation.org), a former palace given to the US government by the Sultan Moulay Slimane, and preserved today as the only American historic landmark abroad. Morocco was the first overseas power to recognize an independent United States and this was the first American ambassadorial residence, established in 1777. A fascinating three-storey palace, bridging an alleyway (the Rue d'Amérique) below, it houses excellent exhibits on the city's history – including the correspondence between Sultan Moulay Ben Abdallah and George Washington – and has displays of paintings by, mainly, Moroccan-resident American artists. Malcolm Forbes's military miniatures of the Battle of Songhai and the Battle of Three Kings are also on display having been donated by the Forbes family when the Forbes Museum was closed (see box, p.96). Downstairs, by the library, a room dedicated to Paul Bowles features photographs of Bowles and his contemporaries, including a shot of him by Beat poet Allen Ginsberg. Separate from the downstairs library, there is a research library (Mon–Thurs 9am–4pm, Fri 9am–2pm) containing an interesting selection of books on Moroccan history and archeology which you can peruse if you call ahead and book an appointment.

Over to the southeast of the Grand Socco, off the Rue de la Plage, is another interesting relic of Tangier's international past, the **Gran Teatro Cervantes** – the old Spanish theatre. Located on a side street still labelled in Spanish as Calle Esperanza Orellana (the wife of its architect), it is an unmistakeable building, with its tiled, Art Nouveau front and impressive glass dome. The facade was restored with the help of EU and Spanish funds, though it is starting to show signs of wear again and sadly the interior remains derelict.

The Medina

The Grand Socco offers the most straightforward **approach to the Medina**. The arch at the northern corner of the square (probably on the site of a Roman gate) opens onto Rue d'Italie, which becomes Rue de la Kasbah, the northern entrance to the kasbah quarter. Through an opening on the righthand side of the square is Rue es Siaghin, off which are most of the souks and at the end of which is the Petit Socco, the Medina's main square. An alternative approach to the Medina is from the seafront: follow the American steps, west of the port, up from Avenue Mohammed VI, walk round by the Grand Mosque, and Rue des Postes (Rue Mokhtar Ahardane) will lead you into the Petit Socco.

Rue es Siaghin

Rue es Siaghin – Silversmiths' Street – follows the course of a Roman street, and was Tangier's main thoroughfare into the 1930s. Halfway along from the

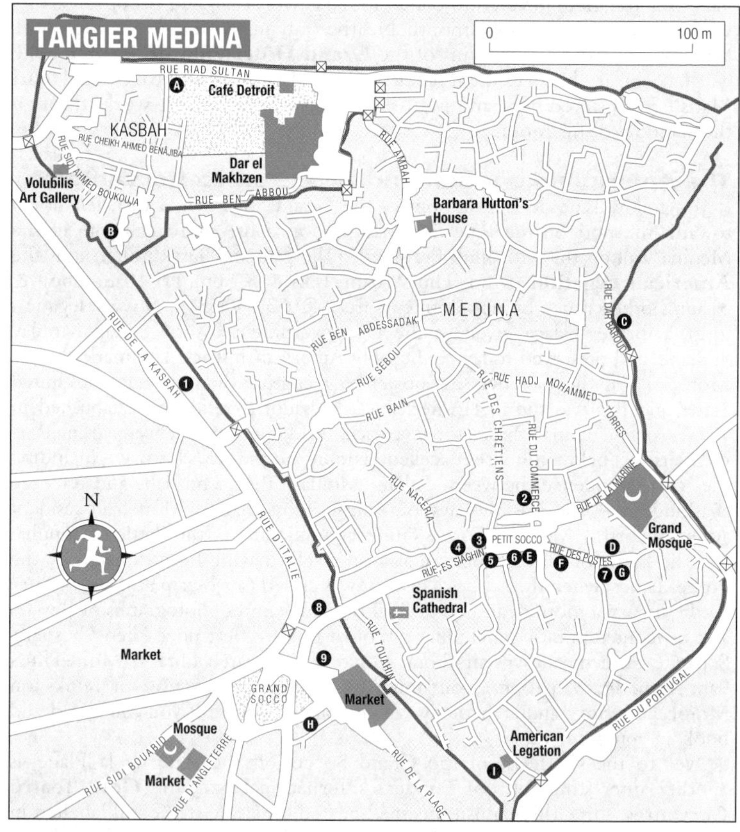

ACCOMMODATION			
Dar Nour	B	La Tangerina	A
Hôtel Continental	C	Pension Fuentes	E
Hôtel du Grand Socco	H	Pension Palace	F
Hôtel Mamora	D	Riad Tanja	I
Hôtel Olid	G		

RESTAURANTS & CAFÉS			
Café Tingis	3	Mamounia Palace	8
Chez Hammadi	1	Ray Charly	5
Chez Hassan	4	Restaurant Ahlen	7
Falafel Café Petit Socco	6	Restaurant Andaluz	2
Les Passagers de Tanger	9	Riad Tanja	I

Grand Socco (on the right) is the **old Spanish Cathedral** and **Mission**. The area behind here was formerly the **Mellah**, or Jewish quarter, centred around Rue des Synagogues.

The Petit Socco

The **Petit Socco**, or Zoco Chico, (Little Market) seems too small ever to have served such a purpose, though in Roman times this was probably the site of the forum. In the nineteenth century the square was almost twice its present size, and it was only at the beginning of the twentieth century that the hotels and cafés were built. There's a seedy and rather conspiratorial atmosphere, and yet the square remains alluring, having been a central location in many of the Moroccan stories of artist, storyteller and friend of Paul Bowles, Mohammed Mrabet, who still frequents it.

In the heyday of the "International City", with easily exploited Arab and Spanish sexuality a major attraction, it was in the alleys behind the Socco that the straight and gay brothels were concentrated. William Burroughs used to hang out around the square: "I get averages of ten very attractive propositions a day", he wrote to Allen Ginsberg. The Socco cafés (the now decidedly chic, *Café Central* was once the prime Beat location) lost much of their appeal at independence, when the sale of alcohol was banned in the Medina, but they remain diverting places to sit around, people-watch, talk and get some measure of the town. Today the reek of hashish pervades the square, but foreigners are strongly advised not to smoke it in the Petit Socco's cafés. The fact that Moroccans all seem to be partaking does not make it safe.

The area around the Petit Socco has an important place in Morocco's **postal history**. During the days of the International Zone, Britain, Spain, France and – until World War I – Germany all had post offices in Tangier. Spain's was at no. 3 in the square itself, Britain's at 23 Rue de la Marine. A few doors towards the square, 37 Rue de la Marine was the office of Morocco's first ever postal service back in the nineteenth century, a pony-express-like horseback relay service between Tangier and Fes. Number 76, opposite, was the site of Morocco's first national bank.

Towards the kasbah

Walking up from the Petit Socco, you can follow **Rue des Chrétiens** and its continuation **Rue Amrah** and emerge, with luck, around the lower gate to the kasbah. Heading past the Socco towards the sea walls are two small streets straddled by the Grand Mosque. If you want to get down to the beach, follow **Rue des Postes** and you'll hit the flight of steps (known as the "American Steps") down to the port. If you feel like wandering, take the other one, **Rue de la Marine**, which curls into **Rue Dar el Baroud** and the entrance to the *Hôtel Continental* – another fine place to sit and drink tea.

The **Grand Mosque** itself is screened from public view – and, as throughout Morocco, entrance is strictly forbidden to non-Muslims.

The kasbah and beyond

The **kasbah**, walled off from the Medina on the highest rise of the coast, has been the palace and administrative quarter since Roman times. It was the Brits who destroyed the city's medieval fortifications, including a great upper castle which covered the entire site of the present-day kasbah. It is a strange, somewhat sparse area of walled compounds, occasional colonnades, and a number of luxurious villas built in the 1920s, when this became one of the Mediterranean's chicest residential sites. Richard Hughes, author of *A High Wind in Jamaica* (and of a book of Moroccan tales), was the first European to take a house here – his address fabulously titled "Numéro Zéro, La Kasbah, Tangier".

Among those who followed was the eccentric Woolworths heiress, Barbara Hutton, who reputedly outbid General Franco for her mini palace, Sidi Hosni. Her parties were legendary – including a ball where thirty Reguibat racing camels and their drivers were brought 1000 miles from the Sahara to form a guard of honour.

The kasbah's main point of interest is the former **Sultanate Palace**, or **Dar el Makhzen**, now converted to an excellent **museum**. It stands near the main gateway to the Medina, the **Bab el Assa**, to the rear of a formal court, or *mechouar*, where the town's pashas held public audience and gave judgement well into the twentieth century. The entrance to the palace, a modest-looking porch, is in the left-hand corner of the court as you enter from the Medina.

Just before the entrance to the palace, you pass (on your left) the ramshackle clubhouse of the Orquesta Andalusi de Tanger, a fine group of musicians who play Andalous music with a lot of swing. If they're around practising, they may well invite you in to watch them play.

The Dar el Makhzen and Café Detroit

The **Dar el Makhzen** – built, like the Grand Mosque, by Moulay Ismail – last saw royal use in 1912, with the residence of the Sultan Moulay Hafid and his entourage of 168, who was exiled to Tangier after his forced abdication by the

Malcolm Forbes: Tangier's last tycoon

The American publishing tycoon **Malcolm Forbes** bought the **Palais du Mendoub** in 1970. His reason, ostensibly at least, was the acquisition of a base for launching and publishing an Arab-language version of *Forbes Magazine* – the "millionaires' journal". For the next two decades, until his death in 1990, he was a regular visitor to the city, and it was at the Tangier palace that he decided to host his last great extravagance, his **seventieth birthday party**, in 1989.

This was the grandest social occasion Tangier had seen since the days of Woolworths heiress Barbara Hutton (see above), whose scale and spectacle Forbes presumably intended to emulate and exceed. Spending an estimated $2.5m, he brought in his friend Elizabeth Taylor as co-host and chartered a 747, a DC-8 and Concorde to fly in eight hundred of the world's rich and famous from New York and London. The party entertainment was on an equally imperial scale, including six hundred drummers, acrobats and dancers, and a *fantasia* – a cavalry charge which ends with the firing of muskets into the air – by three hundred Berber horsemen.

Malcolm's party was a mixed public relations exercise, with even the gossip press feeling qualms about such a display of American affluence in a country like Morocco, and, despite Liz Taylor's presence at Forbes' side, using the choice of location to hint at the tycoon's sexual preferences (a story that broke in full cry after Forbes' death). However, Forbes most likely considered the party a success, for his guests included not just the celebrity rich – Gianni Agnelli, Robert Maxwell, Barbara Walters, Henry Kissinger – but half a dozen US state governors and the chief executives or presidents of scores of multinational corporations likely to advertise in his magazine. And, of course, it was tax deductible.

His former home on Rue Mohammed Tazi, in the 1990s was used to house personal guests of King Hassan II. Until recently, it was open as a museum but has now been returned to a royal residence and is off limits to the public.

French. The extraordinary negotiations which then took place are chronicled in Walter Harris's *Morocco That Was*, (see p.601).

The design is centred on two interior courtyards, each with rich arabesques, painted wooden ceilings and marble fountains. Some of the flanking columns are of Roman origin, particularly well suited to the small display of **mosaics and finds from Volubilis** (see p.196). The palace is home to a **museum of crafts and antiquities** (daily 9am–4pm, closed Tues; 10dh; ⓣ0539 932097, ⓦwww.maroc.net/museums) which has been completely revamped and contains within its rooms well-presented artefacts discovered in and around Tangier, with origins dating from the Palaeolithic era up until Portuguese occupation. Other exhibits include a map depicting international trade routes, a section dedicated to the Islamization of Tangier, and an interesting room concerned with Roman religion and funeral rites.

At the entrance to the main part of the palace is the **Bit el Mal**, the old treasury, and adjoining is a small private **mosque**, near to which is the entrance to the herb- and shrub-lined palace **gardens**, shaded by jacaranda trees. If you leave this way, along Rue Riad Sultan, you will pass under the **Café Detroit** (*Détroit* is French for "strait"). The café, originally called *1001 Nights*, was set up in the early 1960s by Beat writer Brion Gysin, partly as a venue for the **Master Musicians of Jajouka**, drummers and pipe-players from a village in the foothills of the Rif who achieved cult fame when they worked with Rolling Stone Brian Jones, a friend of Gysin's. The café has recently re-opened (daily except Tues 10am–12:30pm) and besides being a café, restaurant and bar, is used as a venue for fusion dance performances (usually held on Sat). There are fantastic views of the Straits from the terrace and meals are served in the main salon.

Café Hafa, Palais du Mendoub and Jews' Beach

Leaving the Medina by Bab el Kasbah, a ten- to fifteen-minute stroll along Rue Asad Ibn Farrat and then Rue Shakespeare (Rue Mohammed Tazi), will bring you to the area known as La Marshan, an exclusive residential quarter with a rich spread of villas, consulates and royal properties. You will pass on your right the small Marchan Art Gallery (daily except Fri 10am–1pm & 3–6pm) owned by local artist Rachid Alaoui. After no. 118, and just before the sports stadium, a rock on a concrete pedestal and a series of columns on the north side of the street lead down to a group of **Punic rock-tombs**, not very exciting in themselves, but a lovely spot where Tanjawis come to smoke a pipe of *kif*, or just admire the view across the Straits to the Spanish town of Tarifa. On a clear day, you can also see the Rock of Gibraltar over to the right. The next turning, bearing left down a narrow lane, leads to the rustic **Café Hafa**. The steep hillside is terraced and from the café, shaded by shrubs and trees, there are stunning views over the Straits (despite the new highway below). Serving coffee, mint tea, sandwiches and cakes, this is just the place to spend the late afternoon – as was the habit of Paul Bowles and his friends, Tennessee Williams, Truman Capote and Jack Kerouac.

Continuing along Rue Mohammed Tazi you come to the **Palais du Mendoub** on the right which is currently being used as a private royal residence. From the 1920s, this was the home of the Mendoub, the sultan's representative during the international years, and more recently was owned by Malcolm Forbes (see box opposite). Continuing past the palace for a further 1km, you reach *Camping Miramonte*, and a track down to the **Jews' Beach** – so called from its role as the landing stage for Spanish Jews fleeing the Inquisition. There is a pleasant little **beach café** open here in summer.

La Montagne and Villa Josephine

The two most prestigious addresses in Tangier are **La Marshan**, the area west of the Palais du Mendoub, and **La Montagne**, the "Mountain" behind the Spanish Consulate, on the inland route to Cap Spartel (see p.106). The Mountain is home to two vast royal palaces and is peppered with villas, most with stunning gardens and views of the bay.

In the Sidi Masmoudi area below La Montagne is the iconic **Villa Josephine** built by the writer Walter Harris (see p.601), and former residence of Pasha el Glaoui (see p.362). The villa is now a top-end *maison d'hôte* (see p.100) and the whole estate is in impeccable condition, retaining the Mediterranean, Arab and African influences from its original owner. There is a restaurant (open to the public Mon–Sat) and bar as well as an outdoor terrace with fantastic views of both the Straits of Gibraltar and Bay of Tangier. To reach Villa Josephine take a petit taxi from the Grand Socco (20dh).

Eating, drinking and nightlife

Over the last few years, the local **restaurant** scene has been rejuvenated and there is currently an impressive selection of restaurants serving various international cusines, ranging from inexpensive to top end, scattered around the city centre. The possibilities for films, theatre, the occasional concert and, at the right time of year, festivals are also surprisingly varied. The same can't really be said for most of the **bars** and **discos** which seem to be either stuck in a time warp or grossly expensive.

Restaurants

Alcohol is not served in the **Medina** (except in upscale guesthouses and *Hôtel Continental*. For late-night snacks, several of the cafés around the Grand Socco stay open all night.

Medina

All these restaurants are shown on the map on p.94, unless otherwise stated.

Chez Hammadi 2 Rue de la Kasbah ⓣ0539 934514. Just outside the west wall of the Medina, this is a rather kitsch salon, where traditional Moroccan dishes – and good pastilla – are served to entertainment from a worthwhile band of Andalous musicians. Moderate.

Chez Hassan 22 Rue es Siaghin. Small, unpretentious restaurant (with Arabic/English name sign up high) on the main street of the Medina, not far from the Petit Socco, serving decent Moroccan fare. Cheap.

Falafel Café Petit Socco. A small café serving falafel, hummus, and tabouleh; a welcome change of pace to café-grill lunches. Cheap.

Mamounia Palace 4 Rue es Siaghin. A nicely done-out place, not quite achieving the palatial style it aspires to, but laid-back, with comfortable seating, unobtrusive musicians and decent food. The only options are two set menus, at 115dh each.

Les Passagers de Tanger Grand Socco ⓣ0619 000250. A roof-top brasserie overlooking the square, run by a French couple, popular with an affluent expat crowd and known for delicious *tartines* (open sandwiches) and indulgent desserts. Licensed. Closed Sun evening and Mon. Expensive.

Ray Charly Corner of Petit Socco. A hole-in-the-wall diner – just a counter and a row of seats – serving burgers, chicken, egg and chips. Very cheap.

Restaurant Ahlen 8 Rue des Postes. Simple but well-cooked food – roast chicken, grilled beef, *harira* – and a warm welcome. Cheap.

Restaurant Andaluz 7 Rue du Commerce. In the first alley to the left off Rue de la Marine (the street running from the Petit Socco to the Grand Mosque). With a trio of tables, it is about as simple as it's possible to be – and excellent, serving impeccably fried swordfish steaks and grilled brochettes. Cheap.

Restaurant Marhaba 26 Palais Ahannar, off Rue de la Kasbah at no. 67, just outside the Medina; see map, p.84 ⓣ0539 937927. A splendid old palace, stacked with antiques, and with music and good food. Set menus for 150dh and 190dh. Open lunch and dinner. Moderate to expensive.

Riad Tanja 2 Rue Amar Alilech, turn off Rue de Portugal near the American Legation ⓣ0539 333538. Small and intimate restaurant, stylishly and simply decorated, whose signature *nouvelle cuisine Marocaine* includes light vegetable salads, fish tajines and caramelized fruit desserts. Open to non-residents. Lunch and dinner, closed Mon. Reservation recommended. Expensive.

Ville Nouvelle

All these restaurants are shown on the map on p.89, unless otherwise stated.

Anna e Paolo 17 Av Price Heritier, see map, p.85, ⓣ0539 944617. Quite simply the best Italian cuisine in Tangier. Open lunch and dinner. Closed Sun. Moderate.

Casa España 11 Rue Jebha el Ouatania, by the *Rembrandt Hôtel*. Tangier's Spanish club, with a 20 percent surcharge for nonmembers, but still reasonably good value with three different paellas (Valencian, seafood and vegetarian), plus such Iberian standards as kidneys in sherry, tortilla and, in season, Andalucian gazpacho. Moderate.

El Dorado 21 Rue Allal Ben Abdallah, near the *Hôtel Chellah*; see map, p.85. Dependable Moroccan–Spanish cooking, with couscous on Fri and paella on Sun. Moderate.

El Korsan in the *Hôtel el Minzah*, 85 Rue de la Liberté ⓣ0539 935885. The hotel's Moroccan restaurant has a reputation as one of the country's best, serving authentic and traditional specialities to the accompaniment of a group of musicians. Expensive.

El Pescador 39 Rue Allal Ben Abdallah; see map, p.85. A swanky Spanish restaurant with an inviting tapas bar at the rear. Lunch and dinner, closed Sun. Moderate to expensive.

Le Mangana Complex Dawliz, 42 Rue de Hollande ⓣ0539 333377. A stylish modern dining room serving mainly French cuisine with 80dh and 140dh set menus. Not as intimate as *Relais de Paris* next door, but with fantastic sea views. Moderate to expensive.

Otori Sushi 41 Av de la Résistance, see map, p.85 ⓣ0539 325533. Though lacking atmosphere, sushi lovers will be pleased to find Tangier's international reputation manifest in quality maki rolls and by-the-piece sushi. Fresh fish arrives daily. Takeaway and delivery available. Expensive.

Relais de Paris Complex Dawliz, 42 Rue de Hollande ⓣ0539 331819, ⓦwww.relaisdeparis.com. The current meeting place of choice for Tangier's wheelers and dealers. Fine French cuisine including succulent grills and a set menu of 120dh. The Medina and sea views may make the expense worthwhile. Open lunch and dinner. Expensive.

Restaurant Africa 83 Rue de la Plage at the bottom of the hill, opposite *Hôtel Valencia* ⓣ0539 935436. A simply decorated and peaceful dining room known for its excellent value 55dh four course set menu. Licensed. Moderate.

Restaurant Agadir 21 Rue Prince Héritier, off Place de France. This small and friendly restaurant, run by a Tafraouti, with accomplished French and Moroccan cooking, is a particular favourite. Licensed. Moderate, with a 70dh set menu.

Restaurant Hassi Baida 83 Rue de la Plage. Recently renovated, bright, tiled restaurant serving fish, couscous, tajine and pizza. Moderate.

Restaurant le Coeur de Tanger 1 Rue Annoual, off Place de France (it's above the *Café Paris*, though the entrance is on a side street). Moroccan dishes served in some style. Set menus of 140dh. Moderate to expensive.

Restaurant Number One 1 Bd Mohammed V, across the side street from the *Rembrandt Hôtel* ⓣ0539 941674. A restaurant and cocktail bar, with a French–Moroccan menu that attracts a business crowd at lunchtime (noon–3pm) and tends to be fairly quiet in the evenings (6.30–11pm). Expensive.

Restaurant Pagode Rue el Boussiri, just off Rue Prince Héritier ⓣ0539 938086. Possibly the best Chinese food in Tangier, though the service is pretty joyless. Expensive.

Restaurant Populaire Saveur Mediterannée On the steps leading down from Rue de la Liberté to the Fondouk Market. A small and popular diner specializing in fish. Closed Fri. Cheap.

Restaurant San Remo 15 Rue Ahmed Chaouki, a side street opposite the terrace-belvedere (see map, p.89) on Bd Pasteur. Credible, good-value Spanish, French and Italian cooking, and with a cheaper pizzeria across the road. Moderate.

Rubis Grill 3 Rue Ibn Rochd, off Av Prince Moulay Abdallah. Long established, serving Spanish and other European cuisines; the candle-lit hacienda decor is a bit over the top, but the food and service are exemplary. Moderate.

Seafront

All restaurants are marked on the map on p.85 unless otherwise stated.

Hôtel Biarritz 104 Av Mohammed VI, (see map, p.89). One of the nicer hotel restaurants, with old-style service and a limited but reliable menu which consists mostly of Moroccan and French cuisine. Moderate.

Hôtel Marco Polo corner of Av Mohammed VI and Rue el Antaki. Very noisy ground-floor bar, with restaurant on the first and top floors, and views of the bay. Serves generous helpings of Moroccan cuisine and often has seafood specials. Moderate.

L'Marsa *Hôtel L'Marsa*, 92 Av Mohammed VI (see map, p.89). Superb pizzas and spaghetti, with home-made ice cream to follow, served (slowly) on a roof terrace, patio or inside. Moderate, with an 80dh set menu.

Restaurant Miramar Av Mohammed VI, opposite the *Hôtel Rif* ⓣ0539 944033. A beach restaurant with a varied menu of Moroccan, Spanish and seafood dishes. There's a separate lively tapas bar at the rear. Noon–midnight. Moderate to expensive.

Restaurant Sable d'Or Av Mohammed VI, on the beach opposite the *Hôtel Solazur* ⓣ0539 946441. Tangier's only curry house, with Indian dishes for vegetarians and meat-eaters, including a pretty good chicken tikka masala. Expensive.

Restaurant Valencia 6 Av Youssef Ben Tachfine ⓣ0539 945146. A simply furnished fish restaurant, very popular with locals and tourists. Closed Tues. Moderate.

Out of town

You'll need a car to get to all the below recommendations.

Chez Abdou 17km out of town, on the coast road leading south towards Asilah, in the so-called Fôret Diplomatique. Handy for lunch, and recommended for seafood. Expensive.

Club Le Mirage near the Caves of Hercules (see p.106) in the area known as Ashakar, 5km south of the Cap Spartel lighthouse ⓣ0539 333332, ⓦwww.lemirage-tanger.com. An international-style restaurant located within a long-established and popular resort. The food is excellent – saffron flavoured *soupe de poisson* and curried langoustine brochettes are amongst the signature dishes – and so are the views. Expensive.

Le Riad Restaurant 7km along the Malabata road, amid the trees to the right. Serves a selection of tajines and brochettes and makes for a pleasant lunchtime stop. Moderate.

Villa Josephine 231 Rue de la Montagne, Sidi Masmoudi ⓣ0539 334535, ⓦwww.villajosephine-tanger.com. Fantastic Straits views from the outdoor terrace, and serving up some of the best French and Moroccan cuisine in Tangier. There are also 11 opulent guest rooms, each with their own fireplace and balcony, starting from 2500dh per double. See box, p.98.

Cafés

Tangier has a wealth of attractive cafés. There are also some excellent **patisseries**, among which three in particular are rated by the cognoscenti: *Matisse* at Rue Allal Ben Abdallah (near *Hôtel Chellah*; map p.85), which is the poshest; *Rahmouni*, at 35 Rue du Prince Moulay Abdallah (see map, p.89), which is the oldest; and the upstart *Traiteur al Mouatamid Bnou Abbad*, at 16 Rue al Mouatamid Ibn Abadd (see map, p.85). All the following are shown on the Tangier City Centre map on p.89, unless otherwise stated.

Café de Paris Place de France. Tangier's most famous café, from its conspiratorial past. Still a staple meeting place for expats and usually a good place to track down English newspapers in the morning.

Café Hafa La Marshan; see map, p.84 & directions p.97. This clifftop café is the perfect late-afternoon locale to gaze across the Straits and write your postcards.

Café Metropole 27 Bd Pasteur, next to the synagogue. This serves the best *café au lait* in town and pastries can be bought across the road at *Pâtisserie Le Petit Prince* and consumed at your table.

Café Tingis Petit Socco; see map, p.94. A favorite haunt of Tennessee Williams with its shaded terrace and atmospheric interior and a more attractive choice than next door *Café Central*, where refurbishment has replaced the dingy charm that attracted Burroughs with characterless modern decor.

Cafeteria Katerina Rue Lafayette, behind *Hôtel Chellah*; see map, p.85. A relaxed spot for snacks and refreshments on a quiet street. Their delicious *croque monsieur* is particularly recommended.

Dolcy's On the eastern end of Bd Pasteur. Central and friendly, a great spot for breakfast with eggs, toasted sandwiches, and fresh juices.

Bars

A decadent past has taken its toll on Tangier's **bars** and most of those that do survive have fallen into a rather bland seediness. The better options are in or alongside the older hotels, supplemented in summer by the beach bars, which stay open till 1am or so (though take care in this area after dark). All these are shown on the Tangier City Centre map on p.89, unless otherwise stated.

▲ Café culture, Tangier

Atlas Bar 30 Rue Prince Héritier, across the road from the *Hôtel Atlas*. Small, friendly tapas pub open nightly. Proudly in business since 1928 and has barely changed since – the intimate dive-bar atmosphere is still fully intact.

Caid's Bar in the *Hôtel el Minzah*, 85 Rue de la Liberté. Long the chi-chi place to meet over very pricey drinks. Over the bar is the centrepiece of the ritzy décor, a grand painting of Caid Sir Harry Maclean, former commander in chief of the sultan's army (see p.93).

Carrousel Bar 6 Rue Khalil Metrane, off Rue Prince Héritier. Comfortable British-run wine bar, in business since 1936.

Dean's Bar Rue d'Amérique du Sud. The closest bar to the Medina – a tiny shop-room that was once the haunt of Tennessee Williams, Francis Bacon and Ian Fleming. It is now frequented more or less exclusively by Moroccans although tourists are welcomed. For more on Dean himself, see p.93.

Hôtel Marco Polo Av Mohammed VI; see map, p.85. The ground floor is popular with tourists, especially hard-drinking Scandinavians and Germans getting through its range of European beers.

Mondial 52 Av Mohammed VI; off map, p.85. Beachside tapas bar with a separate entry from the adjoining nightclub. A not-so-intimidating place for women travellers, though the drinks are expensive. Noon–midnight.

Tanger Inn 16 Rue Magellan, below the *Hôtel el Muniria* (see p.90). One of Tangier's last surviving International Zone relics, with photos on the wall of Burroughs, Ginsberg and Kerouac while they were staying at the hotel above. Daily 9pm–2am, but liveliest Thurs, Fri and Sat nights.

The Pub 4 Rue Sorolla. A British-themed pub, with hunting scenes on the walls and bar food, but it's not quite the real thing. Daily 9pm–1am.

Discos and clubs

The principal areas for **discos** is the grid of streets south of Place de France and Boulevard Pasteur and the beach. Admission is usually 100dh, drinks are two or three times regular bar prices and be careful leaving late at night as the streets hereabouts are none too safe; the best idea is to tip the doorman 5dh to call a taxi. All these venues are shown on the Tangier City Centre map on p.89, unless otherwise stated.

Borsalino 30 Rue du Prince Moulay Abdallah. A small and usually quite lively disco, with a mixed crowd, and loud pop music.

Mondial 52 Av Mohammed VI, on the beach; off map, p.85. Catering to a young, modern crowd of twenty-something Moroccans and weekender Europeans, with two resident DJs and regular guest DJs. Open nightly 11pm–5am.

Morocco Palace 13 Rue du Prince Moulay Abdallah. A clear winner among Tangier's nightspots, this strange, sometimes slightly manic place puts on traditional Moroccan music and dance (sometimes belly-dancing) nightly from around 9pm until 4am. Customers are predominantly Moroccan and expect a good show.

Radio Club 30 Rue du Prince Moulay Abdallah. Slightly seedy club sometimes featuring Moroccan bands.

Regine Club Rue el Mansour Dahbi (opposite the Roxy Cinema); see map, p.85. Mainstream disco, larger and a little cheaper than most. Open from 10pm.

Scott's Rue el Moutanabi (Rue Sanlucar). Traditionally (though not exclusively) a gay disco, this is worth a look if only for its very particular choice of paintings – Berber boys in Highland military uniform. Usually quiet until after midnight.

Snob Av Mohammed VI, on the beach, across from *Hôtel Ramada*; (off map, p.85). A new stylish lounge club with state-of-the-art audio and lighting catering to a trendy crowd.

Concerts and films

Both traditional and pop/rock **concerts** come to Tangier from time to time. Check with the tourist office and look out for posters advertising the larger events. The old Spanish bullring, out beyond the bus station in the Ville Nouvelle, has been converted into an open-air concert hall and is a venue for occasional large events. Cultural events are also hosted by the **American Legation** (see p.93) and the **Institut Français de Tangier**; the latter organizes the Tangier Music Festival (see "Listings", opposite) as well as various concerts and theatrical performances at the small Salle Beckett theatre on Rue Ibn Naffiy off Rue Allal Ben Abdallah. You can pick up a programme for Institut Français events from Galerie Delacroix (see below).

One of only a few **cinemas** still operating in Tangier is the Cinema Rif (Ⓦ www.cinemathequedetanger.com), on the Grand Socco, which has been renovated and reborn thanks to the not-for-profit organization Cinémathèque de Tanger, the dream of Moroccan-born photographer and artist Yto Barrada. The cinema aims to become the focal point for cinema culture for all of North Africa. Currently there are weekly showings of new releases, documentaries and classics.

Up-to-date **information** on local events can be found in the weekly publication, *Les Nouvelles du Nord*, available in cafés and hotel receptions on Friday or Saturday.

Galleries, shops and stalls

Besides from the Galerie d'Art Contemporain (see p.93) and Marchan Art Gallery (see p.97) other notable galleries include: The **Galerie Delacroix**, 86 Rue de la Liberté (Tues–Sun 11am–1pm & 4–8pm), which usually has interesting exhibitions of contemporary art and, for local artists, the **Volubilis Art Gallery**, 6 Sidi Boukouja (in the kasbah; Tues–Sun 10.30am–1pm & 3.30–7pm), under the very friendly management of Mohamed and Karla Raiss el Fenni, who also manage the Volubilis Boutique in the Petit Socco. Up-to-date listings and information on various other small galleries can be found in the window of Bab el Fen, a well stocked art supply shop at 25 Rue ibn Rochd across from the *Rembrandt Hôtel*.

Many of the Tangier **market stalls and stores** are eminently avoidable, geared to selling tourist goods that wouldn't pass muster elsewhere. But a few are worthwhile, unique, or both; a half-hour preliminary browse at the more "fixed price" outlets on Boulevard Pasteur is useful for establishing roughly what you should pay for things. Threre's a massive flea market (daily, but best on Sundays), out of town at **Casa Barata**, reached by shared grand taxi from the Grand Socco or bus #16 from the bus and train stations. For supermarkets see p.104.

Crafts and souvenirs

Bazaar Tindouf 64 Rue de la Liberté, opposite the *Hôtel el Minzah*. One of the better-quality junk/antique shops, with a good array of cushion-carpets and old postcards. Bargaining is essential.
Chakkara Bazaar Rue Amarh, below the kasbah. Little more than a hole in the wall, but Chakkara has folders full of old photos, postcards, and various other visual artefacts, even a few rare etchings.
Ensemble Artisanal Rue Belgique (left-hand side, going west from the Place de France). A government-run store displaying modern Moroccan crafts. Prices are (more or less) fixed – a useful first call to get an idea of quality and costs before bargaining elsewhere. Open daily except Fri, 9am–1pm & 3–7pm.
Marrakech la Rouge 50 Rue Siaghin. Large and not-too-pushy bazaar selling rugs, jewellery, pottery, antique weaponry and leather, wood and metal crafts. Open daily.
Rue Touahin first right off Rue Siaghin, entering the Medina from the Grand Socco. This line of jewellery stalls may turn up something appealing, though don't take silver, gold or most stones at face value: judge on aesthetics.
Volubilis Boutique 15 Place Petit Socco. A usually interesting mix of traditional Moroccan and Western fashion.

Listings

Airlines Royal Air Maroc, 1 Pl de France ⓣ0539 379507 or 0900 00800. Air France ⓣ0539 936477. KLM ⓣ0539 938926 and Lufthansa ⓣ0539 931327 all have offices at 7 Rue du Mexique.
Banks Most are grouped along Bd Pasteur/Bd Mohammed V. BMCE has branches at 21 Bd Pasteur and in the Grand Socco, both with ATMs. SGMB also has a Grand Socco branch with ATM. WAFA Bank has a *bureau de change* at 22 Bd Pasteur, (Mon–Fri 8am–6pm, Sat 9am–1pm). WAFA also represents Western Union, as does the post office. Most banks in Tangier will cash travellers' cheques, a service not widely offered in many other parts of the country.
Books The long-established Librairie des Colonnes at 54 Bd Pasteur (Mon–Sat 9.30am–1pm & 4.30–7pm) has some good French books on Tangier and Morocco, and a small selection of English-language books.
Car rental Avis, 54 Bd Pasteur ⓣ0539 934646; Budget, Gare de Ville ⓣ0539 901045; Europcar, 87 Bd Mohammed V ⓣ0539 941938; Hertz, 36 Bd Mohammed V ⓣ0539 322165; National, Résidence Lina, Bd Mohammed V ⓣ0539 325159. Avis, Budget, Europcar, Hertz and National also have desks at the airport. Local agencies are scattered around Av Mohammed V.
Car repairs Most repairs can be undertaken – or arranged – by Garage Lafayette, 27 Rue Mohammed Abdou (ⓣ0539 932887).
Consulates UK, Trafalgar House, 9 Rue Amerique du Sud ⓣ0539 936939. There is no US consulate in Tangier (nearest US diplomatic representation is in Rabat).
Ferry companies Comanav, 43 Av Abou Aala el Maari ⓣ0539 934096 (to Algeciras, Sète and sometimes Genoa); Comarit, Av Mohammed VI ⓣ0539 320032 (to Algeciras and Sète); EuroFerrys, 31 Av de la Résistance ⓣ0539 322253 (to Algeciras); FRS, 18 Rue el Farabi ⓣ0539 942612 (to Algeciras, Tarifa and Gibraltar); IMTC, 2 Bd Pasteur ⓣ0539 336002 (to Algeciras); Limadet, 13 Rue Prince Moulay Abdallah ⓣ0539 933621 (to Algeciras); LME c/o Comarit (to Algeciras); Nautas, in the port ⓣ0539 934463 (to Algeciras); Trasmediterranea c/o Limadet (to Algeciras).
Festivals Tanjazz Festival features more than 100 international artists for four days in June; see ⓦwww.tanjazz.org. For other events check with the tourist office or pick up an Institut Français programme.
Golf Tangier Royal Golf Club, BP 41, Tangier ⓣ0539 944484, (18 holes); and Cabo Negro Royal Golf, BP 696 G Tetouan ⓣ0539 978303.
Hammam The *Hôtel el Minzah*'s Wellness Centre is open to non-residents. For 150dh you get a traditional wash and scrub from an attendant and can indulge yourself in steam and soap all day long.
Hospitals Clinique Assalam, 10 Av de la Paix (ⓣ0539 322558), is regarded as the best private clinic in Tangier for medical emergencies. The government-run Hospital Mohammed V (ⓣ0539 938056) is on the road to the airport. Closer to the

city centre is *Hôpital Espagnol* ⓣ0539 931018 on Rue de l'Hôpital Espagnol near Place Oued El Makhazine. For a private ambulance, call ⓣ0539 954040 or ⓣ0539 946976.

Internet access Cybercafé Adam, 4 Rue Ibn Rochd (off Bd Pasteur); Euronet, 5 Rue Ahmed Chaouki (off Bd Pasteur); Club Internet 3000, 27 Rue el Antaki (also sells computer accessories); ViaWeb, 48 Rue Allal ben Abdallah, in a teléboutique opposite the *Hôtel Chellah*.

Newspapers English-language newspapers are sold outside the post office, in various stores along Bd Pasteur or Av Mohammed VI, and by vendors around the *Café Paris*.

Pharmacies There are several English-speaking pharmacies in the Pl de France (try the Pharmacie Pasteur, next door to the *Café Paris*, or the Pharmacie de Paris opposite) and along Bd Pasteur. A roster of all-night and weekend pharmacies is displayed in every *pharmacie* window. Pharmacists will recommend local doctors.

Photographic equipment and developing Studio Flash, 79 Rue de la Liberté.

Police The Brigade Touristique has its HQ at the former train station by the port (ⓣ0539 931129). There are smaller police posts on the Grand Socco and in the kasbah. Emergency ⓣ19.

Post The main PTT is at 33 Bd Mohammed V and has a *poste restante* service (Mon–Fri 8am–6pm & Sat 8am–noon).

Supermarkets Acima, with a liquor outlet, is on Rue al Hariri (off Pl des Nations). Open daily 9am–9pm. Marjane Hypermarket, selling everything from groceries (including bacon) and alcohol to clothing and household goods, is on the edge of the city on the N1 road to the airport and Asilah.

Travel agencies Voyages Marco Polo, 72 Av Mohammed VI ⓣ0539 934345; and Koutoubia, 112 bis Av Mohammed VI ⓣ0539 935540. American Express is represented by Voyages Schwartz, 54 Bd Pasteur ⓣ0539 374837 (Mon–Fri 9am–5pm).

Moving on

Travelling on **into Morocco** from Tangier is simplest either by **train** (the lines run to Meknes–Fes–Oujda or to Rabat–Casablanca–Marrakesh; all trains stop at Asilah en route), or, if you are heading east to Tetouan, by **bus** or shared **grand taxi**. Leaving the country, **ferries** run to Algeciras, Gibraltar, Tarifa, Genoa (Italy) and Sète (France). Note that Tarifa is not an international port and therefore only accepts passengers holding EU passports.

By train

Tangier's train station, **Tanger Ville**, is 2km east of town on the continuation of Boulevard Mohammed V, and only 300m or so off the eastern end of the beach. Services inside the station include an ATM, Budget car rental desk, small bookshop and a café. The best way to get to it is by petit taxi (15dh or so); it is also served by bus #16 from the bus station but not by any buses from the city centre. Alternatively, bus #13 from the port goes to Tangier's second station, **Tanger Morora**, 4km down the Tetouan road, which is served by all trains out of Tanger Ville.

The best train service from Tangier by far is the **night train to Marrakesh**, with very comfortable couchettes – a great way to arrive refreshed the next morning. For further information on destinations and frequencies see "Travel Details", p.138.

By bus and grand taxi

CTM long-distance buses leave from the port entrance (see map, p.85), including those for Tetouan and Chefchaouen. If you have missed their daily (noon) direct bus to Chefchaouen but still want to push on, an alternative is to go to Tetouan and then find a bus or grand taxi going to Chefchaouen. All other long-distance services start from the **gare routière**, 2km from the centre of town and easily reached by petit taxi (15dh from the port). Useful departures include, again, Tetouan and Chefchaouen (the latter doesn't involve a change of bus, though you stop in Tetouan for twenty minutes; don't pay extra to hustlers there who might just suggest your ticket covers only a "reservation fare" for the Chefchaouen stage).

Grands taxis also mostly leave from the *gare routière*. Regular shared runs (ask for a *plassa*) are to Asilah, Tetouan and Fnideq. Occasionally you may find a taxi direct to the Ceuta border, 2km beyond Fnideq. Shared grands taxis to Fnideq and Ksar es Seghir also depart from Rue du Portugal off Rue de la Plage at the southernmost corner of the Medina.

For destinations in the immediate **vicinity of Tangier**, you may need to charter a grand taxi at the rank on the Grand Socco, though it's possible to get to places like the Caves of Hercules or Cap Malabata by shared grand taxi or city bus (see p.88).

By ferry and hydrofoil

Although **ferries** often depart an hour or so late, you should **check in** at the port at least one hour before official sailing time to get through the chaos of official business. **Hydrofoil** departures, on the other hand, are usually on time.

At the ferry and hydrofoil terminal (Gare Maritime Ouest), you have to get an embarkation card and departure card from the *départ* desk of the ferry companies. Arrival and departure information is displayed on screens in the terminal building. Should your ferry or hydrofoil depart from terminals 1 or 2, present your cards, along with your passport, to the *Controle Police et Douane* (immigration and customs police) at the far end of the building. If you are departing from terminals 3, 4 or 5 you need to present yourself at a separate, smaller immigration and customs building located about 50m outside, alongside the port wall. Arrive later than an hour before official departure time and you may find the visa police have already left – which means waiting for the next ferry.

Two **periods to avoid** the ferries from Tangier are the end of the **Easter week** (Semana Santa) holiday, and the **last week of August**, when the ferries can be full for days on end with Moroccan workers returning to northern Europe. During these periods, reservations are essential.

Details of **ferry and hydrofoil routes** are to be found in the "Basics" section of this book (see pp.30–31). **Tickets and timetables** can be obtained from any travel agent in Tangier or from the ferry company's agents (listed on p.31).

By air

Tangier's **airport**, Ibn Batouta, is 15km west of the city (information ⓣ0539 393720). Some hotels will organize a transfer for you, otherwise the best way to reach the airport is by grand taxi from the Grand Socco (120dh is the standard rate, though you may need to bargain hard to get it).

West of Tangier: the Caves of Hercules and around

The **Caves of Hercules** (Grottes d'Hercule) are something of a symbol for Tangier, with their strange sea window, shaped like a map of Africa. The name, like Hercules' legendary founding of Tangier, is purely fanciful, but the caves, 16km outside the city and above the Atlantic Beach, make an attractive excursion. If you feel like staying for a few days by the sea, the beach can be a pleasant base, too; outside of July and August only stray groups of visitors share the long surf beaches. Take care with currents, however, which can be very dangerous even near the shore.

Cap Spartel and the caves

The most interesting route to the caves and Cap Spartel runs around and above the coast via the quarter known as La Montagne (see box, p.98). Follow this road for around 14km and you'll reach a short turn-off to the lighthouse at Africa's most northwesterly promontory, **Cap Spartel**, a dramatic and fertile point, known to the Greeks and Romans as the "Cape of the Vines". You can visit the lighthouse and sometimes, if the keeper is around, enter and climb it. There is a pleasant restaurant here (open summer only) with ocean views.

To the south of Cap Spartel begins the vast and wild Atlantic Beach , known locally as **Robinson Plage**. It is broken only by a rocky spit – 5km from the Cape, and home to the **Caves of Hercules**. Natural formations, occupied in prehistoric times, they are most striking for a man-made addition – thousands of disc-shaped erosions created by centuries of quarrying for millstones. There were still people cutting stones here for a living until the 1920s, but by that time their place was beginning to be taken by professional guides and discreet sex hustlers; it must have made an exotic brothel. Today, there's a standard admission charge of 5dh (9am–sunset), and you'll probably get some would-be guide attaching themselves to you in the hope of payment too. There are a number of restaurants surrounding the car park, serving grilled fish caught from the rocks below.

Practicalities

If you have your own **transport**, you can head out to the caves via La Montagne and make a round trip by continuing along the coast road, and then taking either the minor road through Jabila or the faster main road (N1), back to Tangier. If you don't, it shouldn't cost you more than 100dh including waiting time to charter a **grand taxi** from the Grand Socco. Alternatively, the #2 **bus**, from St Andrew's Church by the Grand Socco, goes there on summer weekends only; at other times it stops at the nearby village of Jabila, a long walk from the caves – but you're better off alighting before then, at Ziyatin on the old airport road, from where there are connecting taxis to the caves. You can also get to Ziyatin in shared grands taxis from St Andrew's Church.

Close by the caves, on the same rocky spit is the *Le Mirage* (Ⓣ0539 333332, Ⓦwww.lemirage-tanger.com; ⑧), an upmarket clifftop complex of 27 bungalows with full facilities including swimming pool and satellite TV. The restaurant and piano bar are open to non-residents and make a very pleasant, albeit expensive, lunch stop if you are on a day's outing from Tangier. Across from Le Mirage is a **campsite**, *Camping Ashakar* (Ⓣ0674 719419), a pleasant, well wooded site with 13 small bungalows (④), showers, café, restaurant and small shop, but really only for those with transport.

East of Tangier: Cap Malabata and Ksar es Seghir

The best beaches in the immediate vicinity of Tangier are to be found at **Cap Malabata**, where much wealthy villa development has been taking place, but long open swathes of sandy beach can still be found. Beyond here, **Ksar es Seghir** offers a pleasant day by the sea, or a stop on the coast road to Ceuta.

The Port Tanger Mediterranée near the village of Dalia, 20km from Ceuta is the new commercial-only port that, together with a new road and rail network, has transformed the rugged coastline into a busy trade hub.

Cap Malabata

The bay east of Tangier is flanked by long stretches of beach and a chain of elderly villas and new apartment blocks until you reach the "*complexe touristique*" of **Cap Malabata**, accessible on bus #15 or #16, or by petit taxi, which has a couple of intermittently open hotels and some attractive stretches of beach. Further on, an old Portuguese fort on an outcrop makes a good destination for coastal walks. Plans to build a rail tunnel between Cap Malabata and Punta Paloma in Spain have been in foetal stages for over a decade and despite continuing opposition from the EU, the proposed tunnel remains a major interest on Morocco's international agenda.

Ksar es Seghir and Djebel Moussa

KSAR ES SEGHIR, halfway to Ceuta, makes a pleasant stop, and can be reached by shared grand taxi from Rue de Portugal in Tangier, or on any bus running between Tangier and Fnideq. The picturesque little fishing port attracts a fair number of Moroccan beach campers in summer, but few Europeans. The centre of town is the junction where the roads to Tangier, Tetouan and Fnideq all meet, and where grands taxis from Tangier will drop you. Just across the river from the junction lie the remains of a medieval Islamic town and Portuguese fortress (there's a plan of the site posted up by the west side of the bridge). Legend has it that Tariq Ibn Ziyad invaded Spain from here in 711. Ksar es Seghir has been of specific interest to archeologists, being positioned at the meeting point of three distinct terrains: The Habt (Atlantic lowlands), Jabala (sandstone hills), and the Rif mountains, and consequently remained an important settlement throughout the region's early history.

The *Café-Restaurant Diamant Bleu* (open summer only) has **rooms** overlooking the sea, and there's a campsite (also summer only) by the beach just east of the ruins. More upmarket accommodation can be found 12km before the town at the *Hôtel Tarifa*. There are a few café-restaurants by the beach, but the best places in town to **eat** are the *Restaurant L'Achiri* by the taxi station, *Restaurant el Ghoroub* just up the hill and *Restaurant Borj Wad Ghalala* on the eastern edge of town overlooking the beach. Banque Populaire is the only **bank** in town and has an ATM.

From Ksar es Seghir the road to Fnideq climbs around the windy **Djebel Moussa** – the mountain that, with Gibraltar, forms the so-called Pillars of Hercules. According to legend, Hercules separated Europe from Africa with a blow of his sword during his fight with the giant Antaeus, and seen from a plane Gibraltar and Djebel Moussa really do look like two pillars. They also produce remarkable thermal currents, speeding passage for **migratory birds** at this, the shortest crossing between Africa and Europe. A spring or autumn visit should ensure sightings, as up to two hundred species make their way across the Straits.

Asilah

The first town south of Tangier – and first stop on the train line – **ASILAH** is one of the most elegant of the old Portuguese Atlantic ports, small, easy to manage, and exceptionally clean. First impressions are of wonderful square stone ramparts, flanked by palms, and an outstanding beach – an immense sweep of sand stretching to the north halfway to Tangier. The town's Medina is one of the most attractive in the country, colourwashed in pastel shades, and with a series of murals painted for the town's **International Festival**, first held in 1978. It takes place in August, attracting performers from around the world with a programme usually including art, dance, film, music and poetry over the course of three to four weeks.

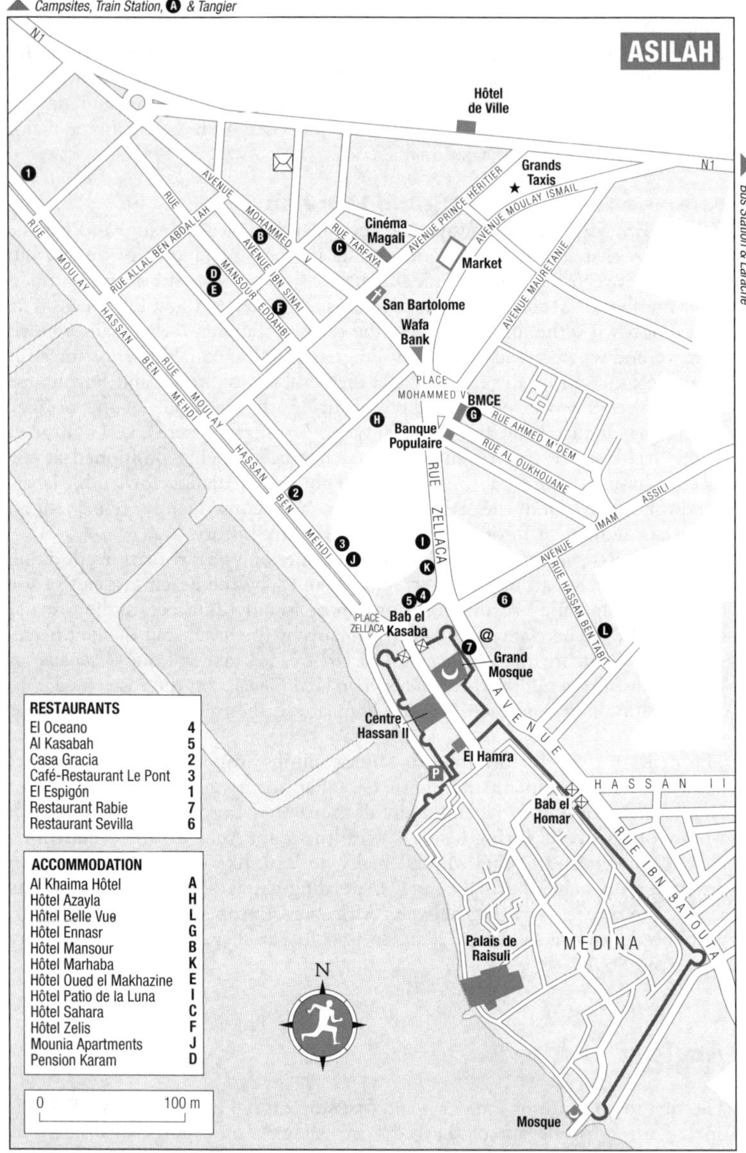

Arrival and information

The **train station** is 2km north of the town; there is occasionally a taxi to meet arrivals but don't count on it. It's an easy enough walk into town, so long as you're not weighed down with bags. **Buses** arrive at the *gare routière* on the road to Larache (N1) just on the edge of town, while coming from Tangier or Larache by **grand taxi**, you'll probably be dropped nearby, on

Avenue Moulay Ismail. From either of these, it's a short walk to **Place Mohammed V**, a small square in the centre of town, not far from the Medina's main gate, **Bab el Kasaba**.

Internet access is available on Avenue Hassan II opposite the al fresco eateries. Finally, ask directions to the town's small **hammam**, tucked down an alleyway in the north of the Medina. Unusually, the keeper charges Westerners a group rate and gives you the place to yourselves.

Accommodation

Asilah can be packed during its festival but at other times, even high season, there's usually space in the dozen or so *pensions* and hotels. Campsites, open in summer only, are usually found in the area around the train station, but many have recently closed due to vague governmental zoning laws. Campervans are also usually allowed to park for the night in an open parking area just outside the Medina wall at the end of Rue Moulay Hassan Ben Mehdi – tip the *gardien* 10dh.

Al Khaima Hôtel Route de Tanger, 1km north of town on the Tangier road, across from the beach ⓣ0539 417428, ⓕ0539 417566. An efficient, modern hotel built around a pool. It has a pleasant bar, open to non-residents, which can be a little noisy in high season. ❺

Hôtel Azayla 20 Rue Ibn Rochd ⓣ0539 416717. The newest hotel in town and just a short stroll from the Medina or the beach. Good-value bright, clean rooms with a/c, and some extra large rooms with a sitting area. Free wi-fi. Breakfast included. ❹

Hôtel Belle Vue Rue Hassan Ben Tabit ⓣ&ⓕ0539 417747. A well-located hotel with slightly bizarre decor, but reasonably priced, with clean, en-suite rooms. ❷

Hôtel Ennasr 3 Rue Ahmed M'dem (no phone). The cheapest option in town. Simple rooms around a palmed courtyard. ❷

Hôtel las Palmas 7 Rue Imam Assili ⓣ0534 267648 . A cheap hotel with slightly grubby rooms, all en suite and some with balconies. ❷

Hôtel Mansour 49 Av Mohammed V ⓣ0539 417390. Has long been one of the better mid-range hotels in town, with immaculate rooms and an English-speaking owner who also runs a handy travel agency, Jaouharat el Haram Voyages. Breakfast included. ❷

Hôtel Marhaba 9 Rue Zellaca ⓣ0539 417144. A friendly place, close to the town gate, with small, simple rooms. Good value for money, though prices increase in summer. ❷

Hôtel Oued el Makhazine Av Melilla ⓣ0539 417090, ⓕ0394 17500. A pleasant and comfortable hotel, it may not be the most exciting in town, but it's close to the seafront. ❹

Hôtel Patio de la Luna 12 Rue Zellaca ⓣ0539 416074, ⓕ0539 416540. A small house, beautifully converted into a tastefully decorated guesthouse, with a peaceful patio and garden – very central. ❹

Hôtel Sahara 9 Rue Tarfaya ⓣ0539 417185. A little way from the action, behind the Cinéma Magali, and not all rooms have external windows, but it's quiet, clean and comfortable. Hot showers 5dh extra. ❷

Hôtel Zelis 10 Rue Mansour Eddahbi ⓣ0539 417029, ⓕ0539 417098. Still one of the better hotels in town but not especially attractive. Bright, airy rooms, some with ocean views. Has a swimming pool, café and internet access. The restaurant, however, is not recommended. Breakfast included. ❺

Mounia Apartments 14 Rue Moulay Hassan Ben Mehdi ⓣ0539 417815. A range of apartments with kitchenettes, next to *Restaurant Casa Garcia* on the promenade. The owner has other apartments elsewhere. ❹–❻

Pension Karam 40 Rue Mansour Eddahbi ⓣ0539 417626. A small, homely *pension* close to the seafront (and behind the prominent *Hôtel Oued el Makhazine*). ❸

The Town

Before the tourists and the International Festival, Asilah was just a small fishing port, quietly stagnating after the indifference of Spanish colonial administration. Whitewashed and cleaned up, it now has a prosperous feeling to it: the Grand Mosque, for example, has been rebuilt and doubled in size, there's a new paved seaside promenade and property developments, including a marina and golf course estate, are popping up either side of the town. As with Tangier, the **beach** is the main focus of life in summer. The most popular stretches are to the north of the town, out towards the train station. For more isolated strands, walk south, past the Medina ramparts.

The ramparts and Medina

The Medina's circuit of **towers and ramparts** – built by the Portuguese military architect Botacca in the sixteenth century – are pleasant to wander around. They include two main gates: **Bab el Homar**, on Avenue Hassan II, and **Bab el Kasaba**. If you enter by the latter, you pass the **Grand Mosque** and the **Centre Hassan II des Rencontres Internationales**, an arts venue and accommodation centre for the festival, with a cool open courtyard.

Further on is a small square overlooked by the "red tower", **El Hamra**. This is used for exhibitions, particularly during the festival. Turn right past here, along a tiny network of streets, and down towards the platform overlooking the sea, and you'll come upon at least a half-dozen **murals** painted (and subsequently repainted) during the festivals; they form an intriguing mix of fantasy-representational art and geometric designs. Keep an eye out for the small art galleries of local artists which are scattered around the Medina.

Palais de Raisuli

The town's focal sight – stretching over the sea at the heart of the Medina – is the **Palais de Raisuli**, built in 1909 with forced tribal labour by one Er Raisuli, a local bandit. One of the strangest figures to emerge from what was a bizarre period of Moroccan government, he began his career as a cattle rustler, achieved notoriety with a series of kidnappings and ransoms (including the British writer Walter Harris and a Greek-American millionaire, Perdicaris, who was bailed out by Teddy Roosevelt), and was eventually appointed governor over practically all the tribes of northwest Morocco. Harris described his captivity in *Morocco That Was* as an "anxious time", made

▲ Art for sale in the Asilah Medina

more so by being confined in a small room with a headless corpse. Despite this, captor and 'captive formed a friendship, Harris finding Raisuli a "mysterious personage, half-saint, half-blackguard", and often entertaining him later in Tangier.

Another British writer, Rosita Forbes, visited Raisuli in his palace in 1924, later writing his biography. Raisuli told Forbes that he made murderers walk to their death from the palace windows – a 27-metre drop to the rocks. One man, he said, had turned back to him, saying, "Thy justice is great, Sidi, but these stones are more merciful."

The palace overhangs the sea ramparts towards the far end of the Medina (away from the beach). It is not officially open to visitors but if you're interested – the interior is worth seeing – knock or enlist the help of a local and you may strike lucky with the caretaker.

Church of San Bartolome and around

At the junction of Avenue Mohammed V and Avenue Prince Héritier, is the **Church of San Bartolome**, built by Franciscan priests from Galicia, in northwest Spain. The cool and airy colonial-Spanish-style interior is complemented by the nuns' own small chapel in Moorish style, with prayers common to Islam and Christianity carved in Arabic. One of the few church bells allowed to be used in Morocco is rung for Mass at 11am on Sundays and the sisters, from a teaching order founded by Mary Ward in Yorkshire in 1585, train local girls in dressmaking, embroidery and literacy. Visitors are welcome at any time – ring the bell by the door alongside the church.

There's a villagers' **market**, at its liveliest on Thursday and Sunday held on Avenue Moulay Ismail below the grand taxi stand.

Eating, drinking and nightlife

The town's most prominent **restaurants** are *El Oceano* (also called *Casa Pepe*) and *Al Kasabah*, side by side in the Place Zellaca, just outside the ramparts and further along the seafront, *Casa Gracia*. *All* have outdoor tables and Spanish-style fish and seafood dishes. *Café-Restaurant Le Pont* and *El Espigón*, also on the seafront and again specializing in fish, are slightly cheaper. In the town, the *Restaurant Sevilla*, near the *Hôtel Las Palmas* at 18 Av Imam Assili, serves generous helpings of Spanish-style dishes, and there is a string of small eateries, including *Restaurant Rabie*, on Avenue Hassan II opposite the Grand Mosque, with tables outside under the shade of large eucalyptus trees.

In summer, there are **discos** at the *Al Khaima Hôtel*.

Mzoura

If you have an interest in ancient sites, you might devote a half-day to explore the prehistoric **stone circle of Mzoura**, south of Asilah. The site, whose name means "Holy Place" in Arabic, originally comprised a tumulus, assumed to be the tomb of some early Mauritanian king, enclosed by an elliptical circle of some 167 standing stones. It was excavated in 1935 and the mound is now reduced to a series of watery hollows. There are photographs of Mzoura, pre-excavation, in the archaeological museum in Tetouan.

To reach Mzoura, follow the N1 south of Asilah for 16km, then turn left along the R417 towards Tetouan. After crossing the railway line, and 4km from the junction with the N1, turn left by the Somepi petrol station and onto a side road signposted El Yamini (Tnine Sidi Lyamani). From here the site is 5km northeast, across a confusing network of sandy tracks; it's a good idea to enlist a guide at El Yamini.

Larache and Lixus

LARACHE is a relaxed, easy-going town, its summer visitors primarily Moroccan tourists who come to enjoy the beaches to the north of the estuary of the River Loukos. You'll see as many women around as men – a reassuring feeling for women travellers looking for a low-key spot to bathe. Nearby, and accessible, are the ruins of **ancient Lixus**, legendary site of the Gardens of the Hesperides.

Larache was the main port of the northern Spanish zone and, though the central Plaza de España has since become Place de la Libération, it still bears much of its former stamp. There are faded old Spanish hotels, Spanish-run restaurants and Spanish bars, even an active Spanish cathedral (Mass Sat 7pm, Sun 11am) for the small colony who still work at the docks. In its heyday it was quite a metropolis, publishing its own Spanish newspaper and journal, and drawing a cosmopolitan population that included the French writer Jean Genet, who spent the last decade of his life here and is buried in the old Spanish cemetery found to the southwest of town.

Before its colonization in 1911, Larache was a small trading port. Its activities limited by dangerous offshore sandbars, the port-town eked out a living by building pirate ships made of wood from the nearby Forest of Mamora for the "Barbary Corsairs" of Salé and Rabat.

Today, there are major building projects underway on the outskirts of town including a government-sponsored resort, Port Lixus. This and similar projects in Asilah are demonstrative of a new initiative (Vision 2010) to reinvent Morocco's Atlantic coast as a holiday hot spot.

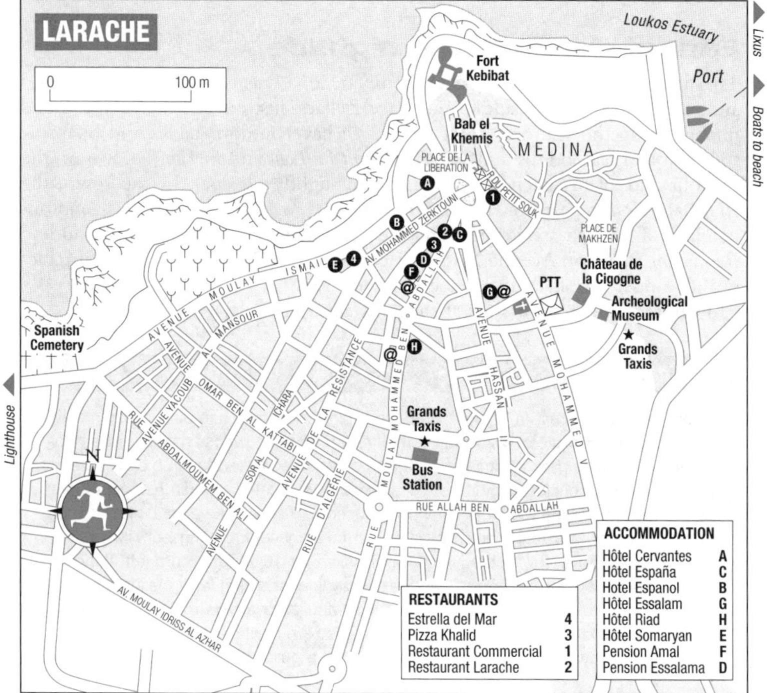

Arrival and information

Long-distance **buses**, including CTM, use the town bus station, just off Rue Moulay Mohammed Ben Abdullah. There are a few **banks** around Place de la Libération with ATMs, but no tourist office.

Accommodation

Larache has some decent accommodation and in summer, it's a good idea to book ahead. Caravans and campervans are accommodated at *Centre d'Acceuil* or *Aire de Repos* (Ⓣ0539 521069), on the N1 road towards Ksar el Kebir (the main road into town coming from the toll road) the latter of which has showers, toilets and a restaurant.

Hôtel Cervantes 3 Rue Tarik Ibnou Ziad, off Pl de la Libération Ⓣ0539 910874. Don't be put off by the unappealing paintwork – this is a friendly little place, with comfortable enough rooms and shared hot showers. ❷

Hôtel España Pl de la Libération/entrance at 6 Av Hassan II Ⓣ0539 913195, Ⓕ0539 915628. *The Grand Hôtel* in Spanish days – recently renovated with a touch of elegance. Offers a range of rooms including excellent value suites. Wi-fi available. ❸

Hôtel Espanol Av Mohammed Zerktouni Ⓣ0539 912650. A large new hotel with comfortable, attractive rooms, many with bathtubs and balconies. ❹

Hôtel Essalam 9 Av Hassan II Ⓣ0539 916822, Ⓕ0539 916822. One of our readers described this place as "the best budget hotel in Morocco", and we'd be hard-pressed to disagree: the rooms, some of which are en suite, are spacious and immaculate, with constant hot water and even a TV. ❷

Hôtel Riad Av Moulay Mohammed Ben Abdallah Ⓣ0539 912626, Ⓕ0539 912629. The former mansion of the Duchesse de Guise, mother of the current pretender to the French throne, and supposedly the best hotel in town, with gardens, a restaurant and café. Retains an attractive old-world colonial ambience, though with major renovation plans in the pipeline, this could change. ❹

Hôtel Somaryan 68 Av Mohammed Zerktouni Ⓣ0539 910116. Another recently opened modern hotel which, despite the slightly bizarre decor in the lobby, offers large attractive rooms. ❹

Pension Amal 10 Rue Abdallah Ben Yasin Ⓣ0539 912788. Basic, with simple but decent rooms, this is signposted – off to the left down an alleyway – on the street from the bus station to Place de la Libération. Hot showers 10dh extra and there is a public shower in the same little side street. ❷

Pension Essalama 50 Av Moulay Mohammed Ben Abdallah Ⓣ0676 994747. Welcoming, budget hotel with basic rooms. Hot showers 10dh. ❶

The town and beach

The town's circular main square, **Place de la Libération**, is a striking piece of Spanish colonial architecture, set just back from the sea and a straightforward 400-metre walk from the bus station and grand taxi stand.

A high archway, **Bab el Khemis**, at the centre of the square leads into the **Medina**, a surprisingly compact wedge of alleys and stairways leading down towards the port. The colonnaded market square, just inside the archway, was built by the Spanish in the seventeenth century.

If you carry on through the Medina, you can reach the small Place de Makhzen, below the **Château de la Cigogne** (Castle of the Stork), a hulking, three-sided fortress from the original Spanish occupation. Standing back from here, to the right, is a palace, built by the Spanish in 1915 and now used as a music school. Opposite, overlooking the Oued Loukos and across to Lixus, is a fine esplanade and a small **archeological museum** (daily except Mon 9am–noon & 3–6pm; 10dh), converted from a prison and containing a few Roman coins and other relics from Lixus.

The beach and coastline

If you walk from the Place de la Libération, directly to the seafront, you find yourself on another, longer promenade, Avenue Moulay Ismail. The shore below here is wild and rocky, but cross the estuary of the Oued Loukos and there are miles of fine sandy **beach** sheltered by trees and flanked by a handful of café-restaurants. You can get there by bus (#4 from the port, every 20min – some buses start from the square), a circuitous seven-kilometre route, or, more fun, from the port in a flotilla of small **fishing boats** (5–15dh per person depending on whether you haggle), which shuttle across leaving from the base of a flight of stone steps. From the square, the quickest route down to the **port** is along the promenade and under the crumbling ruins of the **Fort Kebibat** (Little Domes), built by Portuguese merchants in the sixteenth century.

In summer, an oddity on the beach is the variety of foreign languages you hear – yet with so few foreigners around. The explanation is the number of migrant families who return to the town for their holidays. People from Larache make up a big part of the Moroccan community in London, and on the beach you're likely to come upon kids with disarming English accents.

Eating

Meals in Larache, except at the Medina cafés, or the **sardine grills** down by the port, remain resolutely Spanish. The cheapest **cafés** are in Place de la Libération around Bab el Khemis, the entrance archway of the Medina. The *Restaurant Commercial* here serves fine paella, fish and chicken tajine.

A little more upmarket, and worth trying for seafood, are *Restaurant Larache* at 18 Av Moulay Mohammed Ben Abdallah, and the *Estrella del Mar* at 68 Av Mohammed Zerktouni (the other end from Pl de la Libération). For a quick late-night snack, *Pizza Khalid* on Rue Moulay Mohammed Ben Abdallah serves pizza by the slice. The seafront tea rooms also serve snacks and lunches.

Ancient Lixus

Ancient Lixus is one of the oldest – and most continuously – inhabited sites in Morocco. It had been settled in prehistoric times, long before the arrival of Phoenician colonists around 1000 BC, under whom it is thought to have become the first trading post of North Africa. Later, it was in turn an important Carthaginian and Roman city, and was deserted only in the fifth century AD, two hundred years after Diocletian had withdrawn the empire's patronage. There are remains of a church from this period, and Arabic coins have also been found.

Lixus and Hercules

The legendary associations of Lixus – and the site's mystique – centre on the Labours of Hercules. For here, on an island in the estuary, Pliny and Strabo record reports of the palace of the "Libyan" (by which they meant African) King Antaeus. Behind the palace stretched the Garden of the Hesperides, to which Hercules, as his penultimate labour, was dispatched.

In the object of Hercules' quest – the Golden Apples – it is not difficult to imagine the tangerines of northern Morocco, raised to legendary status by travellers' tales. The site, too, seems to offer reinforcement to conjectures of a mythic pre-Phoenician past. Megalithic stones have been found on the Acropolis – they may have been linked astronomically with those of Mzoura (see p.111) – and the site was known to the Phoenicians as Makom Shemesh (City of the Sun).

As an archaeological site, then, Lixus is certainly significant, and its legendary associations with Hercules (see box opposite), add an element of mythic allure. The ruins lie upon and below the summit of a low hill on the far side of the Oued Loukos estuary, at the crossroads of the main Larache–Tangier road and the narrow lane to Larache beach. A track, worth climbing for the panoramic view alone, wends up to the amphitheatre area, where there are mosaics. The ruins are interesting rather than impressive, and only around a quarter of the site has been excavated.

It's a four- to five-kilometre walk to the ruins from either the beach or town, or you can take bus #6 which runs between the two or bus #5 from town; alternatively, for about 100dh you could charter a boat to row you over from Larache, wait an hour or so, and then row you back to the town or beach.

The site

The site is not effectively enclosed, so there are no real opening hours. A notice by the roadside at the entrance explains the site with a useful map board. The Lower Town, spreading back from the modern road, consists largely of the ruins of factories for the production of salt – still being panned nearby – and *garum* fish sauce. The factories seem to have been developed in the early years of the first century AD and they remained in operation until the Roman withdrawal.

A track, some 100m down the road to Tangier, leads up to the Acropolis (upper town), passing on its way eight rows of the Roman **theatre** and **amphitheatre**, unusually combined into a single structure. Its deep, circular arena was adapted for circus games and the gladiatorial slaughter of animals. Morocco, which Herodotus knew as "the wild-beast country", was the major source for these Roman *venations* (controlled hunts), and local colonists must have grown rich from the trade. Until 1998, the **baths** built into the side of the theatre featured a remarkable **mosaic** depicting Neptune's head on the body of a lobster; unfortunately, the mosaic was irreparably damaged when the *gardien*'s son tried to dig it up to sell, and just about a third of it remains.

Climbing above the baths and theatre, you pass through ramparts to the main fortifications of the **Acropolis** – a somewhat confused network of walls and foundations – and **temple sanctuaries**, including an early **Christian basilica** and a number of **pre-Roman buildings**. The most considerable of the sanctuaries, with their underground cisterns and porticoed priests' quarters, were apparently rebuilt in the first century AD, but even then retained Phoenician elements in their design.

South from Larache

Heading **south from Larache**, the main road and most of the buses bypass **Ksar el Kebir** on their way towards Meknes, Fes or Kenitra/Rabat. You'll probably do likewise, though the town does have one of the largest weekly markets in the region (on Sundays). Just past here, you cross the old border between Spanish and French colonial zones. Beyond, **Moulay Bousselham** has miles of sandy beach, some attractive accommodation options and is a hot spot for birdwatchers.

Ksar el Kebir and around

As its name – in Arabic, "the Great Enclosure" – suggests, **KSAR EL KEBIR**, an eleventh-century Arab power base 36km southeast of Larache, was once a place of some importance. It was 12km north of here where, in August 1578, the Portuguese fought the disastrous **Battle of the Three Kings**, the most dramatic and devastating in their nation's history – a power struggle disguised as a crusade, which saw the death or capture of virtually the entire nobility and which ultimately resulted in 62 years of Spanish rule.

The town fell into decline in the seventeenth century, after a local chief incurred the wrath of Moulay Ismail, though its fortunes were revived to some extent under the Spanish protectorate, when it served as a major barracks.

The **Sunday souk** is held right by the *gare routière* and Moulay el Mehdi station. On any morning of the week, however, there are lively **souks** around the main **kissaria** (covered market) of the old town – in the quarter known as Bab el Oued (Gate of the River). Beyond Ksar el Kebir, a decaying customs post at **Arbaoua** marks the old colonial frontier between the Spanish and French zones. South again, **Souk el Arba Du Rharb** is the first settlement of any size, though it is little more than its name suggests (Wednesday Market of the Plain), a roadside sprawl of market stalls, with some grill-cafés and a few **hotels**, the best of which is the *Gharb Hôtel* (no phone; ❷).

Practicalities

The easiest way to get to Ksar el Kebir is by train, but for the town centre get off at Moulay el Mehdi station, one stop south of Ksar el Kebir station, which is way out on the northern edge of town. As the motorway bypasses the town, few long-distance buses come here; grands taxis from Larache operate to and from a station just across the tracks from the *gare routière*, and those from Ouezzane and Souk el Arba du Rharb operate from one 500m further south. For those heading to Chefchaouen by car see the box on p.136.

Hôtel Ksar al Yamama, 8 Bd Hassan II (Ⓣ0539 907960, Ⓕ0539 903838; ❷), is good value, with nice, large, airy rooms, some en suite with a bathtub, and some with balconies overlooking a town square. To get to it, head south from the Moulay el Mehdi station and turn right after 300m. There's a trio of cheaper and more basic hotels just across the square on Boulevard Mohammed V. For **meals**, there isn't much, but try the grill-café *Khay Ibd Rahim* on Boulevard Mohammed V, across the square from *Hôtel Ksar al Yamama*.

Moulay Bousselham

MOULAY BOUSSELHAM, 55km from Ksar el Kebir, is a very low-key resort, popular almost exclusively with Moroccans. It comprises little more than a single street, crowded with grill-cafés and sloping down to the sea at the side of a broad lagoon and wetland area, known as **Merdja Zerga**. This is one of northern Morocco's prime **birdwatching** locations (see box opposite), and any foreign visitor will be accosted by the growing number of resident guides to see the lagoon's flamingo and other bird colonies.

The **beach** itself is sheltered by cliffs – rare along the Atlantic – and has an abrupt drop-off, which creates a continual crash of breaking waves. While a lot of fun for swimming, the currents can be highly dangerous and the beach is strictly patrolled by lifeguards. Take care.

For Moroccans, the village is part summer resort, part pilgrimage centre. The saint from whom the village takes its name, the **Marabout Moulay Bousselham**, was a tenth-century Egyptian, whose remains are housed in a *koubba* prominently positioned above the settlement. In July this sees one of the largest **moussems** in the region.

Moulay Bousselham has a **post office** (east of town on the Souk el Arba road), branches of the **banks** Banque de Populaire and Credit Agricole, the latter with an ATM, and a **téléboutique**.

Wetland wildlife

Adjoining the Moulay Bousselham lagoon is a large wetland area – awarded protected wildlife status – known as **Merdja Zerga** ("Blue Lake"). This open barren space is used for grazing by nomadic herds of sheep, cattle and goats, while around the periphery are lines of dwarf palm and the giant succulent agave.

This diversity of habitat, and the huge extent of the site, ensures rewarding **birdwatching** at all times of year. There are large numbers of waders, including a large colony of flamingos, plus little ringed plovers, black-winged stilts and black-tailed godwits.

For serious birdwatchers, it is the **gulls and terns** that roost on the central islands which are worthy of the closest inspection, as, among the flocks of lesser black-backed gull and black tern, it is possible to find rarer species such as **Caspian tern**. However, the campsite (*Camping Caravaning International*) at Moulay Bousselham is probably the best place in Morocco to see pairs of North African **marsh owl** which usually appear hunting over the adjacent grassland ten to fifteen minutes after sunset, and the same vantage point is also a good spot for seeing **Barbary partridge**. One bird you'll certainly see wintering here, usually around cattle (and sometimes sitting on their backs), is the **cattle egret**. For rarity-spotters, the grail is the **slender-billed curlew**, an endangered species, spotted once or twice in recent years; it is smaller than the European curlew with distinct spade-like markings on its flanks.

The *Café Milano* in Moulay Bousselham keeps a **bird log** and will put you in touch with English speaking, local ornithologist Hassan Dalil (ⓣ0668 434110) who comes highly recommended as a guide to the area and its birdlife. Hassan charges 100dh per hour for a tour around Merja Zerga by boat and his expertise is immediately evident. These tours are best taken in early morning or at dusk, depending on the tides.

Accommodation and eating

Moulay Bousselham has two **campsites**: the ageing *Camping Caravanning International* (ⓣ0537 432477), 500m east of town on the lagoon and consequently plagued by mosquitoes; and the nearby curiously named *Flamants Loisirs*, or "spare flamingos" (ⓣ0537 432539) which is in slightly better condition and has a swimming pool and bungalows for rent. **Accommodation** includes the *Villa Nora* (ⓣ0537 432071; ❹), a family-run villa on the coast road at the northern end of town, about 1.5km from the centre. Overlooking the beach and the Atlantic rollers, it's an attractive place, with an English owner, Jean Oliver, who is knowledgeable on local birdlife and in summer exhibits works of Moroccan art. Down by the lagoon is *La Maison des Oiseaux*, "the house of the birds" (ⓣ0661 301067, ⓔmaisondesoiseaux@hotmail.com; ❹), a whitewashed villa with a pleasant garden and a homely family atmosphere. There's a variety of rooms including some family suites that sleep up to four adults. Themed courses such as cooking and yoga can also be arranged. On the town's main road and with fantastic views over the lagoon is the *Hôtel Le Lagoon* (ⓣ0537 432650, ⓕ0537 432649; ❹) with comfortable rooms and a restaurant. The *Hôtel Mirimar* (no phone; ❷), in the middle of town and overlooking the beach, has very basic rooms with separate showers and toilets at the back of a busy café.

Most of the **grill-cafés** will fix you a mixed platter of fish – served in copious amounts and at very reasonable prices. For **restaurants**, *Firdaous*, *Normandie* and *Restaurant Milano*, all on the main street, are good bets. The *Milano* is also a good place to contact bird guides (see box above).

Ceuta (Sebta)

A Spanish enclave since the sixteenth century, CEUTA (Sebta in Arabic) is a curious political anomaly. Along with Melilla, east along the coast, it was retained by Spain after Moroccan independence in 1956 and today functions largely as a military base, its economy bolstered by a limited duty-free status. It has been an autonomous city, with a large measure of internal self-government for its 80,000 inhabitants, since 1995. The city makes for an attractive stop when en-route either to or from Morocco with its relaxed European atmosphere, pristine squares, tapas bars, coastal walks, and pleasant accommodation options. However, you will need no more than a day or two here to experience most of what is on offer.

Note that Ceuta works to Spanish time, an hour ahead of Morocco (two hours ahead between the times when Europe and Morocco change to daylight saving). When phoning Ceuta from Morocco (or anywhere else outside Spain), you must prefix phone numbers with the international code (Ⓣ00 34). Dialling numbers within Ceuta you must include the old local code Ⓣ956 as part of the new nine-digit number. To phone Morocco from Ceuta, you need to dial Ⓣ00 212, followed by the local code (minus the initial zero) and number. Ceuta uses the euro.

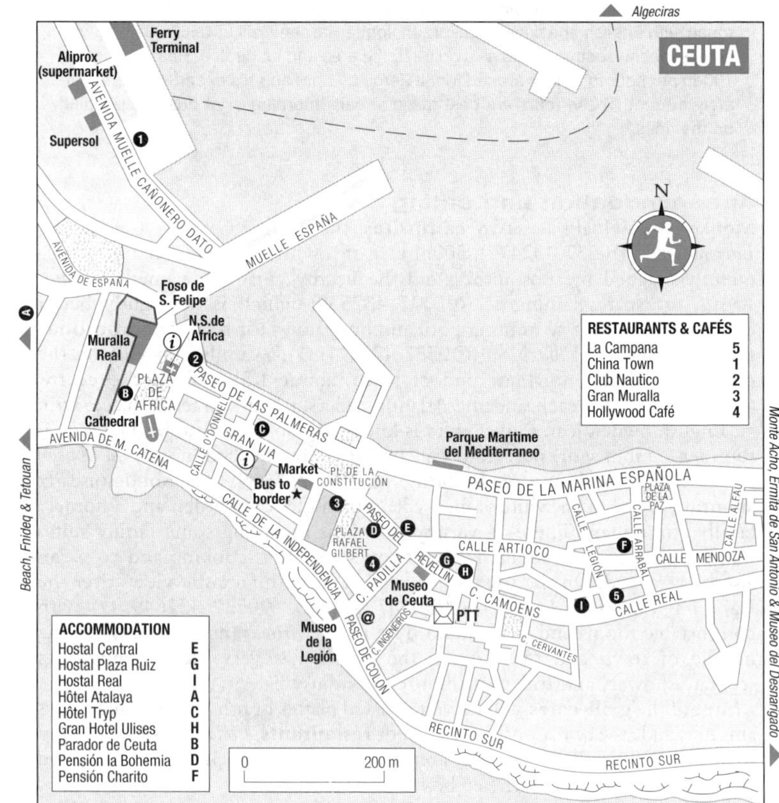

Crossing the border at Ceuta

Since the Algeciras–Ceuta ferries and hydrofoils are quicker than those to Tangier (and the ferries significantly cheaper for cars or motorbikes), Ceuta is a popular **point of entry and exit**. Coming over on a first visit to Morocco, however, try to arrive early in the day so that you have plenty of time to move on to Tetouan – and possibly beyond. There is no customs/passport check at the port as you don't officially enter Morocco until the border, 3km out of town. This can be reached by local bus #7 from the centre of Ceuta (turn left as you come off the ferry or hydrofoil and it is about 800m away, in Plaza de la Constitución). Coming from the Moroccan side, most buses and grands taxis drop you off in **Fnideq**, 2km short of the border (see p.130). If so, just head down to the coastal highway, where you can pick up a grand taxi to the border post for 5dh a place or you can simply walk.

At the border, formalities are brief on the **Spanish side** – at least, if you are leaving Spain: searches are common for those coming back, and there are often tailbacks of cars on Sunday evenings, though the main customs check (complete with dogs and X-ray machines) is across the Straits at Algeciras. On the **Moroccan side**, the procedure can be time-consuming, especially for drivers. You need a registration form (yellow or photocopied white) for yourself, and, if you have a car, an additional green form; these are available – if you ask for them – from the security *chefs* outside the frontier post. The car form requires inconvenient details such as chassis number and date of registration. If you despair of getting a form and having it processed, you can always enlist an official porter (they have badges – ask to see it) for a 10dh tip; try and avoid unofficial touts (and ignore touts trying to charge you for immigration forms, which are free). The whole business can take ten minutes on a good day, an hour or two on a bad one, and the noise and chaos can be a bit unsettling. Just try to keep a steady head and if you are in doubt as to where and what you should do, ask one of the (sometimes over-stressed) officials for assistance or directions.

Once across and into Morocco proper, you can take a shared **grand taxi** to Fnideq, 2km away (5dh per place), where you'll find connecting services to **Tetouan** (15dh) or **Tangier** (30dh); buses also run from Fnideq to both towns. Coming into Ceuta, local bus #7 departs directly from the border post (€0.70) as do metered taxis (€2.90 to the town centre).

On the Moroccan side of the border there are branches of BMCE and Banque Populaire, which accept cash and travellers' cheques, and on the Spanish side there are a couple of travel agencies that will change Moroccan dirhams for you.

Drivers should note that **petrol** in Ceuta is about forty percent cheaper than in mainland Spain, so stock up as best you can. It is tempting to fill up spare tanks too, but be aware that Spanish customs officers at Algeciras could sting you for duty if you do.

Arrival and information

Ceuta's tourist office is off the southern end of Paseo de las Palmeras (Mon–Fri 8.30am–8.30pm, Sat/Sun 9am–8pm). There are also a few information kiosks, the main one on Grand Via across from *Hotel Tryp* (daily 10.30am–1.30pm and 6–9pm in theory, but often closed). Currency exchange is available on the Spanish side of the border and at most banks on Paseo Del Revellin. There is also a currency exchange booth in the ferry terminal. Internet access is available at Cyber Ceuta on Paseo Colón.

Border trade: people and drugs

Over the last few decades, the economies on both sides of the border seemed to benefit from the enclave, spurred on by Ceuta's duty-free status. However, the border is also the frontier between Africa and Europe and inevitably the EU is increasingly concerned about traffic in drugs and illegal immigrants, financing a £15m ($22m) hi-tech "wall" with closed-circuit TV and sensors along the eight-kilometre boundary.

The money to be made from outflanking these defences has attracted equally hi-tech smugglers, trading in hash, hard drugs, disadvantaged Moroccans, and refugees from as far south as Liberia and Rwanda. More affluent refugees have been sent over to Spain by night, often in small boats unsuited to the short but difficult crossing. The more desperate try to swim across to Ceuta from Fnideq's beach or scale the six-metre high border fence. Most recently, there has been growing dissent in the impoverished residential areas of Ceuta where Moroccan residents have come into conflict with the Spanish authorities over a severe lack of employment and poor living conditions.

Accommodation

Accommodation problems are compounded at **festival times**, the main events being Carnival (Feb), Holy Week, the Fiesta de Nuestra Señora de Monte Carmel (July 16), and the Fiesta de Nuestra Señora de Africa on August 5, though it's advisable to book ahead at all times of the year.

Most of the dozen or so hotels and *hostales*, and cheaper *pensións, casas de huespedes* and *fondas* are to be found along the main thoroughfare, Paseo del Revellín, or its extensions, Calle Camoens and Calle Real. Some of the cheaper places are easy to miss, distinguished only by their blue and white signs (H for *Hostal*; P for *Pension*; CH for *Casa de Huespedes*; F for *Fonda*).

Hostal Central 15 Paseo del Revellín ⓣ&ⓕ 956 516716, ⓦ www.hostalesceuta.com. An excellent new option with comfortable modern rooms and all the mod-cons. Wi-fi available. ❻

Hostal Plaza Ruiz 3 Plaza Teniente Ruiz ⓣ&ⓕ 956 516733, ⓦ www.hostalesceuta.com. Under the same ownership as *Hostal Central*, this offers slightly larger rooms, some with balconies. Wi-fi available. ❻

Hostal Real c/Real 1, third floor ⓣ&ⓕ 956 511449. A pleasant, comfortable little *pensión*, a cut above the average, though most rooms lack outside windows. ❺

Hotel Atalaya Avda Reyes Catolicos 6 ⓣ 956 504161. A quiet two-star hotel on the way into town from the border, on bus route #7. All rooms are en suite. ❻

Hotel Tryp Gran Via 2 ⓣ 956 511200. A new four-star hotel with a gleaming white atrium and quite luxurious rooms. ❼

Gran Hotel Ulises c/Camoens 5 ⓣ 956 514540, ⓦ www.hotelceuta.com. A recently refurbished and respectable four-star business hotel on a pedestrian mall. Breakfast included. ❼

Parador de Ceuta (*Gran Hôtel La Muralla*) Pl de Africa 15 ⓣ 956 514940, ⓦ www.parador.es. Ceuta's characterful old *Parador* remains the prime choice if you can afford it. ❼

Pensión la Bohemia Paseo del Revellín 12, first floor ⓣ 956 510615. Best deal among the cheapies, clean and comfortable though most rooms lack outside windows. ❺

Pensión Charito c/Arrabal 5 ⓣ 956 513982. One of the best and most welcoming among a number of small, cheap lodgings in this area. Located on the second floor of an unmarked building, one door down the hill from *Limite* bar. Cold showers. ❺

The Town

Ceuta has a long and eventful history, with occupation by Phoenicians, Romans, Visigoths, Byzantines, Moors, Portuguese, and finally the Spanish. Despite this tumultuous history, there's not a great deal to see – or do. The town is modern, functional and provincial in the lacklustre Spanish manner, and its most attractive part is within several hundred metres of the new ferry dock, where the **Plaza de Africa** is flanked by a pair of Baroque churches, **Nuestra Señora de Africa** (Our Lady of Africa – open most days) and the **cathedral** (usually locked). Bordering the square, to the west, are the most impressive remainders of the city walls – the walled moat of **Foso de San Felipe** and the adjacent **Muralla Real** (daily 10am–2pm & 4–8pm; free). The oldest sections of the fortifications were built by the Byzantines.

To the east of Plaza de la Constitución, an oldish quarter rambles up from the bottom of the long **Paseo del Revellin**. There's an interesting little municipal museum here, the **Museo de Ceuta** (June–Aug Mon–Sat 10am–2pm & 7–9pm, Sun 10am–2pm; Sept–May, same except evenings 5–8pm only; free), displaying archeological finds from Stone Age and Roman times through to the Islamic era, well laid out and with good explanations, but in Spanish only. There is also a section dedicated to contemporary art exhibitions on the ground floor. To the south of here, the **Museo de la Legión** (Mon–Sat 10am–1.30pm; free), on Paseo de Colón, offers a glimpse of Spanish–African military history, crammed with uniforms, weapons and paraphernalia of the infamous Spanish Foreign Legion.

From the museum, if you have a couple of hours to spare, you can continue along a round circuit of the peninsula by heading east on Recinto Sur. As the buildings gradually disappear from view, the land swells into a rounded, pine-covered slope, known as **Monte Acho**, crowned by a Byzantine-era fort offering fine views out to the Rock of Gibraltar. Around midway, signs direct you to the **Ermita de San Antonio**, an old convent rebuilt during the 1960s and dominated by a monument to Franco. At the very eastern end of the peninsula is another military museum, the **Museo del Desnarigado,** (Sat & Sun 11am–2pm & 4–6pm; free), housed in a fort that is mainly nineteenth-century though with remnants from the sixteenth and seventeenth centuries.

Other Ceuta attractions include a **town beach**, 1km southwest of the moat, and a seafront leisure and amusement complex, the **Parque Maritime del Mediterráneo** (daily 11am–8pm; closed Thurs in winter; €5, children €3), complete with swimming pools, restaurants, and a casino.

The duty-free status of the port draws many Tangier expats on day-trips to buy cheap spirits, and Spanish day-trippers to buy radios and cameras, but, besides buying a cheap bottle, these aren't very compelling pursuits for casual visitors. If you do want to stock up on booze, stop at either of the Supsersol or Aliprox supermarkets just outside the ferry terminal on Avenida Muelle Cañonero Dato.

Eating and drinking

Ceuta's main concentration of restaurants is around the Plaza de la Constitución. For tapas bars, check the smaller streets off Calle Camoens.

China Town Av Muelle Canonero Dato. Just south of the ferry terminal. A busy and cheerful Chinese restaurant. Cheap to moderate.

Club Nautico c/Edrissis ⓣ956 514400. A small fish restaurant within the town's boat club, just off Paseo de las Palmeras and overlooking the fishing harbour. Serves up some of the best seafood dishes in Ceuta. Open Mon–Sat 9am–3pm & 5pm–midnight, Sun 10am–3pm. Moderate.

Gran Muralla Plaza de la Constitución 4. A popular, long-established Chinese restaurant with extensive menu and sweeping views over the harbour, located up the steps from the square. Moderate.

Hollywood Café c/Padilla 4. Very friendly, family-run café with toasted sandwiches, paella and other Spanish dishes. Daily 10am–9pm. Cheap.

La Campana c/Real 13. A smoke-filled bar-café with a reasonable €6 set menu (though no choice for non-pork eaters), plus tapas, spaghetti, sandwiches, beer and wine from the barrel. The hilariously grumpy service alone makes it worth the visit. It also has a great patisserie next door. Cheap.

Moving on

Leaving Ceuta **by ferry** for Algeciras, you can normally turn up at the port, buy tickets, and board a ferry within a couple of hours, though you can only travel with the company from which you have purchased your tickets. The two periods to avoid, as at Tangier, are the end of the **Easter week** (Semana Santa) holiday and the **last week of August**, when the ferries can be full for days on end with Moroccan workers and their families returning to northern Europe.

If you plan to use the quicker **hydrofoil service** to Algeciras, it's best to book the previous day – though you should be fine outside the high season.

Shipping companies represented at the ferry terminal include Acciona Trasmediterránea (Ⓣ956 522215), Balearia Nautus (Ⓣ956 205190), Buquebus (Ⓣ956 501113) and Euroferrys (Ⓣ956 521529). For details of services, see p.30. Be aware that all arrivals from Ceuta need to go through customs at Algeciras, where searches of suspected drug-runners can be extremely thorough.

A more expensive way across the Straits is via a helicopter service run by Inaer (Málaga Ⓣ952 048700, Ceuta Ⓣ956 504974, Ⓦwww.grupoinaer.com), between Ceuta and Málaga. This service runs five times daily on weekdays, twice on Saturdays and Sundays, and costs €134 per person one way.

Tetouan

If you are new to Morocco, coming from Ceuta, **TETOUAN** will be your first experience of a Moroccan city with its crowded streets and noisy souks. You do need to keep your wits about you, especially arriving with baggage at the bus station, as hustlers try to latch on to new arrivals. Despite the hustle, a new university in nearby Martil has relaxed the general atmosphere and promoted a more open-minded attitude towards foreigners.

Approaching Tetouan from the landward side it looks strikingly beautiful, poised atop the slope of an enormous valley against a dark mass of rock. Its name (pronounced *Tet-tá-wan*) means "open your eyes" in Berber, an apparent reference to the town's hasty construction by Andalucian refugees in the fifteenth century. The refugees, both Muslims and Jews, brought with them the most refined sophistication of Moorish Andalucía, reflected in the architecture of the Medina. Their houses, full of extravagant detail, with tiled lintels and wrought-iron balconies, seem much more akin to the old Arab quarters of Cordoba and Seville than those of Moroccan towns. With its excellent local beaches, Tetouan is a popular Moroccan resort that attracts mostly Moroccan families who flock to the beach in the summer to escape the heat.

Arrival, orientation and information

Buses arrive at the new bus station 1km south of the city. CTM buses arrive at a separate station below Boulevard Sidi Driss on the edge of the Ville Nouvelle. Built by the Spanish in the 1920s, this quarter of town follows a straightforward grid. At its centre is **Place Moulay el Mehdi**, with the Spanish consulate, post office and main banks. From there the pedestrianized Boulevard Mohammed V runs east **to Place Hassan II** and the **Royal Palace**, beyond which lies the Medina, still partially walled and entered through the Bab er Rouah gateway.

Official guides can be enlisted at the helpful **tourist office** (Mon–Thurs 8.30am–4.30pm, Fri 8.30–11:30am & 2–4.30pm; Ⓣ0539 961915, Ⓕ0539 961402), a few metres from Place Moulay el Mehdi at 30 Bd Mohammed V. There are various internet points scattered throughout the town centre. Try the first floor internet café on the corner of Rue Mohammed Ben Larbi Torres and Rue De La Luneta on the southern end of Place Hassan II.

Accommodation

Ignore all offers from touts and head for one of the recommendations below. You're likely to get the best deal at the **hotels**, as most of the thirty-or-so **pensions** (including the few we've listed) raise their prices well above basic rates in summer when rooms can be in short supply.

The nearest **campsites** are on the beach or nearby at **Martil**, 11km out (see p.129 for transport details), which can be useful fallbacks if you have problems finding a room.

El Reducto 38 Zankat Zawya, in a lane off Bd Mohammed V ⓣ0539 968120, ⓦwww.riadtetouan.com. Tetouan's most upmarket accommodation, this small riad used to be the home of the Spanish governor, and has been lovingly brought back to life by the current owner. Four individually furnished suites overlook a central courtyard and (excellent) restaurant. Book ahead. Includes breakfast. ❺–❻

Hôtel Bilbao 7 Bd Mohammed V (no phone). This is one of the cheapest *pensions* and is centrally placed. Reasonably clean, with cold showers in the rooms. ❷

Hôtel Chams Rue Abdelkhaleq Torres ⓣ0539 990901, ⓕ0539 990907. Still one of Tetouan's best hotels, 3km out of town on the road to Martil. Comfortable – with a pool, a/c and satellite TV – but hardly worth the out-of-town inconvenience. ❺

Hôtel Oumaima Av 10 Mai ⓣ0539 963473. Central and functional, with small rooms, each with a TV, and a ground-floor café for breakfast. ❸

Hôtel Principe 20 Av Youssef Ben Tachfine ⓣ0533 113128. Midway from the bus station to Place Moulay el Mehdi, just off the pedestrianized strip of Bd Mohammed V. A decent cheapie but with gloomy rooms, some boasting a shower. There's a café for breakfast and snacks. ❷

Hôtel Regina 8 Rue Sidi Mandri ⓣ0539 962113. A small hotel with en-suite rooms, cheaper and rather better value than the *Oumaima* and the *Paris*. A small café serves breakfast. ❷

Hôtel Trebol 3 Av Yacoub el Mansour ⓣ0539 962093. Very basic but clean and cheap (especially for singles), but has no showers at all. ❶

Hôtel Victoria 23 Av Mohammed V ⓣ0539 965015. Good-value, clean and very cheap with shared bathroom facilities. ❷

Paris Hôtel 31 Rue Chkil Arssalane ⓣ0539 966750, ⓕ0539 712654. Not dissimilar to the *Oumaima* (even the price was identical at last check), with slightly nicer rooms, those at the back being quietest. The restaurant is open in summer only. ❸

Pensión Iberia 5 Pl Moulay el Mehdi, third floor ⓣ0539 963679. Above the BMCE bank, central, clean, and excellent value for money. Hot showers (10dh). ❷

Riad Dalia 25 Rue Ouessaa Mtamar ⓣ0539 964318, ⓦwww.riad-dalia.com. An atmospheric riad nestled in the Medina with variety of rooms and suites, all very reasonably priced. The view from the terrace may well be the best in Tetouan. ❹–❻

The Medina

Two cities rose and fell in the vicinity of Tetouan before the present-day city was built. Tamuda, the scant ruins of which can still be seen on the south side of Oued Martil 4km southeast of town, was founded by the Berber Mauritanians in the third century BC, and razed by the Romans in 42 AD; and the original Tetouan, built by the Merenids in 1307, on the same site as today's Medina, destroyed by a Castilian raiding party in 1399. The present town was established in 1484 by Muslims and Jews fleeing the Christian reconquest of Andalucía in southern Spain. Jewish merchants – able to pass relatively freely between Muslim North Africa and Christian Europe – brought prosperity to the city, and ramparts were put up in the seventeenth century under Moulay Ismail.

Tetouan has since been occupied twice by the Spanish. It was seized briefly, as a supposed threat to Ceuta, from 1859 to 1862, a period which saw the **Medina** converted to a town of almost European appearance, complete with street lighting. Then, in 1913 a more serious, colonial occupation began. Tetouan served first as a military garrison for the subjugation of the Rif, later as the

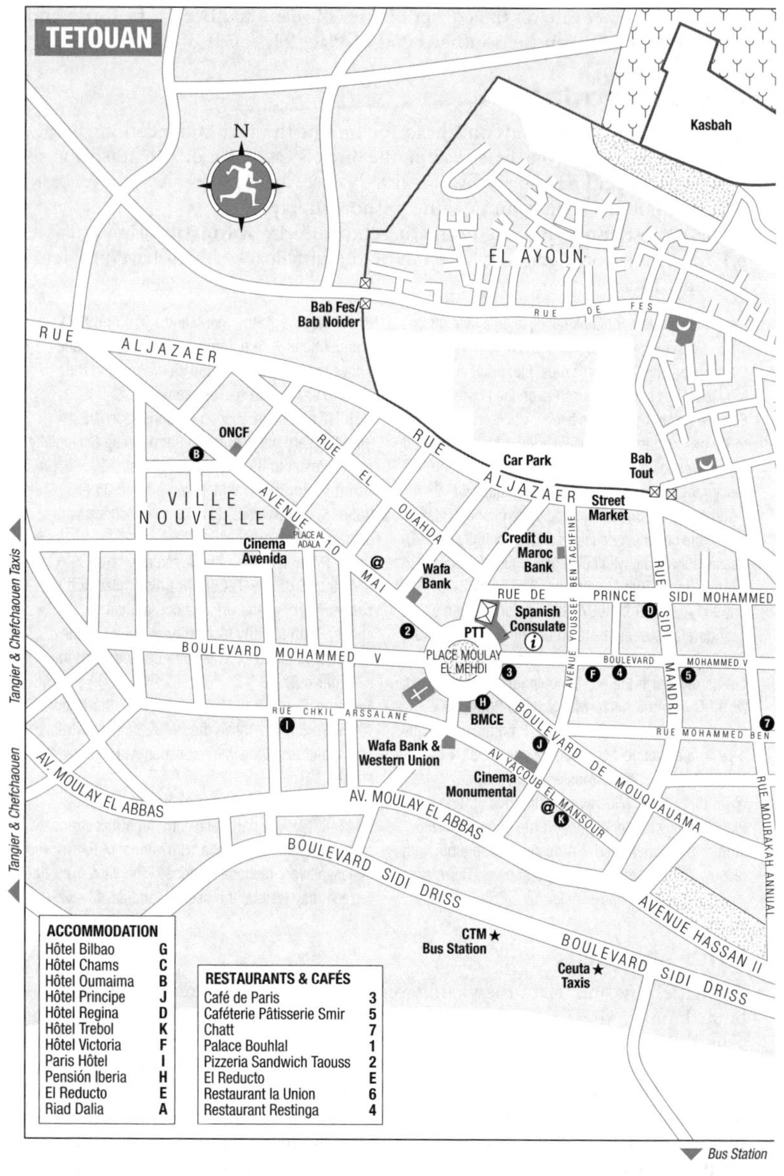

capital of the **Spanish Protectorate Zone**. As such it almost doubled in size to handle the region's trade and administration, and it was here in 1936 that **General Franco** declared his military coup against Spain's elected Liberal–Socialist coalition government, thus igniting the Spanish Civil War.

For Tetouan's Moroccan population, there was little progress during the colonial period. Spanish administration retained a purely military character and only a handful of schools were opened throughout the entire zone. This legacy

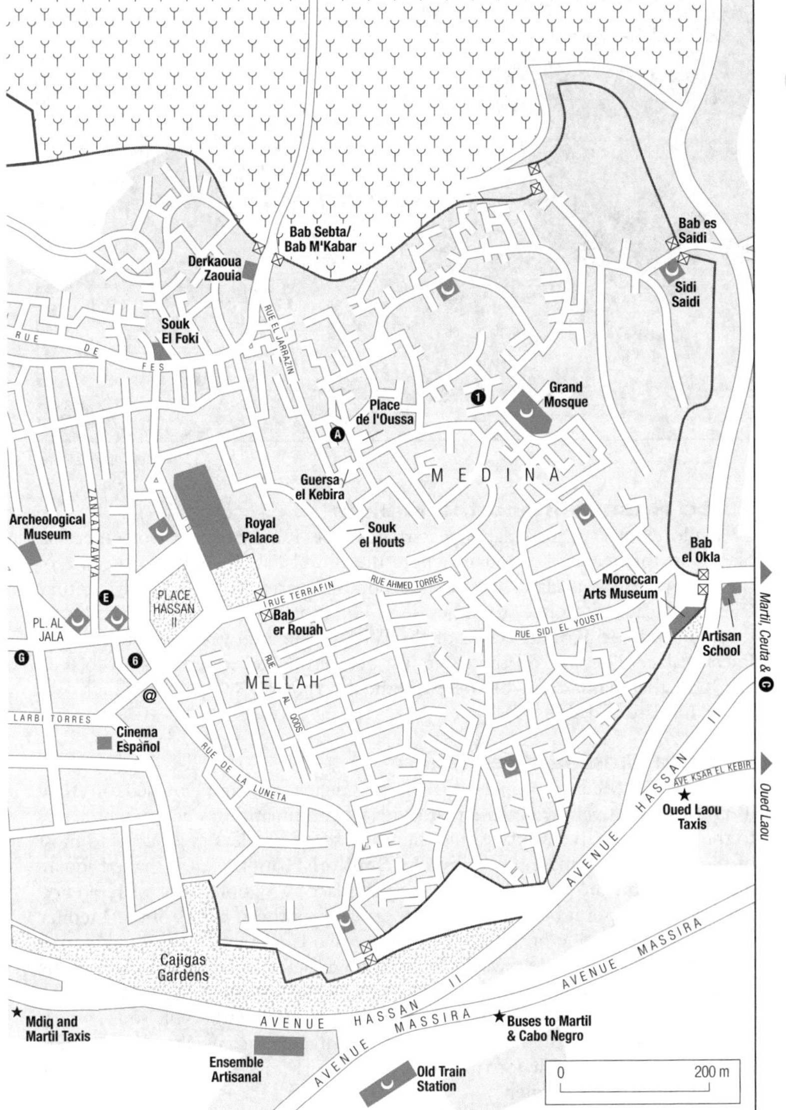

had effects well beyond independence in 1956, and the town, alongside its Rif hinterland, adapted with difficulty to the new nation and was at the centre of anti-government rioting as recently as 1984. Aware of this undercurrent, the new king, **Mohammed VI**, made it his business to visit the former Spanish protectorate almost as soon as he ascended the throne in 1999, a gesture that has helped to give Tetouan and its region a much stronger sense of nationhood than it had under the previous monarch.

▲ View over Tetouan

Place Hassan II and the Mellah

To explore Tetouan, the place to start is **Place Hassan II**, the old meeting place and former market square where the Royal Palace (built on the site of the old Spanish consulate) stands, incorporating parts of a nineteenth-century Caliphal Palace that once stood beside it. The usual approach to the Medina is through **Bab er Rouah** (Gate of the Winds), the archway just south of the Royal Palace. The lane on the right, just before the archway, opens on to Rue al Qods, the main street of the **Mellah**, the old Jewish quarter which was created as late as 1807.

Into the Medina: the souks

Entering the Medina proper, at Bab er Rouah, you find yourself on **Rue Terrafin**, a relatively wide lane that (with its continuations) cuts straight across to the east gate, Bab el Okla. Along the way a series of alleys give access to most of the town's food and craft souks. The **Souk el Houts**, a small shaded square directly behind the grounds of the Royal Palace is a good point of reference, being a central point between the northern and southern halves of the Medina.

From the north side of the Souk el Houts, two lanes wind up through a mass of alleys, souks and passageways towards Bab Sebta. Following the one on the right (east) for about twenty metres, you'll see an opening to another small square. This is the **Guersa el Kebira**, essentially a cloth and textile souk, where a number of stalls sell the town's highly characteristic *foutahs* – strong and brilliantly striped lengths of rug-like cotton, worn as a cloak and skirt by the Djebali and Riffian women.

Leaving the Guersa at its top right-hand corner, you should emerge more or less on **Place de l'Oussa**, another beautiful little square, easily recognized by an ornate, tiled fountain and trellises of vines. Along one of its sides is an imposing nineteenth-century **Xharia**, or almshouse; on another is an artisania shop, elegantly tiled and with good views over the quarter from its roof.

Beyond the square, still heading up towards Bab Sebta, are most of the specific **craft souks** – among them copper and brass workers, renowned makers of *babouches* (pointed leather slippers), and carpenters specializing in elaborately carved and painted wood. Most of the shops along the central lane here –

Rue el Jarrazin – focus on the tourist trade, but this goes much less for the souks themselves.

So, too, with the nearby souks around **Rue de Fès**, which is reached most easily by following the lane beside the Royal Palace from Place Hassan II. This is the main thoroughfare of an area selling ordinary everyday goods, with the occasional villagers' **Joutia**, or flea market. At its main intersection – just to the right as you come out onto the lane up from Place Hassan II – is **Souk el Foki**, once the town's main business sector, though it's little more than a wide alleyway. Following this past a small perfume souk and two sizeable mosques, you meet up with Rue el Jarrazin just below **Bab Sebta** (also known as Bab M'Kabar).

Walk out this way, passing (on your left) the superb portal of the **Derkaoua Zaouia** (no admission to non-Muslims), headquarters of the local Derkaoua brotherhood, and you enter a huge **cemetery**, in use since at least the fifteenth century and containing unusually elaborate Andalucian tombs. Fridays excluded, non-Muslims are tolerated in most Moroccan cemeteries, and walking here you get illuminating views over the Medina and across the valley to the Rif.

On the west side of the Medina, and most easily accessed from the Ville Nouvelle, there is a regular **street market** by Bab Tout, spilling out of the gates and along Rue Aljazaer. This is well worth a stroll and is only a couple of blocks north of Boulevard Mohammed V.

The Moroccan Arts Museum and Artisan School

The **Moroccan Arts Museum** (Tues–Sat 10am–6pm; 10dh), the entrance to which is just inside Bab el Okla, is housed in a former arms bastion and has an impressive collection of traditional crafts and ethnographic objects.

Across the road, outside the Medina's walls, is the **Artisan School** (École des Métiers; Mon–Thurs & Sun 8am–4.30pm; 10dh), where you can see craftsmen working at new designs in the old ways, essentially unmodified since the fourteenth century. Perhaps owing to its Andalucian heritage, Tetouan actually has a slightly different zellij (enamelled tile mosaics) technique to other Moroccan cities – the tiles are cut before rather than after being fired. A slightly easier process, it is frowned upon by the craftsmen of Fes, whose own pieces are more brittle, but brighter in colour and closer fitting. Many of the workshops have items for sale if you enquire.

The Ensemble Artisanal and Archeological Museum

The **Ensemble Artisanal** (Mon–Sat 9.30am–1pm & 3.30–7pm) on the main road below the town has regular exhibits on the ground floor which can be worth a look if you're planning to make purchases in the souks and want to assess prices and quality first. However, the main point of interest is upstairs, where you will find a fascinating array of carpet and embroidery workshops and outside the building, where there are metalwork, basketry and musical instrument artisans at work. This is a unique opportunity to get up close to the craftsmen and women and their work without feeling pressured into buying anything. Nearby, the **Old Train Station**, which looks like an Oriental palace, will soon (dates are vague) house a modern art museum.

The **Archeological Museum** (Tues–Sat 10am–6pm; 10dh) is off Place al Jala at the eastern end of Boulevard Mohammed V. It was founded during the Spanish protectorate, so it features exhibits from throughout their zone, including rock carvings from the Western Sahara. Highlights, as so often in North Africa, are the Roman mosaics, mostly gathered from Lixus and the oft-plundered Volubilis.

Other than these, the most interesting exhibits are concerned with the stone circle at Mzoura (see p.111), including a model and aerial photographs.

Eating, drinking and entertainment

Tetouan is not exactly a gourmet's paradise, with nowhere really worth going out of your way for. As ever, the cheapest food is to be found in the **Medina**, particularly the stalls inside Bab er Rouah and along Rue de la Luneta in the old Mellah quarter. For variety, try one of the many places on or around Boulevard Mohammed V or Rue Mohammed Ben Larbi Torres in the **Ville Nouvelle**. Two good **cinemas** are the Avenida, on Place al Adala (off Av 10 Mai) and the Monumental, near the *Hôtel Principe*. The Español, near the *Restaurant La Union*, mainly shows "*l'histoire et la géographie*" (a double bill of Bollywood and kung fu). The Institut Francais (ⓣ0539 961212), a cultural arts foundation, frequently puts on concerts and theatre performances at various venues in Tetouan. Check with the tourist office and keep an eye out for flyers.

Restaurants

El Reducto 38 Zankat Zawya, in a lane off Bd Mohammed V ⓣ0539 968120, ⓦwww.riadtetouan.com. Open to non-residents daily 8am–late. The menu is mainly Moroccan with some inventive Spanish and seafood dishes, all very reasonably priced. Licensed. Moderate.

Palace Bouhlal 48 Jamaa el-Kebir, a lane north of the Grand Mosque ⓣ0539 998797. A palace restaurant which serves indulgent Moroccan meals in a richly decorated salon. Open daily, lunch only. Moderate.

Restaurant la Union (formerly known as *Restaurant Moderno*), 1 Pasaje Achaach, off Rue Mohammed Ben Larbi Torres – to find it, go through the arcades opposite Cinema Español. Popular with locals, this budget eatery serves up standard Moroccan fare, including *harira*, brochettes and a reasonable meat tajine. Open daily noon–9.30pm. Cheap.

Restaurant Restinga 21 Bd Mohammed V. Eat indoors or in a courtyard at this very pleasant restaurant that's been serving tajine, couscous and fried fish twelve hours a day (11.30am–11.30pm) since 1968. Beer available with meals. Moderate.

Cafés and snack bars

Café de Paris Place Moulay el Mehdi. A large café on the main square, which has become quite a fashionable and relatively female-friendly hangout.

Caféterie Patisserie Smir 17 Bd Mohammed V. Rich gateaux, sweets and soft drinks. Daily 11am–11.30pm.

Chatt Rue Mourakah Annual. Popular spot with pretty much everything you'd need for breakfast, plus tea, coffee, burgers, omelettes and snacks. Daily; opens early and closes very late.

Pizzeria Sandwich Taouss 3 Rue 10 Mai. Pizzas, sandwiches and snacks to eat in or take out.

Moving on

From the main **bus station** there are regular departures to Chefchaouen, Meknes, Fes and Tangier; ask around for times at the various windows. CTM buses leave from a separate CTM station just below the Boulevard Sidi Driss (see map, p.124).

Heading for Tangier, Chefchaouen, Ceuta or the nearby coast resorts, it's easiest to travel by **grand taxi**; these are routine runs – just go along to the ranks and get a place. Collective grands taxis for Tangier and Chefchaouen leave

The Orquesta Andalusi de Tetouan

The **Orquesta Andalusi de Tetouan** is one of the best-known groups playing Moroccan-Andalous music, a seductive style awash with Oriental strings. It was founded, and is still conducted, by Abdessadaq Chekana, and his brother Abdellah leads on lute. The orchestra has recorded with Spanish flamenco singer Juan Peña Lebrijano and has toured with British composer Michael Nyman (best known for his soundtracks for Peter Greenaway's films – and for *The Piano*). Despite such collaborations, none of them reads music; everything is committed to memory. They often play in Tetouan and you may be able to catch them locally at an official reception, or at a wedding or festival; ask at the tourist office, where staff may be able to help.

from Avenue Khaled Ibnou el Oualid, west of town, a twenty-minute walk or 15dh petit taxi ride. For the Ceuta border at Fnideq, they leave from Boulevard Sidi Driss). Grands taxis to Mdiq, Martil and Cabo Negro leave from the junction of Boulevard Sidi Driss with Avenue Hassan II; those for Oued Laou leave from the beginning of Avenue Ksar el Kebir, which is the Oued Laou turn-off from Avenue Hassan II, not far from Bab el Okla.

The Tetouan beaches: Mdiq to Oued Laou

Despite the numbers of tourists passing through, Tetouan is above all a resort for Moroccans, rich and poor alike – a character very much in evidence on the extensive beaches to the east of the town. Throughout the summer whole villages of family tents appear at **Martil**, **Mdiq** and, particularly, around **Restinga-Smir**, further north. **Oued Laou**, 40km southeast of Tetouan, is the destination of a younger, more alternative crowd in summer. All these places are accessible by bus and shared grand taxi from Tetouan (see above).

Martil

Martil, essentially Tetouan's city beach, was its port as well until the river between the two silted up. Today it is a small, slightly ramshackle seaside town which takes on a resort-like feel in summer when Moroccan families flood the beach to escape the heat. The beach, stretching all the way around to the headland of Cabo Negro, is superb – an eight-kilometre stretch of fine, yellow sand that is long enough to remain uncrowded, despite its summer popularity and colonization by *Club Med* and other tourist complexes.

There are various options for **accommodation**. Arriving from Tetouan, there is a small hotel on the right, *Hôtel Los Mares* (Ⓣ0539 688706; ❸), a little tatty, but adequate for the price, as is *Hostal Nouzha* (no phone; ❷), at the southern end of Avenue Moulay Rachid, the main road in town running parallel to the seafront road. Somewhat more expensive, but good value, is the *Hôtel Etoile de la Mer* (Ⓣ0539 979276; ❸; closed in winter), on the seafront by the grand taxi stand; known locally as the *Nejma el Bahr*, it has a popular café and restaurant.

Of the **campsites**, *Camping al Boustane*, a kilometre north (Ⓣ0539 688822), is well maintained and friendly, with plenty of shade, decent facilities, quite a classy restaurant and a pool. *Camping Oued el Maleh* is further out to the north (signposted from town), reached along a riverbank. It's a dusty site but safe enough and has some shade and a useful shop; the beach is just 200m away.

There are many **cafés and restaurants**, though the majority are closed during the winter; recommended for refreshments and sea views is *Café Rio Martil*, on Avenue Prince Héritier nearly opposite *Hôtel Etoile de la Mer*. For meals try *Café Restaurant Avenida* at 102 Av Mohammed V or Restaurant Andalous, a pleasant restaurant specializing in fish, further north on the same road. Five kilometres towards Mdiq is the *Restaurant La Lampe Magique* (Ⓣ0539 970822), an extraordinary place complete with cupolas, one of which is made up of nine thousand Heineken bottles and illuminated at night. For pasta and pizza, try the friendly and popular *Aux Vitamins de la Mer*, 9 Av Moulay Rachid, next door to *Hostal Nouzha*.

Mdiq

Mdiq is a lovely coastal resort and semi-active fishing port, which can be approached via Martil or direct from Tetouan (18km on the N13). A popular, though slightly overdeveloped, promenade overlooks the superb town beach and there are a handful of nice places to stay nearby. The best hotel is the *Golden Beach* (Ⓣ0539 975077, Ⓕ0539 975096; ❺), a four-star beach holiday hotel with nightclub, swimming pool and all mod cons (*demi-pension* only in high season). *Hotel Playa* (Ⓣ0539 975166; ❹) on Boulevard Lalla Nezha overlooking the beach is new and friendly and offers bright airy en suites, the majority of which have uninterrupted sea views. There is also a bar and restaurant on the ground floor. The town's only budget option is the *Narjiss* opposite the police station on Avenue Lalla Nazha, the main road to Martil (Ⓣ0668 248095; ❸). There is no campsite but campervans are usually allowed to stay overnight in the car park next to the promenade.

Restinga-Smir and Fnideq

Restinga-Smir is more a collective name for a length of beach than for an actual place or village: an attractive strip of the Mediterranean, dominated by package hotels and holiday villages. Many Moroccan families still camp in the woods between here and Fnideq. The rather spartan but inexpensive *Al Fraja* **campsite**, opposite the *El Andalouz* tourist complex and 15km from Fnideq, makes a good first or last stop in the country in summer; in winter it's closed.

In addition, there are several **hotels** in **Fnideq,** just 2km from the Ceuta border, scattered along the town's main road, Avenue Mohammed V. The best of these is *Hôtel Fnideq* (Ⓣ0539 675467; ❸) whose en-suite rooms are basic but clean. *Hôtel Alouiam* (Ⓣ0539 76140; ❸) further south, is a similar choice. *Hôtel Nador* (Ⓣ0539 675345; ❸) is the cheapest of the bunch. For meals, try *La Costa* at 232 Av Mohammed V, an excellent seafood restaurant. Fnideq, however, has little to recommend it except a busy market for cheap Spanish goods.

Oued Laou

Travelling southeast from Tetouan, the coastline almost immediately changes and you come under the shadow of the **Rif**. The road (N16, formerly S608) follows the coast initially, but then begins to climb into the foothills of the Rif, a first taste of the zigzagging Moroccan mountain roads. Alongside the beach, near Cap Mazari, is the nicely shaded *Camping Azla* (14km from Tetouan; open summer only) with a small café/shop.

When you finally arrive in **Oued Laou**, 44km to the southeast, (served by local **bus** and **grand taxi)**, you're unlikely to want to return immediately. It's not an especially pretty place – Riffian villages tend to look spread out and lack any core – but it has a near-deserted beach, which extends for miles on each side, particularly to the southeast, where the river has created a wide, fertile bay down to Kâaseras, 8km distant. Equally important, Oued Laou is one of the best parts of the Rif to meet and talk with local people. Hustlers have nothing to hustle except *kif* and rooms, and aren't too bothered about either.

On Saturdays, there is a **souk**, held 3km inland from Oued Laou, which draws villagers from all over the valley.

Practicalities

For **accommodation** try the friendly *Hôtel-Restaurant Oued Laou* (Ⓣ0648 064435; ❷–❸) one block from the beach on Boulevard Massira. It is open all year round (large reductions off-season) with hot water and clean, sunny rooms. A few doors down is *Hôtel Laayoune* (no phone; ❸) which has a few basic rooms but is only open in summer. *Camping Oued Laou* (no phone) alongside the municipal building, is a secure site, shaded with olive trees, with hot showers and washing facilities, a small shop and a café. Camping fees are reasonable and there are three two-bedroom bungalows (300dh a night) that will comfortably house four adults or a family. *Hôtel Mares Norstrum* (Ⓣ0664 375056, ❻–❼) 4km north, signposted off the N16 is the area's upmarket option, situated on a cliff overlooking the sea. Guests are accommodated in comfortable bungalows and there is a swimming pool and restaurant.

For **meals**, head to *Chez Raes*, a small fish restaurant across from *Hôtel Laayoune*. The fish is very fresh, being caught fifty metres in front of the restaurant. Walking northwards down the beach you will eventually come to a rocky outcrop where *Café Picasso* is built into the rock, made from driftwood and reeds, like something out of *Robinson Crusoe*. This café restaurant, whose owner has been cooking up tajines on the beach for over a decade, is a great place to relax.

If you want to continue from Oued Laou to Chefchaouen the easiest way, without your own transport, is to take a taxi to **Kâaseras**, a small village on the beach twenty minutes drive from Oued Laou, where there is one bus daily (check with locals) to Chefchaouen at 6am.

Chefchaouen (Chaouen, Xaouen) and around

Shut in by a fold of mountains, **CHEFCHAOUEN** (pronounced "shef-**sha**-wen", sometimes abbreviated to Chaouen) had, until the arrival of Spanish troops in 1920, been visited by just three Westerners. Two were missionary explorers: Charles de Foucauld, a Frenchman who spent just an hour in the town, disguised as a rabbi, in 1883, and William Summers, an American who was poisoned by the townsfolk here in 1892. The third, in 1889, was the British journalist Walter Harris (see p.601), whose main impulse, as described in his book, *Land of an African Sultan*, was "the very fact that there existed within thirty hours' ride of Tangier a city in which it was considered an utter impossibility for a Christian to enter".

This impossibility – and Harris very nearly lost his life when the town was alerted to the presence of "a Christian dog" – had its origins in the foundation of the town in 1471. The region hereabouts was already sacred to Muslims due to the presence of the tomb of Moulay Abdessalam Ben Mchich – patron saint of the Djebali tribesmen and one of the "four poles of Islam" – and over the centuries acquired a considerable reputation for pilgrimage and *marabouts* – "saints", believed to hold supernatural powers. The town was actually established by one of Moulay Abdessalam's *shereefian* (descendant of the Prophet) followers, Moulay Rachid, as a secret base from which to attack the Portuguese in Ceuta and Ksar es Seghir. In the ensuing decades, as the population was boosted by Muslim and Jewish refugees from Spain, Chefchaouen grew increasingly anti-european and autonomous. For a time, it was the centre of a semi-independent emirate, exerting control over much of the northwest, in alliance with the Wattasid sultans of Fes. Later, however, it became an almost completely isolated backwater. When the Spanish arrived in 1920, they were astonished to find the Jews here speaking medieval Castilian.

These days, a major hotel disfigures the twin peaks (*ech-Chaoua*: the horns) from which the town takes its name, but local attitudes towards visitors are relaxed, the Medina *pensions* are among the friendliest and cheapest around, and staying here a few days and walking in the hills remains one of the best possible introductions to Morocco.

As the centre of so much *maraboutism*, Chefchaouen and its neighbouring villages have a particularly large number of **moussems**. The big events are those in Moulay Abdessalam Ben Mchich (40km away: usually in May) and Sidi Allal el Hadj (in Aug).

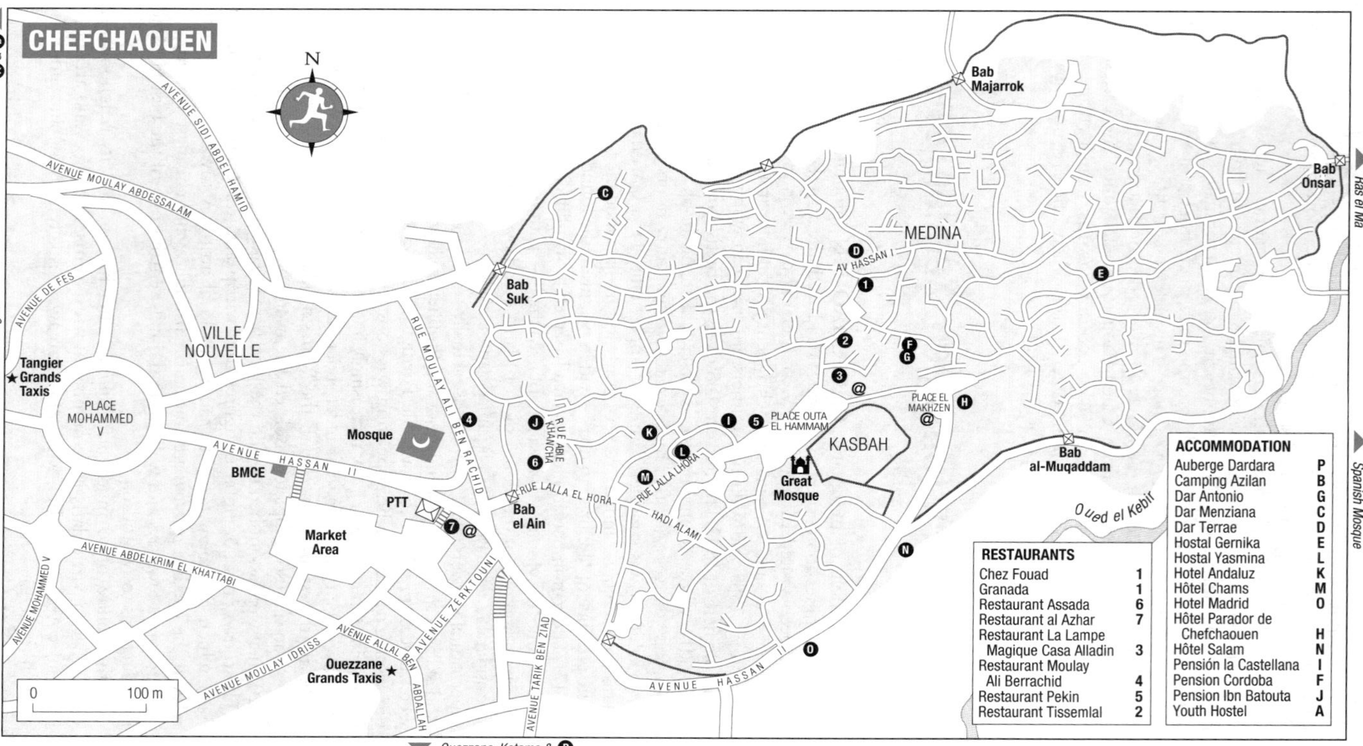
CHEFCHAOUEN
N
A & B
Tetouan & Tangier
Gare Routière
Ras el Ma
Spanish Mosque
Ouezzane, Ketama & P
MEDINA
KASBAH
VILLE NOUVELLE
Bab Majarrok
Bab Onsar
Bab Suk
Bab el Ain
Bab al-Muqaddam
Great Mosque
Mosque
PTT
BMCE
Market Area
Tangier Grands Taxis
Ouezzane Grands Taxis
PLACE MOHAMMED V
PLACE OUTA EL HAMMAM
PLACE EL MAKHZEN
AV HASSAN I
AVENUE HASSAN II
AVENUE HASSAN II
RUE MOULAY ALI BEN RACHID
RUE LALLA EL HORA
RUE LALLA LHORA
RUE ABIE KHANCHA
HADI ALAMI
AVENUE SIDI ABDEL HAMID
AVENUE MOULAY ABDESSALAM
AVENUE DE FES
AVENUE ABDELKRIM EL KHATTABI
AVENUE MOHAMMED V
AVENUE MOULAY IDRISS
AVENUE ALLAL BEN ABDALLAH
AVENUE ZERKTOUNI
AVENUE TARIK BEN ZIAD
Oued el Kebir
0 100 m
RESTAURANTS
Chez Fouad 1
Granada 1
Restaurant Assada 6
Restaurant al Azhar 7
Restaurant La Lampe Magique Casa Alladin 3
Restaurant Moulay Ali Berrachid 4
Restaurant Pekin 5
Restaurant Tissemlal 2
ACCOMMODATION
Auberge Dardara P
Camping Azilan B
Dar Antonio G
Dar Menziana C
Dar Terrae D
Hostal Gernika E
Hostal Yasmina L
Hotel Andaluz K
Hôtel Chams M
Hotel Madrid O
Hôtel Parador de Chefchaouen H
Hôtel Salam N
Pensión la Castellana I
Pension Cordoba F
Pension Ibn Batouta J
Youth Hostel A

Arrival, orientation and information

With a population of around 45,000, Chefchaouen is more like a large village than a town in size and feel, and confusing only on arrival. **Buses** drop you at the *gare routière*, 15dh by petit taxi to Place Outa el Hammam or twenty to thirty minutes' walk to the town centre: take Avenue Mohammed Abdou eastward (and upward) for 300m to the next main junction, where you turn left up Avenue Mohammed V, which leads into the centre of town. **Grands taxis** from Tetouan and Ouezzane drop much more centrally on Avenue Allal Ben Abdallah. The marketplace is in the Ville Nouvelle alongside Avenue Hassan II, which is dominated by the Ben Rachid mosque. There's a **PTT** here, plus Wafa, BMCE and Banque Populaire **banks**, all with ATMs. Banque Populaire also has a bureau de change, open daily, up in Place Outa el Hammam. **Internet access** is available at outahammam.com (daily 9am–10pm, later in summer), located between Place Outa el Hammam and Place el Makhzen, and upstairs by *Café Mondial* (same hours) on Avenue Hassan II, nearly opposite Bab el Ain. There is also a small internet café across from *Hôtel Parador*.

The main gateway to the Medina, Bab el Ain, is a tiny arched entrance at the junction of Avenue Hassan II with Rue Moulay Ali Ben Rachid. Through the gate a clearly dominant lane winds up through the town to the main square, **Place Outa el Hammam** (flanked by the gardens and towers of the **kasbah**) and, beyond, to a second, smaller square, **Place el Makhzen**.

Accommodation

Along and around the main route in the Medina there are a number of small **pensions**, most of them converted from private houses; rooms can be a bit cell-like, but most are exceptionally clean and remarkably inexpensive. For more comfort (though less community interaction), several of the **hotels** in the Ville Nouvelle are good value, and there's also an old Spanish *parador* in the heart of the Medina.

The recommendations below are in the Medina or just outside. Chefchaouen can get bitterly cold during winter and all of those listed proclaim to have hot water, though few have en-suite bathrooms.

Auberge Dardara 11km from Chefchaouen at the junction of the N2 to Al Hoceima and the P28 to Ouezzane ⓣ0539 707007. Guests, including King Mohammed VI, come here to experience a unique blend of rustic getaway and agri-tourism. The brain-child of local man El Hababi Jaber ("Jabba"), the *auberge* has twelve comfortably furnished rooms – each named after an influential woman in Jabba's life – and focuses on environmentally friendly practices and community involvement. The restaurant serves fresh, hearty food. Compulsory half-board ❻

Camping Azilan Located on a hill above the Medina, follow signs for the *Atlas Riad Chaouen Hotel* ⓣ0539 986979, ⓦwww.campingchefchaouen.com. Shaded and inexpensive, with a café, small shop, and internet café but can be crowded in summer. A good place to enquire about mountain treks.

Dar Antonio Rue Garnata ⓣ0552 278569. Owner Hicham's imagination has touched every tiny detail of this cosy guesthouse. Each room is unique, colorful and warm. There's even one with a working fireplace. Guests have access to a kitchen for self catering and showers are in a cave-like grotto. ❷

Dar Menziana Rue Zagdud ⓣ0539 987806, ⓦwww.darmezianahotel.com.The Medina's most luxurious guesthouse with comfortable and tastefully decorated en-suite rooms and suites overlooking an open-plan courtyard and kitchen. Panoramic views from the terrace and a hammam to top it off. ❺

Dar Terrae Av Hassan I ⓣ0539 987598. Chefchaouen's first riad, in a charming old Andalucian-style house. There's a homely atmosphere and though not all rooms are en suite, each is different and comes with a fireplace, and there are three roof terraces. Breakfast included. ❹

Hostal Gernika 49 Onsar ⓣ0539 987434. This old house has been superbly converted by its female Basque owner. It's in the higher quarter of the Medina, going up towards Bab Onsar. Some rooms are en suite. ❷

Hostal Yasmina 12 Rue Lalla el Hora ⓣ0539 883118. Small, bright and clean with only six rooms, but very conveniently located, just off the

Medina's main square, modern in style, and a very pleasant little place to stay. Hot showers 10dh. ❷

Hôtel Andaluz 1 Rue Sidi Salem ⓣ0539 986034. Small, functional *pension*, whose rooms face an inner courtyard with a friendly management, shared showers and a kitchen. It's signposted off to the left at the near end of Pl Outa el Hammam. ❷

Hôtel Chams Rue Lalla el Hora ⓣ0539 987784. A new option and a good compromise between *pension* price and hotel comfort. Centrally located with large clean en-suite rooms and a pleasant terrace. ❷

Hôtel Madrid Av Hassan II just outside the Medina ⓣ0539 987496, ⓕ0539 987498. Tastefully decorated, with a fine panoramic rooftop breakfast terrace and most rooms en suite with four-poster beds and slightly garish decor. Breakfast included. ❺

Hôtel Parador de Chefchaouen Pl el Makhzen ⓣ0539 986136, ⓦwww.hotel-parador.com. The former Spanish "grand hotel", once part of the Parador chain, now reconstructed for the package-tour trade. The bar and swimming pool help justify the expense and there are stunning views from the terrace. However, if you're only having an occasional splurge, this isn't special enough. ❺

Hôtel Salam 39 Av Hassan II ⓣ0539 986239. A friendly place just below Bab el Hammam, and long a favourite with individuals and groups. Back rooms and a shady roof terrace overlook the valley. Bathrooms are shared and meals are served in a salon or on the terrace. Breakfast included. ❷

Pension la Castellana 4 Rue Bouhali ⓣ0539 986295. Just to the left at the near end of Place Outa el Hammam – follow the signs. Aficionados return loyally to the *Castellana* each year, creating a distinctly laid-back and youthful atmosphere; others take one look at the poky rooms and leave. The key is the manager, Mohammed Nebrhout, who arranges communal meals and excursions on request. There's also a hammam right next door. ❷

Pension Cordoba Rue Garnata ⓣ0664 430044. Lovely rooms and tasteful decor in a charming old Andalucian-style house, beautifully done out. Not quite a riad, but a lot cheaper than one. Breakfast included. ❷

Pension Ibn Batouta 31 Rue Abie Khancha ⓣ0539 986044. One of the quietest of the *pensions*, with less of a "travellers' hangout" feel; located in an alley to the left, about 70m along from Bab el Ain, beyond the *Restaurant Assada*. Rooms are very cheap if a little dingy, bathrooms shared (hot showers 5dh). ❶

Youth Hostel Next to *Camping Azilan*. Very basic rooms available for 30dh per person per night, bedding not provided. Showers cost 10dh.

The town and river

Like Tetouan, Chefchaouen's architecture has a strong Andalucian character: less elaborate (and less grand), perhaps, but often equally inventive. It is a town of extraordinary light and colour, its whitewash tinted with blue and edged by soft, golden, stone walls – and it is a place which, for all its present popularity, still seems redolent of the years of isolation.

The souks and Mellah

Souks are held on Mondays and Thursdays in the market square and are worth browsing. The town's carpet and weaving workshops remain active and many of their designs unchanged.

Since the Medina is so small, it is more than ever a place to enjoy exploring at random. It's interesting to observe the contrasts in feel between the main, Arab part of Chefchaouen and the still modestly populated Jewish quarter of the **Mellah**. This is to be found behind the jewellers' souk, between the Bab el Ain and the kasbah.

Place Outa el Hammam and the kasbah

Place Outa el Hammam is where most of the town's evening life takes place. On the northern end, on Zankat el Targui, in amongst the run-of-the-mill tourist stalls are a few **souvenir shops** that typify the place's relaxed feel. Further up beyond Zankat el Targui at 75 Rue Adarve Chabu, also known as Rue Granada, is the tiny shop of the local hat man who sells distinctive woollen beanies, berets and leg-warmers, all great for fending off the evening chill.

On one side of the square is the town's **kasbah** (daily except Tues 9am–1pm & 3–6pm; 10dh), a quiet ruin with shady gardens and a little museum of crafts and old photos. The kasbah was built, like so many others in northern Morocco, by

Moulay Ismail. Inside, and immediately to the right, in the first of its compounds, are the old town prison cells, where Abd el Krim (see pp.144–145) was imprisoned after his surrender in nearby Targuist in 1926. Five years earlier, he had driven the Spanish from the town, a retreat that saw the loss of several thousand of their troops. Next to the kasbah is the Great Mosque, with a fifteenth-century octagonal tower.

Place el Makhzen and Ras el Ma

Place el Makhzen – the old "government square" – is an elegant clearing with an old fountain and souvenir stalls. Next to *Hôtel Parador* and not particularly interesting, is the Ensemble Artisanal.

If you leave the Medina at this point, it's possible to follow **the river**, the Oued el Kebir, around the outside of the walls, with Bab Onsar up to your left. Here, past a couple of traditional flour-mills, **Ras el Ma** (head of the water) lies outside the top, eastern side of the town, where water, clear and freezing cold (tapped for the town's supply) cascades from the gorge wall. Local women come here to do laundry and it has long been a favourite picnic spot, as well as being a holy place, due to the nearby *marabout*'s tomb of Sidi Abdallah Habti.

Over to the southeast of the town, an enjoyable, half-hour walk brings you to the ruined "**Spanish Mosque**". It is set on a hilltop, with exterior patterned brickwork and an interior giving a good sense of the layout of a mosque – normally off-limits in Morocco.

Into the hills

Alongside the path to the Spanish Mosque are some spectacular rock-climbing pitches, frequented by European climbers (ask at *Dar Antonio* or *Camping Azilan* for trekking and climbing information); and in the limestone hills behind there are active cave systems – the source of local springs.

Further afield, a good **day's hike** is to head east, up over the mountains behind Chefchaouen. As you look at the "two horns" from town, there is a path winding along the side of the mountain on your left. A four-hour (or more) hike will take you up to the other side, where a vast valley opens up, and if you walk further, you'll see the sea. The valley, as even casual exploration will show, is full of small farms cultivating *kif* – as they have done for years. Walking here, you may occasionally be stopped by the military, who are cracking down on foreign involvement in the crop. For more ambitious hikes – and there are some wonderful paths in the area – ask at the *pensions* (or *Camping Azilan*) about hiring a **guide**. Someone knowledgeable can usually be found to accompany you, for around 150dh a day; the harder the climb, the more it costs.

Eating

Most of Chefchaouen's better **restaurants** are in the back streets of the Medina. **Place Outa el Hammam** is one of the prime spots for a meal, and its restaurants are surprisingly cheap, though not all of them are that great – be particularly wary of any which have pre-fried fish lying out. Alcohol is only available in the larger hotels and upscale guesthouses.

Medina

Chez Fouad Rue Adarve Chabu. A poky little place known for its tajines and fish kebabs. Cheap.

Granada opposite *Chez Fouad* on Rue Adarve Chabu. Extremely cheap, with quite reasonable food (chicken and chips, tajines), but nothing tremendously exciting.

Restaurant Assada on a nameless lane just north of Bab el Ain, opposite the *Hôtel Bab el Ain*. This has long been a favourite and has recently extended across the lane and above to an open terrace. Very friendly, and serves food all day from breakfast through to tajine or couscous at dinner. Cheap.

Restaurant La Lampe Magique Casa Alladin Zenkat el Targui. Two floors and a terrace, beautifully done out in Arabian Nights style, as its name suggests, serving great tajines, couscous (including vegetarian) and other staple fare (set menus 75dh & 100dh). Moderate.

Restaurant Pekin Pl Outa el Hammam. The middle of three restaurants (the other two are *Morisco* and *Bab Kasba*) in a row on the square, directly opposite the kasbah. All three serve fairly standard Moroccan food and are open from breakfast till late. Moderate.

Restaurant Tissemlal Zenkat el Targui ⓣ0539 986153. A beautifully decorated old house with French-Moroccan set menu (60dh). There are a few rooms here, too; a double room with half-board (❺).

Ville Nouvelle

Restaurant al Azhar At the bottom of the steps on Av Moulay Idriss. Popular local eatery with good food and friendly and efficient service. Cheap.

Restaurant Moulay Ali Berrachid Rue Moulay Ali Ben Rachid – just up from Bab el Ain. A popular restaurant, specializing in fresh fish. Cheap.

Moving on

The **gare routière** is a fifteen-minute walk southwest from the town centre – head south from Place Mohammed V down Avenue Mohammed V, cross Avenue Abdelkrim el Kattabi, and turn right after 200m down Avenue Mohammed Abdou (no street sign at the junction). A petit taxi from Bab el Ain shouldn't cost much more than 15dh.

Unfortunately, CTM and most other lines start their Chefchaouen routes elsewhere so that buses can (despite promises) arrive full, with no available space. The best advice is to visit the bus station the evening before you plan to leave and, if possible, book a ticket in advance.

Availability tends to be best on the routes to Tetouan, Tangier or Fnideq – indeed, Tetouan has at least one departure every hour between 6am and 6pm, and sometimes as many as four. Services to Fes and Meknes are more likely to be full, and you may have to take a grand taxi to Ouezzane and another to Jorf to pick up onward transport there.

Grands taxis for Ouezzane and Bab Berred (connecting there for Issaguen and points east) leave from around the junction of Avenue Allal Ben Abdallah with Avenue Zerktouni near the market. For Tangier and Tetouan, they leave from Avenue Jamal Dine el Afghani, off the west side of Place Mohammed V. To reach Fes or Meknes, you can change vehicles at Ouezzane and again at Jorf (where, be warned, grands taxis to Fes and Meknes are sparse, and you'll probably end up having to wait for a bus) or travel in style by chartering a grand taxi – you'll need to bargain hard, but the trip should cost around 450dh for up to six passengers.

Ouezzane (Wazzan)

Few tourists stay in **OUEZZANE**, 60km southwest of Chefchaouen, but there are worse places to be stranded. Situated at the edge of the Rif , it traditionally formed the border between the *Bled es-Makhzen* (the governed territories) and

The R410

If you have your own transport and wish to head towards the west coast from Chefchaouen, the R410 to Ksar el Kebir is a highly recommended scenic route and shortcut. The road is signed off the N13 to Ouezzane on your right coming from Chefchaouen. The route wends its way through wooded high country following the Oued Loukos to the Barrage Oued el Makhazine, where there are magnificent vistas, and on to Ksar el Kebir.

the *Bled es-Siba* (those of the lawless tribes). As such, the town was an important power base, and particularly so under the last nineteenth-century sultans, when its local sheikhs became among the most powerful in Morocco.

The sheikhs – the *Ouezzani* – were the spiritual leaders of the influential **Tabiya brotherhood**. They were *shereefs* (descendants of the Prophet) and came in a direct line from the Idrissids, the first and founding dynasty of Morocco. This however, seems to have given them little significance. In the eighteenth century, Moulay Abdallah es-Shereef established a *zaouia* at Ouezzane, which became a great place of pilgrimage.

Until the beginning of the twentieth century Jews and Christians were allowed to take only temporary residence in the town. However, in 1877, an Englishwoman, Emily Keane, married the principal *shereef*, Si Abdesslem. The marriage was, of course, controversial. For several decades she lived openly as a Christian in the town, and is credited with introducing vaccinations to Morocco. Her *Life Story*, published in 1911 after her husband's death, ends with the balanced summing up: "I do not advise anyone to follow in my footsteps, at the same time I have not a single regret." She is commemorated in the Anglican church in Tangier (see p.93)

Ouezzane is also a place of pilgrimage for Moroccan Jews, who come here twice a year (April & Sept) to visit the tomb of Rabbi Amrane ben Diwane, an eighteenth-century Jewish *marabout* buried in a Jewish cemetery north of town.

Arrival, information and accommodation

The bus and grand taxi terminal is about 50m below the **Place de l'Indépendance**, where you'll also find three small **hotels**. The best of these, though it's by no means deluxe, is the *Grand* (no phone; ❶). The *Marhaba* (❷) and *Horloge* (❶) are more basic. *Hôtel Bouhlal* (ⓣ0553 7907154, ❷), signposted off the main road (N13) and located below **Place de l'Indépendance,** is a family home with a few rooms and currently the town's most comfortable option. The only other choice is *Motel Rif*, 4km out on the Fes road (ⓣ0537 907172), which offers en-suite rooms, camping facilities, and a swimming pool. A farm supplies all the food for its large restuarant. There is a **hammam** on Avenue Mohammed V and a handful of **grill-cafés** on the square.

The Town

The **Zaouia**, distinguished by an unusual octagonal minaret is the site of a lively spring **moussem**, or pilgrimage festival. As in the rest of Morocco, entrance to the *zaouia* area is forbidden to non-Muslims.

The main **souks** climb up from an archway on the main square, Place de l'Indépendance, by the *Grand Hôtel*. Ouezzane has a local reputation for its woollen rugs – most evident in the weavers' souk, around Place Rouida near the top end of the town. Also rewarding is the metalworkers' souk, a covered lane under the Mosque of Moulay Abdallah Shereef; to find it, ask directions for the pleasant (and adjacent) *Café Bellevue*. The town has an Ensemble Artisanal on Place de l'Indépendance, and there is a large Thursday souk down the hill from here, near the bus station.

Moving on

Ouezzane provides a useful link if you're travelling by **public transport** (bus or grand taxi) between Chefchaouen and the Atlantic coast. There are also a fair number of **buses** to Meknes and Fes, but if you're stopping or staying, buy onward tickets in advance; as with Chefchaouen it's not unusual for them to arrive and leave full. Grands taxis occasionally run direct to Fes, but usually you have to take one to the truck-stop village of Jorf and pick up onward transport there. If you arrive early in the day, you should find grands taxis from Jorf to Fes, but otherwise, and for Meknes, you will have to take a bus.

Travel details

Trains

Tangier to: Asilah (6 daily; 40min); Casablanca Voyageurs (3 direct & 3 connecting daily; 5hr 15min); Fes (1 direct & 5 connecting daily; 5hr 10min); Marrakesh (1 direct & 5 connecting daily; 9hr 40min); Meknes (1 direct & 5 connecting daily; 4hr 15min); Oujda (1 direct & 2 connecting daily; 11hr 40min); Rabat (3 direct & 3 connecting daily; 4hr 15min); Souk el Arba (5 daily; 2hr); Taza (1 direct & 3 connecting daily; 7hr 50min).

Buses

Asilah to: Larache (25 daily; 1hr); Tangier (25 daily; 40min).
Chefchaouen to: Al Hoceima (1 CTM daily; 4hr 30min); Casablanca (3 daily; 9hr); Fes (3 CTM and 8 others daily; 5hr); Fnideq (4 daily; 2hr 30min); Meknes (4 daily; 5hr 30min); Rabat (5 daily; 8hr); Tangier (1 CTM and 9 others daily; 3hr 30min); Tetouan (2 CTM daily & others at least hourly 6am–6pm; 2hr).
Larache to: Asilah (3 CTM & 22 others daily; 1hr); Ksar el Kebir (8 daily; 40min); Meknes (2 daily; 5hr 30min); Rabat (20 daily; 3hr 30min); Souk el Arba (8 daily; 1hr).
Ouezzane to: Chefchaouen (4 daily; 2hr); Fes (3 daily; 5hr 30min); Meknes (2 daily; 4hr); Tangier (1 daily; 5hr).
Souk el Arba to: Moulay Bousselham (5 daily; 35min); Ouezzane (3 daily; 1hr 30min).
Tangier to: Agadir (1 CTM & 1 other daily; 16hr); Al Hoceima (7 daily; 6hr); Asilah (3 CTM & 22 others daily; 40min); Casablanca (4 CTM & 35 others daily; 6hr 30min); Chefchaouen (1 CTM & 9 others daily; 4hr 30min); Fes (3 CTM & 9 others daily; 5hr 45min); Fnideq (for Ceuta) (13 daily; 1hr); Larache (3 CTM & 22 others daily; 1hr 30min); Marrakesh (1 CTM & 6 others daily; 10hr); Meknes (3 CTM & 9 others daily; 7hr); Nador (6 daily; 12hr); Rabat (5 CTM and 35 others daily; 5hr); Tetouan (2 CTM and over 50 others daily; 1hr 30min).
Tetouan to: Agadir (1 CTM bus daily; 15hr); Al Hoceima (2 CTM and 9 others daily; 5hr 30min); Casablanca (2 CTM & 23 others daily; 6hr); Chefchaouen (2 CTM & 20 others daily; 1hr 30min); Fes (3 CTM & 4 others daily; 5hr 20min); Fnideq (for Ceuta) (12 daily; 1hr); Larache (6 daily; 3hr); Marrakesh (1 CTM & 7 others daily; 10hr); Meknes (2 CTM & 5 others daily; 6hr); Nador (1 CTM & 7 others daily; 9hr 30min); Oued Laou (5 daily; 1hr 30min); Rabat (2 CTM & 18 others daily; 5hr); Tangier (1 CTM & some 50 others daily; 1hr 30min).

Grands taxis

Asilah to: Larache (40min); Tangier (40min).
Chefchaouen to: Bab Berred (50min); Ouezzane (1hr 15min); Tangier (2hr); Tetouan (1hr).
Fnideq to: Ceuta border (10min); Mdiq (20min); Tangier (1hr); Tetouan (20min).
Ksar el Kebir to: Larache (30min); Ouezzane (1hr); Souk el Arba (30min).
Larache to: Asilah (40min); Ksar el Kebir (30min).
Mdiq to: Fnideq (for Ceuta) (30min); Martil (15min); Tetouan (20min).
Ouezzane to: Chefchaouen (1hr 15min); Jorf (change for Fes) (45min); Ksar el Kebir (1hr); Souk el Arba (1hr).
Souk el Arba to: Ksar el Kebir (30min); Moulay Bousselham (30min); Ouezzane (1hr).
Tangier to: Asilah (40min); Chefchaouen (2hr); Fnideq (for Ceuta) (1hr); Ksar es Seghir (30min); Tetouan (1hr).
Tetouan to: Chefchaouen (1hr); Fnideq (for Ceuta) (20min); Martil (15min); Mdiq (20min); Oued Laou (1hr); Tangier (1hr).

Ferries

Ceuta to: Algeciras (12–30 daily; 45min–1hr 30min).
Tangier to: Algeciras (12–22 daily; 1hr 30min–2hr 30min); Genoa (1 weekly; 48hr); Gibraltar (1 weekly; 1hr 20min); Sète (1–2 weekly; 36hr); Tarifa, passage for EU passport holders only (4–10 daily; 35min).

Flights

Tangier to: Casablanca (RAM 1–3 daily; 50min).

The Mediterranean coast and the Rif

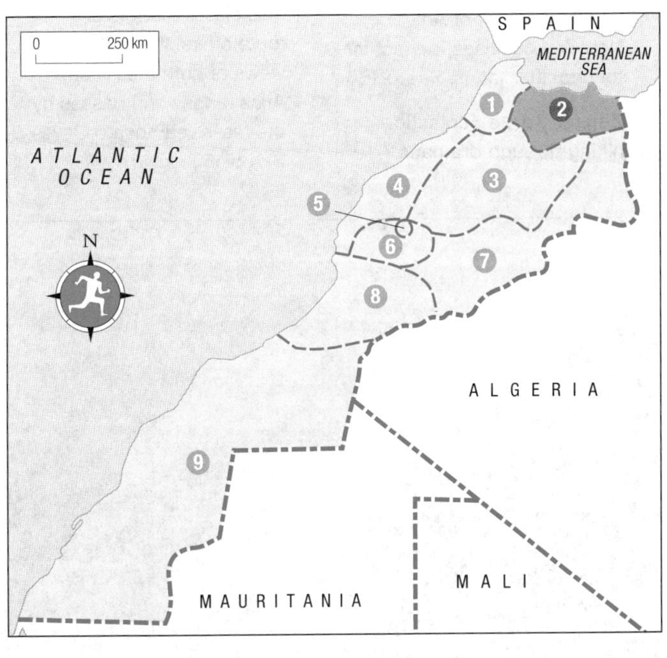

CHAPTER 2

Highlights

* **Chefchaouen to Al Hoceima** The scenic and sometimes vertiginous drive along the northern slopes of the Rif is simply spectacular. See p.142

* **The coast road** There are rich pickings for birdwatchers amongst the dunes, deserted coves and a few very low-key resorts. See p.146

* **Melilla** The Spanish enclave boasts a wealth of Art Nouveau buildings, perfect for touring after tapas. See p.154

* **Zegzel Gorge** Fantastic hiking through dramatic limestone cliffs, terraced fruit groves and magnificent cedar and oak forests. See p.161

* **Saïdia** Close to the Algerian border, this enjoyable beach resort comes alive in summer, hosting a Raï music and popular arts festival in August. See p.162

* **Cirque du Djebel Tazzeka** This classic car-driver's route offers stupendous views of both the Rif and Atlas ranges and passes by the massive Friouato Caves. See p.168

▲ Route from Chefchaouen to Al Hoceima

2

The Mediterranean coast and the Rif

Morocco's Mediterranean coast extends for nearly 500km, from the Spanish enclave of Ceuta east to Saïdia on the Algerian border. Much of it lies in the shadow of the Rif Mountains, which restrict access to the sea to a very few points. Such beaches as there are here remain mostly undeveloped; for a seaside stop head for the fishing harbour and holiday resort of Al Hoceima, or (better) to Saïdia at the end of the road. If you're making a loop east of the Rif, you'll find Oujda a pleasant, relaxed city, with a scenic side-trip through the Zegzel gorge, and further gorges, cutting into the Middle Atlas, at Taza, on the Fes–Oujda road.

Between Al Hoceima and Oujda is a second Spanish enclave, **Melilla**, an attractive town offering an authentic slice of Spanish life which will tempt bird-watchers as the dunes and lagoons spreading around nearby **Nador** are among the richest sites in Morocco.

The **Rif Mountains** themselves are even less on the tourist trail than the coast – and with some reason. This is wild, isolated country with a tradition of dissent from central government and with the authorities. A vast, limestone mass, over 300km long and up to 2500m in height, the Rif is the natural boundary between Europe and Africa. Its economy is based very largely on cannabis; even where uncultivated, the plants grow wild around the stony slopes, and with prices bringing growers five times that of other crops, it is not surprising that it has taken over so much of the farmland, despite the government criminalizing its cultivation in 2004. Moroccan law also forbids its sale, purchase and possession (see p.63). These laws are enforced on occasion with some vigour, so don't be seduced by the locals: police roadblocks are frequent, informers common. Cannabis in the Rif is big business and potentially dangerous for casual visitors to get mixed up in.

If you want a look at some dramatic Riffian scenery, you can take a bus or grand taxi between Chefchaouen and Fes, via **Ketama**, or Al Hoceima or Nador and Taza, via **Aknoul**. **Driving** through Ketama in a foreign-registered or rented vehicle is perfectly possible and if you drive in daylight you are unlikely to be the only car on the road for any length of time. However, common sense applies; you should on no account stop for hitchhikers or people who appear to be asking for help and never stop if a car pulls over to the side of your vehicle - local gangsters sometimes try to pressurize drivers into buying

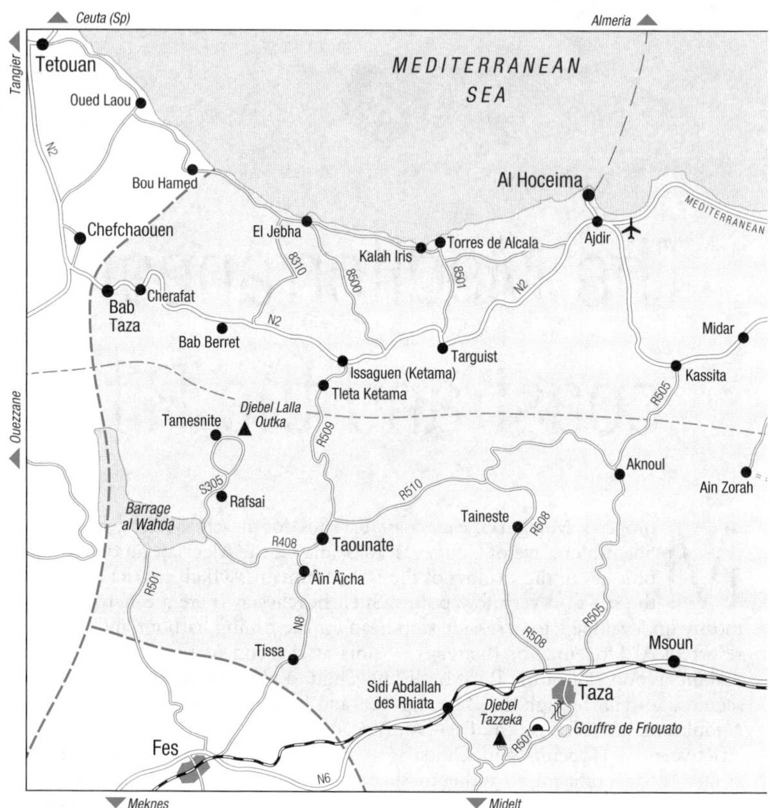

low-grade hash or simply rob them at knifepoint. As an alternative, you can opt to drive between Fes and Al Hoceima or Melilla using the main road (N6) via Taza and cross over the Rif via Aknoul (R505) or make a detour further east via Guercif and Saka (N15). Between Fes and Chefchaouen, go via Ouezzane (N4/N13); and between Chefchaouen and Al Hoceima, you could take the long way round via Ouezzane, Fes, Taza and Aknoul (N13/N4/N6/R505/N2).

Chefchaouen to Al Hoceima

One of Morocco's most memorable journeys is the 210-kilometre mountain road from **Chefchaouen** (see p.131) to **Al Hoceima** which weaves along high on the crests of the Rif Mountains. Driving requires some confidence; bends are endless and some are tight, the road is prone to subsidence in places and meeting buses and lorries can be alarming. Snow may occasionally block the road in winter but snow ploughs soon restore the flow of traffic. The views for most of the year, however, are spectacular. Paul Bowles describes the route well in "The Rif, to Music" chapter of *Their Heads Are Green* – "mountains covered with olive trees, with oak trees, with bushes, and finally with giant cedars". And, of course, cannabis plants.

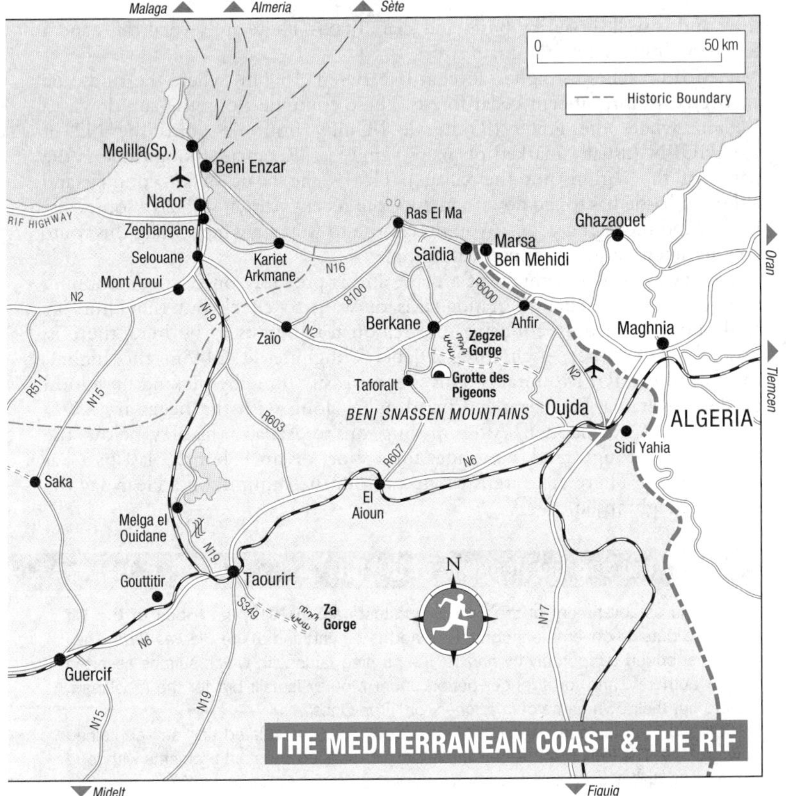

From Chefchaouen to Ketama

Leaving Chefchaouen (via its lower, southern exit for the panoramic view of the town from across the valley), you join the N2 near the Dardara junction for Ouazzane where there's a notable eco-friendly auberge. The road sweeps steadily upwards through attractive countryside with olive farms, cork oaks and flowery hedgerows to reach the village of **Bab Taza**, 23km from Chefchaouen, where, suddenly, the feeling of being at altitude kicks in. There is a bank (with ATM), a petrol station and a Wednesday souk.

Ten kilometres on, the village of **Cherafat** deserves a pause. Waterfalls tumble down to flow beneath the road bridge, and steps nearby lead up to a vigorous spring where three jets rush out, into an irrigation channel. Buses travelling through to Al Hoceima, Nador and Oujda make a stopover here and shops and cafés line the road.

Fifteen kilometres further on is **Khamis Medik**, where an inviting Thursday souk attracts a multitude of Berber villagers from this part of the *Djebala*. Beyond here the road runs through woods of various oak species with the richest cultivation in the Rif on the impressively deep slopes below, dotted with farms and the expensive and isolated villas that are testimony to the wealth generated by the cannabis trade.

About 60km from Bab Taza is the only big town on the route, **Bab Berret**. A bustling administrative centre since the Spanish days, it has a lively Monday souk and is well served by buses and shared taxis. There are several cafés and a few basic hotels along the main street.

The road reaches its highest level at Bab Besen (1600m) where the landscape is covered in magnificent cedar forests. These continue along the run down to Ketama where the R509 (Route de l'Unité) from Fes joins the N2, at ISSAGUEN (usually marked on maps simply as "Ketama", though that is the name of the region, not the village). This is the heart of *kif* country, and although hassle has toned down somewhat in recent years, it still has a somewhat lawless and menacing edge; if you do choose to stop anywhere along this route you are likely to get unwanted attention.

Issaguen itself is not much of a place and is probably only worth stopping at if you have to change grands taxis or want to check out the Thursday souk. Locals can only conceive one reason for tourists to be here; there is, however, one other – climbing Djebel Tidighine, at 2448m the highest summit in the Rif Mountains. This is most easily done by picking up a local guide in Ketama, best arranged in advance, along with the necessary 4WD vehicle, in Chefchaouen. After driving on to Azila, a hamlet below the mountains, a rough track continues for a short distance, but the last part has to be walked. There are extensive views from the summit; on a clear day the sea can be glimpsed.

Abd el Krim and the Republic of the Rif

Until the establishment of the Spanish protectorate in 1912, the **tribes of the Rif** existed outside government control – a northern heartland of the *Bled es Siba*. They were subdued temporarily by *harkas*, the burning raids with which sultans asserted their authority, and for a longer period under Moulay Ismail; but for the most part, bore out their own name of *Imazighen*, or "Free Ones".

Closed to outside influence, the tribes developed an isolated and self-contained way of life. The Riffian soil, stony and infertile, produced constant problems with food supplies, and it was only through a complex system of alliances (*liffs*) that outright wars were avoided. Blood feuds, however, were endemic, and a major contributor to maintaining a viably small population. Unique in Morocco, the Riffian villages are scattered communities, their houses hedged and set apart, and where each family maintained a pillbox tower to spy on and fight off enemies. They were different, too, in their religion: the *salat*, the prayers said five times daily – one of the central tenets of Islam – was not observed. *Djinns*, supernatural fire spirits, were widely accredited, and great reliance was placed on the intercession of local *marabouts*.

It was an unlikely ground for significant and organized rebellion, yet for over five years (1921–27) the tribes forced the Spanish to withdraw from the mountains. Several times they defeated whole Spanish armies, first and most memorably at **Annoual** in 1921 (see p.575), which with later disasters led to General Primo de Rivera becoming – with the king's blessing – the virtual dictator of Spain. It was only through the intervention of France, and the joint commitment of nearly half a million troops, that the Europeans won eventual victory.

In the intervening years, **Abd el Krim el Khattabi**, the leader of the revolt, was able to declare a **Republic of the Rif** and to establish much of the apparatus of a modern state. Well educated, and confident of the Rif's mineral reserves, he and his brother, Mohammed, manipulated the *liff* system to forge an extraordinary unity among the tribes, negotiated mining rights in return for arms with Germany and Britain, and even set up a Riffian State Bank. Still more impressive, the brothers managed to impose a series of social reforms – including the destruction of family pillboxes and the banning of *kif* – which allowed the operation of a fairly broad administrative system. In their success, however, was the inevitability of defeat. It was the first nationalist

If you need to stay here, your choice is limited to the *Hôtel Saada* (☎0539 813061; ❶) south of the N2/R509 junction near the Taounate taxi stand, or the old Spanish *parador*, the *Hôtel Tidghine* (☎0539 813132; ❻), just south of the junction. Its four-star facilities are somewhat incongruous considering the setting but it makes a novel lunch stop.

Continuing east from Ketama the cedar forests give way to a more barren, stony landscape. The road continues to wend down the southern flank of the hills then twists down to bypass **Targuist.** The town itself is a new conglomeration of ugly buildings and far removed from being the site of Abd el Krim's headquarters (see box below). There are a few basic hotels (❶), and a lively Saturday souk, but no real reason to stay. Long-distance buses stop 2km beyond the centre at the Shell petrol station, where there is a restaurant.

It is only 46km before the village of Ajdir that the sea finally comes into view, and that distance descends the flank of a single long ridge; rather an anticlimax if it wasn't for the payoff of reaching the coast. **Other roads to the coast** lead off the N2 23km before and 12km beyond Ketama, cutting through the mountains to the village of El Jebha. Both are memorable trips (the roads are in bad condition and the going is slow) but there are much better beaches at Torres de Alcala and Kalah Iris, accessible from the next junction (see p.148).

movement in colonial North Africa, and although the Spanish were ready to quit the zone in 1925, it was politically impossible for the French to allow that. Intervention by French troops tipped the balance against the rebels.

Defeat for the Riffians – and the capture of Abd el Krim at Targuist – brought a virtual halt to social progress and reform. **The Spanish** took over the administration en bloc, governing through local *caids* (district administrators), and although they exploited some mineral deposits there was no road-building programme nor any of the other "civilizing benefits" introduced in the French zone. There were, however, two important changes: migration of labour (particularly to French Algeria) replaced the blood feud as a form of population control, and the Riffian warriors were recruited into Spain's own armies. The latter had immense consequences, allowing General Franco to build up a power base in Morocco. It was with **Riffian troops** that he invaded Andalucía in 1936, and it was probably their contribution that ensured the Fascist victory in the Spanish Civil War.

Abd el Krim was a powerful inspiration to later nationalists, and the Riffians themselves played an important guerrilla role in the 1955–56 **struggle for independence**. When, in April 1957, the Spanish finally surrendered their protectorate, however, the Berbers of the former Spanish zone found themselves largely excluded from government. Administrators were imposed on them from Fes and Casablanca, and in October 1958, the Rif's most important tribe, the Beni Urriaguel, rose in open **rebellion**. The mutiny was soon put down, but necessitated the landing at Al Hoceima of then-Crown Prince Hassan and some two-thirds of the Moroccan army.

The Rif is still perhaps the most unstable part of Morocco, remaining conscious of its under-representation in government and its historical underdevelopment. However, King Mohammed VI seems sympathetic to this situation and in recent years the region has witnessed substantial school-building programmes, improved road, air and ferry accessibility, large agricultural projects in the plains south of Nador and Al Hoceima and massive tourism developments near the Algerian border. Labour **emigration** remains high – with Western Europe replacing Algeria as the main market – and (as in the rest of Morocco) there is widespread resentment at the difficulty of obtaining a passport and then a visa for this outlet.

Torres de Alcala and Kalah Iris

Torres de Alcala and **Kalah Iris** are accessible via a good road (signposted Beni Boufrah and Torres de Alcala) 5km west of Targuist, and can be reached by grand taxi from Targuist or Al Hoceima. They are both temptingly low key, but this may change now that the new coast road makes them easily accessible from Al Hoceima. The road from Targuist winds up terraced slopes peppered with prickly pear cacti, almond trees and giant, mushroom-shaped haystacks – it's a very grand drive. Nearer the sea, the road periodically disappears under the debris of flash floods as it crosses and recrosses the *oued* beyond the hamlet of Beni Boufrah.

Torres de Alcala

TORRES DE ALCALA is a simple, whitewashed hamlet, 250m from a small, pebbly beach. Cliffs frame its beach, and on the western headland is a deserted fort, probably Spanish, with stunning views along the Mediterranean coast. There's just a bakery, the smallest of shops and a tiny café on the beach – it's about as laid back as you can get. There are currently no hotels or campsites, though somebody will offer you a room if you ask around.

Kif in Morocco

Although many of the Riffian tribes in the **mountains** had always smoked *kif*, it was the Spanish who really encouraged its cultivation – probably as an effort to keep the peace. This situation was apparently accepted when Mohammed V came to power, though the reasons for his doing so are obscure. There is a story, probably apocryphal, that when he visited Ketama in 1957, he accepted a bouquet of cannabis as a symbolic gift.

Whatever, Ketama continued to supply the bulk of the country's cannabis, and in the early 1970s it became the centre of a significant drug industry, exporting to Europe and America. This sudden growth was accounted for by the introduction, by an American dealer, of techniques for producing hash resin. Overnight, the Riffians had access to a compact and easily exportable product, as well as a burgeoning world market for dope. Inevitably, big business was quick to follow and now Morocco is reckoned to be the world's leading producer of cannabis, supplying the vast majority of Europe's demand, and contributing an estimated US$2bn (£1.2bn) to the Moroccan economy. Even bigger money, however, is made by the dealers – mainly British, Dutch, Spanish and Italians – who organize the shipments and sell the hash on the streets at prices fifty times higher than those paid to the Riffian growers.

The Moroccan authorities are caught between a rock and a hard place over the cannabis industry. They are pressured by Western European governments – and the UN – to take action against growers and dealers, and, given their aspirations to join the EU, have made efforts to cooperate. But the cultivation and sale of cannabis are important items in the local economy; well over a million people are said to depend on the crop for their existence.

The government, with help from EU grants, has tried to reduce cultivation – a project near Rafsai has replaced cannabis with 600,000 olive trees, for example – and the authorities claim that cultivation has reduced from 134,000 hectares in 2003 to 60,000 hectares in 2008. However, these figures are estimations gleaned from satellite photographs and are reckoned by European experts to be highly dubious. The bare fact is that farmers earn at least five times the income from cannabis than they would from growing legal crops.

The government's stated aim to eradicate cannabis cultivation by 2008 has clearly failed. The best they can hope for is to encourage farmers to rotate cannabis with other crops to avoid ruining their land with overuse of chemical fertilisers – whatever European hippies might like to think, cannabis grown in the Rif is anything but "organic".

Along a rocky cliff-path, 5km to the west, are the **ruins of Badis**, which from the fourteenth to the early sixteenth century was the main port of Fes, and used for trade with the western Mediterranean states, in particular Venice. A once-considerable caravan route ran across the Rif, following the course of the modern R509 road, the so-called Route de l'Unité (see p.163).

Kalah Iris

At **KALAH IRIS**, 4km west of Torres de Alcala along a paved road, there's a longer beach, with a natural breakwater, formed by a sandspit that runs out to one of two islets in the bay. There are a couple of sleepy cafés by the small fishing harbour at the western end of the beach but few other facilities. Again, there are no hotels or campsites, but if you want to stay, ask at the cafés and somebody might offer you a bed. It is not totally undiscovered, with excursions being offered to European holidaymakers in Al Hoceima, but it's still a delightful spot.

Al Hoceima

Coming from the Rif, **AL HOCEIMA** can be a bit of a shock. It may not be quite the "exclusive international resort" the tourist board claims, but it is truly Mediterranean and has developed enough to have little in common with the farming hamlets and tribal markets of the mountains around. It is at its best in late spring, or September, when the beaches are quiet. In midsummer, the town and beaches get pretty crowded under the weight of Moroccan families and French and German tourists, and rooms can be difficult to find.

The peaceful atmosphere of the town was tragically disturbed, not for the first time, in the early hours of February 24, 2004, by an earthquake measuring 6.5 on the Richter scale. Although most of the buildings in town are built to withstand earthquakes, it was the smaller communities around Al Hoceima, particularly Imzouren and Aït Kamra, that were badly hit by the quake; the final death toll was 572. Al Hoceima was also very near the epicentre of Morocco's previous big earthquake in 1990. Physical evidence of either quake, in Al Hoceima at least, is minimal.

Arrival and information

Buses arrive at Place du Rif, from where it is very easy to locate food and lodgings situated around the square or on Avenue Mohammed V, a short stroll away. Arriving by **grand taxi** from Nador, Oujda or Taza you will be dropped off just east of Place du Rif on Rue Alouien. From other destinations such as Issaguen and Kalah Iris you alight west of Avenue Mohammed V on Rue Raya al Maghriba.

The local **airport**, Aeroport Charif al Idrissi (Ⓣ0539 982005), is 17km southeast of Al Hoceima on the Nador road (N2), just before the village of Imzouren. It caters largely for charter flights from France and Germany – used as much by Moroccan workers as tourists.

A small passenger **ferry** terminal, catering for the annual summer onslaught of holidaying Riffians returning from their European work bases, has been built between Plage Quemado and the fishing harbour. The twice-daily crossings to the Spanish port of Almería operate from the end of June to the beginning of September only.

The ONMT office has closed down; instead go to Chafarinas Tours at 109 Bd Mohammed V (Ⓣ0539 840202, Ⓦhttp://rifitours.tripod.com), which has very

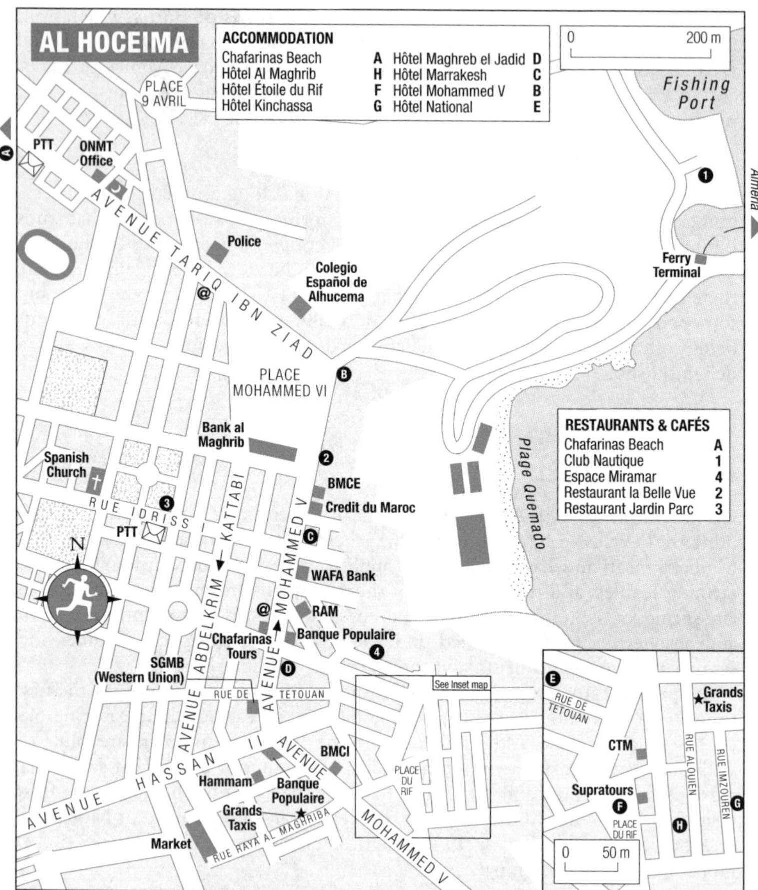

helpful staff who also organize **walking tours** and **pony trekking** in the Rif mountains, the logistics for which typically include accommodation in rural Berber houses and luggage relay either by 4WD, or mules in more rugged terrain.

There are plenty of **banks** with ATMs in town, all on Avenue Mohammed V. Various internet cafés and pharmacies also line the avenue. The most convenient **hammam** is at 12 Rue Azzalaga, parallel with Avenue Hassan II behind the Banque Populaire. It's near the centre and easy to find (women daily 9am–6pm, men daily 6–9pm & Sat 5–9am) – a picture hung outside tells you which sex is in occupation.

Accommodation

Most of the cheaper *pensions* are grouped in and around the Place du Rif; many are pretty dire. Those mentioned below are the best of them, and advance booking is advisable. Mid-range places are generally shabby and overpriced. Note that *Charafinas Beach* is the only hotel with a pool.

Al Maghrib 23 Rue Imzouren ⓣ0616 246429. Basins, tables, balconies and hat-stands make nice additions to the large tiled rooms. Facilities are shared but spotless and have copious hot water. Great value. ❶

Chafarinas Beach Plage Tala Youssef (Plage Chafarinas) ⓣ0539 841601, ⓦwww.complexchfarinasbeach.com. If you are after upmarket accommodation and a peaceful setting, this is the only choice. Five kilometres from town, the far-reaching views over the Mediterranean from the eye-popping reception hall and adjacent restaurant – open to non-residents – are unmatched by any hotel in town, and these same views can be enjoyed from the 38 self-catering apartments (sleeping up to 4 people) dotted on the slopes above the main building. Shuttle service to and from town. BB ❼

Hôtel Étoile du Rif 40 Pl du Rif. Currently undergoing major refurbishment, this has a prime location overlooking the square and when it reopens could well be the best mid-range place to stay in this part of town.

Hôtel Kinchassa Rue Imzouren ⓣ0670 786978. Bright, clean rooms with shared toilets and showers. Ahmed, the friendly owner, runs a tight ship and is clearly popular as this is often the first place to get booked up in summer. ❷

Hôtel Maghreb el Jadid 56 Av Mohammed V ⓣ0539 982504, ⓔhotelmagrebjadid@yahoo.fr. Very much past its prime, its top-floor bar and restaurant open only at the height of summer. En-suite rooms are clean and all have a/c but the general air is drab. ❸

Hôtel Marrakesh Av Mohammed V ⓣ0539 983025, ⓕ0539 981058. Clean rooms, all en suite and with reliable hot water, are adequate but somewhat gloomy. ❸

Hôtel Mohammed V Pl Mohammed VI ⓣ0539 982233 or 34, ⓕ0539 983314. The old state-run grand hotel, privatized and reopened in 1997, has slightly dated decor but the rooms are decent and have all mod cons, and there are beach views to be enjoyed from the terrace restaurant and bar. ❺

Hôtel National 23 Rue de Tetouan ⓣ0539 982141, ⓕ0539 982681. A central location, close to the buses in Pl du Rif. The rooms are en suite and have a/c and heating but are a bit musty. ❹

The Town

Al Hoceima's compact size is one of its charms. Until the 1950s, it consisted of just a small fishing port to the north of the bay, and a fringe of white houses atop the barren cliffs to the south. At the heart of this older quarter is the **Place du Rif**, enclosed by café-restaurants and *pensions*, and the terminal for CTM and private-line buses.

The newer part of town, with its neat grid of boulevards and occasional palms, occupies the land sloping down from the cliffs above the town beach, **Plage Quemado** – between the harbour and the original village – and at every turn you can see either the wooded hills behind the town, or the sea. If this quarter can be said to have a heart, it is the **Place Mohammed VI**, a squeaky-clean square on the cliff top.

From some vantage points, you get a view of the **Peñon de Alhucemas**, another of the Spanish-owned islands off this coast (and former penitentiary), over in the bay to the east of town. It's a pretty focal point, topped with sugar-white houses, a church and tower. The Spanish took it in 1673 and have held it ever since – a perennial source of dispute between Morocco and Spain.

Al Hoceima itself was developed by the Spanish after their counter-offensive in the Rif in 1925 (see p.145), and was known by them as **Villa Sanjuro**. The name commemorated the Spanish General José Sanjuro, who landed in the bay, under the cover of Spanish and French warships, with an expeditionary force – and it is still occasionally used for the old part of town around the Place du Rif. Coincidentally, it was at Al Hoceima, too, that the then Crown Prince Hassan led Moroccan forces to quell the Riffians' revolt in 1958, following independence.

Names aside, the Spanish left little to distinguish their occupation. The only notable architectural feature is the **Spanish College**, the **Colegio Español de Alhucema**, which, until 1956, was the provincial headquarters of the *Misión Cultural Española* in Morocco. It's the custard-cream-and-chocolate building, with blue and white *azulejos* tiles, on the north edge of town, beyond the main square.

▲ Plage Quemado, Al Hoceima

Beaches

Swimming – and walking in the olive-groved hills if you want a change – is the main attraction of Al Hoceima. Plage Quemado is clean enough but gets very crowded. Four kilometres west of town is **Plage Tala Youssef**, best known by the name of the exclusive and expensive resort *Chafarinas Beach* (see below) at its far end. You can walk in about an hour, otherwise, it's a rather steep 70dh by grand taxi. Far nicer are the beaches to the southeast. **Calle Bonita** is the first, down an unmarked road 1km out of town. It is a small bay with pedaloes, a couple of cafés and the *Restaurant Bellevue*, where you can sit with tapas and a beer on the balcony overlooking the beach. Three kilometres from town is **Plage Izly**, a long shingle beach with a café and very basic free accommodation in bamboo shacks. Another 2km along the main road is **Souani**, a long sandy beach with cafés and good sun loungers to cater for the many who flock here in the summer – try the sardine tajine at *Café Mediterranée*. A major new resort complex is being planned here but no building work was in evidence at the time of writing; enjoy the low-key vibe while you can.

There are beaches further west at **Torres de Alcala** and **Kalah Iris** (see p.146), which, although 60km away, are nevertheless thought of as Al Hoceima beaches.

Eating and nightlife

Al Hoceima has quite a lot of good, cheap **eateries**, though nothing very upmarket, nor much in the way of nightlife. Cafés around Place du Rif and Place Mohammed VI offer standard fare at decent prices and there are some good **patisseries** in town – try the one opposite *Espace Miramar*.

Chafarinas Beach Plage Tala Youssef (Plage Chafarinas) ☎0539 841601. Classic Moroccan dishes are well executed but costly (120dh main course); service is slick and the restaurant is licensed. Plan a long lunch to take full advantage of the coastal views and use of the spotless pool. Book ahead in the summer.

Club Nautique by the fishing port ☎0539 981641. Unmissable for huge plates of fresh fish, beer and lots of local colour in this lively joint;

expect to share your table with local drinkers when things get busy. Good fun. Closed during Ramadan. Daily 2pm–1am.

Espace Miramar Rue Moulay Ismail. Decent pizzas as well as Moroccan staples in this large place with terraces overlooking Plage Quemado. Open from all day until midnight; occasional live music.

Restaurant Jardin Parc 3 Mars, opposite the PTT. Relaxing spot with outdoor tables on the southeast corner of the square. Basic but well-cooked tajine and chicken dishes. Daily 7.30am–midnight.

Restaurant la Belle Vue Av Mohammed V by Pl Mohammed VI. A café all year, and a fully fledged restaurant in summer, with fish, meat, tajines and paella, plus views over the beach. Daily 6am–midnight. Grubby but cheap.

Moving on

Buses tend to leave Al Hoceima early, especially those heading eastwards. All depart from Place du Rif, where CTM and various other companies have offices. A CTM bus for Oujda leaves at 12.30am, while the last bus for Nador departs at 2.30pm. Note that some of the Nador buses continue to the Melilla border. For Targuist, Ketama, Chefchaouen, Tetouan and Tangier, there are departures both morning and evening, while there's just one daily bus to Casablanca, leaving at 8pm and calling at Fes, Meknes and Rabat en route. **Grands taxis** gather in Rue Alouien, just east of Place du Rif. For Chefchaouen, you have to change at Issaguen, a place that you can avoid if travelling to Fes by going via Taza instead, though the latter is the less scenic route. Travelling to Nador the N2 cuts back into the mountains and passes through Kassita, where you can branch off south to Aknoul and Taza, before reaching Nador via the unremarkable towns of Midar and Driouch. The more attractive, and faster, route is along the N16, the Mediterranean Highway which offers easy driving with spectacular sweeping views along the coast.

Nador and the coast

Entering or leaving Morocco at the Spanish enclave of Melilla, you may have to pass through **NADOR**. If you're a birdwatcher, you will be attracted to the marshes and dunes east of the town, (see box, p.153). Nador itself has little to offer, but you could break your journey here to walk on the seaside promenade by the lagoon, and unwind at one of the many cafés.

When the Spanish left in 1957, Nador was just an ordinary Riffian village, given work and some impetus by the port of Melilla. Its later designation as a provincial

Al Hoceima National Park

The **Al Hoceima National Park**, the entrance to which is on the N16 about 20km east of Al Hoceima, is a fantastic spot for **walking** and **mountain biking**. Covering 285 square kilometres, the park's majestic rocky canyons and pine forests harbour several rare species of birds and reptiles as well as jackals and wild boar. Thirty kilometres of well-marked tracks criss-cross the park, most negotiable by a tourist vehicle, and you can scramble down to a few isolated beaches where you may be lucky enough to spot dolphins. A few Berber settlements are dotted around the park, where you can see traditional crafts such as pottery and basket weaving in action. Accommodation is offered in four attractive houses (❶–❷) organized by the very helpful Anissa el Khattabi (Ⓣ0662 101279) who can also arrange guides and suggest itineraries. Without your own transport, you'll have to take a grand taxi from Al Hoceima, about 150dh. For more on the park, see Ⓦwww.parquenacionalalhucemas.com.

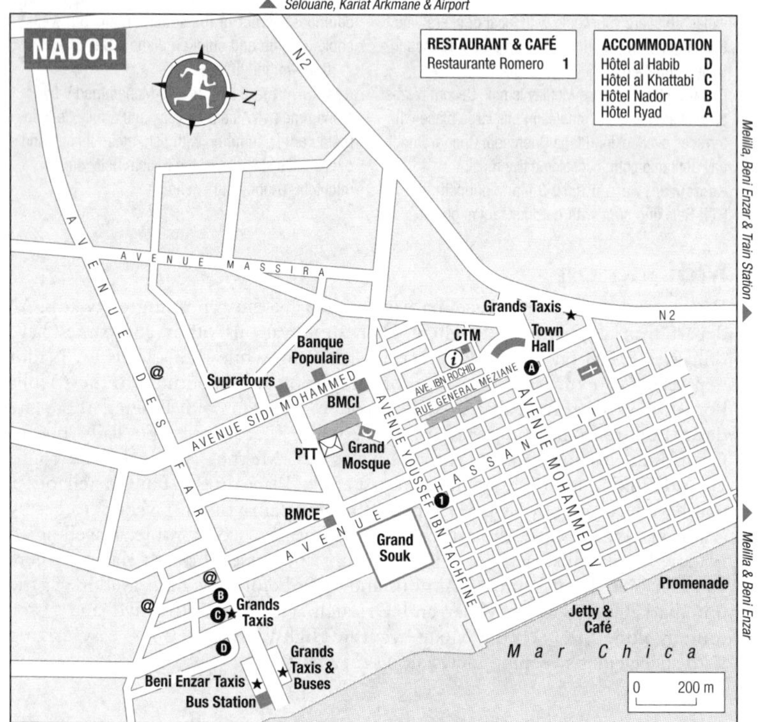

capital led to extensive growth based on the cement industry and the legal and illegal traffic passing through its busy port. It is now an ugly, sprawling city, which, despite some current redevelopment, won't tempt many tourists to linger.

Arrival and information

If you're arriving by **bus** or **grand taxi**, you'll likely be dropped at the ranks on Avenue des Far near the Grand Souk. Arriving by ferry, you disembark at **Beni Enzar**. Three hundred metres west of where you disembark is the main roundabout from where shared grands taxis constantly ply the route to Nador, 8km to the south (5dh). **Trains** from Taourit take you to the new train station, which lies 500m north of the centre.

Nador's ONMT **tourist office** is at 88 Bd Ibn Rochid (Mon–Fri 8.30am–4.30pm; Ⓣ0536 330348), next to the Rif cinema. There are numerous **banks** in town, all with ATMs and foreign exchange facilities, and **internet** access is available from various cafés near the bus and grand taxi station.

Nador's Taouima **airport** (Ⓣ0536 361075, Ⓕ0536 361072) is located 10km south of the city and caters mainly for international flights, although RAM operates daily flights to Casablanca.

Accommodation and eating

There are a surprising number of **hotels**, many of them built in the more optimistic climate of the late 1980s/early 1990s and now looking sadly rundown.

For **meals**, besides the hotel restaurants, the *Restaurante Romero* at 48–50 Av Youssef Ibn Tachfine, overlooking the Grand Souk (noon–10pm; cheap), is recommended for fish dishes. Roast chicken or fried fish and chips is the order of the day in the many cafés lining Boulevard Hassan II. For an early evening drink and a slice of cake, head to the **café** on the jetty over the Mar Chica.

Hôtel al Habib 17 Rue Hay el Khattabi ⓣ0536 332924. A grand marble staircase leads to upper floors, each with a small lounge/reading area and airy, light en-suite rooms. ❸

Hôtel el Khattabi Rue Hay el Khattabi, opposite *Hôtel Nador* ⓣ0536 330390. Clean and functional budget hotel with occasional hot water. ❶

Hôtel Nador 49 Rue Hay el Khattabi ⓣ0536 607071. The best cheap hotel in town with clean rooms, shared facilities and hot water. Rooms at the front can be noisy however. ❶

Hôtel Ryad Av Mohammed V ⓣ0536 607717, ⓔhotelryad@menara.ma. A once shiny and spectacular wedding cake of a hotel, this is now looking tarnished and drab. Not really worth the splurge, though it does have a restaurant, a bar and a nightclub. ❺

Birds and dunes

The coast east of Nador offers compelling sites for birdwatching – and plant wildlife – with a series of highly frequented freshwater and saline sites.

At **Kariet Arkmane** a path leads out, opposite the village mosque, past salt pans and a pumping station (right-hand side) to an **extensive area of salt marsh**. This is covered by the fleshy-stemmed **marsh glasswort** or *salicornia*: a characteristic "salt plant" or *halophyte*, it can survive the saline conditions through the use of glands which excrete the salt. The **insect life** of the salt marsh is abundant, including damselflies, brightly coloured grasshoppers and various ants and sand spiders. The **birds** are even more impressive, with black-winged stilt, greater flamingo, coot, great-crested grebe, and various gulls and terns wheeling overhead.

Further along the coast, a walk east of the resort of **Ras El Ma** demonstrates the means by which plants invade **sand dunes**: a sequential colonization is known as "**succession**", where one plant community gradually cedes to the next as a result of its own alteration of the environment. Typical early colonizers are marram grass and sea couch, which are eventually ousted by sea holly and sea spurge and finally by large, "woodier" species such as pistacihu, juniper and cistus species. Whole sequences can be seen occurring over time along the beach. The area attracts a variety of interesting **sea birds** as well, including the internationally rare slender-billed curlew and **Audouin's gull** (thought to breed on the adjacent offshore Chafarinas Islands; see below). Other more familiar birds include dunlin, Kentish plover and oystercatcher.

Even further along the coast is the freshwater lagoon system which marks the mouth of the **Oued Moulouya**. The lagoons here are separated from the sea by a remarkable series of sand spits, no more than fifty metres across, and the **birdlife** is outstanding. Secluded among the reedbeds, it is possible to locate grey heron, white stork and little egret while the water's surface is constantly patrolled by the ever-alert black terns and kingfishers. Other varieties which you should manage to spot, wading in the shallows, are redshank, spotted redshank (in summer) and black-tailed godwit. The mouth and adjacent wetlands are under serious threat from government-encouraged and European-financed tourism developments a couple of kilometres to the east. In response to local and international pressure, a small parcel of wetland encompassing the mouth has been declared a protected area funded by, amongst others, the Global Environmental Fund and UNDP. Bird hides and information signboards have been erected along a marked walking path.

The Spanish-owned **Islas Chafarinas**, incidentally, are another important wildlife site, which has been declared a nature reserve. The three small islets support the Mediterranean's largest sea-bird colonies; sadly, the endangered monk seals disappeared from the islands in the 1990s and haven't been seen since.

Moving on

As Nador is a duty-free port, buses between here and Fes are invariably used for smuggling and therefore subject to numerous police and even customs checks and subsequent delays. Therefore, if you are heading for Fes, Taza or Oujda, the best course is to go by rail - three trains a day leave for Taourit where you connect to the Oujda-Fes line.

CTM and some private **buses** to most destinations leave from a terminal on Rue General Meziane, across the avenue from the *Hôtel Ryad*. Other buses leave from the main bus station opposite the grand taxi stand.

Details of the Nador–Almería and Nador–Sète (summer only) **ferries** appear on p.176.

The coast

The village of **Kariet Arkmane (Qariet Arekmane)**, 30km from Nador, gives access to a sand-and shell-packed road along the spit of the lagoon. This is a desolate area but picturesque in its own way, with salt marshes that provide manifold attractions for birdwatchers. The road out follows the edge of the lagoon from Kariet, passing an old Spanish lookout post en route to a shell-beach – a popular weekend spot with Spaniards from Melilla – before giving out at a tiny fishing village. There is no accommodation here, just expensive holiday homes of wealthy Moroccans and a ribbon of easy and relaxed café-restaurants.

The road **east of Kariet** is a pleasant drive, twisting into the hills, never far from the sea, and eventually bringing you to **Ras el Ma** (or Ras Kebdana, as it is also known), 70km from Nador. Facing another of Spain's offshore island possessions on this coast, the three tiny **Islas Chafarinas**, this charming fishing village has a clean shingly **beach**, a smattering of decent cafés and restaurants and good rocks for swimming from by the harbour. Rooms can be rented from Mohsin (☎0658 256462) or you could camp discreetly on the beach. On the eastern edge of town on the road to Saïdia is the jolly *Auberge de Cap de L'eau* (☎0536 640264; ❶) with en-suite rooms sleeping up to four people and a large restaurant.

If you have your own transport, you could complete a loop back towards Nador from Ras el Ma, trailing the **Oued Moulouya** on road R612 to the small town of Zaïo on the N2 – or take the road across the river (once the border between the French and Spanish Protectorates) to the beaches around Saïdia (see p.162). If you're depending on public transport, there's a daily bus from Nador to Kariet Arkmane and Ras el Mar. It turns around on arrival at Ras el Mar and heads back to Nador, so you'll have to sleep over if you want to spend any time here.

Along this road the dunes used to run virtually undisturbed to the Algerian border but have now been levelled, some would say desecrated, for a massive residential golf resort developed as part of the king's strategy to attract tourism to the region.

Melilla (Mlilya)

Spanish-occupied **MELILLA** is a friendly little place, much more so than Ceuta (see p.118), with a pride in its **mix of cultures** and an interesting selection of early twentieth-century **modernist architecture**. Pleasures are to be found, too, in an exploration of the walled old town, **Medina Sidonia**, with its stunning views out across the Mediterranean. And if you're here in August,

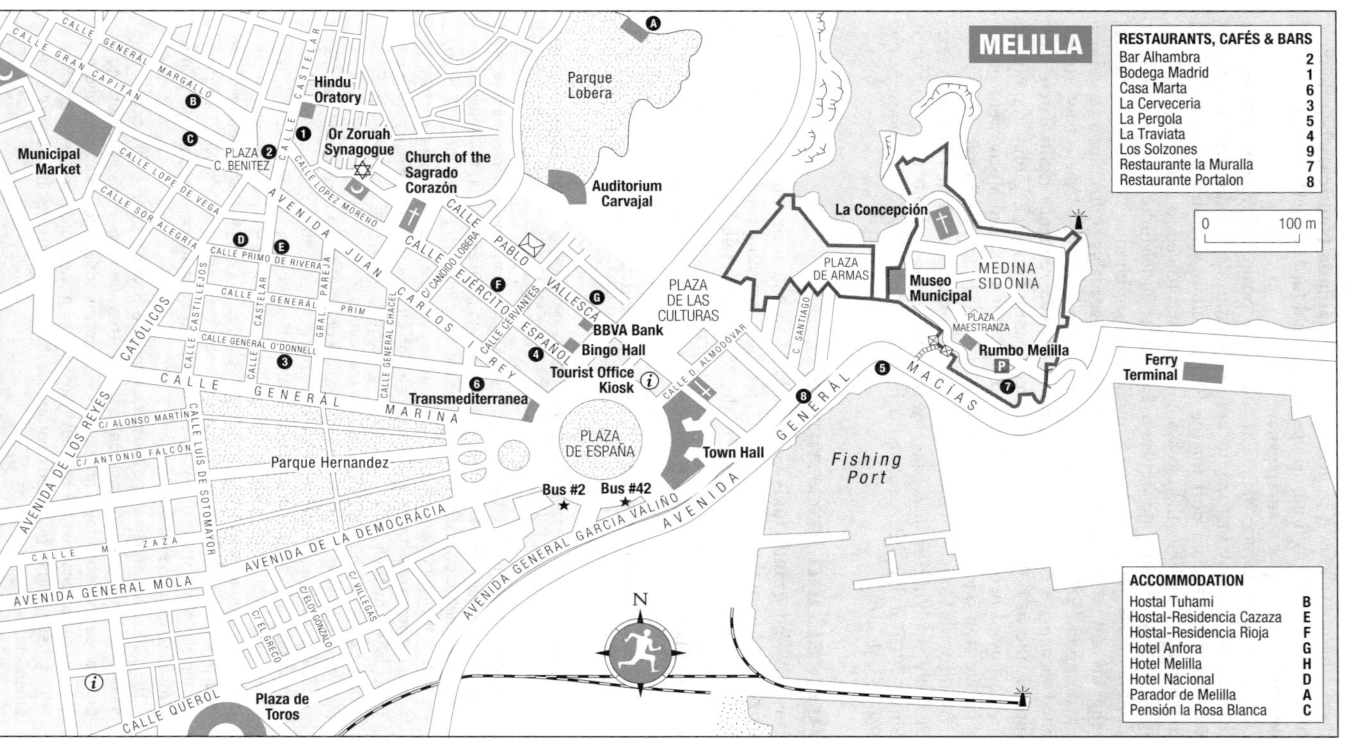
MELILLA
RESTAURANTS, CAFÉS & BARS
Bar Alhambra 2
Bodega Madrid 1
Casa Marta 6
La Cerveceria 3
La Pergola 5
La Traviata 4
Los Solzones 9
Restaurante la Muralla 7
Restaurante Portalon 8
ACCOMMODATION
Hostal Tuhami B
Hostal-Residencia Cazaza E
Hostal-Residencia Rioja F
Hotel Anfora G
Hotel Melilla H
Hotel Nacional D
Parador de Melilla A
Pensión la Rosa Blanca C
0 100 m
Municipal Market
Hindu Oratory
Or Zoruah Synagogue
Church of the Sagrado Corazón
Parque Lobera
Auditorium Carvajal
La Concepción
PLAZA DE ARMAS
Museo Municipal
MEDINA SIDONIA
PLAZA MAESTRANZA
Rumbo Melilla
Ferry Terminal
PLAZA DE LAS CULTURAS
BBVA Bank
Bingo Hall
Tourist Office Kiosk
Transmediterranea
PLAZA DE ESPAÑA
Town Hall
Fishing Port
Parque Hernandez
Bus #2
Bus #42
Plaza de Toros
PLAZA C. BENITEZ
CALLE GENERAL MARGALLO
CALLE GRAN CAPITAN
CALLE LOPE DE VEGA
CALLE SOR ALEGRÍA
CALLE CASTELAR
CALLE LOPEZ MORENO
AVENIDA JUAN CARLOS I REY
CALLE PABLO VALLESCA
CALLE EJÉRCITO ESPAÑOL
C/ CANDIDO LOBERA
CALLE CERVANTES
CALLE PRIMO DE RIVERA
CALLE GENERAL PRIM
GRAL PAREJA
CALLE GENERAL CHACEL
CALLE GENERAL O'DONNELL
CALLE CASTILLEJOS
CATÓLICOS
CALLE GENERAL MARINA
C. SANTIAGO
CALLE D. ALMODOVAR
AVENIDA GENERAL MACÍAS
AVENIDA DE LOS REYES
C/ ALONSO MARTÍN
C/ ANTONIO FALCÓN
CALLE LUÍS DE SOTOMAYOR
CALLE M. ZAZA
AVENIDA DE LA DEMOCRÁCIA
AVENIDA GENERAL GARCIA VALIÑO
AVENIDA GENERAL MOLA
C/ VILLEGAS
C/ ELOY GONZALO
C/ EL GRECO
CALLE QUEROL
N
H, 9 & Nador

there's the marvellous, if misleadingly titled **Semana Naútica**, when the port fills with sailing boats from mainland Spain and further afield for a fortnight of maritime extravaganzas and regattas.

Together with Ceuta, Melilla is the last of Spain's Moroccan enclaves – a former penal colony that saw its most prosperous days under the Protectorate, when it was the main port for the Riffian mining industry. Since Moroccan independence in 1956, the city's population has halved to a little over 65,000, split roughly two-to-one between Christians and Muslims (mostly Berber), along with 750 Jews and about a hundred Indian Hindus. The enclave's various religious and ethnic communities get along reasonably well, despite an episode of rioting in 1986, after the enactment of Spain's first real "Aliens Law" threatened to deprive certain Muslim families of their residence rights. There were further riots in 1996, when four hundred Spanish Foreign Legionnaires, a tough bunch posted here by the Madrid authorities out of harm's way, went on the rampage after one of their number had been killed in a bar brawl.

Along with Ceuta, Melilla achieved autonomous status in 1995 after years of shilly-shallying on the issue by Madrid for fear of offending Morocco. Since 2007 it has been ruled by Juan José Imbroda Ortiz's conservative People's Party.

Arrival and information

Bus #19 and **grands taxis** from Nador drop you at the border post of **Beni Enzar**, and from there, once the often time-consuming process of crossing the border is out of the way, buses on the Melilla side will take you to the main square, Plaza de España. Melilla's **ferry terminal** is at the far end of Avenida Generál Macías, a short walk from the Plaza. Within the terminal is an office for Acciona Trasmediterraneas and there are a couple of travel agencies just outside. Arriving at the **airport**, 3km southwest of the town, means a €6.50 taxi ride into the centre.

The Nador-Melilla border

On a good day you can cross the **Nador–Melilla border** in ten or fifteen minutes. At other times, you may need considerable time and patience. During the summer it's often extremely crowded, with Moroccans returning from (or going to) jobs in Europe, as well as travellers off the ferry. If you want to avoid the queues, it is a good idea to spend a couple of hours in Melilla after arriving off a ferry, to let the main traffic get through. Alternatively, travel on the next morning: Melilla is worth a stay. Early mornings are very busy on both sides of the border.

If you are **driving**, be aware that smuggling goes on at the border, with periodic police crackdowns; in recent years, trading has included both drugs and people, with Moroccans (and sub-Saharan Africans) attempting to cross illegally into mainland Spain. Driving at night, keep an eye out for road checks – not always well lit but usually accompanied by tyre-puncturing blockades. If driving to Nador, beware of the local police, eager to pounce and demand large "fines" from newly arrived foreigners for the slightest infraction. If you've rented a car in Morocco, you can take it into Melilla but not into mainland Spain.

The 200m that separate the Moroccan and the Spanish sides of the border are much more than just a geopolitical anomaly. They are a no-man's land isolating a prosperous European town from an unemployment-ridden Moroccan one, and the sharp contrast between the two illustrates why so many Moroccans risk – and lose – their lives trying to reach the Spanish coast on makeshift rafts in search of better prospects.

The **tourist office** (Mon–Fri 10am–2pm & 5–8.30pm; ⓣ952 681635, ⓦwww.melillaturismo.com) is in the Palacio de Exposiciones y Congresos, c/ Fortuny 21, near the Plaza de Toros, and in the more conveniently located kiosk by the town hall (Mon–Sat 9am–2pm & 4–8.30pm, Sun 10am–2pm). When **phoning Melilla** from Morocco (or anywhere else outside Spain), you must prefix numbers with the international code (ⓣ00 34). Dialling numbers within Melilla you must include the old local code 952 as part of the new nine-digit number. To **phone Morocco from Melilla**, you need to dial ⓣ00 212, followed by the local code (minus the initial zero) and number. Note that Melilla works to Spanish time, which is one hour ahead of Morocco.

There are a number of **banks** on or near Avenida Juan Carlos I Rey, all of which have ATMs and will change cheques, sterling, dollars or dirhams. It's worth shopping around to get the best exchange rates. Bear in mind that, as part of Spain, Melilla uses euros. Apart from taxis and buses to and from the border, dirhams are not generally accepted. In case of medical emergency, head to the **Hospital Comarcal** at c/Remonta 2 (ⓣ952 670000) or the **Hospital Militar** at c/General Polavieja s/n (ⓣ952 674743).

Accommodation

Accommodation in Melilla is not easy to find; rooms tend to be in short supply – and are expensive by Moroccan standards. If you have problems, the tourist offices (see above) might be able to help.

Hostal-Residencia Cazaza c/Primo de Rivera 6 ⓣ952 684648. The rooms are a little scruffy, but it's a friendly, well-maintained place, with TV and large bathroom in all rooms, and there's a small café on the ground floor for breakfast. ❺

Hostal-Residencia Rioja c/Ejército Español 10 ⓣ952 682709. Good location, big rooms with basins and clean, shared bathrooms. ❺

Hostal Tuhami c/General Margallo 13 ⓣ952 686045, ⓔhostaltuhami@hotmail.com. More a hotel than a hostel, with spotless en-suite a/c rooms and friendly staff. ❻

Hotel Anfora c/Pablo Vallesca 16 ⓣ952 683340, ⓕ952 683344. Current refurbishment should smarten things up a bit; good a/c rooms, bar and a top-floor restaurant with panoramic views. ❼

Hotel Melilla Puerto Esplanada de San Lorenzo s/n, 200m from town centre ⓣ952 695525, ⓦwww.hotelmelillapuerto.com. Dull, upmarket hotel, geared towards the business traveller. No pool, despite the price ❼

Hotel Nacional c/Primo de Rivera 10 ⓣ952 684540, ⓕ952 684481. Small but comfortable rooms with TV, a/c and newly refurbished bathrooms. It also has the only kosher restaurant in town, open to nonresidents. Guests can arrange car rental here for day-trips to Morocco. ❻

Parador de Melilla Avda de Candido Lobera – overlooking the Parque Lobera ⓣ952 684940, ⓦwww.parador.es. Rather dated but with large and well-appointed rooms and fine views over the town but the food and service leave something to be desired. Swimming pool for residents only. ❼

Pensión la Rosa Blanca c/Gran Capitan 7 ⓣ952 682738. A charming, quiet little *pension* worth booking ahead as it is often full in summer. Rooms are large and come with basins; some have balconies. Shared bathrooms. ❺

The Town

Melilla centres on **Plaza de España**, overlooking the port, and **Avenida Juan Carlos I Rey**, leading inland off it. This is the most animated part of town, especially during the evening *paseo*, when everyone promenades up and down, or strolls through the neighbouring **Parque Hernandez**.

To the northeast, occupying a walled promontory, and adjacent to the ferry terminal, is the old part of town, **Medina Sidonia,** which is a must. The marina and the long sandy beach to the south see the usual Spanish seaside action but there are few places to stay here.

Medina Sidonia

Until the beginning of the twentieth century, the walled "Old Town" of **Medina Sidonia**, wedged in above the port, was all there was of Melilla. This was the site of the original Phoenician colony of Rusadir around the tenth century BC, which the Spanish took in 1497, a kind of epilogue to the expulsion of the Moors from Spain after the fall of Granada in 1492. As an enclave, its security was always vulnerable, and at various periods of expansionist Moroccan rule – it was blockaded throughout the reign of Moulay Ismail – the Spanish population was limited to their fortress promontory and its sea approaches. The quarter's streets were laid out along the lines of a Castilian fort, following a major earthquake in the sixteenth century.

Steps near the fishing port lead up to the quarter's main square, **Plaza Maestranza**, entered by the Gothic **Puerta de Santiago**, a gate flanked by a chapel to St James the Apostle – known to Spaniards as *Matamoros*, "the Moor-Slayer". Beyond the recently restored square you come to an old barracks and armoury, and, if you follow the fortifications round from here, a small fort, below which is the church of **La Concepción**, crowded with Baroque decoration, including a revered statue of *Nuestra Señora de Victoria* (**Our Lady of Victory**), the city's patroness. Back on Plaza Maestranza is the **Museo Municipal (Museo de la Ciudad Autonoma de la Melilla**, Tues–Sat 10am–2pm & 4–8.30pm winter; 10am-1.30pm & 5-9.30pm summer, Sun 10am–2pm; free), which houses a miscellany of historical documents, coins and ceramics. Also interesting is the nearby **Rumbo Melilla** museum (same hours as above; free), which shows a fifteen-minute audiovisual projection on the history of the various peoples to have occupied and influenced the town. These and other places of interest are all signposted and numbered as part of a short circular self-guided walk within the Medina.

The New Town

In the new town, many of the buildings around **Plaza de España** were designed by **Enrique Nieto**, a *modernista* (Art Nouveau) disciple of the renowned Catalan architect, Antoni Gaudí. Nieto arrived in 1909 at the age of 23 and, over the next four decades, transformed Melilla's architecture. The tile and stucco facades left

▲ Medina Sidonia, Melilla

by Nieto and his imitators – in a style more flowery than Gaudí's – are a quiet delight of the New Town if you cast your eyes above the shops.

A short, circular **walk** taking in these delights starts in Plaza de España with Melilla's most famous Art Deco building, the town hall, a Nieto building of 1947. Avenida Juan Carlos I Rey, leading away from the Plaza de España, begins with the 1917 Trasmediterranea building on the left, followed by another fine piece of Art Nouveau at no. 9, built in 1915. From here head for Calle Ejército Español to have a look at no.16 and continue up Calle Lopez Moreno, checking out the *modernista* buildings on the right-hand side, among them Nieto's **Or Zoruah (Holy Light) Synagogue**, built in 1924, the ground floor of which bizarrely houses a cheap trinket shop. Visits can be arranged via the tourist office. Opposite is the Polygon Mosque, also by Nieto, and dating to 1945. Back on Avenida Juan Carlos I Rey, there is quite a selection around Plaza Comandante Benitez and, just down Calle Reyes Catolicos, check out those on Calle Sor Alegría, before heading along Avenida General Prim to see the building on the corner of Castelar. The last building, the **bingo hall** on the corner of Comandante Emperador and Ejército Español, just off Plaza de España, has another fine stucco facade, in Art Deco style this time.

Eating and drinking

Melilla has some great **tapas bars**, but not much in the way of **restaurants**; the main concentration lies in the area east of Avenida Juan Carlos I Rey, between the Plaza de España and the Municipal Market. There is also a cluster of cafés and restaurants in the new marina to the south of the fishing port. Coming from Morocco, the easy availability of alcohol and open drinking culture are refreshing in more ways than one.

Bar Alhambra c/Castelar 3. A fairly large bar, popular with locals, serving cold beers, tapas and *bocadillos*. Daily except Sun 10.30am–3pm & 8.30–11pm.

Bodega Madrid c/Castelar 6. Functional seating, bright lights and huge rations of freshly cooked fish and seafood (you may want to go for a half-portion). Daily 11.15am–3pm & 8.30–10.45pm. Cheap to moderate.

Casa Marta c/Justo Sanchez. Great little tapas bar/restaurant with tables on the street and barrels to stand at inside. Daily noon-5pm & 8pm-2am.

La Cerveceria c/General ODonnell. Popular tapas bar with whacky *modernista* decor, good food and decent wines available by the glass. Service is very friendly, too. Daily 12.30–4pm & 8.30–midnight.

La Pergola Avda Generál Macias, alongside the fishing port. Enjoy coffee or cocktails on the waterside terrace then tackle the huge restaurant menu which includes plenty of fish. Packed at weekends. Daily noon–midnight.

La Traviata c/Ejercito Espanol 5 ⓣ952 681925, ⓔlatraviatamelilla@hotmail.com. Swanky new bar/restuarant serving gourmet modern Spanish food at top end prices. Daily 12.30–3pm & 8pm–1am.

Los Salazones c/Conde de Alcaudete 15 ⓣ952 673652. Established in 1967 and still going strong, this large tapas bar/restaurant located a block back about halfway down the beach, serves traditional Spanish fare with great aplomb. Daily 12.30-3pm & 8pm-midnight.

Restaurante la Muralla c/Mirador de Florentina s/n, near the southeast corner of Medina Sidonia ⓣ952 681035. Fantastic views over the port from this restaurant that's also a chef school. Thurs–Sat 12.30–3pm & 8–11.30pm

Restaurante Portalon Avda Generál Macias 9. Popular eatery across from the fishing port serving tapas, pizza, and average seafood. Good coffee though. Open for breakfast, lunch and dinner.

Moving on

Ferries from Melilla (see pp.30–31) run most days to **Málaga** and **Almería**, twice daily to Almería in summer. Making advance bookings is essential in August – with waits of up to three days possible if you just turn up for a boat – and the period at the end of Semana Santa (Easter week) is also best avoided.

Alternatively, there are Iberia **flights** to **Málaga**, **Mallorca, Valencia**, **Almería**, **Granada** and **Madrid**. Again, reserve ahead of time if possible, and be warned that flights don't leave in bad weather. The Iberia/Air Nostrum office is at the airport (Ⓣ902 341342) and there is an Iberia Airlines agency in town at 20 c/Generál Marina. You can find more detailed information on flights from and to Melilla on Ⓦwww.iberia.es or www.aena.es (official site of the Spanish airport authority), both of them available in English. A helpful **travel agency** for information and reservations is Viajes Mariaire, Avda Juan Carlos I Rey 30 (Mon–Fri 9am–1pm & 4.30–8pm; Ⓣ952 681017, Ⓕ952 690023).

Travelling into Morocco you can usually pick up collective grands taxis for **Nador** just over the border, but if there are none, or if they try to make you charter a whole taxi and you don't want to, then walk 100m to the roundabout and pick one up there. There are also city buses (#19) to Nador.

Berkane, the Zegzel Gorge and Saïdia

The **route east** from Nador to Oujda along the N2 is well served by buses and grands taxis. It holds little of interest along the way, but if you've got the time (and ideally a car), there's a pleasant detour around Berkane into the **Zegzel Gorge**, a dark limestone fault in the Beni Snassen mountains – the last outcrops of the Rif. The new coast road, the N16, is faster, more attractive and has the considerable appeal of **Saïdia**, one of the country's most pleasant and relaxed seaside resorts at its finish.

The gorge route

The **Oued Zegzel** is a tributary of the Moulouya, which as it runs south of Berkane has carved out a fertile shaft of mountain valleys. For centuries, these marked the limits of the Shereefian empire.

The route through these valleys is easily accessible with your own car; from Berkane take the N2 east out of town and, after 10km, turn south onto the R607, climbing up to Taforalt, 10km from the turn-off. If you're using public transport, get a seat in a grand taxi from Berkane to Taforalt and negotiate another one back, this time via the gorge road.

Berkane

BERKANE is a strategic market town, French-built and prosperous, set amid an extensive region of orchards and vineyards. If you stay, you're likely to be the only tourist in the town – so there aren't any hustlers.

The town's main square is at the top end of town on the N2 road. Buses and Oujda grands taxis hang out in the street running south from here. There are good eating places on the long, unpaved street running uphill from Boulevard Hassan II, along with lots of very dark, tented souks.

The best place to stay is the *Hôtel Rosalina* on Boulevard Mohammed V (Ⓣ0536 618992, Ⓔrosalina_hotel@hotmail.fr; ④), which has good en-suite rooms and a ground-floor café. There isn't much to see in Berkane, but worth a glance is the now disused **church**, (closed Wed afternoon) just north of the main road, 50m east of the main square, painted in red ochre, with a row of strange grimacing faces picked out in yellow along the top of its facade.

Moving on from Berkane is straightforward, with frequent buses and grands taxis to Nador, Oujda and Saïdia; the CTM service to Casablanca (via Fes, Meknes and Rabat) departs at 7pm. Buses leave from just off the main square, as do grands taxis for Oujda. Grands taxis for Nador are to be found 200m west along the main road, while those for Saïdia leave from just north of the roundabout 300m east of the main square.

Taforalt, the caves and the gorge

TAFORALT (Tafoughalt) is a quiet mountain village, active only for the **Wednesday souk**, but serves as a good base for hikers or birdwatchers; it has a reliable supply of grands taxis (though it's not served by any buses), and you should be able to move on rapidly towards the Zegzel Gorge. As well as a smattering of roadside cafés, there is a very good hotel, *Auberge de Taforalt*, (T 0661 347398, W www.taforaltclub.com) which has quirky rooms, (BB 5) Berber tents on the roof (BB 4) and kitchens, if you want to self-cater. Across the street, and with the same owner, is *Club Taforalt*, a complex with a pool, bar and restaurant where locals come at the weekends to relax over long lunches.

Two kilometres from Taforalt are the **Grottes des Pigeons**. Currently being excavated by a team from Oxford University, some of the earliest human remains in the world have been found here, as well as jewellery – pierced shells which date back a staggering 90,000 years. Information is displayed on a board in the picnic area below the caves. A further 8km on, signed off the gorge road to Berkane, is the **Grotte du Chameau**, a cavern of vast stalactites, one of which is remarkably camel-like in shape. This has been closed to visitors for years and now houses a herd of goats. Local boys stationed just before the cave will charge 5dh per vehicle for the use of the car park at the end of the road where you can enjoy the picnic area underneath towering limestone buttresses and dense cedar trees.

The **Zegzel Gorge**, or rather **gorges**, begins about a kilometre beyond the cave. A rough track branches off the main road, only suitable for 4WD vehicles

A note on Algeria

Throughout the 1990s and into the early 2000s Algeria was effectively off limits to all foreign visitors. During the civil war between 1992 and 1998 over 150,000 people were killed in attacks and reprisals by Islamic fundamentalists and the army; foreigners, as well as Algerian intellectuals, journalists and musicians, were particular targets. After elections in 1999 the situation improved somewhat, although there were still occasional skirmishes with militant Islamic extremists. 2007 saw a worrying resurgence of violence, with Al-Qaeda implicated in attacks in Algeria and Morocco that left many dead.

Algeria and Morocco have disputed their borders since Algerian independence in 1963. The border was closed in 1975 following Morocco's "Green March" into Spain's former colony of Western Sahara – the Algerians supported Polisario, the Saharan independence movement. The border reopened some years later but was closed again in 1994 when Morocco imposed strict visa restrictions on Algerians following a terrorist attack in Marrakesh.

In 2004, in an attempt to improve relations, Morocco lifted all visa entry requirements for Algerians and in 2008, citing their "common past and shared destiny", called on Algeria to normalize relations and reopen the border – it is estimated that the border closure costs Morocco $1bn a year in lost trade and tourist revenues. There was a brief breakthrough in the impasse in February 2009 when the border was opened to allow the passage of an aid convoy heading for the Gaza Strip, but it seems unlikely the situation will change until the Western Sahara issue is resolved to Algeria's satisfaction. It's possible for non-Moroccans to obtain entry visas for Algeria, and there is a consulate at Oujda (see p.172), but entry to Algeria from Morocco is only possible by air flying out of Casablanca.

and perennially subject to rock avalanches and flash-floods. The gorges are terraced and cultivated with all kinds of citrus and fruit trees. As the track criss-crosses the riverbed, the gorges progressively narrow, drawing your eye to the cedars and dwarf oaks at the summit, until you eventually emerge (22km from Taforalt) onto the Berkane plain.

Saïdia

Only a few years ago, **SAÏDIA** was a low-key resort, rambling back from the sea in the shadow of a still-occupied nineteenth-century kasbah, and fronted by one of the best beaches on the Mediterranean. Recent years, however, have seen massive development along the coast to the west of the town, co-funded by the Moroccan government and two of the country's largest corporations. The growth is enormous – hundreds of new apartment blocks stretching along the beach, the largest marina in Morocco, a shopping complex and, 10km from Saïdia town, the Palmeral Golf Club, managed by the world-renowned Troon Golf group.

Arrival and information

Buses and **grands taxis** will drop you by the northwest corner of the kasbah, from where the beach is a couple of blocks to the north. Down by the beach are two main thoroughfares running parallel to each other: beachfront Boulevard Mohammed V and Boulevard Hassan II. The town's small square, Place du 20 Août, connects the two towards the eastern end. On Boulevard Hassan II, close to Place du 20 Août, are branches of Banque Populaire and Wafa, both **banks** with ATMs, as well as the **post office** (Mon–Fri 8am–6pm, Sat 8am–noon), two blocks west of *Hôtel Atlal*. Note that there is no official petrol station in town; take the second left travelling west off Boulevard Hassan II after *Hôtel Atlal* and ask for "l'homme avec essence".

Accommodation

For a town of its size, Saïdia has a fair number of mid-range hotels. The views from the sea-facing rooms in any of the places on Mohammed V are simply fantastic. The only campsite, *Camping Chams* (Ⓣ0667 178941) at the eastern edge of town, has good pitches for 50dh.

Hôtel Atlal 44 Bd Hassan II Ⓣ0536 625021, Ⓔatlalben@menara.ma. Ask for a west-facing balcony where you can sit with a beer and some tapas from the bar next door and watch the sun go down over a very pleasing skyline. Great bed linen, large bathrooms and nice lighting are added bonuses. Good family rooms available, too. Worth a splurge. BB ❺

Hôtel Hannour Place du 20 Août Ⓣ0536 625115, Ⓕ0536 624343. A lively three-star establishment, rooms are a bit dark but have fans. ❸

Hôtel Manhattan Bd Mohammed V Ⓣ0536 624243. One of a trio of seafront hotels, located above its own popular café-restaurant. All rooms are en suite with TV and are tiled throughout. ❹

Hôtel Paco Bd Hassan II opposite the *Atlal* Ⓣ0536 625110. A rather spartan hotel with good-value en-suite rooms, hot showers and an agreeably insalubrious bar. ❷

Hôtel Rimal Bd Mohammed V Ⓣ0536 624141, Ⓕ0536 624142. Very similar in style to the neighbouring *Manhattan*, including the ground-floor café-restaurant, but better value. Also has some larger suites. ❸

Hôtel Titanic Bd Mohammed V Ⓣ&Ⓕ0536 624071. A large poster of the blockbuster movie presides over the reception of this blue-and-cream hotel, the best of the three neighbouring seafront choices. The modern, airy rooms lead onto good-sized balconies offering unbeatable sea views. Closed during winter. ❸

Hôtel Barceló Mediterránea Saïdia Station Balnéaire Saïdia-H1 Ⓣ0536 630063, Ⓦwww.barcelo.com. Located out by the Palmeral Golf Club, this is a five-star number with all the requisite creature comforts, including six pools and three bars. ❼–❽

The Town

The new development functions as a separate resort from the town itself and so far has no hotel accommodation other than the two five-star complexes – most of the apartments are privately owned and at the time of writing there were none available to rent to the short-term visitor. Saïdia proper is very relaxed and has some decent hotels along with sunny cafés and good, simple restaurants. It has been spared the high-rise monstrosities found elsewhere along this coast and it offers a really chilled-out beach vibe with plenty of summer visitors to keep things lively. The main square becomes particularly animated when the town hosts the August **Festival du Raï et des Arts Populaires**. The two-week festival is an opportunity to listen to some indigenous *chaâbi*, *raï* and *amazigh* music, and see *raggada* and *laäoui* folk-dancing ensembles.

If you prefer birds to beaches, there are rewarding bird sites in the marshes and woodland stretching behind the beach towards the Oued Moulouya (see box, p.153).

Eating and drinking

There are a few lively **café-restaurants** by the market and kasbah and, during the holiday season, on the beach. The best restaurants, however, are around Place du 20 Août and are open all year round. Both *Hôtel Atlal* and *Hôtel Paco* have **bars**, whilst next door to *Hôtel Hannour* is the relaxed *Mediterrania Club* with pool tables, café and *shisha* pipes. There's a great patisserie at the back of *Hôtel Atlal*.

Chez Saïd Bd Hassan II, opposite *Hôtel Hannour* ⓣ0536 625411. Small, well-established restaurant serving seafood specialities as well as Moroccan staples. Lunch & dinner daily.

Hôtel Atlal 44 Bd Hassan II ⓣ0536 625021. The best restaurant in town, with cosy dining room and a pretty terrace; spanking fresh fish and hearty tajines are served with charm and there's also a good selection of Moroccan wines. Open all day.

Café Royal Place du 20 Août. Cheap and cheerful café serving huge portions of grilled fish, rotisserie chickens and salads. Open all day.

The Route de L'Unité: Ketama to Fes

At the end of the Spanish Protectorate in 1957, there was no north–south route across the Rif, a marked symbol both of its isolation and of the separateness of the old French and Spanish zones. The Route de l'Unité, a road cutting right across the range from Ketama to Fes, was planned to provide working contact between the Riffian tribes and the French-colonized Moroccans.

The Route (more prosaically known as the R509), completed in 1963, was built with volunteer labour from all over the country – Hassan II himself worked on it at the outset. It was the brainchild of Mehdi Ben Barka, first president of the National Assembly and the most outstanding figure of the nationalist Left before his exile and subsequent "disappearance" in Paris in 1965. Ben Barka's volunteers, 15,000-strong for much of the project, formed a kind of labour university, working through the mornings and attending lectures in the afternoons.

Today the Route de l'Unité sees relatively little traffic – travelling from Fes to Al Hoceima, it's quicker to go via Taza and the R505; from Fes to Tetouan, via Ouezzane. Nevertheless, it's an impressive and very beautiful road, certainly as dramatic an approach to Fes as you could hope for. However, see the **warning** about driving through here on p.141.

Taounate, Tissa and Rafsaï

TAOUNATE is a pleasantly bustling little town with sweeping views over the plains to the south. If you can make it for the huge **Friday market**, you should be able to organize a lift out to any number of villages in the region. There's a cheap but dirty hotel, the *Entente* (☎0535 688291; ❶), halfway down the hill on the left-hand side or *Hôtel du Lac* (☎0535 689367; ❷) in the middle of town up an alley opposite the market entrance. Numerous cafés and banks, a petrol station and a good daily market line the main road through the town. Continuing south along the Route, 33km from Taounate, is a left-hand turn that takes you to **TISSA**. The region around Tissa is known for its thoroughbred Hayani horses. Here, in late September/early October, horses and riders from the region gather to compete at the annual **horsefair**. The climax is the competitive **fantasias** judged on speed, discipline and dress. Elsewhere, *fantasias* – traditional cavalry charges culminating in firing of muskets in the air – are put on largely for tourists, but these are the real thing, for aficionados.

To the west of Taounate lies **RAFSAÏ**, the last village of the Rif to be overrun by the Spanish, and the site of a December **Olive Festival**. Rafsaï is reached by taking the R408 to the Barrage al Wahda, and then turning northwards on the S305. The lake formed by the dam is 34km long, designed to irrigate 2000 square kilometres of the **Gharb** coastal plain and protect them from floodwaters. It also contributes ten percent to the national electricity grid. If you are into scenic roads and have transport, you might consider taking a forty-kilometre dirt road out from Rafsaï to the **Djebel Lalla Outka**, the peak reputed to offer the best view of the whole Rif range. The road is reasonable as far as the village of Tamesnite, but thereafter is very rough *piste* – accessible only in summer.

Going **east from Taounate**, an attractive though less spectacular route winds towards the village of **Aknoul**, from where you can pick up a daily bus or grand taxi down to Taza, or catch the daily bus to Nador and Al Hoceima.

Taza and the Djebel Tazzeka

TAZA was once a place of great importance: the capital of Morocco for periods of the Almohad, Merenid and Alaouite dynasties, and controlling the Taza Gap, the only practicable pass from the east. It forms a wide passage between the Rif and Middle Atlas and was the route to central power taken by Moulay Idriss and the first Moroccan Arabs, as well as the Almohads and Merenids, both of whom successfully invaded Fes from Taza. However, the local Zenatta tribe were always willing to join an attack by outsiders and in the nineteenth century, managed to overrun Taza completely, with centralized control returning only with the French occupation of 1914.

After the French occupation Taza was an important centre of the resistance movement; troops fought long and hard in the Rif mountains in skirmishes which occurred sporadically right up to independence.

Modern Taza seems little haunted by this past, its monuments sparse and mostly inaccessible to non-Muslims. The town splits into two parts, the **Medina** and the French-built **Ville Nouvelle**, distinct quarters separated by 2km of road. The Ville Nouvelle is of little interest, though it has the usual facilities, but the Medina, with its magnificent hilltop site, is steeped in history and has a quiet charm.

Taza is best used as a base from which to explore the national park of **Djebel Tazzeka**, a treat for drivers and hikers alike

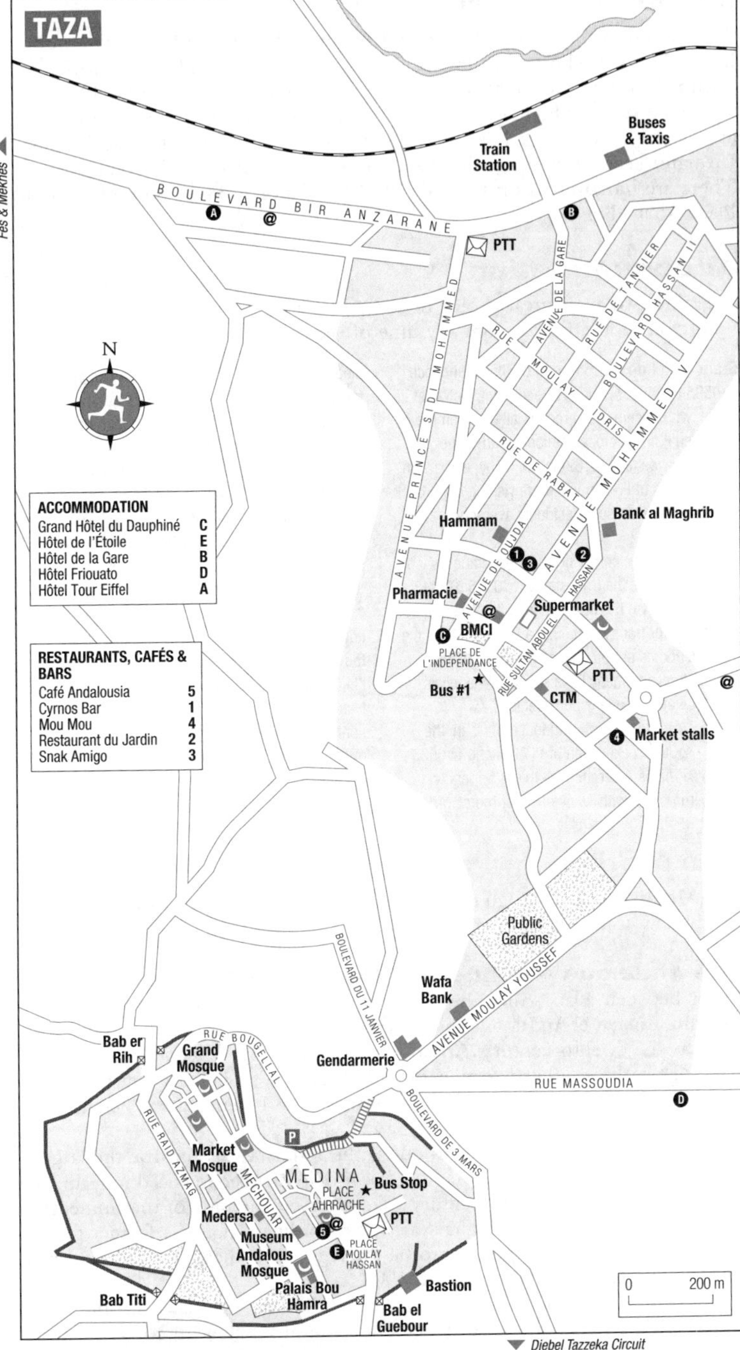
TAZA
Fes & Meknes
Al Hoceima, Nador & Oujda
Djebel Tazzeka Circuit
Train Station
Buses & Taxis
BOULEVARD BIR ANZARANE
PTT
AVENUE PRINCE SIDI MOHAMMED
AVENUE DE LA GARE
RUE DE TANGIER
BOULEVARD HASSAN II
RUE MOULAY IDRIS
RUE DE RABAT
AVENUE MOHAMMED V
Hammam
Bank al Maghrib
AVENUE DE OUJDA
AVENUE HASSAN
Pharmacie
Supermarket
BMCI
RUE SULTAN ABOU EL
PLACE DE L'INDEPENDANCE
Bus #1
CTM
Market stalls
ACCOMMODATION
Grand Hôtel du Dauphiné C
Hôtel de l'Étoile E
Hôtel de la Gare B
Hôtel Friouato D
Hôtel Tour Eiffel A
RESTAURANTS, CAFÉS & BARS
Café Andalousia 5
Cyrnos Bar 1
Mou Mou 4
Restaurant du Jardin 2
Snak Amigo 3
Public Gardens
BOULEVARD DU 11 JANVIER
Wafa Bank
AVENUE MOULAY YOUSSEF
Gendarmerie
RUE MASSOUDIA
BOULEVARD DE 3 MARS
Bab er Rih
RUE BOUGELLAL
Grand Mosque
RUE RAID AZMAG
Market Mosque
MECHOUAR
MEDINA
PLACE AHRRACHE
Bus Stop
Medersa
Museum
Andalous Mosque
PLACE MOULAY HASSAN
Palais Bou Hamra
Bastion
Bab Titi
Bab el Guebour
0 200 m
www.roughguides.com

Arrival and information

Several buses run between **Place de l'Indépendance** and **Place Ahrrache**, in the Medina. The **train station** and adjacent **bus stand** and **grand taxi** terminals are at the north end of the Ville Nouvelle, 1km from Place de l'Indépendance, which is where CTM services will drop you. Petits taxis are available for rides between the stations, Ville Nouvelle and Medina. **Internet** access is available at several places around Place de l'Indépendance. There are **hammams** off Place de l'Indépendance at 34 Av d'Oujda and off Place Ahrrache.

Accommodation

Taza doesn't have a great choice of accommodation – and there's no campsite – but you should find a room any time of year.

Grand Hôtel du Dauphiné Pl de l'Indépendance ⓣ0535 673567. An old Art Deco hotel, well past its prime, with decent-sized rooms, all of which are en suite. You'll find a cross-sectional plan of the Friouato caves (see p.169) in the lobby, along with some photos of French explorers visiting them back in 1951. There's also a decidedly average restaurant. ❸

Hôtel de la Gare corner of Bd bir Anzarane & Av de la Gare, opposite the train station ⓣ0535 672448, ⓕ0535 670844. The best option in the Ville Nouvelle and handy for transport though a long haul from the Medina. Rooms are off a small courtyard with a banana tree, and many have showers and toilets, and hot water mornings and evenings. ❷

Hôtel de l'Étoile Pl Moulay Hassan, the southern extension of Pl Ahrrache ⓣ0535 270179. This is a bargain cheapie – a friendly, family-run place with twelve decent rooms off a tiled courtyard. The nearby hammam compensates for the absence of showers. There's not much in the way of places to eat round here but there are kitchen facilities for self-catering. ❶

Hôtel Friouato Rue Massoudia ⓣ0535 672593, ⓕ0535 672244. A charmless concrete outpost, set in its own grounds amid the scrubland between the Ville Nouvelle and Medina. Still, there's a functional swimming pool, a bar and a restaurant. ❹

Hôtel Tour Eiffel Bd bir Anzarane ⓣ0535 671562, ⓕ0535 671563. A slightly overpriced three-star hotel, with a scale model of the Parisian icon above the front door, located a petit taxi ride from Pl de l'Indépendance. The rooms boast all mod cons but lack character. However, the restaurant, open to nonresidents is worth a try, with a good selection of fish specialities, like *friture de poisson*. Taxi circuits of Djebel Tazzeka can be arranged from here, starting at 250dh. ❹

The Medina

The **Medina** is easy enough to navigate, though you may need to ask directions for the few scattered sites.

The Andalous Mosque and Palais Bou Hamra

From between Place Ahrrache and its southern extension, **Place Moulay Hassan**, Zenqat el Andalous, which starts roughly opposite the post office, runs west to the twelfth-century **Andalous Mosque**. The mosque is the largest building in the southern section of the Medina – though its courtyards are characteristically well concealed from outside view. The minaret is best viewed from the Mechouar.

To the rear of the Andalous Mosque is the **Palais Bou Hamra**, the largely ruined residence of Bou Hamra, the *Rogui* or pretender to the throne in the early years of the twentieth century. Like most protagonists of the immediate pre-colonial period, Bou Hamra was an extraordinary figure, a former forger, conjurer and saint, who claimed to be the legitimate Shereefian heir and had himself proclaimed Sultan at Taza in 1902.

The name Bou Hamra – "man on the she-donkey" – recalled his means of travel round the countryside, where he won his followers by performing "miracles". One of these involved talking to the dead, which he perfected by the timely burying of a disciple, who would then communicate through a concealed straw; the pronouncements over, Bou Hamra flattened the straw with his foot (presumably not part of the original deal) and allowed the amazed villagers to dig up the by-then-dead witness.

Bou Hamra's own death – after his capture by Sultan Moulay Hafid – was no less melodramatic. He was brought to Fes in a small cage on the back of a camel, fed to the court lions (who refused to eat him), and was eventually shot and burned. Both Gavin Maxwell and Walter Harris give graphic accounts (see "Books" in Contexts, p.601 & p.603).

You can get a taste of more recent history at the museum on the Mechouar (daily 10am–5pm; free), a small but poignant collection of photos, newspaper cuttings and artefacts.

The souks and Grand Mosque

Taza's **souks** branch off to either side of the main street (by now Rue Koubet), midway between the Andalous and Grand Mosque. Since there are few tourists, these are very much working markets, free of the artificial "craft" goods so often found. The **granary** and the covered stalls of the **kissaria** are also worth a look, in the shadow of the **Market Mosque** (Djemaa es Souk).

Taza's **Grand Mosque** is historically one of the most interesting buildings in the country, though, like that of the Andalous, it is so discreetly screened that it's difficult for non-Muslims to gain any glimpse of the interior. Founded in the twelfth century by the Almohad sultan Abd el Moumen, it is probably the oldest Almohad structure in existence, predating even the partially ruined mosque at Tin Mal (see p.407), with which it shares most stylistic features.

Bab er Rih and the bastions

Above the Medina, at **Bab er Rih** (Gate of the Winds), it is possible to get some feeling for Taza's historic and strategic significance. You can see up the valley towards the Taza Gap: the Djebel Tazzeka and the Middle Atlas on one side, and the reddish earth of the Rif behind on the other.

The actual gate now leads nowhere and looks somewhat lost below the road, but it is Almohad in origin and design. So, too, is most of the circuit of walls, which you can follow round by way of a **bastion** (added by Moulay Ismail, in Spanish style) back to Place Moulay Hassan.

Eating and drinking

Most of the **cafés and restaurants** are around **Place de l'Indépendance**. The *Restaurant du Jardin*, a block northeast at 46 Rue Sultan Abou el Hassan, opposite the Bank al Maghrib (daily noon–midnight) offers pizzas as well as tasty tajines. Similar menus are available at *Snak Amigo*, next door to the *Cyrnos Bar*, and *Mou Mou*, which also serves panini and shawarma, on Boulevard Moulay Youssef. Good street food is to be had from stalls in the market around the mosque and there are several good **patisseries** near the centre. Rue de Fes has a small **supermarket**.

In the **Medina**, you won't find any restaurants as such, though shops around Place Ahrrache will sort you a sandwich. A good place for a mint tea or a coffee-and-croissant breakfast is the *Café Andalousia*, above *Laiterie Ahrrache* on the south side of Place Ahrrache, overlooking the square and next door to *La Paix* **patisserie**. Nearer the Grand Mosque, you will find a couple of cafés with fantastic views overlooking the town and beyond.

The rather forlorn *Hôtel Friouato* has a bar, as does the *Hôtel du Dauphiné*. The latter has off-putting mirrored windows, and women may feel uncomfortable, but there are a few tables on the pavement outside. You could also try *Cyrnos Bar*.

Moving on

Taza is quite a transport junction, with good connections west to Fes, east to Oujda and north to Nador and Al Hoceima. Grands taxis and all buses other than CTM services leave from right by the train station.

For **Fes** there are a wide choice of options. Grands taxis run throughout the day (just ask and wait for a place), arriving in Fes at Bab Ftouh. Fes is also served by four daily trains, plus a number of buses. **Oujda** and **Nador** are easiest reached by train, though there are buses, too.

For the **Rif**, most buses leave very early in the morning. There are plenty to **Nador** via Taourirt, **Al Hoceima** via Aknoul and to Oujda. From Aknoul you can catch sporadic grands taxis across the southern slopes of the Rif to Taounate on the Route de l'Unité.

CTM buses leave from Place de l'Indépendance with daily services to Al Hoceima and Nador (9pm), Oujda (2.30pm) and Tangier (10.30pm); plus two to Rabat and Casablanca and four to Fes.

The Cirque du Djebel Tazzeka and beyond

A loop of some 123km around Taza, the **Cirque du Djebel Tazzeka** is really a car-driver's route, with its succession of mountain views, marking a transition between the Rif and Middle Atlas. However, it has a specific "sight" in the immense **Gouffre du Friouato** (**Friouato Caves**), 22km from Taza, and the whole route is fertile ground for bird-watching and other wildlife (see box below). If you don't have transport, a place in a grand taxi from Taza will cost 15dh each way.

The **road** starts out curling around below Taza's Medina before climbing to a narrow valley of almond and cherry orchards. Twelve kilometers out of Taza, the *Café Ras el Ma* is worth a pit-stop not so much for its workaday menu of Moroccan staples and sandwiches as for the aerial views of the village afforded by its shaded terrace. Beyond here, the road, prone to rock avalanches but generally in good condition, loops towards the first pass (at 1198m), passing some great picnic spots and eventually emerging onto the Chiker Plateau. Here, in exceptionally wet years, the **Dayat Chiker** appears as a broad, shallow lake.

Wildlife in the Djebel Tazzeka

The **Djebel Tazzeka National Park** is one of northern Morocco's most rewarding wildlife sites, positioned, as it is, at the point where the Rif merges with the Middle Atlas. The range's lower slopes are covered in cork oak, the prime commercial crop of this area, and interspersed with areas of mixed woodland containing holm oak, the pink-flowered cistus and the more familiar bracken.

These woodland glades are frequented by a myriad of **butterflies** from late May onwards; common varieties include knapweed, ark green fritillaries and Barbary skippers. The forest floor also provides an ideal habitat for **birds** such as the multi-coloured hoopoe, with its identifying crest, and the trees abound with the calls of wood pigeon, nuthatch, short-toed treecreeper and various titmice. The roadside telegraph lines also provide attractive hunting perches for such brightly coloured inhabitants as rollers and shrikes, both woodchat and great grey, who swoop on passing insects and lizards with almost gluttonous frequency.

More often than not, though, it is just a fertile saucer, planted with cereals; geographers will recognize its formation as a classic limestone polje.

At this point, the road divides; to reach the Friouato caves, take the right fork – the left leads to Meghraoua and Midelt (see below). After 4km, midway along the polje, you'll pass a sign to the **Gouffre du Friouato** (daily 6am–10.30pm), 500m to the right of the road. The cave complex, starting 300m below ground level, is said to be the deepest in North Africa – and it feels it, entered by descending into a huge naturally lit "pot", over 30m wide, with five hundred wall-clinging steps down to a scree-filled base. The sense of descending into the entrails of the earth is exhilarating. The charming Youness Kassimi (☎0613 267185) is the official guide and is usually found hanging around near the cave's entrance. He charges 200dh for an exploratory trip 2km into the cave, for a maximum of five people, and rents out waterproofs, including shoes and a hard hat, for 50dh per person. Warm clothing is essential. Alternatively, you can go as far as the base of the steps unaccompanied for 5dh and come back. The complex has hardly been developed but there is a small café, and a map of the system is on sale. You can stay in simple tents nearby for 100dh.

At **Bab Bou Idir**, a low-key *éstivage* site 8.5km from Friouato, there is an office, café and campsite (open July–Aug) for the **Djebel Tazzeka National Park** (see box opposite). There are several good walks from here, from twenty-minute rambles to eight-hour hikes.

The most dramatic and scenic stretch of the cirque is undoubtedly the **ascent of Djebel Tazzeka** itself. It can be reached by driving 9km up the *piste* that turns off 15km beyond Bab Bou Idir and serves a communication mast at the summit. The view from the top, encased in forests of cedars, stretches to the Rif and to much of the eastern Middle Atlas. Slightly further on from the turn-off is a picnic site, *Vallée des Cerfs* (Valley of the Stags), set in amongst the cork trees. The road wends on pleasantly, through cork oak forests where cork production is much in evidence, to rejoin the Fes–Taza road at Sidi Abdallah Des Rhiata.

A route to Midelt

For anyone with sturdy transport, there is an adventurous route **through the Middle Atlas to Midelt**. The start of this is the left fork (R507) at the beginning of the Chiker Plateau described opposite and above; it is paved road as far as Meghraoua, where a very rough dirt road takes over. This road eventually hits the R502 a few kilometres south of Boulemane; from here you follow the road all the way south to Midelt (see p.252).

Taza to Oujda

The route from **Taza to Oujda** is as bare as it looks on the map: a semi-desert plain, broken by little more than the odd roadside town. Nonetheless, if you've got time to spare, and transport, there are a couple of recommendable detours.

Msoun

MSOUN, 29km east of Taza, and 3km north of the main road, is the first point of interest. The village, inhabited by a hundred or so members of the semi-nomadic Haoura tribe, is built within a **kasbah**, dating to the reign of Moulay Ismail (1672–1727), which is still turreted and complete on three sides. You can view its original rainwater cistern and grain silos, alongside the settlement's shop, post office and mosque.

Back on the main road, just opposite the track to Msoun, is the *Motel La Kasbah* (☎0535 674651; ❶), a friendly place for a meal or overnight stop.

Guercif, and the Bou Mazouz Cascades

At the agricultural centre of **Guercif**, 37km from Taza, is another small **hotel**, the *Hôtel Howary* (☎0535 625062; ❷); it's a modest, friendly place with a reasonable restaurant at street level. There are also a number of grill café-restaurants surrounding the main roundabout.

The **Bou Mazouz Cascades** are reached by turning north for 9km along the N19 towards the Melga el Ouidane barrage. In contrast to the barren landscape either side of the main Taza road, this takes you past orange and olive orchards watered by the Oued Za. Look for a small mosque on the right; leave the road at this point and follow a rough track 100m to the waterfalls – you can swim in a natural pool here, and camp beside it if you want. A proposed new railway bridge may eventually mar its peace but in the meantime it's a great place for a dip.

Taourirt

TAOURIRT, the largest town along the route, was the crossroads between the old north–south caravan route linking Melilla and the ancient kingdom of Sijilmassa (see p.471), and the Taza corridor between Morocco and Algeria.

For travellers it is a useful transport junction, with trains north to Nador connecting reasonably well with arrivals from Oujda or Fes. If you need to break your journey here, try the *Hôtel Mansour*, just off the roundabout in the centre of town (☎0536 694003; ❶). Taourirt itself is of little interest, save for its large **Sunday souk**, but you might like to explore the peaceful **Za Gorges**, about 6km southeast from the centre. The road isn't marked so you'll have to ask for directions.

Oujda

Open and easy-going, with a large and active university, **OUJDA** has that rare quality in Moroccan cities – nobody makes demands on your instinct for self-preservation. After the Rif, it is a surprise to see women in public again, and to re-enter a Gallic atmosphere – as you move out of what used to be Spanish Morocco into the old French Protectorate zone. Morocco's easternmost town, Oujda was the capital of French Maroc Orient and an important trading centre.

With its strategic location at the crossroads of eastern and southern routes across Morocco and Algeria, Oujda, like Taza, was always vulnerable to invasion and has frequently been the focus of territorial claims. Founded in the tenth century by Berber chieftain Ziri Ben Attia, it was occupied for parts of the thirteenth and fourteenth centuries by the Ziyanids, whose capital at Tlemcen is today just across the Algerian border. From 1727 until the early nineteenth century Oujda was under Turkish rule – the only town in present-day Morocco to have been part of the Ottoman Empire. Following the French defeat of the Ottomans in Algeria, France twice occupied the town prior to its incorporation within the Moroccan Protectorate in 1912, an early and prolonged association, which remains tangible in the streets and attitudes.

In more recent years, the town's proximity to the Algerian border and distance from the government in Rabat led to a reputation for dissidence and unrest.

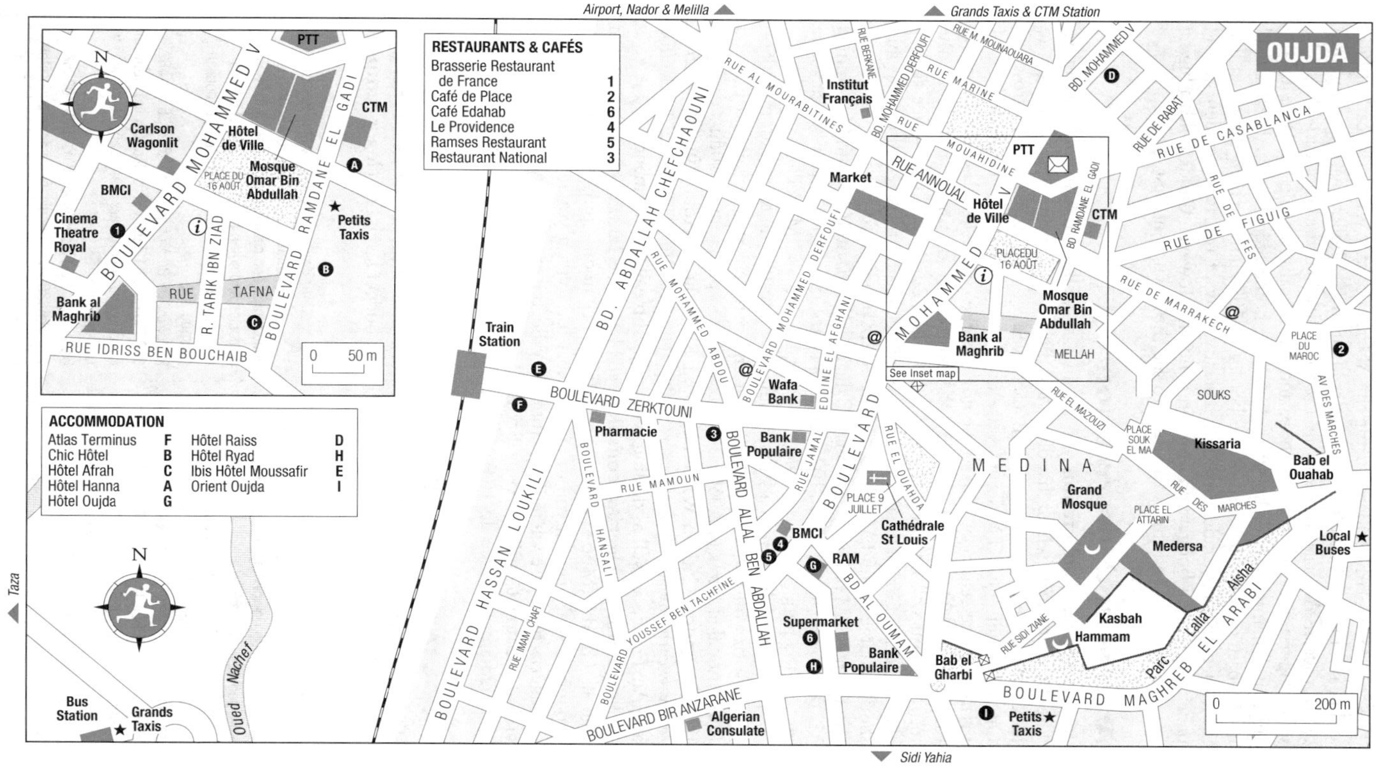

OUJDA

Airport, Nador & Melilla
Grands Taxis & CTM Station
Sidi Yahia
Taza

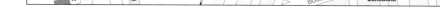

RESTAURANTS & CAFÉS

Brasserie Restaurant de France	1
Café de Place	2
Café Edahab	6
Le Providence	4
Ramses Restaurant	5
Restaurant National	3

ACCOMMODATION

Atlas Terminus	F	Hôtel Raiss	D
Chic Hôtel	B	Hôtel Ryad	H
Hôtel Afrah	C	Ibis Hôtel Moussafir	E
Hôtel Hanna	A	Orient Oujda	I
Hôtel Oujda	G		

PTT
CTM
Hôtel de Ville
Mosque Omar Bin Abdullah
Place du 16 Août
Carlson Wagonlit
BMCI
Cinema Theatre Royal
Petits Taxis
Bank al Maghrib
Boulevard Mohammed V
Boulevard Ramdane El Gadi
R. Tarik Ibn Ziad
Rue Tafna
Rue Idriss Ben Bouchaib
0 50 m

Train Station
Institut Français
Market
Wafa Bank
Bank Populaire
Pharmacie
Supermarket
RAM
Cathédrale St Louis
Place 9 Juillet
Algerian Consulate
Bus Station
Grands Taxis
Oued Nachef
Medina
Mellah
Souks
Kissaria
Grand Mosque
Medersa
Kasbah
Hammam
Bab el Gharbi
Bab el Ouahab
Local Buses
Place du Maroc
Place Souk el Ma
Place el Attarin
Parc Lalla Aisha
See Inset map
Rue Al Mourabitines
Rue Berkane
Bd. Mohammed Derfoufi
Rue M. Mounaouara
Rue Marine
Bd. Mohammed V
Rue de Rabat
Rue de Casablanca
Rue de Figuig
Rue de Fes
Rue de Marrakech
Av des Marches
Rue des Marches
Rue Annoual
Mouahidine
Bd. Abdallah Chefchaouni
Rue Mohammed Abdou
Boulevard Mohammed Derfoufi
Eddine el Afghani
Boulevard Zerktouni
Boulevard Allal Ben Abdallah
Rue Jamal
Rue el Ouahda
Rue el Mazouzi
Rue Sidi Ziane
Bd Al Oumam
Rue Mamoun
Boulevard Hansali
Boulevard Youssef Ben Tachfine
Rue Imam Chafi
Boulevard Hassan Loukili
Boulevard Bir Anzarane
Boulevard Maghreb el Arabi
0 200 m

This was particularly evident during the Algerian border war in the early 1960s, and again, in the 1980s, in a series of student strikes. Following the restoration of Moroccan–Algerian relations in 1988 the city became truly pan-Maghrebi, with Algerians coming in to shop, and Moroccans sharing in some of the cultural dynamism of neighbouring Oran, the home of *raï* music. Alas, this is all in the past since the closure of the border in 1994, after which the town lost most of its passing trade, including a steady flow of tourists – evident in the paucity of decent budget and mid-range hotels. However, Oujda holds a big *raï* festival each July and this is the time to see the town at its best.

Arrival and information

Arriving at the **train station** you are in easy walking distance of the centre. The **bus station**, which handles most services, is more of a walk (or an inexpensive petit taxi ride), 500m southwest of the train station, across the Oued Nachef, but CTM services use their own terminal on Boulevard Omar Errifi near the cemetery, 1km to the north of the centre. Oujda–Angad **airport** (Ⓣ0536 682084, Ⓕ0536 684462) is 12km north of Oujda and inside the terminal you will find desks for Avis, Hertz and Europcar, a post-office agency and an ATM. Grands taxis are usually waiting outside to meet all arrivals and should charge around 150dh to take up to six people into the city.

In town, RAM has an office alongside the *Hôtel Oujda* on Boulevard Mohammed V (Ⓣ0536 683909, Ⓕ0536 710227), and operates daily flights to Casablanca. There are also less frequent direct services to Paris, Brussels and Marseilles.

For **car rentals** there is a Budget office just outside the train station (Ⓣ0660 174120) or you could try the efficient and privately run Benahmed Cars on Rue Anoual el Baraka (Ⓣ0661 363600; expect to pay around 300dh a day). The **travel agency** Carlson Wagonlit, facing Place du 16 Aout (Ⓣ0536 682520, Ⓦwww.carlsonwagonlit.com), acts as the agent for Europcar, Royal Air Maroc and Air France as well as dealing with general travel arrangements.

There is still an **Algerian consulate** at 11 Rue de Taza, about 300m west of Bab el Gharbi (Mon–Thurs 8am–3.30pm, Fri noon–2pm; Ⓣ0536 710452), though its staff may tell you to go to Rabat for a visa if you're intending to fly to Algeria from elsewhere. The Hôtel de Ville, the **post office**, several **banks** and the **tourist office** (Mon–Fri 8.30am–5.30pm; Ⓣ0536 682036) are all grouped around Place du 16 Août. **Internet** access is widely available.

Accommodation

There are many hotels to choose from; sadly, most of them have seen better days and good value is hard to find, particularly at budget level. The closest **campsite** is in Saïdia (see p.162).

Atlas Terminus Pl de la Gare Ⓣ0536 711010, Ⓦwww.hotelsatlas.com Top-notch five star with all the facilities you'd expect for the price including spa, pool and gym. ❼

Chic Hotel 34 Bd Ramdane el Gadi Ⓣ0539 690566. The name is wildly optimistic but the rooms are fairly clean, if noisy. ❷

Hôtel Afrah 15 Rue Tafna Ⓣ0536 686533. Located on a busy pedestrianized street, this has comfortable en-suite rooms, heated in winter, and great views across the Medina from its rooftop terrace. ❷

Hôtel Hanna 132 Rue de Marrakech Ⓣ&Ⓕ0536 686003. The best budget option; neat and clean rooms, some of them with balconies and some en suite. The vast terrace overlooks the minaret of the Omar Bin Abdullah mosque. ❶

Hôtel Oujda Bd Mohammed V Ⓣ0536 684482, Ⓕ0536 685064. Funky '70s decor in the lobby and a rooftop bar. Rooms are a bit shabby but have TVs, a/c and baths. ❸

Hôtel Raiss Bd Mohammed V Ⓣ0536 703058, Ⓕ036 688008. A friendly, clean and comfortable hotel with TVs and heating in all rooms – those at the back are quietest. ❸

Hôtel Ryad Av Idriss al Akbar ☎0536 688353. Clean rooms and very friendly staff, there is a restaurant, piano bar and a disco, all open to nonresidents. Good fun. ❹

Ibis Hôtel Moussafir Bd Abdellah Chefchaouini, near the train station ☎0536 688202, Ⓦwww.ibishotel.com. Spotless but dull rooms, swimming pool, bar and pleasant gardens in this reliable chain hotel. ❹

Orient Oujda Bd Maghreb el Arabi ☎0536 700606, Ⓦwww.hotelsatlas.com. Chic rooms, large pool, two bars and a hammam/spa; this offers good value, but the food is mediocre. The *Alcazar* nightclub next door (daily 11pm–3am) is open to nonresidents. ❻

The Town

Oujda consists of the usual **Medina** and **Ville Nouvelle**, the latter highly linear in its layout, having started out as a military camp. The **Medina**, walled on three sides, lies right in the heart of town and is largely a French reconstruction – obvious by the ease with which you can find your way around. It has an enjoyably active air, with **Place du 16 Août**, the town's main square, at its northwest corner.

Entering from **Bab el Ouahab**, the principal gate, you'll be struck by the amazing variety of food – on both café and market stalls. Olives are Oujda specialities, and especially wonderful if you're about after the September harvest. In the old days, more or less up until the French occupation, Bab el Ouahab was the gate where the heads of criminals were displayed.

Exploring the quarter, a good route to follow from the gate is straight down the main street towards **Place el Attarin**, flanked by a *kissaria* (covered market) and a grand *fondouk*. At the far end of the souks you come upon **Souk el Ma**, the irrigation souk, where the supply of water used to be regulated and sold by the hour. Walking on from here, you'll arrive back at Place du 16 Août.

Running along the outside of the Medina walls, the **Parc Lalla Aisha** is a pleasant area to seek midday shade. Following it round to the west takes you to the Bab el Gharbi from which Rue el Ouahda runs north to the old French **Cathédrale Saint Louis** (Mass Sat 6.30pm & Sun 9am). The fonts are dry, and the statue niches empty, but there is a beautiful chapel; for admission, ring at the door of the presbytery at the back, on Rue d'Azila.

Sidi Yahia

SIDI YAHIA, 6km east of Oujda, is a rather unimpressive little oasis for most of the year, with only a rundown park area and a few cafés. However, it's a place of some veneration, purportedly housing the tomb of John the Baptist. There are spectacular **moussems** held here in August and September when almost every shrub and tree in the oasis is festooned with little pieces of cloth, a ritual as lavish and extraordinary as anything in the Catholic Church. There are no regular bus services; take a grand taxi and haggle over the price depending on how long you want to stay.

Eating, drinking and entertainment

Oujda has a strong cultural life and is one of the most enjoyable Moroccan cities in which to while away an evening. Hustlers don't really feature here and the bars and restaurants are sociable and open places. Most of the town's **bars** are in the hotels. For **cafés/patisseries**, there's the *Café Edahab*, next to *Hôtel Ryad* on Avenue Idriss al Akbar; *Le Providence*, on Boulevard Mohammed V, serves possibly the best espresso in town – and fresh pastries to match. For groceries, there is an unnamed, but well-stocked, **supermarket** on Avenue Idriss al Akbar, opposite *Café Edahab*.

The Theatre Royal **cinema** on Rue Okba Ibn Nafia, opposite the Banque al Maghrib on the other side of Boulevard Mohammed V, has daily showings of foreign and Moroccan films in French. The Institut Français at 3 Rue de Berkane (ⓣ0536 684404, ⓦwww.ambafrance-ma.org/institut/oujda) organizes an eclectic selection of **cultural events** – from audiovisual talks to exhibitions, theatre and musical performances by local and visiting artists.

The focus of evening activity is **Bab el Ouahab**, around which you can get all kinds of grilled food from stalls. On the other side of the Medina there are plenty of eating places on, or just off, **Boulevard Mohammed V** and **Boulevard Zerktouni**.

Brasserie Restaurant de France Bd Mohammed V. This is one of the fancier places in town, offering a selection of mostly French fish and meat dishes. It's located upstairs from a café-patisserie, and with a nightclub attached. Licensed. Daily 6–11pm. Moderate.

Café de Place Pl du Maroc. Busy café/restaurant serving good coffee and decent food. Daily 8am–10pm.

Ramses Restaurant 2 Bd Mohammed V. The downstairs restaurant (daily noon–11pm) serves mainly pizza and panini whilst the upstairs café and patisserie (daily 5am–11pm) has a great breakfast menu and fresh juices. Cheap to moderate.

Restaurant National Bd Zerktouni, corner of Bd Allal Ben Abdallah. A good place for tajines and meat dishes; things get lively here at weekends. Daily 7am–11pm. Cheap.

Moving on

Various companies run services to most destinations from the main **bus station** across the Oued Nachef. You are unlikely to wait more than an hour or so for a bus to the most immediate destinations regardless of the time of day. CTM runs daily buses to Casablanca via Rabat and Tangier – both go via Taza, Fes and Meknes. Their ticket office is just off Place du 16 Août. Four **trains** daily leave for Fes via Taourirt and Taza with connections on to Nador, Meknes, Marrakesh, Rabat, Casablanca and Tangier.

Grands taxis for Ahfir, Berkane, Nador, Al Hoceima and the airport leave from the junction of Boulevard Mohammed Derfouti and Rue Ibn Abdelmalek; those for Taourirt and Taza leave by the main bus station – you'll have to change at Taza for Fes, and there for most points beyond.

The **airport**, Oujda–Angad, is 12km north, off the N2 (ⓣ0536 682084, ⓕ0536 684462). In town, RAM has an office alongside the *Hôtel Oujda* on Boulevard Mohammed V (ⓣ0536 683909, ⓕ0536 710227), and operates daily flights to Casablanca. There are also less frequent direct services to Paris, Brussels and Marseilles.

South to Figuig

In past years, before the eruption of civil war in Algeria, there was a well-established travel route from Oujda, south to the ancient date palm oasis of **Figuig**, and across from there into the Algerian Sahara. Whilst the latter is no longer a possibility, those into isolated journeys might still want to consider the route from **Oujda** to **Figuig** – and on from here to the southern Moroccan oasis town of **Er Rachidia** (see p.464).

If you're on for the trip, be warned it's a long, hot haul: 369km from Oujda to Figuig, and a further 393km to Er Rachidia. You can travel by bus – there is a bus every other day, returning to Oujda the following day or, if you have transport, you can drive: the road is sealed all the way. Whichever way you travel, expect to explain yourself at a number of military checkpoints: this is a sensitive border area. See p.37 for tips in dealing with checkpoint police.

The route

En route between Oujda and Figuig there are just a few roadside settlements and mining towns – for coal, copper, manganese and zinc. If you are driving, **Aïn Benimathar**, 83km from Oujda, is a good point to break the journey: the village has a group of kasbahs, an important (and ancient) **Monday souk**, and some grill-cafés. About 4km to its west is a small oasis, **Ras el Aïn**, with a highly seasonal waterfall.

Another possible stop could be **Tendrara**, 198km from Oujda, a larger settlement with an important **Thursday souk**; it has a traditional marketplace in the centre and sheep and goats corralled on the outskirts. Again, there are grill-cafés.

At 241km, you reach **Bouarfa**, the region's administrative centre and transport hub, with buses to Er Rachidia (as well as Figuig and Oujda), and a couple of hotels. For details of **Figuig and the route to Er Rachidia**, see pp.478–479.

Travel details

Trains

Oujda to: Casablanca (3 direct & 1 connecting daily; 10hr); Fes (4 daily; 5hr 30min); Guercif (4 daily; 2hr 30min); Marrakesh (2 connecting daily; 14hr); Meknes (3 daily; 7hr); Rabat (2 direct & 2 connecting daily; 9hr); Tangier (1 direct & 2 connecting daily; 12hr); Nador (1 connecting daily; 4hr 15min); Taourirt (4 daily; 1hr 45min); Taza (4 daily; 3hr 30min). There are no longer any passenger services from Oujda to Bouarfa; nor currently across the border to Algeria.

Taza to: Casablanca (3 direct & 1 connecting daily; 7hr); Fes (4 daily; 2hr); Guercif (4 daily; 1hr); Marrakesh (2 connecting daily; 10hr); Meknes (3 direct & 1 connecting daily; 3hr 15min); Nador (2 connecting daily; 4hr); Rabat (2 direct & 2 connecting daily; 6hr); Tangier (1 direct & 2 connecting daily; 8hr 20min);

Nador to: Casablanca (3 connecting daily; 10hr); Fes (2 connecting daily; 6hr); Meknes (3 connecting daily; 7hr); Oujda (1 connecting daily; 4hr 15min); Rabat (3 connecting daily; 11hr); Tangier (2 connecting daily; 12hr); Taourirt (3 direct daily; 2hr).

Buses

Berkane to: Casablanca (1 CTM daily; 12hr 15min); Fes (1 CTM daily; 7hr 15min); Meknes (1 CTM daily; 8hr 15min); Nador (19 daily; 1hr 30min); Oujda (20 daily; 1hr 30min); Rabat (1 CTM daily; 10hr 45min); Saïdia (4 daily; 1hr).

Al Hoceima to: Aknoul (1 daily; 1hr 30min); Casablanca (1 CTM daily; 12hr) via Rabat (9hr); Fes (2 CTM & 6 others daily; 5hr); Meknes (2 CTM & 1 other daily; 6hr); Nador (2 CTM & 6 others daily; 3hr); Oujda (2 CTM & 1 other daily; 4hr 30min); Tangier (2 CTM & 5 others daily; 6hr); Tetouan (2 CTM & 8 others daily; 5hr 30min) via Issaguen (3 daily; 2hr 30min) and Chefchaouen (2 CTM & 5 others; 4hr 30min).

Nador to: Aknoul (1 daily; 3hr 30min); Casablanca (2 CTM & 10 others daily; 12hr); Fes (2 CTM & 17 others daily; 5hr 30min); Guercif (at least one every hour; 3hr); Al Hoceima (3 CTM & 16 others daily; 3hr); Meknes (2 CTM & 5 others daily; 6hr 30mins; Oujda (1 CTM & 16 others daily; 2hr 30min); Rabat (1 CTM & 16 others daily; 9hr); Er Rachidia (2 daily; 14hr); Rissani (1 daily; 16hr); Saïdia (1 daily; 2hr); Tangier (1 CTM & 7 others daily; 12hr) via Tetouan (9hr 30min); Taourirt (4 ONCF/Supratours daily; 1hr 30min; connecting with train service to Fes, Meknes, Kenitra, Rabat & Casablanca); Taza (at least one every hour; 4hr).

Oujda to: Bouarfa/Figuig (every other day; 5hr/7hr); Casablanca (1 CTM & at least 7 others daily; 11hr) via Rabat (9hr 30min); Al Hoceima (1 CTM & 1 other daily; 8hr); Fes (3 CTM & 18 others daily; 6hr 15min); Meknes (1 CTM & 15 others daily; 7hr 15min); Nador (12 daily; 2hr 30min); Saïdia (2 daily; 1hr 30min); Taza (1 CTM & 15 others; 4hr).

Taza to: Aknoul (1 daily; 1hr 30min); Casablanca (2 CTM & 9 others daily; 7hr 30min) via Meknes (2hr 45min) and Rabat (6hr 15min); Fes (4 CTM daily & others roughly hourly; 2hr 30min); Al Hoceima (1 CTM & 1 other daily; 3hr 30min); Meknes (2 CTM & 3 others daily; 3hr 15min); Nador (at least one every hour; 4hr); Oujda (1 CTM daily & others roughly hourly; 3hr 30min); Tangier (1 CTM daily; 8hr).

Grands taxis

Berkane to: Nador (1hr 30min); Saïdia (45min); Oujda (50min); Taforalt (45min).
Al Hoceima to: Issaguen (2hr); Kalah Iris (1hr); Kassita (1hr); Nador (3hr); Oujda (5hr 30min). Occasionally direct to Fes (4hr); Targuist (1hr 30min); Taza (4hr 30min).
Bab Berret to: Issaguen (45min); Chefchaouen (1hr).
Issaguen (Ketama) to: Bab Berret (45min); Al Hoceima (1hr 45min); Taounate (1hr 20min); Targuist (45min).
Nador to: Beni Enzar (15min); Berkane (1hr 30min); Al Hoceima (2hr 45min); occasionally direct to Oujda (2hr 30min).
Oujda to: Ahfir (45min); Berkane (50min); Al Hoceima (5hr 30min); Taza (3hr). Occasionally direct to Nador (2hr).
Saïdia to: Ahfir (30min); Berkane (30min).
Taounate to: Fes (1hr 30min); Issaguen (1hr 20min).
Targuist to: Al Hoceima (1hr 30min); Issaguen (45min); Kalah Iris (45min).
Taza to: Aknoul (1hr); Fes (1hr 30min); Guercif (45min); Kassita (2hr); Oujda (3hr). Occasionally direct to Al Hoceima (2hr 45min).

Ferries

Al Hoceima to: Almería (2 daily June–Sept; 5hr).
Nador (Beni Enzar) to: Almería (13 weekly in winter, 3–4 daily in summer; 6–7hr); Sète (every four days in summer only; 36hr).
Melilla to: Málaga (1–2 daily; 8–9hr); Almería (1 daily, 2 daily in summer; 6hr).
For further details on ferry services, see pp.30–31.

Flights

Nador to: Casablanca (1 daily; 1hr 35min).
Oujda to: Casablanca (1–3 daily; 1hr 10min).

3

Meknes, Fes and the Middle Atlas

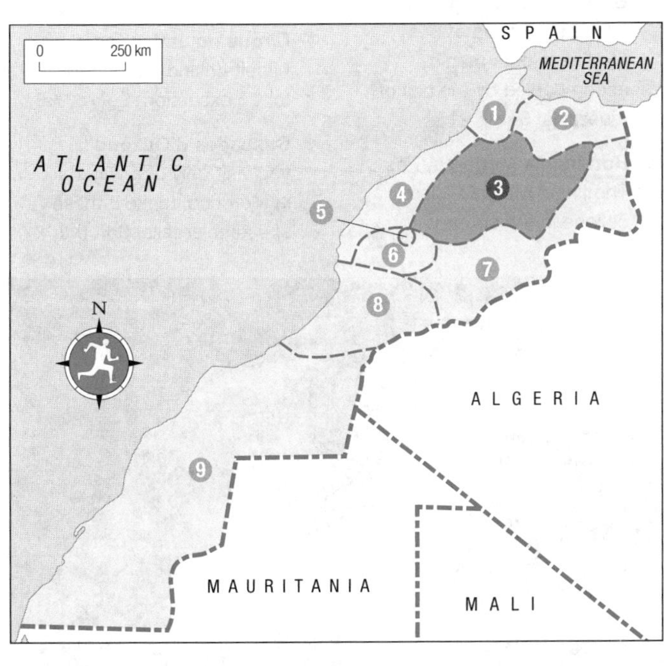

CHAPTER 3 **Highlights**

- **The souks of Meknes** Hassle-free and a pleasure to browse – don't miss the spice and sweet stalls. See p.191

- **Volubilis and Moulay Idriss** Remarkable Roman and Islamic sites that can be combined on an easy day-trip from Meknes. See p.195

- **Borj Nord at sunset** The fabled panorama of Fes Medina is pure magic accompanied by the call of muezzins. See p.215

- **Bou Inania Medersa, Fes** The finest Merenid Islamic college in the country, looking better than ever after renovation. See p.215

- **The tanneries, Fes** A little voyeuristic, but the view of these leather-tanning vats can have barely changed since medieval days. See p.223

- **Mibladene and El Ahouli** The off-road drive to these derelict mines is an adventure in itself. See p.255

- **Cirque du Jaffar** The classic Midelt driving route, perfect for an excursion. See p.256

- **Cascades d'Ouzoud** If you visit only one waterfall in Morocco, make it these spectacular falls. See p.263

▲ Meknes souk

3

Meknes, Fes and the Middle Atlas

The undoubted highlight of this chapter is **Fes**, the city that has for the past ten centuries stood at the heart of Moroccan history as both an imperial capital and intellectual as well as spiritual centre. Unique in the Arab world, preserving the appearance and much of the life of a medieval Islamic city, it boasts as many monuments as Morocco's other Imperial capitals combine, while the souks, extending for over a mile maintain the whole tradition of urban crafts. Neighbouring Meknes has an allure of its own, found throughout the city's pleasant souks and the architecturally rich streets of the sprawling imperial district. Just north of Meknes, the holy mountain town of Moulay Idriss and the impressive Roman ruins of Volubilis make for a rewarding day-trip.Heading south through the cedar-covered slopes and remote hinterlands of the **Middle Atlas**, there are two main routes. The most popular passes through the Berber market town of **Azrou** to emerge, via Beni Mellal and the dramatic **Cascades d'Ouzoud**, at Marrakesh. The second climbs southeast from Azrou towards **Midelt** before passing through great gorges to Er Rachidia and the vast date-palm oasis of Tafilalt – the beginning of a tremendous southern circuit (see p.463). A third route leaves the main Azrou–Marrakesh highway at **El Ksiba** and makes its tortuous way **across the Atlas** via Imilchil and the Todra Gorge to Tinerhir (see p.458).

Meknes

Cut in two by the wide river valley of the Oued Boufekrane, **MEKNES** is a prosperous provincial city with a notably relaxed and friendly atmosphere, due in part to a large student population. Monuments from its past – particularly the extraordinary creations of Moulay Ismail (see p.187) – justify a day's rambling exploration, as do the varied and busy souks of its Medina.Visitors en route to Fes will find Meknes a good introduction to the drama of its illustrious neighbour, whilst those arriving from Fes are sure to enjoy the reduced tempo. In addition, nearby **Volubilis** and **Moulay Idriss** can easily be reached by grands taxi.

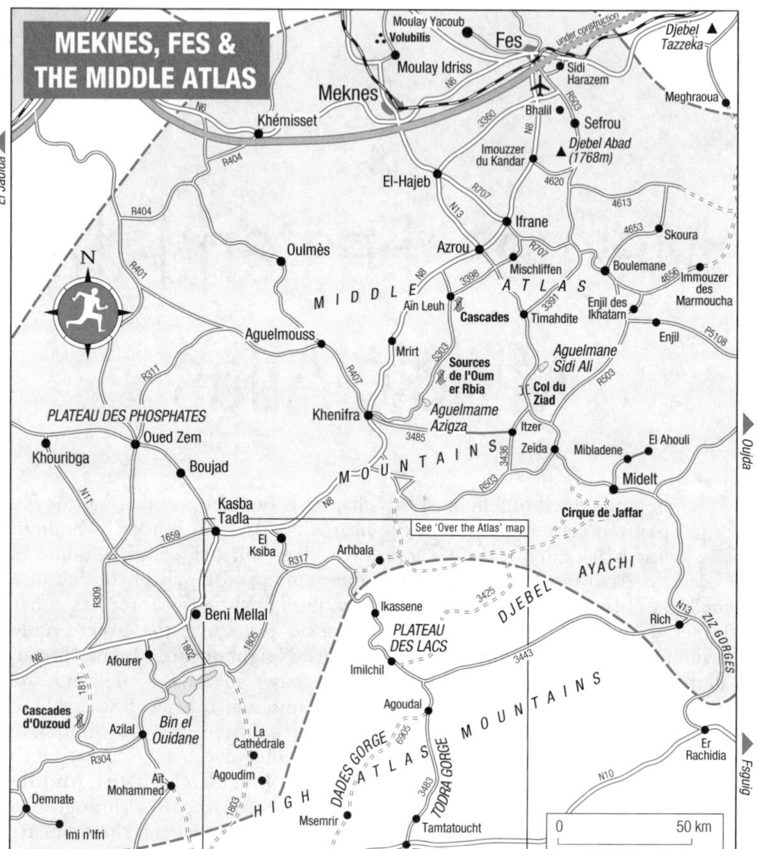

Orientation and information

Meknes is simpler than it looks on the map. Its **Ville Nouvelle** (*Hamriya* in Arabic) stretches along a slope above the east bank of the river; the **Medina** and its neighbouring **Mellah** (the old Jewish quarters) occupy the west bank, with the walls of Moulay Ismail's **Ville Impériale** edging away, seemingly forever, to their south. The focal point of the Medina – and a good place to fix your bearings – is **Place el Hedim**, remodelled in the 1990s into a pedestrian plaza with fountains, decorated arcades and shops. As an idea of distances, the walk between Place Administrative, at the heart of the Ville Nouvelle, and Place el Hedim takes around twenty minutes (12dh in a petit taxi).

The **tourist office** is at 27 Pl Administrative (Mon–Fri 8.30am–4.30pm; ⓣ0535 516022, ⓦwww.meknes-net.com), with unusually helpful staff and considerable, if sometimes dated, information on the noticeboard.

Arrival

Arriving by **bus** you'll be dropped either at the main **bus station** on the north side of the New Mellah just outside Bab el Khemis, or (if coming by CTM) at the **CTM bus station** on Avenue de Fes, east of the Ville Nouvelle.

The town's two **train stations** are both in the Ville Nouvelle. The **main station** is a kilometre away from the central area; a smaller, more convenient one, the **Gare el Amir Abdelkader**, is a couple of blocks from the centre (behind the *Hôtel Majestic*). Not all trains stop at the latter, so check first if you want to get on or off there.

Grands taxis from most destinations use a yard alongside the CTM bus station. Grands taxis from one or two local destinations use a yard below Place el Hedim in the Medina, and on Rue Omar el Moutahida in the Ville Nouvelle.

If you are **driving**, it's worth noting that traffic on Avenue Mohammed V and Avenue Allal Ben Abdallah is one-way, circulating anticlockwise. Parking near the Medina is available just west of Place el Hedim.

Accommodation

Meknes' hotels are concentrated in the **Ville Nouvelle**, which is the best choice for comfort (unless you opt for one of the riads in the **Medina** or the **Ville Impériale**) and proximity to most bars and restaurants. It's only a twenty-minute walk from there to the Medina, monuments and souks.

Booking accommodation is really only a necessity around the time of the Ben Aissa Mousseum (see box, p.192).

Medina and Ville Impériale

As ever, all the cheapies have pretty basic facilities, although the trade-off is their location just a few minutes from the sights.

Hôtel Agadir 9 Rue Dar Smen ⓣ0535 530141. Clean and friendly, with small, basic rooms mostly tucked away in odd crannies of an eccentric rambling building. Hot showers are available on the terrace (7dh), and there's a hammam nearby (see p.195). ❶

Hôtel Meknes 35 Rue Dar Smen ⓣ0535 535198. Down-to-earth hotel with rooms on two floors arranged around an inner courtyard. It's between *Hôtel Nouveau* and *Hôtel Regina*, and best as a fall-back if both are full. Cold showers. ❶

Hôtel Nouveau 65 Rue Dar Smen ⓣ0535 679317. Opposite the Banque Populaire, this claims to be the first hotel in the Medina (despite the name) and is certainly the cheapest. Helpful, basic facilities and no external windows. Hot showers available for 5dh. ❶

Hôtel Regina 19 Rue Dar Smen ⓣ0535 530280. This old hotel is a mite more expensive than its neighbours and has slightly larger, though just as basic, rooms with washbasins. Hot showers are available for 5dh. ❶

Maison d'hôte Riad 79 Ksar Chaacha ⓣ0535 530542, ⓦwwww.riadmeknes.com. Seven rooms in a modern but antique-filled complex attached to the *Restaurant Riad* (see p.193 for directions), individually decorated by theme – from sumptuous Arabic via a traditional tent to rustic Berber cottage. The style throughout is purest Moroccan, and created with traditional techniques and materials. There is also a decent sized pool in the garden. Includes breakfast. ❻

Maroc Hôtel 7 Rue Rouamzine ⓣ0535 530075. Cleanest and quietest of the Medina hotels; most rooms are pleasantly furnished and look onto a patio garden full of orange trees. There are hot showers (7am–noon & 7–11pm) and a hammam nearby (see p.195). Rooftop sleeping in summer for 50dh. ❷

Palais Didi 7 Dar el Kebira ⓣ0535 558590, ⓦwww.palaisdidi.com. A seventeenth-century palace tucked away in the Ville Impériale through Bab er Rih (follow signs), now an upmarket courtyard hotel from the owner of the *Restaurant Riad* (see p.193). Whiffs of chiffon on four-posters and zellij-tiled baths add romance to colourful rooms, all with a/c. Also has small pool. Includes breakfast. ❻

Riad Bahia Rue Tiberbarine, behind Dar Jamaï ⓣ0535 554541, ⓔcontact@ryad-bahia.com. Not as glamorous as those in Fes, this Medina riad is charming nevertheless, restored by local artisans following strict aesthetic and architectural guidelines. All rooms are en suite and have a/c, many are furnished with antique painted woodwork, yet the vibe is one of laid-back luxury. There's a small restaurant, open to nonresidents by reservation (see p.193). Includes breakfast. ❺

Riad Yacout 22 Pl Lalla Aouda ⓣ0535 533110, ⓦwww.riad-yacout-meknes.com. A slick new addition to the growing number of upscale riads in and around the Ville Impériale, well priced, tastefully decorated and equipped with a plunge pool and restaurant. Convenient for parking. ❺

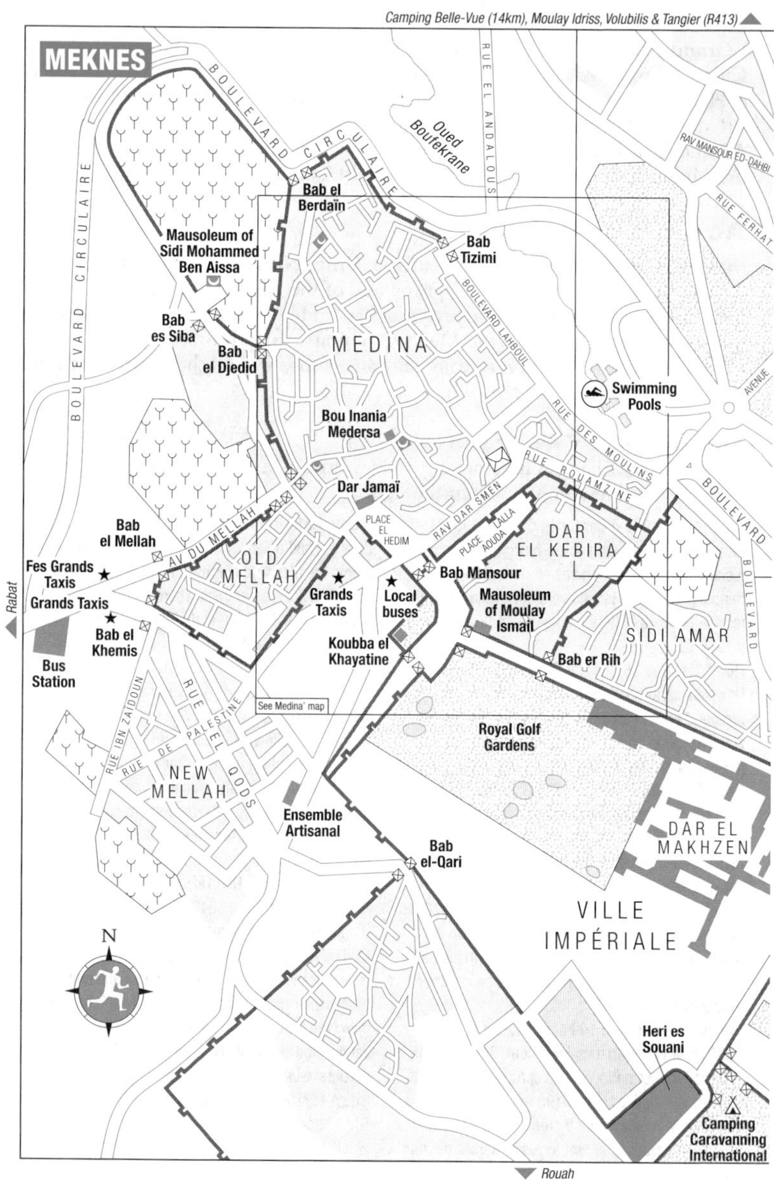
MEKNES
Camping Belle-Vue (14km), Moulay Idriss, Volubilis & Tangier (R413)
Rabat
Rouah
BOULEVARD CIRCULAIRE
RUE EL ANDALOUS
Oued Boufekrane
RAV MANSOUR ED-DAHBI
RUE FERHAT
AVENUE
Bab el Berdaïn
Bab Tizimi
Mausoleum of Sidi Mohammed Ben Aissa
Bab es Siba
Bab el Djedid
MEDINA
BOULEVARD LAHBOUL
Swimming Pools
RUE DES MOULINS
RUE ROUAMZINE
BOULEVARD
Bou Inania Medersa
Dar Jamaï
PLACE EL HEDIM
RAV DAR SMEN
PLACE LALLA AOUDA
DAR EL KEBIRA
Bab el Mellah
AV DU MELLAH
OLD MELLAH
Fes Grands Taxis
Grands Taxis
Grands Taxis
Local buses
Bab Mansour
Mausoleum of Moulay Ismail
SIDI AMAR
Bab el Khemis
Bus Station
Koubba el Khayatine
Bab er Rih
See Medina' map
RUE IBN ZAIDOUN
RUE DE PALESTINE
RUE EL QODS
Royal Golf Gardens
NEW MELLAH
Ensemble Artisanal
Bab el-Qari
DAR EL MAKHZEN
VILLE IMPÉRIALE
N
Heri es Souani
Camping Caravanning International

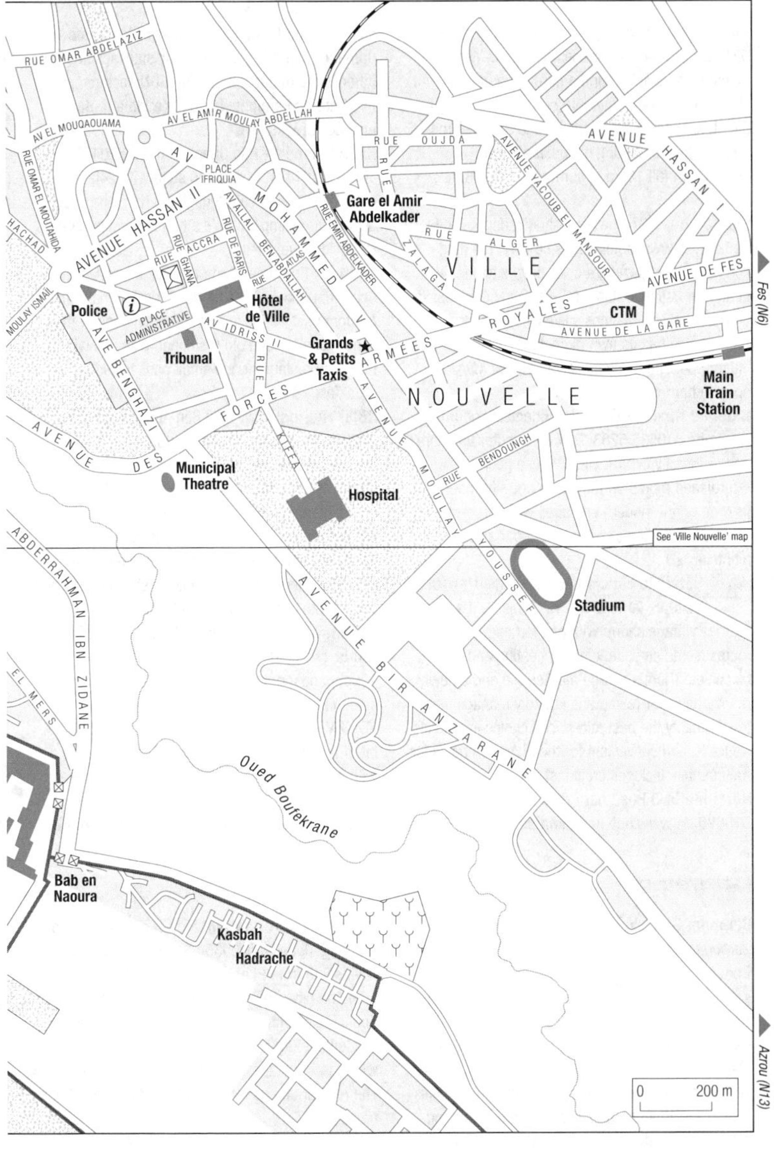
RUE OMAR ABDELAZIZ
AV EL MOUQAOUAMA
AV EL AMIR MOULAY ABDELLAH
RUE OMAR EL MOUTAHIDA
PLACE IFRIQUIA
AVENUE HASSAN II
MOHAMMED V
RUE ACCRA
RUE GHANA
RUE DE PARIS
AV ALLAL BEN ABDALLAH
RUE ATLAS
RUE EMIR ABDELKADER
Gare el Amir Abdelkader
RUE OUJDA
RUE ZALAGA
RUE ALGER
AVENUE YACOUB EL MANSOUR
AVENUE HASSAN I
VILLE
NOUVELLE
AVENUE DE FES
AVENUE DE LA GARE
ROYALES
CTM
Main Train Station
Fes (N6)
Police
PLACE ADMINISTRATIVE
Hôtel de Ville
Tribunal
AV IDRISS II
Grands & Petits Taxis
ARMÉES
AVE BENGHAZI
AVENUE DES FORCES
RUE KLEFA
AVENUE MOULAY YOUSSEF
RUE BENDOUNGH
Municipal Theatre
Hospital
See 'Ville Nouvelle' map
Stadium
AVENUE BIR ANZARANE
ABDERRAHMAN IBN ZIDANE
EL MERS
Oued Boufekrane
Bab en Naoura
Kasbah Hadrache
Azrou (N13)
0 200 m
MOULAY ISMAIL
HACHAD

Ville Nouvelle

Some of the prominent hotels in the Ville Nouvelle are fairly unsavoury; grubby or even used as brothels. Budget travellers may want to stick to the Medina's pensions, as a number of recent closures have made slim pickings of the cheap options.

Auberge de Jeunesse Av Okba Ibn Nafi ⓣ0535 524698, ⓔauberge_meknes@yahoo.fr. Well-maintained hostel around a garden courtyard, with single beds shoehorned into dorm rooms (50dh), plus functional doubles, triples and four-bed rooms and hot showers (5dh). It's open all year: 8am–10pm (till 11pm in summer; closed Sun 10am–6pm).

Hôtel Akouas 27 Rue Amir Abdelkader ⓣ0535 515967, ⓦwww.hotelakouas.com. All the mod cons – double-glazing, a/c, heating, satellite TV – in an international-standard business hotel near the CTM station and Meknes's lively nightlife; the *Akouas* also has its own nightclub. There's a small indoor pool and a decent restaurant, *El Menzeh*, open to nonresidents. ❹

Hôtel de Nice Cnr Omar Ben Chemssi and Rue Antsirabé ⓣ0535 520318, ⓔnice_hotel@menara.ma. A friendly central place whose good-value refurbished rooms on the fourth and fifth floors provide bright modern en suites with three-star facilities, including a/c. Also has a bar and nightclub. ❹

Hôtel Majestic 19 Av Mohammed V ⓣ0535 522035, ⓕ0535 527427. This 1930s hotel marries vintage charm with comfortable, clean rooms (some en suite) offering heating and balconies. There's a large roof terrace and a newly renovated salon-restaurant. Friendly management, too. Probably the best mid-priced choice in the Ville Nouvelle, and convenient for the El Amir Abdelkader train station. Includes breakfast. ❸

Hôtel Malta 3 Rue Charif el Idnssi ⓣ0535 515020, ⓦwww.hotelmaltamaroc.com. A spacious and friendly newcomer to Meknes's upmarket hotel scene, with four-star facilities in its en-suite rooms, each with ISDN sockets, plus two bars and a nightclub (daily midnight–3am). Includes breakfast. ❼

Hôtel Palace 11 Rue Ghana ⓣ0535 520407, ⓕ0535 401431. Rooms (en suite with 24hr hot water) are well priced, though spartan, and could do with a revamp. There's a handy parking garage for resident vehicles. ❸

Hôtel Rif Rue Omar Ben Chemssi, formerly Rue Accra ⓣ0535 522591, ⓔhotel_rig@menara.ma. An upmarket 1950s tour-group hotel bang in the centre, comfy in an old-fashioned way and with a bar, good restaurant and small pool. Includes breakfast. ❺

Hôtel Touring 34 Av Allal Ben Abdallah ⓣ0535 522351. A central cheapie with pretty average facilities; a little threadbare in places, functional in others. Hot showers. Some rooms en suite. ❷

Hôtel Transatlantique Rue el Marinyen ⓣ0535 525050, ⓔtransat01@menara.ma. Meknes's luxury hotel, with two wings: a characterful older arm, with tiled floors in Moroccan-styled rooms and patio doors opening on to lovely gardens, and a modern wing, comfy if bland. There are tennis courts, two outdoor pools (open to nonresidents for 100dh) and a new nightclub and terrace bar with astounding views to the Medina. ❻

Hôtel Volubilis 45 Av des FAR ⓣ0535 525082. A bit of faded grandeur from the 1930s, complete with Art Deco lobby and facade. One of the oldest hotels in the quarter, and still decent, with hot showers, but located at a noisy road junction. ❸

Camping

Camping Belle-Vue Also called *Camping Zerhouane*, on the road to Moulay Idriss, 14km from Meknes ⓣ0535 544168. A shaded site with a small café and a few rooms to let. Not as good as *Camping Aguedal* and inconvenient unless you have a car, though buses to and from Moulay Idriss (9km away) will drop or pick you up here. Can also be found 11km along the direct road from Volubilis to Meknes, though roads here are poorly marked – it's easiest located by asking directions to the nearby *Refuge Zerhouane*.

Camping Caravaning International Also called *Camping Aguedal* ⓣ0535 551828. A half-hour walk south from Pl el Hedim (or a 13dh petit-taxi ride), the city campsite is sited opposite the Heri es Souani. Although a little pricey, it's a pleasant, shaded site (*aguedal*, or *agdal*, means "garden"), with good facilities (hot water showers available). The restaurant has menus from 60dh (reservations required).

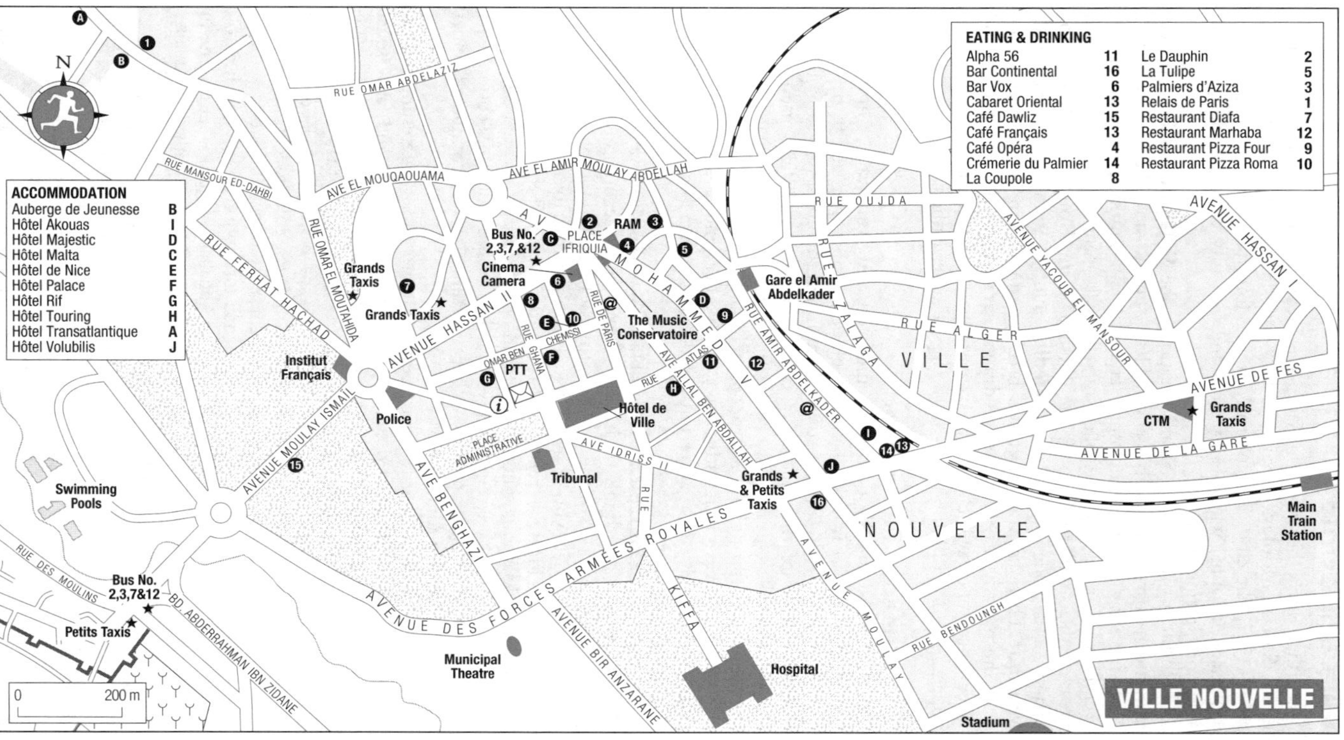
VILLE NOUVELLE
EATING & DRINKING
Alpha 56 11
Bar Continental 16
Bar Vox 6
Cabaret Oriental 13
Café Dawliz 15
Café Français 13
Café Opéra 4
Crémerie du Palmier 14
La Coupole 8
Le Dauphin 2
La Tulipe 5
Palmiers d'Aziza 3
Relais de Paris 1
Restaurant Diafa 7
Restaurant Marhaba 12
Restaurant Pizza Four 9
Restaurant Pizza Roma 10
ACCOMMODATION
Auberge de Jeunesse B
Hôtel Akouas I
Hôtel Majestic D
Hôtel Malta C
Hôtel de Nice E
Hôtel Palace F
Hôtel Rif G
Hôtel Touring H
Hôtel Transatlantique A
Hôtel Volubilis J
N
RUE OMAR ABDELAZIZ
RUE MANSOUR ED-DAHBI
AVE EL MOUQAOUAMA
AVE EL AMIR MOULAY ABDELLAH
RUE FERHAT HACHAD
RUE OMAR EL MOUTAHIDA
Grands Taxis
Grands Taxis
Bus No. 2,3,7,&12
PLACE IFRIQUIA
RAM
AV MOHAMMED V
Cinema Camera
AVENUE HASSAN II
RUE DE PARIS
The Music Conservatoire
RUE CHEMSSI
RUE GHANA
OMAR BEN
PTT
RUE ATLAS
AVE ALLAL BEN ABDALLAH
Hôtel de Ville
Institut Français
Police
PLACE ADMINISTRATIVE
AVE IDRISS II
Tribunal
AVENUE MOULAY ISMAIL
AVE BENGHAZI
Grands & Petits Taxis
Swimming Pools
RUE DES MOULINS
Bus No. 2,3,7&12
Petits Taxis
BD. ABDERRAHMAN IBN ZIDANE
AVENUE DES FORCES ARMÉES ROYALES
Municipal Theatre
AVENUE BIR ANZARANE
RUE KIFFA
Hospital
AVENUE MOULAY
RUE BENDOUNGH
Stadium
NOUVELLE
VILLE
Gare el Amir Abdelkader
RUE AMIR ABDELKADER
RUE ZALAGA
RUE OUJDA
RUE ALGER
AVENUE YACOUB EL MANSOUR
AVENUE HASSAN I
AVENUE DE FES
CTM
Grands Taxis
AVENUE DE LA GARE
Main Train Station
0 200 m

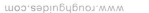

Ville Impériale

More than any other town in Morocco, Meknes is associated with a single figure, **Sultan Moulay Ismail** (see box opposite). During his 55-year reign (1672–1727), the city was tranformed from a forgettable provincial centre into a spectacular capital with twenty gates and over fifty palaces enclosed within 45km of exterior walls.

The principal remains of Ismail's creation – the **Ville Impériale** of palaces and gardens, barracks, granaries and stables – sprawl below the Medina amid a confusing array of walled enclosures, and it's a long morning's walk to take in everything. Starting from the Ville Nouvelle, make your way down to the main street at the southern edge of the Medina (**Rue Rouamzine/Rue Dar Smen**), and along to **Place el Hedim** and its immense gateway, **Bab Mansour**. There are usually **guides** hanging around here if you want to use one. Alternatively, drivers of **horse-drawn carriages** in Place el Hedim and Place Lalla Aouda will take up to six passengers on an hour-long tour of the imperial city for 120dh – easier on the legs if rather rushed.

Bab Mansour and around

Place el Hedim ("Square of Demolition and Renewal") immediately recalls the reign of Moulay Ismail. Seeking a grand approach to his palace quarter, the *Dar el Kebira*, the sultan demolished the houses that formed the western corner of the Medina to create the square. He also used it as a depot for marble columns and construction material he had gathered from sites and cities throughout Morocco, including Roman Volubilis. From late afternoon, it takes on a festive air as storytellers and astrologers, acrobats and traditional doctors gather until mid-evening, like Marrakesh's Djemaa el Fna in miniature.

The centrepiece of the city's ensemble of walls and gateways is the great **Bab Mansour**, startlingly rich in its ceremonial decoration and almost perfectly preserved. Its name comes from its architect, one of a number of Christian renegades who converted to Islam and rose to a high position at Ismail's court. A local tale relates that the sultan inspected the completed gate, then asked El Mansour whether he could do any better, a Catch 22 for the hapless architect, whose response ("yes") led to his immediate execution. That said, the story may be apocryphal because the gate was completed under Ismail's son, Moulay Abdallah.

Whatever the truth, the gate is the finest in Meknes and an interesting adaptation of the classic Almohad design, flanked by unusual inset and fairly squat bastions which are purely decorative and whose marble columns were brought from Volubilis – indeed, they are more impressive than any that remain at the site itself. The decorative patterns on both gate and bastions are elaborations of the Almohad *darj w ktaf* motif (see *Moroccan Architecture* colour section), the space between each motif filled out with a brilliant array of zellij created by a layer of cutaway black tiles, just like the ornamental inscription above, which extols the triumph of Ismail and, even more, that of Abdallah, bragging that no gate in Damascus or Alexandria is its equal. Alongside Bab Mansour is a smaller gateway in the same style, **Bab Djemaa en Nouar**.

Nowadays, traffic passes through neither gate – indeed, the inside of Bab Mansour is used as an arts and crafts market, sometimes displaying work from the Ensemble Artisanal (see p.189). To the left of Bab Mansour (when facing the gate) on Rue Dar Smen is the **Musée de Meknès** (Tues–Sun 9am–6.30pm; 20dh), containing various artisanal artefacts; though interesting, your time is better spent at the Musée Dar Jamaï (see p.189). Heading

The Sultan Moulay Ismail (1672–1727)

"The **Sultan Moulay Ismail**," wrote his chronicler, Ezziani, "loved Mequinez, and he would have liked never to leave it." But leave it he did, ceaselessly campaigning against the rebel Berber chiefs of the south, and the Europeans entrenched in Tangier, Asilah and Larache, until the entire country lay completely under government control for the first time in five centuries. His reign saw the creation of Morocco's strongest ever – and most coherent – army, which included a crack Negro guard, the Abid regiment, and, it is reckoned, a garrison force of one in twenty of the male population. The period was Morocco's last golden age, though the ruthless centralization of all decisions, and the fear with which the sultan reigned, led to a slide into anarchy and weak, inward-looking rule.

Ismail's achievements were matched by his **tyrannies**, which were judged extreme even by the standards of the time – and contemporary Europeans were burning their enemies and torturing them on the rack. His reign began with the display of 400 heads at Fes, most of them of captured chiefs, and over the next five decades it is estimated that he was responsible for over 30,000 deaths, not including those killed in battle. Many of these deaths were quite arbitrary. Mounting a horse, Ismail might slash the head off the eunuch holding his stirrup; inspecting the work on his buildings, he would carry a weighted lance, with which to batter skulls in order to "encourage" the others. "My subjects are like rats in a basket," he used to say, "and if I do not keep shaking the basket they will gnaw their way through."

Yet the sultan was a tireless **builder** throughout Morocco, constructing towns and ports, and a multitude of defensive kasbahs, palaces and bridges. By far his greatest efforts were focused on Meknes, where he sustained an obsessive building programme, often acting as architect and sometimes even working alongside the slaves and labourers. Ironically, time has not been kind to his constructions in Meknes. Built mainly of *tabia*, a mixture of earth and lime, they were severely damaged by a hurricane even in his lifetime, and were left to decay thereafter, as subsequent Alaouite sultans shifted their capitals back to Fes and Marrakesh. Walter Harris, writing only 150 years after Ismail's death, found Meknes "a city of the dead… strewn with marble columns and surrounded by great masses of ruin". Thankfully, more recent city authorities have tackled the restoration of the main monuments with more energy.

through the nearby gateway and across Place Lalla Aouda brings you to an open square, in the far right corner of which is the green-tiled **Koubba el Khayatine** (daily: June to mid-Sept 9am–6.30pm; mid-Sept to June 9am–5.30pm; 10dh), an anonymous zellij-covered reception hall for ambassadors to the imperial court. More intriguing is a vast series of subterranean vaults – lit only by the skyholes that stud the lawn above – that are reached via a stairway behind and which are, by popular tradition, known as the **Prison of Christian Slaves** (same ticket). This was more likely a storehouse or granary, although there were certainly several thousand Christian captives at Ismail's court. The story goes that any who died were simply buried in the walls they were building, although no human remains have come to light even though most of the walls have crumbled away.

Ahead of the *koubba*, set within the long wall and at right angles to it, are three modest **gates**. The one in the centre is generally closed and is at all times flanked by soldiers from the royal guard; within, landscaped across a lake and the sunken garden of Ismail's last and finest palace, are the **Royal Golf Gardens** – private and strictly *interdit* unless you play a round on one dedicated section (p.195).

Mausoleum of Moulay Ismail

Together with the tomb of Mohammed V in Rabat, and the Medersa Bou Inania in Fes, the **Mausoleum of Moulay Ismail** (daily 9am–12.30pm & 3–6pm, closed Fri morning, tomb open to Muslims only; free) is the only active Moroccan shrine that non-Muslims may visit. Modest dress, for both women and men, is required.

The mausoleum has been a point of reverence since Ismail's death (it was constructed in his own lifetime) and is still held in high esteem. Given tales of the ruler's excesses, this seems puzzling to Westerners, but in Morocco Ismail is remembered for his achievements: bringing peace and prosperity after a period of anarchy, and driving out the Spanish from Larache and the British from Tangier. His extreme observance of orthodox Islamic form and ritual also conferred a kind of magic on him, as, of course, does his part in founding the ruling Alaouite dynasty – although, technically, the dynasty began with his brother, Moulay Rachid, Ismail is generally honoured as the founder.

Entering the mausoleum, you are allowed to approach the **sanctuary** in which the sultan is buried, though cannot go beyond this annex. Most interesting is the reverance with which the shrine is treated. You will almost invariably see villagers here, especially women seeking *baraka* (charismatic blessing) and intercession from the saintly sultan's remains.

Dar el Kebira

Beyond the mausoleum, a gate on your left leads into the dilapidated quarter of **Dar el Kebira**, Ismail's great palace complex. The imperial structures – there were originally twelve pavilions within the complex – can still be seen above and between the houses here: ogre-like creations of massive scale compared with the modest dwellings. They were completed in 1677 and dedicated at a midnight celebration, when the sultan personally slaughtered a wolf so its head could be displayed at the centre of the gateway.

Some later commentators saw a conscious echo of Versailles – its contemporary rival – in the grandeur of Ismail's plan, though it would be another decade until the first reports of Louis XIV's palace reached the imperial court. When they did, however, Ismail's interest was pricked. In 1699, he sent an ambassador to Paris to negotiate the addition of Louis' daughter, Princess Conti, to his harem. The ambasssador returned without the girl, but bearing some magnificent clocks, offered as a conciliatory gesture by the Sun King and now on display in the mausoleum.

Dar el Makhzen and Heri es Souani

On the opposite side of the long-walled corridor, beyond the Royal Golf Gardens, more immense buildings are spread out, making up Ismail's last great palace, the **Dar el Makhzen**. The most you can get are a few brief glimpses over the heads of the guards posted by occasional gates in the crumbling, twenty-foot walls. The corridor itself was a favourite drive of the sultan – according to several sources, he was driven around in a bizarre chariot drawn by his women or eunuchs – and runs for a mile from Moulay Ismail's mausoleum. It eventually brings you out by the **Heri es Souani** (or Dar el Ma), the chief sight of the Ville Impériale, which is often introduced by local guides as "Ismail's stables" (closed at time of writing due to flood damage; otherwise daily 9am–noon & 3–6pm; 10dh). In fact, the stables are further south, and the startling series of high-vaulted chambers here were storerooms and granaries, filled with provisions for siege or drought. They give a powerful impression of the complexity of seventeenth-century Moroccan engineering.

Each of Ismail's palaces had underground plumbing (well in advance of Europe), and here you can find a remarkable system of chain-bucket wells built between each of the storerooms. One on the right, near the back, has been restored.

Just as worthwhile is the view from the **roof** of the Heri es Souani, which is accessed through the second entrance on the right, although frequently closed to visitors. From its garden, you can gaze out over the Dar el Makhzen and the still **Agdal Basin**, built as an irrigation reservoir and pleasure lake where families picnic in summer.

The Rouah

The ramshackle ruins of Moulay Ismail's stables, the **Rouah** are officially closed to visitors and not really worth the thirty-minute walk from the Heri es Souani unless you have a serious interest in archaeology. If you are committed, turn up and ask around for the *gardien,* who will usually let you have a quick look. It is a massive complex, perhaps twice as large as the Heri es Souani. In contemporary accounts, the Rouah is often singled out as the greatest feature of all Ismail's building projects: some three miles in length, traversed by a long canal, with flooring built over vaults used for storing grain, and space for over 12,000 horses. More than anything else in Meknes, it recalls the scale and madness of Moulay Ismail's vision.

The Medina

Although taking much of its present form and size under Moulay Ismail, the Medina bears far less of his stamp. Its main sights, in addition to the extensive **souks**, are a Merenid *medersa* (an Islamic college; see box, p.217) – the **Bou Inania** – and a nineteenth-century palace museum, the **Dar Jamaï**, both rewarding and easy to find.

Dar Jamaï

The Dar Jamaï (daily except Tues 9am–5pm; 10dh) stands discretely down a stairway at the back of Place el Hedim. One of the finest examples of a late nineteenth-century Moroccan palace, it was built in 1882 by the same family

Arts and crafts

The **Ensemble Artisanal** on Avenue Zine el Abidine Riad (Mon–Thurs 8.30am–noon & 2.30–6.30pm, Fri 8.30–11am & 3–6.30pm; ⓣ0535 530929) is found above the local bus station, up the hill from the grands taxis park west of Place el Hedim. It is large and trains apprentices, but there is little to buy. However, there is a lot to be seen, including the work of young craftsmen making **zellij** tiles. The building also houses several active cooperatives, including **La Cooperative Féminine de Céramique**.

In the Medina, **Espace Berbère** at 32 Rue Tiberbarine has an interesting and eclectic collection of craft items. For a genuine Meknesi product, head for **Kissaria Lahrir** (see p.191), where you can buy traditional **silver damascene** tableware and other items.

The **Music Conservatoire** of Meknes is the impressive French-style building near Place Ifriquia, between avenues Mohammed V and Allal Ben Abdallah. Students study classical Arab-Andalous music, together with *milhûn* and, less so, *gharnati*, and the *conservatoire* gives occasional concerts. The **Institut Français**, Place Farhat Hachad (ⓣ0535 524071, ⓦwww.ambafrance-ma.org/institut/fes-meknes), has a programme of music, theatre, cinema and literature events, plus a popular student café. Its cultural activities are more comprehensive than those in Fes, and well priced at 30dh per adult, or 15dh for the cinema.

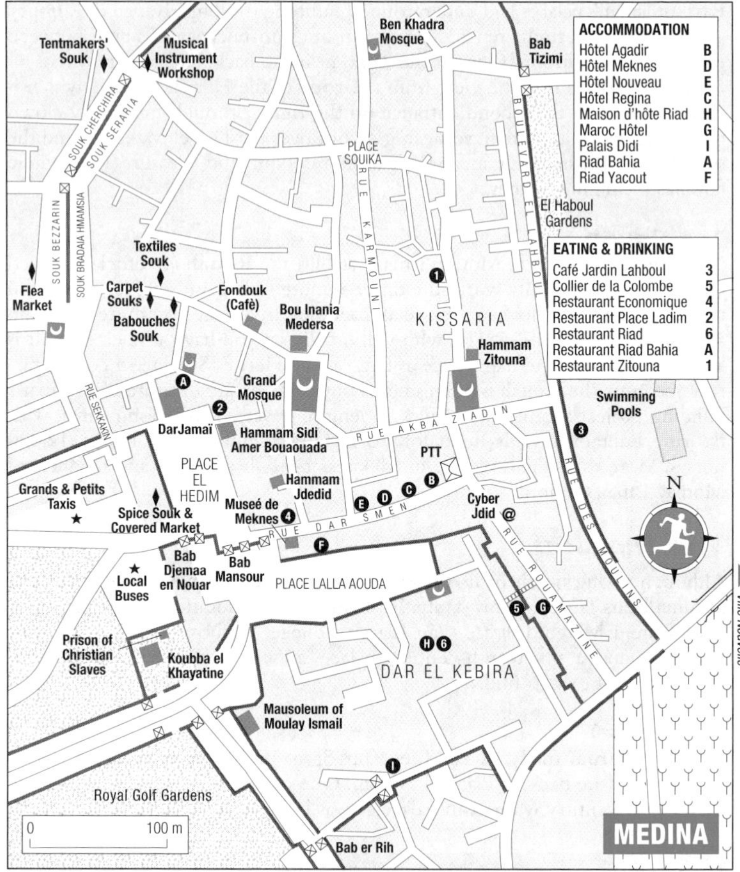

of viziers (high government officials) who erected the Palais Jamaï in Fes. After 1912, it was used as a military hospital, becoming the Museum of Moroccan Art in 1920.

Today, it houses one of the best museums in Morocco. Its exhibits, some organized to recreate the gloriously cluttered reception rooms of nobility in the late-1800s, are predominantly of the same age as the palace, though some pieces of **Fes** and **Meknes pottery** date back to around Ismail's reign. These ceramics – elaborate polychrome designs from Meknes and strong blue-and-white patterns from Fes – make an interesting comparison, with Fes's strong handicrafts tradition coming out as superior. A display of Berber jewellery also catches the eye, though the best is that of **Middle Atlas carpets**, in particular the bold geometric designs of the Beni M'guild tribe.

Artefacts and antiques aside, the museum is worth a visit as much for the building, boasting a gorgeous upper-floor reception room with intricate wood carvings on the ceiling. The viziers' **Andalusian Garden** has also been preserved, a lush courtyard with palm, banana, lemon and orange trees, as well as papyrus, roses and cypresses, usually twittering with birds.

The souks

The most accessible souk from Place el Hedim is **Souk Atriya** (Covered Market; closed Fri), which runs all along the west side of the square. This is the produce market where locals do their shopping; row upon row of multicoloured vegetable and spice stalls, olives piled into pyramids, butchers (not for the squeamish), and sweet stalls so loaded with cakes you can hardly reach the stallholder to pay.

A lane immediately behind the Dar Jamaï (Rue Tiberbarine) from Place el Hedim leads into other souks. Follow it and you emerge in the middle of the Medina's major market street; on the right, leading to the Grand Mosque and Bou Inania Medersa, is **Souk es Sebbat**, on the left **Souk en Nejjarin**. Turning first to the left, you enter an area of textile stalls, which give way to the carpenters' (*nejjarin*) workshops after which the souk is named. Shortly after this, you pass a mosque on your left, beyond which is an entrance to a parallel arcade. The **carpet market**, or **Souk Joutiya es Zerabi**, is just off here to the left. Quality can be very high, as can prices, though because Meknes lacks the constant stream of tourists of Fes or Marrakesh, dealers are more willing to bargain; don't be afraid to start low.

At the end of Souk en Nejjarin you come to another souk, the **Bezzarin**, which runs up at right angles to the Nejjarin, on either side of the city wall. This looks an unpromising, rundown neighbourhood, but things get more interesting if you follow the outer side of the wall to an assortment of craftsworkers, grouped in trade guilds and often fronted by an old *fondouk* or warehouse. There are **basketmakers**, **ironsmiths** and **saddlers**, and at the top near **Bab Djedid** you'll find **tent-makers** – although they rarely sew any traditional tents these days – and a couple of **musical instrument workshops** in the gate itself.

Going the other way beyond the Dar Jamaï, on **Souk es Sebbat**, you reach a classier section of the market – starting off with *babouche* vendors and moving on to the fancier goods aimed at tourists near the medersa, before finally exiting into a covered **kissaria** dominated by kaftan sellers. From here it's easy to find your way to the Bou Inania Medersa, whose imposing portal is on the left-hand side of the street. If you want a tea break, a nineteenth-century **fondouk**, a short way back, doubles as a café and carpet/crafts emporium – look for its open courtyard. Incidentally, Meknes mint is reputed to be the best in Morocco.

Near the Bou Inania Medersa (see below) is the **Kissaria Lahrir**, where you can see traditional **silver damascene** being made, the hair-thin silver thread slowly engraved in steel and used to decorate plates, jugs and other items. The family of Essaidi M'barek has passed on the skills for such delicate work from one generation to the next; his English-speaking son, Saidi, will explain the process if you're interested. To find the *kissaria* turn right as you face the entrance of Bou Inania, then take the lane first on the right; after 30m you will see the entrance of the souk on your left.

Bou Inania Medersa

The **Bou Inania Medersa** (daily 9am–5:30pm; 10dh) was built around 1340–50, so is more or less contemporary with the great medersas of Fes. It takes its name from the notorious Sultan Abou Inan (see p.216), though it was founded by his predecessor, Abou el Hassan, the great Merenid builder behind the Chellah *zaouia* in Rabat and Salé medersa.

A modest and functional building, the medersa follows the plan of Hassan's other principal works in that it has a single **courtyard** opening onto a narrow **prayer hall**, and is encircled on each floor by the students' **cells**, with exquisitely carved cedar screens. It has a much lighter feel to it than the Salé medersa, and in its balance of wood, stucco and zellij achieves a remarkable combination of intricacy – no area is left uncovered – and restraint. Architecturally, the most unusual feature is a ribbed dome over the **entrance hall**, an impressive piece of craftsmanship that extends right out into the souk.

From **the roof**, generally open to visitors, you can look out – and feel as if you could climb across – to the tiled pyramids of the **Grand Mosque**; you can just catch a glimpse of the interior. The souk is mainly obscured from view, but you can get a good, general panorama of the town and the mosques of each quarter. Inlaid with bands of green tiles, the minarets of these distinctive mosques are unique to Meknes; those of Fes or Marrakesh tend to be more elaborate and multicoloured.

North from Bou Inania

North of the medersa, the Medina is largely residential, dotted with the occasional fruit and vegetable market, and featuring the **Ben Khadra Mosque**, which has beautiful polychrome doors and some exquisite coloured stucco, and a carpenters' souk. If you continue this way, you'll eventually come out in a long, open square, which culminates in the monumental **Bab el Berdaïn** (Gate of the Saddlers). This was another of Ismail's creations, a rugged, genuinely defensive structure, which looks like a more muscular version of the central section of Bab Mansour.

Outside, the city walls extend along the main road to Rabat. Follow it and you will catch occasional glimpses on your left of an enormous **cemetery** – almost half the size of the Medina in extent. Non-Muslims are not permitted to enter the enclosure near the centre, home to the *zaouia* and shrine of one of the country's most famous and curious saints, **Sidi Mohammed Ben Aissa**. Reputedly a contemporary of Moulay Ismail, Ben Aissa conferred on his followers the power to eat anything, even poison or broken glass, without suffering any ill effects. His cult, the Aissaoua, became one of the most important in Morocco, and certainly the most violent and fanatical. Until prohibited by the French, some 50,000 devotees regularly attended the saint's annual moussem (see box below). Entering into a trance, they were known to pierce their tongues and cheeks with daggers, eat serpents and scorpions – a scene vividly described by Victorian traveller Joseph Thomson – or devour live sheep and goats. The only other confraternity to approach such frenzy was the Hamadcha of Moulay Idriss, whose devotees were known to cut each other's heads with hatchets or, during more extreme rites, toss heavy stones or cannonballs into the air, so they landed on their heads. Both cults continue to hold moussems, though successive Moroccan governments have effectively outlawed the more outrageous activities.

The Sidi Ben Aissa Moussem

The **Sidi Ben Aïssa Moussem**, or Moussem Cheikh el Kamal, is held on the eve of Mouloud (see p.51 for dates), and includes a spectacular **fantasia** (a charge of horses with riders firing guns at full gallop) if weather conditions permit, held near Place el Hedim. Along with the enormous conical tents, and crowds of country people in white *jellabas* beneath the city walls, it has the appearance of a medieval tournament, plus an adjoining fairground, with illusionists and various performers.

The moussem was the principal gathering of the **Aissaoua** brotherhood, an occasion for them to display powers of endurance under trance (see p.583), though their activities today are more subdued. Their focus is the *marabout* tomb of Ben Aissa, near the road to Rabat.

Restaurants, bars and nightlife

Meknes is a small town compared with Fes or even Tangier. In the **Ville Nouvelle**, most of the action is within a few blocks of the central **Place Administrative**.

Restaurants

In the **Ville Nouvelle** you'll find a dozen or so good restaurants, most serving a daily three-course menu. Eating in the **Medina** is largely at basic café-grills; as well as those listed here, cheap hole-in-the-wall joints with fried fish and brochettes line Rue Rouamazine, near the *Maroc Hôtel*. However, there are also palatial restaurants – the *Collier de la Colombe*, the *Restaurant Riad* and the *Riad Bahia* – where you can tuck into excellent food at a fraction of the price you'd pay in the touristy equivalents in Fes. All smarter options, and a few of the moderates, are licensed to serve alcohol.

Medina

Collier de la Colombe 67 Rue Driba ⓣ0535 55 5041. A smart but far from costly restaurant in the ornate mansion of "Sultan" Lakhal, a non-Alaouite pretender to the throne on the death of Moulay Youssef in 1927. Night and day, the views across the valley to the Ville Nouvelle are stunning, especially from the roof terrace. Atlas trout stars alongside tajines with fruit and olives on an à la carte menu or reasonable set menus (from 110dh). There are also a number of specialty dishes that require advance notice. Daily 11.30am–4pm & 7–11pm. Moderate to expensive.

Restaurant Economique 123 Rue Dar Smen. A long-established café-restaurant serving all the standard fare. Daily 11am–9pm. Cheap.

Restaurant Place Lahdim Pl El Hedim, head for the terraces in the back right-hand corner of the square. A pleasant spot for lunch, with tajines and brochettes served on multi-level terraces. The aerial view of Pl Lahdim is great for people watching, especially at sunset. Daily 9am–9pm. Cheap.

Restaurant Riad 79 Ksar Chaacha, Dar el Kebira ⓣ0535 530542. A lovely little place snug in the last of Moulay Ismail's original twelve pavilions, the only one to have survived the 1755 earthquake. It's tricky to find (follow green arrows from the entry to Dar el Kebira by Bab er Rih), but well worth the effort to sample refined traditional cuisine – the best in town, say some locals – in beautifully restored salons or in the patio garden that's magic in the evening. As well as very reasonable à la carte eating (*mechoui* needs to be ordered up to 3hr in advance), set menus start at 110dh. Daily 12am–3pm & 6.30–10.30pm. Moderate to expensive.

Restaurant Riad Bahia Rue Tiberbarine, just behind the Dar Jamaï museum ⓣ0535 554541. Heavenly pastilla and tanjia, the beef stew cooked in an old clay pot in the low heat of a hammam's embers. Rachid, the chef and owner's brother, personally takes the pots to the nearby hammam, where they simmer for over five hours. Daily noon–3pm & 7–10pm. Reservations required. Moderate to expensive.

Restaurant Zitouna 44 Jamaâ Zitouna. All the usual Moroccan dishes, served in the courtyard and rooms of a renovated late-nineteenth-century palace; often swamped by tour groups during lunch, so best left to evenings. Unlicensed. Daily 12am–3pm & 7–10pm. Moderate.

Ville Nouvelle

La Coupole corner of Av Hassan II and Rue du Ghana. Popular with locals for an extensive range of reasonably priced Moroccan and European dishes and a set menu (110dh); grilled meats are the house special. There's also a bar and a noisy nightclub. Daily noon–3pm & 6–11pm. Moderate.

Le Dauphin 5 Av Mohammed V, entrance at side. Managed by the *Hôtel Bab Mansour*, this is a smart, old-fashioned French place, with reliable cooking and a reputation for excellent seafood; the fish is guaranteed fresh each day. Decent wine list, too. Daily noon–3pm & 7–11pm. Expensive.

Relais de Paris 46 Rue Oqba, across from the *Auberge de Jeunesse*. This new bistro has opened following the success of its counterpart in Tangier. Delicious French cuisine, from foie grais to sea bream, an extensive wine list, and a trendy bar-lounge downstairs. Daily 11am–3pm & 7–11pm. Expensive.

Restaurant Diafa 12 Rue Badr el Kobra. What looks like a private house has extremely good and reasonably priced cooking, with two set menus, though not a vast choice of dishes. Daily noon–3pm & 7pm–midnight. Moderate.

Restaurant Marhaba 23 Av Mohammed V, not to be confused with the café *Glacier Marhaba* that fronts Av Mohammed V. A no-nonsense eating house, popular with locals for a budget serving of thick *harira* soup (from 4dh), brochettes and tajines. Daily noon–9pm. Cheap.

Restaurant Pizza Four 1 Rue Atlas, near *Hôtel Majestic*, off Av Mohammed V. Omelettes, pizzas and tenuously Italian food in a bizarre – and rather gloomy – mock Italian-Tudor interior. Daily 11am–3pm & 6.30pm–midnight. Moderate.

Restaurant Pizza Roma 8 Rue Accra, alongside the *Hôtel de Nice*. Limited menu, beyond the pizzas, but good value, and handy for out-of-hours snacks. Open 24hr. Cheap.

Cafés and patisseries

Meknes's finest patisseries are in the Ville Nouvelle, the classiest located near Place Ifriquia.

Alpha 56 16 bis Av Mohammed V. A heavenly *tarte tatin* and a few profiteroles make this patisserie a favourite haunt in Meknes. Scrumptious, although at prices to match. Daily 6am–9pm.

Café Dawliz Av Moulay Ismail, behind *McDonald's*. A smart café with panoramic views over the Medina to the west – especially atmospheric at sunset. Daily 8am–11pm.

Café Jardin Lahboul Bd El Lahboul, outside the Medina walls near El Lahboul gardens. Pleasant café on the river's edge and shaded by trees.

Café Opéra 7 Av Mohammed V. A blend of café and patisserie, which attracts a young crowd and stays open daytime during Ramadan. Daily 6am–11pm.

Crémerie du Palmier 53 Av des FAR, next to the *Hôtel Excelsior*. Another excellent patisserie, with good *rayeb* (set yoghurt in a glass) and fresh fruit juices. Daily 3am–10pm.

La Tulipe Pl Maarakat Lahri. A semi-smart place to indulge yourself with ice cream, which you can eat in a fondant-hued interior, a quiet terrace or take away. Daily 6am–9.30pm.

Palmiers d'Aziza 9 Rue de Tarfaya, near Place Ifriquia. The chicest option of Meknes's café scene, the palm tree on its terrace is to honour the owner's origins in Figuig, south Morocco. There's a choice of terraces, all ruled by waiters in black and whites and frequented by a trendy clientele. Daily 6.30am–10pm.

Bars

Many of the Ville Nouvelle hotels have bars and nightclubs, often quite lively in the evenings. The stylish bar of the *Hôtel Transatlantique* is your best bet for a mellow drink, especially recommended for Medina views at sunset; or the nightclub of the *Hôtel Rif* is a mite more lively, and kicks off with a Scheherezade-style floor show. The bars below are more boisterous, and although some have female staff, women may find the raucous, all-male clientele intimidating.

Bar Continental By the *Hôtel Continental*, on the opposite side of Av des FAR. Outside tables are blighted by traffic, so go inside. A rather seedy dive, but fun if you're in the mood for a no-nonsense boozey vibe. Daily 6am–10.30pm.

Bar Vox Av Hassan II, next to Cinema Camera. A straight-forward drinker, considerably less intimidating than most, with a varied clientele. Daily 6am–midnight.

Cabaret Oriental Av des FAR (next to *Café Français*). Occasionally hosts bands into the small hours. Daily 9pm–3am.

Café Français (also called *Club de Nuit*). By the *Hôtel Excelsior*, on Av des FAR. A rather bunker-like bar behind a brick facade, pepped up with funky 1970s mirrors. Bar daily 6am–11pm, club 9pm–2am.

Listings

Airlines Royal Air Maroc, 7 Av Mohammed V ⓣ0535 520963.

Banks Concentrated around Pl Administrative, and along Av Mohammed V (the Crédit du Maroc is at no. 28, Banque Populaire at no. 17, BMCE at no. 9) and Av des FAR (BMCE is at no. 98). In the Medina, the Banque Populaire on Rue Dar Smen, near Bab Mansour, has exchange facilities and an ATM, as does BMCE in Rue Rouamazine. BMCI by Dar Jamaï in Pl el Hedim has a bureau de change (Sun 10am–noon & 3–5pm). The *Hôtel Rif* (see p.184) will exchange cash round the clock.

Bookshops The best in town, with a vast selection of literature in French, is Librairie Papeterie des

Ecoles at 10 Av Allal Ben Abdellah (Mon–Fri 9am–12.30pm & 3–8.30pm, Sat 9am–12.30pm, 4–8.30pm), 50m southeast of the Cinema Camera.

Car rental None of the major companies have offices in Meknes. Try Meknes Car, on the corner of Av Hassan II and Rue Safi (Ⓣ0535 512074, Ⓦwww.meknescar.net), or friendly Serenite Car, 19 Rue Mansour Ed-Dahbi at the bottom of the hill leading up to *Hotel Transatlantique* (Ⓣ0535 525375), both with small three-doors from 250dh per day.

Cinemas The Camera on Pl Ifriquia shows a varied programme of Bollywood, American and French movies, and has two daily screenings at 2.45pm and 8.45pm, each offering a double-bill for the price of a single ticket. Cinema Dawliz on Av Moulay Ismail is handy for the Medina and shows Bollywood and Western films.

Festivals The Ben Aïssa Moussem (see box, p.192) is the country's most impressive. Also worth planning for are the Beni Rached Moussem (at the village of Beni Rached, out of town on the Moulay Idriss road; 7 days after Mouloud) and the Moulay Idriss Moussem (at Moulay Idriss, second week of August).

Golf The Meknes Royal Golf Club at Bab Belkari Jnane Lbahraouia (Ⓣ0535 530753, Ⓕ0535 557934), has a nine-hole, par-36 course within the confines of the Royal Palace Golf Gardens.

Hammams In the Medina, the Hammam Sidi Amer Bouaouada (women 1–9pm; men 9pm–1am & 6am–1pm) is one of a very few where you can see the basement heating system; the hammam is 20m on the right on the lane off the northeast corner of Pl el Hedim.

Medical services English-speaking doctors include Dr Mohammed Dbab at 4 Rue Accra (Ⓣ0535 521087).

Pharmacies The emergency night pharmacy in the *Hôtel de Ville* on Pl Administrative (Ⓣ0535 523375) is open daily 8.30pm–8.30am

Police The local HQ is at Pl Ferhat Hached, at the western end of Av Hassan II (Ⓣ19). There's a smaller station next to Bab Djemaa en Nouar in the southwest corner of Pl el Hedim.

Post office The PTT is just off Pl de France (mid-July to Sept 8am–3.30pm; Oct to mid-July Mon–Fri 8am–6.30pm & Sat 8–11.30am; Ramadan 9am–3.30pm).

Swimming pools There are two public pools down by the Oued Boufekrane, reached along a lane from Bd el Haboul or from the intersection of avenues Hassan II and Moulay Ismail, both open June–Sept only. The first is very cheap at 5dh; just to its north is CODM Natation – classier, less crowded, and six times the price.

Moving on

The **CTM** terminal is on Avenue de Fès, at the eastern end of Ville Nouvelle. There's a handy CTM ticket office on Rue Rouamazine in a tèlèboutique across from *Hôtel de Paris*. **Private buses** leave from the *gare routière* on Avenue du Mellah, west of the Medina. For a run-down of frequencies and destinations, see "Travel Details" on p.268.

The most convenient **train station** is Gare el Amir Abdelkader, near the *Hôtel Majestic* in the Ville Nouvelle, but not all trains stop here, so you may need to use the Gare de Ville on the eastern edge of town.

Grands taxis use a yard alongside the bus station but some for Fes and Oujda may also leave from next to the CTM bus station. Grands taxis for one or two local destinations use the yard below Place el Hedim in the Medina, and on Rue Omar el Moutahida in the Ville Nouvelle, though it is unlikely that you will need to use these. There's also a **taxi** rank (grands and petits taxis) at the junction of Avenue des FAR and Avenue Mohammed V.

Volubilis and Moulay Idriss

An easy excursion from Meknes, **Volubilis** and **Moulay Idriss** embody much of Morocco's early history: Volubilis as its Roman provincial capital, Moulay Idriss in the creation of the country's first Arab dynasty. Their sites stand 4km apart, at either side of a deep and very fertile valley, about 30km north of Meknes.

Getting there

You can take in both sites on a leisurely day-trip from Meknes. **Grands taxis** make regular runs to **Moulay Idriss** (10dh a place) from near the new bus station by Bab el Khemis in the Medina and from near the French Cultural Centre just off Avenue Hassan II in the Ville Nouvelle. For **Volubilis**, you can take an Ouezzane **bus** and ask to be set down by the site (which is a five-hundred-metre walk downhill from the N13 – formerly P28 – road), or you could charter a grand taxi. The whole taxi (*une course*) should cost 60dh (drivers are likely to try and charge more), which can be split between up to six passengers; if you pay more, the driver will wait at Volubilis and take you on to Moulay Idriss, where you can look round at leisure and then get a regular place in a grand taxi back to Meknes. To charter a private taxi for a half-day tour, expect to pay 380dh.

You could also **walk** between Volubilis and Moulay Idriss, which are only around 4km apart – ask the grand taxi driver to drop you at the junction of the N13 and the Moulay Idriss road, which will save you about 1km. The walk from the junction (known to taxi drivers as "*le carrefour*") to Volubilis is a scenic and safe fifty-minute stroll, particularly enjoyable in the early morning when locals join you on their way to the olive groves. If you're **driving** to Volubilis from the north, turning east after Sidi Kacem, note that the route might be signposted only to Oualili, the Arabic for Volubilis (which is a corruption of *oualili*, meaning oleander).

Accommodation and eating

Until recently, non-Muslims were not permitted to stay overnight in Moulay Idriss, the last place in Morocco to keep this religious prohibition. But after King Mohammed VI decreed this unfair following a visit in 2005, a number of family-run *maison d'hôtes* have appeared. Prices generally include breakfast, and evening meals can be ordered and enjoyed in an authentic family atmosphere. Two of the most well established are *La Colombe Blanche* (21 Derb Zouak Tazga, Ⓣ0535 544596, Ⓔlacolombe_blanche@yahoo.fr, ❸; on Saturdays, a tour group of around ten stay here, so book ahead), an intimate family home, and the upscale but more impersonal *Dar Al Andalousia* (Derb Zouak 169, Ⓣ0535 544749, Ⓔandalous@maisondhote-volubilis.com; ❸). The most hotel-like accommodation in town is *Diyar Timnay* (7 Rue Aïn Rjal, Ⓣ0535 544400, Ⓦwww.diyar-timnay.com; ❸), found below the grand taxi rank, which offers en-suite rooms and has a decent restaurant with panoramic views.

Upscale accommodation is found 3km from Moulay Idriss at the *Volubilis Inn*, 1km north of the site (Ⓣ0535 544405, Ⓕ0535 544280; ❼). Reopened in 2006 after renovation into a smart four-star, it is geared towards tour groups and justifies its high prices with a pool and astounding views over the ruins from every room. For camping, head to *Camping Belle-Vue*, 11km from Volubilis and 9km from Moulay Idriss (see p.201). A **café** at the site entrance serves basic food and drink.

Volubilis

A striking sight, visible for miles on the bends of the approach roads, **VOLUBILIS** occupies the ledge of a long, high plateau. Below its walls, towards Moulay Idriss, stretches a rich river valley; beyond lie dark, outlying ridges of the Zerhoun mountains. The drama of this scene – and the scope of the ruins – are undeniably impressive, so much so the site was a key location for Martin Scorsese's film *The Last Temptation of Christ*.

Some history

Except for a small trading post on the island off Essaouira, Volubilis was the Roman Empire's most remote and far-flung base. It represented – and was, literally – the end of the imperial road, having reached across France and Spain, then down from Tangier, and despite successive emperors' dreams of "penetrating the Atlas", the southern Berber tribes were never effectively subdued.

In fact, direct Roman rule here lasted little over two centuries – the garrison withdrew early, in 285 AD, to ease pressure elsewhere. But the town must have taken much of its present form well before the official annexation of North African Mauretania by Emperor Claudius in 45 AD. Tablets found on the site, inscribed in Punic, show a significant Carthaginian trading presence in the third century BC, and prior to colonization it was the western capital of a heavily Romanized, but semi-autonomous, Berber kingdom that reached into northern Algeria and Tunisia. After the Romans left, Volubilis experienced very gradual change. Latin was still spoken in the seventh century by the local population of Berbers, Greeks, Syrians and Jews; Christian churches survived until the coming of Islam; and the city itself remained alive and active well into the eighteenth century, when its marble was carried away by slaves for the building of Moulay Ismail's Meknes.

What you see today, well excavated and maintained, are largely the ruins of second- and third-century AD buildings – impressive and affluent creations from its period as a colonial provincial capital. The land around here is some of the most fertile in North Africa, and the city exported wheat and olives in considerable quantities to Rome, as it did wild animals from the surrounding hills. Roman games, memorable for the sheer scale of their slaughter (9000 beasts were killed for the dedication of Rome's Colosseum alone), could not have happened without the African provinces, and Volubilis was a chief source of their lions. Within just two hundred years, along with Barbary bears and elephants, they became extinct.

The site

The entrance to the site (daily 8am–sunset in theory, in practice around 5.30pm; 10dh) is through a minor gate in the city wall (or through a break in the wall further uphill, depending on construction work), built along with a number of outer camps in 168 AD, following a prolonged series of Berber insurrections. Just inside are the **ticket office** and *Café Bazar* on a hillside spur. A new administrative office is slowly being built below and will house a small **museum**. From time to time, funds permitting, there are further excavations and discoveries – and attempts at the restoration of the fallen structures.

The best of the finds – which include a superb collection of bronzes – have been taken to the Rabat museum, which is worth a visit for that reason alone. Volubilis, however, has retained *in situ* the great majority of its **mosaics**, some thirty or so, which are starting to show the effects of being exposed to the elements. Bar those subject to heavy-handed restoration, the once-brightly coloured tiles have faded to a subtle palette of ochres and greys. Similarly, the site requires a bit of imagination to reconstruct a town from the jumble of low walls and stumpy columns. Nevertheless, you leave with a real sense of Roman city life and its provincial prosperity, while it is not hard to recognize the essentials of a medieval Arab town in the layout.

Guides hang around by the ticket office and café (120dh per hour) or you can explore at leisure on the following **itinerary**; most showpiece buildings are demarcated with a plaque. Until the new administrative centre is finished, turn left off beyond the café on a path that leads across a bridge over the Fertassa

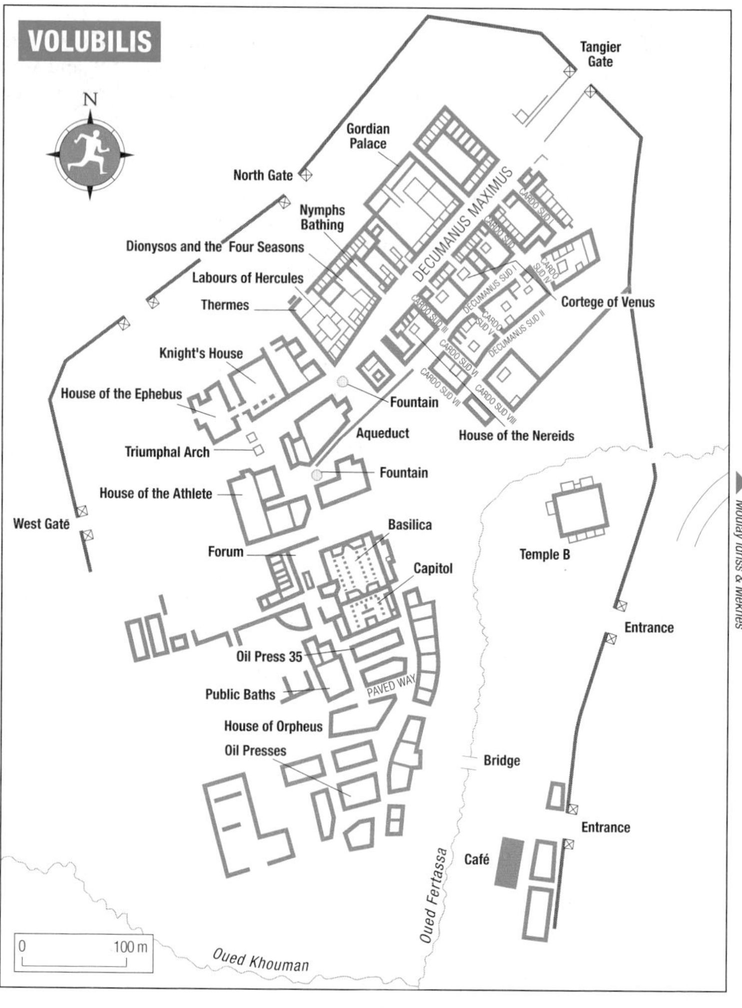

stream, and you climb up a hillside to a mixed area of housing and industry, each of its buildings containing the remains of at least one **olive press**. The extent and number of these presses, built into even the grandest mansions, reflect the olive's central importance to the city and indicate perhaps why Volubilis remained unchanged for so long after the Romans' departure. A significant proportion of its 20,000 population must have been involved in some capacity in the oil's production and export.

Somewhat isolated in this suburban quarter is the **House of Orpheus**, an enormous complex of rooms just beside the start of a paved way. Although substantially in ruins, it offers a strong impression of its former luxury – an opulent mansion, perhaps for one of the town's richest merchants. Its two main sections – public and private – each have their own separate entrance and interior court. The private rooms, which you come to first, are grouped around a small patio, which is decorated with a more or less intact **dolphin mosaic**. You can also make out the furnace and heating system (just by the entrance), the kitchen, and the **baths**, an extensive system of hot, cold and steam rooms.

A little further inside, the house's public apartments are dominated by a large **atrium**, half reception hall, half central court, and again preserving a very fine mosaic, **The Chariot of Amphitrite Drawn by a Seahorse**. The best mosaic here, however, from which the house takes its name, is that of the **Orpheus Myth**, located to the south in a room that was probably the *tablinium*, or archives.

Just north of the House of Orpheus, you pass first through the remains of the city's main **Public Baths**. Restored by the Emperor Gallienus in the second century AD, these are clearly monumental in their intent, though sadly the mosaics are only fragmentary. Immediately after the baths is **Oil Press 35**, restored in 1990 and featuring a reconstruction of the grinding mechanism, including both grinding stones.

Above the Orpheus House, a broad, paved street leads up towards the main group of public buildings – the Capitol and Basilica, whose sand-coloured ruins dominate the site. The arrangement of the **Forum** is typical of a major Roman town: built on the highest rise of the city and flanked by a triumphal arch, market, capitol and basilica.

Inscriptions date the **Capitol**, the smaller and lower of the two main buildings, to 217 AD, when this public nucleus seems to have been rebuilt by the African-born Severian emperors. Adjoined by small forum **baths**, it is a simple building with a porticoed court that leads on to a small temple and altar dedicated to the official state cult of Capitoline Jove, Juno and Minerva. The large five-aisled **Basilica** to its side served as the courthouse, while immediately across the **forum** were the small court and stalls of the central market. Storks have colonized some columns of the Capitol and Basilica; on a quiet day, you will hear their clacking noises and will almost certainly see a few circling above or gliding on and off their nests.

The **Triumphal Arch**, right in the middle of the town, had no purpose other than to create a ceremonial proscenium for the principal street, the Decumanus Maximus. It was erected to honour the Severian emperor Caracalla and was once topped with a bronze chariot, according to a weathered inscription. The heavy eroded medallions on either side presumably depict Caracalla and his mother, Julia Donna, who is also named in the inscription.

Mansions and mosaics

The finest of Volubilis's mansions – and its mosaics – line the **Decumanus Maximus**, fronted in traditional Roman and Italian fashion by the shops built in tiny cubicles. Before you reach this point, however, take a look at the remains of an **aqueduct** and **fountains** across from the triumphal arch; these once supplied yet another complex of public baths. Opposite them is the **House of the Athlete** (also called House of the Acrobat), which retains an impressive **Mosaic of an Athlete** or "chariot jumper" – depicted receiving the winner's cup for a *desultor* race, a display of great skill which entailed leaping on and off a horse in full gallop.

First of the Decumanus Maximus mansions, the **House of the Ephebus** takes its name from the bronze of a youth found in its ruins (and today displayed in Rabat). In general plan it is very similar to the House of Orpheus, once again containing an olive press in its rear section, though this building is on a far grander scale – almost twice the size of the other – with pictorial mosaics in most of its public rooms and an ornamental pool in its central court. Finest of the mosaics is a representation of **Bacchus Being Drawn in a Chariot by Panthers** – a suitable scene for the *cenacula*, or banqueting hall, in which it is placed.

▲ Mosaic of an Atlas lion, Volubilis

Separated from the Ephebus House by a narrow lane is a mosaic-less mansion, known after its facade as the **House of Columns**, and adjoining this, the **Knight's House** with an incomplete mosaic of **Dionysos Discovering Ariadne** asleep on the beach at Naxos; both houses are largely ruins. More illuminating is the large mansion which begins the next block, similar in plan, but with a very complete mosaic of the **Labours of Hercules**. Almost comic caricatures, these give a good idea of typical provincial Roman mosaics. The next house along, the **House of Dionysos**, holds the site's best preserved mosaic, **Dionysos and the Four Seasons**, which still hints at the exuberant original colours. In the neighbouring house is a mosaic of the **Nymphs Bathing**, severely deteriorated around its central area.

Beyond this area, approaching the partially reconstructed **Tangier Gate**, stands the **Palace of the Gordians**, former residence of the procurators who administered the city and the province. Despite its size, however, and even with evidence of a huge **bath house** and pooled courtyards, it is unmemorable, stripped of its columns and lacking any mosaics. Its grandeur may have made it a target for Ismail's building mania. Indeed, how much of Volubilis remained standing before his reign is an open question; Walter Harris, writing at the turn of the twentieth century, found the road between here and Meknes littered with ancient marbles, left as they fell following the announcement of the sultan's death.

Back on the Decumanus, cross to the other side of the road and walk down a block to a smaller lane below the street, heading for the isolated cypress tree opposite the Palace of the Gordians. In the house by the tree is the most exceptional ensemble of mosaics in Volubilis – the **Cortege of Venus**. You cannot enter the house but most of the fine mosaics can be seen by walking round the outside of the ruins. Around the central court is a small group of mosaics, including an odd, very worn representation of a **Chariot Race** – with birds instead of horses. The villa's most outstanding mosaics lie beyond, in the "public" sections. On the left, in the corner, is a geometrical design, with medallions of **Bacchus Surrounded by the Four Seasons**; off to the right are **Diana Bathing** (and surprised by the huntsman Acteon) and the **Abduction of Hylas**

by Nymphs. Each of these scenes – especially the last two – is superbly handled in stylized, fluid animation. They date, like that of the **Nereids** (two houses further down), from the late second or early third century AD, and were a serious commission. It is not known who commissioned the house, but its owner must have been among the city's most successful patrons; bronze busts of Cato and Juba II were also found here and now form the centrepiece of Rabat's museum.

Leaving the site by a path below the forum, you pass close by the ruins of a **temple** on the opposite side of the stream. The Romans dedicated it to Saturn, but it seems to have previously been used for the worship of a Carthaginian god; several hundred votive offerings were discovered during its excavation.

Moulay Idriss

MOULAY IDRISS takes its name from its founder, Morocco's most venerated saint and the creator of its first Arab dynasty. His tomb and *zaouia* lie right at the heart of the town, the reason for its sacred status and the object of constant pilgrimage – a trip here is worth a fifth of the *hajj* to Mecca – not to mention an important summer **moussem** in the third week of August. For most Western tourists, there is little specific to see and certainly nothing that may be visited – non-Muslims are barred from the shrines. But you could lose a happy day exploring the tangled lanes that shimmy between the sugar-cube houses scattered over two hills, enjoying delightful window-views or just absorbing the easy-going holiday atmosphere. Few tourists bother to stay overnight – another reason to linger.

The Town

Grands taxis and buses for Moulay Idriss drop you at a square at the very base of the town. From here, walk up the steep road to another square – almost directly ahead are the green-tiled pyramids of the shrine and *zaouia*, flanked on either side by the hillside residential quarters of Khiber and Tasga. Locals say the town looks like a Bactrian camel, with the shrine and *zaouia* as the saddle between the two humps.

Moulay Idriss and the foundation of Morocco

Moulay Idriss el Akhbar (The Elder) was a great-grandson of the Prophet Mohammed; his grandparents were Mohammed's daughter Fatima, and cousin and first follower, Ali. Heir to the Caliphate in Damascus, he fled to Morocco around 787, following the Ommayad victory in the great civil war which split the Muslim world into Shia and Sunni sects.

In Volubilis, then still the main centre of the north, Idriss seems to have been welcomed as an *imam* (a spiritual and political leader), and within five years had succeeded in carving out a considerable kingdom. At this new town site, more easily defended than Volubilis, he built his capital, and he also began the construction of Fes, continued and considerably extended by his son Idriss II, that city's patron saint. News of his growing power filtered back to the East, however, and in 792 the Ommayads had Idriss poisoned, doubtless assuming that his kingdom would crumble.

They were mistaken. Alongside the faith of Islam, Idriss had instilled a sense of unity among the region's previously pagan (and sometimes Christian or Jewish) Berber tribes, which had been joined in this prototypical Moroccan state by increasing numbers of Arab Shiites loyal to the succession of his *Alid* line. After his assassination, Rashid, the servant who had travelled to Morocco with Idriss, took over as regent until 807, when the founder's son, Idriss II, was old enough to assume the throne.

The **souks**, such as they are, line the streets of the **Khiber** (the taller hill) above the *zaouia*. They offer a variety of religious artefacts for Muslim visitors, especially plain white candles for the shrines, together with excellent local nougat and, in autumn, *arbutus* (strawberry tree) berries.

Rebuilt by Moulay Ismail, **Moulay Idriss's shrine and zaouia** are cordoned off from the street by a low, wooden bar to keep out Christians and beasts of burden. To get a true sense of its scale, you have to climb up towards one of the vantage points near the pinnacle of each quarter. It's not easy to find your way up through the winding streets (most end in abrupt blind alleys), and, unless you enjoy the challenge of it all, you'd do better to enlist the help of a guide (around 40dh). Should you decide to venture on your own, from the entrance of the shrine (as you face its courtyard) take the left passageway and climb the steps towards a fountain, 50m beyond, where the lane splits in two; take the right fork for another 30m or so and then turn left up another flight of steps; continue up the steps (150 of them), negotiating some switchbacks on the way, until you (hopefully) find yourself at the *grand terrase*.

On your way up, aim for the unusual modern minaret of the **Idriss Medersa**, now a Koranic school. The Medersa was built with materials taken from Volubilis and the cylindrical minaret was built in 1939 by a *hadji* who had been inspired by those he had seen in Mecca. A *surah* (chapter) from the Koran is inscribed in Kufic script in green mosaics.

Eating

Restaurants are scarce as the majority of the town's guesthouses cook up evening meals for guests. For a quick bite, the best bet is the grill **cafés** on the square by the shrine and *zaouia*. For more substantial fare, head for *Restaurant Baraka* (lunchtime only; moderate) found in a small white building, near the *fantasia* ground on the way into the town. *Diyar Timnay*'s pleasant panoramic restaurant is also a good option for inexpensive tajines and brochettes. Unfortunately, the popular *Restaurant Trois Boules d'Or*, with its premium position on the *terrase* overlooking the mausoleum, was closed due to management problems but will hopefully reopen soon.

Fes (Fez)

The history of Fez is composed of wars and murders, triumphs of arts and sciences, and a good deal of imagination.

Walter Harris: *Land of an African Sultan*

The most ancient of the Imperial capitals and the most complete medieval city of the Arab world, **FES** stimulates all the senses: a barrage of haunting and beautiful sounds, infinite visual details and unfiltered odours. It has the French-built Ville Nouvelle of other Moroccan cities – familiar and modern in looks and urban life – but a quarter or so of Fes's 950,000 inhabitants continue to live in the extraordinary Medina-city of **Fes el Bali**, which owes little to the West besides electricity and tourists. More than any other city in Morocco, the old town seems suspended in time somewhere between the Middle Ages and the modern world.

Like much of "traditional" Morocco, the city was "saved" then recreated by the French, under the auspices of General Lyautey, the Protectorate's first Resident-General. Lyautey took the philanthropic and startling move of declaring the city a historical monument; philanthropic because he certainly saved Fes el Bali from destruction (albeit from less benevolent Frenchmen), and startling because until then Moroccans were under the impression that Fes was still a living city – the Imperial Capital of the Moroccan empire rather than a preservable part of the nation's heritage. More conveniently for the French, this paternalistic protection helped to disguise the dismantling of the old culture. By building a new European city nearby – the Ville Nouvelle – then transferring Fes's economic and political functions to Rabat and the west coast, Lyautey ensured the city's eclipse along with its preservation.

To appreciate the significance of this demise, you only have to look at the Arab chronicles or old histories of Morocco – in every one, Fes takes centre stage. The city had dominated Moroccan trade, culture and religious life – and usually its politics, too – since the end of the tenth century. It was closely and symbolically linked with the birth of an "Arabic" Moroccan state due to their mutual foundation by Moulay Idriss I, and was regarded as one of the holiest cities of the Islamic world after Mecca and Medina. Medieval European travellers describe it with a mixture of awe and respect, as a "citadel of fanaticism" yet the most advanced seat of learning in mathematics, philosophy and medicine.

The decline of the city notwithstanding, **Fassis** – the people of Fes – continue to head most government ministries and have a reputation throughout Morocco as successful and sophisticated. What is undeniable is that they have the most developed Moroccan city culture, with an intellectual tradition and their own cuisine, dress and way of life.

The development of Fes

When the city's founder, Moulay Idriss I, died in 792, Fes was little more than a village on the east bank of the river. It was his son, **Idriss II**, who really began the city's development, at the beginning of the ninth century, by making it his capital and allowing in refugees from Andalucian Cordoba and from Kairouan in Tunisia – at the time, the two most important cities of western Islam. The impact on Fes of these refugees was immediate and lasting: they established separate, walled towns (still distinct quarters today) on either riverbank, and provided the superior craftsmanship and mercantile experience for Fes's industrial and commercial growth. It was at this time, too, that the city gained its intellectual reputation. The tenth-century Pope Silvester II studied here at the Kairaouine University, technically the world's first, where he is said to have learned the Arabic mathematics that he introduced to Europe.

The seat of government – and impetus of patronage – shifted south to Marrakesh under the Berber dynasties of the **Almoravides** (1068–1145) and **Almohads** (1145–1250). But with the conquest of Fes by the **Merenids** in 1248, and their subsequent consolidation of power across Morocco, the city regained its pre-eminence and moved into something of a "golden age". Alongside the old Medina, the Merenids built a massive royal city – **Fes el Djedid**, meaning "New Fes" – which reflected both the wealth and confidence of their rule. Continued expansion, once again facilitated by an influx of refugees, this time from the Spanish reconquest of Andalucía, helped to establish the city's reputation as "the Baghdad of the West".

After the fall of the Merenids, Fes became more isolated under the Saadians and Alaouites, and French colonial rule allowed the city little more than a provincial existence. Despite the crucial role the Fassis played in the struggle for independence (a time brought to life in Paul Bowles' novel *The Spider's House*), Mohammed V retained the French capital of Rabat, condemning the city to further decline. If UNESCO had not moved in with its Cultural Heritage plan for the city's preservation, it seems likely that much of the old city would have been threatened by extensive physical collapse.

Orientation, information, arrival and guides

Even if you felt you were getting to grips with Moroccan cities, Fes is bewildering. The basic layout is simple enough, with a Moroccan **Medina** and French-built **Ville Nouvelle**, but here the Medina comprises two separate cities: **Fes el Bali** (Old Fes), in the pear-shaped bowl of the Sebou valley, and **Fes el Djedid** (New Fes), established on the edge of the valley during the thirteenth century.

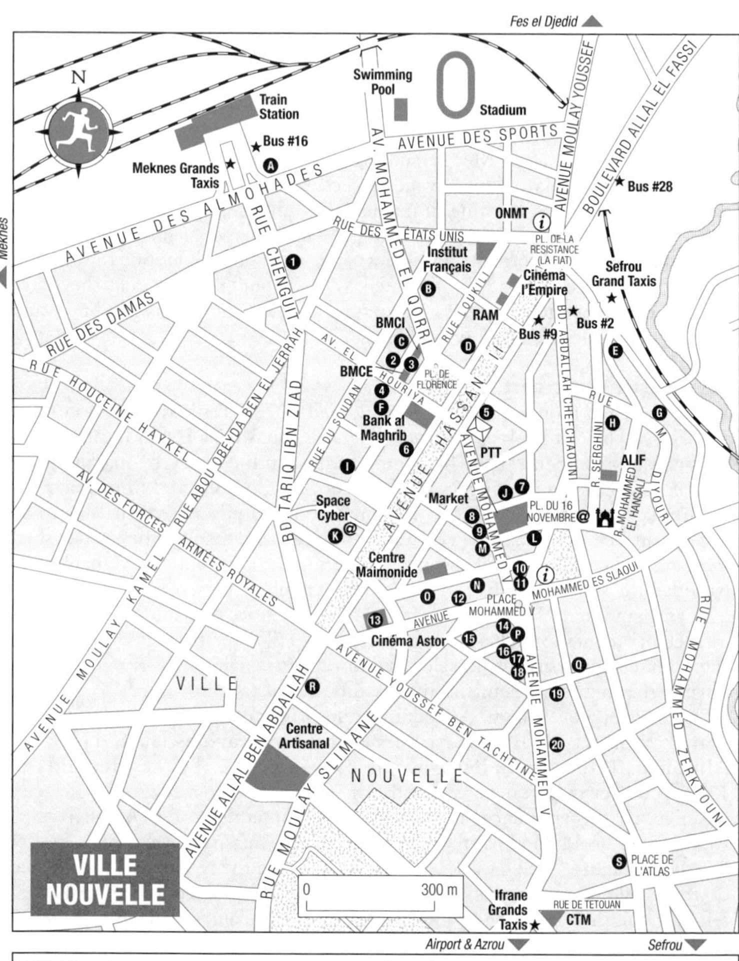

ACCOMMODATION

Auberge de Jeunesse	H
Grand Hôtel	L
Hôtel al Fath	M
Hôtel Amor	F
Hôtel Central	P
Hôtel de la Paix	D
Hôtel Kairouan	B
Hôtel Menzeh Zalagh	E&G
Hôtel Mounia	Q
Hôtel Olympic	J
Hôtel Renaissance	N
Hôtel Rex	S
Hôtel Royal	C
Hôtel Sofia	I
Hôtel Volubilis	R
Hôtel Wassim	K
Ibis Moussafir Hôtel	A
Splendid Hotel	O

EATING & DRINKING

Astor	13
Brasserie le Marignon	9
Café 24/24	7
Café Chope	17
Café de la Renaissance	11
Café Floria	5
Café-Restaurant al Mousaffir	18
Chez Vittorio	16
Dalila	8
Gelatitalia	2
Le Filet Bleu	3
Le Nautilus	D
Le Progrès	15
Number One	10
Pâtisserie Crystal	14
Restaurant la Cheminée	1
Restaurant Isla Blanca	6
Restaurant Marrakesh	19
Restaurant Ten Years	17
Tivoli	12
Venezia Sandwich	4
Zagora Restaurant	20

Petits taxis and city buses

Petits taxis in Fes use their meters, so offer good value. Useful petit taxi ranks include:

Pl Mohammed V (Ville Nouvelle).
Main PTT on Ave Hassan II (Ville Nouvelle).
Pl des Alaouites (Fes el Djedid).
Pl Baghdadi (north of Bab Boujeloud, Fes el Bali).
Dar Batha (south of Bab Boujeloud, Fes el Bali).
Bab Guissa (north gate, by Palais Jamaï, Fes el Bali).
Bab er R'cif (central gate, south of the Kairaouine Mosque, Fes el Bali).
Bab Ftouh (southeast gate, Fes el Bali).

City buses Useful city bus routes are detailed, where relevant, in the text. As a general guide, these are the ones you're most likely to want to use:

#2 Av Mohammed V to Bab Smarine (by Av Hassan II and Pl des Alaouites).
#3 Pl de la Résistance (La Fiat) via Bd Allal el Fassi to Bab Ftouh.
#9 Pl Mohammed V to Route de Sefrou via Dar Batha.
#10 Train station via *gare routière* to Bab Ftouh.
#12 Bab Boujeloud to Bab Ftouh.
#16 Train station to the airport.
#17 Pl de Florence, opposite Banque al Maghrib, to Aïn Chkeff.
#18 Dar Batha to Sidi Boujida via Bab Ftouh.
#19 Train station to Pl er R'cif, south of the Kairaouine Mosque.
#20 Pl de Florence to the Arms Museum.
#27 Dar Batha to Pl er R'cif, south of the Kairaouine Mosque.
#28 Pl de la Résistance (La Fiat) via Bab Ftouh to Sidi Harazem.
#29 Pl de l'Atlas to Pl er R'cif, south of the Kairaouine Mosque.
#38 From Pl de l'Atlas to Ain Bedia via the *Camping International* (see p.211) on the Sefrou road.
#45 Hay Adarissa to Pl R'cif via Pl l'Istiqlal

Note: These **numbers are marked on the sides** of the buses; those on the back are completely different.

Fes el Djedid, dominated by a vast enclosure of royal palaces and gardens, is relatively straightforward. But **Fes el Bali**, where you'll want to spend most of your time, is an incredibly intricate web of lanes, blind alleys and souks. It takes two or three days before you even start to feel confident of where you're going.

Fes's **tourist office**, the Direction Régionale du Tourisme, on the east side of Place Mohammed V, is open Monday to Friday 8.30am to 4.30pm. Though not very helpful, it's a convienient place to arrange an official guide for the Medina.

Arrival

By train

The new train station (ⓣ0890 203040), under construction at the time of writing, is in the Ville Nouvelle, ten minutes' walk from the concentration of hotels around Place Mohammed V. If you prefer to stay in Fes el Bali, either take a petit taxi or bus #10 or #47 to Bab Boujeloud, where most of the old city's hotels are to be found; if you walk to Avenue Hassan II, you can pick up the #9 bus to nearby Dar Batha (pronounced *dar baat-ha*). From the train station, the #10 bus passes the main bus station and the #16 bus runs to the airport. Other buses from the train station run to outlying suburbs.

Beware of **unofficial taxi drivers**, who wait at the station and charge very unofficial rates for the trip into town; in a petit taxi during daytime (prices increase after dark), the fare to Bab Boujeloud is around 10dh (supplements for more than one person will increase this by a few dirhams).

By bus

Coming in by bus can be confusing, since there are terminals in the Ville Nouvelle and by the various gates to the Medina. From most destinations, however, you will arrive at the main **bus station** or *gare routière* just north of Bab Mahrouk, between Kasbah Cherada and Borj Nord (see map, p.212). CTM has its own principal station on the corner of Rue Tetouan and Avenue Mohammed V in the Ville Nouvelle (ⓣ0535 732984; see map, p.204); buses call here before, in theory, continuing on to the main bus station. The other exception is if you're coming from **Taza and the east**: buses stop at the Medina's southeast gate, **Bab Ftouh**, before continuing to the main bus station.

By grands taxis

Like buses, grands taxis mostly operate from the *gare routière* outside Bab Mahrouk. Exceptions are those from **Immouzer**, **Ifrane** and **Azrou** (and sometimes Marrakesh), which use a rank opposite the CTM office, 100m west of Place de l'Atlas (see Ville Nouvelle map, p.204) and those from/to **Sefrou** (and sometimes Immouzer), which use a rank 100m down southeast of Place de la Résistance (La Fiat). **Meknes** grands taxis arrive outside the train station. Grands taxis from **Sidi Harazem**, **Taza**, and **Taounate** arrive at **Bab Ftouh**.

By air

Fes's Saïs **airport** is 15km south of the city, off the N8 (formerly P24) to Immouzer. From here you can reach town by grand taxi – ranks are just outside the terminal building on the left. Prices have been fixed at 120dh for up to six people from the airport to the town centre. If you are alone, you will be required to pay the full fare so it is worth finding others to share the cost with. Alternatively, bus #16 to the train station leaves the airport at least every hour.

By car

Central options for **parking** in the Ville Nouvelle include: Place de Florence; the square backed by *Hôtel Sofia* one block south; and Place du 16 Novembre. If you intend to stay in Fes el Bali (or just drive there for the day), you can leave your car in car parks around Bab Boujeloud; west on the wasteground opposite the Lycée or south by the Dar Batha Museum, from where it is only a short walk to the Medina and its hotels. Other useful carparks are off Route du Tour de Fes, near the centre of Talâa Kebira (just south of *Maison Blue 'Le Riad'* hotel on the map p.212) and by Bab el Guissa. Expect to pay the *gardien* at each around 10dh per day, 20dh overnight.

Maps

The **maps** in this guide provide functional overviews of the city. On p.204 is a plan of the Ville Nouvelle, showing the outline of Fes el Djedid and edge of Fes el Bali; on pp.212–213 is a general plan of Fes el Bali (with enlargements of the Bab Boujeloud area on p.214 and the Kairaouine Mosque area on p.221). An additional map of Fes el Djedid is on p.226. Inevitably, all maps of Fes el Bali are hugely simplified: more than any other Medina in Morocco, the old city is composed of an impenetrable maze of lanes and blind alleys whose precise orientation and localized names do not exactly lend themselves to cartography.

However, there are two maps of the Medina for sale that are worth noting. Sold at most newsstands and Bureau de Tabacs (check those across from the Dar Batha Museum) is the *Fes: The Thematic Tourist Circuits*, a green booklet that includes a large fold-out map of the Medina. The guide will cost you 100dh and provides information on a variety of different itineraries using colour-coded routes that correspond with the star-shaped tourist signs scattered throughout the Medina. The second is a simple map entitled *Plan de Fes*, which details both the Ville Nouvelle and the Medina (unfortunately, the current edition is marred by badly placed photographs of monuments), free from the tourist office or 10dh from most newsstands.

Guides

A tour from an **official guide** is a useful introduction to Fes el Bali; no matter how many people are in your group, the fee is 150dh for a half-day and 250dh for a whole day, although it is always a good idea to clarify in advance exactly what is meant by a "full" day. Official guides identify themselves by laminated identity cards around their necks and can be engaged at the Direction Régionale du Tourisme on the east side of Place Mohammed V or through the more upmarket hotels in the Medina.

Guides who tout their services are likely to be **unofficial** and technically illegal. This doesn't necessarily mean they're to be avoided – some who are genuine students (as most claim to be) can be excellent. But you have to choose carefully, ideally drinking a tea together before settling a rate or declaring interest. One of the downsides of taking an unofficial guide is that in order not to be spotted by their official counterparts, they sometimes follow convoluted and ill-frequented routes around the Medina, or call out directions from a few metres in front of or behind you, so they don't look like they are at your service – not a good way to gain information about the places you are walking by. More disreputable guides play an unpleasant trick of leading you into Fes el Bali and, once you're disorientated, maybe with dusk descending, demand more than the agreed fee to take you back to your hotel. Don't be intimidated – appeal to passers-by, who will be happy to direct you back to your hotel.

Whether you get an official or unofficial guide, it's essential to work out in advance the **main points you want to see** and make it absolutely clear if you are not interested in **shopping**. If you enter a shop with a guide, official or otherwise, they will take a commission from the shopkeeper on anything you buy, which will be added to the price you pay. For some hints on shopping on your own, see "Shopping for Crafts" on p.233.

Security

Despite what some *faux guides* may say, the Medina is not a dangerous place. However, some female visitors report experiencing unwanted attention from teenage touts. If a stern word does not work, appeal to older Fassis nearby, who will be as shocked as you at their lack of respect. In the Ville Nouvelle, locals warn that robbery is a problem at night on Boulevard Allal El Fassi, the isolated main road between Dar Batha and Place de La Résistance in the Ville Nouvelle; if you must walk it, do so only in groups of at least three people. Also, avoid the overgrown hillside east of Place de la Résistance, between the *McDonald's* and the train track, where muggings have occurred even during daytime.

Accommodation

Staying in Fes used to mean either comfort (and a reliable water supply) in modern **Ville Nouvelle** hotels or roughing it in the Medina hotels of

Fes el Bali and **Fes el Djedid**. No longer. Not only has plumbing in the Medina improved somewhat, the rise and rise of Fes's riad scene means there's class and character in renovated palaces – if you are prepared to pay for it. Either way, hotel space is at a premium in all categories, so be prepared for higher prices than usual and reserve in advance if possible.

Fes el Bali

With the notable exceptions of the *Hôtel Batha*, *Palais Jamaï*, a few mid-range options that have cropped up on the edge of Bab Boujloud and a fast-growing number of pricey riads (currently nearing one hundred), the majority of hotels in Fes el Bali are basic *pensions*, most of which could do with a makeover and better plumbing. Some are also overpriced, charging the equivalent of one-star prices when they can get away with it in peak season. So long as your expectations are modest, most are adequate, and the group around Bab Boujeloud are an ideal launchpad from which to explore the old city's sights and souks. The problem of water – or rather lack of it in summer – in many of the bargain-basement hotels can be overcome by taking a steam bath in the nearby hammam.

Bab Boujeloud

Bab Boujeloud is the western gateway to Fes el Bali and offers pedestrian access to Fes el Djedid. Bus and petit taxi ranks for getting to and from the Ville Nouvelle are in nearby **Place de l'Istiqlal**. Unless otherwise stated, the hotels listed below are keyed on the "Around Bab Boujeloud" map on p.214. There is also a hammam nearby (see p.238).

Dar Bouânania 21 Derb Ben Salem (off Talâa Kebira) ⓣ&ⓕ 0535 637282. See map, p.212. Not as classy as the riads yet a cut above other Bab Boujeloud cheapies. Simple characterful rooms (two en suite) are arranged around an intimate courtyard of painted woodwork and zellij that hints at riad charm at a fraction of the price. ❹

Hôtel Bab Boujloud 49 Rue Isesco, off to the left of the square outside Bab Boujloud ⓣ0535 637625, ⓔhotelbabboujloud@gmail.com. A new hotel intended to satisfy the lack of mid-range options in the Boujloud area. Most rooms are en suite with a/c and offer comfort at the expense of character. Excellent views of the Medina from the large terrace. Wi-fi available. ❸

Hôtel Batha Pl de l'Istiqlal ⓣ0535 741077, ⓔhotelbatha@menara.ma. A tour-group favourite next to the Dar Batha museum, this three-star is comfy if a little bland, its character concealed in the bar of the older block behind, formerly the British consulate. Also has a small swimming pool. Breakfast included. ❺

Hôtel Cascade 26 Rue Serajine ⓣ0535 638442. Usually full by mid-day during high season, a busy Boujloud favourite frequented by a young international crowd. Offers small simple rooms, hot showers, and the best terrace in Bab Boujeloud (where you can sleep for 50dh). Breakfast is also available. ❷

Hôtel Erraha Signposted by Boujeloud Mosque ⓣ0535 633226. Rooms in the "*Relax*" are basic and a little tatty but a better choice than nearby *Hotel National*. Hot showers available. Good terrace, too. ❷

Hôtel Lamrani Talâa Seghira, opposite the Hammam Sidi Azouz ⓣ0535 634411. A friendly place with small but clean rooms, most with double beds. Hot showers available. ❷

Hôtel Mauritania 20 Rue Serajine ⓣ0535 633518. A fall back to – and overpriced compared with – the *Hôtel Cascade* next door. Washbasins in cell-like rooms, hot showers in the corridor. ❷

Pension Batha 8 Sidi Lkhayat Batha ⓣ0535 741150. Close to Place de l'Istiqlal and away from the hustle around the gateway, this has pleasant old-fashioned decor in the rooms – rooms 4 and 5 feature nice stuccowork on the ceiling – and some en-suite hot showers. Breakfast included. ❸

Pension Kawtar 25 Derb Tarjana, signposted off Talâa Seghira ⓣ0535 740172. A homely, family-owned Moroccan townhouse with various-sized rooms scattered over two floors. Great value for money. ❸

Pension Talâa Talâa Seghira (opposite Medersa Bou Inania) ⓣ0535 633359. A warm welcome in a well-maintained and well-located *pension*, with pleasant doubles, though singles are rather hutch-like. A mellower alternative to the *Cascade*. Shared hot showers. ❷

Riads and upmarket hotels in Fes el Bali

Staying in style in Fes el Bali means the best of both worlds, but it doesn't come cheap. Fes's riad scene is fast catching up with that of Marrakesh as owners cotton on that period atmosphere means high prices – some are overpriced, so it pays to be choosy (most riads have one smaller room available to suit restricted budgets). Due to the sheer number of immaculately restored riads that provide accommodation in every corner of the Medina, the recommendations below are far from all-encompassng, though they do include a selection of well-established riads in a variety of different locations. Reservations are recommended and breakfast is included in all prices.

Dar el Hana 22 Rue Ferrane Couicha ⓣ0535 635854, ⓦwww.darelhana.com. See map, p.212. Tastefully renovated by the same minds behind *Dar Seffarine*, this intimate dar offers three comfortable rooms and an instantly homely, sociable atmosphere. Home-cooked meals are served in the snug courtyard or terrace, which offers views not easily rivalled. Cooking lessons are available. Whether booking rooms or the whole place, do so well in advance. ⑤

Dar Seffarine 14 Derb Shoa Lougote (alley 20m north of Pl Seffarine) ⓣ0535 635205, ⓦwww.darseffarine.com. See map, p.221. In the old heart of Fes el Bali, with some of the oldest zellij and stucco of Fes's riads and rooms styled in a sort of Moroccan minimalism by its designer-architect owners; the Koba suite is a knock-out. Add in a community spirit that sees guests breakfast together and you have one of the most appealing – and well-priced – options. ⑥

La Maison Bleue 2 Pl de l'Istiqlal ⓣ0535 741843, ⓦwww.maisonbleue.com. See map, p.214. The first riad in Fes and still one of the best, an intimate world of luxury opposite the Dar Batha museum where rooms, some with a private terrace, are named after female members of the family who built and still own it. Style is a mix of Moroccan and classy European pieces and there's excellent traditional dining in its expensive restaurant (open to non-guests). More romantic still is the sister house *La Maison Bleue* "*Le Riad*", across a car park north of Talâa Kebira at 33 Derb el Miter (ⓣ0535 741873, ⓦwww.maisonbleue.com; see map, p.212). This has the added appeal of a garden and a swimming pool in the courtyard, plus a hammam hidden away among its many levels. Both ⑧

Riad al Bartal 21 Rue Sournas ⓣ0535 637053, ⓦwww.riadalbartal.com. See map, p.212. The light touch of French owners Mireille and Christian Laroche abounds in this *maison d'hôte*, from the arty, pared-down decor in a plant-filled courtyard to individually styled rooms with painted ceilings and *tadelakt* walls. Suites are worth the extra 150dh. ⑥

Riad Fes Derb Ben Slimane ⓣ0535 947610, ⓦwww.riadfes.com. See map, p.212. Less a *maison d'hôte* than a boutique hotel, architecturally the grandest in Fes. With a third extension now open, guests stay in Baroque, traditional, or modern themed accommodation. There's a stylish bar, a plunge pool in the garden and immaculate service throughout. ⑧

Riad Laaroussa 3 Derb Bechara off Talâa Seghira ⓣ0674 187639, ⓦwww.riad-laaroussa.com. See map, p.212. A popular contender with a modern twist on traditional decor. The grassy courtyard and spacious furnishings provide a calming retreat from the commotion of the Medina. There's also a hammam and spa. ⑦

Riad Louna 21 Derb Serraj off Talâa Seghira ⓣ0535 741985, ⓦwww.riadlouna.com. See map, p.214. One of the best-value riads, traditionally restored by its Belgian owner, with six rooms and three suites set around a lovely garden of palms, orange trees and a fountain. It is easiest located from Pl de l'Istiqlal: leaving the PTT on your left, take the first right down steps then right down a narrow alley. A windowless room is available at a bargain price and is just about worth it for the charm outside; others from ⑤

Riad Norma 16 Derb Sornas ⓣ0535 634781, ⓦwww.riadnorma.com. See map, p.212. Charming riad, simpler than others and elegantly furnished with antiques, with more modern style in five suites and a plunge pool in the garden. ⑦

Ryad Mabrouka 25 Derb el Miter ⓣ0535 656345, ⓦwww.ryadmabrouka.com. See map, p.212. Through a door in an unassuming dead-end alley, Moroccan style is paired with French antiques and modern art, a reflection of the eclectic tastes of French owner Michel Trezzy. There's also a plunge pool in an idyllic garden and great views of the Medina from the terrace to boot. ⑥

Sofitel Palais Jamaï Bab Guissa ⓣ0535 634331, ⓦwww.sofitel.com. See map, p.213. Along with Marrakesh's *Mamounia*, this is the most famous and historic hotel in Morocco, a five-star number founded on a nineteenth-century vizier's palace. It also served as a principal setting for Paul Bowles' novel *The Spider's House*. Unless you pay upwards of 6000dh for a palace suite, you're in the modern block behind; the best of the smallish rooms offer excellent views of the Medina. There are three restaurants, two spas, and a large pool. ⑧

Fes el Djedid

An alternative to the backpacker hostels around Bab Boujeloud, these are within a ten- to fifteen-minute walk of Fes el Bali and less frequented by tourists (and hustlers). See map on p.226 for locations.

Hôtel du Parc Off Grand Rue des Merenides ⓣ0535 941698. Overlook squalid toilets, grubby rooms and cold-water showers and this friendly place has a certain shabby appeal, plus a terrace with views of the ramparts. ❷

Hôtel Glacier Near Pl des Alaouites ⓣ0535 626261. Located at the bottom of an alleyway off Rue des Merenides, this brightly painted hotel has clean and basic rooms arranged around an interior courtyard. Run by two friendly women, who speak only Arabic. Best budget choice in this part of town; shared cold-water showers. ❶

Hôtel Juane S'bile Across from the Jardins de Boujloud ⓣ0535 638635, ⓦwww.hoteljuanesbile.com. Newly opened two-star offering comfortable, if slightly pokey, mod-con rooms. A good option for those looking for proximity to the Medina without the noise. ❹

The Ville Nouvelle

As cheap rooms can be tricky to obtain in Fes, it's wise to book ahead. The places below are marked on the map on p.204.

Cheap

Auberge de Jeunesse 18 Rue Abdeslam Seghrini ⓣ0535 624085, ⓦwww.fesyouth-hostel.com. One of the best Moroccan youth hostels; easy-going, friendly and refurbished to provide spotless dorms from 55dh and doubles from 130dh; free hot showers 8.15–10am. It's set in a small garden in a quiet backwater near the *Hôtel Zalagh*, which usually allows guests to swim in its pool for a reduced fee. Its enthusiastic Fassi manager is also a mine of local information. Doors close at 10pm.

Hôtel al Fath Formerly the *Excelsior*, corner of Av Mohammed V and Rue Larbi el Kaghat ⓣ0535 944650. Spartan but friendly. Hot showers mornings and evenings. ❷

Hôtel Amor 31 Rue Arabie Saoudite, previously Rue du Pakistan ⓣ0535 622724. One block from Av Hassan II, behind the Bank al Maghrib. Attractive tiled frontage; reasonably priced accommodation with restaurant. ❷

Hôtel Central 50 Rue Brahim Roudani, also called Rue du Nador ⓣ0535 622333. Good-value, popular one-star that's often full. Rooms are clean and bright, heated in winter, some with small en-suite shower cubicles. ❷

Hôtel Kairouan 84 Rue de Soudan ⓣ0535 623590. A simple, well-kept hotel with large rooms (all with hot showers) but sited somewhat in no-man's-land between the train station and town centre. ❷

Hôtel Renaissance 29 Rue Abdelkrim el Kattabi ⓣ0535 622193. Despite a rather gloomy entrance and only functional rooms, the *Renaissance* is a friendly and clean billet in a central position with shared hot showers. ❷

Hôtel Rex 32 Pl de l'Atlas ⓣ0535 642133. A basic place offering large rooms. Shared facilities throughout. Handy for CTM departures (or late arrivals). ❷

Hôtel Royal 36 Rue de Soudan ⓣ0535 624656. Convenient for the train station. Its simple rooms vary somewhat; those on the first floor with shared facilities are cheaper, but better en suites are worth the extra. ❷

Moderate

Grand Hôtel Bd Abdallah Chefchaouni ⓣ0535 623245, ⓔgranotel@hotmail.ma. An old colonial hotel with an Art Deco facade and similarly impressive proportions in refurbished rooms, somewhat spartan though all with a/c, heating and en suite; many have a bath. Facilities include a bar, restaurant, nightclub and garage. ❹

Hôtel de la Paix 44 Av Hassan II ⓣ0555 625072, ⓔhoteldelapaix@iam.net.ma. An old-established tour-group hotel, well worth a call. Red-carpeted corridors lead to modern(ish) spotless rooms with full bathroom suite, TV, a/c and heating. The hotel's good seafood restaurant, *Le Nautilus*, is open to nonresidents. ❹

Hôtel Mounia 60 Bd Zerktouny ⓣ0535 624838, ⓦwww.hotelmouniafes.ma. A friendly, modern hotel that has been recently refurbished to provide smart rooms, all with central heating, a/c and satellite TV. One of the best mid-range choices in the Ville Nouvelle. ❺

Hôtel Olympic Rue Houman el Fatouaki, off Av Mohammed V, facing one side of the covered market ⓣ0535 932682, ⓕ0535 932665. A keenly priced option, clean and reliable with a reasonable restaurant. Recently refurbished throughout – all rooms now have bathroom, TV, and heating in winter. ❸

Hôtel Wassim Rue du Liban, off Av Hassan II ⓣ0535 654939, ⓦhotelwassim.ifrance.com. Classy in an understated kind of way, this four-star has been recently renovated. Fully equipped rooms are tasteful and spotless. Downside is that it can be overrun by tour groups. Also has a nightclub (free for residents but open to all). ❼

Ibis Moussafir Hôtel Pl de la Gare/Av des Almohades ⓣ0535 651902, ⓔH2035@accor .com. An always-busy member of Accor's international Ibis chain, modern and bright if rather impersonal. Smallish pleasant rooms. Also has a so-so restaurant, a bar and small swimming pool. ❺

Splendid Hôtel 9 Rue Abdelkrim el Khattabi ⓣ0535 622148, ⓔsplendid@menara.ma. An efficient modern hotel in the heart of the Ville Nouvelle, with newly refurbished and very pleasant en-suite rooms, a good restaurant, bar and small swimming pool. One of the best-value options in the Ville Nouvelle when not booked out by tour groups. ❹

Expensive

Hôtel Menzeh Zalagh 10 Rue Mohammed Diouri ⓣ0535 625531, ⓦwww.menzeh-zalagh.ma. A formerly state-owned hotel, now privatized, with quite a chic clientele (even the tour groups are select), and a new annexe on Rue Diyouri at the corner of Rue de Ravin, the *Hôtel Menzeh Fes*. Facilities include the hotel's own hammam. The swimming pool is open to nonresidents, but expensive at 70dh. On the other hand, the fine views across to Fes el Djedid are anyone's for the cost of an orange juice. ❼

Hôtel Sofia 3 Rue Arabie Saoudite ⓣ0535 624265, Four-star standards in a central modern chain hotel with a pool and all the works, frequented almost exclusively by tour groups; bar and nightclub open to nonresidents. Reasonably priced for a quality hotel. ❻

Hôtel Volubilis Av Allal Ben Abdallah next to the Centre Artisanal ⓣ0535 623098, ⓔvolubilis @fram.fr. Another four-star, whose main attraction is a central garden with two pools. The rooms are rather functional but most enjoy views over the garden. Nightclub is free to residents (100dh for nonresidents). ❺

Camping

Camping International Route de Sefrou ⓣ0535 618061. A relatively new site next to the new football stadium 4km from the city centre, accessible by bus #38 from Pl de l'Atlas. Well kept, with plenty of greenery, shade and constant hot water, it's pricey as campsites go, although for your money you get a pool, a bar, tennis courts and horseriding. The pool is also open to nonresidents (daily 9am–5pm; 15dh).

Fes el Bali

With its mosques, medersas and *fondouks*, combined with a mile-long labyrinth of souks, there are enough sights in **Fes el Bali** to fill three or four days just trying to locate them. In this – the apparently wilful secretiveness – lies part of Fes's fascination and there is much to be said for Paul Bowles' somewhat lofty advice to "lose oneself in the crowd – to be pulled along by it – not knowing where to and for

Getting in and out of Fes el Bali

There are four principal entrances and exits to Fes el Bali. **Bab Boujeloud**, the western gate, is easily identified by its bright polychrome decoration and the hotels and cafés grouped on either side. **Bab er R'cif** is a central gate by the square (and car park) beside the Mosque er R'cif, and is a convenient entrance, just a few blocks below the Kairaouine Mosque. Bus #19 and bus #29 run between the square and Avenue Mohammed V in the Ville Nouvelle, #19 continuing to the train station, #29 to Place de l'Atlas. Bus #27 runs between the square and Dar Batha. **Bab Ftouh** is the southeast gate at the bottom of the Andalous quarter, with cemeteries extending to the south. Bus #18 runs between here and Place de l'Istiqlal (near Bab Boujeloud) and there is also a petit taxi rank. Finally, **Bab Guissa**, the north gate, is up at the top of the city by the *Hôtel Palais Jamaï*: it's a convenient point to enter (or leave) the city from (or heading to) the Merenid tombs. Petits taxis are available by the gate.

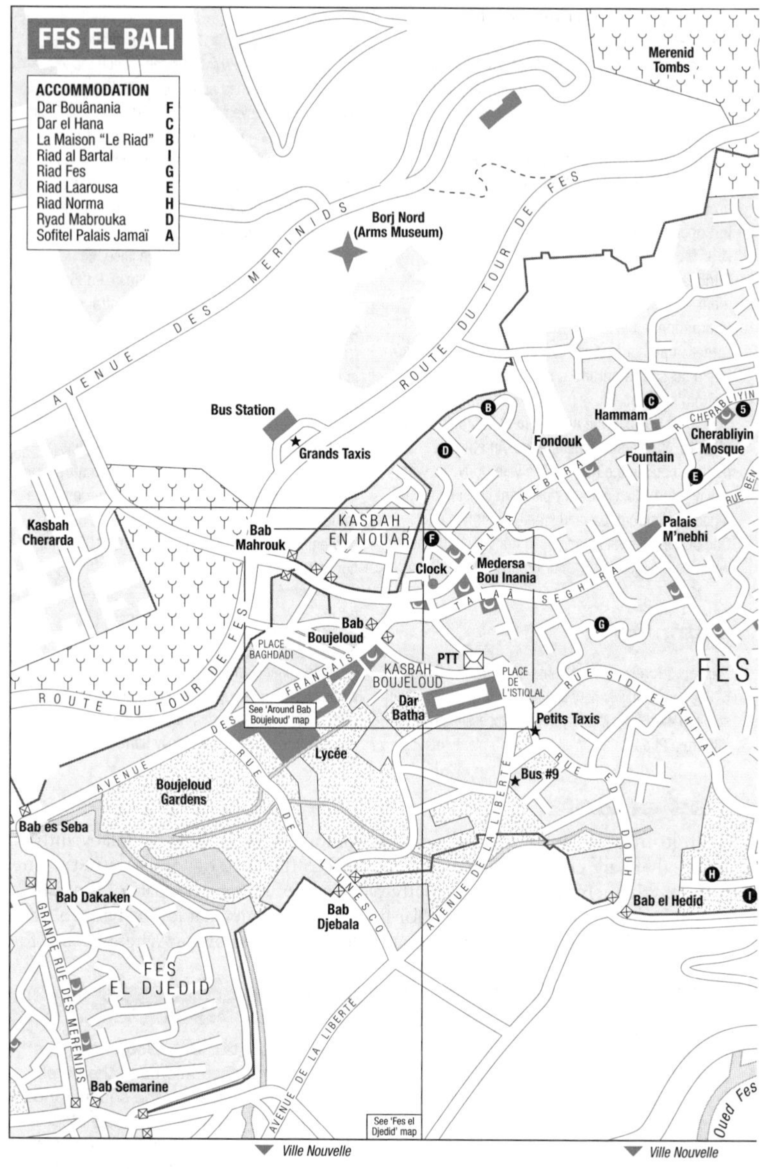

how long…to see beauty where it is least likely to appear". Do the same and you must be prepared to get really lost. However, the Medina is not a dangerous place despite what some hustlers say, and there's always someone around to ask for directions or to lead you towards a landmark: Bab Boujeloud, Talâa Kebira, the Kairaouine Mosque, Bab er R'cif or Bab Ftouh, for example. The flow of life eases considerably on Friday, when much of the Medina takes a day off and crowds thin.

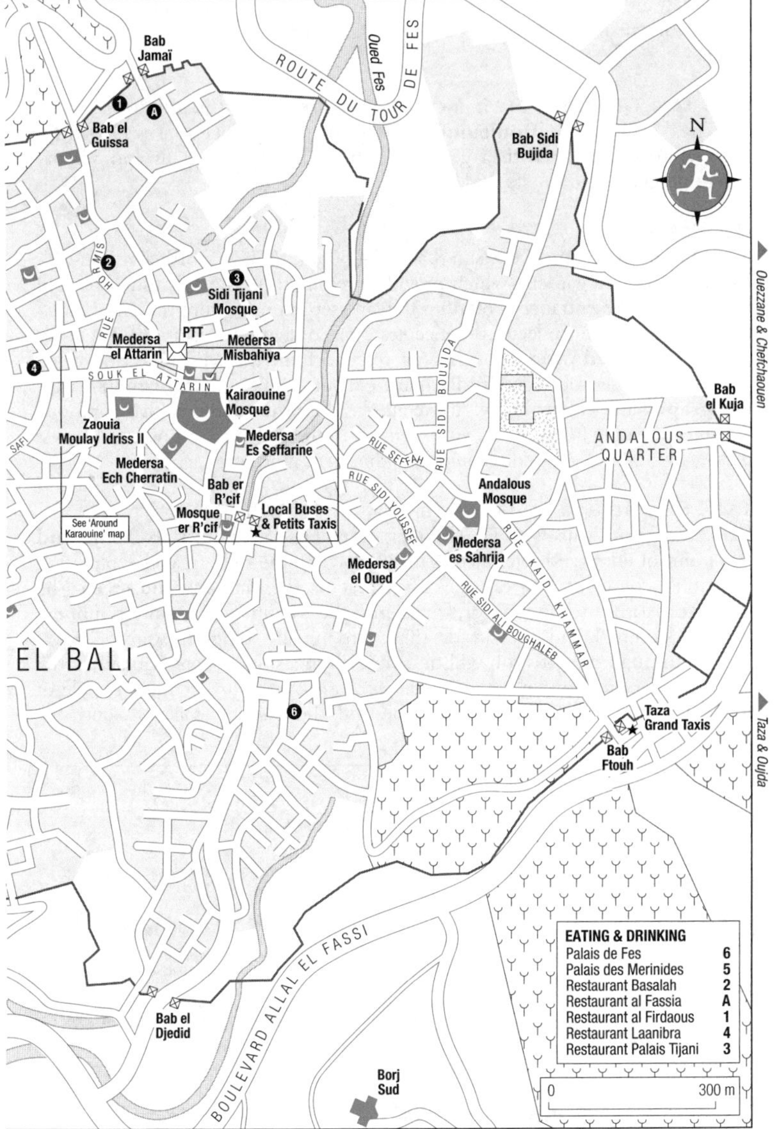

To help visitors, tourism masterminds have scattered star-shaped signs throughout Fes el Bali, directional markers for colour co-ordinated routes that correspond with those highlighted in *Fes: The Thematic Tourist Circuits* map and guide produced by the tourist board (see p.207). Although it's best not to rely on them blindly, the signs at door-top height, often indicating simply the direction of a landmark such as Bab Boujeloud or Place er R'cif, will at least confirm your own in-built compass.

If you want to avoid coinciding with tour groups, especially in summer, try visiting the main sights between noon and 2pm, when the groups stop for lunch.

Into the Medina: Bab Boujeloud and Dar Batha

The area around **Bab Boujeloud** is the principal entrance to Fes el Bali for most visitors; a place with a great concentration of cafés, stalls and activity where people come to talk and stare.

Dar Batha

The **Dar Batha** (Mon,Wed–Sun 8.30am–4.30pm; 10dh) is worth a visit just for its courtyards and gardens, which provide a respite from the exhausting pace of the Medina. The entrance is 60m up the lane separating it from the *Hôtel Batha*.

The art and crafts collections concentrate on local artisan traditions. There are displays of **carved wood**, much of it rescued from the Misbahiya and other medersas; another room of **Middle Atlas carpets**; and examples of **zellij-work**, **calligraphy** and **embroidery**. Above all, it is the **pottery** rooms that stand out. The pieces, dating from the sixteenth century to the 1930s, are beautiful and stress the preservation of age-old techniques rather than innovation.

Talâa Seghira and Talâa Kebira

Until you get to grips with Fes el Bali, it's useful to stick with **Bab Boujeloud** as a point of entry and reference. With its polychrome tiled facades – blue (the traditional colour of Fes) on the outside, facing the ramparts, and green (the colour of Islam) on the interior, facing into the Medina – it is a pretty unmistakeable landmark and once inside, things are initially straightforward.

Once through the gate you will find yourself in a small square, flanked by the *Hôtel Cascade* on your right, the *Restaurant Kasbah* on your left and a couple of minarets almost directly ahead. Just beyond the *Hôtel Cascade*, an entrance

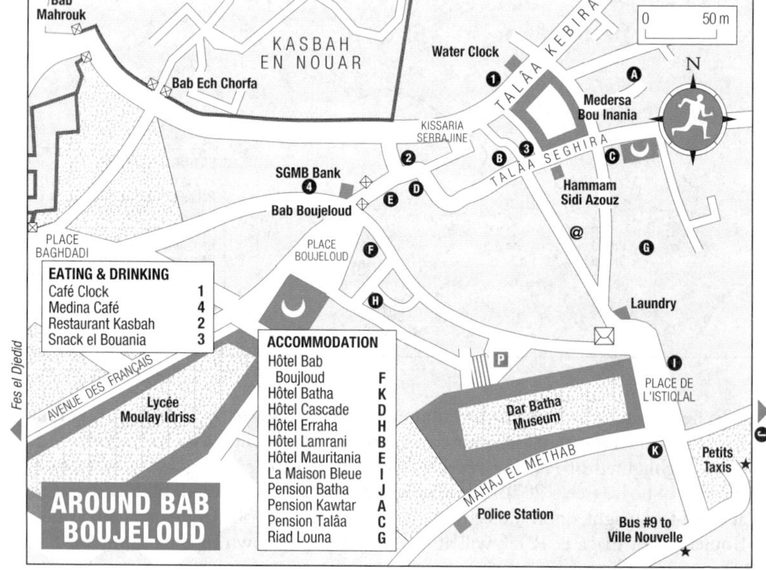

The Merenid tombs and a view of Fes

On the hillside overlooking Bab Boujeloud, the fortress of Borj Nord and, further east, the crumbling remnants of the Merenid tombs stand vigil over the sprawling Medina. **Borj Nord** and its southern counterpart across the valley were built in the late sixteenth century by the Saadians to control the Fassis rather than to defend them. Carefully maintained, the Borj now houses the country's **arms museum** (in theory, daily except Tues 8.30am–noon & 2.30–6pm; 10dh) – daggers encrusted with stones and an interminable display of row upon row of muskets, most of them confiscated from the Riffians in the 1958 rebellion. The pride of place is a cannon 5m long and weighing twelve tonnes, said to be used during the Battle of the Three Kings (see p.569).

Clambering along the hillside to the **Merenid tombs** is worth the effort especially at dawn or dusk when the call to prayer sweeps across the Medina. From this superb vantage point you can delineate the more prominent of Fes's reputed 365 mosque minarets. At sunset, the sky swarms with a frenzy of starlings, egrets, and alpine swifts adding further spectacle to the scene. All around you are spread the Muslim cemeteries which flank the hills on each side of the city, whilst below, the city's major monuments protrude from the hubbub of rooftops. The pyramid-shaped roof of the Zaouia of Moulay Idriss II is easily defined. To its left are the two minarets of the Kairaouine Mosque: Burj an-Naffara or the Trumpeter's Tower (the shorter of the two) and the original minaret. The latter, slightly thinner in its silhouette than usual – most minarets are built to an exact 5:1 (height:width) ratio – and with an unusual white-washed dome, is the oldest Islamic monument in the city, built in the year 956.

The sounds of the city, the stillness and the contained disorder below all seem to make manifest the mystical significance which Islam places on urban life as the most perfect expression of culture and society.

From the tombs you can enter Fes el Bali either through **Bab Guissa** (which leads to the Souk el Attarin), or by returning to **Bab Boujeloud**. There is a petit taxi stand by Bab Guissa.

straight ahead leads into the Kissaria Sejjarin, a small yard of craft shops. The road chicanes around sharply to the right, then the left, past a handful of small foodstalls where you can buy chunks of pastilla, the great Fassi delicacy of pigeon pie, then leads under an arch to begin its descent into the Medina.

This is **Talâa Seghira**, the lower of two lanes that run into the Medina in parallel for much of their length, traversed by dozens of alleys. Further down, en route to where the lane (renamed Rue Ben Safi) rejoins the continuation of Talâa Kebira at the Souk el Attarin is the **Palais M'nebhi**. It was here the agreement for the France-Morocco protectorate was signed in 1912. The palace now operates as a venue for private functions, though you can usually look inside for a small fee.

The upper lane, **Talâa Kebira** (Rue du Grand Talâa), is the major artery of the Medina, a route lined with craft shops and stalls which runs right through to the Kairaouine Mosque (albeit under different names). From Bab Boujeloud it is reached through the Kissaria Sejjarin or from an entrance opposite the *Hôtel Cascade*.

Medersa Bou Inania and around

About a hundred metres down the Talâa Kebira, on the right, is one of the most brilliant of all the city's monuments, the **Medersa Bou Inania** (Mon–Thurs, Sat & Sun 8.30am–noon & 1–6pm, Fri 8.30–11am & 1–5pm, daily 9am–3pm during Ramadan; 10dh). If there is just one building you seek out in Fes – or, not to put too fine a point on it, in Morocco – this should be it. The most elaborate, extravagant and beautiful of all Merenid monuments, immaculate after renovation, it comes close to perfection in every aspect of its construction; its dark cedar is fabulously carved, the zellij tilework classic, and the stucco a revelation.

In addition, the medersa is the city's only building still in religious use that non-Muslims are permitted to enter. Of course, non-believers cannot enter the prayer hall, which is divided from the main body of the medersa by a small canal, but they can gaze across to it from the exquisite marble courtyard. Set somewhat apart from the other medersas of Fes, the Bou Inania was the last and grandest built by a Merenid sultan. It shares its name with the one in Meknes, which was completed (though not initiated) by the same patron, **Sultan Abou Inan** (1351–58). But the Fes version is infinitely more splendid. Its cost alone was legendary – Abou Inan is said to have thrown the accounts into the river on its completion because "a thing of beauty is beyond reckoning".

At first, Abou Inan doesn't seem the kind of sultan to have wanted a medersa – his mania for building aside, he was more noted for having 325 sons in ten years, deposing his father, and committing unusually atrocious murders. The *Ulema*, the religious leaders of the Kairaouine Mosque, certainly thought him an unlikely candidate and advised him to build his medersa on the city's garbage dump, on the basis that piety and good works can cure anything. Whether it was this or merely the desire for a lasting monument that inspired him, he set up the medersa as a rival to the Kairaouine itself and for a while it was the most important religious building in the city. A long campaign to have the announcement of the time of prayer transferred here failed in the face of the Kairaouine's powerful opposition, but the medersa was granted the status of a Grand Mosque – unique in Morocco – and retains the right to say the Friday *khotbeh* prayer.

The medersa

The basic **layout** of the medersa is quite simple – a single large courtyard flanked by two sizeable halls and opening onto an oratory – and is essentially the same design as that of the wealthier Fassi mansions. For its effect it relies on the mass of decoration and the light and space held within. You enter the **courtyard** – the medersa's outstanding feature – through a stalactite-domed entrance chamber, a characteristic adapted from Andalucian architecture.

Off to each side of the courtyard are stairs to the upper storey (closed to the public), which is lined by student cells. In the courtyard, the **decoration**, startlingly well preserved, covers every possible surface. Perhaps most striking in terms of craftsmanship are the wood carving and joinery, an unrivalled example of the Moorish art of *laceria*, "the carpentry of knots". Cedar beams ring three sides of the courtyard and a sash of elegant black Kufic script wraps around four sides, dividing the zellij (ceramic tilework) from the stucco, thus adding a further dimension; unusually, it is largely a list of the properties whose incomes were given as an endowment, rather than the standard Koranic inscriptions. Abou Inan is bountifully praised amid the inscriptions and is credited with the title caliph on the foundation stone, a vainglorious claim to leadership of the Islamic world pursued by none of his successors.

The water clock

More or less opposite the medersa entrance, just across Talâa Kebira, Bou Inania's property continued with an extraordinary **water clock**, built above the stalls in the road. This was removed over a decade ago for research and possible restoration; the woodwork has now been restored, but the metal parts have yet to be replaced. An enduring curiosity, it consisted of a row of thirteen windows and platforms, seven of which retained their original brass bowls. Nobody has

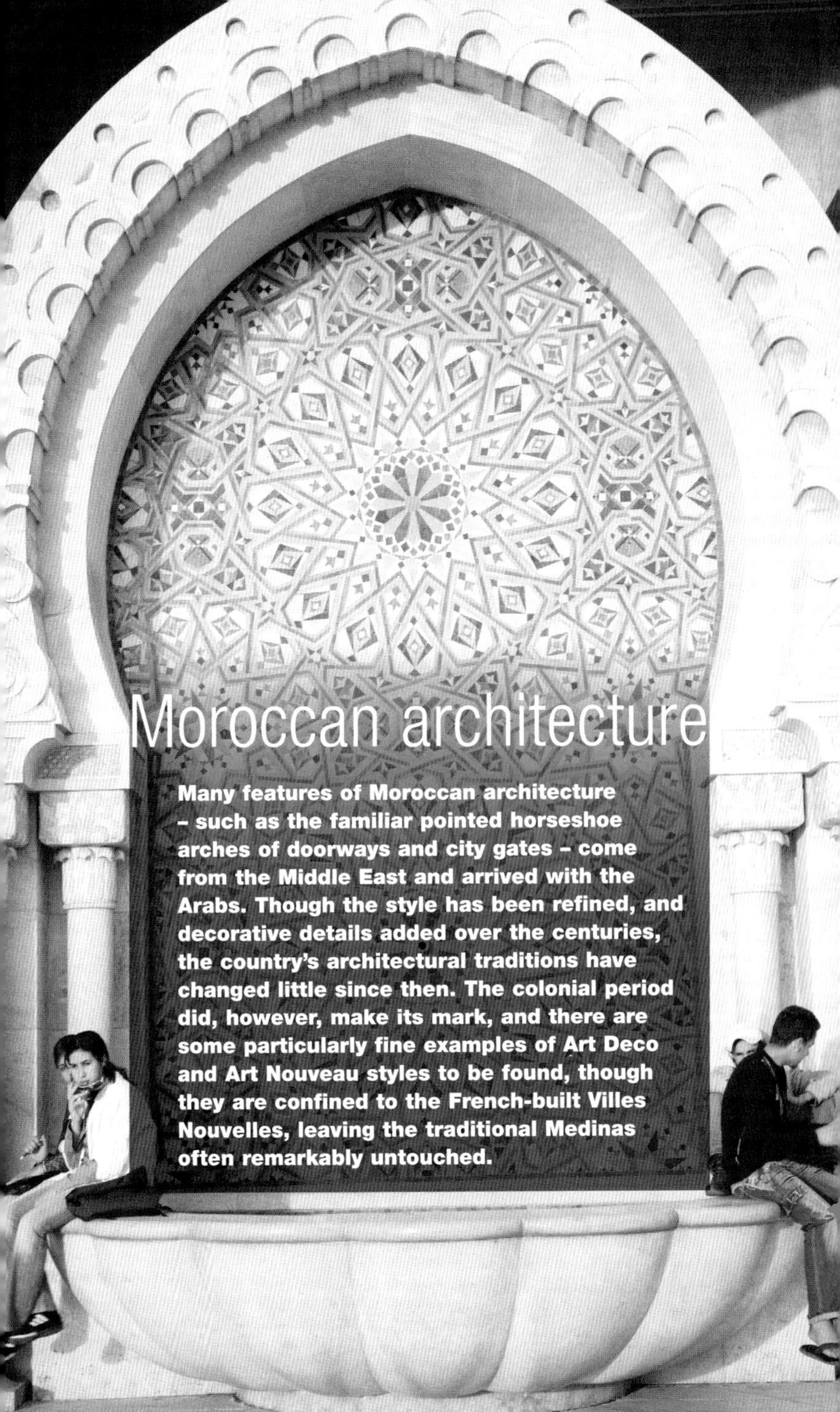

Moroccan architecture

Many features of Moroccan architecture – such as the familiar pointed horseshoe arches of doorways and city gates – come from the Middle East and arrived with the Arabs. Though the style has been refined, and decorative details added over the centuries, the country's architectural traditions have changed little since then. The colonial period did, however, make its mark, and there are some particularly fine examples of Art Deco and Art Nouveau styles to be found, though they are confined to the French-built Villes Nouvelles, leaving the traditional Medinas often remarkably untouched.

Moulay Idris Mosque, Fes ▲

Ben Youssef Medersa, Marrakesh ▼

Some history

It was the Almoravids who first used many of the decorative elements that have become so typical of the country's architecture. The Almohads introduced the classic Moroccan square minaret, and the Merenids and the Saadians brought in techniques of zellij tilework and carved stucco and cedarwood. The next big change came with the colonial period, when European styles began to appear in the Villes Nouvelles of larger cities.

Mosques

Mosques follow the same basic plan regardless of their age or size. All mosques face Mecca, the birthplace of Islam and the direction in which all Muslims pray. This direction is indicated by an alcove called the **mihrab**, set in the Mecca-facing *qibla* wall. Next to the mihrab in larger mosques is a pulpit, usually wooden, called the **minbar**. Larger mosques will also have a courtyard, often with a fountain for ablutions, but the *qibla* end is taken up by a covered **prayer hall**. The **minaret** is a tower from which, back in the day, the *muezzin* would climb to call the faithful to prayer. Moroccan mosques invariably have only one minaret, and since the days of the Almohads in the twelfth century, almost all Moroccan minarets have been square in shape, with a ratio of 5:1 height to width.

A **zaouia** is a mosque built around the tomb of a *marabout*, or Islamic saint; typically the saint's tomb will be located next to the prayer hall, and surmounted by a dome or **koubba**.

Morocco's most important mosque architecture includes the Koutoubia in

Marrakesh, the Kairaouine Mosque and the Zaouia of Moulay Idriss in Fes, the Hassan Tower in Rabat, and the Mosquée Hassan II in Casablanca. Non-Muslims, unfortunately, are not allowed inside most mosques.

Medersas

A **medersa** (or *madrasa*) is a religious school where students come to study Islam, and unlike mosques, medersas are open to non-Muslims. Typically they consist of a large courtyard, with rooms around it for teaching, and rooms upstairs where the students sleep. The medersas of Fes in particular, such as Bou Inania and the Attarin, are richly decorated with carved stucco and cedarwood, and zellij mosaic tilework. Because Islam is suspicious of representational art (lest it lead to idol worship), religious buildings such as medersas are decorated with geometric designs and calligraphy, the latter almost always consisting of quotations from the Koran. Other architecturally interesting medersas include the Abou el Hassan in Salé, and the Ben Youssef in Marrakesh.

▲ Kasbahs, Aït Benhaddou

▼ Traditional riad courtyard

Kasbahs

A **kasbah** can be a walled residential district (as in Fes), or the citadel of a walled city (as in Tangier and Marrakesh), but in southern Morocco, most impressively in Telouet, Tamdaght and the Skoura Oasis, a kasbah is a fortified citadel, something like a castle, where everyone in a village could take refuge in times of trouble (see box, p.428). Built of mud bricks, these kasbahs are rectangular structures with turrets at each corner, usually decorated with Berber motifs.

Darj w ktaf ▲

Stucco ▼

Zellij ▲

Carved cedarwood ▼

Painted wooden ceilings ▼

Merlons ▼

Architectural motifs

Darj w ktaf This fleur de lys-like pattern, used on Marrakesh's Koutoubia and the Moulay Idriss mosque, has been a favourite in Moroccan architecture since the time of the Almohads.

Stucco Intricate decorative designs are carved into plaster on lintels, cornices and walls.

Zellij A mosaic of specially shaped pieces of tile put together to form a geometric pattern, usually based on a star with a specific number of points.

Carved cedarwood Especially in the form of panels and lintels, cedarwood with inscriptions and stylistic designs carved into it surmounts walls, doorways and recessed fountains.

Painted wooden ceilings The cedarwood ceilings of mansions and palaces in cities such as Fes and Marrakesh are adorned with beautiful hand-painted traditional designs.

Merlons The battlement-like castellations seen atop so many city gates and palaces are decorative as much as defensive.

Traditional homes

People's houses in Morocco do not look outward, like a Western home, but rather inward, to an enclosed patio, an arrangement that guards privacy, particularly for women, who traditionally observed purdah and did not allow men outside the family to see them. Rooms are arranged around the patio, usually on two floors with a roof terrace. At one time, most homes would have had a well in the middle of the patio to supply drinking water. A grand house or mansion might have a whole garden in the patio, typically with orange trees, and sometimes a second patio too. The ceilings would be wooden and often beautifully painted.

The function of medersas

Medersas – student colleges and residence halls – were by no means unique to Fes. Indeed, they originated in Khorassan in eastern Iran and gradually spread west through Baghdad and Cairo, where the Al Azhar Medersa was founded in 972 and became the most important teaching institution in the Muslim world. They seem to have reached Morocco under the Almohads, although the earliest ones still surviving in Fes are Merenid, dating from the early fourteenth century.

The word medersa means "place of study" and there may have been lectures delivered in some of the prayer halls. However, most medersas served as little more than dormitories, providing room and board to poor (male) students from the countryside, so that they could attend lessons at the mosques. In Fes, where students might attend the Kairaouine University for ten years or more, rooms were always in great demand and "key money" was often paid by the new occupant. Although medersas had largely disappeared from most of the Islamic world by the late Middle Ages, the majority of those in Fes remained in use right up into the 1950s. Non-Muslims were not allowed into the medersas until the French undertook their repair at the beginning of the Protectorate, and were banned again (this time by the colonial authorities) when the Kairaouine students became active in the struggle for independence.

Since then, restoration work, partly funded by UNESCO, has made them more accessible, although several restored medersas are accommodating students again. This means visitors are sometimes welcome only at certain times; as restoration continues, accessibility is impossible to predict.

yet been able to discover exactly how it functioned, though a contemporary account detailed how at every hour one of its windows would open, dropping a weight down into the respective bowl.

Clocks had great religious significance during the Middle Ages in establishing the time of prayer, and it seems probable that this one was bought by Abou Inan as part of his campaign to assert the medersa's pre-eminence; there are accounts of similar constructions in Tlemcen, just across the border in Algeria. Fassi conspiracy theories are told to account for its destruction – most of them revolve round the miscarriage of a Jewish woman passing below at the time of its striking and a Jewish sorcerer casting the evil eye on the whole device. The building to which the clock is fixed, once owned by a rabbi, is popularly known as "The House of the Magician".

Further down Talâa Kebira

Making your way down the **Talâa Kebira**, you eventually emerge at the labyrinth of lanes round the Kairaouine Mosque and Zaouia Moulay Idriss II. It's a straightforward route to follow that is interesting less for specific sights than the accumulation of stimuli that barrage the senses.

Along the first stretch, heading down from the Bou Inania Medersa, you pass a number of old **fondouks**. Before the advent of French-style cafés in Morocco at the beginning of the twentieth century, the *fondouks* – or caravanserais as they were called in the East – formed the heart of social life outside the home. They provided rooms for traders and richer students, and frequently became centres of vice, intrigue and entertainment. There were once around two hundred in Fes el Bali and many of those that survive now serve as small factories or warehouses, often graced with beautiful fourteenth- and fifteenth-century decorations. The most interesting of the five or so in the area is fondouk *Qa'at Sman*, at no. 89, which was originally a **Merenid prison**, fitted out with solid colonnades and arches.

Rue ech Cherabliyin

A little way beyond the *fondouks*, the street twists round to the right, past a small mosaic fountain, and changes name to become **Rue ech Cherabliyin (Road of the Slippermakers)**. Continuing past the **hammam** Bourous, the oldest hammam still in use in Fes (men only), you find yourself in a district of **leather stalls and shoemakers**. This is one of the best areas for buying handmade traditional *babouches* (leather slippers). Look out for the sophisticated-looking grey and black pairs that are unique to Fes. Before you buy, examine the different versions on offer and bargain hard. Prices vary (60–600dh) depending on the quality of the leather (the best type is goat skin called *Ziouani*) and stitching.

Souk el Attarin and around

Beyond the Cherabliyin district, the street again changes name to Rue de Tarafin and continues to Souk Tiyalin, lined by more leatherworkers. Just past the *Palais des Merinides* restaurant (see p.232), lower arterial street Talâa Seghira links up at last (see p.215), while further along Rue de Tarafin an arched gateway leads to **Souk el Attarin**, the "Souk of the Spice Vendors". This was the formal heart of the old city and its richest and most sophisticated shopping district. It was traditionally around the grand mosque of a city that the most expensive commodities were sold and kept, a pattern more or less maintained as you approach the Kairaouine.

There are a few small cafés inside the spice souk, and on the main street on the left is **Dar Saada**, a nineteenth-century mansion now housing an expensive restaurant (see p.232), opposite which is one entrance to Souk el Henna (see p.220). Just beyond the restaurant, this time on the right of the street, is a covered market, again dominated by textiles and modern goods and nothing very special – most of its character went up in smoke during a fire in the 1950s.

Reaching the end of Souk el Attarin you come to a **crossroads of lanes** lying slightly askew from the direction of the street. On your right (and ahead) are the walls of the **Kairaouine Mosque**; in front of you is the magnificent **Medersa el Attarin** (see p.220). Beforehand, however, take a look at the area below the Souk el Attarin, dominated as it has been for five centuries by the **shrine and zaouia of Moulay Idriss II**, the city's patron saint.

Zaouia of Moulay Idriss II and around

The principal landmark south of the Souk el Attarin is the **Zaouia Moulay Idriss II**, one of the holiest buildings in the city. Although enclosed by a confusing web of lanes, it is not difficult to find: take the first lane on the right – Rue Mjadliyin – as soon as you have passed through the arch into the Attarin and you will find yourself in front of a wooden bar that marks the beginning of its *horm*, or sanctuary precinct. Until the French occupation of the city in 1911, this was as far as Christians, Jews or mules could go, and any Muslim who went beyond it had the right to claim asylum from prosecution or arrest. These days, non-Muslims are allowed to walk around the outside of the *zaouia*, and although they are not permitted to enter, it is possible to glimpse discreetly inside the shrine and even see the saint's tomb.

Passing to the right of the bar, and making your way around a narrow alley, you emerge on the far side of the *zaouia* at the **women's entrance**. Looking in from the doorway, the **tomb** of Moulay Idriss II is on the left amid a scene of intense and apparently High Baroque devotion all around. Women – Idriss's principal devotees – burn candles and incense here, then proceed around the corner of the precinct to touch or make offerings at a round brass grille that opens directly onto the tomb. A curious feature, common to many *zaouias* but rarely visible

The fez

The red cylindrical hat with its black tassel, more correctly known as a Fassi tarbouche, is not only worn and manufactured in Fes, but as far afield as Egypt and Syria. In the eighteenth and nineteenth centuries, **the fez** became associated with the Ottoman Empire and in some places it was donned as a mark of support, a gesture that led to it being banned by Kemal Atatürk when he took power in Turkey and abolished the empire. The fez is also going out of fashion in its home town, and tends to be worn only by older men – most young men now prefer the Tunisian *chechia* or baseball caps.

from outside, are the numerous European clocks – prestigious gifts and very popular in the nineteenth century, when they were shipped from Manchester by Fassi merchant families (their main export base for the cotton trade).

There is no particular evidence that Moulay Idriss II was a very saintly *marabout*, but as the effective founder of Fes and the son of the founder of the Moroccan state, he has considerable *baraka*, the magical blessing that Moroccans invoke. Originally, it was assumed that Idriss had been buried near Volubilis, like his father, but in 1308 an uncorrupted body was found on this spot and the cult was launched. Presumably, it was an immediate success, since in addition to his role as the city's patron saint, Idriss has an impressive roster of supplicants. This is the place to visit for poor strangers arriving in the city, for boys before being circumcized and for women wanting to facilitate childbirth. For some long-forgotten reason, Idriss is also the protector of Morocco's sweetmeat vendors. The shrine itself was rebuilt in the eighteenth century by Sultan Moulay Ismail – his only act of pious endowment in this city.

Round the other side of the *zaouia* is a tight network of lanes called the Kissaria, full of clothes shops. If you want a **fez** hat, this is the place to come – the best shop is a small, plain-looking stall next to the kissaria entrance by the southeast corner of Moulay Idriss's *zaouia*.

Place en Nejjarin

Head downhill via Rue Bab Moulay Ismail, the lane directly in front of the women's entrance to the *zaouia* and full of stalls selling candles and silverware for devotional offerings, and follow this around to the wooden bar, go under it (turning to the right), and then, keeping to your left, you should come out in the picturesque square of **Place en Nejjarin** (Carpenters' Square).

Here, a beautiful canopied fountain, the **Nejjarin Fountain**, best known of several mosaic fountains in the Medina, stands next to the imposing **Nejjarin Fondouk**, built at the same time in the early eighteenth century. The *fondouk* was in pretty bad shape but still used until a few years ago as a hostel for students at the nearby Kairaouine University. It is currently open to the public as a woodwork museum (daily 10am–5pm; 20dh). Of particular interest are the fourteenth- to eighteenth-century cedarwood friezes exhibited on the middle floor, and, on the top floor, a *rabab* (string instrument) beautifully inlaid with mother-of-pearl. However, it is the interior of the building itself that is worth the entrance fee, wonderfully restored after six years of work – a small exhibit on the roof terrace covers the renovation, where there's also a café and fine views over the city.

In the alleys that lead off the square, you'll find the **Nejjarin souk**, best located by the sound and smell (one of Morocco's finest) of its carpenters chiselling away at sweet-smelling cedarwood.

South of Place en Nejjarin is the **Belghazi Museum**, tucked away in a maze of narrow lanes at 19 Rue Guerniz Derb el Ghorba (daily 10am–6.30pm;

40dh); to find it, trust the signs either around Place en Nejjarin, near the Karaouine Mosque or after the Banque Populaire on Talâa Seghira – keep your eyes peeled because, depending on where you start from, you will be following them for more than 300m. Housed in a traditonal riad built in the seventeenth century, the museum explains the basic layout and features of this type of architecture.

At the end of the Nejjarin souk, a passage leads off to the right; at the end of that, turn left to get back to Souk el Attarin.

Souk el Henna

Just off Souk el Attarin via an arch opposite the *Dar Saada* restaurant – and also accessible from the passage that leads to the Place en Nejjarin (first left off it) 50m further down – is the **Souk el Henna**, a quiet, tree-shaded square adjoining what was once the largest madhouse in the Merenid empire, said to be the first asylum in the world to implement musical therapy as a method for treating patients, an imposing building now in use as a storehouse. Stalls here continue to sell henna and other traditional cosmetics such as *kohl* eyeliner (traditionally antimony but usually now lead sulphide, which is cheaper but also toxic), and lip reddener made from crushed poppy petals; on one side of the square there is a huge pair of scales used for weighing the larger deliveries. In addition, several outlets here offer the more esoteric ingredients required for medical cures, aphrodisiacs and the odd magical spell.

That said, they are in a minority because **pottery stalls** are gradually encroaching on this traditional pharmacological business. Cheap but often striking in design, the pieces include Fassi pots, which are usually blue and white or simple black on earthenware; those from Safi, the pottery most commonly exported from Morocco, distinguished by heavy green or blue glazes; and from Salé, often elaborate modern designs on a white glaze.

Medersa el Attarin

The Medersa el Attarin, whose entrance is at the far end of the Souk el Attarin, at the northwest corner of the Kairaouine Mosque, is the building most worth visiting here if, finally, the extensive renovation is complete. After the Bou Inania, the **Medersa el Attarin** (before renovation daily 8.30am–5pm; 10dh) is the finest of the city's medieval colleges, graced by an incredible profusion and variety of patterning. For all the startling richness of its zellij, wood and stucco, the decoration retains an air of ease, and the building's elegant proportions are never threatened with being overwhelmed.

The medersa was completed in 1325 by the Merenid sultan, Abou Said, and is thus one of the earliest in Fes. Its general lightness of feel is achieved by the simple device of using pairs of symmetrical arches to join the pillars to a single weight-bearing lintel – a design repeated in the upper storeys and mirrored in the courtyard basin.

If it has reopened, on your way in, stop a while in the **entrance hall**, whose zellij decoration is perhaps the most complex in Fes. Its circular pattern, based on an interlace of pentagons and five-pointed stars, perfectly demonstrates the intricate science – and philosophy – employed by the craftsmen. As Titus Burckhardt explains in *Moorish Art in Spain*, it is directly opposed to the pictorial representation in Western arts:

> **...with its rhythmic repetitions, [it] does not seek to capture the eye to lead it into an imagined world, but, on the contrary, liberates it from all the pre-occupations of the mind. It does not transmit specific ideas, but a state of being, which is at once repose and inner rhythm.**

Burckhardt also notes how the patterns radiate from a single point as a pure simile for the belief in the oneness of God, manifested as the centre of every form or being.

Around the second floor, usually out of bounds to visitors, are **cells** for over sixty students; these operated as an annexe to the Kairaouine University until the 1950s. If you can get onto it, one of the most complete possible **views of the Kairaouine Mosque** is available from the medersa's roof.

The Kairaouine Mosque

Djemaa el Kairaouine – the **Kairaouine Mosque** – was the largest mosque in Morocco until the construction of the new Hassan II Mosque in Casablanca – and vies with Cairo's Al-Azhar for the title of world's oldest university. It remains today the fountainhead of the country's religious life, governing, for example, the timings of Ramadan and the other Islamic festivals. An old Fassi saying goes that all roads in Fes lead to the Kairaouine, a claim which retains some truth.

The mosque was founded in 857 by the daughter of a wealthy refugee from the city of Kairouan in Tunisia, but its present dimensions, with 16 aisles and room for 20,000 worshippers, are essentially the product of tenth- and twelfth-century reconstructions: first by the great Caliph of Cordoba, Abd Er Rahman III, and later under the Almoravids.

For non-Muslims, who cannot enter the mosque's courts and prayer halls, the Kairaouine is a rather elusive sight. The building is so thoroughly enmeshed into the surrounding houses and shops that it is impossible to get any clear sense of its shape, and at most you can get only partial views of it from the adjoining rooftops or through the four great entrances to its main courtyard. Nobody seems to object to tourists gaping through the gates, though inevitably the centrepieces that would give order to all the separate parts – the main aisle and the main mihrab

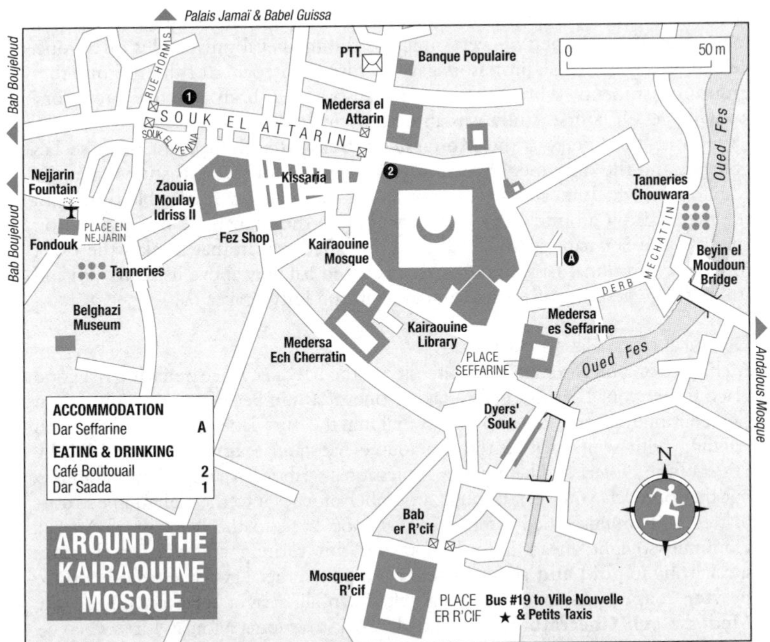

– remain hidden from view. The overall layout was inspired by the Great Mosque of Cordoba in Spain. The courtyard is open to the sky, with a large fountain at its centre and two smaller ones under porticoes at each side, added in the seventeenth century and based on originals in the Alhambra at Granada.

The best way to avoid getting lost in the vicinity of the mosque is to try to keep it on one side as you circumnavigate (on your right if you go clockwise), picking up glimpses of the Kairaouine's interior as you go.

Place Seffarine and around

Moving around the Kairaouine Mosque via the passage to the right of the Medresa el Attarin past *Café Boutouail* (see p.232) and Bab Wouroud, where, if the gates are open, you will have a direct view of one of the Kairaouine's peripheral courtyards, the alley pinches tighter before you emerge into a wedge-shaped square. This is **Place Seffarine**, almost wilfully picturesque with its metalworkers hammering away surrounded by immense iron and copper cauldrons for weddings and festivals, and a gnarled tree at its centre.

The tall, simple entrance in the whitewashed walls on your right leads into the **Kairaouine Library (closed to the public)**. Established by the Kairouan refugees in the ninth century, then stocked by virtually the entire contents of Cordoba's medieval library, it once held the greatest collection of Islamic, mathematical and scholarly books outside Baghdad. That much of the library was lost or dissipated in the seventeenth century is a pointed marker of Fes's decline. Restored and in use again by scholars hunched over texts in the large study hall, it is one of the most important in the Arab world.

Despite the studious atmosphere of the library, the **university** here has been largely usurped by modern departments around Fes el Djedid and the Ville Nouvelle, and dispersed throughout Morocco. However, until recent decades it was the only source of Moroccan higher education. Entirely traditional in character, studies comprised courses on Koranic law, astrology, mathematics, logic, rhetoric and poetry – very much as the medieval universities of Europe. Teaching was informal; professors gave lectures in a corner of the mosque to a group of students who contrived to absorb the body of the professors' knowledge. Of course, study was an entirely male preserve.

Opposite the library is the **Medersa es Seffarine**, the earliest of these Fes colleges and the only medersa still used as a hostel for students studying at the Kairaouine, which means you can pop in for a look at any reasonable time with no charge. Built around 1285 – 20 years before the Attarin, 42 before the Bou Inania – the Seffarine is unlike all the other medersas in that it takes the exact form of a traditional Fassi house, with an arched balcony above its courtyard and still with suggestions of former grandeur in the lofty prayer hall.

Onward from Place Seffarine

A chance for a breather after the intensity of the Medina, Place Seffarine is a good place to get your bearings before taking one of a number of onward routes. You can continue around the mosque by taking the first lane to the right (when standing with your back to the Kairaouine Mosque) – **Sma't el Adoul** (The Street of the Notaries). The notaries, professional scribes, have gone out of business, but the route lets you peek through a number of gates into the Kairaouine's rush-matted and round-arched interior as you loop back to the Medersa el Attarin. Continue straight ahead instead of taking this turning and you enter souks specializing in **gold and silver jewellery** and used metal goods, especially ornate **pewter teapots**. As this route veers left downhill, a right turn leads up to the **Medersa ech Cherratin** then eventually back to Zaouia Moulay Idriss.

Medersa Ech Cherratin

Very different from the Seffarine (and indeed all the previous medersas), the recently restored **Medersa ech Cherratin** (daily 9am–4:30pm; 10dh) dates from 1670 and the reign of Moulay Rachid, founder of the Alaouite dynasty. The design represents a shift in scope and wealth to an essentially functional style, whereby the student cells are grouped around three corner courtyards and latrines/ablutions around the fourth.

Continuing down the lane beyond the entrance to the Medersa es Seffarine, swinging down the hill to the right, you reach **Rue des Teinturiers** and a bridge over the Oued Fes, below which you can leave the Medina by the square beside the **Mosque er R'cif.**

South and east of the Kairaouine: the Dyers' Souk and tanneries

The antidote to the medieval prettiness of the central souks and medersas is the region just below the Kairaouine – the dyers' and tanners' souks on which the city's commercial wealth from the tenth to the nineteenth century was founded and the prosaic, often smelly, underside of everything you've seen until now.

The Dyers' Souk

Souk Sabbighin (Dyers' Souk or Rue des Teinturiers in French) – is directly below the Medersa es Seffarine. Continue past the medersa to your left, then turn right immediately before the bridge ahead. Short but bizarre, the souk is draped with fantastically coloured yarns and cloth drying in the heat. Below, workers in grey overalls toil over ancient cauldrons of multicoloured dyes in an atmosphere that is thick and mysterious, and not a little disconcerting so close to one of the city's main entrances.

At the end of the Dyers' Souk you come to a second bridge, the humpbacked **Qantrat Sidi el Aouad**, almost disguised by the shops built on and around it. On the other side is the **Andalous Quarter** (see p.225), and if you follow the main lane up to the left, Rue Sidi Youssef, you'll come out at the Andalous Mosque. Staying on the Kairaouine side of the river and taking the lane down to your right at the end of the souk you emerge at the open square by the Mosque er R'cif; take buses #19, #29 or #45 – or a petit taxi – if you want to return to the Ville Nouvelle.

The tanneries Chouwara

For the main tanneries quarter – the **Souk Dabbaghin** – return to Place Seffarine and take the right-hand lane at the top of the square (the second lane on your left if you're coming from the Palais de Fes). This lane is known as **Derb Mechattin** (Combmakers' Lane), and runs more or less parallel to the river for 150m or so until it reaches a T-junction. The right-hand branch leads down to the river and **Beyin el Moudoun Bridge** – another approach to the Andalous Mosque. The left winds up **Derb Chouwara**, through a maze of eighteenth-century streets, for 150 to 200m until you see the tanneries on your right. It sounds a convoluted route but is actually one that's plied constantly by tourists to visit the **tanneries Chouwara**, the biggest tanneries in Fes and the most striking sight in the Medina. The best time to visit is in the morning, when the tanneries are at their most active. You will be asked to pay a small fee – 10dh is usual – to one of the *gardiens*. Shops overlooking the tanneries will often invite you for a look in return for the opportunity to show you what they have for sale (generally at high prices).

▲ The tanneries

There is a compulsive fascination about the tanneries. Cascades of water pour through holes that were once the windows of houses, hundreds of skins lie spread out on the rooftops to dry, while amid the vats of dye and pigeon dung (used to treat the leather), an unbelievably gothic fantasy is enacted as tanners treat the skins. The rotation of colours in the honeycombed vats follows a traditional sequence – yellow (supposedly "saffron", in fact turmeric), red (poppy), blue (indigo), green (mint) and black (antimony) – although vegetable dyes have largely been replaced by chemicals, to the detriment of workers' health.

This innovation and the occasional rinsing machine aside, there can have been little change here since the sixteenth century, when Fes replaced Cordoba as the pre-eminent city of leather production. As befits such an ancient system, the ownership is also intricately feudal: the foremen run a hereditary guild and the workers pass down their specific jobs from generation to generation.

For all the stench and voyeurism involved, there is a kind of sensuous beauty about the tanneries. However, it is a guilty pleasure. Look across at the gallery of camera-touting foreigners snapping away and there are few more pointed exercises in the nature of comparative wealth. Like it or not, this is tourism at its most extreme.

North to Bab Guissa

From Souk el Attarin you can wend your way northward through a web of lanes towards Bab Guissa, the *Sofitel Palais Jamaï* hotel, and the Merenid tombs. The sights en route are more curiosities than monuments, and are troubled by few tourists, but this is part of the area's appeal. The best starting point is Rue Hormis, the first lane on your left just inside the entrance to Souk el Attarin, 15m before the *Dar Saada* restaurant. From here, make your way through a series of produce markets and start heading north away from Souk el Attarin. Eventually, depending on the trustworthiness of your inner compass, you should emerge below Bab Guissa. A quick right before the gate threads to the *Sofitel Palais Jamaï*, whose luxury comes as quite a shock to the Medina below. The view from the *Al Mandar* bar terrace merits the drink prices if you can afford a splurge. Petits taxis to Bab Boujloud or the Ville Nouvelle can be caught just outside the hotel. Alternatively, from Bab Guissa you can take a short cut through the cemetery to the Merenid tombs, an astounding spot to watch dusk descend over the Medina (see box, p.215).

The Andalous Quarter

The eastern side of Fes el Bali across the **Bou Khareb** river is known as the Andalous Quarter. Crossing the river from the Kairaouine – now by the Tarrafine Bridge south of Place Seffarine or the Bein el Moudoun Bridge ("The Bridge Between the Cities") near the main tanneries – to the **Andalous bank** is hardly the adventure it once was. For the first three centuries of their existence, the two quarters were separate walled cities and the intense rivalry between them often erupted as factional strife. It still lingers enough to give each area a distinct identity, although since the thirteenth century this has been a somewhat one-sided affair: according to Fassis, the Andalousis had more beautiful women and braver soldiers, but the Kairaouinis have always had the money.

Whatever the truth of the tale, nearly all of the most famous Andalucian scholars and craftsmen lived and worked on the other side of the river and as a result the atmosphere in the quarter has a somewhat provincial character. Monuments are few and comparatively modest, and the streets are quieter and predominantly residential. As such, it can be a pleasant quarter to spend the early evening and get caught up in the rhythms of daily life in Fes el Bali. Most street trading here (and in the southern quarters of the Kairaouine side, too) revolves around daily necessities, providing a link between the "medieval" town and continuing urban life. And your relationship with the city changes accordingly as you cease to be a consuming tourist – there is a near-total absence of "guides" and hustlers.

As well as from the Kairaouine area, you can reach the Andalous Mosque from Place er R'cif (**bus**: #19, #29 or #45 from the Ville Nouvelle; #27 from Dar Batha) or more directly from Bab Ftouh (**bus**: #3 from Place de la Résistance (La Fiat), #12 from Bab Boujeloud or #18 from Place l'Istiqlal, by the Dar Batha).

The Medersa es Sahrija and Andalous Mosque

A goal for your wanderings in the Andalous Quarter, the **Medersa es Sahrija** (daily 8am–6pm; 10dh), is the quarter's most interesting monument and is generally rated the third finest medersa in the city after the Attarin and Bou Inania. Anywhere else but Fes it would be a major sight. But such is the brilliance of the more accessible monuments, it rarely receives the attention it deserves.

What makes it worth the visit is the considerable range and variety of the original decoration, looking better than ever after restoration. The zellij is among the oldest in the country, and the palmettes and pine cones of the cedarwood carving hark back to Almohad and Almoravid motifs. Built around 1321 by Sultan Abou el Hassan, it is slightly earlier than the Attarin and a more or less exact contemporary of the medersa in Meknes, which it resembles in many ways.

There is little to be seen of the nearby **Andalous Mosque** other than the monumental entrance gates because it is built at the highest point of the valley. Like the Kairaouine, it was founded in the late ninth century and saw considerable enlargements under the Almoravids and Merenids.

Towards Bab Ftouh

Going south from the Andalous Mosque – out towards **Bab Ftouh** – you emerge into a kind of flea market: clothes sellers at first, then household and general goods and odds and ends. At the top of the hill, on the edge of a cemetery area, entertainers – storytellers and the occasional musician – sometimes perform to large audiences.

This region of the city, a strange no-man's-land of **cemeteries** and rundown houses, was once a leper colony, and is traditionally known as a quarter of necromancers, thieves, madmen and saints. At its heart, close by Bab Ftouh, is the whitewashed **koubba of Sidi Ali Ben Harazem**, a twelfth-century mystic who has been adopted as the patron saint of students and the mentally ill. The saint's moussem, held in the spring, is one of the city's most colourful; in past centuries it was often the cue for riots and popular insurrections. At **Bab Ftouh** you can pick up a petit taxi to any part of town or take bus #18 to the Ville Nouvelle.

Fes el Djedid

Unlike Fes el Bali, whose development and growth seems to have been almost organic, **Fes el Djedid** – "New Fes" – was a planned city, built by the Merenids at the beginning of their rule, under Sultan Abou Youssef around 1273, as a practical and symbolic seat of government.

The chronicles present the Merenids' decision to site their city some distance from Fes el Bali as a defence strategy, though this would seem less against marauders than to safeguard the new dynasty against the Fassis themselves – and it was only in the nineteenth century that the walls between the old and new cities were finally joined. It was not an extension for the people in any real

sense, being occupied largely by the vast royal palace of **Dar el Makhzen** and a series of garrisons. This process continued with the addition of the **Mellah** – the Jewish ghetto – at the beginning of the fourteenth century. Forced out of Fes el Bali after one of the periodic pogroms, the Jews provided an extra barrier (and scapegoat) between the sultan and his Muslim faithful, not to mention a source of ready income conveniently located by the palace gate.

In the immediate aftermath of independence in 1956, concerned about their future status-their position-was-made untenable by the Arab-Israeli war, the Mellah's 17,000 **Jewish population** emigrated to Israel, Paris or Casablanca virtually en masse. Today, the future of the Jewish community in Fes is more fragile than ever with just a handful of Jewish families living here and in the Ville Nouvelle. The Jewish Community Centre, Centre Maimonide, is at 24 Rue el Houssine el Khaddar (Ⓣ0535 620503; Mon–Fri 8.30am–noon, 2.30–6pm), opposite the copse that faces the *Splendid Hôtel*. Rabbi Abraham Sabbagh (Ⓣ0535 623203), who officially accompanies predominantly Jewish visiting parties around the Mellah and other Jewish sites, is a mine of information on Jewish history in Fes.

Fes el Djedid can be reached in a ten-minute walk from **Bab Boujeloud** (outlined below); walking from the Ville Nouvelle, be aware that locals advise against taking the isolated route between the two cities at night unless in a large group. **Bus** #2 from Place de la Résistance (also called La Fiat) goes to **Place des Alaouites** and **Bab Semarine** beside the Mellah.

West from Bab Boujeloud

The scale shifts as you walk to Fes el Djedid from Bab Boujeloud. Gone are the labyrinthine alleyways and souks of the Medina, to be replaced by a stretch of massive walls. Within them, on your left, are a series of gardens: the private **Jardins Beïda**, behind the Lycée, then the public **Jardins de Boujeloud**, Jnane Sbil (under renovation at the time writing), their pools diverted from the Oued Fes. The latter have an entrance in the middle of Avenue des Français (or at the far end if that's closed) and are a vital lung for the old city. If everything gets too much, wander in, lounge on the grass and spend an hour or two at the tranquil **café-restaurant** (see p.232) by an old waterwheel, at their west corner.

The Petit Mechouar

Continuing west along Avenue des Français, you pass through a twin-arched gate to reach an enclosed square, the **Petit Mechouar**, once the focus of city life and a stage for the sort of snake charmers, jugglers and storytellers that are still found in Marrakesh's Djemaa el Fna. They were cleared out when the Mechouar was closed for repairs in the mid-1970s and have not been allowed back.

The Petit Mechouar has five exits. One of the two on its eastern side leads onto Avenue des Français; through the other, just south and beyond another double archway, **Bab Baghdadi**, Fes el Djedid proper begins as the **Grande Rue** (see p.228). On the west flank of the Petit Mechouar, **Bab Moulay Abdallah** leads to the eponymous Quartier Moulay Abdallah (see p.228), while to the south **Bab Mechouar** opens onto the grounds of the Royal Palace. From here, ordinary citizens would approach the palace to petition the king – the mechouar was where they would wait for admission.

The northern gate is the monumental **Bab Dekkakine** (Gate of the Benches), more correctly known as **Bab es Seba**, a Merenid structure that was the main approach to the Royal Palace and Fes el Bali until King Hassan realigned the site in 1967–71. It also served as a gallows for the Infante Ferdinand of Portugal, who was hanged here, head down, for four days in 1443.

He had been captured during an unsuccessful raid on Tangier and was doomed after his country failed to raise the ransom. As a further, salutary warning, his corpse was cut down, stuffed and displayed beside the gate, where it remained for the next three decades.

The Vieux Mechouar

Once through the three great arches on the north side of the Petit Mechouar, you enter a much larger courtyard, the **Vieux Mechouar**. Laid out in the eighteenth century, this is flanked along the whole of one side by the **Makina**, an arms factory built by Italians in 1886 and today partially occupied by a rug factory and local clubs.

A smaller gate, the nineteenth-century **Bab Segma**, stands at the far end of the court, forcing you into an immediate turn as you leave the city through the Merenid outer gateway, whose twin octagonal towers slightly resemble the contemporary Chellah in Rabat.

If you are walking to the **Merenid tombs** from here, you can either turn sharp right and scramble up the hillside after the Borj Nord, or go straight ahead along the longer Route du Tour de Fes. The latter takes you past the huge **Kasbah Cherada**, a fort built by Sultan Moulay Rashid in 1670 to house – and keep at a distance – the Berber tribes of his garrison. The partially walled compound is now the site of a hospital, a school and an annexe of the Kairaouine University.

Quartier Moulay Abdallah and the souks

Back at the Petit Mechouar – and before turning through the double arch onto the Grande Rue de Fes el Djedid – a smaller gateway leads off to the right at the bottom of the square. This enters the old *quartier reservé* of **Moulay Abdallah**, once home to cafés, dance halls and brothels; a red-light district established by the French Protectorate. The prostitutes were mostly young Berber girls, lured by the chance of a quick buck; most returned to their villages after they had earned enough to marry or keep their families. The quarter today has a slightly forlorn feel about it on a main street that twists to Fes el Djedid's 1276 **Grand Mosque**. West of this, on the way to Bab Bou Jat, is the **Moulay Abdallah Mausoleum**, a mosque and medersa complex that also contains the tombs of four sultans of the current Alaouite dynasty, from the eighteenth and twentieth centuries. To get here from the Grand Mosque, follow the street to the west for 50m onto a small square with fountains; cross the square and take the right fork at the far end. You will see the minaret of the mausoleum shortly after, from which you can reach Bab Bou Jat by heading northwest. Bab Bou Jat leads on to the **Grand Mechouar**, a large open space that can also be entered from the main road to its north.

East of the Quartier Moulay Abdallah and through the main gateway, the **Grand Rue** zigzags slightly before leading down to the Mellah. There are **souks**, mainly for textiles and produce, along the way but nothing much to detain you long. Just by the entrance, though, immediately to the left after you go through the arch, a narrow **lane** curves off into an attractive little area on the periphery of the Jardins de Boujeloud. There's an old **waterwheel** here that used to supply the gardens, and adjacent, the *Café-Restaurant la Noria* (see p.232).

The Mellah and Royal Palace

Once home to Jewish families, few of which remain, the **Mellah** has been largely resettled by poor Muslim emigrants from the countryside. Although the quarter's name came to be used for Jewish ghettos throughout Morocco, it originally applied only to this one in Fes, christened from the Arabic word for "salt" (*mellah*) perhaps in reference to the Fassi Jews' job of salting the heads of criminals before they were hung on the gates.

The enclosed and partly protected position of the Mellah fairly accurately represents the historically ambivalent position of Moroccan Jews. Arriving for the most part with compatriot Muslim refugees from Spain and Portugal, they were never fully accepted into the nation's life. Yet nor were they quite rejected as in other Arab countries. Inside the Mellah, they were under the direct protection of the sultan (or the local *caid*) and maintained their own laws and governors.

Whether the creation of a ghetto ensured the actual need for one is debatable. Certainly, it greatly benefited the reigning sultan, who could depend on Jewish loyalties and also manipulate the international trade and finance that they came to dominate in the nineteenth century. But despite their value to the sultan, even the richest Jews led extremely circumscribed lives. In Fes before the French Protectorate, no Jew was allowed to ride or even to wear shoes outside the Mellah, and they were severely restricted in their travels elsewhere.

Houses, cemeteries and synagogues

Since the Protectorate ended, whereupon many of Fes's poorer Jews left to take up an equally ambivalent place at the bottom of Israeli society (although this time above the Arabs), memories of their presence have faded rapidly. What remains are their eighteenth- and nineteenth-century **houses**, conspicuously un-Arabic, with their tiny windows and elaborate ironwork. Cramped even closer together than the houses in Fes el Bali, they are interestingly designed if you are offered a look inside.

The **Hebrew Cemetery** (Mon–Fri & Sun 7.30am–sunset, closes slightly earlier on Fri for Jewish Sabbath) lies east of the Place des Alaouites on the edge of the Mellah, its iron gate just up from a car park, between the Garage Sahar and the start of the flea market on the side street. Inside, white, rounded gravestones extend to the edge of the valley of the Oued Zitoun; 12,000 have names, around 600 are anonymous, mostly victims of a typhus epidemic in 1924, and none are more pitiful than the tiny tombs of children. Visitors leave a pebble on the gravestone to mark their visit or burn a candle in the recess provided. The most visited tombs are those of former chief rabbis, notably that of eighteenth-century Rabbi Yehuda Ben Attar, which is covered in green and black mosaic tiles, and that of Lalla Solika Hatchouel, topped by three vase-like turrets. She caught the eye of Prince Moulay Abderrahman, who asked her to convert to Islam, so he could marry her. She refused and was promptly imprisoned and executed for the affront, and has since been venerated as a martyr.

At the northeast corner of the cemetery is the **Em Habanim Synagogue** (same hours), built in 1928 and until fairly recently in regular use for services and as a religious school. It has been restored by the Jewish-Moroccan Heritage Foundation and the Moroccan Ministry of Culture, and opened as a museum, containing a massive clutter of bric-a-brac, much of it only tangentially related to Fes's Jewish community. During opening hours, there is always someone to show you round the cemetery and museum. There is no charge but a donation is expected. The *gardien* of the cemetery can also direct you to other synagogues on or just off the Grande Rue des Merenides.

The Royal Palace

At the far end of the Mellah's main street – Grand Rue des Merenides (or Grand Rue de Mellah) – you come into **Place des Alaouites**, fronted by the new ceremonial gateway to the **Royal Palace**. The palace, which has been constantly rebuilt and expanded over the centuries, is one of the most sumptuous complexes in Morocco, set amid vast gardens, with numerous pavilions and guest wings.

Today, the palace complex is strictly off limits to all except official guests.

Eating and drinking

By day, there's little to keep you in the **Ville Nouvelle**, the new city established by Lyautey at the beginning of the Protectorate. Unlike Casa or Rabat, where the French adapted Moroccan forms to create their own showplaces, this is a pretty lacklustre European grid. However, the Ville Nouvelle is home to most of the faculties of the city's university, and is the city's business and commercial centre. If you want to talk with Fassis on any basis other than guide or tout to tourist, your best chance will be in the cafés here, and it's more likely that the students you meet are exactly that. The quarter is also the centre for most of the city's restaurants, cafés, bars, bookshops and other facilities.

Fes el Bali and **Fes el Djedid** are quieter at night, except during Ramadan (when shops and stalls stay open till two or three in the morning). As with Medina quarters throughout Morocco, they are bereft of bars and, with the exception of the smarter palace-restaurants, some of which only open for lunch, or those in hotels, their eating places are on the basic side.

Ville Nouvelle

The Ville Nouvelle has a decent selection of restaurants, though few justify the city's reputation as the home of Morocco's finest cuisine. Cafés, at least, are plentiful – and there are a few bars. The following are all on the map on p.204.

Restaurants

The majority of **restaurants** are scattered around Avenue Mohammed V, many of which serve wine and beer; booking is rarely necessary.

Café-Restaurant al Mousaffir 47 Bd Mohammed V ☎0535 620019. This delicately tiled establishment, which prides itself on not depending on tour groups and agencies for its survival, offers a wide selection of meat and fish dishes, and local wines from 60dh to 180dh; menu 100dh. Daily 11am–3pm & 6pm–midnight. Moderate.

Café 24/24 Pl 16 Novembre, by *Hôtel Olympique*. A café-restaurant worthy of note for its claim to supply a meal (burgers, steak, brochettes) at any time of the day or night, so handy if you get the munchies in the wee hours. Open 24hr. Cheap.

Chez Vittorio 21 Rue du Nador (Brahim Roudani), almost opposite the *Hôtel Central*. Reliable place whose decor makes a decent stab at a trattoria and whose chef prepares a small menu of pizzas and pasta dishes. Daily noon–3pm & 6.30–11.30pm. Moderate.

Le Filet Bleu Rue de Libie, just off Rue el Houria near Pl de Florence ☎0535 941972. A new, stylish fish restaurant with Mediterranean flair, friendly service and a varied menu, from fish tajine to paella. Fresh fish is delivered daily. Moderate.

Le Nautilus First floor of the *Hôtel de la Paix*, 44 Av Hassan II. A rather classy restaurant renowned for its fish and seafood. Mon–Sat noon–3pm & 7pm–midnight. Moderate to expensive.

Restaurant la Cheminée 6 Rue Chenguit (Av Lalla Asma), on way to train station ☎0535 624902. Small and friendly licensed restaurant specializing in meat grills. Daily 7pm–midnight. Moderate.

Restaurant Marrakesh 11 Rue Omar Amkhtar, between Av Mohammed V and *Hôtel Mounia*. Small, with a limited menu, but the food is well cooked and tasty. Menus from 115dh. Daily 10am–midnight. Moderate.

Restaurant Isla Blanca 32 Av Hassan II. "Atlas trout" and seafood specialities plus Italian dishes, a Moroccan menu at 150dh and à la carte from 100dh. Good wine list, too. Daily noon–3pm & 6pm–1am. Moderate to expensive.

Restaurant Ten Years Formerly *Roi de la Bière*. 61 Av Mohammed V. A reasonable but not tremendously exciting restaurant whose set menu (90dh) includes options for couscous, lamb tajine with prunes or chicken tajine with lemon and olives.

Also prepares so-so Italian dishes. Daily 10am–3pm & 6–11pm. Cheap.

Venezia Sandwich 7 Av el Houria, formerly Av de France, round the corner from the *Hôtel Amor*. A superior fast-food joint with grilled sausages, fish and *kefta*, plus a range of salads. Daily 11am–midnight. Cheap.

Zagora Restaurant 5 Bd Mohammed V ⓣ0535 940686. In a shopping mall off the main street, this classy place serves French dishes à la carte or a set menu (130dh) of Moroccan cuisine; service is immaculate and helpful. Daily noon–3pm & 6.30–11pm. Moderate.

Cafés and bars

Cafés and **patisseries** are scattered throughout the Ville Nouvelle, with some of the most popular around Place Mohammed V. The *Café de la Renaissance* was an old Foreign Legion hangout, now a popular gathering point for weekend football matches on TV; the *Patisserie Crystal*, opposite the tourist office, has a vintage 1960s vibe in a split-level interior ruled by uniformed waiters and is a good place for a quiet drink. Just up the road, the *Brasserie le Marignon*, screened by fig trees opposite the market, is a mite more stylish and suffers less traffic fumes. Another cluster of decent cafés can be found along Avenue Mohammed es Slaoui, Avenue Hassan II and Boulevard Mohammed V. Two of the most popular of these are the *Café Floria*, a block north of the PTT on Avenue Hassan II, boasting excellent croissants (and very clean toilets), and the *Number One* in Avenue Lalla Asma, with mirror-tile decor dating from the disco era. Good **ice creams** are to be had at the *Gelatitalia* on Rue Libya, just off Rue el Houria near Place de Florence.

For **bars**, you have to look a little harder. Some might enjoy the seedy but cheap *Dalilla* at 17 Bd Mohammed V, decorated with futuristic metal panels and whose upstairs bar is a place for serious drinking. The *Astor*, by the old cinema of the same name at 18 Av Mohammed es Slaoui, has a cellar bar that doubles up as the city's only **kosher restaurant**, while at the *Tivoli* just 50m to its east at no. 46, the back bar is more relaxed than the loud front bar. Around the corner, on Boulevard Mohammed V, the *Café Chope*, with its neon-illuminated interior, does decent bar snacks. *Le Progrès* at 21 Av Mohammed es Slaoui, with a pool table and a crowd of regulars, is a dark, boozy place that seems permanently stuck at 2am. Beyond these options (none likely to feel very comfortable for women), you're left with the handful of **hotel bars**: in the *Ibis*, *de la Paix*, *Mounia*, *Lamdaghri*, *Splendid* and *Grand*, and the upmarket and rather dull *Royal Mirage Hôtel* and *Sofia*. Alternatively, an off-licence opposite *Hôtel Olympic* by the market sells a large selection of wine, beer plus some spirits.

Fes el Bali and Fes el Djedid

Fes el Bali has possibilities for budget meals and, at greater cost, for sampling (relatively) traditional cuisine in some splendid old palaces. **Fes el Djedid** has a few basic café-restaurants, although none worth specially recommending, save for *Café Restaurant la Noria* in the Jardins de Boujeloud (see p.232), a relaxing and usually quiet spot for a meal. Drinking around these parts is restricted to hotels and riads, with the only exception being *Mezzanine* (see p.232) a bar and restaurant that has recently opened on Avenue des Francais facing the Boueloud gardens.

Cafés and café-restaurants

There are two main areas for **budget eating** in Fes el Bali: just inside Bab Boujeloud; and along Rue Hormis, which runs up from Souk el Attarin towards Bab Guissa in the north and has good hole-in-the-wall places. The outdoor **café-restuarants** around Bab Boujeloud all serve decent meals and have little to distinguish between them. There are plenty of small **cafés** all over the Medina, but few worthy of special mention. Unless otherwise stated, the following are marked on the map on pp.212–213.

Café Boutouail Northwest corner of the Kairaouine Mosque, opposite Medersa el Attarin (see map, p.221). At the very heart of the old city, *Café Boutouail* does a good line in coffee and pastries – extra seating is hidden away upstairs – but its speciality is *panachi*, a mixture of milk, almond milk and raisins, with a blob of ice cream on top for good measure. Mon–Thurs & Sat–Sun 6am–10pm, Fri 6am–12.30pm & 7–9.30pm.

Café Clock 7 Derb el Magana, signposted of Talâa Kebira near the waterclock Ⓦwww.cafeclock.com. This café-restaurant cum cultural centre housed in a restored dar is a popular hangout for students and tourists alike. Check the website for weekly schedules that include yoga and film nights. The food is inventive and delicious, especially the camel burger. Moderate.

Café Restaurant la Noria By the waterwheel off the Jardins de Boujeloud, accessible from Av des Français and Grande Rue des Merenides Ⓣ0535 654 255. A good spot to have breakfast or stop for a coffee. Daily 6.30am–10.30pm. Moderate to expensive.

Medina Café Bab Boujeloud, just up from SGMB bank. A more laid-back option in Bab Boujeloud, with the obligatory pastilla, veggie coucous and tajines, though a little more expensive, too, and not all dishes merit the extra few dirhams. Daily 11am–midnight. Cheap to moderate.

Restaurant Basalah Rue Hormis, almost opposite the Cine Hillal. Simple but tasty Moroccan staples in a very popular but unsignposted joint. Mon–Thurs & Sat–Sun noon–7pm. Cheap.

Restaurant Kasbah Bab Boujeloud, opposite *Hôtel Cascade*. The most appealing option in Bab Boujeloud due to two terraces with views and zellij-covered walls. The 70dh menu is acceptable if uninspiring; à la carte brochettes, *kefta* and pastilla are better. Daily 11.30am–midnight. Cheap.

Mezzanine 17 Av des Français, across from the Jardins de Boujloud and next to *Hotel Jnan Sbil* Ⓣ0535 638668, Ⓦwww.restaurantfez.com. A super-chic new restaurant/lounge bar that serves a unique variation of tapas platters including sushi, which can be washed down with anything from frozen cocktails to vintage champagne. Besides the hotels, the closest bar to the Medina. Expensive.

Snack el Bouania Tâlaa Seghira, 10m below *Hotel Lamrani*. New and clean, with a sit-down restaurant at the back – a good option for standard fare without the tourist hustle. Cheap.

Restaurants

For a Fassi banquet in an appropriate palace setting, most restaurants charge around 150–200dh a head. Some places, particularly those in the heart of Fes el Bali, serve lunch only because they are tricky to find even in daylight. Unless otherwise stated, the following are marked on the map on pp.212–213.

Dar Saada 21 Rue el Attarin Ⓣ0535 637370. See map, p.221. Tasty pastilla or (ordered a day in advance) *mechoui*, all in vast portions – two people could order one main dish and a plate of vegetables – in another century-old palace whose fine carving was renewed after a fire in 1972. Lunch only. Daily 8am–5.45pm. Expensive.

Palais de Fes 15 Makhfia er R'cif, off Pl er R'cif behind the Cinéma el Amal Ⓣ0535 761590. Delicious pastilla and fine Medina views are the specialities of this highly regarded restaurant and *maison d'hotes*, both served on the best terrace in town. There's a choice of set-menus, and reservation is recommended if only to request a free car to pick you up from your hotel. Daily 10am–midnight. Expensive.

Palais des Merinides Ⓣ0535 634028, 100m east of the Cherabliyin Mosque. Beautifully restored palatial decor inside and good views from the terrace out. There's a choice of themed set menus from 195dh – the Fassi menu features chicken pastilla (pigeon if ordered 24hr in advance) – or à la carte eating from around 230dh. Daily noon–11.30pm or the last customer. Expensive.

Restaurant al Fassia *Sofitel Palais Jamaï hotel*, Bab Guissa Ⓣ0535 634331. A distinguished Moroccan-cuisine restaurant (favourite of King Mohammed VI) with a terrace overlooking the Medina, and a belly-dancing floorshow and musicians. There are few more stylish ways to spend an evening, but count on at least 400dh each, more if you order (24hr in advance) one of the specials such as *mechoui* or stuffed sea bass. Daily 8–11pm. Expensive.

Restaurant al Firdaous 10 Rue Zenjifour, Bab Guissa, just down from the *Hôtel Palais Jamaï* Ⓣ0535 634343. A rich merchant's house of the 1920s. Meals, with music and a floorshow (featuring

Shopping for crafts

Fes has a rightful reputation as the centre of Moroccan traditional crafts, but if you're buying rather than looking bear in mind that it also sees more tourists than almost anywhere bar Marrakesh. However much you bargain, **rugs and carpets** will probably be cheaper in Meknes, Midelt or Azrou, and although the **brass, leather and cloth** here are the best you'll find, you will need plenty of energy, a good sense of humour and a lot of patience to get them at a reasonable price. Fassi dealers are expert hagglers – making you feel like an idiot for suggesting a ludicrously low price, jumping up out of their seats as if to push you out of the shop or lulling you with mint tea and elaborate displays.

This can be all good fun, but it requires confidence and some idea of what you're buying and how much you should be paying for it. For some guidelines on **quality**, look at the historic pieces in the **Dar Batha** museum – keeping in mind, of course, that exhibits here are the best available. If you want to check on the **prices** of more modest and modern artefacts, browse the shops along Avenue Mohammed V in the **Ville Nouvelle**, which have fairly fixed prices (and are easy to leave). Alternatively, visit the government-run and strictly fixed-price **Centre Artisanal**, out past the *Royal Mirage Hôtel Fes* on the left-hand side of Avenue Allal Ben Abdallah (daily 9am–12.30pm & 2.30–6.30pm; ⓣ0535 621007). It's not the best in the country but it's worth a visit, time permitting.

Two shops that deserve a quick look are Tissage Berbère and Chez Hamidou, both on the way to the main tanneries on Derb Chouwara. Contrary to what you might expect in a street so frequently plied by tourists, these carpet and cushion shops, respectively, are generally overlooked by tour groups in the rush to visit the tanneries and continue with their itinerary. **Carpet** prices at **Tissage Berbère** are reasonable, and bartering with the informative owner enjoyable; to find it, follow the signs on Derb Chouwara near the main entrance to the tanneries. **Chez Hamidou** is a few metres before Tissage Berbère and consists of no more than a hole in the wall stacked with **cushion covers**, the speciality of the shop and reputedly the best in the Medina.

mock weddings, fire dancing and belly-dancing) in the evenings. Choice of several set menus costing from 290dh. Daily 8.30am–11.30pm. Expensive.

Restaurant Laanibra 61 Aïn Lkhail ⓣ0535 741009. A wonderful seventeenth-century palace that's home to a friendly restaurant, one that's more intimate than the grander *Palais des Merinides* nearby (see opposite). Only open for lunch, it serves à la carte dishes and a choice of menus from 200dh. Find it west of the *Palais de Merinides*, signposted down a lane on the left. The entrance is under a little archway on the right – look for a heavy wooden door. Daily noon–4pm. Expensive.

Restaurant Palais Tijani 51–53 Derb Ben Chekroune, east of Sidi Ahmed Tijani Mosque ⓣ0535 741128. Less grandiose than the other palace-style eateries and without the floorshow, but better value for money. The emphasis here is on the food ("Fes seen through its cuisine"), and the diners as likely to be Moroccan as foreign. Menus start at 120dh. Daily 11am–midnight. Moderate.

Listings

Airlines Royal Air Maroc, 54 Av Mohammed V ⓣ0535 948551.

Arabic Language Institute in Fes (ALIF) At 2 Rue Ahmed Hiba near the youth hostel and the *Hôtel Menzeh Zalagh* (ⓣ0535 624850, ⓦwww.alif-fes.com). This American initiative offers a range of courses plus private/specialized lessons. There are three-week (60hr) and six-week (120hr) courses in Colloquial Moroccan Arabic or Modern Standard Arabic at all levels. ALIF also has its own residence for students, or the option of a homestay with a Moroccan family. Since ALIF doubles as an English school, the American Language Center, it is also a good place to meet up with Moroccans.

Banks Most banks are grouped along Bd Mohammed V. As always, the BMCE (branches at Pl Mohammed V, Pl Florence and Pl de l'Atlas) is best for exchange and handles Visa/Mastercard transactions, as well as travellers' cheques. There is a BMCI office a few metres beyond BMCE in Pl Florence. Others include: Banque Populaire (Av Mohammed V), with quick service for currency and travellers' cheques, and opposite the Royal Palace on Rue Bou Khessissat in Fes el Djedid, with change facilities and cashpoint; Crédit du Maroc (Av Mohammed V) and SGMB (at the intersection of Rue el Houria and Rue Soudan). Banque Populaire also has three branches in Fes el Bali: halfway down Talâa Seghira, north of Medersa el Attarin by Sidi Tijani, and on Rue Kaid Khammar by Bab Ftouh. Outside banking hours you can change money at Karima Voyages at 106 Bd Mohammed V (Mon–Sat 8.30am–12.30pm & 2.30–8pm, Sun 8.30am–12.30pm; ⓣ0535 650 247). Most of the four- or five-star hotels also change money and cheques.

Bookshops The Librairie du Centre, 134 Bd Mohammed V (near the post office), has a good selection of books in French, including some poetry, and a small shelf of books in English, mostly classic novels.

Car rental Fes has quite a number of rental companies, though none are as cheap as the best deals in Casa. Call around the following, which all allow return delivery to a different centre: Avis, 50 Bd Abdallah Chefchaoueni ⓣ0535 626969, ⓔavis.fes@iam.net.ma; Budget, 6 Rue Chenguit also called Av Lalla Asmae ⓣ0535 940092; Europcar, 45 Av Hassan II ⓣ0535 626545, ⓕ022 310360; First Car, Av des FAR ⓣ0359 30909, also

Two nearby spas: Moulay Yacoub and Sidi Harazem

The spa villages of **Moulay Yacoub** and **Sidi Harazem**, 20km northwest and 15km southeast of Fes respectively, are largely medicinal centres, offering cures for the afflicted as they have for centuries. They are local rather than tourist attractions, loved by Moroccan families, but Moulay Yacoub, in particular, makes a pleasant day-trip for a swim and hot bath. Either site can be reached by grand taxi from the *gare routière* to Moulay Yacoub (10dh) and from Bab Ftouh to Sidi Harazem (5dh). Buses to Moulay Yacoub run hourly from the main bus station and bus #28 runs to Sidi Harazem at least every hour from the stand 400m northeast of Place de la Résistance, on Boulevard Allal el Fassi.

Moulay Yacoub

The trip to **MOULAY YACOUB** takes you across pleasant, rolling countryside, with wonderful views south over the plain of Saïss to the Middle Atlas beyond. Legend relates that the village was named either after Sultan Moulay Yacoub Ben Masour – cured after his first bath, they say – or from the corruption of Aquae Juba, the spring of a local Berber king, Juba, who was envious of Roman hot baths. Either way, the hillside village's fame is founded on its 36–40°C sulphur-rich spa waters. Cars and taxis park at the top of the village, leaving you to descend flights of steps past stalls whose bathing goods add a chirpy resort atmosphere. The **swimming pool** (daily 6am–10pm; separate areas for men and women; 7dh), as well as most of the hotels, is near a square halfway down the hill. The old **thermal baths** (or *baignoires or anciennes thermes*; daily 6am–10pm) are a short walk from the pool, and have a more medicinal purpose – albeit fairly basic to Western eyes – and are usually busy, but you can enjoy a hot bath on your own (*baignoire individuelle*; 15dh for 30min) or with a friend (25dh for 30min). Massage and jacuzzi are also available for 35dh each, or masseurs in the thermal baths charge around 15–20dh for a hammam-style scrub. Beware that both facilities – baths and pool – are only cleaned once a week on Tuesday, when they close at 6pm, so you're probably best not swimming that afternoon.

Continue down the steps to the foot of the hill and you reach the newer and more upmarket baths of the **Thermes de Moulay Yacoub** (ⓣ0535 694064, ⓦwww.moulayyacoub.com), a spa for serious medical treatment – mostly rheumatism and respiratory problems – and serious self-indulgence that is as exclusive as it gets in Morocco. Not surprisingly, prices rise accordingly: a thirty-minute dip in the pool starts at 90dh, albeit including a bathrobe, towel and cloakroom. The main reason to come, however, is that the main pool is mixed – a rare chance for male/female couples to bathe together. Prices for the various massages, manicures, pedicures and facials average 150dh.

at the *Royal Mirage Hôtel*; Hertz, Bd Lalla Maryem, 1 Kissariat de la Foire ⓣ0535 622812; Tourvilles, 13 Bis Rue Mokhtar Soussi, off Bd Mohammed V ⓣ0535 626635, ⓔreservation@tourvilles.net. First Car, Avis, Europcar, Budget and Hertz have desks at the airport. One of the best local companies is Les Almohades-Auto, Pl du 16 Novembre ⓣ0535 940447, with small cars available from 250dh a day.

Car repairs Mechanics can be found in the vicinity of the train station. The garage on Rue Soudan (ⓣ0535 622232) is good for Renault repairs.

Cinemas Several in the Ville Nouvelle show foreign films – mainly dubbed into French; the Empire, on Av Hassan II near Pl de la Résistance, has showings at 3.20pm & 9pm.

Festivals and cultural events Since 1995, Fes has hosted a **Festival of World Sacred Music**, held each June, which has developed into the country's most interesting and inspiring cultural festival. Recent years have seen Sufi chanters from Azerbaijan, Tibetan dancers, dervishes from Kurdistan, a Javanese gamelan and a Byzantine choir from Greece. Concerts take place at Pl Moulay Hassan north of the Mechouar by Bab Makina, at the Dar Batha, and sometimes further afield, such as amid the ruins of Volubilis. Details are available from the secretariat (ⓣ0535 740535, ⓔinfo@fesfestival.com), or on the festival's website at ⓦwww.fesfestival.com. The **Fes Festival of Sufi Culture** (ⓦwww.par-chemins.com) usually held over a week in April, is

Among the selection of generally good hotels in town – most located just above or along the steps that go downhill – are the following:

Grand Hôtel ⓣ0535 694160. A cheapie just past the public baths, with basic but clean en suites. Arabic only spoken. ❷

Hôtel Aleonard ⓣ0535 694020. At the top of steps, with all the mod cons of a newly built hotel. Friendly, too. ❹

Hôtel Fadoua ⓣ0535 694050. Bright, sunny rooms are on the small side, but the location opposite the public baths is excellent. ❸

Hôtel Hanae ⓣ0535 694191. Not quite as modern as the nearby *Aleonard*, but clean and comfy rooms, all with a/c. ❹

Hôtel Moulay Yacoub ⓣ0535 694035, ⓦwww.sogatour.com. The smartest place in town, by the turn-off to the village, has bright, spacious rooms that face the hills and marble floors in its en-suite bathrooms. Bungalows for four to six people are also available. ❻

Sidi Harazem

The eucalyptus-covered shrine of **SIDI HARAZEM** was established by Sultan Moulay er Rachid in the seventeenth century, though the centre owes its current fame to its bestselling mineral water, said to treat kidney conditions and high cholesterol as well as arthritis. At the weekend, Fassi families come to stock up on the sodium- and calcium-rich water. Around the central **fountain**, the hub of activity of the spa, you give a few dirhams to any of the attendants who are authorized to dispense the venerated liquid – the fountain is chained all-round and you are not allowed to step inside.

The other focal point of a visit is the **Piscine du Palmier** (daily 8am–5pm; 17dh). There are two pools, one for men and women (although in practice only men use it) and another smaller one for women only, cleverly out of sight but still in the open air. Both pools are clean and well maintained, particularly the latter, and there's a café by the pool, often animated in the evening by local bands.

For anyone not seeking a cure or a swim, the reason to visit is for one of the biggest **moussems** in the Fes region (see p.236).

The refurbished four-star *Sidi Harazem* **hotel** (ⓣ0535 690135, ⓦwww.sogatour.com; ❺) of the Sogatour group offers bright, tastefully decorated rooms, plus a private pool and garden. Just below it, apartment blocks (ⓣ0535 690047; ❸) also run by Sogatour – known locally as the *pension* – are fairly spartan, with squat toilets and cold showers, but offer very good value; they sleep up to six people and are fitted with cooker, fridge and a private lawned area.

For a **meal**, there's the pricey hotel restaurant or you could walk 600m to the grill complex beyond the hotel; follow the charcoal smoke and smell of brochettes.

comprised of a number of performances that take place each night in the courtyard of the Dar Batha (organized discussions are held during the day); it's a rare opportunity to experience the music of the world's most renowned Sufi musicians and vocalists. Major local festivals are the students' moussem of Sidi Harazem (held outside the city in Sidi Harazem at the end of April) and the Moulay Idriss II Moussem (held in Fes; Sept). There are other moussems held locally – ask at the tourist office for details – and some good events a little further out, such as the Fête des Cerises at Sefrou (see p.238) in June. Cultural events in the city are relatively frequent, both Moroccan- and French-sponsored. Again, ask for details at the tourist office, where you can buy tickets, or at the Institut Français on Rue Loukili (☎0535 623921). A *Son et Lumière* show is presented from March to October (daily except Sun 7.15pm, May–Sept 9.30pm).

Golf The Fes Royal Golf Club, 15km from Fes on the Route d'Ifrane (☎0535 665210), was designed by Cabell B Robinson and has an 18-hole, par 72 course.

Hammams Hammam Sidi Azouz is on Talâa Seghira opposite *Hôtel Lamrani*; there are separate hours for men and women, Fri–Sun are the busiest days. If you are unfamiliar with the routine, and since the staff may well speak Arabic and Berber only, it is best, especially for women, to ask someone at your hotel to escort you. The oldest hammam in Fes (Hammam Kantarte Bourous – men only) is on Rue ech Cherabliyin. Don't forget to take your towel, soap, shampoo and swimsuit (or change of underwear).

Internet access The best option in Bab Boujloud is the internet café just up from the Boujloud Mosque on the right. In Ville Nouvelle, try *Cyber* above the teleboutique a few doors down from Hotel de la Paix on Avenue Hassan II.

Laundry In the Ville Nouvelle, try Pressing Dallas, 44 Rue Asilah near *Hôtel Mounia*; near Bab Boujeloud, there's a laundry, Blanchisserie Batha, at the northern end of Pl de l'Istiqlal facing the local post office (daily 7.30am–10pm).

Left luggage/baggage A deposit is available at the bus and train stations.

Newspapers Some British dailies are usually on sale at newsagents stalls on Av Mohammed V (for example, on the corner of Rue Abdelkrim el Khattabi); otherwise, try the newsagent at 16 Pl 16 Novembre for the *USA Today* and the British *Guardian Weekly*, as well as *Time*, *Newsweek* and *The Economist*; the *International Herald Tribune* is sometimes sold at 34 Av Hassan II.

Petrol stations Several around Pl de l'Atlas, near the beginning of the road to Sefrou and Midelt, and off Bd Abdallah Chefchaoueni.

Pharmacies There are numerous pharmacies throughout the Ville Nouvelle, one just outside Bab Boujeloud, another at the northern end of Pl de l'Istiqlal, and another on Grande Rue des Merenides in the Mellah. The Pharmacie du Municipalité, just up from Pl de la Résistance, on Av Moulay Youssef, stays open all night.

Police There are *commissariats* by the post office on Av Mohammed V and off Pl de l'Istiqlal on the road to the right of the post office that leads to Cinéma Boujeloud. The police emergency number is ☎19.

Post office The main PTT is on the corner of Bd Mohammed V/Av Hassan II in the Ville Nouvelle (Mon–Fri 8.30am–6.30pm, Sat 8–11am); the **poste restante** section is inside the main building; the **phones section** (daily 8.30am–9pm) has a separate side entrance when the rest is closed. Just outside Fes el Bali there is a PTT at Pl de l'Istiqlal; there are also branch post offices on Pl des Alouites on the edge of the Mellah, and in the Medina just north of Medersa el Attarin.

Swimming pools There's a municipal pool (mid-June to mid-Sept) on Av des Sports, just west of the train station. The upmarket *Hôtel Menzeh Zalagh* (see p.211) has an open-air pool, although at 80dh for non-residents, this is a little pricey.

Moving on

Buses for most destinations leave from the main **bus station** or *gare routière* just north of Bab Mahrouk, between Kasbah Cherada and Borj Nord. Most CTM services now leave from here, too, before calling at the CTM station in the Ville Nouvelle, on the corner of Rue Tetouan and Avenue Mohammed V. For frequencies and destinations, see "Travel Details" on p.268.

Like buses, **grands taxis** mostly operate from the *gare routière*. Exceptions are those for **Immouzer**, **Ifrane** and **Azrou** (and sometimes Marrakesh), which use a terminal across from the *Hôtel Mounia*, on Boulevard Mohammed V, and those to **Sefrou** (and sometimes Immouzer), which use a rank 100m southeast of Place de la Résistance (also called La Fiat). **Meknes** grands taxis depart from outside the train station. Grands taxis based at Bab Ftouh run to

Sidi Harazem, **Taza**, **Taounate** and other points east and north of Fes. Leaving Fes by bus for **the south**, note that convenient **night buses** cover most routes – to Marrakesh and Rissani, for example.

Fes's tiny **airport** is 15km south of the city, at Saïs, off the N8 to Immouzer (Ⓣ0535 624800), and is most easily reached by chartering a grand taxi from the *gare routière*, though you can also get to it on bus #16 from the train station.

The Middle Atlas

Most people heading south from Fes take a bus straight to either **Marrakesh** or **Er Rachidia**, the start of the great desert and *ksour* routes. However, both journeys involve at least ten to twelve hours of continuous travel, which in summer is reason enough to stop off along the way.

A second, better reason if you have the time (or, better still, a car), is to get off the well-trodden tourist routes and into the mountains. Covered in forests of oak, cork and giant cedar, the **Middle Atlas** is a beautiful and relatively little-visited region. The brown-black tents of nomadic Berber encampments immediately establish a cultural shift away from the European north, the plateaux are pockmarked by dark volcanic lakes, and, at **Ouzoud** and **Oum er Rbia**, there are some magnificent waterfalls. If you just want a day-trip from Fes, the Middle Atlas is most easily accessible at **Sefrou**, a relaxed market town, 28km southeast of the city.

On the practical front, **bus** travellers may find a few problems stopping en route between Fes and Marrakesh, as many of the buses arrive and depart full. The solution is flexibility – take the occasional grand taxi or stop for a night to catch an early bus and you will never be stuck for long. This is especially true of the Fes–Azrou–Midelt–Er Rachidia route, where buses are plentiful. This is the old *Trek es Sultan*, or Royal Road, an ancient trading route that once carried salt, slaves and other commodities with caravans of camels across the desert from West Africa.

Sefrou and around

The fate of **SEFROU** is to be just 28km south of Fes. Anywhere else in Morocco, this ancient walled town at the foothills of the Middle Atlas would receive a steady flow of visitors, just as it did when it served as the first stop on the caravan routes to the Tafilalet; until the Protectorate, it marked the mountain limits of the Bled el Makhzen – the governed lands. Instead, the pull of the larger city leaves Sefrou, once known as the Jardin du Maroc, virtually ignored by most tourists, a source of some local resentment and the reason, perhaps, for the extreme persistence of the few hustlers here.

To add insult to injury, Sefrou actually predates Fes as a city and might well have grown into a regional or imperial capital if Moulay Idriss I and II had not acted differently. Into the 1950s, at least a third of the then 18,000 population were Jews. There seems to have been a Jewish-Berber population here long before the coming of Islam and, although most converted, a large number of Jews from the south settled again in the town under the Merenids. Today, only a handful remain, most having left for Israel, Paris or Casa.

From Fes, the town can be reached in less than an hour by **bus** or **grand taxi**; the former leave from Bab Ftouh in Fes el Bali (9dh), the latter from just below Place de la Résistance (La Fiat) in the Ville Nouvelle. Situated some 880m above sea level, it makes a cool day-trip in summer, and in winter is at times covered in snow, and there are decent walks in the area, which you'll usually have to yourself.

The town draws sizeable crowds during the annual **Fête des Cerises**, a cherry festival in June, usually over the last weekend, with music, folklore and sports events, and whose climax is the crowning of the Cherry Queen on Saturday evening.

The Town

Although Sefrou is not a large place – the population today is only around 40,000 – its layout is a little confusing. If you are coming in by bus or grand taxi, you are usually dropped in the landscaped **Place Moulay Hassan**, off which is **Bab M'kam**, the main entrance to the Medina. On the other side of Place Moulay Hassan, the old cemetery has been transformed into the **Jardin 3 Mars**, a rather scruffy park whose southernmost section contains the massive modern **Tribunal** (High Court) building.

Beyond the square, the road – and some of the buses – continues round a loop above the town and valley, crossing the **Oued Aggaï** and straightening out onto **Boulevard Mohammed V**, the principal street of the modest Ville Nouvelle.

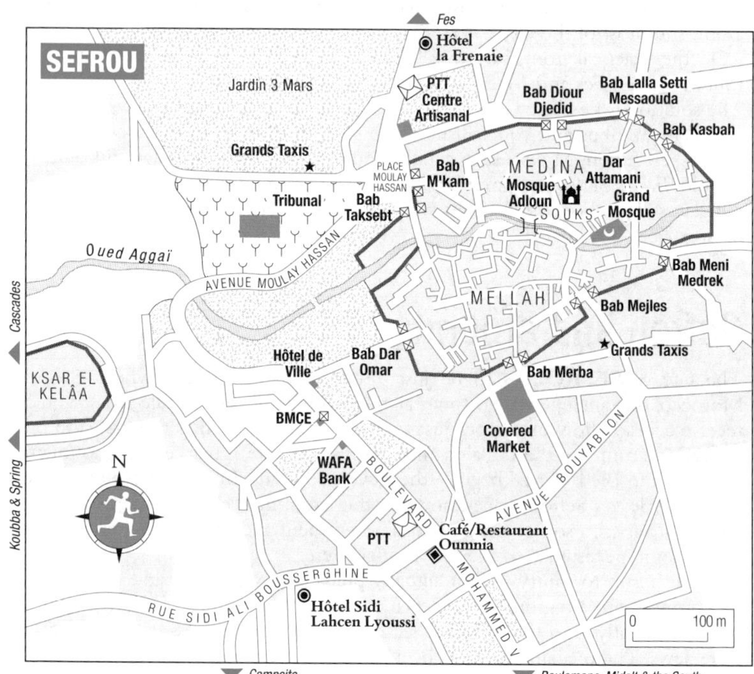

The Medina

In comparison with Fes, the Medina of Sefrou inevitably feels rather low-key. However, it is equally well preserved on its modest scale – a pocket-size version of Fes el Bali that is far less intimidating for many visitors – and the untouristy atmosphere makes it a pleasant place to explore by instinct. The **Thursday souk**, for example, remains a largely local affair, drawing Berbers from neighbouring villages to sell garden produce and buy basic goods.

Enclosed by its nineteenth-century ramparts and split in two by the **Oued Aggaï**, the Medina isn't difficult to find your way around, not least because the river provides a handy reference if you get lost. The most straightforward approach is through **Bab M'Kam**, the old main gate on the *place*. Beyond Bab M'Kam, the main street of the old Arab town winds clockwise down to the river, passing through a region of **souks**. When you reach the first bridge across the river you will find the **Mosque Adloun** on your left. Following the north bank of the river east from here, you soon emerge at the **Grand Mosque,** with its domed minaret. A second bridge here lets you cross the river and head right (southwest) for Bab el Merba, or left (southeast) to come out of the Medina via Bab Mejles.

The Mellah

A dark, cramped conglomeration of tall, shuttered houses and tunnel-like streets, the **Mellah** lies across the river from the Grand Mosque. Even though many of the Jews only left for Israel after the June 1967 Six-Day War and the population is now largely Muslim, the district still seems distinct.

The Sefrou Jewish community had become quite well-off during the French Protectorate thanks to the good agricultural land they owned in the environs. But living conditions must have been pretty miserable when most of their houses were built in the mid-nineteenth century. Edith Wharton, visiting in 1917, (see p.602) found "ragged figures…in black gabardines and skull-caps" living one family to a room in most of the mansions, and the alleys were lit even at midday by oil lamps. "No wonder," she concluded sanctimoniously,

▲ Gateway to the Mellah

"[that] the babies of the Moroccan ghettos are nursed on date-brandy, and their elders doze away to death under its consoling spell".

From the Mellah, you can return, still clockwise, to the *place* by way of the Mosque Adloun.

Into the hills

High enough into the Middle Atlas to avoid the suffocating dry heat of summer, Sefrou is a good base for some modest walking. Dozens of **springs** emerge in the hills above the town and a few waterfalls are active for part of the year.

For a relatively easy target, take the road up behind the Ville Nouvelle post office on Boulevard Mohammed V, which will divide into a fork after about a kilometre. The left-hand branch goes up past the campsite; the right leads to a small, deserted, French military post, known as the **Prioux**, and to the **koubba** of one Sidi Bou Ali Serghin. The views from around here are exciting: in winter, the snow-capped Mischliffen; in summer, the cedars and holm oaks cresting the ridges to infinity.

You can also reach the *koubba* and French fort on a road that forks left in front of the fortified **kelâa** (settlement), quite interesting in itself and reached on **Rue de la Kelâa** west of the sharp bend in the main road across the **Oued Aggaï**. However, go right in front of the *kelâa* and you'll get to a junction signposted "Cascades". From here a single-lane tarmac road continues up beside the river, flanked by some expensive holiday homes. After a short distance you'll pass a small hydroelectric power station on your right, then 250m beyond, below imposing rocky outcrops, are the waterfalls, at their best in spring. Flash floods regularly wash away the path here, so repair work may bar your access to a pool beneath for a paddle.

Practicalities

Though Sefrou can be easily reached from Fes by **grand taxi**, one reason for its lack of visitors may be its lack of **hotels**. The upscale choice is *Dar Attamani*, with immaculate and tastefully decorated rooms, located in the heart of the Medina (ⓣ0535 969174, ⓦwww.darattamani.com; ❸). Otherwise, *Hôtel Sidi Lahcen Lyoussi* (ⓣ0535 683428; ❸) is Sefrou's longest running accommodation option with its Alpine-chalet feel, en-suite rooms with balconies (grubby bathrooms and often no hot water, though), erratic restaurant, popular cellar bar and swimming pool – sometimes even full of water in summer (20dh nonresidents). *Hôtel la Frenaie* (no phone; ❷) is on the left as you enter town, with seven functional rooms and shared facilities above a bar that prepares snacks. Alternatively, a couple of kilometres to the west of town, there is a well-maintained **municipal campsite** (no phone), with plenty of shade, stunning views, hot showers and friendly staff (a new restaurant was under construction at time of writing).

For **food and drink**, in addition to the hotels, hole-in-the-wall grills flank either side of the covered market by Bab Merba. Otherwise, you are limited to *Café-Restaurant Oumnia* on Boulevard Mohammed V (daily 8.30am–11.30pm; cheap), whose dining room is beyond a smokey cafe.

Internet access is available at a cyber-café (daily 8.30am–midnight) adjacent to *Hôtel la Frenaie*. The town's two **banks** are on Boulevard Mohammed V.

Just up from Bab M'kam on Place Moulay Hassan, the tiny **Centre Artisanal** (Mon–Fri 8am–7pm), though small beer compared with those in Fes or Marrakesh, with just a handful of shops that open in rotation, is worth a visit, and you can usually see woodcarvings, brassware and carpets being created by hand.

Around Sefrou

Signposted off the Fes road, 6km northwest of Sefrou, **Bhalil** claims pre-Islamic Christian origins. Locals say it was founded by emigrants from Roman Volubilis, who introduced red hair and blue eyes into the village's gene pool, apparently. More visibly, Bhalil retains a number of troglodyte dwellings. The **cave houses** are to the rear of the village, reached by a dirt road; ask directions from Mohammed Chraibi, the official guide, who will show you his own cave home.

The village itself – or at least the old part of it – is charming, its whitewashed houses tumbling down a hillside connected by innumerable bridges. Coming from Fes by car, it is signposted off on the right 6km before Sefrou. Without your own transport, grands taxis for Bhalil (3dh) depart from just off Place Moulay Hassan in Sefrou.

South and east of Sefrou are some of the most attractive swathes of the Middle Atlas: dense, wooded mountains, with great scope for hiking or *piste* driving, and not a hint of tourism. Immediately south of the town is the **Massif du Kandar**, which loops round to Imouzzer du Kandar. To the east, further afield, are the Bou Iblane mountains – an exploration of which could be combined by drivers with the Djebel Tazzeka circuit, near Taza (see p.168).

Heading south, there's a daily **bus to Midelt**, via the quiet roadside town of **Boulemane**, but none to Ifrane or Azrou on the Fes–Marrakesh road. Short of returning to Fes, the only way to cross onto this route is by grand taxi to Immouzer du Kandar (11dh). Boulemane itself can be worth a stop for its Sunday souk, which serves a wide and diverse area.

The Djebel Bou Iblane

East of Sefrou – and southeast of Fes – is a huge area of high country, culminating in the two mountains of **Djebel Bou Iblane** (3190m) and **Djebel Bou Naceur** (3340m). It is an extraordinarily varied landscape: the northern aspects rise from the cedar forests, while the south is stark and waterless, although demarcated by the great Oued Moulouya. The whole area is sparsely populated and trekkers are almost unknown, yet it's a rewarding area and has relatively easy access. From either Sefrou or Fes, you could arrange a grand taxi to take you to the centre of the range, dropping you either at the forestry hut of **Tafferte** or at the largely abandoned ski resort under Djebel Bou Iblane, where the local *caid* has an office; he is responsible for this great empty quarter.

Grands taxis run to **Skoura** (on route 4653) and **Immouzer des Marmoucha** (on route 4656) giving access from the east. As with so many lesser-known ranges, the best sources of information are the Peyron Guides (see p.71) and AMIS (see p.54).

Imouzzer du Kandar and Ifrane

The first hills you see of the Middle Atlas, heading directly south from the plains around Fes, seem distinctly un-Moroccan thanks to their lush forests. The towns en route feel different, too, their flat, gabled European-style houses lending an Alpine-resort feel. The French colonial chiefs retreated from the heat at the "hill station" resort of **Ifrane**, where the king now has a summer palace. En route is another small French-built hill station, **Immouzer du Kandar**, easy-going but rather mundane, and, in the wet season, a gorgeous freshwater lake, the **Dayet Aaoua**.

Imouzzer du Kandar

IMOUZZER DU KANDAR, 36km south of Fes at 1345m high, is a one-road, one-square kind of place. There's nothing specific to see, but it's a relaxed, friendly resort where Fassis come to swim, picnic and spend a few days when the summer heat becomes overbearing. There are a large number of hotels if you feel like doing the same and some good restaurants, too.

A small Monday **souk** is held just off the central square within the ruined kasbah, location for music and dance events during a Fête des Pommes **festival** in August. The kasbah itself is reduced to crumbling walls, although it conceals a couple of the troglodyte dwellings that were once common in the area – most were filled in by local French governors, who were appalled at the idea of people living in caves. You'll find them, both private, on the lane on the immediate right as you enter the kasbah gate.

Three kilometres west of town is the **Aïn Soltane** spring, a tranquil spot among grassy hillocks and old pine trees; it's a pleasant stroll from town, particularly in the late afternoon or early evening when locals do likewise. To get here, head through the park (southeast) by the *Hôtel Royal* and across the canals beyond, then turn right on the tarmac lane and continue for about 500m, past some villas and holiday homes. Alternatively, take a petit taxi (5dh).

Grands taxis for Azrou and Ifrane leave by the market; those for Fes and Sefrou leave from a parking area 100m north, on the main road. **Buses** pass regularly en route between Fes and Azrou. Immouzer has one **bank**, a Banque Populaire with an ATM, located behind *Hôtel la Chambotte*.

Around the town centre, there are several decent **restaurants**, the best of which is *Le Rose des Vents* (ⓣ0535 663766; daily 11am–3pm & 7–10pm; moderate), which serves up heavenly lamb chops in tomato and rosemary sauce and some elaborate fish dishes. A rather ritzy **patisserie** downstairs does delicious cakes and French pastries.

Accommodation

Immouzer has a good choice of **hotels**, except at the very bottom of the scale, where options are limited.

Hôtel Chaharazed 2 Pl du Marché ⓣ0535 663012, ⓕ0535 663445. On the main road, opposite the square. Comfortable rooms with heating, a/c, TV and a balcony, plus a reasonable restaurant, two bars, and friendly, efficient staff. Reservations are advisable in summer. ❸

Hôtel des Truites 200m north of the main square on the Fes road ⓣ&ⓕ0535 663002. A delightful, old-fashioned place with a quirky, rustic French-style bar and restaurant, and great views north towards Fes. Rooms in the annexe are en suite. Charming owners, too. ❷

Hôtel du Rif 500m south of main square on the Ifrane road ⓣ0535 663392. Sombre and basic en suites, although cheapest in town and a quiet location. No central heating, and cold showers. ❷

Hôtel la Chambotte Bd Mohammed V ⓣ&ⓕ0535 663374. A French-style *auberge* with a good restaurant and smallish, characterful rooms; rooms 6 and 7 are en suite. Showers are hot (on demand), and there's central heating when called for. Also has six duplex apartments in an annexe. Rooms ❷, apartments ❸

Hôtel Royal Bd Mohammed V ⓣ0535 663080. A large three-star with bland en-suite rooms, bar, disco, restaurant and café. More expensive and less attractive than nearby *Hôtel Chaharazed*. ❹

Hôtel Saamara On the main square, opposite the *Chaharazed* ⓣ0535 663464. The best cheapie in town, basic but clean and friendly, with a lively café-restaurant attached. Shared hot showers. ❷

Dayet Aaoua

A good excursion from Immouzer, or an alternative place to break the journey south, is the lake of **Dayet Aaoua**; it is sited just to the east of the N8, 9km

Birdlife in the Dayet Aaoua and Middle Atlas lakes

Like other freshwater lakes in the Middle Atlas, when it's full **Dayet Aaoua** has a good mosaic of habitats and supports a wide variety of animals. Green frogs take refuge from the summer drought within the lake's protective shallows, and a multitude of dragonflies and damselflies of shimmering reds, blues and greens patrol the water's surface.

The **birdlife** is similarly diverse, attracting all kinds of waders and wildfowl. Waders include **black-winged stilt**, **green sandpiper**, **redshank** and **avocet** (one of Morocco's most elegant birds), and the deeper waters provide food for flocks of **grebes** (great-crested, black-necked and little varieties), and in the spring the magnificent **crested coot** (which has spectacular bright red knobs on either side of its white facial shield, when in breeding condition). The reedbeds provide cover for **grey heron** and **cattle egret** and ring with the songs of hidden **reed-** and **fan-tailed warbler**.

The water's edge is traced by passage grey and yellow wagtails and in summer the skies are filled with migrating swallows and martins – the sand martin especially. This abundance of life proves an irresistible draw for resident and migrant **birds of prey** – there are regular sightings of the acrobatic **red kite** at **Aaoua**, usually circling overhead. You may also see flocks of collared pratincole, whose darting flight is spectacular, and, quartering overhead, the **Montagu's harrier**, ever alert for any unsuspecting duck on the lake below.

If the lake is dry, there are still birds to be seen alongside – or close to – the seventeen-kilometre stretch of the N8 between Ifrane and Azrou. Here you will find the endemic Levaillant's green **woodpecker**, **firecrest**, **nuthatch**, short-toed **tree creeper** and local variants of the **jay** and **blue tit**.

White storks, **ravens** and a colony of **lesser kestrels** have been recorded in the low hills behind the *Hôtel Panorama* in **Azrou**.

south of Immouzer. You can camp around the lakeside, but, like other lakes in the Ifrane area, Aaoua is often dry due to the prevalence of limestone and sometimes to climatic changes. On the other hand, when it is full of water, it has a rewarding **birdlife habitat** – see box above.

The N8 continues past the lake to Ifrane, climbing through ever-more dense shafts of forest. If you are driving, it's possible to reach Ifrane by a longer and more scenic route, following a *piste* (4627) up behind the Dayet Aaoua, then looping to the right, past another (often dry) lake, **Dayet Hachlef**, on *piste* 3325, before joining the S309 back to Ifrane.

Since the *Restaurant Chalet du Lac* (ⓣ0535 663197; summer only) on the north bank of the lake stopped providing rooms, accommodation is restricted to a couple of *gîtes*. *Le Gîte Dayet Aoua* (ⓣ0535 604880; includes breakfast; ❸) is an inviting chalet-style house with wood-panelled rooms, a cosy licensed restaurant, and a rustic Alpine feel. Treks and horseriding excursions can be arranged and there are mountain bikes for rent from 100dh per day. The second choice is Gîte de la Montagne, signposted off the western side of the lake and tucked up in the hills above, 3km up a winding track from the lake road (ⓣ0662 586472; own transport needed; ❸). A simple compound offers basic but comfortable rooms (heated), homecooked meals, refreshing walks and peaceful seclusion.

Ifrane

With its globe lights in manicured parks, its fountains in ornamental lakes, or its pseudo-Alpine villas on broad leafy streets, **IFRANE** is something of an anomaly among Moroccan towns: a little prim, even perhaps a little smug. Although the name reveals the site has long been inhabited – "*yfran*" are the "caves" in which local Berbers once lived – the modern town was created by the Protectorate in 1929 as a self-conscious "poche de France" (pocket of France), then adopted enthusiastically after independence by Moroccan government ministries and the wealthier bourgeoisie, who own the gleaming top-of-the-range marques parked throughout town from June to September. In recent times, the town won extra prestige with the addition of a **Royal Palace**, whose characteristic green tiles (a royal prerogative) can be seen through the trees on the descent into a valley.

Ifrane is also the site of another royal initiative. On January 16, 1995, King Hassan II inaugurated the **Al Akhawayn University**, on the northern edge of town, beyond the *Hôtel Mischliffen*. Its chalet-style buildings, cream walls and russet-tiled roofs were designed by Michel Pinseau, the architect behind the king's showpiece Hassan II Mosque in Casablanca. The name Al Akhawayn ("Brothers" in Arabic) denotes it as the brainchild (and beneficiary) of the Moroccan king and his "brother" King Fahd of Saudi Arabia; it has also been funded by the United States and, to a lesser extent, by the British Council. The undergraduate and postgraduate curricula are modelled on the American system of higher education, and English is used for lectures.

King Hassan was keen to underpin his creation with the religious and cultural values of Christianity and Judaism as well as of Islam. The university is dedicated to "practical tolerance between faiths" and a mosque, church and synagogue are on campus to provide, as the king put it, "a meeting place for the sons of Abraham", a concept endorsed by the Prince of Wales when he visited Ifrane in 1996.

Inevitably, there have been criticisms of the new university, not least that it is an elite initiative restricted to those who can pay. There is also something of an anti-French feel, too; Moroccan academics are trying to escape the French educational straitjacket and have begun to "Arabize" science teaching in the established universities. Should you want to visit the campus, try to go on a weekday afternoon when the students are about.

As befits a royal resort and aspiring academia, **Ifrane town** is no average Moroccan settlement – its Alpine resort-style centre is squeaky clean and spacious, and there's a steady growth of costly new houses. Unsurprisingly, it is also expensive – even provisions in the shops are pricier than elsewhere – and being a relatively new resort, it rather lacks the human touch. In summer, a policeman is even posted to stop anyone clambering onto the resort's landmark **stone lion** – located in a copse by the central *Hôtel Chamonix*, it was carved by an Italian prisoner of war, apparently – and when the court is in residence in summer, security is very tight.

Usually, however, Ifrane retains an easy-going, affluent air. A walk by the river, below the Royal Palace, is pleasant, as is the cool summer air, and there's an excellent municipal swimming pool (summer only) signposted off the main road 250m north of the turning for the *Hôtel Mischliffen*.

Arrival and information

Ifrane has a *Delegation du Tourisme* **tourist office** in Place du Syndicat, on the corner of avenues Mohammed V and Prince Moulay Abdallah (Ⓣ0535 566821, Ⓕ0535 566822; Mon–Fri 8.30am–4.30pm). The **bus station** is behind the municipal market off the Meknes road, 400m from the town centre, with frequent services to Fes and Azrou, but fewer to Meknes, Rabat, Casablanca and Marrakesh. CTM destinations include Casa, Meknes, Rabat, Marrakesh and

Agadir. **Grands taxis** gather just beside the bus station, and ply routes to Fes, Azrou and Immouzer on a regular basis, and, less frequently, Meknes.

Accommodation

To help maintain its air of exclusivity, Ifrane doesn't do cheap **accommodation**, nor is it always easy to obtain in summer, when reservations are recommended. Those on a budget should consider rooms in Immouzer du Kander or Azrou. However, there is a municipal **campsite** (ⓣ0535 566025) on Boulevard Mohammed V (the Meknes road), near the market, with a little shop open in summer.

Grand Hôtel Av de la Marche Verte ⓣ0535 567531, ⓔgrandhotelifrane@hotmail.com. Recent restoration has buffed up this 1941-vintage hotel into the best and most stylish in the region – stone walls, recycled 1930s cedarwood beams and fireplaces sit comfortably with modern hardwood floors and furnishings to create an Alpine lodge feel. Also has a bar and nightclub (daily midnight–3am). 7

Hôtel Chamonix Av de la Marche Verte ⓣ0535 566028, ⓕ0535 566826. A good-value hotel in the centre of town, with light, spotless rooms done out in pastel green, and heating, a/c and TV in each. There's also a nightclub (Fri & Sat 11pm–3am), open to nonresidents. 5

Hôtel Mischliffen Route de Fes ⓣ0535 566607, ⓕ0535 566622. When doors reopen after renovation at the end of 2009, this hotel should offer modern luxury facilities and two pools. Views from its hilltop 800m north of the centre will be just as superb. 6

Hôtel Perce-Neige Rue des Asphodelles ⓣ0535 566350. An upmarket place, friendly and efficiently run, its small but comfortable carpeted rooms refurbished in early 2007, some with a terrace, and all with satellite TV, heating and a/c. There's also a good restaurant and cosy bar. Breakfast included. 5

Restaurants

Café Restaurant La Rose Rue de la Cascade, behind *Hôtel Chamonix*. Newly refurbished with an artsy refit, the menu includes various forms of Atlas trout, grillades and pizzas. Daily 9am–11pm. Moderate.

Grand Hôtel Av de la Marche Verte. International cuisine and upmarket Moroccan dishes served in a rustic-chic dining room decorated with Alpine antiques. Menus 170dh. Daily 11am–3pm & 6.30–11pm. Expensive.

Hôtel Chamonix Av de la Marche Verte. A decent if unspectacular option, with reasonably priced menus at 80dh and 130dh. Daily noon–3pm & 7pm–11pm. Moderate.

Rendezvous des Skieurs Av de la Marche Verte. Pizzas cooked in a wood-fired oven, plus well-priced dishes such as rabbit tajine or menus in a café-style option. Daily 6am–11pm. Cheap.

Restaurant Pizzeria la Paix Av de la Marche Verte, next to *Hôtel Chamonix*. An upmarket modern place, where à la carte meals start at 110dh. An attached café-cum-patisserie provides cheaper sandwiches and pizzas. Daily 9am–11pm. Expensive.

Azrou

The first real town of the Middle Atlas, **AZROU** grew at the crossroads of two major routes – north to Meknes and Fes, south to Khenifra and Midelt. As might be expected, it's an important market centre (the main souk is on Tuesday) and it has long held a strategic role in controlling the mountain Berbers. Moulay Ismail built a **kasbah** here, the remains of which survive, while more recently the French established the prestigious **Collège Berbère** – one plank in their policy to split the country's Berbers from the urban Arabs.

The college, now the **Lycée Tarik Ibn Ziad** and still a dominant building in the town, provided many of the Protectorate's interpreters, local administrators

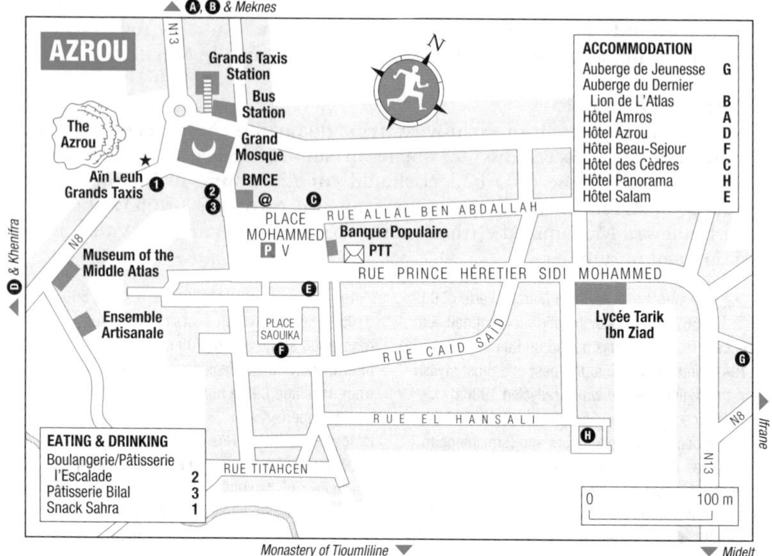

and military officers. But in spite of its ban on using Arabic and any manifestation of Islam, the policy was a failure. Azrou graduates played a significant role in the nationalist movement – and were uniquely placed to do so, as a new French-created elite. However, since independence their influence has been minor outside of the army, in part because many Berber student activists of the 1950s and 1960s pledged allegiance to Mehdi Ben Barka's ill-fated socialist UNFP party (see p.576).

The town's relaxed atmosphere (bar one or two over-persistent touts) and the possibilities for walks and treks nearby make Azrou a pleasant spot to break your journey or even spend a few days.

Arrival and information

The **bus station** is just north of the central Grand Mosque, the **grand taxi** station just behind and downstairs from it. **Petits taxis** wait on streets north and east of the mosque.

Two **banks** (BMCE and Banque Populaire) are in Place Mohammed V; both have change facilities for travellers' cheques and cashpoints. The **PTT** is just east of the square, behind the Banque Populaire. **Internet** access is available at Internet Abrid (daily 9am–midnight) and Cyber Canadien (same hours), both on the first floor of a mall to the left of the BMCE, or Cyber Kawtar (daily 9am–midnight) at the bus station is a convenient place to email while you wait for a bus. There's a handy **laundry** 50m south of Place Saouika, by the army garrison – ask for directions at the *Hôtel des Cèdres*.

Accommodation

Azrou's position at a major road junction means that there are plenty of **hotels** in town; bear in mind that the nights are cold, particularly in winter, and central heating is only provided in dearer (and more distant) places.

Auberge de Jeunesse Route de Midelt-Ifrane ⓣ0535 563733. On the outskirts of town, about 1km from the centre and before the road forks to Midelt/Er Rachidia (N13) and to Ifrane/Fes (N8). Friendly and well run, with good views, too. A bed in the dorm costs 30dh but a YHA card (100dh) may be required depending on how strict the guardian is feeling.
Auberge du Dernier Lion de L'Atlas 16 Route de Meknes ⓣ0535 561868, ⓔa.elkhaldi@menara.ma. Proprietor Aziz is a wealth of information on the region and promotes cultural awareness from his *auberge*-cum-cultural centre. Most of the twenty comfortable rooms are en suite and meals can be arranged in the cafeteria. Wi-fi access. ❸
Hôtel Amros 6km out on the Meknes road ⓣ0535 563663, ⓕ0535 563680. An upmarket hotel, for which you will need a petit taxi. The rooms (mostly en suite) are comfortable though many are looking a bit tired. According to the season, there is a nightclub and a swimming pool, as well as a newly renovated restaurant – which gets mixed reports – and bar. ❺
Hôtel Azrou Route du Khenifra, 300m downhill southwest of Pl Mohammed V ⓣ0535 562116, ⓕ0535 564273. A good-value place, with pleasant rooms, some en suite, a good restaurant and bar, and English spoken. ❷
Hôtel Beau-Sejour 45 Pl Sauika ⓣ0535 560692. Recently re-opened under new management, the rooms are clean and some come with balconies overlooking the square. In summer, you can sleep on the terrace for 50dh. Hot showers 10dh. ❷
Hôtel des Cèdres Pl Mohammed V ⓣ&ⓕ0535 562326. The best value in central Azrou. Spacious, comfortable rooms are enjoyably old fashioned, all with high ceilings and washbasins, and a shared balcony overlooks the square. Heating in winter and shared hot showers (10dh). ❷
Hôtel Panorama Rue el Hansali ⓣ0535 562010, ⓦwww.hotelpanorama.ma. There's a solid old-fashioned hotel feel to this minor pile 10min walk north of the centre. Rooms are spacious but somewhat spartan, but the entrance hall, with a working fireplace, is bright and relaxing. Some rooms en suite; hot water, central heating, a good restaurant and bar. ❸
Hôtel Salam Off Pl Saouika ⓣ0535 562562, ⓔhotel.salam@gmail.com. Boxy rooms in a central, clean hotel, with shared facilities and free hot showers. ❷

The town and its souk

Once the defining feature on arrival in Azrou was the massive knobble of rock on its western edges – the *azrou* ("rock" in Berber) after which it is named. Now, your view is somewhat impeded by the impressive new Grand Mosque that adjoins the main square, **Place Mohammed V**.

In summer, Azrou's public swimming pool, signposted 300m along the Khenifra road, is almost reason enough to stop. The opening of the large **Museum of the Middle Atlas** is long overdue, but when it does open, it should offer an interesting array of artefacts from the region. One of the most compelling reasons to visit Azrou is its Tuesday souk, which draws Berbers from surrounding mountain villages. It is held a little above the main part of town – just follow the crowds up to the quarter across the valley. At first it appears to offer little more than fruit and vegetable stalls, but keep going and you'll see a stretch of wasteland – often with a few musicians and storytellers performing – beyond which is a smaller section for carpets, textiles and general goods.

On other days, the **craft stalls** in the old quarter of town around Place Saouika (Place Moulay Hachem Ben Salah) and Place Mohammed V can turn up some beautiful items, fairly priced if not exactly bargains. There's less hard sell at a **carpet shop** by the *Hôtel des Cèdres*, which has a comprehensive selection of carpets and rugs from the various Beni M'Guild tribes in the Middle Atlas, most with bright, geometric designs based on traditional tribal patterns. Affable owner Amraoui Saïd is a knowledgeable *chasseur des tapis* (carpet hunter), as he calls himself, who will explain the difference between good Berber carpets and mere souvenirs if you show enough interest. Another source of rugs and carpets is the **Ensemble Artisanale** (Mon–Fri 8.30am–noon & 2.30–6.30pm), on the Khenifra road; it's seen better days – it's a bit sleepy compared with other cooperatives – but some decent modern rugs, plus stone and cedar carvings, are still produced.

The Benedictines of Tioumliline

The functional **monastery of Tioumliline** was built in 1926 by French Benedictines, and until the mid-1990s played an important role in the life of the local Berber community. The focus of the monastery's life was its *dispensaire* or clinic, outside the walls of the complex and by the road to Aïn Leuh. The clinic offered free medical treatment and medicines to any passer-by; Berber families in isolated mountain villages used to bring their sick relatives to be treated and looked after by the monks. As well as free medical care, the monastery supplied the poorest Berber families – and generally anyone whose harvests failed – with basic foodstuffs.

The end of the monastery came in the mid-1990s as a result of increasing animosity against Christians in the area. Most of the monks of Tioumliline were relocated to the Abbey of Calcat in France, while their superior, Father Gilbert, went to the Abbey of Saint Benoît de Koubiri, near Ouagadougou in Burkina Faso. The Benedictines of Tioumliline are affectionately remembered by many of the locals, including Monsieur Boudaoud, who lives with his family in the former dispensary. He can tell you stories about the monastery and show you around the ruins.

Azrou is an excellent staging post for exploring the dense cedar forests of the **Parc National d'Ifrane** (see box, p.250). If you don't have your own transport, good walks are to be had in the surrounding hills – lush when watered by seasonal springs and home to Barbary apes – or down to the river, which is reputedly well stocked with trout. A pleasant afternoon stroll goes to the derelict twentieth-century **Benedictine Monastery of Tioumliline** (see box, above), 3km away in the hills above Azrou, reached along the road to Aïn Leuh, which branches off the N13 to Midelt. On your way back to town you can cut across the hills south of the monastery on any of the footpaths that crisscross the area. Further afield are extensive **cedar forests** (see box, p.250); for guides to the area contact Moulay Abdellah Lahrizi (Ⓣ0662 190889 or 0663 772687, Ⓔlahrizi37@yahoo.co.uk), president of the Ifrane and Azrou branch of the Association of Mountain Guides, or Boujemâa Boudaoud (Ⓣ0663 760825, Ⓔboujemaa_boudaoud@yahoo.com), an unofficial but knowlegable guide whose family live in the monastery dispensary. Both speak good English and charge around 200dh per day.

Eating

The best place to **eat** in town – though it tends to be colonized by drinkers in the evening – is the restaurant of the *Hôtel Azrou* (daily 11.30am–3pm & 6–11pm; cheap to moderate), where the trout in particular is recommended. After that, the best choice is the restaurant of the *Hôtel Panorama* (daily noon–3pm & 7–11pm; expensive) with a gourmet menu from 130dh. Another reasonable restaurant is that of *Hôtel des Cèdres* (daily noon–3pm & 7–10pm; cheap to moderate), which is warmed by a log fire in winter.

For even cheaper eating, basic grills line the roads around the Grand Mosque and prepare the usual brochettes, tajines and spit-roast chicken; as ever, doublecheck that the birds were not left on the spit overnight if you choose the latter for lunch. The stalls towards the *azrou* rock tend to be better than those towards the bus station – *Snack Sahra* serves a generous portion of *kefta*, fries and salad for 25dh.

The town has a few classy **patisseries** near Place Mohammed V: *Patisserie Bilal* (summer 24hr, winter 5am–midnight) has a sitting area inside and a small terrace by the road, while *Boulangerie/Patisserie l'Escalade*, just round the corner, sells a variety of French bread as well as cakes and pastries, some of them savoury.

Moving on

There are several daily **bus** services to Fes, Meknes, Khenifra, Beni Mellal, Midelt and Er Rachidia, fewer to destinations such as Marrakesh, Casablanca and Rabat, and only one to Aïn Leuh. CTM also has several daily services, the most frequent being to Fes, Meknes and Midelt. If you don't want to get the only night-time bus to Er Rachidia and Rissani, take the Midelt bus and change there. Similarly, to reach Marrakesh, you may have to change at Beni Mellal. Because most bus services are just passing through, tickets sometimes only go on sale when the bus arrives and the conductor tells the people in the ticket office how many places are available – cue a mad scramble if seats are scarce. Arrive early and set up a place by the ticket window, and you'll be at the front of the queue if that happens.

Grands taxis run regularly to Midelt, Meknes, Ifrane and Fes, and occasionally to Khenifra and sporadically Beni Mellal. Grands taxis for Aïn Leuh have their own station at the beginning of the Khenifra road opposite the Grand Mosque and the *azrou*.

Aïn Leuh and the Oum er Rbia sources

South of Azrou lies some of the most remote and beautiful country of the Middle Atlas: a region of cedar forests, limestone plateaus and polje lakes that is home to some superb wildlife (see box, p.250), including Barbary apes.

It's rewarding countryside for a few days' exploration, either by car or on foot. At the heart of the region – an obvious focus for a trip – are the **waterfalls of Oum er Rbia**, the source of Morocco's largest river. If you don't have transport, you can get a daily **bus** from Azrou to **Aïn Leuh**, 30km along the route (and with some minor falls of its own), or, if you have the money or can round up a group, you could charter a **grand taxi** from Azrou.

Aïn Leuh

AÏN LEUH, 17km from Azrou along the main Khenifra road, then 13km up the S303, is a large Berber village, typical of the Middle Atlas, with its flat-roofed houses tiered above the valley. As at Azrou, there are ruins of a kasbah built by Moulay Ismail, and in the hills behind the town there are **springs** and a more or less year-round waterfall.

Aïn Leuh's **souk** is held on Wednesday, though it can extend a day in either direction. It serves as the weekly gathering of the **Beni M'Guild** tribes, still semi-nomadic in this region – you may see them camping out with their flocks in heavy, dark tents. As a colonial *zone d'insécurité*, this part of the Atlas was relatively undisturbed by French settlers, and the traditional balance between pasture and forest has remained largely intact.

There are a couple of decent **accommodation** options. *Auberge Le Magot De L'Atlas*, signposted just below the Aïn Leuh on the road to Azrou (Ⓣ0535 569517; ❷), has eight rooms in a country house, an enclosed camping area and a restaurant. Alternatively, homely chalets can be rented from *Site Touristique Ajjaabou* on the other side of town on the road towards the Oum er Rbia sources (Ⓣ0535 433596). Starting from 500dh a night and sleeping up to six people, the one- or two-bedroom chalets contain a kitchen, salon and bathroom and are heated by woodfires. There's also a restaurant and swimming pool.

Into the forest: barbary apes and Gouraud cedar

The **cedar forests** that lie to the **south of Azrou** are a unique habitat in Morocco, their verdant atmosphere contrasting starkly with the surrounding aridity and barrenness of the Middle Atlas range. They shelter several troupes of **Barbary apes**, a glimpse of which is one of the wildlife highlights of a visit to Morocco. They can be found feeding along the forest margins – sometimes on the outskirts of Azrou itself. You are almost guaranteed to see them 8km from Azrou on the road to Midelt (N13) at a junction known locally as Moudmane and identified by a cluster of fossil shops and a picnic area. Here the apes laze around the picnic area in search of food and are fairly accustomed to the approaches of humans. From here a road branching off the N13 to the right is signposted as the **Circuit Touristique des Cedres** and heads towards Aïn Leuh and ultimately, the sources de l'Oum er Rbia (see below), through swaths of dense cedar forest and barren plateaus. Further information on the region can be found on the Parc National d'Ifrane maps posted in the *Hotel Beau-Sejour* and *Auberge du Dernier Lion de L'Atlas*.

The forest **birdlife in this area is particularly interesting and** includes Morocco's two species of woodpecker (pied and red great spotted) and green and yellow Levaillant's varieties. Other avian highlights include the splendid **booted eagle** and Kestrels who nest in the Oum er Rbia gorge, near the falls in spring.

Turning left off the N13 at the fossil stands in Moudmane takes you to the **Gouraud cedar**, singled out among others of much the same stature by a sign nailed to the tree. The 130-foot giant, with a girth of around 25ft, is reputed to be at least eight hundred years old. The history of its name is a mystery – Colonel Gouraud was Lyautey's second in command from 1912 to 1914 and some locals say Lyautey's cedar is nearby, but why two soldiers should lend their names to trees is not clear, the confusion confounded by a recent authority that claims Gouraud's cedar was actually felled at the turn of the century, when it was at least 980 years old. Maybe the sign is moved from tree to tree, possibly by the **Barbary apes** you will see hereabouts.

Details of two local guides who know the Cedar forests inside out – one official the other not, but both well informed about the Azrou region – are provided on p.248.

Oum er Rbia and Aguelmane Azigza

The road to the **Oum er Rbia sources** continues just south of Aïn Leuh, signposted "Aguelmane Azigza/Khenifra". Though paved along its entire course, with several new bridges over the Rbia, it can still become waterlogged and impassable in winter, when you should ask about conditions in Azrou or Khenifra before you set out. For the most part, it runs through mountain forest, where you're almost certain to come across apes.

About 20km south of Aïn Leuh, to the left of the road, there's a small lake, **Lac Ouiouane**, and beside it a couple of farms and a large *maison forestière*. A stretch of more open country, dotted with grazing sheep and odd pitched-roof farmsteads, leads to the descent to the Oum er Rbia valley. Here, the road twists down, bends through a side valley and round to a concrete bridge over the Rbia, with a small parking area by the river. (Coming from the south, the descent to the Oum er Rbia – around 45km from Khenifra – is unmistakeable.)

Guides may offer to lead you to the **walk to the falls** but they are unnecessary because a clear path leads up to the gorge – a ten- to fifteen-minute walk. Along the river's edge, the water comes out in forty or more springs (*sources*), many of them marked with café-shelters. Beyond, where the gorge is barred, a small waterfall flows down the rocks, with a fish hatchery below. Swimming is not advisable as the currents are extremely strong.

Aguelmane Azigza

On past the bridges, the main road heads off to the west, crossed by a confusing array of *pistes*. After 18km, a turn-off on the left leads to the **Aguelmane Azigza**, a dark and deep lake, secluded among the cedar trees. You can camp and swim here, as many Moroccans do. Azigza has terrific **wildlife**: the wooded slopes of the lake throng with insect life, including the brilliant red and black grasshopper and the small Amanda's blue butterfly, while the forest provides nesting and feeding areas for woodland finches and titmice, including the elusive hawfinch, identified by a heavy bill. There's more birdlife in the waters, too, notably diving duck (mainly grebes and coot) and marbled teal in autumn and winter.

Improved *pistes* and often surfaced roads wend through this huge area of cedar forest, offering tours unlike anything else in Morocco. The Atlas cedar (*Cedrus atlantica*) can soar to over 40m, often flat-topped, the trees are carefully nurtured and rejuvenating successfully. The best **west–east routes** are as follows: from just south of Aïn Leuh across the R13 to the Mischliffen; from just south of the Azigza turn-off on to Itzer, from where either the R13 or R503 can be reached; and, almost 20km south of Khenifra, an excellent road by El Kbab (Monsouk) up the Oued Serou to Kerrouchen and the Tizi Rechou to the R503. A web of *pistes* link these and are popular with bikers and 4WDs.

South to Midelt and Er Rachidia

If you're travelling the southern circuits of the *ksour* and *kasbahs* of the south, you're almost certain to take this route in one direction or the other. It's 125km from **Azrou to Midelt** and a further 154km to **Er Rachidia** – feasible distances to cover in a single bus trip or a day's driving, but more satisfying when made in a couple of stages. You cross passes over both Middle and High Atlas ranges, catch a first glimpse of the south's fabulous *pisé* architecture and end up in the desert.

Azrou to Midelt

Climbing up from Azrou, the Midelt road (R13, which becomes the N13) follows a magnificent stretch of the Middle Atlas, winding through the forests to emerge at the **valley of the Oued Gigou**, the view ahead taking in some of the range's highest peaks. By bus, you have little alternative but to head straight to Midelt, reached in around two hours, via the market village of Timadhite (large **Thursday souk**). With a car, there are two very brief and worthwhile detours.

The first of these comes 52km from Azrou, as the road levels out on a strange volcanic plateau littered with dark pumice rock. A turn-off to the left directs you to **Aguelmane Sidi Ali**, the largest of the region's many mountain lakes that pooled in extinct craters; long, still and eerily beautiful yet only a kilometre from the road. Besides an occasional shepherd's tent and flock, there is unlikely to be anything or anyone in sight, and the lake itself is reputed to be teeming with trout, pike and perch.

The other point where you might want to leave the road is 24km further down, past the **Col du Ziad**, a 2178-metre pass across the Middle Atlas; superb trekking country lies west of the col, leading to the Oued Sefrou. South of the col, a road leads for 6km to the small village of **ITZER**, whose **market** (Mon & Thurs) is one of the most important in the region, and can be a good source of Berger rugs and carpets.

Back on the main road, you pass road junctions near Boulôjul (the R503 – formerly P20 – from Boulemane) and Zeïda (with the R503 from Khenifra). A few kilometres south of Zeïda is a small, but good, tourist complex, the *Centre Timnay* (see opposite), including a shop, café-restaurant, swimming pool (in summer) and a clean **campsite**, with shared accommodation available for those without tents. The centre has been developed by its owner, Aït Lemkaden Driss, as a base for **Land Rover**, **mountain bike** and **walking** expeditions in the region.

Midelt

At **MIDELT**, reached through a bleak plain of scrub and desert, you have left behind the Middle Atlas. As you approach from the north, the greater peaks of the High Atlas appear suddenly through the haze, rising behind the town to a massive range, the **Djebel Ayachi**, at over 3700m. The sheer drama of the site – tremendous in the clear, cool evenings – is one of the most compelling reasons to stop over. Though the town is comprised of little more than a street with a few cafés and hotels and a small souk, it's a pleasant place to break a journey, partly because so few people do, partly because of its easy-going (and predominantly Berber) atmosphere. Indeed, there is a hint of the frontier town about Midelt, a sense reinforced by the **derelict mines** at Mibladene and El Ahouli, northeast of Midelt, in the nearby gorge of Oued Moulouya (see box, p.255), which are well worth a visit.

Midelt is so far inland that it has a microclimate of extremes: bitterly cold in winter and oppressively hot in summer. Consequently, one of the best times to visit is autumn, particularly at the start of October, when the town hosts a modest **apple festival**. And year-round, if you get the chance, try to

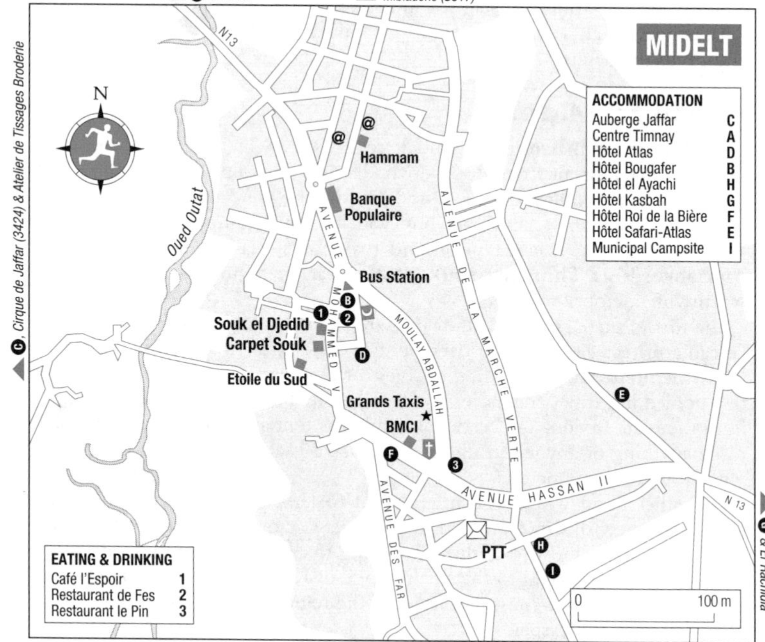

arrive for the huge **Sunday souk**, which spreads back along the road towards Azrou.

Arrival and information

Midelt's **bus station**, in the centre of town, has regular departures to Azrou, Meknes, Fes, Er Rachidia and Rissani, with fewer services to Casablanca and Rabat. During our last visit a new bus station was under construction on the road to Er Rachidia, a short taxi ride from the town centre. The **grand taxi** stand on Avenue Moulay Abdallah, has regular runs to Azrou, Fes, Meknes, Zeïda, Khenifra and Er Rachidia. There is a small men-only **hammam** on Avenue Tarik Souk Jamâa (daily 7am–9pm; 6dh). For **internet** access, *Cyber Panorama* opposite the bus stop (daily 9.30am–1pm & 2.30–10.30pm) is handy to knock off an email while waiting for a bus; otherwise, *Cybre Melouya* at 3 Av Moulay Idriss, and *Cyber el Ayachi*, at 43 Av Tarik Souk Jamâa, are both open daily from 9am to midnight.

The hotel *Safari-Atlas* arranges **4WD excursions** to the El Ahouli mines, the Djebel Ayachi and Cirque Jaffar; a Land Rover for up to six people costs from 1200dh per day, including driver service and food.

Accommodation

Midelt has a reasonable spread of accommodation, but **hotels** are often full by mid-afternoon in peak season, so arrive early or make a reservation in advance. There is a **municipal campsite** (closed for renovation at the time of writing) behind the *Hôtel el Ayachi*, rather bare and stony, but with a pool in summer and hot showers. The *Centre Timnay,* 30km northwest of Midelt on the N13 to Azrou (see opposite), is a better place to camp if you have your own transport.

Auberge Jaffar 5km west of town on the Cirque du Jaffar road ⓣ0535 583415. Fantastic views over the Djebel Ayachi, friendly management and the bonus of a pool. ❸

Centre Timnay signposted on the N13 30km northwest of Midelt ⓣ0535 360188, ⓔtimnay@menara.ma. A very popular spot, with friendly management and excellent facilities including a restaurant and swimming pool. There's a pleasant camping area with a Berber tent where you can sleep for 30dh. Rooms are in either a motel-style block or a new luxury faux-kasbah. Treks and 4WD excursions can also be arranged. Room price includes breakfast. ❸–❹

Hôtel Atlas 3 Rue Mohammed Amraoui ⓣ0535 582938. Lovely – and popular – small *pension* run by a charming Berber family, their ten rooms spotless and cosy. Homecooked meals are prepared on the ground floor. You can sleep on the terrace for 30dh. Hot showers 10dh. ❶

Hôtel Bougafer 7 Av Mohammed V ⓣ&ⓕ0535 583099. A friendly, modern place above a café with rooms distributed over two floors, some newly renovated and en suite, others more basic with shared facilities (hot showers 10dh). There are great views from the roof terrace, where you can sleep out for 35dh or in a Berber tent for 50dh, and a restaurant. ❶–❸

Hôtel el Ayachi Rue Agadir ⓣ0535 582161, ⓕ0535 583307. Midelt's main upmarket hotel, once chockablock with tour groups, now rather frayed at the edges. The best rooms are comfy but dated – those at the rear look over the garden to High Atlas peaks. A 1990 *International Gastronomy Award* remains on display in the restaurant (menu 100dh) – still the best in town when it pulls out the stops. ❹

Hôtel Kasbah 2km south on the Er Rachidia road ⓣ0535 580405, ⓕ0535 583945. Styled after a traditional kasbah but has three-star facilities: a/c in rooms, a flamboyantly decorated restaurant and a pool. Recent reports of poor management make *Hôtel el Ayachi* the better choice. ❹

Hôtel Roi de la Bière corner of Av Hassan II and Av des FAR ⓣ&ⓕ0535 582675. A pleasant and comfortable place founded in 1938, clean and well kept – some rooms have en-suite (hot) showers. No beer in the bar anymore, mind. ❷

Hôtel Safari-Atlas 118 Bd Palestine ⓣ&ⓕ0535 580069, ⓔsafariatlas_hotel@yahoo.com. One of the better mid-range hotels, this has spacious and comfortable en-suite rooms, all fairly modern and with a/c. It has a restaurant – usually open to residents only – with menus from 60dh; just below the hotel there's also a patisserie. Arranges 4WD excursions. Includes breakfast. ❸

The Town

The most interesting section of town, meriting at least a stop between buses, is the area around the old souk – **Souk Djedid**, behind the stalls facing the bus station. Just to the south of the main souk, a daily fruit and vegetable market, is an arcaded **carpet souk**. This is a relaxed place for shopping, and the rugs are superb – mostly local, geometric designs from tribes of the Middle Atlas. Ask to see the "antique" ones, few of which are actually more than ten or twenty years old, but which are usually the most idiosyncratic and inventive. Good examples can also be seen at the **Etoile du Sud** carpet shop, behind the *Hôtel Occidental* just south of the souk, or at the smaller **Maison Berbère** a few doors up from the *Hôtel Atlas*. Be prepared to bargain hard to secure a decent price – it goes without saying, don't turn up with a guide.

A worthier place to buy carpets – plus blankets and beautiful traditional embroidery – is the **Atelier de Tissages et Broderie** (Mon–Thurs & Sat 8am–noon & 2–5.30pm; ⓣ0535 582443), also known as Kasbah Myriem, in a former convent building; the entrance is just beyond that to the convent itself (see opposite). The *atelier* is run by six Franciscan nuns, who welcome visitors to see carpets and textiles being made from start to finish by local women. Girls learn techniques from as young as five years old, and women who choose to continue after marriage, rather than focus on domestic duties, are paid for their work. Consequently, the women practise and pass on traditional skills and designs, and also contribute to their own domestic economies.

The nuns operate this programme in conjunction with literacy courses; up to twelve local women spend two years labouring in the workshop for part of the day, then attending Arabic lessons. Admittedly, this is not the cheapest place to buy a carpet, but your money contributes directly to the local economy – next to no intermediaries are involved – and the pieces are of high quality; all "*fait avec amour*", as the nuns put it. The *atelier* is located on the western outskirts of Midelt, to the left past a new mosque on the road to **Tattiouine**, where a **Coopérative de Tissages** is run by semi-nomadic families, also assisted by the Franciscan community.

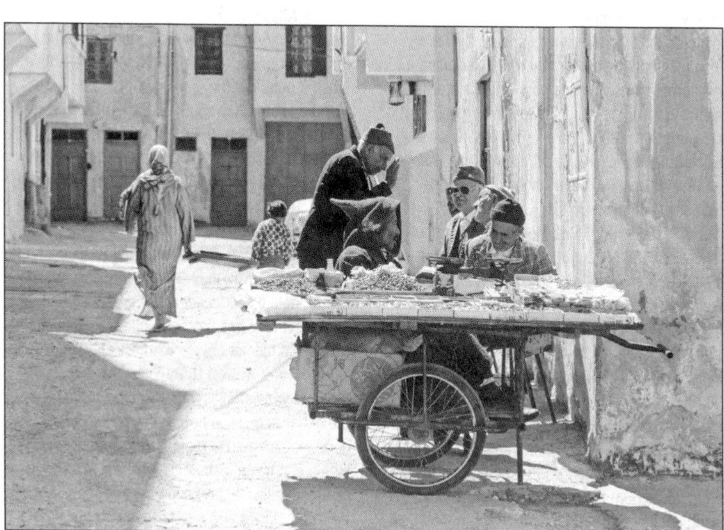

▲ Craft stall, Midelt

El Ahouli: Moroccan klondike

Less than an hour's drive from Midelt, on the banks of the **Oued Moulouya** where it emerges from its spectacular gorge, is the deserted mining settlement of **El Ahouli**. You can reach it by car from Midelt – leave by Avenue Moulay Idriss – first along the S317, past **Mibladene** (11km from Midelt) and then, by the 3419, to El Ahouli (another 14km). Alternatively, 4WD and fossicking excursions run by *Hôtel Safari-Atlas* (see p.253) costs between 200d and 300dh per person per day.

Once past Mibladene (appropriately, "Our Mother Earth" in Berber), where modest excavations are still being worked, the road deteriorates and the tarmac virtually disappears as you approach El Ahouli. In some respects, the barren and tortuous route from Mibladene, and the desolate landscape around it, are reason enough to do the trip. The bleak plateau where Mibladene is located leads to a narrow and picturesque gorge, which you negotiate with frequent crossings of the river on rattling wooden bridges. On a clear day, the reddish landscape provides a dramatic contrast with the blue sky.

Soon, you reach the mining ruins on both sides of the river. From the turn of the twentieth century, and long before on a more modest scale, the locals mined **lead**, which contained **silver**. In 1979, around three thousand people still worked here but all had gone by the mid-1980s. You don't have to be an industrial archeologist to be impressed by the tunnels, aqueducts, aerial ropeways, barrack-like living quarters and, above all, the mine buildings, pressed high against the cliff face like a Tibetan monastery. Tracks cut across the sides of the gorge – first used by mules, then a mineral-line railway passing through the tunnels – and everywhere there is rusting ironmongery.

Beyond El Ahouli, a rough track continues downstream to **Ksabi** from where you can complete the circuit to Midelt by the N15 and N13. Realistically, most of the route beyond Mibladene needs a 4WD because the track is regularly subjected to flash floods. If you find a grand taxi whose driver agrees to do the trip – not everyone will, because of the poor condition of the track – expect to pay between 200dh and 300dh for a return trip to the mines, including a two-hour stopover at the site.

The convent building itself, **Nôtre Dame de l'Atlas**, is home not to the nuns – who live in a house opposite – but to five elderly Trappist monks, among them Frère Jean-Pierre, one of only two survivors of the massacre of seven Jesuit monks in Tibhirine, Algeria, in 1996. Mass is held at the convent (times are posted on the metal gate at the entrance) and visitors are welcome to join in.

If you follow the Tattiouine road a few kilometres further, you enter very different countryside from that around Midelt, where eagles soar above the hills and mule tracks lead down to valleys dotted with an occasional kasbah. For more on this area – and the Cirque Jaffar beyond – see p.256.

Eating

A clutch of café-restaurants south of the bus station on Avenue Mohammed V prepare simple **meals**; try the *Café L'Espoir* (no phone; daily 10am–9pm; cheap), or opposite on Rue Lalla Aïcha, the *Restaurant de Fes* (*Chez Fatima et Fils*)–daily noon–3pm & 6–9pm; moderate–which offers a generous *menu du jour* for 80dh, with vegetarian tajines, and quince stewed in sugar and cinnamon for afters. Outside the hotels, other options include the *Restaurant Le Pin*, part of a tourist complex on Avenue Moulay Abdallah (June–Sept 8am–6.30pm; Oct–May 10am–4pm; moderate), with a good-value 80dh menu, the choice of five different tajines, as well as brochettes and omelettes. More relaxing than its hall-like dining room are the bar and tent-syled café in the gardens – a pleasant spot for breakfast.

The Cirque Jaffar, Djebel Ayachi and beyond

The classic route around Midelt is the **Cirque Jaffar**, a good *piste* that leaves the Midelt–Tattiouine road to edge its way through a hollow in the foothills of the **Djebel Ayachi** (see box opposite). The views of the Atlas Mountains are truly dramatic and the rugged road ensures an element of adventure. The route eventually loops back to the Midelt–Azrou road after 34km (turn right, onto the 3426, near the *Maison Forestière de Mitkane*); it is only 79km in all back to Midelt, but takes a good half-day to complete. If you are taking your own vehicle, the reputable Garage El Ayachi (18 Route de Meknes ⓣ0661 354745) is on hand for repairs and recovery assistance.

Across the Atlas

Standard cars make it over the Atlas from Midelt to Tinerhir in summer, though it's a lot easier with a 4WD; everyone needs a pick and spade for the occasional very rough detour (beware of scorpions when shifting rocks), some warm clothes and a tent for sleeping out at night – Atlas nights are chilly, even in summer. If you don't have a vehicle, you can use Berber lorries over the various stages, which provide a kind of bus service most days. Travelling this way, you should reckon on up to three days for the journey to Imilchil (though you might make it in one), and a similar number from there down to the Todra Gorge and Tinerhir (see p.453). Note that you can also reach Imilchil on daily minibuses from Rich (see opposite).

South to Er Rachidia

There's less adventure in continuing **south from Midelt to Er Rachidia**, though the route is a striking one, marking the transition to the south and the desert. The area was long notorious for raids upon caravans and travellers carried out by the Aït Haddidou, a nomadic Berber tribe, fear of whom led the main spring along this route to be known as *Aïn Khrob ou Hrob* – "Drink and Flee". The tribe were pacified with great difficulty by the French, with skirmishes only fizzling out as late as the 1930s, and as a result traditional *ksour* (fortified villages) are often shadowed by old Foreign Legion posts.

The Tizi n'Talrhmeht and Rich

Around 30km south of Midelt, you heave up across one of the lower passes of the High Atlas, the **Tizi n'Talrhmeht** (Pass of the She-Camel), before descending onto a sparse desert plain. At Aït Messaoud, just beyond the pass, there's a distinctly *Beau Geste*-like Foreign Legion fort, and a few kilometres further down, you come across the first southern *ksar*, Aït Kherrou, a river oasis at the entrance to a small gorge. After this, the *ksour* begin to dot the landscape as the road follows the meanders of the great Ziz River.

The main settlement in these parts is **RICH**, a dusty, red-washed market town and administrative centre, spread on a plain between mountains. Enclosed by palms that are watered by a *seguia* or *khettera* (irrigation channel) from the Oued Ziz, the town developed around a *ksar* and was an important fort during the Protectorate. There is a lively Monday **souk**, and several **hotels** lie just off the main square, the best of which is *Hôtel Isli* (ⓣ0535 368191; ❶), which has clean rooms and free hot showers above a café-restaurant. In the unlikely event that it's full, on the same street are the basic *Hôtel Salama* (ⓣ0535 589343; ❶) and *El Massira* (ⓣ0535 589340; ❶), marginally preferable and which has hot showers and a restaurant.

Djebel Ayachi and Tounfite

Djebel Ayachi can be climbed from Midelt, either returning to the town, or as part of a through-trek to Tounfite. From Midelt, a taxi or pick-up can be arranged to the springs 2km beyond Tattiouine, and from here you can follow the **Ikkis valley** (the col at the end leads to the Cirque du Jaffar). An easy ascent leads to the many summits of this huge range, which was long thought to be the highest in Morocco (it is 3700m – compared to Toubkal at 4167m). A descent south to the Oued Taarart valley brings you to several villages and a Wednesday truck out to Tounfite.

At **Tounfite**, rooms are available and buses and taxis link it with **Boumia** (with a Thurs souk), Zeïda and Midelt. The village also gives access to the **Djebel Masker** (3265m) – a long day's climb, rising from cedar forests. Ayachi and Masker are long wave-crests; seen from a distance, they appear to curve over the horizon such is the scale.

Serious expeditions

From Tounfite, an interesting *piste* runs west, between the Toujjet and Oujoud peaks to the head of the Melwiya plains and Arghbala, beyond which lies the main *piste* across the Central Atlas via Imilchil. South of Djebel Masker lies a chaos of spectacular peaks, little visited. The only information in English at present is in Michael Peyron's *Grand Atlas Traverse* guide, which details the whole zone between Midelt and the Toubkal massif.

Over the Atlas from Rich

West of Rich, the Atlas mountains stretch into the distance, skirted by a road up behind the town that trails the last section of the Oued Ziz. The R317 (formerly 3443) road west from Rich begins as the R706 (formerly 3442) and is surfaced all the way to **Imilchil**. Minibus taxis ply this impressive route daily, a wonderful three-hour trip through great gorges and ever-more barren valleys. They depart in the morning from a *place* one block east of the bus station, by the road sign to Imilchil, then head to the bridge across the Ziz; you can pick them up at either place, usually from around 7am.

The route can also be travelled in stages by **Berber lorries** (*camions*), which head for the Imilchil souk on Fridays. Land Rover taxis also cover the route and, if there are enough customers, you will be able to pay for a *place* rather than chartering the whole vehicle. The most promising day to set out from Rich by *camion* or Land Rover is Friday (or early Sat morning), when you might get a shared vehicle all the way to Imilchil for its Saturday souk; make enquiries at the Rich hotels.

The Ziz Gorges

The scenic highlight of the regular Midelt–Er Rachidia route is the dramatic **Ziz Gorges**, tremendous erosions of rock that carve a passage through the Atlas. The route follows the Ziz valley from **Aït Krojmane** (7km from Rich) onwards, just past the Ziz ("gazelle" in Berber) filling station. About 20km from Rich, you will see a cluster of modern buildings on the right between the road and the river, signposted **Hammat Moulay Ali Cherif**. This is a small but well-known spa, whose outdoor hot springs (over 36°C), rich in magnesium and sulphates, are said to cure rheumatic disorders and kidney problems. You will see the afflicted hopefuls in steamy thickets nearby. Men and women bathe on alternate days, and there is a café and some primitive rooms to rent.

A further 5km on, you enter the gorges proper, around 25km from Rich, shortly after the **Tunnel du Légionnaire**, built by the French in 1930 to open up the route to the south and still guarded by drowsy soldiers. The gorges are truly majestic, especially in late-afternoon, when they are lit by great slashes of sunlight and the mountain landscape reveals sudden vistas of brilliant green oasis and red-brown *ksour*.

You emerge from the gorges near the vast **Barrage Hassan Addakhil**, built in 1971 to irrigate the valley of the Tafilalt beyond, and to supply electricity for Er Rachidia. The dam also regulates the flow of the Oued Ziz, preventing the serious flooding that occurred frequently before it was built, as witnessed by the deserted *ksour* in the gorges above and below the lake.

Azrou to Kasba Tadla

The **main route from Azrou to Marrakesh** – the **N8** – skirts well clear of the Atlas ranges. The towns along the way are dusty, functional market centres, unlikely to tempt you to linger, and the interest is all in the subtle changes of land, cultivation and architecture as you move into the south. In addition, the Middle Atlas is close at hand if you leave the main road and take to the *pistes*. A great network of them spreads out behind the small town of **El Ksiba**, itself 4km off the N8, but easily reached by bus from Kasba Tadla.

Khenifra

With long-distance buses regularly passing through the provincial centre of **KHENIFRA**, you are unlikely to get stranded here. Nor are you likely to want to: the modern quarters, bisected by the Fes-Marrakesh road (N8), are not very enticing and the town's small Medina contains little of interest.

Indeed, Khenifra now seems far too mundane to have been a focus of resistance under Moha ou Hammou. Yet in the early years of the Protectorate, the French suffered a costly victory here, losing six hundred men when they took the town in 1914. Khenifra also played an important part in the struggle for independence, which climaxed on August 20, 1955 when mass rioting broke out on its streets.

Prehaps the best reason to visit is in order to pick up the scenic route that connects Khenifra to the Sources de l'Oum er Rbia (see p.250). Should you decide to stay, there are a number of small **hotels** along Avenue Zerktouni. The best budget option is *Hôtel Jaouharat al Atlas* (☎0535 588030; ❷), which offers modest though clean and comfortable rooms. For mid-range digs, both *Hôtel Najah*, just north of the junction (☎0535 588331; ❸), with pleasant heated en-suite rooms and satellite TV and *Hôtel de France* (Quartier des FAR, ☎0535 586114; ❸), cheaper with clean old-fashioned en-suite rooms, are good options. Otherwise, 500m east above the junction, newly renovated *Hotel Atlas Zayane* (☎0535 586020; ❺) is the upscale choice: all the mod-cons plus a swimming pool.

The best place to **eat** is the reputable restaurant of the *Hôtel de France* (noon–3.30pm & 7pm–midnight; moderate), offering the usual dishes plus good steaks and 80dh menus. The easiest way to get there is by petit taxi (around 8dh) from the bus station. Otherwise, there are a number of cafés and restaurants around the junction of avenues Zerktouni and Mohammed V: the *Hôtel Najah* (12.30–5pm & 7–9pm; moderate), which prepares well-cooked menus for 90dh, and *La Tente Berbere* (7am–10pm; cheap) just north, which serves charcoal-oven pizza and a selection of Moroccan and international dishes.

A BMCE bank and the PTT are on Avenue Mohammed V. Internet cafés are scattered along Avenue Zerktouni. The **bus station** is located at the southern end of Avenue Zerktouni on the right, and is served by frequent daily services to all major destinations both north and south. Southbound **grands taxis** –

including those for El Ksiba – leave behind the bus station, those for Fes and Meknes leave from a station in the Medina.

El Ksiba, Arhbala and across the Atlas

EL KSIBA is a busy Berber village lying 4km south of the N8 Fes–Marrakesh road, enclosed by apricot, olive and orange groves and with a **Sunday souk**. Two buses arrive daily from Kasba Tadla, as do **grands taxis** from Khenifra and Kasba Tadla. The village, dusty and not terribly inspiring, has a **bank** and a passable small **hotel**, the *Henri IV*, in the Quartier Administrative (Ⓣ&Ⓕ0523 415002; ❷); from the centre of the village, head uphill from opposite the petrol station and bear left after about 300m – if coming by car from the N8, take the left before you enter the village. The hotel is in attractive surroundings, with plenty of scope for day walks or overnight treks. The **PTT** is next door.

South of El Ksiba, the road crosses the Atlas by way of Imilchil and the Todra Gorge to Tinerhir. Once a challenging *piste*, this is now mostly tarmac and measures are being taken to avoid past wash-out danger spots.

From El Ksiba, the R317 road twists through forest to a panoramic col, then descends to a river and a junction with the R306 to Ouaouizaght and Azilal via the Bin el Ouidane reservoir (see p.264), a fine scenic drive. **Ouaouizaght** has a busy Wednesday souk, and one hotel, the *Hôtel Atlas*, at the top end of town (Ⓣ0523 442042; ❶).

The R317, meanwhile, turns upwards by a gorge and continues through varied forest to cross the **Tizi n'Isli** pass (a village of the same name is just off the road). From here, it snakes down to a junction, at which an unnamed road branches off eastward to **Arhbala**, (see p.462) a busy market town with a Wednesday souk, and cafés that have rooms to rent. This road continues to meet the R503 Beni Mellal–Midelt road, an attractive circuit, surfaced but in a poor state. Heading south from the junction, route R317 (also known here as the Trans-Atlas road) crosses a girder bridge and continues on a rough road to **Ikassene**, something of a staging post on this route, with several cafés, and rooms available. Beyond Ikassane, a new line leads on to Tassent, then hauls upwards on many bends (periodic landslides may block it) to a high valley and a col, giving a view to the Tislit lake, beyond which lies **Imilchil**.

Kasba Tadla

KASBA TADLA takes its name from a fortress Moulay Ismail built here, strategically positioned beside the Oum er Rbia river. It remains a military town, not that you'd know it, in a surprisingly sleepy, leafy town centre. The only site – such as it is – is a walled **kasbah** at the southern end of the main street, Avenue Mohammed V. This features an impressive derelict Grand Mosque with a crumbling brick minaret, and an interesting smaller mosque, whose minaret has the same protruding perches as that of the Great Mosque in Tiznit.

As you enter town, keep an eye open for four tall, square pillars near the turn-off on the N8 Fes–Marrakesh road (about 1km from the town centre). This is a **memorial** to the French soldiers killed hereabouts from 1912 to 1933, and affords a fine view of the *bidonville* by the river and the town beyond. The town's other main feature is a sizeable **souk** held on Mondays.

For anyone stranded, there are two cheap and very basic **hotels** off Avenue Mohammed V, a few blocks north of the kasbah. The better of the two is the ramshackle *Hôtel des Alliés* at 38 Av Mohammed V (Ⓣ0523 418587; cold showers; ❶), with iron bedsteads in rooms and a barn-like bar that could have been transported from 1930s pastoral France, but with no alcohol, though.

The only other option is the cheaper and even more basic *Hôtel Atlas*, round the block at 46 Rue Majjati Obad (no phone; ❶).

Your best bet for **eating** is the *Restaurant Kordouba* (daily 8am–10pm; cheap), a couple of blocks south of the *Alliés* at the corner of Avenue Mohammed V and Rue Tarik Ibn Ziad, serving chicken, brochettes and steak.

The **bus station** is 500m north of the centre and has frequent departures for Beni Mellal and Khenifra, two a day to El Ksiba, and more to Marrakesh, Fes, Meknes, Midelt and Casablanca, with even one daily departure each for Tangier and Agadir. The **grand taxi** yard opposite offers regular runs to Beni Mellal, El Ksiba, Khenifra and Marrakesh.

Beni Mellal

Ideally sited between Marrakesh and Fes, and on the main routes to Casablanca and Rabat, **BENI MELLAL** is one of Morocco's fastest-growing towns, whose haphazardly planned new suburbs nibble deeper into the surrounding olive groves with every year. A largely modern town, it has few specific sights – and even fewer tourists – but makes a break en route to Marrakesh or a good transit point for other destinations; it is well connected by bus services. Serving as a market centre for the broad, prosperous flatlands to the north, the town hosts a large **Tuesday souk,** which is good for woollen blankets that feature unusual Berber designs. Olives are grown on the lower slopes of the Djebel Tassemit and the plain is well known for its oranges.

Moulay Ismail's **kasbah** in the old Medina has been restored to the point of no interest. Your time is better spent walking to the smaller **Kasbah Ras el Aïn** and the nearby spring of **Aïn Asserdoun**, both south of town. The latter is a pleasant spot, feeding a series of artificial falls amid well-tended gardens. A petit taxi (8dh) or bus #3 from the Medina (summer only) will take you to the *source*, from where you can walk to the kasbah, fifteen minutes up the footpath behind the car park – start from the steps at the far left.

If you're in Beni Mellal on a Saturday, it's worth a trip to what is traditionally the Middle Atlas's largest weekly **market**, held 35km southwest of the town at **Souk Sebt des Oulad Nemâa**, and linked by regular buses.

Arrival, orientation and information

The main road from Fes to Marrakesh (the N8) cuts into the northern suburbs of Beni Mellal as the N8a and leads to the **bus station**; if you can't face the twenty-minute walk to the centre, a petit taxi will cost around 7dh.

For details of local **guides** – and adventure tours – into the Atlas from Beni Mellal, see box, p.262.

Accommodation

If the hotels listed below are full, try more basic options on Place de la Liberté.

Hôtel Aïn Asserdoun Av des FAR Ⓣ&Ⓕ0523 483493. A friendly place, with a small restaurant (menu 80dh), comfortable accommodation and en-suite bathrooms; popular with Moroccans passing through. ❷

Hôtel Chems Ⓣ0523 483460, Ⓕ0523 488530. One of two garden hotels on the original Marrakesh road, this is less flash than the nearby *Hôtel Ouzoud* but also more friendly. Accommodation is modern, facilities include a pool, tennis courts and a nightclub. Includes breakfast. ❻

Hôtel de Paris Hay Ibn Sina, New Medina Ⓣ0523 482245, Ⓕ0523 484227. A 1950s-style hotel, 15min from the town centre. Pleasant rooms, all with a/c, have a country vibe thanks to pine furniture. Good restaurant, too. ❸

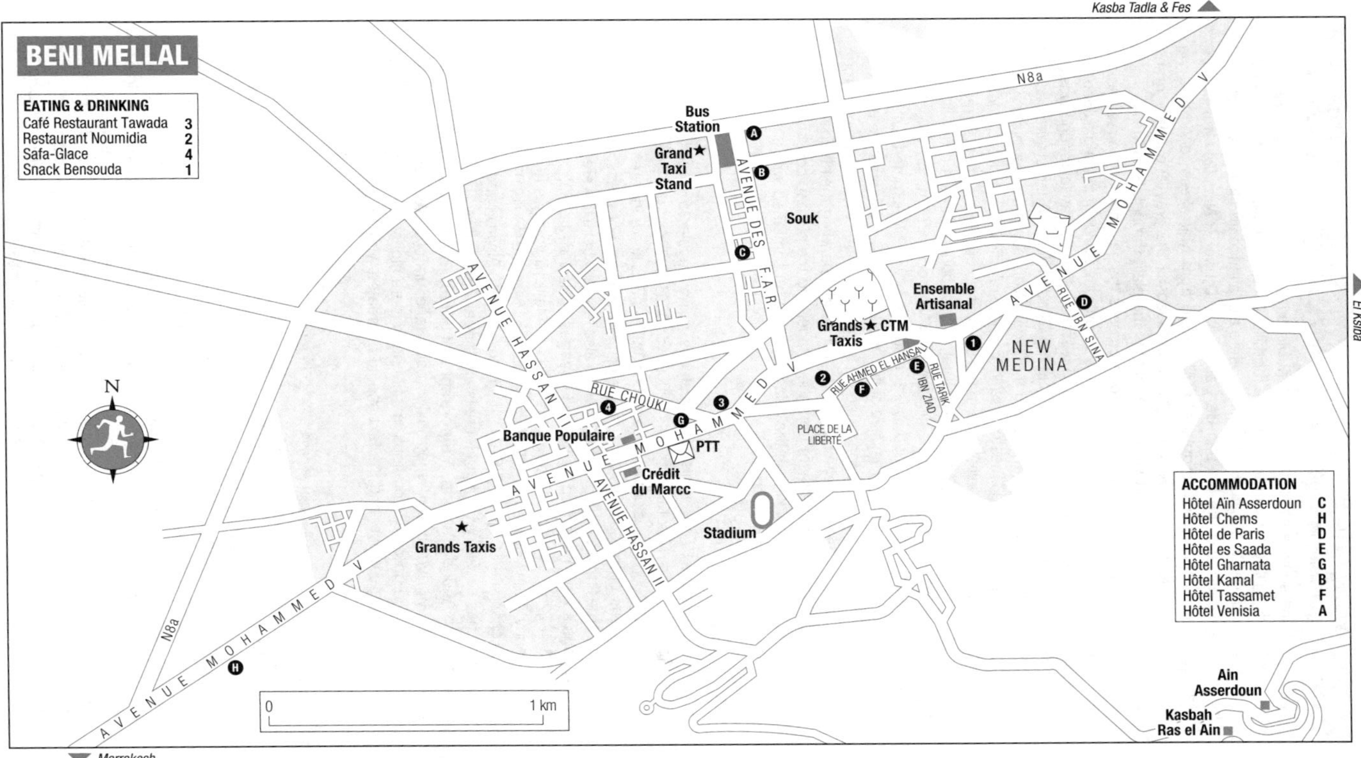
BENI MELLAL
EATING & DRINKING
Café Restaurant Tawada 3
Restaurant Noumidia 2
Safa-Glace 4
Snack Bensouda 1
ACCOMMODATION
Hôtel Aïn Asserdoun C
Hôtel Chems H
Hôtel de Paris D
Hôtel es Saada E
Hôtel Gharnata G
Hôtel Kamal B
Hôtel Tassamet F
Hôtel Venisia A
Kasba Tadla & Fes
El Ksiba
Casablanca
Marrakesh
N8a
Bus Station
Grand Taxi Stand
Souk
AVENUE DES F.A.R.
Ensemble Artisanal
Grands Taxis
CTM
NEW MEDINA
RUE IBN SINA
RUE AHMED EL HANSALI
RUE TARIK IBN ZIAD
PLACE DE LA LIBERTÉ
AVENUE MOHAMMED V
AVENUE HASSAN II
RUE CHOUKI
Banque Populaire
PTT
Crédit du Marcc
Stadium
Grands Taxis
Ain Asserdoun
Kasbah Ras el Ain
N
0
1 km

South of Beni Mellal: Atlas hikes and pistes

The mountains south and southeast of Beni Mellal and the Bin el Ouidane reservoir are ideal trekking and 4WD country. In the foothills, **Djebel Tassemit** (2248m) – which towers like a high wall behind Beni Mellal – offers a challenge and fine views; reached by Aïn Asserdoun and the Kasbah de Ras el Aïn. **Djebel R'Nim** (2411m) can be climbed from the pass to **Ouaouizaght**. The road from Marrakesh to Arhbala via Azilal, Bin el Ouidane and Ouaouizaght is surfaced all the way and offers grand scenery, far more interesting than the N8 across the plain through Beni Mellal.

The real mountains lie to the south. A road crosses the east end of the reservoir to wend its way through to Tillouguite (which has a Saturday souk), becoming a Jeepable *piste* at the col. It continues spectacularly to reach the Oued Ahansal (bridge washed out in 1999), from where one branch goes up the Oued Mellal to Anergui (*gîte*), access for **Morik** (3223m), Laqroun (3117m) and the **Mellal Gorges**. The other branch goes to Tamga, facing the soaring limestone walls of the peak nicknamed "*La Cathédrale*" (a spectacular goat path actually leads to the summit dome). The *piste* then makes a high and tortuous ascent to **Zaouia Ahansal**, a *marabout's* shrine at the village of **Agoudim** in what are known as "the Dolomites of Morocco" (70km from Tillouguite).

Zaouia Ahancal is also reached by a *piste* from Aït Mohammed and Azilal, descending under Aroudane's massive cliffs. Agoudim's tower architecture is unique north of the Atlas, and it has long been a religious centre, besides being strong enough to stop the Glaoui chieftains (see p.410) from expanding their fiefdom further east. The Taghia gorges upstream from the village, and the plateau country beyond, offer some of the best trekking in the Atlas, and can be combined with a start/finish in the more popular Bou Guemez.

Practicalities

It would be possible to cover this route in stages, using irregular local Berber lorries or jeeps. Abderrahman Tissoukla (Ⓣ0523 420899 or 0668 962883), the president of the local Guides Association, is one of several local **guides** who know the area well, and can organize means of transport such as mules or Land Rovers. For **maps**, contact Atlas Maps, the same firm as AMIS (see p.54), which also regularly treks this area. **Land Rover expeditions** are also arranged by **Imilchil Voyages** in Beni Mellal (333 Av Mohammed V; Ⓣ0523 487259). Across and down the road from Imilchil Voyages is another helpful travel agency, Torin Voyages at 412 Bd Mohammed V (Ⓣ0523 480191), which is also a *bureau de change* and agent for RAM, Air France, Bristish Airways and Alitalia.

Agoudim has several *gîtes*, and there is another at Amezraï, by the perched *agadir* a kilometre to Agoudim's north. A **topographical guide**, *Randonnées Pédestres dans le Massif du Mgoun*, is published in Morocco (and unobtainable anywhere else). While useful, the gorge explorations mentioned in it are highly dangerous scrambles rather than sedate walks, and the text should be treated with caution.

Hôtel es Saada 129 Rue Tarik Ibn Ziad Ⓣ0523 482991. The cheapest option with cleanish rooms, some windowless; hot showers for 7dh next door. ❶

Hôtel Gharnata Cnr Rue Chouki and Av Mohammed V Ⓣ0523 483482, 0523 422427. Nothing special, and two-star rooms are on the small side, but well placed in the town centre. ❷

Hôtel Ouzoud Av Mohammed V, Ⓣ0523 483752, Ⓦwww.sogatour.ma. Beni Mellal's swish international-standard business hotel. Rooms have all the mod cons though some are a bit motel-like. There's a good restaurant, bar, tennis courts and swimming pool. ❻

Hôtel Tassamet 186 Rue Ahmed el Hansali, just off the street Ⓣ0523 421313. A cut above the usual Medina cheapie, clean and welcoming, with constant hot water and en-suite rooms, and good views from front-facing rooms – ask for a balcony – and the roof terrace. ❷

Hôtel Venisia Bd du 20 Août Ⓣ0523 482348. Newest and best of the trio of similarly priced hotels facing the bus station, with well-kept and comfortable en-suite rooms. If it's full, the *Hôtel Kamal* (Ⓣ0523 486941; ❷) on the main road is a better bet than the twinned *Hôtel Zidania/Hôtel Charaf* nearby. ❷

Eating

Beni Mellal is not blessed with choices for eating out, and many options are choked by exhaust fumes on Avenue Mohammed V. For upmarket **meals**, try *Hôtel Ouzoud* (daily 11.30am–3pm & 6.30–11pm; moderate to expensive), whose smart restaurant serves international and Moroccan dishes, or *Hôtel de Paris* (daily 10.30am–3pm & 6.30–11.30pm; moderate), which offers a self-service buffet and à la carte. In the town centre, tasty fare at lower prices is rustled up at the *Café Restaurant Tawada* (11.30am–3pm & 7–11pm; cheap) adjacent to the Total garage on Avenue Mohammed V – the rabbit tajine with raisins and cinnamon takes some beating.

As ever, the cheapest eats are in the Old Medina, where *Restaurant Noumidia* at 141 Rue Ahmed el Hansali (daily 10am–midnight; cheap) is the best of a trio of popular eateries doing roast chicken, brochettes and *kefta* kebabs. Another popular, unpretentious place, offering exotic fare such as liver and brain kebabs alongside the usuals, is *Snack Bensouda* at 136 Av Mohammed V (daily noon–midnight; cheap), though outside tables are blighted by traffic. *Safa-Glace* at 40 Rue Chouki (11.30am–4pm & 6–11.30pm; cheap) has a more pleasant location, plus tasty pizzas and ice cream.

Moving on

Beni Mellal is at a strategic crossroads, so is served by a wealth of **buses**.

Grands taxis to Fes and Azrou leave from the esplanade opposite the CTM office; those to Marrakesh, Azilal, Ouzoud, Casablanca and Rabat, as well as Kasba Tadla and El Ksiba, leave from a parking area behind the bus station.

The Cascades d'Ouzoud

The **Cascades d'Ouzoud** are the most spectacular in Morocco, their ampitheatre of waterfalls falling into pools in a lush valley that remains invisible till the last moment. The wide spread of cataracts at the top isn't entirely natural – water from the *oued* is channelled through a variety of irrigation channels towards the rim of the falls – but the result is an image that is not too far removed from the Muslim idea of Paradise depicted on gaudy prints throughout the nation. Nor has the site been overcommercialized – despite the cascades appearing in every national tourism brochure, the atmosphere remains laid-back and relaxing. Camping spots and cafés abound, and the good paths, high summer apart, are never too busy; the site is at its best from March until mid-June. That there are pleasant walks in the locale is just another reason to stay overnight – to swim in pools below the cascades by moonlight (technically forbidden) is something special, and in late-afternoon, arching rainbows appear in the mist around the falls.

Ouzoud lies 18km down a surfaced road off the R304 Marrakesh–Azilal road, 21km before Azilal. There are regular **grands taxis** to the falls from Azilal (17dh a *place* or 100dh for the whole taxi). Getting back to Azilal is generally no problem, with grands taxis regularly shuttling from the falls. From Beni Mellal, a grand taxi to the falls should cost around 360dh (60dh per person if you can fill it). From Marrakesh, tourist agencies offer day-long **tours**.

Bin el Ouidane and Azilal

The quickest road from Beni Mellal to Azilal heads off 20km along the N8 through Afourer and hauls uphill, providing a vast panorama of the huge plain that sweeps east into the distance, then crests a pass to descend zigzagging through the hills to the **Bin el Ouidane reservoir**. This was one of the earliest (1948–55) and most ambitious of the country's irrigation schemes and has changed much of the land around Beni Mellal – formerly as dry and barren as the phosphate plains to the northwest. It also supplies much of central Morocco's electricity.

A new modest **campsite** beside the barrage, *L'eau Vive* (ⓣ05523 44931; ❷), has three homely rooms and camping on a beautiful grassy terrace overlooking the river downstream of the dam and is an idyllic place to stop for a coffee or even lunch. There are a few other accommodation options scattered around the area, including *Gite Chez Les Berbers* (beyond the dam) and the dysfunctional *Hotel Bin el Ouidane* (5km down the road that forks left before the dam), though neither are of particular repute. Once completed, the 89-room *Hotel Chems du Lac* found on the edge of the lake on the Azilal side of the dam will provide the region's upscale accommodation.

AZILAL, 27km further on, **feels** more oversized village than provincial capital, yet its loose affiliation of streets have a garrison, banks and hotels, and a Thursday souk, and there are good transport links. Buses drop you on a patch of wasteground behind the main square (backed by a large mosque) near the budget **hotels** on Avenue Hassan II. The best of these is the friendly *Hôtel Dades* (ⓣ0523 458245; ❶), 300m east (left) of the bus station and with colourful rooms around a plant-filled courtyard. On the way, you'll pass the *Tissa* (ⓣ0523 458589; ❶), the *Ouzoud* (ⓣ0523 458482; ❶) and the *Souss* (no phone; ❶). The smartest option in town – still rather shabby – is the *Hôtel Assounfou*, 200m west of the town square on Avenue Hassan II (ⓣ0523 459220, ⓕ0523 458442; ❷). The only places to **eat** are simple café-restaurants, among them the down-to-earth *Ibnou Ziad Restaurant* (daily 7.30am–9.30pm; cheap), 50m west of the town square on Avenue Hassan II. The Banque Populaire opposite the main square has an **ATM**, and there's a Crédit Agricole 200m east of it, beyond which, about 800m out of town, are the **PTT** and Complexe Artesanal. **Internet** access is widely available on the main drag; try *Cyber Adrar* beside *Hôtel Assounfou* (daily 8am–midnight).

Buses from Azilal serve Marrakesh four times daily, two continuing to Agadir. There are also five direct buses to Beni Mellal, three morning buses to Casablanca and two departures to Demnate, although most Marrakesh and Agadir buses also call here. **Grands taxis** from a rank beside the bus yard mostly serve Beni Mellal, plus some to the Cascades d'Ouzoud. You may also be able to get one 45km west to Tanant, and one from there to Demnate. The Bou Guemez valley is reached by a surfaced road, with a daily bus service from Azilal. Should you need a guide, seek advice at the *Hôtel Dades*.

The Cascades

The **Cascades d'Ouzoud** are a popular destination in summer, with both Moroccan and foreign tourists attracted by the falls and an easy-going ambience that is refreshingly uncommercialized – for now. The falls face northwest, so are shrouded in darkness for much of the morning and early afternoon; for the best photos, visit from mid- to late-afternoon and bring a wide-angle lens if you have one. The largest rainbows are best seen from the first of the outlook spots, halfway down the path to the bottom of the falls.

Before you descend, however, have a look at the lip of the falls just past the *Riad Cascades d'Ouzoud* at the top of the village. The over-sized hutches here shelter small **watermills**, some still grinding wheat into flour as the river is diverted through the wheels before it plunges over the edge. The path starts from the top of the village, to the left of the *Dar Essalam* hotel, then zigzags past **cafés and souvenir stalls to** the great basins below the **cascades**, where boatmen in rickety rafts offer to row visitors to the main pool. Although strictly speaking it's not permitted, you can swim in one of the lower natural pools – currents are dangerous in the main pool beneath the falls – and you might spot the occasional Barbary ape under the oak and pomegranate trees; your best chance is at daybreak or an hour or so before dusk, when they come to drink in the river.

For a memorable short **hike**, go beyond the lower pools to the so-called "Mexican village" (officially named Tanaghmelt, though some guides prefer "Berber village"), a fascinating place connected by semi-underground passages. To get there, follow the path past the lower pools and you will see a path climbing up on the left, past a farmhouse and up to the top of the plain. Follow this west and the village is sited on the slopes of the wooded hills, about 1km along the path, which drops to a stream before climbing up to the houses. Allow four hours for a circuit. Another path follows the river valley beyond the falls, at its narrowest and most impressive after 7km at the Gorges de l'Ouzoud-el-Abid. With your own transport, you could see this on the road north towards the N8, or unofficial guides tout their services for dayhikes; ask in hotels or at the café at the top of the village, by the turn-off towards *Hôtel Restaurant de France*.

Accommodation options start 100m beyond the taxi stand with the friendly *Dar Essalam* (no phone; ❶), built around a courtyard; you can rent bare rooms or sleep on the roof (20dh). Nearby *Relais De Titrite* (no phone; ❸) is a pleasant restaurant, handy for breakfast, with a few decent rooms for rent upstairs. More comfortable is newly renovated *Hôtel Chellal d'Ouzoud* (Ⓣ0523 429180; ❹) at the start of the path downhill, clean and cool, and with its own terrace to sleep on (25dh). The restaurant offers a menu of Moroccan staples for about 85dh. For something more tranquil, the *Hôtel Restaurant de France* (Ⓣ0523 459017; ❸) is among olive groves 500m from the top of the village, and has bright rooms, some en suite, and a pleasant garden. The only upmarket choice is the *Riad Cascades d'Ouzoud* (Ⓣ0523 429173, Ⓦwww.ouzoud.com; includes breakfast; ❺), at the top of the village, a beautifully restored house whose rustic chic sits comfortably alongside traditional features and which has open fires in rooms in winter. Several **campsites** lie at the top of the village, all fairly basic but offering shady spots for tents and motorhomes; the first you come to is *Camping Amalou*. Closer to the waterfalls, cafés on the path downhill have spaces where you can camp for a small fee. On the other side of the falls there are a number of pleasant sites – facing the falls, *Camping Tafna* has a particularly stunning location. All tend to attract a young backpacking clientele.

On from Ouzoud

Continuing to Marrakesh from Ouzoud on local transport, it's easiest to backtrack to Azilal, picking up a bus there to Beni Mellal or (if you time it right) direct to Marrakesh. However, if you are driving, you could head down to **Khemis des Oulad** on the Beni Mellal–Marrakesh road (N8) – 51km of tarred road.

Bou Guemez valley and Ighil Mgoun

The **Bou Guemez valley** ("La Vallée Heureux") is second only to Djebel Toubkal in popularity among mountain-lovers, not only for its own unique beauty, but also as a base for **Ighil Mgoun** (4068m), Morocco's second highest summit (see box, p.266). There are also some astonishing gorges and passes on the southward trek through the mountains to exit at El Kelâa des Mgouna.

A highly spectacular road turning off near Aït Mohammed gives access to the lower end of the Bou Guemez and Bou Willi valleys. Most visitors arrive by Land Rover from Marrakesh, but a daily minibus service operates from Azilal (see p.264), and more infrequently from Aït Mohammed via the old *piste*, which enters over an eastern pass that is often blocked in winter. Trekkers are recommended to tackle the two-day walk in to the Bou Guemez from Aït Mohammed via the pretty hamlet of **Srempt** (where theres a *gîte)* and the **Tizi n'Aït Ouriat** (2606m), which has great views of the mountain ranges. Another possible approach is via Demnate (see opposite), from where trucks go on to the road end at **Imi n'Wakka** (Tarbat n'Tirsal) under the bulk of Djebel Rhat. A spectacular trek of several days heads down the Bou Willi valley to connect with the Bou Guemez. On the **Tizi n'Tirghyst** (2390m) are prehistoric rock-carved pictures of battles and symbols from 4000 years ago.

A longer circuit goes round the west flank of **Djebel Rhat** (3797m) and **Djebel Tignousti** (3825m) to reach the **Oued Tessaout**, which is followed to its head under Ighil Mgoun to rejoin the Bou Guemez. East from the Bou Guemez, the seasonal lake of **Izoughar** is dominated by Djebel Azourki and other big hills. A *tizi* leads to Arouadane and the Zaouia Ahansal area of spectacular gorges. **Agoudim**, a village of remarkable architecture, has several *gîtes* (see box, p.262), as has **Taghia**, which faces the finest gorge and cliff scenery in the country, a rock-climbers' playground of Dolomitic scope.

Several of the Bou Guemez valley villages have *gîte* accommodation, meals and mule hire (see lists in the ONMT Atlas guide). The *Auberge Dar Itrane* (Ⓣ0523 459312; ❷) in **Imelghas** is a more expensive option than the village *gîtes* but

Ighil Mgoun and around

Ighil Mgoun, at 4068m, is Morocco's only summit above 4000m outside the Toubkal massif, and a popular target for hill-goers, giving an easy but long ascent from a base on the Tessaout Sources/Tarkeddid plateau, itself most easily reached from the Bou Guemez valley. This remote spot is the start of the Oued Tessaout, which descends the spectacular Wandras gorge (climbing involved) and also the Arouss gorge (climbing) to the Bou Guemez and, eastwards then south, drains out to Imi n'Wakka and El Kelâa des Mgouna; three to four days including many hours of wading gorges (flash-flood risk), easy but dramatic. **Tarkeddid** (3565m) gives excellent climbing on its traverse. West of Mgoun, two rarely visited peaks of 3883m and 3877m are the highest between Mgoun and the Toubkal area. Several *gîtes* make walking in the Bou Guemez itself worthwhile, while east, between **Azourki** (3677m) and **Ouaougoulzat** (3763m), both skiers' objectives in winter, is the seasonal **Lac Izoughar** (Izourar), beyond which lies the vast nomad plateau and gorges between Zaouia Ahansal and the Dadès (see p.262).

The Tessaout Valley

Demnate is the gateway into the **Tessaout Valley**, and to **Imi n'Wakka** and **Tarbat n'Tirsal**, below vast Djebel Rhat and near Tizi n'Tirghyst, with the finest area of **rock carvings** in Morocco (and the continuation to the Bou Willi/Bou Guemez valleys). From the Tuesday souk at **Aït Tamlil**, the **Oued Tessaout** gives high-class trekking to its source under Mgoun. **Djebel Rhat** (3781m) and **Djebel Tignousti** (3825m) to the north, and a whole crest of peaks to the south, are all worth climbing. Passes south from **Toufghine/Aït Tamlil** (surfaced), **Magdaz** (the most beautiful village in the Atlas, now also accessible by *piste*) and **Amezri** (reached by *piste* from the south) allow exits to the south, with *piste* routes covered by a daily truck except from Magdaz (mule pass only). From Aït Tamlil, trekking links can also be made to Telouet (see p.410), either north or south of Djebel Anghomar (3610m).

worth considering if you plan to make a stopover in the village. Mohammed Achari (Donar Iskattefen, Aït Bou Guemez, Bureau Tabant, par Azilal ⓣ0523 459327) is an experienced mountain guide who has helped many British parties, and offers a full range of services, including Land Rover rental.

Azilal to Marrakesh: Demnate

Having come as far as Azilal and the cascades, it is easier to continue along the R304 road to Marrakesh rather than the descent to the N8 main road from Beni Mellal, in any case the more interesting route.

You may have to change buses along the way at **DEMNATE**, a walled market town with a Glaoui-era kasbah, an old Mellah (half the population were Jews until the 1950s) and a **Sunday souk**, held 2km out of town on the Sidi Rahal road. The souk is by far the largest in the region, an interesting and unaffected event and worth rejigging your travel plans to see. There is also a small daily souk just outside the ramparts and along the nearby streets, as well as a central market with butchers, bakers and fruit and vegetable stalls.

The surrounding area is renowned for **olives** and attractive glazed **pottery**, which is made at out-of-town Bougrhat – signposted and also worth a visit. Another trip, possible by grand taxi (3dh per *place*) from a square 300m beyond the town gate, is to an impressive natural bridge, **Imi n'Ifri**, around 6.5km from Demnate. The arch spans a yawning gorge, the result of the partial collapse of an underground cave system, and guaranteed to unnerve anyone of a vertiginous disposition. It's a quiet untouristed spot, with a seasonal restaurant to sit in and little to do but watch the aerobatic displays of choughs and swifts, with their white rumps and square tails, or the *sibsib* (ground squirrels) on roadside walls.

Demnate sees few tourists and makes for a relaxed stopover. **Buses** drop you at a stop 400m to the right of the old town gate Bab el 'Arabi (the Gate of the Arabs); **grands taxis** to and from Azilal, Marrakesh and Beni Mellal stop and leave from the gate. The **PTT** just inside the gate has an ATM. **Accommodation** is in one of two basic but extremely cheap establishments: the *Hôtel Imi-Nifri*, just inside the gate (ⓣ0523 506003; ❶), and the friendly and slightly better *Hôtel Ouzoud*, 150m or so back down the street outside the gate (ⓣ0661 241099; ❶). Both can be grubby in places, so ask to see several rooms. Superior to anything in the town is a delightful **gîte**, run by a mountain guide, Ezzaari Thami, situated 500m beyond Imi n'Ifri (ⓣ&ⓕ0523 506473, mob 0662 105168; ❷). The *gîte* enjoys a beautiful garden setting and offers delicious Berber dishes; you can also camp here.

From Demnate, **buses to Marrakesh** are frequent (1hr 30min).

Travel details

Trains

Fes to: Casablanca (9 daily; 4hr 15min); Kenitra (9 daily; 2hr 45min); Marrakesh (7 daily; 7hr 40min); Meknes (10 daily; 45min); Oujda (3 daily; 5hr 25min); Rabat (9 daily; 3hr 20min); Tangier (6 daily; 5hr 30min); Taza (4 daily; 2hr).
Meknes to: Casablanca (9 daily; 3hr 30min); Fes (11 daily; 55min); Kenitra (9 daily; 2hr); Marrakesh (7 daily; 7hr); Oujda (3 daily; 7hr 15min); Rabat (9 daily; 2hr 20min); Tangier (6 daily; 4hr 40min); Taza (4 daily; 3hr 20min).

Buses

Azilal to: Agadir (2 daily; 7hr); Beni Mellal (5 daily; 1hr 30min); Casablanca (3 daily; 5hr); Demnate 2 daily; 1hr); Marrakesh (4 daily; 3hr).

Azrou to: Agadir (1 CTM & 1 other daily; 13hr); Aïn Leuh (1 daily; 40min); Beni Mellal (2 CTM & 9 others daily; 5hr); Casablanca (2 CTM & 2 others daily; 5hr 30min); Fes (2 CTM & 17 others daily; 1hr 30min) via Ifrane (20min) and Immouzer (45min); Khenifra (2 CTM & over 18 others daily; 1hr 40min); Marrakesh (2 CTM & 6 others daily; 9hr); Meknes (4 CTM & 18 others daily; 1hr); Midelt (3 CTM & 18 others daily; 3hr); Rabat (2 CTM & 7 others daily; 4hr); Er Rachidia (2 CTM & 14 others daily; 6hr); Rissani (1 CTM & 4 others daily; 9hr); Tangier (1 daily; 8hr); Tetouan (2 daily; 7hr).
Beni Mellal to: Agadir (1 CTM & 6 others daily; 8hr); Azilal (3 daily; 1hr 30min); Azrou (2 CTM & 9 others daily; 5hr); Casablanca (1 CTM & over 2 others daily; 3hr 30min); Demnate (6 daily; 3hr); Essaouira (1 daily; 6hr); Marrakesh (1 CTM & 27 others daily; 4hr); Fes (1 CTM & 9 others daily; 6hr); El Jadida (2 daily; 5hr 30min); Midelt (2 daily; 4hr 30min); Meknes (6 daily; 5hr); Rabat (4 daily; 2hr 30min); Er Rachidia (1 daily; 6hr); Safi (2 daily; 6hr).
Demnate to: Azilal (2 daily; 1hr); Marrakesh (9 daily; 1hr 30min).
Fes to: Agadir (1 CTM & 4 others daily; 12hr); Azrou (2 CTM & 16 others daily; 1hr 30min); Beni Mellal (2 CTM & 9 others daily; 6hr); Casablanca (9 CTM & 24 others daily; 5hr 30min) via Rabat (4hr); Chefchaouen (4 CTM & 8 others daily; 5hr); Al Hoceima (1 CTM & 6 others daily; 5hr); Ifrane (2 CTM & 16 others daily; 1hr 30min); Immouzer (hourly; 45min); Khenifra (2 CTM & 12 others daily; 4hr); Marrakesh (1 CTM & 12 others daily; 10hr) via Beni Mellal (7hr); Meknes (3 CTM daily & others hourly 7am–7pm; 50min); Midelt (2 CTM, 7 others daily; 5hr 30min); Moulay Yacoub (roughly hourly; 30min); Nador (2 CTM & 17 others daily; 5hr 30min); Oujda (3 CTM & 18 others daily; 5hr 30min); Er Rachidia (7 daily; 8hr 30min); Rissani (2 CTM & 5 others daily; 10hr 30min); Sefrou (17 daily; 30min); Tangier (3 CTM & 7 others daily; 5hr 45min); Taza (3 CTM daily & others roughly hourly; 2hr 30min); Tetouan (3 CTM & 12 others daily; 5hr 20min).
Meknes to: Agadir (2 CTM & 2 others daily; 12hr); Azrou (1 CTM & 16 others daily; 1hr 30min); Beni Mellal (6 daily; 6hr); Casablanca (1 CTM & 7 others daily; 4hr 30min); Chefchaouen (5 daily; 5hr 30min); Fes (7 CTM daily & others hourly 7am–7pm; 50min); Al Hoceima (2 CTM & 1 other daily; 6hr); Larache (3 CTM & 8 others daily; 5hr 30min); Marrakesh (1 CTM & 8 others daily; 9hr); Midelt (2 CTM & 12 others daily; 5hr 30min); Nador (2 CTM & 5 others daily; 6hr 30min); Ouezzane (7 daily; 4hr); Oujda (2 CTM & 15 others daily; 6hr 30min); Rabat (7 CTM & 15 others daily; 3hr); Er Rachidia (1 CTM & 4 others daily; 8hr 30min); Rissani (1 CTM & 1 other daily; 10hr 30min); Tangier (3 CTM & 6 others daily; 7hr); Taza (4 CTM & 9 others daily; 3hr 15min); Tetouan (2 CTM & 7 others daily; 7hr).
Midelt to: Azrou (2 CTM & 18 others daily; 3hr); Beni Mellal (3 daily; 4hr 30min); Casablanca (1 CTM & 2 others daily; 8hr); Khenifra (5 daily; 3hr); Marrakesh (2 CTM & 5 others daily; 8hr 30min); Meknes (1 CTM and 9 others daily; 5hr 30min); Nador (2 daily; 6hr); Ouarzazate (2 daily; 9hr 30min); Rabat (1 CTM & 8 daily; 7hr); Er Rachidia (2 CTM & 8 others daily; 3hr); Rissani (2 CTM & 8 others daily; 6hr); Tangier (3 daily; 12hr).

Grands taxis

Azilal to: Beni Mellal (1hr); the Cascades d'Ouzoud (40min).
Azrou to: Aïn Leuh (20min); Fes (1hr 30min); Meknes (45min); Midelt (2hr 30min); Ifrane (20min); occasionally Beni Mellal (3hr 30min) and Khenifra (1hr 30min).
Beni Mellal to: Azilal (1hr); Azrou (3hr 30min); Kasba Tadla (40min); Khenifra (2hr); Marrakesh (3hr).
Fes to: Azrou (1hr 30min); Casablanca (3hr 30min); Ifrane (1hr); Immouzer (40min); Meknes (40min); Moulay Yacoub (30min); Rabat (2hr 30min); Sefrou (30min); Sidi Harazem (30min); Taounate (1hr); Taza (1hr 15min).
Ifrane to: Azrou (20min); Fes (1hr); Immouzer (30min); Meknes (1hr).
Imouzzer du Kandar to: Azrou (45min); Fes (40min); Sefrou (40min); Ifrane (30min).
Khenifra to: Beni Mellal (2hr).
Meknes to: Azrou (45min); Fes (40min); Kenitra (1hr 30min); Khenifra (1hr 30min); Moulay Idriss (35min); Ouezzane (2hr 30min); Sidi Slimane (1hr).
Midelt to: El Ahouli mines (1hr); Azrou (2hr 30min); Fes (4hr); Meknes (4hr); Khenifra (2hr 30min); Er Rachidia (2hr).

Flights

Fes to: Casablanca (RAM 1–3 daily; 45min–1hr).

The Atlantic coast: Rabat to Essaouira

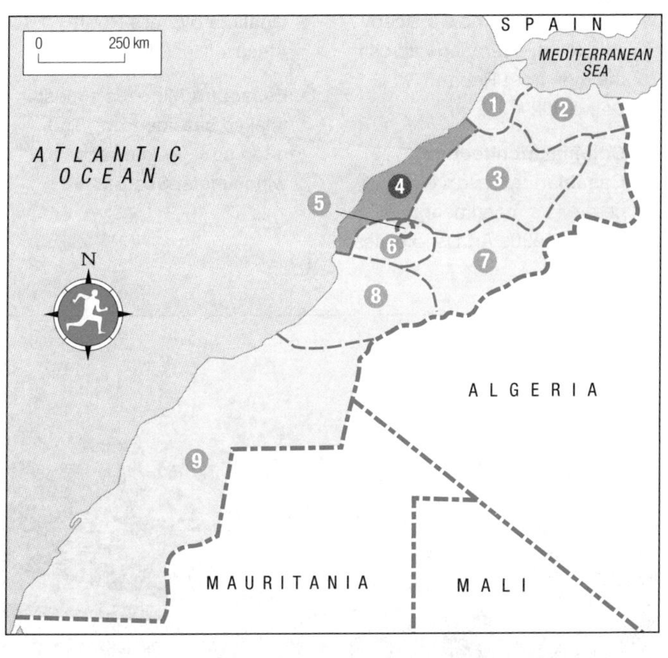

CHAPTER 4

Highlights

* **Hassan Mosque, Rabat** Never completed, the minaret of this Almohad mosque is a masterpiece of Islamic architecture. See p.284
* **Chellah, Rabat** As beautiful a ruin as you could imagine, with Roman remains and royal tombs from the Merenids. See p.286
* **Salé** Once the capital of a pirate republic, now a sleepy little town, a ferry ride across the river from Rabat. See p.292
* **Colonial architecture, Casablanca** Casa's city centre is a monument to French 1930s Art Deco styles. See p.305
* **Mosquée Hassan II, Casablanca** Second in size only to Mecca, Hassan II's great mosque can (unusually) be visited by non-Muslims. See p.308
* **Cité Portugaise, El Jadida** Walk round the ramparts or check out the cistern where Orson Welles filmed *Othello*. See p.318
* **Oualidia oysters** North Africa's finest. See p.321
* **Essaouira** Morocco's most relaxed seaside town, and a top spot for kite- and windsurfers. See p.326

▲ Essaouira

The Atlantic coast: Rabat to Essaouira

The five hundred-kilometre stretch of Atlantic coastline from Kenitra to Essaouira includes Morocco's urban heartland, comprising the cities of Rabat and Casablanca – the respective seats of government and of industry and commerce – and the neighbouring towns of Kenitra, Salé (alongside Rabat) and Mohammedia (alongside Casablanca). Together, this area accounts for close on a fifth of the whole country's total population. It's an astonishingly recent growth along what was, until the French Protectorate, a neglected strip of coast. The region is dominated by the country's elegant, orderly administrative capital, Rabat; and the dynamic commercial capital, Casablanca, which looks more like Marseille than a Moroccan city. This is the most Europeanized part of the country, where you'll see middle-class people in particular wearing Western-style clothes (even shorts) and leading what appear on the surface to be quite European lifestyles.

The fertile plains inland from Rabat (designated *Maroc Utile* by the French) have been occupied and cultivated since Paleolithic times, with Neolithic settlements on the coast to the south, notably at present-day Temara and Skhirat, but today it is French and post-colonial influences that dominate in the main coastal cities. Don't go to Casa – as Casablanca is popularly known – expecting some exotic movie location; it's a modern city that looks very much like Marseilles. Rabat, too, which the French developed as a capital in place of the old imperial centres of Fes and Marrakesh, looks markedly European, with its cafés and boulevards, though it also has some of Morocco's finest and oldest monuments, dating from the Almohad and Merenid dynasties. If you're on a first trip to Morocco, Rabat is an ideal place to get to grips with the country. Its westernized streets make an easy cultural shift and it's an excellent transport hub, well connected by train with Tangier, Fes and Marrakesh. Casa is maybe more interesting after you've spent a while in the country, when you'll appreciate both its differences and its fundamentally Moroccan character.

Along the coast are a large number of beaches, but this being the Atlantic rather than the Mediterranean, tides and currents can be strong. Surfing is a popular sport along the coast, increasingly with Moroccans as well as foreigners, and Essaouira is Morocco's prime resort for windsurfing.

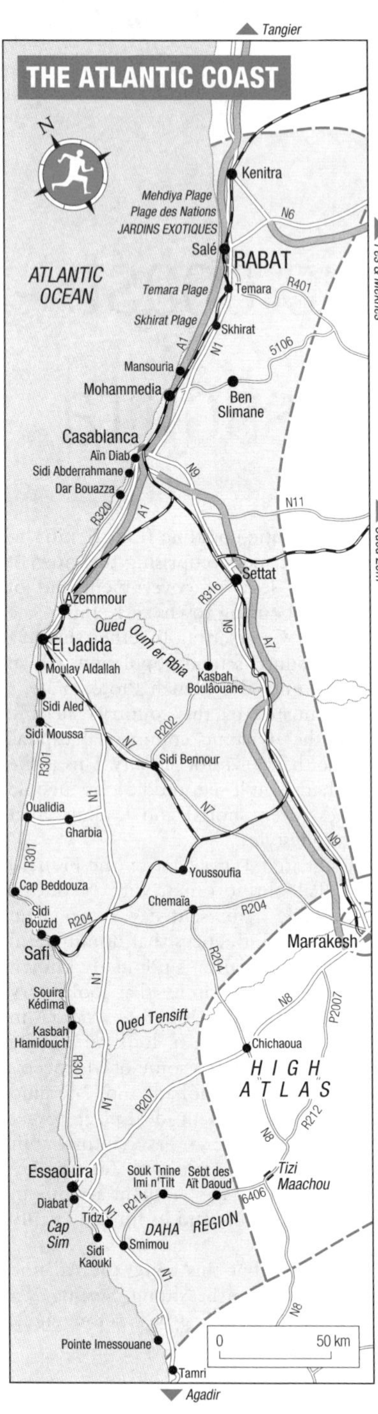

Kenitra and the coast to Rabat

KENITRA was established by the French as Port Lyautey – named after the Resident General – with the intention of channelling trade from Fes and Meknes. It never quite took off, however, losing out in industry and port activities to Casablanca, despite the rich farming areas of its hinterland. It has a population today of nearly 400,000, employed mainly in paper mills and a fish cannery. It's livelier than most Moroccan towns of its size, with a noticeably friendly atmosphere that goes some way to make up for the paucity of sights. There are also several **beaches** within easy reach.

Kenitra has two main streets: **Avenue Mohammed V**, the town's main artery, which runs east to west, and **Avenue Mohammed Diouri**, running north to south. The central square, dominated by the *baladiya* (town hall – *hôtel de ville* in French), is **Place Administrative**, two blocks north of Avenue Mohammed V and three blocks east of Avenue Mohammed Diouri. There are two **train stations**: Kenitra station, the most central, at the southern end of Avenue Mohammed Diouri; and Kenitra Medina (or Kenitra Ville), one stop north, off the eastern end of Avenue Mohammed V and near the **bus station** on Avenue John Kennedy.

The main **post office** is on Avenue Hassan II, just off Place Administrative, and **banks** can be found along Avenue Mohammed V. One of the best places for **internet access** is Acces Pro at 12 Rue Amira Aïcha, next door to *Hôtel de Commerce* (daily 8.30am–midnight; 5dh per hr).

Accommodation

There's a reasonable selection of **hotels** in town and a **campsite**, *Camping La Chenaie* on the edge of town (approaching from Rabat, look for signs to the left for the *Complexe Touristique*; ⓣ0537 363001), rather overgrown and rundown, although prices are pretty low and there's tennis, a pool and a football pitch. An alternative for campervans is the *Aire de Repose*, 8km out of town on the road to the motorway (see p.46), and there's also a campsite at Mehdiya (see below).

Hôtel Ambassy 20 Av Hassan II ⓣ0537 379978, ⓕ0537 377420. Comfortable and central; each room has a little laundry room as well as a bathroom, and there are two bars (one with a pool table) and a mediocre fish restaurant. BB ❹

Hôtel de la Poste 307 Av Mohammed V ⓣ0537 377769. Friendly little place about halfway up the avenue. Simple rooms, but bright and well kept, some with private shower. ❷

Hôtel du Commerce 12 Rue Amira Aïcha ⓣ0537 371503. A small hotel near the town hall. Simple, but adequate rooms with shared showers (5dh). ❷

Hôtel Jacaranda (formerly Hôtel Farah) Pl Administrative ⓣ0537 373030. The most upmarket place in town, with a swimming pool, restaurant and nightclub. Ask for a room at the back, overlooking the pool. BB ❺

Hôtel la Rotonde 60 Av Mohammed Diouri ⓣ&ⓕ0537 371401. A little gloomy inside but rooms are large and clean, if a bit basic. Hot water evenings only. The downstairs bar and reception area is popular with locals, and it also has a good restaurant next door. BB ❸

Hôtel Mamora northern end of Av Hassan II, opposite the town hall ⓣ0537 371775, ⓦwww.hotelmamora.ma. Comfortable three-star with a good swimming pool, comfortable bar and reasonable restaurant, albeit with a limited menu. Popular with business travellers. BB ❺

Eating, drinking and nightlife

There are a few good **restaurants** in addition to the hotel ones mentioned: *Restaurant Chez Ouidad*, 52 Rue de la Maâmora, serves traditional dishes at low prices; *Café Restaurant Ouazzani*, 8 Av Hassan II, near *Hôtel Ambassy*, offers tajine and other Moroccan standards; *El Dorado*, 64 Av Mohammed Diouri, is clean and pleasant with a good range of dishes, plus couscous on Fridays and chocolate mousse for afters.

For **bars** and **nightlife**, try the area around the triangular garden at the junction of Avenue Mohammed V and Avenue Mohammed Diouri, but don't expect too much. Look for: *Mama's Club*, attached to *Les Arcades* bar at the corner of avenues Mohammed V and Mohammed Diouri; *Le Village* at the corner of Avenue Mohammed V and Rue de la Maâmora; and *007* at 93 Av Mohammed Diouri.

Mehdiya

MEHDIYA, 9km west of Kenitra, is a dull **beach** (bus #15 from Kenitra) with a ruined **kasbah**, overlooking the Oued Sebou estuary (bus #9 from Kenitra). Originally Portuguese but rebuilt under Moulay Ismail, it shelters the remains of a seventeenth-century governor's palace. A couple of kilometres inland is the birdlife-rich **Lac Sidi Boughaba**, a narrow freshwater lake divided by a central causeway and flanked by a *koubba* that is the site of an August **moussem**. At the southern edge of the lake, the National Centre for Environmental Education (CNEE; ⓣ0661 074779, ⓔspana@spana.org.ma) is focused mainly on environmental education for local schoolchildren but is open to visitors on weekends and public holidays (winter noon–4pm; summer noon–5pm). The best viewing points for the lake's birdlife are from the causeway or the viewing deck at the education centre.

Plage des Nations

The **Plage des Nations** (22km south of Kenitra, also called Sidi Bouknadel) was named after the foreign diplomats and their families who started swimming here – and continue to do so. Unlike the capital's Kasbah or Salé beaches, it has a very relaxed, friendly and cosmopolitan feel about it and is unusual in that young Moroccan women feel able to come out here for the day. The beach itself is excellent, with big, exciting waves – but dangerous currents, and is patrolled by lifeguards along the central strip. It's flanked by a couple of beach cafés and the *Hôtel Firdaous* (Ⓣ0537 822131, Ⓕ0537 822143; BB ❺), which has a swimming pool (non-residents 70dh), plus a bar, restaurant and snack bar. It's a good place to stay, too – all rooms have a sea view, you can get a suite for not much more than the price of a room, and the 1970s decor manages to seem charmingly period rather than just outdated.

The beach lies 2km along a surfaced track from the N1 coast road. Directly opposite the turn-off, the **Museé Dar Belghazi** (daily 8am–5pm; 50dh for a simple tour, 100dh for a complete tour including the reserve collection; Ⓣ0537 822178) has a wealth of manuscripts, nineteenth-century carpets and textiles, eighteenth- and nineteenth-century ceramics, and examples of woodwork, armour and jewellery. The more tightly packed reserve collection holds further treasures including a reproduction eighteenth-century cedarwood carriage, and the 1812 *minbar* from the Grand Mosque in Tangier, which was removed by the Ministry of Islamic Affairs (to the great outrage of many Tanjawis) and subsequently resurfaced here. There's not much by way of explanatory text in the museum other than a small booklet in French and Arabic, but if you have a particular interest in Moroccan or Islamic art, then the trip out here is worthwhile.

In summer, there are regular grands taxis to the Plage des Nations from Rabat's satellite town of Salé, while throughout the year local bus #28 runs from Rabat's Avenue Moulay Hassan (via Bd Al Alaouiyne and Salé's Bab Khemis, almost opposite the train station).

Jardins Exotiques

The **Jardins Exotiques** (daily: winter 9am–5pm; summer 9am–7pm; 10dh), 6km south of the Plage des Nations and also served by bus #28, were laid out by one M. François in the early 1950s, fell into decline in the 1980s and were rescued in 2003 by the king's "Fondation Pour la Protection de l'Environnement", being assiduously renovated before the grand reopening in November 2005. If you can visit in spring or early summer, the gardens are a delight.

Entering the gardens, you find yourself directed across a series of precarious bamboo bridges and dot-directed routes (they suggest a one-and-a-half hour red route, or a forty-five-minute blue route) through a sequence of regional creations. There's a **Brazilian rainforest**, dense with water and orchids, a formal **Japanese garden**, a Mexican cactus garden, and a piece of **French Polynesia**, with rickety summerhouses set amid long pools, turtles paddling past, palm trees all round and flashes of bright-red flowers. The last of the series, returning to a more local level, is an **Andalucian garden** with a fine collection of Moroccan plants. A map and information leaflet is available (1dh) at the entrance. There's also a **terrarium** (5dh) featuring a few snakes and tortoises.

Rabat

Capital of the nation since 1912, **RABAT** is elegant and spacious, slightly self-conscious in its civilized modern ways, and, as an administrative centre, a little bit dull. If you arrive during Ramadan, you'll find the main avenues and boulevards an astonishing night-long promenade, but at other times, it's hard to find a café open much past ten at night; Rabat, as they tell you in Casa, is provincial. What it does have – along with neighbouring **Salé** – are some of the most interesting historic and architectural monuments in the country, but the fact that the local economy does not depend on tourist money makes it a whole lot more relaxed from a tourist's point of view than cities such as Fes or Marrakesh.

Some history

The Phoenicians established a settlement at Sala, around the citadel known today as **Chellah**. This eventually formed the basis of an independent Berber state, which reached its peak of influence in the eighth century, developing a code of government inspired by the Koran but adapted to Berber customs and needs. It represented a challenge to the Islamic orthodoxy of the **Arab** rulers of the interior, however, and to stamp out the heresy, a *ribat* – the fortified monastery from which the city takes its name – was founded on the site of the present-day kasbah.

The *ribat*'s activities led to Chellah's decline – a process hastened in the eleventh century by the founding of a new town, **Salé**, across the estuary. But the **Almohads** rebuilt the kasbah and **Yacoub el Mansour** created a new Imperial capital here, whose legacy includes the superb **Oudaïa Gate** of the kasbah, **Bab er Rouah** at the southwest edge of town, and the early stages of the **Hassan Mosque**. He also erected over 5km of fortifications, though it is only in the last sixty years that the city has expanded to fill his circuit of *pisé* walls.

After Mansour's death, Rabat's significance was dwarfed by the imperial cities of Fes, Meknes and Marrakesh, and the city fell into neglect. Sacked by the Portuguese, it was little more than a village when, as New Salé, it was resettled by seventeenth-century Andalucian refugees. In this revived form, however, it entered into an extraordinary period of international piracy and local autonomy. Its corsair fleets, the **Sallee Rovers**, specialized in the plunder of merchant ships returning to Europe from West Africa and the Spanish Americas, but on occasion raided as far afield as Plymouth and the Irish coast – Daniel Defoe's Robinson Crusoe began his captivity "carry'd prisoner into Sallee, a Moorish port".

The Andalucians, owing no loyalty to the Moorish sultans and practically impregnable within their kasbah perched high on a rocky bluff above the river, established their own pirate state, the **Republic of the Bou Regreg**. They rebuilt the Medina below the kasbah in a style reminiscent of their homes in the Spanish city of Badajoz, dealt in arms with the English and French, and even accepted European consuls, before the town finally reverted to government control under Moulay Rashid, and his successor, Moulay Ismail. Unofficial piracy continued until 1829 when Austria took revenge for the loss of a ship by shelling Rabat and other coastal towns. From then until the French made it their colonial capital, Rabat-Salé was very much a backwater.

Arrival

Rabat Ville train station is right in the middle of the Ville Nouvelle, a few minutes' walk from hotels. Other stations in the Rabat–Salé area are less useful. Business visitors and diplomats may have cause to alight at **Rabat Agdal**, which

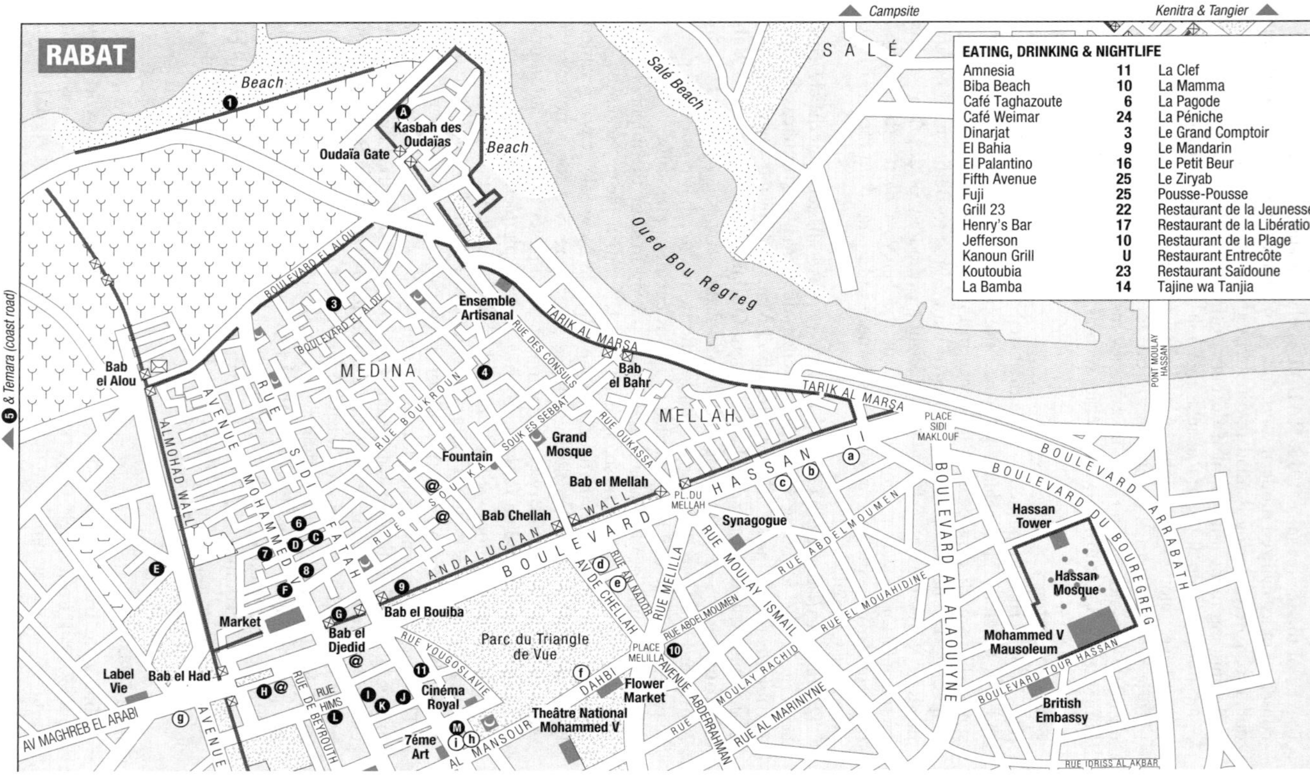
RABAT
EATING, DRINKING & NIGHTLIFE
Amnesia 11
Biba Beach 10
Café Taghazoute 6
Café Weimar 24
Dinarjat 3
El Bahia 9
El Palantino 16
Fifth Avenue 25
Fuji 25
Grill 23 22
Henry's Bar 17
Jefferson 10
Kanoun Grill U
Koutoubia 23
La Bamba 14
La Clef 19
La Mamma 13
La Pagode 21
La Péniche 2
Le Grand Comptoir 12
Le Mandarin 5
Le Petit Beur 15
Le Ziryab 4
Pousse-Pousse 25
Restaurant de la Jeunesse 8
Restaurant de la Libération 7
Restaurant de la Plage 1
Restaurant Entrecôte 25
Restaurant Saïdoune 18
Tajine wa Tanjia 20
Campsite
Kenitra & Tangier
Airport, Meknes, Magic Park (Fair Ground), B & 2
5 & Temara (coast road)
SALÉ
Salé Beach
Oued Bou Regreg
Beach
Kasbah des Oudaïas
Oudaïa Gate
Ensemble Artisanal
MEDINA
MELLAH
Bab el Alou
Bab el Bahr
Bab el Mellah
Bab Chellah
Bab el Bouiba
Bab el Djedid
Bab el Had
Grand Mosque
Fountain
Market
Label Vie
Synagogue
Hassan Tower
Hassan Mosque
Mohammed V Mausoleum
British Embassy
Parc du Triangle de Vue
Flower Market
Théatre National Mohammed V
Cinéma Royal
7éme Art
PLACE SIDI MAKLOUF
PL. DU MELLAH
PLACE MELILLA
PONT MOULAY HASSAN
TARIK AL MARSA
BOULEVARD EL ALOU
RUE DES CONSULS
RUE BOUKROUN
SOUK ES SEBBAT
RUE OUKASSA
SOUIKA
RUE SIDI FATAH
AVENUE MOHAMMED V
ALMOHAD WALL
ANDALUCIAN WALL
BOULEVARD HASSAN II
BOULEVARD AL ALAOUIYNE
BOULEVARD DU BOUREGREG
BOULEVARD ARRABATH
BOULEVARD TOUR HASSAN
RUE ABDELMOUMEN
RUE EL MOUAHIDINE
RUE MOULAY ISMAIL
RUE MOULAY RACHID
RUE AL MARINIYNE
AVENUE ABDERRAHMAN
RUE MELILLA
RUE AN NADOR
AV DE CHELLAH
DAHBI
RUE YOUGOSLAVIE
AL MANSOUR
RUE HIMS
RUE DE BEYROUTH
AV MAGHREB EL ARABI
RUE IDRISS AL AKBAR

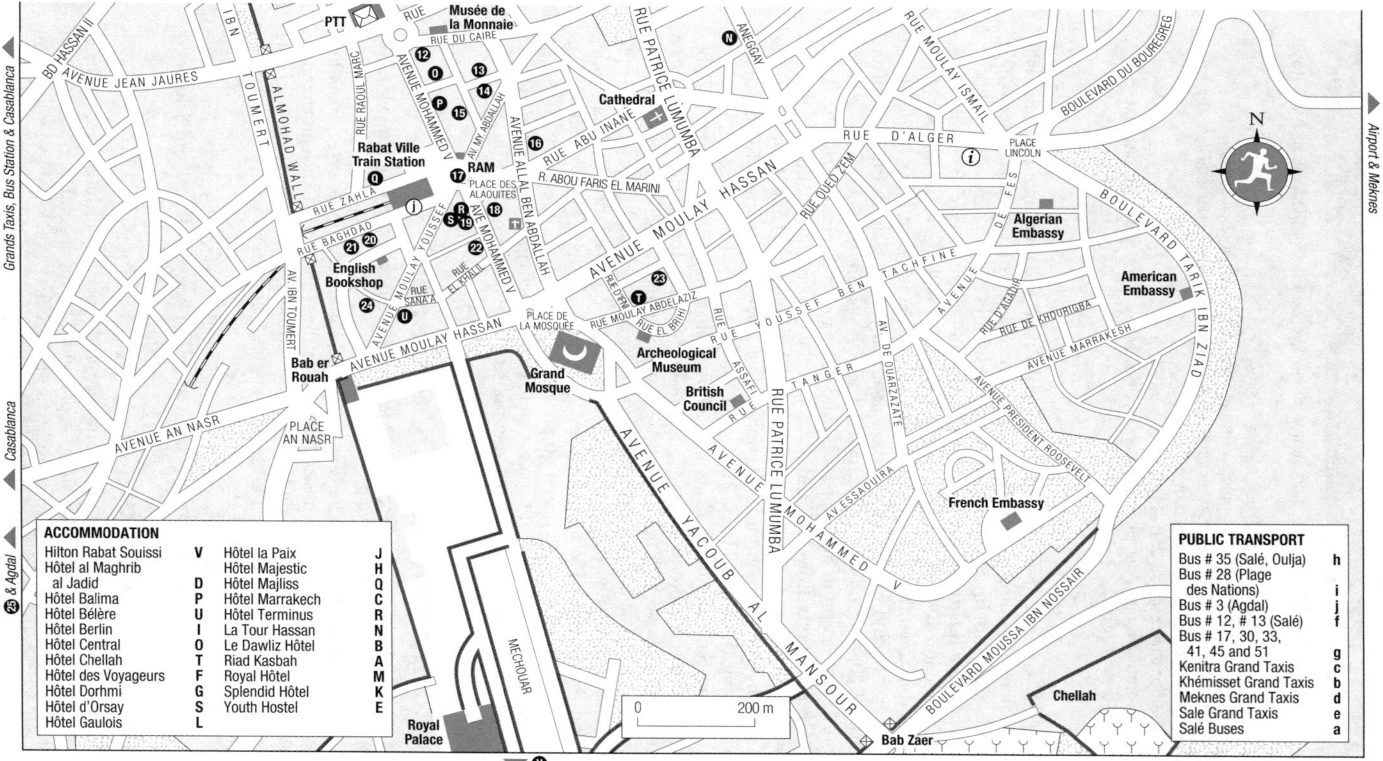

Airport & Meknes
Grands Taxis, Bus Station & Casablanca
Casablanca
25 & Agdal
V
N
PUBLIC TRANSPORT
Bus # 35 (Salé, Oulja) h
Bus # 28 (Plage des Nations) i
Bus # 3 (Agdal) j
Bus # 12, # 13 (Salé) f
Bus # 17, 30, 33, 41, 45 and 51 g
Kenitra Grand Taxis c
Khémisset Grand Taxis b
Meknes Grand Taxis d
Sale Grand Taxis e
Salé Buses a
ACCOMMODATION
Hilton Rabat Souissi V
Hôtel al Maghrib al Jadid D
Hôtel Balima P
Hôtel Bélère U
Hôtel Berlin I
Hôtel Central O
Hôtel Chellah T
Hôtel des Voyageurs F
Hôtel Dorhmi G
Hôtel d'Orsay S
Hôtel Gaulois L
Hôtel la Paix J
Hôtel Majestic H
Hôtel Majliss Q
Hôtel Marrakech C
Hôtel Terminus R
La Tour Hassan N
Le Dawliz Hôtel B
Riad Kasbah A
Royal Hôtel M
Splendid Hôtel K
Youth Hostel E
0 200 m
PTT
Musée de la Monnaie
RUE DU CAIRE
Cathedral
Rabat Ville Train Station
RAM
PLACE DES ALAOUITES
English Bookshop
Bab er Rouah
PLACE AN NASR
Grand Mosque
PLACE DE LA MOSQUÉE
Archeological Museum
British Council
Royal Palace
MECHOUAR
French Embassy
Algerian Embassy
American Embassy
Chellah
Bab Zaer
PLACE LINCOLN
BD HASSAN II
AVENUE JEAN JAURES
IBN TOUMERT
ALMOHAD WALL
RUE RAOUL MARC
AVENUE MOHAMMED V
AV. MY. ABDALLAH
AVENUE ALLAL BEN ABDALLAH
RUE ABU INANE
RUE PATRICE LUMUMBA
ANEGGAY
RUE MOULAY ISMAIL
BOULEVARD DU BOUREGREG
RUE D'ALGER
R. ABOU FARIS EL MARINI
RUE ZAHLA
RUE BAGHDAD
AVENUE MOULAY YOUSSEF
AVE MOHAMMED V
RUE EL KHALIL
RUE SANA'A
AV. IBN TOUMERT
AVENUE MOULAY HASSAN
AVENUE AN NASR
RUE D'IFNI
RUE MOULAY ABDELAZIZ
RUE EL BRIHI
RUE ASSAFI
RUE YOUSSEF BEN TACHFINE
RUE TANGER
RUE OUED ZEM
AV. DE OUARZAZATE
AVENUE YACOUB AL MANSOUR
AVENUE MOHAMMED V
AV. ESSAOUIRA
AVENUE DE FES
RUE D'AGADIR
RUE DE KHOURIGBA
AVENUE MARRAKESH
AVENUE PRESIDENT ROOSEVELT
BOULEVARD TARIK IBN ZIAD
BOULEVARD MOUSSA IBN NOSSAIR

Useful local bus routes

#3 from just by Rabat Ville train station down Avenue Fal Ould Ouemir in Agdal to Avenue Atlas.
#12 and #13 from just off Place Melilla to Salé.
#17, #30 and #41 from just outside Bab el Had to the intercity bus station.
#28 from Avenue Allal Ben Abdallah to Salé, Jardins Exotiques, Museé Dar Belghazi and the Plage des Nations turn-off.
#33 from just outside Bab el Had to Temara Plage.
#35 from Avenue Allal Ben Abdallah to Salé, Magic Park and the Complexe des Potiers in Oulja.

serves the southern suburbs and the Royal Palace; the royal train is occasionally seen here in a siding. **Salé Ville** station serves Salé, across the estuary (see p.292), with **Salé Tabriquet** serving its northern suburbs.

The main **bus terminal** is in Place Zerktouni – 3km west of the centre by the road junction for Casa and Beni Mellal. Local buses will take you from here to Bab el Had in town (bus #30 picks up right outside the terminal, buses #17 and #41 stop just behind it), or you can get a petit taxi (carrying up to three passengers; around 20dh into town on the meter). Easier, if you are coming by bus from the north, is to get off in **Salé** (see p.292) and take a grand taxi from there into Rabat.

Grands taxis from Fes and Casablanca will deposit you outside the bus station. Those from Meknes usually arrive on Boulevard Hassan II opposite Bab Chellah, while those from Salé leave you one block east, and from Kenitra 300m east along Boulevard Hassan II.

Rabat–Salé airport is 7km northeast of Rabat, and grands taxis are the only public transport into town from here. The current tariff for the ride is 150dh into the city centre (500dh to Casablanca – a sign in the terminal displays the official rates, and is worth checking before you approach a taxi), for up to six people. The airport has a bureau de change and desks for the main car rental companies. From **Mohammed V airport** near Casablanca, your best bet is to take a train (hourly 6am–9pm – later trains do not make the connection unless you're lucky with delays) and change at Casa Voyageurs or Aïn Sebaa for a connecting service to any of the four train stations mentioned above. The fare from the airport to Rabat is 65dh and the journey takes an hour and forty minutes.

Information and city transport

The ONMT **tourist office** is at 22 Rue d'Alger, near Place Lincoln (Mon–Fri 8.30am–4.30pm; ⓣ0537 660663).

Local bus services can be very useful, and some bus stops are clearly marked, with the numbers of the buses that stop at them posted up, though there are still places where you're simply expected to know the location of the stop. The most useful routes are listed in the box above. A new **tram** system is now being built that will link central Rabat and Salé.

Petits and **grands taxis** can be found on Boulevard Hassan II and by the train stations; petits taxis are not allowed to run between Rabat and Salé.

Accommodation

Hotel space can be tight in midsummer, and especially in July, when budget-priced rooms in particular are at a premium, so it's a good idea to book in advance. A couple of cheapies aside, all of the better hotels are to be found in the Ville Nouvelle and there's little to gain from staying in the Medina, which is in any case only a stroll across the boulevard. The **campsite** in Salé has closed, though campervans still park up off Avenue de la Plage (tip the parking attendant to keep en eye on them).

Ville Nouvelle Hotels

Hilton Rabat Souissi ⓣ0537 675656, ⓔrbahitw@meganet.net.ma. This deluxe five-star set among pleasant gardens has all the standard facilities and is wheelchair accessible, with a free shuttle service to the golf course, but it is rather inconveniently located in the suburb of Souissi, southwest of town, beyond the royal palace. ⑨

Hôtel Balima Corner of Rue Jakarta and Av Mohammed V ⓣ0537 708625, ⓦwww.hotel-balima.net. Once Rabat's top hotel but long overtaken by the competition. It has been refurbished and still has quite reasonable prices, not least for its suites; T'hami el Glaoui, Pasha of Marrakesh (see p.362), stayed in one of these on his visits to the city in the early 1950s. The open-air café between the hotel and the avenue is shaded and popular. BB ⑤

Hôtel Bélère 33 Av Moulay Youssef ⓣ0537 203301, ⓦwww.belerehotels.ma. Comfortable, a/c tour-group hotel, well positioned for the train station. Rooms are attractively done out and there's a good breakfast. BB ⑥

Hôtel Berlin 1st floor, 261 Av Mohammed V ⓣ0537 703435. Centrally located and good value, with bright, refurbished en-suite rooms. ③

Hôtel Central 2 Rue Al Basra ⓣ0537 707356, ⓔhotel.central.rabat@gmail.com. Best of the cheapies, conveniently located for restaurants, banks and Rabat Ville station and, with 34 rooms, likely to have space. Most rooms have patterned colonial floor tiles, and some have showers (otherwise they're 10dh), with hot water mornings and evenings. ②

Hôtel Chellah 2 Rue d'Ifni ⓣ0537 668300, ⓦwww.helnan.com. An upmarket tour-group hotel run by the Danish *Helnan* chain in a rather characterless block, handy for the archeological museum, with a good grill-restaurant, *Le Kanoun* (see p.289). BB ⑧

Hôtel d'Orsay 11 Av Moulay Youssef, on Pl de la Gare ⓣ0537 701319. Comfortable in a well-worn kind of way, and convenient for the train station, though it's seen better days. ③

Hôtel Gaulois corner of Rue Hims and Av Mohammed V ⓣ0537 723022, ⓕ0537 738848. Friendly old hotel with a spacious grand entrance and both shared-shower and en-suite rooms, the former especially being pretty good value for money. ②

Hôtel la Paix 2 Rue Ghazza, on corner with Av Allal Ben Abdallah ⓣ0537 722926. Friendly staff and comfortable, if sombre, rooms with good en-suite bathrooms. ③

Hôtel Majestic 121 Av Hassan II ⓣ0537 722997, ⓦwww.hotelmajestic.ma. Friendly old hotel, refurbished with bright, spotless rooms, some overlooking the Medina, but often full (you'll be lucky to find a room much after midday). Sporadic hot water. ③

Hôtel Majliss 6 Rue Zahla ⓣ0537 733726, ⓦwww.majlisshotel.ma. A modern four-star, overlooking the platforms of the Rabat Ville station. There's a choice of room styles, and standard rooms are equipped with orthopaedic beds. The more expensive ones at the back have views over the roof of the parliament building to the Atlantic Ocean. BB ⑦

Hôtel Terminus 384 Av Mohammed V ⓣ0537 700616, ⓕ0537 701926. Round the corner from the *Hôtel d'Orsay* and a possible alternative if that's full. Once quite a posh joint, it's been going downhill for many years, and could do with some looking after. Some rooms are a lot better than others, so it's worth checking out a few. ④

La Tour Hassan 26 Rue Chellah ⓣ0537 239000, ⓦwww.latourhassan.com. Rabat's plushest offering, with exquisite, palatial decor in the public areas and several grades of rooms and suites (mostly priced according to the views available from them) peaking at a whopping 17,500dh a night (plus tax). The rooms, however, are not huge, and in fact the *Majliss* has the edge on it comfort-wise. ⑨

Royal Hôtel 1 Rue Amman, on corner with Av Allal Ben Abdallah ⓣ0537 721171, ⓦwww.royalhotelrabat.com. A two-star hotel with comfortable and reasonable rooms – not huge, but refurbished, clean and well maintained. The best ones overlook the attractive Parc du Triangle de Vue. BB ⑤

Splendid Hôtel 8 Rue Ghazza ⓣ0537 723283. The best rooms at this nice old hotel overlook a pleasant courtyard with flowers and banana trees, and some have their own showers (hot water evenings only). Opposite, the *Café-Restaurant Ghazza* is good for breakfast and snacks. ②

Youth Hostel 43 Rue Marrassa ⓣ0537 725769, ⓔauberge.jeunes.rbt@hotmail.fr. Conveniently sited just west of the Almohad walls of the Medina and to the north of Bd Hassan II. It's clean and there's a nice courtyard, but the dorms (65dh per person with breakfast) are a bit cramped and there are no self-catering facilities. Open 8am–11pm (till midnight in summer).

Medina hotels

Hôtel al Maghrib al Jadid 2 Rue Sebbahi ⓣ0537 732207. Basic and clean, though the decor is a garish combination of candy pink and bright blue. Hot showers are available 8am–9.30pm at 7.50dh a go. The *Hôtel Marrakech*, down the street at no.10, is run by the same people, with exactly the same prices and colour scheme. ❷

Hôtel des Voyageurs 8 Souk Semarine, by Bab Djedid (no phone). Cheap, popular and often full. Clean, airy rooms but no showers, and no public ones nearby. The same stretch of street has several similar places. ❶

Hôtel Dorhmi 313 Av Mohammed V ⓣ0537 723898. Refurbished to a decent standard, and nicely positioned, just inside Bab el Djedid above the *Café Salam*. Hot showers (7am–10pm) are external, and cost 10dh. Rooms cannot be reserved here in advance. ❷

Riad Kasbah In the kasbah at 39 Rue Zirara, on your left as you enter through Bab Oudaïas ⓣ0537 702392, ⓦwww.riadoudaya.com. This small riad oozes simplicity and authenticity. It's nicely furnished and the staff are overwhelmingly attentive. There's 24hr hot water and breakfast is included. Minimum two-night stay and pre-booking is required. The same people also run a slightly plusher and pricier riad, the Oudaya, off Rue Sidi Fateh in the Medina proper. BB ❼

The Medina and souks

Rabat's **Medina** – all that there was of the city until the French arrived in 1912 – is a compact quarter, wedged on two sides by the sea and the river, on the others by the twelfth-century Almohad and seventeenth-century Andalucian walls. It's open and orderly in comparison to those of Fes or Marrakesh, and still essentially the town created by Muslim refugees from Badajoz in Spain, but with its external features intact, its way of life seems remarkably at odds with the government business and cosmopolitanism of the Ville Nouvelle.

That this is possible – here and throughout the old cities of Morocco – is largely due to **Marshal Lyautey**, the first of France's Resident Generals, and the most sympathetic to local culture. In colonizing Algeria, the French had destroyed most of the Arab towns, and Lyautey found this already under way when he arrived in Rabat, but, realizing the aesthetic loss – and the inappropriateness of wholesale Europeanization – he ordered demolition to be halted and had the Ville Nouvelle built outside the walls instead. His precedent was followed throughout the French and Spanish zones of the country, inevitably creating "native quarters", but preserving continuity with the past. Lyautey left Morocco in 1925 but when he died in 1934 he was returned and buried in a Moorish monument in Rabat until 1961, when his body was "repatriated" to Paris.

Into the Medina

The grid-like regularity of its Medina, cut by a number of long main streets, makes Rabat a good place to get to grips with the layout of a Moroccan city. Its plan is typical, with a main market street – **Rue Souika** and its continuation **Souk es Sebbat** running beside the Grand Mosque, and behind it a residential area scattered with smaller souks and "parish" mosques. The buildings, characteristically Andalucian, like those of Tetouan or Chefchaouen, are part stone and part whitewash, with splashes of yellow and turquoise and great, dark-wood studded doors.

From **Boulevard Hassan II**, half a dozen gates and a series of streets give access to the Medina, all leading more or less directly through the quarter, to emerge near the kasbah and the hillside cemetery. On the west side, the two main streets – **Avenue Mohammed V** and **Rue Sidi Fatah** – are really continuations of Ville Nouvelle avenues, though, flanked by working-class café-restaurants and cell-like hotels, their character is immediately different. Entering along either street, past a lively, modern food market and a handful of stalls selling fruit, juice and snacks, you can turn right along **Rue Souika**, which is dominated by textiles and silverware along the initial stretch, giving way to shoe stalls as you approach the Grand Mosque. The shops are all fairly everyday, and not, for the most part, geared to tourists.

There are few buildings of particular interest, as most of the medieval city – which predated that of the Andalucians – was destroyed by Portuguese raids in the sixteenth century. The **Grand Mosque**, founded by the Merenids in the fourteenth century, is an exception, though it has been considerably rebuilt – its minaret, for example, was completed in 1939. Entry to the mosque is forbidden to non-Muslims. Opposite, there is a small example of Merenid decoration in the stone facade of a public **fountain**, which now forms the front of an Arabic bookshop.

The Mellah and Joutia

To the east of Rue Oukassa is the **Mellah**, the old Jewish quarter, still the poorest and most rundown area of the city. It was designated as a Jewish quarter only in 1808 – Jews previously owned several properties on Rue des Consuls, to the north – and no longer has a significant Jewish population. If you can find a local guide, you may be able to look into some of its seventeen former **synagogues**. None of these function: the only active synagogue in the city is a modern building, one block from here, at the bottom end of Rue Moulay Ismail.

With its meat and produce markets, the Mellah looks a somewhat uninviting and impenetrable area, but it is worth wandering through towards the river. A **joutia**, or **flea market**, spreads out along the streets below Souk es Sebbat, down to Bab el Bahr. There are clothes, pieces of machinery, and general bric-a-brac, with the odd bargain occasionally to be found.

Towards the kasbah: Rue des Consuls

Beyond the Mellah, heading towards the kasbah, you can walk out by **Bab el Bahr** and follow an avenue (Tarik al Marsa) near the riverside up to Bab oudaïa. The river's shoreline has now been made into a pleasant promenade. For crafts, there's also an **Ensemble Artisanal** on the west side of Tarik al Marsa.

Rue des Consuls, a block inland, is not so busy and is a more interesting approach to the kasbah; like the Mellah, this, too, used to be a reserved quarter – the only street of the nineteenth-century city where European consuls were permitted to live. Many of the residency buildings survive, as do a number of impressive merchants' *fondouks* – most in the alleys off to the left (the French consul's residence, now rather rundown, is at the end of an alley called Impasse du Consulat de France). Shopping is pleasantly hassle-free, and there are some good **jewellery shops**, with a mix of Middle Eastern and European designs at good prices. The upper end of the street in particular is a centre for **rug and carpet shops**, and on Monday and Thursday mornings Rue des Consuls and Souk es Sebbah host a **souk** for carpets new and old.

Rabat carpets, woven with very bright dyes (which, if vegetable-based, will fade), are a traditional cottage industry in the Medina, though they're now often made in workshops, one of which you can see on the kasbah's *plateforme* (see p.283). Some of the traditional carpets on sale, particularly in the shops, will have come from further afield. They are officially graded at a special centre just off Rue des Consuls – to the right as you climb towards the kasbah.

The Kasbah des Oudaïas

The site of the original *ribat* and citadel of the Almohad, Merenid and Andalucian towns, the **Kasbah des Oudaïas** is an evocative, village-like quarter. Ignore the

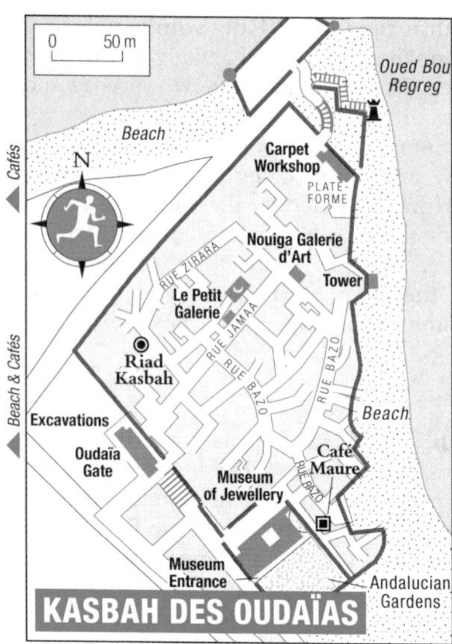

petty hustlers hovering around the entrances to mislead you with tales of the museum and galleries being closed.

Bab Oudaïa

The Kasbah's main gate, **Bab Oudaïa**, is Almohad, like so many of Morocco's great monuments. Built around 1195, it was inserted by Yacoub el Mansour into a line of walls already built by his grandfather, Abd el Moumen. The walls in fact extended well to its west, leading down to the sea at the edge of the Medina (excavations are now revealing some of these), and the gate cannot have been designed for any real defensive purpose – its function and importance must have been ceremonial. It was to be the heart of the kasbah, its chambers acting as a courthouse and staterooms, with everything of importance taking place nearby. The **Souk el Ghezel** – the main commercial centre of the medieval town, including its wool and slave markets – was located just outside the gate, while the original sultanate's palace stood immediately inside.

The gate impresses not so much by its size as by the strength and simplicity of its decoration, based on a typically Islamic rhythm, establishing a tension between the exuberant, outward expansion of the arches and the heavy, enclosing rectangle of the gate itself. Looking at the two for a few minutes, you begin to sense a kind of optical illusion – the shapes appear suspended by the great rush of movement from the centre of the arch. The basic feature is, of course, the arch, which here is a sequence of three, progressively more elaborate: first, the basic horseshoe; then, two "filled" or decorated ones, the latter with the distinctive Almohad *darj w ktaf* patterning (see the *Moroccan Architecture* colour section), a cheek-and-shoulder design somewhat like a fleur-de-lys. At the top, framing the design, is a band of geometric ornamentation, cut off in what seems to be an arbitrary manner but which again creates the impression of movement and continuation outside the gate. The dominant motifs (scallop-shell-looking palm fronds) are also characteristically Almohad, though without any symbolic importance.

Inside the kasbah

You can enter the **kasbah** through the small gateway to the right of Bab oudaïa itself (which is sometimes used for exhibitions), or by a lower, horseshoe arch at the bottom of the stairway. This leads (straight ahead) through a door in the palace wall to Rue Bazo, where a right turn will take you down to the **Café Maure**, a fine place to retreat, high on a terrace overlooking the river, serving mint tea, brewed up on an ancient brazier, and trays of pastries – *corne de gazelle* is their speciality.

Inside the Oudaïa Gate, **Rue Jamaa** (Street of the Mosque), runs straight down to a broad terrace commanding views of the river and sea. Along the way,

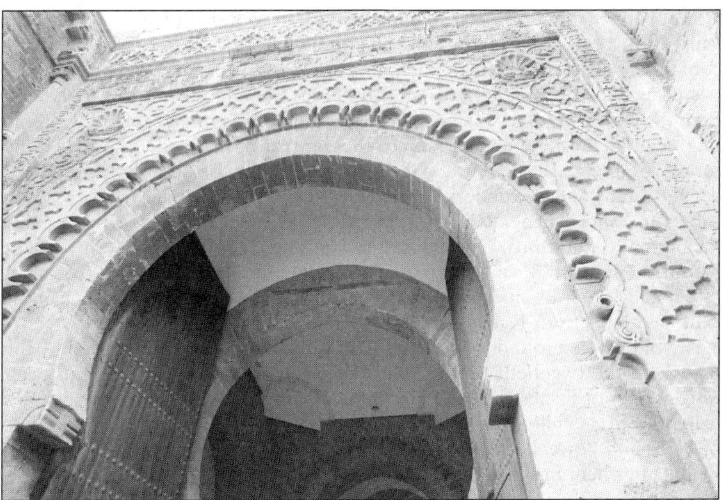

▲ Bab Oudaïa, Rabat

you pass by the **Kasbah Mosque**, the city's oldest, founded in 1050, though rebuilt in the eighteenth century by an English renegade known as Ahmed el Inglisi – one of a number of European pirates who joined up with the Sallee Rovers.

El Inglisi was also responsible for several of the forts built below and round the seventeenth-century **plateforme**, originally a semaphore station, on which was built an eighteenth-century warehouse, now housing a carpet cooperative workshop. The guns of the forts and the *plateforme* regularly echoed across the estuary in Salé. The Bou Regreg ("Father of Reflection") River is quite open at this point and it would appear to have left the corsair fleets vulnerable, harboured a little downstream, where fishing boats today ferry people across to Salé. In fact, a long sandbank lies submerged across the mouth of the estuary – a feature much exploited by the shallow-keeled pirate ships, which would draw the merchant ships in pursuit, only to leave them stranded within the sights of the city's cannon. The sandbank proved a handicap in the early twentieth century and diverted commercial trade to the better-endowed Casablanca.

From the *plateforme*, it's possible to climb down towards the **beach**, crowded throughout the summer, as is the Salé strip across the water, though neither is very inviting, and you'd be better off at the more relaxed (and less exclusively male) sands at the Plage des Nations or Temara Plage (see p.274 & p.295).

The Jewellery Museum and Andalucian Garden

The horseshoe gate (turning right as you enter) leads to the palace and the Andalucian Gardens, which are also accessible from within the kasbah via *Café Maure*.

The seventeenth-century **palace** was built for Moulay Ismail, the first sultan since Almohad times to force a unified control over the country. Ismail, whose base was at Meknes, gave Rabat – or New Salé, as it was then known – a relatively high priority. Having subdued the pirates' republic, he took over the kasbah as a garrison for Saharan tribesmen who accepted military service in return for tax exemption, and who formed an important part of his mercenary army.

The palace now houses a **Museum of Jewellery** (daily except Tues 9am–4pm; 10dh); explanations are in Arabic, French and Spanish. **Room 1** contains prehistoric jewellery, including some semi-fossilized ivory bracelets, as well as Phoenician gold, a scarab from Lixus (showing that it had trade with Egypt), and medieval jewellery, including a dinky little finger-ring in very fine filigree gold. From here you pass into the **central courtyard**, from which the rooms of the palace led off. Going round clockwise, **Room 2** contains daggers, guns and a wonderful nineteenth-century gold tiara from Fes with rubies and aquamarines. **Room 3** shows the jewellers' manufacturing process, including a traditional jeweller's furnace, and **Room 4** was the palace hammam. **Room 5**, once the palace mosque, displays jewellery typical of different Moroccan cities and regions, including some beautiful nineteenth-century pieces from Rabat.

The old palace grounds contain an **Andalucian Garden** constructed by the French in the twentieth century, but true to Andalucian tradition, with deep, sunken beds of shrubs and flowering annuals. Historical authenticity aside, it's a delightful place, full of the scent of tree daturas, bougainvillea and a multitude of herbs and flowers. It has a modern role too, as a meeting place for women, who gather here in small groups on a Friday or Sunday afternoon.

The Hassan Mosque and Mohammed V Mausoleum

The most ambitious of all Almohad buildings, the **Hassan Mosque** (daily 8.30am–6.30pm; free) and its vast minaret dominates almost every view of the capital. If it had been completed, it would (in its time) have been the second largest mosque in the Islamic world, outflanked only by the one in Smarra, Iraq. Even today its size seems a novelty.

The mosque was begun in 1195 – the same period as Marrakesh's Koutoubia and Seville's Giralda – and was designed to be the centrepiece of Yacoub el Mansour's new capital in celebration of his victory over the Spanish Christians at Alarcos, but construction seems to have been abandoned on El Mansour's death in 1199. The tower was probably left much as it appears today; the mosque's hall, roofed in cedar, was used until the Great Earthquake of 1755 (which destroyed central Lisbon) brought down its central columns. Its extent must always have seemed an elaborate folly – Morocco's most important mosque, the Kairaouine in Fes, is less than half the Hassan's size, but served a much greater population. Rabat would have needed a population of well over 100,000 to make adequate use of the Hassan's capacity, but the city never really took off under the later Almohads and Merenids; when Leo Africanus came here in 1600, he found no more than a hundred households, gathered for security within the kasbah.

The minaret is unusually positioned at the centre rather than the northern corner of the rear of the mosque. Some 50m tall in its present state, it would probably have been around 80m if finished to normal proportions – a third again the height of Marrakesh's Koutoubia. Despite its apparent simplicity, it is arguably the most complex of all Almohad structures. Each facade is different, with a distinct combination of patterning, yet the whole intricacy of blind arcades and interlacing curves is based on just two formal designs. On the south and west faces these are the same *darj w ktaf* motifs as on Bab oudaïa (see p.282); on the north and east is the *shabka* (net) motif, an extremely popular form adapted by the Almohads from the lobed arches of the Cordoba Grand Mosque – and still in contemporary use.

The Mohammed V Mausoleum

Facing the tower – in an assertion of Morocco's historical independence and continuity – are the **Mosque and Mausoleum of Mohammed V**, begun on the king's death in 1961 and inaugurated six years later. Hassan II and his brother, Moulay Abdellah, are buried here too, alongside their father. The **mosque**, extending between a stark pair of pavilions, gives a somewhat foreshortened idea of how the Hassan Mosque must once have appeared, roofed in its traditional green tiles.

The **mausoleum** was designed by Vietnamese architect Vo Toan. Its brilliantly surfaced marbles and spiralling designs seem to pay homage to traditional Moroccan techniques, but fail to capture their rhythms and unity. Visitors file past fabulously costumed royal guards to an interior balcony; the tomb of Mohammed V, carved from white onyx, lies below, an old man squatting beside it, reading from the Koran. If possible, plan a morning or afternoon visit as the mausoleum usually closes for midday prayers in the adjoining mosque.

The Ville Nouvelle

French in construction, style and feel, the **Ville Nouvelle** provides the main focus of Rabat's life, above all in the cafés and promenades of the broad, tree-lined Avenue Mohammed V. There's a certain grandeur, too, in some of the *Mauresque* colonial public buildings around the main boulevards, which were built with as much desire to impress as those of any earlier epoch.

Numismatists will enjoy the **Musée de la Monnaie** (Tues–Fri 3–5.30pm, Sat 10am–5.30pm, Sun 10am–1pm; 30dh), with its entrance at the side of the Bank al Maghrib in Rue du Caire. It's quite plush and very well laid-out, with coins dating back to the Phoenicians and the Berber kingdom of Mauretania, but the constant background musak starts to grate after a while.

One pleasant spot to relax in the Ville Nouvelle is the **Parc du Triangle de Vue** (daily 7am–7pm, Ramadan 7am–3.30pm), opposite the south wall of the Medina, with an open-air café that's a popular afternoon meeting place.

The walls and gates

More-or-less complete sections of Yacoub el Mansour's **Almohad walls** run right down from the kasbah to the Royal Palace and beyond – an extraordinary monument to Yacoub el Mansour's vision. Along their course four of the original **gates** survive. Three – **Bab el Alou**, **Bab el Had** and **Bab Zaer** – are very modest. The fourth, **Bab er Rouah** (Gate of the Wind), is on an entirely different scale, recalling, and in many ways rivalling, the Oudaïa.

Contained within a massive stone bastion, **Bab er Rouah** again achieves the tension of movement – with its sun-like arches contained within a square of Koranic inscription – and a similar balance between simplicity and ornament. The west side, approached from outside the walls, is the main facade, and must have been designed as a monumental approach to the city; the shallow-cut, floral relief between arch and square is arguably the finest anywhere in Morocco. Inside, you can appreciate the gate's archetypal defensive structure – the three domed chambers aligned to force a sharp double turn. They're used for exhibitions and are usually open.

From Bab er Rouah, it's a fifteen-minute walk down towards the last Almohad gate, the much-restored **Bab Zaer**, and the entrance to **Chellah**. On the way, you pass a series of modern gates leading off to the vast enclosures of the **Royal Palace** – which is really more a collection of palaces, built mainly in the nineteenth century and decidedly off-limits to casual visitors.

The Archeological Museum

Rabat's **Archeological Museum** on Rue el Brihi (daily except Tues 9am–4.30pm, but sometimes closed so call ahead; 10dh; ⓣ0537 701919) is the most important in Morocco. Although small – surprisingly so in a country which saw substantial Phoenician and Carthaginian settlement and three centuries of Roman rule – it houses an exceptional collection of Roman-era bronzes.

The bronzes are displayed in a special annex with a separate entrance; although included in the entry fee, it's sometimes closed. If so, ask one of the attendants at the museum's entrance to open it up for you. The bronzes date from the first and second centuries AD and were found mainly at the provincial capital of Volubilis (near Meknes), together with a few pieces from Chellah and the colonies of Banasa and Thamusida. Highlights include superb figures of a guard dog and a rider, and two magnificent portrait heads, reputedly those of Cato the Younger (Caton d'Utique) and Juba II – the last significant ruler of the Romanized Berber kingdoms of Mauretania and Numidia before the assertion of direct imperial rule. Both of these busts were found in the House of Venus at Volubilis.

Back in the main building, there are showcases on two floors; each contains finds from different digs, of little interest unless you have already visited the area – or plan to do so. Captions are in French and, if you ask, you may be provided with a guide to the museum – also in French.

Chellah

The most beautiful of Moroccan ruins, **Chellah** (daily 8am–6pm; 10dh) is a startling sight as you emerge from the long avenues of the Ville Nouvelle. Walled and towered, it seems a much larger enclosure than the map suggests. The site has been uninhabited since 1154, when it was abandoned in favour of Salé across the Bou Regreg. But for almost a thousand years prior to that, Chellah (or *Sala Colonia*, as it was known) had been a thriving city and port, one of the last to sever links with the Roman Empire and the first to proclaim Moulay Idriss founder of Morocco's original Arab dynasty. An apocryphal local tradition maintains that the Prophet himself also prayed at a shrine here.

Under the Almohads, the site was already a royal burial ground, but most of what you see today, including the gates and enclosing wall, is the legacy of 'The Black Sultan', **Abou el Hassan** (1331–51), the greatest of the Merenids. The **main gate** has turreted bastions creating an almost Gothic appearance. Its base is recognizably Almohad, but each element has become inflated, and the combination of simplicity and solidity has gone. An interesting technical innovation is the stalactite (or 'honeycomb') corbels which form the transition from the bastion's semi-octagonal towers to their square platforms; these were to become a feature of Merenid building. The Kufic inscription above the gate is from the Koran and begins with the invocation: "I take refuge in Allah, against Satan."

To your left if coming from the entrance, signposted "Site Antique", are the main **Roman ruins**. They are of a small trading post dating from 200 BC onwards, are well signposted and include a forum, a triumphal arch, a Temple of Jupiter and a craftsmen's quarter.

The Sanctuary

From the main gate, the **Islamic ruins** are down to the right, within an inner sanctuary approached along a broad path through half-wild gardens. The most prominent feature is a tall stone-and-tile **minaret**, a ludicrously oversized stork's nest usually perched on its summit. Indeed, Chellah as a whole is a good spot for **birdwatching**, especially in nesting season.

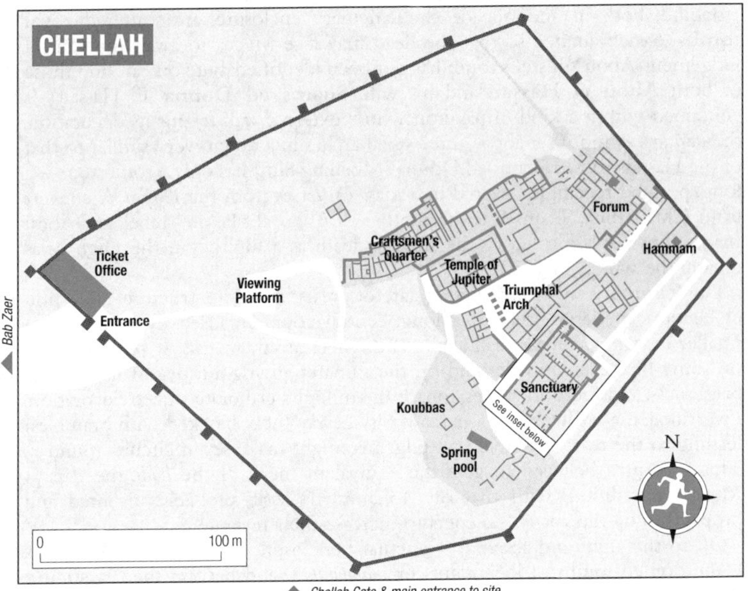

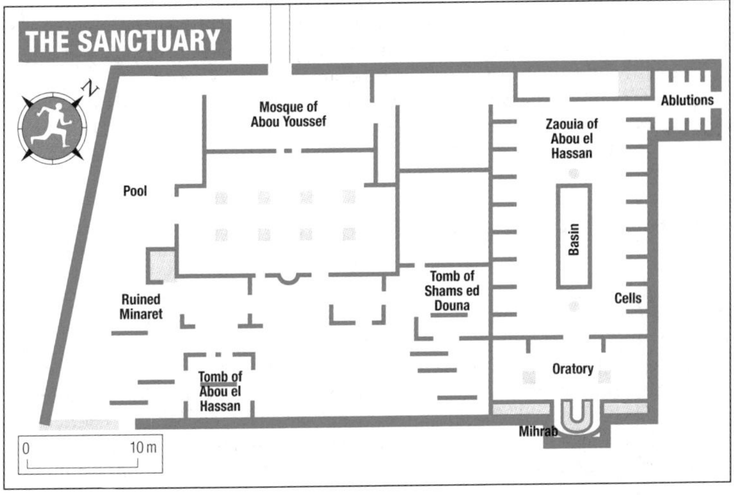

The **sanctuary** itself appears as a confusing cluster of tombs and ruins, but it's essentially just two buildings: a mosque, commissioned by the second Merenid sultan, Abou Youssef (1258–86), and a *zaouia*, or mosque-monastery, added along with the enclosure walls by Abou el Hassan. You enter directly into the *sahn*, or courtyard, of **Abou Youssef's Mosque**, a small and presumably private structure built as a funerary dedication. It is now in ruins, though you can make out the colonnades of the inner prayer hall with its mihrab to indicate the direction of prayer. To the right is its minaret, now reduced to the level of the mosque's roof.

Behind, both in and outside the sanctuary enclosure, are scattered **royal tombs** – each aligned so that the dead may face Mecca to await the Call of Judgement. Abou Youssef's tomb has not been identified, but you can find those of both **Abou el Hassan** and his wife **Shams ed Douna**. El Hassan's is contained within a kind of pavilion whose external wall retains its decoration, the *darj w ktaf* motif set above three small arches in a design very similar to that of the Hassan Tower. Shams ed Douna (Morning Sun) has only a tombstone – a long, pointed rectangle covered in a mass of verses from the Koran. A convert from Christianity, Shams was the mother of Abou el Hassan's rebel son, Abou Inan, whose uprising led to the sultan's death as a fugitive in the High Atlas during the winter of 1352.

The **Zaouia** is in a much better state of preservation, its structure, like Abou el Hassan's medersas, that of a long, central court enclosed by cells, with a smaller oratory or prayer hall at the end. There are fragments of zellij tilework on some of the colonnades and on the minaret, giving an idea of its original brightness, and there are traces, too, of the mihrab's elaborate stucco decoration. Five-sided, the **mihrab** has a narrow passageway (now blocked with brambles) leading to the rear – built so that pilgrims might make seven circuits round it. This was once believed to give the equivalent merit of the *hadj*, the trip to Mecca: a tradition, with that of Mohammed's visit, probably invented and propagated by the *zaouia's* keepers to increase their revenue.

Off to the right and above the sanctuary enclosure are a group of **koubbas** – the domed tombs of local saints or *marabouts* – and beyond them a **spring pool**, enclosed by low, vaulted buildings. This is held sacred, along with the eels which swim in its waters, and women bring hard-boiled eggs for the fish to invoke assistance in fertility and childbirth. If you're here in spring, you'll get additional wildlife, with the storks nesting and the egrets roosting.

At the far end of the sanctuary, you can look down a side-valley to the Bou Regreg estuary. From here, you can appreciate that this site was destined, from early times, to be settled and fortified. The site was easy to defend and the springs provided water in times of siege.

Eating, drinking and nightlife

For a capital city, Rabat is pretty quiet, but it does have some excellent restaurants – many of them moderately priced or inexpensive – plus loads of good cafés, some reasonable bars and, as Moroccan nightlife goes, some not-too-terrible clubs. As ever, the cheapest places to eat are to be found in the **Medina**. In the **Ville Nouvelle** you can pick from a fine selection of Moroccan and French restaurants, plus a few East Asian places for a change of cuisine. The suburb of **Agdal**, about 3km southwest of the city centre and favoured by Rabat's expat residents, has some fine restaurants and a reasonable variety of cuisines, though it's a bit of a haul if you're not already based there.

Medina restaurants

Café Taghazoute 7 Rue Sebbahi. This café serves simple dishes, including tasty fried fish, and also omelettes, which makes it a good option for breakfast. It tends to be busy with office workers at lunchtime. Cheap.

Dinarjat 6 Rue Belgnaoui, off Bd el Alou ⓣ0537 704239. This palatial eatery with fine Moroccan dishes and musical entertainment, in a seventeenth-century mansion at the northern end of the Medina, makes a good choice if you wish to spoil yourself. Expensive.

El Bahia Bd Hassan II, built into the Andalucian wall, near the junction with Av Mohammed V. Tajines, kebabs and salads, in a pleasant courtyard, upstairs or on the pavement outside, though service can be slow. Moderate.

Le Ziryab 10 Impasse Ennajar, off Rue des Consuls ⓣ0537 733636, ⓦwww.restaurantleziryab.com. Very popular among execs, diplomats and politicians, with good reason: the 500dh set menu is first-class Moroccan fare. Dinner only, closed Sun.

Restaurant de la Jeunesse 305 Av Mohammed V. One of the city's better budget eateries, with generous portions of couscous, and decent tajines. Cheap.

Restaurant de la Libération 256 Av Mohammed V. Another good cheapie, serving couscous (including a vegetarian one), stews and brochettes. Cheap.

Ville Nouvelle restaurants

Café Weimar Goethe Institute, 7 Rue Sana'a. Considered by some expats to serve the best food in Rabat, with pasta, meats and salads accompanied by German wine and beer. Moderate.

Grill 23 386 Av Mohammed V. Shawarma, burgers and big salads. Near the station, so handy for carry-out food to take on a train journey, though there is a pleasant shaded seating area. Conveniently open 7am–1am daily. Cheap.

Kanoun Grill 6th floor, *Chellah Hôtel*, 2 Rue Ifni, ⓣ0537 701051. The best place in town to sink your teeth into a good steak, or any other meat grilled over charcoal. Open for dinner daily except Sun, reservation recommended. Expensive.

Koutoubia 10 Rue Pierre Parent, off Rue Moulay Abdelaziz, and near the *Hôtel Chellah* ⓣ0537 720125. There's an upmarket bar and, with a separate entrance through a quaint wood and glass extension, an old-style restaurant, serving excellent food. It claims the late King Hassan among past clientele an elderly patron who knew his father, Mohammed V. Moderate to expensive.

La Bamba 3 Rue Tanta, a small side street behind the *Hôtel Balima* ⓣ0537 709839. European and Moroccan dishes, with good-value set menus for 80–110dh. Licensed. Moderate.

La Clef Rue Hatim, a narrow side street just off Av Moulay Youssef, and near the *Hôtel d'Orsay*. There's serious drinking in the bar downstairs, but the restaurant upstairs is quiet and serves good French and Moroccan dishes such as tajines, brochettes and pastilla, with a 75dh set menu. Moderate.

La Mamma 6 Rue Tanta ⓣ0537 707329. Opposite *La Bamba* and its Italian-style rival, with a range of good pizzas and pasta dishes. *La Dolce Vita*, next door to *La Mamma*, is owned by the same patron and provides luscious Italian-style ice cream. Moderate.

La Pagode 13 Rue Baghdad, parallel to (and south of) the train station ⓣ0537 709381. Has been around for a while now and is still one of the more popular Asian – mainly Chinese and Vietnamese – restaurants in town. Recently refurbished, they also have a take-out and home delivery service. Moderate to expensive.

Le Grand Comptoir 279 Bd Mohammed V ⓦwww.legrandcomptoir.ma. A classy brasserie with live light music in the evenings. Serves excellent seafood and a decent selection of wines. Expensive.

Le Mandarin 100 Av Abdel Krim Al Kattabi ⓣ0537 724699. Popular Chinese restaurant in L'Océan quarter, 250m from Bab el Alou. Closed Wed. Moderate to expensive.

Le Petit Beur 8 Rue Damas. A small but well-appointed little place serving very tasty tajines and excellent pastilla. *Beur* is French backslang for 'Arab'. Closed Sun. Licensed. Moderate.

Restaurant Saïdoune In the mall at 467 Av Mohammed V, opposite the *Hôtel Terminus*. A good Lebanese restaurant run by an Iraqi, serving mezze (tabbouleh, hummus, moutabel), falafel, kubbe and shawarma, with a 55dh set menu, Closed Fri lunchtime. Licensed. Moderate.

Tajine wa Tanjia 9 Rue Baghdad ⓣ0537 729797. Great little restaurant with a nice atmosphere accompanied most nights by live *oud* playing. The menu is mainly Moroccan fare, well presented, with a range of tajines (including vegetarian), tanjia (jugged beef or lamb), and, on Fridays, couscous. Closed Sun. Licensed. Moderate.

Beach area restaurants

La Péniche Av du Bou Regreg, on the Salé side of the Bou Regreg river between the Royal Nautical Club and the Magic Park ⓣ0537 785661. This floating restaurant in a canal boat serves excellent seafood, and is licensed. Expensive.

Restaurant de la Plage On the beach below the Kasbah des Oudaïas ⓣ0537 202928. A fine fish restaurant overlooking the beach, offering the latest catch, well cooked. Expensive.

Agdal restaurants

Fuji 2 Av Michliffen, at the western end of Av Atlas ⓣ0537 673583. This upmarket Japanese restaurant favoured by Rabat's Japanese community (such as it is), was closed for renovations at last check, but is widely considered to have the best Oriental food in Rabat: sushi, sashimi, tempura and bento lunch boxes. Closed Tues and lunchtime Wed. Expensive.

Pousse-Pousse 41 Av Atlas ⓣ0537 683435. Reasonable Vietnamese- and Chinese-style food to eat in, take out or have delivered. Moderate.

Restaurant Entrecôte 74 Av Fal Ould Ouemir ⓣ0537 671108. A well-established restaurant with a good French menu and excellent fish dishes. Wi-fi connected. Expensive, with a 255dh tourist menu.

Cafés, bars and nightlife

Avenues Mohammed V and Allal Ben Abdallah have some excellent **cafés**, for coffee, soft drinks and pastries. Particularly pleasant spots include the *Hôtel Balima* outdoor café, which is very popular with locals and something of a gay male cruising spot, the *Café Maure* in the kasbah (see p.282), and the café in the shady Parc du Triangle de Vue, just south of Boulevard Hassan II, which is usually full of students working or arguing over a mint tea, but opens in the daytime only.

Bars – outside the main hotels – are few and far between. The bar and adjoining courtyard inside the *Hôtel Bouregreg* is pleasant enough, though it's a little out of the way if you're not staying there. The one inside the *Hôtel Balima* is a trifle seedy and smoky, and closes at 10pm, but it has a terrace and attracts an interesting crowd of Moroccan drinkers.

The restaurants *La Clef*, *De la Paix* and *Koutoubia* all have bars. *Henry's Bar* on Place des Alaouites, pretty much opposite the train station, is a decent enough place as Moroccan city bars go, though it closes at 9pm. *El Palantino* at 133 Av Allal Ben Abdallah is a Spanish-style tapas bar where you can order individual tapas or a selection.

Most of Rabat's **discos**, notably those around Place de Melilla, are little more than pick-up joints, though they expect you to dress up in order to get in. *Biba Beach* and *Jefferson* at 1 and 3 Patrice Lumumba, just off Place de Melilla, are open until the early hours by which time, frankly, you don't want to be there. One reasonable place for a dance is *Amnesia* at 16 Rue de Monastir, which attracts quite a mixed crowd. Another popular dance-club is *5th Avenue*, near the Moulay Youssef Sport complex, in the Agdal quarter, south of the centre, easiest reached by petit taxi.

Listings

Airlines Royal Air Maroc, Av Mohammed V opposite the train station ⓣ0537 709710; Air France, 281 Av Mohammed V, just north of *Hôtel Balima* ⓣ0537 707580.

Banks Most are along avenues Allal Ben Abdallah and Mohammed V. BMCE's main branch at 340 Av Mohammed V has a bureau de change (daily 8am–8pm), and two ATMs, with a third round the corner at 5 Rue Alexandrie.

Bookshops The English Bookshop, 7 Rue Al Yamama (Mon–Sat 9am–12.30pm & 3–6pm; ⓣ0537 706593; see map, p.277), stocks new titles plus a wide selection of secondhand paperbacks. You can get coffee-table books on Morocco and phrasebooks from several of the bookshops along Av Mohammed V – Kalila Wa Dimna, no. 344, and Éditions La Porte, just north of *Hôtel Balima*, both have a good selection.

Car rental Cheaper deals are available in Casablanca, but there are twenty or so rental agencies in Rabat. Main companies include: Avis, 7 Zankat Abou Faris al Marini ⓣ0537 721818, ⓕ0537 767503; Budget, 469 Av Mohammed V ⓣ0537 705789; Europcar, 25 bis Rue Patrice Lumumba ⓣ0537 722328; Hertz, 467 Av Mohammed V ⓣ0537 707366, ⓕ0537 709227; National, corner of Rue de Caire and Rue Ghandi ⓣ0537 722731, ⓕ0537 722526. Avis, Budget, Europcar, Hertz and National have desks at Rabat–Salé airport.

Children Youngsters may appreciate a visit to the riverside Magic Park on Av du Bou Regreg, on the Salé side of the river (bus #35 from Bd Al Alaouiyne in Rabat via Salé's Bab Mrisa). There are carousels and other gentle fairground rides, as well as bumper cars, and the park is open Wed 2–9pm, Sat, Sun and daily in school holidays 11am–9pm (Ramadan Mon–Fri 8pm–1am, Sat & Sun noon–1am); entry is 5dh for children, 10dh for accompanying adults, 25dh for adults with no children, and a 45dh ticket gives access to all rides.

Cinemas and theatres Cinéma Royal, Rue Amman, diagonally opposite *Royal Hôtel* (mostly Kung Fu and Bollywood); Salle de 7ème Art, Av Allal Ben Abdallah, also near *Royal Hôtel* (smaller, more an arts cinema). The Théâtre National Mohammed V on Rue du Caire (ⓣ0537 208316, ⓦwww.tnmv.ma) puts on a range of concerts (Arabic and Western classical music) and films.

Embassies Algeria, 46 Bd Tariq Ibn Ziad ⓣ0537 661574 (but note that the land border with

Morocco is still closed at present); Canada, 13 bis Rue Jaâfar as Sadiq, Agdal ⓣ0537 687400, ⓦwww.morocco.gc.ca; Mauritania, 6 Rue Thami Lamdouar, Souissi ⓣ0537 656678, ⓦwww.ambarimrabat.ma, visa applications Mon–Fri 9–11am (collect Mon–Thurs 3–4pm, Fri noon–1pm, application form and conditions available on website); South Africa, 34 Rue des Saadiens ⓣ0537 706760; UK, 28 Av SAR Sidi Mohammed, Souissi ⓣ0537 633333; USA, 2 Av Mohammed el Fassi (Av Marrakech) ⓣ0537 762265, ⓦrabat.usembassy.gov. Australia is represented by the Canadian embassy and New Zealanders by their embassy in Madrid (ⓣ00-34/91 523 0226), though they may get help from the Brits in cases of dire emergency. The nearest Irish representation is in Casablanca (see p.313).

Golf The Dar es Salaam Royal Golf Club, 7km out of Rabat on Zaers Rd (ⓣ0537 755864, ⓦwww.royalgolfdaressalam.com) is one of the country's finest, with two eighteen-hole and one nine-hole course designed by Robert Trent-Jones.

Internet access The cheapest places (4dh per hr) are in the Medina, including Cyber at 8 Impasse Bechkaoui (off Rue Souika; daily 9.30am–midnight), and Téléboutique Baghdad on Rue Souika opposite Impasse Bechkaoui (daily 10am–midnight). Slightly comfier but pricier are Ville Nouvelle places such as: sacar@.net, 83 Av Hassan II (daily 8.30am–9pm); Phobos, 113 Bd Hassan II by *Hôtel Majestic* (daily 8am–11pm). If you're in Salé, there's a good and cheap internet station, Perfect Computer, just inside Bab Djedid (Mon–Sat 9am–11pm).

Medical aid Dr Youssef Alaoui Belghiti, 6 Pl des Alaouites ⓣ0537 708029; Dr Mohammed el Kabbaj, 8 Rue Oued Zem ⓣ0537 764311. For emergencies call the Service Médical d'Urgence on ⓣ0537 737373. The US embassy maintains a list of useful medical contacts online at ⓦcasablanca.usconsulate.gov/rabat2.html. Pharmacies include Rennaissance, 352 Av Mohammed V, just north of the post office. **A reliable dentist is** Dr Karim Yahyaouti, 5 Rue Tabaria ⓣ0537 702582.

Police The main station is on Av Tripoli, near the cathedral (ⓣ0537 720231), with a police post at Bab Djedid and another at the northern end of Rue des Consuls, near the Kasbah.

Post office The central PTT is at the junction of avenues Mohammed V and Jean Jaurès, opposite the Bank Al Maghrib (Mon–Fri 8am–6pm, Sat 8am–noon).

Supermarkets Label Vie, 4 Av Maghreb el Arabi, about 100m west of Bab el Had, and at the junction of Av Fal Ould Oumeir & Bd Ibn Sina (500m west of Agdal train station) is open daily 8.30am–9pm. There is also a Marjane hypermarket off the main road to Salé.

Moving on

Leaving town by **train** is easy, with Rabat Ville station slap-bang in the city centre. Services to Casa are extremely frequent, and most run to the more convenient Port station rather than the less central Voyageurs.

The main **bus terminal** is at Place Zerktouni, 3km out from the centre by the road junction for Casa and Beni Mellal (around 20dh by petit taxi, or 3dh by #17 or #30 bus from just outside Bab el Had; it will eventually be served by tram line 2 from Boulevard Hassan II). To Casa in particular, though private firms have departures every few minutes, it's worth taking the CTM, which drops you right in town. Private services to Fes on the other hand (which leave hourly, via Meknes) drop you at the *gare routière* near Bab Boujeloud, generally more convenient than the CTM station in the Ville Nouvelle.

Grands taxis for Fes and Casa leave from outside the bus terminal. For Meknes, they leave from Boulevard Hassan II at the corner of Avenue Chellah, while those for Kenitra and Khémisset also leave from just off Boulevard Hassan II, a few blocks to the east.

Rabat–Salé Airport (ⓣ0537 808090) is 7km northeast of Rabat, served by no public transport other than privately hired grands taxis (150dh for up to six people). Casablanca's **Mohammed V Airport** (ⓣ0522 539040), is an easy run from Rabat, with hourly trains (currently leaving on the hour till 9pm), changing at Aïn Sebaa (or sometimes Casa Voyageurs), a total journey time of an hour and forty minutes.

Salé

Though now essentially a suburb of Rabat, **SALÉ** was the pre-eminent of the two right through the Middle Ages, from the decline of the Almohads to the pirate republic of Bou Regreg (see p.275). Under the Merenids, as a port of some stature, it was endowed with monuments such as its superb **Medersa Bou Inan**.

In the twentieth century, after the French made Rabat their capital and Casablanca their main port, Salé became a bit of a backwater. The original Ville Nouvelle was just a small area around the bus station and the northern gates, but recently it has been spreading inland and along the road to Kenitra. Nevertheless, Salé still looks and feels very different from Rabat, particularly within its medieval walls, where the souks and life remain surprisingly traditional.

The Medina

The most interesting point to enter Salé's Medina is through **Bab Mrisa**, near the grand taxi terminal. Its name – "of the small harbour" – recalls the marine arsenal that used to be sited within the walls, and explains the gate's unusual height. A channel running here from the Bou Regreg has long silted up, but in medieval times it allowed merchant ships to sail right into town. Robinson Crusoe was brought into captivity through this gate in Daniel Defoe's novel. The gate itself is a very early Merenid structure of the 1270s, its design and motifs (palmettes enclosed by floral decoration, bands of Kufic inscription and *darj w ktaf*) still inherently Almohad in tone.

The souks

Inside Bab Mrisa you'll find yourself in a small square, at the bottom of the old **Mellah** (Jewish quarter). Turning to the left and continuing close to the walls for around 350m, you come to another gate, **Bab Bou Haja**, beside a small park. If you want to explore the souks – the route outlined below – veer right and take the road – Rue Bab el Khebaz – which runs along the left-hand side of the park. If not, continue on just inside the walls to a long open area; as this starts to narrow into a lane (about 40m further down) veer to your right into the town. This should bring you out more or less at the **Grand Mosque**, opposite which is the **Medersa of Abou el Hassan.**

The park-side street from Bab Bou Haja is **Rue Bab el Khebaz** (Street of the Bakers' Gate), a busy little lane that emerges at the heart of the **souks** by a small **kissaria** (covered market) devoted mainly to textiles. Most of the alleys here are grouped round specific crafts, a particular speciality being the pattern-weave mats produced for the sides and floors of mosques – to be found in the **Souk el Merzouk**. There is also a wool souk, the **Souk el Ghezel**, while wood, leather, ironware, carpets and household items are in the **Souk el Kebir** – the grand souk.

Close by the *kissaria* is a fourteenth-century hospice, the **Fondouk Askour**, with a notable gateway (built by Abou Inan), and beyond this the Medina's main street, **Rue de la Grande Mosque**, leads uphill through the middle of town to the Grand Mosque. This is the simplest approach, but you can take in more of the souks by following **Rue Kechachin**, parallel. Along here are the carpenters and stone-carvers, as well as other craftsmen. In **Rue Haddadin**, a fairly major intersection which leads off to its right up towards Bab Sebta, you'll come upon gold- and coppersmiths.

The Grand Mosque and Medersa

The area around the **Grand Mosque** is the most interesting part of town, with lanes fronting a concentration of aristocratic mansions and religious *zaouia*

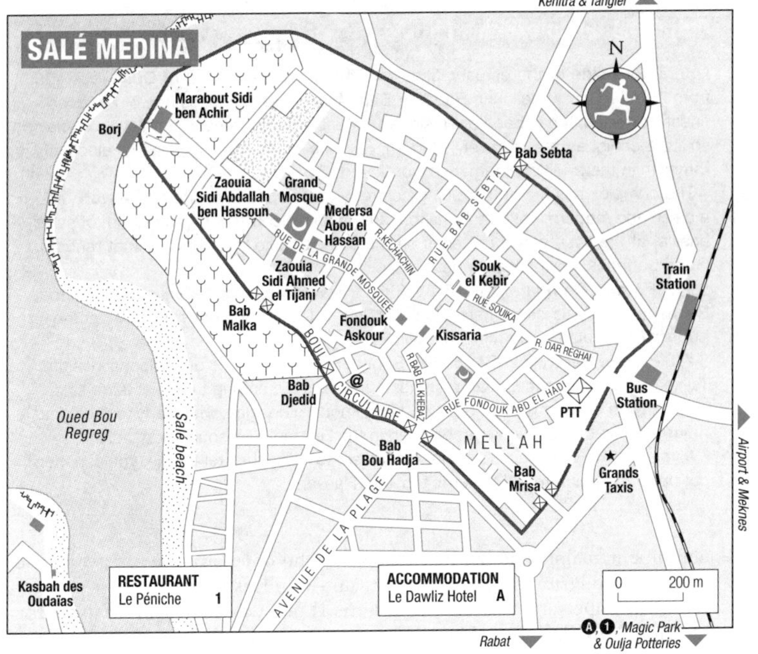

foundations. Almohad in origin, the mosque is one of the largest and earliest in Morocco. Unfortunately, non-Muslims can only see the gateway and minaret, which are recent additions, though Muslims can enter to see the prayer hall and mihrab, which are original.

Everybody can visit the recently restored **Medersa** (daily 8.30am–5pm, but sometimes closes early; 10dh), opposite the mosque's monumental, stepped main entrance. The medersa was founded in 1341 by Sultan Abou el Hassan, and is thus more or less contemporary with the Bou Inania medersas in Meknes and Fes. Like them (though rather smaller), it is intensely decorated with carved wood, stucco and zellij, leaving hardly an inch of space which doesn't draw the eye into a web of intricacy.

The patterns, for the most part, derive from Almohad models, with their stylized geometric and floral motifs, but in the latter there is a much more naturalistic, less abstracted approach. There is also a new stress on calligraphy, with monumental inscriptions carved in great bands on the dark cedarwood and incorporated within the stucco and zellij. Almost invariably these are in the elaborate cursive script, and are generally passages from the Koran. Close to its entrance there is a stairway up to the former cells of the students (now partially renovated to look almost livable) and to the **roof**, where, looking out across the river to Rabat, you sense the enormity of the Hassan Tower.

Zaouias, moussems and marabouts

Round the Grand Mosque, and over to the northwest, you can view (but only enter if you are Muslim) a trio of interesting buildings.

The first is the **Zaouia Sidi Ahmed el Tijani**, whose elaborate portal faces the Grand Mosque and Medersa. *Zaouias* are a mix of shrine and charitable

Oulja: the Complexe des Potiers

On the Salé side of the estuary, 3km from the town, the suburb of **Oulja** (bus #35 from Av Allal Ben Abdallah in Rabat or Bab Mrisa in Salé) houses one of Morocco's finest **potteries**. It has been open since 1980, established around a rich vein of clay, so its techniques are relatively modern, its kilns fired mostly by gas or electricity rather than the traditional tamarisk wood.

The complex has a craft shopping centre, an area specializing in basketwork, and a clean and modern restaurant. Visitors are made welcome, with a minimum of sales hassle, at the twenty-odd potteries on the complex and you could pick at random. Good potteries, however, include:

#12 **Poterie Demnate** ⓣ0537 813629, ⓦwww.poteriedemnate.fr.st. The patron, Bennami Abdelaziz came here after working in Demnate. Wares include ashtrays, butter dishes, plates and miniature tajines.

#10 **Poterie Hariky** ⓣ0664 756662. Superb modern versions of traditional designs. Tajines, cups and saucers, lamp stands and vases are among the objects for sale.

#9 **Poterie el Attar** ⓣ0537 807435. Light, modern designs, with many tea sets and mugs – some of their work can be seen in the Hassan II Mosque in Casablanca.

If you want to walk back to Rabat, head east to cross the first bridge; you can then cut up to the high ground towards the Tour Hassan.

establishment, maintained by their followers, who once or more each year hold a moussem, a pilgrimage festival, in the saint-founder's honour.

The most important of Salé's **moussems** is the 'wax moussem' of its patron saint, **Sidi Abdallah Ben Hassoun**, whose **zaouia** stands at the end of the Rue de la Grande Mosquée, a few steps before the cemetery. The saint lived in Salé during the sixteenth century and plays a role like St Christopher for Muslim travellers. His moussem, held on the eve of Mouloud (the Prophet's birthday; see p.51), involves a spectacular procession through the streets of the town with local boatmen, dressed in corsair costumes, carrying huge and elaborate wax candles in the form of lanterns mounted on giant poles. The candle bearers (a hereditary position) are followed by various brotherhoods, dancing and playing music. The procession starts about 3pm and goes on for three or four hours; the best place to see it is at Bab Bou Hadja, where the candles are presented to local dignitaries.

At the far end of a cemetery (again forbidden to non-Muslims), which spreads down to the river, is a third revered site, the white *koubba* and associated buildings of the **Marabout of Sidi Ben Achir**. Sometimes known as 'Al Tabib' (The Doctor), Ben Achir was a fourteenth-century ascetic from Andalucía.

His shrine, said to have the ability to attract ships onto the rocks and quell storms – good pirate virtues – reputedly effects cures for blindness, paralysis and madness. Enclosed by nineteenth-century pilgrim lodgings, it, too, has a considerable annual moussem on the eve of Mouloud.

Practicalities

From Rabat you used to be able to cross the river to Salé by rowing-boat ferry but these have diminished somewhat since the riverside promenade was completed, and you may well not find any in operation. Otherwise you can take one of the many **buses** (#12, #13, #14, #16, #34, #38 & #42) that pick up from the eastern end of Boulevard Hassan II; some can be picked up further west – #12 and #13 for example, which start on Rue al Mansour Dahbi in front of the entrance to the Parc du Triangle de Vue. The buses drop you just outside **Bab Mrisa**.

Grands taxis from various points on Boulevard Hassan II and Rue An Nador serve specific places in Salé: those for Bab Mrisa leave from the corner of Rue An Nador with Zenkat Deldou.

Salé's **campsite** has closed, though you can still park campervans up near where it used to be, tipping the parking attendant to keep an eye on them. To the east of the Medina and overlooking the river, the top-end *Le Dawliz Hôtel* (ⓣ0537 883277, ⓦwww.ledawliz.com; BB ❼) boasts 45 large rooms with all mod cons plus a complex of bars, restaurants and a nightclub. The neighbouring *Le Péniche* **restaurant** (see p.289) serves excellent seafood. In the evenings, you can eat reasonably at one of the many **cafés** along Rue Kechachin, but the streets empty even earlier than those in Rabat.

The coast from Rabat to Casa

It's a little over an hour by grand taxi from Rabat to Casa (under an hour by express train). If you're driving, the **coast road** (R322) is more scenic than the inland N1. Leaving Rabat, follow Tarik al Marsa past the Kasbah des Oudaïas for the coast road, or take Boulevard Misr alongside the Medina wall, then bear left onto Avenue Al Moukaouma and its continuation Avenue Sidi Mohammed Ben Abdallah for the N1.

Temara and Ech Chiana

TEMARA VILLE (served by bus #17 from outside Bab el Had in Rabat, and by some trains between Casa and Rabat) has a **kasbah** dating from Moulay Ismail's reign. Its beach, **Temara Plage**, is about 4km from the town, served by bus #33 from outside Bab el Had in Rabat, and in summer by grands taxis from Boulevard Hassan II, or take the road that leads west off the N1 about 500m north of Temara Ville train station.

A slightly plusher resort, **ECHCHIANA**, or Rose Marie Plage, is 9km south of Temara, with a luxury beachside **hotel**, *La Kasbah* (ⓣ0537 749116, ⓦwww.hotelkasbahclub.com; ❻), and on the inland side of the road, the cheaper *Hôtel Les Gambusias* (ⓣ0537 749525, ⓕ0537 749008; ❹), which has a swimming pool and does good meals, especially fish dishes.

Skhirat Plage

The **Royal Palace** at **SKHIRAT PLAGE** (served by eight daily trains between Casa Port and Rabat) was the site of a coup attempt by Moroccan generals during King Hassan II's birthday celebrations in July 1971. The coup was mounted using a force of Berber cadets, who took over the palace, imprisoned the king and killed a number of his guests. It was thwarted by the apparently accidental shooting of the cadets' leader, General Mohammed Medbuh, and by the strength of personality of Hassan, who reasserted control over his captors. Among the guests who survived was Malcolm Forbes (see p.96). The palace still stands, though it has understandably fallen from royal favour. Right next door, the *Amphitrite Palace* (ⓣ0537 621000, ⓦwww.lamphitritepalace.net; ❽) is one of Morocco's most deluxe beach hotels.

Getting to the resort by public transport, take any of the eight daily **trains** between Casa Port and Rabat which stop at Skhirat Ville, a small farming town a couple of kilometres up from the beach.

Mohammedia

Formerly known as Fedala, but renamed following the death of Mohammed V in 1961, the port of **MOHAMMEDIA** has a dual identity, as the site of Morocco's main oil refineries, and the base of its petrochemical industry, and as a holiday playground for Casablanca, with one of the best beaches on the Atlantic, a racecourse, and the Mohammedia Royal Golf Club (☎0523 324656) where the game was played in the sand in the 1920s, before a Frenchman, Pierre Uruguayen, shaped the present eighteen holes. In July, the week-long **Mohammedia Festival** encompasses all kinds of cultural activities and exhibitions.

With its friendly, easy-going atmosphere, and a fine selection of restaurants, Mohammedia makes a very pleasant stopover, or a base for Casablanca; it's only

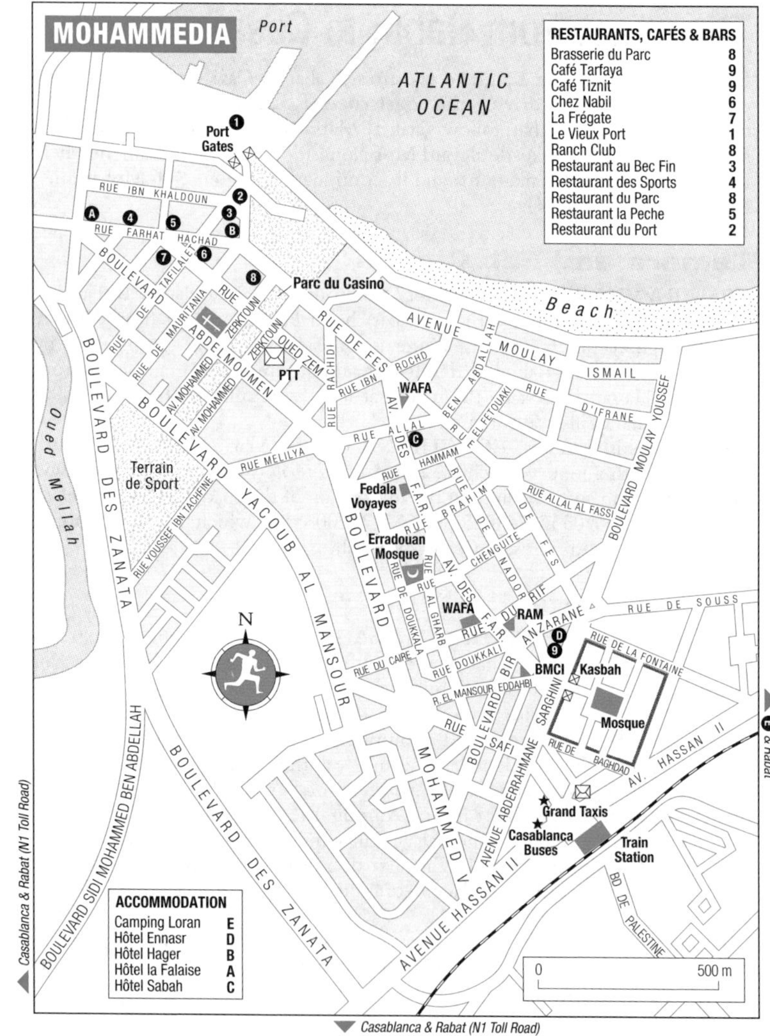

twenty minutes by rail from Casa Port and there are trains every half-hour for most of the day. Between the **train station** and the **Ville Nouvelle**, there is a small square **kasbah**, built during a period of Portuguese occupation and still preserving its original gateway. **Buses** and **grands taxis** operate from Avenue Hassan II, just in front of the train station. Travelling to Casablanca, the best bus to take is #900, which drops you in the city centre.

There are a few banks with ATMs. The **travel agency** Fedala Voyages at 35 Av des FAR (ⓣ0523 327390) is helpful for confirming flights and arranging car rental. Royal Air Maroc has an office on the corner of Avenue des FAR and Rue du Rif. Rue Baghdad near the station is the place for car repairs, with a slew of mechanics and spares shops. There is a Marjane **supermarket** on the way out to the N1 toll road from the port end of town.

Accommodation

The **campsite**, *Camping Loran*, 2km north of town on the Rabat road (ⓣ0523 324946), is closed in winter, and sometimes even in summer, so sites up or down the coast are better options (see p.273 & p.305).

Hôtel Ennasr Bd Moulay Youssef (no phone). This basic hotel with cubicles (no outside windows) off a first-floor corridor has shared showers and a ground-floor café that is lively or noisy, depending on your point of view. Make sure you are clear from the outset how much you have agreed to pay for the room. ❷

Hôtel Hager Rue Farhat Hachad ⓣ0523 325921, ⓔhotelhager@menara.ma. Modest but modern hotel, with bright, sparkling rooms, two excellent restaurants (one on the roof), and a patisserie next door. BB ❹

Hôtel la Falaise Rue Farhat Hachad ⓣ0523 324828. A lovely little place run by an energetic Frenchwoman, with eight spotless rooms, (only one is en suite), a tree-shaded central courtyard and a bar. It's often full so worth booking ahead. ❷

Hôtel Sabah 42 Av des FAR ⓣ0523 321454, ⓦwww.hotelsabah.net. A modern, expensive hotel, halfway between the kasbah and the port, it caters more for businesspeople than tourists. BB ❺

Eating and drinking

For its size, Mohammedia's choice of **restaurants** is impressive, especially for fish. As well as the options listed below, the *Hôtel Hager*'s two eateries are both worth trying (the downstairs one is something of an oasis during Ramadan). **Breakfast and snacks** are available from several pavement cafés facing the main entrance to the kasbah: the *Tiznit* and *Tarfaya* both serve grills and brochettes. Just inside the main gate of the kasbah, on the right, there are a number of similar café-restaurants worth a try. **Bars** include the *Ranch Club* on Rue de Fes facing the Parc du Casino, and *Brasserie du Parc* just around the corner; the bar at the *Hôtel la Falaise* is also not bad.

Chez Nabil Rue de Tafilalet. A café-restaurant with fried fish and paella to eat in or take away. Cheap.

Restaurant au Bec Fin Rue Cheikh Chouaib Doukali, near the port gates ⓣ0523 324429. A small, but highly recommended restaurant with a truly Spanish flavour. Moderate.

Restaurant du Parc Rue de Fes, facing the Parc du Casino and next to the *Ranch Club* ⓣ0523 322211. Excellent place, with fish specialities such as sole au roquefort or St Peter fish (tilapia) with orange and raisins. Expensive.

Restaurant du Port 1 Rue du Port, opposite the port gates ⓣ0523 325895. The town's best-known restaurant, with nautical decor and a flower-strewn garden, renowned for its charcoal grills. Same patron as Casablanca's *La Brasserie Bavaroise* (see p.310). Expensive.

Restaurant des Sports Rue Farhat Hachad ⓣ0523 323532. Large and classy, with excellent seafood and "folkloric spectacles" at weekends in the season. Dinner only. Moderate to expensive.

Restaurant la Frégate Rue Oued Zem, near the *Hôtel Hager* ⓣ0523 324447. Lobster, prawns and all manner of seafood in generous helpings, particularly of shellfish paella. There's a takeaway and delivery service too. Moderate to expensive.

Restaurant la Peche Rue Farhat Hachad. Unpretentious and popular seafood restaurant serving some of the best calamari, fish, oysters and paella in town. Can get very busy on Sundays with well-to-do Casablancans enjoying their weekly seafood feast. Lunch and dinner. Cheap to moderate.

Restaurant le Vieux Port In the fishing port ☎0523 321931. Oysters, paella, fish and seafood, fresh as can be, well cooked and not outrageously priced (many items, including lobster, are priced by weight). Moderate.

Casablanca (Casa, Dar el Baida)

Morocco's biggest city and commercial capital, **CASABLANCA** (Dar el Baida in its literal Arabic form) is the Maghreb's largest port, and busier than Marseilles, on which it was modelled by the French. Its development, from a town of 20,000 in 1906, has been astonishing but it was ruthlessly deliberate. When the French landed their forces here in 1907, and established their Protectorate five years later, Fes was Morocco's commercial centre and Tangier its main port. Had Tangier not been in international hands, this probably would have remained the case. However, the demands of an independent colonial administration forced the French to seek an entirely new base. Casa, at the heart of *Maroc Utile*, the country's most fertile zone and centre of its mineral deposits, was a natural choice.

Superficially, with a population of over three million, Casa today is not unlike a large southern European city. Arriving here from the south, or even from Fes or Tangier, most of the preconceptions you've been travelling round with will be happily shattered by the city's cosmopolitan beach clubs or by the almost total absence of the veil. But these "European" images shield what is substantially a first-generation city – and one still attracting considerable immigration from the countryside – and perhaps inevitably some of Morocco's most intense social problems.

Alongside its wealth and its prestige developments – notably the Mosquée Hassan II – Casablanca has had a reputation for extreme poverty, prostitution, crime, social unrest and the *bidonvilles* (shanty towns) which you will see both sides of the train track as you come into town. In fact, the French word *bidonville* – literally "tin-can town" – was coined in Casablanca in the 1920s, when construction workers on a building project in the Roches Noires district, east of the port area, knocked up some temporary accommodation next to their main quarry. Over the decades, other migrant workers followed suit, and the *bidonvilles* escalated, partly from the sheer number of migrants – over a million in the 1960s – and partly because few of them intended to stay permanently. Most sent back their earnings to their families in the country, meaning to rejoin them as soon as they had raised sufficient funds for a business at home.

The pattern is now much more towards permanent settlement, and this, together with a strict control of migration and a limited number of self-help programmes, has eased and cleared many of the worst slums. Also, *bidonville* dwellers have been accorded increasing respect during recent years. They cannot be evicted if they have lived in a property over two years, and after ten years they acquire title to the land and building, which can be used as collateral at the bank for loans. The dread of every *bidonville* family is to be evicted and put in a high-rise block, regarded as the lowest of the low on the housing ladder.

The problem of a concentrated urban poor, however, is more enduring and represents, as it did for the French, an intermittent threat to government stability. Through the 1940s and 1950s Casa was the main centre of anti-French rioting, and post-independence it was the city's working class that formed the base of Ben Barka's Socialist Party. There have been strikes here sporadically in subsequent decades, and on several occasions they precipitated rioting, most violently in the food strikes of 1982. More recently, the *bidonvilles* also proved a fertile recruiting ground for *jihadi* extremists – one *bidonville*, Sidi Moumen, was home to perpetrators of bomb attacks in Casablanca in 2003, and Madrid the following year, and also to a suicide bomber who blew himself up in a Casablanca internet café in 2007.

Arrival

The best way to arrive in Casa is by **CTM bus**, which will drop you on Rue Léon l'Africain, in the centre of town. Second best is on a **local train** from Kenitra or Rabat, most of which run into the relatively central **Casa Port** station (Gare du Port), near the end of Boulevard Félix Houphouët Boigny, 150m from Place des Nations Unies. **Intercity trains** stop at the less convenient station of **Casa Voyageurs** (Gare des Voyageurs), 2km from the centre at the far end of Boulevard Mohammed V. Few trains run from Voyageurs to Port station, so if there isn't one in the offing, you'll have to either take a taxi into town (about 10dh), or walk (20 minutes – straight ahead down Boulevard Mohammed V, curving slightly to the left as you come to the next main square, Place el Yassir), or take bus #2 from outside the station. Alternatively, change trains at Rabat on the way.

Private **buses** (except CTM) and most grands taxis (exceptions detailed below) arrive at the **Ouled Ziane gare routière**, 4km southeast of the city centre. The easiest way to get into town from here is by petit taxi (about 20dh on the meter). Buses #10 and #11 go into town (Bd Mohammed V by Marché Central) from the other side of Route des Ouled Ziane, the crossing of which is rather hazardous (best turn left down it and cross at the next junction). The *gare routière* has a 24-hour left-luggage office (*consigne*), which costs 7dh per item for every twelve hours.

Most **grands taxis** arrive in front of the Ouled Ziane *gare routière*. The main exceptions include those from Rabat, which deposit passengers in town on Boulevard Hassan Seghir, very near the CTM terminal, and those from Mohammedia, which go to Rue Zaid ou Hmad, close to Casa Port train station. Grands taxis from El Jadida, Safi and Essaouira leave you on Boulevard Brahim Roudani, by the junction with Boulevard Bir Anzarane, 2km southeast of the city centre. From here it's a twenty-minute walk into town, or take a petit taxi (about 15dh), or hop on bus #7 to Place des Nations Unies.

From the **Aéroport Mohammed V**, there is an hourly train service (6am–10pm then midnight) to Casa Voyageurs (35 min; 35dh).

The CTM airport shuttle bus is no longer operating, so if you don't want to take the train you will need to organize a transfer with your hotel or take a grand taxi, located outside the entrance of the terminal. The official rate is 230dh for up to six people, but it often seems to depend on how many passengers and the time of day. There are numerous bank ATMs and bureaux de change in the arrivals terminal. You could also rent a car on arrival (see pp.312–313), though driving in Casablanca is pretty nightmarish, and you'd be better off waiting until you leave town.

Orientation and information

Casa can be a bewildering place to arrive, but once you're in the centre, orientation is relatively straightforward. It's focused on a large public square,

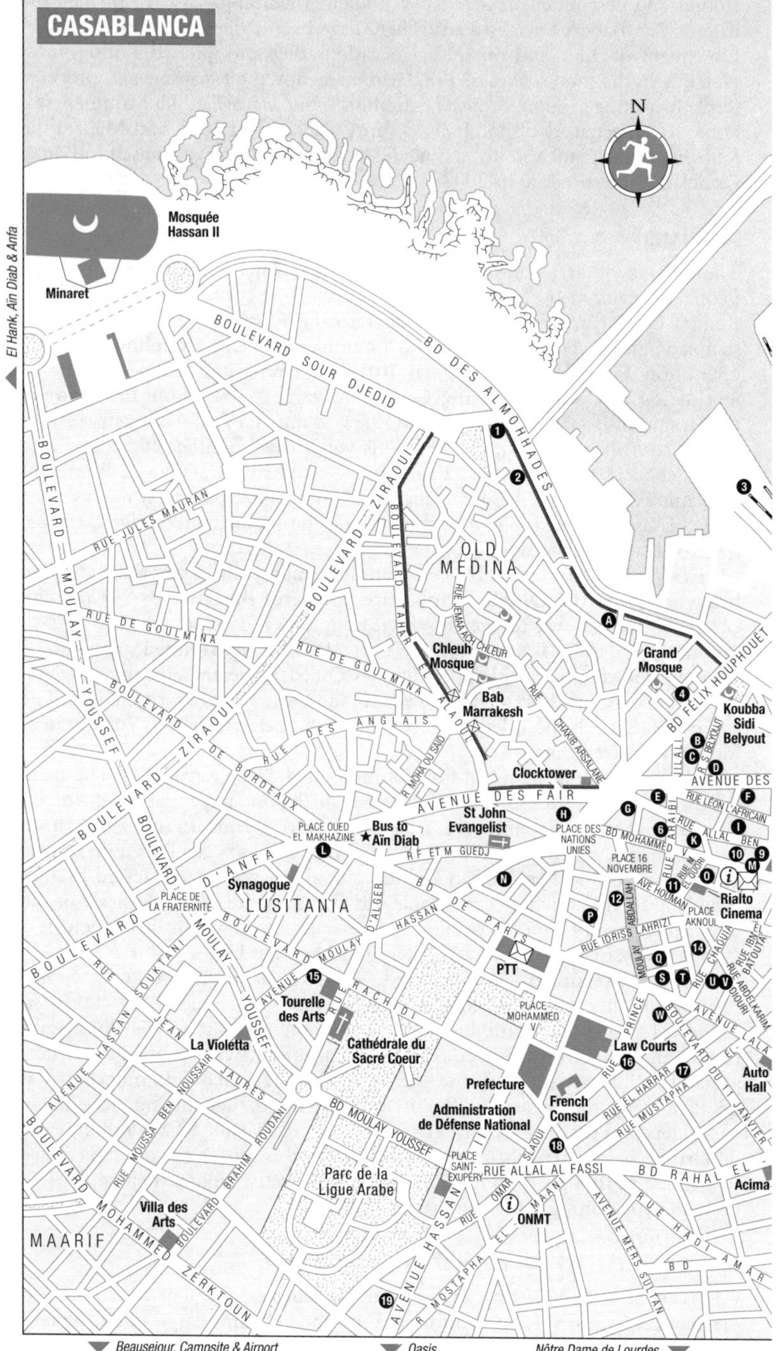
CASABLANCA
N
Mosquée Hassan II
Minaret
El Hank, Aïn Diab & Anfa
BOULEVARD SOUR DJEDID
BD DES ALMOHHADES
BOULEVARD
RUE JULES MAURAN
BOULEVARD ZIRAOUI
BOULEVARD TAHAR EL ALAOUI
OLD MEDINA
RUE JEMAA ACH CHLEUH
MOULAY
RUE DE GOULMINA
RUE DE GOULMINA
Chleuh Mosque
Grand Mosque
BD FÉLIX HOUPHOUET
Bab Marrakesh
RUE CHAKIB ARSALANE
Koubba Sidi Belyout
YOUSSEF
BOULEVARD ZIRAOUI
RUE DES ANGLAIS
BOULEVARD DE BORDEAUX
R. MOHA OU SAID
Clocktower
JILALI
R. S. BELYOUT
AVENUE DES
AVENUE DES FAIR
RUE LÉON L'AFRICAIN
BOULEVARD
BOULEVARD
St John Evangelist
PLACE OUED EL MAKHAZINE
Bus to Aïn Diab
PLACE DES NATIONS UNIES
BD MOHAMMED V
RUE ARAIBI
RUE ALLAL BEN
RF ET M GUEDJ
PLACE 16 NOVEMBRE
RUE M EL QUORI
D'ANFA
Synagogue
BD
AVE HOUMAN
Rialto Cinema
PLACE DE LA FRATERNITÉ
LUSITANIA
D'ALGER
HASSAN
DE PARIS
MOULAY ABDALLAH
PLACE AKNOUL
RUE IDRISS LAHRIZI
RUE CHAOUIA
RUE IBN BATOUTA
BOULEVARD
BOULEVARD MOULAY
MOULAY
RUE SOUKTANI
PTT
RUE ABDELKARIM DIOURI
RUE
AVENUE
RUE RACHIDI
Tourelle des Arts
YOUSSEF
PLACE MOHAMMED V
RUE PRINCE
BOULEVARD DU 11 JANVIER
AVENUE LALA
RUE JEAN JAURES
La Violetta
Cathédrale du Sacré Coeur
Law Courts
AVENUE HASSAN
RUE BEN NOUSSAIR
Prefecture
Auto Hall
RUE EL HARRAR
RUE MUSTAPHA EL
French Consul
Administration de Défense National
BOULEVARD
RUE MOUSSA BEN
BRAHIM ROUDANI
BD MOULAY YOUSSEF
RUE SLAOUI
PLACE SAINT-EXUPÉRY
RUE ALLAL AL FASSI
BD RAHAL EL
Acima
Parc de la Ligue Arabe
AVENUE HASSAN II
RUE OMAR EL
RUE MAANI
AVENUE MERS SULTAN
RUE HADI
Villa des Arts
ONMT
MOHAMMED
BOULEVARD
MAARIF
BD ZERKTOUN
R. MOSTAPHA
BD AMAR
Beausejour, Campsite & Airport
Oasis
Nôtre Dame de Lourdes

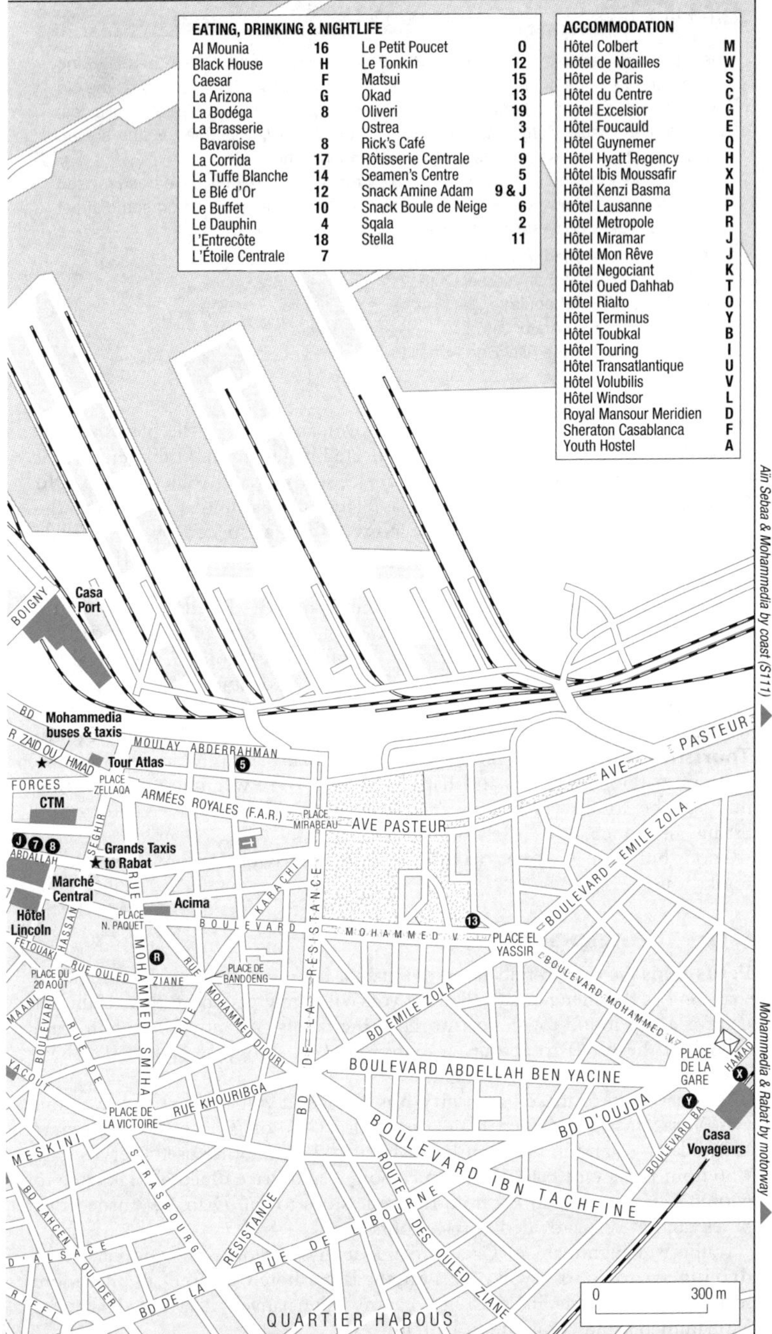
EATING, DRINKING & NIGHTLIFE
Al Mounia 16
Black House H
Caesar F
La Arizona G
La Bodéga 8
La Brasserie Bavaroise 8
La Corrida 17
La Tuffe Blanche 14
Le Blé d'Or 12
Le Buffet 10
Le Dauphin 4
L'Entrecôte 18
L'Étoile Centrale 7
Le Petit Poucet 0
Le Tonkin 12
Matsui 15
Okad 13
Oliveri 19
Ostrea 3
Rick's Café 1
Rôtisserie Centrale 9
Seamen's Centre 5
Snack Amine Adam 9 & J
Snack Boule de Neige 6
Sqala 2
Stella 11
ACCOMMODATION
Hôtel Colbert M
Hôtel de Noailles W
Hôtel de Paris S
Hôtel du Centre C
Hôtel Excelsior G
Hôtel Foucauld E
Hôtel Guynemer Q
Hôtel Hyatt Regency H
Hôtel Ibis Moussafir X
Hôtel Kenzi Basma N
Hôtel Lausanne P
Hôtel Metropole R
Hôtel Miramar J
Hôtel Mon Rêve J
Hôtel Negociant K
Hôtel Oued Dahhab T
Hôtel Rialto O
Hôtel Terminus Y
Hôtel Toubkal B
Hôtel Touring I
Hôtel Transatlantique U
Hôtel Volubilis V
Hôtel Windsor L
Royal Mansour Meridien D
Sheraton Casablanca F
Youth Hostel A
Casa Port
BOIGNY
BD Mohammedia buses & taxis
R ZAID OU HMAD
MOULAY ABDERRAHMAN
Tour Atlas
FORCES
PLACE ZELLAQA
CTM
ARMÉES ROYALES (F.A.R.)
PLACE MIRABEAU
AVE PASTEUR
AVE PASTEUR
SEGHIR
ABDALLAH
Grands Taxis to Rabat
Marché Central
KARACHI
Acima
Hôtel Lincoln
HASSAN
PLACE N. PAQUET
BOULEVARD MOHAMMED V
PLACE EL YASSIR
BOULEVARD EMILE ZOLA
FETOUAKI
RUE
MOHAMMED SMIHA
PLACE DE BANDOENG
PLACE DU 20 AOÛT
RUE OULED ZIANE
BD DE LA RÉSISTANCE
BOULEVARD MOHAMMED V
BD EMILE ZOLA
RUE MOHAMMED DIOURI
MAANI
BOULEVARD
RUE DE
YACOUT
BOULEVARD ABDELLAH BEN YACINE
PLACE DE LA GARE
HAMAD
Casa Voyageurs
PLACE DE LA VICTOIRE
RUE KHOURIBGA
BD D'OUJDA
BOULEVARD BA
MESKINI
STRASBOURG
BOULEVARD IBN TACHFINE
ROUTE DES OULED ZIANE
BD LAHCEN OU IDER
D'ALSACE
RÉSISTANCE
RUE DE LIBOURNE
RIFFI
BD DE LA
QUARTIER HABOUS
0 300 m
Aïn Sebaa & Mohammedia by coast (S111)
Mohammedia & Rabat by motorway
Ouled Ziane Gare Routière

Old and New Street Names

The names of Casa's chief squares – **Place Mohammed V** and **Place des Nations Unies** - are a source of enduring confusion. In 1991, Hassan II declared that the old Place des Nations Unies (around which are grouped the city's main public buildings) be known as Place Mohammed V, while the old Place Mohammed V (the square beside the Medina) was renamed Place des Nations Unies.

As elsewhere in Morocco, many of the old French street names have been revised to bear Moroccan names, but many people use the old names – as do some street maps. Significant conversions include:

Rue Branly – Rue Sharif Amziane
Rue Claude – Rue Mohammed el Qorri
Rue Colbert – Rue Chaouia
Rue Foucauld – Rue Araibi Jilali
Rue de l'Horloge – Rue Allal Ben Abdallah

Place Mohammed V (but note box above), and most of the places to stay, eat, or (in a rather limited way) see, are located in and around the avenues that radiate from it. A few blocks to the north, still partially walled, is the **Old Medina**, which was all there was of Casablanca until around 1907. Out to the south is the **Habous** quarter – the **New Medina**, created by the French, while to the west, along the Corniche past the Mosquée Hassan II, lies the beach suburb of **Aïn Diab**.

Casablanca's **tourist offices** include the **Syndicat d'Initiative** at 98 Bd Mohammed V (Mon–Fri 8.30am–4.30pm, Sat 8.30am–noon; ⓣ0522 221524), which is central and very helpful. The Conseil Regional du Tourisme have a kiosk in the corner of Place Mohammed V, and another next to the Mosquée Hassan II (Mon–Sat 8.30am–12.30pm & 2.30–6.30pm), with a website at ⓦwww.visitcasablanca.ma. The ONMT **Délégation du Tourisme** is south of the centre at 55 Rue Omar Slaoui (Mon–Fri 8.30am–4.30pm; ⓣ0522 271177), and happy enough to answer questions. Further info can be found via ⓦwww.casablanca.ma, a portal for Casa news and listings in French.

Good but pricey street **maps** of greater Casablanca are available at bookshops.

City transport

Petits taxis are easy to find along the main avenues and are invariably metered – as long as the meter is switched on you will rarely pay more than 15dh per taxi for a trip round town. For Aïn Diab the fare is currently 20dh (5dh extra if you get the driver to detour en route round the Mosquée Hassan II). There is a fifty-percent surcharge at night.

You may want to make use of **city bus** services if you arrive at or leave from Casa Voyageurs (#2), Ouled Ziane *gare routière* (#10 or #11), or the Essaouira/El Jadida taxi stand in the suburb of Maarif (#7). The other useful services are #56 from Boulevard Félix Houphouët Boigny and Place Oued el Makhzine to Mosquée Hassan II, and #9 from the same stops to Aïn Diab. Be warned that buses can get very crowded at rush hours.

Traffic is a nightmare in Casa, and frequently gridlocked: if you can avoid **driving**, try to do so. If you have a car, the larger hotels at Aïn Diab offer more security than those in the city centre. Alternatively, stay in Rabat or Mohammedia and commute in by train.

Accommodation

Although there are a large number of hotels in Casa, they operate at near capacity for much of the year and can fill up at short notice for conferences. If possible, phone ahead for a room, or at least arrive fairly early in the day. Even if you have a reservation, it's wise to phone ahead the day before to confirm. If there is a royal-patronage event on, your hotel may well be commandeered.

Hôtel Colbert 38 Rue Chaouia (Rue Colbert) ⓣ0522 314241. Conveniently located – one block from the CTM – and surprisingly large. Rooms are a bit gloomy, but clean and friendly, some with showers. There are several grill-cafés alongside for a quick snack or meal. ②

Hôtel de Noailles 22 Bd du 11 Janvier, just off Av Lalla Yacout ⓣ0522 202554, ⓕ0522 220589. Though starting to show its age, this is a pleasant and tasteful hotel with a *salon de thé* and a touch of class. ③

Hôtel de Paris 2 Rue Sharif Amzian, on the corner with the pedestrianized length of Rue Prince Moulay Abdallah ⓣ0522 273871, ⓕ0522 298069. In the centre of town and highly recommended, though rooms at the front can be noisy; it's often full, so book or arrive early. ④

Hôtel du Centre 1 Rue Sidi Belyout, corner of Av des FAR ⓣ0522 446180, ⓕ0522 446178. Old-fashioned hotel with a creaky antique lift, but some nice Art Deco ironwork on the staircase, and rooms cheered up by a lick of paint and sparkling en-suite bathrooms. ②

Hôtel Excelsior 2 Rue el Amraoui Brahim, off Pl des Nations Unies ⓣ0522 200263, ⓕ0522 262281. A once-grand hotel, opened in 1915 and thus Casa's oldest surviving hotel. It's seen better days, and is a dusty old place, but it retains a certain faded elegance and has a central and very convenient location. BB ③

Hôtel Foucauld 52 Rue Araibi Jilali ⓣ0522 222666. A good-value hotel with nice stuccowork in the lobby, and clean, if bare, salmon-pink rooms, some en suite. ②

Hôtel Guynemer 2 Rue Mohammed Belloul (Rue Pegoud) ⓣ0522 27 57 64, ⓦwww.geocities.com/guynemerhotel. Well-appointed, family-run hotel just off Rue Prince Moulay Abdellah in the most architecturally interesting part of town. Great Art Deco touches on the exterior and a refurbished interior – ask for one of the newer, larger rooms. It has a licensed restaurant and the staff are very friendly, helpful and speak good English. Free internet and wi-fi. Airport (and sometimes bus) pick-ups if pre-arranged. BB ⑤

Hôtel Hyatt Regency Pl des Nations Unies ⓣ0522 431234, ⓦwww.casablanca.regency.hyatt.com. Casablanca's most prominent deluxe hotel, where facilities include a pool (summer only), gym, sauna, basketball court, squash courts, private hammam, guarded parking, three restaurants, a bar and a nightclub. Service is impeccable and the rooms are modern and spacious. ⑨

Hotel Ibis Moussafir Casablanca Bd Ba Hamad, Pl de la Gare ⓣ0522 401984, ⓦwww.ibishotels.com. As with most hotels in this popular chain, it's situated by the train station; in this case Casa Voyageurs, so it's hardly central, though convenient for a late arrival (book in advance) or early departure. Restaurant, (sometimes noisy) bar, and car park. ⑤

Hôtel Kenzi Basma 35 Av Moulay Hassan I, just off Pl des Nations Unies ⓣ0522 223323, ⓕ0522 268936. Efficient and comfortable, this newish four-star business hotel is in a horrible-looking building, but some of its rooms have great views over the Medina and towards the Mosquée Hassan II. BB ⑧

Hôtel Lausanne 24 Rue Tata (Rue Poincaré), off Av Idriss Lahrizi, opposite the Cinéma Lusitania ⓣ0522 268690, ⓕ0522 268083. The owner has lived in Switzerland where, according to Bernard Shaw, they know all about hotels. The *Hôtel Lausanne* illustrates his point: it's efficient and well managed, with a *salon de thé* next door, but the elevator is not safe for children. ③

Hôtel Metropole 89 Rue Mohammed Smiha ⓣ0522 301213, ⓕ0522 305801. Off Bd Mohammed V, this is quite a comfortable hotel, with a bar and restaurant, and rather kitsch decor in the rooms. Reduced rates usually available. ④

Hôtel Miramar 22 Rue León l'Africain ⓣ0522 310308. Only 50m from the CTM, this is currently the cheapest of the little hotels in the city centre. It has an old-fashioned feel, and bathroom facilities are shared (shower 10dh), but the rooms are fine for the price. ②

Hôtel Mon Rêve 7 Rue Chaouia (Rue Colbert) ⓣ0522 311439. A friendly little place, and one that has long been a favourite with budget travellers, though some of the rooms are way up the steep spiral staircase, and the cheaper ones have shared bathroom facilities. ②

Hôtel Negociant 116 Rue Allal Ben Abdallah ⓣ0522 314023. Opposite *Hôtel Touring* (see p.304), and very similar, though currently priced slightly higher, with clean, comfortable rooms

You must remember this...

One of the best-known facts about Casablanca is that it wasn't the location for Michael Curtiz's movie, all of which was shot in Hollywood. Warner Bros, upset by the Marx Brothers filming *A Night in Casablanca*, wanted to copyright the very name Casablanca – which could have been inconvenient for the city.

The film of course owes its enduring success to the romantic tension between Humphrey Bogart and Ingrid Bergman, but at the time of its release it received a major publicity boost by the appearance of Casablanca and Morocco in the news. As the film was being completed, in November 1942, the Allies launched **Operation Torch**, landing 25,000 troops on the coast north and south of Casablanca, at Kenitra, Mohammedia and Safi. The troops, under General Eisenhower, consisted mainly of Americans, whom Roosevelt believed were less likely than the British to be fired on by the Vichy French colonial authorities. An even more fortunate coincidence took place in the week of the film's première in Los Angeles in January 1943, as Churchill and Roosevelt had arranged an Allied leaders' summit, and the newsreels revealed its location: the **Casablanca Conference**, held in Anfa, out beyond Aïn Diab. Such events – and the movie – are not, it has to be said, evoked by modern-day Casa, though the movie is commemorated in the city at the American-owned *Rick's Café* (see p.311).

(some en suite), and a popular choice with Moroccan families. ❷

Hôtel Oued Dahhab 17 Rue Mohammed Belloul (Rue Pegoud) ⓣ0522 223866, ⓔhotelguynemer@yahoo.com. Owned by the same family as the nearby *Hôtel Guynemer*, this is a rare budget option in this area of the city centre with basic but large, airy rooms, some en suite. Airport (and sometimes bus) pick-ups if prearranged. ❷

Hôtel Rialto 9 Rue Salah Ben Bouchaib ⓣ0522 275122. Opposite the Cinema Rialto and just off Bd Mohammed V. All rooms have a shower, some have toilets too; there's hot water 6am–noon in the rooms, and 24/7 in showers on the corridor. ❷

Hôtel Terminus 184 Bd Ba Hamad ⓣ0522 240025. Close to Casa Voyageurs, so quite convenient: clean, decent rooms with hot showers on the corridor. It's not in the same league as the nearby *Hôtel Ibis Moussafir* (see p.303) but then it's less than half the cost. ❷

Hôtel Toubkal 9 Rue Sidi Belyout, off Av des FAR ⓣ0522 311414, ⓦwww.bestwestern.com/ma/hoteltoubkal. One of the Best Western chain, centrally located with a/c rooms, restaurant, bar, cabaret and safe parking, but nothing very special for the price, though discounts are usually available. ❼

Hôtel Touring 87 Rue Allal Ben Abdallah ⓣ0522 310216. A friendly old French hotel that's been refurbished and is excellent value, with clean, comfortable rooms, some with their own shower, and hot water all day (bar a couple of hours around noon). It's even got its own little mosque. Definitely the first choice on this street. ❷

Hôtel Transatlantique 79 Rue Chaouia (Rue Colbert) ⓣ0522 294551, ⓦwww.transatcasa.com. Founded in 1922 in a Lyautey colonial building, and recently refurbished with a great mix of colonial decor (including two big brass lions in the foyer) and traditional stucco, tilework and stained glass, the *Transatlantique* boasts very comfortable rooms, a bar, restaurant and nightly cabaret. Past guests include Edith Piaf. ❻

Hôtel Volubilis 20/22 Rue Abdelkrim Diouri ⓣ0522 272771 or 2, ⓦwww.volubiliscasa.com. Built In 1919, the *Volubilis* re-opened in 2006 after a complete refurbishment, with a suitably Roman-themed reception area. There are 45 (mostly small) rooms, some with balcony and adjoining doors, good for families, and there's a small lift. ❹

Hôtel Windsor 93 Pl Oued el Makhazine ⓣ0522 200352. Large rooms with either a large bathroom or (cheaper) just a shower. There's also a decent bar and the staff are generally friendly and helpful. BB ❺

Sheraton Casablanca 100 Av des FAR ⓣ0522 439494, ⓦwww.sheraton.com/casablanca. A very modern and central state-of-the-art five-star hotel with every conceivable facility, including a pool (summer only), three restaurants and a nightclub (see p.312). The rooms (including one wheelchair-adapted) are comfortable but unexciting, and many of the staff speak English. ❾

Youth Hostel 6 Pl Ahmed el Biolaoui, previously Amiral Philibert ⓣ0522 220551. A friendly, airy place, just inside the Medina, and well maintained. Cards are not required. There are dorms (60dh BB) and double rooms, and internet service, but hot water can be iffy. Reservation is advisable. There's a good café, small post office and hammam on the leafy square. BB ❷

1914, but already exceeded by the time he left in 1923. Prost was keen to combine traditional Moroccan forms with current European town planning ideas, and was more than anyone else responsible for Casablanca's shape, and much of its architectural style.

The effect of the central ensemble in Place Mohammed V is very impressive indeed, the only feature out of place being a clocktower in the old **Préfecture**, on the south side of the square. The **law courts** on the east side of the square, and the **Bank al Maghrib** on the north are both solidly imposing too, and unlike much of the city's architecture, barely seem to have aged at all, probably because so many more recent buildings are modelled on them. On the west side of the square, the 1919 **post office** incorporates lots of surprisingly traditional features, in the tilework around the door for example, as well as the ceiling and brass chandelier within.

To the south of the square, at the junction of Avenue Hassan II with Rue d'Agadir and Rue Allal el Fassi, check out the building at 2 Place Saint-Exupéry, an imposing edifice with an impressive semicircular facade. Opposite, across Avenue Hassan II, the Administration de Défense Nationale building, dating from 1916, represents an earlier and much simpler style of Mauresque, reminiscent of buildings in the Spanish zone of northern Morocco. Off Avenue Hassan II, you'll find some fine 1920s buildings along **Avenue Mers Sultan**, especially around *L'Entrecôte* restaurant and the next main junction, Place Mers Sultan.

The cathedral and around

From Avenue Hassan II, Boulevard Moulay Youssef heads west towards Casablanca's most classic piece of colonial architecture, the **Cathedral of Sacré Cœur**, at the far end of the **Parc de la Ligue Arabe**. More European in style, though adopting African forms, the cathedral was built to a wonderfully balanced and airy design, paying genuine homage to its Moroccan setting. Most days you should be able to have a look around inside and if you're lucky, the *gardien* may escort you to the top of the tower for a brilliant view of the city and port.

Some 500m south of the cathedral at 30 Bd Brahim Roudani, an Art Deco villa has been lovingly restored and now houses the **Villa des Arts** (Tues–Sat 9am–7pm, except Ramadan 10am–3pm & 8.30pm–10.30pm; free; Ⓣ0522 295087 or 94, Ⓦwww.fondationona.ma), an exhibition centre concentrating on contemporary art. Other Art Deco villas, now derelict, include **La Violetta** on Boulevard Moulay Youssef, and the **Tourelle des Arts** on Rue d'Alger, opposite the cathedral. Heading north along **Rue d'Alger**, there are more fine colonial-era buildings especially nos. 54 and 78, which, despite their numbering are pretty much next to each other, and the Art Deco balconies on the Radiology Clinic at no. 12.

The Old Medina

The **Old Medina** dates largely from the late nineteenth century. Before that, it was little more than a group of village huts, half-heartedly settled by local tribes after the site was abandoned by the Portuguese in 1755. Casa Branca, the town the Portuguese founded here in the fifteenth century after the expulsion of the pirates, had been virtually levelled by the great earthquake of that year. Only its name ("White House": *Casablanca* in Spanish; *Dar el Baida* in Arabic) survives.

The Medina has a slightly disreputable air (it's said to be the place to go to look for any stolen goods you might want to buy back) but it isn't sinister, and it can be a good source for cheap snacks and general goods. A single main street, which starts from the top end of Boulevard Félix Houphouët Boigny by a restored clocktower as **Rue Chakib Arsalane**, becomes

Rue Jemaa Ach Chleuh halfway along. A small eighteenth-century bastion, the **Skala**, has been restored, with some old cannons and an upmarket café-restaurant (see p.311).

The one other building of interest nearby is the **Koubba of Sidi Belyout**, on the east side of Boulevard Félix Houphouët Boigny. It's closed to non-Muslims, but the white domed tomb can be seen through the door to the enclosure. Sidi Belyout is the patron saint of Casablanca and lent his name to the district southeast of the port. Legend has it that he despaired of mankind, blinded himself and went to live with animals who took care of him.

Quartier Habous – the New Medina

About a kilometre southeast of the city centre, at the end of Avenue Mers Sultan, is the **New Medina** – or **Quartier Habous** – which displays a somewhat bizarre extension of Mauresque. Built in the 1930s, it was intended as a model quarter, and it still has a kind of Legoland look, with its neat little rows of streets. What's most unreal, perhaps, is the neighbourhood mosque, flanked by a tidy stretch of green just as if it were a provincial French church.

South again from the New Medina, at the junction of avenues Mers Sultan and 2 Mars, alongside the Rond-point de l'Europe, the **Church of Notre-Dame de Lourdes** was completed in the 1950s. It's smaller than the cathedral and still in use. Its beautiful stained-glass windows, the work of Gabriel Loire, a master craftsman from Chartres, are its pride and joy.

Mosquée Hassan II

In a speech on July 9, 1980 (his birthday and Youth Day), King Hassan II said

> I wish Casablanca to be endowed with a large, fine building of which it can be proud until the end of time...I want to build this mosque on the water, because God's throne was on the water. Therefore, the faithful who go there to pray, to praise the creator on firm soil, can contemplate God's sky and ocean.

Work on the **Mosquée Hassan II** duly commenced the same year, and the mosque was inaugurated on August 30, 1993. Raised on a rocky platform reclaimed from the ocean, it was designed by French architect Michel Pinseau, and is open to non-Muslims on accompanied one-hour visits which also visit the mosque's huge and elaborate basement hammam (Sat–Thurs 9am, 10am, 11am, & 2pm in winter, 2.30pm in summer, Fri 9am & 2pm/2.30pm; 120dh, students 60dh).

From the city centre, the mosque's huge size tricks you into thinking it's nearer than it is. The minaret is 200m high, making it by far the tallest structure in the country, and the tallest minaret in the world. A laser on its summit projects a beam towards Mecca. It has space for 25,000 worshippers within, and 80,000 more in the courtyard. A glass floor in the mosque reveals the ocean below, a reminder of the Koran's statement (11:7), reiterated by Hassan II, that God's throne is upon the water. In order that the faithful can "contemplate God's sky", the enormous roof of the mosque rolls open on occasions. The mosque is second only to mecca's in size, and St Peter's in Rome could fit comfortably inside it.

The facts of the mosque's construction are almost as startling as its size. During the early 1990s, when it was being readied for opening, 1400 men worked by day and a further 1100 by night. Most were master-craftsmen, working marble from Agadir, cedar from the Middle Atlas, granite from Tafraoute, and (the only

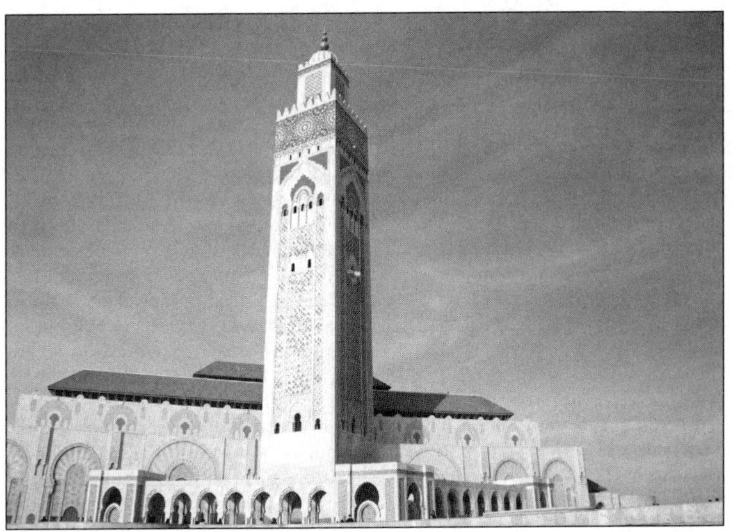

▲ Mosquée Hassan II, Casablanca

import) glass from Murano near Venice. Its cost is reckoned to have exceeded £500m/US$750m, raised by not entirely voluntary public subscription.

A brisk twenty-minute walk from the city centre along Boulevard Moulay Youssef, the mosque can also be reached by petit taxi (less than 10dh on the meter), or by bus #56 from Boulevard Félix Houphouët Boigny.

Aïn Diab: the beach

You can get out to the beach suburb of **Aïn Diab** by bus #9 from Boulevard Félix Houphouët Boigny, by petit taxi (about 20dh on the meter from Place des Nations Unies) or – if you fancy a long walk (30–45min) – on foot. The beach starts around 3km out from the port and Old Medina, past the Mosquée Hassan II, and continues for about the same distance.

A beach within Casa may not sound alluring – and it's certainly not the cleanest and clearest stretch of the country's waters – but Aïn Diab's big attraction is not so much the sea, in whose shallow waters Moroccans gather in phalanx formations, as the **beach clubs** along its front, each with one or more pools, usually of filtered seawater, a restaurant and a couple of snack bars. The prices and quality of the clubs vary – most locals have annual membership and for outsiders a day or weekend ticket can work out expensive (65–200dh) – so it's worth wandering round to check out what's available.

Out beyond Aïn Diab, along the Corniche and inland from it, is the suburb of **Anfa**, where the city's wealthy have their villas, and companies their corporate headquarters – including the striking shiny black block of the **OCP** (Office Chérifien des Phosphates).

The Jewish Museum

Five kilometres south of town, in the suburb of Oasis, the **Jewish Museum of Casablanca** at 81 Rue Chasseur Jules Gros (Mon–Fri 10am–6pm; 20dh, or 40dh with a guided tour; wheelchair accessible; Ⓣ0522 994940, Ⓦwww.casajewishmuseum.com) is Casablanca's one museum, and the only

Jewish museum in any Muslim country. It is also an important resource of information on Morocco's massive Jewish heritage, one that rather dwarfs the country's 5000-strong Jewish population, of whom more than sixty percent live in Casablanca.

The museum, set up and run jointly by the Jewish-Moroccan Cultural Heritage Foundation and the Ministry of Culture, is housed in a bright, modern building. It exhibits photographs of synagogues, ancient cemeteries and Jewish holy sites nationwide, many of which are covered in this book, as well as reconstructed synagogue interiors, books and scrolls, traditional costumes, both full- and doll-size, and sacramental items, mostly made of silver and some hailing from Manchester, England. In fact, since silverwork was once the preserve of Morocco's Jews – even today, you'll find the jewellery souk in the Mellah (Jewish quarter) of many Moroccan towns – there are exhibits of Jewish-made silver jewellery, and a reconstructed jeweller's workshop. There are also photos of ancient synagogues such as the Ibn Danan in Fes and others in Ifrane de l'Anti-Atlas (see p.517) and elsewhere.

You can get to the museum by petit taxi from the city centre (about 20dh – it's worth asking your driver to wait for you, as taxis locally are scarce), or by train from Casa Voyageurs. From Oasis station, turn left and head towards a motorway bridge across the road. Take the last street on the right before the bridge (Rue Abu Dhabi, though it isn't signposted), turning left after about 300m by no. 53, and the museum is just ahead on your left.

Eating, drinking and nightlife

If you can afford the fancier restaurants, Casa has the best dining in Morocco. On a budget, your choice is more limited, but there are plenty of chicken rôtisseries and snack joints, so you won't starve.

The city is also well known for its **patisseries**, of which the most famous by far is *Gâteaux Bennis*, 2 Rue Fkih el Gabbas in the Quartier Habous (Ⓣ0522 303025). In town, one of the more renowned is *Le Blé d'Or* at 38 Rue Prince Moulay Abdallah. **Ice-cream parlours** are also popular: one of the best is *Oliveri*, 132 Av Hassan II, which is also quite a refined café. More central, though it's takeaway only, is *Stella*, at the corner of Rue Mohammed el Quorri and Avenue Houman Fetouki, boasting over eighty flavours (though only about twenty are available at any time), and waffle cones freshly made on the premises.

Restaurants

In addition to the places listed here, there are inexpensive hole-in-the-wall eateries in the **Old Medina**, and if you're putting together a picnic, the **Marché Central** (daily 6am–2pm) on Rue Chaouia groans under the weight of the freshest and best produce in Morocco.

Downtown

Al Mounia 95 Rue du Prince Moulay Abdallah Ⓣ0522 222669. Excellent traditional Moroccan cuisine served in a salon or out in the garden. You can eat well for 250dh. Closed Sun. Moderate to expensive.

La Bodéga 127 Rue Allal Ben Abdallah Ⓣ0522 541842, Ⓦwww.bodega.ma. Spanish cuisine, including various seafood tapas, fajitas, burritos and grilled steaks in a lively taverna-style setting. It can get very busy, and there's a downstairs bar and dancefloor (salsa night Tues). You come here for the vibe and alcohol (including sangría) more than the food on its own. Closed Sun. Moderate to expensive.

La Brasserie Bavaroise 129–131 Rue Allal Ben Abdallah Ⓣ0522 311760, Ⓦwww.bavaroise.ma. A fine selection of fish and meat dishes at this French-style brasserie, with a daily special. Closed Sat lunchtime & Sun. Expensive.

La Corrida 35 Rue el Arrar (Rue Gay Lussac) ⓣ0522 278155. Spanish restaurant run by a Spanish-French couple, serving gazpacho, Spanish omelette, stuffed squid, fish brochettes, and *zarzuela* (fish stew). In summer, you can eat in the garden. Closed Sun and the whole of August. Moderate with a 55dh lunchtime set menu.

La Tuffe Blanche 57 Tahar Sebti. One of the few remaining Jewish eating places, it serves kosher dishes and alcohol. Convenient for the *Hôtel Guynemer* and *Hôtel de Paris*. Cheap to moderate.

Le Buffet 99 Bd Mohammed V. Quick, bright and popular, with a reasonable 65dh *menu du jour*. Cheap to moderate

Le Dauphin 115 Bd Félix Houphouët Boigny ⓣ0522 221200. Long-established and very popular fish restaurant. You may need to queue, or you could make a reservation. Moderate to expensive, with a 115dh set menu.

L'Entrecôte 78 Av Mers Sultan. French cuisine in a relaxed setting. Licensed. Moderate to expensive.

Le Petit Poucet 86 Bd Mohammed V. A slice of old Casablanca, a French restaurant dressed up like a 1920s Parisian salon (which is what it was), where French aviator and writer Saint-Exupéry used to recuperate between his mail flights south to the Sahara; a couple of framed sketches by him grace the walls. You come for the decor rather than the food, which is fine but nothing special, though the *soupe à l'oignon* is pretty good. Prices are moderate and there is a (much cheaper) snack bar next door.

L'Étoile Centrale 107 Rue Allal Ben Abdallah ⓣ0661 637524. The most "local" of the resturants on this street, with a spartan interior but good atmosphere, serving a choice of four pastillas and thirteen lamb or chicken tajines (or pigeon, rabbit or fish tajine if ordered in advance). Moderate.

Le Tonkin 34 Rue Prince Moulay Abdallah ⓣ0522 221913. First-floor restaurant on the pedestrianized length of the street, serving Chinese and Vietnamese food, including pork dishes, in an "exotic setting". Moderate, with set menus (including one vegetarian) at 80–125dh.

Matsui *JM Suites* hotel, 161 Av Moulay Hassan I ⓣ0522 229874. More a sushi bar (complete with conveyor; sushis 29–59dh) than a restaurant, though it also serves dishes such as tempura, teriyaki, and beef in wasabi sauce. Moderate.

Okad 433 Bd Mohammed V. A new place serving fresh fish at very reasonable prices, including seafood salad, prawn pili-pili, and fried sole, hake, squid, prawns or a mixture. Daily noon–10pm. Cheap to moderate.

Ostrea Port de Pêche ⓣ0522 441390, ⓦwww.ilove-casablanca.com/ostrea. This place, tucked away in the port area, deserves to be better known, especially for its Oualidia oysters. Other fabulous fresh fish dishes include lobster or crayfish sold by weight, and even frogs' legs *à la provençale*. Moderate to expensive.

Rick's Café 248 Bd Sour Jdid, off Bd des Almohades ⓣ0522 274207, ⓦwww.rickscafe.ma. A varied menu with a fusion of Moroccan, French and Californian cuisine, including chicken pie, and fish and chips. The pianist (Issam rather than Sam) creates a Forties and Fifties musical ambience every night except Mon, and apparently never tires of playing the inevitable "As Time Goes By". Expensive, with tacky souvenirs available.

Rôtisserie Centrale 36 Rue Chaouia. The best of a bunch of cheap chicken-on-a-spit joints on this little stretch of road opposite the Marché Central. Chicken, chips and salad here won't set you back much more than 30dh.

Snack Amine Adam 5 & 22 Rue Chaouia. Café-restaurant with two locations, no. 22 specializing in seafood dishes like paella or fried fish, no. 5 in brochettes and spit-roast chicken. Cheap.

Snack Boule de Neige 72 Rue Araibi Jilali. Tasty, cheap dishes including chicken, liver, heart, shawarma, and, on Fridays, couscous.

Sqala Bd des Almohades. An upmarket café-restaurant amid pleasant gardens in an eighteenth-century bastion of the Medina wall, complete with cannons. There are set breakfasts (75dh) 8.30am–noon, juices, coffees, teas and infusions all day, and meals noon–4pm and 7pm–midnight. Expensive.

On the coast

A Ma Bretagne Sidi Abderrahmane, 2km west of Aïn Diab ⓣ0522 397979. French gastronomes visit Casablanca purely to eat at this restaurant, run by André Halbert, one of just three *Maître Cuisiniers de France* working in Africa and recipient of an award for the best French cooking in the continent. Specialities include *huîtres au Champagne* and *salade de l'océan au foie gras*; the site is delightful, close to the little island *marabout* of Sidi Abderrahmane (see p.315). Naturally, it's not cheap and you should anticipate upwards of 350dh a head. Licensed. Closed Sun and throughout Aug.

Essad 39 Bd de la Corniche, Aïn Diab. Mainly meat including liver, heart or steak, but they'll do you fried fish if you want. Licensed. Cheap to moderate.

Le Poisson 59 Bd de la Corniche, Aïn Diab. A good place for fish and seafood, offering a whole range of different prawns (ordinary, king, Dublin Bay), not to mention bivalves (mussels, oysters, razor shells), or a seafood hot pot, or cold plate. Expensive, with a 150dh set menu.

Notre Alsace 59 Bd de la Corniche, Aïn Diab ⓣ0522 367191. A very pleasant bar-restaurant-brasserie with a good choice of fish and meat dishes. Moderate.

Bars and nightclubs

Casa has a surprisingly elusive nightlife, at least in the centre, where the clubs tend to be tacky cabaret joints. **Bars** are plentiful, but as usual they're all-male preserves, and women wanting a hassle-free drink are going to be hard-put. Two notable exceptions offering a place to socialize and drink no matter what your gender are *La Bodéga* (Mon–Sat noon–4pm & 7pm–12.30am; see p.310), and the rather more refined *Rick's Café* (see p.311). The *Seamen's Centre* on Boulevard Moulay Abderrahman (ⓣ0522 309950) is really only for members and mariners, but they'll usually admit and serve foreigners, and as bars go, it's a good one, with a pool table and space to relax. Hotel bars worth a try include the *Transatlantique*, the *Windsor* and the *Noailles*. Of ordinary bars around town, *Au Petit Poucet*, 86 Bd Mohammed V, attached to the restaurant of the same name is quite relaxed and there are also a few around the Rialto Cinema. If you want to check out some typical all-male hard-drinking dens, you'll find a row of them next to *La Bodéga*, along Rue Allal Ben Abdallah behind the Marché Central.

Nightclubs generally open around 11pm, close about 3am, and charge around 100dh to get in. The term in general use for a dancefloor nightclub is "disco", while "nightclub" usually means a place with tables and a cabaret floorshow, such as the very sleazy *La Arizona* on Rue el Amraoui Brahim, next to the *Hôtel Excelsior* (women will probably want to avoid this one). Of the dance clubs, those attached to five-star hotels, such as the *Black House* at the *Hyatt Regency* and *Caesar* at the *Sheraton*, are pricey and attract a well-heeled crowd. In summer especially more happens out at Aïn Diab on the coast, where the top clubs include *Le Tube* at 1 Bd de la Corniche, *Velvet* next door at no. 3, *Le Village* at no. 11 (which has quite a large gay contingent), the quite upmarket *La Notte* at no. 31, and *Metropolis* in the *Hôtel Suisse* at the junction of Boulevard de la Corniche with Boulevard Biarritz. *Calypso* at 61 Bd de la Corniche is more relaxed, a bar with a dancefloor rather than a disco as such.

Listings

Airlines Air France, 11 Av des FAR ⓣ0522 431818; British Airways, Centre Allal Ben Abdallah, 47 Rue Allal Ben Abdallah ⓣ0522 433300; Emirates, Sania Building, 140 Bd Zerktouni, fourth floor ⓣ0522 439900; Iberia, 17 Av des FAR ⓣ0522 439542; KLM c/o Air France; Lufthansa, Tour Habous, Av des FAR near the *Sheraton* hotel ⓣ0522 421200; Regional Air Lines, 41 Av des FAR ⓣ0522 543417; Royal Air Maroc, 44 Av des FAR ⓣ0522 489702.

Banks Most banks have main branches with ATMs along Av des FAR between Pl des Nations Unies and Pl Zellaqa, and other branches with ATMs on Bd de Paris east of Pl Mohammed V. There are also foreign exchange bureaux keeping longer hours on and around Bd Félix Houphouët Boigny and at 353 Av Mohammed V; most close Sun, but Currency Exchange Point by the clock tower on Av des FAR opens daily 9am–9pm.

Books and newspapers For English-language books try the American Language Center Bookstore, 1 Pl de la Fraternité just off Bd Moulay Youssef (Mon, Tues, Thurs & Fri 9am–noon & 3–7pm, Wed & Sat 9am–noon), with a small selection of fiction. British newspapers and the *International Herald Tribune* are available from stands around Pl des Nations Unies (and in the *Hyatt Regency* on the square) and at the Gare du Port.

Car rental Competition is stiff and it's worth phoning around. One of the best local firms is Afric Cars, 33 Rue Mohammed Radi Slaoui

☎0522 24 21 81. Others include: Ennasr Car, 18 Bd Anfa ☎0522 220813; First Car, 30 Rue Sidi Belyout ☎0522 300007, ©reservations@firstcar.ma; Goldcar, 5 Av des FAR ☎0522 202509; Weekend Cars, second floor, 39 Rue Omar Slaoui ☎0522 472558. The international franchises (all with desks at the airport too) are: Avis, 19 Av des FAR ☎0522 312424, ⓕ0522 311135; Budget, Tour des Habous, Av des FAR, near the *Sheraton* hotel ☎0522 313124; Europcar, Tour des Habous, Av des FAR, near the *Sheraton* hotel ☎0522 313737; Hertz, 25 Rue Al Oraibi Jilali ☎0522 484710, ⓕ0522 294403; National, 12 Rue Araibi Jilali ☎0522 472540, ⓕ0522 471566. Cheaper deals may be had from local firms.

Children Small people may appreciate a visit to Parc des Jeux Yasmina, an amusement park with children's fairground rides on Bd Moulay Youssef in Parc de la Ligue Arabe (daily 10am–7pm, Ramadan 11am–4pm; entry 1.50dh). Out in Aïn Diab, beyond the hotels on the Corniche, there is the Sindibad amusement park, with a huge cut-out of Sinbad the Sailor, plus pedalos, dodgems, roundabouts and slides.

Cinemas Cinéma Rif, Av des FAR at Rue Araibi Jilali (Rue Foucault); Leutitia, 19 Rue Tata, opposite *Hôtel Lausanne*; Rialto, Rue Mohammed el Quorri at Rue Salah Ben Bouchaib (see p.306), and the Ritz, opposite; Lynx, 55 Av Mers Sultan.

Consulates Algeria, 159 Bd Moulay Idriss I ☎0522 864175 (but the land border with Morocco is still closed); Ireland (Honorary Consul), Copragń Building, Bd Moulay Ismail, km 6-3, Route de Rabat, Aïn Sebaa ☎0522 660366; UK, 36 Rue de la Loire, Polo ☎0522 857400, ©british.consulate2@menara.ma; USA, 8 Bd Moulay Youssef ☎0522 264550.

Internet access Internet stations are surprisingly sparse in downtown Casablanca, with the largest concentration in the little streets around the pedestrianized part of Rue Prince Moulay Abdallah. Current options include: Soukaina.net, 38 Rue Mouftaker Abdelkader, near *Guynemer* hotel (daily 9am–10pm; 6dh/hr); G@.net, 29 Rue Mouftaker Abdelkader (daily 9am–10pm; 8dh per hr); LG Net, 81 Bd Mohammed V, first floor (Mon–Sat 9am–midnight, Sun 10am–midnight; 10dh per hr).

Laundry Lavomatic, 24 Rue Salah Ben Bouchaib, near Rialto Cinema.

Medical aid Dial ☎15 for emergency services or call SOS Médecin (☎0522 44 44 44) or SOS Médecins Maroc (☎0522 989898) for a doctor, or SAMU (☎0522 252525) for an ambulance. Clinics open round the clock for emergency treatment include: Clinique Badr, 35 Rue el Alloussi Bourgogne (☎0522 492380–84) and Clinique Yasmine, Bd Sidi Abderrahman Hay el Hana (☎0522 396960). English-speaking doctors include: Dr Mohammed Bennani, 45 Rue Atlas Maarif ☎0522 994799; Dr Alain Guidon, 4 Rue Mohammed Ben Ali (Rue Jean Jaurès), Gauthier ☎0522 267153. Large hotels should also have addresses for doctors. There's an all-night pharmacy (9pm–8am) in the Préfecture in Pl Mohammed V (☎0522 269491); details of other pharmacies open out of hours appear in the local press, or on lists displayed by all pharmacies. The US Consulate maintains a list of useful medical contacts online at ⓦcasablanca.usconsulate.gov/casablanca2.html. Dentists include Dr Hassan Belkady, 305 Bd Bir Anzarane ☎0522 36 10 39 and Dr Hicham Benhayoun, 3 Bd Mohammed Abdou ☎0522 273314.

Photographic supplies and developing Chez Faugra, 36 Av Mers Sultan; Studio Restinga, 27 Rue Tahar Sebti.

Police Main station is on Bd Brahim Roudani (☎0522 989865). For emergencies call ☎19.

Post office The main PTT is on Pl Mohammed V (Mon–Fri 8am–6pm & Sat 8am–noon). The most useful branch office is at 116 Bd Mohammed V, on the corner of Rue Chaouia (Rue Colbert) (Mon–Fri 8am–4.15pm, Sat 9am–noon).

Shopping Casablanca is not the place to buy crafts, but there are shops on Bd Félix Houphouët Boigny for last-minute purchases before you fly home; beware of *trafika* (phoney fossils for example), and expect to pay higher prices for lower quality than elsewhere in Morocco. The Exposition Nationale d'Artisanat at Av Hassan II with Rue Maarakat Ohoud (across from the *Hyatt Regency*), has crafts from around the country. Amazonite, 15 Rue Prince Moulay Abdallah has upmarket jewellery, objets d'art and antiques. For music, the Comptoir Marocain de Distribution de Disques at 26 Av Lalla Yacout has Moroccan and Middle Eastern sounds on CD and vinyl, but nothing recent. Supermarkets include Acima at 21 Rue Pierre Parent, at Pl Nicolas Paquet (Pl Georges Mercie) by the junction of Bd Mohammed V with Rue Mohammed Smiha, and on Bd Rahal el Meskini at the corner of Bd Lahcen Ouider.

Sports Casa is the best place in Morocco to see football; the city's rivals, Raja and Wydad (also known as WAC) both play at the Complexe Mohammed V on Rue Socrate in Maarif; check the local press for fixtures. The complex also houses an Olympic-size indoor swimming pool, and has facilities open to the public (☎0522 362309). The city also boasts a racecourse, the Hippodrome, at Anfa (alternate Sun in winter) and, beside it, a nine-hole Royal golf course (closed Mon; ☎0522 365355); there are eighteen-hole courses along the coast at Mohammedia (see p.103) and El Jadida (see p.316). As well as the beach clubs on the Corniche, and the Complexe Mohammed V, you can swim in the open-air Piscine Océanique in Aïn Sebaa. The pool at the *Hyatt Regency* hotel costs 200dh for non-residents.

Moving on

For destinations, frequencies and journey times, see pp.339–340.

CTM buses run from their city-centre terminal (☎0522 268061); some services to Fes are now non-stop.

All **private bus** firms operate out of the Ouled Ziane *gare routière,* 4km southeast of the city centre. To get there, you can take a petit taxi, or a #10 or #11 bus from Boulevard Mohammed V opposite the Marché Central. For Mohammedia, you can alternatively take local bus #900, which leaves from Rue Zaid ou Hmad, as do Mohammedia grands taxis.

Grands taxis for Fes, Meknes and Tangier operate from outside the Ouled Ziane *gare routière*. Those for Rabat leave from the Boulevard Hassan Seghir, very near the CTM terminal, but get sparse after midday, while the grand taxi station for El Jadida, Safi and Essaouira is on Boulevard Brahim Roudani in Maarif, some 2km from the city centre, served by #7 bus from Place des Nations Unies.

Trains for El Jadida, Mohammedia, Rabat and Kenitra are best caught at Casa Port station (☎0522 271837; currently in a temporary building as the terminal is being rebuilt), but for Marrakesh, Tangier, Meknes, Fes and Oujda, you'll need to get to Casa Voyageurs station (☎0522 243818), a long walk, a short taxi ride, or a hop on a #2 bus from Place des Nations Unies or Boulevard Mohammed V.

Casablanca's **airport** (☎0522 539040) is around 25km and 230dh from town by grand taxi (taking up to six people), or 35dh by train from Casa Voyageurs (hourly 6.07am–10.07pm; 35min) or Casa Port (hourly 6.30am–9.30pm, changing at Aïn Sebaa, 1hr 10min). All flights depart from terminal 2 other than Myair to Italy and Royal Air Maroc flights to Canada, Germany, the Netherlands, Italy and USA, which leave from terminal 3. There is a free shuttle service between the terminals. All airport bureaux de change claim they will exchange your unused Moroccan dirhams back into euros or US dollars, but don't count on it. You cannot use dirhams in duty-free shops. Both a pharmacy and post/fax bureau operate on the upper level between the departure and arrival areas.

South of Casablanca

The road and train line run side by side, south across the plains from **Casa** to **Marrakesh**. To the east lies the desolate and dusty phosphate-mining region, the Plateau des Phosphates. **SETTAT**, 60km south of Casablanca, is the only major town on the way to Marrakesh, the centre of Morocco's **cotton industry**, and has the nine-hole Settat University Golf Club (☎0523 400755).

Fifty kilometres west of Settat, halfway to El Jadida, is the impressive **Kasbah de Boulaoune** and the vineyards famous for **Gris de Boulaoune**, Morocco's best-known rosé, rarely visited due to lack of public transport, though possible by car or chartered grand taxi. The kasbah, high on a rocky outcrop above a great loop of the Oum er Rbia River, was commissioned by

Moulay Ismail in 1710 as a control post on the inland route from the Sahara to the Mediterranean, and appears today very much as it did in the eighteenth century. The high crenellated walls are complete with seven bastions, and the square minaret still stands, though the mosque below is not in such good shape.

Sidi Abderrahmane

Heading south from Casa on the R320 coast road, the first bay that you come to after passing through Aïn Diab, 10km from central Casa, has a beach facing the picturesque little island **Marabout of Sidi Abderrahmane**. The island is a tiny outcrop of rock, under 50m from the rock shore, from which it's possible to walk across at low tide, but non-Muslims may not enter the shrine, dedicated to Sidi Abderrahmane, a Sufi from Baghdad. It is visited by people suffering from mental illnesses (or their relatives), for whom the saint has supposedly curative powers. *A Ma Bretagne* (see p.311) overlooks the beach.

Azemmour

Despite its strategic site at the mouth of the great Oum er Rbia river, **AZEMMOUR** has always been a backwater, and sees fewer tourists than any other Moroccan coastal town, making it a quiet, rather sedate place to visit, and perhaps stay in one of the riads in its whitewashed clifftop Medina.

Practicalities

The town is easily reached from El Jadida by **bus** (#101 from the roundabout 200m south of the bus station) or **grand taxi** (from Rue Abdelmoumen el Mouahidi by the bus station). It's also served by seven daily **trains** from Casa Voyageurs and El Jadida, though the station is inconveniently located 2km out of town, on the far side of the N1.

Once in town, getting your bearings is pretty straightforward. The main thoroughfare is **Avenue Mohammed V**, which leads to the main square, **Place du Souk**, with the **Medina** straight ahead.

The Medina has two magical little six-room **riads**. *L'Oum Errebia* at 25 Derb Chtouka (ⓣ0523 347071, ⓦwww.azemmour-hotel.com; BB ❻), once the kitchen and servant quarters for the town's *caid*, has been renovated with a distinctly modern touch, and bright, abstract paintings adorning almost every spare bit of wall space. The river view from the terrace is unequalled. *Riad Azama*, 17 Derb Ben Tahar (ⓣ0523 347516, ⓦwww.riadazama.com; BB ❺), has been restored with a more traditional feel. Meals can be taken on the terrace overlooking the medina or in the intricately decorated dining, or *douiria*, room. Outside the Medina is the basic *Hôtel de la Poste* at 78 Av Mohammed V, on Place du Souk (ⓣ0523 357702; ❶). The town also has several **café-restaurants**, best of which is the *Café el Manzeh* on Place du Souk. There are also two café-restaurants down at the beach (see p.316).

The Medina

The Portuguese remained in Azemmour long enough to build a circuit of walls, directly above the banks of the river and dramatically extended by the white **Medina**. The best view of all this – and it is impressive – is from across the river, on the way out of town towards Casablanca.

To look round the Medina, make your way to Place du Souk, on the landward side of the ramparts, where you will see a sixteenth-century **gate** with an unusual, European-style, semicircular arch. Through it extends the old **kasbah**

– largely in ruins but safe enough to visit. If you wait around, the local *gardien* will probably arrive, open things up and show you round; if he doesn't turn up, you might find him by asking at the cafés. Once inside the ruins, you can follow the parapet wall round the ramparts, with views of the river and the gardens, including henna orchards, along its edge. You'll also be shown **Dar el Baroud** (The House of Powder), a large tower built over the ruins of an old gunpowder store; note also the ruined Gothic window.

The old **Mellah** – Azzemour had a substantial Jewish population until the 1960s – lies beyond the kasbah at the northern end of the Medina. Here, beside ramparts overlooking the Oum er Rbia, you will be shown the old town synagogue which is still well maintained and visited occasionally by practising Jews from Casablanca and El Jadida. It's cared for by a local family and you can – for an additional tip – look inside to see the tomb of Rabbi Abrahim Moul Niss, a shrine for Jewish pilgrims and the focus of an August moussem.

Haouzia beach

The river currents at Azemmour are notoriously dangerous, but there's a nice stretch of **beach** half an hour's walk through the eucalyptus trees beyond the town. If you go by road, it's signposted to the "Balnéaire du Haouzia", a small complex of cabins and camping occupying part of the sands. There are two **restaurants** here: *La Perle* (Ⓣ0523 347905), which is good but fairly expensive (around 150dh per person), serving paella and other fish dishes; and the newer *Cap Blanc* (Ⓣ0523 357000), with similar fare. In summer, you can camp in the private complex; in winter, you can safely camp alongside the restaurants.

For **birdwatchers**, the scrub dunes around the mouth of the river should prove rewarding territory.

El Jadida Royal Golf Club

The coast between Azemmour and El Jadida is showing signs of development, the most ambitious complex being the **El Jadida Royal Golf Club** (Ⓣ0523 352251), beside the sea, 10km from Azemmour and 7km from El Jadida. The eighteen-hole golf course was designed by the American Cabell B. Robinson and is one of the most attractive in Morocco, with mimosa, sand dunes, a large lake and, across the bay, the skyline of El Jadida. Alongside is the four-star *Sofitel Royal Golf Hôtel* (Ⓣ0523 379100, Ⓦwww.sofitel.com; ❽) set among beautiful gardens and with all mod cons including two restaurants, a swimming pool and tennis court.

El Jadida and around

EL JADIDA is a stylish and beautiful town, retaining the lanes and ramparts of an old Portuguese Medina. It was known as Mazagan under the Portuguese, who held it from 1506 until 1769. The city was taken from the Portuguese by Sultan Sidi Mohammed Ben Abdallah and then in the nineteenth century was renamed El Jadida – "The New" – after being resettled, partly with Jews from Azemmour, by Sultan Abd er Rahman. Under the French, it grew into a quite sizeable administrative centre and a popular beach resort.

Moroccans from Casablanca and Marrakesh, even Tangier or Fes, come down to the beach here in summer; when the bars are crowded, there's an almost frenetic evening promenade and – as in Casa – Moroccan women are visible and active participants.

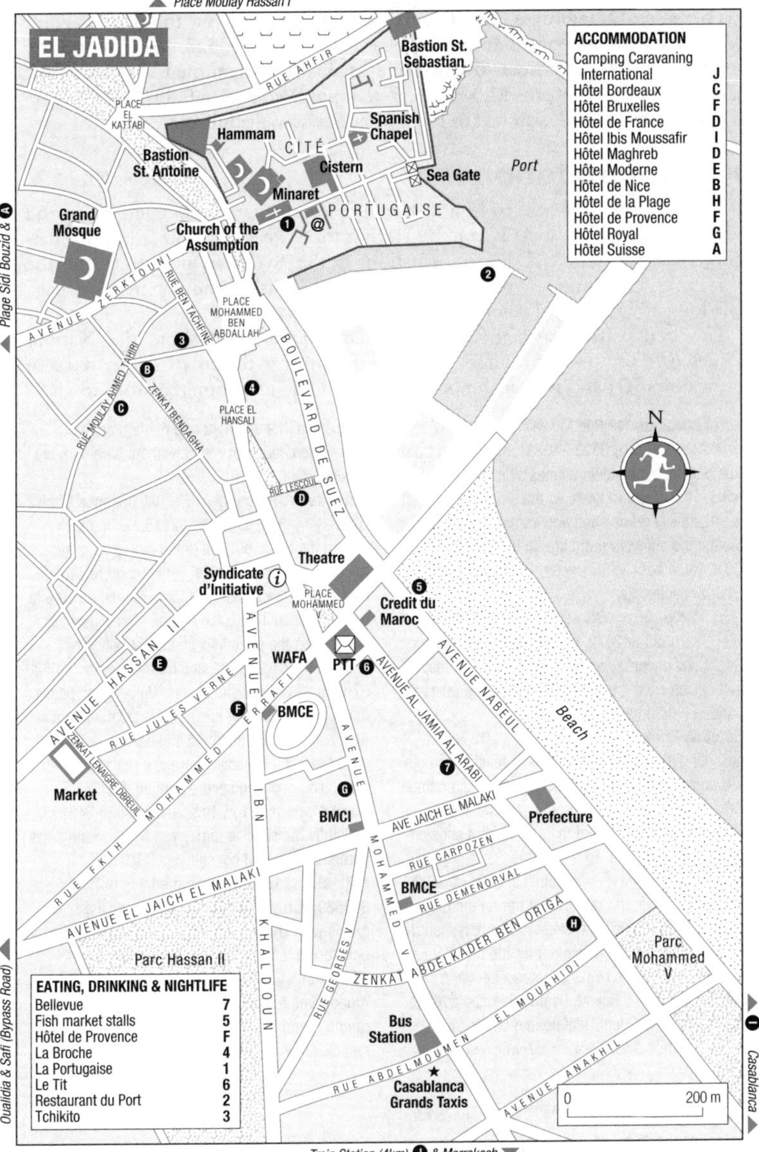

Arrival and information

The **bus station** is at the southern end of town, from where it's a fifteen-minute walk to the Medina or to most hotels. The **train** station is 4km south of town on the Marrakesh road (N1); petits taxis are usually available (about 15dh). **Grands taxis** from Casa drop you by the bus station, while those from Oualidia leave you by the lighthouse, about 1km up the Oualidia road from the city centre.

There's a **Délégation de Tourisme** east of town at the Rond Point Marrakech roundabout (Mon–Fri 8.30am–4.30pm; ⓣ0523 344788) and the more accessible **Syndicat d'Initiative** at 33 Pl Mohammed V (Mon, Tues, Thurs, Fri & Sat 9.30am–12.30pm & 3–6.30pm, Wed & Sun 9.30am–12.30pm). There's also a useful website (in French) at ⓦwww.eljadida.ma.

Accommodation

Rooms can be very hard to find in summer, so prices are higher and it's a good idea to book in advance. If you are staying for a week or more, there are flats and villas for rent: ask for information at the Syndicat, or check out the Locations Saisonnières website, with both English- and French-language versions, at ⓦwww.jadidalocations.com.

The **campsite**, *Camping Caravaning International*, on Avenue des Nations Unies (ⓣ0523 342755), offers moderate facilities with lots of shade, and also bungalows (❷) and is near the beach, but a couple of kilometres from town.

Hôtel Bordeaux 47 Rue Moulay Ahmed Tahiri ⓣ0523 373921, ⓕ0523 340691, signposted from Rue Ben Tachfine, down a small side street. An old hotel – the oldest in town, so the patron claims – it is attractively refurbished and immaculately clean, though the showers (5dh) are on the corridor. Good-value but slightly pricier than some of the other cheapies. ❷

Hôtel Bruxelles 40 Av Ibn Khaldoun ⓣ0523 342072, next to *Hôtel de Provence*. Bright and cheerful, with pleasant, clean rooms, and balconies at the front. For drivers, the guarded parking (10dh) here is a big plus. ❷

Hôtel de France/Hôtel Maghreb 12/16 Rue Lescoul ⓣ0523 342181. This is in reality one hotel – though with two entrances, stairways and names. Great value and creaking with character, it's old and roomy, with views of the sea and hot showers on the landing (5dh). ❶

Hôtel de la Plage 3 Av al Jamia al Arabi ⓣ0523 342648. Despite the rather grim bar on the ground floor, this is friendly, with clean rooms and shared bathroom facilities. Convenient for the bus station, and the *patron* also owns the campsite. ❷

Hôtel de Nice 15 Rue Mohammed Smiha ⓣ0523 352272. Off Rue Ben Tachfine and on the same street as the *Tchikito restaurant*, which is well signposted. Not as bright and modern as the nearby *Bordeaux*, but rooms without bathroom are cheaper. ❷

Hôtel de Provence 42 Av Fqih Mohammed Errafi ⓣ0523 342347, ⓕ0523 352115. Getting a bit long in the tooth, but this grand old dame is still the best mid-range choice, with a good restaurant, a garden for breakfast, and large rooms. Be sure to reserve ahead, particularly in the high season; in low season the price falls by almost half. ❹

Hôtel Ibis Moussafir Place Nour el Kamar ⓣ0523 379500, ⓦwww.ibishotel.com. Unlike most hotels in this chain, this one has a prime location right on the beach. Rooms have a/c and heating, and two are wheelchair-friendly. There is a restaurant, bar, swimming pool and secure parking. BB ❻

Hôtel Moderne 31 Av Hassan II ⓣ0523 343133. A slightly ramshackle family-run hotel, with a small garden and shared hot showers. ❷

Hôtel Royal 108 Av Mohammed V ⓣ0523 342839, ⓔroyal_hotel@menara.com. Large, airy rooms with erratic plumbing, a garden and lively bar. Convenient for the bus station. ❷

Hôtel Suisse 175 Av Zerktouni ⓣ0523 342816. A good-value cheapie, small and friendly, with rooms round a patio; some have en-suite facilities. ❷

The Cité Portugaise

El Jadida's **Medina** is the most European-looking in Morocco: a quiet, walled and bastioned seaside village, with a handful of churches. It was founded by the Portuguese in 1513, and retained by them until 1769, and it is still popularly known as the **Cité Portugaise**. As they withdrew, the Portuguese blew up several of the churches and other important buildings. The Moors who settled here after the Portuguese withdrawal tended to live outside the walls. Budgett Meakin, writing in the 1890s (see p.603), found an "extensive native settlement" spreading back from the harbour, while European merchants had re-established

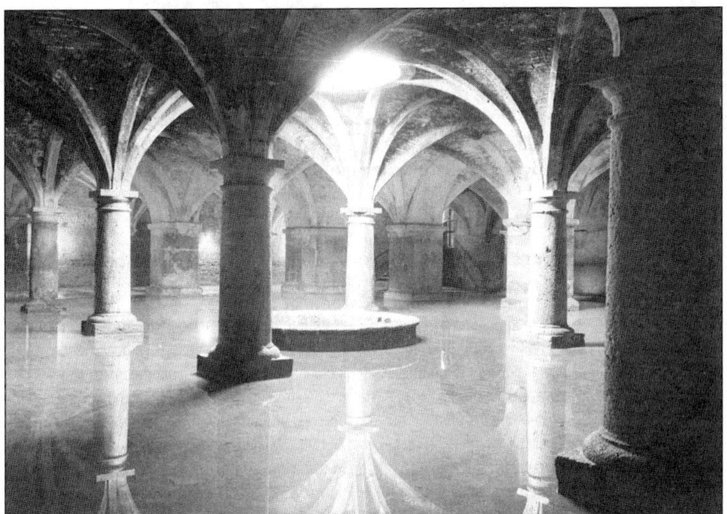

▲ Inside the Portuguese Cistern, El Jadida

themselves in the "clean, prosperous and well-lighted streets" of the Medina. As in all the open ports on this coast, there was also an important Jewish community handling the trade with Marrakesh; uniquely, old Mazagan had no separate Jewish Mellah.

The beautiful old **Portuguese Cistern** (daily 9am–1pm & 3–6pm, open until 7.30pm in summer; 10dh) is a subterranean vault that mirrors its roof and pillars in a shallow film of water covering the floor. It is midway along the Medina's main street, Rua Carreira (now renamed Rue Mohammed Ali Bahbai), and was used to startling effect in Orson Welles's film of *Othello*; he staged a riot here and filmed it from within and above. It also featured in a Moroccan TV ad for Samar coffee and locals associate it with that, rather than Orson Welles.

At the entrance to the cistern there is a useful model of the Cité Portugaise, and if you continue up Rua Carreira you'll come to its most prominent feature – the **Sea Gate** (Bab el Bahr), the original gate onto the port. From here you can climb onto the ramparts (daily 9am–6.30pm; free), and walk all the way round and onto all the bastions, should you so desire. By Bastion St Sebastian, the restored former **synagogue** has an interesting crescent and Star of David on its back wall. The Christian churches and chapels of the Portuguese City are generally closed; but, if you have time, you can look for the small **Spanish chapel**, now closed and bricked up bar a small section used as a shop. More impressive is the seventeenth-century Portuguese **Church of the Assumption** by the entrance to the Cité Portugaise, which was restored and used as a cultural centre, but is now empty. The minaret of the **Grand Mosque** was once a five-sided watchtower or lighthouse, and is said to be the only pentagonal minaret in Islam.

The beaches

El Jadida's town **beach** spreads northeast from the *cité* and port, well beyond the length of the town. It's a popular strip, though from time to time polluted by the ships in port. Three kilometres further north along the coastal road, past the **Phare Sidi Ouafi** (lighthouse), is a broader strip of sand where Moroccan families set up tents for the summer. Good swimming is to be had and there are makeshift beach cafés in the summer.

Plage Sidi Bouzid, 2km southwest, is more developed, flanked by some fancy villas and with a few restaurants well-known for their seafood, *Le Requin Bleu* (Ⓣ0523 348067, Ⓦwww.requinbleu.com) and (same management, phone and website) *l'Alligator*. The beach can be reached on bus #2 from alongside Place Mohammed Ben Abdallah, or by grand taxi.

Eating and drinking

Many hotels have **bars** – try the lively one at *Hôtel de la Plage*, *Hôtel de Provence*'s pleasant bar or *Le Tit*, 2 Av Al Jamia el Arabi.

Bellevue 5th floor, 46 Av Al Jamia Al Arabi. French cuisine in a stylish setting, with a 150dh set menu, but in case of a fire or power cut, you're on the fifth floor, and the only way out, apparently, is by very slow elevator. Daily noon–3pm & 6pm–midnight. Licensed. Expensive.

Fish market stalls Av Nabeul. Freshly caught, freshly grilled sardines served with enough bread to make a meal of it. Cheap.

La Broche 46 Pl el Hansali. Offers the usual meat or chicken dishes and omelettes. The menu lists all kind of exciting-sounding things (rabbit in mustard sauce, squid stuffed with fish), but that's just to pull in the punters – don't expect them to actually be available. Daily 11.30am–3.30pm & 7–11pm. Moderate.

La Portugaise Rua Carreira (Rue Mohammed Ali Bahbai), Cité Portugaise. A very pleasant little restaurant with red-and-white check tablecloths, serving French rather than Portuguese dishes, including prawn bisque, sole meunière and chocolate mousse. The food is good but the portions are not huge. Daily noon–3.30pm & 7–11pm. Moderate.

Restaurant du Port at the northern end of the port Ⓣ0523 342579. This first-floor restaurant in an unprepossessing building has a great view of the sea and serves good and plentiful seafood. Mon–Sat 9am–3.30pm & 7–11pm, Sun 9am–3.30pm. Moderate to expensive.

Tchikito Rue Mohammed Smiha. A hole-in-the-wall (and quite *chiquito*) fish restaurant, with generous helpings at low prices, decorated with photos of the proprietor, the royal family and saints' tombs, and some koranic calligraphy. Cheap.

Listings

Airlines Royal Air Maroc, Marhaba Centre, Av Mohammed VI (at Av el Jaich el Malaki) Ⓣ0523 379300.

Banks Plenty around town, including several branches of BMCE with ATMs (marked on the p.317 map). There's also a Currency Exchange Point (daily 8am–10pm) opposite the Syndicat d'Initiative.

Car rental Local agencies include Narjisscar, shop 2, Central Market, N° 2, Zenkat Le Maigre du Breuil (Aristide Briand) Ⓣ0523 340261, Ⓔnarjisscarloc@menara.ma.

Car spares and repairs Mechanics' workshops are grouped behind the bus station, on and around Rue Abdelmoumen el Mouahidi, with tyre changers and spare parts shops to its north and south on Av Mohammed V.

Hammam There's one in the Cité Portugaise at 1 Rue No. 45 (enter the double gate, turn left along Rua do Arco and it's 50m along on your right), open 7.30am–8pm with separate entrances for women and men.

Internet access Mellah Net, 11 Rue No. 11, off Rua Carreira, Cité Portugaise (daily 10am–10pm; 5dh per hr); Akil Tec, 1st floor, 62 Pl el Hansali (daily 9am–10pm; 6dh per hr).

Post office The main PTT is on Pl Mohammed V (Mon–Fri 8am–6pm, Sat 8am–noon).

Souk A Wednesday souk takes place by the lighthouse northwest of town.

Travel agency Fedala Voyages, Av des FAR Ⓣ0523 343426.

Moulay Abdallah and Ribat Tit-n-Fitr

MOULAY ABDALLAH (also called Tit), 11km south of El Jadida on the R301 coast road, is a tiny fishing village, dominated by a large *zaouia* complex and partially enclosed by a circuit of ruined walls. An important **moussem** in late August attracts thousands of devotees – and almost as many horses in the parades and *fantasias*.

The village walls span the site of a twelfth-century **ribat**, or fortified monastery, known as **Ribat Tit-n-Fitr**, which was built as a base for Sufi mystics, and to defend the coast from a possible Norman invasion – a real threat at the time, the Normans having launched attacks on Tunisia. Today, there is little to see, though the minaret of the modern **zaouia** (prominent and white-washed) is Almohad; behind it, through the graveyard, a second, isolated minaret is thought to be even older. If so, then it is the only one surviving from the Almoravid era – a claim considerably more impressive than its simple, block-like appearance might suggest.

Sidi Abed and Sidi Moussa

The first good beach beyond Cap Blanc is at the village of **SIDI ABED**. Two kilometres north of the village, on the seaward side, *Le Relais* (Ⓣ0523 345498; ❺) is an auberge and restaurant (year-round, except for Ramadan), with its own small beach, worth a stopover if only to enjoy a mint tea and the view from the terrace.

The coast hereabouts is an alternation of sandy beach and rocky outcrops, and past **SIDI MOUSSA**, 36km from El Jadida, it's backed by huge dunes, then, towards Oualidia, cut off by a long expanse of salt marshland. From here on south, for the next 70km or so, birdwatchers are in for a treat (see box below) but there's also an estuary-like lagoon, a beach and a very pleasant **hotel**, the *Villa la Brise* (Ⓣ0523 346917; ❸), with French cooking, a bar and a swimming pool that's full in summer. It's a popular base for fishing parties.

Oualidia

OUALIDIA, 78km from El Jadida, is a stunningly picturesque little resort – a fishing port and lagoon beach, flanked by a kasbah and a royal villa. The **kasbah** is seventeenth century, built under the Saadian Sultan el Oualid (after whom the village is named) as a counterweight and alternative to Portuguese-held El Jadida. Until Sultan Sidi Mohammed took El Jadida, the lagoon made an excellent harbour and, as late as 1875, a French geographer thought that "by a little dredging the place would again become the safest shipping station on the whole Moroccan seaboard". The **royal villa**, now empty, was built for Mohammed V, who celebrated many birthdays and other family events here.

Today, most Moroccans know Oualidia for its **Japanese oysters**; Morocco's first oyster farm was launched here in 1957 and nowadays it harvests some 200 tonnes a year, mostly sold locally. But the town really deserves to be better known as a resort: its beach is excellent for surfing and windsurfing, and

Bird habitats around Oualidia

The 70km of coast between Sidi Moussa (36km south of El Jadida) and Cap Beddouza (34km south of Oualidia) is one of the richest **birdlife habitats** in Morocco. The coastal wetlands, sands and saltpans, the jagged reefs, and the lagoons of Sidi Moussa and Oualidia shelter a huge range of species – flamingos, avocets, stilts, godwits, storks, terns, egrets, warblers and many small waders. Numerous country-side species come in, too; golden oriole and hoopoe have been recorded, and flocks of shearwaters are often to be seen not far offshore. The best watching locations are the two **lagoons** and the rocky headland at **Cap Beddouza**.

swimming is safe and easy thanks to the shielded lagoon. The atmosphere for most of the year is very relaxed, aside from August when the place is jam-packed with Moroccan holidaymakers.

Arrival and information

Buses and collective **grands taxis** stop across the street near the road that leads down to the beach. There's one **bank** in town, the Banque Populaire, with an ATM. A **post office** with a **pharmacy**, and a **doctor's surgery** are next door. The lagoon and beach are both a ten-minute downhill walk from the main road.

Accommodation

The **campsite** (Ⓣ0523 366556; open all year but very full in August) is off the beach, opposite *Motel-Restaurant à l'Araignée Gourmande*. The hotels down by the lagoon are mostly very good too, and offer excellent seafood meals. Up on the main road, *Hôtel Restaurant Thalassa* has set menus for 60dh, and 2km north of town, *Ostrea II* (run by the same people as *Ostrea* in Casablanca; see p.311) serves and sells oysters.

Hôtel Hippocampe Ⓣ0523 366108, Ⓔhotelhippocampe@hotmail.com. A delightful place, halfway up the slope from the lagoon to the village at the top. Immaculate rooms off a flower-filled garden and steps down to a "private" beach; also has a pool and a good restaurant, but in high season guests have to take half-board. HB ❽

L'Initiale Hôtel Restaurant Oualidia Plage Ⓣ0523 366246. A family-run place that's the last along the beach road, with a mixture of food on offer in the restaurant. Most of the six rooms have a sea view. Booking advisable. BB ❺

Motel-Restaurant à l'Araignée Gourmande Ⓣ0523 366144. This stands alongside the lagoon beach, and offers well-kept rooms and an excellent fish restaurant with set menus starting at 135dh, or a lobster set menu for 300dh. BB ❹

Kasbah Gharbia

The Doukkala plains, inland from the El Jadida–Safi coast have long been a fertile and fought-over region, and there are scattered forts and kasbahs at several villages. One of the most interesting and accessible is at **GHARBIA**, 20km from Oualidia on a road that takes you across an undulating limestone plateau. The **kasbah** here is a vast enclosure, four kilometres long on each side, bastioned at intervals, and with a gate at each point of the compass, giving onto roads to Oualidia, Safi, El Jadida and Marrakesh: a strategic site. Within, a few houses remain in use and there's a large white house in the centre, occupied by the *caid* in the days of the Protectorate.

Cap Beddouza and Lalla Fatna

South of Oualidia, the road climbs a little inland and above the sea, which is hidden from view by sand dunes. At **Cap Beddouza**, the rocky headland gives way intermittently to sandy beaches, sheltered by cliffs. The best of the cliff-sheltered beaches is **Lalla Fatna**, 15km north of Safi (connected by local bus #10 or #15), a steep two-kilometre descent from the road, with a **koubba**, but little else, so bring provisions; if camping be sure to pitch your tent far enough back from the tides. There is a **moussem** at the *koubba* on the thirteenth of Shaban (the month before Ramadan).

Beyond Cap Safi, you pass **Sidi Bouzid beach** – Safi's local strand – where on November 8, 1942, American troops under General Patton landed as the southernmost thrust of *Operation Torch* (see box, p.304), the Vichy French position offering little resistance. **Hotels** here include the sprawling *Hôtel Atlantique Panorama* (ⓣ0524 668490; ❺), which has a huge swimming pool overlooking the sea. Good local **restaurants** include *La Corniche* and *Le Refuge*, both on the Route de Sidi Bouzid.

Safi and around

SAFI, with an old **Medina** in its centre, walled and turreted by the Portuguese, has a strong industrial-artisan tradition, with a whole quarter devoted to **pottery workshops**. These have a virtual monopoly on the green, heavily glazed roof tiles used on palaces and mosques, as well as providing Morocco's main pottery exports, in the form of bowls, plates and garden pots. For a beach escape, local buses #10 and #15 run to **Lalla Fatna** and **Cap Beddouza** (see opposite) from the Place de l'Indépendance. In summer there are also local buses to **Souira Kedima** (see p.328).

Arrival, orientation and information

Buses and shared **grands taxis** arrive at the bus station, around 1.5km south of the Medina. The **train station** – Safi has two trains a day to and from Benguerir, where they connect for Marrakesh and Casa – is a similar distance. The town has two main squares, **Place de l'Indépendance**, just south of the Medina, or **Place Mohammed V** on the higher ground (known by the French as the *Plateau*). Most **banks** are around Place de l'Indépendance, while **internet** offices include Club Internet at 29 Rue du R'bat (daily 8.30am–midnight; 5dh per hr), and Lascala opposite the post office on Avenue Sidi Mohammed Abdallah (daily 8am–midnight), which is also a pool hall and café, and a great place to meet young Moroccans. Two nearby cafés – *Café Plateau* and *Glacier Assala* – have free wi-fi. Rue du R'bat becomes a bustling **street market** in the late afternoon and evening.

The ONMT **tourist office** is south of the bus station at 26 Rue Imam Malik (Mon–Fri 8.30am–4.30pm; ⓣ0524 624453). Safi also has an information website, mostly in French but with some English, at ⓦwww.safi-ville.com.

Accommodation

The **campsite**, *Camping International Safi*, is 2km north of town, signposted to the right of the road to Oualidia (ⓣ0524 463816; summer only). Spacious and well shaded, with a shop, pool and usual facilities, it has some great views over the town and towards the sea and is 1km from the beach at Sidi Bouzid.

Golden Tulip Farah Safi (formerly Hôtel CMKD) Av Zerktouni ⓣ0524 464299, ⓦwww.goldentulipfarahsafi.com. Supposedly a five-star; rooms are spacious, with all mod cons, and there are three restaurants, two bars, a nightclub, secure parking and commanding views over the city. ❻

Hôtel Anis Corner of Rue du R'bat and Rue de la Falaise ⓣ0524 364078. Cheerless but reasonably central place with en-suite facilities and a few "apartment" suites. Also has car parking. ❸

Hôtel Assif Av de la Liberté ⓣ0524 622940, ⓦwww.hotel-assif.ma. The best mid-range hotel, with small but homely rooms, some (for not very much more) with a/c, heating and balcony, and there's an underground car park and a good restaurant. ❸

Hôtel Atlantide Rue Chaouki ⓣ0524 462160, ⓔimsa-atlantide@menara.com. Built in 1919, this place still has quite a bit of character, with views over the town from the balconies, a swimming pool and good restaurant. ❸

Hôtel de l'Avenir 1 Impasse de la Mer ⓣ0524 131446. The best of a trio of cheap hotels tucked just inside the Medina (the *Essaouira* and *Paris* are

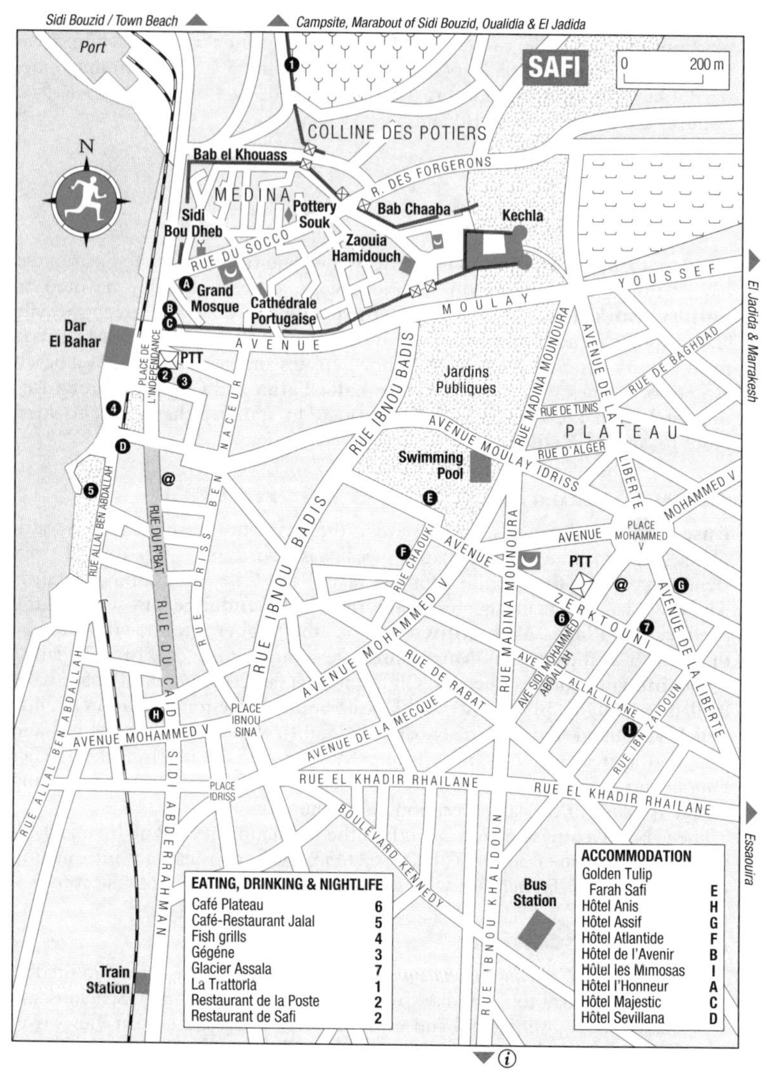

tolerable fall-backs). Hot showers (7dh) on the first floor, grand views of the sea from some rooms and a busy café downstairs. ❷

Hôtel les Mimosas Rue Ibn Zaidoun ⓣ0524 623208, ⓕ0524 625955. An old hotel, now moved into a new wing, with good-size rooms, the *Golden Fish* disco/nightclub (10pm–4am) and a bar across the street. It is good value for money, but not central. ❸

Hôtel l'Honneur (Foundouq esh Shraf) 56 Pl Douane (no phone). At the beginning of Rue du Socco, a homely little place with plain but clean rooms around a central patio (most windows only opening inward, the top floor gets most light). Shared showers, and hot water if you're lucky. ❷

Hôtel Majestic Place de l'Indépendance ⓣ0524 464011, ⓕ0524 462490. Fine views of the Dar el Behar and the sea, from fairly spacious, clean and pleasant rooms, and shared hot showers. Marginally the best of the cheapies. ❷

Hôtel Sevillana 1 Rue Ben Hassan ⓣ0524 462391. The blue-painted rooms are clean but a bit cramped, with shared hot showers (7dh), and a terrace with views over the Medina. ❶

Dar el Bahar, Kechla and the Medina

The **Dar el Bahar**, or Château de la Mer (daily 8.30am–noon & 2.30–6pm; 10dh), is the main remnant of Safi's 1508–41 Portuguese occupation. Built in the Manueline style of the day as the governor's residence, it was later a fortress and a prison. Within, you can see the old prison cells at the foot of a spiral staircase to the ramparts, where a line of Dutch and Spanish cannon is ranged pointing out to sea.

The old Medina walls climb north, enclosing the Medina, to link with another and larger fortress known as the **Kechla**, also Portuguese in origin, and entered from the east side, outside the Medina walls. Until 1990 it housed the town's prison, but is now the National Ceramics Museum (Mon–Fri 8.30am–noon & 2.30–6pm, Sat & Sun 8.30am–6pm; 10dh ⓣ0524 463895) with a not too exciting collection of local ceramics, plus cannons (British this time), garden courtyards and Portuguese coats-of-arms.

Another relic of the Portuguese is the **Cathédrale Portugaise** in the Medina (daily 8.30am–noon & 2.30–6pm; 10dh), actually just the choir gallery of what was to be the cathedral, left uncompleted when the Portuguese withdrew, and again adorned with Manueline motifs. It's most easily found by heading up the Rue du Socco – the Medina's main street – for about 100m, until it opens out a little; there on your right, by the entrance to the Grand Mosque, a sign painted on the wall points the way through a small doorway. Beyond here, Rue du Socco leads uphill past a series of **souks** (markets) selling food and domestic-goods, to the old city gate of **Bab Chaaba** and, through it, to the Colline des Potiers. On the way, you pass (on your left) the **Souk de Poterie**. If you are looking to buy goods, you are likely to find better pieces here than in the showrooms at the foot of the Colline des Potiers itself.

If you are Muslim, you can enter two important Sufi shrines in the Medina: the **Marabout Sidi Bou Dheb** (at the bottom end of Rue du Socco) and the **Zaouia of Hamidouch** (near the Kechla). Sidi Bou Dheb is perhaps the best-known Sufi saint in Morocco and both his *marabout* and the Hamdouchia *zaouia* host **moussems** (held in May in recent years) attended by their respective brotherhoods; these feature music, dervish-type dancing and, often, trance-induced self-mutilation with hatchets and knives.

Colline des Potiers

The **Colline des Potiers** (potters' quarter) sprawls above the Medina, with its dozens of whitewashed beehive-kilns and chimneys. The processes here remain traditional – electricity and gas have made scarcely an inroad on the tamarisk-fired kilns – and the quarter is worth at least the time it takes to wander up the new concrete steps and pathways. At the foot of the hillside is a street of

And the sardines?

Safi's famed **sardines** are caught in the deeper waters of the Atlantic from Boujdour in the south to Safi in the north. There are around five hundred 18-to 20-metre wooden trawlers in the town fleet and you can still see them being made in the boatyards at Safi, Essaouira and Agadir. The fleet lands 350,000 tonnes of sardines annually and most of them are canned in Safi. Increasingly, those caught further south are landed at the nearest port and brought to Safi in refrigerated trucks. Most of the tins get sold abroad – Morocco being the **world's largest exporter** of sardines.

showrooms. The products on display are of interest, but you are as likely to see U-bends for toilets being fired here as anything else. Unofficial guides may hustle you for business (they'll want you to buy stuff so that they can get a commission), and while the kilns are easily located without assistance, some guides may take you to more remote kilns and make it easier to take photographs and ask questions. If you do accept an offer of a guided "tour" make sure you agree a price beforehand (perhaps 10dh per person) and don't be intimidated into buying anything.

Eating

The hotels *Assif*, *Atlantide* and *Golden Tulip Farah Safi* have good restaurants, as does the city's beach, Plage Sidi Bouzid (see p.323).

Café-Restaurant Jalal Rue Allal ben Abdallah. A café with a children's play area (making it handy for families) and a terrace overlooking the sea, serving tea, coffee and Moroccan staples (tajines and brochettes) as well as pizzas and burgers. Moderate.

Fish grills sea front near Dar el Bahar. A row of small restaurants serving grilled or fried fresh fish. Cheap.

Gégéne 8 Rue de la Marine, just off Pl de l'Indépendance ☎0524 463369. A lively restaurant with separate bar and a limited but satisfying menu. Moderate.

La Trattoria 2 Route de l'Aouinate ☎0524 463176 or 620959. Near the Délégation des Pêches Maritime de Safi, follow the signs to *La Trattoria*. Upmarket and very pleasant Italian restaurant. Moderate to expensive.

Restaurant de la Poste 40 Pl de l'Indépendance. The upstairs restaurant serves French cuisine, particularly fish and seafood (not to mention chocolate mousse). Licensed. Mon–Sat noon–3pm & 8.30–11pm. Moderate.

Restaurant de Safi 3 Rue de la Marine, next to *Gégéne*. Friendly little restaurant serving up soup, brochettes and grilled meat or fish. Cheap.

Safi to Essaouira

Buses from **Safi to Essaouira** take the inland N1, but the R301 coast road passes **Souira Kedima**, a fine beach around 30km south of Safi used by people from Safi and Marrakesh on summer holidays. Nearby, on a windswept headland, there is an old Portuguese fortress known as **Agouz**. A little beyond Souria Kedima, a new bridge allows you to cross the Oued Tensift to reach, along a stretch of good but sandy *piste*, the large and isolated fortress of **Kasbah Hamidouch**, commissioned by Moulay Ismail to control the mouth of the Tensift. South of the kasbah, a new and quite **scenic road** (R301) heads off along the coast towards Essaouira via **Cap Hadid**.

Essaouira (Mogador)

ESSAOUIRA is by popular acclaim Morocco's most likeable resort: an eighteenth-century town, enclosed by medieval-looking battlements. Its whitewashed and blue-shuttered houses and colonnades, wood workshops and art galleries, boat-builders and sardine fishermen and feathery Norfolk Island pines, which only thrive in a pollution-free atmosphere, all provide a colourful and very pleasant backdrop to the beach. Many of the foreign tourists making their own way to Essaouira are drawn by the wind, known locally as the *alizee*, which in spring and summer can be a bit remorseless for sunbathing but creates much-sought-after waves for **windsurfing** and, increasingly, **kitesurfing**. The same winds make Essaouira pretty terrible for **surfing** – those in the know head down the coast to Taghazout (see p.499)

Some history

A series of forts were built here from the fifteenth century but it was only in the 1760s that the town was established and the present circuit of walls constructed. It was known to Europeans as **Mogador**, possibly from the prominent *koubba* of Sidi Mgdoul, used for navigating entry to the bay. Less likely is the legend that the town's patron saint was a Scotsman named McDougal who was shipwrecked here in the fourteenth century. To Moroccans it was known as Seurah, from the Berber "little picture".

The walls were commissioned by sultan **Sidi Mohammed Ben Abdallah**, and carried out by a French military architect, Theodore Cornut, which explains the town's unique blend of Moroccan Medina and French grid layout. The original intention was to provide a military port, as Agadir was in revolt at the time and Sultan Mohammed Ben Abdallah needed a local base. Soon, however, commercial concerns gained pre-eminence. During the nineteenth century, Mogador was the only Moroccan port south of Tangier that was open to European trade, and it prospered greatly from the privilege. Drawn by protected trade status, and a harbour free from customs duties, British merchants settled in the kasbah quarter, and a large Jewish community in the Mellah, within the northeast ramparts.

Decline set in during the French Protectorate, with Marshal Lyautey's promotion of Casablanca. Anecdote has it that he arrived in Essaouira on a Saturday when the Jewish community was at prayer; he cast a single glance at the deserted streets and decided to shift to the port of Casablanca further up the coast. The decline was accelerated after independence, by the exodus of the Jewish community. These days, however, the town is very much back on its feet, as a fishing port, market town and ever-more-popular resort. Orson Welles' 1952 film **Othello** was largely shot in Essaouira, and opens with a tremendous panning shot of the Essaouira ramparts, where Welles placed a scene-setting "punishment" of Iago, suspended above the sea and rocks in a metal cage.

Arrival

CTM and private **buses** arrive on the outskirts of the town, about 500m north of Bab Doukkala. Especially at night, it's worth taking a petit taxi into town (about 7dh to Bab es Sebaa). Taxis cannot enter the Medina city walls, but you can hire one of the barrow boys who are usually on hand to meet arriving buses and wheel your luggage to a hotel for you – bargain for the price (about 20dh). **Supratours** buses from Agadir and Marrakesh arrive and depart from their office at the end of a short cul de sac by the south bastion (off Av Lalla Aicha).

Grands taxis operate from a yard by the bus station. There is a **petit taxi rank** by the car park at the southern end of Avenue Oqba Ibn Nafia, and taxis serving the Medina also run to and from Bab es Sebaa and Bab Doukkala.

If you are driving, it's worth making use of the **car parking** space, guarded round the clock (20dh for 24hr) in front of the harbour offices, south of Place Prince Moulay el Hassan.

The best way into town from the **airport**, 15km south of town, is by grand taxi (200dh for up to six passengers). If you're on a really tight budget, you can take local bus #2 for 6dh (8 daily; 1hr). A new terminal building is being built but at present there is no ATM or bureau de change, or much else for that matter, and it is wise to call ahead and have your hotel send a taxi, or you may find there are none around when you arrive.

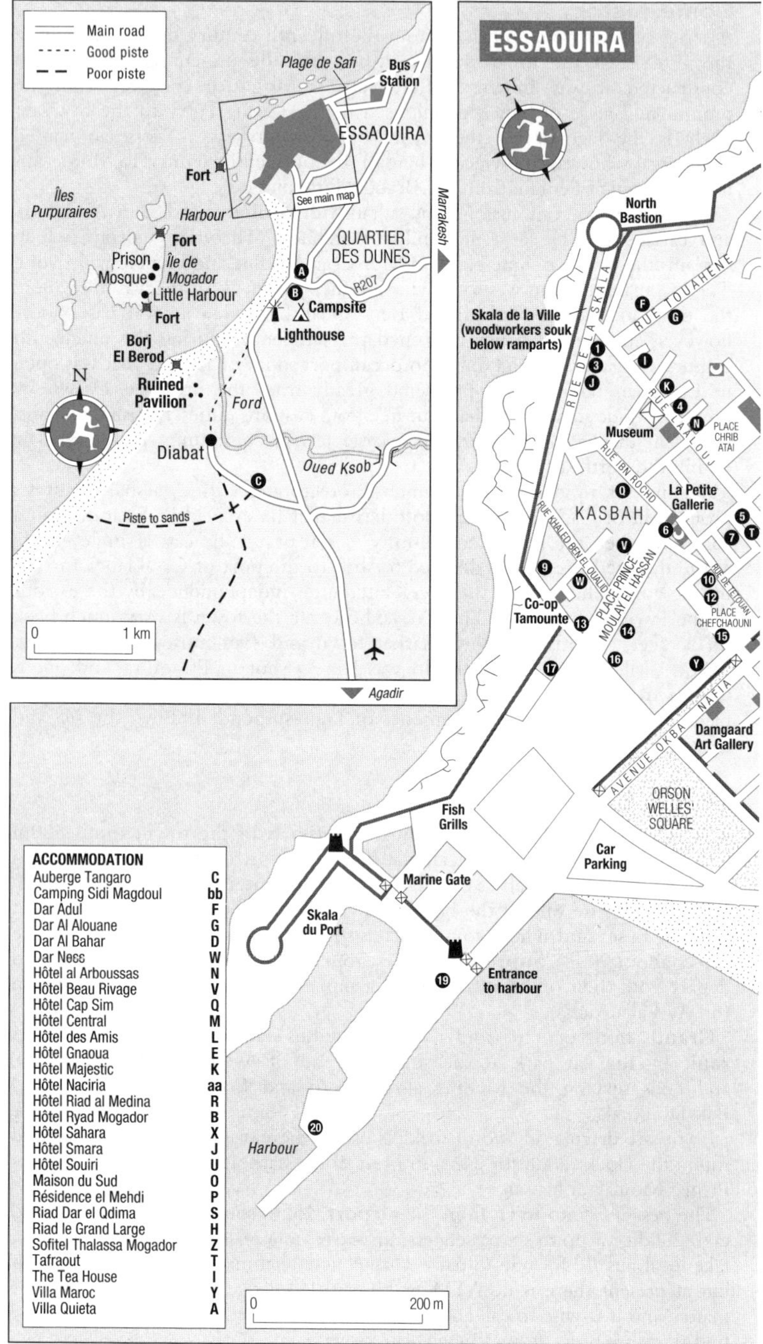
Main road
Good piste
Poor piste
Plage de Safi
Bus Station
ESSAOUIRA
Fort
Îles Purpuraires
Harbour
See main map
Marrakesh
QUARTIER DES DUNES
Fort
Prison
Mosque
Île de Mogador
Little Harbour
Fort
R207
Campsite
Lighthouse
Borj El Berod
Ruined Pavilion
Ford
Diabat
Oued Ksob
Piste to sands
0
1 km
Agadir
N
ESSAOUIRA
N
North Bastion
RUE TOUAHENE
Skala de la Ville (woodworkers souk below ramparts)
RUE DE LA SKALA
RUE LAALOUJ
Museum
PLACE CHRIB ATAI
RUE IBN ROCHD
La Petite Gallerie
KASBAH
RUE KHALED BEN EL OUALID
PLACE PRINCE MOULAY EL HASSAN
RUE DE TETOUAN
Co-op Tamounte
PLACE CHEFCHAOUNI
NAFIA
AVENUE OKBA
Damgaard Art Gallery
ORSON WELLES' SQUARE
Fish Grills
Car Parking
Marine Gate
Skala du Port
Entrance to harbour
Harbour
0
200 m
ACCOMMODATION
Auberge Tangaro C
Camping Sidi Magdoul bb
Dar Adul F
Dar Al Alouane G
Dar Al Bahar D
Dar Ness W
Hôtel al Arboussas N
Hôtel Beau Rivage V
Hôtel Cap Sim Q
Hôtel Central M
Hôtel des Amis L
Hôtel Gnaoua E
Hôtel Majestic K
Hôtel Naciria aa
Hôtel Riad al Medina R
Hôtel Ryad Mogador B
Hôtel Sahara X
Hôtel Smara J
Hôtel Souiri U
Maison du Sud O
Résidence el Mehdi P
Riad Dar el Qdima S
Riad le Grand Large H
Sofitel Thalassa Mogador Z
Tafraout T
The Tea House I
Villa Maroc Y
Villa Quieta A

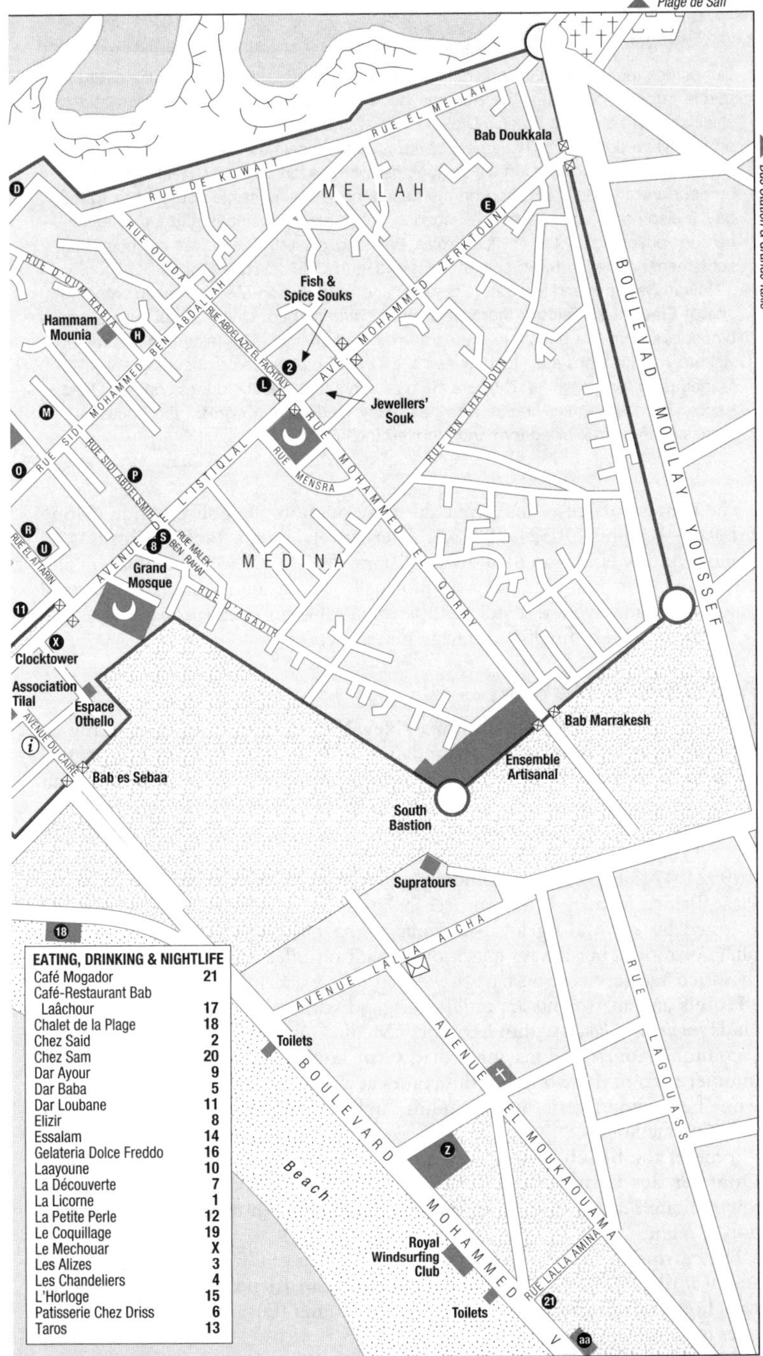
Plage de Safi
Bus Station & Grands Taxis
Rue el Mellah
Rue de Kuwait
Bab Doukkala
MELLAH
Rue Oujda
Rue d'Oum Rabia
Hammam Mounia
Fish & Spice Souks
Jewellers' Souk
Rue Mohammed Ben Abdallah
Rue Abdelaziz el Fachtaly
Ave Mohammed Zerktouni
Rue Ibn Khaldoun
Boulevard Moulay Youssef
Rue Sidi Mohammed Ben Abdallah
Rue Sidi Abdelsmih
Rue Mensra
Rue Mohammed el Qorry
Avenue de l'Istiqlal
Rue Malek Ben Rahal
Rue el Attarin
MEDINA
Grand Mosque
Rue d'Agadir
Clocktower
Association Tilal
Espace Othello
Avenue du Caire
Bab es Sebaa
Bab Marrakesh
Ensemble Artisanal
South Bastion
Supratours
Avenue Lalla Aicha
Rue Lagouass
Toilets
Avenue el Moukaouama
Boulevard Mohammed V
Beach
Royal Windsurfing Club
Rue Lalla Amina
Toilets
Quartier des Dunes, bb, Agadir & Marrakesh
EATING, DRINKING & NIGHTLIFE
Café Mogador 21
Café-Restaurant Bab Laâchour 17
Chalet de la Plage 18
Chez Said 2
Chez Sam 20
Dar Ayour 9
Dar Baba 5
Dar Loubane 11
Elizir 8
Essalam 14
Gelateria Dolce Freddo 16
Laayoune 10
La Découverte 7
La Licorne 1
La Petite Perle 12
Le Coquillage 19
Le Mechouar X
Les Alizes 3
Les Chandeliers 4
L'Horloge 15
Patisserie Chez Driss 6
Taros 13

The Île de Mogador

Out across the bay from Essaouira lie the **Îles Purpuraires**, named from the dyes for purple imperial cloth that the Romans once produced on the islands from murex shellfish. Here also, Sir Francis Drake ate his Christmas lunch in 1577, commenting on the "verie ugly fish". The largest of the islands, known as the **Île de Mogador**, is flanked on each side by a fort which, together with the fort on the islet just off the town harbour and the Bord el Berod on the beach, covers all possible approaches to the bay. It also has a small harbour, a mosque, a few rusting cannons and a nineteenth-century prison used for political exiles but long closed. There was a Phoenician settlement on the landward side of the island in the late seventh century BC.

Nowadays the island is a nature reserve, and the only non-Mediterranean breeding site of **Eleonora's falcon**, Morocco's most dramatic bird, which is best seen with binoculars from the beach, in the early evening half-light. The falcons are summer visitors to Morocco, staying between May and October before heading south to Madagascar for the winter. They are often seen hunting over the dunes south of Oued Ksob. The nearby river course also has many **waders** and **egrets** and occasional rarities such as gull-billed tern and Mediterranean gull.

The **tourist office** is on Avenue du Caire opposite the police station (Mon–Fri 9am–4.30pm; ⓣ0524 783532). Alternatively there's **Jack's Kiosk**, 1 Pl Prince Moulay el Hassan (daily 10am–10pm; ⓣ0524 475538), a newsagent and bookshop that has long served informally as an information booth and accommodation agency. It still lets apartments, has an international phone and fax centre, and sells English-language newspapers.

Accommodation

At holiday times (summer, Christmas/New Year), you need to arrive early or book ahead to ensure the accommodation of your choice; if you plan to stay for a week or more, it can be worth renting an **apartment** or a villa. You can do this through Jack's Kiosk (see above, or check its website at ⓦwww.essaouira.com/apartments), through Karimo, whose office is just off the north end of Place Prince Moulay el Hassan in the passage through to Rue Ibn Rochd (ⓣ0524 474500, ⓦwww.karimo.net), or through the *Restaurant Essalam* on Place Prince Moulay el Hassan (see p.336; ⓣ0524 475548). You may also be accosted by key-waving local residents at the bus station as you arrive with offers of rooms, but always check out what's on offer carefully, and be sure of the price and services you have agreed on before accepting.

Hotels and apartments are proliferating as Essaouira's popularity grows, as are **riads** (*maisons d'hôte*), within Essaouira's Medina to meet the rise in demand for accommodation. A riad may offer that warm, homely feel associated with B&Bs in other parts of the world but this comes at a price, whereas the hotels perhaps won't be as atmospheric, but the rooms can be considerably cheaper with much the same facilities.

Some of the **beach hotels** are very near town, others are 2km south in the **Quartier des Dunes** district. This removes you somewhat from the life of the town, though it's an easy enough walk along the beach by day, or a short taxi hop at night.

The **campsite**, *Camping Sidi Magdoul*, is 3km out of town on the Agadir road and near the lighthouse (ⓣ0524 472196). It's clean, friendly and well-managed, with hot showers, bungalows in spring and summer (❷), and an area of soil and trees for pitching tents in.

In town

Hôtel al Arboussas 24 Rue Laâlouj, in a small alley opposite the museum ⓣ0524 472610, ⓔarboussashotel@yahoo.fr. A large house, nicely converted. The rooms are small, but impeccably clean, en suite and comfortable. BB ❹

Hôtel Beau Rivage 4 Pl Prince Moulay el Hassan ⓣ0524 475925, ⓔbeaurivage@menara.ma. A prime location on the square and clean, modern en-suite rooms each with its own balcony. Those overlooking the square, however, can be a bit noisy. There is a popular restaurant down below and a terrace up top with fantastic Medina and sea views. ❹

Hôtel Cap Sim 11 Rue Ibn Rochd ⓣ0524 78534, ⓔhotelcapsim@menara.ma. Central, clean and popular with a fourth-floor terrace. Some rooms are en suite and the water is partly solar-heated. BB ❷

Hôtel Central 5 Rue Dar Dheb, off Av Mohammed Ben Abdallah ⓣ0524 783623, ⓔsi2007@live.fr. Cheap and cheerful basic rooms and friendly staff in a nice old house around a patio with a fig tree. Shared hot showers (8dh). ❷

Hôtel des Amis 24 Rue Abdelaziz el Fachtaly (no phone). Basic and rather musty but very cheap travellers' hotel in the middle of the Medina with shared hot showers (8dh); there's an inexpensive restaurant next door offering various set menus, one of them vegetarian. ❷

Hôtel Gnaoua 89 Av Zerktouni ⓣ0524 475234, ⓕ0524 475236. Near Bab Doukkala and away from the more touristy parts of the Medina, spick and span but a little bit overpriced. All rooms are en suite but not all have outside windows. ❸

Hôtel Majestic 40 Rue Laâlouj ⓣ0524 474909. The former French colonial courthouse (opened in 1914, according to the plaque on the side of the building), and not bad value with decent-sized rooms and hot showers, though only two rooms are en suite. ❷

Hôtel Riad al Medina 9 Rue Attarine ⓣ0524 475907, ⓦwww.riadalmadina.com. A former palatial mansion built in 1871, which had by the 1960s fallen on hard times and become a budget hotel for hippies – guests supposedly included Jimi Hendrix, Frank Zappa, Jefferson Airplane and Cat Stevens. Now refurbished with 49 rooms and suites, it gets mixed reports: some people love it, and it's certainly friendly with bags of character; others hate it, largely because it's quite basic by package-tour standards, and expensive for what you get. BB ❻

Hôtel Sahara Av Okba Ibn Nafia ⓣ0524 475292, ⓕ0524 476198. Centrally located, with large rooms around a central well, en suite with central heating. It's worth asking for one of the newly refurbished rooms, which are smarter and brighter than the older ones. ❸

Hôtel Smara 26 Rue Skala ⓣ0524 475655. A small hotel with small rooms, but the sea view from the terrace and the front rooms is a bonus, though they cost almost twice as much as the rooms at the back. ❷

Hôtel Souiri 37 Rue Attarine ⓣ0524 475339, ⓦwww.hotelsouiri.com. Very central and deservedly popular, with a range of rooms, the cheaper ones having shared bathroom facilities. Rooms at the front are considered the best, though those at the back are quieter. BB ❸

Hôtel Tafraout 7 Rue de Marrakesh ⓣ0524 476276. Recently renovated with friendly staff and comfortable rooms, some en suite, but lacking character, and not all rooms have outside windows. ❸

Résidence el Mehdi 15 Rue Sidi Abdelsmih ⓣ0524 475943, ⓦwww.residenceelmehdi.com. A modernized old house with nice, airy rooms, two patios (one covered, one open), two terraces and a reliable kitchen, plus a couple of apartments and a suite. BB ❹

Riads

Dar Adul 63 Rue Touahene (near the Skala) ⓣ&ⓕ0524 473910. Lashings of whitewash give this place a bright, airy feel, and help to keep it cool in summer. It's French-run, with a selection of different-sized rooms, some split-level, and the largest with a fireplace to make it cosy in winter. BB ❻

Dar al Alouane (also called La Maison des Couleurs) 66 Rue Touahene ⓣ0524 476172, ⓔdar_al_alouane@yahoo.fr. Simple and stylish, done out in very original decor and beautiful colours, with a range of rooms and suites at different prices, some with shared bathrooms but still excellent value. ❸

Dar al Bahar 1 Rue Touahene ⓣ0524 476831, ⓦwww.daralbahar.com. Wild sea views, especially from the terrace, cool whitewashed rooms and paintings and window blinds by some of the best local artists make this an excellent choice, though it's a bit tucked away. BB ❺

Dar Ness 1 Rue Khalid ben Oualid ⓣ0524 476804, ⓦwww.darness-essaouira.com. A nineteenth-century house turned into an attractive place to stay by its French owner, though it's a little bit impersonal for a riad. BB ❻

Maison du Sud 29 Rue Sidi Mohammed Ben Abdallah ⓣ0524 474141, ⓦwww.maisondusud.net. An eighteenth-century house built around a covered patio with fountain. Most rooms are split-level with a sitting area and bathroom below the sleeping area. BB ❺

Riad Dar el Qdima 4 Rue Malek Ben Rahai ⓣ0524 473858, ⓦwww.darqdima.com. A small riad in an eighteenth-century house with a variety of rooms around a covered patio, or adjoining the roof terrace. BB ❺

Riad le Grand Large 2 Rue Oum Rabii ⓣ0524 472866, ⓦwww.riadlegrandlarge.com. Despite its name, a small, cosy place with ten smallish rooms, lovely staff, a restaurant and a roof terrace café. Good value, with reductions off-season. BB ❺

The Tea House 74 Rue Laâlouj, in an alley off the street ⓣ0524 783543, ⓦwww.theteahouse.net. Two self-contained and well-equipped apartments, each sleeping four adults, comprising two bedrooms each with own shower, a sitting room, kitchen and bathroom, in an old house run by a British woman and her Marrakshi husband. There is also a new upper terrace with sea views. Among services offered are help with souvenir shopping, and a neighbour who'll come in and cook a Moroccan meal. BB ❻

Villa Maroc 10 Rue Abdallah Ben Yassin, just inside the Medina wall near the clocktower ⓣ0524 476147, ⓦwww.villa-maroc.com. Established long before riads became trendy, from two old houses converted into a score of rooms and suites, heated in winter and decorated with the finest Moroccan materials. It even has its own hammam. Most of the year you will need to book several months ahead, though it's always worth a call on the off-chance. Nonresidents can dine here if they reserve before 4pm. Though accessible only on foot, they have porters on hand to carry your luggage from the car park. BB ❻

Near the beach

Hôtel Naciria 58 Bd Mohammed V ⓣ0524 784504, ⓦwww.darnaciria.net. A kilometre south of the old town, facing the beach, the decent-sized rooms are nicely done out in sky blue or sunny yellow. There's a good restaurant, *La Petite Algue*, and a bar, both open to nonresidents. BB ❹

Hôtel Ryad Mogador where Bd Mohammed V leaves the seafront and turns inland to become the R207 ⓣ0524 783555, ⓦwww.ryadmogador.com. A four-star beach hotel (though some 200m off the beach) with a good-sized pool, quite spacious rooms and nice decor. Better value for money than the *Sofitel*. ❼

Windsurfing around Essaouira

Essaouira and its nearby beaches are Morocco's prime **wind- and kitesurfing** destination, drawing enthusiasts throughout the year. The trade wind at Essaouira is northwesterly and blows year-round; it's stronger in summer – if you're inexperienced try to get out early in the morning – but the swell is bigger in winter. The winds can be quite strong (sails required are 5.03.5) but the curved shape of Essaouira's bay, along with a gently sloping sandy bottom that creates a wide shallow area along the shoreline, makes it ideal for novices. Even during summer the water temperature rises only to 20 degrees maximum, so a wetsuit is required all year. There are numerous **surf shops** and schools in Essaouira, as well as one or two in Sidi Kaouiki and Point Imessouane (see pp.338–339) further south. **Surfers** should be warned that for most of the year Essouaria's non-stop winds, though great for windsurfing, can be a disappointment for board surfing and you might be better off down at Point Imessouane with its easterly facing bay.

Surfing supplies

Gipsy Surfer 14 Rue de Tetouan ⓣ0524 783268. Sells surfing and windsurfing equipment, and surfwear.

Hotel Ocean Vagabond (Club Mistral) ⓣ0524 479222, ⓦwww.oceanvagabond.com. Has a surf school at the far southern end of the beach where it also offers kitesurfing lessons and posts the weather forecast.

Magic Fun Afrika Av Mohammed V, 100m south of *Hôtel Tafoukt* ⓣ0524 473856, ⓦwww.magicfunafrika.com. Rents out kayaks, kitesurfing, surfboards and windsurfing equipment, offers surf lessons and posts the weather forecast outside daily.

No Work Team 2 Rue Skala & 7 Rue Houmam el Fatouki ⓣ0524 475272. This British-owned place sells surfwear and surfing equipment from its two shops.

The Royal Windsurfing Club (*Royal Club de Planche à Voile*), next to Magic Fun ⓣ0670 577411. Offers windsurfing lessons.

Sofitel Thalassa Mogador Bd Mohammed V ⓣ0524 479000, ⓦwww.sofitel.com. The most expensive hotel in Essaouira by a very long chalk, and possibly the best, though certainly not by the same kind of margin. It has a pool, two bars, two restaurants, a thalassotherapy centre (if a swim in the sea isn't sufficient), and – which might make it worth the price if you need it – a room adapted for wheelchair users. BB ⑨

Villa Quieta 86 Bd Mohammed V, Quartier des Dunes ⓣ0524 785004, ⓦwww.villa-quieta.com. A luxurious mansion built in semi-traditional style by the current owner's father in the 1950s, some 2km south of town. The rooms are tasteful and comfortable, and the place retains the feel of an upscale guesthouse rather than a hotel. There's no pool, but it's only 150m to the beach. BB ⑦

The Town

The ramparts are the obvious place to start a tour of Essaouira. At the top of the **Skala de la Ville**, the great sea bastion that runs along the northern cliffs (daily sunrise–sunset; free) are a collection of European cannon, presented to Sultan Sidi Mohammed Ben Abdallah by nineteenth-century merchants. At its northern end is the circular **North Bastion**, with panoramic views across the Medina and out to sea.

Along the Rue de Skala, built into the ramparts, are a number of **marquetry and wood-carving workshops**, long established in Essaouira. Here – and in workshops around town – artisans produce amazingly painstaking and beautiful marquetry work from **thuya** (also spelt *thuja*; *arar* in Arabic), an aromatic mahogany-like hardwood from a local coniferous tree, from which they adapt both the trunk and the roots (or *loupe*). With total justice, they claim that their produce is the best in the country, and this is the best place to buy it. To gauge quality and prices before you come to make a purchase, visit Afalkay Art at 9 Pl Prince Moulay el Hassan (opposite the *Hôtel Beau Rivage*), a vast emporium where you can browse with no commitment to buy.

The **Musée Sidi Mohammed Ben Abdallah**, on Rue Laâlouj next to the post office (daily except Tues 8.30am–6.30pm; 10dh), is in a nineteenth-century mansion that served as the town hall during the Protectorate, and is now used to display a collection of traditional jewellery, coins, carpets, costumes and Gnaoua musical instruments decorated with marquetry, along with a gallery of pictures of old Essaouira.

Spice and jewellery souks and the Mellah

The town's **other souks** spread around and to the south of two arcades, on either side of Rue Mohammed Zerktouni, and up towards the Mellah. Worth particular attention are the **Marché d'Epices** (spice market) and **Souk des Bijoutiers** (jewellers' market).

The jewellery business was one of the traditional trades of Essaouira's Jewish community, who have long since deserted the **Mellah**, in the northwest corner of the ramparts. The **Jewish community** in the last quarter of the nineteenth century may have comprised as much as half of the town's population. **Sir Moses Montefiore**, the nineteenth-century leader of Britain's Jewish community, was born here.

At the northeast corner of the Medina, **Bab Doukkala** leads to a small Christian cemetery dating from colonial times (100m on the left). Some 400m beyond Bab Doukkala there is further evidence of the former Jewish community in the extensive Jewish cemetery – two vast grey lanes of tombstones, carefully tended and well ordered, in a site on both sides of the road. The principal entrance is on the right.

Essaouira art galleries

Essaouira has become quite a centre for painting and sculpture, and many of its artists have made a name for themselves in both Morocco and Europe. Artists with their own distinctive styles tend to have an entourage of second-rate imitators, so it's worth checking that the artist whose works you're looking at really is the one whose work you were interested in, as it should be in any of the galleries listed here.

Association Tilal 4 Rue du Caire ⓣ0524 475424. A gallery exhibiting the work of half a dozen or so local painters with quite distinctive styles. Many of the pieces exhibited here have been knocked up quickly to sell at low prices: to buy some of the artists' better work, you'll have to speak to them personally and perhaps commission something. The association should be able to put you in touch.

Espace Othello 9 Rue Mohammed Layachi, behind the *Hôtel Sahara* (daily 9am–1pm & 3–8pm). This gallery was opened in 1993 by the *patron* of the nearby *Restaurant el Minzah* to display paintings and sculptures by local artists.

Galerie d'Art Frederic Damgaard on Av Oqba Ibn Nafia ⓣ0524 784446. Paintings and sculptures by twenty or so locally based artists, in a gallery run by a Danish furniture designer, who uses the traditional thuya techniques in a highly imaginative, modern context. There's also an atelier at 2 Rue el Hijalli, just off Pl Chefchaouni.

La Petite Galerie Just off the north end of Pl Prince Moulay el Hassan in the passage through to Rue Ibn Rochd. A small but well-chosen selection of works by local painters.

The port

Essaouira is Morocco's third fishing port after Agadir and Safi, and the port area bustles with life for most of the day, with the local wooden fishing boats being built or repaired, and the fishing fleet bringing in the day's catch. Some boats also offer rides. The sea bastion by the harbour, the **Skala du Port**, is open to the public (daily 9am–5.30pm; 10dh), and worth popping in to climb on the ramparts and enjoy the views.

Just outside the port area, is a line of **fish grill-cafés**, a meal at which is considered *de rigeur* for a stay in Essaouira (see opposite).

The beach

The main town beach, **south** of the Medina, extends for miles, often backed by dunes, out towards Cap Sim. On its early reaches, the main activity, as ever in Morocco, is football. There's virtually always a game in progress and at weekends a full-scale local league, with a dozen matches side by side and kick-offs timed by the tides. If you're a player, you'll be encouraged to join in, but the weekend games are fun just to watch, and on occasions half the town seems to turn out.

The southern beach also has a dozen or so **camel** men, offering rides up and down the sands, or out to the dunes. If you fancy a ride (or have children who do), watch the scene for a while and be sure to pick someone you feel confident about – it's a long way to fall. You'll need to bargain for rates.

The beach to the north of town, known as the **Plage de Safi**, is good in hot weather and with a calm sea, but the water can be dangerous if the wind is up. It's reached from the north end of town by skirting left through a malodorous area, the reward being miles of often delightfully empty sand.

Bordj el Berod and Diabat

Walking further along the beach to the south, past the football and the crowds, you pass the riverbed of the Oued Ksob (impassable at high tide) and come

▲ *Chez Sam*, Essaouira

upon the ruins of an old fort, the **Bordj el Berod**. According to local mythology, this was the original Castle Made of Sand that inspired the track of that name on Jimi Hendrix's *Axis Bold As Love* album, and it is said that Hendrix played impromptu concerts here for his fellow hippies back in the day. Nice though it would be to believe this, Hendrix stories in Essaouira want taking with a pinch or two of salt – *Axis Bold as Love*, for example, was released in January 1968, but Hendrix didn't visit Morocco until July 1969; he spent a week touring the country, of which a few days at most were in Essaouira. The fort is nonetheless an excellent viewing spot for the Iles Purpuraires, offshore, and their birdlife (see box, p.330). Inland you can see the ruins of a royal summer pavillion.

A little further south, inland through the scrub, is the small Berber village of **Diabat**. This was once a legendary hippy hangout, and local mythology has it that both Jimi Hendrix and Cat Stevens (a favourite in Morocco for having converted to Islam) spent time in the colony. These days, it has reverted to an ordinary Berber farming village but is about to be overwhelmed by a residential golf development.

Few venture beyond the Oued Ksob, from which an aqueduct once carried water to Essaouira, but a walk to Cap Sim and back is an all-day challenge. The majority of the walk is quite isolated and two tourists were attacked here in 2005. This may be a one-off incident but it's worth bearing in mind. Take plenty of water, and be careful of the tides. You can visit the *Auberge Tangaro* on the way back (see p.338).

Eating and drinking

For an informal lunch, or early evening meal, you can't do better than eat at the line of **grills** down at the port, an Essaouira institution, with fish as fresh as can be. You choose from the fish displayed in front of your stall, and have it grilled there and then. Prices are fixed and displayed, but unfortunately some of the stalls have been getting rather hassly of late, and also overcharging (needless to say, it's the same ones that hustle for business who try to pull a fast one), so check prices first, and choose a stall that doesn't try to accost you. Chez Said in the retail fish souk is cheaper and as good, though there's less choice. Finish off with a scoop of excellent Italian-style **ice cream** from *Gelateria Dolce Freddo*, on the corner of Place Prince Moulay el Hassan, at a mere 10dh a pop.

Essaouira doesn't have much by way of nightlife – it's a café more than a bar scene – but there are a few places where you can have a **drink**, namely the restaurants *Les Chandeliers* and *Chalet de la Plage*, (though they prefer customers to eat as well), *Le Mechouar* (next to *Hôtel Sahara*) and the seafront *Café Mogador*. *Taros* at 2 Rue de la Skala, just off Place Prince Moulay el Hassan, has a good terrace bar that's popular with local expats, and stays open till midnight. *Dar Ayour*, at 16 Rue de la Skala, is a relaxed café and *salon de thé* where young locals gather to play **billiards and pool**.

Café-Restaurant Bab Laâchour Bab Laâchour, by Pl Prince Moulay el Hassan ⓣ0524 473572. A café favoured by locals downstairs, with a more tourist-oriented restaurant on the floor above, overlooking the square. The menu includes fish and tajines. Moderate.

Chalet de la Plage Bd Mohammed V, on the seafront, just above the high-tide mark ⓣ0524 475972. Built entirely of wood by the Ferraud family in 1893, the building is now a little gloomy and barnacled with marine mementos, but the seafood and sea views are truly memorable. Avoid lunchtime when day-trippers overwhelm the place. Licensed. Moderate to expensive, with 150dh and 180dh set menus.

Chez Sam in the harbour ⓣ0524 476513. An Essaouira institution – a wooden shack, built like a boat, set seductively right by the waterfront in the harbour. Service can be a bit hit-and-miss but the portions are generous, the fish is usually cooked pretty well, there's beer and wine available, and fishing boats to watch through the portholes. Moderate to expensive, with set menus at 85dh, or 250dh with lobster.

Dar Baba 2 Rue de Marrakech, on the corner with Rue Sidi Mohammed Ben Abdallah (same street as *Hôtel Tafraout*, on 1st floor). Italian dishes, including pizza, but most especially their own fresh pasta. Cheap.

Dar Loubane 24 Rue du Rif, a stone's throw from Pl Chefchaouni ⓣ0524 476296. Upmarket restaurant on the ground-floor patio of an attractive eighteenth-century mansion. Moroccan and French cuisine, friendly service, interesting exhibits and semi-kitsch decor. Live Gnaoua music takes place on Saturday evenings when it's advisable to make a booking. Moderate.

Elizir 1 Rue d'Agadir ⓣ0524 472103, ⓦwww.elizir.com. Eclectic retro decor and a harmonious fusion of Italian and Moroccan cuisine using locally sourced ingredients in this pioneering little restaurant. Dishes include inky black cuttlefish risotto, swordfish brochettes with ginger, or gnocchi with fromage frais and almond pesto. Moderate to expensive.

Essalam 23 Pl Prince Moulay el Hassan. The cheapest set menus in town (30–65dh), and certainly value for money, though the choice is a little bit limited. Good for breakfast too. On the walls, you will see small watercolours by Charles Kérival who often visits and paints in Essaouira. Born in Brittany, he discovered Morocco when the oil-tanker on which he was working visited Casablanca in 1956. Cheap.

Laayoune 4 bis Rue Hajjali. A good place for Moroccan staples in a relaxed setting with friendly service, but with back-breakingly low tables. Moderate, with tajine- and couscous-based menus at 68–88dh.

La Découverte 8 bis rue Houmane el Fetaouki ⓣ0524 473158, ⓦwww.essaouira-ladecouverte.com. French-Moroccan cuisine at this little place run by a French couple (she does the cooking, he greets and serves the customers) with a short but sweet menu of excellent food including seafood pasta, vegetables stuffed with minced fish or meat, an excellent pastilla, and on Mondays, camel couscous. Open 10am–10pm except Sat. Moderate.

La Licorne 26 Rue Skala ⓣ0524 473626. An upmarket Moroccan restaurant serving some of the best traditional French and Moroccan food in town. The chocolate mousse is particularly recommended, but doesn't feature on the 150dh set menu. Expensive.

La Petite Perle 2 Rue el Hajjalli ⓣ0524 475050. A small place with low divan seating and generous servings of good traditional Moroccan cooking. Moderate, with set menus for 60–95dh.

Le Coquillage (Restaurant du Port) in the harbour ⓣ0524 476655. A seashell-bedecked competitor to the older *Chez Sam*, and offering a similar menu in slightly more refined surroundings. Moderate to expensive, with a three-course set menu at 120dh, four-course at 150dh, and four-course with lobster for 250dh.

Les Alizes 26 Rue Skala ⓣ0524 476819. Next to the *Hôtel Smara* and away from the mainstream, this restaurant has built up a good reputation for Moroccan dishes – choice is limited to an 99dh set menu, but everything is delicious. Wine is available; booking advised. Closed Nov.

Les Chandeliers 14 Rue Laâlouj ⓣ0524 475827, ⓦwww.leschandeliers.net. A well-established restaurant and wine bar run by a French family and offering both Continental and Moroccan options. Licensed; evenings only. Moderate to expensive, with a 95dh vegetarian set menu, and meat or fish set menus at 125–135dh.

L'Horloge Pl Chefchaouni. Moderately priced Moroccan meals, standard and lacking imagination, but good value for money. Housed in a one-time synagogue.

Patisserie Chez Driss 10 Rue Hajjali, just off Pl Prince Moulay el Hassan. Long established and one of the town's most popular meeting places. Delicious fresh pastries and coffee in a quiet leafy courtyard. Ideal for a leisurely breakfast. Cheap.

Listings

Banks BCM, Banque Populaire and Crédit du Maroc are in the big open area just south of Pl Prince Moulay el Hassan; BMCE is just off the square to the north; Société Générale is on Av Okba Ibn Nafia; and WAFA is at 60 Av de l'Istiqlal, all with ATMs.

Bookshops Galerie Aide, 2 Rue Skala, run by a former New Yorker, has a small and overpriced selection of secondhand English-language books, and some nice antiques and bric-a-brac. There's a secondhand book store on Rue Sidi Mohammed Ben Abdallah by the turning for the *Hôtel Central* with a few used books in English, mostly pulps.

Car rental Of the big international firms, only Avis has an office here, at 28 bis Av Oued el Makhazine (ⓣ0524 475270), and at the airport (ⓣ0524 474926). Smaller, local firms include Dzira Location, 50 Bd Mohammed V (ⓣ&ⓕ0524 473716); and Isfaoun Rent-a-Car, 62 Bd Mohammed V (ⓣ0524 474906, ⓦwww.essaouiracar.com).

Festivals A dozen or so local moussems, fairs and festivals are held between March and October. The main event is the Festival d'Essaouira in late June, the main focus of which is Gnaoua music. For further information, check the festival website at ⓦwww.festival-gnaoua.co.ma. In October, the air rally commemorating the Aéropostale Service of the 1920s passes through Essaouira. An annual music festival is held each spring.

Hammam Hammam Mounia on Rue d'Oum Rabia near *Riad le Grand Large* is clean and tourist-friendly: women daily 12.30–6.30pm, men 6.30–10.30pm.

Internet access There are numerous internet cafés on Av de L'Istiqlal, some open all day, every day. There is also Internet Club on Av du Caire, next to the tourist office (daily 9am–11pm; 10dh per hr).

Post office The PTT is outside the ramparts on Av Lalla Aicha (Mon–Fri 8am–6pm; Sat 8am–noon), with branch offices in Rue Laâlouj and by the bus station.

Shopping Despite its size, Essaouira rivals Marrakesh and Fes as a centre for attractive items, and it's relatively hassle-free. As usual, however, beware of tourist emporiums selling *trafika* (simulated antiques and fossils) – tiles with Hebrew lettering, supposedly old tiles from the Mellah, are a favourite scam here, and any shop selling them is probably worth avoiding. Hippy-style clothing is a good buy in Essaouira – a couple of shops on Rue el Hajjali are good for tunics and drawstring trousers. Thuya wood crafts are also good value (see p.333), and paintings by local artists are worth a look if you feel like spending a bit more. Argan oil (see box, p.498) and its associated beauty products are widely sold but relatively pricey: Co-operative Tamounte at 6 Rue Souss is a good place for argan oil and thuya wood crafts, both made by local co-operatives.

Moving on

Most **buses** and shared **grands taxis** leave from the bus station 500m north of Bab Doukkala (about 7dh by petit taxi from Bab es Seba or Place Orson Welles). The best direct bus to **Casablanca** is the overnight CTM, which leaves Essaouira daily at 1am, arriving at 6am in the centre of Casablanca (private services leave you at the much less convenient *gare routière*). Supratours buses for **Marrakesh** leave from a lane off Avenue Lalla Aicha

(Ⓣ0524 475317), arriving at Marrakesh train station to connect with trains for Casa and beyond; tickets are best bought the day before, and you can get through tickets for the train too.

Royal Air Maroc run **flights** to Casablanca and Paris-Orly from Essaouira's airport, 15km south of town on the Agadir road (Ⓣ0524 476704), reached by grand taxi (200dh for up to six people) or by bus #2 from Bab Doukkala (8 daily; 6dh). RAM's office is on Rue du Caire (Ⓣ0524 785384).

South of Essaouira

The main road south from Essaouira crosses the river Oued Ksob upstream before joining the N1 to Agadir. A turning to the right just before this junction takes you to Diabat by a metalled side road (see inset map, p.328).

En route to **Diabat** and signposted from the main road is the *Auberge Tangaro* (Ⓣ0524 784784, Ⓦwww.auberge-tangaro.com; HB ❻), an Italian-owned place that provides an alternative to staying in Essaouira if you have transport. Half-board is compulsory though it serves excellent meals, and the place is little used except at weekends, when groups of French and German windsurfers arrive from Casablanca and Marrakesh. Prices are steep however, especially considering that there isn't any electricity. Bus #5 from Bab Doukkala serves Diabat.

Sidi Kaouki

Further south, the beach at **SIDI KAOUKI** (also served by bus #5) attracts **windsurfers** virtually year-round, and wind generators have been installed to supply up to 95 percent of the village's electricity. For a village of only 120 or so inhabitants, it has an astonishing amount of **accommodation**, including *Résidence La Kaouki* (Ⓣ0524 783206, Ⓦwww.sidikaouki.com; BB ❸), its neighbour *La Pergola* (Ⓣ0524 785831, Ⓦwww.pergola-maroc.com; BB ❸), the solar-powered *Hotel Villa Soleil* (Ⓣ0650 229473, Ⓦwww.hotelvillasoleil.com; BB ❹) and the newer *Auberge de la Plage* (Ⓣ0524 476600, Ⓦwww.kaouki.com; BB ❸). All have restaurants serving lunch and dinner, though non-residents are advised to book ahead. Light meals are also available at the Sidi Kaouki Surfclub (Ⓦwww.sidi-kaouki.com), which rents out gear for surfers, windsurfers and kitesurfers. Near the beach is the original **Marabout of Sidi Kaouki**, which has a reputation for curing female sterility, and beyond that is **Cap Sim**, backed by long expanses of dunes.

Twenty-six kilometres south of Essaouira, accessible by local bus #3 (6 daily) from Bab Doukkala in Essaouira, at **Tidzi**, the Commune Rurale de Tidzi was the first of what are now a handful of women's co-operatives making argan oil, forming an association called Targanine with another co-op at Tamanar.

On towards Agadir

For off-road vehicles, the *pistes* south along the coast from Sidi Kaouki offer a mix of long strands, dunes and scenic headlands, with occasional blue-painted fishing boats. Eventually the main road (N1) is rejoined north of **SMIMOU**, a one-street town with a petrol station and a couple of café-restaurants. A few kilometres before Smimou, a metalled road which soon turns to *piste* leads west to **Ifrane**, one of the finest beaches.

Just south of Smimou, inland, lies the forested whaleback of **Djebel Amsittene** (905m). A challenging *piste* climbs to traverse the crest of this grand viewpoint, and descends not far from **Imi n'Tilt**, a busy Monday souk, and a recommended venture if you have 4WD. A little further south of Smimou, another scenic *piste* leads westward to **Cap Tafelney**, below which lies a curious village and a bay full of fishing boats.

The coast is rockier if approached from **Tamanar**, a larger town with a few restaurants. Fifteen kilometres south, a surfaced road leads to **POINTE IMESSOUANE**, which used to be a picturesque little harbour with a few fishermen's cottages, but now has a grand complex of apartments and shops around a large square and modern fish market. No matter what swell, tide or wind condition prevails, its two bays should offer something for all surfers and windsurfers. Two **surf schools**, Kahina and Planet Surf Morocco, and the unimaginatively named Surf Shop, which rents out secondhand surf gear, are all within fifty metres of each other down near the market. There are a number of **cafés** offering, among other things, excellent grilled sardines. **Accommodation** is presently limited to *Kahina l'Auberge* (Ⓣ0528 826032, Ⓦwww.kahinasurfschool.com; ❸), which has a prime site overlooking **Imoucha,** the east bay, and a restaurant with good seafood, open to nonresidents. Three kilometres to the north is the *Auberge Tasra* (Ⓣ0528 820597; ❷), and opposite is a track leading to a large, open campsite overlooking the west bay. There are also many **caves** in this limestone region. Forty-nine kilometres beyond Tamanar, you reach the roadside settlement of **TAMRI**, where bananas on sale by the roadside give a sense of arrival in the south. The route from here on to Taghazout and Agadir is covered (in a south–north direction) on p.500.

Travel details

Trains

Note that Supratours buses connect at Marrakesh for Essaouira, Agadir, Laayoune and Dakhla, at Tnine Sidi Lyamani (on the Tangier line) for Tetouan, and at Taourirt (on the Oujda line) for Nador, with through tickets available from any train station.

Casablanca Port to: El Jadida (7 daily; 1hr 35min); Kenitra (26 daily; 1hr 30min) via Mohammedia (20min) and Rabat (1hr); Rabat (half-hourly 6.30am–8.30pm, plus one at 9.30pm; 1hr).

Casablanca Voyageurs to: Mohammed V airport (hourly 6.07am–10.07pm, plus one early morning; 33min); Asilah (4 direct & 1 connecting daily; 5hr); Fes (15 daily; 3hr 55min); Kenitra (19 direct daily; 1hr 30min); Marrakesh (9 daily; 3hr 15min); Meknes (14 daily; 3hr 15min); Oujda (3 direct & 1 connecting daily; 9hr 45min); Rabat (19 direct daily; 1hr); Settat (17 daily; 55min); Tangier (4 direct & 1 connecting daily; 5hr 40min).

El Jadida to: Casa Port (7 daily; 1hr 35min) via Casa Voyageurs (1hr 21min). Six services connect at Casa Voyageurs for Meknes and Fes, one for Tangier (plus one more changing again at Sidi Kacem), and all connect for Marrakesh with a one-hour wait at Casa Voyageurs.

Kenitra to: Asilah (4 direct & 1 connecting daily; 3hr 25min); Casa Port (26 daily; 1hr 30min); Casa Voyageurs (19 direct and 19 connecting daily; 1hr 35min); Fes (15 daily; 2hr–2hr 30min); Marrakesh (9 daily; 4hr 55min); Meknes (14 daily; 1hr 25min–1hr 50min); Oujda (3 direct & 1 connecting daily; 8hr 50min); Rabat (45 daily; 25min); Tangier (4 direct & 1 connecting daily; 4hr 10min).

Rabat Ville to: Asilah (4 direct & 1 connecting daily; 4hr); Casa Port (half-hourly 6.30am–8pm, last at 9pm; 1hr); Casa Voyageurs (19 direct daily; 1hr); Casablanca Mohammed V airport (2 early morning then hourly 7am–9pm, changing at Aïn Sebaa; 1hr 40min); Fes (15 daily; 3hr); Kenitra (44 daily; 30min); Marrakesh (9 daily; 4hr 20min); Meknes (14 daily; 2hr); Oujda (3 direct & 1 connecting daily; 9hr); Settat (9 direct & 7 connecting daily; 2hr 30min); Tangier (4 direct & 1 connecting daily; 4hr 40min).

Safi to: Benguerir (2 daily; 1hr 50min) via Youssoufia (1hr 5min); connecting at Benguerir for Casablanca (4hr 50min), Fes (8hr 40min), Marrakesh (4hr 15min) and Rabat (5hr 25min).

Buses

Casablanca to: Agadir (6 CTM and 34 others daily; 9hr); Beni Mellal (2 CTM daily & others roughly every half-hour; 3hr 30min); Essaouira (2 CTM & 24 others daily; 6hr); Fes (10 CTM & 18 others daily; 5hr 30min); El Jadida (6 CTM daily & others every 15min; 2hr 30min); Er Rachidia (1 CTM & 1 other daily; 12hr); Kenitra (3 CTM & 14 others daily; 2hr); Laayoune (2 CTM daily; 20hr); Marrakesh (9 CTM daily & others half-hourly 4.30am–9pm; 4hr); Meknes (5 CTM & 11 others daily; 4hr); Nador (1 CTM & 12 others daily; 12hr); Ouarzazate (2 CTM daily; 9hr); Oujda (1 CTM & 15 others daily; 12hr); Rabat (5 CTM daily & others at least half-hourly 6am–8.30pm; 1hr 20min); Safi (7 CTM & 22 others daily; 4hr 45min); Settat (half-hourly 9am–6.30pm; 2hr); Tangier (5 CTM & 36 others daily; 6hr 30min); Tetouan (4 CTM & 27 others daily; 6hr); Tiznit (4CTM & 6 others daily; 11hr).

Essaouira to: Agadir (1 CTM & 26 others daily; 3hr 30min); Casablanca (2 CTM & 24 others daily; 6hr); Marrakesh (2 CTM, 5 Supratours & 18 others daily; 3hr); Rabat (13 daily; 8hr 30min); Safi (2 CTM & 25 others daily; 3hr 30min); Tangier (1 daily; 14hr).

El Jadida to: Casablanca (6 CTM daily & others every 15min; 2hr 30min); Marrakesh (12 daily; 4hr); Oualidia (3 daily; 1hr 30min); Rabat (14 daily; 4hr); Safi (6 CTM & 13 others daily; 2hr 30min); Settat (4 daily; 2hr 30min).

Rabat to: Agadir (3 CTM & 23 others daily; 11hr); Casablanca (5 CTM daily & very frequent private services; 1hr 20min); Essaouira (13 daily; 8hr 30min); Fes (6 CTM daily & others hourly 5am–7pm; 4hr); El Jadida (14 daily; 4hr); Marrakesh (2 CTM daily & others hourly 8.30am–11.30pm; 5hr 30min); Meknes (4 CTM daily & others hourly 5am–7pm; 3hr); Nador (1 CTM & 4 others daily; 9hr 30min); Ouarzazate (5 daily; 9hr 30min); Safi (8 daily; 6hr); Salé (frequent; 15min); Tangier (4 CTM daily & 35 others; 5hr); Tetouan (2 CTM & 18 others daily; 5hr).

Safi to: Agadir (1 CTM & 16 others daily; 5hr); Casablanca (7 CTM & 22 others daily; 4hr 45min); Essaouira (2 CTM & 25 others daily; 3hr 30min); El Jadida (6 CTM & 13 others daily; 2hr 30min); Marrakesh (15 daily; 2hr); Oualidia (1 CTM & 13 others daily; 1hr 25min); Rabat (8 daily; 6hr); Tangier (1 daily; 11hr).

Grands Taxis

Casablanca to: Fes (3hr 30min); El Jadida (2hr); Mohammedia (30min); Rabat (1hr 20min); Safi (3hr 30min); Tangier (5hr).

Essaouira to: Casablanca (5hr); Inezgane (2hr 30min); Marrakesh (2hr 30min); Safi (2hr 30min).

El Jadida to: Casablanca (2hr); Oualidia (1hr); Safi (2hr).

Rabat to: Casablanca (1hr 20min); Fes (2hr 30min); Kenitra (1hr); Meknes (1hr 50min); Salé (15min).

Safi to: Casablanca (3hr 30min); Essaouira (2hr 30min); El Jadida (2hr); Marrakesh (2hr 30min).

Flights

Casablanca Mohammed V to: Agadir (RAM 5–6 daily; 1hr); Dakhla (RAM, RAL 7 weekly; 2hr 20min); Essaouira (RAM 4 weekly; 1hr 10min); Fes (RAM 1–3 daily; 55min); Laayoune (RAM, RAL 6 weekly; 1hr 45min–2hr 30min); Marrakesh (RAM 5–6 daily; 40min); Ouarzazate (RAM 1–3 daily; 55min–1hr 10min); Oujda (RAM 1–3 daily; 1hr 30min); Tangier (RAM 1–3 daily; 50min–1hr 5min).

Essaouira to: Casablanca (RAM 4 weekly; 50min).

Marrakesh

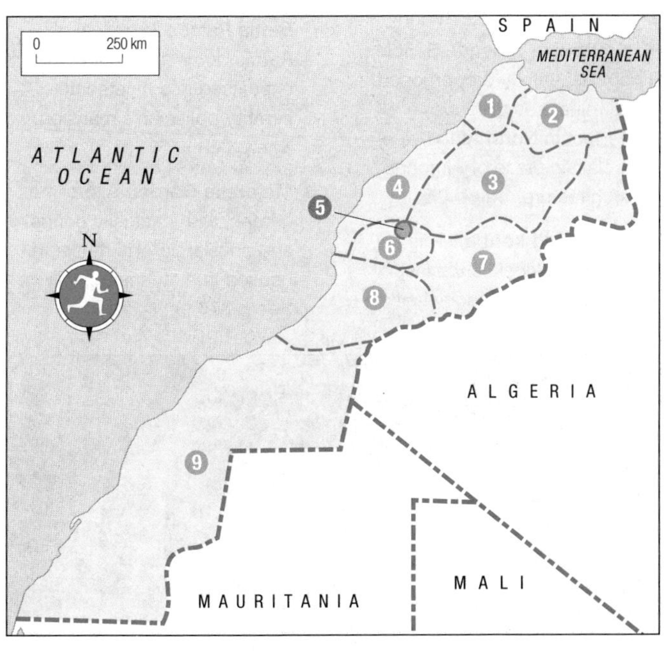
0
250 km
SPAIN
MEDITERRANEAN SEA
ATLANTIC OCEAN
N
1
2
3
4
5
6
7
8
9
ALGERIA
MALI
MAURITANIA

CHAPTER 5 Highlights

* **Riads** One of the joys of Marrakesh is a stay in a well-chosen riad, a beautiful old house imprinted with the personality of its *patron*. See p.350

* **Djemaa el Fna** The world's most amazing city square: an open-air circus of snake charmers, acrobats, musicians and storytellers. See p.353

* **Koutoubia Mosque** Simple but beautifully proportioned, its minaret is the most perfect in North Africa, and a classic piece of Almohad architecture. See p.354

* **Almoravid koubba** This tiny ablutions kiosk is the last remnant of the original city, and the only intact Almoravid building in Morocco. See p.359

* **Ben Youssef Medersa** Stucco, zellij tilework, and carved cedarwood mark this beautiful medersa. See p.360

* **El Badi Palace** The "Incomparable Palace", now an incomparable ruin. See p.366

* **Bahia Palace** The ideal of Arabic domestic architecture expressed in a nineteenth-century politician's mansion. See p.368

* **Majorelle Garden** A sublime garden, with cacti, lily ponds, and an Islamic Arts museum housed in a stunning pavilion. See p.370

▲ Ben Youssef Medersa

5

Marrakesh

Marrakesh – "Morocco City", as early foreign travellers called it – has always been something of a pleasure city, a marketplace where the southern tribesmen and Berber villagers bring in their goods, spend their money and find entertainment. For visitors it's an enduring fantasy – a city of immense beauty, low, red and tent-like before a great shaft of mountains – and immediately exciting. At the heart of it all is a square, Djemaa el Fna, really no more than an open space in the centre of the city, but the stage for a long-established ritual in which shifting circles of onlookers gather round groups of acrobats, drummers, pipe musicians, dancers, storytellers, comedians and fairground acts. However many times you return there, it remains compelling. So, too, do the city's architectural attractions: the immense, still basins of the Agdal and Menara gardens, the delicate Granada-style carving of the Saadian Tombs and, above all, the Koutoubia Minaret, the most perfect Islamic monument in North Africa.

It won't take you long to see why Marrakesh is called the **Red City**. The natural red ochre pigment that bedecks its walls and buildings can at times seem dominant, but there's no shortage of other colours. Like all Moroccan cities, it's a town of two halves: the ancient walled **Medina**, founded by Sultan Youssef Ben Tachfine in the Middle Ages, and the colonial **Ville Nouvelle**, built by the French in the mid-twentieth century. Each has its own delights – the Medina with its ancient palaces and mansions, labyrinthine souks and deeply traditional way of life, and the Ville Nouvelle with its pavement cafés, trendy boutiques, gardens and boulevards.

Marrakesh has become Morocco's **capital of chic**, attracting the rich and famous from Europe and beyond. Though the vast majority of its residents are poor by any European standard, an increasing number of wealthy visitors are taking up residence and their influence on the tourist experience is evident.

Marrakesh has **Berber** rather than Arab origins, having developed as the metropolis of Atlas tribes – Maghrebis from the plains, Saharan nomads and former slaves from beyond the desert. Once upon a time, Marrakesh was the entrepôt for goods – slaves, gold, ivory and even "Morocco" leather – brought by caravan from the ancient empires of Mali and Songhay via their great desert port of Timbuktu. All of these strands of commerce and population shaped the city's souks and its way of life, and even today, in the crowds and performers of the Djemaa el Fna, the nomadic and West African influence can still seem quite distinct.

Some history

Marrakesh was founded near the onset of **Almoravid** rule, founded by the first Almoravid dynasty ruler, **Youssef Ben Tachfine**, around 1062–70. It must at first have taken the form of a camp and market with a *ksour*, or fortified town, gradually developing round it. The first seven-kilometre **circuit of walls** was raised in 1126–27, replacing an earlier stockade of thorn bushes. These, many times rebuilt, are essentially the city's present walls – made of *tabia*, the red mud of the plains, mixed and strengthened with lime.

Of the rest of the Almoravids' building works, hardly a trace remains. The dynasty that replaced them – the **Almohads** – sacked the city for three days after taking possession of it in 1147, but they kept it as their empire's capital.

With the 1184 accession to the throne of the third Almohad sultan, **Yacoub el Mansour**, the city entered its greatest period. *Kissarias* were constructed for the sale and storage of Italian and Oriental cloth, a new kasbah was begun, and a succession of poets and scholars arrived at the court. Mansour's reign also saw the construction of the great **Koutoubia Mosque** and minaret.

By the 1220s, the empire was beginning to fragment amid a series of factional civil wars, and Marrakesh fell into the familiar pattern of pillage, ruination and rebuilding. In 1269, it lost its status as capital when the Fes-based **Merenids** took power, though in 1374–86 it did form the basis of a breakaway state under the Merenid pretender Abderrahman ibn Taflusin.

Taking Marrakesh, then devastated by famine, in 1521, the **Saadians** provided a last burst of imperial splendour. Their dynasty's greatest figure, **Ahmed el Mansour**, having invaded Mali and seized control of the most lucrative caravan routes in Africa, had the **El Badi Palace** – Marrakesh's largest and greatest building project – constructed from the proceeds of this new wealth, and the dynasty also of course bequeathed to Marrakesh their wonderful mausoleum, the **Saadian Tombs**.

Under the **Alaouites** Marrakesh lost its status as capital to Meknes, but remained an important imperial city, and the need to maintain a southern base against the tribes ensured the regular presence of its sultans. But from the seventeenth to the nineteenth century, it shrank back from its medieval walls and lost much of its former trade.

During the last decades prior to the Protectorate, the city's fortunes revived somewhat as it enjoyed a return to favour with the Shereefian court. **Moulay Hassan** (1873–94) and **Moulay Abd el Aziz** (1894–1908) both ran their governments from here in a bizarre closing epoch of the old ways, accompanied by a final bout of frantic palace building. On the arrival of **the French**, Marrakesh gave rise to a short-lived pretender, the religious leader El Hiba, and for most of the colonial period it was run as a virtual fiefdom of its pasha, **T'hami el Glaoui** – the most powerful, autocratic and extraordinary character of his age (see p.362).

Since **independence**, the city has undergone considerable change, with rural emigration from the Atlas and beyond, new methods of cultivation on the Haouz plain and the development of a sizeable tourist industry. After Casablanca, it's Morocco's second largest city, with slightly over a million inhabitants, and its population continues to rise. It has a thriving industrial area and is the most important market and administrative centre of southern Morocco.

Arrival

The **train station** is a ten- to fifteen-minute walk from the centre of Guéliz, or a longer walk or bus ride to the Medina; the taxi fare should be around 15dh to the Medina, less to hotels in Guéliz. Buses #3, #4, #8, #10, #14 and #66 run to the Place Foucauld, alongside Place Djemaa el Fna, from Avenue Hassan II opposite the old station exit (halfway down platform 1 – if it's closed, exit via the Supratours office).

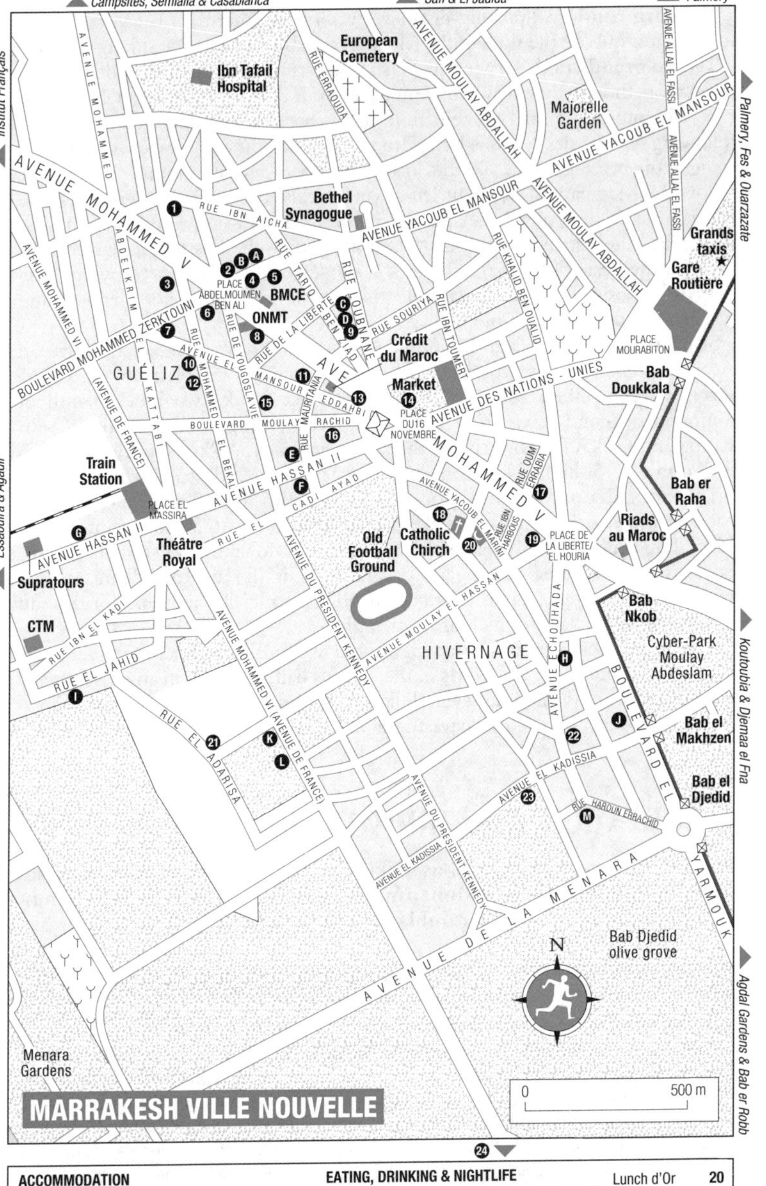

ACCOMMODATION

- Hôtel Atlas Medina K
- Hôtel du Pacha C
- Hôtel Farouk E
- Hôtel Fashion F
- Hôtel Franco-Belge A
- Hôtel le Grand Imilchil H
- Hôtel Ibis Moussafir Marrakech Centre Gare G
- Hôtel Ryad Mogador Menara L
- Hôtel Sofitel Marrakech M
- Hôtel Toulousain D
- Hôtel des Voyageurs B
- The Red House J
- Youth Hostel I

EATING, DRINKING & NIGHTLIFE

- African Chic 17
- Al Bahriya 16
- Al Fassia 5
- Amandine 10
- Café-Bar de l'Escale 11
- Café du Livre D
- Café des Negotiants 4
- Chesterfield Pub 8
- Chez Lamine Hadj 1
- Comptoir Darna 22
- Diamant Noir 17
- Grand Café de la Poste 13
- Hôtel Agdal 7
- Hôtel Farouk E
- Katsura 17
- La Taverne 6
- La Trattoria 12
- Le Cantanzaro 9
- Le Jacaranda 2
- Lunch d'Or 20
- Pacha Marrakech 24
- Paradise Disco 21
- Puerto Banus 18
- Resto Primo 14
- Rôtisserie de la Paix 15
- Samovar 3
- Theatro 23
- VIP Club 19

The **gare routière** (for long-distance bus services other than CTM or Supratours) is just outside the walls of the Medina by Bab Doukkala. Most long-distance collective **grands taxis** arriving in Marrakesh terminate immediately behind this bus station, though they may drop you off in front of it on Place Mourabiton. You can walk into the centre of Guéliz from the *gare routière* in around ten minutes by following Avenue des Nations Unies (to the right as you exit the bus station, then straight on bearing right). To the Place Djemaa el Fna it's around 25 minutes: follow the Medina walls (to your left as you exit the bus station) down to Avenue Mohammed V, then turn left. A petit taxi is about 10dh to the Djemaa el Fna, less to Guéliz. Alternatively, catch bus #16, from outside the bus station, which runs through the heart of Guéliz, or buses #3, #8, #10, #14, #16 or #66, which stop directly opposite Bab Doukkala itself (though the bus stop is not obvious), and head south to Place Foucauld.

Supratours services from Essaouira, Agadir, and the Western Sahara arrive on Avenue Hassan II next to the train station (accessed via platform 1). **CTM** services stop at their office on Rue Aboubaker Sedik, two blocks south of Supratours. Grands taxis from the **High Atlas villages** of Asni, Imlil, Setti Fatma and Oukaïmeden arrive at their own *gare routière*, 2km southwest of Bab er Robb – a 15dh taxi ride from the Djemaa el Fna, 20dh to Guéliz.

The city's **airport** is 4km southwest of town. Bus #19 (20dh one-way, 30dh for a round trip within two weeks) leaves half-hourly (6.30am–midnight) for Place Foucauld (by the Koutoubia) and Avenue Mohammed V (Guéliz). Petits taxis (for up to three passengers) or grands taxis (for up to six) are a more comfortable option, though they have fixed an artificially high fare for the run (currently 80dh, half as much again at night).

Arriving at the airport late at night, you won't always find the **exchange** kiosks open, but there are ATMs in the arrivals hall; taxis will in any case usually accept euros, and sometimes even dollars or sterling, at more or less the equivalent dirham rate, or you can have them call at an ATM en route (see p.379).

Orientation and information

Despite its size and the maze of its souks, Marrakesh is not too hard to navigate. The main artery is **Avenue Mohammed V**, leading from the Medina's unmistakeable landmark of the **Koutoubia** minaret to **Guéliz**, the downtown area of

Sightseeing bus tours

If you don't have much time and you want to scoot around Marrakesh's major sights in a day or two, the **hop-on hop-off Marrakech Tour bus** (☎0525 060006) could be for you. Using open-top double-deckers, with a commentary in several languages including English, the tour follows two circular routes: the first tours the Medina and Guéliz, calling at Place Foucauld (for the Djemaa and Koutoubia), Place des Ferblantiers (for the Bahia and El Badi Palaces, plus the Mellah), and the Menara Gardens; the second tours the palmery, following the Circuit de la Palmeraie. The Medina/Guéliz bus departs from outside *Boule de Neige* café in Place Abdelmoumen Ben Ali every 30min from 9am till 5pm (7pm April–July, 8pm Aug); the palmery bus leaves from the same place five times a day (afternoons only). You can get on and off where you like, and tickets (130dh) can be bought on board, or at Place Abdelmoumen Ben Ali or Place Foucauld. They are valid for 24 hours, so even if you start your tour after lunch, you can finish it the following morning.

Local bus routes

The following buses leave from Avenue el Mouahidine alongside Place Foucauld, opposite *Hôtel de Foucauld*:

#1 along Avenue Mohammed V to Guéliz, then up Avenue Mohammed Abdelkrim el Khattabi (Route de Casablanca) to Semlalia.

#3, #4, #8, #10, #14, #16 & #66 all go to Bab Doukkala (for the bus station), then on down Avenue Hassan II past the train station.

#6 and **#20** to Bab Ighli and the entrance to the Agdal gardens.

#16 to Guéliz via Bab Doukkala.

#17 and #26 to the Route de Fes for the palmery.

#19 circular route from the airport to Place Foucauld, then north up Avenue Mohammed V, south down Avenue Mohammed VI and back to the airport.

the Ville Nouvelle. You might want to consider hiring a guide to explore the Medina, but given a decent map, it really isn't necessary.

The ONMT **tourist office**, on Place Abdelmoumen Ben Ali in Guéliz (Mon–Fri 8.30am–4.30pm; ⓣ0524 436239), keeps a dossier of useful information with listings of hotels, campsites, car-rental firms and other contacts, and staff are generally happy to answer any questions. The I Love Marrakesh **website** at ⓦwww.ilovemarrakesh.com has listings of upmarket hotels, riads and restaurants, plus write-ups and some photos of the main tourist sights. Marrakech Travel Guide at ⓦwww.travelmarrakech.co.uk has advice and recommendations but hasn't been updated for a while.

Our own Rough Guide **city map** of Marrakesh, printed on tear-proof paper, is frankly the best you'll get. It's most easily obtained abroad, though local bookshops such as Librairie Chatr (see p.379) have been known to stock it. Otherwise, the free Marrakech Evasions map, produced by Éditions Bab Sabaa and given away in some upmarket shops, hotels, restaurants and riads, is better than any other maps you'll pay for.

City transport

It is a fairly long walk between Guéliz and the Medina, but there are plenty of **petits taxis**, which will take you between the two for around 10–15dh. There are taxi ranks at most major intersections in Guéliz, and in the Medina in the northwest corner of Place Djemaa el Fna, outside the *Grand Hôtel Tazi*, and at the Place des Ferblantiers end of Avenue Houman el Fetouaki. **Bus** #1 and #16 also run along Avenue Mohammed V between Guéliz and the Koutoubia in the Medina (for other bus routes, see box above).

Petits taxis have meters, which they should use; most trips should cost around 10–15dh during the day, or 15–20dh at night, when there is a surcharge on the meter price. If a taxi driver doesn't want to use the meter, it is because they intend to overcharge you. To and from the airport, and from the Hivernage hotels, taxi drivers have agreed amongst themselves an artificially high fixed price, and won't use the meter. If you get a petit taxi out to somewhere on the periphery, such as the palmery or one of the golf courses, and especially if the driver doesn't try to pull any stunts over the fare, it's worth getting a phone number to call them for the return journey.

In addition to taxis, there are **calèches**, horse-drawn cabs which line up on Place Foucauld near the Koutoubia, and at some of the fancier hotels. These can take up to five people and are not much more expensive than petits taxis, but be sure to fix the price in advance, especially for a tour of the town.

An alternative for exploring the more scattered city sights, such as the Agdal and Menara gardens or the palmery, is renting a **bicycle** or **moped** (see p.379); bicycles will cost around 100dh a day, mopeds more like 300dh. **Grands taxis** can also be chartered by the day for around 250dh – very reasonable if split between four people (the taxis take up to six passengers, but four is comfortable). Negotiate at the ranks in Djemaa el Fna or by the post office in Guéliz. By law grands taxis have to display prices for specified trips; these prices are per trip, not per person.

Accommodation

The **Medina** has the main concentration of small, budget hotels, especially in the area around the Djemaa el Fna. It is also where you'll find most of Marrakesh's **riads**, usually hidden away deep in its backstreets. **Guéliz**, whose hotels tend to be concentrated in the mid range, is handier for transport, especially for the train station. Hotels in **Hivernage** and **Semlalia** are upmarket, in modern buildings with swimming pools, but they're pretty soulless.

Advance bookings are a wise idea, especially for the more popular places in the Medina. The worst times are the **Easter** and **Christmas/New Year** holiday periods, when virtually every decent place can be full to capacity.

Medina hotels

Most of the Medina's budget hotel accommodation is concentrated in the small area south of the Djemaa el Fna, though more deluxe hotels are further afield. Those reviewed below are shown on the map on p.354, unless otherwise stated.

Dar les Cigognes 108 Rue de Berrima, Medina ⓣ0524 382740, ⓦwww.lescigognes.com; see map, p.365. A luxury boutique hotel run by a Swiss–American couple in two converted Medina houses that gets consistently good reports. It's done up in traditional fashion around the patio, but with modern decor in the rooms and suites. There's a library, a hammam, a jacuzzi, a salon and a terrace where you can see storks nesting on the walls of the royal palace opposite (hence the name, which means "house of the storks"). BB ❽

Dar Salam 162 Derb Ben Fayda off Rue el Gza near Bab Doukkala, Medina ⓣ0524 383110, ⓦwww.dar-salam.com; see map, 364. A Moroccan family home which takes in guests, this is a true *maison d'hôte* as opposed to a riad, a place to relax and put your feet up rather than admire the decor. The food is similarly unpretentious – tasty home-style Moroccan cooking, like your mum would make if she were Marrakshi. BB ❹

Hôtel Aday 111 Derb Sidi Bouloukat ⓣ0524 441920. Friendly budget hotel, well kept, clean and pleasantly decorated. The rooms, grouped around a central patio, are small and most have only inward-facing windows. Shower facilities are shared, with hot water round the clock. Single rooms are half the price of doubles, making them a very good deal for lone travellers, and you can sleep on the roof for 30dh. ❷

Hôtel Ali Rue Moulay Ismail ⓣ0524 444979. Used by groups heading to the High Atlas, so a good source of trekking (and other) information; also changes money, and can arrange car, minibus or 4WD rental, but sometimes has the air of a transport terminal. Booking ahead is advisable, but so is checking your room before taking it (all are en-suite with a/c, but some are a bit whiffy). There's cheap dorm accommodation (70dh BB) and a restaurant with all-you-can-eat buffet suppers, served on the rooftop terrace in summer. BB ❸

Hôtel Central Palace 59 Derb Sidi Bouloukat ⓣ0524 440235, ⓔhotelcentralapace@hotmail.com. A choice of simple rooms, or en-suite or a/c rooms, at this clean and well-kept budget hotel very usefully located just off Rue Bab Agnaou, a stone's throw from the Djemaa el Fna. ❷

Hôtel CTM Pl Djemaa el Fna ⓣ0524 442325. The hotel is above the old bus station (hence its name), now used as a car park, and handy if you're driving. The hotel is gradually being modernized, and there are currently three categories of rooms: old, unmodernized rooms with shared bathroom (no hot water); en-suite rooms, clean but drab, with hot-water showers; and modernized en-suite rooms with a/c in summer, heating in winter. The last category includes rooms 1–4, which overlook the square, though this does of course make them noisy. Breakfast (included in the room rate) is served on the roof terrace, which also overlooks the square. ❷

Hôtel Essaouira 3 Derb Sidi Bouloukat ⓣ0524 443805. One of the most popular cheapies in Marrakesh – and with good reason. It's a well-run, safe place, with thirty rooms, communal hot showers, a laundry service, baggage deposit and rooftop café. ❷

Hôtel de Foucauld Av el Mouahidine, facing Pl de Foucauld ⓣ0524 440806, ⓕ0524 441344. Rooms are a little sombre and some are a bit on the small side, but they're decent enough, with a/c, heating and constant hot water (with a choice of tub or shower). There's a roof terrace with views of the Koutoubia, and a restaurant with buffet suppers. The staff can arrange tours, help with local information, and put you onto guides for High Atlas trekking. BB ❹

Hôtel Gallia 30 Rue de la Recette ⓣ0524 445913, ⓔhotel.gallia@menara.ma. Beautifully kept hotel in a restored Medina mansion with immaculate en-suite rooms off two tiled courtyards, one with fountain, palm tree and caged birds. There's central heating in winter and a/c in summer. A long-time favourite and highly recommended. Book online, at least a month ahead if possible. Not strictly wheelchair accessible, but staff are very helpful to chair users and there are rooms with more-or-less level access. BB ❺

Hôtel Ichbilia 1 Rue Bani Marine ⓣ0524 381530. Near the Mabrouka cinema, and well placed for shops, banks and cafés, with rooms off a covered gallery, some plain and simple (but still clean and comfortable), others with a/c and private bathroom. Sometimes referred to as *Hotel Sevilla (Ichbilia* is the Arabic for Seville). ❷

Hôtel la Gazelle 12 Rue Bani Marine ⓣ0524 441112, ⓔhotel_lagazelle@hotmail.com. Well-kept if slightly dull hotel on a street with foodstalls and small grill cafés, with rooms around a covered patio – windows of downstairs rooms open onto the patio, those upstairs open to the outside. Some rooms have bathrooms, and there's a discount on the room price after three nights. ❷

Hôtel la Mamounia Av Bab Jdid ⓣ0524 388600, ⓦwww.mamounia.com; see map, p.365. Marrakesh's most famous hotel, in palatial grounds, with full facilities, including a hammam and sauna, a pool (of course), several bars and restaurants, and a casino, plus 1920s Art Deco touches by Jacques Majorelle (of Majorelle Garden fame), but despite the history, the fame and all the trimmings, standards of service have not always matched the price, though the hotel has recently reopened after a long renovation, so things may have changed. For a description of the gardens and some history of the hotel, see p.355. ❾

Hôtel Medina 1 Derb Sidi Bouloukat ⓣ0524 442997. Clean, friendly and very good value, with an English-speaking proprietor, hot shared showers, and a rooftop café (especially handy for breakfast). In summer there's also the option of a cheaper (30dh) bed on the roof. ❷

Hôtel Sherazade 3 Derb Djama, Rue Riad Zitoun el Kedim ⓣ0524 429305, ⓦwww.hotelsherazade.com. Before riads took off big time, this place was already on the scene, an old merchant's house, prettily done up, that gets rave reviews from our readers. Besides a lovely roof terrace, the hotel offers a wide variety of well-maintained rooms at different prices, not all en suite. Run very professionally by a German-Moroccan couple, it's extremely popular, so book well ahead. ❸

Jnane Mogador Hôtel Derb Sidi Bouloukat by 116 Rue Riad Zitoun el Kedim ⓣ0524 426323, ⓦwww.jnanemogador.com. Set in a beautifully restored old house, with charming rooms around a lovely fountain patio, its own hammam, and a roof terrace where you can have breakfast, or tea and cake. It's run by the same management as the *Essaouira*, rather more upmarket, but still great value. ❹

La Maison Arabe 1 Derb Assebbe Bab Doukkala, behind the Doukkala mosque ⓣ0524 387010, ⓦwww.lamaisonarabe.com; see map, p.364. Though not as famous as the *Mamounia*, this is Marrakesh's classiest hotel, boasting high standards of service in a gorgeous nineteenth-century mansion restored with fine traditional workmanship. The furnishings are sumptuous, as is the food (this was a restaurant before it was a hotel, and it even offers cookery classes –1600dh 1–2 people, 500–600dh per person for small groups). There are two beautifully kept patios and a selection of rooms and suites, all with TV, minibar, a/c and heating, some with private terrace and jacuzzi. There is no pool on the premises, but a free shuttle bus can take you to the hotel's private pool nearby. ❽

Les Jardins de la Medina 21 Derb Chtouka, Kasbah ⓣ0524 381851, ⓦwww.lesjardinsdelamedina.com; see map, p.365. A beautiful old palace transformed into a luxury hotel, its rooms set around an extensive patio garden with hammocks slung between the trees and a decent-sized pool. What the hotel really plugs, however, is its hammam-cum-beauty-salon where you can get manicured, pedicured, scrubbed and massaged till you glow. BB ❽

Villa des Orangers 6 Rue Sidi Mimoun, off Pl Youssef Ben Tachfine ⓣ0524 384638, ⓦwww.villadesorangers.com; see map, p.365. This gorgeous luxury establishment is officially a hotel, but it's a riad in the true sense of the word: an old house around a garden patio – three in fact – with orange trees and lots of lovely carved stucco. There's a range of rooms and suites, many with their own private terrace. Rates include breakfast and light lunch. ❾

Riads

Marrakesh is where the **riad** craze started, and the number is growing all the time. There are some sumptuous riads in Marrakesh, especially at the top end of the market, and some very friendly and homely places at the lower end of the market too, but some riads are overpriced and nothing special, so it pays to shop around. Most places offer low rates in July and August. All those listed here are shown on the Medina map on pp.364–365, unless otherwise stated. Though not officially classified as riads, the *Dar les Cigognes*, *Gallia*, *Jnane Mogador*, *Sherazade* and *Villa des Orangers* (see pp.348–349 & above) are all worth considering too.

Dar Ihssane 14 Derb Chorfa el Kebir, near Mouassine Mosque; see map, p.365 ⓣ0524 387826, ⓦwww.darihssane.com. A good-value riad in an eighteenth-century mansion with many original features (some of which were only discovered during renovation). It's owned by the nephew of painter Georges Bretegnier, and decorated with some of Bretegnier's original paintings and drawings. BB ❻

Le Clos des Arts 50 Derb Tbib, off Rue Riad Zitoun el Djedid ⓣ0524 375159, ⓦwww.leclosdesarts.com. A beautiful riad, full of the works of one of the proprietors, who is a painter and sculptor as well as an interior designer. Each room has its own style and colour, and the whole effect is warm and delightful, as are the owners, who give it a real personal touch. Facilities include a rooftop pool and free wi-fi throughout. BB ❼

Noir d'Ivoire 31 Derb Jedid, Bab Doukkala ⓣ0524 381653, ⓦwww.noir-d-ivoire.com. A magnificent riad, impressive from the moment you walk in, owned by an English interior designer, who's done it out in cream, brown and black (the name refers to the colour scheme), with a feel that manages to be classy yet cosy at the same time. There's a well-equipped gym, two pools and a bar, and service is punctilious, reflecting the fact that there's almost one staff member per guest. BB ❽

Riad 72 72 Derb Arset Aouzal ⓣ0524 387629, ⓦwww.riad72.com. A very sleek and stylish Italian-owned riad, with sparse but extremely tasteful modern decor, palms and banana trees in the courtyard and its own hammam (but no pool). The catering is Moroccan. The riad is part of a group called "Ouvo" (Italian for "egg") with two similarly stylish sister establishments, *Riad 12* and *Riad Due*. BB ❽

Riad Bayti 35 Derb Saka, Bab el Mellah ⓣ0524 380180, ⓦwww.riad-bayti.com. A great old house, formerly owned by a family of Jewish wine merchants in the Mellah, with that quarter's

Riad-booking agencies

Marrakesh Medina 102 Rue Dar el Bacha, Northern Medina ⓣ0524 442448, ⓦwww.marrakech-medina.com. A firm that's actually in the business of doing up riads as well as renting them out, with a reasonable selection in all price ranges.

Marrakech Riads Dar Cherifa, 8 Derb Charfa Lakbir, Mouassine, Northern Medina ⓣ0524 426463, ⓦwww.marrakech-riads.net. A small agency with only eight riads; committed to keeping it chic and authentic.

Riads au Maroc 1 Rue Mahjoub Rmiza, Guéliz ⓣ0524 431900, ⓦwww.riadomaroc.com. One of the first and biggest riad agencies with lots of choice in all price categories.

distinctive high ceilings and wide verandah, giving a spacious feel. Run by a dynamic young French couple, with warm modern decor that perfectly complements the classic architecture, and the smell of spices wafting in from the market below. Facilities include childcare and wi-fi, and just a few doors away they also run the smaller but very cool, ultra-modern *Riad Inaki* (ⓦwww.riadinaki.com). BB ⑦

Riad Jonan 35 Derb Bzou, off Rue de la Kasbah ⓣ0524 386448, ⓦwww.riadjonan.com. Laid-back and very friendly British-run riad in the Kasbah with lots of brick and terracotta tiles, stylish room decor, especially in the new wing, a/c in all but one room, a plunge pool, British TV, and a very easy-going atmosphere. BB ⑥

Riad Kniza 34 Derb l'Hotel, near Bab Doukkala ⓣ0524 376942, ⓦwww.riadkniza.com. Owned by a top antique dealer and tour guide (whose clients have included US presidents and film stars), this is one classy riad, with beautiful rooms, and a state-of-the-art pool, not to mention a sauna, hammam and massage room, genuine antiques for decoration, and solar panels for ecologically sound hot water, yet it still manages to feel like a real Moroccan family home. The family themselves (all English-speaking) are always on hand to make you feel welcome, the food is excellent and the service absolutely impeccable. BB ⑨

Riad Sahara Nour 118 Derb Dekkak ⓣ0524 376570, ⓦwww.riadsaharanour-marrakech.com. More than just a riad, this is a centre for art, self-development and relaxation. Art workshops in music, dance, painting and calligraphy are held here, and self-development programmes in meditation and relaxation techniques are available. Guests who wish to hold artistic happenings are encouraged, but you don't need to take part in these activities in order to stay here and enjoy the calm atmosphere on the patio, shaded by orange, loquat and pomegranate trees. BB ⑦

Riad Zolah 114–116 Derb el Hammam, near Mouassine Mosque; see map, p.356 ⓣ0524 387535, ⓦwww.riadzolah.com. An extremely well-run British-owned riad, with all sorts of little touches that make you feel like a special guest ("the most generous range of extras in Marrakesh", so they claim). Facilities include wi-fi, in-house hammam and massage room, tasteful decor with lots of white, generous splashes of colour, original features, and wonderful use of carpets and drapes. BB ⑧

Riyad al Moussika 17 Derb Cherkaoui, off Rue Douar Graoua ⓣ0524 389067, ⓦwww.riyad-al-moussika.ma. A gem of a riad, formerly owned by Thami el Glaoui (see p.362), with absolutely gorgeous decor, all designed to exact specifications in traditional Moroccan style by its Italian owner. The resulting combination of Moroccan tradition and Italian flair is harmonious and beautiful – like a traditional Marrakshi mansion, but better. The walls are decked with contemporary paintings by local artists, and the owner's son, a cordon bleu chef, takes care of the catering – in fact, the riad claims to have the finest cuisine in town. BB plus lunch and afternoon tea ⑨

Riyad el Cadi 86–87 Derb Moulay Abdelkader, off Rue Dabachi ⓣ0524 378098, ⓦwww.riyadelcadi.com. The former home of a German diplomat who was ambassador to several Arab countries, embellished with his wonderful collection of rugs and antiques and incorporating five patios, three salons, a pool, a hammam, free wi-fi and excellent standards of service. As well as ordinary guest rooms, there are two wonderful suites, and the "blue house", a patio with two double rooms, which is rented in its entirety. The riad is closed in July. BB ⑧

Guéliz

Hotels listed here are shown on the map on p.345.

Hôtel des Voyageurs 40 Bd Mohammed Zerktouni ⓣ0524 447218. This long-established budget hotel has rather an old-fashioned feel, but it's well kept, with spacious if rather sombre rooms and a pleasant little garden. ②

Hôtel du Pacha 33 Rue de la Liberté ⓣ0524 431327, ⓔhoteldupacha@wanadoo.net.ma. A 1930s-built hotel with large if rather drab rooms, most around a central courtyard, with a/c and satellite TV. There's a good restaurant, but no pool. ④

Hôtel Farouk 66 Av Hassan II ⓣ0524 431989, ⓔhotelfarouk@hotmail.com. Owned by the same family as the *Ali* in the Medina, and housed in a rather eccentric building, with all sorts of branches and extensions, it offers a variety of rooms – have a look at a few before choosing – all with hot showers. Staff are friendly and welcoming, and there's an excellent restaurant. BB ③

Hôtel Fashion 45 Av Hassan II ⓣ0524 423707, ⓔfashionhotel@menara.ma. Terracotta-tiled rooms and bathrooms, nicely carved black-painted wooden furnishings, reliable hot showers with a strong jet, and large windows grace the rooms at this tastefully designed three-star with a pool. A rooftop restaurant is planned but not yet open. BB ⑤

Hôtel Franco-Belge 62 Bd Mohammed Zerktouni ⓣ0524 448472. Decent but rather drab ground-floor rooms, some with shower, around a courtyard in what claims to be the oldest hotel in Guéliz, with hot water 8am–6pm. ❷

Hotel Ibis Moussafir Marrakech Centre Gare Av Hassan II/Pl de la Gare ⓣ0524 435929 to 32, ⓦwww.ibishotel.com. Tasteful chain hotel located right by the train station, not the most exciting accommodation in town, but good value, with efficient service, a swimming pool, a restaurant, a bar in the lobby and good buffet breakfasts available. It's worth asking for a room that's been recently renovated (currently those on the first floor). ❺

Hôtel Toulousain 44 Rue Tariq Ben Ziad ⓣ0524 430033, ⓦwww.geocities.com/hotel_toulousain. Excellent budget hotel originally owned by a Frenchman from Toulouse (hence the name); has a secure car park and a variety of rooms, some with shower, some with shower and toilet, some with shared facilities. BB ❷

Hivernage

Hivernage is completely uninteresting but contains several upmarket hotels, mostly used by package tours. The chain four- and five-stars have frankly amateurish standards of service in comparison with their equivalents abroad, and few people travelling independently bother with them nowadays as there are so many excellent deluxe riads in the Medina which are far more attractive. What some upmarket Hivernage hotels do offer, however, that riads do not, is wheelchair access, and they're also more child-friendly, and have large pools. The hotels listed here are shown on the map on p.345.

Hôtel Atlas Medina Av Moulay el Hassan ⓣ0524 339999, ⓦwww.hotelsatlas.com. The Atlas chain's top offering in Marrakesh, set amid extensive gardens and best known for its spa facilities, but service is mediocre, and certainly not five-star. Three rooms are adapted for wheelchair users. BB ❽

Hôtel Le Grand Imilchil Av Echouhada ⓣ0524 447653, ⓔhotel.imilchil@hotmail.com. This well-run three-star is an oasis of tranquillity in a location near Place de la Liberté that's handy for both the Medina and the Ville Nouvelle. The swimming pool is small but service is punctilious and the hotel is good value for the price. ❺

Hôtel Ryad Mogador Menara Av Mohammed VI (Av de France) ⓣ0524 339330, ⓦwww.ryadmogador.com. Five-star (though really more like a four-star) whose facilities include a health club and three restaurants, but alcohol is banned from the premises. The lobby is done out in classic style, with painted ceilings, chandeliers and a very Moroccan feel, and the receptionists wear traditional garb. Rooms, on the other hand, are modern, light and airy. There's a babysitting service, and four rooms are adapted for wheelchair users. ❽

Hôtel Sofitel Marrakech Rue Harroun Errachid ⓣ0524 425600, ⓦwww.sofitel.com. Definitely not up to five-star standards, but not too bad as package hotels go, done out in royal red, with 61 suites, and four rooms adapted for wheelchair users, plus two restaurants, two bars, three pools and a fitness centre with a sauna, jacuzzi and hammam. ❾

The Red House Bd el Yarmouk opposite the city wall ⓣ0524 437040 or 41, ⓦwww.theredhouse-marrakech.com. A beautiful nineteenth-century mansion (also called *Dar el Ahmar*) full of fine stucco and zellij work downstairs, where the restaurant offers gourmet Moroccan cuisine. Accommodation consists of eight luxurious suites – extremely chic and palatial – though European imperial rather than classic Moroccan in style. BB ❾

Camping and youth hostel

Camping Caravanning Ferdaous 13km from the city centre on the Casablanca road (N9, formerly P7) ⓣ0524 304090, ⓕ0524 302311. Good facilities and fine for an overnight stay if using a car or campervan, but not really convenient as a base for exploring Marrakesh on foot.

Relais de Marrakech 10km from the city centre on the Casablanca road, opposite Grand Stade football ground ⓣ0564 717328, ⓦwww.lerelaisdemarrakech.com. Upmarket campsite, with a pool, and also permanent tents and rooms (❹) as well as the option of pitching your own, or parking a campervan.

Youth Hostel Rue el Jahid, Guéliz; see map, p.345 ⓣ0524 447713. Friendly, quiet and sparkling clean, with a small garden. Very near to the train station, and even nearer to the CTM office, with dorm beds for 70dh BB.

The Djemaa el Fna

There's nowhere in Morocco like the **Djemaa el Fna** – no place that so effortlessly involves you and keeps you coming back for more. By day it's little more than a market, with a few snake charmers, storytellers and an occasional troupe of acrobats. In the evening it becomes a whole carnival of storytellers, musicians and entertainers. Come on down and you'll soon be immersed in the ritual: wandering round, squatting amid the circles of onlookers, giving a dirham or two as your contribution. If you want a respite, you can move over to the rooftop terraces of the *Argana* or the *Café du Grand Balcon* for a vista over the square.

As a foreigner in the Djemaa el Fna, you can feel something of an interloper. Sometimes the storyteller or musician will pick on you to take part or contribute generously to the end-of-show collection and, entering into the spectacle, it's best to go denuded of the usual tourist trappings such as watches, belt-wallet or too much money; **pickpockets** and scam artists operate (giving a "present" and then demanding payment for it is an old scam to beware of, asking tourists to change counterfeit euro coins is a more recent one). The crowds around performers are sometimes used as an opportunity to grope female foreigners, and by male Moroccans and gay male tourists for cruising.

In the evening, the food stalls set up and the real performers get going, in particular **musicians** playing all kinds of instruments: the *Aissaoua*, playing oboe-like *ghaitahs* next to the snake charmers; Andalous groups, with their *ouds* and violins; and the Gnaoua trance-healers who beat out hour-long hypnotic rhythms with iron clanging castanets, and pound tall drums with long curved sticks. Late at night, when only a few people are left in the square, you still encounter individual players, plucking away at their *ginbris,* the skin-covered two- or three-string guitars.

For refreshment, stalls offer orange and grapefruit juice (but have it squeezed in front of you if you don't want it adulterated), while neighbouring handcarts are piled high with dates, dried figs, almonds and walnuts, especially delicious in winter when they are freshly picked in the surrounding countryside. As dusk falls, the square becomes a huge open-air dining area, packed with stalls lit by gas lanterns, and the air is filled with wonderful smells and plumes of cooking smoke spiralling up into the night (see box, p.372).

The development of the Djemaa el Fna

Nobody is entirely sure when or how the Djemaa el Fna came into being – nor even what its **name** means. The usual translation is "assembly of the dead", a suitably epic title that may refer to the public display here of the heads of rebels and criminals (the Djemaa was a place of execution until well into the nineteenth century). The name might alternatively mean "the mosque of nothing" (djemaa means both "mosque" and "assembly" – interchangeable terms in Islamic society), recalling an abandoned Saadian plan to build a new grand mosque on this site.

Either way, as an open area between the original kasbah and the souks, the square has probably played its present role since the city's earliest days. It has often been the focal point for **rioting** and the authorities have plotted before now to close it down and move its activities outside the city walls. This happened briefly after independence in 1956, when the government built a corn market on part of the square and tried to turn the rest into a car park, but the plan lasted barely a year. Tourism was falling off and it was clearly an unpopular move. As novelist Paul Bowles observed, without the Djemaa, Marrakesh would be just another Moroccan city.

ACCOMMODATION			
Hôtel Aday	J	Hôtel la Gazelle	K
Hôtel Ali	B	Hôtel Medina	F
Hôtel Central Palace	C	Hôtel Sherazade	I
Hôtel CTM	A	Jnane Mogador Hôtel	H
Hôtel Essaouira	G		
Hôtel de Foucauld	E		
Hôtel Gallia	L		
Hôtel Ichbilia	D		

RESTAURANTS			
Argana	3	Grillade Chez Sbai	1
Café du Grand Balcon	6	Hôtel Ali	B
Café Restaurant Iceberg	13	Hôtel CTM	A
Chez Bahia	9	Les Prémices	8
Chez Chegrouni	4	Marrakchi	5
Earth Café	14	Pâtisserie des Princes	10
El Bahja	11	Restaurant Oscar Progrès	12
Grand Hôtel Tazi	15	Snack Café Toubkal	7
		Terrasses de l'Alhambra	2

The Koutoubia and around

The absence of architectural features on the Djemaa el Fna serves to emphasize the drama of the **Koutoubia Minaret**. Nearly 70m high and visible for miles on a clear morning, this is the oldest of the three great Almohad towers (the others are the Hassan Tower in Rabat and the Giralda in Seville) and the most complete. Its pleasing proportions – a 1:5 ratio of width to height – established the classic Moroccan design.

Completed under Sultan Yacoub el Mansour (1184–99), work on the minaret probably began shortly after the Almohad conquest of the city, around 1150. It displays many of the features that were to become widespread in Moroccan architecture – the wide band of ceramic inlay near the top, the pyramid-shaped, castellated *merlons* (battlements) rising above it, the use of *darj w ktaf* ("cheek and shoulder"; see *Moroccan architecture* colour section and other motifs – and it also established the alternation of patterning on different faces. Here, the top floor is similar on each of the sides but the lower two are almost eccentric in their variety. The semicircle of small lobed arches on the middle niche of the southeast face was to become the dominant decorative feature of Almohad gates. The three great copper balls at the top are the subject of numerous legends, mostly of supernatural interventions to keep away thieves. They are thought to have originally been made of gold, the gift of the wife of Yacoub el Mansour, presented as penance for breaking her fast for three hours during Ramadan.

Close to the arches, the stones of the main body of the tower become slightly smaller, which seems odd today, but not originally, when the whole minaret was covered with plaster and painted, like that of the Kasbah Mosque (see p.363). There was talk about restoring this on the Koutoubia back in 2000, but the authorities settled for a straight clean-up – to stunning effect, especially when it's floodlit at night. At the same time, archeologists excavated the original mosque, which predates the tower, confirming that it had had to be rebuilt to correct its alignment with Mecca.

Alongside the mosque, and close to Avenue Mohammed V, is the **tomb of Fatima Zohra**, now in a white *koubba*. She was the daughter of a seventeenth-century religious leader and tradition has it that she was a woman by day and a white dove by night; women still dedicate their children to her in the belief that her blessing will protect them.

To the south and west of the Koutoubia are the **Koutoubia Gardens**, attractively laid out with pools and fountains, roses, orange trees and palms, very handy for an afternoon stroll, and giving excellent views of the Koutoubia.

Hôtel la Mamounia

West of the Koutoubia, it's worth having a look round the gardens of the luxurious **Hôtel la Mamounia**, once royal grounds, laid out by the Saadians with a succession of pavilions. Today they're slightly Europeanized in style but have retained the traditional elements of shrubs and walkways. You can admire the gardens for the not cripplingly exorbitant cost of a tea on the terrace (though visitors are not supposed to enter wearing shorts or jeans).

Usually open only to hotel residents, the **Winston Churchill suite** is preserved as visited by its namesake. The hotel has been rebuilt and enlarged since his day, but decoratively, it is of most interest for the 1920s Art Deco touches of **Jacques Majorelle** (see p.370), and their enhancements, in 1986, by King Hassan II's then-favourite designer, **André Paccard**.

The souks and northern Medina

It is spicy in the souks, and cool and colourful. The smell, always pleasant, changes gradually with the nature of the merchandise. There are no names or signs; there is no glass...You find everything – but you always find it many times over.

Elias Canetti: The Voices of Marrakesh

The **souks** north of the Djemaa el Fna seem vast the first time you venture in, and almost impossible to navigate, but in fact the area that they cover is pretty compact. A long, covered street, **Rue Souk Smarine**, runs for half their length and then splits into two lanes – **Souk el Attarin** and **Souk el Kebir**. Off these

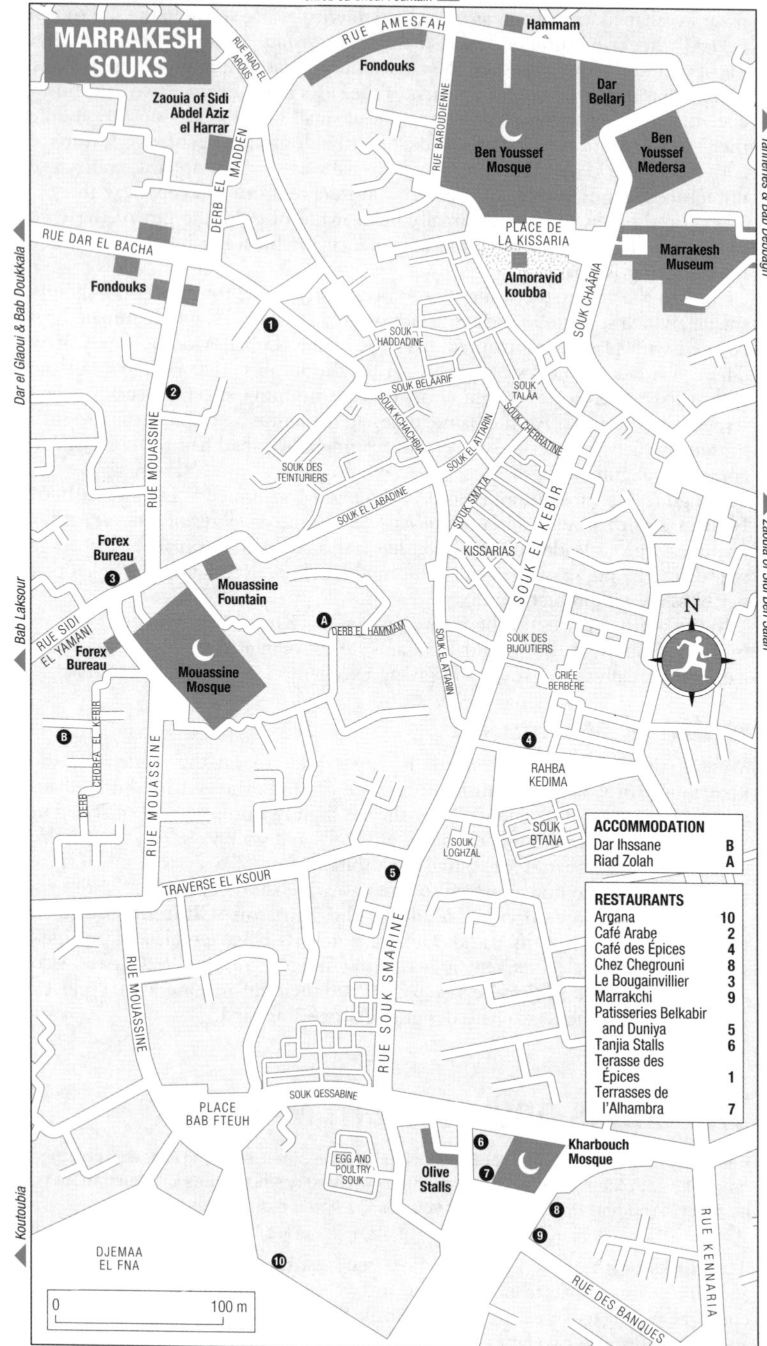
MARRAKESH SOUKS
Bab Moussoufa
Chrob ou Chouf Fountain
Tanneries & Bab Debbagh
Zaouia of Sidi Ben Salah
Dar el Glaoui & Bab Doukkala
Bab Laksour
Koutoubia
Rue Riad Zitoun el Kedim
Rue Riad Zitoun el Djedid
RUE AMESFAH
RUE RIAD EL AROUS
Hammam
Fondouks
Dar Bellarj
Zaouia of Sidi Abdel Aziz el Harrar
DERB EL MADDEN
RUE BAROUDIENNE
Ben Youssef Mosque
Ben Youssef Medersa
RUE DAR EL BACHA
PLACE DE LA KISSARIA
Marrakesh Museum
Almoravid koubba
SOUK CHAÂRIA
Fondouks
SOUK HADDADINE
SOUK BELAARIF
SOUK TALÂA
SOUK KCHACHBIA
SOUK EL AITARIN
SOUK CHERRATINE
RUE MOUASSINE
SOUK DES TEINTURIERS
SOUK EL LABADINE
SOUK SMATA
SOUK EL KEBIR
KISSARIAS
Forex Bureau
Mouassine Fountain
RUE SIDI EL YAMANI
DERB EL HAMMAM
SOUK EL AITARIN
SOUK DES BIJOUTIERS
Forex Bureau
Mouassine Mosque
CRIÉE BERBÈRE
N
DERB CHORFA EL KEBIR
RUE MOUASSINE
RAHBA KEDIMA
SOUK BTANA
SOUK LOGHZAL
TRAVERSE EL KSOUR
RUE SOUK SMARINE
RUE MOUASSINE
ACCOMMODATION
Dar Ihssane B
Riad Zolah A
RESTAURANTS
Argana 10
Café Arabe 2
Café des Épices 4
Chez Chegrouni 8
Le Bougainvillier 3
Marrakchi 9
Patisseries Belkabir and Duniya 5
Tanjia Stalls 6
Terasse des Épices 1
Terrasses de l'Alhambra 7
SOUK QESSABINE
PLACE BAB FTEUH
EGG AND POULTRY SOUK
Olive Stalls
Kharbouch Mosque
RUE KENNARIA
DJEMAA EL FNA
RUE DES BANQUES
0
100 m

are virtually all the individual souks: alleys and small squares devoted to specific crafts, where you can often watch part of the production process.

If you are staying for some days, you'll probably return often to the souks – and this is a good way of taking them in, singling out a couple of specific crafts or products to see, rather than being swamped by the whole. To get to grips with the general layout, you might find it useful to walk round the whole area once with a **guide**, but it's certainly not essential: with a reasonable map, you can quite easily navigate the souks on your own, and besides, getting a little bit lost is all part of the fun.

The most interesting **times** to visit are in the early morning (6.30–8am) and late afternoon, at around 4 to 5pm, when some of the souks auction off goods to local traders. Later in the evening, most of the stalls are closed, but you can wander unharassed to take a look at the elaborate decoration of their doorways and arches; those stalls that stay open, until 7 or 8pm, are often more amenable to bargaining at the end of the day. For more on shopping, see p.378.

The easiest approach to the main souks from the Djemaa el Fna is by the *Terrasses de l'Alhambra* (see p.372), where a lane to the left of the restaurant leads to Souk Ableuh, dominated by stalls selling olives. Continue through here and you will come out opposite the archway that marks the beginning of Rue Souk Smarine.

Souk Smarine and the Rahba Kedima

Busy and crowded, **Rue Souk Smarine** is an important thoroughfare, traditionally dominated by textiles and clothing. Today, tourist "bazaars" are moving in, but there are still dozens of shops in the arcades selling and tailoring traditional shirts and kaftans. The street is covered by an iron trellis with slats across it that restrict the sun to shafts of light; this replaces the old rush (*smar*) roofing, which along with many of the souks' more beautiful features was destroyed by a fire in the 1960s.

Just over 100m up Souk Smarine, you can pass through the passageways to the right (on the east side that is) into **Rahba Kedima**, a square with stalls set up in the middle selling baskets, hats and souvenirs. Immediately to the right, as you go in, is **Souk Loghzal**, once a slave market, then a wool market, now given over to second-hand clothes.

The most interesting aspect of Rahba Kedima are the **apothecary stalls** around the southwest entrance to the square. These sell traditional cosmetics – earthenware saucers of cochineal (*kashiniah*) for lip-rouge, powdered *kohl* (traditionally made of stibnite, a mineral form of antimony trisulphide, but commonly substituted with cheaper lead sulphide – both are toxic) for darkening the edges of the eyes, henna (the only cosmetic unmarried women are supposed to use) and the sticks of *suak* (walnut root or bark) with which you see Moroccans cleaning their teeth. The same stalls also sell herbal and animal ingredients still in widespread use for spells and medicinal cures. As well asaphrodisiac roots and tablets, you'll see dried pieces of lizard and stork, fragments of beaks, talons and other bizarre animal products. Some shops (to be avoided) also sell gazelle skulls, leopard skins and other products from illegally poached endangered wild animals. The *Café des Épices* (see p.373) overlooks the square and is a good place to take a breather.

La Criée Berbère

At the end of Rahba Kedima, a passageway to the left gives access to another, smaller square – a bustling, carpet-draped area known as **La Criée Berbère** (the Berber auction), also called the **Souk Zrabia**.

It was here that the old **slave auctions** were held, just before sunset every Wednesday, Thursday and Friday, until the French occupied the city in 1912.

▲ Marrakesh souks

They were conducted, according to travel writer Budgett Meakin's 1900 account (see p.602), "precisely as those of cows and mules, often on the same spot by the same men…with the human chattels being personally examined in the most disgusting manner, and paraded in lots by the auctioneers, who shout their attractions and the bids". Most had been kidnapped and brought in with the caravans from Mali, travelling on foot – those too weak to make it were left to die en route.

These days, the souk specializes in **rugs and carpets**, and if you have the time and willpower you could spend the best part of a day here while endless (and often identical) stacks are unfolded and displayed before you. Some of the most interesting are the Berber rugs from the High Atlas – bright, geometric designs that look very different after being laid out on the roof and bleached by the sun. The dark, often black, backgrounds usually signify rugs from the Glaoui country, up towards Telouet; the reddish-backed carpets are from Chichaoua, a small village nearly halfway to Essaouira, and are also common.

Around the kissarias

Just north of the passages leading to Rahba Kedima, Souk Smarine forks, with Souk el Attarin leading off to the left, while the main street changes its name to **Souk el Kebir**, and continues past (on your left) the **kissarias**, the covered markets at the heart of the souks, mostly selling blankets, clothes and leather goods. Off Souk el Kebir to the right, **Souk des Bijoutiers** is a modest jewellers' lane, less varied than the one established by Jewish craftsmen in the Mellah (see p.367).

At the northern end of Souk el Kebir is a convoluted web of alleys that comprise the **Souk Cherratine**, essentially a leather workers' souk, with dozens of purse-makers and sandal cobblers. If you bear left through this area and then turn right (or vice versa), you should arrive at Place de la Kissaria (see opposite).

The Dyers' Souk and around

The other road leading north from the fork in Souk Smarine (see above) is **Souk el Attarin**, originally the spice and perfume souk, which passes along the west side of the *kissarias*, before itself forking. The right-hand fork is **Souk Smata**, also called the **Souk des Babouches** (slipper market), lined with shops selling Moroccan slippers (though actually the best shop for these is Ben Zarou Frères at 1 Kissariat Drouj, off Souk el Attarin by no. 116); Souk Smata eventually leads through to Souk Cherratine (see opposite).

The left-hand fork from Souk el Attarin is **Souk Kchachbia**, which contains some interesting shops including Femmes de Marrakech (see p.379) and, directly behind it, Moulay Larbai's mirror shop. A right turn just past Femmes de Marrakech, by Moulay Larbai's shop, leads to **Souk Haddadine**, the blacksmiths' souk, whose banging and clanging you'll hear long before arriving. Before you get that far, the first or second left off Souk Kchachbia if coming from Souk el Attarin both lead through to **Souk des Teinturiers**, the dyers' souk, the area's main attraction, and always colourful, hung with bright skeins of wool or fabric drying in the sun,You can also usually catch some of the dyers at work, pounding cloth in their big vats of coloured liquid.

West of the dyers' souk, the street widens out into a square opposite an elaborate triple-bayed **fountain** adjoining the Mouassine Mosque. Built in the mid-sixteenth century under the prolific Saadian builder, Abdallah el Ghalib, it is one of many such fountains in Marrakesh with a basin for humans set next to two larger troughs for animals; its installation was a pious act, directly sanctioned by the Koran in its charitable provision of water for men and beasts. To get back to the Djemaa el Fna from here, continue on past the Mouassine Mosque and take a left down Rue Mouassine.

Around Place de la Kissaria

At the northern end of the souks area, is **Place de la Kissaria**, an open space surrounded by important public buildings. Its north side is dominated by the **Ben Youssef Mosque**, successor to an original put up by the city's Almoravid founders. The mosque was completely rebuilt under the Almohads, and several times since, so that the building you see today dates largely from the nineteenth century.

The Marrakesh Museum

On the east side of Place de la Kissaria is the **Marrakesh Museum** (daily 9am–6.30pm; 40dh ticket includes entry to the Almoravid *koubba*, combined ticket with Ben Youssef Medersa 60dh), housed in a magnificent late-nineteenth-century palace, **Dar Mnebbi**. The palace was built for Mehdi Mnebbi, defence minister of Moulay Abdelziz (1894–1908), who later became Moroccan ambassador in London. Nearly derelict after years of neglect, the palace was bought up and restored by local arts patron Omar Benjoullan, and reopened in 1997. It houses exhibitions of Moroccan art and sculpture, both traditional (in the main hall and surrounding rooms), and contemporary (in what were the palace kitchens). It is the restoration itself, however, that is most remarkable, especially in what was the hammam, and in the now-covered inner courtyard with its huge brass lamp hung above a central fountain.

Almoravid koubba

On the southern side of Place de la Kissaria, opposite the Ben Youssef Mosque, the **Almoravid koubba** (Koubba Ba'adiyn; daily 9am–6pm; same ticket as Marrakesh Museum) is just a small, two-storey kiosk, but as the only Almoravid building to survive intact in Morocco (excepting possibly a minaret in Tit near El Jadida; see p.321), its style is at the root of all Moroccan architecture. Its motifs – such as pine cones, palms and acanthus leaves –appear again in later buildings such as the nearby Ben Youssef Medersa (see p.360). The windows on each of the different sides became the classic shapes of Almohad and Merenid design – as did the merlons, the complex "ribs" on the outside of the dome, and the square and star-shaped octagon on the inside, which is itself repeated at each of its corners. It was probably just a small ablutions annex to the Ben Youssef Mosque, but its architecture gives us our only clue as to what that mosque might originally have looked like.

Excavated only in 1952, the *koubba* had previously been covered over amid the many rebuildings of the Ben Youssef Mosque. It is well below today's ground level, and you have to go down two flights of stairs to get to the level it was built at, now uncovered once again thanks to recent excavations. Once down there, you can also look around the attendant facilities, including a large water cistern, and remains of latrines and fountains for performing ablutions, much like those you will still find adjacent to many Moroccan mosques.

Ben Youssef Medersa

Just 30m north of the museum is the entrance to the **Ben Youssef Medersa** (daily 9am–6pm; 40dh, combined ticket with Marrakesh Museum and Almoravid *koubba* 60dh), a koranic school attached to the Ben Youssef Mosque, where students learned the Koran by rote.

Like most of its counterparts up in Fes (see p.217 for a description of their development and function), the Ben Youssef was a Merenid foundation, established by the "Black Sultan" Abou el Hassan (1331–49), but rebuilt in the 1560s, under the Saadians. As with the slightly later Saadian Tombs, no surface is left undecorated, and the overall quality of its craftsmanship, whether in carved wood, stuccowork or zellij tilework, is startling.

The **central courtyard**, its carved cedarwood lintels weathered almost flat on the most exposed side, is unusually large. Along two sides run wide, sturdy, columned arcades, which were probably used to supplement the space for teaching in the neighbouring mosque. Above them are some of the windows of the **dormitory quarters**, which are reached by stairs from the entry vestibule, and from which you can get an interesting perspective – and attempt to fathom how over eight hundred students were once housed in the building. One room is furnished as it would have been when in use.

At its far end, the court opens onto a **prayer hall**, where the decoration, mellowed on the outside with the city's familiar pink tone, is at its best preserved and most elaborate, with a predominance of pinecone and palm motifs.

The tanneries and northern gates

The main souks – and the tourist route – stop abruptly at Place de la Kissaria. Beyond them, in all directions, are ordinary **residential quarters** of the Medina.

North of the entrance to the Ben Youssef Medersa, you quickly reach a fork in the side street. Bear right and keep going as straight as possible, and after about fifteen minutes, you'll reach the tanneries and the ramparts by Bab Debbagh. Before the tanneries you'll cross a small square and intersection, **Place el Moukef**, where a busy street to the left leads to Bab el Khemis (see opposite). Turning right instead, you arrive within ten minutes at Place Ben Salah and the **Zaouia of Sidi Ben Salah** with a very fine prominent minaret, commissioned by a fourteenth-century Merenid sultan.

Bab Debbagh and the tanneries

Bab Debbagh is supposedly Almoravid in design, though over the years it must have been almost totally rebuilt. Passing through the gate, you become aware of its very real defensive purpose: three internal chicanes are placed in such a manner as to force anyone attempting to storm it to make several turns. Just before the gate, several shops on the left give good views over the quarter from their roofs, and shopkeepers will let you up (for a small fee – agree it first or you'll be mercilessly overcharged).

Looking out, you get partial views over the **tanneries**, more scattered and thus less interesting to look at than those at Fes. They were built here at the edge of the city not only because of the smell, but also for access to water: a stream, the Oued Issil, runs just outside the walls. If you want to take a closer look at the tanning process, come in the morning, when the cooperatives are at work. The smell comes largely from the first stage, where the hides are soaked in a vat of pigeon droppings. The natural dyes traditionally used to colour the leather have largely been replaced by chemicals, many of them carcinogenic – a fact to remember when you see people standing waist-deep in them. One tannery that's easy to find is on the north side of the street about 200m before Bab Debbagh, opposite the blue-tiled stand-up fountain, with another one about 200m further west. Ignore hustlers trying to persuade you that you have to pay them for entry.

Bab el Khemis

The road north from Bab Debbagh, outside the ramparts, takes you up to **Bab el Khemis**, another reconstructed Almoravid gate. Built at an angle in the walls, it is surrounded by concentric rings of decoration and topped with Christmas-tree-like castellations. Its name, means "Thursday Gate", a reference to the market held outside, 400m to the north, past a *marabout's* tomb and a former cemetery, now landscaped as a little park. Although the main market is held on a Thursday morning, there are stalls out most days. It is really a local produce market, though odd handicraft items do occasionally surface.

North of the Ben Youssef Mosque

The area immediately **north of the Ben Youssef Mosque** is cut by two main streets: Rue Assouel (which leads up to Bab el Khemis) and Rue Bab Taghzout, which runs up to the gate of the same name and to the Zaouia of Sidi Bel Abbes. These were, with Bab Doukkala, the principal approaches to the city until the twentieth century and along them you find many of the old **fondouks** used for storage and lodging by merchants visiting the souks.

One of these *fondouks* is sited just south of the mosque and a whole series can be found along **Rue Amesfah**, which, if you bear left under the archway north of the entrance to the Ben Youssef Medersa and continue to the junction with **Rue Baroudienne**, is the street more or less directly ahead of you. Most of the *fondouks* are still used in some commercial capacity, as workshops or warehouses, and the doors to their courtyards often stand open. Some date from Saadian times and have fine details of woodcarving or stuccowork. So long as they are not people's homes, nobody seems to mind tourists wandering in for a quick look.

The Zaouia of Sidi Bel Abbes

If you follow Rue Baroudienne north from its junction with Rue Amesfah, and turn right at the end, you pass another *fondouk*, opposite a small sixteenth-century recessed fountain known as **Chrob ou Chouf** ("drink and look"), which is worth a second glance for its carved cedarwood lintel. Take the next left, and around 500m further north is the old city gate of **Bab Taghzout**. This marked the limits of the Medina from Almoravid times until the eighteenth century, when Sultan Mohammed Abdallah extended the walls to enclose the **Zaouia of Sidi Bel Abbes,** the most important of Marrakesh's seven saints – seven holy men whose tombs were established as a circuit for pilgrims under

El Glaoui: the Pasha of Marrakesh

T'hami el Glaoui, Pasha of Marrakesh during the French Protectorate, was the last great southern tribal leader, a shrewd supporter of colonial rule (see box, p.410) and personal friend of Winston Churchill. Cruel and magnificent in equal measure, he was a spectacular party-giver in an age where rivals were not lacking. At the extraordinary *difas* or banquets held at the Dar el Glaoui for his Western friends, "nothing", as Gavin Maxwell wrote, "was impossible." Hashish and opium were freely available, and "to his guests T'hami gave whatever they wanted, whether it might be a diamond ring, a present of money in gold, or a Berber girl or boy from the High Atlas".

He was so hated that, on his death in 1956, a mob looted the palace, destroying its fittings and the cars in its garages, and lynching any of his henchmen that they found. However, passions have burnt out over the years, and the family has been rehabilitated. One of T'hami's sons, Glaoui Abdelssadak, rose to high rank in the Moroccan civil service and became vice president of Gulf Oil.

the Alaouite ruler Moulay Ismail in the seventeenth century to bring tourists into Marrakesh. The **zaouia**, as a cult centre, often wielded great influence and served as a refuge for political dissidents.

The present buildings date largely from the time of Moulay Ismail, who had them rebuilt, an act probably inspired more by politics than piety. Non-Muslims are not allowed to enter, but may see something of the complex and its activities from outside the official boundary, but they should not try to enter the main courtyard. The *zaouia* has always prospered and still owns much of the quarter to the north and continues its educational and charitable work, distributing food each evening to the blind.

West to Bab Doukkala: Dar el Glaoui

West from Ben Youssef towards **Bab Doukkala**, the route, once you've found your way down through Souk Haddadine to **Rue Bab Doukkala**, is a sizeable thoroughfare and very straightforward to follow. Midway, you pass the **Dar el Glaoui**, the old palace of the pasha who ruled Marrakesh on behalf of the French during the colonial period, when he was feted by Europeans, and hated by Marrakshis (see box above). His palace now houses the offices of the UMT trade union federation, but you can usually pop in to look at the patio.

The southern Medina

The area south of Djemaa el Fna is quite different from that to the north of it, generally more open and containing **Dar el Makhzen** (the royal palace), the **kasbah** (old inner citadel), and the **Mellah** (former Jewish quarter). The two obvious focal sights, not to be missed, are the **Saadian Tombs**, preserved in the shadow of the Kasbah Mosque, and **El Badi**, the ruined palace of Ahmed el Mansour. Also worth seeing are the **Bahia Palace** and the nearby Dar Si Said and Tiskiwin **museums**.

The Saadian Tombs and around

The **Saadian Tombs** (Sat–Thurs 8.30–11.45am & 2.30–5.45pm, Fri 8.30–11.30am & 2.45–5.45pm; 10dh), belonging to the dynasty which ruled Morocco from 1554 to 1669, escaped plundering by the rapacious Alaouite sultan Moulay Ismail, probably because he feared bad luck if he desecrated them. Instead, he blocked all access bar an obscure entrance from the Kasbah Mosque. The tombs lay half-ruined and half-forgotten until they were rediscovered by a French aerial survey in 1917, and a passageway was built to give access from the side of the Kasbah Mosque. Restored, they are today the kasbah's main "sight", housed in a quiet, high-walled enclosure, shaded with shrubs and palms. The best time to see them is first thing in the morning, before the crowds arrive, or late in the afternoon when they, and the heat, have largely gone.

There was probably a burial ground behind the royal palace before the Saadian period, but the earliest tomb here dates from 1557, and the main structures were built under Sultan Ahmed el Mansour, around the same time as the Ben Youssef Medersa and the El Badi Palace. A few prominent Marrakshis continued to be buried in the mausoleums after Saadian times: the last, in 1792, was the "mad sultan", Moulay Yazid, whose 22-month reign was one of the most violent and sadistic in the nation's history. Named as the successor to Sidi Mohammed, Moulay Yazid threw himself into a series of revolts against his father, waged an inconclusive war with Spain, and brutally suppressed a Marrakesh-based rebellion in support of his brother. A massacre followed his capture of the city, though he had little time to celebrate his victory – a bullet in the head during a rebel counterattack killed him soon after.

The simplest route to the tombs from the Djemaa el Fna is to follow **Rue Bab Agnaou**. At its southern end you come to a small square flanked by two gates. Directly ahead is **Bab er Robb**, leading out of the Medina towards the High Atlas mountains. To its left, somewhat battered and eroded, is **Bab Agnaou**, one of the two original entrances to the kasbah, though the magnificent blue granite gateway which stands here today was built in 1885. The name actually means "black people's gate", a reference to its use by swarthy commoners, while the fair-complexioned aristocracy had their own entrance into the kasbah (now long gone). The gate is surrounded by concentric arches of decoration and topped with an inscription in decorative script, which reads: "Enter with blessing, serene people." Notice how the semicircular frieze above the arch creates a three-dimensional effect without any actual depth of carving.

Passing through the gate, the **Kasbah Mosque** is in front of you: its minaret looks gaudy and modern but is, in fact, contemporary with both the Koutoubia and Hassan towers – it was restored to its exact original state in the 1960s. The narrow passageway to the Saadian Tombs is well signposted, at the right-hand corner of the mosque.

The mausoleums

There are two main **mausoleums** in the enclosure. The finest is on the left as you come in – a beautiful group of three rooms, built to house Ahmed el Mansour's own tomb and completed within his lifetime. Continuing round from the courtyard entrance, the first hall is a **prayer oratory**, a room probably not intended for burial, though now almost littered with the thin marble stones of Saadian princes. It is here that Moulay Yazid was laid out, perhaps in purposeful obscurity.

Architecturally, the most important feature of this mausoleum is the **mihrab**, its pointed horseshoe arch supported by an incredibly delicate arrangement of columns. Opposite this is another elaborate arch, leading to the domed **central chamber** and **Ahmed el Mansour's tomb**, which you can glimpse through the next door in the court. The tomb, slightly larger than those surrounding it, lies right in the middle, flanked on either side by those of the sultan's sons and successors. The room itself is spectacular; faint light filtering onto the tombs from an interior

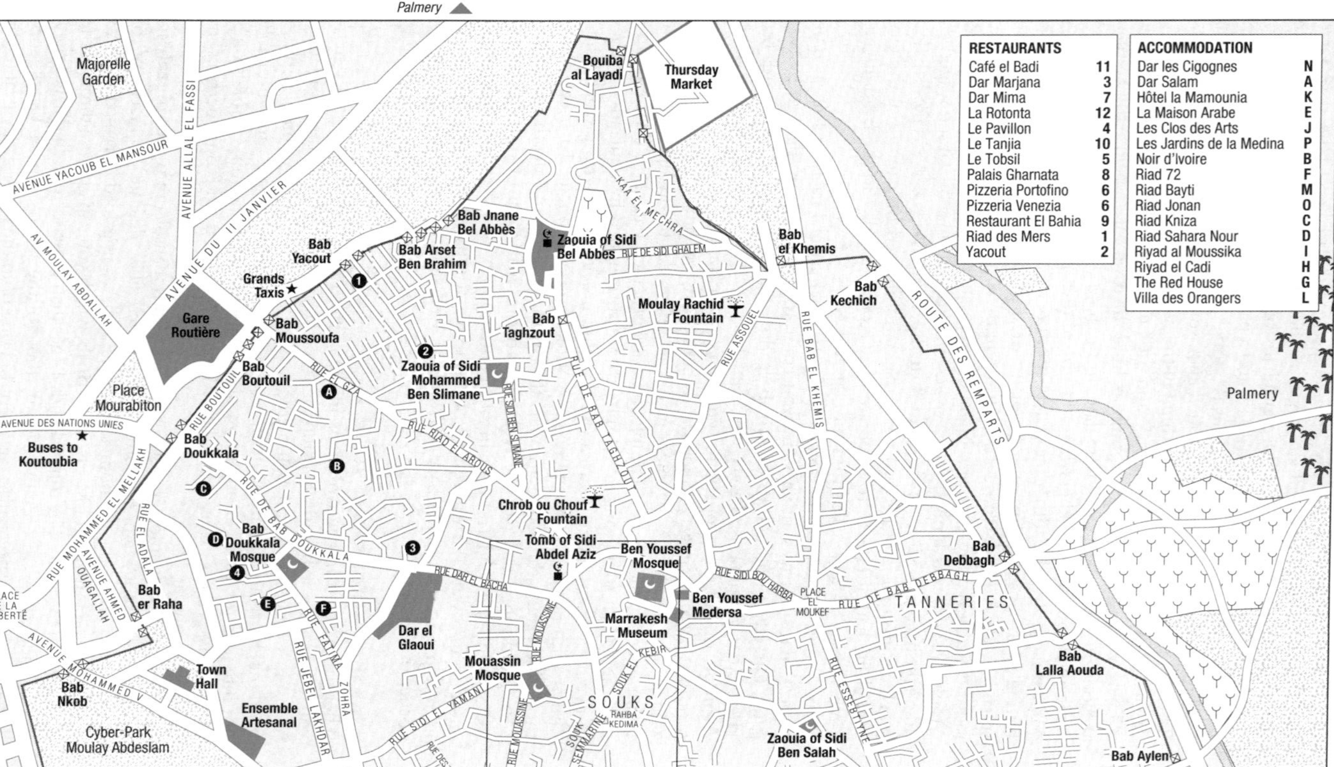
RESTAURANTS
Café el Badi 11
Dar Marjana 3
Dar Mima 7
La Rotonta 12
Le Pavillon 4
Le Tanjia 10
Le Tobsil 5
Palais Gharnata 8
Pizzeria Portofino 6
Pizzeria Venezia 6
Restaurant El Bahia 9
Riad des Mers 1
Yacout 2
ACCOMMODATION
Dar les Cigognes N
Dar Salam A
Hôtel la Mamounia K
La Maison Arabe E
Les Clos des Arts J
Les Jardins de la Medina P
Noir d'Ivoire B
Riad 72 F
Riad Bayti M
Riad Jonan O
Riad Kniza C
Riad Sahara Nour D
Riyad al Moussika I
Riyad el Cadi H
The Red House G
Villa des Orangers L
Palmery
Guéliz
Majorelle Garden
Thursday Market
Bouiba al Layadi
Bab Jnane Bel Abbès
Zaouia of Sidi Bel Abbes
Bab el Khemis
Bab Kechich
Bab Yacout
Bab Arset Ben Brahim
Grands Taxis
Gare Routière
Bab Moussoufa
Bab Boutouil
Bab Doukkala
Place Mourabiton
Buses to Koutoubia
Bab Taghzout
Moulay Rachid Fountain
Zaouia of Sidi Mohammed Ben Slimane
Chrob ou Chouf Fountain
Tomb of Sidi Abdel Aziz
Ben Youssef Mosque
Ben Youssef Medersa
Marrakesh Museum
Bab Doukkala Mosque
Dar el Glaoui
Mouassin Mosque
SOUKS
TANNERIES
Bab Debbagh
Bab Lalla Aouda
Bab Aylen
Zaouia of Sidi Ben Salah
Bab er Raha
Town Hall
Ensemble Artesanal
Bab Nkob
Cyber-Park Moulay Abdeslam
PLACE DE LA LIBERTÉ
ROUTE DES REMPARTS
AVENUE YACOUB EL MANSOUR
AVENUE ALLAL EL FASSI
AVENUE DU 11 JANVIER
AV MOULAY ABDALLAH
AVENUE DES NATIONS UNIES
RUE MOHAMMED EL MELLAKH
RUE EL ADALA
AVENUE AHMED OUAGALLAH
AVENUE MOHAMMED V
RUE BOUTOUIL
RUE EL GZA
RUE RIAD EL AROUS
RUE SIDI BEN SLIMANE
RUE DE BAB TAGHZOUT
RUE DE BAB DOUKKALA
RUE DAR EL BACHA
RUE FATIMA ZOHRA
RUE JEBEL LAKHDAR
RUE SIDI EL YAMANI
RUE MOUASSINE
SOUK SEMMARINE
RAHBA KEDIMA
SOUK EL KEBIR
RUE DE SIDI GHALEM
KAA EL MECHRA
RUE ASSOUEL
RUE BAB EL KHEMIS
RUE SIDI BOU HABBA
PLACE EL MOUKEF
RUE DE BAB DEBBAGH
RUE ESSEBTIYNE
RUE DES-

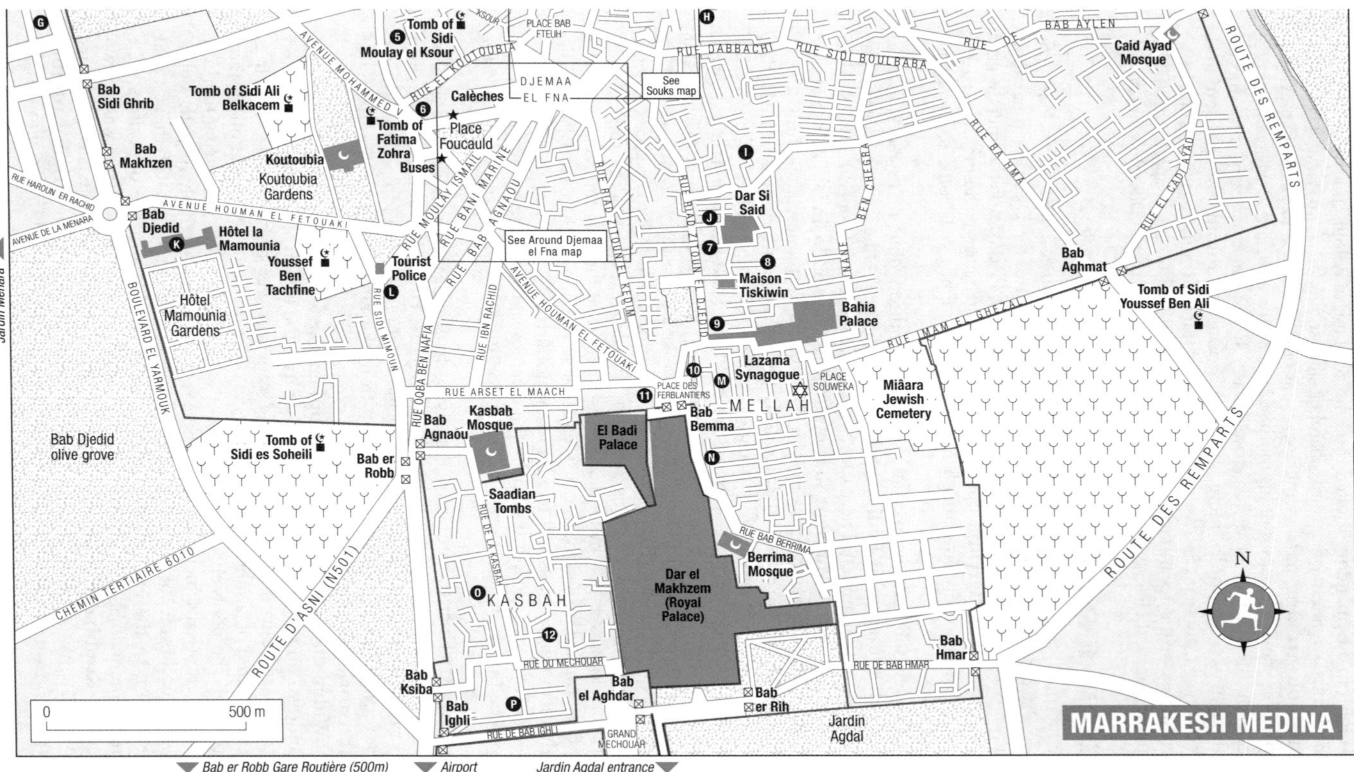
MARRAKESH MEDINA
N
0
500 m
Bab er Robb Gare Routière (500m)
Airport
Jardin Agdal entrance
Jardin Menara
Tomb of Sidi Moulay el Ksour
Caid Ayad Mosque
Bab Sidi Ghrib
Tomb of Sidi Ali Belkacem
Calèches
Tomb of Fatima Zohra
Place Foucauld
Buses
Bab Makhzen
Koutoubia
Koutoubia Gardens
Bab Djedid
Hôtel la Mamounia
Youssef Ben Tachfine
Tourist Police
Hôtel Mamounia Gardens
Dar Si Said
Maison Tiskiwin
Bahia Palace
Bab Aghmat
Tomb of Sidi Youssef Ben Ali
Lazama Synagogue
PLACE SOUWEKA
Miâara Jewish Cemetery
PLACE DES FERBLANTIERS
MELLAH
Bab Bemma
Kasbah Mosque
El Badi Palace
Bab Agnaou
Bab er Robb
Bab Djedid olive grove
Tomb of Sidi es Soheili
Saadian Tombs
Berrima Mosque
Dar el Makhzem (Royal Palace)
KASBAH
Bab Hmar
Bab Ksiba
Bab el Aghdar
Bab er Rih
Bab Ighli
GRAND MECHOUAR
Jardin Agdal
DJEMAA EL FNA
See Souks map
See Around Djemaa el Fna map
PLACE BAB FTEUH
KSOUR
BAB AYLEN
RUE DABBACHI
RUE SIDI BOULBABA
RUE DE
RUE BA HMA
RUE EL CADI AYAD
BEN CHEGRA
INANE
ROUTE DES REMPARTS
AVENUE MOHAMMED V
RUE EL KOUTOUBIA
RUE HAROUN ER RACHID
AVENUE DE LA MENARA
AVENUE HOUMAN EL FETOUAKI
RUE MOULAY ISMAIL
RUE BANI MARINE
RUE BAB AGNAOU
RUE RIAD ZITOUN EL KEDIM
RUE RIAD ZITOUN EL DJEDID
RUE IBN RACHID
RUE SIDI MIMOUN
RUE OQBA BEN NAFIA
RUE ARSET EL MAACH
RUE IMAM EL GHEZALI
BOULEVARD EL YARMOUK
CHEMIN TERTIAIRE 6010
ROUTE D'ASNI (N501)
RUE DE LA KASBAH
RUE BAB BERRIMA
RUE DU MECHOUAR
RUE DE BAB IGHLI
RUE DE BAB HMAR
G
H
I
J
K
L
M
N
O
P
5
6
7
8
9
10
11
12

lantern in a tremendous vaulted roof, the zellij full of colour and motion and the undefined richness of a third chamber almost hidden from view. The **other mausoleum**, older and less impressive, was built by Ahmed in place of an existing pavilion above the tombs of his mother, Lalla Messaouda, and of Mohammed ech Sheikh, the founder of the Saadian dynasty. It is again a series of three rooms, though two are hardly more than *loggias*. Outside, **round the garden and courtyard**, are scattered the tombs of over a hundred more Saadian princes and members of the royal household. Like the privileged 66 given space within the mausoleums, their gravestones are brilliantly tiled and often elaborately inscribed.

El Badi Palace

The ruins of the **El Badi Palace** (daily 8.30–11.45am & 2.30–5.45pm; 10dh) are off Place des Ferblantiers (see opposite), 700m south of the Djemaa el Fna along Rue Riad Zitoun el Kedim. On the south side of Place des Ferblantiers, a gate known as **Bab Berrima** opens onto a long rectangular enclosure, flanked on either side by walls; go through it, and on your right you'll come to the Badi's entrance.

Though substantially in ruins, and reduced throughout to its red *pisé* walls, enough remains of **El Badi** to suggest that its name – "The Incomparable" – was not entirely immodest. The palace was originally commissioned by the Saadian sultan **Ahmed el Mansour** shortly after his accession in 1578. The money for it came from the enormous ransom paid by the Portuguese after the Battle of the Three Kings (see p.571). It took his seventeenth-century successor **Moulay Ismail** over ten years of systematic work to strip the palace of everything valuable, and there's still a lingering sense of luxury and grandeur. The scale, with its sunken gardens and vast, ninety-metre-long pool, is certainly unrivalled, and the odd traces of zellij and plaster still left evoke a decor that was probably as rich as that of the Saadian Tombs. The most enduring account of the palace concerns its state opening, a fabulous occasion attended by ambassadors from several European powers and by all the sheikhs and *caids* of the kingdom. Surveying the effect, Ahmed turned to his court jester for an opinion on the new palace. "Sidi," the man replied, "this will make a magnificent ruin".

What you see today is essentially the ceremonial part of the **palace complex**, planned on a grand scale for the reception of ambassadors, and not meant for everyday living.

The palace's **entrance** was originally in the southeast corner of the complex, but today you enter from the north, through the Green Pavilion, emerging into a vast **central court**, over 130m long and nearly as wide. In its northeast corner, you can climb up to get an overview from the ramparts, and a closer view of the **storks** that nest atop them.

Within the central court are four **sunken gardens**, two on the northern side and two on the southern side. **Pools** separate the two gardens on each side, and there are four smaller pools in the four corners of the court, which is constructed on a substructure of vaults in order to allow the circulation of water through the pools and gardens. When the pools are filled – as during the June folklore festival which takes place here – they are an incredibly majestic sight.

On each side of the courtyard were summer pavilions. Of the Crystal Pavilion, to the east, only the foundations survive. On the opposite side, a monumental hall that was used by the sultan on occasions of state was known as the **Koubba el Hamsiniya** (The Fifty Pavilion), after its size in cubits. You can pay another 10dh (at the main gate) to see the original **minbar** (pulpit) from the Koutoubia Mosque (see p.354), housed in a pavilion in the southwest corner of the main courtyard. It may not sound like much, but this *minbar* was in its day one of the most celebrated works of art in the Muslim world. Commissioned from the Andalucian capital Cordoba in 1137 by the last Almoravid sultan, Ali Ben Youssef, it took eight years to complete, and was covered with the most exquisite inlay work, of which, sadly, only patches remain. When the Almohads took power, they installed the *minbar* in their newly built Koutoubia Mosque, where it remained until it was removed for restoration in 1962, and eventually brought here. Unfortunately, members of the public are not usually allowed to walk around it and inspect the surviving inlay work, but the *gardien* may relent if you show a particular interest. Photography is not usually allowed.

South of the courtyard, accessed just to the right of the building housing the *minbar*, are ruins of the palace **stables**, and beyond them, leading towards the intriguing walls of the present royal palace, a series of **dungeons**, used into the last century as a state prison.

The Mellah

Marrakesh's **Mellah** (Jewish quarter) was created in 1558. There is no record of why it was done at this particular time. It may have been to use the Jews as a buffer zone (and scapegoat) between the palace and the populace in times of social unrest, but more likely it was simply to make taxation easier. The Jews of Marrakesh were an important financial resource – they controlled most of the Saadian sugar trade, and comprised practically all of the city's bankers, metal-workers, jewellers and tailors. In the sixteenth century, at least, their quarter was almost a town in itself, supervised by rabbis, and with its own souks, gardens, fountains and synagogues.

The present-day Mellah, now known officially as **Hay Essalam**, is much smaller in extent and almost entirely Muslim – most Marrakshi Jews left long ago for Casablanca, France or Israel. The few who remain, outwardly distinguishable only by the men's small black skullcaps, are mostly poor, old or both. The quarter, however, is immediately distinct: its houses are taller than elsewhere, the streets are more enclosed, and even the shop cubicles are smaller. Until the Protectorate, Jews were not permitted to own land or property – nor even to ride or walk, except barefoot – outside the Mellah. Today, though not a sought-after neighbourhood, its air of neglect and poverty is probably less than at any time during the past three centuries.

Around the quarter

The easiest approach to the Mellah is from **Place des Ferblantiers** – the tinsmiths' square. Formerly called Place du Mellah, this was itself part of the old Jewish souk, now prettied up into quite a pleasant little square, surrounded by the workshops of lantern makers. North of here, off the street leading up to Rue Riad Zitoun el Djedid, is a **jewellers' souk**, where one of the traditional Jewish trades has pretty much been taken over by Muslim craftsmen.

The main road into the Mellah leads east from here, leading along the southern side of the Bahia Palace. The first left (under a low arch) takes you to **Place Souweka**, a small square at the centre of the Mellah, very much like the goal in a maze. If you ignore that turning, the main road does a twist, and the next left (Derb Ragraga) takes you after 100m to the unmarked **Lazama Synagogue**, the last door on the left before the street widens out (no. 36; no sign, just knock on the door; Sun–Thurs 9am–6pm, Fri 9am–1pm, closed Sat and Jewish hols; free, but a tip is expected). The synagogue is still in use but the interior is modern and not tremendously interesting. Like all the Mellah's synagogues, it forms part of a private house, which you'll notice is decorated with Star of David zellij tiling. Would-be guides may offer (for a tip, of course) to show you this, and some of the Mellah's other, smaller synagogues, now disused. Even when in use, these were as much private houses as places of worship.

Some 200m to the east is the **Jewish cemetery**, the **Miâara** (Sun–Thurs 7am–6pm, Fri 7am–3pm; closed Sat and Jewish holidays; no charge but tip expected), reckoned to date from the early seventeenth century. More sprawling than the cemetery in Fes (see p.229), it is well tended and boasts eleven Jewish *marabout* (*tsadikim* in Hebrew) shrines.

Just outside the Mellah, on Rue Arset el Mâach (Rue de l'Electricité), the first-floor **Bitoun Synagogue** is out of use and closed to the public, but it's worth checking out the unusual exterior, up above a herb shop, in mustard yellow with, naturally, a Star of David motif.

The Bahia Palace and around

By far the most ambitious and costly of these mansions was the **Bahia Palace** (Sat–Thurs 8.45–11.45am & 2.45–5.45pm, Fri 8.45–11.30am & 3–5.45pm; 10dh), at the southern end of Rue Riad Zitoun el Djedid, originally built in 1866–7 for **Si Moussa**, a former slave who had risen to become Moulay Hassan's chamberlain, and then grand vizier. His son, **Bou Ahmed**, who himself held the post of chamberlain under Moulay Hassan, became kingmaker in 1894 when Hassan died while returning home from a *harka* (tax-collecting expedition). In something of a coup, Ahmed managed to conceal news of the sultan's death until he was able to declare Hassan's fourteen-year-old son Moulay Abd el Aziz sultan in his place, with himself as grand vizier and regent (see p.574). The wily Bou Ahmed thus attained virtually complete control over the state, which he exercised until his death in 1900.

Ahmed began enlarging the Bahia (meaning "brilliance") in the same year as his coup, and added a mosque, a hammam and even a vegetable garden; much of the palace has been restored to its original glory. Visitors enter the palace from the west, through an arcaded courtyard which leads to a **small riad** (enclosed garden), part of Bou Ahmed's extension. The riad is decorated with beautiful carved stucco and cedarwood, and salons lead off it on three sides. The eastern salon leads through to the **council room**, and thence through a vestibule – where it's worth pausing to look up at the lovely painted ceiling – to the **great courtyard** of Si Moussa's original palace. The rooms surrounding the courtyard are also all worth checking out for their painted wooden ceilings.

South of the great courtyard is the **large riad**, the heart of Si Moussa's palace, fragrant with fruit trees and melodious with birdsong, approaching the very ideal of beauty in Arabic domestic architecture. To its east and west are halls decorated with fine zellij fireplaces and painted wooden ceilings. From here, you leave the palace via the **private apartment** built in 1898 for Ahmed's wife, Lalla Zinab, where again you should look up to check out the painted ceiling, carved stucco, and stained-glass windows.

When Bou Ahmed died, the servants ransacked the palace. For some years during the Protectorate, it was used to house the Resident General, and it is still called into use when the royal family is in the city, usually during the winter months, at which times there is no public admission.

Maison Tiskiwin

The **Maison Tiskiwin** at 8 Rue de la Bahia (daily 9.30am–12.30pm & 2.30–5.30pm; 20dh) is an early twentieth-century townhouse built in Spanish-Moroccan style. It's easy to find: 200m north of the Bahia Palace on Rue Riad

Zitouan el Djedid, where the street opens out to the left, take a right turn (under an arch), and it's 100m ahead on the right (look for the yellow sign).

Within lies a unique collection of Moroccan and Saharan artefacts, billed as "a journey from Marrakesh to Timbuktu and back". They come from the collection of Dutch anthropologist Bert Flint, a Morocccan resident since 1957. Each room features carpets, fabrics, clothes and jewellery from a different region of the Sahara, and explanatory notes in French describe the exhibits room by room. The exhibition illustrates the longstanding cultural links across the desert, a result of the centuries of caravan trade between Morocco and Mali.

Dar Si Said

The next left after the Maison Tiskiwin brings you to **Dar Si Said** (daily except Tues 9am–11.45pm & 2.30–5.45pm; 10dh), a smaller version of the Bahia Palace, built for a brother of Bou Ahmed, who, though something of a simpleton, nonetheless gained the post of royal chamberlain. It's a pleasurable building, with beautiful pooled courtyards, scented with lemons, palms and flowers, and it houses an impressive **Museum of Moroccan Arts** (though not all its exhibits will necessarily be on show at any one time).

The museum is particularly strong on its collection of eighteenth- and nineteenth-century **woodwork**, some of it from the Glaoui kasbahs and most of it in cedarwood. There are also (upstairs, but not always on display) a number of traditional **wedding palanquins** – once used for carrying the bride, veiled and hidden, to her new home. Today, such chairs are still made, and used symbolically, to carry the bride from her womenfolk in one room to the groom's menfolk in the next room. On the top floor, four **fairground ride seats** were part of a contraption like a small wooden Ferris wheel, in which children commonly rode at moussems until the early 1960s. A photograph shows the apparatus as it was when in use.

One of the museum's most important exhibits (at the end of the passage from the entance) is a rectangular marble **basin**, dating from around 1005. Originally from the Andalucian capital, Cordoba, it is decorated along one side with what seem to be heraldic eagles and griffins. Although most Islamic artwork eschews images of plants and animals, the Andalucian Ummayad caliphs who commissioned it had few reservations about representational art. What is more surprising is that it was brought over to Morocco by the highly puritanical Almoravid sultan Ali Ben Youssef, placed in his mosque, and left untouched by the dynasty's equally iconoclastic successors, the Almohads.

The Ville Nouvelle, gardens and palmery

Marrakesh's **Ville Nouvelle** radiates out from **Guéliz**, its commercial centre. Though it's hardly chock-a-block with attractions, it does have one must-see: the **Majorelle Garden**. South of Guéliz, the **Hivernage** district, built as a garden suburb, is where most of the city's newer tourist hotels are located. The city's two large gardens – the **Agdal** and **Menara** – are a little further afield, as is Marrakesh's **palmery**.

To get to the Agdal or Menara gardens, or to the palmery, you will want **transport** – either a petit taxi or calèche. If you are considering a calèche trip at any stage, the Agdal, Menara and palmery are perfect destinations. Alternatively, to take in both gardens and tour the ramparts and palmery, you could rent a **bike** or charter a grand taxi for the day.

Guéliz

The heart of modern Marrakesh, Guéliz has a certain buzz that the sleepy old Medina rather lacks. Its main thoroughfare, **Avenue Mohammed V**, runs all the way down to the Koutoubia, and it's on and around this boulevard that you'll find the city's main concentration of upmarket shops, restaurants and smart pavement cafés. Its junctions form the Ville Nouvelle's main centres of activity: Place de la Liberté, with its modern fountain; Place 16 Novembre, by the main post office; and Place Abdelmoumen Ben Ali, epicentre of Marrakesh's modern shopping zone. Looking back along Avenue Mohammed V from Guéliz to the Medina, on a clear day at least, you should see the Koutoubia rising in the distance, with the Atlas mountains behind.

Another remnant of the colonial era is the **European Cemetery** on Rue Erraouda (daily: April–Sept 7am–7pm; Oct–March 8am–6pm; free). Opened in 1925, it's a peaceful plot with lots of wild flowers, and some quite Poe-esque French family mausoleums. The first thing you'll notice on entry is the large white obelisk dedicated to the soldiers who fell fighting in Africa for Free France and democracy during World War II; 333 of these men have their last resting places in the cemetery's section H. Section B is devoted to children who died in infancy, and the oldest part, to the left of the obelisk as you come in, contains the tombs of colonists from the 1920s and 1930s, most of whom seem to have been less than forty years old when they died. The cemetery is nowadays also home to a colony of cats.

The Majorelle Garden

The **Majorelle Garden**, or Jardin Bou Saf (Ⓦwww.jardinmajorelle.com; daily Oct–March 8am–5.30pm, May–Sept 8am–6pm, Ramadan 9am–5pm; 30dh; no dogs, no unaccompanied children, no picnics, no smoking), is a meticulously planned twelve-acre botanical garden, created in the 1920s and 1930s by French painter Jacques Majorelle (1886–1962), and subsequently owned by fashion designer Yves Saint Laurent. The entrance is on a small side street off the jacaranda-lined Avenue Yacoub el Mansour.

The feeling of tranquillity here is enhanced by verdant groves of bamboo, dwarf palm and agave, the cactus garden and lily-covered pools. The Art Deco pavilion at the heart of the garden is painted in a striking cobalt blue – the colour of French workmen's overalls, so Majorelle claimed, though it seems to have improved in the Moroccan light. This brilliantly offsets both the plants – multicoloured bougainvillea, rows of bright orange nasturtiums and pink geraniums – and also the strong colours of the pergolas and concrete paths – pinks, lemon yellows and apple greens. The enduring sound is the chatter of the common bulbuls, flitting among the leaves of the date palms, and the pools also attract other bird residents such as turtle doves and house buntings. The garden became better known abroad when it was featured by Yves Saint Laurent in a brilliant reproduction at London's 1997 Chelsea Flower Show. Pierre Bergé and Madison Cox's *Majorelle, A Moroccan Oasis* is a superbly photographed coffee-table book on the garden, sometimes available at Librairie d'Art (see p.379).

In Majorelle's former studio, housed within the pavilion, a **Museum of Islamic Arts** (15dh) exhibits Saint Laurent's fine personal collection of North African carpets, pottery, furniture and doors; Saint Laurent was himself born in Algeria. It also has many of Jacques Majorelle's engravings and paintings – mainly of Atlas scenes fifty years ago, including the fortified village of Anemiter and the Kasbah of Aït Benhaddou, near Ouarzazate.

When leaving, ignore the taxi drivers waiting outside, who run a cartel and will not take you unless you pay well over the odds. The answer is simply to walk down to the main road and hail a cab there.

The Menara and Agdal gardens

Southwest of Hivernage, the **Menara Gardens** (bus #11 from Place Youssef Tachfine; daily 8am–6pm; free) are a popular picnic spot for Marrakshi families, as well as tourists, centred on a rectangular pool providing a classic postcard image beneath a backdrop of the High Atlas mountains. Originally dating from the twelfth century, it was restored and its pavilions rebuilt in the mid-nineteenth century. The poolside *minzah* (daily 8.30am–noon & 2.30–5.45pm; 10dh) replaced an earlier Saadian structure. Aside from the pool, the garden is largely filled with olive trees. There's usually someone by the park entrance offering camel rides.

The **Agdal gardens** (bus #6 from Place Foucauld; Fri & Sun 8am–5pm; free) are much larger but less well kept. They were originally watered by a system of wells and underground channels, known as *khettera,* from the base of the Atlas in the Ourika Valley and dating, in part, from the earliest founding of the city. These fell into disrepair and the gardens largely abandoned untilk the nineteenth century, when they were restored. At the heart of the gardens are a series of pools, the largest of which is the **Sahraj el Hana** (Tank of Health – now a green, algae-clogged rectangle of water), which was probably dug by the Almohads and is flanked by a ramshackle old *minzah*, or summer pavilion, where the last few precolonial sultans held picnics and boating parties.

The palmery

Marrakesh's **palmery**, or oasis, is northeast of town between the Route de Fes (N8) and the Route de Casablanca (N9). It's far from being the most spectacular in the country, but it does make a change from the urban landscape if you're spending time in town. Dotted with the villas of prosperous Marrakshis, the palmery also boasts a golf course and a couple of luxury hotels. The clumps of date palms look rather windswept, but the palmery does have a certain tranquillity, and it's 5°C cooler than the Medina, which could make it a particular attraction in summer. The most popular route through the oasis is the five-kilometre **Circuit de la Palmeraie**, which meanders through the trees and villas from the Route de Fes to the Route de Casablanca. The classic way to see it is by calèche, but you'll need to bargain hard to get a good price. To do the Circuit de la Palmeraie on foot, take bus #17 or #26 to the Route de Fes turn-off, and bus #1 back from the Route de Casablanca (or vice versa). It's also possible to ride around the palmery on a camel – men by the roadside offer rides.

Eating, drinking and nightlife

Guéliz has most of the city's French-style cafés, bistros and restaurants, and virtually all the bars. In the **Medina**, there are the Djemaa el Fna food stalls, many inexpensive café-restaurants, and a number of upmarket palace-restaurants.

Medina cafés and restaurants

Recommendations for the Medina span the range: from a bench in the Djemaa el Fna to the most sumptuous palace setting. Only the more expensive places are licensed to sell alcohol.

Djemaa el Fna foodstalls

Even if you don't eat at one of them, at some stage you should at least wander down the makeshift lane of food stalls on the Djemaa el Fna, which look great in the evening, lit by lanterns. As well as couscous and pastilla, there are spicy merguez sausages, *harira* soup, salads, fried fish, or, for the more adventurous, stewed snails (over towards the eastern side of the square), and sheep's heads complete with eyes. To partake, just take a seat on one of the benches, ask the price of a plate of food and order all you like. It's probably worth avoiding places that try to hustle you, and it's always wise to check the price of a dish before you order. Stalls patronized by Moroccans are invariably better than those whose only customers are tourists. If you want a soft drink or mineral water with your meal, the stallholders will send a boy to get it for you. Guides often suggest that the stalls aren't very healthy, but, as the cooking is so visible, standards of cleanliness are doubtless higher than in many hidden kitchens. On the southern edge of the food stalls, a row of vendors sell a hot, spicy ginseng drink (*khoudenjal*), said to be an aphrodisiac, and taken with a portion of nutty cake. Orange and grapefruit juice stalls line both sides of the foodstall area at all hours of the day, but check the price first, and insist on having the juice pressed in front of you – if they pull out a bottle of ready-pressed juice, it'll most likely be watered down, and quite possibly mixed with squash.

Overlooking the Djemaa

All these places appear on the map on p.354.

Argana The closest vantage point over the Djemaa, right on top of the action, and not at all a bad place to eat. Menus are 90–150dh, and dishes include lamb tajine with prunes, and seafood pastilla, a new-fangled variation on the traditional Fassi dish.

Café du Grand Balcon Next door to the *Hôtel CTM*, this place has the fullest view over the Djemaa, taking it all in from a perfect vantage point, but it isn't as close-up as the *Argana*. You can come up for just a drink (tea, coffee or soda), but they also do food, including salads, pizzas and tajines.

Chez Chegrouni Come at a quiet time if you want to bag one of the seats on the upstairs terrace that actually do overlook the square. Popular with tourists, this place does decent couscous and good tajines at moderate prices (mostly 50dh a throw, 10dh less if you forego the scenic terrace), though the portions are on the small side.

Hôtel CTM The rooftop café here gives a view onto most of the square and does a very good-value continental breakfast (7.30–11am; 22dh), but otherwise serves only drinks.

Marrakchi 52 Rue des Banques ⓣ0524 443377. High up above the square, with imperial but intimate decor, impeccable service and superb food, including delicious pastilla, and several couscous and tajine options, including vegetarian. Expensive (main dishes are mostly around 130dh).

Les Prémices Good Moroccan and European food including tasty gazpacho, well-prepared tajines, steaks, fish, pizzas and even crème brûlée. It's on the very southeastern corner of the square, but close enough for a view of the action, and very moderately priced (you can eat well for 100dh, very well for 150dh).

Terrasses de l'Alhambra A tourist trap, yes, and the food is a little overpriced and not consistently good, but it does have a great location overlooking the northeastern arm of the Djemaa, with two covered terraces, menus at 150dh and lots of pizzas, pasta and salad, plus teas, infusions, juices and ice cream.

Cheap cafés and restaurants

Apart from the Djemaa itself (see box above), there's a a concentration of cheap and basic eateries on Rue Bani Marine, a narrow street that runs south from the post office and Bank al Maghrib on Djemaa el Fna, between and parallel to Rue Bab Agnaou and Rue Moulay Ismail. Another street of cheap eats, with grills on one side and fried fish on the other, is the small street that runs from Arset el Maach alongside Place des Ferblantiers to the entrance of the El Badi

Palace (see map, p.365). There's also a row of places just outside the walls at Bab Doukkala, between the bus station and the grand taxi stand. All the following are on the map on p.354, unless stated.

Café des Épices Pl Rahba Kedima, north side; see map, p.356. A small café offering refuge from the hubbub, with orange juice, mint tea, coffee in various permutations, including spiced with cinnamon, and views over the Rahba Kedima from the upper floor and the roof terrace.

Café el Badi by Bab Berrima; see map, p.356. On a rooftop looking out over Place des Ferblantiers and towards the Mellah, this is one place to get close to the storks nesting on the walls of the El Badi Palace. It serves a range of hot and cold (non-alcoholic) drinks, and set menus (80–120dh) featuring soup, salad, couscous, and Moroccan sweetmeats for afters.

Café Restaurant Iceberg Av el Mouahidine. Formerly an ice-cream parlour, hence its name, this place is central and popular with Marrakshis. Downstairs, it serves the best coffee in the Medina; upstairs there's a restaurant serving reasonable Moroccan food, with a 55dh set menu.

Chez Bahia Rue Riad Zitoun el Kedim, 50m from Djemaa el Fna. A café-diner offering pastilla, wonderful tajines and low-priced snacks, plus excellent set breakfasts. You can eat well here for 50–60dh.

El Bahja 24 Rue Bani Marine. This place (whose patron has appeared on a British TV food programme) is popular with locals and tourists alike. It's a good-value but generally unexciting cheap eatery, but don't miss the house yogurt for afters. Set menus 60–70dh.

Grillade Chez Sbai 91 Rue Kassabine. The tables are upstairs but you order downstairs at this tiny hole-in-the-wall eatery. It isn't much to look at, but the food is good, the portions are ample and the prices are low. Most customers go for the spit-roast chicken, but the best deal is a big plate of chicken brochettes with chips and salad, a snip at 23dh.

Patisserie Belkabir and Patisserie Duniya 63–65 Souk Smarine, by the corner of Traverse el Ksour; see map, p.356. Two shops, side by side, specializing in traditional Moroccan sweetmeats, stuffed with nuts and drenched in syrup, and particularly popular during the holy month of Ramadan, when of course they are eaten by night. A kilo of assorted sticky delights costs 100dh.

Pâtisserie des Princes 32 Rue Bab Agnaou. A sparkling patisserie with mouth-watering pastries at prices that are a little high by local standards but worth the extra. They also have treats like almond milk and ice cream. The *salon de thé* at the back is a very civilized place to take breakfast, morning coffee or afternoon tea.

Restauant Oscar Progrès 20 Rue Bani Marine. One of the best budget restaurants in town, with friendly service, excellent-value set menus, and large servings of couscous (go for that or the brochettes in preference to the tajines, which are rather bland). You can fill up here for around 55dh, or be a real pig and go for the 100dh set menu.

Snack Café Toubkal in the far corner of Djemaa el Fna, beyond *Hôtel CTM* and best recognized by its backdrop of a dozen colourful carpets for sale. As well as fruit juices, home-made yogurts, and patisseries, there are salads, tajines and couscous, set menus (45–50dh) and good-value breakfasts (18dh).

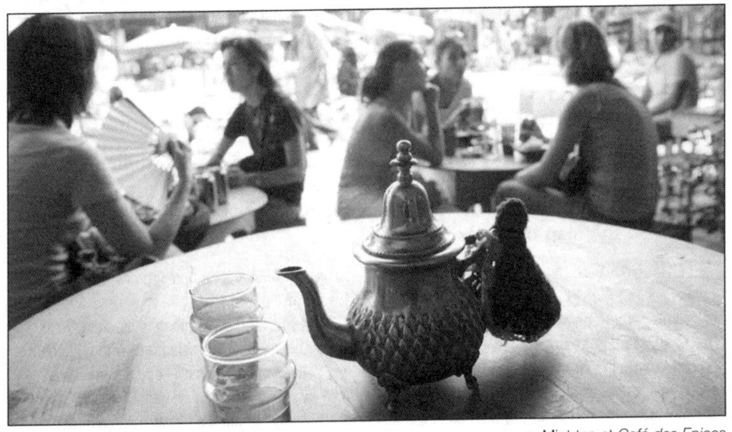

▲ Mint tea at *Café des Epices*

Moderate cafés and restaurants

Le Bougainvillier 33 Rue Mouassine, see map, p.356. An upmarket café and quiet retreat in the middle of the Medina, handy for a break after a hard morning's shopping in the souks. There are salads, sandwiches, cakes, juices, coffee and tea, but most of all it's a pleasant space to relax in.

Café Arabe 184 Rue Mouassine ⓦwww.cafearabe.com; see map, p.356. A sophisticated bar and eatery in the heart of the Medina, very handy for the souks, with excellent Moroccan and European cooking and snappy service, plus juices, teas, cocktails and mocktails, served on the terrace, in the patio or in the salon.

Dar Mima 9 Derb Zaouia el Khadiria, off Rue Riad Zitoun el Djedid ⓣ0524 385252, ⓦdarmima.ifrance.com; see map, p.365. A modest nineteenth-century townhouse converted into a simple but comfortable restaurant, open evenings only. The à la carte menu represents what guests might be served in the home of a well-to-do Marrakshi family. Expect to pay around 250dh per person plus wine, and be sure to book in advance (they may even arrange for somebody to meet you and show you the way).

Earth Café 1 Derb el Zouaq, off Rue Riad Zitoun el Kedim ⓦwww.earthcafemarrakech.com; see map, p.354. Marrakesh's first vegetarian restaurant, offering six dishes (at 60dh a throw), of which four are vegan. The portions are generous, and the food is well prepared and delicious, enough to tempt any carnivore to a veggie meal, and a nice change from the usual Moroccan fare. They also serve excellent juices and herbal infusions, and the atmosphere is intimate and relaxed.

Hôtel Ali Rue Moulay Ismail; see map, p.354. Justifiably popular restaurant with à la carte lunches, and a great-value buffet every evening, featuring *harira*, salads, couscous and ten or more tajine-style dishes – eat as much as you like for 80dh (residents 70dh).

Pizzeria Portofino 279 Av Mohammed V. see map, p.365. Quite a posh ambience, tablecloths and all, and wood-oven pizzas that are well cooked, but slightly bland, though this is easily remedied with a splash of the garlic-and-chilli olive oil they thoughtfully provide.

Pizzeria Venezia 279 Av Mohammed V; see map, p.365. Rooftop restaurant whose main attraction is its unparalleled view of the Koutoubia rather than its so-so pizzas, but it isn't a bad place for breakfast.

Restaurant el Bahia 1 Rue Riad Zitoun el Djedid, by the Bahia Palace ⓣ0524 378679; see map, p.365. A proper palace restaurant, but with bargain-priced menus (lunch 100dh, supper 150dh) in a beautifully restored mansion, all finely carved stucco and painted wooden ceilings, which used to offer meals with a floorshow at three times the price.

Le Tanjia 14 Derb Djedid, Hay Essalam/Mellah, near Pl des Ferblantiers ⓣ0524 383836; see map, p.365. Stylish bar-restaurant billed as an "oriental brasserie" serving well-cooked Moroccan dishes, including vegetarian options, in an old mansion done out in modern decor, and not outrageously expensive (count on around 250dh per head plus wine).

Terrasse des Épices 15 Souk Cherifa ⓦwww.terrassedesepices.com; see map, p.356. Above the souks, a terrace restaurant run by the same people as *Café des Épices* (see map, p.356). It has separate bays for each table giving diners their own space and a bit of privacy – handy if you want to use the free wi–fi – while still allowing you to enjoy the great views. There's pastilla or a trio of Moroccan salads to start, and things like turkey in ginger or lamb served as at the Eïd el Kebir festival to follow. Afters include crème brûlée or chocolate mousse.

Expensive restaurants

Many **palace-restaurants** are well hidden away and can be difficult to find, especially at night; if in doubt, phone in advance and ask for directions – sometimes the restaurant will send someone to meet you. All the following are marked on the map on pp.365–365.

Dar Marjana 15 Derb Sidi Ali Tair, off Rue Bab Doukkala ⓣ0524 385110. Housed in an early nineteenth-century palace – look for the sign above the entrance to a passageway diagonally across the street from the corner of the Dar el Glaoui; take the passage and look for the green door facing you before a right turn. The set menu costs 726dh. Advance booking only; daily except Tues from 8pm.

La Rotonta 39 Derb Lamnabha, Kasbah ⓣ0524 385549. A bi-national restaurant, with two chefs – one Italian, one Moroccan – and set menus at 350–500dh, that's made a name for itself very quickly serving fine food from both countries amidst beautifully ornate decor from the owner's collection of antiques, or with a view of the Atlas should you care to eat on the roof terrace. Evenings only, closed Tues.

Le Pavillon 47 Derb Zaouia ⓣ0524 387040. Best approached from Rue Bab Doukkala, round the back of the Bab Doukkala Mosque – look for the sign over the first archway on the right, head down the passage and it's the last door on the right. Among the specialities whipped up by Michelin-starred French chef Laurent Tarridec are duck breast with peaches or turbot tronçon with carrots and cumin, and a Grand Marnier or ginger soufflé. There's a 600dh menu, including wine, or you can eat à la carte.

Le Tobsil 22 Derb Abdellah Ben Hessaien, near Bab Ksour ⓣ0524 444052. Sumptuous Moroccan cuisine in an intimate riad, considered by many to be the finest restaurant in town, though the wine (included in the price) doesn't match the quality of the food. Open evenings only (7–11pm) and closed Tues; worth booking ahead; set menu 600dh.

Palais Gharnata 5–6 Derb el Arsa, off Rue Riad Zitoun el Djedid ⓣ0524 389615, ⓦwww.gharnata.com. Popular with foreign visitors, though unfortunately the food (the 550dh menu features pastilla, couscous, lamb tajine) is merely so-so, and individual diners play second-fiddle to groups. However the decor is splendid, as the building is a magnificently decorated sixteenth-century mansion, with an Italian alabaster fountain at its centre; scenes from *The Return of the Pink Panther* were shot here. Past patrons have included Jacqueline Kennedy and the Aga Khan. Although it's open lunchtime, evenings are best as there's a floorshow (music and dancing) from 8.30pm.

Riad des Mers 411 Derb Sidi Messaoud ⓣ0524 375304. They bring their own supplies in from the coast for this French fish and seafood restaurant in a patio garden (covered in winter), run by the proprietors of the neighbouring *Riad Sindibad*. You can start with oysters or razor shells, continue with sea bass, king prawns or monkfish brochettes, and finish with chocolate pudding. There's a 295dh or 345dh set menu, or you can eat à la carte. Daily noon–2pm & 7pm–midnight.

Yacout 79 Sidi Ahmed Soussi ⓣ0524 382900 or 29. In a gorgeous old palace, with columns and fireplaces in super-smooth orange- and blue-striped *tadelakt* plaster, designed by acclaimed American interior designer Bill Willis, whose use of *tadelakt* here and elsewhere made it massively trendy in Moroccan interior design. The classic Moroccan tajine of chicken with preserved lemon and olive is a favourite here, but the fish tajine is also rated very highly. The cuisine has received Michelin plaudits in the past, though standards are beginning to slip as the tour groups move in. The menu costs 700dh per person.

Guéliz cafés and restaurants

All these are shown on the map on p.345.

Al Bahriya 69 Bd Moulay Rachid, Guéliz. The best and most popular of a trio of cheap fried fish joints on this block. For 30dh you get a big plate with a selection of fish plus bread, olives and sauce. Unbeatable value. Daily 11am–midnight. Cheap.

Al Fassia Résidence Tayeb, 55 Bd Mohammed Zerktouni ⓣ0524 434060. Truly Moroccan – both in decor and cuisine – specializing in dishes from the country's culinary capital, Fes. Start with that great classic, pigeon pastilla, followed by a choice of five different lamb tajines, among other sumptuous Fassi offerings. There's a lunchtime set menu for around 150dh, but dinner will cost twice that. The ambience and service are superb. Daily noon–2.30pm & 7.30–11pm. Expensive.

Amandine 177 Rue Mohammed el Bekal. If you're on a diet, look away now, because this is a double whammy: a café-patisserie, stuffed full of scrumptious almond-filled Moroccan pastries and French-style cream cakes, and right next-door, a plush ice-cream parlour where you can sit and eat in comfort. You can have a coffee with your choice of sweetmeat in both halves, but the ice-cream section is more spacious. Daily 7am–9pm.

Café des Negotiants Pl Abdelmoumen Ben Ali. Slap bang on the busiest corner in Guéliz, this grand café is the place to sit out on the pavement and really feel that you're in the heart of modern Marrakesh. It's also an excellent venue in which to spend the morning over a coffee, with a choice of set breakfasts, or an omelette or sandwich to accompany your caffeine fix. Daily 6.30am–11pm.

Café du Livre 44 Rue Tariq Ben Ziad, by *Hôtel Toulousain*, ⓦwww.cafedulivre.com. A very elegant space, serving tea and coffee, breakfasts, salads, sandwiches and brochettes, even tapas (30dh a go, or a selection of three for 65dh) and cold cuts (100dh for a selection). There's also draught beer, but only with food. Most importantly, the café has a library of second-hand English books to read or buy, and free wi-fi too. Mon–Sat 8am–midnight.

Chez Lamine Hadj 19 Résidence Yasmine, Rue Ibn Aïcha, corner of Rue Mohammed Bekal. Unpretentious, inexpensive restaurant (main dishes 25–38dh) and very poplar with Marrakshis for *mechoui* (roasts), grills, tajines, sheep's head, brochettes and other indigenous, mainly lamb-based dishes. Daily 9am–11pm. Cheap.

Comptoir Darna Av Echouada, Hivernage ⓣ0524 437702, ⓦwww.comptoirdarna.com. Downstairs it's a restaurant serving reliably good Moroccan and international cuisine, with dishes like chicken curry, salmon steak, or weeping tiger (steak in ginger sauce), as well as one or two vegetarian options. Upstairs it's a chic lounge bar, very popular with Marrakesh's young and rich. The bar opens at 4pm, with meals served from 8pm, and cabaret entertainment starting at 10.30pm. Expensive.

Grand Café de la Poste Rue el Imam Malik, just off Av Mohammed V behind the post office ⓣ0524 433038. More grand than café, this is in fact quite a posh restaurant serving international cuisine (duck breast with olives, for example, wok-fried chicken fricassee, or even English-style roast beef). Main courses go for 100–160dh. Wash it down with a cup of Earl Grey, or a choice of rums, tequilas and fine brandies if you prefer something harder. Daily 8am–1am. Expensive.

Hôtel Farouk 66 Av Hassan II. From noon the hotel restaurant offers an excellent-value 60dh set menu with soup, salad, couscous, tajine or brochettes, followed by fruit, ice cream or home-made yogurt. Alternatively, tuck in to one of their excellent wood-oven pizzas (35–50dh). Daily 6am–11pm. Cheap to moderate.

Katsura 1 Rue Oum Errabia ⓣ0524 434358. Billing itself as a "Thai wok and sushi restaurant", this is Marrakesh's first Thai eatery, and not at all bad, with the usual Thai standards including tom yam soup and green or red curries (plus sushis – not very Thai, but good). Main courses cost around 95–140dh, or you can pay roughly the same for a lunchtime set menu. The food's fresh and tasty, and the service is pleasant and efficient. All in all, a nice change from the usual Moroccan fare. Expensive.

La Taverne 22 Bd Mohammed Zerktouni ⓣ0524 446126. As well as a drinking tavern, this is a pretty decent restaurant – in fact, it claims to be the oldest in town – where you can dine on French and Moroccan fare indoors or in a lovely tree-shaded garden. The 130dh four-course set menu is great value. Daily 12.30–2.30pm & 6.30–10.30pm. Moderate.

La Trattoria 179 Rue Mohammed el Bekal ⓣ0524 432641, ⓦwww.latrattoriamarrakech.com. The best Italian food in town, with impeccable service and excellent cooking, located in a 1920s house decorated by Bill Willis (as in *Yacout*; see p.375). As well as freshly made pasta, steaks and escalopes, there's the house speciality – beef medallions in parmesan – plus a wonderful tiramisu to squeeze in for afters. Daily 7–11.30pm. Expensive.

Le Cantanzaro 50 Rue Tarik Ibn Ziad ⓣ0524 433731. One of the city's most popular Italian restaurants, crowded at lunchtime with Marrakshis, expats and tourists. Specialities include *saltimbocca alla romana* and rabbit in mustard sauce, and there's crème brûlée or tiramisu to round it off with. You're strongly advised to book, but you can also just turn up and queue for a table. Licensed. Mon–Sat noon–2.30pm & 7.15–11pm. Moderate.

Le Jacaranda 32 Bd Mohammed Zerktouni, on Pl Abdelmoumen Ben Ali ⓣ0524 447215, ⓦwww.lejacaranda.ma. Reliably good traditional French cuisine, starting with the likes of locally renowned oysters from Oualidia on the coast, beef carpaccio, or snails in garlic butter, followed by duck confit with baked apples and wild mushrooms, or perhaps a fish trilogy tajine. À la carte eating will set you back around 350dh a head plus wine, or there are lunchtime set menus for 85–105dh, and a dinner menu for 190dh. The restaurant doubles as an art gallery, with different exhibits on its walls each month. Expensive.

Lunch d'Or Rue de l'Imam Ali, opposite the church. It can be hard to find an honest-to-goodness cheap Moroccan eatery in the Ville Nouvelle, but this place (and its neighbour, called *Nismaq*) serves tasty tajines at 15–25dh a shot, great value and very popular with workers on their lunch break. Daily 7.30am–8pm. Cheap.

Puerto Banus Rue Ibn Hanbal, opposite the police headquarters in the Royal Tennis Club ⓣ0524 446534. A Spanish fish restaurant – though French-managed – with specialities such as gazpacho, paella and Oualidia oysters. There's also a good selection of French and Moroccan dishes, including seafood pastilla. Count on 200dh per head without wine eating à la carte, though at lunchtimes there's a good-value 95dh buffet including a serve-yourself salad bar. Daily noon–3pm & 7.30pm–midnight. Expensive.

Rôtisserie de la Paix 68 Rue de Yougoslavie, alongside the former cinema Lux-Palace ⓣ0524 433118, ⓦwww.restaurant-diaffa.ma/rotisserie. An open-air grill, established in 1949, specializing in mixed grills barbecued over wood, usually with a fish option for non-meat-eaters. It's all served either in a salon with a roaring fire in winter, or in the shaded garden in summer. Couscous served on Fridays only. Daily noon–3pm & 7–11pm. Moderate to expensive.

Crafts and souvenirs

Handicrafts are big in Morocco, and pretty much every part of the country has its speciality. In cities like Fes and Marrakesh, different parts of the Medina produce different goods, from furniture to ironwork to sandals to musical instruments. Jewellery and carpets tend to come in from the countryside, where each region – each village even – has its own style and its own techniques. The advantage of shopping in a big city is that you'll have a huge range to choose from, but there's a very special pleasure in tracking the souvenir you want down to the place where it's made, and even seeing the artisans at work making it.

Carpets for sale, Essaouira ▲

Potter at work, Safi ▼

The distinctive blue-and-white pottery of Fes ▼

Carpets, rugs and blankets

Morocco produces some lovely carpets, in wonderful warm colours – saffron yellow, cochineal red, antimony black – that look great flung across the floor in any living space. Nowadays most carpets are coloured with synthetic dyes, but their inspiration remains the natural dyes with which they were traditionally made. The most expensive carpets are hand-knotted, but there are also woven rugs called kellims.

Knotted carpets are not cheap – you can pay €1500 and more for the finer Arab designs in Fes or Rabat – but **rugs and kellims** come in at more reasonable prices, with a range of strong, well-designed weaves from €50–70. Most of these kellims will be of Berber origin and the most interesting ones usually come from the High and Middle Atlas. You'll find a big selection in Marrakesh, but if you're looking seriously, try to get to the town souk in Midelt or the weekly markets in Azrou and other villages in the region.

On a simpler and cheaper level, the **Berber blankets** (*foutahs*, or *couvertures*) are imaginative, and often very striking with bands of reds and blacks; for these, Tetouan and Chefchaouen, on the edge of the Rif, are promising.

Ceramics

Pottery is colourful if fairly crudely made on the whole, though the blue-and-white designs of Fes and the multicoloured pots of Chefchaouen (both produced largely for the tourist trade) are highly attractive. The essentially domestic pottery of Safi – Morocco's major pottery centre – is worth a look, too, with its colourful

Leatherware

Morocco leather is famously soft and luxurious. In towns like Fes, Marrakesh and Taroudant you can even visit the **tanneries** to see it being cured. It comes in a myriad of forms from belts, bags and clothing to pouffes and even book covers, but Morocco's best-known leather item is the *babouche*, or slipper. Classic Moroccan **babouches**, open at the heel, are immensely comfortable, and produced in yellow (the usual colour), white, red (for women) and occasionally grey or (for the truly fetishistic) black; a good pair – and quality varies enormously – can cost between €9 and €22. Marrakesh and Tafraoute are especially good for *babouches*.

plates, **tajines** and **garden pots**. Safi tajines are nice to look at, but for practical use, the best are those produced by the Oulja pottery at Salé, near Rabat, in plain red-brown earthenware.

▲ Tanneries, Fes

▼ Babouches, Marrakesh souks

Jewellery

Arabic-style **gold** jewellery tends to be a bit fussy for Western tastes, but **silver** is another story. In the south particularly, you can pick up some fabulous Berber necklaces and bracelets, always very chunky, and characterized by bold combinations of semiprecious (and sometimes plastic) stones and beads. Women in the Atlas and the Souss Valley regions in particular often wear chunky silver bracelets, belts embellished with old silver coins, or heavy necklaces with big beads of **amber**, **coral** and **carnelian**. Silver brooches are used to fasten garments, and many of the symbols found in Moroccan jewellery, such as the "hand of Fatima" and the five-pointed star, are there to guard against the evil eye. Essaouira, Marrakesh and Tiznit have particularly good jewellery souks.

▼ Traditional Berber silver jewellery

Wood

Marquetry is one of the few crafts where you'll see genuinely old pieces – inlaid tables and shelves – though the most easily exportable objects are boxes. The big centre for marquetry is Essaouira, where cedar or thuya wood is beautifully inlaid with orange-tree wood and other light-coloured woods to make trays, chess and backgammon sets, even plates and bowls, and you can visit the workshops where they are made.

Fes, Meknes, Tetouan and Marrakesh also have souks specializing in carpentry, which produce not only furniture, but also chests, sculptures, and kitchen utensils such as the little ladles made from citrus wood that are used to eat *harira* soup.

Minerals and fossils

You'll see a variety of **semiprecious stones** on sale throughout Morocco, and in the High Atlas they are often aggressively hawked on the roadsides. If you're lucky enough to be offered genuine amethyst or quartz, prices can be bargained to very tempting levels. Be warned, however, that all that glitters is not necessarily the real thing. Too often, if you wet the stone and rub, you'll find traces of dye on your fingers.

Fossils too are widely sold in Morocco, and can be as beautiful as they are fascinating. The fossil-rich black marble of the Erfoud region, for example, is sold in the form of anything from ashtrays to table tops. But again, things aren't always what they seem, and a lot of fossils are in fact fakes, made out of cement. This is particularly true of trilobites, or any black fossil on a grey background. For more on fossils and minerals, see the box on p.473.

Bars and nightlife

Entertainment and nightlife in the **Medina** revolve around Djemaa el Fna. For a drink in the Medina, choices are limited; apart from the *Tazi* (see below), you can get a beer in the *Café Arabe* (see p.374). In the **Ville Nouvelle**, there's more variety; some of the bars are rather male, but women should be all right in the *Chesterfield*, and also in the bars of the *Agdal* and *Ibis* hotels. **Nightclubs** can be fun too: most play a mix of Western and Arabic music, but it's the latter that really fills the dancefloor. None of them really gets going until around midnight (in fact, some don't open until then), and they usually stay open until 3 or 4am.

Unless otherwise stated, all the places listed below are in Guéliz, and shown on the map on p.345.

Bars

African Chic 5 Rue Oum Errabia ⓦwww.african-chic.com. One of Marrakesh's most congenial bars, informal and relaxed, with cocktails, wines and beers, tapas (four for 110dh, eight for 180dh), salads, pasta, or even meat or fish dishes, not to mention live Latin and Gnaoua music every night from 10pm. Daily 6pm–1.30am.

Café-Bar de l'Escale Rue Mauritanie. This place has been going since 1947 and specializes in good bar snacks, such as fried fish or spicy merguez sausages – you could even come here for lunch or dinner (there's a dining area at the back). It isn't recommended for unaccompanied women, especially in the evening, but there's family-friendly terrace eating out front by day.

Chesterfield Pub 119 Av Mohammed V. Upstairs in the *Nassim Hôtel*, this supposedly English pub – it's nothing of the sort – is one of Marrakesh's more sophisticated watering holes, with a comfortable if rather smoky bar area, all soft seats and muted lighting. There's also a more relaxed, open-air poolside terrace to lounge about on with your draught beer or cocktail of a summer evening. Daily 11am–midnight.

Grand Hôtel Tazi Corner of Rue Bab Agnaou and Rue el Mouahidine, Medina; see map, p.354. Once, this was the only place in the Medina where you could get a drink, and it's still the cheapest (beers from 25dh). There's nothing fancy about the bar area – squeezed in between the restaurant and the lobby, and frequently spilling over into the latter – but it manages to be neither rough nor pretentious (a rare feat among Marrakesh drinking dens) and women should have no worries about drinking here.

Resto Primo Marrakech Plaza, off Rue des Nations Unies by Place 16 du Novembre. A lively tapas bar with an easy-going crowd, Spanish bodega atmosphere, and music from 9.30pm nightly. Daily 6am–1am.

Nightclubs

Diamant Noir Rue Oum Errabia, behind *Hôtel Marrakesh* ⓣ0524 446391. Look for the signpost on Av Mohammed V to find this lively dance club where Western pop and disco alternate with Algerian and Moroccan *raï* music. There are two bars, quite a sophisticated range of drinks (the 100dh entry ticket includes one), and a mainly young crowd, with a gay contingent.

Pacha Marrakech Av Mohammed VI (southern extension), Nouvelle Zone Hôtelière de l'Aguedal ⓣ0524 388400, ⓦwww.pachamarrakech.com. The Marrakesh branch of the famous Ibiza club claims to have the biggest and best sound system in Africa, and it's certainly the place to come if DJing skills, acoustics and visuals are important for your clubbing experience. Big-name DJs from abroad regularly play here – check the website for current line-ups. Sun–Thurs 100–150dh; Fri & Sat 200–250dh; occasionally as much as 350dh for a big event; entry includes one drink.

Paradise Disco *Hôtel Kempinski*, Bd el Mansour Eddahbi, Hivernage ⓣ0524 448222. A plush and trendy club that tries to be reasonably exclusive (so dress smartly). The clientele of well-heeled Moroccans, with a sprinkling of expats, plus a few tourists staying at the attached five-star hotel, dance to some well-mixed sounds, mostly at the commercial – or at least, the more tuneful – end of house and techno. The drinks list is impressively long, and impressively expensive. Entry is 150dh weekdays, 200dh weekends.

Theatro *Hôtel es Saadi*, Av el Kadassia (also spelt Qadassia), Hivernage ⓣ0524 448811, ⓦwww.theatromarrakech.com. One of Marrakesh's more interesting nightclubs, located in, as its name suggests, an old theatre. Nights are themed, the atmosphere is sophisticated, big on ladies' nights and other offers to entice female revellers (details on the website).

VIP Club Pl de la Liberté ☎0524 434569. The gullet-like entrance leads down to the first level, where there's an "oriental cabaret" (meaning a belly-dancing floor-show), and then further down to the deepest level, where there's what the French call a *boîte*, meaning a sweaty little nightclub. It's got a circular dancefloor and a small bar area, but despite its diminutive size, the place rarely seems to be full. Entry 150dh.

Shopping

There are a massive number of shops in Marrakesh selling all kinds of crafts, but nothing you won't get cheaper elsewhere. Marrakesh's attraction is that you don't have to go elsewhere to get it, and if you're flying home out of Marrakesh, then buying your souvenirs here means you won't have to lug them round the country with you.

Before setting off into the souks, it's worth taking a look at the **Ensemble Artisanal** (Mon–Sat 8.30am–7pm, Sun 9am–1pm), on Avenue Mohammed V, 200m south of Bab Nkob. This government-run complex of small arts and crafts shops holds a reasonable range of goods, notably leather, textiles and carpets. Shopping here is hassle-free, and the prices, which are supposedly fixed (though actually you can haggle here too), are a good gauge of the going rate if you intend to bargain elsewhere. At the back are a dozen or so workshops where you can watch young people learning a range of crafts including carpet-weaving. Another place with supposedly fixed prices is **Entreprise Bouchaib Complexe d'Artisanat** at 7 Derb Baissi Kasbah, on Rue de la Kasbah near the Saadian Tombs (daily 9am–7pm). The "fixed" prices here are only slightly higher than what you might pay in the souks, and, though you won't be allowed to browse freely, the sales assistants who follow you round are generally quite charming and informative. In particular it's a good place to check out carpets and get an idea of the absolute maximum prices you should be paying.

Otherwise, the best place to buy **carpets** is, naturally enough, in the carpet souk (Souk des Tapis), just off Rahba Kedima by the Criée Berbère, with old rugs and carpets on sale at Bazar du Sud (nos.14 & 117), and new ones at Bazar Jouti (nos.16 & 119). The carpets here come from all over the south of Morocco, and most are coloured with natural dyes such as saffron (yellow), cochineal (red) and indigo (blue). A large carpet might cost 4000dh, but you might be able to find a small rug for around 500dh.

For **jewellery**, there's a souk for the kind of gaudy gold variety favoured by Moroccan women just off Souk el Kebir, but tourists tend to favour chunkier silver pieces. Boutique Bel Hadj, at 22 & 33 Souk Fondouk Louarzazi, off the north side of Place Bab Fteuh, is a good place to look for those. Abdellatif Bellawi, 56 & 103 Kissariat Lossta (one of the passages in the *Kissaria* between Souk el Kebir and Souk Attarine) also has big silver Berber bangles, and beads from West Africa, the Sahara and Yemen as well as Morocco. For something smarter, not to mention a lot pricier, you need to head to Guéliz, where shops like Amazonite (94 Bd El Mansour Eddahbi) and Bazar Atlas (129 Av Mohammed V) have some lovely pieces.

Plenty of places sell **clothes**, of course, mostly aimed at Moroccans rather than tourists. For ordinary Moroccan kaftans, gandoras (sleeveless kaftans) and such like, try the covered souk just to your left as you come into Souk Smarine from the Djemaa el Fna. For something smarter, Maison du Kaftan Marocain at 65 Rue Sidi el Yumani has some beautiful but pricey robes, tunics and kaftans in shimmering silks and velvets, and sells to celeb customers like Mick Jagger and Samuel L. Jackson, whose photos are displayed on the wall. Not far away, Kulchi, at 1 Rue des Ksour, is a chic little boutique selling Moroccan clothes aimed at Western women, while in the heart of the souks, Femmes de Marrakech, at 67 Souk el Kchachbia, is a fair-trade co-op selling excellent hand-made cotton and linen dresses and kaftans.

Other good buys include **babouches** (Moroccan slippers), for which there's a whole souk (Souk Smata; see p.359) dedicated to nothing else, or there are tin, brass and iron **lanterns**, made and sold in several places, but especially in Place des Ferblantiers. For decorated **mirrors**, there's Moulay Larbai at 96 Souk el Kchachbia, in the heart of the souks, where Souk el Kchachbia meets Souk Belâarif. At the southern end of Rue Riad Zitoun el Kedim, shops that originally sold buckets and flip-flops for hammam use now sell all sorts of goods made from **recycled rubber tyres**, including tuffets and picture frames. For **musical instruments**, the place to look is Rue Riad Zitoun el Djedid. **Wooden kitchen implements** (including wooden scissors for cutting home-made pasta) can be found around the junction where Souk Smarine forks to become Souk el Kebir and Souk el Attarine (Omar Siam, just before the fork at 39 Souk Nejjarine has fixed and marked prices), while the main shop in town for **tajines** – practical rather than decorative ones – is Herman at 3 Rue Moulay Ismail, just off Place Foucauld. In the way of **foodstuffs**, the shops in the olive souk, just off Djemaa el Fna by *Terrasses de l'Alhambra*, has not only lots and lots of olives, but also lemons preserved in brine – very handy if you want to try your hand at a chicken tajine at home.

The municipal market on Rue Ibn Toumert, in Guéliz, is convenient for **food supplies**, as is the little covered market off the east side of the Djemaa el Fna. There are a couple of hypermarkets on the outskirts, but the best supermarket actually in town is Aswak on Avenue 11 du Janvier at the junction with Avenue Prince Moulay Abdallah, across the street from the bus station (daily 8am–10pm).

Listings

Airlines Atlas Blue, Terminal 2, Menara airport ⓣ0524 424200; British Airways, Menara airport ⓣ0524 448951; Royal Air Maroc, 197 Av Mohammed V ⓣ0524 425500.

Banks The main area for banks in the Medina is off the south side of the Djemaa el Fna on Rue Moulay Ismail. In Guéliz, the main area is along Av Mohammed V between Pl Abdelmoumen Ben Ali and the market. Most major branches have ATMs. BMCE's branch in the Medina (Rue Moulay Ismail on Pl Foucauld) has a bureau de change open Mon–Fri 8.30am–1.30pm & 2.30–8pm, Sat & Sun 9am–12.30pm & 3–7pm, and their branches in Guéliz (144 Av Mohammed V) and Hivernage (Av de France, opposite *Hôtel Atlas*) have bureaux de change open Mon–Fri 8.30am–12.30pm & 3.30–6.30pm. The post office on Pl 16 du Novembre has an office (to the left of the main entrance; Mon–Fri 8am–7pm, Sat 8.30am–7pm, Sun 10am–5.30pm) that will change cash, as will the post office at the train station (daily 8am–8pm), and the Djemaa el Fna post office has a bureau de change round the back, by the telephones (Mon–Sat 8am–8pm, Sun 10am–8pm). There are also a number of private foreign exchange bureaux, including Global Cash at 13 Rue de la Liberté in Guéliz (daily 9am–8pm) and a handful around the Mouasine Mosque in the Medina (similar hours). Even outside these hours, the *Hotel Ali* (see p.348) and *Hotel Central Palace* (see p.348) will change money. The *Hotel Ali* often has the best rates in town in any case.

Bicycles, mopeds and motorbikes You can rent bicycles on Pl de la Liberté and a number of roadside locations in Hivernage. Mopeds and scooters from these places will probably not be properly insured, and it is better to rent them from a reputable firm such as Loc2Roues on the upper floor of Galerie Élite, 212 Av Mohammed V (ⓣ0524 430294, ⓦwww.loc2roues.com). Expect to pay around 100dh a day for a bicycle, 250dh for a moped or scooter.

Bookshops The best bookshop in town is Librairie Chatr 19 Av Mohammed V, Guéliz, with lots of books on Morocco in French, including books on trekking and off-roading, plus a small selection of titles in English. Librairie d'Art in *Résidence Taïb*,

55 Bd Mohammed Zerktouni, Guéliz, has lots of art and coffee-table books on Marrakesh and Morocco. In the Medina, there's a small bookshop which sells French books and a range of stationery, Librairie Ghazali, 51 Rue Bab Agnaou.

Car rental Concorde Cars, 154 Av Mohammed V ⓣ0524 431116, ⓦconcordecar.ifrance.com, comes highly recommended. Other local firms include: First Car, 234 Av Mohammed V ⓣ0524 438764, ⓕ0524 438749; Najm Car, shop 9, Galerie Jakar, 61 Av Mohammed V ⓣ0524 437891, ⓦwww.najmcar.com. International franchises include: Avis, 137 Av Mohammed V ⓣ0524 432525, ⓕ0524 431265; Budget, 66 Bd Mohammed Zerktouni ⓣ0524 431180; Europcar, 63 Bd Mohammed Zerktouni ⓣ0524 431228; Hertz, 154 Av Mohammed V ⓣ0524 439984, ⓕ0524 439983; National, 1 Rue de la Liberté ⓣ0524 430683, ⓕ0524 430503; most have desks at the airport, or will meet arrivals by arrangement. Many hotels can also arrange car rental, often at competitive rates. For minibus or 4WD rental, try Sahara Expeditions on the corner of Rue el Mouahdine with Rue Bani Marine (ⓣ0524 427977, ⓦwww.saharaexpe.ma).

Cinemas Colisée, alongside *Café Le Siroua* on Bd Mohammed Zerktouni, Guéliz; Cinéma Mabrouka, Rue Bab Agnaou, Medina; Cinéma Eden, off Rue Riad Zitoun el Djedid, is more downmarket, but watching a film at the Eden is a real Moroccan experience. American and Hong Kong films are dubbed into French, Indian films are in Hindi with Arabic and sometimes French subtitles, French and Arabic films are shown without subtitles. Cheap cinemas traditionally show a Bollywood/Kung Fu double bill, known affectionately as "*l'histoire et la géographie*".

Consulates UK Honorary Consul: Mohammed Zkhiri, Résidence Taib (entrance A, mezzanine floor), 55 Bd Mohammed Zerktouni ⓣ0524 420846, ⓔmatthew.virr@fconet.fco.gov.uk.

Dentist Dr Abdel Jouad Bennani, 112 Av Mohammed V (first floor), opposite the ONMT office, Guéliz (ⓣ0524 449136), speaks some English and has been recommended.

Doctors Dr Abdelmajid Ben Tbib, 171 Av Mohammed V, Guéliz (ⓣ0524 431030), is recommended and speaks English. Dr Frédéric Reitzer, Immeuble Berdaï (entrance C, 2nd floor), 1 Av Moulay el Hassan (at Place de la Liberté), Guéliz ⓣ0524 439562, also speaks some English. There's also an emergency call-out service, SOS Médecins (ⓣ0524 404040), which charges 400dh per consultation. See also "Hospitals".

Festivals and events The two-week Festival National des Arts Populaires (ⓦwww.marrakechfestival.com), held in June or July each year, is the country's biggest and best folklore and music festival, with musicians and dancers coming in from across Morocco and beyond, spanning the range of Moroccan music; shows start around 9pm and are preceded by a fantasia at Bab Djedid, with Berber horsemen at full gallop firing guns into the air. Marrakesh also has an annual Marathon, run on the third or fourth Sunday in January (see ⓦwww.marathon-marrakech.com for details), and the Marrakesh Film Festival in November or early December (ⓦwww.festivalmarrakech.info), in which the featured movies are shown at cinemas across town, and on large screens in the El Badi Palace and the Djemaa el Fna.

Gay Marrakesh For gay men, a certain amount of cruising goes on in the crowds of the Djemaa el Fna in the evening, and there's a gay presence at the *Diamant Noir* nightclub (see p.377). The gay male tourist scene in Marrakesh is growing, and a number of riads are run by gay couples, but there is no easily perceptible lesbian scene in Marrakesh as yet.

Golf There are three eighteen-hole golf courses in Marrakesh: the Marrakesh Royal Golf Club (ⓣ0524 404705), 10km out of town on the old Ouarzazate road, once played on by Churchill and Eisenhower; the Palmeraie Golf Club (ⓣ0524 301010), built, as the name suggests, in the palmery, off the Route de Casablanca, northeast of town; and the Amelkis Golf Club, 12km out on the Route de Ouarzazate (ⓣ0524 404414). All courses are open to non-members, with green fees at 400–600dh per day.

Hammams There are plenty of hammams in the Medina. The three closest to the Djemaa el Fna are Hammam Polo on Rue de la Recette, Hammam Bouloukate on the same street as *Hôtel Afriquia*, and one at the northern end of Rue Riad Zitoun el Kedim. All are marked on our map on p.354, and open simultaneously for men and women with separate entrances for each. Expensive hammams for tourists include Hammam Ziani, 14 Rue Riad Zitoun el Djedid (ⓣ0662 715571, ⓦwww.hammamziani.ma), open for both sexes (separate areas) daily 8am–10pm, costing 50dh for a simple steam bath, or 270dh for an all-in package with massage; even dearer is Les Bains de Marrakech, 2 Derb Sedra, down an alley by Bab Agnaou in the kasbah (ⓣ0524 381428, ⓦwww.lesbainsdemarrakech.com), where prices start at 150dh; despite this, you won't (unless you're gay) be able to share a steam bath experience with your partner – if you want to do that, you'll have to stay at one of the many riads with their own in-house hammam.

Hospitals Private clinics that have high standards and are accustomed to settling bills with insurance companies include: Clinique Yasmine, 12 Rue Ibn

Toumert, Guéliz ⓣ0524 439694; and Polyclinique du Sud, at the corner of Rue de Yougoslavie and Rue Ibn Aïcha, Guéliz ⓣ0524 447999.

Internet access The best place to get online is at the Moulay Abdeslam Cyber-Park, on Av Mohammed V opposite the Ensemble Artisanal (daily 9.30am–6pm, closed Sat & Sun noon–2pm); there's a super-modern internet office, with fast connections and low rates (5dh per hr). Also, almost the entire park, especially the area near the fountain in the middle, is a free wi-fi zone. Internet cafés around the Djemaa el Fna include Cyber de la Place in an arcade off Rue Bani Marine by the *Hôtel Ichbilia* (daily 8.30am–11.30pm; 7dh per hr) and Hanan Internet at the southern end of Rue Bab Agnaou (daily 9am–midnight; 7dh per hr), but you get a cheaper deal at Cyber Internet Riad, 62 Rue Riad Zitoun el Kedim (daily 9am–10pm; 5dh per hr). In Guéliz, internet cafés are surprisingly thin on the ground; try Jawal, in a yard behind the old CTM office at 12 Bd Mohammed Zerktouni (daily 9am–11pm; 6dh per hr), the Café Siraoua a block to the east (daily 8.30am–11.30pm; 7dh per hr), or Espace Internet, in the basement at 183 Av Mohammed V (daily 8.30am–10pm; 10dh per hr).

Laundry In Guéliz, Pressing Oasis, 44 Rue Tarik Ibn Zaid, two doors from *Hôtel Toulousain*; in the Medina, Pressing du Sud, 10 Rue Bab Agnaou, near the Djemaa el Fna (entrance on Rue de la Recette).

Newspapers The best newsstand for American and British newspapers is outside the ONMT office on Av Mohammed V, though you'll find *USA Today*, the *International Herald Tribune*, and various British dailies on sale at stalls elsewhere, especially around the south side of Place Djemaa el Fna.

Pharmacies Several along Av Mohammed V, including Pharmacie de la Liberté, just off Pl de la Liberté, which will call a doctor for you if necessary. In the Medina, try Pharmacie de la Place and Pharmacie du Progrès on Rue Bab Agnaou just by Pl Djemaa el Fna. There's an all-night pharmacy by the Commissariat de Police on Djemaa el Fna and another on Rue Khalid Ben Oualid near the fire station in Guéliz. Other all-night and weekend outlets are listed in pharmacy windows.

Photography Photographic equipment, film and batteries can be obtained from Wrédé, 142 Av Mohammed V (ⓣ0524 435739).

Police The tourist police (*brigade touristique*) are based in Pl Youssef Tachfine at the northern end of Rue Sidi Mimoun, just south of the Koutoubia gardens (ⓣ0524 384601). There's also a police station on the west side of the Djemaa el Fna.

Post office The main post office, which receives all *poste restante* mail, is on Pl 16 du Novembre, midway down Av Mohammed V in Guéliz (Mon–Fri 8am–4.30pm for full services; Mon-Fri 8am–5.45pm & Sat 8am–noon for stamps; Mon–Fri 8am–7pm in an office to the left of the main entrance for Western Union and money changing). The Medina post office on Pl Djemaa el Fna is open similar hours, with a bureau de change round the back (Mon–Sat 8am–8pm, Sun 10am–8pm). The post office in the train station is open daily 8am–8pm.

SPANA Visitors are welcome at the clinic for calèche horses, mules and donkeys run by British animal welfare charity SPANA (see p.55) directly north of the Medina in Cité Mohammadi, Daoudiat ⓣ0524 303110.

Swimming pools Many hotels (but, alas, not the *Mamounia*) allow non-residents to use their pools if you have a meal, or for a fee. Useful if you're staying in the Medina is the *Grand Hôtel Tazi* (50dh). Also handy, especially if you're with kids who hate sightseeing is Oasiria, at km4, Route du Barrage, on the Asni/Oumnass road (daily 10am–6pm; 180dh full day, 140dh half-day, children under 1.5m and senior citizens 100dh/80dh ⓣ0524 380438, ⓦwww.oasiria.com); it even runs free shuttle buses from town mid-June–Aug, and offers a 10 percent discount to readers presenting a copy of this book at reception.

Moving on

The **train** station (ⓣ0524 203040) is on Avenue Mohammed VI at Avenue Hassan II, a ten-minute walk west of Guéliz (served by buses #3, #4, #8, #10, #14 and #66 from Place Foucauld). If you're heading to **Tangier** it's possible to do the trip in one go, most easily by booking a couchette on the night train (350dh), preferably on the morning of the day of travel.

Buses to most **long-distance destinations** leave from the main terminal at **Bab Doukkala**, a ten-minute walk from Guéliz, fifteen minutes from the Djemaa el Fna (ⓣ0524 433933; served by the same buses that go to the train station, plus #16, #17 and #26). Buy tickets a day in advance – or turn up early

– for the more popular destinations such as Fes, El Jadida, Tizi n'Test or Zagora. The main CTM office is west of Guéliz on Rue Aboubaker Seddik (Ⓣ0524 448328), where all CTM buses stop.

Supratours express buses for Essaouira, Agadir, Ouarzazate and the Western Sahara leave from an office on Avenue Hassan II near the train station (with direct access from platform 1), though they only sell tickets if there is space after the allocation for train passengers from Casablanca/Rabat. Grands taxis are generally on hand to pick up the overflow at these times and are good value, a place to Agadir costing around 100dh.

Collective grands taxis can also be useful for other destinations and run from behind Bab Doukkala bus station, or (for High Atlas destinations) from the Bab er Robb *gare routière*, which is actually 2km beyond Bab er Robb. To Oukaïmeden, shared taxis operate during the skiing season only, heading up in the morning and back in the evening, and you will have to pay for the round trip, even if staying the night, which may also leave you without any sure transport back.

Marrakesh's **airport** (Ⓣ+0524 447865 or 447910) is 4km southwest of town, past the Menara Gardens. It's not advisable to walk it (muggings are not unheard of), but you can take a petit taxi (they won't use the meter; expect to pay 80dh by day, 120dh by night), or bus #19 from Place Foucauld half-hourly 6.15am to 12.15am (20dh; 30min), via Avenue Mohammed V and Boulevard Mohammed VI (it can be joined at any bus stop en route).

Travel details

Trains

Marrakesh to: Casablanca Voyageurs (9 daily; 3hr 10min); Fes (8 daily; 7hr 10min); Kenitra (9 daily; 4hr 45min); Meknes (8 daily; 6hr 35min); Oujda (3 daily changing at Casa or Fes; 13–14hr); Rabat (9 daily; 4hr 15min); Safi (1 daily changing at Benguerir; 3hr); Settat (9 daily; 2hr 5min); Tangier (1 direct & 3 connecting daily; 9hr 35min).

Buses

Marrakesh to: Agadir (10 CTM, 9 Supratours & 12 others daily; 4hr); Aoulouz via Tizi n'Test (2 daily; 9hr); Asni (10 daily; 1hr 30min); Azilal (2 daily; 3hr); Beni Mellal (2 CTM & some 30 others daily; 4hr); Casablanca (9 CTM daily and others roughly half-hourly 4am–9pm; 4hr); Dakhla (1 CTM, 1 Supratours and 3 others daily; 24hr); Demnate (9 daily; 1hr 30min); El Jadida (12 daily; 4hr); Essaouira (2 CTM, 5 Supratours & 18 others daily; 3hr); Fes (2 CTM & 9 others daily; 10hr); Goulimine (3 CTM, 5 Supratours & 10 others daily; 9hr 30min); Laayoune (3 CTM, 2 Supratours & 2 others daily; 15hr); Meknes (1 CTM & 7 others daily; 9hr); Ouarzazate (4 CTM, 3 Supratours & 11 others daily; 5hr); Rabat (2 CTM & others hourly; 5hr 30min); Rissani (2 daily; 12hr); Safi (15 daily; 2hr); Smara (1 CTM & 1 Supratours daily; 13hr 15min); Taliouine (1 daily; 10hr); Tafraoute (4 daily; 10hr); Taroudant (1 CTM & 7 others daily; 6hr 30min); Tangier (1 CTM & 10 others daily; 10hr); Tetouan (3 daily; 10hr); Tiznit (3 CTM, 2 Supratours & 10 others daily; 7hr); Zagora (2 CTM & 8 others daily; 9hr 30min).

Grands taxis

Bab Doukkala to: Azilal (2hr 30min); Casablanca (2hr 30min); Essaouira (2hr 30min); Inezgane (3hr); Ouarzazate (3hr); Taroudant (4hr).

Bab er Robb station to: Asni (1hr); Moulay Brahim (1hr); Oukaïmeden (winter only; 2hr); Setti Fatma (2hr).

Flights

Marrakesh to: Casablanca (RAM 4–6 daily; 40min).

6

The High Atlas

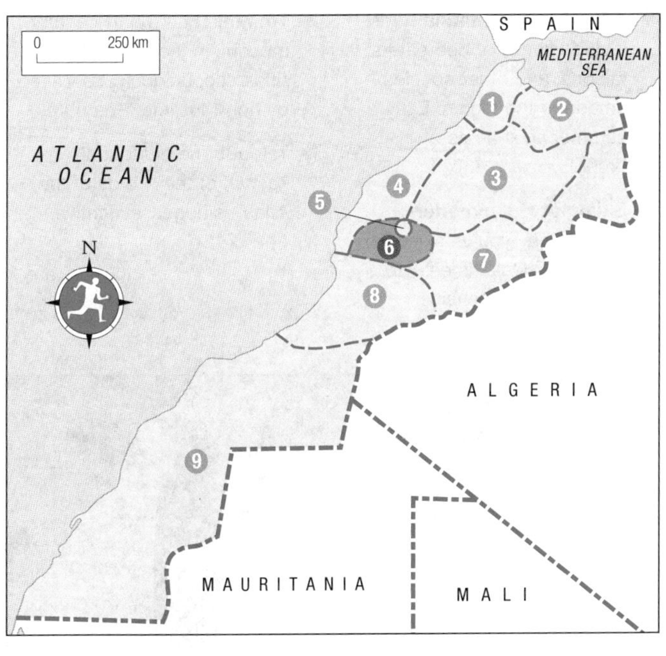

CHAPTER 6

Highlights

* **Atlas Berbers** The High Atlas is a beautiful mountain area, populated mainly by Berbers who have a unique culture, dress and traditions. See p.386

* **Ourika Valley** An easy day-trip from Marrakesh, the valley is a delight, with its waterfalls and riverside cafés. See p.387

* **Atlas flora and fauna** Birds include flocks of bee-eaters, falcons, and other species unique to the region. Early summer sees acres of orchids. See p.389

* **Skiing at Oukaïmeden** Want to say you've skied in Morocco? Ouka is easy to reach and inexpensive. See p.390

* **Imlil and Aroumd** These Toubkal trailhead villages are remote enough to get a taste of Berber mountain life, even if you go no further. See p.394 & p.398

* **Djebel Toubkal** North Africa's highest peak is the goal for most Atlas trekkers, offering summer walks and winter mountaineering. See p.398

* **Tin Mal** This twelfth-century mosque in the heart of the Atlas can, uniquely, be visited by non-Muslims. See p.407

* **Telouet** The old feudal kasbah of the "Lords of the Atlas" is hugely evocative. See p.411

▲ Skiing at Oukaïmedan

6

The High Atlas

The **High Atlas**, North Africa's greatest mountain range, contains some of the most intriguing and beautiful regions of Morocco. A historical and physical barrier between the northern plains and the pre-Sahara, its Berber-populated valleys feel – and indeed are – very remote from the country's mainstream or urban life. For visitors, it is, above all, **trekking country**, with walks to suit all levels of ability and commitment, from casual day-hikes to weeks of serious expedition routes combining a series of peaks (*djebels*) and passes (*tizis* or, in French, *cols*). One of the joys of Atlas trekking is that you can walk unencumbered: mules are available to hire, along with muleteers and mountain guides, who are invaluable if you are doing anything off the main routes. Rock-climbing and ski mountaineering are other options, and mountain biking, too, is increasingly popular on the dirt tracks (*pistes*) and mule paths. There are horses for hire at Ouirgane for organized local treks, and there are also a number of treks to study the alpine flora, bird life and geology of the region.

Despite the forbidding appearance of its peaks, these are surprisingly populated mountains; their slopes drop away to valleys and streams, with Berber

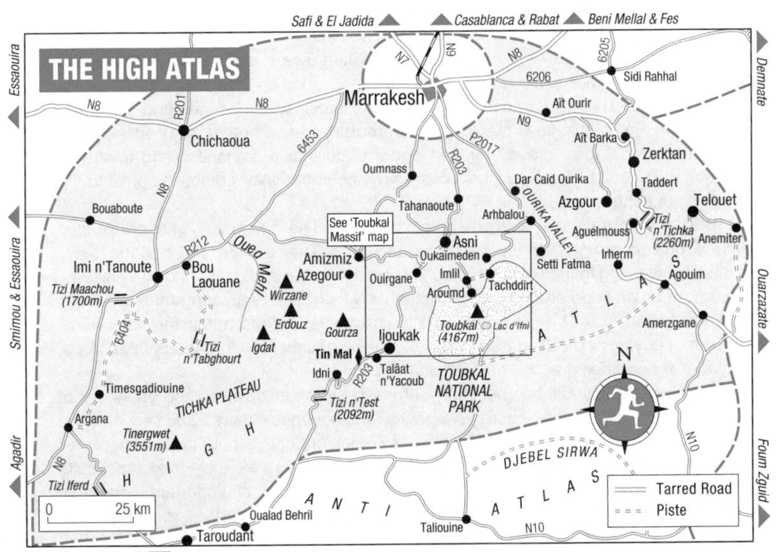

villages terraced into their sides. At many of the **villages** – particularly in the two main hiking centres around Morocco's highest peak **Djebel Toubkal** (4167m) and the **Bou Guemez Valley** (see p.265) – *gîte*-style accommodation is offered in local houses, and there is an established infrastructure of guides and mules. It must be stressed, though, that part of the attraction of Atlas trekking is that it remains so undeveloped in comparison with, say, the Pyrenees or Alps. However, roads and electricity are now reaching more remote areas, and will continue to do so, markedly changing the nature of the region. This chapter – although entitled "The High Atlas" actually covers only the **Western part of the range**; for more on **easterly peaks and routes**, which offer four-wheel drive or travel on local Berber trucks, as well as trekking, see Chapter Seven.

Routes and passes

The **Djebel Toubkal** massif provides the focus for most trekking expeditions and can be reached easily from Marrakesh by driving, or taking a bus or taxi, to **Asni** – just over an hour's journey – and then up to the trailhead at **Imlil**. The region can also be approached from **Ouirgane** or **Ijoukak**, a little further west, the **Ourika Valley** from the east, or the ski resort of **Oukaïmeden**. Some

High Atlas Berbers

Until recent decades, the High Atlas region – and its **Berber inhabitants** – was almost completely isolated. When the French began their "pacification" in the 1920s, the way of life here was essentially feudal, based upon the control of the three main passes (*tizis*) by a trio of "clan" families, "the Lords of the Atlas". Even after the French negotiated the cooperation of these warrior chiefs, it was not until the spring of 1933 – 21 years after the establishment of the Protectorate – that they were able to subdue them and control their tribal land, and only then with the cooperation of the main feudal chief, **T'hami el Glaoui**, who continued to control the region as pasha of Marrakesh (see p.362).

These days, the region is under official government control through a system of local *caids*, but in many villages the role of the state remains largely irrelevant, and if you go trekking you soon become aware of the mountains' highly distinctive culture and traditions. The longest established inhabitants of Morocco, the Atlas Berbers, never adopted a totally orthodox version of Islam (see "Contexts", p.586) and the Arabic language has, even today, made little impression on their indigenous **Tachelhaït** dialects. Their **music** and **ahouache** dances (in which women and men both take part) are unique, as is the village **architecture**, with stone or clay houses tiered on the rocky slopes, craggy fortified **agadirs** (collective granaries), and **kasbahs**, which continued to serve as feudal castles for the community's defence right into the twentieth century.

Berber women in the Atlas go about unveiled and have a much higher profile than their rural counterparts in the plains and the north. They perform much of the heavy labour – working in the fields, herding and grazing cattle and goats and carrying vast loads of brushwood and provisions. Whether they have any greater status or power within the family and village, however, is questionable. The men retain the "important" tasks of buying and selling goods and the evening/night-time irrigation of the crops, ploughing and doing all the building and craftwork.

As an outsider, you'll be constantly surprised by the friendliness and openness of the Berbers, and by their amazing capacity for languages – there's scarcely a village where you won't find someone who speaks French or English, or both. The only areas where you may feel exploited – and pestered by kids – are the main trekking circuits around Djebel Toubkal, where tourism has become an all-important source of income. Given the harshness of life up here, its presence is hardly surprising.

trekkers, with time to spend, also approach from the south, through the Tifnoute valley and Lac d'Ifni.

Asni, Ouirgane and Ijoukak all lie on the dramatic **Tizi n'Test road**, which climbs over an Atlas pass to connect Marrakesh with Taroudant: a switchback of hairpin curves to be driven with care. As well as its scenic appeal and trekking possibilities, the route has an easily accessible historic attraction in the ruins of the twelfth-century mosque of **Tin Mal**.

Southeast of Marrakesh is the **Tizi n'Tichka**, a more substantial road pass, and a spectacular piece of engineering. It was built to replace the old caravan route to the Drâa and the South, which was controlled during the nineteenth century and for much of the twentieth by the legendary **Glaoui family**, "the Lords of the Atlas" (see p.410). Their kasbah, a bizarre cluster of crumbling towers, still stands at **Telouet**, just an hour from the main road.

To the west, the **Tizi Maachou** has less drama, unless you leave the main road to get into the attractive Western Atlas. For most the pass simply offers a fast route between Marrakesh and Agadir; it is cluttered with lorries, and can be dangerous though ongoing work is upgrading it. The older *piste* road runs parallel, slightly east, and offers an attractive alternative; it is also in the process of being upgraded.

Seasons and dangers - snow and floods

The High Atlas is subject to **snow** from **November to April**, and even the major Tizi n'Tichka and Tizi n'Test passes can be closed for periods of a day or more. If so, the south can be reached from Marrakesh by the Tizi Maachou pass (the N8 Agadir road) then the N10 through Taroudant and Taliouine, but the passes are seldom blocked for long and notices outside Marrakesh on the roads inform if they are open or closed.

The **thaw** can present problems, too, when the snow melts in spring, causing swollen rivers which are dangerous to cross. And the possibility of spring/summer **flash floods** must be taken seriously, as they can erupt suddenly and violently and are extremely dangerous. In August 1995, summer storms caused devastating flooding in the Atlas; dozens of buildings and bridges were washed away and more than a thousand lives lost. Always camp on high ground, avoiding any spot where water can lie or might become a course for the torrent. This includes (although it's hard to believe in summer) dried up and apparently terminally inactive riverbeds.

For more on **trekking seasons** – and be aware that winter activities above the snow line are a serious endeavour here – see the box on pp.396–397.

The Ourika Valley and Oukaïmeden

The **Ourika Valley** is an enjoyable and popular escape from the summer heat of Marrakesh, with the village of **Setti Fatma** a big weekend resort for young Marrakshis, who ride out on their mopeds or BMWs to lie around beside the streams and waterfalls. The village lies at the end of the road, but a *piste* (to Timichi) and then a mule track continues up the valley to passes to **Tachddirt** and **Oukaïmeden**, which has the best skiing in Morocco and interesting prehistoric rock carvings, and through to Imlil and Toubkal, making it a useful starting/finishing point for trekkers. A high pass also leads to the **Oued Zat Valley**, dominated by Taska n'Zat, a peak and valley offering demanding treks best left to the experienced.

Getting to the Ourika Valley

Setti Fatma is an easy drive from Marrakesh (67km), and there is a regular service of **buses**, **minibuses** and **grands taxis** leaving from the terminus 2km out on the Asni road (see p.382); the buses take a little under two hours. The Ourika Valley proper begins at **SOUK TNINE DE L'OURIKA** (30km from Marrakesh), a small roadside village, which, as its name proclaims, hosts a Monday **souk** – an excursion offered by many of the tour hotels in Marrakesh. Just beyond, across the river, is **DAR CAID OURIKI**, with a picturesque *zaouia* set back in the rocks, near the ruins of an old *caidal* **kasbah**.

Beyond here, scattered at intervals over the next forty kilometres, are a series of tiny hamlets, interspersed with a few summer homes and the occasional hotel or café-restaurant. The one sizeable settlement is **ARHBALOU** (50km from Marrakesh), where most of the local people on the buses get off. The village has a "palace-restaurant", *Le Lion d'Ourika* (Ⓣ0524 445322), and basic rooms to let in the village. A road west into the mountains leads to the trekking trailhead and ski resort of Oukaïmeden.

Moving on through the valley towards Setti Fatma, those with transport might want to stop at the **antiques/crafts shop**, Le Musée d'Arhbalou, 4km south of Arhbalou, which often has interesting stock. A further 2km on, there are pleasant **rooms** at the *Hôtel Amnougar* (Ⓣ0524 445328; ❹), and there are a number of tempting riverside cafés, too. From the village of **TAZZIDFOUNT** a track leads up east to Adrar Yagour – a good trekking area, where you can see prehistoric rock carvings; see "Treks from Setti Fatma" (below) for more on this.

Setti Fatma

SETTI FATMA is a straggly riverside village, substantially rebuilt, expanded and made safer after its 1995 devastation by floods. The setting, with grassy terraces and High Atlas peaks rising to over 3600m, feels like a real oasis after the dry plains around Marrakesh, and in the rocky foothills above the village are a series of six (at times, seven) **waterfalls**. To **reach the falls** you first have to cross the stream by whatever bridge has been thrown up after the last floods; near the beginning of the climb are several cafés, where you can order a tajine for your return. The first waterfall is a fairly straightforward clamber over the rocks, and it is flanked by another café, the *Immouzer*. The higher ones are a lot more strenuous, and quite tricky when descending, requiring a head for heights and solid footwear. Returning, from the first of the falls you can loop back to Setti Fatma via the village's twin, **Zaouia Mohammed**, a few hundred metres further down the valley.

The **Setti Fatma Moussem** – one of the three most important festivals in the country – takes place for four days around the middle of August, centred on the **Koubba of Setti Fatma**, some way upstream from the *Café des Cascades*. Entry to the *koubba* is forbidden to non-Muslims, but the festival itself is as much a fair and market as it is a religious festival and well worth trying to coincide with.

Treks from Setti Fatma

Ourika cuts right into the **High Atlas**, whose peaks begin to dominate as soon as you leave Marrakesh. At Setti Fatma these mountains provide a startling backdrop that, to the southwest, include the main **trekking/climbing zone of Toubkal**. The usual approach to this is from Asni (see p.393) but it is possible to set out from Setti Fatma, or from Oukaïmeden (see p.390).

Approaching Toubkal from Setti Fatma, one route is to trek via **Timichi** and **Oukaïmeden** and take the trail from there to Tachddirt. It is around five hours'

High Atlas wildlife

The High Atlas has unique flora and fauna, which are accessible even to the most reluctant rambler if you base yourself at **Oukaïmeden**, **Imlil** or **Ouirgane**.

The spring bloom on the lower slopes comprises aromatic thyme and thorny caper, mingling with golden spreads of broom. Higher slopes are covered by more resilient species, such as the blue tussocks of hedgehog broom. The passes ring to the chorus of the painted frog and the North African race of the green toad during their spring breeding seasons, while some species of reptile, such as the **Moorish gecko**, have adapted to the stony walls of the area's towns and villages. **Butterflies** which brave these heights include the Moroccan copper and desert orange tip, and painted ladies heading from West Africa to western England. Other inhabitants include the almost invisible praying mantis, the scampering ground squirrel and the rare elephant shrew.

Birds to be found among the sparse vegetation include Moussier's redstart and the crimson-winged finch, which prefers the grassy slopes where it feeds in flocks; both birds are unique to North African mountains. The rocky outcrops provide shelter for both chough and alpine chough and the mountain rivers are frequented by dippers who swim underwater in their search for food. Overhead, darting Lanner falcon or flocks of brilliantly coloured bee-eaters add to the feeling of abundance which permeates the slopes of the High Atlas. In the cultivated valleys look out for the magpie which, uniquely, has a sky-blue eye mark; there are also storks galore. Other High Atlas birds, as the snow melts, include shore larks, rock bunting, alpine accentor, redstarts and many species of wheatear.

Flora is impressive, too. The wet meadows produce a fantastic spread of hooped-petticoat daffodils, *romulea* and other bulbs, and Oukaïmeden in May/June has acres of orchids.

walk along the *piste* from Setti Fatma to Timichi (which has several *gîtes*; see p.401). From Timichi, it is about five to six hours on a mule track to Oukaïmeden, including a steep ascent to the Tizi n'ou Attar. (The long day-trek direct from **Timichi to Tachddirt** is ideally done in the opposite direction, so is thus described on p.401).

Other **adventurous treks** from Setti Fatma – all of them requiring proper equipment, supplies and planning – include **Adrar Yagour**, with its many prehistoric rock carvings; **Adrar Meltzen**, via **Tourcht**; and the secluded **Oued Zat** region reached by the demanding Tizi n'Tilst. The **Taska n'Zat–Arjoût peaks** require scrambling (up gorges and on the crests) while the way down the Oued Zat offers some days of splashing through gorges to reach the *piste* out. An ancient route climbs to the **Tizi Tazarzit** and reaches the N9 at **Agouim** south of the range. These are some of the hardest options in the Atlas and it is a good idea to enlist one of the guides from Imlil (such as Aït Idir Mohammed; see p.395), or Hosain Izahan (who can be contacted through the *Café Azapza* in Setti Fatma).

Practicalities

Setti Fatma has an ever-growing number of **places to stay** and outside of weekends, or at festival time (when there'll be nothing going – but a huge impromptu campsite), you should have little problem finding a room. For **meals**, the *Asgaour* and *Restaurant Le Noyer* are the best bets.

Café des Cascades The first café on the route to the falls, it has decent if basic rooms. ❷

Café-Restaurant Asgaour This is in Setti Fatma village proper, and though the rooms are a bit basic, they are spotless, and overlook the river. The patron, Chebob Lahcen, also cooks excellent meals. ❷

Hôtel Gare One of a row of little hotel-restaurants that line the concrete road by the taxi turning area

– and marginally more appealing than its neighbours. ❷

Hôtel Tafoukt and **La Perle d'Ourika** These two modest and modern hotels are in Asgaour – once a separate village (and labelled as such on most maps) but now basically the beginning of Setti Fatma. They both have en-suite rooms. ❸

Oukaïmeden

The village and ski centre of **OUKAÏMEDEN** is a much easier trekking base than Setti Fatma from which to set out towards Toubkal – and a good target in its own right. In summer, there are some attractive day-hikes, and the chance to see prehistoric rock carvings (see box below), while in winter, of course, there is the chance to **ski** – and it's hard to resist adding Africa to a list of places you have skied. "Ouka", as it is known, is reached via a good road that veers off from the Ourika road just before Arhbalou. **Grands taxis** sometimes go up from Marrakesh in the winter for the skiers or you can charter a whole taxi for yourself. The resort has a 10dh entrance fee in winter; a snowplough keeps the road open.

Skiing

The slopes of **Adrar-n-Oukaïmeden** offer the best **skiing** in Morocco, and up until the war the resort could boast the highest ski lift in the world – which, at 3273m, still remains impressive (it was re-strung in 2003). It gives access to good *piste* and off-*piste* skiing, while on the lower slopes a few basic drag lifts serve nursery and intermediate runs. For **cross-country skiers**, several crests and *cols* are accessible, and ski mountaineers often head across to Tachddirt.

Snowfall and snow cover can be erratic but the **season** is regarded as February to April; the lifts close at the end of April (even if there are perfect skiing conditions). **Equipment** can be rented from several shops around the resort, at fairly modest rates but quality fluctuates so ask around. Ski passes are cheap (around US$5), and there are modest charges if you want to hire a **ski guide**, or instructor.

Trekking: Oukaïmeden to Tachddirt

The **walking trails** from Oukaïmeden are strictly summer only: routes can be heavily snow-covered late into spring. However, weather conditions allowing,

Prehistoric rock carvings in the Atlas

Details of the fascinating **prehistoric rock carvings of the Atlas**, showing animals, weapons, battle scenes and various unknown symbols, can be found in an indispensable guidebook (on sale in the Oukaïmeden CAF chalet and in Marrakesh bookshops), *Gravures Rupestres du Haut Atlas*, though unfortunately it is only available in French. Several sites are located near Oukaïmeden and (in summer) a local will guide you to the better sites for a small tip.

A puzzling related feature of prehistoric rock sites in the Atlas and elsewhere are **cupmarks** – groups of small circular hollows (Peter Ustinov suggested they were egg-cups) with no apparent pattern carved into exposed rock surfaces at ground level. They had been noted down the western side of Scotland and Europe, but were unknown in Africa until recently, when Atlas explorer and *Rough Guide to Morocco* co-author Hamish Brown discovered them. Since then, he has come across them several times in his wanderings. Unlike the usual rock art, they appear in granite (in the western Atlas) and conglomerate (at Tinerhir) as well as sandstone (in the Middle Atlas). If anyone discovers further sites in Morocco, we would be grateful to hear from them so that the information can be passed on.

the **trail to Tachddirt** (3hr) is pretty clear, being a *piste* as far as the pass, **Tizi n'Eddi** (2928m), reached in about two hours. On the descent, the trail divides in two, with both branches leading down into Tachddirt. For more details of this route, described in reverse, and routes on from Tachddirt, see p.401.

Practicalities

There are several **hotels** in the resort, as well as a rather basic **campsite**. The hotels cater mainly for the ski season, but most stay open year-round.

Chalet-Hôtel de l'Angour (also called *Chez Juju*) ☎0524 319005. An excellent little *auberge*, owned by a Canadian couple, with decent French cooking and a bar. Open all year. ❹

Club Alpine Chalet ☎0524 319036 (50dh per night for members, 100dh non-members). Open for both members and non-members. Well equipped, with a bar and restaurant, which does substantial meals. The warden usually has Atlas trekking guidebooks for sale. ❷

Kenzi Louka ☎0524 319080. This 100-room, four-star hotel has terrific views from its pyramid-tiered rooms. Facilities include two restaurants, a bar, an indoor swimming pool, a hammam, a gym and even conference rooms. ❻

The Djebel Toubkal Massif

The **Toubkal Massif**, enclosing the High Atlas's highest peaks, is the goal of almost everyone who goes trekking in Morocco. You can reach its trailhead villages in just two to three hours from Marrakesh, and its main routes are well charted. Walking even fairly short distances, however, you feel transported to a very different world. The Berber mountain villages look amazing, their houses stacked one on top of another in apparently organic growth from the rocks, and the people are immediately distinct from their city compatriots, with the women dressed in brilliant costumes even when working in the fields.

From late spring to late autumn (see note on seasons, p.396), the region's trails are accessible for anyone reasonably fit. Mule tracks round the mountain valleys are well contoured and kept in excellent condition, and there's a network of village *gîtes*, houses and CAF refuges (huts) for accommodation, which makes camping unnecessary unless you're going well away from the villages.

In summer, **Djebel Toubkal** (4167m), the highest peak in North Africa, is walkable right up to the summit; if you're pushed for time, you could climb it and be back in Marrakesh in three days – though at the risk of altitude sickness. Alternatively, if you feel unable to tackle an ascent of Toubkal, it's possible to get a genuine taste of the mountains by spending days exploring the beautiful valleys accessible from Imlil or Aroumd.

More committed trekkers will probably want to head further afield, away from the busy Toubkal trail. A tempting target is **Lac d'Ifni**, over a demanding pass, but there are infinite variations on **longer treks**, from local circuits to the two-to-three-week trek to Ighil Mgoun (see p.266).

Moulay Brahim

MOULAY BRAHIM is a picturesque village, off the main Marrakesh–Asni road and dominating the gorges leading up from the plains. The **Kik Plateau** and its escarpment, which runs above the main road towards Ouirgane, is botanically rich and offers perhaps the best panorama of the Atlas and can be reached from the top end of the town, on a *piste* past marble quarries (see pp.393–394). A good road crosses the plateau to descend to Amizmiz.

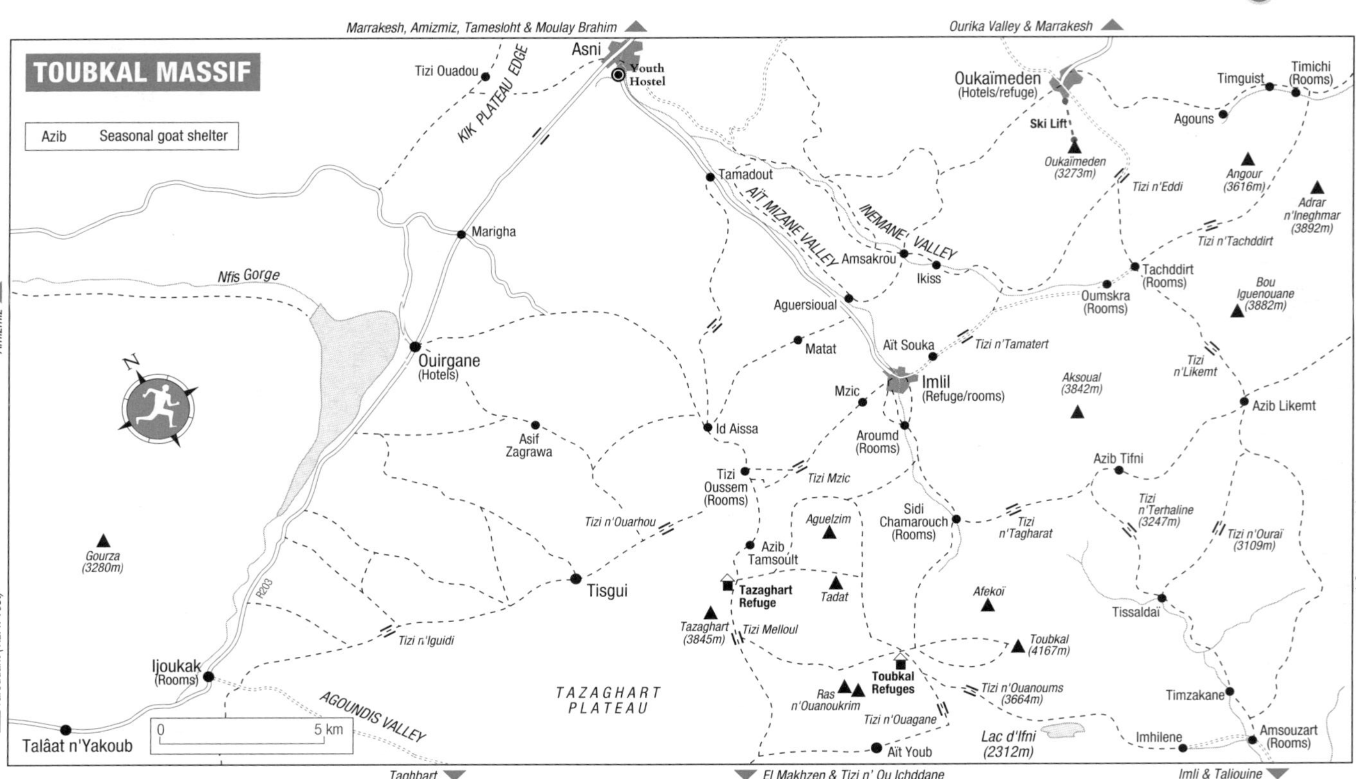
TOUBKAL MASSIF
Azib Seasonal goat shelter
Marrakesh, Amizmiz, Tamesloht & Moulay Brahim
Ourika Valley & Marrakesh
Setti Fatma & Ourika Valley
Difficult route to Ourika Valley (Kissaria Gorge)
Imli & Taliouine
El Makhzen & Tizi n' Ou Ichddane
Taghbart
Taroudant (Tizi n'Test)
Amizmiz
Asni
Youth Hostel
Tizi Ouadou
KIK PLATEAU EDGE
Marigha
Nfis Gorge
Ouirgane (Hotels)
Asif Zagrawa
Gourza (3280m)
Ijoukak (Rooms)
Talâat n'Yakoub
R203
AGOUNDIS VALLEY
0 5 km
Tizi n'Iguidi
Tisgui
Tizi n'Ouarhou
TAZAGHART PLATEAU
Tamadout
AÏT MIZANE VALLEY
INEMANE VALLEY
Amsakrou
Ikiss
Aguersioual
Matat
Id Aissa
Tizi Oussem (Rooms)
Tizi Mzic
Mzic
Aït Souka
Imlil (Refuge/rooms)
Aroumd (Rooms)
Tizi n'Tamatert
Azib Tamsoult
Aguelzim
Tazaghart Refuge
Tadat
Tazaghart (3845m)
Tizi Melloul
Ras n'Ouanoukrim
Toubkal Refuges
Tizi n'Ouagane
Aït Youb
Sidi Chamarouch (Rooms)
Afekoï
Toubkal (4167m)
Tizi n'Ouanoums (3664m)
Lac d'Ifni (2312m)
Oukaïmeden (Hotels/refuge)
Ski Lift
Oukaïmeden (3273m)
Tizi n'Eddi
Oumskra (Rooms)
Tachddirt (Rooms)
Tizi n'Tachddirt
Agouns
Timguist
Timichi (Rooms)
Angour (3616m)
Adrar n'Ineghmar (3892m)
Bou Iguenouane (3882m)
Aksoual (3842m)
Tizi n'Likemt
Azib Likemt
Azib Tifni
Tizi n'Tagharat
Tizi n'Terhaline (3247m)
Tizi n'Ouraï (3109m)
Tissaldaï
Timzakane
Imhilene
Amsouzart (Rooms)

The village is a popular weekend spot for Marrakshis and an alternative base for a first night in the Atlas, with several **hotels** – mostly cheapies such as the central *Alfouki* and the *Talfoukt* at the entrance to the town (both ❷) plus the better equipped and larger *Star's Hôtel* and the uninspiring *Haut Rocher* (both ❸) above the town. There are plenty of good eating places, and regular **buses** and **taxis** to and from Asni and Marrakesh. The village hosts a large **moussem** two weeks after Mouloud.

Asni

The end of the line for most buses and grands taxis, **ASNI** is little more than a roadside village and marketplace, from where you can head straight on to Imlil, though a night here is quite pleasant – at least once the touts have left off. You may find it pays to make some small purchase and take a mint tea with one of the sellers; after all, they have little else to do, and you may as well stay relaxed. The most interesting time to be here before heading on to Toubkal is for the **Saturday souk**, when the enclosure behind the row of shop cubicles is filled with local produce (this is a big fruit-growing region) and livestock stalls.

Accommodation and eating

Accommodation is limited in Asni, so it's worth considering moving straight on to Imlil or Ouirgane. For **meals**, most of the café-stalls by the souk will fix you a tajine or *harira*.

Auberge de Jeunesse At the south end of the village. Asni's youth hostel is open all year and to all-comers, with slightly higher charges for non-IYHF members. There are cold showers and you'll need your own sleeping bag, though blankets can be rented; the location by the river can be very cold in winter. Nonetheless, it is a friendly place and good meeting point. They will store luggage if you want to go off trekking unencumbered. ❶

Villa de l'Atlas near the top end of the long straight road heading for Imlil Ⓣ&Ⓕ 0524 484855 or 061 667736. A pleasant new guesthouse, some way out of town, so worth taking a taxi if you have much luggage. ❸

Moving on

Transport from Asni on **to Imlil** is pretty straightforward, with minibuses and taxis shuttling back and forth along the 17km of road, with larger lorries on Saturdays for the souk. All normally wait until they fill their passenger quota, though they can be chartered.

Buses from Asni run to Marrakesh, Moulay Brahim or Ijoukak and – at around 6am – over the Tizi n'Test for Taliouine (change at Ouled Berhil for Taroudant; see p.508), but check in advance as the service changes occasionally. From Asni a place in a **grand taxi** can be negotiated to Marrakesh, Moulay Brahim or Ouirgane, and (in stages but unreliably) over the Tizi n'Test.

Buses and taxis leave from the souk entrance area (main destinations); from the roadside up from the petrol station (for up-valley destinations); and from the smaller souk entrance (on Sat).

Walks around Asni and Moulay Brahim

There's no need to rush up to Toubkal, and there are many local walks in the fruit-growing areas around Asni and Moulay Brahim, which will get you acclimatized for the higher peaks. They are not much explored and so have a charm of their own. The forested slopes above Asni are dominated by a rocky scarp which is the edge of the hidden limestone **Kik Plateau**. In spring a walk up here is a delight, with a spread of alpine flowers and incomparable views. To get the best from it, set off early in the day and carry water; four hours' walking will bring you over the plateau if you take a bus or taxi up to the start.

If you are walking from Asni, follow the Tizi n'Test road to where it swings out of sight (past the red conical hill). Just past a souvenir stall, a *piste* breaks off and can be seen rising up the hillside. Take this to reach the pass, then turn right again, through fields, to eventually join the plateau edge, which you can follow to **Moulay Brahim**; leave the crest to join a *piste* down to the left, which passes big marble quarries just before the village. You can also cut down to Asni by a zigzag path leaving the route midway along.

There's also a spectacular surfaced road across the Kik Plateau. Crossing from Asni, you descend towards the reservoir of Lalla Takerkoust, and you will eventually emerge on the Amizmiz–Marrakesh road. The western (Aguergour) scarp is a prime site for paragliding.

Valley approaches

The valleys of Asni, Imlil (Mizane), Tachddirt (Imenane) and Tizi Oussem/Ouirgane (Azzadene) offer fine walks, which you might do to acclimatize yourself before tackling Toubkal or other high mountains. They are all much easier if you walk them downhill – back to Asni/Ouirgane, from which it is easy enough to return to Imlil by taxi. Note there are a number of new *piste*s being driven up these valleys, some of which are surfaced.

Imlil to Asni. This is a pleasant half-day walk. From Imlil, walk back down the road, then, after about an hour, swap over to the old mule track on the east side of the valley. Follow this for about two hours, then at an area of purple, yellow and red soils, climb up to a pass and end by the lower Imenane; or go out to the last bump of the crest for a grand view.

Tachddirt to Asni. There is a long but straightforward *piste*/trail from Tachddirt down-valley to Asni, taking seven to nine hours. It's an enjoyable route through a fine valley – a good (and neglected) exit from the mountains. You could also do this route from Imlil, heading off down from the Tizi n'Tamatert (1hr from Imlil) to the bottom of the valley at Tinhourine. If you want to camp out at night, there are possible places to pitch a tent below Ikiss or Arg, and there are also **gîtes** at Ikiss and Amsakrou. A fine pass rises opposite Ikiss to cross a *tizi* to Aguersioual and so back to Imlil, an excellent round trip.

Imlil

The trip from Asni to **IMLIL** is a startling transition. Almost as soon as it leaves Asni, the road begins to climb; below it the valley of the Oued Rhirhaia unfolds, while above, small villages crowd onto the rocky slopes. Early on, you pass a palatial hotel, *Kasbah Tamadot*, which is owned by Richard Branson who started several of his balloon flights nearby. Half way up the valley, at a roadside café, there is a sudden good view of Toubkal. As you emerge at Imlil the air feels quite different – silent and rarefied at 1740m. Paths head off in all directions among the valleys, making this a walker's paradise.

If you want to make an early start for the Toubkal refuges and the ascent of Toubkal, Imlil village is a better trailhead than Asni, as is Aroumd (the next village on towards Toubkal – see p.398). It is not advisable to try and reach the Toubkal Refuge from Asni or Marrakesh in one day; the altitude effects can kick in and spoil your chances of climbing the peak.

Accommodation

Imlil has many provisions shops and a fair choice of accommodation including a CAF refuge, a fast-growing cluster of **hotel-cafés** and *gîtes,* and a kasbah treat.

Atlas Tichka ⓣ0524 485223, ⓕ0524 485628. One of the best of the new village-run hotels, with charming atmosphere and service. ❹

CAF refuge ⓣ0524 485122 or 0677 307415. This old-established French Alpine Club refuge has been refurbished to a high standard and is now run by a French cook/guardian Madame Letiche. ❸

Chez Lahcen Askary ⓣ&ⓕ0524 485617. A fine *gîte*, set above the village, managed by Lahcen Askary (who runs the "Shopping Centre" facing the Imlil refuge). ❹

Hôtel-Café Aksoual ⓣ0524 485612. Facing the CAF refuge and with clean, comfortable rooms. ❸

Hôtel-Café Soleil ⓣ0524 485622, ⓕ0524 485622. On the square by the river, this place offers decent rooms and does superb tajines. It also offers camping, self-catering, and rooms at the *Auberge La Vallée* (ⓣ0524 485216), at the top of the village. ❸

Hôtel El Aïne ⓣ0524 485625. Further down the main street, this has reasonable rooms around an attractive courtyard. ❸

Hôtel Etoile de Toubkal ⓣ0524 485618. Decent enough, but without much care or character. ❹

Kasbah du Toubkal ⓣ0524 485611, ⓕ0524 485636; or through Discover Ltd in the UK ⓣ01883 744392, ⓦwww.kasbahdutoubkal.com. This *caid*'s kasbah above Imlil was restored by the British company Discover using local crafts and workers, and offers a treat unlike any other in the area. Accommodation ranges from shared Berber-style hostel rooms to luxury private rooms. The setting is tremendous, as is the decor, and the cooking. The kasbah can organize treks and guides, and has a small reception office by the car park in Imlil. ❺

Trekking resources and guides

Good sources of **information** include the CAF refuge and its *gardiens* (wardens), the *Kasbah du Toubkal*, and the long-established "Shopping Centre" facing the refuge, run by Lahcen Askary, an experienced, English-speaking guide. Also helpful is the *Hôtel-Café Soleil*'s owner, Aziam Brahim, who works for part of the year for a French trekking company, and his brother, Ibelaid Brahim.

Lahcen and the Brahim brothers and Aït Idir Mohammed (who runs *Chez Mohammed*) are among Imlil's **qualified guides** listed in the guides' office in the corner of the car park near the CAF Refuge. They can all arrange treks, ascents, mules, camping, guides and *gardiens* for your baggage and food.

Imlil to Djebel Toubkal

Most trekkers leaving Imlil are en route for the **ascent of Djebel Toubkal** – a walk rather than a climb after the snows have cleared, but a serious business nonetheless. The route to the ascent trailhead, however, is fairly straightforward, and is enjoyable in its own right, following the Mizane Valley to the village of **Aroumd** (4km from Imlil; 1hr–1hr 30min) and from there on through the pilgrim hamlet of **Sidi Chamarouch** to the **Toubkal Refuges** (3200m; 12km from Imlil; 5–6hr in all), at the foot of Toubkal's final slopes.

Most trekkers set out early to mid-morning to stay the night at a Toubkal refuge, starting out at first light the next morning for Toubkal in order to get the clearest possible panorama from its heights – afternoons can be cloudy. Arriving at the Toubkal refuge early in the day also gives you time to acclimatize and rest: many people find the hardest bit of the experience is the last hour's trek up to the hut, so it's important to take it easy.

Imlil to Aroumd

To **walk from Imlil to Aroumd**, you basically follow the flank of the Mizane river. On the west side there's a well-defined mule track that zigzags above the river for about 2km before dropping to the floor of the valley, just after a crossing point to Aroumd; there is also a more circuitous *piste*, driveable in a reasonably hardy vehicle. On the east bank, there's a rough path – much the same distance but slightly harder to follow.

Atlas trekking practicalities

Equipment and experience

Unless you're undertaking a particularly long or ambitious trek – or are here in winter conditions – there are no technical problems to hold anyone back from trekking in the Toubkal area, or climbing the peak itself. However, the mountain needs to be taken seriously. You must have decent **footwear and clothing** – it's possible to be caught out by summer storms as well as bad winter conditions – and you should be prepared to camp out if you are going on longer treks (or find the Toubkal refuges full). It's important to keep to a gentle pace until you are properly acclimatized as altitudes of 3000–4000m can be quite demanding, especially when combined with the midday heat and walking over long sections of rough boulders or loose scree.

Seasons

Toubkal is usually under **snow** from November until June, and experienced mountaineers can enjoy some classic climbs, ski ascents and treks in winter, though be cautious of storms, which can last up to three days. In spring, the best trekking lies below the snowline, and less experienced trekkers should only aim for the summit when the snow has gone. In all cases, take local advice before you climb; ice axes and crampons can be rented in Imlil.

Altitude

Toubkal is 4167m above sea level and much of the surrounding region is above 3000m, so it's possible that you might get **acute mountain sickness (AMS)**, also called altitude sickness. Aspirin can help, but just sucking on a sweet or swallowing is often effective, as is resting. Most people experience some symptoms of AMS but serious cases are rare. Hurrying is a major cause so it's important to pace your ascent, allowing your body time to acclimatize. If you do develop more than slight breathlessness and really feel like vomiting, going down straight away is the best, and almost immediate, cure.

Accommodation

At most Atlas villages, it is usually possible to arrange a room in a local house; just turn up and ask. At some of the villages on more established routes, there are official *gîtes*, often the homes of mountain guides, who can provide mules and assistance – as well as food, showers, toilets and sometimes hammams. All *gîtes* are graded by the tourist authorities, who sometimes have lists of them available. Most charge 80–120dh per person for a night and for a further 60–75dhs will provide meals.

There are also three CAF refuge **huts**, Toubkal (formerly known as *Neltner*), Tazaghart (formerly known as *Lépiney*) and Tachddirt, run by the *Club Alpin*; they charge about 85dh for a bed (less for members of Alpine Clubs). Toubkal, the best appointed, is often heavily booked and is always crowded in March/April (ski-touring season) and July–September (trekking season). A new independent refuge, *Les Mouflons* (ⓣ0663 763713), has been built, with over one hundred beds in smaller rooms, and all facilities.

If you are planning to **camp**, there are designated areas. You will need a tent and warm sleeping bag – nights can be cold, even in summer, and you must use the official water sources and toilet facilities.

Guides and mules

Guides can be engaged at Imlil and at a number of the larger villages in the Toubkal region; **mules**, too, can be hired, usually in association with a guide or porter. Rates are around 250dh a day for a guide, 100dh for a mule. One mule can usually be shared among several people – and if you're setting out from Imlil, say, for Lac d'Ifni, or the Toubkal or Tazaghart refuges, it can be a worthwhile investment. In addition, you will be expected to pay a small fee to the car park supervisor in Imlil and a tip to the muleteer at the end. (Payment to all parties, incidentally, is best made at the end of a trip.) Note that guides are more reluctant – and reasonably so – to work during the month of **Ramadan** (see p.50).

Water

Bottled **waters** Sidi Ali, Aïn Saïs and Sidi Harazem are spring sourced. If you are heading off main routes, a litre bottle of water is enough because you can refill it regularly. However, Giardiasis **bacteria** is present in many of the streams and rivers downriver from human habitation (including the Toubkal huts), so purification tablets are highly advisable, as, of course, is boiling the water to make it safe.

Clothes

Even in the summer months you'll need a warm sweater or jacket and a windbreaker. Hiking boots are ideal, although you can get by with a decent pair of trainers. The sun is very strong here, making a hat, sunblock and sunglasses essential.

Other things to bring

You can buy **food** in Asni, Imlil and some of the other villages – or negotiate meals – though it gets increasingly expensive the higher and the more remote you get. Water purification tablets or filtering systems are worthwhile on longer trips, as are stomach pills, insect repellent and wet wipes (which should be used on hands before meals).

Children constantly ask you for cigarettes, bonbons and *cadeaux* – but it's better for everyone if you don't give in; limit **gifts** to those who offer genuine assistance. A worthwhile contribution trekkers can make to the local economy is to trade or give away some of your gear – this is always welcomed by guides.

Guidebooks and maps

There are almost limitless Atlas trekking routes, only a selection of which are detailed in these pages. For other ideas, either engage a guide at Imlil, or invest in one of the Atlas Mountain trekking guidebooks such as *Trekking in the Moroccan Atlas* by **Richard Knight** (Trailblazer), or *The Atlas Mountains: A Walking and Trekking Guide* by **Karl Smith** (Cicerone Press).

Large-scale survey **maps** are available for the region; most are 1:100,000, though Toubkal is also mapped at 1:50,000. These, like the guidebooks above, are best obtained in advance from specialist map/travel shops outside of Morocco, though occasionally guides or shops at Imlil or Oukaïmeden (or the *Hôtel Ali* in Marrakesh, see p.348) may have some maps to sell.

Ski-touring

The Toubkal Massif is popular with **ski-mountaineering** groups from February to April. Most of the *tizis* (*cols*), and Djebel Toubkal and other peaks, can be ascended, and there is an *Haute Route* linking the huts. The descent from Toubkal summit to Sidi Chamarouch must rank as fine as you'll find. The Toubkal refuges can get pretty crowded at these times, and the Tachddirt refuge (or, for a serious approach in winter, Tazaghart refuge) can make better bases.

AROUMD (also called Around or Aremd) is the largest village of the Mizane Valley, an extraordinary looking place, built on a huge moraine spur above the valley at 1840m. Steep-tiered fields of potatoes, onions, barley and various kinds of fruit line the valley sides, their terraces edged with purple iris. The village is used as a base or overnight stop by a number of trekking companies, and several houses have been converted to well-equipped **gîtes**; among them are *Restaurant Résidence Aremd* (❸), overlooking the school, and the *Atlas Toubkal/Chez Omar le Rouge* (Ⓣ0524 485750; ❸), by the west bank of the river, which has a tented restaurant and also offers camping. There's only one small shop, so if you're cooking for yourself it's best to bring supplies with you.

Aroumd to Sidi Chamarouch and Toubkal Refuge

From Aroumd, the **Toubkal trail** goes up the flood plain, with unavoidable river crossings, which are only sometimes problematic (hitch a mule ride over them if so). At the end of the flood plain the track zig zags up to make its way along, high above the gorge. If you have been following the main mule trail on the west side of the valley from Imlil, you can continue without going round into Aroumd.

The river is crossed once more by a bridge just before you arrive at the hamlet of **SIDI CHAMAROUCH** (1hr 30min–2hr from Aroumd). Set beside small waterfalls, this is a disordered row of houses, all built one into another. Its seasonal population of ten or twelve run grocery shops for trekkers and Moroccan pilgrims, who come to the village's *marabout* shrine – a boulder sited across the river from the village and reached by a concrete bridge which non-Muslims are strictly forbidden to cross. The shrine is probably a survival of a very ancient nature cult – in these parts often thinly veiled by the trappings of Islam; on the approach to the village you may notice a tree, sacred to local tradition, where the Berbers hang strips of cloth and make piles of stones. Basic **rooms** (❶) are available and **camping** is possible – below the hamlet down by the stream. Do not drink untreated water here, or around the Toubkal huts.

Beyond Sidi Chamarouch, the Toubkal trail climbs steeply in zigzags and then traverses the flank of the valley well above the Mizane. The trail is clear the whole way to the **Toubkal Refuges**, which, at 3207m, is often the spring snow line. In winter the snow line can drop to Sidi Chamarouch and mules have to be replaced by porters if you want assistance to the Toubkal Refuges.

The Toubkal Refuges

Even in mid-August it feels pretty cold at the two 3200m **refuges** (**Toubkal** and **Les Mouflons**; Ⓣ0663 763713; both ❷) once the sun has disappeared behind the ridge. The refuges are open all year and have hot showers, sitting rooms and self-catering kitchens; meals can also be ordered from the *gardiens*. A separate building houses local guides and mules. See box on p.396 for further information on accommodation in the Atlas.

Climbing Toubkal

At the Toubkal Refuge you're almost bound to meet people who have just come down from **Djebel Toubkal** – and you should certainly take advantage of talking to them and the refuge *gardiens* for an up-to-the-minute description of the routes and the state of the South Cirque (Ikhibi Sud) trail to the summit. If you don't feel too confident about going it alone, take a guide – they are usually available at the refuge – but don't let them try to rush you up the mountain. See box on pp.396–397.

The **South Cirque** (Ikhibi Sud) gives the most popular and straightforward ascent of Toubkal and, depending on your fitness, should take between

2hr 30min and 3hr 30min (2–2hr 30min coming down). There is a worn path, which is easy enough to follow. More of a problem is finding the right track down through the upper slopes of loose scree.

The **trail** begins above the Toubkal Refuge, dropping down to cross the stream and then climbing to reach the first of Toubkal's innumerable fields of boulders and scree. These are the most tiring (and memorable) features of the trek up, and gruelling for inexperienced walkers. The summit, a sloping plateau of stones marked by a tripod, is eventually reached after a lot of zigzagging up out of the cirque to walk the edge of the spectacular southern cliffs. It should be stressed that **in winter** even this easiest of routes is a **snow climb** and not for walkers. Slips can and have had fatal consequences. If you are properly equipped, check out the start the night before, and set off early. Ice axes and crampons are essential. For those capable it is also a splendid ski route.

An alternative ascent – though longer (4hr 30min) and best for more experienced climbers – is the **North Cirque** (Ikhibi Nord). En route you will pass the remains of an aircraft that crashed while flying arms to Biafra, and the cairn of the small peak of Tibherine dominating the valley is actually one of its engines. The final ridge to the summit area calls for some scrambling. You should descend by the South Cirque.

Toubkal Refuge to Lac d'Ifni and beyond

Lac d'Ifni is one of the rare mountain lakes in the Atlas – and the only one of any size in the Toubkal region. From the refuge it's about a four-to-five hour trek, again involving long, tedious stretches over loose rock and scree, and with odd stretches of snow remaining into July. On the way back, the scree demands are even more pronounced. To make the trip worthwhile, take along enough food for a couple of days' camping; there are no facilities of any kind en route.

The **trail** begins at the Toubkal Refuge, climbing up a rough, stony slope and then winding round to the head of the Mizane Valley towards the

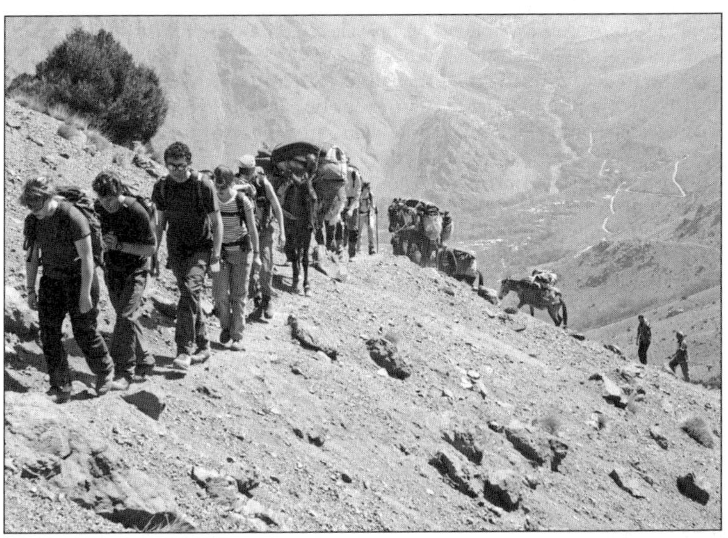

▲ Trekking in the Toubkal

imposing **Tizi n'Ouanoums**. The path is reasonably easy to follow, zigzagging until you reach the pass (3664m), a narrow gap in the rocky wall, which takes about an hour.

The views from the *tizi* are superb, taking in the whole route that you've covered and, in the distance to the south, the outline of the lake (which disappears from view as you descend). At this point the hard work seems over – but this is a false impression. The path down the valley to Lac d'Ifni is steep, the scree apparently endless, and the lake doesn't come back into sight until you are almost there, being enclosed by the mountains that look like demolished heaps of rubble. All of which makes **Lac d'Ifni** a memorable sight, its only human habitations a few shepherds' huts (*azibs*), and the only sound that of water idly lapping on the shore; it is unusually deep (50m over much of its area) and stocked with trout.

Sadly, the lakeside is a poor place to camp in summer, as it's very hot and somewhat fly-ridden by day, and often with no drinking water source (the lake waters are polluted and springs do exist but can run dry). You can camp much more enjoyably by carrying on for another hour until you reach the first patches of irrigated valley, high above the village of Imhilene. Incredibly there is often a small café (closed winter) functioning by the lake, which offers minimal but welcome refreshments.

Taxis and minibuses operate from all the villages south of Toubkal down the Tifnoute valley to **Aoulouz** (see p.508), passing a big reservoir at the lower end.

On from Lac d'Ifni: a loop to Sidi Chamarouch or Tachddirt

Most people return from Lac d'Ifni to the Toubkal refuge by the same route but it's quite feasible to make a longer, anticlockwise, loop towards **Sidi Chamarouch** or **Tachddirt**.

From the lake, you can strike east to the valley above Imhilene, and beyond it to the kasbah-like village of **Amsouzart**, reached in around three hours. There is a café/campsite here and *gîte* accommodation (❷) and meals at Omar's house; ask for him at the café or shop, which is your last chance of supplies on this route. From Amsouzart, follow the up-valley path to reach **Tissaldaï** in about four hours (camping possible). From here, it's at least four hours of strenuous trekking to get up the **Tizi n'Terhaline** (3247m), worth all the effort as you descend into a beautiful valley. After about two hours' descent you reach **Azib Tifni**, a collection of *azibs*, few more than a metre or two high. You then follow the valley west over another high pass, Tizi n'Tagharat, for the long, steep, hard descent to **Sidi Chamarouch**, or you can loop to **Tachddirt**. From Azib Tifni you can descend a small but impressive gorge, or a pass to avoid it, down the **Tifni valley** to reach Azib Likemt – a region of intense cultivation and magnificent spring flowers. About 2km further down the Tifni, climb up to the village of **Azib Likemt**, from which a mule track climbs steeply to the **Tizi Likemt** (3555m), the spot from which Joseph Thomson noted Toubkal as the highest Atlas peak in 1888. From here there's a reasonably clear path down across some of the worst screes of the region. The large spring at the foot of the descent makes a good campsite, or you can cross over to the **CAF refuge**, or rooms, at **Tachddirt**. The upper valley here is notorious for scorpions.

The country east of Azib Likemt, the **Kissaria Gorges**, is wild in the extreme, and too hard even for mules. However, there is a magnificent, if very demanding (on people or mules) route over to the Ourika Valley by the splendid Tizi n'Oumchichka that sidesteps the Kissaria, one of the best walks in the massif.

Tachddirt and beyond

TACHDDIRT (2000m), 8km east of Imlil, is an alternative and in many ways more attractive base for trekking expeditions. As at Imlil, there is a CAF refuge, and a fine range of local treks and onward routes. But despite its comparatively easy access – a pleasant mule track up the valley to the Tizi n'Tamatert (more direct than the tortuously winding *piste*) – the village sees only a handful of the trekkers who make it up to Toubkal.

You can walk here **from Imlil** in three to four hours, or there is a daily Berber **lorry** along the *piste*. There is only one small shop in Tachddirt, so you may want to bring provisions. The **CAF refuge** (❶) has soft drinks and cooking facilities, and its *gardien* will provide meals on request; it is sited at the down-valley edge of the village and is kept locked, though the *gardien* does not usually take too long to appear. He can arrange a guide and mules. **Rooms** (❶) are also available in the village. The next village down, **Oumskra**, has a couple of **gîtes** (❷), and following the valley from here to Imlil is an enjoyable option.

Tachddirt to Setti Fatma

This is one of the best routes for anyone contemplating more than a simple day-trip into the hills. Taken at a reasonable pace, the route takes two days. There is a well-defined mule track all the way, so no particular skills are needed beyond general fitness. Several sections of the trail are quite exposed and steep. You'll probably want to carry some food supplies with you. However, meals are offered at the village of Timichi, so cooking gear and provisions are not essential. You might want to hire mules at Tachddirt or Imlil.

Tachddirt to Timichi is a superb day's walk. The first three hours or so are spent zigzagging up to the Tizi n'Tachddirt (3616m), a route with ever more spectacular views. Green terraced fields give way to rough and craggy mountain slopes, then the path down gives one of the more barren sections. As you approach Timichi the valley again becomes more cultivated.

TIMICHI has several *gîtes* (❷) and makes a good overnight stop. A hard but impressive pass, **Tizi n'ou Attar** (3050m), leads to Oukaïmeden and it is possible to follow the valley up and out under the peak of Angour. Another three-day recommended circuit is Oukaïmeden–Tachddirt–Timichi–Oukaïmeden.

Timichi to Setti Fatma is another beautiful day-trek. At first you follow the river fairly closely, passing several villages before you follow the *piste* up to avoid a gorge, with a great view from the last spur before it zigzags down to the flood plain of the Ourika Valley about 2km north of Setti Fatma.

The Angour Traverse

The ridge of Angour is pretty demanding, taking a full day from Tachddirt and requiring basic climbing skills; a guide is useful for this.

From the **Tizi n'Tachddirt** (see above) head north up a rough, grassy slope, to break through crags onto the sloping **plateau**, which can be followed to the **summit of Angour** (3616m). This plateau is an unusual feature on a peak with such dramatic cliffs as it is split by a valley. With care, you can scramble along an exposed ridge down from here to **Tizi n'Eddi** (to pick up the Oukaïmeden trail, see p.391), or cut down to Tachddirt once you are onto easy but still very steep ground.

Tachddirt to Oukaïmeden

This is a fairly straightforward route – a three- to four-hour walk on a steep mule track by way of the 2960m **Tizi n'Eddi/Tizi nou Addi**.

Tachddirt to Imlil via Tizi n'Aguersioual

An alternative route back from **Tachddirt to Imlil** is by way of **Tizi n'Aguersioual**. This takes you down-valley to the hamlets of Tinerhourhine (1hr) and Ikiss (15min further down; soft drinks/rooms). From Ikiss a good path on the other side of the valley leads up to the Aguersioual pass and then zigzags down to the village of **Aguersioual**, from where you can follow the Asni road back up to Imlil. Aguersioual has a **gîte**, *Le Mont Blanc* (Ⓣ0524 85647; ❸).

West of Imlil: Tizi Oussem and the Tazaghart Refuge

The area west of Imlil offers a good acclimatization trek to **Tizi Oussem** village. A harder trek climbs to the **Tazaghart Refuge** (❶), accessible also from the Toubkal Refuge and Aroumd, and the possibility of one- or two-day treks out to **Ouirgane** or **Ijoukak** on the Tizi n'Test road, or back to the Asni–Imlil road at **Tamadout**.

Tizi Oussem and on to Ouirgane or Ijoukak

The village of **TIZI OUSSEM**, in the next valley west of Imlil, is reached in about four hours over the **Tizi Mzic**; the track is not that easy to find, so ask for directions. The most interesting section is the path down from the pass to Tizi Oussem. If you are heading for the **Tazaghart Refuge**, another path from the pass follows round the hillside to Azib Tamsoult, and then to the gorge for the ascent to the refuge.

Once at Tizi Oussem, you could follow its **valley** in a long day's trek down to Ouirgane on the Tizi n'Test road. From the village you need to keep initially to the east bank and then drop onto the flood plain to gain the west bank at a narrowing. The path keeps high then zigzags down to cross the river to gain height on the east side, passing the walled farm of Azerfsane. Beyond there, the path swings west and drops to the river where a mule track on the left bank helps you cross to pull up to a spur with a commanding view to the rich Ouirgane Valley. You can follow a stretch of *piste* from here, turning off where it heads to Marigha, and following cultivation paths on the left bank to reach Ouirgane, at the *Auberge Au Sanglier Qui Fume* (see p.404).

Experienced walkers could make a three-day expedition to reach **Ijoukak** (see p.404), with two camps en route, one just below the Tizi Ouarhou (2672m) and the second before the Tizi n'Iguidi.

The Tazaghart Refuge area

The **Tazaghart Refuge** (formerly known as the *Refuge Lépiney*; ❶) is essentially a climbing base for the fine cliffs of **Tazaghart**. To get access, you (or a porter) may have to go down to the village of Tizi Oussem to get the hut *gardien*, Omar Abdallah, who is also a very good (and extremely pleasant) guide; he can arrange a room in the village, too.

To **reach the refuge** from Imlil (6hr 30min–7hr 30min) follow the routes described above. Alternatively, you can follow a mule path (summer only) which leads from Aroumd over the Tizi n'Tizikert, north of Aguelzim.

To the south of the Tazaghart Refuge, **Tizi Melloul** (3–4hr) allows access to **Tazaghart** (3843m), an extraordinary plateau and fine vantage point. From here, you could cross over the pass and, with a night's camping, walk down the **Agoundis Valley to Ijoukak**. A hair-raising *piste* now reaches the highest Agoundis villages and a lift out to Ijoukak might be possible.

Tizi n'Test: Ouirgane, Ijoukak and Tin Mal

Tizi n'Test (2092m), the road pass that crosses the Atlas to Taroudant or Taliouine, is unbelievably impressive. Cutting right through the heart of the Atlas, the road was blasted out of the mountains by the French from 1926 to 1932 – the first modern route to link Marrakesh with the Souss plain and the desert, an extraordinary feat of pioneer-spirit engineering. Until then, passage had been considered impracticable without local protection and knowledge: an important pass for trade and for the control and subjugation of the south, but one that few sultans were able to make their own.

Through much of the nineteenth century – and the beginning of the twentieth – the pass was the fief of the **Goundafi** clan, whose ruined kasbahs still dominate many of the crags and strategic turns along the way. Much earlier it had served as the refuge and power base of the Almohads, and it was from the holy city of **Tin Mal**, standing above the Oued Nfis, that they launched their attack on the Almoravid dynasty. As remote and evocative a mountain stronghold as could be imagined, Tin Mal is an excursion well worth making for the chance to see the partially restored ruins of the twelfth-century mosque, a building close in spirit to the Koutoubia Mosque in Marrakesh.

Practicalities

The Tizi n'Test is not for the faint-hearted. If you are **driving**, some experience of mountain roads is advisable. The route is well contoured and paved, but between the pass and the intersection with the N10, the Taliouine–Taroudant road, it is extremely narrow (one and a half times a car's width) with almost continuous hairpin bends and blind corners. As you can see for some distance ahead, this isn't as dangerous as it sounds – but you still need a lot of confidence.

Using public transport, a **shared taxi** is your best option, negotiated either at Marrakesh, Asni or (coming in the other direction) Taliouine or Taroudant. **Buses** over the pass are erratic, though there is one service most days between Marrakesh and Taliouine, with a change at Oulad Berhil if you are heading for Taroudant. From November to the end of April, the pass is occasionally blocked with **snow**. When this occurs, a sign is put up on the roadside at the point where the Asni–Test road leaves Marrakesh and on the roadside past Tahanaoute.

The road to the pass

Leaving Marrakesh, the Tizi n'Test road runs over the Haouz plain to **Tahanaoute** (Tuesday souk) – a fairly monotonous landscape until you reach the gorges of the Moulay Brahim, leading to Asni. Twisting endlessly over a watershed, thereafter there is some impressive "Badlands" scenery, with salt leaking from the soil before the rich basin of Marigha is reached. Here a road right runs down past saltworks and over the hills to Amizmiz (see p.404). Continuing over a rise, the main road drops to the large green valley basin of Ouirgane and the extensive lake formed by damming the Oued Nfis.

Ouirgane

OUIRGANE is a tiny place and a wonderful spot to rest up after a few days of trekking around Toubkal. It's also a very pleasant base in itself for day walks, mountain-bike forays or horseriding in its beautiful valley. The village hosts a small Thursday souk.

Accommodation

La Bergerie ⓣ0524 485716, ⓔbergerie@rediscover.co.uk. Sited in the Marigha valley, this place is French-run and has a nice garden setting, a (modest) pool and good French food. ❺

Café Badaoui This village café has a few simple rooms. ❶

Chez Momo ⓣ0524 485704, ⓦwww.aubergemomo.com. Another garden-set hotel – attractive, quiet, and with a small pool, though somewhat overpriced. Its restaurant does classic Berber dishes. ❼

Le Moufflon ⓣ0524 485722. A small roadside inn, half way between the Nfi's bridge and the souk. ❶

Résidence Ouirgane Adama ⓣ0524 319207, ⓕ0524 432095. A nice hotel, magnificently sited above the village and the lake. ❺

Résidence de la Roseraie ⓣ0524 432094, ⓕ0524 432095. Ouirgane's top hotel is a luxury retreat with 45 rooms scattered around a rose garden. It has a swimming pool, sauna, tennis, an equestrian centre (horseriding 350dh for a half-day – bring your own helmet), and a renowned restaurant. Most people are on half-board, which ranges from 220dh to 300dh according to season. ❼–❽

Au Sanglier Qui Fume ⓣ0524 485707, ⓕ0524 485709. A very attractive, long established French-run *auberge*, with excellent food and a delightful garden and pool. Prices are a lot lower than at the *Roseraie*, and in summer you usually need to book well in advance. ❺–❻

Amizmiz

The small town of **AMIZMIZ** can be reached direct from Marrakesh – on a minor road with regular bus and grand taxi connections. A low-key, very pleasant Atlas base, it is the site of a long-established **Tuesday souk** – one of the largest Berber markets of the Atlas, and not on the tourist route. The town comprises several quite distinct quarters, including a *zaouia,* kasbah and former Mellah, separated by a small, usually dry, river. **Accommodation** is available at the *Rahha*, a simple hotel in the centre of town (❷), or at the classier, women-run *Restaurant Le Source Bleu* (ⓣ0524 454595; ❸), a nice *auberge* 4km above the town (ask for directions).

Amizmiz is a good base for some challenging **trekking**, as well as for **mountain biking** (see box opposite). High Country (ⓣ0524 332182, ⓦwww.highcountry.co.uk), a **trekking/adventure company** run by Englishman Matthew Low, arrange trekking, climbing, skiing, kayaking and off-road 4WD expeditions.

Treks around Amizmiz

The mountains backing Amizmiz offer some of the best trekking in the Atlas, little known and almost entirely unspoilt save for the intrusion of a few *pistes*.

The **Anougar valley** from Amizmig leading up to the neighbouring peaks of **Imlit** (3245m) and **Gourza** (3280m) is beautiful and various passes can be crossed to the Nfis or Ougdemt valleys. A British party (Hooker and Ball) made the first foreign ascent of a 3000-metre peak on climbing Gourza in 1871.

Southwest beyond Azgour, rolling country rises to the **Wirzane-Erdouz crest** (3579m), so prominent from Marrakesh rooftop views, which is prime trekking country with several magnificent passes over to the Ougdemt valley, a number crossed by Joseph Thomson who ascended Igdat (3616m) in 1888. There is also a fine descent to the plains by the Oued Wadaker, north of Azegour.

Ijoukak

IJOUKAK is an important shopping centre where the Agoundis Valley joins the Nfis. Buses stop at its many cafés, and there are **rooms** available at the *Café Ounaine* (*Chez Saïd*; ⓣ062 036364; ❷), the last café at the Tizi n'Test end of the

Mountain biking – and some routes from Amizmiz

Morocco offers some of the best adventure riding in the world with routes suitable for all abilities. The High Atlas has jeep and mule tracks that cover the countryside and several **adventure companies** offer mountain biking as a pursuit. Travelling independently, it's important to be aware of local sensibilities; ride slowly through villages, giving way to people where necessary, especially those on mules and children tending livestock. If **renting a bike**, negotiate essential extras like a pump, puncture repair kit and/or spare inner tube. A helmet is recommended, and carry plenty of water. For general information on planning and problems see pp.41–42.

Of the **three routes** detailed below, the first two can be done by a novice with a rented bike, while the third is best left to the proficient, preferably on their own bike. All routes begin and end at *Restaurant Le Source Bleu* (see opposite) above Amizmiz. As few roads are signposted, the Amizmiz 1:100,000 **topographical map** is highly recommended, and best obtained from specialist map shops (see p.71) before you leave home.

Route 1 The Oued Anougal Circuit

From *Le Source Bleu*, descend to the *piste* road running from Amizmiz to Azegour and then head on uphill past the *Maison Forestière*. About 1.5km beyond, a narrow *piste* branches off left, taking you down the west side of the valley to pass through the village of Aït Ouskri, from where there are tremendous views up the valley, to Djebel Gourza and Djebel Imlit. The *piste* continues, passing the villages of Tizgui, Toug al Kheyr and, after 10km, Imi-n-Isli and Imi-n-Tala ("big spring"), before crossing the Anougal river below **Addouz** to the eastern side of the valley. Care should be taken **in spring**, when the river can become swollen from melted snow. Following the *piste* through Imzayn, and sticking to the lower track, leads to Igourdan and, after about 12km, uphill, to **Aït Hmad**.

Leaving Aït Hmad behind, the road widens to become a full-width *piste* jeep track allowing a fast but safe downhill back into Amizmiz.

Route 2: Djebel Timerghit Circuit

Follow the Route 1 description to Imi-n-Tala then take a *piste* westwards through the forest to reach the Oued Erdouz road from Azegour, with Djebel Timerghit towering above. Turn left and circuit the hill to Toulkine and on through the granite landscape towards Azegour. Five hundred metres before Azegour you come to a junction – turn left here, crossing a bridge over the Oued Wadakar, and continue past the remains of a mining site. The route then runs through forest and, after a gentle crest run, descends in numerous bends to Amizmiz, passing the *Maison Forestiere*.

Route 3: Toulkine Descent

Begin the route in the same way as those above, but don't break off left as in Route 1. Keep on ahead for the long toil through the forest to gain the gentler crest before descending into the Erdouz-Wadakar valley where there are extensive ruins from the mining that once took place here. Cross the bridge and turn right to circuit round to Toulkine. A *piste* heads northwest from the village but instead follow the mule track that heads due north over the crest to circuit the valley heads with Adghous perched in the middle. This then wends through the Djebel Aborji forest before a rather brutal descent to the plains at Tiqlit. Note that it's advisable to check the route at Toulkine.

village, which is a nice place serving good tajine, and at *Café Badaoui* (☎068 164591; ❷), at the lower end of the street.

Walking from Ijoukak, you can easily explore Tin Mal and Talâat n'Yacoub (see p.407 & p.408) or try some more prolonged **trekking in the Nfis and**

Agoundis valleys. The Agoundis can also be enjoyable just as a day's wandering, or you can take the winding forestry road up the hill dominating the village for its commanding view.

Agoundis Valley

East from Ijoukak winds the **Agoundis Valley**, which offers an alternative access to Toubkal; it takes two days of serious trekking to reach the Toubkal Refuge. From Ijoukak head out on the Marrakesh road, cross the Oued Agoundis and turn right onto the up-valley road passing several *gîtes.* The scenery grows ever grander yet fields will cling wherever possible and there are a surprising number of villages. After an hour's walking you reach the wreck of an old mineral processing plant, a gondola still high in the air on a cable stretched across the valley to mines that closed decades ago. After passing **Taghbart** there is a fork; the right branch crosses the river and makes an impressive ascent to the 2202-metre **Tizi-n-Ou-Ichddane** on the Atlas watershed. Over the pass, branches lead to Aoulouz or to the R203 10km east of the Tizi n'Test turn-off, which are highly recommended **4WD routes**. The Agoundis *piste* soon passes **El Makhzen** and a prominent house in wedding-cake style before becoming progressively narrower, exposed and rough, passing perched villages and ending at Aït Youl. Enquire at *Chez Saïd* in Ijoukak (see p.404) about public transport up the valley, as **Aït Youl** is a long day's walk. From there strong walkers can reach the Toubkal refuge in a day, crossing the **Tizi n'Ougane** (risk of snow on the final slopes until May) passing through wild gorges and screes on the way.

Ougdemt Valley

West from Ijoukak and the Agoundis Valley lies the **Ougdemt**, a long, pleasant valley filled with Berber villages surrounded by walnut groves.

A surfaced road ascends from **MZOUZIT** (3km beyond Tin Mal and 8km from Ijoukak) up to **ARG** at the head of the valley (6–7hr walking). From Arg you could aim for **Djebel Erdouz** (3579m) to the north of Tizi n'Tighfist (2895m), or the higher **Djebel Igdat** to the south (3616m), by way of Tizi n'Oumslama. Both are fairly straightforward when following the mule paths to the passes and can be reached in five to six hours from Arg. Be sure to take your own water in summer as the higher elevations can be dry. A two- to three-day traverse of these peaks on to Djebel Gourza (3280m) and down to Tin Mal is a challenging adventure. The east ridge of Erdouz gives serious scrambling as does the east ridge of Igdat.

For the very adventurous, a further expedition could be undertaken all the way to the **Tichka plateau** – summer grazing pastures at the headwaters of the Nfis River – and across the other side to the Marrakesh–Agadir road. This takes at least six days from the Tizi n'Test road and requires you to carry provisions for several days, or hire mules. A brief summary of this trail, taken from the opposite direction, follows in the "Tichka Plateau" section on p.416.

Idni and the Tizi n'Test

At **IDNI**, well up on the pass, the small *Café Igdet* has very basic rooms with bed mats (❶), hot meals and tea. From the hamlet, a path zigzags down to the Nfis which can then be followed out to the main road again.

The **Tizi n'Test** (2092m) itself is eighteen tortuous kilometres beyond Idni. There's a small **café** on the col and another excellent one just down on the south side (with rooms); buses will stop on request. From the summit of the pass a *piste* rises up towards a platform mounted by a TV relay station, where the views down to the Souss Valley and back towards Toubkal can be stunning. Experienced climbers could backpack along the crest west from here to descend into the Nfis Valley later with the massive cliffs of Flillis dominating the view. There is also a *piste* (with a path direct from the *tizi* to join it) leading down to Souk Sebt Ghbalou on the Nfis. Descending to the souk and following the Nfis east is a good trek, with one bivouac.

Over the Tizi n'Test pass, the descent towards the **Taroudant–Taliouine road** is dramatic: a drop of some 1600m in little over 30km. Throughout, there are stark, fabulous vistas of the peaks, and occasionally, hundreds of feet below, a mountain valley and cluster of villages. Taroudant is reached in around two and a half to three hours by car or bus, Taliouine in a little more; coming up, needless to say, it all takes a good deal longer. For details on Taroudant and Taliouine, see p.502 & p.508.

Tin Mal Mosque

The **Tin Mal Mosque**, quite apart from its historic and architectural importance, is a beautiful monument – isolated above a lush reach of river valley, with harsh mountains backing its buff-coloured walls. It has been partially restored and is a highly worthwhile stop if you're driving the Tizi n'Test. If staying at Ijoukak, it's an easy eight-kilometre walk, passing the riverside Goundafi kasbah near Talâat n'Yacoub (see p.408). You can return on the opposite side of the Nfis if a bridge (replaced seasonally) is in place – check before you set off from Ijoukak.

The mosque is set a little way above the modern village of Tin Mal (or Ifouriren) and reached by wandering uphill from the road bridge. The site is kept locked but the *gardien* will soon spot you, open it up and let you look round undisturbed (10dh admission, tip is expected). The mosque is used for the Friday service, so is closed to non-Muslims on that day.

The mosque

The **Tin Mal Mosque** was built by Abd el Moumen around 1153–54, partly as a memorial and cult centre for Ibn Toumert and also as his own family mausoleum. Obviously fortified, it probably served also as a section of the town's defences, since in the early period of Almohad rule, Tin Mal was entrusted with the state treasury. Today, it is the only part of the fortifications – indeed, of the entire Almohad city – that you can make out with any clarity. The rest was sacked and largely destroyed in the Merenid conquest of 1276.

That Tin Mal remained standing for that long, and that its mosque was maintained, says a lot about the power Ibn Toumert's teaching must have continued to exercise over the local Berbers. Even two centuries later the historian Ibn Khaldun found Koranic readers employed at the tombs, and when the French began restoration in the 1930s they found the site littered with the shrines of *marabouts.*

Architecturally, Tin Mal presents a unique opportunity for non-Muslims to take a look at the interior of a traditional Almohad mosque. It is roofless, for the most part, and two of the corner pavilion towers have disappeared, but the mihrab (or prayer niche) and the complex pattern of internal arches are substantially intact. The arrangement is in a classic Almohad design – the T-shaped plan with a central aisle leading towards the mihrab – and is virtually identical to that of the Koutoubia in Marrakesh, more or less its contemporary. The one element of eccentricity is in the placing of the **minaret** over the mihrab: a weakness of

Ibn Toumert and the Almohads

Tin Mal's site seems now so remote that it is difficult to imagine a town ever existing in this valley. In some form, though, it did. It was here that **Ibn Toumert** and his lieutenant, **Abd el Moumen**, preached to the Berber tribes and welded them into the **Almohad** ("unitarian") movement; here that they set out on the campaigns which culminated in the conquest of all Morocco and southern Spain; and here, too, a century and a half later, that they made their last stand against the incoming Merenid dynasty.

Known to his followers as the *Mahdi* – "The Chosen One", whose coming is prophesied in the Hadith (Sayings of The Prophet) – Toumert was born in the High Atlas, a member of the Berber-speaking Masmouda tribe, who held the desert-born Almoravids, the ruling dynasty, in contempt. He was an accomplished theologian and studied at the centres of eastern Islam, a period in which he formulated the strict Almohad doctrines. For Toumert, Almoravid Morocco contained much to disapprove of and, returning from the East with a small group of disciples, he began to preach against all manifestations of luxury and against women mixing in male society.

After being exiled from the Almoravid capital, Marrakesh, in 1124, Ibn Toumert and Abd el Moumen set out to mould the Atlas Berbers into a religious and military force. They also stressed the significance of the "second coming" and Ibn Toumert's role as *Mahdi*. Hesitant tribes were branded "hypocrites" and massacred – most notoriously in the Forty-Day Purge of the mountains – and within eight years none remained outside Almohad control.

engineering design that meant it could never have been much taller than it is today. In terms of decoration, the most striking feature is the variety and intricacy of the **arches** – above all those leading into the mihrab, which have been sculpted with a stalactite vaulting. In the **corner domes** and the **mihrab vault** this technique is extended with impressive effect. Elsewhere, and on the face of the mihrab, it is the slightly austere geometric patterns and familiar motifs (the palmette, rosette, scallop, etc), of Almohad decorative gates that are predominant.

The Goundafi kasbahs

The **Goundafi kasbahs** don't really compare historically, or as monuments, with Tin Mal – nor with the Glaoui kasbah in Telouet (off the Tizi n'Tichka; see p.410). But, as so often in Morocco, they provide an extraordinary assertion of just how recent the country's feudal past is. Despite their medieval appearance, the buildings are all nineteenth- or even twentieth-century creations.

The more important of the kasbahs is the former Goundafi stronghold and headquarters near the village of **TALÂAT N'YACOUB** (which has an interesting mountain **souk** on Wed). The kasbah is reached off to the right of the main road, down a very French-looking, tree-lined country lane; 6km from Ijoukak, 3km from Tin Mal, and clearly visible from the roadside at Talâat. Decaying, partially ruined and probably pretty unsafe, the **kasbah** stands by the river. Nobody seems to mind if you take a look inside, though beware its crumbling state – and the dogs near its entrance. The inner part of the palace-fortress, though blackened from a fire, is reasonably complete and retains traces of its decoration.

It is difficult to establish the exact facts with these old tribal kasbahs, but it seems that it was constructed late in the nineteenth century for the next-to-last Goundafi chieftain. A feudal warrior in the old tradition, he was constantly at war with the sultan during the 1860s and 1870s, and a bitter rival of the neighbouring Glaoui clan. His son, Tayeb el Goundafi, also spent most of his life in tribal campaigning, though he finally threw in his lot with Sultan Moulay Hassan, and later with the French. At the turn of the twentieth century, he could still raise some five thousand armed tribesmen with a day or two's notice, but his power and fief eventually collapsed in 1924. The writer, Cunninghame Graham, was detained here by the Goundafi in the 1890s, and describes the medieval scene well in his book, *Mogreb el-Acksa* (see p.601).

Another dramatic-looking Goundafi kasbah, **Agadir n'Gouj**, stands above the road overlooking the Kasbah Goundafi and is worth the climb up to its hilltop site. The interior has been cleared and some decorative details can still be seen. The structure is well preserved – as indeed it should be, having been built only in 1907, mainly to stable the Goundafi horses.

When the road begins to turn up and away from the river, another stark ruin lies high up, left. This is the **Tagoundaft**, the most imposing but seldom visited of the Goundafi kasbahs. It retains its vast cistern, though the aqueduct that once served this has gone. The walk up is worthwhile, if only to get a sense of its setting.

Telouet and the Tizi n'Tichka

The **Tizi n'Tichka** – the direct route from Marrakesh to Ouarzazate – is not so remote or spectacular as the Tizi n'Test pass. As an important military (and tourist) approach to the south, the road is modern, well constructed and relatively fast. At **Telouet**, however, only a short distance off the modern highway, one feels ambushed by a medieval world – though much of it was a late nineteenth to twentieth-century creation – for this pass and the mountains to the east of it were the stamping ground of the extraordinary **Glaoui** brothers, the greatest and the most ambitious of all the Berber tribal leaders.

Their kasbah-headquarters, a vast complex of buildings abandoned only in 1956, are a rewarding detour (21km from the main road). And for trekkers, bikers or four-wheel-drivers, Telouet has an additional and powerful attraction, offering an alternative and superb *piste* to the south, following the old tribal **route to Aït Benhaddou**.

The Tizi n'Tichka

Telouet aside, it is the engineering of the Tichka road, and the views from its switchback of turns, that are the main attraction between **Marrakesh and the Tizi n'Tichka** – at 2260m. If you are driving north to Marrakesh, and want to stop for the night before reaching the city, the French-run **auberge**, *Le Coq Hardi* (Ⓣ0524 480056; ❹), set in gardens beside the **Zat river** bridge near Aït Ourir is a good bet. It has a bar, restaurant and pool (though not always filled).

The **road out from Marrakesh** runs through the **Haouz Plain**, but once across the Oued Zat it begins to contour forest slopes high above the Oued Ghdat valley. From **ZERKTAN**, a Sunday souk, it is possible to drop down and head east over the Tizi n'Igli to Demnate: the road is part paved, part *piste*. Staying on the main road, constant twists and turns, passing small villages and fields in the river bends, leads to **TADDERT**, the last significant village on the north side of the pass. There are cafés and craft shops and one rather gloomy overpriced **auberge**, *Les Noyers* (Ⓣ0524 484575; ❸). Most traffic now stops a kilometre on at upper Taddert, which has dozens of places to eat but is busy and noisy.

The road thereafter climbs in an amazing array of hairpin bends to reach pastureland – "Tichka" means high pasture – before a final pull up to the **Tichka pass** (2260m), marked by cafés and tourist stalls. Not far down on the south side of the pass is the **turning to Telouet**.

If you keep on the main road south, you might want to stop at **IRHERM** (10km on), where there is a well-restored **agadir**. To find someone to unlock it, ask at the café or at the roadside **hotel**, *Chez Mimi* (Ⓣ024 880056; ❷), which has basic garden rooms and a bar. Further on, at **AGOUIM** a road heads west below the mountains to reach the Lac d'Ifni area (see p.399) and, 19km before Ouarzazate, a turning to the left leads to **Aït Benhaddou** and its kasbahs (see p.428).

Telouet: the Glaoui kasbah

The **Glaoui kasbah** at **TELOUET** is one of the most extraordinary sights of the Atlas – fast crumbling into the dark red earth, but visitable, and offering a peculiar glimpse of the style and melodrama of Moroccan political government and power still within living memory. There's little of aesthetic value – many of the rooms have fallen into complete ruin – but nevertheless, even after over a half-century of decay, there's still vast drama in this weird and remote site, and in the decorated salon walls, often roofless and open to the wind.

The Dar Glaoui

Driving through Telouet village you bear off to the right, on a signposted track, to the kasbah, **Dar Glaoui**. The road twists round some ruins to a roughly paved courtyard facing massive double doors. Wait a while and you'll be joined by a caretaker-guide (tours 20dh per group), necessary in this case since the building is an unbelievable labyrinth of locked doors and connecting passages;

The Glaoui

The extent and speed of **Madani** (1866–1918) and **T'hami el Glaoui**'s (1879–1956) rise to power is remarkable enough. In the mid-nineteenth century, their family were simply local clan leaders, controlling an important Atlas pass – a long-established trade route from Marrakesh to the Drâa and Dadès valleys – but lacking influence outside of it. Their entrance into national politics began dramatically in 1893. In that year's terrible winter, **Sultan Moulay Hassan**, on returning from a disastrous *harka* (subjugation/burning raid) of the Tafilalt region, found himself at the mercy of the brothers for food, shelter and safe passage. With shrewd political judgement, they rode out to meet the sultan, feting him with every detail of protocol and, miraculously, producing enough food to feed the entire three thousand-strong force for the duration of their stay.

The extravagance was well rewarded. By the time Moulay Hassan began his return to Marrakesh, he had given *caid*-ship of all the lands between the High Atlas and the Sahara to the Glaouis and, most important of all, was forced to abandon vast amounts of the royal armoury (including the first cannon to be seen in the Atlas) in Telouet. By 1901, the brothers had eliminated all opposition in the region, and when the **French** arrived in Morocco in 1912, the Glaouis were able to dictate the form of government for virtually all the south, putting down the attempted nationalist rebellion of El Hiba, pledging loyalty throughout World War I, and having themselves appointed **pashas of Marrakesh**, with their family becoming *caids* in all the main Atlas and desert cities. The French were content to concur, arming them, as Gavin Maxwell wrote, "to rule as despots, [and] perpetuating the corruption and oppression that the Europeans had nominally come to purge".

it is said that no single person ever fully knew their way around the entire complex. Sadly, these days you're shown only the main halls and reception rooms but if you climb up to the roof (generally allowed) you can look down upon some of the courts and chambers, the bright zellij and stucco enclosing great gaping holes in the stone and plaster.

The **reception rooms** – "the outward and visible signs of ultimate physical ambition", in Maxwell's phrase – at least give a sense of the quantity and style of the decoration, still in progress when the Pasha died and the old regime came to a sudden halt. They have delicate iron window grilles and fine carved ceilings, though the overall result is once again the late nineteenth- and early twentieth-century combination of sensitive imitation of the past and out-and-out vulgarity. There is a tremendous scale of affectation, too, perfectly demonstrated by the use of green Salé tiles for the roof – usually reserved for mosques and royal palaces. The really enduring impression, though, is the wonder of how and why it ever came to be built at all.

Practicalities

Getting to Telouet is straightforward if you have transport: it is an easy 21-kilometre drive from the Tizi n'Tichka (N9) road, along the paved 6802. Using **public transport**, there is a daily **bus** from Marrakesh, departing from Bab Rhemat (daily at around 2–3pm), to Telouet and on to Anemiter (see p.412); it returns from Anemiter at 6.30am (7am from Telouet). Alternatively, there are shared **grands taxis** from Marrakesh to Anemiter, via Aït Ourir and Telouet.

Telouet itself is no more than a village; it has a Thursday **souk**, and makes a pleasant stopover at any time. Finding a **room** should be no problem. At the turn-off for the Dar Glaoui is the *Auberge Telouet* (ⓣ0524 890717; ❸), with its nomad tent outside and kasbah building across the road. It has good food and ambience, and the owner, Mohammed Boukhsas, can also arrange interesting accommodation in village houses. Alternatively, there is *Chez Benouri* (❷), run by Mohammed Benouri (a trekking guide) and his father in part of an old *ksar*, and the simple *Auberge Le Pin* (ⓣ0524 890709; ❷) at the west end of the village. There are also several **cafés**, which serve meals.

Telouet to Aït Benhaddou

The **Tizi n'Tichka road** will bring you from the pass to Aït Benhaddou or Ouarzazate in a couple of hours (see p.409 for this route). However, if you have four-wheel drive (or a mountain bike), or want a good two-day walk, it is possible to reach Aït Benhaddou down the **Oued Ounila** from Telouet. This is now a rather minor *piste* road but before the construction of the Tichka road it was the main route over the Atlas. Indeed, it was the presence in the Telouet kasbah of T'hami's xenophobic and intransigent cousin, Hammou ("The Vulture"), that caused the French to construct a road along the more difficult route to the west. This route is being upgraded and the major river crossing at the south end is bridged.

The Ounila Valley

All in all, it is 35km from Telouet to Aït Benhaddou by the **Ounila Valley**. If you are walking or biking, the route offers tranquillity and unparalleled views of green valleys, with a river that splashes down its whole length and remarkable coloured scree slopes amid the high, parched hillsides. Despite the absence of settlements on most of the maps, there are scattered communities here, all making abundant use of the narrow but fertile valley. This unveils a wealth of dark red and crumbling **kasbahs** and **agadirs**, cliff dwellings, patchworks of wheatfields, terraced orchards, olive trees, date palms and figs – and everywhere children calling to each other from the fields, the river or the roadside.

If you are walking, you will need to take provisions for the trip but mules can be hired at Telouet or Anemiter.

Telouet to Anemiter

There are shared taxis (and the daily bus) between Telouet and **ANEMITER** (12km), one of the best-preserved fortified villages in Morocco. It is well worth a visit, even if you go no further along this route, and has some atmospheric **places to stay**. Mohammed Elyazid (Ⓣ0524 890780; ❶–❷) offers simple nomad tent accommodation, camping, village house options, and meals, and can organize local treks.

Another possible stopover is at **TIGHZA**, 10km further on, up the Ounila Valley, where the brothers Bouchahoud, both mountain guides, have a fine **gîte** (Ⓣ0524 445499; ❷). They arrange local walks to the turquoise **Tamda lakes**, into the mountains, and to Anemiter and Telouet (by the crest of hills to the south). It is also possible to take mule tracks beyond the Tamda lakes to reach a new tarmac road over the Atlas from Demnate to Skoura, via the Oued Tessaout valley.

Anemiter to Aït Benhaddou

There are occasional truck-taxis south of Anemiter, along the *piste*, but if you're setting out without transport it would be best to accept that you'll walk most of the way to Tamdaght, which will take around ten hours.

Leaving Anemiter, the main track clings to the valley side, alternately climbing and descending, but with a general downhill trend as you make your way south. After three kilometres you cross a sturdy bridge; beyond here the *piste* follows the left bank of the river to the hamlet of **ASSAKO** (2hr 30min walk from Anemiter), where it climbs to the left round some spectacular gorges and then drops steeply.

Walkers should aim to get beyond this exposed high ground before camping. At Tourhat, around six or seven hours from Anemiter, you might be able to find a room in a village home. Another three hours south of Tourhat, the trail brings you to **TAMDAGHT**, a scattered collection of buildings with a classic **kasbah**. This was used as a setting in the film *Gladiator* – and retains some of its Hollywood decor, along with ancient and rickety storks' nests on the battlements.

From **Tamdaght** the road continues to **Aït Benhaddou** (see p.428), where there are cafés and hotels, as well as taxis on to Ouarzazate.

Marrakesh to Agadir and Essaouira

The direct route from **Marrakesh to Agadir** – the **Imi n'Tanoute** or **Tizi Maachou** pass – which was only built in the 1970s, lacks the spectacular nature of the high passes but is still impressive with its sweeping scale and is the main artery between Marrakesh and Agadir and the far south. Extremely busy with endless slow lorries and sweeping curves, it sees many accidents. Work to upgrade the road is ongoing and the journey from Marrakesh to Agadir should take about four hours. The hinterland of the pass also offers some exciting trekking, well off the beaten track (see "Tichka Plateau treks", opposite). Not far off the main road lies the old tribal **kasbah of the Mtouggi**, the third of the "Lords of the Atlas", alongside the Glaoui and Goundafi, and a ruin almost as impressive as Telouet.

Chichaoua, Imi n'Tanoute and the pass

Leaving Marrakesh, most Agadir traffic (including the majority of buses) follows the Essaouira road (N8) as far as **CHICHAOUA**, a small town and administrative centre set at a junction of routes, known for its **carpets**. Brightly coloured and often using stylized animal forms, they are sold at the local **Centre Coopératif** and also at the **Thursday market**. The village is a pleasant stop along the road to break your journey, though there's no reason to stay – and no great appeal in its basic souk hotels. Beyond Chichaoua, the **road to Essaouira** (R207) extends across the drab Chiadma plains. **Sidi Mokhtar**, 25km on from Chichaoua, has a **Wednesday souk** with an attractive array of carpets; a road from here (and another from Imi n'Tanoute) leads to Kasbah Mtouggi (see below).

Heading for Agadir, the N8 begins a slow climb from Chichaoua towards **IMI N'TANOUTE**, another administrative centre, with a **Monday souk**, and then cuts through the last outlying peaks of the High Atlas. Imi n'Tanoute is of little interest, though if you need to stay before setting out on a trek, there are **rooms** at a couple of the cafés, and provisions. A few kilometres further along the N8 from Imi n'Tanoute is the **Tizi Maachou** (1700m). The road south of the pass is often lined with locals selling bottles of golden argan oil (see p.498) and runs by the **dams of Tanizaourt** before descending to the fertile **Souss Valley**, with its intensive greenhouse cultivation.

There is also a minor tarred road, the **R212**, which breaks off the Essaouira road 23km west of Marrakesh, just after a bridge over the Nfis, and goes direct to Imi n'Tanoute. It's no faster but pleasantly unbusy. And if you have 4WD transport, you might alternatively want to consider the **old Tizi Maachou road**, a *piste* which runs east of the current N8; you can rejoin the main road at **Argana**, or head over the dramatic Tizi Iferd (Tizi Babaoun) to the Souss Valley, nearer Taroudant, a road now being surfaced.

Kasbah Mtouggi

The Mtouggi dominated this western Atlas pass, just as the Goundafi and Glaoui did the eastern routes, and their **kasbah** near the village of **BOUABOUTE** looks, in its ruinous state, almost as large as Telouet. You can gain access to the ruins and see something of their one-time splendour, and the site is not hard to reach, either from Imi n'Tanoute on the Agadir road, or from Sidi Mohhtar on the Essaouira road. The road is paved.

Western High Atlas: Tichka Plateau treks

Exploring the **Tichka Plateau** and the **western fringes of the Atlas**, you move well away from established tour-group routes and pass through Berber villages that scarcely ever see a foreigner. You'll need to carry provisions, and be prepared to camp or possibly stay in a Berber village home if you get the invitation – as you almost certainly will. Sanitation is often poor in the villages and it's a good idea to bring water purification tablets (see box, p.397). Eating and drinking in mountain village homes, though, is surprisingly safe, as the food (mainly tajines) is thoroughly cooked and the drink is invariably mint tea.

There are approaches to the mountains from both north and south: **Imi n'Tanoute**, **Timesgadiouine** and **Argana**, on the main Marrakesh–Agadir bus route (north and west), and **Taroudant–Ouled Berhil** (south) or the Tizi n'Test road (east). From the north and west approaches, taxis, or rides on trucks bound for mines or markets at trailheads, could be used; from the south, *camionettes* ply up daily to Imoulas, the Medlawa Valley and Tigouga. For eastern access by the Oued Nfis, take the *piste* down from the Tizi n'Test and follow up the south bank of the river. If you can afford it, hiring **Land Rover transport** to take you, and possibly a **guide**, to meet prearranged mules and a muleteer is the most efficient procedure. **El Ouad Ali** in Taroudant (see p.504) is the recognized expert on the region and could make all arrangements. Or you could arrange a **small group trek** through the UK-based trekking company Walks Worldwide Ⓦwww.walksworldwide.com, who organize all levels of treks with El Ouad Ali. The IGN 1:100,000 **maps** for the area are *Tizi n'Test* and *Igli*.

Imi n'Tanoute to the Tichka Plateau

A dirt road leads up into the mountains from Imi n'Tanoute to **Afensou**, where a Thursday market (Al Khemis) is held, making your best chance of a lift up on Wednesday with one of the lorries. The road (not really suitable for ordinary cars) crosses the **Tizi n'Tabghourt** at 2666m, from where you can ascend Djebel Tabghourt offering a magnificent panorama of the Western Atlas, often white with snow until early summer.

At Afensou you are in the **Haut Seksawa** with some of the highest mountain walks and climbs in the Atlas lying to the south and holding the romantic **Tichka Plateau** in their midst. **Moulay Ali** (3349m) dominates; the ridge from it to the main chain was only climbed for the first time in 2001. The **Tizi Asdim** gives almost the only northern access to the Tichka Plateau, passing under **Djebel Ikkis** (3183m) and other climbers' peaks.

Timesgadiouine approaches

The second access point to the mountains along the Marrakesh–Agadir road is **TIMESGADIOUINE**, about 50km south of Imi n'Tanoute. A signposted road leads off the N8 beside a café/petrol station. The actual village is 3km further on. From here a good *piste* heads into the mountains to Souk Sebt Talmakant (Saturday souk) after which the road twists up to run along a long ridge to the mining area above Afensou to which the road drops in endless loops. The views are spectacular. Another *piste* heads up the Aït Driss valley giving access to the Awlim–Tinergwet peaks. In fact this area particularly lends itself to the growing pastime of Land Rover "trekking" (exploring and camping with 4WD instead of mules). It is possible to go right along, against the grain, under the north slopes of the Atlas to exit by the Oued Mel or reach Demnate, routes of real challenge for the cyclist as well.

Southern approaches to the Tichka Plateau

The Western High Atlas and "lost world" of the Tichka Plateau (and the beautiful valleys leading up to the heights) offer trekking of high quality. Going it your own way, *camionettes* from Taroudant and Ouled Berhil ply up to **Imoulas**, **Tagmout** and **Souk Tnine Tigouga**, from where mule trails lead over the mountain wall to the secretive Tichka Plateau. From the east the Ouad Nfis can be followed up to reach the Tichka Plateau in one or two days by dropping down to the valley from the Tizi n'Test and working upstream. The main routes from the south are outlined below. The roads from Tizi n'Test to Souk Sebt and to Imoulas from the south are now surfaced, the others being upgraded.

Imoulas

IMOULAS is the most westerly market town of the foothills, with a Sunday souk. From here a *piste* extends to Tinighas, for a dramatic route through a gorge to high *azibs* and a hard ascent to **Djebel Tinergwet** (3551m), the highest peak in the area, and **Awlim** (3482m). East of Awlim extends the "**Ridge of a Hundred Peaks**", running on to the distant Tichka Plateau. A branch *piste* circles west to Tasguint and the Tizi n'Ifguig which gives access to the Asif Tichka, Arg and the north of the range.

Tagmout

Houses may offer accommodation here or at the end of the *piste*, up the beautiful Medlawa Valley. A long zigzag mule track reaches the Tizi n'Targa, at the head of the Tichka Plateau. Tagmout/Tigouga *camionettes* leave from east of Taroudant. El Ouad Ali in Taroudant (see p.504) can arrange local treks staying in local houses, which are especially popular with family groups.

Souk Tnine Tigouga

As the name suggests, **SOUK TNINE TIGOUGA** has a **Monday souk**, the easiest time to get a lift up, or out. Mule tracks west and east of Awlim give access to the **Tichka Plateau** and the only pass out north, the Tizi Asdim, to Aguersaffen, Afensou and Souk Khemis in the Seksawa. A *piste* curls east to several villages and the Tizi n'Wadder mule track onto the lower Tichka Plateau. Djebel Flillis (3083m) in the ridges jutting to the south, is a worthy objective for experienced hill-goers, as is the granite Takoucht.

The Tichka Plateau

However you approach it, the **Tichka Plateau** is a delight. Grazing is controlled so the meadows, in spring, are a mass of early daffodils and flowers.

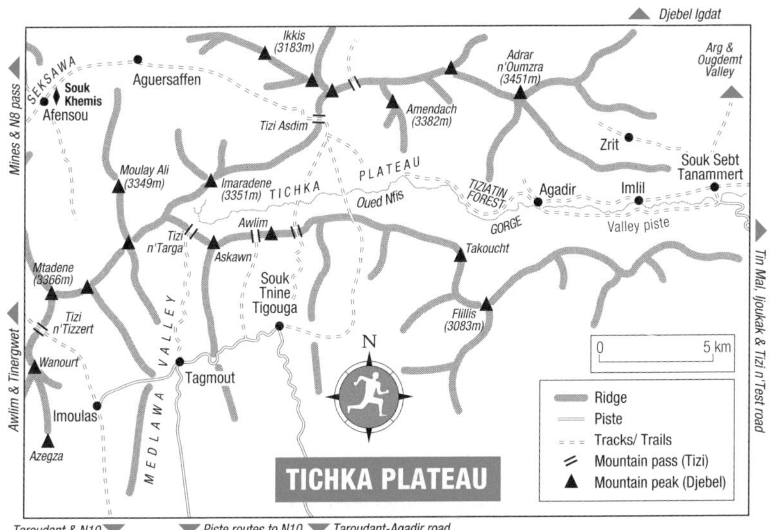

Imaradene (3351m) and **Amendach** (3382m) are the highest summits, west and east, and are superlative viewpoints. The plateau is drained by the Oued Nfis, first through the Tiziatin oak forest, using or bypassing gorges, then undergoing a series of villages, one of which, another Imlil, has a shrine to Ibn Toumert, the founder of the Tin Mal/Almohad dynasty.

A two-day trek from the plateau will take you to **SOUK SEBT GHBALOU**. From this Saturday market, a lorry road climbs up to the Test road, not far from the pass itself. You can hitch out here or continue trekking for two more days to Mzouzit, near Tin Mal, or go one day north to Arg via Tizi n'Aghbar (2653m) and Tizi n'Tiddi (2744m), and the exit by the long **Ougdemt Valley** to Mzouzit (see p.406). Passes from the Ougdemt Valley north over to Amizmiz are some of the hardest and finest in the Atlas. An excellent trail also descends the **Oued Nfis Valley** from Souk Sebt Tanammert, going through beautiful gorges and forested countryside. The ultimate trek is a ten-day one from Tichka Plateau to Djebel Toubkal.

Travel details

Buses

Marrakesh (Bab Doukkala terminal) to: Agadir via Imi n'Tanoute (20 daily; 4hr); Amizmiz (6 daily; 2hr); Ouarzazate via Tizi n'Tichka (6 daily; 4–5hr); Taliouine via Imi n'Tanoute (4 daily; 6hr).
Buses to Ourika, Asni (very irregular; 1hr 30min), and Moulay Brahim, leave from the bus station 2km out on the Asni road; some buses also run to Asni from the Bab Doukkala bus station.

Grands taxis

Marrakesh to: Ourika, Asni, Amizmiz and other Atlas trailhead towns – negotiate for these by the bus station 2km out on the Asni road.

7

The southern oasis routes

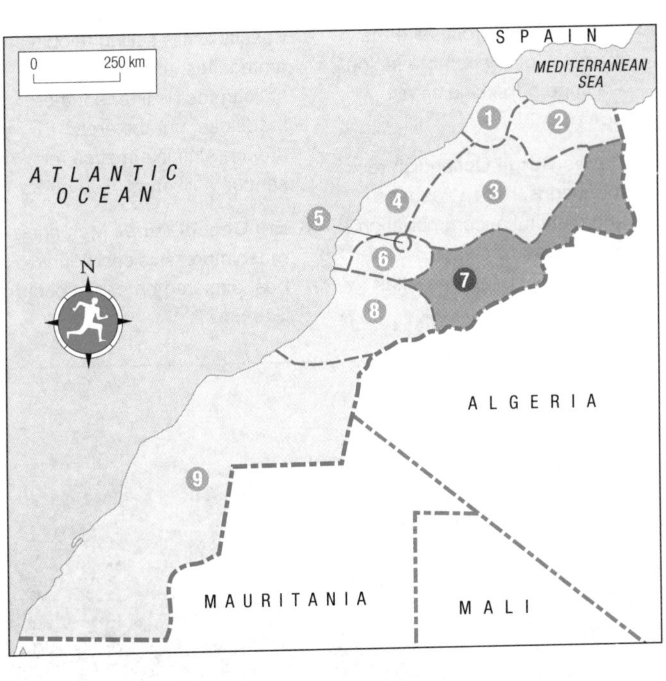

CHAPTER 7

Highlights

* **Kasbahs** Made with mud and straw *pisé*, some of these imposing traditional structures now house atmospheric hotels. See p.423, p.430 & p.432
* **Aït Benhaddou** The cream of the Deep South's desert architecture, used as a location for numerous movies. See p.428
* **Vallée des Roses** Used to make perfume, roses are the mainstay of this remote region – a superb trekking area. See p.445
* **Dadès Gorge** Outlandish rock formations, ruined kasbahs and plentiful accommodation at the head of a valley winding deep into the Atlas watershed. See p.450
* **Palmeries** Fed by ancient water courses, the great palmeries of Morocco's southern oases form an astounding contrast with the desert. See p.455
* **Todra Gorge** This dramatic cleave in the High Atlas range is simply one of the great natural spectacles of Morocco. See p.456
* **Fossils** Stalls selling trilobites, ammonites, and other striking fossils litter southern roadsides, but the area around Alnif is a mecca for serious collectors. See p.473
* **Erg Chebbi dunes** Morocco's most impressive sand dunes, best explored on camel back. See p.477

▲ Camels at the Erg Chebbi dunes

The southern oasis routes

The Moroccan pre-Sahara begins as soon as you cross the Atlas to the south. It is not sand for the most part – more a wasteland of rock and scrub which the Berbers call *hammada* – but it is powerfully impressive.

There is, too, an irresistible sense of wonder as you catch a first glimpse of the great southern river valleys – the **Drâa**, **Dadès**, **Todra**, and **Ziz**. Long belts of date palm oases, scattered with the fabulous mud architecture of kasbahs and fortified *ksour* villages, these are the old caravan routes that reached back to Marrakesh and Fes and out across the Sahara to Timbuktu, Niger and old Sudan, carrying gold, slaves and salt well into the nineteenth century. They are beautiful routes, even today, tamed by modern roads, and if you're travelling in Morocco for any length of time, they are a must. The simplest circuits – **Marrakesh–Zagora–Marrakesh**, or **Marrakesh–Tinerhir–Midelt**-can be covered in around five days, though to do them any degree of justice you need a lot longer. With ten days or more to spare, the loop from Ouarzazate to Merzouga (via Boumalne and Tinerhir), and thence southwest to Zagora and M'hamid, becomes a possibility, stringing together the region's main highlights via good roads and dependable transport connections.

The **southern oases** were long a mainstay of the pre-colonial economy. Their wealth, and the arrival of tribes from the desert, provided the impetus for two of the great royal dynasties: the Saadians (1154–1669) from the Drâa Valley, and the current ruling family, the Alaouites (1669–present) from the Tafilalt. By the nineteenth century, however, the advance of the Sahara and the uncertain upkeep of the water channels had reduced life to bare subsistence even in the most fertile strips. Under the French, with the creation of modern industry in the north and the exploitation of phosphates and minerals, they became less and less significant, while the old caravan routes were dealt a final death blow by the closure of the Algerian border in 1994.

Today, there are a few urban centres in the south; **Ouarzazate** and **Er Rachidia** are the largest and both were created by the French to "pacify" the south; they seem only to underline the end of an age. Although the date harvests in October, centred on **Erfoud**, can still give employment to the *ksour* communities, the rest of the year sees only the modest production of a handful of crops – henna, barley, citrus fruits and, uniquely, roses – the latter developed by the French around **El Kelâa des Mgouna** for the production

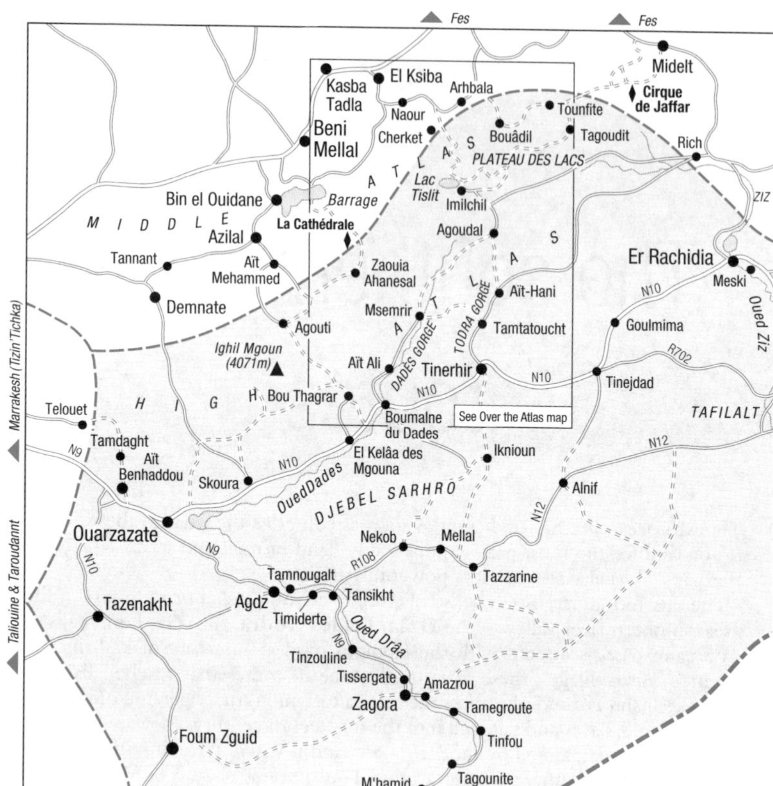

of rose-water and perfume in May. Severe drought in the 1990s had a devastating effect on crops, including dates, and forced many of the male population to seek work further north, but since 2007 the water levels have greatly improved and the palmeries are returning to their picture-book lushness.

Ouarzazate and the Drâa

Ouarzazate – four or five hours by bus from Marrakesh – is the main access point and crossroads of the south. To the northeast of the town, the dramatic desert scenery and kasbahs of the Dadès Valley and gorges provide a compelling introduction to the region. South, on the other side of a tremendous ridge of the Anti-Atlas, begins the **Drâa Valley** – 125km of date palm oases, which eventually merge into the Sahara near the village of M'hamid.

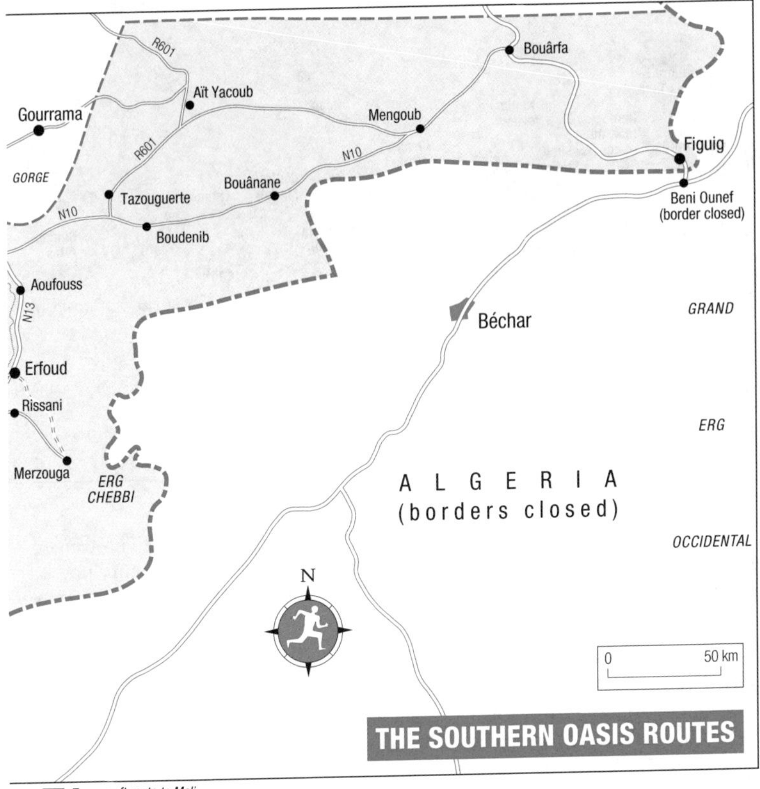

It is possible to complete a circuit through and out from the Drâa, heading from the valley's main town, **Zagora**, across *piste* roads west through Foum Zguid and Tata to the Anti-Atlas, or north into the Djebel Sarhro (a trekking area from October to April– see pp.447–450 for details), or east across to Rissani in the Tafilalt. However, most visitors content themselves with a return trip along the main **N9** between Ouarzazate and Zagora: a great route, taking you well south of anywhere in the Tafilalt, and flanked by an amazing series of turreted and creamy pink *ksour.*

Ouarzazate

At some stage, you're almost bound to spend a night in **OUARZAZATE** and it can be a useful base from which to visit the *ksour* and kasbahs of Aït Benhaddou or Skoura. Like most of the new Saharan towns, it was created as a Foreign Legion garrison and administrative centre by the French in the late 1920s. An underwhelming line of functional buildings and modern hotels stretches along the straggling main highway, but the town nevertheless has a buzzy, almost cosmopolitan feel which contrasts with the sleepier settlements found elsewhere in this region.

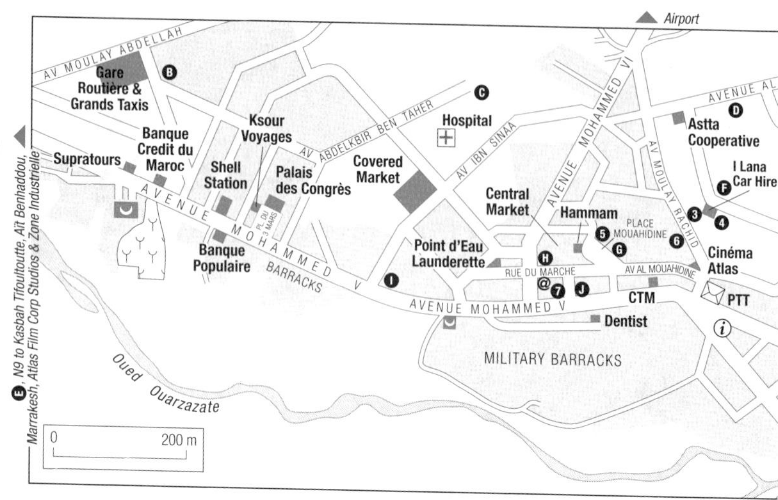

During the 1980s, Ouarzazate was something of a boom town. The tourist industry embarked on a wildly optimistic building programme of luxury hotels, based on Ouarzazate's marketability as a staging point for the "Saharan Adventure", and the town was given an additional boost from the attentions of filmmakers. The region first came to prominence in the film world in 1930 when Joseph von Sternberg filmed Marlene Dietrich in *Morocco*. David Lean shot *Lawrence of Arabia* in 1962 at nearby Aït Benhaddou and in the Tafilalt, and since then numerous directors have followed in their footsteps – most famously Bernardo Bertolucci, filming Paul Bowles's novel, *The Sheltering Sky* (1990), and Ridley Scott, who shot *Gladiator* here in 1999 and *Kingdom of Heaven* in 2005. A BBC-sponsored mini series about Ben Hur will be hitting our screens sometime in 2010.

Ouarzazate holds a mystic attraction for Moroccans, too – similar to the resonance of Timbuktu for Europeans – and recent years have seen renewed expansion. Vast residential building projects are already underway in response to the growing demand from young people unwilling to live with their parents, as well as an influx from rural areas. An ill-fated golf course development to the north of the city has, unsurprisingly, been abandoned, but there are plans afoot to build yet more five-star hotels and a slew of casinos. Whether the region will attract enough visitors in the future to sustain all this development remains to be seen.

Arrival and information

The **CTM bus station** more or less marks the centre of town, with the **PTT** alongside. Private long-distance **buses** operate from the Mahta *gare routière*, 2km on the bypass to the northwest. It's a fifteen-minute walk to the centre from here, or take a petit taxi (10–15dh). Most **grands taxis** also arrive outside the *gare routière*, but some work from the CTM bus station just off the main street. Ouarzazate's **airport** is 2km north of town and served by local taxis (20dh). The **tourist office** (Mon–Fri 8.30am–6.30pm; ⓣ0524 882485) is on Avenue Mohammed V, just across from the PTT but it's remarkably unhelpful – better to ask advice from your (or any other) hotel.

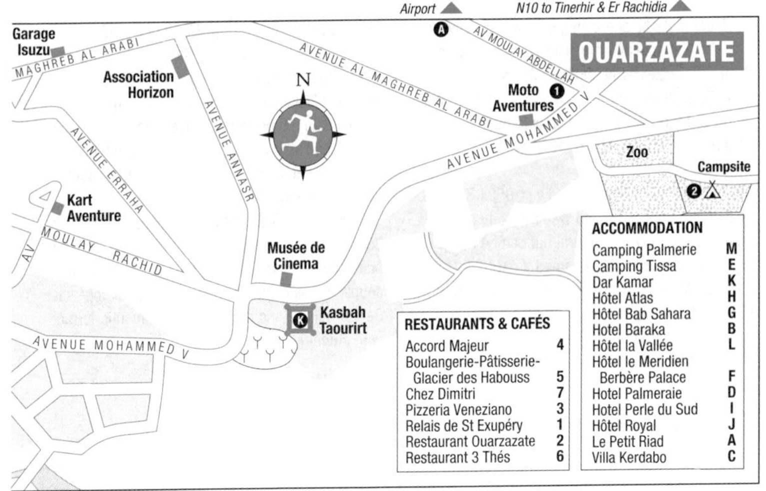

Accommodation

Finding a hotel room should present few problems. Most of the cheaper and unclassified places are grouped in the centre of town; the more upmarket chain hotels are mainly set back on the plateau to the north. Roughly 2km south across the river, the suburb of Tabounte holds some of the mid-range places; with your own vehicle, these are worth considering but otherwise lie inconveniently far from the centre. A more picturesque alternative would be to stay out at Aït Benhaddou (see p.428)

Camping La Palmeraie Tabounte ⓣ0524 854237/0676 666064, ⓦwww.camping-ouarzazate.com. All the usual facilities plus a few simple rooms and a wonderfully camp pink dining room where produce from the garden is served and music is occasionally laid on.

Camping-Restaurant Ouarzazate 2km east of the centre, signposted to the right about 500m after the Kasbah Taorirt ⓣ0524 888322. A welcoming enough place, but has limited shade and in the evenings noise from the adjacent tourist complex can be a nuisance.

Camping Tissa 20km west of town near the Aït Benhaddou junction ⓣ0524 890430. Basic but cheap and very friendly.

Dar Kamar Kasbah Taourirt ⓣ0524 888733, ⓦwww.darkamar.com. Wonderfully romantic and glamorous hotel hidden in the heart of the kasbah, plush rooms, wall-to-wall candles, deluxe hammam and a dreamy terrace. Tailor-made excursions can be arranged to the desert and beyond. ❼

Hôtel Atlas 13 Rue du Marché ⓣ0524 887745, ⓕ0524 886485. The best-value budget option. Some rooms have showers, others use showers on the corridor; in both cases hot water in the evenings. ❶–❷

Hôtel Bab Sahara Pl Mouahidine ⓣ0544 884722, ⓕ0544 884465. Convenient for the CTM bus station, grands taxis and shops. Rooms are available with showers and those that face the square have small balconies. Breakfast and other meals are available in the sunny café. ❷

Hôtel la Baraka Bloc D, Cité la Résistance ⓣ0524 884518. Very basic but right by the Mahta bus station so handy for late arrivals/early departures, and it has a reasonable café. ❷

Hôtel la Vallée 2km south in Tabounte ⓣ0524 854034, ⓕ0524 854043, ⓦwww.hotellavallee maroc.com. Good value and well maintained; the only drawback is the distance from the town centre, though compensations include meals by the pool and dawn from the terrace. Used for overnights by trekking groups, including Exodus and Explore. ❷–❸

Hôtel le Meridien Berbère Palace Quartier el Mansour Eddahbi ⓣ0524 883105, ⓦwww.palaces-traditions.com, ⓔmberberpala@menara.ma.Hang out with the film crews at Ouarzazate's top hotel, a state-of-the-art five star incorporating traditional architectural motifs and a magnificent pool, as well as a hammam and all the usual trimmings. BB ❽

Hotel Palmeraie Av Al Maghreb Al Arabi ⓣ0524 887293, ⓔpalmeraie@iam.net.ma. Drab but clean rooms and friendly service; sup cold beer around the large pool then retire to the bar and shoot some pool. ❹

Hôtel Royal 24 Av Mohammed V ⓣ0524 882258. Clean, well-maintained and with a variety of rooms, priced accordingly; it's central but can be noisy. ❶

La Perle du Sud Bd Mohammed V ⓣ0524 888640. Good value in a central location. Comfy en-suite rooms, large pool, bar and an adjacent nightclub open to non-residents. Ask for a room at the front with a balcony to get the best sunsets. ❹

Le Petit Riad Hay Al Wahda ⓣ0524 885959, ⓦwww.lepetitriad.com A charming and tranquil *maison d'hotes* run by Fatima Agoujil, the first officially-trained female guide in the region. Chic rooms, small pool and fabulous meals cooked by Fatima – help her out in the kitchen and learn some authentic recipes as well as valuable local information. BB ❺

Villa Kerdabo Sidi H'ssain Bennaceur ⓣ0524 887727 ⓦwww.villakerdabo.com. Hard to find but heavenly when you do. Run by a delightful French couple, it has eight airy *pisé* rooms, pool, top-notch Berber cuisine and an impossibly romantic terrace with stunning views. ❹

The town and kasbahs

Ouarzazate is not exactly choc-a-bloc with visitor attractions, but the local Glaoui Kasbah of **Taourirt** deserves a visit. Movie fans may also enjoy tours of the **Atlas Film Corporation Studios** (daily 8.30am–noon & 2.30–6pm), on the western outskirts of town, or the CLA Studios (same hours) further out by the junction of the N9 towards Zagora. Easier to reach is the **Musée de Cinema** (daily 9.00am–6pm) opposite Kasbah Taourirt where you can see dusty props and sets used in several international blockbusters, as well as an interesting collection of movie making paraphanalia. Entrance to each of these is 50dh. For day trips, head to Aït Benhaddou (see p.428) or a little along the Dadès to Skoura – a rambling oasis (see p.441), easily accessible using the Boumalne/Tinerhir buses. Fint, 10km down a *piste* (negotiable by tourist car) heading south off the Ouarzarzate-Tifoultoute road, is a picturebook oasis complete with palms, frogs and a few *pisé* buildings. Book ahead for lunch at *La Terrasse des Delices* (ⓣ0524 854890/0668 515640, ⓦwww.terrassedesdeliceshotelouarzazate.com) where you can also stay in decent rooms (BB ❷). Check out ⓦwww.ouednoujoum.com for details of an award-winning ecotourism scheme nearby.

Kasbah Taourirt

The **Kasbah Taourirt** (8am–6.30pm; 20dh) stands to the right of Avenue Mohammed V, at the east (Tinerhir direction) end of town. It's a dusty, twenty-minute walk from the centre.

Although built by the Glaoui, the kasbah was never an actual residence of its chiefs. However, located at this strategic junction of the southern trading routes, it was always controlled by a close relative. In the 1930s, when the Glaoui were the undisputed masters of the south, it was perhaps the largest of all Moroccan kasbahs – an enormous family domain housing numerous sons and cousins of the dynasty, along with several hundred of their servants and labourers, builders and craftsmen, including Jewish tailors, jewellers and moneylenders.

After being taken over by the government following independence, the kasbah fell into drastic decline. Recent work carried out under the auspices of CERKAS, a government organization devoted to the restoration of kasbahs and *ksour*, has had only partial success – parts of the structure have disappeared, washed away by heavy rains, others are completely unsafe. What you see is just the main reception courtyard and a handful of principal rooms, lavishly decorated but not especially significant or representative of the old order of things. A small section of the original – a kind of village within the kasbah –

Southern practicalities

Transport

All the main road routes in this chapter are covered by regular buses, and often grands taxis. On many of the others, local Berber trucks (*camions*) or pick-ups (*camionettes*) run a bus-type service, charging standard fares for their trips, which are usually timed to coincide with the network of souks or markets in villages en route. The trucks cover a number of adventurous desert *pistes* – such as the direct routes from Zagora to Foum Zguid and Tata – and some very rough roads over the Atlas behind the Dadès or Todra gorges. If you plan to drive on these, you'll need to have a decent vehicle (4WDs are essential for some routes) and be able to do basic mechanical repairs.

Travelling by bus in the desert in summer, the main disadvantage is the sheer physical exhaustion involved: most trips tend to begin at dawn to avoid the worst of the heat and, for the rest of the day, it can be difficult to summon up the energy to do anything. If you can afford to rent a car – even for just two or three days – you'll be able to take in a lot more, with a lot less frustration, in a reasonably short period of time. Many of the *pistes* are navigable in a rental car but be aware that the insurance is invalid when you drive on them. There are numerous rental outlets in Ouarzazate, some of which allow you to return their vehicles to Agadir, Marrakesh, Fes, or even Casablanca.

Petrol stations can be found along all the main routes. It's wise to carry water, too, in case of overheating, and, above all, be sure you've got a good spare tyre – punctures tend to be frequent on all southern roads. As throughout the country, local mechanics are excellent and most minor problems can be quickly dealt with (a puncture can be repaired for around 20dh).

Climate and seasons

Temperatures can climb well above 50°C in midsummer and you'll find the middle of the day is best spent being totally inactive. If you have the option, spring is by far the most enjoyable time to travel – particularly if you're heading for Zagora (reckoned to be the hottest town in the country), or Rissani-Merzouga. Autumn, with the date harvests, is also good. In winter, the days remain hot, though it can get very cold at night, and further south into the desert, it can actually freeze.

Be aware, too, that the Drâa, in particular, is subject to flash floods in spring, as the snow melts in the Atlas. Passes across the Atlas at this time can be difficult or impossible.

Health

Rivers in the south are reputed to contain **bilharzia**, a parasite that can enter your skin, including the soles of your feet, so, even when walking by streams in the oases, take care to avoid contact. Travellers are advised to drink only bottled mineral water in southern Morocco.

remains occupied today and it makes for interesting wandering. Enter down the alley to the left of the entrance to the main door and step back in time.

Kasbah Tifoultoute

Around 10km from Ouarzazate is the **Kasbah of Tifoultoute** (8am–7pm; 10dh), originally owned by the Glaoui clan. It stands majestically on the banks of the Oued Tifoultoute, though it's rather more impressive from a distance than on entry.

In the 1960s, the kasbah was converted into a hotel for the cast of *Lawrence of Arabia*, since which time it has lapsed into a state of disrepair and now there is little of interest to see except the storks nesting on the roof. To reach it, cross the river to the Tabounte district and turn right at the petrol station where you see the sign for Tifoultoute. Another part holds the *Auberge Restaurant Oued Tifoultoute*, which serves delicious mint and herb teas and menus ranging from 80–120dh on a pair of sunny terraces; it may not be open in low-season, however. Photos on the walls testify to Gerard Depardieu's repeated custom when he was filming *Asterix and Obelix: Mision Cleopatra in 2002*. It also has a few simple rooms. ❷.

Craft shopping

Opposite the Kasbah Taourirt is the **Centre Artisanal** (Daily 8.30am–6.30pm), a complex of a dozen or so little shops. Besides stone carvings and pottery, look for two local specialities: the geometrically patterned, silky woollen carpets of the region's Ouzguita Berbers, and the silver jewellery – necklaces and earrings incorporating *tazras* (chunky orange copal beads). There are also musical instruments used for the *ahouach*, a dance usually performed in the light of great fires until the first rays of daylight. The Cooperative Tissage, opposite Kasbah Taourirt, has good-quality carpets with fairly fixed prices.

On the north side of town towards the airport, **Association Horizon** (Mon–Sat 9am–6pm) has a shop selling attractive pottery, weaving and metalwork produced as part of a self-help scheme for less able-bodied craft workers. You can also visit workshops to watch them in action. Astta, a women's cooperative on Av Al Maghreb Al Arabi (Mon–Sat 9am–6pm), sells textiles, jewellery, honey, saffron and herbs.

Avenue Mohammed V and the central market have several small shops selling traditional items, old and new, where you may choose to try your bargaining skills. Better still, but more difficult to find, is the **Maison Berbère** in the Tabounte district, the other side of the river on the road to Zagora.

Eating

Budget travellers should head for the cheap **café-grills** grouped around the central market at Place Mouahidine, Avenue Al Mouahidine and along the nearby Rue du Marché. For breakfast, the sunnier north side of Boulevard Mohammed V is the area to head for, with a row of terrace cafés serving French baguettes, pastries and coffee; the same places also serve tajines, grills and light salads for lunch and dinner from around 35dh.

Accord Majeur opposite *Hotel Berbere-Palace*, ☎0524 882473. Mingle with the film stars and lap up foie gras, duck confit and boeuf bourgignon in this chic French-run restaurant with a pretty roadside terrace. A treat if you're bored of tajines and have a heavy wallet.

Boulangerie-Patisserie-Glacier Des Habouss Pl Mouahidine. Ouarzazate's best bakery-cum-ice-cream parlour is the top spot for a coffee stop, serving several kinds of delicious Moroccan bread, in addition to crusty baguettes, croissants and pains au chocolat. They also do the full gamut of sticky local patisserie (sold by weight).

Chez Dimitri 22 Av Mohammed V (next to *Hôtel Royal*) ☎0524 887346. Founded in 1928 to serve the Foreign Legion, this bar-brasserie is something of an institution. It is licensed and has a wide-ranging menu of mostly Gallic and Moroccan standards (mains from around 65dh), served by wonderfully retro uniformed waiters. Old photographs of the town and desert add to the colonial ambience. The food is a bit hit-and-miss but the vibe is always jovial. Popular with tour groups and film crews so reservations recommended.

Pizzeria Veneziano Av Moulay Rachid ☎0524 887676. Unexpectedly smart little pizza joint serving a wide range of inexpensive salads, European dishes and tajines, in addition to filling, tasty pizzas (from 35dh). They also offer plenty of veggie options.

Relais de St Exupéry 13 Av Moulay-Abadallah ☎0524 887779. Just off the main Tinerhir road, near the airport (turn left as you leave town, before the petrol station). Excellent Moroccan and French cuisine cooked by Jean-Pierre, the indomitable Bordelais chef-proprietor. Memorabilia from the *Aéropostale* days of *Little Prince* author Antoine de

St Exupéry adorns the walls, but the food is the real attraction: try the wonderful pigeon pastilla, sea bass with orange or saffron ice cream. Fixed menus from 110dh plus a la carte.

Restaurant 3 Thés Av Moulay Rachid. Generous portions of classic Moroccan dishes as well as lighter snacks available all day. Popular with locals and expats alike.

Listings

Airport Aéroport Taourirt (Ⓣ0524 899150) is 2km north of town, and served by petits taxis (20dh). There are daily RAM flights to Casablanca and 4 flights a week flights to Paris. RAM has an office at 1 Av Mohammed V (Ⓣ0524 885102, Ⓕ024 886893).
Banks Banks and ATMs are plentiful and are mostly found along Av Mohammed V. They include: Crédit du Maroc, Wafabank, BMCE, BCM and Banque Populaire.
Bikes – including mountain bikes – can be rented from Ksour Voyages, 11 Pl du 3 Mars (see "Tours", opposite).
Car rental Literally dozens of agencies operate in Ouarzazate, most from offices on Bd Mohammed V or out on Pl du 3 Mars. Shop around for the best deals; prices start from 300dh per day if you rent a vehicle for seven days, but it's always worth haggling – at least with local firms – and scrutinize the small print. As ever in Morocco, it's also advisable to opt for additional insurance to cover any damage excess (see p.40); and check the car (front and back lights, petrol gauge and spare tyre) thoroughly before driving away. Best of the local firms is Ilana, tucked behind *Restaurant Accord Majeur* (Ⓣ&Ⓕ0524 884142, Ⓔilanarentcar@gmail.com), which has helpful staff and new cars. Newloc, 30 Rue du Marche Ⓣ0524 887853/0662 836864 has an English speaking owner but the cars are getting on a bit.; International companies are more expensive – Avis, Pl du 3 Mars Ⓣ0524 888000; Budget, Av Mohammed V Ⓣ0524 882892; Europcar/InterRent, Pl du 3 Mars Ⓣ0524 882035; Hertz, 33 Av Mohammed V Ⓣ0524 882084.
Car repairs Garage Raquiq el Habib, Quartier Industriel No. 99 (Ⓣ0524 884933) is recommended, as is Garage Isuzu on Av Al Maghreb al Arabi. Motoaventures (see opposite) has a brilliant English-speaking mechanic who fixes bikes and cars.
Internet There are numerous internet cafés on Rue du Marché and Bd Mohammed V.
Motorcycle rental and tours Motoaventures at the far eastern end of Av Mohammed V (Ⓣ0665 282247, Ⓦwww.motoaventures.com) is an English-run operation that has been here for 13 years, so they really know their stuff. They offer tours to the desert and the High Atlas on KTM bikes with all kit included. All levels of experience are catered for; motorbike licence essential. Kart Aventure on Av Moulay Rachid (Ⓣ0524 88 63 74, Ⓦwww.kart-aventure.com) runs buggy and 4WD trips to the desert, gorges and mountains from 1400dh per vehicle.
Post office The PTT on Av Mohammed V has poste restante facilities, it's open Mon–Fri 8.30am–6pm, Sat 8.30am–noon.
Shopping The Super Marché, 73 Av Mohammed V, opposite *Chez Dimitri*, is well stocked, including beer and wine, and is open until 10pm. Head to the Covered Market on Av Ibn Sinaa for fruit, veg, meat and fish. The Central Market on Rue du Marché is great for street food, spices, and souvenir trinkets. Souk days are Sunday out by the Zone Industrielle and Saturday in Tabounte.
Tours There are countless tour operators offering anything from half-day excursions to two-week treks. Ksour Voyages on Pl du 3 Mars (Ⓣ0524 882840, Ⓕ0524 884899, Ⓦwww.ksour-voyages.com), Cherg Expeditions, Place Al Mouahidine, (Ⓣ&Ⓕ0524 887908, Ⓦwww.cherg.com) and Zbar Travel, also on Place Al Mouahidine (Ⓣ0673 267893, Ⓦwww.zbartravel.com) have good reputations and English-speaking guides.To arrange adventure trips into the High Atlas, including trekking and mountaineering, your best option is Désert et Montagne Maroc at the *Hôtel Dar Daif* in Tabounte (Ⓣ0524 854232, Ⓦwww.desert-montagne.ma), run by French-qualified mountain guides Pierre and Zineb Datcharry.

Moving on

CTM bus services leave from their station near the PTT, to Agadir (via Taliouine, Taroudant and Inezgane), Casablanca, Marrakesh, M'Hamid, Zagora, and Er Rachidia. SATAS and other privately run **long-distance buses** go from the *gare routière* at Mahta 2km from the centre (a 15dh taxi ride away); as ever, they're cheaper, but take longer. For a full rundown of destinations, see "Travel details" on p.480. If possible, book your ticket at least one day before departure.

Some grands taxis leave from alongside the CTM bus station but most operate from the less conveniently situated *gare routière* out at Mahta.

There are regular runs along the Dadès to Boumalne (30dh a place; connections on towards Tinerhir and Er Rachidia), and for Marrakesh, Zagora and points westwards (including Tazenakht, Taliouine, Aloulouz, Ouled Berhil, Taroudant and Agadir), with connections for the Tizi n'Test pass.

Aït Benhaddou

The first thing you hear from the guides on arrival at **AÏT BENHADDOU**, 32km from Ouarzazate, is a list of its movie credits. Though this is a feature of much of the Moroccan south, the Benhaddou *ksar* has a definite edge over the competition. *Lawrence of Arabia* was filmed here, of course; Orson Welles used it as a location for *Sodom and Gomorrah*; and for *Jesus of Nazareth* the whole lower part of the village was rebuilt. In recent years, more controlled restoration has been carried out under UNESCO auspices and film crews have been involved in some "re-modelling".

With its souvenir shops and constant stream of tour groups, Aït Benhaddou is not really the place to catch a glimpse of fading *ksar* life but it is one of the most spectacular sights of the Atlas, piled upon a low hillock above a shallow, reed-strewn river. Its buildings are among the most elaborately decorated and best preserved; they are less fortified than is usually the case along the Drâa or the Dadès, but, towered and crenellated, and with high, sheer walls of dark red *pisé*, they must have been near impregnable in this remote, hillside site.

Ksour and kasbahs

Ksour (**ksar** in the singular), and **kasbahs**, are to be found throughout the southern valleys and, to an extent, in the Atlas. *Ksour* are essentially fortified tribal villages while a kasbah is a fortified home built for the ruling family. They are massive structures built, in the absence of other available materials, out of the mud-clay **pisé** of the riverbanks. A unique and probably indigenous development of the Berber populations, they are often monumental in design and fabulously decorated, with bold geometric patterns incised or painted on the exterior walls and slanted towers. The seasonal rains wash off some of the mud so the buildings need constant maintenance.

Agadirs and *tighremts*, also variants of the *ksar* structure, used to serve as a combination of tribal fortress and communal granary or storehouse in the villages.

The Drâa kasbahs

Ksour and kasbahs line the route more or less continuously from Agdz to Zagora; most of the larger and older ones are grouped a little way from the road, up above the terraces of date palms. Few that are still in use can be more than a hundred years old, though you frequently see the ruins and walls of earlier *ksour* abandoned just a short distance from their modern counterparts. Most are populated by **Berbers**, but there are also Arab villages here, and even a few scattered communities of **Jews**, still living in their Mellahs. All of the southern valleys, too, have groups of **Haratin**, descendants of West African slaves brought into Morocco along these caravan routes. Inevitably, these populations have mixed to some extent – and the Jews here are almost certainly converted Berbers – though it is interesting to see just how distinct many of the *ksour* still appear, both in their architecture and customs. There is, for example, a great difference from one village to the next as regards women's costumes, above all in the wearing and extent of veils.

▲ Kasbahs at Aït Banhaddou

As ever, it's impossible to determine exactly how old the *ksar* is, though there seem to have been buildings here since at least the eleventh century. The importance of the site, which commands the area for miles around, was its position on the trans-Saharan trade route from Marrakesh through Telouet to Ouarzazate and the south. In the twentieth century, the significance of this route disappeared with the creation of the new French road over the Tichka pass, which has led to severe depopulation. There are now only half a dozen families living in the kasbahs, earning a sparse living from the valley's agriculture and rather more from the tourists who pass through. Entry to the **kasbah** is free, although the gateways are "controlled" by people who may try to convince you otherwise (only pay the 10dh or so demanded if you want to see the inside of any houses). Follow the network of lanes uphill and you'll eventually arrive at the ruins of a vast and imposing **agadir**, or fortified granary, from where there are great views over the surrounding desert.

Given how difficult it can sometimes be to find transport out of Aït Benhaddou, you may well end up deciding to spend the night here; if you do, get up at dawn to see the *ksar* at its best.

Arrival and orientation

Getting to Aït Benhaddou is simple enough by car. Leaving Ouarzazate on the N9 (Tizi n'Tichka) road, you turn right after 18km along a surfaced road. A bus or grand taxi to the turn-off will cost 15dh, where you can pick up another for the remaining leg to the village (5dh). At the "new village", on the west bank of the river, the road passes the dreary *Hôtel-Restaurant Le Kasbah*, in front of which there's a parking area where guides hang around hoping to escort visitors across the river: in winter you sometimes have to wade across though the water is rarely more than knee-deep (when it is, donkeys can be ridden across for 20dh each way).

Leaving town by public transport at the end of the day can be tricky: local traffic tends to dry up by 4pm allowing taxis to charge what they think they can get away with. The only cheap alternative is to walk the 5km back to the highway and catch a grand taxi. *Auberge Carrefour* at the junction makes a cheery coffee/food stop and has brightly painted rooms. ❷.

Accommodation and eating

There's no shortage of accommodation options, although cafés and restaurants are somewhat thinner on the ground, with most people opting to eat at their hotel or guesthouse.

Dar Mouna Ⓣ0528 843054, Ⓕ0528 833080, Ⓦwww.darmouna.com. Traditionally furnished rooms (all en suite) in a converted kasbah, on a bluff bang opposite the old village. The hotel is virtually self-sufficient with its own vegetable garden, bread ovens, natural well, and animals. There is also a pool and a hammam. The restaurant offers an adventurous menu, too, with Egyptian *shorbah*, chicken crêpes and flambéed banana in addition to the usual Moroccan standards. (120dh per head). ❻–❼

Defat Kasbah 3km north of Aït Benhaddou, on the riverside Ⓣ0524 888020, Ⓦwww.defatkasbah.com. Occupying a prime, tranquil spot with fine views up the valley and owned by a young French-Moroccan couple, this is a friendly place with helpful staff and a range of attractively furnished rooms (most en suite). Those on the upper floors have access to a terrace, and there's a pool, bar and a ground-floor salon restaurant. Tours can be arranged from here. ❷–❸

La Rose du Sable Ⓣ0524 890022, Ⓦwww.larosedusable.com. Best value in town. A new family-run hotel on the main drag with 18 comfy rooms, decent restaurant, lovely terrace and a big pool. ❶–❷ or sleep on the roof or salon for less.

Riad Ksar Ighnda Ⓣ0524 887644, Ⓦwww.ksar.ighnda.net. Drop-dead gorgeous hotel, oozing luxury chic. Rooms with all mod cons and wonderful mattresses, immaculate gardens, a pool and spa, and a classy restauarant. Divine. ❼

Riad Maktoub Ⓣ0524 888694, Ⓦwww.riadmaktoub.com. Located in the village centre on the main road, an attractive riad-style building with seven small but cool rooms and five suites surrounding a traditional long courtyard. Meals (60–75dh) are served in the salon, around the small pool or on either of the elegant terraces overlooking the kasbah. HB ❹

Tamdaght

Spread across a platform above a bend in the river, its fringes hemmed in by canyon walls, **TAMDAGHT**, 6km further up the valley from Aït Benhaddou, has a more authentic Berber feel than its neighbour. The village, which formerly flourished with the caravan route over the Tizi n'Tichka, is dominated by the remnants of a crumbling Glaoui kasbah, its towers crowned by gigantic storks' nests. Few of the day-trippers that pass through Aït Benhaddou make it this far, but from the river below the *Hôtel Dar Kasbah* you can either follow the road for (another 2km) or walk along the riverbank. Both lead through some spectacular desert scenery (featured by Ridley Scott in *Gladiator* and Oliver Stone in *Alexander*), but on foot you've the added bonus of crossing the lush terraced gardens below the **kasbah**. Visits to the only section of the building still inhabited (one or two wings are on the verge of collapse) are possible; knock at the main door (facing the road) and expect to pay a donation of around 10dh.

From the end of the tarmac at Tamdaght, a *piste* leads 35km further northwest to Telouet and the Tizi n'Tichka pass. This is a popular trekking and mountain bike itinerary, and the road is being upgraded, though at present only advisable for 4WD travelling. The route penetrates increasingly magnificent landscape punctuated at regular intervals by villages, several of which have small *gîtes d'étapes*. At **Anemiter**, there's also a large Glaoui kasbah. Allow a half-day if following the *piste* by car, a full day by mountain bike and two to three days if on foot. (This route is covered in reverse from Telouet in the High Atlas chapter, see p.411.)

Birds and the El Mansour Eddahbi Barrage

The shoreline of the **El Mansour Eddahbi Barrage** is an essential stop on the birdwatchers' itinerary. Throughout the year (especially late July–Nov & March–May) the area attracts a variety of migrants such as ruddy shellduck, other waterfowl and waders. There have also been sightings of a variety of desert-dwelling species such as mourning wheatear, trumpeter finch, blackbellied sandgrouse, thick-billed lark (and other larks) and raptors, including lanner falcon.

Practicalities

Tamdaght has a couple of places to stay, both close to the kasbah on the edge of the village. The cheapest option is the eccentric *Auberge des Cigognes* (Ⓣ0524 890371 or 0662 787354; HB ❷), which offers four very basic rooms (with shared showers and toilets) in a rambling ancestral home. Its sole permanent occupant, owner Adelazize Taoufik, also has a cheap dorm frequented mostly by trekkers en route to or from Telouet (❶).

At the opposite end of the scale, the neighbouring *Kasbah Ellouze* (Ⓣ0667 965483, Ⓦwww.kasbahellouze.com; HB ❹) is a much fancier place run by a couple from Nîmes. Although modern, the building follows traditional lines with cavernous rooms that combine stylish traditional Moroccan design with mod cons such as heaters and bathtubs. Beautifully cooked meals are also served on a lovely rear terrace (open to nonresidents for tea) overlooking the village orchards, river and valley.

South to Zagora: the Drâa oases

The road from **Ouarzazate to Zagora** is well maintained and, for the most part, broad enough for two vehicles, though it does take its toll on tyres. If you're on the bus, get yourself a seat on the left-hand side for the most spectacular views.

Although Zagora is the ostensible goal and destination, the valley is the real attraction. Driving the route, take the opportunity to stop and walk out to one or another of the *ksour* or kasbahs. Using local transport, you might consider hiring a grand taxi for the day – or half-day – from Ouarzazate, stopping to explore some of the kasbahs en route; if you intend to do this, however, be very clear to the driver about your plans.

Along certain stretches of the route you'll notice groups of kids brandishing boxes of **boufeggous dates**, highly prized in Morocco and worth stopping to taste – in some cases, the vendors may encourage you to do so by leaping in front of your car. Another hassle, prevalent throughout the south but refined along this road, are "**fake breakdowns**". People standing next to stationary cars will flag you down, ostensibly for help getting to a garage; but when you arrive at the next town they insist on returning the favour by offering you a "special price" on items from their handicraft shop.

Tizi n'Tinifift

The route begins unpromisingly: the course of the Drâa lies initially some way to the east and the road runs across bleak, stony *hammada*. After 15km, a side road, the P31F, leads 11km down to the **El Mansour Eddahbi Barrage and reservoir** (road closed to vehicles). In 1989 and again in 2009 freak rains flooded the reservoir, and the Drâa, for the first time in recent memory, ran its course to the sea beyond Tan Tan.

On the main road, the first interest comes just beyond Aït Saoun, one of the few roadside villages along this stretch, where a dramatic change takes place. Leaving the plains behind, the road climbs, twists and turns its way up into the mountains, before breaking through the scarp at the pass of **Tizi n'Tinififft** (1660m). From the summit of the pass there are fine views north to the Atlas mountains.

Beyond it the road swings down through a landscape of layered strata, until finally, some 20km from the pass, you catch a first glimpse of the valley and the oases – a thick line of palms reaching out into the haze – and the first sign of the Drâa kasbahs.

Agdz

You descend into the Drâa Valley at **Agdz** (pronounced Ag–dèz), 68km from Ouarzazate, a stopping point for many of the buses and a minor administrative centre for the region. Many of the shops along the main street sell carpets and pottery – and in the few minutes before the bus leaves, prices can drop dramatically. If you stop here, travelling in either direction, you'll probably have to stay overnight to get a place on the Zagora/Ouarzazate bus; however, there are also **grands taxis** (to either destination), which, like the buses, leave from the Grande Place.

It's certainly worth a stop; just to the north of the village begins a beautiful **palmery**. If the river here is low enough (take care to avoid the bilharzia-infested water) you can get across to view a few **kasbahs** on the far side, in the shadow of Djebel Kissane. Also worth a look is the Kasbah du Caïd Ali, reached by turning north off the main square.

Accommodation and eating

The town has a handful of **hotels**. Of the budget options ranged around the Grande Place, *Hôtel des Palmiers* (ⓣ0524 843127; ❷) is the best. By the ceremonial archway at the northern entry to the town is the pricier *Hôtel Kissane* (ⓣ0524 843044, ⓕ0524 843258; ❸), a very pleasant place with obliging staff, a pool and a good salon **restaurant**.

Alongside the Kasbah Asslim, the *Camping Kasbah de la Palmerie* (ⓣ&ⓕ0524 843640) is reached by turning north off the main street just by the Grande Place and continuing for about 2km. The site has plenty of shade, but the swimming pool and toilet blocks are a little grubby. There are also a few rooms for rent in the kasbah itself (❷).

Along this road is *Dar Qamar* (ⓣ0524 843784, ⓦwww.locsudmaroc.com; ❺), one of the nicest hotels in the region, run by a charming French couple. Sumptuous rooms are set around a pretty garden with a small pool, and there's a hammam, library and a cosy fire-lit salon. Delicious food, too. Continue to the end of the road and you'll reach *Kasbah Azul* (ⓣ0524 843931, ⓦwww.kasbah-azul.com; ❺-❻) which has a beautiful terrace around its large pool and classy rooms.

West from Agdz to Tazenakht

Just north of Agdz, a junction marks the start of the wonderfully remote route to **Tazenakht.** Settlements along the way include **Tasla**, which has a small but interesting museum; and **Bou Azzer**, where there are extensive cobalt mines but little else. **TAZENAKHT**, a carpet weaving centre, is at the junction of the Agadir, Ouarzazate and Foum Zguid roads. The town is quite a transport hub, with regular buses and grands taxis to Ouarzazate, plus buses to Foum Zguid, Tissint and Tata. It also has decent rooms and meals: try the *Hôtel Zenaga* (ⓣ0524 841032, ⓔzenaga_hotel@hotmail.com; ❷, roof ❶), on Avenue Moulay-Hassan, or *Hôtel Taghdoute* (ⓣ0524 841393; ❷) also on Avenue Moulay-Hassan, whose owner organizes walking trips into the surrounding countryside. For cheap meals, there are simple cafés opposite the *gare routière*, which knock up freshly grilled kebabs, spicy lentil stew (*ledus*) and fish steaks. There's also a Banque Populaire with an ATM and a couple of petrol stations. If you're going to buy a carpet, this is probably the best place to do so – there are numerous shops and a good cooperative on the road towards Agdz. The Friday souk is also well worth a visit.

Tamnougalt, Timiderte and Tinzouline

Continuing south down the Drâa Valley, the *ksar* at **TAMNOUGALT** – off to the left of the road, about 6km past Agdz – is perhaps the most dramatic and extravagant of any in the locality. The village was once the capital of the region, and its assembly of families (the *djemaa*) administered what was virtually an independent republic. Today, it's a wild cluster of buildings, each fabulously decorated with pockmarked walls and tapering towers, and populated by a Berber tribe, the Mezguita. You can visit the kasbah here – the 50dh entry is well worth it – and stay right next door at the delightful *Chez Jacob* (ⓣ0524 843394, ⓔtamnougalte@yahoo.fr; HB ❸) which has simple but gorgeously cool rooms and a large tented roof terrace where you can bed down (HB ❷). Mohammed, the manager, speaks good English and will give you the lowdown on the area.

Another 15km south, on the opposite side of the river, is the palace-like Glaoui kasbah of **TIMIDERTE**. You'll have to ford the river again, this time on foot – ideally with some local assistance as the best crossing place isn't all that obvious – to reach another superb kasbah, the **Aït Hammou-Saïd**. The back country road from Rissani and Nekob meets the N9 just south of Timiderte (a route described on pp.472–474), where you might be able to pick up a grand taxi in any direction. Beyond the junction, another striking group of *ksour*, dominated by a beautiful and imposing *caid's* kasbah, stands back from the road at **TINZOULINE**, 57km beyond Timiderte (37km north of Zagora). There is a large **Monday souk** held here and, if you're travelling by bus, the village is one of the better places to break the journey for a while. With some guidance, you can also follow a *piste* 7km west of the village to see a group of three-thousand-year-old rock carvings.

Eight kilometres north of Zagora, at **Tissergate,** is a low-key *ksar* and an interesting museum of local history and culture (20dh).

Zagora and around

ZAGORA seems unpromising at first sight: a modern market town with a big crop of hotels and government buildings and few sights of specific interest. As the region's main staging post for trips to the fringes of the Sahara, it attracts more tourist attention than it deserves in itself, not to mention hustlers in search of potential clients for camel treks, but nonetheless makes an agreeable rest stop. Directly behind the town rises the dramatic Djebel Zagora mountains, and at the end of the main street is a mock-serious road sign to Timbuktu ("52 jours" – by camel – if the border were open).

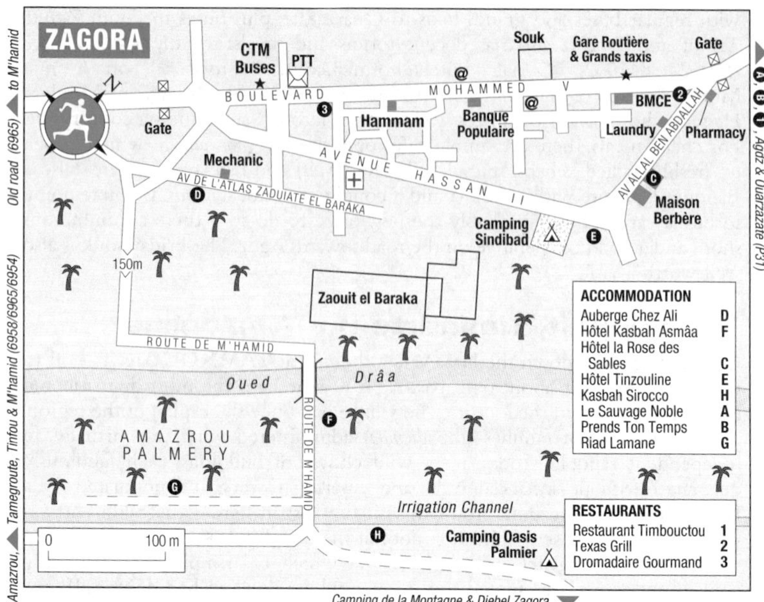

Another draw for Zagora is its festivals. The Drâa's big event, the **Moussem of Moulay Abdelkader Jilali**, is celebrated here during the Mouloud, and like other national festivals here, such as the **Fête du Trône**, is always entertaining.

Though it can seem a bit of a hassle on arrival, and in summer the oven-dry heat is staggering (as are the *frigidaire* nights in winter), Zagora is an easy place to get oriented. Across the river, to the southeast, is the palmery and hamlet of **Amazrou**, a good alternative base, with a fast-growing group of hotels and several campsites.

Accommodation

There is a wide range of **hotels** – in Zagora and Amazrou – and some nicely located **campsites**, especially for those with transport. Travellers on tight budgets should also note that many mid-scale hotels, including the *Sirocco* and *Kasbah Asmâa* (reviewed below) will let you bed down on roof terraces or in nomad tents for 50dh or less. Also, bear in mind that, as elsewhere in the country, most hotels are happy for nonresidents to use their pools, bars and restaurants.

Hotels

Auberge Chez Ali Av Atlas Zaouit el Baraka ⓣ0524 846258, ⓔchez_ali@hotmail.com. A haven of greenery on the edge of town, offering clean, secure and relaxing accommodation in 12 comfortable rooms (8 en suite) or cosy Berber tents. The owner, Ali, is genuinely hospitable and has, over two decades, created a lovely garden filled with flowers, fruit trees and a pair of peacocks. Altogether the nicest option in Zagora, but far from a secret, so book ahead. ❷

Hôtel Kasbah Asmâa 1km from the centre, over the Oued Drâa at Amazrou ⓣ0524 847599, ⓦwww.asmaa-zagora.com. A large kasbah-style hotel, faced with traditional *pisé* and set in a beautiful garden overlooking the palmery, with a shaded swimming pool and top-notch restaurant. The best of the thirty or so rooms are those in the new (and more expensive) block. ❺

Hôtel la Rose des Sables Av Allal Ben Abdellah ⓣ0524 847274. Currently undergoing expansion, this budget hotel has a range of clean and comfortable rooms, and a very friendly owner, Ahmed. The ground-floor restaurant is simple but has some of the best food in town, and is good value, too, with a filling 60dh menu. ❶–❷

Hôtel Tinzouline Av Hassan II ⓣ0524 847252, ⓦwww.zagora-desert.com. Colonial-era charm meets *The Shining*, but not necessarily in a bad way. Zagora's original "grand hotel" is showing its age but its rooms, housed in two huge wings, are plush and most overlook splendid gardens. Avoid the multi-cuisine restaurant; enjoy the hammam, bar and big pool. ❻

Kasbah Sirocco On the road heading northeast at Amazrou towards the Djebel Zagora ⓣ0524 846125, ⓦwww.kasbah-sirocco.com. French-owned place with twenty slightly dreary but a/c rooms that are well heated in winter. Its main attractions are the good-sized pool and bar in a shady garden. You can also sleep in Berber tents on the terrace here for around 50dh, and the patron (a Paris-Dakar veteran) is a mine of information on the region's 4WD possibilities. ❸

Le Sauvage Noble ⓣ0524 838072, ⓦwww.sauvage-noble.org. 5km north of Zagora, this little gem is a Moroccan-German collaboration that also encompasses La Société Bleu Touareg, running social, ecological and tourism projects with local desert tribes. Traditonal decor by local craftsmen (the *tadelakt* bathrooms are particularly fine), sumptuous bedrooms and a very good kitchen. Their excursions are highly recommended, too. ❹

Riad Lamane Amezrou ⓣ0524 848388, ⓦwww.riadlamane.com. Gorgeous top-end hotel hidden behind high walls. With decor looking towards sub-Saharan Africa, the rooms are beautifully appointed with tiled en-suite bathrooms and private balconies. A library, pool and well-stocked bar add to its charm (❼) or bed down in cosy tents in the garden.

Camping

Camping Oasis Palmier Chez Pixa Route Montagne, Amerzou ⓣ0666 569750, ⓔpixameharee@hotmail.com. On the far side of the river, reached via the *piste* turning left off the main M'hamid road after the bridge. A pleasant mix of well-shaded pitches and Berber tents, set at the foot of the mountain, with clean toilet blocks, a relaxing café and friendly management. A pool and hammam are under construction.

Camping Sindibad next to the Hôtel Tinzouline ⓣ0524 847553. A small, friendly site, with adequate shade, a tiny swimming pool (not always in use) and clusters of middle-aged French campers playing boules. Hot showers cost extra and they have a few rooms for rent (60dh). Book ahead for traditional meals, 50dh.

Prends Ton Temps Hay El Mansour Dahbi, ⓣ0524 846543, ⓔf_laalili@yahoo.fr. "Take your time" pretty much sums up this laid-back and slightly eccentric joint. Pitch a tent or sleep in funkily decorated little cabins from 50dh per person. The irrepressible owner Belaid comes from a nomadic tribe and is an accomplished player of the Arabian lute so expect long evenings of music and stories.

Amazrou

Amazrou is a hamlet and palmery just to the southeast of Zagora, across the Drâa, and a great place to spend the afternoon, wandering amid the shade of its gardens and *ksour*. The village is, inevitably, wise to the ways of tourism – children try to drag you into their houses for tea and will hassle you to adopt them as guides – but for all that, the traditional ways of oasis life remain largely unaffected.

The local sight, which any of the kids will lead you towards, is the old Jewish kasbah, **La Kasbah des Juifs**. The Jewish community here was active in the silver jewellery trade – a craft continued by Muslim Berbers after their exodus. It's possible to visit some of the workshops and to buy good new and antique jewellery.

Djebel Zagora

Across the valley from Zagora are two **mountains**. Djebel Zagora is strictly speaking the bulky one, with a military post on top, but the name is also used for the smaller, sugarloaf hill above *Camping de la Montagne*, out past Camping Oasis Palmier.

Watching the sunset from the slopes of the mountain is something of a tradition. Take the road out to the *Hôtel Kasbah Asmâa*, then turn left almost at once at the river to follow the road to *Camping de la Montagne*. Here, swing right on the rough track which leads to a pass between the two peaks, then bends back, rising across the hillside to make an elbow bend on a spur. This popular viewpoint is best reached by 4WD. Just below the road are the remnants of a colossal eleventh-century Almoravid fort, built as an outpost against the powerful rulers of Tafilalt; later it was used to protect the caravans passing below, to and from Timbuktu. The road subsequently goes on to the military fort on the summit (entry forbidden) but the view gains little; from the spur a footpath runs across and down the hillside and can be followed back down to the road.

On foot you can climb the mountain more directly on an old zigzag footpath up from near the *Palais Asmâa*, the sister hotel to Kasbah Asmâa.

Eating

Most of the hotels we've reviewed have dependable restaurants, and many offer competitive half- or full-board deals. For a delightful evening meal, try the garden restaurant at *Auberge Chez Ali* which offers set menus from 80dh; most of the food comes straight from Ali's walled vegetable garden. Those on tighter budgets should head for the *Texas Grill* and other cafés clustered around the intersection of Avenue Allal Ben Abdallah and Boulevard Mohammed V. *Hôtel Rose des Sables* and the *Restaurant Timbouctou* both do inexpensive Moroccan staples, and are as popular with locals as tourists. *Le Dromadaire Gourmand*, a kilometre along the Adgz road, is also recommended.

The **dates** of the Zagora oasis are some of the finest in Morocco and stall-holders at the market sell dozens of varieties: among them, the sweet *boufeggou*, which will last for up to four years if stored properly.

Listings

Banks BMCE and the Banque Populaire on Bd Mohammed V have ATMs and will advance cash against Visa cards.
Camel trips Lots of the hotels and campsites have tie-ins with camel-riding outfits, and in some cases you might find yourself subjected to some pressure to book a ride. Trips range from half-day excursions around the hills and palmeries to the south, to full-blown three-week guided adventures. Rates, as ever, are negotiable; a good way to check out what's on offer is to ask a few of the agencies on Bd Mohammed V, such as Mohammed Chameau Gazelle, Désert et Emotion and Les Amis du Sahara, or Caravane du Sud in Amazrou. *Auberge Chez Ali* arranges recommended overnight trips to various desert locations for 350dh per night per person.
Internet access Boumessaoud Cyber/Cyber Sud on Av Hassan II; Cyber Centre, on Bd Mohammed V near the petrol station, to name two of many.
Petrol There is an Agip station by the Banque Populaire, and others by the exit from town on the Agdz/Ouarzazate road.
Post office The PTT on Bd Mohammed V offers poste restante and phones.
Shopping There's a branch of the Maison Berbère carpet/crafts shop on Av Hassan II. This is one of the best-quality outlets in the south, with other Alaoui family branches at Ouarzazate, Tinerhir and Rissani.
Souk Markets take place on Wed and Sun. There are daily stalls at the entrance for fresh vegetables and fruit.

Moving on

CTM **buses** for Ouarzazate, Marrakesh, Casablanca and, in the other direction, M'Hamid depart from the company's office on Boulevard Mohammed V; private lines leave from the *gare routière*/grand taxi park further along the street. For a rundown of destinations, see p.480.

Grands taxis have regular runs to Ouarzazate, from the rank by the *gare routière*. Grands taxis can also be negotiated for a trip south to Tamegroute and M'hamid (see opposite), and northeast to Nekob; most leave in the morning.

Le Marathon des Sables

A Frenchman, Patrick Bauer, founded the Marathon des Sables in 1986. This annual six-day event is run over 243km and is generally acknowledged as "the toughest foot race in the world". The race, which attracts around 750 runners, 200 or so from the UK, takes place in March/April and the constantly changing route has recently included places such as Tagounite, Foum Zguid and Merzouga.

The best-known British runner to complete the course is probably Chris Moon, who lost his right arm and leg clearing mines in Mozambique in 1995, but went on to run several long-distance races, including the London Marathon and the Marathon des Sables. For further information on the race contact Chris Lawrence at the UK-based company Best of Morocco (see Basics, p.00; ⓦwww.saharamarathon.co.uk), or go to the web page of the MdS organizers (ⓦwww.darbaroud.com).

West from Zagora to Foum Zguid

West from Zagora, maps indicate a *piste* that heads west to **Foum Zguid**, where it joins up with the R111 road north to Tazenakht and the N12 to Tissint and Tata (see p.514). The piste has been upgraded and may become surfaced to complete a good circuit. *Camions* (lorries) or *camionettes* (pick-ups) run daily, more on Sunday and Wednesday (souk days in Zagora), and Monday (souk day in Foum Zguid, and also a good day for onward travel). The *piste* itself is rather monotonous, though the onward roads to Tazenakht and Tata are quite scenic in parts.

Foum Zguid is a tiny town with a few small **hotels** (the best being the *Auberge Iriki*, no phone; ❶) and a few **cafés** opposite a welcome palmery and some *ksour*. It also has a campsite. There are three buses a day to Tazenakht and Ouarzazate, of which two continue to Marrakesh. In the other direction, all three run to Tissint and Tata, with one going on to reach Bou Izakarn, Goulimine and Tan Tan.

South to M'hamid

The **Zagora oasis** stretches for some 30km south of the town, where the Drâa dries up for a while, to resurface in a final fertile belt before the desert. You can follow this route all the way down: the road is now surfaced over the full 98km from **Zagora to M'hamid**, and with a car it's a fine trip with the option of a night's stop near the dunes at Tinfou, or beyond.

If you don't have transport, it's a bit of an effort; there are buses to Tamegroute and further south to M'hamid, but times are inconvenient: the CTM leaves Zagora at 7.30pm, and arrives at M'hamid at 9.30pm, but there are local minibuses which leave every hour or so. It is possible to charter a grand taxi for an early morning departure, however, which would not be too expensive if you can find a group to share costs, and limit your sights to a day visit to **Tamegroute** and the **sand dunes** near Tinfou.

Tamegroute

TAMEGROUTE, 19km from Zagora, is reached by carrying on along the N9 down the east bank of the Drâa. Take care that you get onto this road; the old one to the south (6965 and still marked on some maps) to **Anagam**, on the west bank, is now out of use. It's an interesting and unusual village, a group of *ksour* and kasbahs wedged tightly together and linked by low, covered passageways with an unremarkable Saturday souk and a small potters' cooperative. Despite appearances, it was once the most important settlement in the Drâa valley.

It owes its importance to its ancient and highly prestigious *zaouia*, which was a seat of learning from the eleventh century and, from the seventeenth century, the base of the Naciri Brotherhood. Founded by Abou Abdallah Mohammed Ben Naceur (an inveterate traveller and revered scholar), this exercised great influence over the Drâa tribes until recent decades. Its sheikhs (or holy leaders) were known as the "peacemakers of the desert" and it was they who settled disputes among the *ksour* and among the caravan traders converging on Zagora from the Sudan. They were missionaries, too, and as late as the 1750s sent envoys to preach to and convert the wilder, animist-minded Berber tribes of the Atlas and Rif.

Faux guides will try to show you the way to the **Zaouia Naciri** (daily 8am–12.00pm & 2–6pm; donations expected), at the back of the square, but it's easy enough to find un-aided: look for the tall white minaret. As in centuries past, the sanctuary is a refuge for the sick and mentally ill, whom you'll see sitting round in the courtyard; they come in the hope of miraculous cures and/or to be supported by the charity of the brotherhood and other benevolent visitors. The complex consists of a *marabout* (the tomb of Naceur, closed to non-Muslims), a medersa (theological college – still used by up to eighty students, preparing for university) and – most interesting of all – a small **library**, which welcomes non-Muslim visitors. It was once the richest in Morocco, containing 40,000 volumes,most of which have now been stolen or dispersed to Koranic schools round the country, but Tamegroute preserves a number of very early editions of the Koran printed on gazelle hide, and some rare ancient books, including a thirteenth-century algebra primer featuring Western Arabic numerals, which, although subsequently dropped in the Arab world, formed the basis of the West's numbers, through the influence of the universities of Moorish Spain.

The **potters' cooperative** is on the left as you leave Tamegroute travelling towards Tinfou. Visitors are welcome (Mon–Fri 7am–7pm). Don't be surprised to find the green glaze reminiscent of Fes pottery. This is no accident; the founders of the Naciri Brotherhood wanted to develop Tamegroute. They invited merchants and craftsmen from Fes to settle in Tamegroute and two families, still working in the pottery, claim Fes forebears.

You can stay in Tamegroute at the homely *Jnane-Dar Diafa* (Ⓣ0524 840622 or 0661 348149; Ⓦwww.jnanedar.ch; ❷.), opposite the *zaouia*. Run by a welcoming Moroccan-Swiss couple, its nine rooms are set in a well-tended garden, and you can order traditional meals from 90dh.

Tinfou

Tinfou lies 10km on from Tamegroute. Standing at the edge of a line of sand dunes, it offers the first glimpse of the authentic Sahara. The dunes are a national monument; it is thought that they cover the ruins of the kasbah of Tiguida, which was once used as a bank for the trans-Saharan nomad traders, and rumour has it that there is still gold hidden beneath the sand.

Five hundred metres from Tinfou's large dune stands *Kasbah Hotel Sahara Sky* (Ⓣ0524 848562, Ⓦwww.hotel-sahara.com; ❹). Run by a German astronomer, the small astro-observatory on the hotel's roof attracts astrophotographers and astronomers from all over the world. Guests can gaze at the immense desert sky through one of seven telescopes, the largest of which was, at the time of writing, the most powerful in Morocco (with the ability to view galaxies ten billion light years away). The rooms are comfortable and the traditional Berber food good. Camel and 4WD excursions are also on offer, the best of which will take you east to the Djebel Tadrant or south towards the Djebel Bani.

Tinfou to M'hamid

About 4km south of Tinfou, you cross the Oued Drâa. The great mass of the **Djebel Bani** (1095m) rises up ahead, through which the road winds up and over a high-level pass. The next sizeable village, **TAGOUNITE** (74km from Zagora) has a **Thursday souk**, petrol station and a couple of basic cafés. A *piste* to the west – suitable for 4WD vehicles only – leads off to Foum Zguid (see p.437).

Continuing south, the road crosses another pass of the Djebel Bani, the **Tizi Beni Slimane**, to reach the last fertile belt of the Drâa, the **M'hamid el Gouzlane** – Plain of the Gazelles. A few kilometres on, at the palmery-village of **OULAD DRISS**, the Drâa turns sharply towards the west and the Atlantic; there are some well-preserved *ksour* to explore here, and a small, privately run **museum**, La Musée Big House (daily 8am–6pm; admission free, but donations welcome). Tasteful **accommodation** and camping facilities are available at the renovated *Carrefour des Caravanes* (Ⓣ0661 247929, east of the main road; ❺), which offers rooms, Berber tents, meals, a beautiful terrace and a small pool. Further out of the village in the same direction, the *Auberge Kasbah Touareg* (Ⓣ0254 848678), 800m down a *piste* off the main road, is truly off the beaten track. In business as an *auberge* since the early 1970s, the eccentric decor will charm lovers of naïve art and the warm welcome makes up for lack of luxury. There's a relaxing little garden and meals are available by request (❶) or camp for 60dh.

M'hamid

M'HAMID El DJEDID (new M'hamid), a small administrative centre built around a café-lined square, is the climax of this trip. It was once an important market place for nomadic and trans-Saharan trade, but of this role only a rather mundane **Monday souk** remains. These days, you might, as a visitor, be forgiven for thinking the village's main *raison d'être* is getting tourists onto camels – there are any number of operators, official and unofficial, who offer camel trips into the desert proper. Although smaller than the Erg Chebbi at Merzouga, the **dunes** in this area are worth visiting, the most easily accessible of which are those at **Erg Lehoudi** ("Dunes of the Jews"), 8km north, which can be reached, with guidance, by tourist vehicle via a *piste* just outside the village. They see more than their share of day-trippers and hustlers, and despite reaching a height of over a hundred metres, somehow feel rather mundane. More rewarding, if your budget can stretch to it, are the much larger, three-hundred-metre-high dunes at **Chigaga**, just under 60km away. A return trip there by camel takes around five days; by four-wheel drive you can get there in less than two hours. If you want the desert to yourself, *Carrefour des Caravanes* in Oulad Driss or *Dar Sidi Bounou* (see p.440) organize low-key camel trips to less visited dunes.

Accommodation and eating

Despite most visitors heading off to the desert as quickly as possible, there is a surprisingly wide choice of accommodation, particularly in the higher price brackets. In addition to the places listed, there are a couple of **campsites**: the best is *Hamada du Drâa* (Ⓣ0524 848086, Ⓦwww.hamada-sahara.com) which also has a range of good rooms (❷), Berber tents (50dh), a pool and a restaurant, 500m south of the village on the opposite side of the river bed. Eat at the cafés on the square or at any of the places listed below.

Chez le Pacha ⓣ0524 848696, ⓦwww.chezlepacha.com. A huge pool is at the centre of this attractive complex of romantic en-suite rooms, comfortable tents with spotless shared showers and toilets, a plush salon and lush gardens. HB ❹

Dar Sidi Bounou 4km before you reach the village. ⓣ0524 846330, ⓦwww.darsidibounou.com. This is a real find. Run by a wonderful Canadian-British artist and her Moroccan musician partner, there are four comfortable rooms in the house as well as magical Berber tents in the garden. Guests are treated as part of the family, meaning excellent food, local gossip and impromptu music sessions most nights. HB ❸

Hôtel Sahara On the village square ⓣ0661 871644, ⓔsaharatrek@hotmail.com. Slightly run down but the basic rooms are the best budget option. ❶

Hotel Tabarkat ⓣ0524 848688, ⓦwww.tabarkat.com. Opt for one of the attractive garden rooms around the pool in this well-established and comfortable mid-range hotel run by a friendly Spanish couple. ❹

Camel safaris and other excursions

There is no shortage of opportunities in M'hamid to arrange a camel safari. **Prices** are pretty standard, at around 350dh per day per person, which should include the guide, camel to carry you and your gear, three meals and a tent to sleep in. Note that if you want a longer trip, the day rate quoted may rise dramatically. Heavy rains in 2009 washed away some of the semi-permanent bivouacs around the dunes which may limit future excursions – pre-travel research is advised.

Recommended outfits include Sahara Services, opposite the *Hôtel Sahara* (ⓣ0661 776766, ⓦwww.saharaservices.info), run by Abdelkhalek "Abdul" Benalila (who also has a simple hotel just outside the village) and Zbar Travel on the village square (ⓣ0668 517280, ⓦwww.zbartravel.com) which offers sand boarding as well as camel and 4WD excursions. Ask for Ahmed. Abdulouahab Bounouda of Iguidi Tours (ⓣ0668 579415, ⓦwww.iguiditours.com) is a young man from a local nomad family and has a modest cluster of *nwala* huts and tents 2km west of the village where you get a taste of authentic nomad life (FB ❷) or ask him to take you on a tailor-made excursion.

Moving on

There's a daily CTM **bus** service leaving from the main square at 4.30pm to Casablanca, stopping at Zagora, Ouarzazate and Marrakesh; private services leave twice daily on the same route, the first at 6am and the second around early afternoon. Grands taxis also run to Zagora throughout the day, depending on demand.

The Dadès and Todra

The **Dadès**, stretching northeast from Ouarzazate, is at times harsh and desolate. Along much of its length the river is barely visible above ground, but there is a bleak beauty on the plain between the parallel ranges of the High Atlas and Djebel Sarhro – broken, black-red volcanic rock and limestone pinnacles. This makes the oases and kasbahs (it is also known as the Valley of a Thousand Kasbahs, for obvious reasons), when they appear, all the more astonishing. Each lies along the main bus route from Ouarzazate to Erfoud, offering an excellent and easy opportunity for a close look at a working oasis and, in Skoura, a startling range of kasbahs.

Trans Atlas To Demnate

This spectacular tarred road is an attractive alternative to the Tizi n' Tichka. About 15km east of Ouarzazate and before Skoura (marked as R307 on most road maps) it heads north across the plains to make a dramatic ascent through extremely barren country to reach the Tizi n'Fedrhate (2191m). The road loses this height in the descent to **Oued Tessaout** and the village of Toufrine where there is a small *gîte*. The area is popular with trekkers who use the Oued, which flows to the east, as a way to traverse the rugged terrain. After **Toufrine** there is a long ascent with some tremendous views all round before the road heads down to **Imi n'Ifri** and **Demnate** (see p.267).

Impressive though these are, however, it is the two gorges that cut out from the valley into the High Atlas that steal the show. The **Dadès** itself forms the first gorge, carving up a fertile strip of land behind **Boumalne du Dadès**. To the east is the **Todra Gorge**, a narrowing cleft in high rock walls, which you can trail by car or transit lorry from Tinerhir right into the heart of the Atlas. If you're happy with the isolation and uncertainties of the **pistes beyond**, it is possible, too, to continue across the mountains – a wonderful trip which emerges in the Middle Atlas, near Beni Mellal on the road from Marrakesh to Fes.

To the south of the Dadès, the **Djebel Sarhro** also offers exciting options either trekking on foot, or exploring its network of rough *piste* roads in a 4WD vehicle. Tours and treks can be arranged through AMIS (see p.54) or adventure tour companies abroad for in the trailhead towns of El Kelâa des Mgouna, Boumalne du Dadès and Tinerhir; alternatively, you could approach the massif from the south via Nekob (see p.474).

The Skoura oasis

The **Skoura oasis** begins quite suddenly, around 30km east of Ouarzazate, along a tributary of the Drâa, the **Oued Amerhidl**. It is an extraordinary sight even from the road, which for the most part follows along its edge – a very extensive, very dense palmery, with an incredibly confusing network of

▲ Palmeries

tracks winding across fords and through the trees to scattered groups of *ksour* and kasbahs.

SKOURA village, which lies off the main road, at the east end of the oasis, consists of little more than a souk (Monday is market day) and a small group of administrative buildings, where buses stop. For a quick, cheap bite to eat for those passing through, try one of the no-frills **restaurants** ranged around the junction where the main street peels off the bypass. *La Baraka*, *L'Atlas*, *Café du Sud* and *Restaurant La Kasbah* (also the bus stop for the CTM from Ouarzazate) all serve a standard range of omelettes, salads, tajines, brochettes and local goat's cheese.

Accommodation

Accomodation in and around the area runs the full gamut, from a basic *auberge* to one of the world's most exclusive luxury hideaways.

Auberge les Nomads Follow the main *piste* for 300m heading north from the east end of the main street ⓣ0661 896329. Rather grand for the price, with en-suite showers available and four rooms in turrets that overlook the palmery. ❷

Chez Slimani Signposted off the main road before you enter the village from the west ⓣ0661 746882. Located down a *piste* that meanders over a dry riverbed and through the palmery, this is the best budget option but can be difficult to find, especially at night; follow the orange-painted rocks. A handful of basic rooms and shared washrooms on the ground floor of an old kasbah with a sunny roof terrace overlooking the palmery and a pleasant garden; what this place lacks in comforts it more than makes up for with atmosphere. HB ❷

Dar Ahlam ⓣ0524 85 22 39, ⓦwww.darahlam.com. So exclusive there are no signs to it and nonresidents are not permitted within its walls. Hidden away in the depths of the palmery northeast of the village, amid an oasis that was once the local ruler's private falconry ground, it is as well-appointed as you'd expect for the price – which includes as many Moroccan clay scrubs and Thai massages as you can fit in. Extras such as balloon flights, camel trips and champagne picnics are priced separately. ❽

Dar Lorkam 5km from the village within the palmery ⓣ0524 85 22 40, ⓦwww.dar-lorkam.com. Follow the green triangles painted on trees. Owned by a French family, this has six lovely double rooms around a courtyard with a swimming pool at its centre. The restaurant serves a fusion of French and Moroccan cuisines. Closed Jan and July. HB ❹

Hôtel Palmerie Next to the mosque in the centre of the village ⓣ0670 732175. Also the village's main café; this has adequate rooms. ❶

Kasbah Aït Ben Moro Back on the main bypass road west of the village at *Aït Ben Moro* ⓣ&ⓕ0524 852116, ⓦwww.aitbenmoro.com. An eighteenth-century kasbah beautifully renovated by its Spanish expat owner, it comprises a dozen or so rooms, furnished and decorated in traditional style with an added stone terrace. The food is top-notch. HB ❺. Next door, the original Ben Moro family runs *Auberge Ben Moro* (ⓣ0668 763521), a more low-key operation that's half the price of their neighbour.

Kasbah la Datte d'Or Next door to *Auberge Les Nomads* ⓣ0666 934039, ⓔdattedor@hotmail.com. Run by a pair of sisters, this has decent, if dark, rooms and a roof terrace with views over the palmey. ❷

Kasbahs in the Skoura oasis

Navigating the tiny palmery roads by foot or by car can be quite confusing. If you wish to hire a guide there is no shortage of willing candidates to be found in the village (Mohammed from the *Kasbah Aït Ben Moro* would be a good choice or Skoura-born Mohammed Ouchiar who can be contacted by phone ⓣ0668 885387). In general guides expect around 50dh an hour.

Following the paths behind the *Kasbah Aït Ben Moro*, you pass the half-hidden **Marabout of Sidi Aïssa** and then the (usually dry) riverbed of the Oued Amahidil. Straight across is the **Kasbah Amahidil**, the grandest and most extravagantly decorated in the oasis. It may well look familiar; it's eminently photogenic and features in travel brochures and coffee-table books – and on the

Kasbah maintenance and destruction

Several of the Skoura kasbahs date, at least in part, from the seventeenth and eighteenth centuries, though the majority here – and throughout the Dadès oases – are relatively modern. Most of the older fortifications were destroyed in a vicious tribal war in 1893, and many that survived were pulled down in the French pacification of the 1920s and 1930s. Once a kasbah has been left unmaintained, it declines very fast – twenty years is enough to produce a ruinous state, if the *pisé* walls are not renewed.

The kasbah walls in the Dadès – higher and flatter than in the Drâa – often seem unscalable, but in the course of a siege or war there were always other methods of conquest. A favourite means of attack in the 1890s, according to Walter Harris, who journeyed here in disguise, was to divert the water channels of the oasis round a kasbah and simply wait for its foundations to dissolve.

front of the current fifty dirham note. Show up and someone will be around to let you in. It can also be reached by car, from a turning off the main road travelling west from the village; you can stay in newly refurbished rooms. HB ❸.

Beyond Kasbah Amahidil, a track heads off southwest, past a couple of tumbledown buildings to another impressive-looking kasbah, the **Dar Aït Sidi el Mati**, and from here it's possible to complete a circuit on foot back to the N10 emerging by the ruinous **Kasbah el Kabbaba**.

If you have transport – or a lot of energy – you could search out another kasbah, the isolated **Kasbah Ben Amar**. This is still lived in and well maintained. To find it, backtrack along the N10 towards Ouarzazate, and before the bridge over the Oued Amerhidl, look for a track off to the left/southeast; follow the track for a couple of kilometres and you will see the kasbah ahead. It commands magnificent views of the course of the Oued Dadès.

North of Skoura

There are further impressive kasbahs in the palmery to the north of Skoura village, but they are harder to find; a guide would be invaluable. If you decide to go it alone, drive through Skoura village and turn north following signs to *Dar Lorkham*, crossing the dry riverbed which is quite wide at this point.

After about 4km you should come to a pair of kasbahs, **Dar Aït Sous** and **Dar Lahsoune**; the former, small but once very grand, is in a ruinous state, used only for animals; the latter, once a Glaoui residence, is state-owned, and private. A further 2km drive – and directions from locals – takes you to the magnificent **Kasbah Aït Ben Abou**, which is second in Skoura only to Kasbah Amrhidil. It lies on well-farmed land and is still inhabited. Finally, on the edge of the palmery, you might follow the trail to the imposing **Marabout Sidi M'Barek ou Ali**. A high wall, broken only by a door, encloses the *marabout*, which doubles as a grain store – a powerful twofold protection on both spiritual and military levels.

Skoura to El Kelâa des Mgouna

From **Skoura** village eastwards towards **El Kelâa des Mgouna**, the road runs parallel to the Oued Drâa which flows, out of sight, across this semi-desert plateau. Six kilometres before El Kelâa des Mgouna, is a small hamlet, **Amejgag**, with the riverside *Hôtel Rosa Damaskina* (Ⓣ0524 834913, Ⓦwww.rosadamaskina.com; ❷). a small but brightly furnished place in pretty gardens, it has great charm and is frequented by the artist Charles Kerival, whose watercolours successfully capture the feel of southern Morocco. It also makes a delightful lunch stop.

El Kelâa des Mgouna and the Valée des Roses

Travelling through the Dadès in spring, you'll find Skoura's fields divided by the bloom of thousands of small, pink roses – cultivated as hedgerows dividing the plots – which were probably bought here from Persia by the Phoénicians. At **EL KELÂA DES MGOUNA** (also spelt Qalat Mgouna), 50km east across another shaft of semidesert plateau, there are still more, along with an immense kasbah-style **rose-water factory** with two prominent chimneys. Here, the Capp et Florale company, which you can visit, distils the *eau de rose*. In late May (sometimes early June), a **rose festival** is held in the village to celebrate the new year's crops: a good time to visit, with villagers coming down from the mountains for the market, music and dancing. The rest of the year, El Kelâa's single, rambling street is less impressive, though the shops are always full of rose-related products, and there's an interesting **Wednesday souk**.

Aerial photographs testify to there being 4200km of low hedges; each metre yields up to one kilo of petals and it takes ten tonnes of petals to produce two to three litres of rose oil. The petals are picked by women who start very early in the morning before the heat dries the bloom.

Kelâa also has a tradition of dagger making. The Cooperative Artisan du Poignards Azlag on the eastern edge of town will satisfy all your dagger needs under one roof. There's an interesting Jewish cemetery at Zouit el Bir, 2km east of Kelâa; look for the "Cimetière Juive" sign and knock loudly on the door for directions.

Practicalities

Buses and grands taxis pull into the junction at the centre of town, close to the three **banks** (Banque Populaire, Crédit Agricole and Wafabank), all with ATMs. Of the **hotels**, the cheapest option, on the main street, is the *Hôtel du Grand Atlas* (ⓣ0524 836838; ❶), a nondescript but serviceable little place with a hammam out the back and a simple restaurant on the ground floor. It is run by Lahcen Aaddi and his son, Mustapha, who can put you in touch, if you wish, with guides for trekking in the Djebel Sarhro (see p.447) and Djebel Mgoun. *Kasbah Dar Diafa*, (ⓣ0524 836094, ⓦwww.dardiafa-tourbiste.com; ❷) on the main road 1km west of the town, lacks character but is clean and has a reasonable café. ❷

Much the nicest place to stay, though – and reason enough to break your journey in Kelâa – is the romantic *Kasbah Itran* (ⓣ0524 837103 or 0662 622203, ⓦwww.kasbahitran.com; HB ❺), 4km north up the road from the middle of town to Bou Thrarar. Run by the hospitable Taghda brothers (all seven of them), it's a recent building in traditional style set high on an escarpment overlooking the mouth of the Imgoun river valley, with its spectacular ruined kasbah, *ksour* and irrigated gardens. The stylishly decorated rooms make the most of the views, which extend across the Dadès to the distant Djebel Sarhro and snow-covered Ighil M'Goun (4071m) in the background. Breakfasts are served on a magnificent terrace, and dinner indoors in a conventional Moroccan salon. It has a similarly attractive sister hotel 9km further along the road (ⓣ0524 837392). From Kelâa, walk or hail a grand taxi bound for Hdida.

Vallée des Roses

North of El Kelâa des Mgouna begins one of the most scenic – but least explored – regions of the southern High Atlas. Tourist literature likes to refer to it as "**La Vallée des Roses**", but in fact the famous roses are grown not so much in a single valley as a tangle of different ones, drained by rivers that converge on the village of Bou Thaghrar. Served by regular minibuses, a spectacular 35-kilometre road runs up the Hdida Valley from Kelâa to Bou Thaghrar, traversing a plateau called Imi-n-Louh – where Berber nomads still pass the winter in little caves – to cross the Jbel Ta'Louit at a 2084-metre pass. From there, you can survey the full glory of the M'Goun massif to the north; turn back here unless you have a 4WD, in which case you drop steeply via some hair-raising switchbacks to the valley floor.

An agglomeration of three villages clustered around a broad river confluence, **BOU THRARAR** (pronounced "Boot-Ag-*ra*") holds some impressive ruined kasbahs and a few **auberges**.

Trekking in the Vallée des Roses

Beyond Bou Thrarar, the *pistes* degenerate or disappear altogether, making this prime **trekking** territory, which for the most part remains blissfully beyond the reach of most 4WDs. April and May, while the roses are being harvested, are the best months to walk here, but the routes are practicable in all but the height of summer. Guides charge around 250dh per day and are essential, not just to show the way but also to help relate to local Berber people, few of whom see many trekkers. Walking and other trips are best organized through your hotel – *Kasbah Itran* is recommended for this.

Depending on the amount of time you have, a typical route in the region could range from a day-hike through the satellite villages of Bou Thrarar, to a ten-day trek north through the magnificent **Gorges d'Imgoun** (a real adventure involving hours of wading waist-deep through meltwater). With only three days to spare, the varied (and mostly dry) walk to **Amskar**, via **Iasarm**, **Alemdoun** and **Amajgag** – the conventional approach route for mountaineers bound for the M'Goun summit – would be an ideal sampler, passing through a series of pretty villages and some superb gorges.

Boumalne du Dadès

The main gateway to the Dadès Valley, the town of **BOUMALNE DU DADÈS** holds little of interest in itself and has more than its fair share of hustlers, but it's well poised for exploration of the Djebel Sarhro, as well as the bird-rich Vallée des Oiseaux.

Arrival and information

After crossing the Oued Dadès the road from Ouarzazate passes the straggle of shops and cafés which make up the town centre. To the south is a large market square where the Wednesday souk takes place. At the north of the central square is a mosque and a covered market outside of which is, along with the market square, a departure point for **grands taxis** and pitstop for long distance buses. The CTM office is 150m back towards the river. Past the square and up the hill are several hotels, a Shell petrol station, Banque Populaire and the PTT.

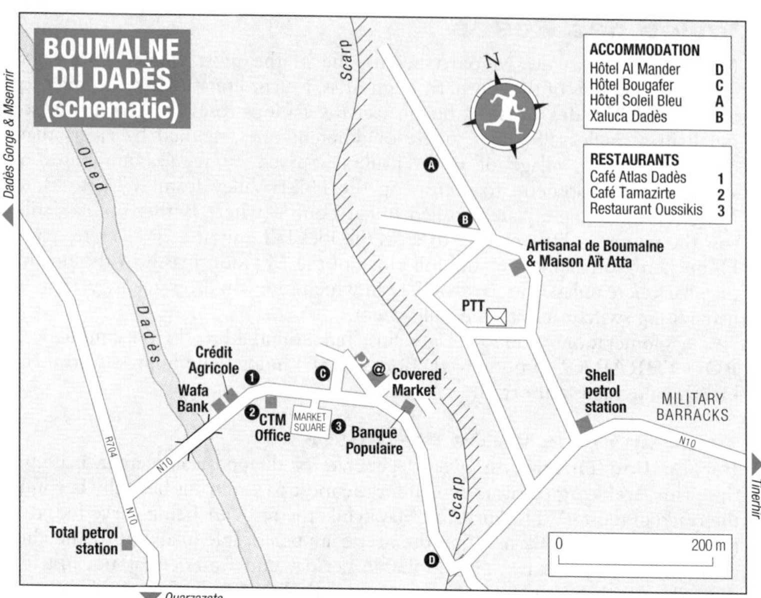

Grands taxis make regular runs to Ouarzazate and Tinerhir. For Msemrir and the Dadès Valley, you can usually get a *camion*; a *camionette* leaves for Msemrir daily between noon and 2pm, returning at dawn the next morning.

Guides for trekking and birdwatching are best contactable through the *Hôtel Soleil Bleu*, or from various hotels up the valley.

Accommodation and eating

There is a reasonable selection of **hotels**, all of which have **restaurants**, though you're generally better off eating at one of the **cafés** at the bottom of town on the main street. *Café Atlas Dadès* has a sunny terrace and smiley waiters; opposite is *Hôtel Tamazirte* which does great brochettes and has a sunny roof terrace. *Restaurant Oussikis* on the market square is good for lunch and people-watching.

Hôtel Al Mander ⓣ0524 830172, ⓔaubergealmander@hotmail.com. A well-kept but drab hotel at the top of the hill with spectacular views. It has eleven rooms with tiny balconies overhanging the escarpment, and a small restaurant. ❸

Hôtel Bougafer ⓣ&ⓕ024 830768. Best of a mediocre bunch of cheapies: small rooms with *pisé* walls, decent beds but dirty toilets. There's also a popular café on the ground floor. ❶

Hôtel Soleil Bleu ⓣ0524 830163, ⓔle_soleilbleu@yahoo.fr. Reached along a *piste*, accessed by turning off the main road at *Hôtel Vallée Des Oiseaux* and continuing through a bland military area, this place is the most appealing in its category. It has sweeping views of the valley, psychedelic decor and two kinds of room: "standard" on the ground floor and more luxurious ones upstairs. There is space for camping and budget travellers are welcome to sleep on the terrace or in the salon for 40dh. Delicious, inventive meals also. The owners, the Najim brothers, specialize in tours and treks (particularly for birdwatchers); day visits to the Vallée des Oiseaux and other promising locations (see box, opposite) are possible, and the hotel maintains an excellent birders' log. ❹

Xaluca Dadès Out towards *Hôtel Soleil Bleu*, ⓣ0524 830060, ⓦwww.xaluca.com. Seriously luxurious, seriously comfortable and seriously expensive, but the staff are friendly and non-residents are welcome to lounge around the beautiful pool drinking beer and enjoying the fine views. ❻

Hammada birds and the Vallée des Oiseaux

Boumalne offers some exceptional birdwatching and wildlife possibilities – as can be seen from the logbook at the *Hôtel Soleil Bleu* (see hotel listings). To the south of the town are abundant and accessible areas of **hammada** or desert fringe, and a grassy valley. The *hammada* provides an austere environment, whose dry, sunny conditions are ideal for cold-blooded reptiles and are frequented by Montpelier snake, Atlas agama and fringe-toed lizard. The **grassy plains** provide food for small herds of Edmi gazelle and Addax antelope and shelter for a variety of bird species such as **cream-coloured courser**, **red-rumped wheatear** and **thick-billed lark**. Predatory **lanner falcon** patrol the skies and the rare and elusive **Houbara bustard** makes an occasional appearance.

The most rewarding birding trip in the region is to the so-called **Vallée des Oiseaux**, which heads off the 6907 from Boumalne to Iknioun in the Djebel Sarhro. This is the Tagdilt track and well known to birdwatchers; it's marked by a line of green shading on the Michelin map. Here, you'll find **Temmink's horned lark**, **bar-tailed desert lark**, **eagle owl** and several **sandgrouse**: pin-tailed, crowned and black-bellied. And, for extra measure, they make traditional pottery at Tagdilt.

The Djebel Sarhro

The **Djebel Sarhro** (or Saghro) lies south of the road from Ouarzazate to Tinerhir and east of that from Ouarzazate to Zagora. It's a starkly beautiful jumble of volcanic peaks, quite unlike the High Atlas or Anti-Atlas, and punctuated by gorges, ruined kasbahs, occasional villages, and the black tents of the semi-nomadic **Aït Atta** tribe. Fiercely independent through the centuries, and never subdued by any sultan, the Aït Atta were the last bulwark of resistance against the French, making their final stand on the slopes of Djebel Bou Gafer in 1933 (see box, p.449).

The Djebel Sarhro is becoming well known through **trekking** operators like Explore and Sherpa Expeditions (Ⓦwww.explore.co.uk, Ⓦwww.sherpaexpeditions.com). They operate here from October to April, when the High Atlas is too cold and snow-covered for walking; in the summer, Sarhro itself is impracticable, being too hot and exposed, and with water, always scarce, quite impossible to find. In fact, Djebel Sarhro means "dry mountain" in Berber.

Independent exploration of the range is possible by **4WD** (many roads on our map are passable by Fiat Uno in reasonable weather, although bear in mind your insurance won't be valid driving on a *piste*). Road signs are rare and flash floods often lead to diversions or worse; navigation is not easy and taking along a local guide would be useful.

A **guide** is certainly recommended for trekking. They can be contacted through the *Hôtel Soleil Bleu* and the *Hôtel Tomboctou* in Tinerhir. Alternatively, if you are approaching the Djebel Sarhro from the south, you could discuss your plans and hire a guide at Nekob, where there's a small *bureau des guides*.

Treks and routes

When planning a trek in the Sarhro, bear in mind the harshness of the terrain and the considerable distances involved. With the exception of the **Vallée des Oiseaux**, off the Boumalne–Iknioun road, which is a feasible destination for day trips (see box above), this is not an area for short treks; nor does it have much infrastructure; you will need to be prepared to camp.

Given ten days, you could set out from El Kelâa des Mgouna, explore the area west of the **Tizi n'Tazazert** and loop back to El Kelâa or Boumalne.

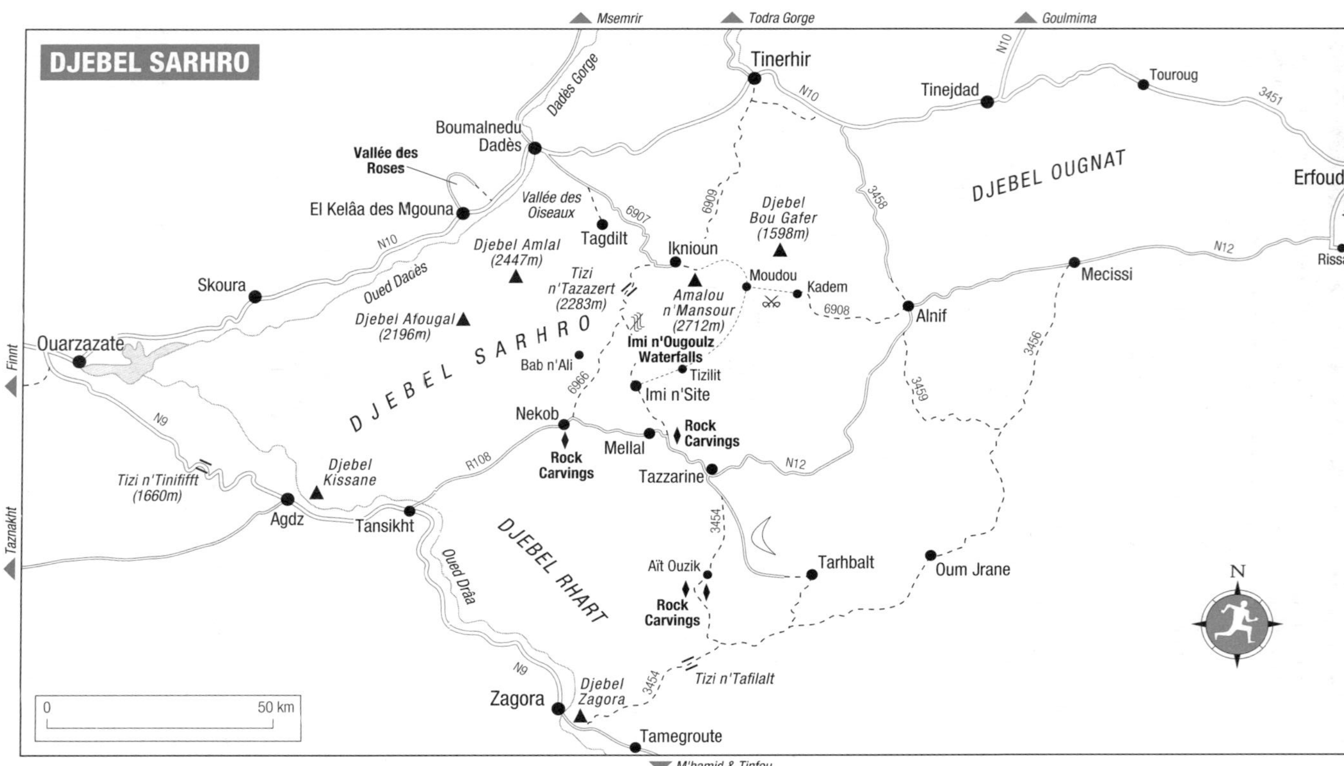
DJEBEL SARHRO
Msemrir
Todra Gorge
Goulmima
Tinerhir
N10
Tinejdad
Touroug
3451
Erfoud
N13
Rissani
N12
Dadès Gorge
Boumalnedu Dadès
Vallée des Roses
El Kelâa des Mgouna
Vallée des Oiseaux
Tagdilt
6907
6909
Iknioun
Djebel Bou Gafer (1598m)
3458
DJEBEL OUGNAT
Mecissi
Djebel Amlal (2447m)
Skoura
Oued Dadès
Tizi n'Tazazert (2283m)
Amalou n'Mansour (2712m)
Moudou
Kadem
6908
Alnif
Djebel Afougal (2196m)
Ouarzazate
Finnt
Imi n'Ougoulz Waterfalls
Tizilit
Imi n'Site
Bab n'Ali
DJEBEL SARHRO
3456
3459
6966
Nekob
N9
Rock Carvings
Mellal
Tazzarine
Djebel Kissane
Tizi n'Tinififft (1660m)
R108
Agdz
Tansikht
Taznakht
DJEBEL RHART
Oued Drâa
3454
Aït Ouzik
Tarhbalt
Oum Jrane
N
Zagora
Djebel Zagora
Tizi n'Tafilalt
Tamegroute
M'hamid & Tinfou
0
50 km

Alternatively, with about five days free, you could travel by local taxi from Boumalne du Dadès or Tinerhir to **Iknioun** and then walk south, by **Djebel Bou Gafer**, to **Imi n'Site** and **Nekob**, taking local transport from there either back to Boumalne or Tinerhir or across to Tansikht on the Ouarzazate–Zagora road. You could also do the latter trip in the opposite direction from the Drâa Valley, arranging a guide at **Nekob**.

Iknioun to Nekob

The easiest access to the range for **trekkers** is a transit taxi from Boumalne to **IKNIOUN**, where the sealed road ends; this runs most days, but Wednesday, after the Boumalne souk, is the most reliable. There are **rooms** in Iknioun, if you wish to stay. Alternatively, you can ask to be dropped at the junction of the *piste* 7km before Iknioun (there is a large sign here, so you shouldn't miss it), which you could follow in two or three days' **walk to Nekob** (35km). The people at the village 1km along the Nekob road will provide rooms for a first night's stop, though walkers should be prepared to camp beyond here. The Nekob souk is on a Sunday so you could plan to pick up a ride on the Saturday.

Following this route – which is also practicable with a 4WD vehicle – it takes about an hour's walk to reach a junction (at 2014m) to Tiouft: turn left here

The battle for Bou Gafer

For three centuries or more, the **Aït Atta** tribe were the great warriors of the south, dominating the Djebel Sarhro and its eastern extension, the Djebel Ougnat. At the beginning of the twentieth century, the British journalist Walter Harris reported seeing the young men at Touroug, one of their tribal strongholds (see map opposite), practising running with galloping horses, holding onto their tails – a breakneck skill which enabled those on foot to travel as fast as the riders.

As guerrilla fighters, the Aït Atta resisted the French occupation from the outset. Led by **Hassou Ba Salem**, they finally retreated, at the beginning of 1933, to the rocky stronghold of the **Djebel Bou Gafer**, a chaos of gorges and pinnacles. Estimates vary, but the Aït Atta had at least a thousand fighting men, who, together with their families, totalled around 7000 people, accompanied by their flocks. They faced vastly superior French forces. Ali, the son of Hassou Ba Salem, says that, according to his father, these included 83,000 troops and four aircraft squadrons.

David Hart in the *Aït 'Atta of Southern Morocco* (1984) concluded that this was "the hardest single battle which the French had ever had to fight in the course of their 'pacification' of Morocco". The French first attacked the stronghold on February 21 and, after that, there were almost daily attacks on the ground and from the air. Many died on both sides but the Aït Atta did not surrender for over a month, by which time they were reduced to half their strength and had run short of ammunition. The victors, moving in on March 25, occupied, according to one of them, "an indescribable charnel house".

Hassou Ba Salem's conditions on surrender included a promise that the Aït Atta could maintain their tribal structures and customs, particularly insofar as law and order were concerned, and that they would not be "ruled" by the infamous T'Hami el Glaoui, the pasha of Marrakesh, whom they regarded as a traitor to their homeland. The French were content to accept, the battle meaning that their "pacification" was virtually complete, and giving them access to the valuable silver and copper mines at Moudou.

Hassou Ba Salem died in 1960 and was buried at Tagia, his birthplace, 5km from Tinerhir. Ali, his son, succeeded him as leader of the tribe, and took part in the 1975 Green March into the Western Sahara. He died in 1992 and is also buried at Tagia. As for the battlefield itself, local guides will show you the sites, including ruins of the fortress. It is still littered with spent bullets, which are covered in spring by colourful clumps of thyme, rockroses and broom.

and climb steadily for an hour to a *faux* col, and then across an easy plateau for half an hour to the true col, **Tizi n'Tazazert** (2283m) where an enterprising family has set up small café and auberge, a handy base for exploring the surrounding peaks. The piste then works down through a harsh landscape with views to tabletop mesas and volcanic cones to the west, and the most notable feature of all, the Bab n'Ali (Gate of the Pinnacles) to the east. There are a couple of small *gîtes* once down from which the Bab n'Ali can be reached in half an hour on foot, and is spectacular at dawn or dusk. The piste runs down a remarkably green valley before climbing out to wander a barren waste to Nekob (see p.474).

Other driving routes

In addition to the **north–south route** over the **Tizi n'Tazazert** to Tansikht, it is possible to drive over a much lower pass, the **Tizi n'Tafilalt**, to Zagora. There are also **east–west routes** between **Tansikht** and **Rissani** (in Tafilalt), which are much better established and are described at the end of the Ziz valley section (see pp.472–474). The road from Iknioun to Tinerhir is very beautiful but only passable in a 4WD.

From these roads, there are astonishing views of the surrounding mountains, of which the most notable are **Djebel Afougal** (2196m), **Djebel Amlal** (2447m) and, the highest, **Amalou n'Mansour** (2712m). All of them are climbed by one or other of the trek operators. **Djebel Bou Gafer** (1598m) is lower and less remarkable but its history (see box, p.449) adds interest; it can be approached on foot from Moudou or Kadem, though either way a guide is again advisable and you may need to camp overnight to make the most of a visit to the battlefield.

Other less demanding attractions include the **Imi n'Ougoulz waterfalls** and **prehistoric rock carvings** near Nekob, Mellal and Tazzarine (local guides are essential for all of these).

The Dadès Gorge

The **Dadès Gorge**, with its high cliffs of limestone and weirdly shaped erosions, begins almost immediately north of Boumalne. Leaving the N10, you follow the R704 road, signposted "Mserhir" (Msemrir). Most travellers cover the first 25km or so by car or taxi, then turn back, which makes for a fine day's trip, but there are so many good hotels in this stretch it would be a shame not to stay in one of them. If you have a 4WD you could try to **loop over to the Todra Gorge** or continue **up and across the High Atlas** to the Beni Mellal–Marrakesh road. Alternatively, a couple of days' walking in and around the gorge from one of its many hotels will reward you with superb scenery, and plenty of kasbahs and *pisé* architecture to admire; there are rooms to rent in several of the villages en route to Msemrir.

The Dadès Gorge is accessible by local transport from Boumalne, with Peugeot taxis, transit vans and Berber pick-ups (*camionettes*) and lorries (*camions*) leaving regularly from the market square for Aït Ali (25km) and less often to Msemrir (63km). Pick-ups run occasionally to Atlas villages beyond but they do so more often on the Todra Gorge route (see p.458), which would make an easier access point if you plan to cross the Atlas on local transport. Returning to Boumalne, a transit/minibus leaves Msemrir daily at 4am. See **map** p.459 for routes.

The road up the **Dadès Gorge** is surfaced all the way to Aït Hani, and beyond to Rich; the route from Aït Hani to Imilchil is under construction.

There is a move to surface existing *pistes* and create new dirt tracks to link all villages of any size so this has opened up trade/transport links to a remarkable extent.

The lower Dadès has gentle slopes, with fields and both modern houses and older *ksour*. In winter, temperatures in the gorge plummet at night and when choosing accommodation it's worth looking into what is on offer in terms of heating.

Boumalne to Aït Oufi

About 8km along the road (R704) into the gorge from Boumalne, you pass the old **Glaoui kasbah** of Aït Youl. There is a garish hotel here, *Kasbah d'Idis* (Ⓣ0524 830003, Ⓦwww.goecities.com/kasbahidis; ④), which commands splendid views from its sunny terrace. Rooms are modern, clean and well appointed and the food is freshly prepared to authentic Berber recipes – the jams at breakfast are particularly good. Shortly after, you climb over a little pass, flanked by the *Café-Restaurant Meguirne,* 14km from Boumalne (Ⓣ0668 763804; ①). The views make this a fine place to stop for lunch (as tour groups do); it also has seven basic, cheap en-suite **rooms** for rent and sleeping space on the terrace. Ali, the unfailingly cheerful owner, also prepares meals – in summer, his breakfast terrace is the first in the valley to catch the sun. Nearby is a hidden side-valley, entered by a narrow gorge, in which Ali takes a proprietary interest, organizing enjoyable half-day hikes and bivouacs.

The most impressive rock formations in this area lie another few kilometres along the road at **Tamnalt**, where an extraordinary cliff known by the locals as the "Body Rocks" rises from the far side of the valley. Geologically the rock is a weathered conglomerate of pebbles which probably lay where a huge river entered a primordial sea. A gorge, in places only a few feet wide, can be followed right through the rocks (ask locally). *Hôtel Tamlalte* (Ⓣ0672 098807, Ⓦwww.hoteltamlalte.com; HB ③) 16 km from Boumalne has great views, dated but clean rooms, couches in the salon for 50dh and camping facilities. They organize a good range of tours, too.

Beyond Tamnalt, the valley floor is less fertile and the hills gentler. The road continues through the hamlet of Aït Ali to a spot known as **Aït Oudinar** (22km from Boumalne), where a bridge spans the river, and the gorge narrows quite dramatically. *Hôtel Les 5 Lunes* (Ⓣ0524 830723, Ⓔles5lunes@hotmail.com; ③) is a delightful place oozing romance; traditionally decorated rooms, excellent home-cooked food and a telescope on the terrace make this one of the nicest places in the gorge. Nonresidents are welcome to eat and star gaze, but book ahead.

Auberge Chez Pierre (Ⓣ0524 830267, Ⓔchezpierre@ifrance.com; HB ⑤) is an altogether more upmarket affair. Situated another 3km further along the road it is owned and run by an expatriate Belgian chef who provides one of the finest tables in Morocco; he is said to hold his own amongst Michelin-starred chefs in London and Paris. Eight tastefully decorated rooms occupy a traditional-style *pisé* building, with its own pool and well-kept gardens. Nonresidents can have dinner for 225dh but must book. Very good wine available, too.

Accommodation in the gorge

The gorge's largest concentration of hotels lies a further 5km up the road (27km from Boumalne), hemmed in by slabs of cliff and are listed here in order of appearance. Note that all offer terrace/riverside camping for significantly less than room prices.

Auberge le Vieux Château ⓣ0524 831261, ⓔlevieuxchateau@gmail.com. A range of rooms (some with balconies, all with excellent towels) and in winter installs heaters on request. The salon restaurant is intimate and cozy and the welcome is warm. There is also a handy supermarket next door. HB ❷

Auberge Tissadrine ⓣ0524 831745, ⓔaguondize@yahoo.fr. Located next to the river, has been recently refurbished in keeping with traditional style. Walks are on offer from here with guides who charge 200dh a day. HB ❷

Hôtel Berbère de la Montagne 34km from Boulmalne, ⓣ0524 830228, ⓦwww.berbere-montagne.ift.fr. One of the best-value mid-scale places in the area – with six tastefully furnished, immaculately clean rooms (some en suite), and carefully prepared meals served on a lovely streamside terrace. The hotel also has a campsite and makes a good base for short walks in and around the gorge. ❸

Hotel Café Timzzillite ⓣ0524 830533. Worth a coffee stop at least. Stupendous views, spotless rooms, various excursions and a souvenir shop. Probably the best budget option. ❷

Hôtel la Kasbah de la Vallée ⓣ&ⓕ0524 831717, ⓦwww.kasbah-vallee-dades.com. A long-established hotel with a friendly English-speaking proprietor, Hammou, who offers comfortable rooms, balconies, hearty food, and open fires in winter. Apart from *Chez Pierre*, this is the only place with a liquor license in the gorge. HB ❷

Sourse Dadès ⓣ0524 831258. Just before the gorge narrows, this ranks among the friendliest and best situated places to stay hereabouts. A traditional building that catches the sun in winter, it comprises only four rooms, all impeccably clean; charm is derived from its striking location and hospitable service. The owners, Ahmed Oussidi and his brother, can point you in the direction of many walks in the area, including one to the ridge above the guesthouse via an old spring. HB ❷

Aït Oufi to Msemrir

After passing the *Hôtel Berbère de la Montagne*, the road climbs by a coil of hairpin bends above the gorge, before squeezing through a tight, narrow gap to reach **Taghia n'Dadès** where there is the small and basic *Café-Hôtel Taghia* (no electricity, no phone and limited toilet facilities; ❶). From here, you can scramble east up the hill to a cave with stalactites, or walk north to a small but impressive gorge, with views down over the Dadès Valley.

Spring floods permitting, it is usually possible to drive on to Msemrir (63km in all from Boumalne). For a distance, the east side of the gorge is dominated by the **Isk n'Isladene** cliffs and then the road follows a canyon to **Tidrit** where it snakes up and crosses the face of one of the huge canyon loops before the final run to Msemrir. Two kilometres before Msemrir, the **Oussikis** valley, to the left, can be visited by an even rougher *piste*.

Msemrir and beyond

MSEMRIR, little more than a scattering of dusty government buildings and cafés, has a desultory, frontier feel to it. The lively Saturday souk provides the only real incentive to stop, but you might want to use the village as a staging post in a longer journey across the mountains. In this case you can find a room at the *El Warda* (ⓣ0524 831609; ❶), a rundown little guesthouse on the main drag or the nearby *Agdal* (no phone; ❶); a shabby café with a few rooms upstairs.

Beyond Msemrir, you've a choice of onward *piste* routes which are presented where the *piste* divides one kilometre outside Msemrir. One route heads east to join the Todra Gorge at Tamtatoucht (6–8hr by 4WD) while the other heads north across the High Atlas.

Over the Atlas

Heading over the High Atlas, the most direct route is to join the road from Todra at Agoudal: 60km or so of very rough driving, over the **Tizi n'Ouano**; it should only be tackled between May and September. Some details of the route beyond are included in the Todra Gorge section (see pp.458–460).

If you are looking for local transport, you may strike lucky with a lorry from Msemrir to Agoudal, but the route isn't driven nearly as regularly as that from Todra, so be prepared for a long wait at Msemrir.

Across to Tamtatoucht

If you are intent on **crossing the Todra Gorge** to Tamtatoucht, there is virtually no chance of a local lorry, though you might just find a lift with fellow tourists. It's a long, uphill haul from the Dadès, and the seventy-odd kilometres of *piste*, often in a shocking state, can take a full day to travel. Most Atlas crossings are made from Tinerhir via the Todra Gorge as the route is considerably easier when driving from the opposite direction.

The Tamtatoucht track keeps on up the dry Oued Tiffaouine valley to reach **Tizi n'Uguent Zegsaoun** (2639m) followed by climbing up the ensuing gorge following the **Tizgui n'Ouaddou** Valley which eventually arrives at a pass where the view opens out to the plains stretching to Aït Hani. The next section is defined by an extremely rugged descent over limestone which finally joins the plain and crosses it to hit the Tamtatoucht/Aït Hani *piste* (see p.460).

Tinerhir (Tinghir)

TINERHIR is largely a base for the trip up into the **Todra Gorge** – but it's also a more interesting place than other administrative centres along this route. It's overlooked by a ruinous but ornamental Glaoui kasbah, and just east of the modern town is an extensive palmery, which feels a world apart, with its groups of *ksour* built at intervals into the rocky hills above. Don't be in too much of a hurry to catch the first lorry up to the Todra Gorge – the Tinerhir and, to the northeast, Todra **palmeries** are major attractions in themselves.

The palmeries seem all the more special after the **journey from Boumalne**: a bleak drive across desolate plains, interrupted by the sudden oases of **Imiter** (with several fine kasbahs) and Timadriouine. The **Djebel Sarhro** (see p.447) looms to the south for the latter part of the trip, dry barren outlines of mountains, like something from the Central Asia steppes; the drama of this part of the range was another memorable backdrop in David Lean's *Lawrence of*

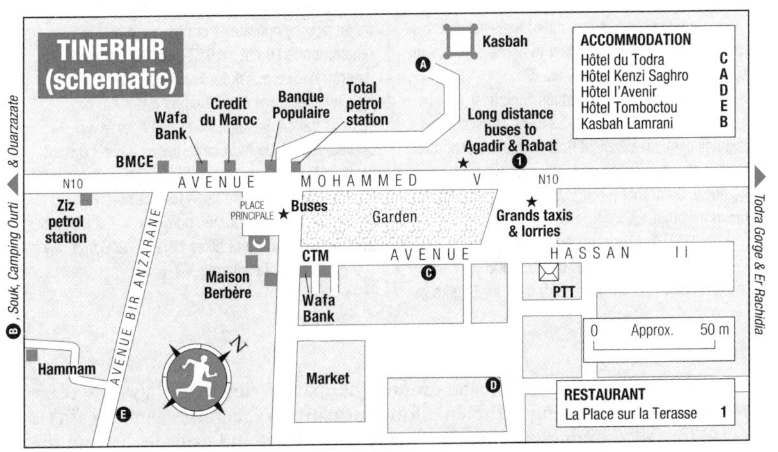

Arabia. There is a heavenly place to stay on this bleak road. *Riad Timadrouine* (27km from Boumalne de Dades, 26km from Tinihir ⓣ0515 933980, ⓦwww.riadtimadrouine.com) is owned by a French sea captain with a fine eye for nautical antiques. A traditional *pisé* riad, it has five exquisite rooms with *tadelakt* bathrooms, a small pool and a stunning roof terrace complete with jacuzzi and hammam. HB ❺, or have a party and rent the whole place for only €200.

Arrival and information

Orientation is straightforward. The centre of Tinerhir is a long **garden square**, flanked by hotels, café-restaurants and the **PTT**; here are to be found the **grands taxis** for standard runs to Boumalne, Er Rachidia and Erfoud and the **lorries** which go up the Todra Gorge to Tamtatoucht and Imilchil. In the **Place Principale** to the southwest of the garden square are the local **buses** and **CTM** office; long-distance buses, passing through Tinerhir en route for Agadir and Rabat, call here or stop on Avenue Mohammed V facing the central garden.

There are now téléboutiques all over town; for **bicycle rental**, try *Hôtel l'Avenir* (see below) or Kasbah Lamrani. If you're interested in buying **crafts**, Tinerhir has a branch of the excellent **Maison Berbère** chain which has high-quality rugs, carpets and especially silver. There are now two shops, both near the Place Principale.

Accommodation

There's a campsite, *Camping Ourti* (ⓣ0524 833205), on the Boumalne road, beyond the souk. The site is enthusiastically managed by a young crowd, open year-round and has a range of facilities – including hot showers and a swimming pool (June–Sept). There's a restaurant (60dh) and a few bungalows, which sleep up to three people (75dh per head). The site can also arrange 4WD transport, driver and guide for the gorge, or other expeditions.

Hôtel du Todra Av Hassan II ⓣ0524 834249, ⓔhaddou64@gmail.com. Open since 1935, this is a cheery, eccentrically decorated place with a range of differently priced rooms. There's also a pleasant terrace and bar. ❷–❸

Hôtel Kenzi Saghro On the hill to the north of the centre ⓣ0524 834181, ⓦwww.bougafer-saghro.com. Dowdy rooms in this dated four-star but it has a huge pool and bar open to nonresidents with suberb views of the palmeries. ❹

Hôtel l'Avenir In the pedestrian zone near the central market ⓣ&ⓕ0524 834599, ⓔavenirhotel@gmail.com. An excellent little budget hotel above a cluster of shops, with good-value rooms but it can be noisy. Great roof terrace where you can bed down for 30dh. ❶

Hôtel Tomboctou Av Bir Anzarane ⓣ0524 834604, ⓕ024 833505, ⓦwww.hoteltomboctou.com. A kasbah built for Sheikh Bassou in 1944, tastefully converted by Moroccophile Spaniard Roger Mimó, this is one of the country's memorable small hotels. There's a range of tasteful and cosy rooms all cool in summer and heated in winter, including some in a separate "riad" style area. There's also a pool in the courtyard, and a small bar. The Suprateam travel agency operates from here – a highly recommended outfit. ⓣ0524 888901, ⓦwww.supratravel.com. Ask for Farid. ❺–❻

Kasbah Lamrani Av Mohammed V, 1 km or so west of the centre ⓣ0524 835017, ⓦwww.kasbahlamrani.com. A large upscale hotel owned by the Alaoui family, in ersatz kasbah style but with all mod cons including huge terraces with fountains, two restaurants, gardens, bar, a big pool, and decent food. Rent bikes here for 200dh a day – a great way of exploring. ❺

Eating

Breakfast well at any of the cafés around the market; this area is also the place to stock up on trekking and picnic food for trips up the gorge. Tinerhir isn't a place for fancy dining but there are many cheap cafés and grillades around the centre where you can fill up at any time of day. *Hôtel du Todra* does reasonable food from its terrace overlooking the action, as does *La Place Sur La Terrasse* opposite the grand taxi station.

Moving on

There are hourly **buses** from Tinerhir to Ouarzazate, many of which go on to Marrakesh, four daily go to Fes and Midelt, two to Meknes (5.30am & 5pm) and two to Rissani and Merzouga (8.30am and 5.15pm). **Grands taxis** in both directions (places available for Ouarzazate/Boumalne/Er Rachidia/occasionally Erfoud and Rissani).

Berber lorries (*camions*) make regular runs to villages in the **Todra Gorge and beyond**; on Mondays, from around noon (following the souk), numerous lorries set out for Atlas villages, including one that goes right over the mountains to Arhbala, driving through the night. Note that you can also arrange transport (and/or trips) for the **Todra Gorge** (or beyond) through the *Hôtel Tombouctou* or *Camping Ourti* (see opposite).

The Tinerhir and Todra palmeries

Palmeries extend southeast and northeast of Tinerhir, lining both sides of the Todra River. The *Hôtel Kenzi Saghro* has the town's best viewing point from its terrace bar. To explore, you're best off renting a **bicycle** from the *Hôtel L'Avenir* in town or *Kasbah Lamrani* – ride on the west side of the valley, where the road is higher, with better views (it's best late in the afternoon when the sun is low and the colours at their most vivid). Alternatively, catch a taxi or hitch out to the group of hotels and campsites at the entrance to the gorge (see pp.456–457),

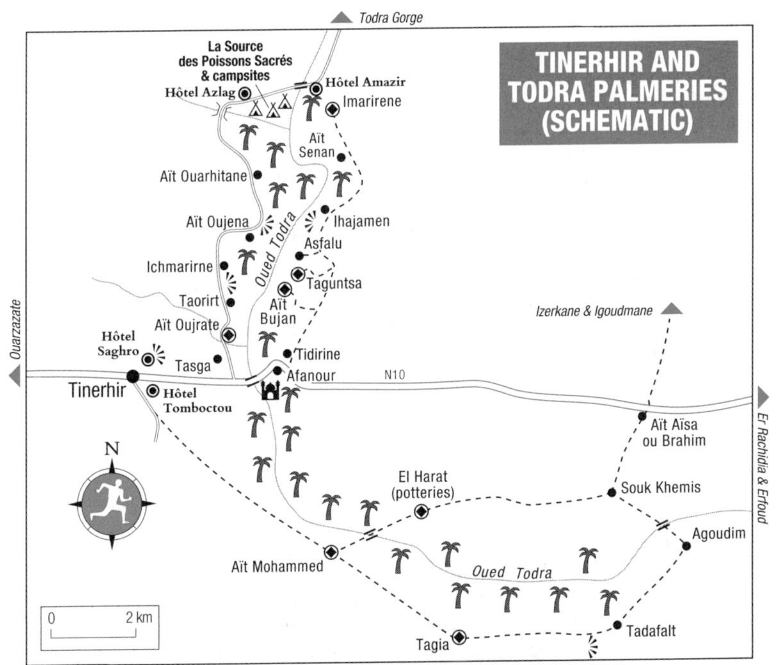

and head south into the palmery on foot from there. Once in the palmery proper, the main paths are easy to follow, and you can peel west at any stage to rejoin the main road, which runs above the houses.

Our map indicates several good viewing points, or **miradors**, and also names the most picturesque villages – many of which have **ksour and kasbahs** with extraordinarily complex patterns incised on the walls. In the small village of **AFANOUR** (see map, p.455) an old earth mosque has been restored; it makes a pleasant destination for an afternoon ramble around the palmeries and provides a rare opportunity to see the interior of ancient mosque architecture (entry 20dh; ask at *Hôtel Tomboctou* for more information).

Southeast of Tinerhir there are potteries at **El Harat**, while at nearby **Tagia** are the tombs of the Aït Atta's chiefs, Hassou Ba Salam, and his son, Ali Ba Salam (see box, p.449). There's a *marabout* near El Harat which is the focus of a June/July moussem; this area was originally settled by black slaves who were known as Haratin. For more on the approach to the gorge – see below.

The Todra Gorge

Most tourist itineraries include a stop at the **Todra Gorge**, and with good reason. At its deepest and narrowest point, only 15km from Tinerhir, this trench through the High Atlas presents an arresting spectacle, its gigantic rock walls changing colour to magical effect as the day unfolds. Taxis drop passengers off at a grouping of budget hotels just before the narrowing of the gorge. For the return journey, you stand a better chance of a taxi if you walk back to the *Zaouia* Sidi Abdelâli, 3km south of the gorge, or hitch a lift with day visitors or other tourists. There are many *faux guides* hanging around the gorge but the hassle is generally low key. At weekends and holidays, there's a cheerfully laid-back vibe – locals more than outnumber tourists; dudes cruise on motorbikes flirting with the girls and families come to picnic by the river. Check hotels' guest books for up-to-date info on reliable guides.

Flash flooding has damaged the road up the Todra to the villages of Tamtatouche, 32km from Tinerhir and Aït Hani, a further 15km, but the road is still easily passable by car. Minibuses run regularly throughout the day to these villages from the eastern end of the municipal gardens in Tinerhir.

Beyond Aït Hani, *pistes* continue **over the Atlas** via the village of **Imilchil** (famed for its annual wedding market; see p.461), while another loops over to the Dadès Valley. You can arrange transport along the Imilchil route, either by chartering it at Tinerhir, or by paying for a place on a series of Berber lorries, which shuttle across for village souks. If you take your time – up to four hours – it is just about passable in a normal car.

Tinerhir to the gorge

En route to the gorge proper, the road climbs along the west flank of the Todra palmery (see map, see p.455), a last, fertile shaft of land, narrowing at points to a ribbon of palms between the cliffs. There are more or less continuous villages, painted the pink-grey colour of the local rock, and the ruins of kasbahs and *ksour* up above or on the other side.

Around 9km from town, you cross a tributary of the Todra, and come to a string of well-established **campsites** and **hotels**, flanking a particularly luxuriant stretch of the palmery. *Auberge Camping de la Source des Poissons Sacrés*

(Ⓣ0668 255309; ❶) is the best choice here, with rooms and shady camping. It also boasts a spring flowing into a pool where a shoal of sacred fish swim, a dip in which is said to cure infertility.

A short way further up the road, 15km from Tinerhir, is the delightfully quirky *Riad Todra* (Ⓣ0676 740341; ❷). Run by a very friendly family, this rambling building has basic but clean rooms, or couches in the tent on the roof for 20dh, a wonderful terrace overlooking the river and plays lots of reggae. Further up, and more upmarket *Dar Ayour* (Ⓣ0524 89527, Ⓔcontact@darayour.com; ❷) is a little gem. Chic, traditionally furnished rooms, a gorgeous terrace and a garden running down to the river, this offers great value for money.

The mouth of the gorge

The really enclosed section of **the gorge** extends for just a few hundred metres; it should certainly be walked, even if you're not going any further, for the drama of the scenery.

It's possible to stay right at the foot of the 300-metre cliffs, where there's a cluster of small **hotels**. Given the traffic and crowds of tourists and hustlers who mill around them through the day, they're far from peaceful, and in winter can be very cold as the sun only reaches them at midday. However, things calm down considerably in the evening after the day-trippers have left, and their rooftops make ideal vantage points from which to admire the escarpments. Climbers congregate at the three budget places just before the entrance to the gorge, which all offer simple rooms with shared facilities from 60–100dh, in addition to dorm beds in salons from 30dh. They also keep log books with useful route descriptions for climbers. Pick of the crop, and generally cleaner than the competition, is the *Hôtel la Vallée* (Ⓣ0524 895126; ❶–❷). Inside the most dramatic section of the gorge, beneath vast overhanging cliffs, are two mid-range places, *Les Roches* (Ⓣ0524 89513, Ⓦwww.les-roches.mezgarne.com; ❸–❹) and *Yasmina* (Ⓣ0524 895118; ❷–❸). Both offer a choice of accommodation, including en-suite rooms, or cheaper beds in the salon or tent dining areas, or out on the terrace. Prices fluctuate according to season and thus demand.

▲ The Todra Gorge

Five kilometres from the mouth of the gorge, situated on a bank opposite the road *Hotel Le Festival* (0661 267251, www.aubergelefestival.com; 2) is the only accommodation option between the mouth of the gorge and the village of Tamtatoucht. This intimate solar-powered hotel and campsite with its solitary location in the middle of the gorge has a truly rustic feel and provides an excellent base for climbers and trekkers with good guides and climbing kit for hire. Apart from the simple, comfortable rooms on the first floor of the hotel there are five inventive en-suites built into the rock below with natural cave-like interiors. A refreshingly different and atmospheric place to spend the night.

Climbing and walking

Having recognized the climbing potential of the gorge, its hotels and excursion agencies have started to cash in on equipment rental and professional climbing excursions, which makes the area ideal for the experienced independent climber. There are now more than 150 bolted routes, French Grade 5+ to 8, of between 25m and 300m, with new ones being added each year. It's worth consulting the logbooks at various hotels in the gorge which will alert you to any **problems** on the rock: over the past few years, kids have tampered with several access bolts, and even fixtures for top ropes. Hassan Mouhajir (0678 364515), has been working on the most comprehensive topographical guide to the bolted routes in the area and can be hired as a climbing guide for 500dh per person per day.

Most of the guides hanging around the gorge try to lead visitors on **walks**, but for the following route, which takes around one and a half to two hours to complete, you won't need help to find the way. It starts just beyond the narrowest section of the gorge. Once through the cliffs, look for a side valley leading quite steeply left (south) from the roadside to a pronounced saddle between two peaks – you'll be able to make out the path climbing on the left flank of the hillside. An easy ascent takes you to the pass in 45 minutes to an hour. From there you could head for the peaks for splendid views over the gorge, or follow the path dropping downhill to your left, keeping to a line of silvery-grey rocks that fringe a dry riverbed. After around thirty minutes, the path then climbs briefly to a second saddle, from which it then descends to the edge of the Todra palmery, near the *Auberge Camping de la Source des Poissons Sacrés* (see p.456).

Beyond Todra: over the Atlas

It's possible to continue via road (recently damaged by flooding) beyond the Todra Gorge to **Tamtatoucht** and Aït Hani and from there across the High and Middle Atlas ranges, to emerge on either the N8 (Azrou–Beni Mellal), or the N13 (Midelt–Er Rachidia), via the beautiful village of **Imilchil**. In between, you are travelling on isolated and at times very rough tracks, for which four-wheel-drive vehicles (or mountain bikes) are essential. With the uncertainty of road conditions in these areas it is important to enquire at Todra Gorge or Tamtatoucht hotels about conditions before attempting the route beyond **Aït Hani**. If you don't have transport, you can travel on a succession of **Berber lorry-taxis** (*camionettes*), timed to coincide with local village souks. The attractions of this journey are considerable, offering a real experience of Berber mountain life – the villagers are generally very open and friendly – and some of the most exciting scenery in Morocco, in a succession of passes, mountains, rivers and gorges.

It's also possible to cross from the Todra Gorge to the **Dadès Valley** via a *piste* starting near Tamtatoucht (see p.460); cutting through sections of unstable

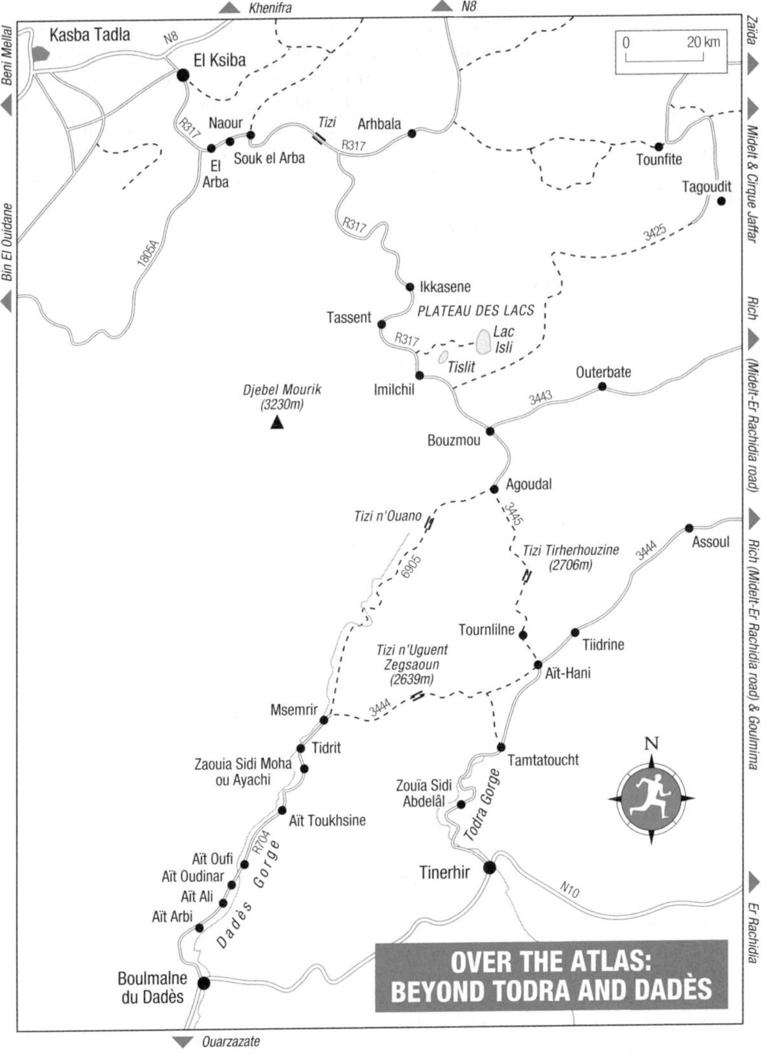

limestone strata and shouldn't be attempted in anything other than a 4WD vehicle or mountain bike.

Practicalities

There are no **banks** between Tinerhir and Khenifra/Kasba Tadla/Rich, so you'll need to have enough cash for the journey. Don't underestimate the expense of buying **food** in the mountains (30–100 percent above normal rates), nor the prices charged for rides in the **Berber lorries**; as a very general guideline, reckon on about 20dh for every 50km. There are police stations at Aït Hani and Imilchil if you need serious help or advice on the state of the *pistes*.

Setting out on the lorries from Todra, the managers of the hotels at the mouth of the gorge usually have an idea of when the next *camionette* will pass through – and will help arrange your first ride. Promising days to start out are Wednesday (to coincide with Aït Hani's Thurs souk) and Friday (for Imilchil's Sat souk), but even at other times there's usually at least one lorry or taxi minibus heading in either direction. Eventually, everyone seems to get across to Arhbala (Aghbala) or Naour (where there are buses down to Kasba Tadla/Khenifra) or to Rich (on the Midelt–Er Rachidia road; see p.256), which is nowadays connected to Imilchil via a good surfaced road served by regular minibuses.

Tamtatoucht and beyond

The road up the Todra Gorge (from the hotels) grows gradually less spectacular as you progress uphill, but with your own vehicle it's worth pressing on to **TAMTATOUCHT**, 17km beyond the gorge, for a taste of the high mountains. A sizeable sprawl with a growing number of attractive hotels and cafés (all of which have well-equipped camping areas), the village is situated beneath a ring of beautiful peaks, and with local guidance you can head off for rewarding day walks in the area. At the entrance a group of new hotels have sprung up; *Les Amis* (Ⓣ0670 234374, Ⓦwww.amistamt.ag.vu; HB ❷) is the nicest, with newly renovated rooms, camping, hearty food and impromptu music sessions. Ali, one of the seven charming brothers who run the place, has over 20 years experience climbing in these parts and he runs excellent climbs and treks. He has full climbing kit to rent but note that he does not recommend this area for beginners. Next door, *Hôtel Essalam* (Ⓣ0524 835843; Ⓔhotel_essalam@yahoo.fr; ❷) has a large pool and a warm welcome.

Next along the road is the friendly, brightly painted *Auberge Baddou* (Ⓣ0672 521389, Ⓦwww.aubergebaddou.co; ❶–❷), with camping, clean rooms, hot showers and a sunny terrace. The owner, Baddou, is one of the most experienced guides in this region. On the opposite side of the road, the *Boule de Neige* (no phone) and *Auberge Bougafer* (Ⓣ0524 702235; ❶) are in a similar mould, offering cheap beds in Berber tents as well as basic rooms. Other options line the roadside on the opposite side of Tamtatoucht, 500m further along the road, including the *Amazigh* (no phone; ❶) and *Auberge Campagnard* (no phone; ❶); the latter has a raised terrace with spectacular views.

Across to the Dadès Gorge

The turning for the *piste* that snakes **over to the Dadès Gorge** (see p.453) lies north of Tamtatoucht, near Aït Hani. This is a particularly rough route; lifts are most unlikely, so it's only an option for 4WD vehicles. The ascent takes you over limestone pavements, after which the track goes over a small pass and then up the long **Tizgui n'Ouaddou** valley towards a huge scarp before the final sweeping bends to the **Tizi n'Uguent Zegsaoun** (2639m). The difficulties then increase; the road is in a bad state with wash-outs and diversions. Only when you edge the final plain and join the Msemrir-Agoudal *piste* does it improve – by which stage Msemrir is just around the corner.

Aït Hani and on to Imilchil

Continuing north from Tamtatoucht into the High Atlas, you reach **Aït Hani**, a strange place of salt mines and waterfalls almost the size of Tamtatoucht. It's just off the main route, and if you're driving you can keep going, turning after the town, rather than into it. On the outskirts, as you approach from the south, there is a police/military post, café and store, but nowhere to stay. This region has a high and barren landscape – the locals travel amazing distances each day

The Imilchil Moussem

Held annually in September, the world-famous **Imilchil Moussem** – the "Fête des Fiancés" or "Marriage Market" – is the mother of all Moroccan mountain souks, a gathering of 30,000 or more Berbers from the Aït Haddidou, Aït Morghad, Aït Izdeg and Aït Yahia tribes. Over the three days of the fair (Fri to Sun), animals are traded, clothes, tools and provisions bought and sold, and distant friends and family members reunited before the first snowfalls isolate their high villages. But what makes it especially highly charged is that it is here the region's youngsters come to decide who they're going to marry.

The tradition derives from colonial times, when the officials from the Bureau des Affaires Indigènes used to insist the Berbers assembled in Agdoul, site of a yearly transhumance fair, to register births, deaths and marriages. After independence the custom was encouraged by the Moroccan tourist office, which the locals blame for propagating the myth that the marriages contracted here were entered into spontaneously. In fact, the matches are nearly all arranged in advance and merely formalized at the moussem. All the same, the fair provides the perfect opportunity for unmarried Berbers – particularly women trapped at altitude for most of the year – to survey their prospects. Dressed in traditional finery, with heavy jewellery and eyes rimmed with heavy black *kohl*, the girls parade around in groups, flirting outrageously with the boys as eagle-eyed elder relatives look on. Later, singing, dancing and drumming give both sexes further opportunities to mingle.

Unfortunately, the influx of tourism has seriously compromised the authenticity of the event, and while local life continues with its serious market and marriage elements, a pure folklore festival for tourists has been shifted up to the Tislit lake. Neither part is actually at Imilchil, of course, and the date is not always easy to discover – contact the ONMT for details. Rates for beds, food and water (which has to be brought in by lorry) tend to be greatly inflated, so fix prices in advance. It is also advisable to bring plenty of warm clothing as the nights at this altitude (over 2000m) can get bitterly cold by the end of September.

to collect wood for fuel. A recently surfaced road leads east from Aït Hani towards Goulmima/Rich.

North of Aït Hani there is a stiff 2700-metre climb up to **Tizi Tirherhouzine**, then down to **AGOUDAL**; it's at least a three hour drive. This is a friendly village, with interesting caves nearby (ask at *Les Amis* in Tamtatoucht, see opposite) and though there's no official hotel, you'll probably be offered a room. You should be able to find a room at **BOUZMOU**, the next village on, and also pick up a *camionette* along the road east to Rich on the Midelt–Er Rachidia road.

The road north improves greatly from Agoudal on, passing beyond Bouzmou through a fertile region to reach **IMILCHIL** (45km from Agoudal). Imichil has lost some of its striking old buildings and has a sorry air these days. Its main function is simply as the regular souk for a wide region, though it's still famed for its September moussem – the so-called **Marriage Market of Aït Haddidou** (see box above) – which these days attracts streams of tourist traffic up the surfaced road from Rich, on the Er Rachidia–Midelt highway, an artery that has spurred development in the village. There are a several simple **hotels** and café-restaurants, including *Hôtel Islane* (Ⓣ0524 442806; ➊) and *Hôtel Atlas* (Ⓣ0524 442828; ➊), both of which can arrange guides and mules for treks in the area. Among the resident trekking guides; Bassou Chabout (Ⓣ0672 521389) is reliable and qualified.

Northeast of Imilchil spreads the **Plateau des Lacs** – flanked by the twin mountain lakes of **Isli** and **Tislit**, named after a couple from Berber folklore, whose love was thwarted and whose tears fell to form the two lakes. At Isli there's a rudimentary *gîte d'étape*; while at Tislit, the kasbah-style *Hôtel Tislit* (no phone; ❶) on the west bank of the lake has basic rooms, shared showers and meals – or sleep in a big nomad tent. A marvellously atmospheric spot.

The main **route north** is surfaced all the way to Arhbala, and provides a spectacular itinerary, with steep drops off the roadside and constant hairpin climbs and descents. This section has few settlements – and certainly nowhere the size of Imilchil. **ARHBALA** itself (see p.259) has a very basic hotel near the marketplace (Wed souk), and a daily bus on to El Ksiba, where you can pick up connections to Khenifra and Beni Mellal. Another surfaced road heads off to join the Khenifra–Midelt road.

Tinerhir to Er Rachidia and Erfoud

East from Tinerhir, there are a couple of interesting stops on the journey to **Erfoud/Er Rachidia** and the Tafilalt. The more attractive route is the minor road (R702) from **Tinejdad to Erfoud**; the **Er Rachidia road** (N10) is a fast but dull highway through barren country that's broken only by the oases of Tinejdad and **Goulmima**. Public transport is easily available from Tinerhir.

Tinejdad

TINEJDAD is one long street, either side of which are the usual services: petrol station, post office, bank and cafés, but it's distinguished by having two of the best museums in this region. Two kilometres before the town is the extraordinary Musée Sources Mimouna (Ⓦwww.sourcesmimouna.com; daily 9am–6pm, 40dh). Owner Zaid has been collecting artefacts including agricultural tools, pottery, jewellery and textiles for nearly 30 years, all displayed here in a beautiful complex of *pisé* buildings set around exposed underground springs. Musée des Oasis (ask for directions, daily 9am–6pm; 20dh), houses a collection of artefacts and photos showcasing local life. Guided visits (included in the ticket price) give you the chance to nose around an immaculate nineteenth century *ksar*, restored by Spanish writer and hotelier Roger Mimó, who also owns the adjacent *Maison d'Hôte el Khorbat* (Ⓣ0535 880355, Ⓦwww.elkhorbat.com; HB ❹), where a handful of rooms have been stylishly converted, with en-suite bathrooms and Berber textiles. You can also eat here at a swish little restaurant, with tasty local and Continental dishes, as well as vegetarian options. Cheaper accommodation can be found on the western outskirts of the town on the Tinerhir road at *Hotel Reda* (Ⓣ0670 675849; ❷), a clean roadside café with half a dozen rooms upstairs. There are other impressive kasbahs and *ksour* around here – ask directions to the Ksar Asrir in the palmery to the northwest of town.

Tinejdad to Erfoud

Covered by daily buses, this alternative route – **direct to Erfoud** – is, in parts, eerily impressive. It's well surfaced all the way, though sections are sometimes submerged with sand. The road branches off from the N10 to Er Rachidia 3km east of Tinejdad; next to the junction itself stands the convenient and welcoming *Café Restaurant Oued Ed-Dahab*.

From here, the road follows a course of lush oases – populated by the Aït Atta tribe, traditional warriors of the south who used to control land and exact tribute as far afield as the Drâa, 175km to the southwest and on the far edge of the Djebel Sarhro (see box, p.449).

You leave the oasis at **Mellab**, which has another fine **ksar**, and from then on it's more or less continuous desert *hammada* until the beginning of the vast palmery of **El Jorf** – the Tafilalt's largest *ksar* (population 6000) – on the approach to Erfoud. There are a few cafés in the modern village, a post office and a petrol station, but no hotel. Beside the road, over much of the distance from Mellab to Erfoud, the land is pockmarked by parallel lines of strange, volcanic-shaped humps – actually man-made entries to the old underground **irrigation channels** or *khettara*. Another curiosity, notable here and elsewhere along the oasis routes, is the Berber **cemeteries** walled off from the desert at the edge of the *ksour*. These consist of long fields of pointed stones thrust into the ground and the occasional cactus and thorn bush, but otherwise unidentified: a wholly practical measure to prevent jackals from unearthing bodies – and in so doing, frustrating the dead's entry to paradise.

Goulmima

GOULMIMA, on the way to Er Rachidia from Tinejdad is a long, straggling palmery, made up of some twenty or so scattered **ksour**. If you are interested in exploring, ask directions along the complex network of tracks to the *ksar* known as **Gheris de Charis**. Saïd Hansali, contactable through *Les Palmiers* (see below), is an excellent English-speaking guide who can show you around the labyrinthine *ksar* and adjacent palmery.

Modern Goulmima, beside the highway, is signalled by the usual "triumphal" entrance and exit arches of the south, and has little more within. There is, however, a Banque Populaire, and a small **hotel**, the *Gheris*, 101 Bd Hassan II (Ⓣ0663 783167; ❶). There' s a small internet café here and an interesting display of herbs in the ground-floor café, whose terrace is much the best place in town for breakfast. You can also stay over in the older end of town, where the *Maison d'Hôtes Les Palmiers* (Ⓣ0535 784004, Ⓦwww.palmiersgoulmima.com; HB ❸) has five pleasantly furnished rooms in the suburban home of a welcoming French-Moroccan couple. The house opens out upon a large walled garden where you can camp. The owner organizes a variety of unique 4WD excursions and treks, the highlights of which include camping in the **Gorges du Gheris** and fossil-finding day-trips in the nearby desert.

Er Rachidia, the Ziz Valley and the Tafilalt

The great date-palm oases of the **Oued Ziz** and **Tafilalt** come as near as anywhere in Morocco to fulfilling Western fantasies about the Sahara. They do so by occupying the last desert stretches of the **Ziz Valley**: a route shot through with lush and amazingly cinematic scenes, from the river's fertile beginnings at the *Source Bleue*, the springwater pool that is the oasis meeting point of **Meski**, to a climax amid the rolling sand dunes of **Merzouga**. Along the way, once again, are an impressive succession of *ksour*, and an extraordinarily rich palmery – historically the most important territory this side of the Atlas.

Strictly speaking, the Tafilalt (or Tafilalet) comprises the oases south of **Erfoud**, its principal town and gateway. Nowadays, however, the provincial capital is the French-built garrison town and administrative centre of **Er Rachidia**. If you're making a circuit of the south, you will pass through here, from or en route to Midelt – a journey through the great canyon of the **Ziz Gorges** (see p.257). Er Rachidia is also a crossroads for the route east to Figuig –which used to be an important crossing point into Algeria when the frontier was open.

Er Rachidia and around

ER RACHIDIA was established by the French as a regional capital – when it was known as Ksar es Souk, after their Foreign Legion fort. Today, it represents more than anywhere else the new face of the Moroccan south: a shift away from the old desert markets and trading routes to a modern, urban centre. The town's role as a military outpost, originally against tribal dissidence, particularly from the Aït Atta (see box, p.449), was maintained after independence by the threat of territorial claims from Algeria, and there is still a significant garrison here.

The town is, nevertheless, a relaxed place to stay, with a large student population.

Arrival and information

All **buses and grands taxis** arrive at the main bus station, on the Place Principale, just south of Avenue Moulay Ali Cherif. Er Rachidia has a functional grid layout, with most facilities – banks, cafés and restaurants, a covered market,

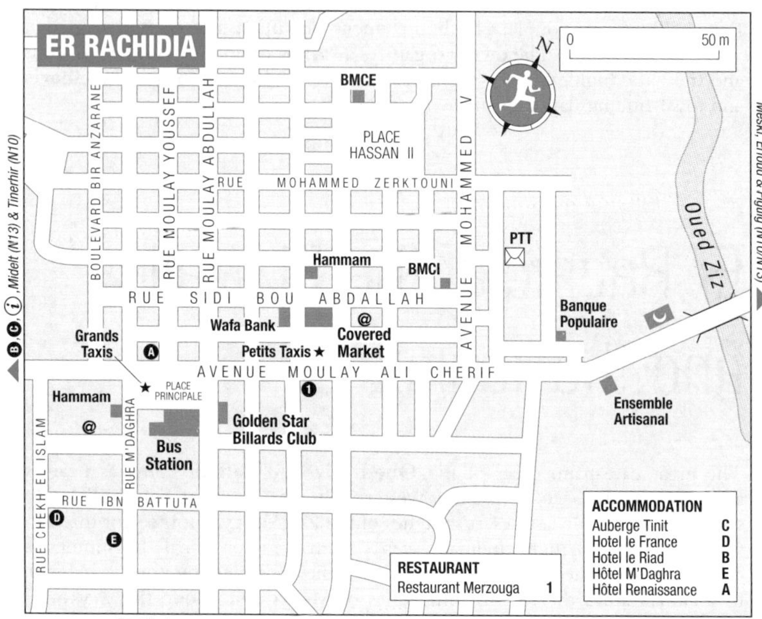

The Tafilalt: past and present

The Tafilalt was for centuries the main Moroccan terminus of the **caravan routes** – the famous **Salt Road** to the south across the Sahara to West Africa, by way of Timbuktu. Merchants travelling south carried with them weapons, cloth and spices, part of which they traded en route at Taghaza (in modern-day Mali) for local **salt**, the most-sought after commodity in West Africa. They would continue south and then make the return trip from the old Kingdom of Ghana, to the west of Timbuktu, loaded with **gold** (one ounce of gold was exchanged for one pound of salt at the beginning of the nineteenth century) and, until European colonists brought an end to the trade, with **slaves**.

These were long journeys: Taghaza was twenty days by camel from Tafilalt, Timbuktu sixty, and merchants might be away for more than a year if they made a circuit via southern Libya (where slaves were still sold until the Italian occupation in 1911). They also, of course, brought an unusual degree of contact with other cultures, which ensured the Tafilalt a reputation as one of the most unstable parts of the Moroccan empire, frequently riven by religious dissent and separatism.

The separatism had a long history, dating back to the eighth century, when the region prospered as the independent kingdom of **Sijilmassa** (see p.471); the dissent began when the *Filalis* – as Tafilalt's predominantly Berber population is known – adopted the **Kharijisite heresy**, a movement which used a Berber version of the Koran (orthodox Islam forbids any translation of God's direct Arabic revelation to Mohammed). Then in the fifteenth century it again emerged as a source of trouble, fostering the *marabout* uprising that toppled the Saadian dynasty.

It is with the establishment of the **Alaouite** (or, after their birthplace, *Filali*) dynasty that the Tafilalt is most closely associated. Mounted from a *zaouia* in Rissani by Moulay Rachid, and secured by his successor Moulay Ismail, this is the dynasty which still holds power in Morocco, through Mohammed VI, the fifteenth sultan in the line. The Alaouites were also the source of the wealth of many of the old kasbahs and *ksour*; from the time of Moulay Ismail, through to the last century, the sultans exiled princes and unruly relatives out here to the edge of the desert.

The Tafilalt was a major centre of resistance to the French, who were limited to their garrison at Erfoud and an outpost of the Foreign Legion at Ouled Zohra until 1931.

The Tafilalt today – and Bayoud disease

The Tafilalt today, deprived of its contacts to the south, is something of a backwater, with a population estimated at around 80,000 and declining, as the effects of drought and Bayoud disease have taken hold on the palms. Most of the population are small-holding farmers, with thirty or so palms for each family, from which they could hope to produce around a thousand kilos of dates in a reasonable year. With the market price of dates around 6dh a kilo there are no fortunes to be made.

It is reckoned that two-thirds of Moroccan palmeries have been infected with **Bayoud disease**. First detected in the Drâa at the beginning of the twentieth century, this is a kind of fungus, which is spread from root to root and possibly by transmission of spores. Palms die within a year of an attack, creating a secondary problem by leaving a gap in the wedge of trees, which allows the winds to blow through. Recent years, howeever, have seen the successful introduction of disease-resistant hybrids which, together with increased rainfall, has led to greatly improved health of the palmeries.

24-hour petrol station, internet cafés and a tourist office – strung along the highway/main street, **Avenue Moulay Ali Cherif**. This runs all the way through town, between the familiar southern ceremonial roadside arches, turning into **Avenue El Massira** after crossing the bridge over the Oued Ziz.

Accommodation and eating

Despite its size, Er Rachidia has a limited choice of decent **hotels** within the city centre and if you want to **camp**, the *Source Bleue* at Meski, 17km south of Er Rachidia (see below), is the nearest possibility.

Several of the hotels listed below host decent restaurants, and there are also many good grillades and cafés clustered around the centre. *Restaurant Merzouga* in an attractive setting opposite the covered market does delicious brochettes.

Auberge Tinit 3km west of the city centre on the Goulmima road ⓣ0535 791759, ⓔtinit_auberge2000@yahoo.fr. A kasbah-style hotel with spotless en-suite rooms and a swimming pool in the courtyard. ❹

Hôtel le France Rue Chekh El Islam ⓣ0535 570997. With a French-style café on the ground floor, the rooms are simple but clean and comfortable. ❷

Hôtel le Riad ⓣ0535 171006, ⓦwww.hotelleriad.com. On the Goulmima road 4km outside the city centre, this is by far the best upscale option; the plush rooms face into a courtyard with a huge swimming pool and bar. Each of the en-suite rooms has a small sitting area and is fitted with all the mod cons. ❻

Hôtel M'Daghra 92 Rue M'Daghra ⓣ0535 574047, ⓕ0535 574049. Much the best deal in this category, with 29 larger-than-average en-suite rooms (avoid the ones at the front of the building), a café and a reasonable restaurant. ❷

Hôtel Renaissance 19 Rue Moulay Youssef ⓣ0666 28 02 35. Cheapest rooms in town, some with showers, and close to the bus station, but grubby. ❶

Listings

Banks There are four banks – Banque Populaire, Wafabank, BMCE and BMCI – all shown on the map.

Car repairs The Renault agent on Pl Hassan II carries a large supply of parts and will order others efficiently from Fes.

Internet access Numerous cyber cafés around the centre – the one on the road parallel to *Hôtel le France* is open 24hr.

Petrol stations There is a Ziz station on the Midelt road, and a 24hr Somepi station on the Erfoud road.

Petits taxis leave from outside the covered market on Av Moulay Ali Cherif.

Post office The PTT on Av Mohammed V has all the usual services; there's a smaller PTT out on the road from Erfoud.

Shopping The covered market is a reliable source of fresh meat, fruit and vegetables. The Ensemble Artisanal (8.30am–6.30pm; closed Sun) is on Av Moulay Ali Cherif just before the bridge; it has a good display of local crafts – pottery, brass, wood and, truly indigenous, basketware made of palm leaves. Souk days are Sun, Tues and Thurs.

Tourist office There's a rather unhelpful Délégation Provinciale du Tourisme at 44 Av Prince Moulay Abdallah (Mon–Fri: summer 7am–2pm; winter 8.30am–noon & 2.30–6.30pm; ⓣ0535 570944), found by leaving town on the Tinerhir road and turning right at the sign opposite the lesser PTT.

Moving on

Buses leave at least six times a day for Erfoud/Rissani, and a similar number head to Ouarzazate and Marrakesh or north to Midelt and Fes or Meknes, via the dramatic Ziz Gorges. It's usually no problem to get a seat in a **grand taxi** to Erfoud or, paying the same price, to the Meski turning.

Meski and the Ziz valley

The small palm grove of **MESKI** is watered by a natural springwater pool – the famous **Source Bleue**, extended by the French Foreign Legion and long a postcard image and favourite campsite for travellers. It's set on the riverbank, below a huge ruined *ksar* on the opposite bank and, with several of the springs channelled into a **swimming pool**. Outside midsummer, you might also consider walking part of the way downstream in the valley bottom, southeast of

Meski. The superb four-hour **trek** along the Oued Ziz will bring you to **Oulad Aïssa**, a *ksar* with fabulous views over the upper Tafilalt.

Shaded by bamboo, palms and tamarisks, the **campsite** is well maintained by the local commune of M'Daghra, with a couple of friendly little café-restaurants that serve meals and the inevitable souvenir/craft shops. The pool itself is safe to swim in, though it's a popular hangout for local boys so women bathers may feel self-conscious. Be warned that the river is likely infected with bilharzia.

Clearly signposted off the main road, the source lies 17km south of Er Rachidia. Coming by bus, ask to get out by the turn-off: from here it's only 400m down to the pool and campsite. **Going on** to Erfoud or back to Er Rachidia from Meski can be tricky, since most of the buses pass by full and don't stop. However, this is an easy place to hitch a lift from other tourists.

South from Meski: the Ziz palmery

Heading south from Er Rachidia and Meski, **towards Erfoud**, the N13 trails the final section of the **Oued Ziz**. Make sure you travel this in daylight, as it's one of the most pleasing of all the southern routes: a dry red belt of desert just beyond Meski, and then, suddenly, a drop into the valley and the great **Tizimi palmery** – a prelude of the Tafilalt, leading into Erfoud. Away from the road, **ksour** are almost continuous – glimpsed through the trees and high walls enclosing gardens and plots of farming land.

If you want to stop and take a closer look at the *ksour*, **Aoufouss**, midway to Erfoud, and the site of a **Thursday souk**, is perhaps the most accessible. There's also a pleasant little guesthouse 2km off the main road here, the *Maison d'Hôtes Zouala* (Ⓣ0661 602890; HB ❸), in a traditional Berber house with en-suite rooms and hot showers. *Auberge Dans la Palmerie* (Ⓣ0661 769804, Ⓦwww.danslapalmeraie.com; ❷) is easier to find, right on the road, and has simple rooms with patchwork quilts, hammocks and shady gardens. **Maadid**, off to the left of the road as you approach Erfoud, is interesting – a really massive **ksar**, which is considered to be the start of the Tafilalt proper.

Erfoud

ERFOUD, like Er Rachidia, is largely a French-built administrative centre, and its desultory frontier-town atmosphere fulfils little of the promise of the Tafilalt. Arriving from Er Rachidia, however, you get a first, powerful sense of proximity to the desert, with frequent sandblasts ripping through the streets,

The Festival of Dates

Erfoud's **Festival of Dates** is held over three days in October and you will be richly rewarded if you can visit at that time. As with all such events, it's a mixture of symbolism, sacred rites and entertainment. Traditionally, dates bring good luck: tied to a baby's arm they ensure a sweet nature, thrown at a bride they encourage fertility, and offered to strangers they signify friendship.

On the first morning of the festival, prayers are said at the mausoleum of Moulay Ali Shereef at Rissani and, the same evening, there is a fashion show of traditional costumes: a pride of embroidered silk, silver and gold headdresses, sequins and elaborate jewellery. Then there are processions, athletics and, on the last night, traditional music and spiritual songs.

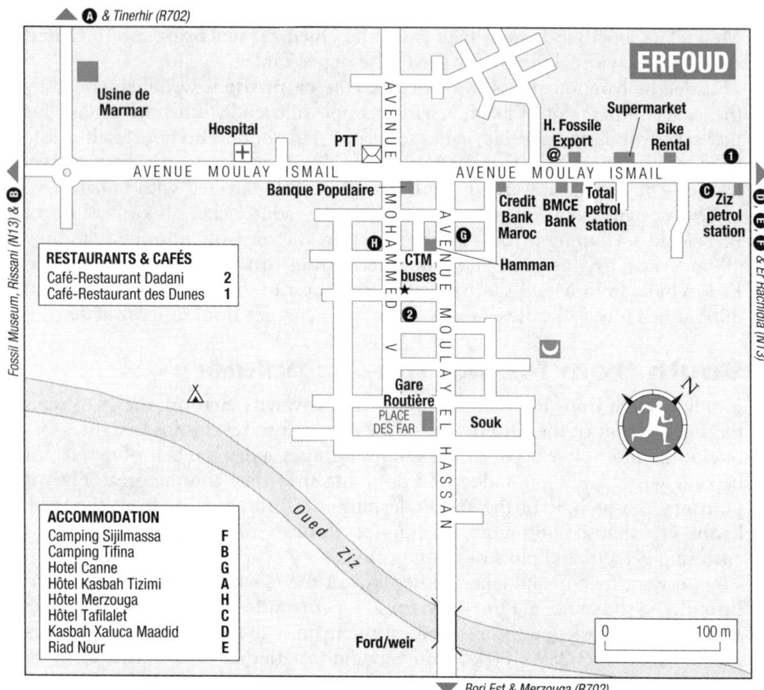

and total darkness in the event of a (not uncommon) electrical blackout. Before the Rissani–Merzouga road was surfaced, Erfoud functioned as a launch pad for trips to the dunes at **Merzouga**. It has, however, been left high and dry since then and tends to be bypassed by travellers who arrive here early enough in the day to pick up onward transport. Its only point of minor interest, aside from the **date festival** (see box, p.467), is the local **marble industry**, which produces a unique, high-quality black marble containing fossils. When polished, it's attractive and can be seen locally on every bar top and reception desk.

You can visit the marble works on the Tinerhir road; look for the Usine de Marmar. A German sculptor, Fred Jansen, and his Arts Natura group, pioneered carving the marble so that the fossils are revealed in 3D and, at its best, this is most impressive. There is also an interesting fossil museum 2km south on the Rissani road (daily 8am–7pm; admission free) with exhibits on the region's extraordinary geology. Conventional sights are thin on the ground, but with time to kill you could walk to a popular viewpoint 1km south of town called **Borj Est**. It's reached by crossing the river towards Merzouga and then turning left after 500m, where a *piste* scales the hillside to a small car park. In addition, some well-preserved **ksour** and fine **palmeries** line the main road 3km north towards Er Rachidia.

Accommodation

There's a surprising number of **hotels** – a legacy of the days when the town served as a staging post for dune trips – but these days budget choices are limited. The town's unmamed campsite is very shabby; best to head for

Camping Sijilmassa, 7km to the north of the town, which has adequate facilities as well as some simple but clean rooms (❶); or to *Camping Tifina* (Ⓣ0610 231415; Ⓦwww.tifina-maroc.com) 8km south on the Rissani road which is a very well appointed new complex with camping, rooms, tents, pool, bar and internet access.

Hôtel Canne Av Moulay el-Hassane Ⓣ0535 578696. Good value, if noisy, and run by a team of efficient women. Dated decor but spotlessly clean with a lively café below. ❷

Hôtel Kasbah Tizimi 2km west of town on the Tinerhir road Ⓣ0535 576179, Ⓦwww.kasbahtizimi.com. A modern *pisé* building featuring traditional wood beams, ironwork and tiles. Ranged around patios and a flower-filled garden, the rooms are attractively decorated, and there's a large pool, bar and spacious terrace. ❺

Hôtel Merzouga 114 Av Mohammed V Ⓣ0535 576532. Reasonably clean en-suite rooms with hot showers; or you can sleep on the terrace for 25dh a head. Best of the rock-bottom options. ❶

Hôtel Tafilalet Av Moulay Ismail Ⓣ0535 576535, Ⓕ0535 576036. One of Erfoud's once-grand old hotels, though in need of renovation. It's very friendly and comfortable nonetheless, with most mod cons, a dusty swimming pool and a shabby bar. ❺

Kasbah Xaluca Maadid 6km north of town on the Er Rachidia road Ⓣ0535 578450, Ⓦwww.xaluca.com. Luxury *pisé* hotel complex, part of a small Spanish-owned chain verging on the tacky, but all comforts are offered and the poolside bar is open to nonresidents. The swish rooms, opening onto small courtyards, are dominated by pastel colours, the furniture, decor and fittings make use of local arts and crafts. Good value at this level. BB ❹

Riad Nour 6km north of town on the Er Rachidia road Ⓣ0535 577748, Ⓔnriad01@menara.ma. This tastefully decorated riad is looking a bit shabby but offers comfortable, cool rooms furnished with wrought iron that open onto a grassy courtyard. There's a large swimming pool, bar, and a pricey dinner menu (120dh). BB ❹

Eating

Most cafés and restaurants are found on Avenue MohammdV and around Place des Far. Try to sample the local specialities, *kalia* – a spicy stew of mutton or kid, flavoured with over forty spices and served in a tajine with vegetables, egg and parsley or southern Morocco's answer to pizza, *madfouna*: griddled-fried wheat-flour bases topped with onions, tomatoes, olives, minced lamb and cheese.

Café-Restaurant Dadani 103 Av Mohammed V Ⓣ0535 577958. A congenial budget restaurant with a large terrace; a range of Moroccan staples prepared with fresh ingredients and served in huge portions. Good coffee, too. Mains from around 40dh. They also have a two-bedroom apartment which they rent for 300dh per night.

Café-Restaurant des Dunes Av Moulay Ismaïl Ⓣ0535 576793. Pizza baked in a wood oven is the house speciality of this established little place, opposite the Zia petrol station. It's cheap and welcoming, and has a shady garden at the rear.

Moving on

CTM and Supratours **buses** leave from their office on Avenue Mohammed V; others, and grands taxis, from the *gare routière* on Place des Far. There are several buses daily to **Tinerhir**, via Tinejdad. A rundown of destinations appears in "Travel Details" on p.480. **For Merzouga**, you can pick up local buses, taxis and minibuses from the Place des Far, although you may have to change at Rissani.

Rissani

RISSANI stands at the last visible point of the Ziz River; beyond it, steadily encroaching on the present town and its ancient *ksour* ruins, begins the desert. From the eighth to the fourteenth centuries, this was the site of the first independent kingdom of the south, Sijilmassa (see box opposite). It was the first capital of the Tafilalt, and served as the last stop on the great caravan routes south. The British journalist Walter Harris reported thriving gold and slave auctions in Rissani as late as the 1890s.

Rissani has a special place in Moroccan lore. It was from the *zaouia* here – which is still an important national shrine – that the ruling Alaouite dynasty launched its bid for power, conquering first the oases of the south, then the vital Taza Gap, before triumphing finally in Fes and Marrakesh.

For visitors, its main interest lies in its proximity to the dunes at Merzouga, accessible via a paved road. If you're driving, you'll probably be tempted to head straight through, but Rissani has some attractions of its own, including well-preserved medieval **ksour**, which the local tourist office have strung together on a waymarked 21-kilometre "**Circuit Touristique**" through the palmeries and a famous thrice-weekly **souk**.

Arrival and information

Private buses pull into a new bus station 500m north of the busy central square and covered market area; CTM services work from their offices in the square. If you're arriving by grand taxi, you'll probably be dropped just to the north of the Place al Massira opposite the *Hôtel Sijilmassa*, (which does reasonable food though the rooms are rather sub par). Rissani has a couple of **banks** (the Banque Populaire and Crédit du Maroc) both ranged around the square and with ATMs. The most convenient petrol station is the Ziz on the main square, where there are also several internet places.

Accommodation

With the dunes only down the road, few travellers choose to stay here, but you can do so at one or other of a grubby and over-priced group of small **hotels** in the centre. The best of these is *Hôtel el Filalia*, next to the CTM office (Ⓣ0672 314193; ❶) which has adequate rooms and a street-side café.

If you can stretch your budget a bit, head for *Kasbah Asmaa*, (Ⓣ0535 774083; Ⓔkasbahotel_asmaa@hotmail.com; ❸) 2km north on the Erfoud road, which is rather dated but has a passé charm, a big pool and a bar, and bargain rooms.

Kasbah Ennasra (Ⓣ0535 774403, Ⓦwww.kasbahennasra.com; BB ❻), 3km outside the town in the direction of Erfoud next to the petrol station, is Rissani's best luxury option; highlights include four-poster beds, an attractive patio, bar, swimming pool, and a first-class restaurant.

Eating options are limited in Rissani. Head for the area around the souk for standard café food.

The town and surrounding ksour

A quarter of Rissani's population still live in a large seventeenth-century **ksar**, in addition to which there is just the Place al Massira and one street, lined by the usual administrative buildings. It's a quiet place, which comes to life for the **souk** – held on Sunday, Tuesday and Thursday. This is more for locals than tourists but often turns up a fine selection of Berber jewellery – including the crude, almost iconographic designs of the desert. Some of the basic products (dried fruits, farming implements and so on) are interestingly distinct from those of the richer north.

Two kilometres from the town centre in the direction of Merzouga there is a sign on the left for **Ksar al Fida**, a nineteenth-century *ksar* that now houses the

Alaouite museum (Mon–Sun 8am–7pm; 20dh), a varied regional collection, where Abdullah will welcome you with open arms and give you a whistle-stop tour in a mixture of French and Arabic; even if you speak neither language, you will get his drift. Two fairly hassle-free **craft shops** might also draw you into an hour or two's browsing: the **Maison Touareg** on the left of the road out to Merzouga, and **Maison Berbère** behind the souk near *Hôtel Panorama*. The Maison Berbère is part of the Alaoui family chain which has a reputation for quality rugs.

Rissani's older monuments are well into the process of erosion – both through crumbling material and the slow progress of the sands. **Sijilmassa**, whose ruins were clearly visible at the beginning of the last century, has more or less vanished (see box below).

There's a collection of *ksour* on the signposted "Circuit Touristique" as you head out of town towards Merzouga. A few people still live in these *ksour* but they are no longer the bustling communities they once were. Nevertheless, the circuit makes an interesting and thought-provoking excursion and is especially beautiful in the golden light of sunset. The first *ksar* you encounter, about 2.5km to the southeast, houses the **Zaouia of Moulay Ali Shereef**, the original Alaouite stronghold and mausoleum of the dynasty's founder. Many times rebuilt – the last time following floods in 1955 – the shrine is now open to non-Muslims.

Sijilmassa: the Berber kingdom

Sijilmassa was founded in 757 by Berber dissidents, who had broken away from orthodox Islam, and for five centuries, until its collapse under civil unrest in 1393, it dominated southern Morocco. The early dominance and wealth of Sijilmassa was due to the fertility of the **oases** south of Erfoud. These are watered by parallel rivers, the Oued Rheris and Oued Ziz, which led to Sijilmassa's description as the "Mesopotamia of Morocco". Harvests were further improved by diverting the Ziz, just south of modern Erfoud, to the west of its natural channel, thus bringing it closer to the Rheris and raising the water table. Such natural wealth was reinforced by Sijilmassa's trading role on the **Salt Road** to West Africa (see box, p.465), which persisted until the west coast of Africa was opened up to sea trade, particularly by the Portuguese, in the fifteenth century. Coins from Sijilmassa in this period have been found as far as Aqaba in Jordan.

Historians disagree about the extent and pattern of Sijilmassa at its height. Some see it as a divided city, comprising several dispersed *ksour*, much as it was after the civil war at the end of the fourteenth century. Others view it as a single, elongated city, spread along the banks of the rivers: 14km from end to end, or half a day's walk.

There is still a gate to be seen on the east side of the Oued Ziz, at the ancient city's northern extremity, just south of El Mansouriya. This is known locally as the **Bab Errih** and may date from the Merenid period (1248–1465), although it has certainly undergone restoration since then. The Alaouites, who brought Sijilmassa to renewed prominence as the provincial capital of the Tafilalt in the seventeenth century, did a major restoration of the garrison. The southernmost point of the ancient city was near the *ksar* of Gaouz, on the "Circuit Touristique".

The (mainly Alaouite) central area is under excavation by a joint team from the Moroccan Institute of Archeology and the Middle Tennessee State University, under the direction of Dr Ronald Messier. The most accessible and visible remains are to be found a little to the west of Rissani, on the east bank of the Oued Ziz, and within the right angle formed by the north–south main road (N13) as it turns east into Rissani. Here can be traced the walls of a mosque with an early mihrab facing south, an adjoining medersa and the walls of the citadel with towers on the length by the river. In Rissani, there is a small museum and study centre where you may get help to explore the site.

With thanks to Dr Ron Messier.

Beside it, dominating this group of buildings, is the nineteenth-century **Ksar d'Akbar**, an awesomely grandiose ruin which was once a palace in exile, housing the unwanted members of the Alaouite family and the wives of the dead sultans. Most of the structure, which still bears considerable traces of its former decoration, dates from the beginning of the nineteenth century. A third royal *ksar*, the **Ksar Oualad Abdelhalim**, stands around 1.5km further down the road. Notable for its huge ramparts and the elaborate decorative effects of its blind arches and unplastered brick patterning, this is one of the few really impressive imperial buildings completed in the twentieth century. It was constructed around 1900 for Sultan Moulay Hassan's elder brother, whom he had appointed governor of the Tafilalt.

You can complete the circuit by passing a further group of *ksour* – **Asserehine**, **Zaouiet el Maati**, **Irara**, **Gaouz**, **Tabassant**, **Tinrheras** and **Ouirhlane** – and then looping back into town past a section of **Sijilmassa**. Tinrheras, a ruined *ksar* on a knoll, has fine views over Tafilalt.

Moving on

Grands taxis and minivans (12dh) for the trip **onwards to Merzouga** leave from the *gare routière* throughout the morning; in the afternoon, they're thinner on the ground and you may have to take a chance on one of the Berber lorries which run the route after the souk finishes; alternatively, walk out of town to the Merzouga road and hitch – there is always a fair bit of tourist traffic. Turn left at the junction past Place al Massira then take the left-hand fork at the next junction.

Heading **northwest** from Rissani, grands taxis and a couple of daily buses run direct to **Tinerhir** (45dh) and Er Rachidia (25dh). An alternative route is the **road west to Zagora, via Alnif**, detailed below. Minivan taxis covering this back road leave from near the CTM daily at 10am.

West from Rissani to the Drâa

Around 3km north of Rissani, a surfaced road (N12) branches west off the main Erfoud highway towards Alnif, Tazzarine, and Nekob. The route sees little tourist traffic, but provides a dependable and scenic link between the Tafilalt and Drâa Valley. There is a basic but pleasant place to stay at Mecissi, 55km east of Rissani. *CampResto Bonne Etape* (Ⓣ0535 884587; ❶) has clean rooms, camping and a cheery café. Aside from the landscape, **fossils** are this region's main attraction. Moujan Fossiles, 64km east of Rissani, is a charming little shop selling fossils found in the area by its elderly owner Mohammed, who will take you off on a rickety old motorbike to look for specimens in distant sites for 200dh or so. The stretch between Alnif and Tazzarine, in particular, has become the centre of a low-scale mining industry whose principal export is large trilobites (see box opposite), sold from dozens of roadside stalls.

Daily **minibuses** and grands taxis run between Rissani and Nekob, which is much the most appealing place to break the trip; a rambling *ksar* set in a palmery with a good choice of accommodation, it also serves as a base for hikes into the Djebel Sarhro and all the hotels listed will be able to arrange excursions.

Alnif and Tazzarine

Trilobites and potatoes are the stock in trade of **ALNIF**, 90km west of Rissani – the former scraped from ancient canyon walls around the town, the latter

Rocks, fossils and minerals

Along roadsides in the High and Anti-Atlas and down into the southeast, boys bound into the paths of oncoming cars to offer crystalline mementos of Morocco, and rocks, fossils and minerals are staples of most tourist shops in the south. Before purchasing, you might want to read these notes:

Geode Tennis-ball-sized specimens of crystals in a hollow geode cost around £12/$24 in Britain or the US; on the Moroccan hard-shoulder, they may cost more. Brilliant orange and red geodes and slices of rock crystal (quartz) look attractive but are unknown to natural science, as are the quartz geodes given an iridescent metal coating by vendors.

Ammonites Attractive spirals of ammonites (from Carboniferous to Jurassic) are common in the limestone areas of Britain but in Morocco they can be bought sliced and polished as well as "raw". Do not rely on the species name you are given by the shopkeeper – look at the centre of the spiral of the ammonite and at the ridge around its shell to check how far natural features have been "enhanced" by a chisel.

Trilobites Slightly older than ammonites, trilobites often appear in shops as identical beige-coloured fossils on grey slate. In nature, they are rarely so perfect – beware plaster casts. The early trilobite *paradoxides* is about the size of a hand, with long whisker-like spines. A deep-sea inhabitant, it is often found looking rather squashed sideways, where the silts on which it lived have been sheared by pressure. The *Calymene* and *Phacops* types of trilobites are about 200 million years younger than *Paradoxides*. They measure about two inches long, with a crab-like outer skeleton. The half-rounded shield-like skull, often found separated from the exo-skeleton, can appear in a shop with the rest of the skeleton carved around it as a tribute to modern Moroccan craftsmanship.

In the black limestone regions near Erfoud, the white crystalline shapes of **belemnites**, **ammonites** and **nautilus** are cross-sectioned and polished to emphasize the internal structure before being formed into ashtrays and even coffee tables, which can of course be transported for you at a cost. They may not look so good back home.

grown in the palmery winding northwards into the hills. It's along the line of this old watercourse that a well-frequented *piste* cuts across a saddle dividing the Djebel Sarhro and Djebel Ougnat ranges to join the main Dadès highway, the N10, 21km southeast of Tinerhir. The route is generally in good condition and passable with a tourist vehicle, though as ever you'd do well to check on its state beforehand, and bear in mind that your insurance won't cover journeys on unsurfaced roads. Basic **accommodation** and meals are available here at *La Gazelle du Sud* (Ⓣ0535 88530) which has a handful of simple rooms and a basic restaurant. The best place in the town centre for a quick meal for those passing through is *Etoile du Sud*, a simple café with friendly staff and reasonably priced traditional food.

Continuing west, the scenery grows wilder as you approach **TAZZARINE**, set in a grassy oasis surrounded by bare mountains. The town hosts a weekly souk on Wednesdays, and there's a petrol station and a straggling row of shops, but little else you'd want to stop for. Tazzarine's budget option is *Bougafer* (Ⓣ0524 839005; ❶) with 20 basic rooms that share showers, toilets and a hammam. Its sister hotel and **campsite** on the edge of town, *Village Touristique Bougafer* (Ⓣ0524 839005; ❹), just past the start of the bridge over the *oued*, is a characterless concrete motel with 70 overpriced rooms, bar, swimming pool, two large restaurants, and a parking lot for campers. RV drivers, however, will prefer the *Camping Amasttou* (Ⓣ0524 839078, Ⓕ0524 839635), which is found down a track to the left on the way out of town at the Nekob junction in a shady patch of palmery. It has a couple of simple **rooms** as well as tents. At the entrance to the site is a **prehistoric rock carving** transported from elsewhere; you can see them *in situ* at Tiouririne (7km) and Aït Ouazik (26km) and one of the camp staff will gladly act as a guide to these or other local sights.

Nekob

NEKOB, 160km west of Rissani and only 38km from the junction with the Drâa Valley road, dominates the most spectacular stretch of this route, its kasbah-studded old quarter looking north from the rim of an escarpment across a large palmery to the peaks of the Djebel Sarhro. The number of grand houses in the town testify to its former prominence as a market hub for the region, but out-migration has taken its toll in recent years. For trekkers, Nekob serves as an important staging post for adventures in the mountains to the north (see below); Mohammed at the Bureau des Guides (⊕0667 487509) speaks very good English and runs various treks. Nekob remains a refreshingly off-track destination which you can explore free of hassle; other than a couple of **prehistoric rock carvings** (*gravures rupestres*) sites across the valley (which you'll need help from your hotel or guesthouse to find), there's nothing much to see, but the traditional *pisé* architecture and fine views from the roof terraces tempt many visitors into staying longer than they intended.

Accommodation

Nekob boasts a surprisingly wide choice of **places to stay**.

Auberge Ait Aata Signed off the main street, ⊕0524 839751. A converted town house, rooms are simple and there is limited running water, but the friendly staff, beautifully painted salon ceilings and character of the place make up for what are quite modest surroundings. ❶

Auberge-Restaurant Enakhil Saghro At the entrance to the town (as you approach from Tazzarine) ⊕0524 839719, ⓦhotel-maroc-nkob.skyrock.com. A pleasant, efficiently run roadside motel with a kasbah-style facade and glorious café-terrace overlooking the palmery. Its rooms, some en suite, are spick-and-span and they run mule and camel treks from 350dh per day. HB ❷

Camping Ouadjou ⊕0661 741508. Near Ksar Jenna, this is the best camping option in the area; you can also sleep in Berber tents or in clean rooms with shared facilities. There's a basic but cheerful café and very welcoming staff. ❶–❷

Kasbah Baha Baha The old quarter ⊕0524 839763, ⓦwww.kasbahabaha.com. This splendid renovated kasbah is owned by an ethnographer from Marrakech with a library of interesting academic papers, a small museum and some lovely rooms in the square towers on the upper floors, decorated with plush Moroccan textiles and carpets. Outside, the garden features a couple of mock-Berber encampments flanking a pool and the whole site enjoys a wonderful panorama over the valley. Mule, camel, 4WD and walking tours can be arranged here. BB ❷–❹

Kasbah Imdoukal The old quarter ⊕0524 839798, ⓦwww.kasbahimdoukal.com. This upscale kasbah hotel has tastefully decorated rooms and a beautiful roof terrace which affords some of the best views of the palmeries in the area. ❻

Ksar Jenna Just beyond the western outskirts of town as you head towards Ouarzazate/Zagora ⊕0671 731976, ⓦwww.ksarjenna.com. Owned and run by an Italian–Moroccan couple, it's a self-consciously chic place whose rooms, high-ceilinged dining hall and salon are stylishly furnished with ceramics and expensive textiles, but the highlight here is a lush garden filled with flowers, fruit trees and water features. HB ❺

Into the Djebel Sarhro

From Nekob, a spectacular *piste* – covered by daily minibuses – heads north to crest the Djebel Sarhro via the **Tazi n' Tazazart**, eventually dropping into the Dadès Valley at Iknioun, near Boumalne du Dadès (see p.449). Winding through dramatic rock formations and gorges, the route rivals the crossing of the main Atlas chain, with superb views from the pass. An added incentive is the spectacular

pinnacles of Bab n'Ali, which you can reach in a half-day's walk from a pleasant, conveniently situated *gîte d'étape* with camping space and dorm beds. You could also use the *gîte* as a base for ascents of several peaks, guided by the *gardien*.

Merzouga and Erg Chebbi

The **Erg Chebbi** dunes at **MERZOUGA** are indisputably one of the great sights of Morocco. Rising to 150m in places, these giant sand hills lining the Algerian border may not be as imposing nor as extensive as some in North Africa, but they come closer than anywhere else in the country (at least, anywhere else that's relatively accessible) to fulfilling most people's expectations of what a true desert should be. A devastating flood in 2006 destroyed many buildings and

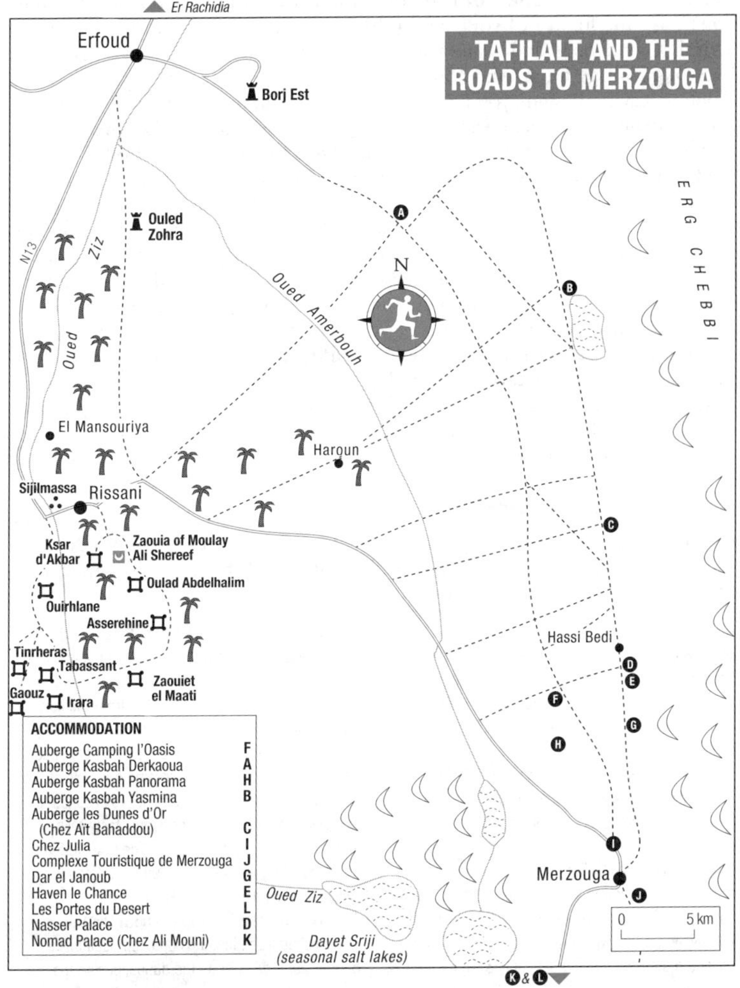

claimed three lives but the village seems to have recovered well and is back on the tourist track. The result is that Merzouga can sometimes feel less like the *désert profond* than a Saharan circus, with groups of luxuriously turbaned tourists posing for photographs with *hommes bleus* under the acacia trees or astride camels. To stand any chance of experiencing the scenery in its essential state, therefore, you should aim to come here out of season (Jan and Feb are the quietest months) and choose your spot very carefully. At the height of summer, the few visitors who brave the fierce heat to reach Merzouga are mostly Moroccans, attracted by the reputed power of the sands to cure rheumatism. Sufferers are buried up to the neck for a minute or two – any longer than that can be fatal.

Arrival, orientation and information

Thanks to the paved road from Rissani, **getting to Merzouga** is easy these days, though when you get there you'll be hassled from *faux guides*; the best tactic, as ever, is to **book your accommodation in advance** and try, if you don't have the luxury of your own vehicle, to get your hotel to meet you on arrival. Grand taxis and *camionettes* regularly ply the route from Rissani to Merzouga village for around 15dh a place.

Before leaving Rissani, you'll also need to get a firm fix on where your chosen hotel actually is (see map). **Places to stay** are strung across a wide area, nestled at the foot of the dunes in a straggling line. *Pistes* to them peel east off the main road at regular intervals (at junctions flagged by signboards), but this final leg across rough *hammada* can be a long one if you stay at the northernmost group of hotels, some of which lie more than 15km off the tarmac. The *pistes* are marked with coloured posts; if you're driving in a standard rental car, don't be tempted to improvise as there are many patches of soft sand where you might easily get stuck. Should this happen, rest assured that help will never be too far away, but expect to pay dearly for a 4WD rescue.

There is a **post office** and **internet café** in Merzouga as well as a few unremarkable **café-restaurants**; you'll get a much better deal if you eat at your hotel, paying an inclusive half- or full-board rate. *Café des Amis* is pleasant enough to while away a little time while you get your head around the place and it rents sandboards and skis for 100dh a day.

Accommodation

Outside high season, rates are surprisingly low, mainly because most places make their real money on camel trips as well as the fact that the steadily increasing number of *auberges* has led to competition.

Auberge Camping l'Oasis ⓣ0661 739041, ⓦwww.auberge-oasis.net. Jolly little set-up with simple en-suite rooms around a central garden and a roof terrace where you can sleep for 25dh. Camping available with light, water and power. Bargain dinner menu for 50dh. ❷

Auberge Kasbah Derkaoua ⓣ0535 577140, ⓦwww.aubergederkaoua.com. Beautiful *pisé* complex in traditional style, set amid olive, almond and fruit orchards on the northern fringes of Erg Chebbi. Ten en-suite rooms traditionally decorated and very comfortable, but you'll probably want to spend more time lazing in the lovely garden, which has a pool and a pretty terrace restaurant. Closed Jan, July & Aug. HB ❺

Auberge Kasbah Panorama ⓣ0662 085573, ⓦwww.kasbahpanorama.c.la. Run by the hospitable Aït Bahaddou family (of *Les Dunes d'Or* fame), this budget *auberge* stands further from the sand than most, at the top of a hill outside Merzouga, but the views are stupendous: the sunset terrace enjoys arguably the best panorama this side of the Atlas. The rooms are well aired, there is space for camping, and the restaurant serves tasty tajines and *madfouna* ("pizza Berber"). They run various tours including visits to hear authentic Gnaoua music at a nearby village. HB ❸

Auberge Kasbah Yasmina ⓣ0661 351667, ⓦwww.hotelyasminamerzouga.com. Established budget *auberge* right on the dunes, beside the seasonal lake where you might see flamingos. The situation is spectacular and views from the sunny rear terrace superb. The rooms, most en suite, are cool and there is a large grouping of Berber tents at the edge of the dunes where you can stay for 50dh per person. Skis and snowboards are available for rent and they offer camel safaris at standard rates (350dh per person all in). Nice pool also, but the food is mediocre. ❷

Auberge les Dunes d'Or (Chez Aït Bahaddou) ⓣ0661 350665, ⓦwww.aubergedunesdor.com. Built around a courtyard, 6km off the road (follow the pink and white posts). Two types of room are on offer – dark standards and brighter, pricier tiled ones, as well as Berber tents. There's a swimming pool in the courtyard and views from the sand hillock behind take in the rusting fuselage of a plane used in a film of Antoine de Saint-Exupéry's fable, *Le Petit Prince*. ❷

Chez Julia ⓣ0535 573182. Situated within the village in a traditional desert house this perennial favourite is defined by an appealing combination of comfort and authenticity. Owned and run by Austrian painter, Julia Günther, the *auberge* has a handful of uniquely decorated colour-themed rooms. The menu features a combination of Moroccan and Austrian dishes, including good vegetarian options, all freshly prepared at reasonable prices. Well-informed guides available for excursions. ❷

Complexe Touristique de Merzouga ⓣ0535 576322, ⓔchez_sadoq@hotmail.com. Close to the centre of the village, this opened in 1980 as Merzouga's original hotel. Simple rooms, a big terrace and a restaurant, this is a bit toruisty but can be a useful place to hook up with other travellers. HB ❸

Dar el Janoub ⓣ0535 577852, ⓦwww.dareljanoub.com. The best of the top-end places, with large rooms, shady courtyard, a lovely pool and the perfect terrace for sundowners, right by the dunes. HB ❺

Haven la Chance ⓣ0535 577269, ⓦwww.haven-la-chance-desert-hotel-merzouga.com. Comprehensive complex of rooms, camping, restaurant, bivouacs and a wide range of excursions and activities. Great views from the terrace, where you can bed down for 30dh. A pool is planned for 2010. HB ❷

Les Portes du Desert 2km south of Merzouga. ⓣ0667 611303, ⓦwww.lesportesdudesert.com. Attractive complex of *pisé* rooms, campsite, salon, pool and gardens. Private bivouacs right in the dunes. HB ❸

Nasser Palace ⓣ0666 039194, ⓦwww.nasserpalace.com. Of the plush hotels between Rissani and Merzouga, this is by far the cheapest. It has a swimming pool, well-decorated rooms (some en suite, some with a/c) and the option of sleeping for less outside. ❸

Nomad Palace (Chez Ali Mouni) 7km south of Merzouga, at Ksar Merzouga ⓣ0661 563611, ⓦwww.nomadpalace.com. The dunes aren't as high at this southern end of Erg Chebbi, but the area's much more peaceful as a result. The *auberge* itself boasts a huge Moroccan salon with open fire, and well-furnished rooms opening onto a quiet courtyard garden. Owner Ali Mouni also runs excellent camel trips to a less frequented area on the far, east side of Erg Chebbi, via a more varied route than normal; and he takes guests out to hear wonderful Gnaoua music at a remote village nearby. ❷

The dunes and camel trips

Compared with the great Erg Occidental of southern Algeria the dunes around Merzouga are relatively modest – 28km from north to south and only 7km across at their widest point – but they still give an impressive taste of the Sahara's grandeur. The highest are those in the centre of the Erg Chebbi, near, or just north of, Merzouga village. Rising dramatically from a plain of blackened *hammada*, they're spectacular at any time of day, but early morning and late afternoon are the best times to view them. To find a relatively peaceful ridge free of footprints, however, you'll have to be prepared to walk for an hour or else arrange a **camel trip** through one of the *auberges* listed opposite and above. These can cost anywhere between 50dh and 100dh for a short amble of one to three hours, to 250–350dh for an overnight excursion taking you deep into the dunes to a camp of Berber tents, where you'll be well placed to enjoy the stars and a memorable sunrise the following day. A guide/cameleer, meals, tea and blankets are included in the price, but it's advisable to bring extra clothes and a sleeping bag – nights out on the sand can get excruciatingly cold.

Desert wildlife

Birdwatchers are well rewarded in this part of the country, with many birds passing through on their spring and autumn migrations as well as native desert-dwelling species. Mourning, red-rumped, white-crowned and desert wheatears, desert sparrows, Tristram's desért warblers, various sandgrouse, thick-billed (and other) larks and Egyptian nightjars can be seen in many parts, the Vallée des Oiseaux near Boulmane de Dadés offering particularly rich pickings. The enormous El Mansour Eddahbi Barrage near Ouarzazate attracts many waders and waterfowl including ruddy shelduck and marbled teal. These can also be found at the **lakes near Merzouga**, along with greater flamingos, but bear in mind that these lakes can disappear to nothing in dry years. The Lanner falcon, eagle owls and Houbara bustards are just a few of the magnificent species which will attract birdwatchers. The desert and *hammada* house **reptiles** such as the Algerian sand lizard, Berber skink, Atlas agama, Montpelier snake and fringe-toed lizard, as well as nocturnal mammals. Jerboa, desert hedgehogs and fennec (desert fox) make their presence felt by leaving footprints in the morning sand.

Acacias, tamarisk and calotropis are the trees of the desert but other **plant life** is generally limited to the lichens and algae that get their modest water from the condensation of dew which clings to the undersides of rocks and stones. When the rains do come there is a glorious, all-too-brief spring bloom, mainly of pink ashphodels, mauve statice and yellow bobonium.

Mohamed Zaki (ⓣ0666 569392, ⓔzakimohamed@yahoo.fr) is probably the most well-qualified wildlife guide in this area. An English-speaking botanist and zoologist based in Agouti in the High Atlas, he runs recommended tours in the mountains and the desert.

Each outfit works its own jealously guarded routes and camps, but it can be a matter of luck whether you hit a crowded section of the dunes or not. Basically, the further from the main agglomeration of *auberges* you go, the more chance you have of avoiding other camel trains and – even more importantly – 4WD drivers whose antics can ruin the peace and quiet. Quad bike activity has also become a real menace, their noise and trackmarks an obnoxious intrusion now discouraging visitors. Whether the authorities will ban this nuisance remains to be seen. The **Paris–Dakar Rally** used to hurtle straight through Merzouga but it was cancelled in 2008 following threats from Al Qaeda and has now, bizarrely, moved to Argentina.

East to Bouarfa and Figuig

The six- to eight-hour desert journey from **Er Rachidia to Figuig** (pronounced F'geeg) is spectacular in its isolation and scenically extraordinary: the real outlands of Morocco, dominated by huge empty landscapes, blank red mountains, mining settlements and military garrisons. It used to be quite a common route for travellers entering Algeria, in the south, but the border has been closed since 1994 and looks unlikely to open any time soon. It is thus a somewhat perverse route to take – a lot of travelling in order to complete a loop via Bouarfa to northern Morocco at Oujda. You can, however, make the journey easily enough by car, the only diversion being the roadside *gendarmerie* who pass the time collecting car numbers and your mother's maiden name. Their concern makes more sense when you note the proximity of the "undefined boundary" with Algeria, shown on some maps and running parallel to the road.

If you take public transport, you'll have to change in Bouarfa. *Hôtel Climat du Maroc* (Ⓣ0535 67796382, Ⓦwww.climatdumaroc.com; ❺) is surprisingly plush and has a pool.

It's 378km from **Er Rachidia** to **Figuig** via **Boudnib** and **Bouarfa**, and a further 386km from **Figuig** to **Oujda** via **Bouarfa** (see p.175), with few sights along the way.

Figuig

The southern oases are traditionally measured by the number of their palms, rather than in terms of area or population. **FIGUIG**, with something like 200,000 trees, has long been one of the largest – an importance enhanced by its strategic border position. The oasis has even less of an administrative town than usual, still basically consisting of its seven distinct villages which in the past feuded almost continuously over water and grazing rights.

At least twice Figuig has been lost by Morocco – in the seventeenth-century wars, and again at the end of Moulay Ismail's reign – and as recently as 1975 there was fighting in the streets here between Moroccan and Algerian troops. Since the border closed in 1994, Figuig's economy has virtually collapsed.

Exploring the ksour

Figuig's **ksour** are signposted off the main road and are spread out round the base of the hill – each enclosing its own palmery within high turreted walls. Their strange, archaic shape – with watchtowers rising above the snaking *feggaguir* (or irrigation channels) – evolved as much from internal tension within the ksour as from any need to protect themselves from the nomadic tribes of the desert. Head for the *platforme*, a man-made lookout poised above the *ksar* of **Zenaga**; the view from here spans a large part of the palmery and its pink-tinged *ksour*, and you can gaze at the weird, multicoloured layers of the enclosing mountains. If you can find the energy – Figuig in summer feels a little like sitting inside a fan-heater – head down into Zenaga, the largest and richest of the seven villages. Going to your left, you should reach its centre, more developed than most in this area, with a couple of shops and a café in addition to a mosque. For a look at the other *ksour*, you would be well advised to hire someone local, preferably through your hotel, to guide you.

Practicalities

Orientation is relatively simple, with almost everything on the road by which you enter the town. *Hôtel Figuig* (Ⓣ0536 899309; ❷), is the only accommodation option. The rooms have hot showers and balconies, the restaurant is good, with menus from 70dh, and the view down the valley to the closed border, and Algeria beyond, is stunning. There is also a secure area for camping and a café that shares the view. There are a couple of **internet cafés** and a branch of the Banque Populaire, in town. The *Café de la Paix* and *Café Oasis* are the only other places to eat.

Buses tend to arrive, and leave from the CTM office on the main street, with services to Oujda leaving early in the morning. Tickets are sold in advance but, as each bus is owned by a different company, you'll need to ask around to find out where to buy the ticket for the bus of your choice. Heading for **Er Rachidia**, there are just two buses a day from Bouarfa (at 9am and 2pm); you will need to catch the 5am bus from Figuig if you want to avoid a long wait at Bouarfa.

Travel details

Buses

Erfoud to: Er Rachidia (5 daily; 1hr 30min); Fes (1 daily; 11hr); Rissani (4 daily; 45min); Tinerhir, via Tinejdad (2 daily; 8hr 30min). Zagora (1 daily; 6hr), Ouarzazate (1 daily; 9hr).
Er Rachidia to: Casablanca (1 CTM daily; 10hr 15min); Erfoud/Rissani (12 daily; 2hr/2hr 45min); Fes (10 daily; 8hr 30min); Figuig (1 daily via Bouarfa; 10hr); Marrakesh (6 daily; 9hr 45min); Meknes (5 daily; 8hr); Midelt (5 daily; 3hr 30 min); Tinerhir (2 daily; 3hr). Ouarzazate (7 daily; 5hr)
Figuig to: Er Rachidia (via Bouarfa; 2 daily; 10hr); Oujda (4 daily; 7hr).
Ouarzazate to: Agadir (4 daily; 8hr 30min); Casablanca (2 daily; 8hr 20min); Er Rachidia (7 daily; 5hr); Marrakesh (8 daily; 4–5hr); M'hamid (2 daily; 7hr); Taliouine/Taroudant (1 CTM daily; 3hr 30 min/5hr); Tinerhir (7 daily; 5hr); Zagora (4daily; 4hr).
Rissani to: Meknes (2 daily: 8hr 30min); Tinejdad/Goulmima (2 daily; 3hr 30min/4hr); Zagora (1 daily; 10hr).
Tazenakht to: Agadir (3 daily; 6hr) via Taliouine (1hr 30min) and Taroudant (3hr 30min); Er Rachidia (1 daily; 6hr) via Tinerhir (3hr); Foum Zguid (4 daily; 1hr 30min); Goulimine (2 daily; 10hr 30min) via Tiznit (8hr); Marrakesh (3 daily; 6hr 30min); Ouarzazate (10 daily; 1hr 30min); Tan Tan (1 daily; 16hr 30min); Tata (3 daily; 4hr), Zagora (1 daily; 4hr 30min).
Tinerhir to: Er Rachidia (2 daily; 3hr); Ouarzazate (7 daily; 5hr); Rissani (2 daily; 4hr).
Zagora to: M'hamid (2 daily; 2hr); Marrakesh (2 daily; 9–11hr); Ouarzazate (4 daily; 4–5hr).

Grands Taxis

Boumalne Minivan taxis at least daily to Msemrir (3hr). Regular runs to Tinerhir (50min).
Erfoud Fairly frequent runs to Rissani (30min) and Er Rachidia (1hr 30min).
Er Rachidia Fairly frequent runs to Erfoud (along the route you can negotiate a ticket to Meski) and to Tinejdad (1hr 30min).
Ouarzazate Regularly to Zagora (3hr). Negotiable for Skoura (1hr) and Aït Benhaddou (1hr 45min, but expensive private trip).
Rissani Regularly to Erfoud (30min) and Merzouga (1hr).
Tinerhir Regular runs to Boumalne (50min) and Tinejdad (1hr; from there on to Er Rachidia).
Zagora Regularly to Ouarzazate (3hr); lorries to Rissani (10hr) and Foum Zguid (8hr).

Flights

Ouarzazate to: Casablanca (1-3 daily; 50min); Paris-Orly (4 weekly; 4hr 10min).

8

Agadir, the Souss and Anti-Atlas

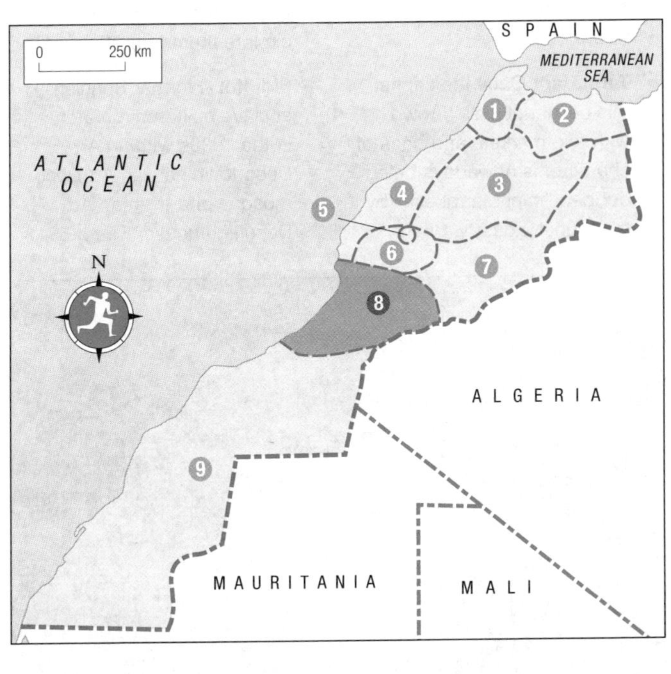

CHAPTER 8

Highlights

* **Agadir beach** Golden sand, top-class hotels and sun pretty much all year round make this the country's number one seaside resort. See p.491

* **Surfing at Taghazout** Morocco's top surfing spot, a village beach resort with a whole series of excellent right breaks attracting tubehounds both local and foreign. See p.500

* **Taroudant** Once the capital, this delightful walled town with two markets and bags of character is nowadays being dubbed "mini Marrakesh" by the tourist industry. See p.502

* **Ancient rock carvings** Across the whole region between Tafraoute and Tata, these prehistoric artworks attest to a time when elephants and giraffes roamed this neck of the woods. See p.515

* **Tafraoute** Tucked away in the Anti-Atlas mountains amid a landscape of strange rock formations, this friendly little town makes a great base to explore them from. See p.522

* **Sidi Ifni** A former Spanish enclave built from scratch in the 1930s with an Art Deco town hall, an Art Deco mosque and even an Art Deco lighthouse. See p.531

▲ Agadir beach

Agadir, the Souss and Anti-Atlas

Southern Morocco's major tourist destination is **Agadir**, a city that was rebuilt specifically as a resort following its destruction by an earthquake in 1960. It became something of a showpiece for the post-Independence "new nation", and these days is an established beach city, with some fine hotels around its great sweep of sand. If you're travelling around Morocco, however, you are unlikely to want to stay for long, for Agadir is very deliberately developed – mainly as a winter resort for Europeans – and feels rather devoid of local, Moroccan culture.

You don't have to travel far to find a very different country. Just north of Agadir is a series of small fishing villages and cove-beaches, among them **Taghazout**, Morocco's number-one **surfing** resort. A short way inland is **Paradise Valley**, a beautiful and exotic palm gorge, from which a mountain road trails up to the seasonal waterfalls of **Immouzer des Ida Outanane** – a superb one- or two-day trip. To the south of Agadir, the beaches are scarcely developed, ranging from solitary campsites at **Sidi Rbat** – one of Morocco's best locations for bird-watching – and **Sidi Moussa d'Aglou**, down to the old port of **Sidi Ifni** – only relinquished by Spain in 1969 and full of splendid Art Deco colonial architecture.

Inland and to the south of Agadir are the **Souss** and the **Anti-Atlas**, easy-going regions whose Tashelhaït (Chleuh) Berber populations share the distinction of having together cornered the country's grocery trade. **Taroudant**, capital of the wide and fertile Souss valley, has massive walls, animated souks and good hotels – a natural place to stay on your way to Marrakesh (which can be reached over the spectacular **Tizi n'Test** pass) or Ouarzazate. Further south, into the Anti-Atlas mountains, **Tafraoute** and its valley are even more compelling – the stone-built villages and villas set amid a stunning landscape of pink granite and vast rock formations.

Agadir

AGADIR was, by all accounts, a characterful port, prior to the terrible earthquake of 1960 that completely destroyed it. Just four years into independence, it was an especially traumatic event, which created a great will to recreate a city

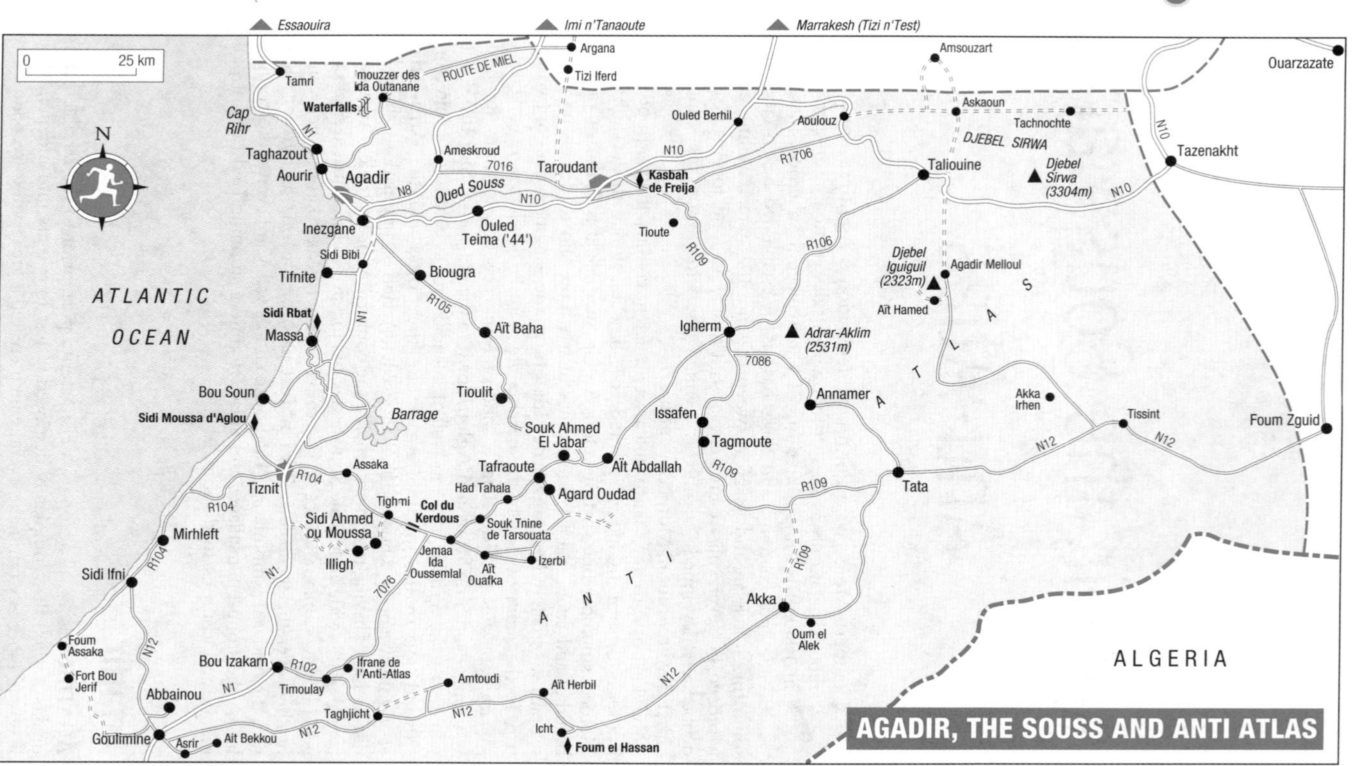
AGADIR, THE SOUSS AND ANTI ATLAS
Essaouira
Imi n'Tanaoute
Marrakesh (Tizi n'Test)
Tan Tan & Laayoune
0
25 km
N
ATLANTIC
OCEAN
ALGERIA
Cap
Rihr
Tamri
Imouzzer des
Ida Outanane
Waterfalls
ROUTE DE MIEL
Argana
Tizi Iferd
Taghazout
Aourir
Agadir
Ameskroud
7016
N8
Oued Souss
Taroudant
Kasbah
de Freija
N10
Ouled Berhil
Aoulouz
R1706
Inezgane
Ouled
Teima ('44')
Tioute
R109
R106
Sidi Bibi
Tifnite
Biougra
R105
N1
Sidi Rbat
Massa
Aït Baha
Igherm
7086
Adrar-Aklim
(2531m)
Bou Soun
Sidi Moussa d'Aglou
Barrage
Tioulit
Souk Ahmed
El Jabar
Issafen
Tagmoute
Annamer
Tafraoute
Aït Abdallah
Agard Oudad
Had Tahala
Tiznit
R104
Assaka
Tighmi
Col du
Kerdous
Souk Tnine
de Tarsouata
Sidi Ahmed
ou Moussa
Illigh
Jemaa
Ida
Oussemlal
Aït
Ouafka
Izerbi
7076
Mirhleft
Sidi Ifni
Foum
Assaka
Fort Bou
Jerif
N12
Bou Izakarn
R102
Ifrane de
l'Anti-Atlas
Timoulay
Amtoudi
Aït Herbil
Abbainou
Taghjicht
Goulimine
Asrir
Aït Bekkou
Icht
Foum el Hassan
Akka
Oum el
Alek
Tata
Amsouzart
Askaoun
Tachnochte
DJEBEL SIRWA
Djebel
Sirwa
(3304m)
Taliouine
Djebel
Iguiguil
(2323m)
Agadir Melloul
Aït Hamed
Akka
Irhen
Tissint
Foum Zguid
Tazenakht
Ouarzazate
A N T I   A T L A S

that showed Morocco in its best, modern face. Half a century on, the result is quite impressive, with swathes of park and garden breaking up the hotel and residential zones. The beach, too, is magnificent and untrammelled by Spanish Costa-style high-rise building, but it's hard to escape the feeling that the city lacks soul, though the lack of bustle has novelty value coming from any other Moroccan town. Despite the air of calm, Agadir is nonetheless the core of Morocco's fifth-biggest urban conglomeration, with a population of some 700,000. Its main industry, as will be immediately apparent to even a casual visitor, is tourism.

Some history

Agadir's **history** closely parallels that of Morocco's other Atlantic ports. It was colonized first by the Portuguese in the fifteenth century, then, recaptured by the Saadians in the sixteenth, carried on its trading with intermittent prosperity, overshadowed, more often than not, by the activities of Mogador (Essaouira) and Mazagan (El Jadida).

Abroad, Agadir's name was known mainly for the **Agadir Crisis** of 1911, when, during the run-up to World War I, Germany sent a warship to Agadir bay to support Moroccan independence against French designs. Germany's real motive – to undermine a Franco-British alliance by using Britain and France's conficting interests in Morocco – failed when Britain cut a deal with France, allowing the French to split Morocco with Spain while the British got a free hand in Egypt and Cyprus.

The really big event in Agadir's history was the devastating **earthquake** of February 29, 1960: a tremor that killed 15,000 and left most of the remaining 50,000 population homeless. In the aftermath, the whole place had to be rebuilt from scratch.

Orientation, information, arrival and city transport

"Downtown" Agadir is centred on the junction of **Boulevard Hassan II** and **Avenue Prince Moulay Abdallah** with **Avenue du Prince Sidi Mohammed**. Rebuilt in 1960s "modernist" style, it has all the trappings of a town centre, with office blocks, a tourist office, post office, Hôtel de Ville (town hall), municipal market and banks. Just to the northeast is an area known as **Talborjt**, with a concentration of budget hotels and small café-restaurants. The fancier hotels are grouped along the avenues parallel to the beach: **Boulevard Mohammed V**, **Boulevard Hassan II** and **Boulevard du 20 Août**.

The best place to go for **tourist information**, if you can catch it open, is the *Syndicat d'Initiative* on Boulevard Mohammed V, opposite the end of Avenue Général Kettani (in principle Mon–Fri 9am–noon & 3–6pm, but sometimes closed if staff are unavailable; ⓣ0528 821821). There is also a *Délégation de Tourisme* in Immeuble Iguenwane, on Avenue Mohammed V west of town towards the port (Mon–Fri 8.30am–4.30pm; ⓣ0528 846377), whose staff are generally happy to answer questions, and a *Conseil Régional du Tourisme* in the Chamber of Commerce building on Avenue Hassan II near the Amazigh Heritage Museum (Mon–Fri 8.30am–noon & 3–6pm, Sat 8.30am–noon; ⓣ0528 842629), which gives out maps and booklets.

Arrival

Agadir's **Al Massira airport** is 25km east of the city. It is well equipped and stays open all night, though the restaurants are closed from around 7pm (a small

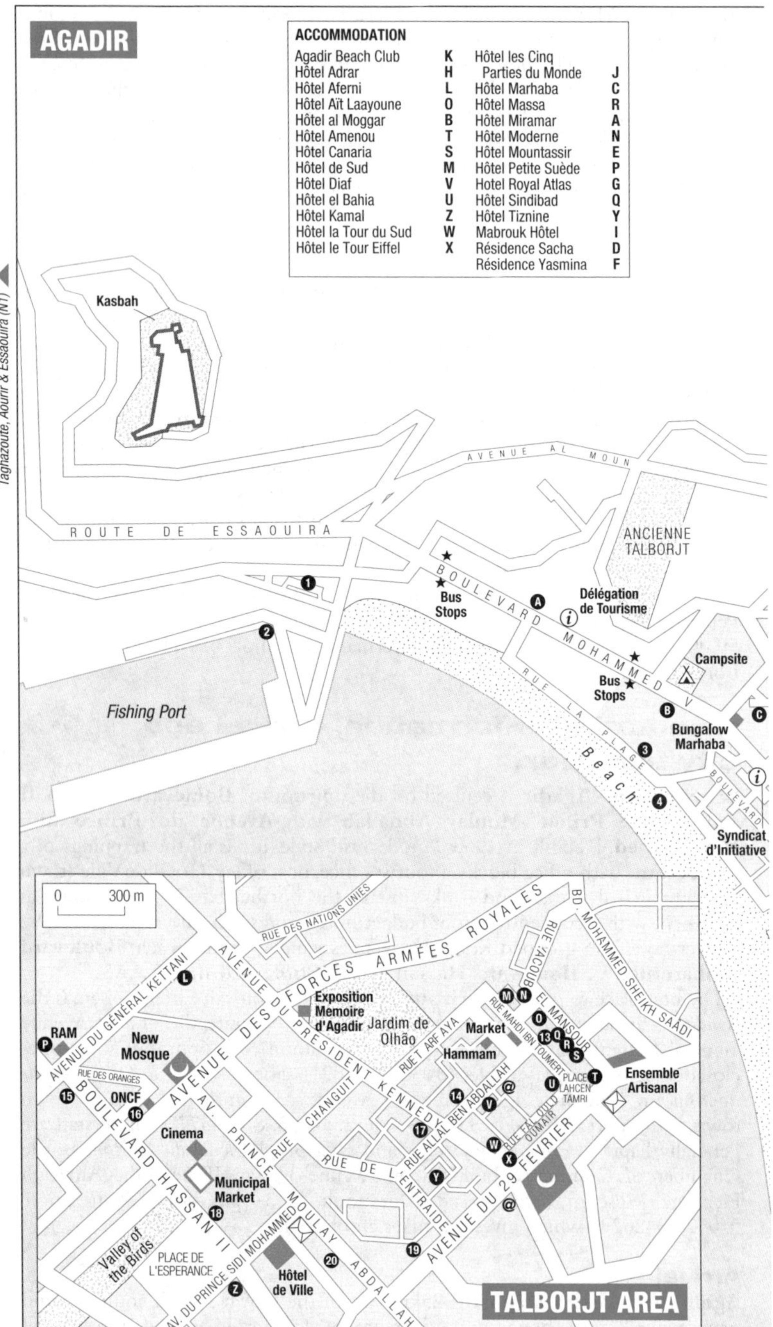
AGADIR
ACCOMMODATION
Agadir Beach Club K
Hôtel Adrar H
Hôtel Aferni L
Hôtel Aït Laayoune O
Hôtel al Moggar B
Hôtel Amenou T
Hôtel Canaria S
Hôtel de Sud M
Hôtel Diaf V
Hôtel el Bahia U
Hôtel Kamal Z
Hôtel la Tour du Sud W
Hôtel le Tour Eiffel X
Hôtel les Cinq Parties du Monde J
Hôtel Marhaba C
Hôtel Massa R
Hôtel Miramar A
Hôtel Moderne N
Hôtel Mountassir E
Hôtel Petite Suède P
Hotel Royal Atlas G
Hôtel Sindibad Q
Hôtel Tiznine Y
Mabrouk Hôtel I
Résidence Sacha D
Résidence Yasmina F
Taghazoute, Aourir & Essaouira (N1)
Kasbah
AVENUE AL MOUN
ROUTE DE ESSAOUIRA
ANCIENNE TALBORJT
Bus Stops
BOULEVARD MOHAMMED V
Délégation de Tourisme
Campsite
Fishing Port
RUE LA PLAGE
Bungalow Marhaba
Beach
BOULEVARD
Syndicat d'Initiative
0 300 m
RUE DES NATIONS UNIES
AVENUE DES FORCES ARMÉES ROYALES
BD. MOHAMMED SHEIKH SAADI
AVENUE DU GÉNÉRAL KETTANI
AVENUE DU PRESIDENT KENNEDY
Exposition Memoire d'Agadir
Jardim de Olhão
RUE YACOUB EL MANSOUR
RUE MAHDI IBN TOUMERT
Market
Hammam
RUET ARF AYA
RAM
New Mosque
RUE DES ORANGES
PLACE LAHCEN TAMRI
Ensemble Artisanal
BOULEVARD HASSAN II
ONCF
AVENUE
RUE CHANGUIT
RUE ALLAL BEN ABDALLAH
RUE FAL OULD OUMAIR
Cinema
AV. PRINCE MOULAY ABDALLAH
RUE DE L'ENTRAIDE
AVENUE DU 29 FEVRIER
Municipal Market
Valley of the Birds
PLACE DE L'ESPERANCE
AV. DU PRINCE SIDI MOHAMMED
Hôtel de Ville
TALBORJT AREA

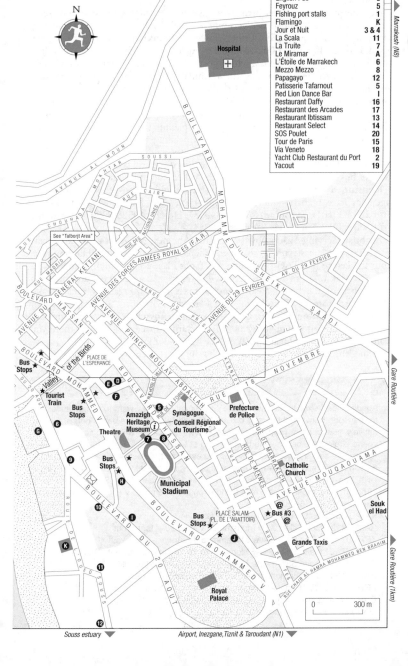

RESTAURANTS, BARS & NIGHTLIFE	
Actor's	G
Disco Tan Tan	10
English Pub	9
Feyrouz	5
Fishing port stalls	1
Flamingo	K
Jour et Nuit	3 & 4
La Scala	11
La Truite	7
Le Miramar	A
L'Étoile de Marrakech	6
Mezzo Mezzo	8
Papagayo	12
Patisserie Tafarnout	5
Red Lion Dance Bar	I
Restaurant Daffy	16
Restaurant des Arcades	17
Restaurant Ibtissam	13
Restaurant Select	14
SOS Poulet	20
Tour de Paris	15
Via Veneto	18
Yacht Club Restaurant du Port	2
Yacout	19

Hospital
Marrakesh (N8)
Boulevard Mohammed Sheikh Saâdi
Avenue Al Moun
Mokhtar Soussi
Rue Caire
Rue Chouhada
Rue des Nations Unies
See "Talborjt Area"
Avenue des Forces Armées Royales (F.A.R.)
Rue Madrid
Boulevard Général Kettani
Avenue du Président Kennedy
Av. du 29 Fevrier
Avenue du 29 Fevrier
Avenue du Hassan II
Avenue Prince Moulay Abdallah
Place de l'Esperance
Rue 18 Novembre
Gare Routière
Bus Stops
Boulevard Mohammed V
Boulevard du 20 Aout
Tourist Train
Boulevard Hassan II
Rue de la Foire
Synagogue
Amazigh Heritage Museum
Conseil Régional du Tourisme
Prefecture de Police
Theatre
Rue de Marrakech
Rue de Meknes
Rue de Fes
Catholic Church
Avenue Mouqaouama
Municipal Stadium
Route de l'Oued Souss
Boulevard du 20 Aout
Place Salam (Pl. de l'Abattoir)
Bus #3
Souk el Had
Grands Taxis
Boulevard Mohammed V
Rue Chair al Hamra Mohammed Ben Brahim
Gare Routière (1km)
Royal Palace
0 300 m
Souss estuary
Airport, Inezgane, Tiznit & Taroudant (N1)

coffee bar stays open till 11pm); car-rental offices open only during office hours. At least one bank is generally open all the time, but taxis will usually accept euros, and sometimes pounds or dollars, or will take you to an ATM en route to your hotel.

Holiday companies run their own buses to meet flights and shuttle passengers to their hotels, and if you've bought a flight-only deal it's worth tagging along with fellow passengers. Otherwise, **grands taxis** waiting outside charge a standard 150dh fare (200dh at night) to Agadir, or 100dh to Inezgane (13km southeast of Agadir; see p.497), which covers up to six passengers. If you plan to share a fare, arrange this inside the terminal. There is no bus to downtown Agadir, but if you don't want to shell out for a grand taxi, you can get to Inezgane on the blue and white GAB #22 bus from outside the airport building (every 30min; 6am–7.20pm; 4dh), and from there take a local ZETRAP bus or shared grand taxi (4dh) to Agadir. If you are planning to move straight on from Agadir, you would in any case be best off heading for Inezgane, from where there's a greater choice of onward transport, especially if you intend to travel by grand taxi. The #22 drops you off right next to the grand taxi stand in Inezgane; for the bus station, just walk across to the other side of the grand taxi stand.

Renting a car at the airport on arrival should be no problem, as several agencies have branches there, including First Car (☎0528 839297), Budget (☎0528 839101), Europcar (☎0528 840337, Hertz (☎0528 839071), National (☎0528 839121) and Avis (☎0528 839244).

All **buses** serving Agadir now terminate at the new *gare routière* on Rue Chair el Hamra at the eastern edge of town. There is no convenient public transport into the centre (RATAG bus #3 goes as far as Place Salam only), so, unless you want to walk (3km to Talborjt), you will have to take a petit taxi (around 10dh to Talborjt or the beach area). **Grands taxis** from Inezgane, Taroudant and Tiznit terminate by Place Salam (aka Place de l'Abattoir), a longish walk or short taxi ride from Talborjt. Grands taxis from anywhere else, and many bus services, will drop you at Inezgane, 13km southeast (see p.497); from there you can get to Agadir by local bus (RATAG #28 and ZETRAP #25 or #30 serve Avenue Mohammed V, where the stop by the *Hôtel Anezi* is the most convenient

City transport

Agadir is for the most part a **walkable** city, though you may want to use petits taxis for transport between the bus or taxi stations and Talborjt or the beach hotels. Alternatively, you can rent **mopeds** or **motorbikes** (see p.495), which would also allow you to explore the beaches north and south of town.

There are also a few useful local bus routes: fares for most of these bus trips are 3.50dh on the municipal RATAG buses, or 5dh on the privately run ZETRAP services; both can be picked up on Avenue Mouqaouama near Place Salam (Place de l'Abbatoir) and most of them also along Avenue Mohammed V (stops are shown on the map on pp.486–487).

RATAG #3 Place Salam – Souk el Had – Gare Rouière
RATAG #12 Place Salam – Av Mohammed V – Aourir – Taghazout
ZETRAP #60 Place Salam – Av Mohammed V – Aourir – Taghazout
ZETRAP #61 Place Salam – Av Mohammed V – Aourir – Taghazout – Tamri
ZETRAP #50 Place Salam – Av Mohammed V – Aourir – Imi Miki
RATAG #28 Port – Av Mohammed V – Place Salam – Inezgane
ZETRAP #25, #30 Port – Av Mohammed V – Place Salam – Inezgane
GAB #17 Inezgane – Sidi Bibi – Tifnite turn-off – Massa
GAB #22 Inezgane – Agadir airport

for Talborjt) or grand taxi (4dh a place to Place Salam, or 24dh to charter a taxi to Agadir for up to six people).

Accommodation

Agadir has a vast number of **hotels**, tourist apartments, "holiday villages" and self-catering *résidences* (in which the rooms are effectively suites with kitchenettes), but in high-season periods – Christmas/New Year, Easter, July and August – it is still worth booking ahead. Out of season, you can often get **discounts** at the large, four-star hotels, but budget hotels are less likely to alter their rates. If you plan to move on more or less immediately, you might be better off staying at **Inezgane** (see p.497), where budget hotels are cheaper, and where you have a greater number of long-distance buses and shared grands taxis.

Talborjt/city centre

Most of the budget hotels are in **Talborjt**, with more upmarket places in the city centre. Talborjt has the advantage of good shops, cafés and street life, whereas the centre is a bit bleak and lifeless.

Hôtel Aferni Av Général Kettani ⓣ0528 840730, ⓦwww.aferni.com. It's worth asking for a room with a bathtub and balcony in this three-star hotel with a pool (heated in winter) and terrace, plus TVs and safes in each room. The only thing lacking is a bar, which you may consider a plus or a minus. ❹

Hôtel Aït Laayoune Rue Yacoub el Mansour ⓣ0528 824375. Cheap and friendly, with shared shower facilities but constant hot water. The rooms are basic but clean. ❷

Hôtel Amenou 1 Rue Yacoub el Mansour ⓣ0528 841556. A plain and simple hotel with showers in some of the rooms, hot water round the clock, and a roof terrace in case you fancy a spot of sunbathing. On the downside, some of the beds are soft and springy, so check yours before taking the room. ❶

Hôtel Canaria 2 Pl Lahcen Tamri ⓣ0528 846727. Rooms (some with en-suite showers) round a sunny central courtyard, so it doesn't matter that most have windows facing inwards only (exceptions are rooms 6 and 10, which have outside windows). ❷

Hôtel de Sud 26 Rue Sidi Sahnoun ⓣ0528 826575. Quiet little hotel hidden away on the edge of Talborjt. The best rooms (6 & 7) overlook a garden, while others overlook the street or open onto an interior patio. On a minus point, the shower is outside the rooms, and you have to ask for the key to use it. ❷

Hôtel Diaf Rue Allal Ben Abdallah ⓣ0528 825852, ⓕ0528 821311. Reliable and comfortable with small but clean rooms. Some rooms have en-suite bathrooms. Reservations are only accepted if taken up before 2pm. Rooms on the first floor are a lot nicer than those on the roof. ❷

Hôtel el Bahia Rue el Mahdi Ibn Toumert ⓣ0528 822724, ⓕ0528 824515. A fine little two-star hotel, beautifully modernized with three categories of room (with shower and toilet, with shower only, and with shared bathroom facilities), all with satellite TV, but not all with outside windows. ❷

Hôtel Kamal Bd Hassan II ⓣ0528 842817, ⓦwww.hotelkamal.ma. Centrally located three-star with quite large, cool, comfortable rooms set round a small swimming pool; of all the hotels in town, this one gets consistently good reports. ❹

Hôtel la Tour du Sud Av Kennedy ⓣ0528 822694, ⓕ0528 824846. Small but immaculate, its en-suite rooms have smoked-glass windows and little balconies, built around two courtyards with large trees growing out of them. It's worth avoiding the ground-floor rooms, however, especially on the side facing the street. ❸

Hôtel le Tour Eiffel 25 Av du 29 Février ⓣ0528 823712. A reasonable place with a café-restaurant downstairs which is handy for breakfast. The bathroom facilities are shared, and the hot water supply a bit iffy, but in theory it's on round the clock. ❶

Hôtel Massa Pl Lahcen Tamri ⓣ0528 822409. Simple rooms but clean, around two upstairs courtyards, with shared bathroom facilities but 24hr hot-water. ❷

Hôtel Moderne Rue el Mahdi Ibn Toumert ⓣ0528 840473. Tucked away in a quiet location, and quite prim and proper. Rooms are done out in salmon pink and blue, and have showers but not toilets en suite. ❷

Hôtel Mountassir Rue de la Jeunesse ⓣ0528 843228, ⓔh.almountassir@menara.ma. A city-centre block that offers good value for money – the rooms are plain but decent enough, with balconies, and there's a small pool and garden as well as a café and restaurant. ❸

Hôtel Petite Suède Bd Hassan II ⓣ0528 840779, ⓦwww.petitesuede.com. One of the first hotels built after the earthquake, and not too far from the beach. All rooms have en-suite showers but most have shared toilets, and some have a balcony. There's also a sun terrace, and a ten percent discount for *Rough Guide* readers. ❸

Hôtel Sindibad Pl Lahcen Tamri ⓣ0528 823477, ⓔsinhot@menara.ma. Comfortable and popular hotel with a restaurant and bar, spotless a/c rooms, and a plunge pool on the roof. ❸

Hôtel Tiznine 3 Rue Drarga ⓣ&ⓕ0528 843925. Bright and gleaming, with pleasant if plain rooms, some en suite. Slightly pricier than the other Talborjt cheapies, but worth the difference. ❷

Résidence Sacha Pl de la Jeunesse ⓣ0528 841167, ⓦwww.agadir-maroc.com. Just off the town centre in a quiet square. French-managed, with a range of good-sized self-catering studios and apartments (some with private gardens), and a small swimming pool. ❹

Résidence Yasmina Rue de la Jeunesse ⓣ0528 842660, ⓦwww.residence-yasmina.com. Self-catering apartments with small bedrooms but large sitting rooms and decent-sized kitchens, plus a lobby and salon done out in traditional zellij tilework, and a café, a swimming pool and a children's pool. There's often a discounted rate of one sort or another available. ❺

Main boulevards – towards the beach

The hotels along the **main boulevards**, and particularly towards the beach, are mostly rather fancy places.

Agadir Beach Club Route de l'Oued Souss ⓣ0528 844343, ⓦwww.agadir-beach-club.net. A very grand four-star at the southern end of the beach, with no less than seven restaurants, four bars, a nightclub, a very large pool, and loads of sports facilities. Rooms are not huge but have a/c, satellite TV and a mini-bar, and there are ramps for wheelchairs, but no specifically adapted rooms. ❼

Hôtel Adrar Bd Mohammed V ⓣ0528 840417, ⓦwww.hoteladrar.com. Not a very imposing building but it has charming staff and a good reputation for service, as well as a full range of facilities including pool and restaurant. The room decor is unconvincingly pseudo-Berber, but strangely pleasing nonetheless. BB ❺

Hôtel al Moggar Bd Mohammed V ⓣ0528 842270 or 72 or 76, ⓦwww.hotelalmoggar.com. A large, well-equipped beach package hotel complex, with a nightclub, a large pool, tennis courts, extensive gardens, and concrete bungalow-style rooms that are ugly without but spacious within and have balconies facing the beach. Discounts often available, especially off-season. ❼

Hôtel les Cinq Parties du Monde Bd Hassan II ⓣ0528 845481, ⓕ0528 842504. Handy for Place Salam bus and grand taxi station, with clean, pleasant rooms off a tiled courtyard, plus a decent restaurant. ❹

Hôtel Marhaba Bd Hassan II ⓣ0528 840670. An excellent-value three-star hotel with large, comfortable rooms, a nice pool and gardens, and promotional deals out of season. The beach isn't too far away, but it's across a busy main road. BB ❹

Hôtel Miramar Bd Mohammed V ⓣ0528 840770. The only hotel to survive the earthquake, a homely, twelve-room place, elegantly redesigned by André Paccard, doyen of the *Hôtel La Mamounia* in Marrakesh and several of King Hassan II's palaces, with a good restaurant (see p.494), but no pool. ❹

Hôtel Royal Atlas Bd du 20 Août ⓣ0528 294040, ⓦwww.hotelsatlas.com. A brand new five-star (though, as always, that's equivalent to a four-star elsewhere), very grand, with well-appointed rooms, friendly but laid-back staff, three restaurants, three bars, and – *de rigeur* nowadays – a spa. Its popularity with rich Saudis doing all the things they can't do at home can make it a bit noisy sometimes. Claims to be wheelchair accessible, but no specially adapted rooms. ❽

Mabrouk Hôtel Bd du 20 Août ⓣ0528 828701 or 2, ⓦwww.hmabrouk.ma. A small, friendly three-star hotel, with an attractive garden and large pool. Promotional prices often available off-season. BB ❺

Between Agadir and Inezgane

There are a handful of good hotels off the road south of town towards **Inezgane** and the airport. The recommendations below, detailed as being on the left or right of the road if travelling from Agadir, can be reached on any local bus or shared grand taxi between Agadir and Inezgane.

Jacaranda off Route de Inezgane, 5km from Agadir, right ⓣ0528 280316, ⓦwww.jacaranda-hotel-agadir.com. A very suave establishment, using ecologically sound thick walls, rather than a/c, to keep out the heat, but otherwise offering the usual four-star luxuries, with a pool, original artworks in the rooms and some beautiful stucco-work in the lobby. ❼

La Pergola Route de Inezgane, 8km from Agadir, left ⓣ0528 271801 or 41, ⓦwww.lapergola.ma. Characterful French-run hotel, formerly a colonial villa, with parking facilities and a restaurant (expensive but with a lunchtime set menu, and deals for full-or half-board) serving classic French cuisine which, when on form, is memorable – the menu changes daily, depending on what they select in the market. ❸

Le Provençal Route de Inezgane, 10km from Agadir, on the edge of Inezgane, right ⓣ0528 832612, ⓔhotel_provencale06@yahoo.com. A French-style *auberge*, with bungalow-style rooms arranged around a medium-sized swimming pool and a well-kept garden with flowers and banana trees, and also a bar. ❸

Camping

Some old hands say that campers are better off staying away from Agadir. There are a lot of "no camping" signs, and one **official campsite**, which gets mixed but mainly negative reports: *Camping International Agadir*, Boulevard Mohammed V (ⓣ0528 841054). It is reasonably well located, within easy walking distance of the centre and beach, open all year and fairly secure, with a snack bar and other facilities but there's limited shade, campervans dominate, prices are relatively high, there are no hot showers and it's pretty crowded.

The town and beach

Agadir has few sights other than its beach. If you have kids to amuse, you might consider a ride on the "**tourist train**", which does a 35-minute run around town starting from Boulevard du 20 Août at the bottom of the Valley of the Birds (every 40min; 9.15am–5pm; 18dh).

Along the beach

Agadir's **beach** is as good as they come: a wide expanse of fine sand, which extends an impressive distance to the south of the town, is swept each morning and patrolled by mounted police. Along its course are a number of cafés which rent out sunbeds and umbrellas. The ocean – it should be stressed – has a **very strong Atlantic undertow** and is definitely not suitable for children unless closely supervised. Even adults are advised not to go out swimming alone. The northern end of the beach has lifeguards on duty from June 15 to September 15 8am to 7pm daily, and a system of flags to tell you how dangerous it is to swim.

Jet-skiing (wet-biking; 300dh for 20min) is available at the northern end of the beach at *Club Royale de Jet-Ski*, and also at the southern end of the beach beyond *Agadir Beach Club*. Surfboards, windsurfing equipment, quad bikes and beach buggies can also be rented.

There are **guarded sections** at the northern end of the beach, mostly run by neighbouring restaurants, where you can rent a sunbed with a parasol. The big beach hotels also have guarded sections for their residents. Toilet and shower facilities (including wheelchair-friendly ones) can be found behind the *Jour et Nuit* restaurant.

The Valley of the Birds

As a break from the beach, you might wander into the **Valley of the Birds** (daily 11am–6pm; 5dh), a small valley which runs down from Boulevard Hassan II, under Boulevard Mohammed V, to Boulevard du 20 Août. It's basically a narrow strip of parkland, with a little aviary of exotic birds, a small herd of Barbary sheep, a waterfall and a children's playground: all very pleasant, and the lush vegetation draws a rich variety of birds throughout the year.

A few blocks to the south is an outdoor theatre – built along Roman odeon lines – and a pedestrian precinct of tourist shops and restaurants where the small **Amazigh Heritage Museum** (Mon–Sat 9.30am–5.30pm; 20dh) has a collection of Berber cultural artefacts, including carpets and jewellery, but nothing wildly exciting.

The Jardim de Olhão

On Avenue Kennedy, just south of Avenue des FAR, a very pleasant outdoor space is the **Jardim de Olhão** (daily 8am–6.30pm; free), a landscaped garden with a café-restaurant and children's playground, opened in 2003 to celebrate the fourth anniversary of Agadir's twinning with the town of Olhão in Portugal. The walls and buildings in the garden are constructed in a traditional Berber style which some claim was inspired by Portuguese architecture, though the influence is hard to see, and could just as easily have been the other way round anyway.

Next to the Jardim de Olhão, at the junction of Avenue Kennedy with Avenue des FAR, the **Exposition Mémoire d'Agadir** (Tues–Sat 9.30am–12.30pm & 3–6pm; 20h) has some interesting photographs of Agadir as it was before and immediately after the 1960 earthquake.

Markets

The **Municipal Market** is a two-storey concrete block in the centre of town between Avenue des FAR and Avenue Prince Sidi Mohammed, with a display of wet fish downstairs cheek by jowl with fossils and handicrafts. Upstairs, it's mostly souvenir shops with rather high prices. **Talborjt** has a plain and simple little food market on Rue Mahdi Ibn Toumert just northwest of Place Lahcen Tamri.

Agadir's most impressive market is the **Souk el Had**, in a massive walled enclosure on Rue Chair al Hamra, selling fruit, vegetables, household goods and clothes, with a few tourist stalls thrown in. Sunday is the big day, when it spreads out over the neighbouring streets, as people come from all over the region to buy and sell their wares.

Signposted off the Inezgane road, 4km out of town, the "**Medina d'Agadir**" (Ⓣ0528 280253, Ⓦwww.medinapolizzi.com; daily except Mon 9am–5.30pm; 40dh) is a complex, purpose-built in traditional style, where crafts are made and sold to tourists. It can be reached by RATAG bus #28 or #40, or ZETRAP bus #25 or #30 from Avenue Mohammed V.

Ancienne Talborjt and the old kasbah

The raised plateau of **Ancienne Talborjt**, which entombs the town demolished in the 1960 earthquake, stands to the west of the city centre. It is marked by a small mosque and unfinished memorial garden. Relatives of the 15,000 dead come to this park area to walk, remember and pray: a moving sight, even after so many years.

For visitors, a more tangible sight of old Agadir is the **kasbah**, on the hill to the north of the port. This is an eight-kilometre trip, worth making if you have transport, or by petit taxi, for a marvellous view of Agadir and the coast. You can see the kasbah quite clearly from central Agadir – and more particularly a vast "Allah–King–Nation" slogan, picked out in Arabic, in white stones, illuminated at night, on the slopes below.

Athough it survived the quake, the kasbah is little more than a bare outline of walls and an entrance arch – the latter with an inscription in Dutch and Arabic recording that the Netherlands began trading here in 1746 (capitalizing on the

The Souss estuary: birds and the palace

If the Oued Souss is flowing (it often dries out), the **estuary** is of interest to **birdwatchers**. The northern banks of the river have good views of a variety of waders and wildfowl including greater flamingo (most evident in Aug and Sept), spoonbill, ruddy shelduck, avocet, greenshank and curlew, while the surrounding scrubby banks also have large numbers of migrant warblers and Barbary partridge. The **Royal Palace**, built in the 1980s in an imaginative blend of traditional and modern forms, can be glimpsed from the riverbank, but is not open to visitors.

To reach the estuary by road, take the Inezgane road out of town (RATAG bus #28 or #40, ZETRAP bus #25 or #30 from Agadir) and turn right after 6km at the traffic lights and signpost for Golf des Dunes, but be warned that there have been reports of robberies, sometimes at knifepoint, so leave your valuables behind.

rich sugar plantations of the Souss plain). It's not much, but it is one of the few reminders that the city has any past at all, so complete was the destruction of the 1960 earthquake.

Eating, drinking and nightlife

For an international resort, Agadir has few bars, clubs or discos, outside of the large hotels. There are plenty of **cafés** and **restaurants**, for all budgets, but most of those lining the beach and the boulevards are tourist traps, with waiters outside trying to hustle in any passing foreigner who shows an interest.

If your hotel doesn't provide **breakfast**, several places in Talborjt will do so (the *Ibtissam* and the *Select* for example), while many cafés around Place Salam bus station – and the café of the *Hôtel Massa*, and its neighbour on Place Lahcen Tamri – have stalls outside selling *harsha* and *msimmen* (Moroccan breads) to eat with a coffee and croissant. The *Hôtel Sindibad* serves breakfast from around 6.30am, handy for early risers.

Restaurants

Inexpensive café-restaurants are concentrated in **Talborjt**, some with bargain set menus. There's also a scattering of cafés and mid-price restaurants on or near the **beach**, including two that stay open 24 hours, along with a fair range of more sophisticated places. Also worth considering if you want something special is the excellent French restaurant at *La Pergola* (see p.491).

Talborjt/city centre

L'Étoile de Marrakech *Studiotel Afoud*, Rue de la Foire ☎0528 843999. Renowned for its traditional Moroccan dishes, the restaurant at the front of the hotel (serving the same food) is open daily 7.30–10.30am for breakfast, noon–3pm for lunch, 7.30–11pm for dinner, with snacks served in between times, while the dinner cabaret, at the back of the hotel, opens at 6pm, gets going with live music at 11pm and continues until 3 or 4am. Moderate.

Restaurant des Arcades Rue Allal Ben Abdallah. The combination of a traditional-style painted stucco ceiling with glass chandeliers and seaside blue-and-white striped walls is a bit jarring, but the food isn't bad for the price, with a good-value 40dh set menu, and snacks such as omelettes. Daily 7am–11pm. Cheap.

Restaurant Daffy Rue des Oranges. Pavement dining or couches around the inside tables, and reasonable set menus (55–60dh), or dishes like pastilla, mechoui or tanjia for two if ordered in advance. Daily 11am–11pm. Cheap to moderate.

Restaurant Ibtissam Pl Lahcen Tamri. The best of a trio of cheapies all next to each other, handy for breakfast as well as for lunch and dinner. Serves Moroccan and international staples, with a bargain set menu (40dh), and vegetarian options if requested. Daily 11am–11pm. Cheap.

Restaurant Select 38 Rue Allal Ben Abdallah. Food varies from mediocre to delicious, but always good for the price. The set menu (40dh) is a great deal, or there are steaks, escalopes, and also juices. Daily 7.30am–10pm. Cheap.

SOS Poulet Av Moulay Abdallah, near the post office. Chicken meals (brochettes, sandwiches, or quarter, half or whole roast chickens with rice or chips), to eat in or take away. Daily noon–midnight. Cheap.

Tour de Paris 40 Bd Hassan II ⓣ0528 840901. Quite a high-quality place, with classic dishes like pastilla, couscous and several tasty tajines (duck confit, for example, or beef noisettes with prawns and Roquefort cheese). Daily noon–midnight. Moderate to expensive.

Via Veneto Bd Hassan II ⓣ0528 841467. This place used to serve the best Italian food in town, and still rustles up a decent wood-oven pizza, *osso bucco* or paella. Daily 11am–midnight. Moderate.

Main boulevards/towards the beach

Feyrouz Bd du 20 Août. Lebanese cuisine, including *mezze*, shish kebab, and *musakhan* (chicken shredded with spices and baked in flat bread – really a Palestinian rather than a Lebanese dish). Daily 3–11pm. Moderate.

Fishing port stalls outside Port d'Agadir. Not on a par with their equivalents in Essaouira (see p.335), but the gathering of stalls here will do you a freshly caught fish grilled over charcoal for not very much money – 34dh for shrimps, squid or whiting, 300dh for lobster, crawfish or king prawns. Daily winter noon–7pm, summer noon–11pm. Cheap.

Jour et Nuit on the beach off Rue de la Plage. International-style dishes such as lamb chops, steaks and roast chicken, and snacks including assorted sandwiches and a range of salads, plus a bar. There's a slightly posher branch in a 1930s-style building just 50m to the north. Both open daily 24hr. Moderate.

La Scala Bd de l'Oued Souss ⓣ0528 846773. Well-regarded upmarket restaurant serving Mediterranean cuisine, including modern dishes such as duck with ginger and orange, or salmon paupiette with aniseed, all served on a large terrace surrounded by trees. Daily noon–3pm & 7pm–midnight. Expensive.

La Truite between Bd Hassan II and Bd Mohammed V, opposite Amazigh Heritage Museum. Bacon and egg breakfasts, draught beer, and a sign that still says "Irish Pub", though the bar inside is decked out with cross of St George flags. It's pretty naff, of course, but it does show live English football, which makes it very handy if you need to catch a game (or if you're pining for a rasher of dead pig). The *English Pub* on Bd du 20 Août is much the same. Daily 8am–10pm. Moderate.

Le Miramar in the *Hôtel Miramar*, Bd Mohammed V ⓣ0528 840770. The city's most chic restaurant – a beautifully decorated place overlooking the fishing port. Fine international cuisine, particularly fish and seafood. Daily noon–2pm & 7.30–10pm. Expensive.

Mezzo Mezzo Bd Mohammed V. Agadir's poshest pizzeria, with a wide selection of pizzas and dishes made with their own fresh pasta, all served in cosy modern surroundings. Daily 7pm–midnight. Moderate to expensive.

Yacht Club Restaurant du Port Port d'Agadir ⓣ0528 843708. An excellent place for fresh fish and seafood – as you'd expect from the location inside the fishing port, though the fish can be overcooked. Specialities include fillet of John Dory with orange sauce, or fish brochettes. Take your passport, as you have to go through customs. Daily noon–3pm & 7–10pm. Moderate to expensive.

Patisseries

Patisserie Tafarnout Bd Hassan II at Rue de la Foire. Agadir's poshest patisserie, to indulge yourself with utterly sinful pastries including blackcurrant mousse on a chocolate cake base, or just a common-or-garden coffee and croissant. Daily 11am–7pm.

Yacout Av du 29 Février between Rue de l'Entraide and Rue Prince Moulay Abdallah. Patisserie selling Lebanese specialities such as *baklava* as well as excellent versions of almond-stuffed Moroccan favourites such as *corne de gazelle*. It also has a café and garden, great for a tea and pastry, or even a pastilla, but don't bother with the set menu (65dh). Daily 7am–10pm.

Bars and nightlife

The *Jour et Nuit* restaurant (see above) has a **bar** open 24 hours. **Nightclubs** get going around 11pm or midnight, and stay open till 4 or 5am; entry tends to be 50dh Monday to Wednesday & Sunday, 100dh Thursday–Saturday (including the first drink). The club scene in Agadir can be quite sleazy – it's a good idea in the more popular clubs to pay for your drinks as you buy them rather than running up a tab to pay at the end of the evening, when you may be too drunk to notice the addition of extraneous items. Prostitution is rife (at the *Flamingo* and the *Papagayo*, for example) but it's illegal, to the extent that girls and punters travel in separate taxis to avoid police attention (if they travel together, the cab driver may flash police en route to alert them), and clampdowns are not unknown.

Shopping in Agadir

Prices for **crafts and souvenirs** in Agadir are generally high. Good first stops are Adrar, on Avenue Prince Moulay Abdallah, through the passageway behind the Crown English Bookshop, and the Uniprix shop at the corner of Boulevard Hassan II and Avenue Prince Sidi Mohammed, which sell goods at fixed prices, as does the chaotic Ensemble Artisanal (Mon–Fri 9am–7pm, though individual shops may open later, close for lunch or shut earlier) on Avenue du 29 Février, just north of Place Lahcen Tamri. There are stalls selling crafts in the Souk el Had (see p.492), and there's also the Medina d'Agadir (see p.492).

For **food and drink**, Sawma Supermarket, 1 Rue Hôtel de Ville, just off Boulevard Hassan II near Rue de la Foire, has a good selection, and the Uniprix shop (see above) also sells the cheapest booze, along with general provisions, hidden away at the back behind the clothes and tourist tat. The biggest supermarket is Marjane, just out of town on the Inezgane road. The Souk el Had and the market in Talborjt (see p.492) are good for fresh produce. The honey shop at 129 Rue Marrakech, by the junction with Avenue Mouqaouama, sells various kinds of honey, and olive and argan oil. In Talborjt, Fromital at 6 Rue Fal Ould Omair (Ⓦwww.fromital.com) purveys its own excellent, locally produced cheeses (also available at big supermarkets elsewhere in the country).

Actor's in the *Hôtel Royal Atlas*, Bd du 20 Août ⓣ0528 294040. Currently Agadir's trendiest disco, with guest DJs, a variety of sounds and a mixed crowd.

Disco Tan Tan in the *Hôtel Almohades*, Bd du 20 Août ⓣ528 840233. Long-established hotel disco, and generally a safe bet, not one of the "in" clubs in Agadir at present, but has the advantage of being nearer to town than most of the others, and usually charges for drinks rather than entry.

Flamingo in the *Agadir Beach Club*, Bd du 20 Août, ⓣ0528 844343. Lively if rather seedy nightclub attached to one of the bigger beach package hotels, and very popular with Moroccans as well as foreigners.

Papagayo in the *Tikida Beach Hotel*, Bd du 20 Août, ⓣ0528 845400. Very lively with a mix of Western and a few Arabic pop sounds. Tacky but fun, though entry is a bit steep at 200dh.

Red Lion Dance Bar in the *Mabrouk Hôtel* ⓣ0528 828701. Not a discotheque, but a bar with an Arabic band – it opens early, around 8pm, but you won't find anyone dancing much before midnight.

Listings

Airlines British Airways, at the airport ⓣ0528 839109; Regional Air Lines, at the airport ⓣ0528 839339; Royal Air Maroc, Av Général Kettani, opposite the junction with Bd Hassan II ⓣ0528 829120.

Banks Many with ATMs on Av Général Kettani between Bd Hassan II and Bd Mohammed V. BMCE and Banque Populaire on Av Kennedy near the junction of Av du 29 Février in Talborjt. Currency Exchange Point foreign exchange bureau at 31 Av Kennedy (daily 8.30am–9.30pm). Tarik Reisen travel agency, 20 Marché Cité Charaf, on the road connecting Bd du 20 Août to Chemin de Oued Souss near the royal palace (daily 9am–9pm).

Bicycle and motorbike rental Various operators rent out motorbikes, scooters and bicycles along Bd du 20 Août south of Route de l'Oued Souss, but many are cowboys. A reliable firm will rent for 24hr rather than just until nightfall, and will show full paperwork (rather than just a receipt) proving that the insurance, minimal though it might be, covers you (and passenger if necessary) and detailing help in the event of a breakdown. Typically, motorbikes are 400dh per day, scooters 250dh, bicycles 100dh.

Car rental Bungalow Marhaba on Bd Mohammed V (see map, p.486) houses Avis (ⓣ0528 841755); Budget (ⓣ0528 848222); Europcar (ⓣ0528 840337), Hertz (ⓣ0528 840939); Lotus Cars (ⓣ0528 840588); Tourist Cars (ⓣ0528 840200); Weekend Cars (ⓣ0528 840667); and local operator Youness Cars (ⓣ0528 840750, Ⓔyouness-cars@hotmail.com), of whom we've had good reports in the past. The main agencies also have branches at the airport. Other companies include: First Car, Immeuble Oumlil,

17 Bd Hassan II, at the corner of Rue de l'Hôtel de Ville (☎0528 826796); National, Immeuble Sud Bahia on Bd Hassan II (☎0528 840026); and recommended local firm Amoudou Cars on Bd Hassan II, at the corner of Av Mouqaouama (☎0528 825010, ⓔamadou.car@laposte.net), who offer a 10 percent discount to Rough Guide readers renting cars for three days or more, and may do special deals in combination with accommodation at the *Petite Suède* hotel.

Cinemas Sahara, Pl Lahcen Tamri in Talborjt (very cheap, mainly Bollywood); Rialto, off Av des FAR behind municipal market (slightly pricier, mainly Hollywood).

Consulates Ireland (honorary consul), *Hôtel Kenzi Europa*, Bd du 20 Août ☎0528 821212; UK (honorary consul), Complet Tours, 26 Immeuble Oumlil, third floor, Bd Hassan II ☎0528 840469, ⓔmichellek.assistant-honcon@fconet.fco.gov.uk.

Festival July's Timitar Festival, dedicated to nomadic music, is not on a par with Essaouira (see p.337), but draws musicians from all over southern Morocco, as well as north and west Africa, France, Spain and, even Latin America.

Golf Agadir has three golf clubs, all southeast of town: Agadir Royal Golf, 12km out on the Route d'Aït Melloul (☎0528 848551), the smallest, with only nine holes and closed Mon, but the oldest-established, and generally considered the finest; Golf des Dunes (☎0528 834690), with three nine-hole courses; and Golf du Soleil (☎0528 337329, ⓦwww.golfdusoleil.com), which is the newest and also has three nine-hole courses.

Hammam To sweat out the grime in Talborjt, the Bain Maure Essalama, on Rue Mahdi Ibn Toumert, is open daily for women 6am–6pm, and for men 6pm–midnight.

Internet access In Talborjt, there's Streamjet at 19 Rue Allal Ben Abdallah (Mon–Thurs 10.30am–1pm & 2–10.30pm, Fri–Sun 2–10.30pm; 5dh per hr), and Futurnet on the first floor of a building on Av Kennedy opposite the mosque at the junction of Av du 29 Février (daily 8am–10pm; 7dh per hr). There are also several places on Rue de Meknes by Pl Salam bus station.

Medical aid Most of the big hotels can provide addresses for English-speaking doctors. Current recommendations include Dr Mustapha Benjelloun, Immeuble Tinmal, Rue des FAR ☎0528 843737, and a dentist – Dr Noureddine Touhami, Immeuble M2, Apt 4, second floor (behind *SOS Pêcheurs*), Av Prince Moulay Abdallah (☎0528 846320), by appointment only. Clinique al Massira, on Av Prince Moulay Abdallah at the junction of Av du 29 Février (☎0528 843238) has 24hr emergency service. There's a night pharmacy at the town hall behind the main post office, and a list of *pharmacies de garde* (chemists open all night) posted in the windows of most town pharmacies.

Post offices The main post office is right at the top of Av Sidi Mohammed, Mon–Fri 8am–6.30pm, Sat 8am–noon. There's a branch post office on Av du 29 Février in Talborjt, opposite the Ensemble Artesanal, with similar hours, and a very small one on Bd du 20 Août near the junction of Chemin de Oued Souss.

Moving on

Agadir is a reasonable **transport terminal**, but for many services, especially in shared grands taxis, you'll need to go to Inezgane. This can be reached by grand taxi from Place Salam (4dh a place), or on RATAG bus #28 or ZETRAP buses #25 and #30 from Avenue Mohammed V.

By air

The **airport** at Al Massira (☎0528 839112) is 25km east of town. The easiest way to get to it without your own transport is by grand taxi (150dh during the day or 200dh at night for up to six people), but there is a cheaper way if you're hard up: get a bus or shared grand taxi (4dh) to Inezgane, and from there take local GAB bus #22 (every 30min; 6am–7.20pm; 4dh).

Driving to the airport from Agadir in your own vehicle, you have a choice of routes. The easiest is to leave Agadir by way of Aït Melloul and the Taroudant (N10) road, turning right at the signposted junction. Alternatively, you can approach from the north, leaving Agadir on the Marrakesh (N8) road, then turning off (left) just after Tikiouine.

Airport staff at Agadir have been known to tell passengers that valuables (such as cameras) are not allowed on as hand baggage and must be carried in the hold. Note that such items are likely to go missing if not securely locked away.

By bus

All **bus** services from Agadir operate from the bleak new concrete *gare routière* at the eastern edge of town on Rue Chair el Hamra (aka Bd Abderrahim Bouabid) at the junction with Avenue Qadi Ayyad (☎0528 822077; around 10–15dh by petit taxi from the city centre, or 3.30dh on RATAG bus #3 from Place Salam), which, despite being brand new, suffers from the usual dearth of departure information. The best services are operated by ONCF/Supratours (10 Rue des Oranges ☎0528 841207) and CTM (Rue Yacoub el Mansour ☎0528 822077), whose schedules can be checked and tickets bought at their offices in town. For journey times and frequencies see p.537.

By grand taxi

Agadir's **grands taxis** leave from a rank a block south of the local bus station at **Place Salam**. They run to Inezgane, as well as direct to Tiznit, Taroudant and sometimes other destinations, but otherwise you'll have to take one to Inezgane and get a connection there, which may be easier even for Taroudant and Tiznit, especially since drivers at Agadir have started trying to charge tourists (not Moroccans, of course) extra for their baggage. The fare in a shared taxi to Inezgane is 4dh, and grands taxis for points beyond will cost 4dh less from Inezgane than direct from Agadir, so you lose nothing by going there, and you could well get a faster connection, with no nonsense about baggage charges. Taxis for Anza and Aourir run from right next to the local bus station itself, and also from outside the fishing port.

Inezgane

INEZGANE, on the north bank of the Oued Souss, is almost a suburb of Agadir, just 13km distant. The two could hardly be more different, though, for Inezgane is wholly Moroccan, and is a major transport hub for the region – much more so than Agadir – with buses and grands taxis going to most southern destinations.

It's connected with Agadir by RATAG bus #28 and ZETRAP buses #28 and #30 (very frequent, all running along Av Mohammed V) and by frequent grands taxis (4dh a place, arriving/leaving Agadir at Place Salam). Each of these, along with intercity buses, have their own section of the *gare routière*, which is off Avenue Mokhtar Soussi, a wide street with arcades on both sides, running from the central Place al Massira to the main Agadir road. Across Avenue Mokhtar Soussi, through the arcades, is a wonderful city **market**, full of fruit, veg, spices, knick-knacks and traditional cosmetics. From Place al Massira, the road makes a ninety-degree turn, and crosses Boulevard Mohammed V, Inezgane's main street, where you'll find the post office and most of the shops.

Accommodation

If you arrive late at Agadir airport, and want to head straight on, you could do a lot worse than stay here, rather than Agadir; you may be able to negotiate a slightly cheaper taxi from the airport, too (around 100dh). There are dozens of **hotels** near the bus station, all pretty basic, but prices are around half what they would be in equivalent Agadir hotels. Hotels on the Agadir–Inezgane road are listed on p.491.

Hôtel al Qods 50 Pl al Massira ⓣ0528 836322. Friendly, reasonably clean (though some rooms are a bit musty), and handy for the market and bus station. Some rooms have an en-suite shower but the cheapest have shared bathroom facilities, and there's hot water round the clock. ❶

Hôtel de Paris 30 Bd Mohammed V ⓣ0528 330571. Extremely cheap, with an inexpensive restaurant too. Some rooms have en-suite shower, and there should be constant hot water. ❶

Hôtel Hagounia 9 Av Mokhtar Soussi ⓣ0528 832783. Right by the bus station on a busy intersection, with reasonable rooms, en-suite showers and 24hr hot water. ❷

North of Agadir

The coast road north from Agadir passes first through the industrial suburb of **Anza**. Beyond that is a great swathe of **beach**, interrupted here and there by headlands and for the most part deserted. RATAG city bus #12, and ZETRAP buses #50, #60 and #61 run regularly up the coast to Aourir, #12 and #60 continuing to Taghazout, #61 to Tamri, while Essaouira-bound intercity buses will take you beyond Tamri and Cap Rhir. The coast is a good target, too, if you rent scooters, mopeds or motorbikes in Agadir.

Eleven kilometres from Agadir, the road reaches **AOURIR**, where it branches inland to Paradise Valley and Immouzer des Ida Outanane (see p.501). Aourir and its sister village of **TAMRAGHT**, a kilometre beyond, are jointly known as "Banana Village" after the thriving banana groves that divide them; the roadside stalls sell bananas in season. Aourir's best **hotel** is the *Littoral* (ⓣ0528 314726, ⓦwww.hotellittoral.com; ❸), just past the Immouzer turn-off, on your right if heading north, with spotless rooms, tiled floors, self-catering suites and a terrace, an amazing bargain compared to Agadir's hostelries. Even more of a bargain is the lovely *Hôtel Riad Imourane*, 2km north of Tamraght on the landward side, beyond a popular surfing spot called Dynamic Beach (ⓣ0528 315419; ❹), with immaculate rooms, beautiful tiled floors, carpets and tasteful traditional decor throughout.

You can **eat** extremely well at the roadside café-restaurants 200m north of the Immouzer turn-off, opposite the Afriquia petrol station, a weekend favourite

Argan trees

One of the stranger sights of the Souss and surrounding coastal region is goats browsing among the branches of spiny, knotted **argan** trees, a species similar to the olive that is found only in this region. Though some younger goatherds seem to have a sideline in charging tourists to take photographs, the actual object of the exercise is to let the goats eat the outer, fleshy part of the argan fruit. The hard, inner nut is then cracked open and the kernel crushed to extract the expensive oil.

Argan **oil** is sweet and rich, and is used in many Moroccan dishes and in salads, or for dunking bread. It is also used to make **amalou**, a delicious dip of honey and almond paste.

An expensive delicacy, argan oil is not easily extracted: whilst one olive tree provides around five litres of olive oil, it takes the nuts from thirty argan trees to make just one litre of argan oil. Plastic **bottles** of argan oil are occasionally sold at the roadside in the Oued Souss area, but are often adulterated with cheaper oils. It is therefore better to buy argan oil or amalou from a reputable source such as the cooperatives at Tidzi (see p.338), Tioute (see p.508), or Tamanar (see p.339), the honey shop in Agadir (see p.495), *Hôtel Tifrit* in Paradise Valley (see p.501), or specialist shops in Marrakesh or Essaouira. Argan oil is also sometimes sold in larger supermarkets.

among Agadiris. The best is the *Baraka* (ⓣ0528 314074; daily noon–midnight; moderate), which offers delicious chicken, beef, lamb or goat tajines, or *mechoui* (you pay by the kilo, around a quarter kilo is fine for one person), but no other options. Otherwise, the restaurant at the *Hôtel Littoral* (daily 11.30am–3pm & 6.30–10pm; moderate) does a variety of fish and pasta dishes, including pesto or Napolitana for vegetarians, and has an 80dh set menu.

Aourir and Tamraght share "Banana Beach", a sandy strip, broken by the Oued Tamraght, the dividing line between the two villages. Banana Beach is used by surfers, and is especially good for the less experienced, with slower, fatter breaks than those at points to the north.

Around 2km north of Tamraght, a prominent rocky headland, **Les Roches du Diable**, is flanked by further good beaches. Shortly beyond (16km from Agadir but opposite a beach which calls itself "Km 17"), a signposted *piste* leads to Ranch R.E.H.A. (ⓣ0528 847549, ⓔreha@wanadoo.net.ma), where you can go **horse trekking** into the mountains.

Taghazout

Eighteen kilometres from Agadir is the fishing village of **TAGHAZOUT** (Tarhazoute, or even Taghagant). At one time Morocco's hippy resort *par excellence*, it is now the country's main surfing resort instead, but the laid-back vibe and friendly relationship between villagers and tourists remains. Several surf shops rent out, sell or repair boards, and sell surfing accoutrements (the longest established is Free Surf on Rue Sidi Said Ouhmed, just opposite the main square).

The main movers and shakers on the surfing scene are British firm Surf Maroc (see p.33), who have a villa between Hash Point and Anchor Point for their clients, with an assortment of terraces and bathroom facilities, offering surf guiding and tuition along with the accommodation. They also rent out apartments at surfing spots further north. If you just want **accommodation** without the rest of the package, the most obvious option (though it's also run by Surf Maroc) is the *Auberge* overlooking the beach on Rue Taiought Atlas (ⓣ0528 200272, ⓦwww.surfmaroc.co.uk/auberge; ❸), with small but pleasant rooms, hot-water showers and a roof terrace, a restaurant downstairs (serving the likes of Thai green curry, and apple crumble) and a juice bar called *Aftas* next door. Local firms rent out apartments, typically at around 250dh a day for a one-bedroom apartment, 350dh for a two-bedroom place, but you may be able to find a cheaper deal by renting a room from a local family – you'll need to haggle, but two people should be able to get a room for 100–150dh a night or less, especially if staying for a week or more. The **campsite** south of the village, used mainly by campervan-driving retired Europeans, has now gone, but is expected to reappear at a new site in the not too distant future, so keep your ear to the ground. Also on the way is a new development called Taghazout Resort, involving a slew of package beach hotels and a golf course, to be built between Tamraght and Taghazout. For **meals**, small restaurants in the village serve up grilled fresh fish at very reasonable prices. Among them are the *Panorama*, overlooking the beach at the south end of the village beach (daily 9am–10pm; cheap), and several restaurants on the main road north of the bus stop, such as the *Café Restaurant Tenerife*, which dish up steak, fish, brochettes or tajines at very reasonable prices.

Taghazout can be reached from Agadir by local bus #12, #60 or #61 (from Place Salam or Boulevard Mouqaouma via Boulevard Mohammed V). In theory the #12 and the #60 run every fifteen minutes, the #61 every half-hour. There are also frequent daily buses in each direction between Agadir and Essaouira, most of which will stop here.

Surfing around Taghazout

For right-footed surfers, the points just north of Taghazout are an absolute paradise, with a cluster of excellent right-hand breaks. Six kilometres north of the village, **Killers**, named after the killer whales which are often seen here, has one of the most consistent breaks, a powerful, perfectly peeling charger which breaks over a cliff shelf. **Source**, just south of Killers, is so called for the fresh water bubbling up underneath it. **Anchor Point**, just north of Taghazout, has long waves and big breaks, while at the north end of the village beach itself, **Hash Point** is supposedly used by those too stoned to make it to the others. A number of places in Taghazout, such as Almugar Surf Shop by the bus stop, rent and repair surfing equipment.

There are also good surf spots north and south of Taghazout, notably at **Banana Beach** between Aourir and Tamraght (see p.499), and **Dynamic Beach** just north of Tamraght (see p.498), and at **Cap Rhir** near Tamri (see below). For further advice on surfing, see p.55. Further information about surf spots around Taghazout can be found on the Surf Maroc website at Ⓦwww.surfmaroc.co.uk.

On to Cap Rhir: beaches and birdwatching

North of Taghazout, **25km Plage** (its distance from Agadir) is an attractive beach by a rocky headland, with good surfing. From here on to Cap Rhir, a stretch also known as **Paradis Plage**, are many little beaches, with caves on the rocky outcrops, including a really superb strand at Amesnaz, 33km from Agadir.

Cap Rhir (41km from Agadir) is distinguished by its 1926 French-built lighthouse and a **surfing** spot called **Boilers**, a powerful right break named after the relic of a shipwreck that's perched on an island: the paddle-out between the wreck and the shore demands good duckdiving or immaculate timing to avoid being washed up by sets. **Draculas**, a fast, shallow right named after its pin-cushion of sea urchins, breaks just inshore of Boilers. The whole area, together with **TAMRI** village and **lagoon**, 3km north (at the end of local bus route #61 from Agadir), is good for **birdwatching** – including the rare bald ibis, Madeiran and Bulwer's petrels, Cory's and Manx Shearwaters, gannets, common scoter and Audouin's gulls – but we've heard of birdwatchers being menaced here by youths, so it's best not to come alone. Tamri's excellent **bananas** are sold at roadside stalls, and there are several **cafés** for other sorts of sustenance.

For the continuation of this route along the N1, see pp.338–339, where it is covered in a north–south direction from Essaouira. For much of the way the road runs inland, with just the occasional *piste* leading down to the sea.

Inland to Paradise Valley and Immouzer

The trip up to **Immouzer des Ida Outanane** – via **Paradise Valley**, a beautiful palm-lined gorge – is a superb excursion from Agadir. It is feasible in a day (Immouzer is 62km from Agadir) but it is more enjoyable to stay at one of the *auberges* or camp in the valley.

The 7002 road to Immouzer leaves the N1 coast road at Aourir, 12km north of Agadir (make sure you take the right-hand fork in the village – the left-hand one is a dead-end). To get there, take a grand taxi or city bus to Aourir, from where there are shared grands taxis to Immouzer, though mostly on Thursday for the weekly souk (other days you may have a long wait, though you should be able to get a paid lift on the way down).

A scenic surfaced road connects Immouzer with the N8 Agadir–Marrakesh road, allowing easy access from Ameskroud, Taroudant or Marrakesh.

Paradise Valley

Paradise Valley begins around 10km east of Aourir, a deep, palm-lined gorge, with a river snaking along the base. There's a well-marked 2.7-kilometre walking trail at around 28km from Aourir, or you can hire a mule to explore the valley's Berber villages, and it's a glorious place to camp, though pitch your tent well away from the riverbed in case of flash floods.

There's an excellent place to stay 3km further, in the form of a small **auberge**, the *Hôtel Tifrit* (Ⓣ0528 826044, Ⓦwww.hotel-tifrit.com; HB ④), set among palms and olives, and run by a charming family, with simple, cool rooms, a swimming pool, and fine Moroccan meals on its terrace (80dh menu or moderate à la carte); they also sell locally made honey and argan oil. The same family run the *Auberge le Panoramic*, 500m further up (Ⓣ0528 216709, Ⓦwww.lepanoramic-auberge.com; HB ④), which lives up to its name, with impressive views down the valley, and a panoramic terrace where you can take lunch. A couple of kilometres further up, in the village of **Aqseri**, and a little bit classier, the *Auberge la Bonne Franquette* (Ⓣ0528 823191; HB ⑥) has five very charming split-level bungalows (sleeping area upstairs, sitting area downstairs), a pool and a French restaurant.

Immouzer des Ida Outanane

A further 20km of winding mountain road takes you to the village of **IMMOUZER DES IDA OUTANANE**, a small regional and market centre (of the Ida Outanane tribe, as its full name suggests) tucked away in a westerly outcrop of the Atlas. The **waterfall**, for which the village was renowned, is nearby, and was best seen at its foot, 4km downhill to the northwest. Unfortunately the falls have been very adversely affected by drought over the last few years; tight control of irrigation now reduces the cascade on most occasions to a trickle, with the villagers "turning on" the falls for special events only. However, the petrified canopy of the falls is of interest in its own right, and there's a full **plunge pool**.

The whole area is perfect for walkers. A four-kilometre surfaced road twists down to the foot of the falls, with cafés and souvenir stalls on both sides of the riverbed. A path from the lowest point in the garden of the *Hôtel des Cascades* follows a water channel across cliffs (it's then possible to scramble down into the olive groves, but it isn't a route for the timid or unfit, and ascending again is harder still). Several of the staff at the hotel can help you spot local birdlife, including golden eagles and crag martins.

In Immouzer village, there's a **souk** every Thursday. The local speciality is honey, made by bees that browse on wild thyme, lavender and other mountain herbs. There's also a five-day honey moussem in late July or early to mid-August.

Accommodation

Hôtel des Cascades (Ⓣ0528 826016; ⑤), signposted from the main square, is delightful, set amid gardens of vines, apple and olive trees, roses and hollyhocks, with a panorama of the mountains rolling down to the coast (all rooms have a balcony and a share of the view), and a spectacular path down to the foot of the falls. The food, too, is memorable and there's a swimming pool (full in summer) and tennis court. The hotel can organize trekking on foot or by donkey, maintains *gîtes* to overnight in, and has arrangements with families further afield to put up guests.

The Massa lagoon

The **Massa lagoon**, on the coast around 40km south of Agadir, is part of the Souss–Massa National Park, and is one of Morocco's most important **bird habitats** (see box below), attracting unusual desert visitors and often packed with flamingos, avocets and ducks. The best times to visit are March to April or October to November.

In the village of **Massa**, *Kasbah Tassila* (ⓣ0528 260047), a restaurant that was originally a market compound built in 1851, is popular with tour groups from Agadir. The only hotel accommodation is the very upmarket *Ksar Massa* (ⓣ0661 280319, ⓦwww.ksarmassa.com; BB ⑧).

Transport of your own is a considerable advantage for getting to and exploring the lagoon area. Otherwise, you could charter a taxi in Agadir or Inezgane for the day, or take GAB bus #17 (every 30min till 7pm) or a grand taxi from Inezgane to Massa. Bus #17 continues to Arbalo, halfway to Sidi Rbat, from where you can walk to the beach along the Oued, an area rich in birdlife. The beach itself is often misty and overcast – even when Agadir is basking in the sun – but on a clear day, it's as good as anywhere else and the walks are enjoyable.

Taroudant and around

With its majestic, tawny-brown circuit of walls, **TAROUDANT** is one of the most elegant towns in Morocco. Its position at the heart of the fertile Souss Valley has always given it a commercial and political importance, and the Saadians briefly made it their capital in the sixteenth century before moving on to Marrakesh. Taroudant is a friendly, laid-back sort of place, with a population of around 60,000 and the good-natured bustle of a Berber market town, and it's a good base for trekking into the Western High Atlas or the Djebel Sirwa as well as for two superb road routes – north over the **Tizi n'Test** to Marrakesh (see pp.403–409), and south to **Tata** (see p.512), Foum el Hassan (see p.515) and beyond.

The Massa lagoon: birdwatching

Oued Massa has a rich mix of habitats and draws a fabulous array of birds. The **sandbars** are visited in the early morning by flocks of sandgrouse (black-bellied and spotted) and often shelter large numbers of cranes; the **ponds** and **reedbed** margins conceal various waders, such as black-tailed godwit, turnstone, dunlin and snipe, as well as the black-headed bush shrike (tschagra) and little crake; the deeper **open waters** provide feeding grounds for greater flamingo, spoonbill, white stork and black-winged stilt; and overhead the skies are patrolled by marsh harrier and osprey. The surrounding **scrubby areas** also hold black-headed bush shrike and a variety of nocturnal mammals such as Egyptian mongoose, cape hare and jackal, while **Sidi Rbat** has a local population of Mauritanian toads.

Twenty kilometres inland, the **Barrage Youssef Ben Tachfine** is an enormous freshwater reservoir where possible sightings include black wheatear and rock dove. By the lake is a car park, where campervans sometimes overnight.

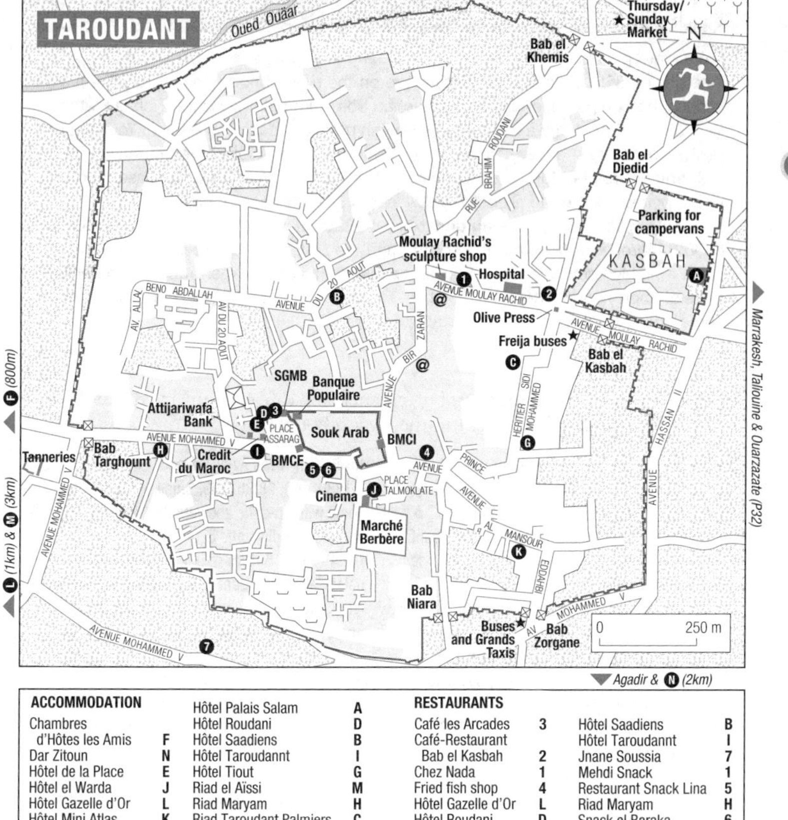

Arrival and orientation

Despite its extensive ramparts and large tracts of open space Taroudant is quite compact, and within the walled "inner city" there are just two main squares – **Place Assarag** (officially renamed Place Alaouyine) and **Place Talmoklate** (officially Place en Nasr) – with the main **souk** area between them to the north. The pedestrianized area of Place Assarag is the centre of activity. **Private buses and grands taxis** will drop you at the **gare routière** outside the walls by Bab Zorgane.

There are **petits taxis** (usually to be found in Place Assarag) and a few horse-drawn **calèches**, with similar tariffs, and you can rent **bicycles** (see p.507), but actually everything is within easy walking distance.

Accommodation

The cheaper **hotels** are on or around Place Assarag or Place Talmoklate; not all have hot water, but public showers are close at hand (Douches Ramoq behind the *Hôtel Roudani*, for example). More upmarket options, as well as those listed below, include *Riad Freija* (see p.508) and the *Arganier d'Or* (see p.508). There's no

Trekking from Taroudant

From Taroudant's rooftop terraces, the fang-like **peaks** of Awlim (3482m) and Tinerghwet (3551m) look temptingly close on the rugged northern skyline. The area is described on p.413, and is easily reached from Taroudant, as is the Tichka Plateau (p.406). The Djebel Sirwa (p.510) is also within practical reach of the town. You should really allow at least a week for a cursory visit, more if possible. One of the very best **trekking routes** in Morocco, nicknamed "The Wonder Walk", is a two-week trip up to the plateau and on to Djebel Toubkal (see p.391), Morocco's highest peak.

If you are interested in a **guided trek**, contact El Aouad Ali (BP127, Taroudant 83000, Morocco ⓣ0666 637972; or through the *Hôtel Roudani* or *Hôtel Taroudant*). He is a highly knowledgeable, English-speaking mountain expert, and can organize treks at short notice if need be. It is best to avoid other agencies as there have been some unpleasant rip-offs by cowboy operators.

campsite as such in Taroudant, but campervans can park up by the walls just north of the *Palais Salam* hotel (tip the *gardien* 20dh a day).

Chambres d'Hôtes Les Amis 800m west of Bab Targhount ⓣ0667 601686, ⓦwww.chambreslesamis.com. More like staying in a Moroccan family home than a hotel, with clean and pleasant rooms, constant hot water, a roof terrace, and use of the kitchen. BB ❷

Dar Zitoun 2km west of town, on the Agadir road ⓣ0528 551141 or 2, ⓦwww.darzitoune.com. Twelve a/c bungalows set in a magnificent garden, with traditional-style decor and a big pool. A good upmarket choice. BB ❼

Hôtel de la Place Pl Assarag ⓣ0528 852623. Grubby and very basic rooms, but OK for the (very cheap) price with hot water showers in the mornings on request, though the nearby public shower (see p.503) is much better. ❶

Hôtel el Warda 8 Pl Talmoklate ⓣ0528 852763. By far the best deal among the cheapies – clean, cosy rooms with en-suite toilets and shared hot showers that don't always work (depending on the water pressure), though there's always hot water in the bathroom taps, and a bucket. Rooms at the front have balconies overlooking the square; those at the back are quieter but get less light. ❶

Hôtel Gazelle d'Or 1km southwest of town, on the Ameskroud road ⓣ0528 852039, ⓦwww.gazelledor.com. An extraordinary place: a hunting lodge created by a French baron in the 1920s, in a Morocco-meets-Provence style. It was converted to a hotel after World War II, and guests (mostly super-rich Brits) stay in bungalows in the lush gardens. Rates – starting at 6149dh for a double, half-board – are among the highest in North Africa, and one dresses for dinner. Facilities include horseriding and croquet. Advance reservation is compulsory, and you won't be allowed past the gate if you don't have it. HB ❾

Hôtel Mini Atlas Av el Mansour Eddahbi ⓣ0528 551880, ⓕ0528 851739. Small but sparkling rooms with en-suite showers (hot water 6–10am & pm) and friendly staff. ❷

Hôtel Palais Salam ⓣ0528 852501, ⓦwww.palaissalamtaroudant.com. A package hotel in a nineteenth-century palace, just inside the ramparts of the kasbah (entrance outside the walls). It's worth asking for a room or suite in the towers or garden pavilions, rather than on the new modern floor. Facilities include two swimming pools, a cocktail bar and three restaurants. BB ❻

Hôtel Roudani overlooking Pl Assarag ⓣ0528 852219. Central and popular with backpackers, though quite basic. Some rooms here have bathrooms but no hot water, and those with shared bathroom facilities are very cheap indeed. There's also a restaurant on the square, and a fine rooftop terrace for breakfast. ❶

Hôtel Saadiens Bordj Oumansour ⓣ0528 852473, ⓔhotsaadi@iam.net.ma. A quiet hotel, north of the two main squares, with a rooftop restaurant, a patisserie and a swimming pool, but hot showers 8–10am only. BB ❸

Hôtel Taroudannt Pl Assarag ⓣ0528 852416, ⓕ0528 851553. A Taroudant institution and the oldest hotel in town, this was run by a grand old French *patronne* up until her death in 1988, and retains her influence (and some of her old poster collection). Very good value, with a patio garden, a generally good restaurant, and a bar which is noisy but closes at 10pm. ❸

Hôtel Tiout Av Prince Héritier Sidi Mohammed ⓣ0528 850341, ⓦwww.hoteltiout.com. Spotless, airy and prettily decorated rooms, all with en-suite showers, some with baths, and most with a balcony, plus a restaurant, a car park, and a pleasant roof terrace with a fountain. BB ❸

Riad el Aïssi Nouayl el Homr, on the Ameskroud road ☎0528 550225, Ⓦwww.riadelaissi.com. A beautifully restful place in a little village 3km southeast of town (past the *Gazelle d'Or*), set amid nineteen hectares of orange, lemon and banana trees in a 1930 pasha's mansion. The rooms are enormous, though the decor is sparse, and there's a restaurant serving Moroccan and Italian food. BB ❺

Riad Maryam 40 Derb Maalem Mohammed, signposted off Av Mohammed V ☎0666 127285, Ⓦwww.riadmaryam.com. Taroudant's first riad, with four smallish rooms (four more under construction) and a suite around a lovely patio garden. The decor isn't exactly tasteful, nor really even kitsch, but it has a certain charm, as do the family who run the place, and the food is wonderful. BB ❻

Riad Taroudant Palmiers Av Prince Héritier Sidi Mohammed ☎0528 854507, Ⓦwww.riadtaroudantpalmiers.com. Not what you'd normally call a riad, though it does have a patio garden, this is a colonial-era convent converted into a hotel, very peaceful, decorated quite simply, with ironwork furniture and the odd rug, rather than heavy with stucco and zellij. Some but not all rooms are en suite. Profits go to help the neighbouring abandoned childen's home. ❸

The Town

Taroudant's twin attractions are its **ramparts** and its two daily **souks**: the **Souk Arab**, immediately east of Place Assarag (and north of Pl Talmoklate), and the **Marché Berbère**, south of Place Talmoklate.

The souks

The **"Arab" souk** – easiest approached along the lane by the BMCE bank (you will probably emerge in Pl Talmoklate; it's a tiny area) – is good for rugs, carpets, leather goods and other traditional crafts, but especially jewellery. This comes mainly from the Anti-Atlas villages (little of it is as "antique" as the sellers would have you believe), though until the 1960s there was an artisan quarter here of predominantly Jewish craftsmen. For good-quality wares, the Antiquaire Haut Atlas, run by Licher el Houcine at 61 Souk el Kebir, is recommended (to find him, if entering the souk from Pl Assarag by the BMCE bank, continue roughly straight ahead, and his shop is on the right after 200m).

The **Marché Berbère** is a more everyday souk, with spices and vegetables, as well as clothing and pottery, and again jewellery and carpets. It is most easily entered from Place Talmoklate. Interesting shops include the Cadeaux de Taroudant, 35 Av Nasr (almost opposite the *Hôtel el Warda*).

On Thursdays and Sundays there is a **souk** by the northeast gate, **Bab el Khemis**, where Berbers from the villages sell farm produce and sometimes craftwork. For something more offbeat, check out the distinctive **sandstone sculptures** sold by eccentric local artist Avolay Moulay Rachid from his shop at 52 Av Moulay Rachid.

The tanneries

The leather **tanneries** are outside the town walls on account of their smell – leather is cured in cattle urine and pigeon droppings – and for the proximity to a ready supply of water. Compared with those in Marrakesh or Fes, they are small, but tidy. Sheep, cow and goat leather articles are all on sale, but don't buy skins of rare or endangered species, also unfortunately on sale: their importation is banned in most Western countries, and buying them encourages illegal poaching of rare animals (in fact, it is best not to patronize any shop which sells them at all). To visit the tanneries, follow the continuation of the main street past *Hôtel Taroudannt* to Bab Targhount, turn left outside, and right after 100m.

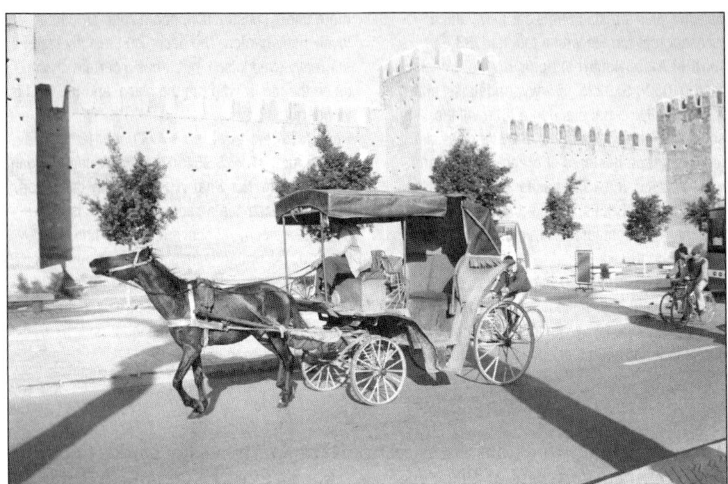

▲ Ramparts, Taroudant

The walls and kasbah

The town's **walls and bastions** make an enjoyable five-kilometre circuit, with stairs up onto them in a couple of places, most notably at **Bab el Kasbah** (also called Bab Essalsla). Some people walk round the outside, but it's easier to rent a bicycle (see opposite) and cycle round, or take a calèche from just inside Bab el Kasbah. The finest stretch runs south from there to Bab Zorgane.

Just to the north of Bab el Kasbah, the **kasbah**, now a kind of village within the town, was originally a Saadian winter palace complex, and contains the ruins of a fortress built by Moulay Ismail.

Eating and drinking

Juice shops around town sell all kinds of concoctions including creamy avocado with almond milk, but for freshly pressed orange and grapefruit juice you can't beat the stalls on Place Talmoklate. The town's main **bar** is in the *Hôtel Taroudannt* (daily 5–10pm).

Café les Arcades Pl Assarag. A restaurant on the square serving reasonable tajines and sometimes couscous, as well as breakfasts. Daily 6.30am–11pm. Cheap.

Café-Restaurant Bab el Kasbah Av Moulay Rachid, opposite the oil press. A 24hr café with a rather incongruous revolving door. The 45–50dh set menu is good value, and they also do pizza and (if ordered in advance) paella. Cheap.

Chez Nada Av Moulay Rachid. Excellent tajines, an 80dh set menu, and even pastilla if ordered three hours in advance, all served upstairs and on the roof terrace. It's open daily noon–3pm & 7–11pm, with a café downstairs open 7am–11pm. Moderate.

Fried fish shop Av Prince Héritier Sidi Mohammed. The best of a handful of shops selling fried fish of different varieties, including prawns and squid rings, sold by weight, to eat in or take out. Always busy, so the fish is freshly cooked. Daily 11am–10pm. Cheap.

Hôtel Gazelle d'Or 1km out of town (☎0528 852039). The tented dining room here is quite a sight, especially at dinner (menu 650dh), when men are required to wear jackets and ties. Lunch by the pool is less costly (450dh). Reservations compulsory. Daily 1–3pm & 8–9.30pm.

Hôtel Roudani Pl Assarag. Simple Moroccan dishes, such as tajines and couscous, but all tasty, fresh and well prepared, with vegetarian options available, served on the *place*, a great place to take in the evening atmosphere or daytime bustle. Daily 9am–10.30pm. Cheap.

Hôtel Saadiens Bordj Oumansour. Top-floor set-menu terrace restaurant, with a view of the High Atlas. You can eat à la carte, or there's a 70dh set menu. Daily 7.30–9.30pm. Moderate.

Hôtel Taroudannt Pl Assarag. Reasonable French and Moroccan meals, and alcohol is served. The cooking is variable, but good if you strike lucky, with 70dh and 90dh set menus. Daily noon–2.30pm & 7–9pm. Moderate.

Jnane Soussia outside the walls, south of town (☎0528 85 49 80). A grandiose would-be tourist restaurant with a pool and promises of evening entertainment, except that there never seem to be enough customers. The food is good (the usual tajines and brochettes, plus dishes like *mechoui* or pastilla if ordered in advance), but it's all a bit soulless. Daily noon–3pm & 7–10pm. Moderate.

Mehdi Snack Directly behind *Chez Nada* (see opposite) and run by the same family, a low-priced fast-food joint, with salads, burgers, fried fish, and set menus (30–50dh) based around those. Daily 11am–11pm. Cheap.

Restaurant Snack Lina Av Sidi Mohammed, just east of Pl Assarag. Shiny tiles and fluorescent lighting make this diner rather stark. The *shawarma* and spit-roast chicken are all right, but make sure they're today's. The tajines are good though, and cheaper than the ones on the square. Daily 10am–midnight. Cheap.

Riad Maryam 40 Derb Maalem Mohammed, signposted off Av Mohammed V ☎0666 127285. The food here is so good that it has featured more than once in the French gourmet magazine *Saveurs*. Non-residents can eat here for 200dh, but must book at least two hours ahead.

Snack el Baraka (Chez Moustapha) Av Sidi Mohammed – between the two squares. A small restaurant serving a variety of kebabs (lamb, chicken, liver, *kefta*), spit-roast chicken and sandwiches. Daily noon–midnight. Cheap.

Listings

Banks Several banks on and around Pl Assarag have ATMs and exchange facilities, as do a trio east of Bab el Kasbah on Av Hassan II.

Bicycles can be rented by the hour, half- or full-day from a little shop on Av Mohammed V just off Pl Assarag between Crédit du Maroc and BCME (5–10dh an hour, 60dh a day).

Cinema Cine Sahara, in a street behind the Berber market.

Car repairs There are garages and spares shops just inside and outside Bab Targhount, and inside Bab Zorgane.

Hammams Hammam Tunsi, 30 Av Mohammed V, 30m along from the *Hôtel Taroudannt*, men 4–11am and 6pm–midnight, women 11am–6pm; 9dh admission (massage extra). There's also a hammam with an entrance for men just next to the *Hôtel el Warda*, and an entrance for women round the back in an alley between 177 and 162 Av Mohammed V (daily 6am–11pm; 9dh).

Internet access Internet surfing is cheap in Taroudant – usually only 3dh or even 2.50dh an hour. Current locales include Club Roudana on Av Bir Zaran (daily 10am till last customer leaves), and the back of a *tabac* on Av Moulay Rachid, opposite Moulay Rachid's sculpture shop (daily 9am–midnight).

Moving on

For frequencies and journey times, see p.538.

Grands taxis and **buses** operate from the *gare routière* outside Bab Zorgane. There are shared grand taxi runs to Agadir or Inezgane – if the Agadir drivers try to give you any nonsense about baggage charges (which Moroccans do not pay), take a taxi to Inezgane and another one on from there. To Tata there are rarely direct shared grands taxis, and you risk getting stranded at Igherm if you take one that's only going that far.

There are no longer any bus services from Taroudant to **Marrakesh via Tizi n'Test**, one of the most exciting mountain roads in Morocco: a series of hairpin bends cutting across the High Atlas, which is described, in the opposite direction, on pp.403–409. There are, however, two daily buses from Aoulouz via Ouled Berhil, one of them leaving Aoulouz at 10am, Ouled Berhil at 11am, the other starting in Taliouine at 4pm, and reaching Ouled Berhil at 6pm, which means that, unless you are travelling in summer, it will be too dark to catch the spectacular scenery. With your own transport, you can drive the route, but be aware that the road is pretty hairy going, and in winter it can occasionally get snowed up. An alternative is to charter a grand taxi to Ijoukak (see p.404), where there is basic accommodation and onward transport to Asni and Marrakesh.

Freija

Freija is an ancient, fortified village, standing on a low hill above (and safe from flooding by) the Souss, and affords sweeping views of the river, the fertile plains beyond, and the High Atlas. A little further to the south, alongside the road in from the R1706, the old kasbah, built of *pisé* (mud and gravel), has been reborn as the *Riad Freija* (Ⓣ0528 851003, Ⓦwww.riadfreija.ma; BB ④), which is owned by the same proprietor as the *Hôtel Tiout* in Taroudant. The decor in the bedrooms isn't as posh as in some riads, but all are en suite with air-conditioning in summer, heating in winter, and the location is superb.

Hourly local buses leave for Freija from Taroudant's Bab el Kasbah, and there are shared grands taxis from the *gare routière* at Bab Zorgane. The shortest driving **route** is to turn south from the Ouarzazate road (N10) at Aït Iazza, 8km out from Taroudant; after a further kilometre, ford the riverbed (this may be impossible in spring if the river is in flood) and follow an abandoned causeway.

Tioute

A rough track leads up to the stone-built Glaoui kasbah at **TIOUTE**, one of the grandest in the south and still owned by the local *caid*. Profiled against the first foothills of the Anti-Atlas, it is a highly romantic sight, and was used as a location in Jacques Becker's 1954 French movie of *Ali Baba and the Forty Thieves*. Equally impressive are its fabulous views over the luxuriant palmery, with the High Atlas peaks beyond. If you want to avoid sharing it with the tour groups (who arrive around lunchtime), be sure to get here early. It is possible to stay in Tioute, at the *Auberge Tigmi*, down by the main road (Ⓣ0528 850555; ③). Just by the *auberge*, at the Taitmatine all-women's argan oil producers' cooperative, you can see argan oil being made, and of course buy some if you wish. El Aouad Ali (see box, p.504) can organize day walks in the hills above Tioute. Tioute can be reached directly from Freija by turning right off the R109 (former 7025) Igherm road 16km beyond Aït Iazza. Shared grands taxis from Taroudant serve Tioute infrequently (mainly mornings and late afternoons).

Taliouine and the Djebel Sirwa

Direct grands taxis from Taroudant to Taliouine take the R1706, which follows the **Oued Souss**. Buses run along the N10, with a halt (and taxi stage) at **OULED BERHIL**, 43km east of Taroudant, where an old kasbah 800m south of the main road (signposted from the centre of the village) has been turned into a sumptuous **hotel-restaurant**, the *Riad Hida* (restaurant open 7am–11pm, food must be ordered 1hr in advance; moderate, with a 120dh set menu), with rooms, suites and spacious grounds (Ⓣ0528 531044, Ⓦwww.riadhida.com; ⑤), scrupulously restored with a magnificent garden. For those with transport, there's alternative upmarket accommodation 20km east of Taroudant on the N10 at the *Complexe l'Arganier d'Or* in Zaouiat Ifergane (Ⓣ0528 550211, Ⓦwww.larganierdor-hotel.com; BB ⑤), with good food and a big pool.

AOULOUZ, 34km east of Ouled Berhil and the starting point for the morning bus to Marrakesh via Tizi n'Test (see p.507), gives onto a **gorge**, rich in birdwatching opportunities. The best **accommodation** is the *Hôtel Sahara* on the main drag (Ⓣ0528 539554; ❷), with nice, fresh rooms and shared but clean bathroom facilities. There are two other small and very basic hotels: the *Oued Souss* (Ⓣ666 311260; ❷), on the main road, and the *Café Restaurant Sa'ada*, down the road from there, by the market (Ⓣ0528 539468; ❶).

East of Aoulouz, a *piste* leads to **Taïssa**, at the southern end of the **Assif n'Tifnout** valley, with a rough *piste* to Amsouzart (see p.400). It is possible to drive this in a sturdy vehicle and you can make a two-day tour, returning to Taliouine (or doing it in the opposite direction. Alternatively, you could walk it. From Aoulouz there are minibuses to Assarag, where you'll find rooms, and from where a few hours' walk north will take you to Amsouzart.

Taliouine and around

TALIOUINE is more a village than a town. Its magnificent **kasbah** (east of the village) built by the Glaoui, is in a much-decayed state and used mainly to house farm animals, though the best-preserved section is still inhabited by a few families. Taliouine is a possible day-trip from Taroudant, or a stop en route to Ouarzazate. There are other kasbahs in the hills round the village, if you have time to explore them.

Taliouine is a centre for **saffron**, harvested in September and October. This is the only area in Morocco in which it is grown. It can be bought in one-gram packets from the Cooperative Souktana de Safran at its office on the eastern edge of town, where they also have a small **museum** (daily 9am–6pm, sometimes later; free). You can buy saffron a lot more cheaply loose elsewhere (in many of the hotels, for example, and even in Casablanca), but note that it is damaged by light, so it's best not to buy if it has been left out in glass jars for any length of time.

Arrival and information

Taliouine has a Monday **souk**, held across the valley behind the kasbah, and a bank, but no ATM. Heading on by **bus** from Taliouine can occasionally be tricky as buses can arrive – and leave – full for Taroudant or Ouarzazate; it's best to go to the main bus stop (buses can pass the *Souktana* full and then leave half empty from the bus stop). **Grands taxis** serve Aoulouz, Taroudant and (less frequently) Tazenakht (see p.432). See p.538 for journey times and bus frequencies.

Accommodation

Auberge Askaoun just east of town Ⓣ0528 534017, Ⓔaubergeaskaoun@yahoo.fr. Friendly with good food and nice big rooms with private bathrooms – a good alternative to the *Souktana*. ❷

Auberge Camping Toubkal 3.5km east of town Ⓣ0528 534343. Run by the same proprietor as the *Auberge Askaoun*, this is in principle a campsite and cheap restaurant, but it also has a/c bungalow rooms (one adapted for wheelchair users), as well as a swimming pool. The campsite is ideal for camper-vans, but not so much for tents, as the ground is rather hard and there isn't much shade. ❷

Auberge Safran just east of town Ⓣ0528 534046, Ⓦwww.auberge-safran.fr.fm. A reasonable fall-back if the *Souktana* is full, with bright, en-suite rooms, some with a/c and heating, solar-supplemented hot water and good food. ❷

Auberge Souktana opposite the kasbah 2km east of town Ⓣ0528 534075, Ⓔsouktana@menara.ma. A wonderful little place, run by Ahmed Jadid, his French wife, Michelle, and their son, Hassan (Ahmed and Hassan are excellent mountain guides – see p.510), offering good meals and a choice of accommodation: en-suite rooms in the main building, or bungalows outside, They have a separate campsite just up the Askaoun road (*Zagmouzen Bivouac Camping Restaurant*), to which they direct campers, and where they have tent bungalows available. ❸

Grand Hôtel Ibn Toumert right next to the kasbah Ⓣ0528 534125. The most comfortable place in town, though rather impersonal, with a pool, a bar, a restaurant, and views of the kasbah from some rooms. ❹

Hôtel Camping Siroua town centre ⓣ0528 534304, ⓦwww.auberge-siroua.com. A good-value place with simple but attractively decorated en-suite rooms, a good restaurant, and a camping ground. It's central, but the surroundings aren't as pretty as in the places east of town. ❸

Hôtel Kasaba by the bus stop (no phone). A basic Moroccan hotel, very low in price and handy for onward transport, but with no showers, no hot water, and not top of the league for comfort. ❶

Djebel Iguiguil

South of Taliouine, **Djebel Iguiguil** is an isolated peak reaching 2323 metres in height and offering a good day's excursion. The road from the N10 (signposted to Agadir Melloul), once it has hauled up the first pass from Taliouine, is surfaced right through to the N12 Tata–Foum Zguid road just west of Tissint, a spectacular drive. From just below Agadir Melloul, a *piste* heads west to pass the village of **Aït Hamed**, whose old *agadir* is worth a visit, before curling up to the lower slopes of the highest peak between Djebel Aklim (the highest peak in the Anti-Atlas, reaching 2531m) and the Sarhro. Detailed information on this area can be obtained from AMIS in Scotland (see p.54).

The Djebel Sirwa (Siroua)

The **Djebel Sirwa** (or Siroua) is an isolated volcanic peak, rising from a high area (3000m-plus, so take it easy) to the south of the High Atlas. It offers trekking as good as you can find anywhere – rewarded by magnificent views, a cliff village and dramatic gorges. It is best in spring; winter is extremely cold. For those with 4WD, one of the great scenic *pistes* of Morocco circles north of Sirwa, a two- to three-day trip from Taliouine via **Askaoun** and **Tachnocht**, rejoining the N10 north of Tazenakht.

A week-long walking circuit taking in Djebel Sirwa is outlined on our map below the numbers being the overnight halts. Mules to carry gear, as well as tent rental, can be arranged by **Ahmed and Hassan Jadid** at the *Auberge Souktana* (see p.509) or by **El Aouad Ali** in Taroudant (see box, p.504), both good cooks who speak fluent English, though they don't operate in the Sirwa in winter. Mules are a worthwhile investment, but having Ali or Ahmed along is the best guarantee of success. If you are going it alone, the

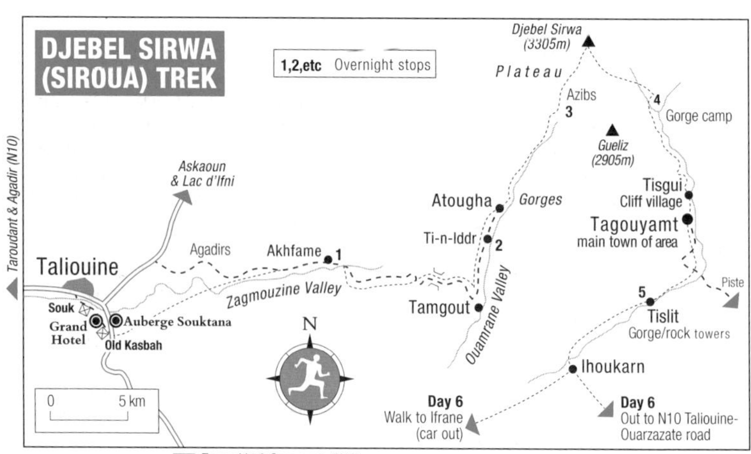

relevant survey maps are the 1:100,000 Taliwine and 1:50,000 Sirwa. Ahmed Jadid can show you these, and dispenses advice whether or not you engage his guiding services.

The circuit

The initial day is a gentle valley ascent along a *piste* to **AKHFAME** where there are rooms and a kasbah. The *piste* actually reaches west of here as far as Atougha but, souk days apart, transport is non-existent and the walk is a pleasant introduction. Beyond Akhfame the *piste* climbs over a pass to another valley at **TAMGOUT** and up it to **ATOUGHA**, before contouring round into the upper valley, where you can stay at *azibs* (goat shelters) or bivouacs.

Djebel Sirwa (3304m) can be climbed from **Atougha** in five to six hours: a pull up from the southern cirque onto a plateau, crowned with rock towers; the nervous may want to be roped for one section of the final scramble. The sub-peak of **Guliz** is worth ascending, too, and a bivouac in the gorge below is recommended.

Beyond Guliz, you should keep to the lower paths to reach **TISGUI** – and don't fail to visit the unique **cliff village** just outside: its houses, ranked like swallows' nests on a 300-metre precipice, are now used as grain stores. Continuing the circuit, past fields of saffron, you reach **TAGOUYAMT**, the biggest village of the Sirwa area and connected by *piste* to the Taliouine road. Trails, however, leave it to pass through a couple of villages before reaching the river, which is followed to the extraordinary conglomerate features of the **Tislit gorges**. This natural sculpture park is amazing; you can camp or get rooms at the village.

On the last day, you can follow the valley to **IHOUKARN** and then to **IFRANE**, where it's possible to get a vehicle out; alternatively, a three-hour trek to the southeast leads to the Taliouine–Ouarzazate road, near its highest point, from where transport back to Taliouine is easier. Ahmed can arrange transport at either point to meet unaccompanied parties.

The Tata circuit

Heading **south** across the **Anti-Atlas** from Taroudant, or east from Tiznit, you can drive, or travel by bus, or a combination of grands taxis and trucks, to the desert oases of **Tata**, **Akka** and **Foum el Hassan** to the west, or **Foum Zguid** to the east. This is one of the great Moroccan routes, still very much a world apart, with its camel herds and lonely, weatherbeaten villages. As throughout southern Morocco, **bilharzia** is prevalent in the oases, so avoid contact with pool and river water.

Transport can be sparse, which means you'll have to think ahead if you want to stop off at various places en route and be somewhere with a reasonable hotel by the time transport dries up. The other problem is that smaller places like Oum el Alek and Aït Herbil have nowhere for visitors to stay and are not served by grands taxis – they'll drop you off, but are unlikely to be passing with a free space and pick you up. One way to solve these problems if you have the money is to rent a car. Hitching is possible but not advisable – we've heard of hitchhikers being robbed by motorists who've picked them up on the N12 road west of Tata.

Taroudant to Tata

Leaving the N10 Taroudant–Taliouine road after 8km at Aït Iazza, the R109 Tata road passes **Freija** and the turning to **Tioute** (see p.508), before winding its way up into the stark Anti-Atlas mountains. Transport is scarce – only three buses a day, the last leaving Taroudant at 6.30am, and direct shared grands taxis between Taroudant and Tata are rare.

Most shared taxis from Taroudant terminate at **IGHERM** (also spelt Irherm, 93km from Taroudant), where there's a **Wednesday souk**. The region was once known for its silver daggers and inlaid rifle butts. If you get stranded here, basic rooms are available at the *Hôtel Restaurant Anzal* (Ⓣ0528 859312; ❶).

Igherm is also a crossroads, with scenic, surfaced roads to Taliouine (see p.509) and Tafraoute (see p.523), as well as the old R109 road to Tata via Issafen. Though buses still continue south on the R109, it has now been superceded by a spectacular new road, climbing over the ragged mountain strata before dropping down into a valley, which it follows to Tata. On this road, at **Annamer** – a blaze of almond blossom in March – you can visit one of the best-preserved *agadirs* in Morocco, a huge walled courtyard with tiers of minute store-rooms reached by ladders made of notched tree trunks. If you want to see inside, ask around for the *gardien*, who will of course expect a tip for his trouble.

If you want to enquire about trucks from Igherm to Taliouine or Tafraoute, try asking around the main square (where there's a petrol station), or in the café-restaurant just off it, where the truck drivers hang out and play cards. Market day (Wednesday in Igherm, Sunday or Thursday in Tata) sees more transport between Tata and Igherm; on other days, you face a long wait and risk getting stuck. There may be transport of some kind to Issafen on the R109, where it should be possible to get transport to Tata (especially on a Thursday, Issafen's souk day). If stranded, there's very basic accommodation at the *Hôtel Restaurant Issafen* (no phone; ❶).

Tata

TATA is a small administrative and garrison town with colonnaded streets, flanking a large oasis, below a steep-sided hill known as **La Montagne** (largely occupied by the military). It's a leisurely place with a friendly (if early-to-bed) air, and distinct desert influences in the dark complexion of the people, the black turbans of the men and the colourful sari-like coverings of the women. Buses terminate in **Place Marche Verte**, shared taxis just to its north.

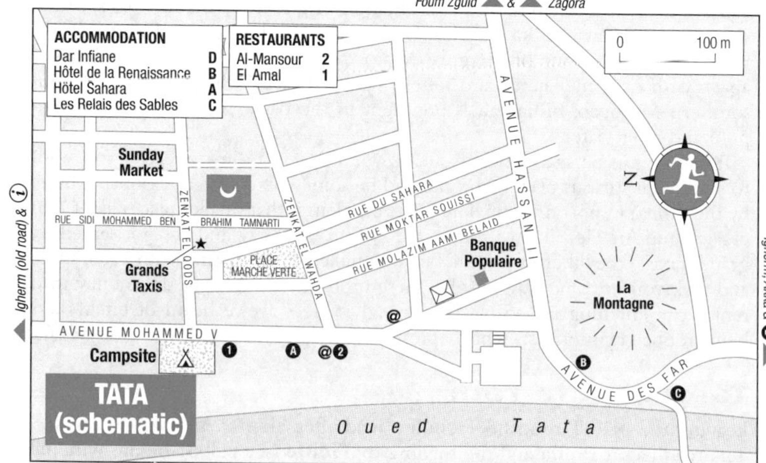

Arrival and information

Tata has a Banque Populaire with an ATM, a post office, a few internet offices (including Cyber de Luxe at 38 Av Mohammed V, open daily 8am–midnight, and Tatanet on the same street near the *Hôtel Essalam*, in theory open daily 10am–10pm) and two fuel stations. There's a Sunday market in town and a very lively Thursday **souk** held at an enclosure – or, more accurately, a series of *pisé* courtyards known as El Khemis, 6km out on the Akka road (N12); the mainstay is dates. The Délégation de Tourisme is on the old Igherm road, 300m north of the campsite (Mon–Fri 8.30am–4.30pm; ⓣ0528 802075).

Accommodation

The **campsite**, *Camping Municipal* (ⓣ0528 803356) is on Avenue Mohammed V, overlooking the *oued*, with clean showers, and a certain amount of shade. Its swimming pool, currently out of use, is due to reopen in 2010 (insha'Allah), along with bungalow accommodation. If you're really pressed for money, they may let you take a mattress in the hall for 20dh.

Dar Infiane off the Akka road, in the palmery ⓣ0524 437370, ⓦwww.darinfiane.com. Upmarket boutique hotel with six rooms and several terraces and patios, in a 500-year-old converted kasbah with palm-frond furnishings and traditional palm-wood ceilings. BB ❼

Hôtel de la Renaissance 9 Av des FAR ⓣ0528 802225, ⓔm.belhassan@hotmail.com. The best-value choice in town, welcoming you with large, gleaming, a/c suites or small, gleaming rooms, the latter at very reasonable prices. The restaurant is good, and licensed, and there's a pool too. ❷

Hôtel Sahara 81 Av Mohammed V ⓣ0672 508229. Basic ultra-cheapy. Rooms here are slightly better than those at the *Essalam*, 100m down the road at no. 41, and are grouped around a covered courtyard, but the hotel is still pretty bare-bones, with no decent washing facilities for example. ❶

Les Relais des Sables Av des FAR ⓣ0528 802301, ⓕ0528 802300. A three-star hotel with a swimming pool, bar and restaurant. The rooms are small but comfortable with en-suite showers and toilets, or there are mini-suites with a/c, sitting area and a complete bathroom. ❸

Eating and drinking

For **meals**, you'll find a handful of grill-cafés under the colonnades on Avenue Mohammed V and on Place de la Marche Verte, the best of which is *Al-Mansour*. There's open-air eating at *El Amal* next to the campsite. For something more fancy (and/or a drink), your only choices are the restaurants in the *Relais des Sables* and *Renaissance* hotels – at the latter it's best to order meals a few hours in advance, if possible – they are reliably good. The *Renaissance* also has a **bar** (daily noon–midnight).

Moving on

A number of **buses** start their journeys in Tata with destinations including Agadir, Bou Izakarn and Casablanca, via Igherm, Taroudant and Marrakesh. For frequencies and journey times see p.538. Waiting for **grands taxis** to get together enough passengers and set off can take quite some time, but there are occasional departures, especially in the morning, to Akka, Foum el Hassan, Bou Izakarn, Issafen, Tissint and Foum Zguid, as well as taxi-trucks to Foum Zguid (especially on Sunday night and Monday morning for Foum Zguid's Monday souk). Note however that transport dries up quickly in the afternoon, buses can easily be fully booked, and they may not let foreigners travel without a seat (it's illegal, and though Moroccan passengers can tip the *gendarmes* to do it, foreigners are out of the *baksheesh* loop). Note if driving westward that the only fuel station before Bou Izakarn is the Ziz station at Aït Herbil, and it's always a good idea to fill your tank before heading west.

East to Foum Zguid

From **Tata**, there is a surfaced road, two daily buses, and regular grands taxis to Foum Zguid (see p.437), the buses continue to Tazenakht (see p.432) and Ouarzazate (see p.421). The route runs through a wide valley, following the course of a seasonal river, amid some extremely bleak landscape, which is now and then punctuated by the occasional oasis and *ksar*, with the wave-like range of the Djebel Bani to the south. At **Tissint**, halfway to Foum Zguid, there's a gorge and waterfall, whose best vantage point is 2km before town on the road from Tata. There's also sometimes a police checkpoint, where you may be asked to show your passport. A surfaced road from Akka-Irhen (25km east of Tata, with a Thurs souk) heads north via Agadir Melloul (see p.510) to join the N10 Taliouine–Tazenakht road just east of Taliouine.

Akka and its oasis

Continuing along the circuit towards Tiznit, the N12 passes through **AKKA**, a roadside town with a large palmery, with a weekly **souk** on Thursdays, where the oasis dates (Akka means "dates" in Teshalhit) are much in evidence. There's a smaller souk on Sundays.

The town has just one **café-hotel**, the *Tamdoult* (☎0528 808030; ❶), with basic rooms, though decent food. If you ask, you may be able to pitch a tent in the municipal garden 200m along the Bou Izakarn road, under the shade of its date palms.

As well as six **buses** a day to Tata (one continuing to Ouarzazate, and one all the way to Meknes and Fes, via Taroudant and Marrakesh), and five the other way to Bou Izakarn (two continuing to Goulimine and Tan Tan, the other three to Tiznit and Inezgane, two to Marrakesh and Casa), there are shared **grands taxis** to Tata and Bou Izakarn, but not usually to Foum el Hassan. Don't leave it too late however if you want onward transport – as at Tata, it dries up early, and given the dearth of accommodation, this is not a place you'll want to get stuck in.

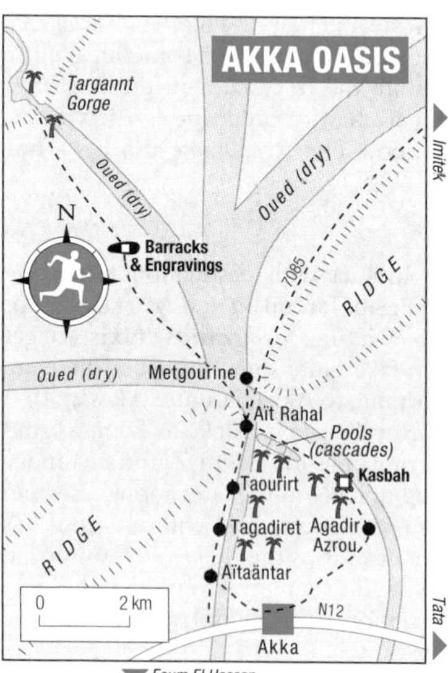

Around the palmery

It's worth taking a morning to explore Akka's palmery. You will probably need to do so on foot, as most of the oasis *pistes* are impossible in a two-wheel drive vehicle. Local sights include a **kasbah** and an **agadir**, southeast of the village of Aït Rahal, and **Les Cascades** – a series of shallow, dammed irrigation pools, enclosed by palms. Local people bathe in these pools, but they are reputed to harbour **bilharzia**, so avoid contact with the water – both here and in the irrigation canals. To reach them on foot, you leave Akka by crossing the dry riverbed by a concrete barrage and then follow a path through the almost continuous palmery villages of Aït Aäntar, Tagadiret and Taouriret.

A three-hour trek to the northwest of Aït Rahal is the **Targannt Gorge**, in which a cluster of oases are tucked between the cliffs. There are ruins of houses, though the place is deserted nowadays, save for the occasional nomadic camel herder. The route is across desert, passable to Land Rover-type vehicles, though the track is poorly defined. En route (and an aid to navigation) is a small hill on which the French built a barracks. There are **rock engravings** of oxen at the eastern end of the hill – some modern, others perhaps up to two thousand years old. Approaching the gorge, a lone palm tempts you to its mouth. A guide from the village would be helpful, while bringing food and a tent would reward you with a gorgeous camping spot.

Oum el Alek

There are more **rock carvings**, said to be prehistoric, near the village of **OUM EL ALEK** (or Oum el Aälague), 7km southeast of Akka, off the Tata road. Anyone with a particular interest is best advised to get in touch with the official *gardien*, Mouloud Taârabet who lives in Oum el Alek and can be contacted in the village, or through the *Café-Hôtel Tamdoult* in Akka. Mouloud knows all the rock carvings in the region, and should be able to take you to any of them you want to see, if you have a car or are prepared to charter a taxi.

West to Foum el Hassan and Aït Herbil: rock carvings

FOUM EL HASSAN (also spelt Fam el Hisn), 90km west of Akka, and 6km off the main road, is basically a military post on the edge of an oasis where there was some fighting with Polisario in the early 1980s. Buses between Tata and Bou Izakarn make the six-kilometre detour to stop here, and you may find grands taxis to Bou Izakarn and Tata. There isn't much else in town aside from a few shops and a couple of cafés on the main square. The nearest accommodation is *Borj Biramane* (ⓣ0528 803566, ⓦwww.borj-biramane.com), just off the main road at Icht, which has shared Berber tents (100dh per person), two-person tents (❸) rooms (❹) and camping facilities as well as food.

Tircht

There are countless **prehistoric rock carvings** in this region, and engaging a guide you will probably be shown the local favourites. Those at **Tircht** can be reached by foot from Foum el Hassan by following the *oued* through the "V" in the mountains behind the town (bear right after 2km where it splits). Tircht is a peaked mountain to the left about 5km from town, but neither it nor the carvings are easy to find: you are best advised to employ someone from town as a guide. The best require a little climbing to get to, but they are among the finest in Morocco – elephants and rhinoceroses, 15cm to 30cm high, dating roughly from 2000–500 BC, a time when the Sahara was full of lakes and swamps. Camping is possible here in the valley and preferable to staying in the town.

Aït Herbil

Less renowned are the rock carvings at the village of **AÏT HERBIL**, 2km off the N12, around 15km west of Foum el Hassan. The junction is easy to recognize, as it's right opposite a Ziz filling station. You can get there by grand taxi from Foum el Hassan, Akka, Tata or Bou Izakarn. For onward travel, however, you'll be lucky to find a passing grand taxi with places free, so short of hitching you'll have to depend on buses, of which there are only

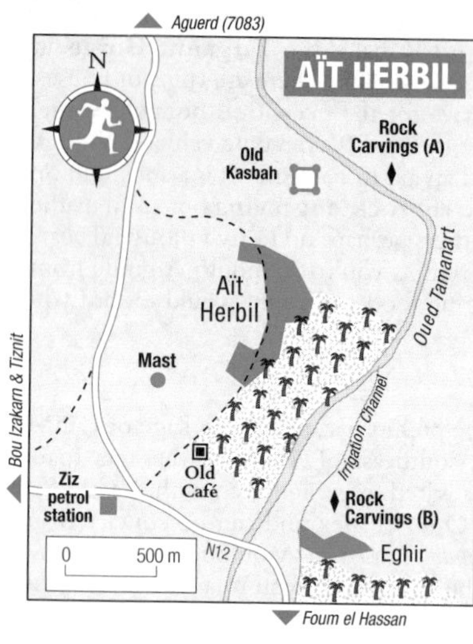

four a day in each direction. There are two series of rock carvings, marked as "A" and "B" on our map opposite, both easily accessible on foot.

"**A**" consists of as many as a hundred small carvings, depicting gazelles, bison, a giraffe and a bird or two, in a steep rock fall, and to the right of a patch of distinctively lighter grey rocks (indicating several deep and dangerous wells). The rock fall looks recent but clearly, with the carvings all in the same place, it has not shifted for centuries, even millennia. "**B**" north of the partly deserted village of Eghir, can be found by following the irrigation channel for 800m from the main road, where a signpost points the way. There are fewer carvings here but they are larger.

West to Bou Izakarn

Beyond Aït Herbil, the N12 continues across a barren patch of *hammada* to the oasis and roadside village of **TAGHJICHT** (or Tarhjijt), where a road heads off north to Amtoudi (see p.516). The village has regular shared taxi runs to Bou Izakarn; in the other direction you might be lucky and pick one up on its way to Foum el Hassan. At **TIMOULAY**, 26km further west, it is usually possible to get a grand taxi to Ifrane de l'Anti-Atlas (see opposite). You should also be able to get a taxi for the final fourteen-kilometre stretch to Bou Izakarn, on the main Tiznit–Goulimine road.

BOU IZAKARN is a larger village with a Friday **souk**, a post office, Banque Populaire, municipal swimming pool (summer only), and a simple but decent **hotel**, the *Anti-Atlas*, in the village centre (Ⓣ0528 788134; ❶). Shared grand taxi runs include Tiznit (for Tafraoute), Ifrane, Inezgane (for Agadir), and Foum el Hassan (from the main taxi rank in the town centre or, in the case of Ifrane, close by), and Goulimine (from a rank on the Goulimine road at the south end of the village).

Amtoudi (Id Aïssa)

If you have transport, it's worth making an excursion from the Bou Izakarn/Tiznit road to visit **AMTOUDI** (or Id Aïssa, as it appears on most maps). This can be reached on a *piste* from Taghicht, or a surfaced road (signposted to Amtoudi) that leaves the N12 14km east of Taghicht. The two roads join at **Souk Tnine D'Adaï**, a village known for its decorative doors.

Amtoudi's **agadir** (fortified granary), with its formidable towers and ramparts, sits on an eyrie-like setting atop the spur of a hill, reached up a steep zig-zag path. A *gardien* shows visitors round. There is a small museum, and parts of the walls and towers have been restored. Make sure the *gardien* is available before tackling the climb, as the *agadir* is kept locked. You should allow around three hours for the visit.

The approach road to the village ends at a parking lot by the *Hôtel Amtoudi* (Ⓣ0528 789394, Ⓦamtoudi.villesaumaroc.com/hotel-amtoudi; ❷), a friendly *auberge* with simple rooms, hot water, a restaurant and a camping area. Alternatively, at the far end of the village, at the mouth of a gorge, *Ondiraitlesud* (Ⓣ0528 789414, Ⓦondiraitlesud.ma.free.fr) is a French-created *auberge* with a lot of character that promotes eco-tourism in the area, and offers dorms (53dh) and shared tents (43dh) as well as a variety of rooms (❷). Both *auberges* can organize excursions in the area's susbtantial gorges. A walk up the gorge at the end of the village leads to another *agadir*, with huge curtain walls, perched high above a cliff, and, 3km on, a spring and waterfall.

You can climb (or ride a mule) up a winding track and walk around the site, providing the *gardien* is there. If by chance you find the place overrun by visitors, you can escape the crowds with a walk down the palm-filled **gorge**; here another imposing but decaying *agadir* is perched on top of the cliff and, after about 3km, you'll come to a spring and waterfall.

Ifrane de l'Anti-Atlas

IFRANE DE L'ANTI-ATLAS is one of the most rewarding oasis detours on the Tata loop. A small Berber settlement in a long oasis, it comprises three surrounding *douar* (villages), each with its own kasbah and endless walls, together

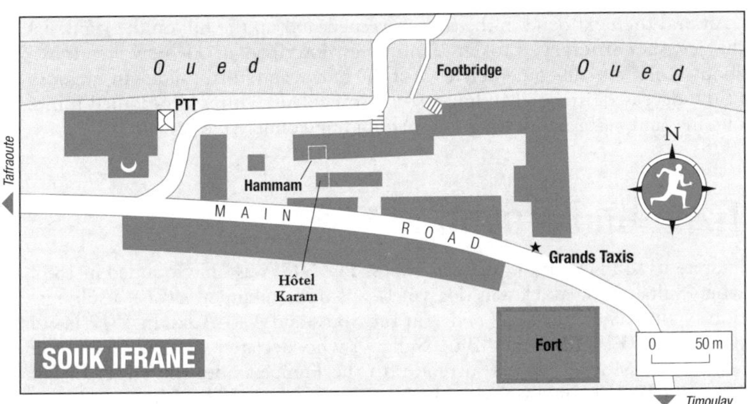

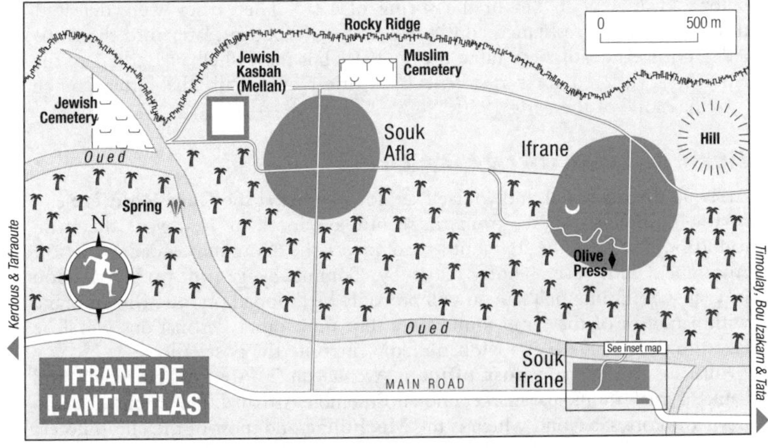

with **Souk Ifrane**, an administrative and market centre (Saturday souk), with a pink, fort-like barracks. Visitors exploring the oasis can expect to be the object of attention, especially from children, but it's worth braving them: there are beautiful walks among the *douar*, springs, and ingenious water channels.

If you have a car, you may want to just stop a few hours, though there are very basic rooms available at the *Hôtel Karam* (Ⓣ0676 717979; ❶). This or a café opposite the mosque should be able to sort a meal out too, though it's best to ask in advance. There is a sealed road north to Tafraoute, but no public transport.

The oasis and Mellah

The Ifrane oasis is the centre of one of the oldest settled regions in Morocco – and was one of the last places in the south to convert to Islam. Across the dry riverbed stand the ruins of the old **Jewish kasbah**, or **Mellah**. Legend holds that Ifrane's Jews settled here in the sixth century BC, and certainly the Jewish community goes back to pre-Islamic days. It endured up until the 1950s, when, as elsewhere in the south, there was a mass exodus to Israel and, to an extent, Casablanca and Rabat. Thanks to a joint initiative by the Ministry of Culture and the Moroccan Jewish community's Heritage Foundation, the synagogue has now been restored, and if you can find the *gardien*, you should be able to have a look inside.

Around the next bend in the stony riverbed, and up the hill on the right, lies the Jewish **cemetery**. Broken tombstones, inscribed in Hebrew, lie strewn about. Relatives still come here to visit the graves and burn candles in memory of the deceased. Ifrane's Muslim past is also evident, with white-domed tombs of saints and *marabouts* dotting the surrounding countryside.

Tiznit and around

Despite its solid circuit of huge *pisé* walls, **TIZNIT** was only founded in 1882, when Sultan Moulay Hassan (Hassan I) was undertaking a *harka* – a subjugation or (literally) "burning" raid – in the Souss and Anti-Atlas. In 1912 it was the base of **El Hiba**, the "Blue Sultan", who declared himself sultan after learning of Moulay Hafid's surrender to the French under the Treaty of Fes. He led a Berber force on Marrakesh – which acknowledged his authority – before advancing on Fes in the spring of 1913. There they were defeated, though El Hiba's resistance continued, first in Taroudant, later into the Anti-Atlas, until his death, near Tafraoute, in 1919, but the Tashelhaït Berbers of the Anti-Atlas suffered their first true occupation only with the bitter French "pacification" of the early 1930s.

Arrival and information

Arriving by **bus** you'll find yourself set down either at the **Gare Routière** east of town (fifteen minutes from the centre on foot), or nearby at the main roundabout where the Tafraoute road meets the Goulimine road (Rue Bir Anzarane), with several hotels close by. Coming by **grand taxi** from Bou Izakarn, Goulimine or Tata you will probably be dropped on Rue Bir Anzarane within metres of the same roundabout, but from other destinations you'll be taken to a yard on Avenue Mohammed V opposite the post office.

Adjacent to the main **post office** is Avenue du 20 Août, where you'll find banks, a small municipal market and an Ensemble Artisanal. The avenue leads to Les Trois Portes, beyond which is the **Mechouar**, and most of the cheap hotels.

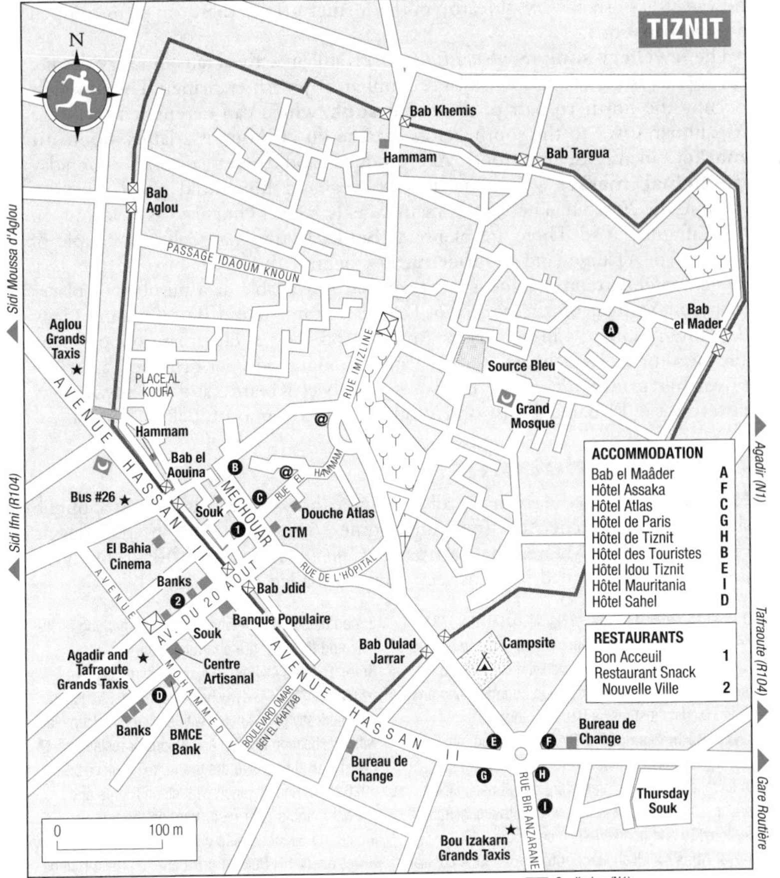

The Town

Tiznit is clean, neat and tidy, and a good staging point en route to Tafraoute, Sidi Ifni or Tata, but perhaps because of its relatively recent origin, it somehow lacks the atmosphere of Morocco's other walled cities. It nonetheless has five kilometres of walls and eight major gates, the most important of which are **Bab Ouled Jarrar** and **Bab Djedid**. The second of these was a French addition, as its name ("New Gate") indicates; it is also called Les Trois Portes ("the three gates"), though in fact it consists of four gateways. The Medina also contains a number of *ksour* which were there before the walls were built.

The walled town's main square, the **Mechouar**, was once a miltary parade ground. The **Great Mosque** in the centre of the Medina has an unusual minaret, punctuated by a series of perches, which are said to be an aid to the dead in climbing up to paradise, and are more commonly found south of the Sahara in Mali and Niger. Alongside the mosque is the **Source Bleue**, a spring dedicated to the town's patroness, Lalla Tiznit, a saint and former prostitute martyred on this spot, whereupon water miraculously appeared (though nowadays it's usually dry). Nearby, in the former prison, there are plans to open a town **museum**.

The **jewellery souk** (*Souk des Bijoutiers*) is still an active crafts industry despite the loss to Israel of the town's large number of Jewish craftsmen. The jewellers occupy the northern part of the **main souk**, which can be entered from the Mechouar. Over to the south, across Avenue du 20 Aôut, is a larger **open-air market**, mainly selling food and produce, and there's a more workaday **municipal market** selling meat, fruit, veg and household goods, just off Avenue du 20 Août. The town's main weekly souk (Thursday) is held out on the Tafraoute road. There are plenty of **banks** in town, as well as a couple of bureaux de change, and a **supermarket** behind the shops next to the *Idou Tiznit* hotel. **Internet access** is cheap, and is available at a number of places including Venmar on the corner of Rue el Hammam and Rue Imizline (daily 8.30am–midnight; 4dh per hr), or Anir, just off Rue el Hammam opposite the alley leading to Douche Atlas (daily 9am–midnight; 3dh per hr). There's a traditional **hammam** just inside the walls at Bab el Khemis, and the town's one **cinema**, the El Bahià, is just off Avenue Hassan II opposite Bab el Aouina.

Accommodation

Hotels in the Medina cannot all guarantee hot water, but there's a public showerhouse, Douche Atlas (men and women 6am–8pm; 9dh) in a cul-de-sac off Rue du Bain Maure. The **campsite**, *Camping Municipal* (ⓣ0528 601354), just outside Bab Ouled Jarrar, is secure but unshaded.

Bab el Maâder 132 Rue el Haj Ali ⓣ0673 907314, ⓦwww.bab-el-maader.com. A small *maison d'hôtes* run by a French couple who've lived in Morocco for years, very homely and located in an interesting area of the Medina just inside Bab el Mader. ❸

Hôtel Assaka Rue Bir Anzarane, on main roundabout ⓣ0528 602286. The best bargain in town, effectively a three-star hotel at backpacker prices. The rooms are impeccable, with a/c, heating, balcony, TV and good en-suite bathrooms. ❷

Hôtel Atlas 42 Mechouar ⓣ0528 862060. A popular hotel with a good café. Newer rooms are slightly nicer than the old ones, and there's access from the official roof terrace to a bit of the roof where you can sit undisturbed and watch the square. ❶

Hôtel Idou Tiznit Av Hassan II ⓣ0528 600333, ⓦwww.idoutiznit.com. Tiznit's poshest option, a four-star that's part of a small nationwide chain, with spacious rooms, a/c, satellite TV, a pool, very professional staff, and usually some kind of promotional rate on offer, but it's a little bit soulless. ❻

Hôtel Mauritania Rue Bir Anzarane ⓣ0528 863632. Best of the cheapies: a well-kept hotel with lovely little rooms, very cosy and beautifully turned out, on top of which there are parking facilities, and the staff are charming, too. ❶

Hôtel de Paris Av Hassan II, by main roundabout ⓣ0528 862865, ⓦwww.hoteldeparis.ma. A friendly and modestly priced hotel, with cosy rooms (complete with a/c, heating and TV) and a popular restaurant. ❷

Hôtel Sahel opposite the grand taxi rank ⓣ0528 602611. A friendly place with clean rooms and showers, and a café-restaurant on the first floor, though no direct outside windows. ❷

Hôtel de Tiznit Rue Bir Anzarane, on main roundabout ⓣ0528 862411, ⓔtiznit-hotel@menara.ma. Formerly the poshest hotel in town, though looking a bit down-at-heel since the *Idou* opened opposite and upstaged it. Nonetheless, it's a decent enough three-star, with a bar and swimming pool, though the rooms are nothing special. They prefer reservations by phone rather than e-mail. ❸

Hôtel des Touristes 80 Mechouar ⓣ0528 862018. A deservedly popular backpacker hotel, with hot showers, friendly staff and old-fashioned iron bedsteads. The communal areas are decorated with pictures of Paris in the 1950s and an impressive collection of banknotes. ❷

Eating

The best of the **café-restaurants** around the Mechouar is the *Bon Accueil*, directly opposite the *Atlas* (meals served daily noon–3pm & 7–10pm; cheap). On Avenue du 20 Aôut, *Restaurant Snack Ville Nouvelle* has a "panoramic terrace" (with huge TV screen but not much of a panorama) and non-smoking saloon on its top floor and offers spaghetti, steaks, brochettes and tajines as well as good-value breakfasts (daily 7am–9pm, meals served from noon; cheap). For a more upmarket meal, or a drink, your best bets are the restaurant of the *Hôtel de Paris* (meals served daily 10am–10pm; moderate), with a good selection of chicken, steak or brochette dishes, or the *restaurant gastronomique* at the *Hôtel Tiznit* (daily 7am–11pm; moderate). The *Hôtel Mauritania*'s modest but decent restaurant (daily 8am–11pm; cheap) is also licensed.

Moving on

Buses that actually begin their journeys in Tiznit are supposed to leave from the *gare routière*, which is just off the Tafraoute road, a couple of hundred metres east of the Thursday souk, but in practice the *gare routière* is little used; most bus companies have their offices on the Mechouar, and departures tend to be from the roundabout where Avenue Hassan II meets the Tafraoute and Goulimine roads. The most important departure is the evening CTM to Tangier via Agadir, Marrakesh, Casablanca and Rabat. Tickets on this, and on two CTM buses southward to Laayoune and Dakhla, can be booked at the CTM office in the Mechouar, but you cannot buy tickets for CTM services that pass through during the night, when the office is closed, nor can you board them, even if there are seats free. Local bus #26 for Mirhleft and Sidi Ifni leaves from opposite Bab el Aouina.

The main **grand taxi** station is opposite the post office, and here you'll find vehicles serving Agadir, Inezgane, Tafraoute, Sidi Ifni and Mirhleft. For Bou Izakarn, Goulimine, Mirhleft, and, less frequently, Tan Tan and Laayoune, they start on Rue Bir Anzarane just south of the roundabout. Those for Sidi Moussa d'Aglou leave from Avenue Hassan II near the southwestern corner of the Medina.

For frequencies and journey times, see p.538.

Sidi Moussa d'Aglou

The beach at **SIDI MOUSSA D'AGLOU** is 17km from Tiznit, along a barren, scrub-lined road. Shared **grands taxis** leave from Avenue Hassan II by the southwestern corner of the Medina, though some only go to Aglou village, 3km short of the beach, an isolated expanse of sand with body-breaking Atlantic surf. It has a dangerous undertow, and is watched over in summer by military police coastguards, who only allow swimming if conditions are safe. **Surfing** can be good but you have to pick the right spots.

Quite a few Moroccans (including migrant workers from France) come down in summer, with a trickle of Europeans in winter. Between times, the place is very quiet. There's a spacious but very basic municipal **campsite** (*Camping Plage Aglou*) about 500m before you get to the beach, on the right if coming from Tiznit. Alternatively, by the beach, at the end of the road, the *Hôtel Aglou Beach* (Ⓣ0528 613034, Ⓔagloubeach@hotmail.com; ④), has comfortable rooms, and a restaurant (daily 11am–3pm & 6.30–11pm; cheap) offering fish tajines and other tasty grub.

There are a couple of *marabout* tombs on the beach and, about 1.5km to the north, a tiny (and rather pretty) **troglodyte fishing village**, with a hundred or so primitive cave huts dug into the rocks. Southwards, a surfaced road follows the coast down to Mirhleft and Sidi Ifni.

Tafraoute and around

Tafraoute is worth all the effort and time it takes to reach, approached by scenic roads through the Anti-Atlas from Tiznit or Agadir (both are beautiful, but the Tiznit approach has the edge, winding through a succession of gorges and a grand mountain valley) or, with your own transport, from Ifrane de l'Anti-Atlas, Igherm or Aït Herbil. The town is a centre for villages built among a wind-eroded, jagged panorama of granite tors – "like the badlands of South Dakota", as Paul Bowles put it, "writ on a grand scale". The best time to visit is early spring, when the almond trees are in full blossom, or in autumn, after the intense heat has subdued; in midsummer, it can be debilitatingly hot.

Buses and **grands taxis** cover the route from Tiznit several times daily, but there is only one bus a day along the road from Agadir via Aït Baha.

Tiznit to Tafraoute

The Tiznit–Tafraoute road (R104, previously numbered 7074) passes a succession of villages, most named after their souk day (see p.616 for the Arabic day names). In winter and spring the road is sometimes crossed by streams but it is generally passable enough; the drive takes around two hours, but leave plenty of time to see (and navigate) the mountains before dusk.

At **ASSAKA** (20km from Tiznit), a bridge has been built over Oued Tazeroualt – the river that causes most difficulty in winter and spring. Nineteen-kilometre further on, a side road heads 10km south to the **Zaouia of Sidi Ahmed ou Moussa**, which in the seventeenth century controlled its own state, the Tazeroualt, its capital at nearby (and now deserted) **Illigh**. The *zaouia* hosts a **moussem** in the second or third week of August, which is worth trying to attend. Sidi Ahmed is the patron saint of Morocco's acrobats, most of whom come from this region – and return to perform.

Just beyond **Tighmi**, 42km from Tiznit, the road begins its ascent of the **Col du Kerdous** (1100m). At the top of the pass, the *Hôtel Kerdous* (Ⓣ0528 862063, Ⓦwww.hotelkerdous.com; ❺), an old fort, deserves at least a stop for a tea and breathtaking views; if you're staying, its worth taking half board, which doesn't cost much more than the room alone. The area is also good for paragliding, though there's not much activity these days.

At the end of the descent, entering the village of **JEMAA IDA OUSSEMLAL** (64km from Tiznit), the road divides. The left fork, which runs downhill through the village, is the direct road to Tafraoute, a picturesque route that drops into the Ameln Valley at Tahala, once a Jewish village. The right fork, a newer road, which skirts round Jemaa Ida Oussemlal, is longer but well surfaced, flatter and faster going, arriving in Tafraoute through a grand spectacle of mountains

Ground squirrels

Along the road from Tiznit to Tafraoute, you may notice children holding little furry animals for sale – live, on a piece of string – by the roadside. These are **ground squirrels**, which are known locally as *anzid* or *sibsib*, and are destined for the **tajine** dish, in which they are considered quite a delicacy, their flesh being sweet since they subsist mainly on a diet of almonds and argan nuts. Recognizable by the prominent stripes down their backs, and by their long tails, ground squirrels are common in the tropics, and have long been ascribed medicinal properties in Morocco. You will not get *anzid* tajine in any restaurant however, unless perhaps you provide the squirrels yourself.

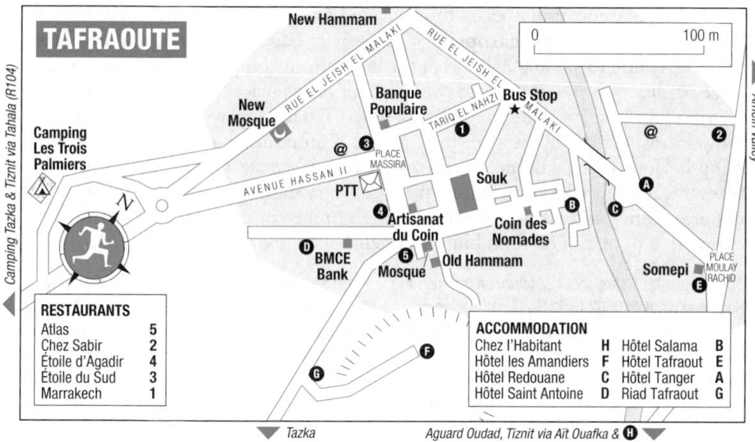

and the lunar landscape around Agard Oudad (see p. 000). Just after Aït Ouafka, it splits again – take the left-hand fork for **IZERBI**, where an ex-housing minister has a Disney-style chateau.

Agadir/Inezgane to Tafraoute via Aït Baha

The R105 road from Agadir to Tafraoute is a bit drab until Aït Baha, but the section from there on to Tafraoute is a highly scenic (and slow and winding) mountain ride past a series of fortified kasbah-villages. There's one daily bus along this route, plus another from Agadir to Aït Baha only.

AÏT BAHA is a lively shopping centre on souk day (Wed). It has a **hotel**, the *Al Adarissa* (Ⓣ0528 254461, Ⓔh.eladarissa@menara.ma; ❷), two cafés and very little shade. More interesting accommodation lies 5km towards Tafraoute, in the thirteenth-century *Kasbah de Tizourgan* (Ⓣ0661 941350, Ⓔtizourganekasbah@yahoo.fr; HB ❹), popular for a last night in Morocco among travellers with transport flying home from Agadir.

The most spectacular fortified village in the region, **TIOULIT**, is to the right of the road, around 35km from Aït Baha (the best views are looking back once you've passed it). Another 25km brings you to a junction of roads, with the left fork heading off to Igherm on the R109 Taroudant–Tata road. Around 5km beyond this junction is the village of **SIDI ABDALLAH EL JABAR**, scene of a small, but lively moussem around its *zaouia* (Oct 20–22).

Tafraoute

TAFRAOUTE, created as an administrative centre by the French, and little expanded since, is one of the most relaxed destinations in Morocco, though a few *faux guides* still make a nuisance of themselves, claiming to be the guides mentioned in this and other books, and spinning all sorts of yarns to coax the unwary into carpet shops where they can be subjected to the old hard-sell routine.

Accommodation

The **hotels** in Tafraoute are generally pretty good value. At the top level, the arrival of competition has made prices even more negotiable than usual, and it's worth shopping around between the *Amandiers*, the *Salama*, the *Saint Antoine* and the *Riad Tafraout* to see who'll give you the best deal (all frequently offer promotional rates).

Further accommodation options can be found 4km north in the Ameln Valley (see p.527). The most central **campsite**, *Camping les Trois Palmiers*, ten minutes' walk from the centre (Ⓣ0666 098403), is a small, secure enclosure with hot showers, and three small rooms (❶). It tends to overflow out of its enclosure and spread onto the surrounding land in winter and spring, when Tafraoute plays host to a swarm of campervans driven by sun-seeking retired Europeans, but there is a second campsite less than a kilometre down the road, *Camping Tazka* (Ⓣ0528 801428, Ⓦwww.campingtazka.com), whose prices are very slightly higher, though its facilities are cleaner and more adequate for the number of campers. Alternative sites, one with a pool, can be found in the Ameln Valley (see p.527).

Chez l'Habitant 1km south of town, on the road to Napoleon's hat Ⓣ0662 029305. Rustic accommodation in a Berber house with views of the Napoleon's hat and lion's face rock formations. You can take a room, rent the whole house, or, in summer, camp out or sleep in a Bedouin-style tent or on the terrace (100dh). ❸

Hôtel les Amandiers on the hill above town Ⓣ0528 800008, Ⓦwww.hotel-lesamandiers.com. Formerly Tafraoute's top hotel, now getting a bit long in the tooth and upstaged by the new kids in town, it still has a certain old-fashioned charm, with a wood-panelled lobby, great views, and large, rather bare rooms. ❹

Hôtel Redouane by the bridge Ⓣ0528 800066. A bit seedy with basic and not very clean rooms at erratic prices, but a possible fall-back if the *Tanger* is full. Has a terrace restaurant on the first floor. ❶

Hôtel Saint Antoine Av Moktar Soussi Ⓣ0528 801497 to 9, Ⓦwww.hotelsaintantoine-tafraout.com. Slick, modern hotel, with efficient, English-speaking staff, cool, spacious rooms and a nice big swimming pool. ❹

Hôtel Salama across the river from the *Redouane* Ⓣ0528 800026, Ⓦwww.hotelsalama.com. A good-value hotel, recently refurbished, offering comfortable rooms, en-suite bathrooms, a roof terrace, a fire in winter, and a good restaurant. They also have a few cheap single rooms on the roof. ❸

Hôtel Tafraout Pl Moulay Rachid, by the petrol station Ⓣ0528 800060. Best of the budget hotels, though not as cheap as the others, with clean and pleasant rooms, a warm welcome, hot showers and very helpful staff. ❷

Hôtel Tanger across the road from the *Redouane* Ⓣ0528 800190. Better rooms than its competitor over the road, and cheaper, with friendly staff, and a good restaurant where you can eat outside. ❶

Riad Tafraout Route de Tazka Ⓣ0528 800031, Ⓦwww.riad-tafraout.com. A very impressive hotel (not really a riad as such), tastefully done out (give or take the odd fox skin on the wall). The first-floor rooms are more attractive than those on the second floor, with straw-and-*pisé*-covered walls, and carved wooden doors from Mali. All rooms have a/c and satellite TV. BB ❹

Eating

In addition to the hotels (of which the *Tanger* and the *Salama* both have good restaurants, the *Tanger* offering a vegetarian tajine among other dishes), there are a few reasonable **restaurants** in town:

Atlas Basic but well presented Moroccan nosh – chicken or lamb brochettes, liver, steak, sandwiches and breakfasts – in spotlessly bright café surroundings complete with blaring TV. Daily 7am–9pm. Cheap.

Chez Sabir 41 Route d'Amelne (100m from Pl Moulay Rachid, then left down a little alley, signposted). A small, intimate place with a good 75dh Moroccan or 90dh French set menu, including vegetarian couscous, but best ordered an hour ahead. It's also possible to eat on the roof terrace. On the downside, tables are at the same level as the seats, making eating a rather back-breaking experience. Daily 8am–10.30pm. Cheap.

Étoile d'Agadir A great little place, serving classic tajines (lamb with prunes and almonds, chicken with lemon and olives) and other Moroccan dishes, all delicious and beautifully presented. Daily 7am–9pm. Cheap.

Étoile du Sud Av Hassan II. A set-menu restaurant (90dh) serving delicious Moroccan food, either indoors or outside in a Bedouin-style tent, with an occasional cabaret and floor show for tour groups. Daily 8.30am--10pm.

Marrakech An unpretentious family-run place with excellent-value meals (55dh set menu) and friendly service. The couscous here is particularly good. Daily 9am–9pm. Cheap.

Tafraoute: village economics

Among Tafraoute villagers, **emigration** to work in the grocery and hotel trade – all over Morocco and France – is a determining aspect of life. The men return home to retire, however, building European-looking villas amid the rocks, and most of the younger ones manage to come back for a month's holiday each year – whether it be from Casablanca, Tangier, Paris or Marseille.

But for much of the year, it is the women who run things in the valley, and the only men to be found are the old, the family-supported or the affluent. It is a system that seems to work well enough: enormously industrious, and very community-minded, the Tafraoutis have managed to maintain their villages in spite of adverse economic conditions, importing all their foodstuffs except for a little barley, the famed Tafraoute almonds and the sweet oil of the argan tree.

Listings

Banks The Banque Populaire is open only on Wed and Thurs mornings for the town's souk, but there's an inconspicuous BMCE behind the post office, with standard opening hours and an ATM.

Car repairs You'll find a few mechanics and tyre repair shops north of the bus stop in the crook where the main road does a sharp bend, and also down towards the Afriquia filling station.

Guides One guide highly recommended for trekking or four-wheel-driving around the region is Mohammed Ouhammou Sahnoun, who lives in the village of Tiouadou and can be contacted by phone or email (Ⓣ0667 095376, Ⓔm_sahnoun@hotmail.com), or via either the *Hôtel Tafraout* or Houssine Laroussi, who runs the Coin des Nomades shop (Ⓣ0661 627921, Ⓔtamayourt1@caramail.com). Brahim Bahou (Ⓣ0661 822677, Ⓔbrahim-izanzaren@hotmail.com) offers tourist information from his kiosk by the souk mosque and two-day treks to Djebel el Kest. Beware, however, of touts falsely claiming to know or to be these people – if someone who accosts you in the street claims to be them, ask to see their state-issued ID cards. For excursions further afield, a recommended firm is Tafraout Adventure on Pl Massira (Ⓣ0528 801368, Ⓦwww.tafraout-aventure.com).

Hammam The old hammam is down a side street by the central mosque. There's another near the bend in the main street (behind the bakery, turn left and it's 100m further, under the arch), and a new one, off Pl Moulay Rachid (50m down the Ameln Valley road, then right and right again after another 50m). All the hammams have entrances for men and women, open from around 5am, but the women's side closes at around 5pm, the men's stays open till about 7.30pm.

Internet access Prices vary quite a bit, but better-value places include Antranet in the same little street as *Chez Sabir* restaurant (daily 8am–midnight; 5dh per hr), and Aday.Net on Av Hassan II by Pl Massira (daily 9am–10pm; 4dh per hr).

Shopping There's a Wednesday souk, held in the centre of town. Worthwhile permanent craft shops include the Coin des Nomades (also called Meeting Place of Nomads) and Artisanat du Coin, both unpressurized. Tafraoute is well known for its *babouches*, and a narrow street of *cordonniers* sells quality slipperwear just below the Coin des Nomades.

Post office The post office is open Mon–Fri 8.30am–4.15pm.

Moving on

Buses leave from the main street where the bus companies have their offices. Departure points and times change frequently, however, so check them in advance. For frequencies and journey times see p.538. **Grands taxis** leave from the same street, opposite the CTM office. The only regular destination for collective taxis is Tiznit.

The Ameln Valley and around

You could spend days, if not weeks, wandering round the 26 villages of the **Ameln Valley** north of Tafraoute. Set against the backdrop of the Djebel el Kest's rock face,

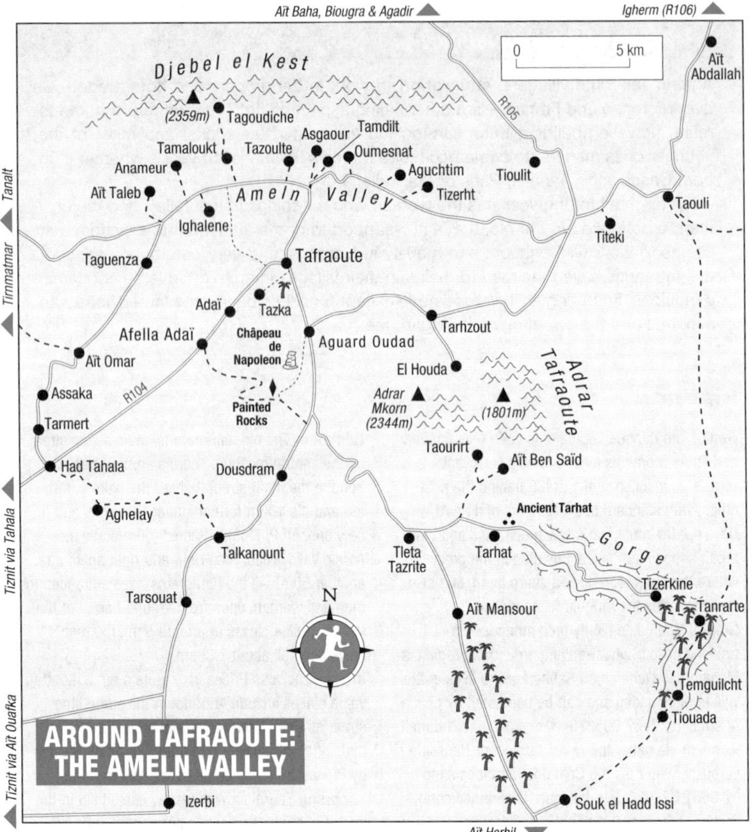

they are all beautiful both from afar and close up – with springs, irrigation systems, brightly painted houses, and mosques. On no account, either, should you miss out on a walk to see the **painted rocks** in their albeit faded glory.

The **Ameln villages** are built on the lower slopes of the Djebel el Kest, between the "spring line" and the valley floor, allowing gravity to take the water through the village and on to the arable land below. Many have basic shops where you can buy drinks, if little else. Getting around them, you can use a combination of taxis and walking, or rent bicycles from Abid (who sets up shop between the Coin des Nomades and the *Hôtel Salama*) or from *Maison de Vacances* on the Agard Oudad road (80dh per day).

Even a casual walker could stroll along the valley from village to village: Oumesnat to Anemeur, for example, is around 12km. More serious walkers might consider making the ascent of the **Djebel el Kest** (2359m) or, best of all, **Adrar Mkorn** (2344m), an isolated peak to the southeast with spectacular twin tops (this involves some hard scrambling). A striking feature on it is the **Lion's Face** at Asgaour – a rock formation which really does look like the face of a lion in the afternoon light when seen from Tafraoute. The area around it (and many other areas scattered on both the southern and northern slopes of the Djebel el Kest) offers excellent rock-climbing on sound quartzite. If you intend doing any rock-climbing in the region, an invaluable source of information is *Climbing in the Moroccan Anti-Atlas* by Claude Davies (Cicerone, 2004), which details each site, showing the ascents on photographs of the rock face. Houssine Laroussi at the Coin des Nomades (see "Guides" p.525) also keeps information on rock-climbing.

A number of **accommodation** options are clustered around the junction of the Ameln Valley road with the road from Tafraoute, 4km north of town (shared taxis from the Ameln road by the street to Chez Sabir restaurant will take you there for 5dh). By the junction, there's a small municipal **campsite** (Ⓣ0666 192626), surprisingly empty compared to the sites in town, and in summer it even has a swimming pool (15dh). Very nearby, *Chez Amaliya* (Ⓣ0528 800065, Ⓦwww.chezamaliya.com; BB ❺) is a hotel with quite a cavernous lobby but small though comfortable rooms (plus four larger ones dubbed "suites") around a pool. Five hundred metres up the road, where the *piste* for Tamdilt and Asgaour branches off, there's the *Hôtel Camping L'Argannnien* (Ⓣ0528 800020, Ⓔargahotel@yahoo.fr; ❸), with small but sweet rooms, each in a different colour, plus camping facilities. Directly opposite, the *Auberge la Tête du Lion* (Ⓣ0528 801165, Ⓦwww.latetedulion.com; ❷) has large rooms, a bar and a panoramic roof terrace, but is not so well kept. All three of the places just mentioned have restaurants as well as air-conditioning in summer and heating in winter. Just 1km up the road to Tamdilt is the *Maison d'Hôte Yamina* (Ⓣ0670 523883, Ⓦwww.yamina-tafraout.com; HB ❹), run by a delightful French-Moroccan couple in a traditional Berber house, upgraded with hot running water, air-conditioning, heating and en-suite bathrooms.

Oumesnat to Anameur – and a loop back to Tafraoute

OUMESNAT, like most Ameln settlements, emerges out of a startling green and purple rockscape, crouched against the steep rock walls of the valley. From a distance, its houses, perched on the rocks, seem to have a solidity to them – sensible blocks of stone, often three storeys high, with parallel sets of windows. Close up, they reveal themselves as bizarre constructions, often built on top of older houses deserted when they had become too small or decrepit; a few of them, with rooms jutting out over the cliffs, are held up by enormous stilts and have raised doorways entered by short (and retractable) ladders.

One of the houses, known as **La Maison Traditionelle**, is owned by a blind Berber and his family, who will show visitors round (tip expected). They give an interesting tour, explaining the domestic equipment – grindstones, water-holders, cooking equipment – and the layout of the house with its guest room with separate entrance, animals' quarters, and summer terrace for sleeping out. To get the most from a visit, you may need to engage an interpreter, such as one of the guides recommended on p.525. The owners of the Maison Traditionelle also offer bed and breakfast (Ⓣ0666 918145, Ⓔmaisonhote@gmail.com; BB ❸) in two adjoining village houses, one with small, simple rooms, the other with more comfortable air-conditioned rooms (heated in winter).

From Oumesnat, you can walk through or above a series of villages to **ANAMEUR**, where there is a *source bleue*, or natural springwater pool, a meandering hike of around three hours. Along the way is **Tazoulte**, one of four local villages with Jewish cemeteries, remnants of a community now completely departed, though Jewish symbols are still inscribed on the region's silverware, which was traditionally made by Jews.

The Ameln's highest village, **TAGOUDICHE** (Tagdichte on the road sign), where the trail up the **Djebel el Kest** (or Lekst) begins, is accessible by Land Rover along a rough *piste*. There is a shop, and a *gîte* (Ⓣc/o Hamid, 0662 891913; ❶) if you want to stay overnight for an early morning ascent. The

Djebel el Kest is a rough and rocky scramble – there's no actual climbing involved – over a mountain of amethyst quartzite. There is a black igneous dyke below the summit pyramid, and the summit, being a pilgrimage site, has shelters on the top, as well as hooped petticoat daffodils blooming in spring. The easiest route is not obvious and a guide may be advisable.

Returning to Tafraoute from the Ameln Valley, you can walk over a pass back from the R104 road near Ighalene in around three hours. The path isn't particularly easy to find but it's a lovely walk, taking you past flocks of sheep and goats tended by their child-shepherds. The route begins as a *piste* (east of the one to Tagoudiche), then you follow a dry riverbed off to the right, up a side-valley, where the zigzags of an old track can be seen. Cross to go up here – not straight on – and, once over the pass, keep circling left till you can see Tafraoute below.

Tirnmatmat

The road west along the Ameln Valley crosses an almost imperceptible watershed, beyond which, at Aït Omar (see map, p.526), a *piste* heads north to **TIRNMATMAT**, a partly abandoned village. Around 200m further, on the north bank of the river, are numerous **carvings** in the rocks, depicting hunters and animals (some of these may be prehistoric), along with more modern graffiti (including a VW Beetle).

The **ridge walk** to the south of this village is taken by some trekking parties and is really special, with Bonelli's eagles circling below, goats climbing the argan trees, and wild boar snuffling round the bushes.

Agard Oudad and the painted rocks

A short but enjoyable walk from Tafraoute is to head south to **AGARD OUDAD** (3km from Tafraoute), a dramatic-looking village built under a particularly bizarre outcrop of granite. Like many of the rocks in this region, this has been given a name. Most of the others are named after animals – people will point out their shapes to you – but this one is known (in good French-colonial tradition) as **Le Chapeau de Napoléon** (Napoleon's hat).

▲ Le Chapeau de Napoléon, Tafraoute

The **Painted Rocks** (Pierres Bleues), 1.5km to the southwest of the village, were executed in 1984 by Belgian artist **Jean Verame** and a team of Moroccan firemen, who hosed some 18 tons of paint over a large area of rocks; Verame had previously executed a similar project in Sinai. The rocks have lost some of their colour over the years but remain weird and wonderful. To reach them on foot, walk through the village and follow the flat *piste* round to the right, behind the Chapeau de Napoléon; you'll see the rocks on your left after a couple of kilometres. You should be able to engage a young guide in the village to help you find them. By car, a smooth *piste* breaks off the Tiznit road 5km further on and wends its way up towards the rocks, leaving a ten-minute walk at the end, but unless you prefer this longer route, don't follow the road sign if you are on foot.

Tazka

Another easy walk from Tafraoute is to **TAZKA**, about 2km southwest, where there is a prehistoric carving of a gazelle. To get there, follow a path through the palmery, arrowed off at the bottom of our Tafraoute map (p.523). When you emerge, past the remains of an old kasbah, you will see on your left the houses of Tazka at the foot of a high granite bluff. Take the lesser path to the right of the bluff and the carvings – a modern one on the rock face and an old one on the tilted surface of a fallen rock – are on your left after around 200m.

A southern circuit from Tafraoute

A beautiful day-trip from Tafraoute is to drive southeast towards Souk el Hadd Issi, a route that takes in some of the most beautiful country of the Anti-Atlas, including some fabulous gorges and palmeries. If you have a sturdy vehicle and a taste for bone-shaking *pistes*, you can make a loop of it, travelling down via Tizerkine, and returning via Aït Mansour. Minibuses (several, but all leaving at the same time) ply each of these routes once daily, leaving Tafraoute around noon, and returning from Souk el Had at 6am next morning. Local guide Mohammed Ouhammou Sahnoun (see Tafraoute "Listings", p.525) lives in **Tiouada** and offers half- or full-board **accommodation** at the *Auberge Sahnoun* (Ⓣ0528 216609, Ⓔm_sahnoun@hotmail.com; HB ❸) for anyone interested in using it as a base to explore the local area. The accommodation is simple, but the setting is lovely, on the edge of Tiouadou's palmery, and hot showers are available; space is limited though, so it's best to call or email ahead. Mohammed can also arrange mule treks in the region, and help locate rock carvings.

Leaving Tafraoute, follow the road out past Agard Oudad, turning left around 3km south of the village. This road climbs over the hills, with superb panoramas back across Tafraoute and the Ameln Valley, to reach **TLETA TAZRITE** (15km from Tafraoute), which has a souk on Friday – not Tuesday as its name implies.

From here, the road continues south to the massive palmery at **Aït Mansour**, and on to **SOUK EL HADD ISSI** (Souk el Had Arfallah Ihrir on the Michelin map), which has a Sunday souk. Five-kiolometres before Souk el Hadd Issi you pass a fine *agadir*. A turn-off shortly after it leads to Aït Herbil (see p.515), passing a number of ancient **rock carvings**, though they are not easy to find and a guide would be advisable. The first and least difficult group of carvings to find are some 700m east of the road, about 6.4km south of the junction, and feature long-horned cattle and elephants, which lived in this part of Africa when the carvings were made.

Alternatively, heading east from Tleta Tazrite along a surfaced but degraded road, you pass the modern village of **TARHAT** (Taghaout) before entering a canyon. Just beyond here, high on your left, are the twelfth-century remains of **ancient Tarhat**, a fortified village and *agadir* perched on the lip of a sheer rock wall. A footpath leads up to it from the modern village. At **TIZERKINE**, a lovely oasis snaking along the canyon, all semblance of paved road comes to an end. A passable *piste* continues (be sure to take the right fork, 5km from Tizerkine) to the village of **TEMGUILCHT**, dominated by the very large and impressive **Zaouia Sidi Ahmed ou Mohammed** (no entrance to non-Muslims), where there is a moussem in honour of the saint every August. The road continues past **TIOUADA** and on to Souk el Hadd Issi (see p.529).

Tiznit to Goulimine – and Sidi Ifni

Heading **south from Tiznit to Goulimine**, you have a choice of routes: a fast inland road across scrubby desert via **Bou Izakarn**, where the road to Tata heads off east (see p.516); or a more circuitous journey along the coast, by way of the splendid former Spanish enclave of **Sidi Ifni**. A lot of people follow one route down and the other back.

Mirhleft

About halfway from Tiznit to Sidi Ifni, **MIRHLEFT** is a friendly, bustling village, set back a kilometre from a series of good beaches with crashing waves and strong currents, that attract surfers and campervans. A 1935 **Spanish fort** overlooks the village from the hill above, which you can climb for beautiful views over the surrounding countryside. The village hosts a Monday **souk**, devoted mainly to secondhand items.

Mirhleft is served by **grands taxis** from Sidi Ifni, and **buses** between Ifni and Tiznit, most particularly the AGB #26 local bus, which passes in each direction at two-hourly intervals. There's an Attijariwafa **bank** on the main road with an ATM. **Internet** facilities include Cyber Tzarzit (daily 9am–midnight; 5dh per hr) and Fara@Mireft (daily 8.30am–past midnight; 5dh per hr), both easy to find in the middle of the village.

Accommodation

Hotels in Mirhleft are generally a little overpriced, especially as most people come here for the beach, and most hotels are at least a kilometre away in the village.

Auberge des Trois Chameaux on the hill above town, just below the fort ⓣ0528 719187, ⓦwww.3chameaux.com. Classy *maison d'hôte* with a choice of "Berber rooms" (not all that special, nor particularly Berber), suites (spacious and well-appointed, for not much more money), and "royal suites" (spacious and well-appointed with private terraces and wonderful views). There's also a swimming pool, parking facilities, an in-house hammam, good food and great vistas over the countryside. HB ❼

Dar Najmat Plage Sidi Mohammed ben Abdallah, 2km south of town ⓣ0528 719056, ⓦwww.darnajmat.com. A beautiful *auberge* with bright modern a/c rooms and a scenic pool, standing all on its own at the end of a small beach dominated by an impressively large rock and overlooked by a mosque and a row of small shops. The beach is unspoiled and not suitable for surfing – which keeps most of the Mirhleft crowd away. BB ❻

Hôtel Abertih on the corner of the main street with the Tiznit–Ifni road ⓣ0528 719304, ⓦwww.abertih.com. The best hotel in the the village, well run and tastefully decorated, with a good restaurant and free wi-fi, constant hot water and some rooms en suite. Also a good place to get paragliding information. ❸

Hôtel Atlas opposite the souk ⓣ0528 719309, ⓦwww.atlas-mirleft.com. Small, clean but simple rooms, some en-suite, with a roof terrace giving views of the fort. Showers and toilets are impressively clean. Not a bad place, but overpriced. BB ❸

Hôtel du Sud opposite the souk ⓣ0528 719407, ⓦwww.hoteldusud.fr. Fresh white rooms, hot-water showers and a splash of paint have turned what was a basic Moroccan hotel into somewhere quite nice to stay. ❷

Hôtel Tafoukt next to the souk ☎0528 719077. Simple hotel charging ordinary Moroccan rates, and in fact the cheapest rooms, with outside windows, are rather better than the slightly pricier ones, which have windows facing inwards. ❶

Maison d'Hôtes Aftas Beach Aftas beach ☎0528 719152, ⓦaftasbeach.ifrance.com. A great location, on its own little beach, but not tremendously well kept, and you may well find, if you turn up unannounced, that there's nobody around. The rooms are also rather poky, and as almost the only building on the beach, it is a prime suspect for the litter and rubble that is unfortunately starting to accumulate there. ❸

Eating

The *Hôtel du Sud*'s **restaurant** *(À la Bonne Franquette)* cooks up some tasty low-priced tajines, though you need to order them an hour ahead. *Hôtel Tafoukt* also serves good tajines at very reasonable prices. The *Hôtel Abertih* offers posher eating, particularly fish, and is licensed. The *Sunset Pub Restaurant* on the Tiznit–Sidi Ifni road is a rather sleazy bar that also serves food.

Legzira Beach

This fine **beach**, with natural sea-worn rock archways, 10km north of Sidi Ifni, is overlooked by an old Spanish fort from the hills above, whose thermal currents attract hang-gliding enthusiasts (tour operators include Welsh Airsports ⓦwww.welshairsports.com). There are three *auberges* on the beach, each with a restaurant and generator (evenings only). The longest-established is *Auberge Legzira* (☎0528 780457, ⓦwww.elgzira.free.fr; HB ❸), which is the best for meals. The other two – *Auberge Sables d'Or* (☎0661 302495; ❷), and *Auberge Beach Club* (☎0528 875013, ⓦwww.legzirabeachclub.com; ❷) – are newer, with brighter rooms, but they don't have the same degree of local knowledge and their food isn't as highly rated. You can get to Legzira on local bus #26 (every two hours) from Tiznit, Mirhleft or Sidi Ifni, or on foot along the coast from Sidi Ifni, a two-and-a-half-hour walk along beach and cliffs, coming into Legzira under the rock archways.

Sidi Ifni

SIDI IFNI is uniquely interesting: an enclave relinquished by Spain only in 1969, after the Moroccan government closed off landward access. Built in the 1930s, on a clifftop site, it is surely the finest and most romantic Art Deco military town ever built. Many of its 1930s buildings have been the victims of neglect, but with a realization by the authorities that they attract tourists, steps are now being taken to conserve the town's heritage, and many are also being bought up by foreigners.

The site, then known as Santa Cruz del Mar Pequeño ("Holy Cross of the Small Sea"), was held by the Spanish from 1476 to 1524, when the Saadians threw them out. In 1860, the Treaty of Tetouan (see p.573) gave it back to them, though they didn't reoccupy it until 1934, after they (or rather, the French) had "pacified" the interior.

In recent years, Sidi Ifni has become something of a base for **surfing and paragliding**. Favourite surfing spots are on the main beach, just in front of the tennis courts, and another beach 100m south of the new port. *Hotel Suerte Loca* runs a small surfing supplies shop. Favourite paragliding spots are the hills behind Ifni, and at Legzira (see above). On Sundays a large **souk** takes place just east of the abandoned airfield, while on June 30 every year there's a **festival** to celebrate Ifni's 1969 reincorporation into Morocco.

Accommodation

Of the three **campsites**, the best is *Camping Sidi Ifni* (Ⓣ0528 876734), run by the proprietors of the *Hôtel Bellevue*, which has simple rooms (1), free wi-fi, a pool (20dh) and restaurant in summer, high walls for security, and gets sunshine most of the day. *Camping el Barco* (Ⓣ0528 780707, Ⓔcampingelbarco@yahoo.fr) is longer established but more open to the elements – it has rooms (3), but isn't good value compared with the hotels. *Camping Municipal* on Avenue Sidi Mohammed (no phone), though slightly cheaper than the other two, is the least attractive, rundown, with little shade and no hot water.

Hôtel Aït Ba Hamram Rue de la Plage – at the bottom of the steps Ⓣ0528 780217. By the beach, with pristine en-suite rooms, a restaurant and bar. (2)

Hôtel Bellevue Pl Hassan II Ⓣ0528 875072, Ⓕ0528 780499. Three categories of room, all clean and well-kept, though some are a bit on the small side, in an original Ifni Art Deco building with sweeping views over the beach, and a good restaurant. (2)

Hôtel Ere Nouvelle Av Sidi Mohammed Abdallah Ⓣ0528 875298. The best of the four cheap hotels in the main part of town, with friendly staff and clean rooms, though not all have outside windows. (1)

Hôtel Houria (aka *Liberté*) 9 Rue Mohammed el Kauzir, off Av Mohammed V; **Hôtel Ifni** Av Mohammed V Ⓣ0528 875807; **Hôtel Wejan** 119 Rue Mohammed el Kauzir. A trio of small, basic hotels very close to each other, and all catering mainly for a Moroccan clientele. Prices are similar to those at the *Ere Nouvelle*, for which these can be considered as fall-back alternative options. (1)

Hôtel Suerte Loca Rue Moulay Youssef Ⓣ0528 875350, Ⓕ0528 780003. A characterful place – the name ("Crazy Luck") and a bodega-style bar (not licensed) reveal its small-town Spanish origins – run by a very welcoming English-speaking family. It has cheap rooms in the old Spanish wing, slightly pricier en-suite ones in a new wing, and is deservedly popular. It also has a good café-restaurant and a terrace overlooking the town and sea, where you can sleep for 50dh. ❷

Maison d'Hôte Xanadu 5 Rue el Jadida (look for the ⵣ symbol on the door) ⓣ0528 876718, ⓦwww.maisonxanadu.com. Bright, cheerful *maison d'hôte* with lots of jolly pastel colours, breezy, modern, en-suite rooms and great views from the roof terrace. BB ❺

Résidence Sidi Ifni 4 Av Moulay Abdellah ⓣ0528 876776. Four apartments, each with two bedrooms, a salon and a bathroom, and a chaos of tiles, not deluxe, but very comfortable, especially if there are four of you. ❸

The Town

Sidi Ifni's main attractions are its Spanish feel and **Art Deco architecture**. The beach, with a *marabout* tomb at its northern end, is not that great (the beaches at Lagzira and Mirhleft, see pp.530 & 531, are better) and is prone to long sea mists.

The heart of the town is **Place Hassan II (Plaza de España)**, its centrepiece an Andalucian garden with Spanish tiled benches and a Moroccan tiled fountain. A plinth in the middle once bore the statue of General Capaz, who took Ifni for Spain in 1934. At the northern end of the square, the now empty **Spanish consulate**, a building straight out of García Márquez, stands next to a Moorish-Art Deco building, which used to be the **church**, and is now the law court. At the other end of the plaza, the candy-striped **town hall**, complete with its town clock, stands next to the former governor-general's residence, now the **royal palace**. Many of these buildings are in immaculate condition, with their stunning pastel shades picked out. More Art Deco splendour is to be seen off the square and along Avenue Hassan II, as well as around the **post office** which was also rather splendid before the top storey was demolished, and from where the town issued its own stamps under Spanish rule, featuring wildlife, traditional costumes and even the town's buildings. Next to the *Hôtel Suerte Loca* and alas sadly dilapidated nowadays, a building in the shape of a ship once housed the **naval secretariat** – its two forward portholes being windows of cells where miscreant sailors were held (it isn't the only ship-shaped building in town: the Banque Populaire, opposite the post office, is another). And there is a whole sequence of monumental **stairways**, rambling down towards the port and beach, and a magnificent Art Deco **lighthouse**. On Rue Moulay Youssef, there's even an Art Deco mosque.

South of town, the **old port**, built by the Spanish, has an odd little concrete island where ships used to dock. It was connected to the mainland by a unique cable car, which hauled goods as well as passengers. The **new port**, further south, has big new sardine- and anchovy-processing factories. On the way is the former Spanish prison, now disused, and an airfield, also disused, whose last landing was an American locust-spraying plane, forced down here on one engine after being shot at by Polisario guerrillas in 1988. The airport building is now a meteorological station.

Eating

Of the hotels, the *Bellevue* has the best **restaurant**; only that and the *Aït Ba Hamram* are licensed. The *Suerte Loca* and *Ere Nouvelle* also have good restaurants.

Chez Mustafa Best of a bunch of hole-in-the-wall eateries on the western side of the municipal market (it's the one nearest Av Hassan II), serving good fish tajines. Daily 9.30am–11pm, except when weather prevents fishing. Cheap.

El Hourria Av el Houria. Eat inside or out in the garden at this attractive new restaurant with options such as osso buco, fried squid, prawn pili-pili or (if ordered 5hr in advance) camel tajine. Daily 9am–11pm. Moderate.

Ocean Miramar 3 Av Moulay Abdellah. Immaculate new place with a scenic terrace specializing in fish and seafood, including fish tajines or paella, and chocolate mousse or banana split for afters. Also does breakfasts. Daily 7am–10pm. Moderate.

Snack Les Fleurs 13 Av Hassan II. Basic spit-roast chicken joint, nothing special but always handy. Daily 11am–1pm. Cheap.

Tagout 2 Av Moulay Abdellah. Good tajines and fish dishes, but probably won't have everything that's on the menu. Daily 8am–11pm. Cheap.

Moving on

Sidi Ifni has two early morning buses to Inezgane, one continuing to Marrakesh. Aside from those, the AGB bus #26 heads up to Tiznit via Legzira Beach and Mirhleft every two hours from 7am to 7pm. **Grands taxis** leave four blocks east of Avenue Mohammed V (see map, p.532). For further details see p.538.

There is little of note on the route south from Sidi Ifni to Goulimine, though the route itself is a pleasant one, especially in spring, when the slopes are green with a mass of euphorbia.

Goulimine and around

Surrounded by some impressively bleak scenery, **GOULIMINE** (also spelt Guelmim or Gulimime) is an administrative town with a distinctly frontier feel and a couple of small, fairly animated souks. The nearest thing it has to a tourist sight is the remains of **Caid Dahman Takni's palace**, in the back streets behind the *Hôtel la Jeunesse*, ruined now but barely a hundred years old. One or two local hustlers indulge in theatrical cons, usually involving invitations to see "genuine *hommes bleus*" (supposedly desert nomads, clad in blue) in tents outside town, inevitably just an excuse to relieve tourists of some money.

Goulimine's Saturday souk, known as the **camel market**, is rather a sham. It has the usual Moroccan goods (grain, vegetables, meat, clothes, silver, jewellery, sheep and goats), but what it doesn't have many of is camels, which have fallen from favour over the years in the wake of lorries and transit vehicles, and the caravan routes are more or less extinct. The few you do see have been brought in for show or to be sold for meat. The market is held a kilometre out of town on the road to Tan Tan; it starts around 6am, and a couple of hours later the first tour buses arrive. There are a couple of quite animated **evening markets**, one off the Route d'Agadir (now officially renamed Boulevard Mohammed VI), mainly selling food, and one off Avenue des FAR, mainly selling clothes.

Arrival and information

The **Délégation de Tourisme** is unsignposted at 3 Résidence Sahara on the Agadir road, by Pharmacie Agadir at the junction of Avenue Houman el Fetaouki (Mon–Fri 8.30am–4.30pm; ⓣ0528 872911). There are plenty of **banks** with ATMs and also a small **supermarket**, Raji, in the centre of town, next to the **post office**. On the other side of *La Poste*, the town **hammam**, with showers as well as steam, is open for both sexes from 6am until 10pm. You can access the **internet** at Horizons next to the Attijariwafa Bank on Avenue Abaynou (daily 8.30am–3am; 4dh per hr).

Accommodation

There are a few very basic **hotels** in town, but not many good ones. Out-of-town alternatives are detailed on pp.536–537.

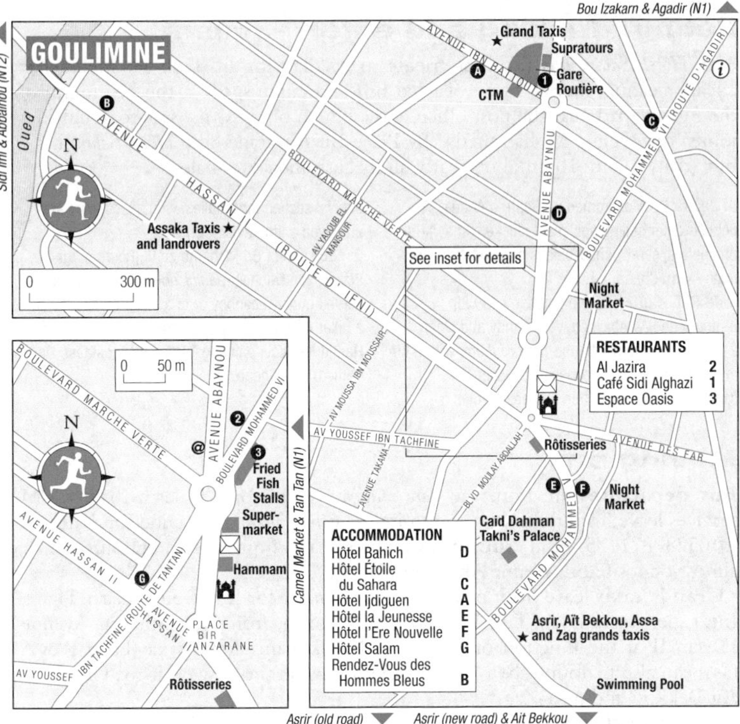

Hôtel Bahich 31 Av Abaynou ⓣ&ⓕ0528 772178, ⓦwww.geocities.com/hotelbahich. An excellent deal, with comfortable rooms, some with en-suite showers, and 3-D paintings in the lobby by local artist, Hamid Kahlaoui. ❷

Hôtel L'Ere Nouvelle 115 Bd Mohammed V ⓣ0662 020817. Best of the ultra-cheapies, basic but clean, with friendly staff and hot showers (4dh) on request. ❶

Hôtel Étoile du Sahara Bd Mohammed VI (Route d'Agadir) ⓣ0528 871095. A tallish building topped by a panoramic terrace (though there isn't much to see), and offering a choice of ordinary rooms with shared bathroom facilities, or big rooms with a shower and a/c, all clean as a whistle, but only worth it if you need that a/c. ❸

Hôtel Ijdiguen Av Ibn Battouta ⓣ&ⓕ0528 771453. Bright, clean, and right opposite the *gare routière*, with shared hot showers (7dh) and friendly staff; great if you've just arrived on a late bus, or need to catch an early one, and a good halfway house between the most basic places and the better hotels, with particularly good rates for single rooms. ❷

Hôtel la Jeunesse 120 Bd Mohammed V ⓣ0670 598106. A possible fall-back if the *Ere Nouvelle* opposite is full. Basic but with shared hot showers (7dh), located up a steep flight of steps. ❶

Hôtel Salam Av Youssef Ibn Tachfine (Route de Tan Tan) ⓣ0528 872057, ⓔhotelsalamguelmim@hotmail.com. Goulimine's top hotel (though not its most expensive), with large en-suite rooms round an open patio, a decent restaurant and the only bar in town. Like the *Bahich*, it has paintings by Hamid Kahlaoui in the lobby. ❷

Rendez-Vous des Hommes Bleus 447 Av Hassan II (Route d'Ifni) ⓣ0528 772821, ⓕ0528 770556. Located 600m up Av Hassan II, nearly at the *oued*, Goulimine's priciest hotel has satellite TV in all its cosy, clean, rather small rooms, but it isn't worth the price difference over the *Bahich* and the *Salam*. Despite the name, *hommes bleus* do not in fact tend to meet up here. ❹

Eating, drinking and entertainment

The *Hôtel Salam* has the best **meals** in town, with an 85dh set menu. For cheaper eating, there's a row of fried fish and tajine spots at the beginning of the Agadir road near the post office, and a bunch of *rôtisseries* (spit-roast chicken joints) on Avenue Mohammed V by Place Bir Anzarane. The *Hôtel Salam* has a **bar** (daily 10am–10pm), but nearly all its customers are male.

Al Jazira Bd Mohammed VI (Route d'Agadir). A popular diner selling spit-roast chicken, shawarma, brochettes, sandwiches, salads and snacks. Daily noon–4am. Cheap.

Café Sidi Alghazi at the junction of Av Ibn Battouta and Av Abaynou. Very handy and clean 24hr café-restaurant by the *gare routière*, with a bit of everything: tajines, couscous, pizzas, sandwiches, juices, coffee and cakes, plus a special section for families, with a kids' play area, and even a little aviary. Cheap.

Espace Oasis Bd Mohammed VI (Route d'Agadir). Pizzas, sandwiches (*panini*, no less) and coffee served under a canopy or in a salon dominated by a pillar disguised as a palm tree and a couple of Hamid Kahlaoui paintings. Good for breakfast. Daily 6am–10pm. Cheap.

Moving on

Bus departures are from the *gare routière* on the Bou Izakarn road. **CTM** services leave from their office opposite the *gare routière* on Avenue Ibn Battouta (Ⓣ0528 871135), and **Supratours** buses leave from the Supratours office, almost opposite on Avenue Abaynou (Ⓣ0528 772650).

Grands taxis leave from next to the *gare routière* for Ifni, Bou Izakarn, Tiznit, Inezgane, Agadir, Tan Tan, Laayoune and Smara, from a station on Avenue Hassan II at the junction of Avenue el Moukouama for Assaka (Land Rover taxis can also be found there), and from stations on the new Asrir road for Asrir, Aït Bekkou and Assa-Zag.

The **airport** is 5km out of town, off the Sidi Ifni road; there's no public transport so you'd have to charter a grand taxi to get there (20dh); arriving by air, you may need to call your hotel to send a taxi. Regional Air Lines are at 218 Avenue Mohammed VI (Route d'Agadir) Ⓣ0528 771269.

For frequencies and journey times see pp.537–538.

Around Goulimine

A large **moussem** is held yearly in early June at **Asrir**, 10km southeast of Goulimine, with lots of camels and the chance to see **Guedra dancing**, a seductive women's dance of the desert, performed from a kneeling position (developed for the low tents) to a slow, repetitive rhythm.

Abbainou

ABBAINOU (Abeïno) is a tiny oasis, 15km northeast of Goulimine, and an easy excursion if you have transport (head up the Sidi Ifni road for a kilometre and it's signposted to the right). If you don't have a vehicle, you could negotiate a grand taxi (from the main rank by the souk). There are hot springs, which have been tapped, and on cool mornings the irrigation channels through the palmery can be seen steaming. There's a basic **campsite**, and a café and bakery in the village centre, but the main interest is the *station thérmale* at the immaculate *Hôtel Abainou* (Ⓣ0528 872892, Ⓕ0528 770424; BB ③), where two indoor pools have been created, one for women at 28°C, the other for men, at a scalding 38°C.

Aït Bekkou

The largest and most spectacular oasis in the Goulimine area is **AÏT BEKKOU** (or Aït Boukka), 10km southeast along the Asrir road, then 7km on *piste*. It can be reached by shared grand taxi from Goulimine (station on the Asrir road). Aït Bekkou is a thriving agricultural community, with an especially lush strip of cultivation along a canal, irrigated from the old riverbed and emerging from a flat expanse of sand. You might even see the odd herd of camels being grazed out here. To reach the canal, head for the thicket of palms about 2km behind the oasis (or pick up a guide on the way).

Fort Bou-Jerif

Fort Bou-Jerif is a truly romantic spot, set beside the Oued Assaka, 13km from the sea, with a wonderful **auberge-campsite** (Ⓣ0672 130017, Ⓦwww.fortboujerif.com) in an old French Foreign Legion camp in the middle of nowhere, with excellent food (including camel tajine), and some superb four-wheel-drive excursions in the area, including trips to the **Plage Blanche** – the "White Beach" that stretches for sixty or so kilometres along the coast southwest of Goulimine. Travellers heading for Mauritania and Senegal should also be able to pick up information here as a lot of overlanders stop over at the fort on their way down. Half-board accommodation is available in a "motel" (❻), a "little hotel" (❻) and a "hotel" (❼) as well as camping (90dh for two people in a campervan), or a nomadic tent to sleep in if you don't have your own (60dh per person), plus power points for caravans, and rows of very clean showers (hot water) and toilets. Most people take half-board, which is a good idea as the food is good and there is nowhere else nearby to eat.

The easiest route to the fort from Goulimine is via a paved road to Tisséguemane which branches left off the Sidi Ifni road a kilometre outside Goulimine, then 20km of *piste*, which you could probably persuade a grand taxi driver to take you along for a small fee, and which can be negotiated, with care, in a car or campervan. The fort can alternatively be approached on a paved road down the coast from Sidi Ifni to Foum Assaka, which leaves only 6km of *piste*. Failing that, you should be able to charter a Land Rover taxi from the junction of Avenue Hassan II with Avenue el Moukaouama.

Travel details

Buses

Agadir to: Beni Mellal (1 CTM & 3 others daily; 8hr); Casablanca (6 CTM & 34 others daily; 9hr); Dakhla (2 CTM, 2 Supratours & 3 others daily; 19hr 30min); Essaouira (1 CTM & 26 others daily; 3hr 30min); Fes (1 CTM & 11 others daily; 12hr); Goulimine (6 CTM, 4 Supratours & 11 others daily; 4hr 30min); Immouzer (1 daily; 2hr 30min); Laayoune (4 CTM, 3 Supratours & 3 others daily; 11hr); Marrakesh (10 CTM, 9 Supratours & 12 others daily; 4hr); Meknes (1 CTM & 5 others daily; 12hr); Ouarzazate (2 daily; 7hr 30min); Rabat (3 CTM & 23 others daily; 11hr); Safi (1 CTM & 16 others daily; 5hr); Smara (1 CTM, 1 Supratours & 1 other daily; 9hr); Tafraoute (5 daily; 5hr); Tangier (1 CTM & 2 others daily; 16hr); Tan Tan (5 CTM, 4 Supratours & 11 others daily; 6hr); Taroudant (5 daily; 1hr 30min); Tata (6 daily; 9hr); Tiznit (6 CTM, 4 Supratours & 17 others daily; 2hr).

Goulimine to: Agadir (6 CTM, 4 Supratours & 11 others daily; 4hr 30min), via Tiznit (2hr 30min); Assa (1 Supratours & 1 other daily; 3hr); Casablanca (3 CTM & 12 others daily; 14hr); Dakhla (2 CTM, 2 Supratours & 3 others daily; 15hr 30min); Laayoune (4 CTM, 5 Supratours & 3 other daily; 7hr); Marrakesh (3 CTM, 5 Supratours & 10 others daily; 9hr 30min); Ouarzazate (2 daily; 15hr) via Tata (9hr 30min), Foum el Hassan (6hr) & Akka (8hr); Rabat (2 CTM & 7 others daily; 16hr); Smara

(1 CTM, 1 Supratours & 1 other daily; 6hr); Tan Tan (4 CTM, 6 Supratours & 15 others daily; 3hr).
Sidi Ifni to: Agadir (1 daily; 3hr 45min); Inezgane (2 daily; 3hr 30min); Marrakesh (1 daily; 8hr 30min); Tiznit (8 daily; 1hr 30min) via Mirhleft (40min).
Tafraoute to: Agadir (5 daily; 5hr); Aït Baha (1 daily; 2hr); Casablanca (5 daily; 14hr); Marrakesh (4 daily; 10hr); Rabat (1 daily; 16hr); Tiznit (5 daily; 3hr).
Taliouine to: Agadir (2 CTM & 2 others daily; 3hr 30min) via Taroudant (2hr); Casablanca (3 daily; 13hr 30min); Er Rachidia (1 daily; 11hr); Marrakesh (1 daily via Tizi n'Test; 10hr); Ouarzazate (2 CTM & 3 others daily; 3hr) via Tazenakht (1hr 30 min); Rabat (1 daily; 15hr 30min); Tinerhir (2 daily; 8hr); Zagora (1 daily; 6hr).
Taroudant to: Agadir (5 daily; 1hr 30min); Casablanca (1 CTM & 10 others daily; 10hr); Marrakesh (1 CTM & 7 others daily; 6hr 30min); Ouarzazate (6 daily; 5hr) via Taliouine (2hr) & Tazenakht (3hr); Rabat (3 daily; 13hr); Tata (3 daily; 4hr 30min) via Igherm (2hr 30min).
Tata to: Agadir (6 daily; 9hr); Bou Izakarn (8 daily; 6hr) via Akka (1hr 30min) and Foum el Hassan (3hr 30min); Casablanca (4 daily; 16hr); Marrakesh (4 daily; 10hr); Ouarzazate (2 daily; 5hr) via Foum Zguid (2hr 30min); Rabat (1 daily; 17hr); Tan Tan (2 daily; 12hr 30min) via Goulimine (9hr 30min); Taroudant (3 daily; 4hr 30min) via Igherm (2hr 30min); Tiznit (6 daily; 7hr).
Tiznit to: Agadir (1 CTM, 4 Supratours & 17 others daily; 2hr); Bou Izakarn (2 CTM & 23 daily; 1hr); Casablanca (4 CTM & 6 others daily; 11hr); Dakhla (2 CTM, 2 Supratours & 3 others daily; 17hr 30min); Goulimine (2 CTM, 5 Supratours & 11 others daily; 2hr 30min); Laayoune (2 CTM, 4 Supratours & 3 others daily; 9hr); Marrakesh (1 CTM, 5 Supratours & 10 others daily; 7hr); Ouarzazate (1 daily; 9hr 30min); Rabat (1 CTM & 7 others daily; 13hr); Sidi Ifni (8 daily; 1hr 30min) via Mirhleft (45min); Smara (1 CTM, 1 Supratours & 1 other daily; 7hr); Tafraoute (5 daily; 3hr); Tata (6 daily; 7hr); Tan Tan (2 CTM, 4 Supratours & 12 others daily; 5hr 30min).

Grands taxis

Agadir to: Aourir (15min); Inezgane (15min); Taroudant (1hr 15min); Tiznit (1hr 15min). Change at Inezgane for most southern destinations.
Aoulouz to: Ouled Berhil (30min); Taliouine (40min); Taroudant (1hr).
Bou Izakarn to: Foum el Hassan (1hr 30min); Goulimine (1hr); Ifrane de l'Anti-Atlas (20min); Inezgane (3hr 30min); Tata (3hr 30min); Tiznit (1hr 30min).
Goulimine to: Agadir (4hr 45min); Aït Bekou (30min); Asrir (15min); Assaka (1hr); Assa-Zag (2hr); Bou Izakarn (1hr); Inezgane (4hr 30min); Laayoune (5hr); Sidi Ifni (1hr); Tiznit (2hr 30min); Tan Tan (2hr 30min).
Inezgane to: Agadir (15min); Essaouira (2hr 30min); Goulimine (4hr 30min); Laayoune (9hr); Marrakesh (3hr); Massa (45min); Ouled Teima (40min); Sidi Ifni (3hr 30min); Tan Tan (6hr 15min); Taroudant (1hr 15min); Tiznit (2hr).
Ouled Berhil to: Aoulouz (30min); Taroudant (40min).
Sidi Ifni to: Goulimine (1hr); Inezgane (3hr 30min); Mirhleft (45min); Tiznit (1hr 30min).
Taliouine to: Aoulouz (40min); Taroudant (1hr 30min); Tazenakht (1hr).
Taroudant to: Agadir (1hr 15min); Aoulouz (1hr); Freija (20min); Igherm (1hr 30min); Inezgane (1hr 15min); Marrakesh (4hr); Ouled Berhil (40min); Taliouine (1hr 30min).
Tata to: Akka (1hr); Bou Izakarn (3hr 30min); Foum el Hassan (2hr); Foum Zguid (2hr 30min); Issafen (2hr); Tissint (1hr).
Tiznit to: Agadir (1hr 15min); Bou Izakarn (1hr 30min); Goulimine (2hr 30min); Inezgane (1hr); Mirhleft (45min); Sidi Ifni (1hr 30min); Sidi Moussa d'Aglou (15min); Tafraoute (2hr).

Flights

Agadir to: Casablanca (RAM 4–5 daily; 1hr–1hr 10min); Dakhla (RAM 1 weekly; 1hr 30min); Laayoune (RAL, RAM 4 weekly; 1hr 25min).
Goulimine to: Casablanca (RAL 3 weekly; 1hr 35min); Tan Tan (RAL 3 weekly; 15min).

9

The Tarfaya Strip and Western Sahara

CHAPTER 9

Highlights

* **Smara** A red ochre desert town, once the seat of local ruler the Blue Sultan, whose palace and great mosque constitute the town's main sights. See p.545

* **Tarfaya** A sleepy fishing village with an offshore fort, which you can walk over to at low tide. See p.549

* **Laayoune** A pioneering boom town built on subsidies and determination, with just a ghost, in its oldest quarters, of a Spanish colonial past. See p.550

* **Dakhla** The furthest south you can go by land from Europe without a visa – 22km from the tropics, with sun all year round, and some lovely beaches within spitting distance of town. See p.558

▲ Casa Mar fort, Tarfaya

9

The Tarfaya Strip and Western Sahara

Few travellers venture south of Goulimine unless bound for Mauritania. The towns – **Tan Tan, Tarfaya**, **Laayoune** and **Dakhla** – are modern administrative centres, with no great intrinsic interest, but the route, across vast tracts of hammada (bleak, stony desert), is another matter, and there is no mistaking that you have reached the **Sahara** proper. Returning, if you don't fancy a repeat of the journey, there are flights from Dakhla and Laayoune to Agadir or the **Canary Islands**.

In colonial times, the Drâa was the border between the French and Spanish protectorates. The land to the south, the **Tarfaya strip**, was part of the Spanish Protectorate in Morocco, along with the area around Tetouan and Al Hoceima in the north. It was not considered part of Spain's two Saharan colonies (together known as the **Spanish Sahara**), of which the northernmost, Seguiat el Hamra, began at the 27°40′ N line just south of Tarfaya, while the southern one, Rio de Oro, began at the 26th parallel, just south of Boujdour. In 1958, two years after the rest of Morocco gained independence, the Spanish gave back the Tarfaya strip, but they kept the Spanish Sahara until November 1975 (see box, pp.552–553).

The region's economic importance was long thought to centre on the phosphate mines at **Boukra**, southeast of Laayoune. However, these have not been very productive in recent years, and the deposits are not especially rich by the standards of the Plateau des Phosphates east of Casablanca. In the long term, the rich deep-water fishing grounds offshore are likely to prove a much better earner. This potential is gradually being realized with the development of fishing ports at Laayoune, Dakhla and Boujdour, together with industrial plants for fish storage and processing.

Throughout the area, Spanish is fast being replaced by French as the dominant second language. Some older residents still speak Spanish, but officials, administrators, and other migrants into the Western Sahara from Morocco proper, as well as younger people in general, are much more likely to understand French.

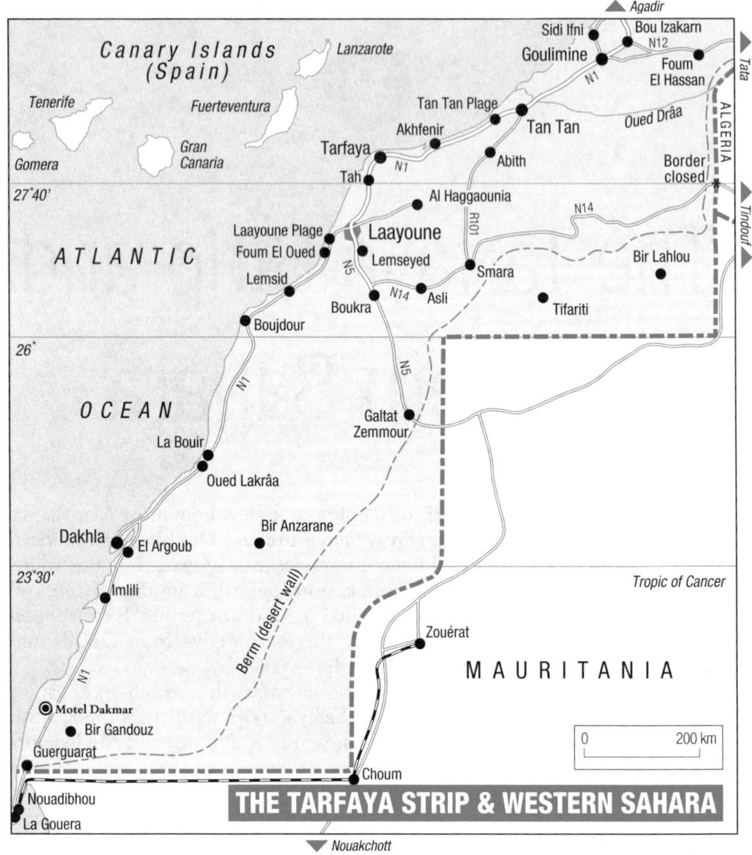

Goulimine to Tan Tan

The approach from **Goulimine to Tan Tan** runs along 125km of straight desert road, across a bleak area of scrub and *hammada*. There are few features to speak of en route: a café and petrol station (55km from Goulimine); a small pass (85km); and finally a crossing of the **Oued Drâa** (109km), invariably dry at this point, where you may be asked to show your passport, as you also may coming into Tan Tan. A *piste* from here heads west to a last French **fort** at the mouth of the Oued.

Tan Tan

TAN TAN is a drab administrative centre of around 70,000 inhabitants, and duty-free zone (the shops are full of radios and electric razors), with a fishing port (25km distant) responsible for a large percentage of Morocco's sardine exports. Its one claim to fame is that it was a departure point for the famous **Green March** (*La Marche Verte*, or *el Massira el Khadra* – see p.552). In early June (or sometimes late May), Tan Tan livens up somewhat for the **Moussem of Sidi Mohammed Ma el Aïnin**, a tribal gathering featuring a camel fair and the sacrifice of a female camel.

Orientation and information

Tan Tan's main artery, the inevitable **Avenue Mohammed V** runs parallel with Oued Ben Khlil, which "flows" north into Oued Drâa. Just off the road's southern end is the **Place de la Marche Verte**, with the **bus** and **grand taxi** rank. At the other end, a smaller square with several cafés and an arcade of shops down one side is referred to locally as **La Poste de la Police** because of the small police post that previously stood in the middle of it (now in the northeast corner – a snack bar has taken over its former location). Beyond the square, the street continues up to meet **Boulevard Hassan II**, the main road in and out of town.

The main **post office** is on Boulevard Hassan II, with a branch office off the Laayoune road. There are a few **banks** on Boulevard Hassan II, as well as the Banque Populaire down near La Poste de la Police, all of which have ATMs. **Internet** access is available at numerous places including Internet Club Yasser at 19 Av Mohammed V (daily 10am–11pm; 3dh per hr) and Cyber Abdou, 17 Rue Ouled Bouaita (daily noon–midnight; 3dh per hr). There's a **hammam** for both sexes just behind the southern end of Place de la Marche Verte, and another at the far end of the street that leads north from the square.

Accommodation

There are a number of unclassified hotels on and around Place de la Marche Verte and La Poste de la Police, most of them grotty if very cheap. Note that many of the cheaper places may balk at letting unmarried couples share a room. Better choices include:

Hôtel Aoubour junction of Av Mohammed V and Bd Hassan II ⓣ0528 877594. Handy for Supratours bus departures, with reasonably clean rooms (upstairs rooms are better than downstairs ones), but not great value compared to the *Bir Anzarane* down the road. ❶

Hôtel Bir Anzarane 154 Bd Hassan II ⓣ&ⓕ0528 877834. The best deal in town, carpeted throughout, with shared bathrooms and very reasonable prices, though not all rooms have outside windows, and it's a bit of a haul from Pl de la Marche Verte. ❶

Hôtel el Hagounia 1 Rue Sidi Ahmed Rguibi ⓣ0528 878561. A cut above the other hotels in this part of town, with bare but large and generally clean rooms, and shared hot showers. ❶

Hôtel el Madina 68 Bd Hassan II ⓣ0528 877171, ⓕ0528 877135. En-suite rooms but no outside windows in this bright little unclassified hotel on the main road through town. ❷

Hôtel Sable d'Or Bd Hassan II ⓣ0528 878069. The best hotel in town, a two-star with large and immaculate en-suite rooms, some with balcony. ❸

Hôtel Tafoukt 98 Pl de la Marche Verte (no phone). Reasonably clean and handy for bus departures, but with no hot water, though for men there's a public shower a block north. ❶

Eating and drinking

There are **cafés** around Place de la Marche Verte (the *Al Amal* on the north side of the square, for example) that claim to offer tajines, though you may well find that they don't actually have any on the go. The Poste de la Police square has a number of snack bars offering sandwiches and spit-roast chicken, newest and cleanest of which is the *Rôtisserie Abi Anass* on the north side (daily noon–midnight; cheap). The *Hôtel Sable d'Or* and the *Hôtel Bir Anzarane* should also be able to produce some food, especially if given notice. The cafés to the north of the square are the best place to sip a mint tea and watch the world go by, in particular, the *Café le Jardin* (daily 7am–9pm), run down but with a garden featuring a slide and swings, which younger travelling companions may appreciate. The two cafés at the fork in the road, though nothing special, are also popular and have a commanding view from their terraces over the comings and goings. The *Le Glacier* café, by the now defunct Renaissance cinema, has a terrace overlooking the oued. A legacy of Spanish rule is a *churros* (fritter) shop at 21 Av Mohammed V.

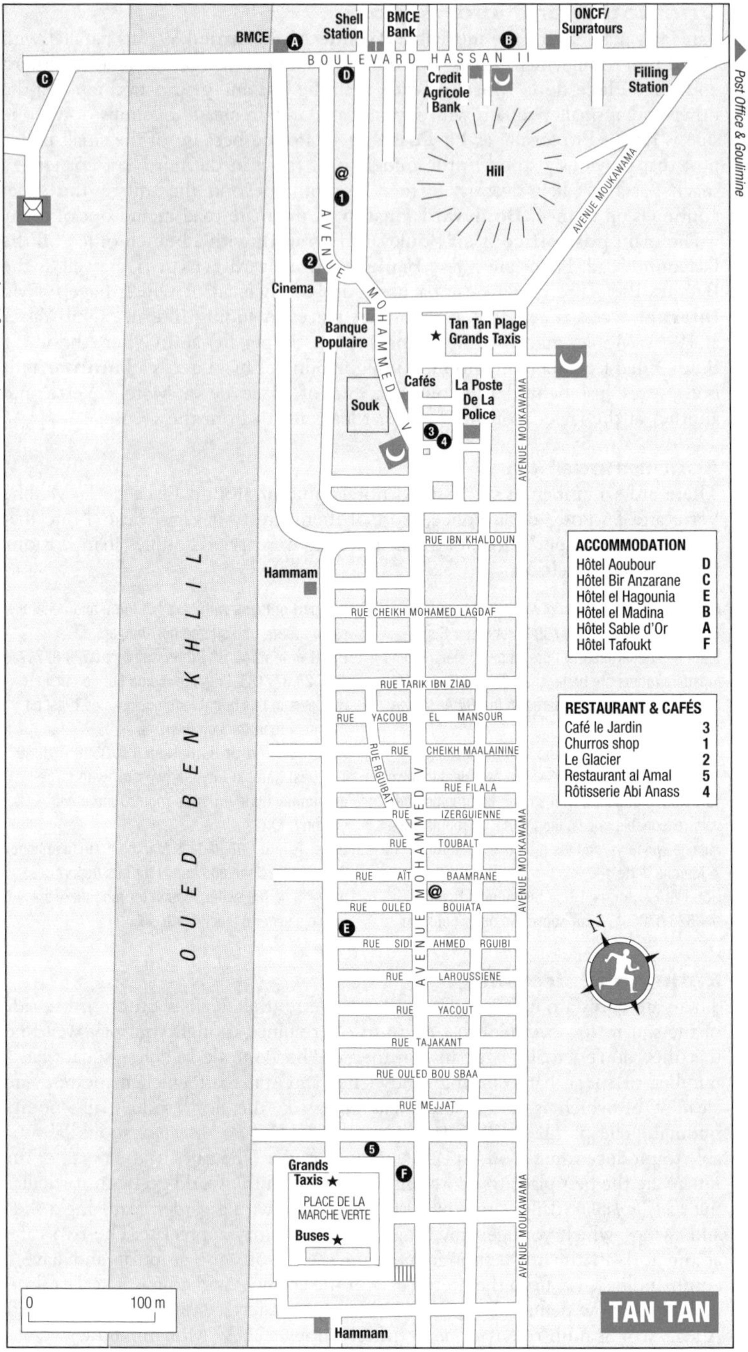

TAN TAN

BOULEVARD HASSAN II
AVENUE MOHAMMED V
AVENUE MOUKAWAMA
OUED BEN KHLIL

BMCE
Shell Station
BMCE Bank
ONCF/ Supratours
Filling Station
Credit Agricole Bank
Hill
Cinema
Banque Populaire
Tan Tan Plage Grands Taxis
Cafés
La Poste De La Police
Souk
Hammam
Grands Taxis
PLACE DE LA MARCHE VERTE
Buses
Hammam

RUE IBN KHALDOUN
RUE CHEIKH MOHAMED LAGDAF
RUE TARIK IBN ZIAD
RUE YACOUB EL MANSOUR
RUE RGUIBAT
RUE CHEIKH MAALAININE
RUE FILALA
RUE IZERGUIENNE
RUE TOUBALT
RUE AÏT BAAMRANE
RUE OULED BOUIATA
RUE SIDI AHMED RGUIBI
RUE LAROUSSIENE
RUE YACOUT
RUE TAJAKANT
RUE OULED BOU SBAA
RUE MEJJAT

CTM, Tan Tan Plage, Laayoune, Smara & Airport
Post Office & Goulimine

0 100 m

ACCOMMODATION	
Hôtel Aoubour	D
Hôtel Bir Anzarane	C
Hôtel el Hagounia	E
Hôtel el Madina	B
Hôtel Sable d'Or	A
Hôtel Tafoukt	F

RESTAURANT & CAFÉS	
Café le Jardin	3
Churros shop	1
Le Glacier	2
Restaurant al Amal	5
Rôtisserie Abi Anass	4

Moving on

All **buses** except Supratours and CTM leave from Place de la Marche Verte. Supratours buses stop outside their office at 118 Boulevard Hassan II (Ⓣ0528 877795). Their southbound services are usually full by the time they get to Tan Tan so you are unlikely to get a seat, except on the 8am bus to Laayoune. CTM buses stop at their office, 200m down the Laayoune road from the main post office. Southbound services all pass through in the wee hours; only the 5.30am service stops at Tarfaya. **Grand taxi** runs include Goulimine, Inezgane, Agadir, Smara and Laayoune; if you strike lucky, you may also find direct taxis for Tarfaya and Tiznit (especially early mornings). They leave from Place de la Marche Verte except for taxis to Tan Tan Plage, which run from just north of La Poste de la Police. The **airport** is 7km out of town on the road to Laayoune and Smara, 20dh by grand taxi; arriving by air however, you may find no taxis at the airport, in which case you'll have to walk 1km down to the main road to find transport.

Tan Tan Plage

TAN TAN PLAGE (also called El Ouatia), 28km from town on the coastal route to Laayoune, is a fishing port with a shadeless and often windswept **beach** that gets quite crowded in summer. Places to **stay** include the clean and cosy *Hôtel Belle Vue*, by the beach (Ⓣ0528 879133; ❸), and the longer-established *Hôtel Marin*, one block inland (Ⓣ0528 879146, Ⓔhotel-lemarin@hotmail.fr; ❸). The *Belle Vue* also has a decent restaurant, specializing in fried fish. At the junction on the main road, 1km out, the *Camping Auberge des 2 Chameaux* (Ⓣ0618 490681; ❸) is a popular stop-off for overlanders heading to West Africa, with space for tents and campervans, or in their own Bedouin tent, as well as pleasant rooms and plenty of hot shower facilities. Next door, there's a restaurant called *Korea House* (daily 10am–10pm; moderate), run by a Korean family and serving a mix of Korean, Moroccan and Spanish dishes.

A loop through Smara

It's possible to make a **loop** from Tan Tan along the R101, to Smara, returning by way of the N1 to Laayoune, and from there across to Tan Tan via Tarfaya – a circuit of some 800km. There are **buses** along each section (though they're not very frequent). If you're driving, you will find **fuel stations** in Tan Tan, Smara and Laayoune; petrol and diesel are subsidized in the Saharan provinces (basically the former Spanish Sahara), and cost about a third less than in Morocco proper, but unleaded fuel is available only in Laayoune and at one station in Dakhla, so if you embark on the trip, be sure to fill up, and to carry good water supplies.

The R101 between Tan Tan and Smara is almost devoid of habitation and features, though you will see some hills and valleys on either side of the road, starting around 20km out of Tan Tan. After 91km more, you enter the Saharan Provinces and a gaggle of petrol stations allow you to take advantage of the lower fuel prices, but they don't sell unleaded fuel.

Smara

SMARA (Es Semara) developed on an important caravan route across the Sahara, but today it is basically a military garrison town, home to both the Moroccan army and the UN, here to supervise the ceasefire and referendum.

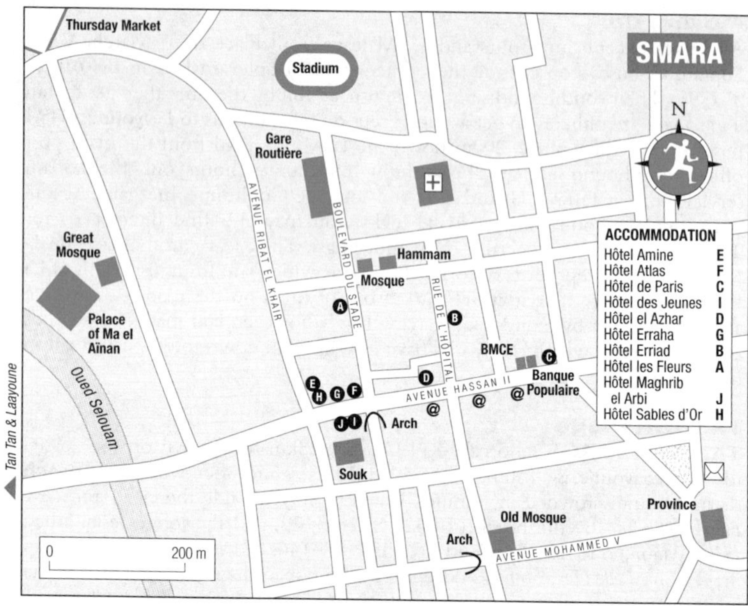

Otherwise, it's a small, sleepy old place, with not a lot going on, though there's a **souk** every Thursday, and a **festival** every April featuring musical and other entertainments.

Information

The **post office** is by the local Province (county hall), at the eastern end of Avenue Mohammed V. There are a couple of **internet** offices on Avenue Hassan II, one opposite the BMCE bank (daily 8.30am–1am; 4dh per hr) and a block east (supposedly 24/7; 4dh per hr). The town also has a couple of **banks** (BMCE and Banque Populaire, both with ATMs), and a couple of **filling stations** (but no unleaded fuel).

The town **hammam** is just off Boulevard de Stade (from Av Hassan II, turn right at the mosque and it's on the left). The first entrance is for women, the third for men, as illustrated above them (the second is for wood to heat the water). If you need a hot shower, the *Hôtel Amine* provides public showers round the back of the hotel.

Accommodation and eating

Smara has a dozen **hotels**, but most are extremely basic, with cold showers or none at all, and only one of the town's hotels has anything approaching comfort. You may have to check out the rock-bottom choices, however, if the more tolerable cheapies are full. There isn't much in the way of **restaurants** in town, though a trio of places along Avenue Hassan II serve basic snacks, and there are open-air grills and fried fish stalls around the souk and on Boulevard de Stade. The best restaurant in town is at the *Hôtel Amine*.

Hôtel Amine 97 Av Ribat el Khair ⓣ0528 887368. The only really decent place to stay in town, with clean rooms and satellite TV, and a restaurant serving spit-roast chicken or tajines. The minus point, if you take a room that isn't en suite, is that you'll have to leave the hotel and go round to the back of the building to take a shower. ❷

Hôtel de Paris 156 Av Hassan II ⓣ0610 780988. Newer and better than the rock bottom options, with friendly staff, bright rooms and hot showers. ❷

Hôtel Maghrib el Arbi 15 Av Hassan II ⓣ0528 899151. Before the *Amine* opened this was Smara's top offering, which isn't saying much. There's no hot water, and no rooms are en suite, but they're a bit bigger and brighter than the ones in the other ultra-cheap places, which are (in order of preference): *Erriad* (49 Rue l'Hôpital – this had hot water showers at last check, 5dh a go); *Atlas* (4 Bd du Stade); *Les Fleurs* (66 Bd du Stade); *Sables d'Or* (1 Av Hassan II, next-door to the *Amine*); *El Azhar* (69 Rue de Figuig); *Erraha* (16 Av Hassan II); *Des Jeunes* (23 Av Hassan II). ❶

The Town

Smara's only link with its past is the remains of the Palace and Great Mosque of **Ma el Aïnin**, the "Blue Sultan", who controlled the region at the beginning of the twentieth century. The **palace**, near the oued, is quite well preserved and contains the residences of Ma el Aïnin's four main wives, one of them now occupied by the *gardien* and his family. If you knock on the door, someone will open up and show you around, usually for a fee. Inside you can see the domed *zaouia*. Though plastered over, it is, like the rest of the palace, built of black basalt from the local hills. What's left of the **Great Mosque**, a separate building further away from the river, is less well preserved, but you can still see the mihrab, and rows of basalt arches.

The **old mosque** marked on our map is also made of local basalt, with a rather pretty stone minaret. This stands in the part of town built under Spanish rule, roughly bounded by the two arches and the *Hôtel Sables d'Or*. A distinctive aspect of the houses here (and elsewhere in the Western Sahara) is the eggshell-like domes which serve as roofs. The domes are said to keep the interior cooler by means of convection currents, but a more likely story is that the Spanish built them like this to prevent build-ups of wind-blown sand on the roofs; the domes are certainly not traditional Saharawi structures, as the Saharawis were always nomads and their traditional homes were tents. Behind the mosque, you'll also find some of the strange tubular barracks put up by the Spanish to house their troops, now private homes. Like most buildings in Smara, they are painted a deep red ochre.

Moving on

All **buses** and **grands taxis** leave from the *gare routière*, a yard on Boulevard de Stade near the stadium, where you'll find the offices of Supratours, SATAS and CTM, the only firms that serve Smara. Supratours run the only daily service to Laayoune.

Smara to Laayoune

Heading towards Laayoune, the desert is black-ish from basalt for the first 5km, before resuming a lighter hue. There are prehistoric rock carvings near **Asli**, 15km out of Smara, but you'd need local help and 4WD transport to find them.

South of the new road, 30km from Smara stands a large brown flat-topped hill called **Gor el Bered** (Hill of the Wind). At the foot of its west side, just north of the road, a small brown cupola-domed building resembling a *marabout* is in fact a structure built by the Spanish in the 1930s to extract chalk from the calcium-rich rock of the hill. A genuine *marabout* is to be found at **Sidi Khatari**, south of the road some 90km from Smara.

Travelling in the Western Sahara

Tourists can now travel freely in most Moroccan-controlled parts of what are called the **Saharan Provinces** (an administrative area created to include the **former Spanish Sahara**, while not coinciding with its boundaries), but do check first on the political situation. The government advisories listed on p.45 will have up-to-date information if any problems have arisen. Apart from this, the only obstacle would be for visitors who admit to being a writer or journalist: a profession not welcome in the region, unless under the aegis of an official press tour.

Otherwise, visiting Laayoune, Smara, Boujdour and Dakhla is now pretty routine, though it does involve answering a series of questions (name, age, profession, parents' names, passport number and date of issue, etc) at numerous **police checkpoints** along the way. This is all usually very amicable, but time-consuming (you'll be asked for these details four times, for example, between Laayoune and Dakhla), and taxi drivers may occasionally, as a result, be unwilling to carry foreigners. To save time it is a good idea to print out and/or photocopy several copies of a sheet with the following information listed, preferably in French (as given here in brackets): family name (*nom*), given names (*prénoms*), date of birth (*date de naissance*), place of birth (*lieu de naissance*), marital status (*situation familiale*), father's name (*nom de père*), mother's name (*nom de mère*), nationality (*nationalité*), occupation (*profession*), address (*addresse* – which should be given in full), passport number (*numéro de passeport*), date of issue (*date de déliverance*), place of issue (*lieu de déliverance*), expiry date (*date d'expiration*), purpose of visit (*motif du voyage – tourisme*, for example), make of vehicle (*marque du véhicule* – you may of course have to leave this one blank), vehicle registration number (*matriculation* – ditto), date of entry into Morocco (*date d'entrée en Maroc*), place of entry (*ville d'entrée*) and police number (*numéro de police* – this is the number stamped in your passport alongside your first entry stamp into Morocco, typically six digits and two letters). For marital status, you could be single (*célibataire*), married (*marié* if male, *mariée* if female), divorced (*divorcé/divorcée*) or widowed (*veuf/veuve*). Armed with this, you can then give your details to police at every checkpoint, which will save them having to ask you for the information point by point.

Continuing south, the **border with Mauritania** is open (see p.561), a good surfaced road reaches the border with Mauritanian-held territory, and officials on both sides are now quite used to travellers passing through, so your only problem should be in finding transport (see p.561).

After the **turn-off to Boukra**, a mining town with a large garrison 25km to the southeast, you become aware of the **Boukra-Laayoune conveyor belt** snaking its way south of the road, bearing phosphates seaward for export. The vast region south of Boukra is a restricted military zone, and inaccessible to casual visitors.

As the road swings west for the last 50km before Laayoune, the canyon of the **Seguiat el Hamra** comes into view on the northern side. Seguiat el Hamra means "Red River" and, though there is no water in it for most of the year, the local clay turns it red when it does flow. The canyon is pretty impressive, but if you stop to take a snapshot be sure you are out of range of anything military. The oasis of **Lemseyed**, 12km before Laayoune, offers fine views over the canyon. Across the Oued, **Fort Dchira**, built by the Spanish in the very early days of their rule, is now occupied by the Moroccan army.

Tan Tan to Laayoune

Between Tan Tan and Tarfaya there is little more than the flyblown roadside settlement of **AKHFENIR** (140km south of Tan Tan) with two 24-hour petrol stations (no unleaded) and a handful of cafés serving fried fish or tajine. South of the village, *La Courbine d'Argent*, (ⓣ0671 422377, ⓦwww.lacourbinedargent.com; BB ❹) offers good accommodation, as well as fishing and bird-watching excursions. Fishing expeditions are also offered by the *Centre de Pêche et de Loisirs* (ⓣ0528 765560, ⓦpeche.sudmaroc.free.fr; BB ❹) at the northern end of the village, which is smaller and a lot homelier, but less well equipped. The only other accommodation is the basic and overpriced *Hôtel Atlas* (ⓣ0666 275111; ❷). **Flamingos** and migratory birds can sometimes be seen in the lagoons and saltpans along the coast to the south.

Tarfaya

TARFAYA is a quiet little fishing town (population 6000) that's probably not far different from its years as a staging post for the Aéropostale Service – when aviators such as **Antoine de Saint-Exupéry** (author of *Night Flight* and *The Little Prince*) used to rest up here on their way down to West Africa.

The air service is commemorated annually in October by a "**Rallye Aérien**", with small planes stopping here on their way south from Toulouse to Dakar. A monument to Saint-Exupéry in the form of a plane stands at the northern end of the beach. Nearby, in the *Maison de l'Initiative* community centre, a **Musée Antoine de Saint-Exupéry** (Mon–Fri 8am–noon & 2–4pm; free) has exhibits on the air mail service that Saint-Exupéry pioneered, but (in the formerly Spanish zone of an Arabic-speaking country) with explanations in French only.

Oddly enough, Tarfaya was actually founded, at the end of the nineteenth century, by a Scottish trader named Donald Mackenzie, and was originally called Port Victoria after Britain's queen. Mackenzie had a fort built, now known as **Casa Mar**, which is just offshore – a few metres' swim at low tide. The Spanish called the town Villa Bens.

These days Tarfaya is a lazy, do-nothing place. Places to stay include two small **hotels** – both quite busy in the fishing season (Dec–March) – of which the better by far is the very welcoming *El Bahja* on a sandy street grandiosely named Boulevard Bir Anzarane (ⓣ0528 895506; ❶). In addition, there's the new *Apart-Hôtel Casamar* (ⓣ0528 895326; ❸), where you can take an apartment with kitchen, bathroom, sitting room and bedroom. For **meals**, the *El Bahja* can whip up a tajine, and the cafés along the north side of the town's main street, Avenue Ahmed el Hayar, have excellent and very cheap fresh fried fish, or fish tajines – the best is the one nearest to the post office by the Maison de la Pêche fishing supplies shop. There is no bank in Tarfaya, so bring as many dirhams as you'll need.

Transport can be tricky; getting to and from Tarfaya, you may have to wait a few hours before anything turns up. Shared grands taxis make the run from both Tan Tan and Laayoune if they can find the passengers – as always, mornings are best. Local firm Najmat Sahara runs a daily bus from Tan Tan and one from Laayoune. Aside from that, some – but not all – Supratours and CTM services between Tan Tan and Laayoune (three or four a day in each direction) call at Tarfaya, but SATAS and SAT services don't, though they will set you down (but not pick up) at the junction on the main road, 3km from town.

South to Laayoune

South of Tarfaya you cross into the Western Sahara just after **Tah**, where a red granite monument flanking the road commemorates the 1975 Green March. From here on you begin to traverse real sand desert – the **Erg Lakhbayta**.

Laayoune

With a population of around 200,000, **LAAYOUNE** (AL AYOUN, sometimes spelt AAIUN in the Spanish colonial period) is the largest and the most interesting town in the Western Sahara, though it was only founded in 1940. The city has the highest per capita government spending in Morocco and soldiers, billeted here for the conflict with Polisario, have been employed in many construction projects. The old **lower town**, built by the Spanish, lies on the southern slope of the steep-sided valley of the **Seguiat el Hamra**, with the new **upper town**, developed since the Green March, on the high plateau beyond.

The population growth – from little more than a village when the Moroccans took over – has been aided by massive subsidies, which apply throughout the Western Sahara, and by an agreement that settlers should initially pay no taxes. The fact that most of Laayoune's residents are here by choice – only a minority of current residents were actually born here – gives the place a dynamism and pioneering feel that contrasts quite sharply with the weight of tradition that hangs heavy on cities like Fes and Marrakesh. The result is that, although Laayoune has little in the way of obvious sights, its atmosphere is quite a change from that of towns in Morocco proper.

▲ Complexe Artisanal, Laayoune

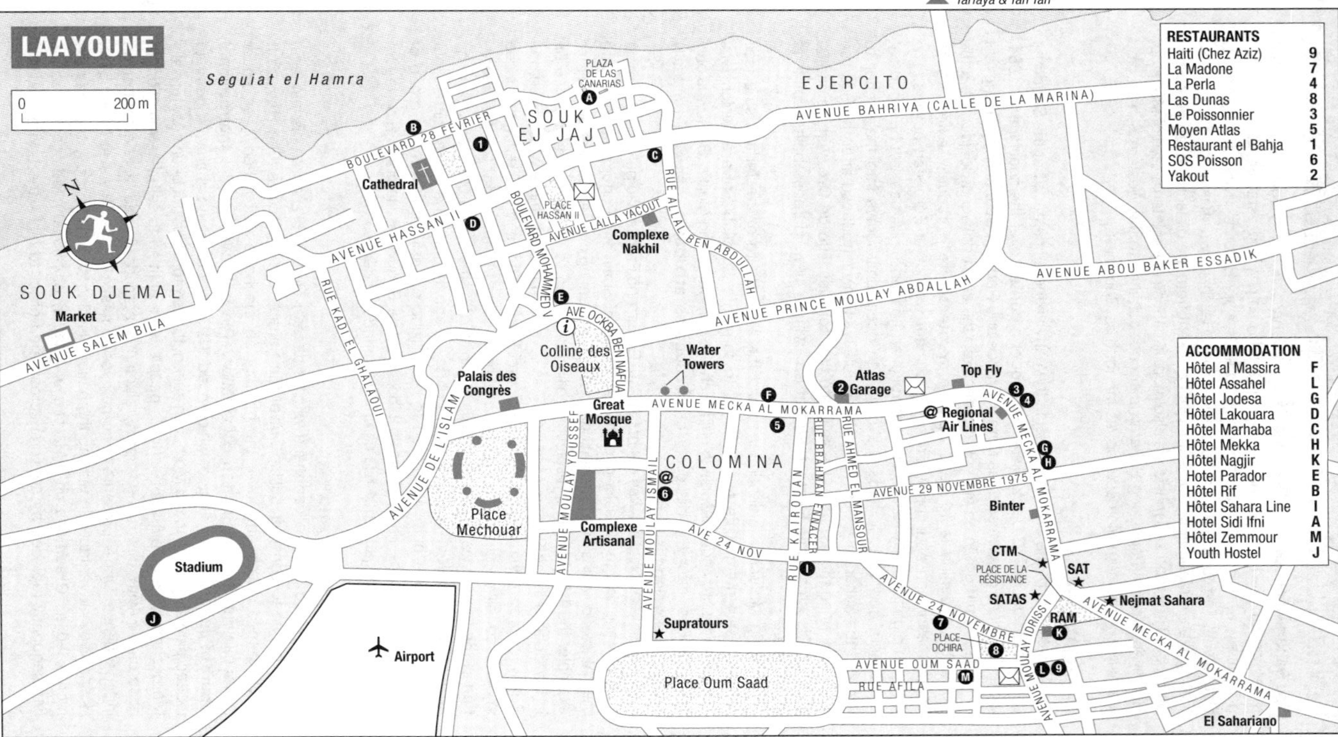
LAAYOUNE
0 200 m
N
Seguiat el Hamra
EJERCITO
SOUK EJ JAJ
SOUK DJEMAL
COLOMINA
Tarfaya & Tan Tan
Grands Taxis (200m)
Smara
Laayoune Plage, Boujdour & Dakhla
RESTAURANTS
Haiti (Chez Aziz) 9
La Madone 7
La Perla 4
Las Dunas 8
Le Poissonnier 3
Moyen Atlas 5
Restaurant el Bahja 1
SOS Poisson 6
Yakout 2
ACCOMMODATION
Hôtel al Massira F
Hôtel Assahel L
Hôtel Jodesa G
Hôtel Lakouara D
Hôtel Marhaba C
Hôtel Mekka H
Hôtel Nagjir K
Hotel Parador E
Hôtel Rif B
Hôtel Sahara Line I
Hotel Sidi Ifni A
Hôtel Zemmour M
Youth Hostel J
PLAZA DE LAS CANARIAS
AVENUE BAHRIYA (CALLE DE LA MARINA)
BOULEVARD 28 FEVRIER
Cathedral
PLACE HASSAN II
AVENUE LALLA YACOUT
RUE ALLAL BEN ABDULLAH
Complexe Nakhil
AVENUE HASSAN II
BOULEVARD MOHAMMED V
AVENUE ABOU BAKER ESSADIK
AVENUE PRINCE MOULAY ABDALLAH
AVE OCKBA BEN NAFUA
Market
AVENUE SALEM BILA
RUE KADI EL GHALAOUI
Colline des Oiseaux
Water Towers
Palais des Congrès
Atlas Garage
Top Fly
AVENUE MECKA AL MOKARRAMA
Regional Air Lines
Great Mosque
AVENUE DE L'ISLAM
AVENUE MOULAY YOUSSEF
AVENUE MOULAY ISMAIL
RUE KAIROUAN
RUE BRAHMAN ENNACER
RUE AHMED EL MANSOUR
AVENUE 29 NOVEMBRE 1975
Binter
Place Mechouar
Complexe Artisanal
AVE 24 NOV
CTM
PLACE DE LA RÉSISTANCE
SAT
SATAS
Nejmat Sahara
AVENUE 24 NOVEMBRE
RAM
PLACE DCHIRA
AVENUE MOULAY IDRISS I
Stadium
Supratours
Airport
Place Oum Saad
AVENUE OUM SAAD
RUE AFILA
El Sahariano

Western Saharan history

The **Saharawi people** who live in the Western Sahara are largely descended from Arab tribes who moved into the area in the fifteenth century, and established themselves definitively with victory over the indigenous Sanhaja Berbers in the 1644–74 Char Bouba war. They speak an Arabic dialect called Hassania, which is much the same as that spoken in Mauritania, and somewhat different from the dialect spoken in most of Morocco. Their food and music are also more like those of Mauritania than of Morocco. However, Hassania-speaking Saharawis are not confined to the Western Sahara, and many live in southern Morocco too, as far north as Goulimine.

Spanish colonial rule

Spain held part of the Saharan coast in the early sixteenth century, but the **Saadians** drove them out in 1524, establishing **Moroccan control** over the coastline. In 1884, while European powers such as Britain, France and Portugal were carving up the rest of Africa, **Spain** got in on the act and declared the coast between Boujdour and the Nouadibhou peninsula to be a Spanish "**protectorate**", gradually extending its boundaries inland and northward by agreement with other European powers. The Spanish didn't actually have much control over the area in practice, but built ports at La Gouera and Villa Cisneros (Dakhla), with occasional forays into the interior to "pacify" the Saharawi tribes. Full colonial rule was only introduced after the Spanish Civil War, when the territory was split into two colonies: **Rio de Oro**, with its capital at Villa Cisneros, and **Seguiat el Hamra**, with a new, purpose-built capital at Laayoune.

Following Moroccan independence and the 1958 return of the Tarfaya strip (see p.541), Spain merged its two colonies to form the **Spanish Sahara**, which was considered a province of Spain itself, much like Ifni, Ceuta and Melilla. But it was only in the 1960s, after the discovery of **phosphates at Boukra**, that Spain actually started to develop the territory.

By that time colonialism was out of fashion. Britain and France had pulled out of most of Africa, and only the Fascist-ruled Iberian states of Spain and Portugal still held onto their African colonies, with international pressure mounting on them to quit. In 1966 for example, the **UN** passed a resolution calling on Spain to organize a referendum on independence in the Sahara. Meanwhile, as education became more widespread, the Spaniards were confronted with the same problem that they and the French had faced in Morocco thirty years earlier – the rise of nationalism. A **Movement for the Liberation of the Sahara** was formed in 1967, and in 1970 it organized a protest in Laayoune against Spanish rule. This was brutally put down, and the Movement was banned, but Spanish repression only succeeded in radicalizing opposition. In 1973, a group of militants formed the Frente para la Liberación de Seguiat el Hamra y Rio de Oro (**Polisario**), and began a guerrilla campaign for independence.

The Green March, and war

Under pressure from Polisario, and with its dictator General Franco on his last legs, Spain began to consider pulling out of the Sahara, but Morocco's King **Hassan II** now claimed sovereignty over the territory on the basis that it had been under Moroccan rule before Spanish colonization. The case went to the **International Court of Justice** in the Hague, which ruled that, though some Saharawi tribes had indeed paid allegiance to the Moroccan sultan, the territory had not been substantially Moroccan before colonization, and its people were entitled to self-determination. In accordance with this ruling, Spain reluctantly agreed to hold a referendum on independence. Under pressure at home over domestic issues, however (see p.578), Hassan saw advantages in waving the nationalist flag as a distraction, and the next month led a "**Green March**" (*Massira el Khadra*) of 350,000 Moroccan civilians (subsequently replaced by soldiers) across the border to claim the territory. At the same time a secret agreement was hatched in Madrid to divide the territory between Morocco and Mauritania as soon as Spanish troops had withdrawn.

The Madrid signatories had however underestimated the Saharawis' determination to fight for their independence. In February 1976, when Spanish forces left, Polisario proclaimed the **Saharawi Arab Democratic Republic (SADR)**, and fought back against Moroccan and Mauritanian occupation, backed by Algeria, and sometimes Libya, who saw the Sahara as a stick with which to beat their regional rival. Thousands of refugees fled into Algeria, where they settled into increasingly unhygienic Polisario-run refugee camps rather than submit to Moroccan or Mauritanian rule. Algeria ceded the territory around the camps to the SADR; 200,000 people still live in them.

Polisario's early military successes were impressive, and Mauritania in particular did not have the resources to beat them. In 1978, the war's destabilization of the Mauritanian economy brought down the government. The new regime made peace with Polisario and pulled out of the Sahara (apart from La Gouera and the western side of the Nouadibhou peninsula, which Mauritania still occupies). The Moroccans moved in to replace them, but by the early 1980s they had been pushed into a small area around Laayoune and Dakhla, and the phosphate mines lay idle. Polisario guerillas even managed to infiltrate into Morocco itself. But the Moroccans fought back and, beginning in 1981, built a series of heavily defended **desert walls** (*berm*) that excluded Polisario forces from successively larger areas. The sixth wall, built in 1987, established Moroccan control over two thirds of the territory, including all its economically important parts and the whole of the coastline. Polisario, now confined to areas behind the *berm*, particularly the region around Bir Lahlou and Tifariti, increasingly turned to diplomacy to gather support, with some success. In 1985, the OAU (now the African Union) admitted the SADR to full membership; Morocco left the organization in protest.

Ceasefire and future prospects

In 1988 a UN plan for a **referendum,** to choose between incorporation or independence, was accepted in principle by both sides, and 1991 saw a ceasefire, with the deployment of a UN peacekeeping force called MINURSO, but the years since have seen the UN aims frustrated, with arguments over the voting list leading to repeated postponement of the referendum; Morocco in particular has brought in large numbers of supporters to vote its way should the promised referendum ever be held. In theory, it will still take place, but observers are sceptical. Having invested so much in the territory – not only in military terms, as subsidies, tax concessions and infrastructure building have all been a heavy drain on the Moroccan economy – it seems inconceivable that Morocco will relinquish its claims. In 2002, Morocco's King Mohammed VI stated that he would never give up any part of the territory, but pro-independence protests are no longer put down by force (though protestors may subsequently get a visit), and the king has tried to be conciliatory, granting a royal pardon to hundreds of Saharawi political prisoners. In 2007 he proposed a new settlement based on limited autonomy under Moroccan sovereignty, which Polisario inevitably rejected. Meanwhile Morocco has started building little villages all along the coast to establish "facts on the ground", and, as an important strategic ally of the West, is unlikely to face much international pressure on the issue. Truth is, prospects for independence are bleak, and limited autonomy is probably the best the Saharawis can hope for.

The case for and against Morocco's claim to the Western Sahara is, of course, keenly argued on the internet. For the pro-independence side (though it may be sensible not to check these while in Morocco), see Ⓦwww.arso.org or Ⓦdspace.dial.pipex.com/suttonlink/334ws.pdf. For the Moroccan case, see Ⓦwww.westernsaharaonline.net or (in French) www.saharamarocain.net.

The **tourist office** is on Avenue de l'Islam, hidden away in a compound opposite the *Hotel Parador* (Mon–Fri 8.30am–4.30pm; ⓣ0528 891694).

Accommodation

Laayoune's best **hotels** are often block-booked by the UN, though most keep rooms aside for non-UN visitors. Unclassified hotels, of which there are maybe a score, are concentrated in the Souk ej Jaj and Souk Djemal districts (the former arguably the most interesting part of town to stay in), but they can be very basic indeed, and none too clean. The **youth hostel** behind the sports stadium (ⓣ0668 388437) is inconveniently located, not especially salubrious, and a dorm bed (30dh) costs the same as a single room at a cheap hotel.

Hôtel al Massira 12 Av Mecka al Mokarrama ⓣ0528 890000, ⓔsahara_hospitality@yahoo.fr. A smart and efficient modern hotel, conveniently located, with a pool, though the rooms are quite small. It's partly block-booked by the UN, but keeps a number of rooms free. ❽

Hôtel Assahel Av Moulay Idriss I ⓣ0528 890170. A good-value choice among the small group of cheapies off Pl Dchira. The upstairs café, where you can smoke a sheesha pipe or drink a freshly squeezed orange juice, overlooks Pl Dchira. Hot showers are available (10dh). ❶

Hôtel Jodesa 223 Av Mecka al Mokarrama ⓣ0528 992064, ⓕ0528 893784. A very pleasant little place, with en-suite rooms, a roof terrace, a downstairs café, and a car rental service. There are often discounts on offer off-season. ❸

Hôtel Lakouara Av Hassan II ⓣ0528 893378. A comfortable two-star with large rooms, en-suite bathrooms, satellite TV and 24hr hot water. Often block-booked by the UN. The upstairs café is used almost exclusively by hotel guests, so it's nice and quiet. ❹

Hôtel Marhaba Av Bahariya, Souk ej Jaj ⓣ0528 893249. A good-value, inexpensive hotel, a cut above most in this price range, but not the cleanest place you'll ever see (make sure your sheets are fresh, to start with). Hot showers available (7dh). ❶

Hôtel Mekka 205 Av Mecka al Mokarrama ⓣ0528 993996. Clean and cosy with en-suite rooms, similar to the neighbouring *Jodesa* except that the rooms are slightly smaller. Discounts usually available off-season. ❸

Hôtel Nagjir 6 Pl Bir Anzarane ⓣ0528 894168, ⓕ0528 890982. Good-value four-star with a good restaurant, and a new wing with spacious suites about to open. Though most rooms are taken by the UN, they keep thirty-odd for casual visitors and generally have promotional rates off-season. ❻

Hôtel Parador Av de l'Islam ⓣ0528 890000, ⓔsahara_hospitality@yahoo.fr. The old Spanish grand hotel, run by the same management as the *Al Massira*, but rather more traditional in style, with larger rooms as well as a pool. The corridors are decorated with photos of the 1975 Green March. ❼

Hôtel Rif 99 Bd 28 Février, Souk ej Jaj, overlooking the Seguiat el Hamra ⓣ0616 116088. Formerly the best of Souk ej Jaj's cheapies, it's become rather run down, and has no hot water, but it's still not a bad place to stay if you need to keep it cheap. ❶

Hôtel Sahara Line Av 24 Novembre at Rue Kairouan ⓣ0528 995454, ⓔsahara_line@menara.ma. A four-star, though it doesn't have a bar or a pool. Efficient management and carpeted rooms, not huge, but equipped with satellite TV and a/c, as well as suites, and even a presidential suite if you need something more spacious. They have a promotional discount of around 30 percent, which they offer on a permanent basis to anyone presenting this guidebook at reception. They are also building a new five-star hotel by the airport. ❻

Hôtel Sidi Ifni 12 Rue Sanhaja, Souk ej Jaj, off Av Bahariya ⓣ0661 720996. This place has to its credit the fact that it's at the heart the oldest part of town, and of Laayoune's original community, with rooms that are decent enough for the price, but it has no hot water, though the Complexe Nakhil (see p.556) is not too far away. ❶

Hôtel Zemmour 1 Av Oum Saad, just off Pl Dchira ⓣ0528 892323. Better, cleaner and brighter than any of the other budget options by a very long chalk; great value with pretty little apple-green and cream rooms, some with a balcony. Bathroom facilities are shared but sparkling, and showers are hot. It costs slightly more than the rock-bottom options, but it's well worth the difference. ❷

The Town

The old **cathedral** is open for Sunday morning mass, and the priest will normally let you have a look inside if you ring on his bell at a reasonable hour. Across the main square, on the east side, the **town hall** was formerly used by the Spanish administration, and is now largely occupied by the Moroccan military (so don't try to photograph it).

The district stretching east from here, **Souk ej Jaj** (Glass Market), is the oldest part of Laayoune, and many of its residents have been here since Spanish days. It's very rundown, but it's undoubtedly Laayoune's most atmospheric quarter. There's a smattering of cheap hotels, and many of the houses still have the eggshell-domed roofs typical of the Western Sahara (see p.547). One that doesn't is **Laayoune's oldest house**, at 16 28 du Février (on the corner of Rue No.18, and opposite the end of Bd Mohammed V), originally constructed in 1933. A few tiled Spanish street signs – or Arabic ones put up by the Spanish – are still in evidence, but most have been replaced by blue metal plaques painted in Arabic and French.

East of Souk ej Jaj, the district of **Ejercito** (Spanish for army) houses Moroccan troops as it did their Spanish predecessors. South of Avenue Bahariya, some of the tubular barracks are now private houses, hemmed in by more modern, box-like, blocks of flats. The other district left from Spanish times is **Colomina**, to the south of Avenue Mecka al Mokarrama. It is nicknamed Colomina Tarduss ("Kick") because, when the Spanish left, Moroccan settlers kicked in the doors to squat their houses. Nowadays, most of the quarter has been rebuilt.

Souk Djemal, with its **municipal market**, represents the first phase of Moroccan settlement, and is now almost as rundown as Souk ej Jaj, though it remains quite animated, especially around dusk. The newer areas are more prosperous, stretching along **Avenue Mecka el Mokarrama**, and radiating outwards from **Place Dchira**.

Most striking of the modern developments is the **Place Mechouar**, at the western end of Avenue Mecka al Mokarrama. Lining one side of the square is a series of tent-like canopies for shade and at each corner are towers to flood-light the square at night. There is also an ambitious **Palais des Congrès**, designed by King Hassan II's favourite architect, André Paccard.

The landscaped gardens of the **Colline des Oiseaux**, whose cages of exotic birds have blinds to be drawn down over the cages in the event of sandstorms, is now closed, and most of the birds gone, but if you go to the entrance on Avenue Ockba Ben Nafaa, and ask the *gardien*, he may let you in for a tip. Of some interest, too, is the **Complexe Artisanal** behind the Great Mosque, where twenty little workshops, capped with cupolas, provide space for metal, wood and jewellery craftsmen.

Eating

Plenty of restaurants in Laayoune serve Moroccan food, but none offer Saharawi food, which is typically meat or fish stew with rice – more like the food of Mauritania than that of Morocco. For an upmarket feed, the hotels *Al Massira*, *Nagjir* and *Parador* all have good **restaurants**. At the other end of the scale, the liveliest place to hang out in the evenings is **Souk Djemal**, where the cafés around the market serve cheap evening meals of tajine or fried fish, and also breakfasts, with *melaoui* and *harsha*, though coffee lovers should check that the coffee they serve is real, since some of them have only instant (and don't warn you of this when you order). *Moyen Atlas* at 50 Av Mecka al Mokarrama, opposite the *Hôtel al Massira*, is a reasonably good patisserie where you can sit in or out and have your pastry with tea, coffee or orange juice.

Haiti (Chez Aziz) 16 Rue No.1 ⓣ0528 994442. A small but pleasant pizzeria-restaurant behind the *Hôtel Nagjir*, with pizza, pasta, fish kebabs, fried squid and roast chicken. The pizzas themselves aren't very good, but their fish dishes aren't bad and the prawn bisque is worth trying. Takeaways and home delivery available. Daily noon–12.30am. Moderate.

La Madone Av 24 du Novembre ⓣ0528 993252. A small pizzeria that's little more than a hole in the wall, but it does have a few tables both inside and out. The pasta dishes are pretty good (try the spaghetti aux fruits de mer), and they also do reasonable fish dishes and pizzas. Takeaways and home delivery available. Daily 11am–1am. Moderate.

La Perla 185 Av Mecka al Mokarrama. The menu looks great, with prawn bisque, chocolate mouse and a fine selection of fabulous-sounding fish dishes, but unfortunately it fails to live up to its promise, though it isn't bad for the price. Daily noon–3pm & 6.30–midnight. Moderate.

Las Dunas middle of Pl Dchira. You can get anything from a coffee and a croissant to a burger or a chicken tajine here, served in a pleasant a/c saloon or outside around a fountain in the square. Very civilized. Daily 11am–8pm. Moderate.

Le Poissonnier 183 Av Mecka al Mokarrama. It looks like *La Perla* next door, and the prices are similar, but the ambience is a bit slicker and the food is far superior, with excellent fish soup and wonderful grilled sea bass. Daily 11am–3.30pm & 7.30–midnight. Moderate.

Restaurant el Bahja 8 Av Mohammed V, Souk ej Jaj. A popular but rather grubby Moroccan greasy spoon offering *kofta* (supposedly camel), lamb chops, and plenty of chips. Daily 10am–midnight. Cheap

SOS Poisson Av Moulay Ismail. Good fish dishes, sometimes including prawn bisque and shark brochettes, though available items depend on what's in the market on a given day. Daily noon–3pm & 6–11pm. Moderate.

Yakout Av Talha Bnou Zubeir, behind Atlas garage. A Moroccan café-restaurant, prettily decorated with tourist souvenirs, and serving tajines and brochettes; it also offers apple-flavoured sheesha pipes and tea or coffee. In theory open 24/7. Cheap.

Listings

Airlines Binter 194 Av Mecka al Mokarrama ⓣ0528 980517; RAM, Pl Bir Anzarane, next to *Hôtel Nagjir* ⓣ0528 995810 to 12; Regional Air Lines, 176 Av Mecka al Mokarrama, opposite *La Perla* and *La Poissonnier* restaurants ⓣ0528 892922; TopFly has an office on Av Mecka al Mokarrama, but all its ticket sales are through El Sahariano on the Smara road ⓣ0528 981212.

Banks There are plenty of banks in town with ATMs and exchange facilities, with one group at the foot of Bd Mohammed V, near Pl Hassan II, and another in Pl Dchira. There's a bureau de change at 83 Av 24 du Novembre near *Hotel Sahara Line* (daily 9am–1pm & 4.30–9pm).

Car rental and fuel The longest-established rental firm is Soubai, on Rue Afila just off Pl Dchira ⓣ0528 893199, ⓕ0528 893661. Unleaded fuel can be hard to find in Laayoune, but the Atlas station on Av Mecka al Mokarrama should have it.

Festival The Rawafid Azawan festival in October is the biggest of the festivals inaugurated by the Moroccan government in the last few years in the main towns of the Western Sahara, with musicians from across the Arab world and beyond.

Hammams The very modern Complexe Nakhil, at the eastern end of Av Lalla Yacout, has hammams or showers for both sexes (6.30am–10pm; 10dh). In Souk Djemal, there's Hammam El Fath off Av Salem Bila (north side) by no.123.

Internet access Loads of places around town, including: Cyber Café Taglabout, 36 Av Mecka al Mokarrama, by Pl de la Résisance (daily 10am–3am; 4dh per hr); Dar el Khair, Av Moulay Ismail (daily 8am–midnight; 4dh per hr); Téléboutique Friouato, 142 Av Mecka al Mokarrama (daily 9am–2am; 5dh per hr).

Post office The main office is on Pl Hassan II. There's a branch office on Pl Dchira.

Supermarket Supermarket Dchira on Av 24 du Novembre by Pl Dchira is small, but well stocked.

Moving on

Bus services mostly depart from Place Bir Anzarane or just off it. The exception is **Supratours**, whose buses (including the only service to Smara) leave from their office on Avenue Moulay Ismail just off Place Oum Saad (Ⓣ0528 893245). **CTM** services leave from outside their office at 198 Av Mecka al Mokarrama (Ⓣ0528 990763), with **SATAS** an **SAT** nearby on Place de la Résistance. All of these do the run down to Dakhla and up to Agadir; CTM, Supratours and SAT also serve Marrakesh (CTM continuing to Casablanca). **Najmat Sahara**'s one daily bus departs at noon from their office by *Café Ibiza* at 237 Av Mecka al Mokarrama (shared with Razma Car) for Tarfaya, connecting there for Tan Tan.

Grands taxis all now leave from a single stand located at the end of Avenue Abou Baker Essadik (roughly a continuation of Av Prince Moulay Abdallah), about 2km east of the town centre.

The **airport** (Ⓣ0528 893346) is about a kilometre out of town, beyond Place Mechouar. For details of frequencies and journey times on internal routes, see p.562. For airline offices see p.556.

Laayoune Plage

LAAYOUNE PLAGE is 20km distant: leave town on the N1 towards Boujdour then, past the airport, turn right off the main road and quickly left at a sign to *Camping Touristique*. At the beach – which is very windy, year-round, with big Atlantic breakers – there is a sporadically open café-restaurant. Places to stay include the *Hôtel Josefina* (Ⓣ0528 998478; ❸) at Laayoune Plage itself and, nearby at **Foum el Oued**, the *Hôtel Nagjir Plage*, a four-star hotel run by the same firm as the *Nagjir* in Laayoune (Ⓣ0528 991018, Ⓕ0528 995270; ❹).

Laayoune to Dakhla

Shared grands taxis and seven daily buses do the run down to Dakhla. The road is reasonably good, though drivers should beware of occasional sand-drifts, and camels grazing by or on the road. Foreigners will need to form-fill at checkpoints along the way, unless they already have the details printed out (see p.548).

The sea is guarded by cliffs most of the way to the fishing port of **BOUJDOUR**, 188km southwest of Laayoune. The beach is dirty with dangerous rocks – the nearest beaches suitable for swimming (if you have the transport to reach them) are 20km south, below the cliffs, and 40km north, just beyond a military checkpoint and fishing settlement. Boujdour has a handful of **hotels**, including the neat and tidy *Al Qods* (Ⓣ0528 896573; ❷), and Laayoue's Hotel Sahara Line runs a bleak and shadeless but well-equipped **campsite** by the shore, with cheerful rooms and quite deluxe bungalows, as well as car wash facilities (Ⓣ0528 892370; ❸). The street from the grand taxi stand down to the campsite comes alive in the evening with restaurants frying up freshly caught fish, and stalls selling charcoal-grilled brochettes and sausages. There are also café-restaurants on the main road, especially around the SATAS and Supratours offices. The area behind these, which makes up most of Boujdour's residential area is a large *bidonville*. The nearest thing to a sight in town is the lighthouse, though it's not open to the public. If you need a bank, the BMCE and Banque

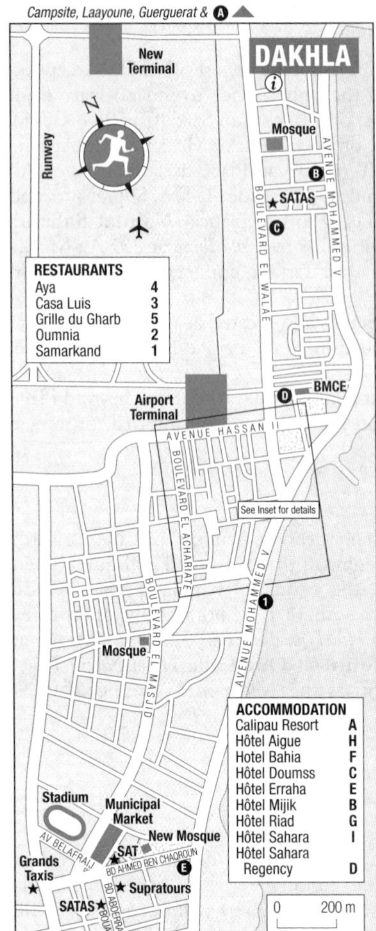

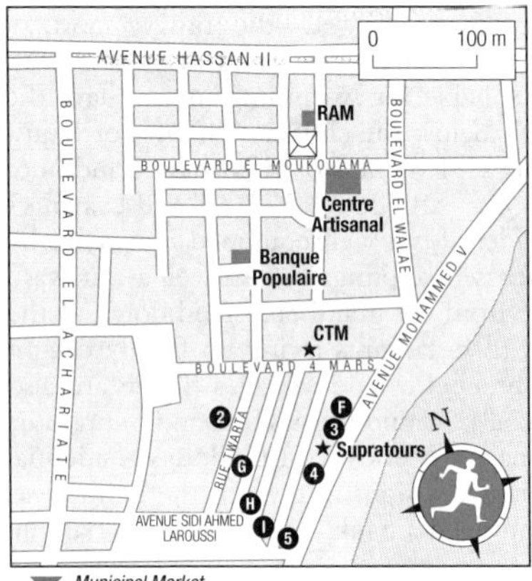

Populaire both have branches with ATMs.

South again from Boujdour the road runs inland, rejoining the coast at a place called **La Bouir** – little more than a filling station and café-restaurant almost midway between Dakhla and Boujdour, where buses may make a halt (if they don't stop 5km further south at Oued Lakrâa). There's a fishing settlement on the beach below the cliffs. The area behind the café at the top of the cliff, beyond the bit that's used as a public toilet, is full of fossilized snail shells.

Dakhla

Some 544km from Laayoune, on a long spit of land, **DAKHLA** (formerly Villa Cisneros, capital of Spain's Rio de Oro colony), is just 22km north of the Tropic of Cancer. Under Spanish rule, only the colonists and people working for them were allowed into town – the Saharawi nomads who lived in the desert were excluded. In 1975, the Spanish left and the Mauritanians moved in, to be replaced four years later by the Moroccans. Since then, Dakhla has grown somewhat, but it retains a lazy, sun-bleached atmosphere, with whitewashed, low-rise buildings and an easy-going feel. Europeans in camper vans head down in winter, drawn by the deserted beaches and year-round sunshine – even in January it's hot, and this is the furthest south you can get by land without needing a visa. Dakhla has also been developing a small **surfing** scene, and there are a couple of surfing supply shops in town. Since 2007, there's been an annual music **festival** every March.

Arrival and information

Should you need it, there is a **tourist office** on the second floor of Immeuble al Baraka, on the east side of Boulevard de Walae, 700m north of Avenue Hassan II (Mon–Fri 8.30am–4.30pm; ⓣ0528 898388 or

9). The main **post office** (Mon–Fri 8am–4.30pm, Sat 8am–noon) is on Boulevard el Moukouama. **Banks** with ATMs include the BMCE off Avenue Hassan II by the *Hôtel Sahara Regency*, and the Banque Populaire, a block south of the post office. There are also a couple opposite the new mosque at the southern end of town. For Moroccan crafts, there's an **Ensemble Artesanal** at the eastern end of Boulevard Moukouama. The only filling station in Dakhla which sells **unleaded fuel** is Atlas on Boulevard Walae, about 3km out of town.

Accommodation

Dakhla has quite a few hotels, and the cheap ones tend to be good value, though one person occupying a double room will have to pay for two places, and not many hotels have single rooms as such. Budget places often fill up early, so you may have to shop around. The main concentration is in the few blocks south of Avenue Hassan II and west of Avenue Mohammed V.

The **campsite**, *Camping Mousafir* (Ⓣ0528 898279), 6km out of town, has a small number of rather bare rooms (❶; lone travellers pay single rates) as well as camping space, and is right by the beach, but inconveniently located for town amenities – the only way into town without your own transport is either to walk, hitch, or wait for a petit taxi to turn up (which should charge 15dh to run you into town).

Calipau Resort 13 Bd Walae, 5km north of town Ⓣ0528 898886, Ⓔinfo@calipau-resort.com. A deluxe five-star done out like a Moroccan riad, with lots of *tadelakt*, a hammam, jacuzzi, scenic pool and private beach, and a suite with its own pool. BB ❼

Hôtel Aigue Rue Laroussiyine, corner of Av Sidi Ahmed Laroussi Ⓣ0528 897395. Bright and clean and friendly, with pleasant rooms, shared showers and supposedly 24hr (but in fact sporadic) hot water, not dissimilar to the neighbouring *Sahara*, for which it's a close second choice. Indeed, a couple of single rooms make it the first choice for budget-minded lone travellers. ❶

Hôtel Bahia 12 Av Mohammed V, corner of Rue Essaouira Ⓣ0528 898263. Dakhla's oldest hotel, but not its best, with bare rooms, though clean. It does have some single rooms, but they tend to be booked up. ❶

Hôtel Doumss Bd Walae, 500m north of Av Hassan II Ⓣ0528 898046 or 7, Ⓕ0528 898045. A comfortable two-star, not very central but handy for SATAS bus arrivals, and a good mid-market choice, with large en-suite rooms with balconies, and a bar. ❹

Hôtel Erraha Av Ahmed Belafrij, at the southern end of town opposite the new mosque Ⓣ0528 898811. A clean and bright hotel, all rooms en suite, some way from the town centre but handy for SAT, Supratours and the grand taxi stand. ❸

Hôtel Mijik (or *Mijak*) on the seafront, behind the *Hôtel Doumss* Ⓣ0655 421112, Ⓔhotelmijik@hotmail.com. Quieter and more seaside-like than most of Dakhla's hotels, with small but well-kept rooms and a restaurant, overlooking a rocky and rather rubbish-strewn shore. Double rooms are en suite with TV, or there are some very cheap single rooms with outside shower. ❷

Hôtel Riad Rue Twarta Ⓣ0528 898419. A jolly little place on a pedestrianized street south of the CTM office, with Spanish tiles in the entrance and corridors, and shared showers with hot water. ❶

Hôtel Sahara Av Sidi Ahmed Laroussi Ⓣ0528 897773. Dakhla's best budget hotel (though not to be confused with the *Sahara Regency*) is friendly and central, with hot showers, though it's getting a little bit grubby. They can arrange transport to Mauritania at competitive prices. ❶

Hôtel Sahara Regency Bd Walae, at the junction with Av Hassan II Ⓣ0528 931555, Ⓦwww.sahararegency.com. The top offering in town. Each room has separate en-suite bathroom and toilet, and a balcony. There are three bars, a rooftop restaurant and a pool (which nonresidents can use for 50dh). They also organize jet skiing, kite surfing, 4x4 rental and visits to an oyster farm, but none of them cheaply. ❻

Eating

In addition to the **eating** places listed below, you'll find a handful of cheap places at the southern end of town on Boulevard Ahmed Ben Chaqroun around the junction with Boulevard Abderrahim Bouabide. The *Hôtel Doumss* has a **bar**, and the three bars in the *Hôtel Sahara Regency* stay open until 10pm.

Aya Av Mohammed V near Av Sidi Ahmed Laroussi. Fast food including swordfish brochettes and octopus (in both cases frozen, not fresh), as well as burgers and *shawarma*. Daily noon–11pm. Cheap.
Casa Luis 14 Av Mohammed V by *Hôtel Bahia*. Good Spanish fare including excellent omelettes and a passable paella (for at least two, order 40min in advance) that makes up in flavour, fish and octopus what it lacks in shelled molluscs and crustaceans. Also does breakfasts. Daily 7am–11pm. Moderate.
Grille du Gharb Av Sidi Ahmed Laroussi, in front of *Hôtel Sahara* (whose own restaurant is very similar) Charcoal-grilled kebabs, served with chips and salad, eaten inside or out on the pavement. Daily noon–3pm & 7pm–midnight. Cheap.

Hotel Bahia 12 Av Mohammed V, corner of Rue Essaouira. Excellent fish and seafood including paella (order 40 minutes in advance), *pulpo alla gallega* (octopus cooked in water, then drizzled with olive oil and sprinkled with paprika), swordfish steak or monkfish kebabs, but no alcohol. Daily noon–4pm & 7.30pm–midnight. Moderate.
Oumnia Rue Twarta. Basically a café but also serves soups, sandwiches, tajines and even fried squid. Nothing fancy, but decent enough. Daily 10.30am–3pm & 6–11.30pm. Cheap.
Samarkand Bd de la Achariate. Café restaurant with a terrace overlooking the sea and serving pizzas, tajines, beef stroganov or fish brochettes, with banana split or peach melba for dessert. Meals served daily noon–3.30pm & 7pm–midnight. Moderate.

Moving on

For **buses**, CTM's office is on Boulevard 4 Mars, three blocks south of Avenue Hassan II (Ⓣ0528 898166). Supratours have their main office on Boulevard Abderrahim Bouabide, at the southern end of town, but their services also call at their old office, which is more conveniently located just around the corner from CTM, on Avenue Mohammed V (Ⓣ0528 897740). SATAS also has an office on Boulevard Abderrahim Bouabide, and one 500m north of Avenue Hassan II on Boulevard de Walae near *Hôtel Doumss*, and SAT is at the southern end of town on Boulevard Ahmed Ben Chaqroun (Ⓣ0528 931123). The **grand taxi** station is also at the southern end of town, southwest of the market and the stadium. Dakhla has an **airport**, very centrally located, just off Boulevard de Walae almost opposite the *Sahara Regency* hotel (Ⓣ0528 897256). The airport is being extended with a new terminal due to open a kilometre or so to the north. RAM's office in town is directly behind the post office (Ⓣ0528 897049); Regional Air Lines is round the side of the *Sahara Regency* hotel (Ⓣ0528 897677). TopFly have in the past served Las Palmas from Dakhla, but at time of writing there were no flights to the Canary Islands.

The road to Mauritania

To travel south from **Dakhla to Mauritania**, you'll need either to have your own transport, or to arrange some. The *Hôtel Sahara* is the best place to start – they can arrange a ride for just about the best rate in town (350dh/€35 to Nouadibhou, or 550dh/€55 to Nouakchott at time of writing). Otherwise, touts around town can put you in contact with Mauritanian drivers but you'll need to bargain hard to get a fair price – try to find out the current rate in advance if possible. Alternatively, try asking around the campsite, a favourite staging post for Europeans doing the run. Many of these will be bypassing Nouadibhou and heading straight for Nouakchott, which you may or may not see as an advantage (Nouakchott will get you to Senegal quicker, but Nouadibhou is where you need to go for the ore train to Choum). The number of European drivers heading in that direction has diminished somewhat since Senegal slapped a massive duty on the import of cars over five years old, thus putting the kibosh on an established trade in second-hand Peugeots from Europe, though these can still be sold in Mauritania, or beyond Senegal in Mali. It should be possible to obtain a **Mauritanian visa** at the border, for the same price as you would pay at the embassy in Rabat (see p.291).

The road south is now surfaced all the way to the border, 370km from Dakhla (including 38km from the town up the spit to the junction with the N1 road from Laayoune and Boujdour). The Mauritanian border post closes at 5.30pm, so set off early if you don't want to spend the night en route. The Moroccans are building settlements along the road, little villages with identikit pretty houses and a mosque. The first is 5km after the military post at **El Argoub**, opposite Dakhla across the lagoon enclosed by the spit; the next is at **Imlili**, some 50km further (124km from Dakhla). The **last fuel** and proper **accommodation** in Moroccan-held territory are at the *Motel Barbas*, approximately 300km from Dakhla (Ⓣ0528 897961; ❸), where you'll find clean rooms, comfortable beds, shared showers and good food. From there, it's 80km to the border post at **Guerguarat**, open daily 8am–7pm on the Moroccan side, 9am–5.30pm on the Mauritanian side (if you arrive after 5pm, you can camp for the night on the Moroccan side).

Five kilometres beyond Guerguarat, the tarmac ends and you enter Mauritanian-held territory. **Guides** are on hand just beyond the frontier to lead you to the **Mauritanian border post**, and you should accept their assistance, as the area is heavily mined. The western side of the Nouadibhou peninsula is part of the Western Sahara, but occupied by Mauritania. Its main town, La Gouera (Lagwira), is used by the Mauritanian military and is off limits to foreigners. The Mauritanian border post is on the eastern side of the peninsula, in Mauritania proper. Formalities completed, you can continue to "**Quarante-Six**", where the road crosses the railway 46km out of Nouadibhou. If your lift is continuing across the desert to Nouakchott and you want to go to Nouadibhou, get off here to wait for a vehicle, but be warned that you may be charged heavily for the journey, especially if it is getting late.

Coming from Mauritania, if you have a vehicle, you will need to get a permit from the Moroccan embassy in Nouakchott (see p.67); you cannot get it from the consulate in Nouadibhou. If you don't have a vehicle, arrange transport at the *auberges* and campsites in Nouadibhou, or in Noukchott. For further information on travelling in Mauritania and points beyond, see the *Rough Guide to West Africa*.

Travel details

Buses

Dakhla to: Agadir (7 daily; 18hr 30min) via Boujdour (5hr 30min), Laayoune (9hr), Tan Tan (13hr 30min) and Goulimine (15hr); Casablanca (2 daily; 28hr); Marrakesh (5 daily; 24hr); Rabat (1 daily; 30hr).
Laayoune to: Agadir (10 daily; 9hr 30min) via Tan Tan (4hr 30min), Goulimine (6hr) and Tiznit (7hr 30min); Dakhla (7 daily; 9hr) via Boujdour (3hr 30min); Casablanca (2 daily; 9hr); Marrakesh (8 daily; 14hr); Rabat (1 daily; 20hr); Smara (1 daily; 3hr); Tarfaya (5 daily; 1hr 30min).
Smara to: Agadir (3 daily; 8hr) via Tan Tan (3hr), Goulimine (4hr 30min) and Tiznit (6hr); Laayoune (1 daily; 3hr); Marrakesh (2 daily; 13hr 15min).
Tan Tan to: Agadir (20 daily; 5hr); Casablanca (10 daily; 16hr); Dakhla (7 daily; 13hr 30min); Goulimine (25 daily; 1hr 30min); Laayoune (9 daily; 4hr 30min); Marrakesh (12 daily; 12hr); Ouarzazate (2 daily; 17hr 30min) via Tata (12hr 30 min); Rabat (5 daily; 17hr 30min); Smara (3 daily; 3hr); Tarfaya (5 daily; 3hr).

Grands taxis

Dakhla to: Boujdour (3hr 30min); Laayoune (9hr); Tan Tan (12hr).
Laayoune to: Inezgane (9hr); Dakhla (9hr); Goulimine (5hr); Laayoune Plage (20min); Smara (3hr); Tan Tan (3hr 30min); Tarfaya (1hr).
Smara to: Goulimine (4hr 30min); Laayoune (3hr); Tan Tan (2hr).
Tan Tan to: Dakhla (12hr); Goulimine (2hr 30 min); Inezgane (6hr); Smara (3hr); Laayoune (3hr 30min); Tan Tan Plage (20min).

Flights

Dakhla to: Agadir (RAM 1 weekly; 1hr 30min); Casablanca (RAM, RAL 7 weekly; 2hr 10min); Laayoune (RAL, RAM 4 weekly; 1hr–1hr 30min).
Laayoune to: Agadir (RAL, RAM 4 weekly; 1hr 25min); Casablanca (RAM, RAL 6 weekly; 1hr 30min–3hr 05min); Dakhla (RAL, RAM 4 weekly; 1hr–1hr 30min); Lanzarote (TopFly 1 weekly; 1hr); Las Palmas (RAL, TopFly, Binter 1–3 daily; 50min).
Tan Tan to: Casablanca (RAL 3 weekly; 1hr 55min); Goulimine (RAL 3 weekly; 15min).

Contexts

Contexts

History

Morocco's emergence as a nation-state is astonishingly recent, dating from the occupation of the country by the French and Spanish at the turn of the twentieth century, and its independence in 1956. Prior to this, it is best seen as a kind of patchwork of tribal groups, whose shifting alliances and sporadic bids for power defined the nature of government. With a handful of exceptions, the country's ruling sultans controlled only the plains, the coastal ports and the regions around the imperial capitals of Fes, Marrakesh, Rabat and Meknes. These were known as Bled el Makhzen – the governed lands, or, more literally, "Lands of the Storehouse". The rest of the Moroccan territories – the Rif, the three Atlas ranges and the outlying deserts – comprised Bled es Siba, "Lands of the Dissidents". Populated almost exclusively by Berbers, the region's original (pre-Arab) inhabitants, they were rarely recognized as being under anything more than local tribal authority.

The balance between government control and tribal independence is one of the two enduring themes of Moroccan history. The other is the emergence, expansion and eventual replacement of the various **sultanate dynasties**. These at first seem dauntingly complicated – a succession of short-lived tribal movements and confusingly similar-named sultans – but there are actually just seven main groups. The first of them, the **Idrissids**, became the model by founding the city of Fes towards the end of the eighth century and bringing a coalition of Berber and Arab forces under a central *makhzen* (government) authority. The last, the **Alaouites**, emerged in the mid-seventeenth century from the great palm oasis of Tafilalt and, continuing with the current king, Mohammed VI, still hold constitutional power. It is around these groups – together with the medieval dynasties of the **Almoravids**, **Almohads**, **Merenids**, **Wattasids** and **Saadians** – that the bulk of the following sections are organized.

Prehistory

Morocco is part of the **Maghreb**, an island of fertile land between the Sahara and the Mediterranean that also includes Algeria and Tunisia. Until around 3000 BC, the Sahara was savannah, fertile enough to support elephants, zebras and a whole range of other wildlife. It seems likely that there were groups of hunter-and-gatherer hominids here as early as a million years ago. Around 15,000 BC there seem to have been **Paleolithic** settlements, and before the Sahara became desert, primitive pastoral and agricultural systems had begun to develop. It is possible also to trace the arrival of two independent Stone-Age cultures in the Maghreb: the **Oranian** or **Mouillian Culture** (from around 12,000 BC), and **Capsian Culture** (from around 8000 BC). These are the people who made the cave and rock drawings of the pre-Sahara and High Atlas, Morocco's oldest archeological sites.

Phoenicians and Carthaginians

Morocco's recorded history begins around 1100 BC with the arrival of the **Phoenicians**, a seafaring people from what is now Lebanon. By the seventh century BC, they had established settlements along the coast, inlcuding Rusadir (Melilla), Tingis (Tangier), Zila (Asilah), Lixis (Larache), Chellah (Rabat), and even Mogador (Essaouira) – of all their colonies, the furthest from their homeland – where they maintained a dye factory on the Îles Purpuraires (see p.330). The settlements were small, isolated colonies, most built on defensible headlands round the coast, and there was probably little initial contact between them and the inhabitants of the interior (known by their Greek name, *Barbaroi*, or **Berbers**). By the fifth century BC, one Phoenician colony, **Carthage** (in Tunisia), had become pre-eminent and gained dominance over the rest. Under Carthaginian leadership, some of the Moroccan colonies grew into considerable cities, exporting grain and grapes, and minting their own coins.

Following Carthage's defeat and destruction by Rome in 146 BC, Morocco's Punic colonies grew in prosperity, taking in hundreds of Carthaginian refugees. Even after Rome had annexed and then abandoned the country, Phoenician was still widely spoken along the coast.

Berber kingdoms and Roman rule

Before Rome imposed direct imperial rule in 24 AD, the "civilized" Moroccan territories for a while formed the Berber **Kingdom of Mauretania**, probably little more than a confederation of local tribes, centred round **Volubilis** (near Meknes) and **Tangier**, which gained a certain influence through alliance and occasional joint rule with the adjoining Berber state of **Numidia** (essentially modern Algeria).

The kingdom's most important rulers, and the only ones of which any substantial records survive, were **Juba II** (25 BC–23 AD) and his son **Ptolemy** (23–41 AD). Juba, an Algerian Berber by birth, was brought up and educated in Rome, where he married the daughter of Antony and Cleopatra. His reign, if limited in its extent, seems to have been orderly and prosperous, and the pattern might have continued under his son, but in 41 AD, Emperor Caligula summoned Ptolemy to an audience in Lyons and had him assassinated – so the story goes, for appearing in a more brilliant cloak than his own. The following year, the new emperor Claudius divided Rome's North African domains into two provinces: Mauritania Caesarensis (the old Numidia) and **Mauritania Tingitana** (essentially, Morocco). Tingis (Tangier) was the capital of Tingitana, while Volubilis became the seat of the provincial governor.

Roman rule

The early years of Rome's new imperial province were taken up with near-constant **rebellions** – the first one alone needing three years and over 20,000 troops to subdue.

Perhaps discouraged by this unexpected resistance, the **Romans** never attempted to colonize Morocco–Mauretania beyond its old limits, and the Rif and Atlas mountains were left unpenetrated, establishing an enduring precedent. But Tingitana had a considerable Roman presence: the second century AD geographer Ptolemy listed more than thirty Roman cities in the province, which provided exotic animals for Roman games, as well as grains, wines, fish sauce (garum), olive oil, copper and purple murex dye. **Volubilis**, the most extensive surviving Roman site in Morocco, was a significant city, at the heart of the north's fertile vineyards and grain fields.

However, as Roman power waned, and Berber uprisings became more frequent, administration was moved from Volubilis to Tingis. When the Romans left in 253 AD, and the **Vandals** took power in southern Spain, the latter were interested only in taking Tingis and the neighbouring port of Ceuta for use as staging posts en route to northern Tunisia. Similarly, the **Byzantine General Belisarius**, who defeated the Vandals and laid claim to the Maghreb for Justinian's Eastern Empire, did little more than replace the Ceuta garrison.

The arrival of Islam

Within thirty years of its foundation (in 622 AD, when the Prophet Mohammed moved with his followers from Mecca to Medina), **Islam** had established itself in the Maghreb at Kairouan in present-day Tunisia, but westward expansion was slowed by Algeria's Berbers – mainly pagans but including communities of Christians and Jews – who put up a strong and unusually unified resistance to Arab control. It was only in 680 that the governor of Kairouan, **Oqba Ibn Nafi**, made an initial foray into Morocco, taking in the process the territory's last Byzantine stronghold at Ceuta. The story goes that Oqba then embarked on a 5000km march through Morocco, all the way to the Atlantic Ocean, but whether this expedition had any real Islamicizing influence on the Moroccan Berbers is questionable. Oqba left no garrison forces and was himself killed in Algeria on his way back to Kairouan.

Islam may, however, have taken root among some of the tribes. In the early part of the eighth century the new Arab governor of the west, **Moussa Ibn Nasr**, returned to Morocco and managed to establish Arab control (and carry out mass conversions to Islam) in both the northern plains and the pre-Sahara, but his main thrust was towards **Spain**. In 711, the first Muslim forces crossed over from Tangier to Tarifa and defeated the Visigoths in a single battle; within a decade the Moors had taken control of all but the remote Spanish mountains in northern Asturias; and their advance into Europe was only halted at the Pyrenees by the victory of Charles Martel at Poitiers in 732.

The bulk of this invading and occupying force were almost certainly **Berber converts** to Islam, and the sheer scale of their military success must have had enormous influence in turning Morocco itself into a largely Muslim nation. It was not at this stage, however, in any way an Arab one. The extent of the Islamic Empire – from Persia to Morocco, and ancient Ghana to Spain – was simply too great for Arab numbers. Early attempts to impose taxes on the Moroccan Berbers led to a rebellion and, once again outside the political mainstream, the Maghreb fragmented into a series of small, independent **principalities**.

The Idrissids (eighth–eleventh century)

Meanwhile the Muslim world was split by the schism between **Sunnis** and **Shi'ites**; when the Sunni Ummayad dynasty took power, the Shi'ites dispersed, seeking refuge both east and west. One of them, arriving in Morocco around 787, was **Moulay Idriss**, an evidently charismatic leader and a great-grandson of the Prophet. He seems to have been adopted almost at once by the citizens of Volubilis – then still a vaguely Romanized city – and by the Aouraba Berber tribe. He was poisoned three years later by order of the Sunni caliph, but had managed to set up the infrastructure of an essentially Arab court and kingdom – the basis of what was to become the Moroccan nation – and his successors, the **Idrissids**, became the first recognizable Moroccan dynasty. His son **Moulay Idriss II**, born posthumously to a Berber woman, was declared sultan in 807, after an apparently orderly regency, and ruled for just over twenty years – something of a golden age for the emerging Moroccan state, with the extension of a central authority throughout the north and even to the oases beyond the Atlas.

Moulay Idriss II's most important achievement was the development of the city founded by his father: **Fes**. Here, he set up the apparatus of court government, and here he also welcomed large contingents of Shi'ite **refugees**, particularly from Western Islam's two great cities, Cordoba and Kairouan. In incorporating them, Fes (and, by extension, Morocco) became increasingly Arabized, and was transformed into a major Arab centre in its own right. The **Kairaouine University** was established, becoming one of the three most important in Islam (and far ahead of those in Europe), and Fes became a vital link in the trade between Spain and the East, and between the Maghreb and Africa south of the Sahara.

After Moulay Idriss's death, the kingdom split again into **principalities**, and the Maghreb (especially Tunisia) was invaded by the **Banu Hilal**, plundering Arabian nomads who destroyed a lot of the infrastructure, including irrigation systems, and devastated agricultural lands with their goats.

The Almoravids (1062–1145)

Morocco was to some extent cushioned from the Banu Hilal, and by the time they reached its southern oases (where they settled), the worst was probably over, but the shattered social order of the Maghreb created an obvious vacuum of authority. Into this stepped the two great Berber dynasties of the Middle Ages – the **Almoravids** and the **Almohads**. Both emerged from the south, and in each case their motivating force was religious: a purifying zeal to **reform** or destroy the decadent ways that had reached Morocco from the wealthy Andalucian Muslims of Spain. The two dynasties together lasted only a century and a half, but in this period Morocco was the pre-eminent power of western Islam, maintaining an **empire** that at its peak reached Spain, Libya, Senegal and ancient Ghana.

The **Almoravids** began as a reforming movement among the Sanhaja Berbers of what is now Mauritania. A nomadic desert tribe like today's Touaregs, they converted to Islam in the ninth century, but the founders of the Almoravid movement, a local sheikh who had returned from the pilgrimage to Mecca and a *fakir* from the Souss plain, found widespread abuse of orthodox practice. In particular, they preached against drinking palm wine, playing licentious music and taking more than four wives, and their movement rapidly took hold among this already ascetic, tent-dwelling people.

Founding a *ribat* – a kind of warrior monastery similar to the Templar castles of Europe – the Almoravids soon became a considerable military force. In 1054, they set out from the *ribat* (from which the word Almoravids derives) to spread the message through a *jihad* (holy war), and within four years they had destroyed the empire of ancient Ghana (mostly in what is now Mali) and captured its capital Koumbi Saleh (now in Mauritania). Turning towards Morocco, they established themselves in Marrakesh by 1062, and under the leadership of **Youssef Ben Tachfine** went on to extend their rule throughout the north of Morocco and, to the east, as far as Algiers.

In 1085, Youssef undertook his first expedition to **Spain**, invited by the princes of Muslim Spain (Andalucía) after the fall of Toledo to the Christians. He crossed over the Straits again in 1090, this time to take control of Spain himself. Before his death in 1107, he restored Muslim control to Valencia and other territories lost in the first wave of the Christian Reconquest. The new Spanish territories reoriented Moroccan culture towards the far more affluent and sophisticated Andalucian civilization, and also stretched the Almoravid forces too thinly. Youssef, disgusted by Andalucian decadence, had ruled largely from **Marrakesh**, leaving governors in Seville and other cities. After his death, the Andalucians proved disinclined to accept these foreign overlords, while the Moroccans themselves became vulnerable to charges of being corrupt and departing from their puritan ideals.

Youssef's son **Ali** was not interested in ceaseless military activity, and in Spain used Christian mercenaries to maintain control. His reign, and that of the Almoravids, was supplanted in the early 1140s by a new movement, the Almohads.

The Almohads (1145–1248)

Ironically, the **Almohads** shared much in common with their predecessors. Again, they were forged from the Berber tribes – this time in the High Atlas – and again, they based their bid for power on an intense puritanism. Their founder **Ibn Toumert** attacked the Almoravids for allowing their women to ride horses (a tradition in the desert), for wearing extravagant clothes, and for being subject to what may have been Andalucian corruptions – the revived use of music and wine. He also claimed that the Almoravids did not recognize the unitary nature of God, the basis of Almohad belief, and the source of their name – the "unitarians". Banished from Marrakesh by Ali, Ibn Toumert set up a *ribat* in the Atlas at **Tin Mal**, waging war on local tribes until they accepted his authority, and he eventually claimed to be the Mahdi, the final prophet promised in the Koran.

Ibn Toumert was aided by a shrewd assistant and brilliant military leader, **Abd el Moumen**, who took over the movement after his death. In 1145, he was strong enough to displace the Almoravids from Fes, and two years later he drove them from their capital, Marrakesh, making him effectively sultan.

The third Almohad sultan, **Yacoub el Mansour** (The Victorious), defeated the Christians at Alarcos in Spain in 1195 and pushed the frontiers of the empire east to Tripoli, and for the first time, there was one single rule across the entire Maghreb and most of Spain, though it did not stretch as far south as under the Almoravids. With the ensuing wealth and prestige, El Mansour launched a great building programme, including a new capital in **Rabat** and magnificent gateways and minarets in Marrakesh and Seville.

Once more though, imperial expansion precipitated disintegration. In 1212, Yacoub's successor, **Mohammed en Nasr**, attempting to drive the Spanish Christians back to the Pyrenees, was decisively defeated at the battle of **Las Navas de Tolosa**; the balance of power in Spain was changing, and within four decades only the Kingdom of Granada remained in Muslim hands. In the

Maghreb, the eastern provinces declared independence from Almohad rule and Morocco itself was returning to the authority of local tribes. In 1248, one of these, the **Merenids** (or Beni Merin), took the northern capital of Fes and turned towards Marrakesh.

Merenids and Wattasids (1248–1554)

The last three centuries of Berber rule in Morocco were marked by increasing domestic **instability** and economic stagnation. The last Andalucian kingdom. Granada, fell to Ferdinand and Isabel in 1492. The Portuguese established footholds on Morocco's Atlantic and Mediterranean coasts, while, to the east, the rest of the Maghreb fell under the domination of the Ottoman Empire. The Portuguese ability to navigate beyond Mauritania also meant the eventual end of the trans-Sahara caravan route.

In Morocco, the main development was a centralized administrative system – the **Makhzen** – maintained without tribal support by standing armies of Arab and Christian mercenaries. It is to this age that the real distinction of Bled el Makhzen and Bled es Siba belongs – the latter coming to mean everything outside the immediate vicinities of the imperial cities.

The Merenids

Perhaps with this background it is not surprising that few of the 21 **Merenid sultans** – or their cousins and successors, the Wattasids – made any great impression. The early sultans were occupied mainly with Spain, at first in trying to regain a foothold on the coast, later with shoring up the Kingdom of Granada. There were minor successes in the fourteenth century under the "Black Sultan", **Abou el Hassan**, who for a time occupied Tunis, but he was to die before being able to launch a planned major invasion of Al-Andalus, and his son, **Abou Inan**, himself fell victim to the power struggles within the mercenary army.

The thirteenth and fourteenth centuries, however, did leave a considerable **legacy of building**, perhaps in defiance of the lack of political progress (and certainly a product of the move towards government by forced taxation). In 1279, the garrison town of **Fes el Djedid** was established, to be followed by a series of brilliantly endowed colleges, or **medersas**, which are among the finest surviving Moorish monuments. Culture, too, saw a final flourish. The historians **Ibn Khaldun** and **Leo Africanus**, and the travelling chronicler **Ibn Battuta**, all studied in Fes under Merenid patronage.

The Wattasids

The **Wattasids**, who usurped Merenid power in 1465, had ruled in effect for 45 years previously as a line of hereditary viziers. After their coup, they maintained a semblance of control for a little under a century, though the extent of the Makhzen lands was by now minimal.

The **Portuguese** had annexed and colonized the seaports of Ceuta, Tangier, Asilah, Agadir and Safi, while large tracts of the interior lay in the hands of religious warrior brotherhoods, or **marabouts**, on whose alliances the sultans had increasingly to depend.

The Saadians and civil war (1554–1669)

The Saadians, the first **Arab dynasty** since the Idrissids, were the most important of the *marabouts* to emerge in the early years of the sixteenth century, rising to power on the strength of their religious positions (they were Shereefs – descendants of the Prophet). They began by setting up a small principality in the **Souss**, where they established their first capital in **Taroudant**. Normally, this would have formed a regular part of Bled el Makhzen, but the absence of government in the south allowed them to extend their power to **Marrakesh** around 1520, with the Wattasids for a time retaining Fes and ruling the north.

In the following decades the Saadians made breakthroughs along the coast, capturing Agadir in 1540 and driving the Portuguese from Safi and Essaouira. When the Wattasids fell into bankruptcy and invited the Turks into Fes, the Saadians were ready to consolidate their power. This proved harder, and more confusing, than anyone might have expected. **Mohammed esh Sheikh**, the first Saadian sultan to control both the southern and northern kingdoms, was himself soon using Turkish troops, and was subsequently assassinated by a group of them in 1557. His death unleashed an incredibly convoluted sequence of factional murder and power politics, which was only resolved, somewhat fortuitously, by a battle with the Portuguese twenty years later.

The Battle of the Three Kings

This event, the 1578 **Battle of the Three Kings**, was essentially a Portuguese crusade, led by the youthful King Sebastião on the nominal behalf of a deposed Saadian king against his uncle and rival. At the end of the day all three were to perish on the battlefield, the Portuguese having suffered one of the most disastrous defeats in Christian medieval history, and a little-known Saadian prince emerged as the sole acknowledged ruler of Morocco.

His name was **Ahmed "El Mansour"** (The Victorious, following this momentous victory), and he was easily the most impressive sultan of the dynasty. Not only did he begin his reign clear of the intrigue and rivalry that had dogged his predecessors, but he was immensely wealthy as well. Ransoms paid for the remnants of their nobility after the battle reduced Portugal to bankruptcy, and the country, with its Moroccan enclaves, even fell, for a time under the control of Habsburg Spain.

Breaking with tradition, Ahmed himself became actively involved in European politics, generally supporting the Protestant north against the Spanish and encouraging Dutch and British trade. Within Morocco he was able to maintain a reasonable level of order and peace, and diverted criticism of his use of Turkish troops (and his own Turkish-educated ways) by embarking on an **invasion of Mali**. This secured control of the Saharan salt mines and the gold and slave routes from Senegal, all sources of phenomenal wealth, which won him the additional epithet of *El Dhahabi* (The Golden One) and reduced his need to tax Moroccans, making him a popular man. His reign was the most prosperous period in the country's history since the time of the Almohads – a cultural and political renaissance reflected in the coining of a new title, the Shereefian Empire, the country's official name until independence in 1956.

Civil war and piracy

Ahmed's death in 1603 caused abrupt and lasting chaos. He left three sons, none of whom could gain authority, and, split by **civil war**, the country once again broke into a number of principalities. A succession of **Saadian rulers** retained power in the Souss and in Marrakesh (where their tombs remain testimony to the opulence and turbulence of the age); another *marabout* force, the **Djila**, gained control of Fes; while around Salé and Rabat arose the pirate **Republic of the Bou Regreg** (see p.275).

Moulay Ismail and the early Alaouites (1665–1822)

Like the Saadians, the **Alaouites** were Shereefs, first establishing themselves as religious leaders – this time in Rissani in the **Tafilalt**. Their struggle to establish power also followed a similar pattern, spreading first to Taza and Fes and finally, under Sultan **Moulay Rashid**, reaching Marrakesh in 1669. Rashid, however, was unable to enjoy the fruits of his labour, since he was assassinated in a particularly bloody palace coup in 1672. It was only with Moulay Ismail, the ablest of his rival sons, that an Alaouite leader gained real control over the country.

Moulay Ismail

The 55-year reign of **Moulay Ismail** (1672–1727) was the country's last stab at imperial glory. In Morocco, where his shrine in Meknes is still a place of pilgrimage, he is remembered as a great and just, if unusually ruthless, ruler; to contemporary Europeans – and in subsequent historical accounts – he is noted for extravagant cruelty (though he was not much worse than the European rulers of his day). He stands out for the grandness of the scale on which he acted. At **Meknes**, his new imperial capital, he garrisoned a permanent army of some 140,000 black troops, a legendary guard he had built up personally through slaving expeditions in Mauritania and the south, as well as by starting a human breeding programme. The army kept order throughout the kingdom – Morocco is today still littered with their kasbah garrisons – and were able to raise taxes as required. The Bou Regreg pirates, too, were brought under the control of the state, along with their increasingly lucrative revenues.

With all this, Ismail was able to build a palace in Meknes that was the rival of its contemporary, Versailles, and he negotiated on equal terms with European rulers. Indeed, it was probably the reputation he established for Morocco that allowed the country to remain free for another century and a half before the European colonial powers began carving it up.

Sidi Mohammed and Moulay Slimane

Like all the great, long-reigning Moroccan sultans, Moulay Ismail left innumerable sons and a terminal dispute for the throne, with the powerful standing army supporting and dropping heirs at will.

Remarkably, a capable ruler emerged fairly soon – Sultan **Sidi Mohammed Ben Abdallah** – and for a while it appeared that the Shereefian empire was moving back into the mainstream of European and world events. Mohammed recaptured El Jadida from the Portuguese, founded the port of Essaouira, traded and conducted treaties with the Europeans, and was the first ruler to recognize the **United States of America**.

At his death in 1790, the state collapsed once more into civil war, Fes and Marrakesh in turn promoting claimants to the throne. When this period drew to some kind of a close, with **Moulay Slimane** (1792–1822) asserting his authority in both cities, there was little left to govern. The army had dispersed; the Bled es Siba reasserted its old limits; and in Europe, with the ending of the Napoleonic wars, Britain, France, Spain and Germany were all looking to establish themselves in Africa.

Moulay Slimane's rule was increasingly isolated from the new realities outside Morocco. An intensely orthodox Muslim, he concentrated the efforts of government on eliminating the power and influence of the **Sufi brotherhoods** – a power he underestimated. In 1818 Berber tribes loyal to the Derakaoui brotherhood rebelled and, temporarily, captured the sultan. Subsequently, the sultans had no choice but to govern with the cooperation of local sheikhs and brotherhood leaders.

Even more serious, at least in its long-term effects, was Moulay Slimane's isolationist attitude towards **Europe**, and in particular to Napoleonic France. Exports were banned; European consuls banished to Tangier; and contacts that might have helped maintain Moroccan independence were lost.

European domination

European powers had from time to time occupied Moroccan ports such as Ceuta, Tangier, El Jadida and Essaouira, but European encroachment in earnest got under way on the nineteenth century. The Moroccan state, still medieval in form, virtually bankrupt and with armies press-ganged from the tribes to secure taxes, was unable to do much about it.

When the **French** occupied Algiers after a victory over the Ottomans in 1830, Sultan **Abd Er Rahman** (1822–59) mustered a force to defend his fellow Muslims but was severely defeated at Isly in 1843. In 1859, the **Spanish** occupied Tetouan, restored to Morocco only after payment of massive indemnities using money borrowed from Britain (for which the sultan had to surrender control of customs administration). The sultan also had to provide Spain with an Atlantic port, which the Spanish later claimed in Sidi Ifni.

Moulay Hassan

By the end of the nineteenth century, both France and Spain had learned to use every opportunity to step in and "protect" their nationals in Morocco. Complaints by **Moulay Hassan**, the last pre-colonial sultan to have any real power, actually led to a debate on this issue at the 1880 **Madrid Conference**, but the effect was only to regularize the practice on a wider scale, beginning with the setting up of an "international administration" in Tangier.

Moulay Hassan could, in other circumstances, have proved an effective and possibly inspired sultan. Acceding to the throne in 1873, he embarked on an ambitious series of modernizing **reforms**, including attempts to stabilize the currency by minting the rial in Paris, to bring in more rational forms of taxation, and to retrain the army under the instruction of Turkish and Egyptian officers. But his social and monetary reforms were obstructed by foreign merchants and local *caids*, while the European powers forced him to abandon plans for other Muslim states' involvement in the army.

Moulay Hassan played off the Europeans as best he could, employing a British military chief of staff, **Caid MacClean**, a French military mission and German arms manufacturers. On the frontiers, he built kasbahs to strengthen the defences at Tiznit, Saïdia and Selouane. But the government had few modern means of raising money to pay for these developments. Moulay Hassan was thrown back on the traditional means of taxation, the *harka*, setting out across the country to subdue the tribes and to collect tribute. In 1894, returning across the Atlas on just such a campaign, he died.

The last sultans

Hassan's son **Abd el Aziz** (1894–1907) was a boy of fourteen at his accession, but for the first six years of his rule the country was kept in at least a semblance of order by his father's chamberlain, **Bou Ahmed**. In 1900, however, Bou Ahmed died, and Abd el Aziz was left to govern alone – surrounded by an assembly of Europeans, preying on the remaining wealth of the court. In the Atlas mountains, the tribal chiefs asserted their freedom from government control, and in the Rif, a pretender to the throne, **Bou Hamra**, led a five-year revolt.

European manipulation during this period was remorselessly cynical. In 1904, the French negotiated agreements on "spheres of influence" with the British (who were to hold Egypt and Cyprus), and with the Italians (who got Tripolitania, or Libya). The following year saw the German kaiser Wilhelm visiting Tangier and swearing to protect Morocco's integrity, but he was later bought off with the chance to "develop" the Congo. France and Spain, meanwhile, reached a secret arrangement on dividing Morocco and simply awaited a pretext to execute it.

In 1907, the French moved troops into **Oujda**, on the Algerian border and, after a mob attack on French construction workers, into Casablanca. Abd el Aziz was deposed by his brother, **Moulay Hafid** (1907–12), in a last attempt to resist the European advance. His reign began with a coalition with the principal Atlas chieftain, **Madani el Glaoui**, and intentions to take military action against the French, but the new sultan first had to put down the revolt of Bou Hamra – who was finally captured in 1909. Meanwhile, supposedly to protect their nationals in Rif mineral mines, the Spanish brought over 90,000 troops to Melilla. Colonial occupation, in effect, had begun.

The Treaty of Fes

Dissidence at home finally drove Moulay Hafid into the hands of the Europeans. With Berber tribesmen at the walls of his capital in Fes supporting a pretender to the throne (one of a number who arose at the time), the sultan went for help to the French, and was forced to accept their terms.

These were ratified and signed as the **Treaty of Fes** in 1912, which gave the French the right to defend Morocco, represent it abroad and conquer the Bled es Siba. A similar document was also signed with the Spanish, who were to take control of a strip of territory along the northern coast, with its capital in Tetouan and another thinner strip of land in the south, running eastwards from Tarfaya. In between, with the exception of a small Spanish enclave in Sidi Ifni, was to be French Morocco. A separate agreement gave Spain colonial rights to the Sahara, stretching south from Tarfaya to the borders of French Mauritania.

The French and Spanish Protectorates (1912–56)

The fates of **Spanish and French Morocco** under colonial rule were to be very different. When **France** signed its Protectorate agreement with the sultan in 1912, its sense of **colonial mission** was running high. The colonial lobby in France argued that the colonies were vital not only as markets for French goods but because they fulfilled France's *mission civilisatrice* – to bring the benefits of French culture and language to all corners of the globe. The Spanish saw themselves more as conquerors than colonists and did little to develop their sector, whose government was described by one contemporary as a mixture of "battlefield, tavern and brothel".

Lyautey and "Pacification"

France's first resident-general in Morocco was **General Hubert Lyautey**, often held up as the ideal of French colonialism with his stated policy: "Do not offend a single tradition, do not change a single habit". Lyautey recommended respect for the terms of the Protectorate agreement, which placed strict limits on French interference in Moroccan affairs. He recognized the existence of a functioning Moroccan bureaucracy based on the sultan's court with which the French could cooperate – a hierarchy of officials, with diplomatic representation abroad, and with its own social institutions.

But there were other forces at work: French soldiers were busy unifying the country, ending tribal rebellion; in their wake came a system of roads and railways that opened the country to further colonial exploitation. For the first time in Moroccan history, the central government exerted permanent control over the mountain regions. The "**pacification**" of the country brought a flood of French settlers and administrators.

In France these developments were presented as echoing the history of the opening up of the American Wild West. Innumerable articles celebrated "the transformation taking place, the stupendous development of Casablanca port, the birth of new towns, the construction of roads and dams…The image of the virgin lands in Morocco is contrasted often with metropolitan France, wrapped up in its history and its routines…".

Naturally, the interests of the natives were submerged in this rapid economic development, and the restrictions of the Protectorate agreement were increasingly ignored.

Spain and revolt in the Rif

The early history of the **Spanish zone** was strikingly different. Before 1920, Spanish influence outside the main cities of Ceuta, Melilla and Tetouan was minimal. When the Spanish tried to extend their control into the Rif mountains of the interior, they ran into the fiercely independent Berber tribes of the region.

Normally, the various tribes remained divided, but faced with the Spanish troops they united under the leadership of **Abd el Krim**. In the summer of 1921, he inflicted a series of crushing defeats on the Spanish army, culminating in the massacre of at least 13,000 soldiers at **Annoual**. The scale of the defeat, at the hands of tribal fighters armed only with rifles, outraged the Spanish public and worried the French, who had Berber tribes of their own to deal with in the Atlas mountains. As the war began to spread into the French zone, the two colonial powers combined to crush the rebellion. It took a combined force of around 360,000 colonial troops to do so.

It was the last of the great tribal rebellions. Abd el Krim had fought for an independent **Rifian state**. An educated man, he had seen the potential wealth that could result from exploiting the mineral deposits of the Rif. After the rebellion was crushed, the route to Moroccan independence changed from armed revolt to middle-class campaigning.

Nationalism and independence

The French had hoped that by educating a middle-class elite they would find native allies in the task of binding Morocco permanently to France. It had the opposite effect. The educated classes of Rabat and Fes were the first to demand reforms from the French that would give greater rights to the Moroccans. When the government failed to respond, the demand for reforms escalated into demands for total independence.

France's first inkling of the depth of nationalist feeling came in 1930, when the colonial government tried to bring in a **Berber dahir** – a law setting up a separate legal system for the Berber areas. This was an obvious breach of the Protectorate agreement, which prevented the French from changing the Islamic nature of government. Popular agitation forced the French to back down.

It was a classic attempt to "divide and rule", and as the nationalists gained strength, the French resorted more and more to threatening to "unleash" the Berber hill tribes against the Arab city dwellers. They hoped that by spreading Christianity and setting up French schools in Berber areas, the tribes would become more "Europeanized" and, as such, useful allies against the Muslim Arabs.

Until World War II, Morocco's **nationalists** were weak and their demands were for reform of the existing system, not independence. After riots in 1937, the government was able to round up the entire executive committee of the small nationalist party. But with French capitulation in the war, the climate changed. In 1943, the party took the name of **Istiqlal** (Independence); the call for complete separation from France grew more insistent.

The loyal performance of Moroccan troops during the war had raised hopes of a fairer treatment for nationalist demands, but postwar France continued to ignore Istiqlal, exiling its leaders and banning its publications. During the postwar period, it steadily developed into a mass party – growing from 10,000 members in 1947 to 100,000 by 1951.

To some extent, the developments of the 1950s, culminating in Moroccan independence in 1956, resemble events in Algeria and Tunisia. The French first underestimated the strength of local independence movements, then tried to resist them and finally had to concede defeat. In Algeria and Tunisia, the independence parties gained power and consolidated their positions once the French had left. But in Morocco, Istiqlal was never uncontested after 1956 and the party soon began to fragment – becoming, by the 1970s, a marginal force in politics.

The decline and fall of Istiqlal was due mainly to the astute way in which Sultan (later King) **Mohammed V** associated himself with the independence movement. Despite threats from the French government, Mohammed became more and more outspoken in his support for independence, paralysing government operations by refusing to sign legislation. Serious rioting in 1951 persuaded the French to act: after a period of house arrest, the sultan was sent into exile in 1953 and a puppet, **Ben Arfa**, installed in his place.

This only increased Mohammed V's popularity. Seeing no way out of the spiralling violence of nationalist guerrillas and French settlers, and unable to simultaneously defend three North African colonies (with economic interests dictating that they concentrate on holding Algeria), France let Mohammed V return in 1955, and the following year 1956, Morocco gained **independence**. Mohammed V then changed his title from sultan to king.

Mohammed V

Unlike his ancestor sultans, **Mohammed V** had inherited a united country with a well-developed industrial sector, an extensive system of irrigation and a network of roads and railways. But years of French administration had left little legacy of trained Moroccan administrators. As leader of the Muslim faith in Morocco and the figurehead of independence, the king commanded huge support and influence. Istiqlal party members held key posts in his first **government**, which established schools and universities, introduced a level of regional government, and launched ambitious public works schemes. There were moves against the Sufi brotherhoods, and also against European "decadence", with a wholesale clean-up of Tangier. But the king did not perceive the Istiqlal as natural allies and instead built links with the army – with the help of Crown Prince Hassan, whose period as commander-in-chief was a defining moment in his political development – and with the police.

Mohammed's influence on the army would prove a decisive factor in the Moroccan state withstanding a series of **rebellions** against its authority. The most serious of these were in the Rif, in 1958–59, but there were challenges, too, in the Middle Atlas and Sahara. The king's standing and the army's efficiency stood the test. In party politics, Mohammed's principal act was to lend his support to the **Mouvement Populaire** (MP), a moderate party set up to represent the Berbers, and for the king a useful counterweight to Istiqlal. In 1959, the strategy paid its first dividend. Istiqlal was seriously weakened by a split which hived off the more left-wing members into a separate party, the **Union Nationale des Forces Populaires** (UNFP) under Mehdi Ben Barka. There had always been a certain tension within Istiqlal between the moderates and those favouring a more radical policy, in association with the unions. A tendency towards parties dividing within and among themselves has been apparent in Moroccan politics ever since, helping to maintain the Palace's leading role in the political arena.

Hassan II (1961–99)

Mohammed V's death in 1961 brought to the throne his son **Hassan II**, whose **autocratic rule** had a very thin veneer of parliamentary politics. But by the time that he died, in July 1999, the monarchy, although still by far the most powerful political institution in Morocco, had begun to engage with other political and social forces – and had established the roots of a more open political culture.

Despite the poverty still apparent in large areas of the country, much was done during Hassan's reign to bring the kingdom into the modern world. It was an achievement in the face of a huge **population explosion** in the 1970s and 1980s, which saw the population rise from eight million at Independence to more than thirty million today.

Elections and coup attempts

In many respects Hassan was a very modern monarch, regularly pictured playing golf, flying a jet fighter, or meeting fellow heads of state. As a power politician he had few peers. But he was also careful to maintain his status as a traditional ruler. **Domestic politics** since independence has centred on a battle of wills between the dominant political forces in the kingdom: the Palace and its allies; a legalized opposition which has at times formed a part of the government; and underground movements such as the Marxist-Leninist Ilal Amam (which has all but disappeared) and, more recently, groups of Islamist radicals.

Even before independence, in a 1955 speech, Mohammed V had promised to set up "democratic institutions resulting from the holding of free elections". The country's first constitution was not ready until after his death, and it was only in 1962, under Hassan II, that it was put to, and approved by, a popular referendum. The constitution was drafted in such a way as to favour the pro-monarchy parties of the centre – setting the pattern that was to prevail up until the end of Hassan's reign.

The 1960s were marked by the fragility of Morocco's political party structure and the authorities' greater enthusiasm for using the bullet and torture chamber rather than the ballot box to handle opposition. This mood was reflected in the **Ben Barka affair**, a notorious incident whose political ramifications endured for the next two decades, when Mehdi Ben Barka, leader of the opposition UNFP party, was assassinated in Paris, with apparent connivance between the governments of Morocco and France.

The opposition subsequently split, with the largest element of the UNFP going on to form the USFP, led by Abderrahim Bouabid until his death in 1992. These parties were largely ineffectual, especially after Hassan announced a new constitution in 1970, following a period of emergency rule. However, the events of 1971–72 showed the real nature of the threat to the monarchy.

In July 1971, a group of soldiers broke into the royal palace in Skhirat in an attempt to stage a **coup**; more than 100 people were killed, but in the confusion Hassan escaped. The following year another attempt was launched, as the king's private jet was attacked by fighters of the Moroccan Air Force. Again, Hassan had a very narrow escape – his pilot was able to convince the attacking aircraft by radio that the king had already died. The former interior minister, General Mohamed Oufkir disappeared (apparently murdered in custody) soon after and the armed forces were restructured.

The Saharan conflict and the UMA

Hassan's great challenge was to give a sense of destiny to the country, a cause similar to the struggle for independence that had brought such prestige to his father. That cause was provided in 1975, when the Spanish finally decided to pull out of their colony in the **Western Sahara** (for more on which, see pp.552–553).

In the 1950s the nationalist Istiqlal party had laid claim to the Spanish Sahara, as well as to Mauritania and parts of Algeria and Mali, as part of its quest for a "Greater Morocco". By 1975, Hassan had patched up the border dispute with

Algeria and recognized the independent government in Mauritania, but he retained a more realistic design – Moroccan control of the Spanish Sahara.

Spanish withdrawal from the Western Sahara in 1975 coincided with General Franco's final illness and Hassan timed his move perfectly, sending some 350,000 Moroccan civilians southwards on **El Massira** – the "**Green March**" – to the Sahara. Spain could either go to war with Morocco by attacking the advancing Moroccans or withdraw without holding a referendum on independence, which they had agreed to call after UN pressure. Hassan's bluff worked, and the popular unrest of the 1960s and the coup attempts of 1971–72 were forgotten under a wave of patriotism. Without shedding any blood, Morocco had "recaptured" part of its former empire. But the Polisario guerillas who had led the fight against Spanish rule now began a campaign against Moroccan occupation. Despite early Polisario successes, the Moroccans managed to assert control over most of the territory, and all of its economically important areas, but in 1988 the two sides agreed a ceasefire under UN auspices, on the principle that a **referendum** would be held on the territory's future.

That promised referendum has yet to take place, but the dispute has damaged Morocco diplomatically; in particular it has left her isolated in African politics since the African Union recognized the Polisario-declared Saharawi Arab Democratic Republic, prompting Morocco to leave. A resolution is also essential if Morocco is to have normal relations with its neighbours, particularly Algeria, which strongly backed Polisario; friction between Morocco and Algeria has hampered efforts towards regional unity.

In February 1989 Algerian, Libyan, Mauritanian, Moroccan and Tunisian leaders, meeting in Marrakesh, had agreed to form the long-awaited regional grouping, the **Arab Maghreb Union**, known by its evocative acronym UMA (from the French Union du Maghreb Arabe but sounding like the Arabic word *'umma*, or community). However, the UMA has been stalled by disputes hinging on longstanding rivalries between the North African states. Chief among the UMA's problems has been Moroccan–Algerian hostility arising largely from the Saharan question. This led in 1994 to the closure of the Algerian–Moroccan border, which has not reopened since.

Economic and social problems

The Saharan war proved to be only a temporary distraction from discontent in Morocco itself. Moreover, the occupation of the Western Sahara and its demands on the economy added to the very problems it was designed to divert attention from. By 1981, an estimated sixty percent of the population were living below the poverty level, unemployment ran at approximately twenty percent (forty percent among the young) and perhaps twenty percent of the urban population lived in shantytowns, or *bidonvilles*.

Popular unrest erupted in the 1984 "**bread riots**" in cities across the country, most notably in Marrakesh, Oujda, Nador and Tetouan. The riots were triggered when the government raised the prices of staple foods following pressure from the International Monetary Fund (IMF) to repay its **burgeoning debt** while phosphate prices were depressed and the country was suffering one of its regular **droughts**. King Hassan had to intervene personally to reverse the decision and, in the opinion of many analysts, save his monarchy from a populist rising.

Dissatisfaction with Hassan's regime in the 1980s and 1990s surfaced in the form of protests by unemployed graduates (despite the dangers of political protest in Hassan's police state), and sometimes violent incidents in the kingdom's universities. In 1990, a general strike called by the CDT trade union federation led to riots in Fes and Tangier. On campus, the student movement linked to Morocco's biggest opposition party, the **Union Socialiste des Forces Populaires** (USFP) went into retreat as a growing Islamist movement took control of student unions.

In the 1990s, Morocco embarked on one of Africa's biggest **privatization** drives as King Hassan firmly nailed his colours to the mast of economic liberalization. New efforts were made to encourage foreign investment in technologically advanced manufacturing industries, **textiles** and, an increasingly important earner, **tourism**. Modern management skills began to take hold with the emergence of a new managerial class independent of the old social loyalties. The decade ended with the Medi Telecom consortium bidding over US$1 billion for a licence to install a GSM mobile telephone system, and privately financed power plants helping to raise energy capacity.

A 1980s application to join the **European Union** was rejected, but in 1996 Morocco's joined the EU's **Euro-Mediterranean Partnership** agreement, intended to create a free trade zone around the Mediterranean, and closer ties with the EU, including preferential trade deals, have followed.

Change and elections

The opposition, which had been quiet through much of the 1980s, started to reassert itself in the 1990s, as traditional opposition parties showed revived enthusiasm for challenging the government – though not the king. The mid-1990s saw Morocco cleaning up its previously appalling **human rights** record. In 1992, a leading dissident, Abraham Serfaty, was one of many well-known figures in a **release of political prisoners** that included many soldiers held, since the 1972 failed coup, in a dungeon prison at Tazmamart in the High Atlas. Several former student radicals who survived imprisonment and torture in the 1960s, '70s and '80s went on to hold positions of responsibility in the local press, universities and even government departments.

In 1996 Hassan judged there to be sufficient consensus on the direction of Moroccan politics to hold a referendum on constitutional reforms, opening the way for a new bicameral parliamentary system. Local and national elections were held in 1997 and for the first time there seemed the prospect of bringing the opposition into government, with genuine power. Disappointingly, the elections produced a lacklustre campaign and much voter apathy, as a three-way split gave right-wing, centrist and left-wing/nationalist groupings a similar number of seats in the lower house of parliament. Hassan appointed as prime minister the USFP leader **Abderrahmane Youssoufi** at the head of a coalition government that included both USFP and Istiqlal ministers.

One notable factor in the 1997 general election was that Islamist deputies were voted into parliament for the first time, under the *Mouvement Populaire Constitutionnel et Démocratique* **(MPCD)** banner. This parliamentary debut for the Islamists came at a time when their calls for a change in views on public morality and private sector development were gaining appeal among those most alienated by increasing social tensions and allegations of corruption, but many have seen the administration's acceptance of the **MPCD**, who stand at the moderate end of the Islamist spectrum, as a classic piece of Moroccan divide-and-rule, aimed at splitting the Islamist movement.

Mohammed VI (1999–)

On Hassan's death in 1999, his son **Mohammed VI** quickly emerged from his father's shadow, ushering in a **new style** of rule with widespread popular support. From the very start he made clear his more inclusive agenda by visiting the **troubled north** (long ignored by Hassan), restoring **civil rights** to those remaining political prisoners not covered by previous amnesties (with over 8,000 released in first-year amnesties), and promising a more **relaxed and consensual** form of rule. He sacked Hassan's powerful but unpopular right-hand man, Minister of State for the Interior **Driss Basri**, and allowed a number of high-profile dissidents to return to Morocco, most notably leftist **Abraham Serfaty**, who he appointed as a personal adviser. In May 2000, he made headlines by freeing his father's most implacable critic, **Abdessalam Yassine**, leader of the banned **Al-Adl wal Ihsane** (Justice and Charity) movement. Dissent is not always tolerated however, and the king's forces have on occasion clamped down rather harshly on street protests, notably a protest by unemployed graduates in Rabat in June 2000, while newspapers are still prosecuted under laws against "undermining" the monarchy or Morocco's "territorial integrity". Nonetheless, the tenor of Mohammed's reign has been to extend democracy, human rights and free speech, albeit in a cautious fashion.

In March 2000, the king announced a **National Action Plan**, whose main feature was a Family Law that radically improved the **position of women** under Moroccan law, banning polygamy and introducing more equal family rights. The proposal sparked a backlash by Islamists, who mustered around a quarter of a million supporters at a march in Casablanca to protest the proposals, and the government responded by setting up a consultative commission to consider the question more carefully. After due consideration, parliament decided to go ahead with the proposals, which came into force in 2004, giving women greater legal rights in Morocco than anywhere else in the Muslim world, and more on a par with those of women in Europe.

The Moroccan government was swift to condemn the September 2001 **attacks by al-Qaida** on the Pentagon and the New York World Trade Center, but the apparent involvement of pro-Islamist Moroccans in those attacks and in the train bombs that killed over 200 people in Madrid in March 2004 severely embarrassed the Moroccan authorities. In Morocco itself, May 2003 saw attacks on Jewish and Western targets by suicide bombers in Casablanca, which resulted in the deaths of 33 people (plus the bombers). The attack severely dented fundamentalist appeal, but a hardcore of support for such actions continues to exist. The authorities reacted to the bombings by rounding up over 1500 people suspected of involvement with militant groups, of whom several hundred were given prison sentences ranging from three months to thirty years.

In the **2002 elections**, the moderate Islamist MPCD, now renamed the PJD (*Parti de la Justice et du Développement*), took thirteen percent of the vote and emerged as Morocco's third biggest political party after the USFP and Istiqlal, which formed an administration together with representatives of four other parties. All the government parties are essentially organizations for the distribution of patronage, and the ministries that they control are largely staffed by their own people. The PJD, which is the only ideologically based political party, is also the only serious opposition in parliament.

The birth of a son and heir, Prince Moulay Hassan, in 2003, gave the king an excuse to release some 9000 prisoners and remit the sentences of thousands more. The same year also saw a major extension of **rights for Berber speakers**, whose languages were taught for the first time in schools in the 2003–4 academic year. Programmes in Berber are also now broadcast on TV.

Elections in 2007 saw Istiqlal regain its position as largest party in parliament – the fact that it could do so with just over a tenth of the vote shows just how fragmented the party system is. Istiqlal leader Abbas el Fassi took over as PM at the head of a four-party coalition including the USFP. The PJD got slightly more votes than Istiqlal, but slightly fewer seats, and remains the main opposition. More significantly, a miserable 37-percent turnout showed how little Moroccans care who sits in parliament. This is partly because, despite his reforms, Mohammed VI's Morocco is still very much dominated by the Palace – where a younger generation of advisers is settling in, but while they talk the language of globalization, their government remains rooted in a political tradition in which they take orders from a king who is both monarch and *Al-Amir Al-Muminin* (commander of the faithful).

To date, the king has proved surprisingly successful in rejuvenating the monarchical and political system. He has needed to do so, if he is now to address the **crucial issues** facing Morocco: unemployment, poverty, a huge young population, the need for a resolution in the Western Sahara, and the spectre of radical Islam. The hope is that the West, and in particular the European Union (where Morocco is seen by some as a buffer against African immigration) will provide support for both the king and system to prosper.

Islam in Morocco

It's difficult to get any grasp of Morocco, and even more so of Moroccan history, without first knowing something of Islam. What follows is a very basic background: some theory, some history and an idea of Morocco's place in the modern Islamic world.

Practice and belief

Islam was founded by **Mohammed** (also spelt Muhammad), a merchant from the wealthy city of Mecca, now in Saudi Arabia. In about 609 AD, he began to receive divine messages, and continued to do so for the rest of his life. After his death, these were collated, and form the **Koran** (*Qur'an*), Islam's Bible. Muslims consider Mohammed to be the final prophet of the same God who is worshipped by Jews and Christians, and Islam recognizes all the prophets of the biblical Old Testament as his predecessors, and also regards Jesus (*Aïssa* in Arabic) as a prophet, but not as the Son of God.

The distinctive feature of Islam is its directness – there is no intermediary between man and God in the form of an institutionalized priesthood or complicated liturgy, as in Christianity; and worship, in the form of prayer, is a direct and personal communication with God.

The Pillars of Faith

Islam has five essential requirements, called **"Pillars of faith":** prayer (*salat*); the pilgrimage to Mecca (*hadj*); the Ramadan fast (*sanm*); almsgiving (*zakat*); and, most fundamental of all, the acceptance that "There is no God but God and Mohammed is His Prophet" (*shahada*). The Pillars of Faith are central to Muslim life, articulating and informing daily existence. **Prayers** are performed five times daily, at sunset (when the Islamic day begins), nightfall, dawn, noon and afternoon, and can be performed anywhere, but preferably in a mosque (*djemaa* in Arabic). In the past, and even today in some places, a *muezzin* would climb his minaret each time and summon the faithful. Nowadays, the call is likely to be prerecorded, but this most distinctive of Islamic sounds has a beauty all its own, especially when neighbouring *muezzins* are audible simultaneously. Their message is simplicity itself: "God is most great (*Allah o Akhbar*). I testify that there is no God but Allah. I testify that Mohammed is His Prophet. Come to prayer, come to security. God is most great." Another phrase is added in the morning: "Prayer is better than sleep".

Prayers are preceded by ritual washing. The worshipper then removes their shoes and, facing Mecca (the direction indicated in a mosque by the mihrab), recites the Fatina, the first chapter of the Koran: "Praise be to God, Lord of the worlds, the Compassionate, the Merciful, King of the Day of Judgement. We worship you and seek your aid. Guide us on the straight path, the path of those on whom you have bestowed your Grace, not the path of those who incur your anger nor of those who go astray." The same words are then repeated twice in the prostrate position, with some interjections of *Allah o Akhbar*. The prostrate position symbolizes the worshipper's submission to God (Islam literally means "submission"), and the sight of thousands of people going through the same motions simultaneously in a mosque is a powerful one. On Friday, believers try to attend prayers in their local grand mosque, where the whole community comes together in worship, led by an *imam* (much like a Protestant pastor), who may also deliver the *khutba*, or sermon.

Ramadan is the name of the ninth month in the lunar Islamic calendar, during which believers must fast between sunrise and sundown, abstaining from food, drink, cigarettes and sex. Only children, pregnant women and warriors engaged in a *jihad* (holy war) are exempt. Though the day is thus hard, nights are a time of celebration.

The pilgrimage, or **hadj**, to Mecca is an annual event, with millions flocking to Mohammed's birthplace from all over the world. Here they go through several days of rituals, the central one being a sevenfold circumambulation of the Kaba, before kissing a black stone set in its wall. Islam requires that all believers go on a *hadj* as often as is practically possible, but for the poor it may be a once-in-a-lifetime occasion, and is sometimes replaced by a series of visits to lesser, local shrines – in Morocco, for instance, to Fes and Moulay Idriss.

Islam's development in Morocco

Morocco was virtually untouched by the Sunni–Shia conflict that split the Muslim world – but the country's unusual geographical and social circumstances have conspired to tip the balance away from official orthodoxy. In the eighth century, many Berbers were attracted to the dissident Kharijite strain of Islam, which rejected the Sunni and Shi'te argument that the leader of the faithful had to be an Arab, and Sijilmasa (Rissani) became the capital of a powerful Kharijite kingdom. Subsequently, Moroccans have in principle been almost universally Sunni, but Sufism and maraboutism became very strong within the religion.

Marabouts

Sufism is the idea that, in addition to following religious rules, people can personally get closer to God by leading a spiritual rather than a materialistic lifestyle, and even by chanting and meditating to achieve a trance-like state. Everywhere in Morocco, as well as elsewhere in North Africa, the countryside is dotted with small domed **koubbas** – the tombs of **marabouts**, Sufi holy men (though the term is also used for the *koubba*) – which became centres of worship and pilgrimage. This elevation of individuals goes against strict Islamic teaching, but probably derives from the Berbers' pre-Islamic tendency to focus worship round individual holy men.

More prosperous cults would also endow educational institutions attached to the *koubba*, known as **zaouias**, which provided an alternative to the official education given in urban medersas (Koranic schools). These inevitably posed a threat to the authority of the urban hierarchy, and as rural cults extended their influence, some became so popular that they endowed their saints with genealogies traced back to the Prophet. The title accorded to these men and their descendants was Shereef, and many grew into strong political forces. The classic example in Morocco is the tomb of Moulay Idriss – in the eighth century just a local *marabout*, but eventually, the base of the Idrissid clan, a centre of enormous influence that reached far beyond its rural origins.

The most influential *marabouts* spawned Sufi **brotherhoods**, whose members meet to chant, play music, meditate, and thus seek personal union with God. This is particularly an important part of the **moussem**, an annual festival associated with each *marabout*. The most famous and flamboyant Moroccan Sufi brotherhood is that of **Sidi Mohammed Bin Aissa**. Born in Souss in the fifteenth century, he travelled in northern Morocco before settling down as a teacher in Meknes and founding a *zaouia*. His powers of mystical healing became famous there, and he provoked enough official suspicion to be exiled briefly to the desert – where he again revealed his exceptional powers by proving himself immune to scorpions, snakes, live flames and other hostile manifestations. His followers tried to achieve the same state of grace. The Aissaoua brotherhood made itself notorious with displays of eating scorpions, walking on hot coals and other ecstatic practices designed to bring union with God.

Towards crisis

With all its different forms, Islam permeated every aspect of the country's pre-twentieth-century life. Unlike Christianity, at least Protestant Christianity, which to some extent has accepted the separation of church and state, Islam sees no such distinction. **Civil law** was provided by the *sharia*, the religious law contained in the Koran, and **intellectual life** by the *msids* (Koranic primary schools where the 6200 verses were learned by heart) and by the great medieval mosque universities, of which the Kairaouine in Fes (together with the Zitoura in Tunis and the Al Azhar in Cairo) was the most important in the Arab world.

At first, Islam brought a great scientific revolution, uniting the traditions of Greece and Rome with those of India and Iran, and then developing them while Christian Europe rejected the sciences of pagan philosophers. As Europe went through its Renaissance, however, it was Islam that started to atrophy, as the religious authorities became increasingly suspicious of any challenge to established belief, and actively discouraged innovation. At first this did not matter in political terms, but as the Islamic world fell behind in science and learning, Europe was able to take advantage of its now superior technology. Napoleon's expedition to Egypt in 1798 marked the beginning of a century in which virtually every Islamic country came under the control of a **European power**. Because East–West rivalry had always been viewed in religious terms, the nineteenth and twentieth centuries saw something of a **crisis in religious confidence**. Why had Islam's former power now passed to infidel foreigners?

Fundamentalism

Reactions and answers veered between those who felt that Islam should try to incorporate some of the West's materialism, and those who held that Islam should turn its back on the West, purify itself of all corrupt additions and thus rediscover its former power. As colonies of European powers, Muslim nations had little chance of putting any such ideas into effective practice. But **decolonization**, and the discovery of oil in the Middle East, brought the Islamic world face to face with the question of its own spiritual identity. How should it deal with Western values and influence, now that it could afford – both politically and economically – almost total rejection? A return to the totality of Islam – **fundamentalism** – is one option. It has a reactionary side, harking back to an imagined time of perfection under the Prophet and the early caliphs, but it is also radical in its rejection of colonialism and materialism, and its most vehement adherents tend to be young rather than old.

Islam in Modern Morocco

In Morocco today, Islam is the official state religion, and King Mohammed's secular status is interwoven with his role as "commander of the faithful". Internationally too, he plays a leading role. Meetings of the Islamic Conference Organization are frequently held in Morocco and students from as far afield as Central Asia come to study Islam at Fes University. For all these indications of Islamic solidarity, though, **state policy** remains distinctly moderate – sometimes in the face of fundamentalist pressure. The 2004 law on the status of women is a good example of this: 100,000 people marched in Rabat to support the new law, and over 200,000 marched in Casablanca against it, a sign of increasing **polarization** on religious questions, not unlike that in the United States.

In the cities, there has long been tension between those for and against secularization, as well as a large body of urban poor, for whom Islamic fundamentalism can seem to offer solutions. In some circles, Islam is becoming very relaxed; in Casablanca, Rabat, El Jadida and Marrakesh, young people of both sexes can be seen socializing together, young women no longer wear the veil, and have exchanged their frumpy cover-alls for flattering, sexy clothes, while young couples visit nightclubs and even drink socially. But against this, the number of people going to pray at mosques is on the up, and among the poor especially, Islam is becoming a mark of pride and respectability. That this is reflected in politics is not surprising, and the moderate Islamist PJD is developing into a serious legal opposition with increasing support, one that could even win an election and form a government in the future, and if that government's programme included the enforcement of religious strictures, it would be strongly resented by secular Moroccans.

In the **countryside**, religious attitudes have changed less over the past two generations. Religious brotherhoods such as the Aissaoua have declined since the beginning of the century, when they were still very powerful, and the influence of mystics generally has fallen. As the official histories put it, popular credulity in Morocco provided an ideal setting for charlatans as well as saviours, and much of this has now passed. All the same, the rhythms of rural life still revolve around local *marabouts*, and the annual moussems, or festivals-cum-pilgrimages, are still vital and impressive displays.

Wildlife

Few countries in the Mediterranean region can match the variety and quality of the wildlife habitats to be found in Morocco. The three bands of mountains – Rif, Middle Atlas and High Atlas – with the Mediterranean coastal strop to the north, and the desert to the south, provide a wide variety of **habitat types**, from coastal cliffs, sand dunes and estuarine marshlands to subalpine forests and grasslands, to the semi-arid Sahel and true desert areas of the south. The **climate** is similarly diverse: warm and humid along the coastal zones, relatively cooler at altitude within the Atlas ranges and distinctly hotter and drier south of the High Atlas. Not surprisingly, the plant and animal life in Morocco is accordingly parochial, species distributions being closely related to the habitat and climate types to which they are adapted.

Birds

In addition to a unique range of **resident bird species**, distributed throughout the country on the basis of vegetation and climatic zonation, the periods of late March/April and September/October provide the additional sight of vast **bird migrations**.

Large numbers of birds which have overwintered south of the Sahara migrate northwards in the spring to breed in Europe, completing their return passage through Morocco in the autumn, and some north European species choose Morocco to avoid the harshness of the northern winter. These movements can form a dramatic spectacle in the skies, dense flocks of birds moving in procession through bottleneck areas such as Tangier and Ceuta where sea crossings are at their shortest.

Among **field guides** to Moroccan birdlife, the definitive tome is Michael Thévenot, Rae Vernon and Patrick Bergier's *The Birds of Morocco* (British Ornithologists' Union, UK), while Patrick and Fédora Bergier's *A Birdwatcher's Guide to Morocco* (Prion Press, UK) is an excellent practical guidebook that includes site-maps and species lists. Pete Combridge and Alan Snook's similarly titled *A Birdwatching Guide to Morocco* (Arlequin Press, UK) covers seventeen sites, with maps, directions and a species checklist.

Resident species

Coastal and marine species include the familiar moorhen and less familiar crested coot, an incongruous bird which, when breeding, resembles its northern European relation but with an additional pair of bright red knobs on either side of its white facial shield. Other species include the diminutive little ringed plover and rock dove.

South of the High Atlas are **desert species**, such as the sandgrouse (spotted, crowned, pin-tailed and black-bellied varieties), stone curlew, cream-coloured courser and Houbara bustard – the latter standing over two feet in height. Other well-represented groups include wheatears (4 varieties), larks (7 varieties) and finches, buntings, warblers, corvids, jays, magpies, choughs and ravens (crow family), tits (primarily blue, great and coal) and owls (barn, eagle, tawny and little).

Raptors (birds of prey) provide an enticing roll call of resident species, including red- and black-shouldered kite, long-legged buzzard, Bonelli's, golden and tawny eagles, Barbary, lanner and peregrine falcons and the more familiar kestrel.

Migrant species

Summer visitors include, among marine and coastal types, manx shearwater, Eleonora's falcon and the bald ibis – for whom Tamri (see p.339) is one of its few remaining breeding colonies in the world. Mountain species include the small Egyptian vulture and several of the hirundines (swallows and martins) and their close relatives, the swifts, such as little swift, red-rumped swallow and the more familiar house martin. A particularly colourful summer visitor in the Sahel regions is the blue-cheeked bee-eater, a vibrant blend of red, yellow, blue and green, unmistakeable if seen close up.

The list of **winter visitors** is more extensive but composed primarily of marine or coastal species. The most common of the truly marine (*pelagic*) flocks include Cory's shearwater, storm petrel, gannet, razorbill and puffin. These are often found congregated on the sea surface, along with any combination of skuas (great, arctic and pomarine varieties), terns (predominantly sandwich) and gulls (including black-headed, Mediterranean, little, herring and the rarer Audouin's) flying overhead. A variety of coastal and estuarine species also arrive during this period, forming large mixed flocks of grebes (great-crested, little and black-necked), avocet, cattle egret, spoonbill, greater flamingo, and wildfowl such as shelduck, wigeon, teal, pintail, shoveler, tufted duck, pochard and coot. Migrant birds of prey during the winter months include the common buzzard (actually a rarity in Morocco), dashing merlin and both marsh and hen harriers.

Many **passage migrants** pass through Morocco en route to other areas. Well-represented groups include petrels (5 varieties) and terns (6 varieties) along coastal areas, and herons (4 varieties), bitterns, cranes, white and black stork and crake (spotted, little, Baillon's and corncrake) in the marshland/estuarine habitats. Further inland, flocks of multicoloured roller, bee-eater and hoopoe mix with various larks, wagtails and warblers (13 varieties), forming large "windfall" flocks when climatic conditions worsen abruptly. Individual species of note include the aptly named black-winged stilt, an elegant black and white wader, with long, vibrant red legs, often found among the disused saltpans; and the nocturnal nightjars (both common and red-necked), which are most easily seen by the reflection of their eyes in the headlamps of passing cars. Birds of prey can also form dense passage flocks, often mixed and including large numbers of black kite, short-toed eagle and honey buzzard. Over open water spaces, the majestic osprey may be seen demonstrating its mastery of the art of fishing.

Finally, Morocco has its share of occasional or **"vagrant" species**, so classified on the unusual or rare nature of their appearances, including such exotic varieties as glossy ibis, pale-chanting goshawk, Arabian bustard and lappet-faced vulture, but they provide few, if any, opportunities for viewing.

Flora

Morocco's flora is remarkably diverse. Plant species have adapted strategies to cope with the Moroccan climate, becoming either specifically adapted to one particular part of the environment (a habitat type), or evolving multiple structural and/or biochemical means of surviving the more demanding seasons. Others have adopted the proverbial "ostrich" philosophy of burying their heads (or rather their seeds in this case) in the sand and waiting for climatic conditions to become favourable – often an extremely patient process. Oleg Polunin and Anthony Huxley's *Flowers of the Mediterranean* (Oxford UP) is the leading field guide.

The type of flowers that you see will obviously depend entirely on where and when you decide to visit. Some parts of the country have very short flowering seasons because of high temperatures or lack of available water, but generally the best times of year for flowering plants are either just before or just after the main temperature extremes of the North African summer.

The very best time to visit is **spring** (late March to mid-May), when most flowers are in bloom. Typical spring flowers include purple barbary nut iris, deep blue germander and the aromatic claret thyme, all of which frequent the slopes of the Atlas ranges. Among the woodland flora at this time of year are the red pheasant's eye, pink viburnum, violet calamint and purple campanula, which form a resplendent carpet beneath the cedar forests. By late spring, huge tracts of the High Atlas slopes are aglow with the golden hues of broom and, secluded among the lowland cereal crops, splashes of magenta reveal the presence of wild gladioli.

By **midsummer** the climate is at its most extreme and the main concern of plants is to avoid desiccation in the hot, arid conditions. Two areas of exception to these conditions are the **Atlantic coastal zones**, where sea mists produce a slightly more humid environment, and the upper reaches of the **Atlas ranges** which remain cool and moist at altitude throughout the year. Spring comes later in these loftier places and one can find many of the more familiar garden rock plants, such as the saxifrages and anemones, in flower well into late July and August. Once the hottest part of the summer is past (September onwards), then a second, autumn bloom begins with later varieties such as cyclamens and autumn crocus.

Habitat varieties

Seashores have a variety of sand-tolerant species, with their adaptations for coping with water loss, such as sea holly and sea stocks. The dune areas contrast starkly with the Salicornia-dominated salt marshes – monotonous landscapes broken only by the occasional dead tamarisk tree.

Arable land is often dominated by cereal crops – particularly in the more humid Atlantic and Mediterranean coastal belts – or olive and eucalyptus groves, which extend over large areas. On the coast around Essaouira and Agadir the indigenous argan tree (see p.498) is common. The general lack of use of herbicides allows the coexistence of many "wild flowers", especially in the fallow hay meadows which are ablaze with the colours of wild poppy, ox-eye daisy, muscali (borage) and various yellow composites.

Lowland hills form a fascinating mosaic of dense, shrubby species, known as *maquis*, lower-lying, more grazed areas, known as *garrigue*, and more open areas with abundant aromatic herbs and shrubs. *Maquis* vegetation is dominated by cistaceae (rockroses) and the endemic argan tree. The lower-lying *garrigue* is more typically composed of aromatic herbs such as rosemary, thyme and golden milfoil. Among these shrubs, within the more open areas, you may find an abundance of other species such as anemones, grape hyacinths and orchids. The orchids are particularly outstanding, including several of the *Ophrys* group, which use the strategy of insect imitation to entice pollinators and as such have an intricate arrangement of flowers.

Flowering later in the year, the slopes of the **Atlas ranges** are dominated by the blue-mauve pitch trefoil and golden drifts of broom. As you travel south through the **Middle Atlas**, the verdant ash, oak, atlantic cedar and juniper forest dominates the landscape. Watered by the depressions that sweep across from the Atlantic, these slopes form a luxurious spectacle, ablaze with colour in spring. Among the glades beneath the giant cedars of the Middle Atlas, a unique flora may be found, dominated by the vibrant pink peony. Other plants which form this spectacular carpet include geranium, anchusa, pink verburnum, saffron mulleins, mauve cupidanes, violet calamint, purple campanula, the diminutive scarlet dianthus and a wealth of golden composites and orchids.

Further south, in the **High Atlas**, the Toubkal National Park boasts its own varieties and spring bloom; the thyme and thorny caper are interspersed with the blue-mauve pit trefoil, pink convulvulus, the silver-blue and pinks of everlasting flowers of cupidane and phagnalon and golden spreads of broom. At the highest altitudes, the limestone Atlas slopes form a bleak environment, either covered by winter snows or scorched by the summer sun. However, some species are capable of surviving even under these conditions, the most conspicuous of these being the widespread purple tussocks of the hedgehog broom.

In the **steppeland** south of the Atlas, temperatures rise sharply and the effect on flora is dramatic; the extensive cedar forests and their multicoloured carpets are replaced by sparse grass plains where the horizon is broken only by the occasional stunted holm oak, juniper or acacia. Commonly known as wattle trees, the acacia were introduced into North Africa from Australia and their large yellow flowers add a welcome splash of colour to this barren landscape. One of the few crop plants grown in this area is the date palm, which is particularly resistant to drought. The steppeland is characterized by the presence of esparto (halfa) grass, which exudes toxins to prevent the growth of competing species. These halfa grass plains are only broken by the flowering of broom in May. Within rocky outcrops, this spring bloom can become a mini-explosion of colour, blending the hues of cistus and chrysanthemum with the pink of rockrose, yellow of milfoil and mauve of rosemary.

Even **desert areas** provide short-lived blooms of colour during the infrequent spring showers; dwarf varieties such as pink asphodels, yellow daisies and mauve statice thrive briefly while conditions are favourable. Under the flat stones of the *hammada* (stony desert) colonies of lichens and microscopic algae eke out an existence; their shade tolerance and ability to obtain sufficient water from the occasional condensation which takes place under these stones allows them to survive in this harshest of environments. No matter how inhospitable the environment or extreme the climate, somewhere, somehow, there are plants surviving – if you take time to look for them.

Amphibians and reptiles

Morocco's few remaining **amphibians** are restricted to scarce watery havens, and more apparent by sound than sight. One of the more common is the green frog, typically immersed up to its eyes in water, releasing the odd giveaway croak. Toads are represented by the Berber toad, another nocturnal baritone, and the Mauritanian toad whose large size and characteristic yellow and brown-spotted coloration make it quite unmistakeable. The painted frog is a common participant in the chorus that emanates from the *oueds* (riverbeds) of the High Atlas, while the wide-ranging whistle of the North African race of the green toad, famed for its ability to change its colour with the surrounding environment, can be heard at altitudes in excess of 2000m.

Key wildlife sites

Features on key Moroccan wildlife, and especially bird habitats are to be found throughout the guide; the main entries are boxed. They include:

- **Agadir/Oued Souss** Riverbank that attracts waders and wildfowl, migrant warblers and Barbary partridge. p.493.
- **Aguelmame Azigza** Middle Atlas occasional inland lake and forest: hawfinch, diving duck and marbled teal in autumn/winter. p.251.
- **Boumalne: Desert Hammada** Atlas agama and fringe-toed lizard; specialist bird species such as cream-coloured courser, red-rumped wheatear and thick-billed lark. **Houbara bustard**. p.447.
- **Cedar forests south of Azrou** Species include green-eyed lizard and chameleon; **butterflies** from April onwards; **Barbary apes**; Moroccan woodpecker and **booted eagle**. p.250.
- **Dayet Aaoua** Another Middle Atlas occasional lake: flocks of grebes, **crested coot**, grey heron and cattle egret; migrant birds of prey include **red kite**. p.242.
- **Djebel Tazzeka National Park** Where the Rif merges with the Middle Atlas: slopes covered in cork oak and woodland; butterflies from late May/early June, and birds such as the hoopoe. p.168.
- **Djebel Toubkal National Park** High Atlas mountains: sights include Moorish gecko, rare butterflies; Moussier's redstart and crimson-winged finch, both unique to North African mountains; hooped-petticoat daffodils, *romulea* and various other bulbs in spring. p.398
- **Essaouira** Coastal dunes, river and offshore islands attract **waders** and **egrets**; also **Eleanora's falcon** between May and October. p.330.
- **Fes** Evening roost of egret and alpine swift; **white stork** on rooftop nests of walls.
- **Lac du Sidi Bourhaba** Freshwater lake, with outstanding **birds of prey**. p.273.
- **Merdja Zerga** Large wetland area guarantees good **bird** numbers at all times of year, especially **gulls and terns** (including the **Caspian tern**). p.117.
- **Merzouga** Sandy (or "true") desert: all-too-brief **spring bloom** of pink asphodels and mauve statice; Algerian sand lizard and Berber skink; **birds** include fulvous babbler, blue-cheeked bee-eater, the rare desert sparrow and even Arabian bustard. p.478.
- **Nador/Kariet Arkmane/Ras el Ma** Salt marshes and coastal sand dunes, good for waders and gulls. p.153.
- **Oualidia** Mix of ragged, rocky coast, sands, lagoon, marshes and salt-pans. Good for small waders. p.321.
- **Oued Massa** Important inland lagoon and reserve that is perhaps the country's number one bird habitat. p.502.
- **Oued Moulouya** Lagoons and sand spits, with outstanding birds. p.153.
- **Todra Gorge** Marsh frog and green toad; ground squirrel; common bulbul, black wheatear, blue rock thrush and rock dove. **Bonelli's eagles** nest in the gorge. p.456.

Reptiles extend from the Mediterranean to the *desert*. Tortoises are now sadly depleted through "craft items" sold to the tourist trade. The blue and green-eyed lizard and the chameleon frequent the **Middle Atlas**, while the Spanish wall lizard is a common basker on the stony **walls** of towns and villages, as is the Moorish gecko.

Further south, the drier, scrub-covered slopes form an ideal habitat for the horseshoe snake (which can exceed 2m in length) and the Montpelier snake, which feeds on birds and rats, as well as the Atlas agama and fringe-toed lizard.

Desert species include the Algerian sand lizard and the Berber skink, also known as the "sand fish", which inhabits the ergs and appears to "swim" through the sand. Morocco's one really poisonous reptile is the horned viper, only half a metre in length, which spends the days buried just below the surface of the sand and feeds by night on jerboas and lizards.

Mammals

Larger animal life in Morocco is dominated by the extensive nomadic herds of goats, sheep and camels which use the most inaccessible and barren patches of wilderness as seasonal grazing areas. One of the most impressive of the wild mammals, however, is the **Barbary ape** – in fact not a true ape but a Macaque monkey. These frequent the cedar forests south of Azrou in the Middle Atlas and can be seen on the ground foraging for food in the glades. Other inhabitants of the cedar forest include **wild boar** and **red fox**. A speciality of the Oued Souss, outside Agadir, is the **common otter**; this is now a rare species in Morocco and can only be seen with considerable patience and some fortune.

The majority of the smaller mammals in Morocco live south of the Atlas ranges in the *hammada*, where the ever-present problem of water conservation plays a major role in the lifestyle of its inhabitants. Larger herbivores include the **Edmi gazelle** and the smaller, and rarer, **Addax antelope,** which graze the thorn bushes and dried grasses to obtain their moisture. Many of the desert varieties reduce the problems of body temperature regulation by adopting a nocturnal lifestyle. Typical exponents of this strategy are the **desert hedgehog** and numerous small rodents such as the **jerboa**. A common predator of the jerboa is the **fennec** (desert fox), whose characteristic large ears are used for both directional hearing (invaluable as a nocturnal hunter) and heat radiation to aid body cooling.

An oddity, found in the Djebel Toubkal area of the High Atlas, is the African **elephant shrew** – a fascinating, mouse-like creature with an elephantine trunk.

Insects and arachnids

Over a hundred species of **butterflies** have been recorded, predominantly in the Middle and High Atlas ranges and are seen from April onwards. The Atlas also witnesses one of the world's most extraordinary butterfly migrations in spring, when waves of painted ladies and Bath whites pass through, having crossed the Sahara from West Africa, en route across the Bay of Biscay to the west of England. Other common groups include grasshoppers, crickets and locusts. In the High Atlas, praying mantis may be seen.

There are three main groups of **arachnids** in Morocco – scorpions, camel spiders and spiders. Scorpions are nocturnal, hiding under suitable covered depressions during the day such as rocks and boulders (or rucksacks and shoes). Some Moroccan species are poisonous (see p.68) but most are harmless and unlikely to sting unless provoked. Camel spiders (or wind-scorpions) lack a poisonous tail but possess huge jaws with which they catch their main source of prey – scorpions. In the Atlas it is possible to see several small species of tarantula (not the hairy South American variety) and the white orb-web spider *Argiope lobata*.

Moroccan music

Traditional music, both folk and classical, remains very much a part of life, evident at every celebration. Every popular or religious festival involves musicians, and the larger **moussems** (see p.52) are always good. Keep an eye out for cultural festivals, too, in particular the summer **Asilah Festival** (p.107), the **Essaouira Gnaoua Festival** (p.377), the **Marrakesh Festival of Popular Arts** (p.380), and the **Festival of Sacred Music** held at the end of May in **Fes** (p.235).

Berber music

Berber music predates the arrival of the Arabs in Morocco, and comes in three main categories: village music, ritual music and the music of professional musicians.

Village music is performed when men and women of a village assemble on festive occasions to dance and sing together. The best-known dances are the **ahouache**, in the western High Atlas, and the **ahidus**, performed by Chleuh Berbers in the eastern High Atlas. In each, drums (*bendirs*) and flute (*naï*) are the only instruments used. The dance begins with a chanted prayer, to which the dancers respond in chorus, the men and women gathered in a large ring in the open air, round the musicians. The *ahouache* is normally performed at night in the patio of the kasbah; the dance is so complicated that the musicians meet to prepare for it in a group called a *laamt* set up specially for the purpose. In the **bumzdi**, a variation on the *ahouache*, one or more soloists perform a series of poetic improvisations. Some of these soloists, such as **Raïs Ajmaa Lahcen** and **Raïs Ihya**, have a national reputation.

Ritual music is rarely absent from celebrations such as moussems or marriages. It may also be called upon to help deal with *djinn*, or evil spirits, or to encourage rainfall. Flutes and drums are usually the sole instruments, along with much rhythmic hand-clapping, although people may engage professional musicians for certain events.

The **professional musicians**, or *imdyazn*, of the Atlas mountains are itinerant, travelling during the summer, usually in groups of four. The leader of the group is called the *amydaz* or poet. He presents his poems, which are usually improvised and give news of national or world affairs, in the village square. The poet may be accompanied by one or two members of the group on drums and *rabab*, a single-string fiddle, and by a fourth player, known as the *bou oughanim*. This latter is the reed player, throwing out melodies on a double clarinet, and also acting as the group's clown. *Imdyazn* are found in many weekly souks in the Atlas.

Rwais

Groups of **Chleuh Berber** musicians, from the Souss Valley, are known as **rwais**. A *rwai* worthy of the name will not only know all the music for any particular celebration, but have its own repertoire of songs – commenting on current events – and be able to improvise. A *rwai* ensemble can be made up of a single-string *rabab*, one or two *lotars* (lutes) and sometimes *nakous* (cymbals), together with a number of singers. The leader of the group, the **raïs**, is in charge of the poetry, music and choreography of the performance. Fine clothes, jewels and elaborate gestures also have an important part to play in this ancient rural form of musical theatre.

A **rwai performance** will start with the *astara*, an instrumental prelude, played on *rabab*, giving the basic notes of the melodies that follow (this also makes it possible for the other instruments to tune to the *rabab*). Then comes the *amarg*, the sung poetry which forms the heart of the piece. This is followed by the *ammussu*, which is a sort of choreographed overture; the *tamssust*, a lively song; the *aberdag*, or dance; and finally the *tabbayt*, a finale characterized by an acceleration in rhythm and an abrupt end. Apart from the *astara* and *tabbayt*, the elements of a performance may appear in a different order.

Andalous music

Morocco's classical music comes from the **Arab-Andaluscian tradition** and evolved in Muslim Spain, though its invention is usually credited to an outstanding musician from Baghdad called **Zyriab**. One of his greatest innovations was the founding of the classical suite called **nuba**, which forms what is now known as **Andalous music**, or **al-âla**. There are, in addition, two other classical traditions, **milhûn** and **gharnati**, each with a distinctive style and form. Andalous music is very popular and greatly loved; during Ramadan, nightly programmes of Andalous classics are broadcast on TV, and people without their own sets gather in cafés to watch them.

The nuba

Originally there were twenty-four **nuba** linked with the hours in the day, but only four full and seven fragmentary *nuba* have been preserved in the Moroccan tradition. Complete *nuba* last between six and seven hours and so are rarely performed in one sitting. Each *nuba* is divided into five main parts, or *mizan*, of differing durations. These five parts correspond to the five different rhythms used within a suite. If a whole *nuba* were being performed then these five rhythms would be used in order: the *basît* rhythm (6/4); *qaum wa nusf* rhythm (8/4); *darj* rhythm (4/4); *btâyhi* rhythm (8/4); and *quddâm* rhythm (3/4 or 6/8).

Traditionally each *mizan* begins with instrumental preludes – *bughya*, *m'shaliya* and *tuashia* – followed by a number of songs, the *sana'a*. There can be as many as twenty *sana'a* within a given *mizan* although for shorter performances an orchestra may only play three or four before going on to the next rhythm.

The words to many *sana'a* deal, though often obliquely, with subjects generally considered taboo in Islamic society like alcohol and sex – perhaps signifying archaic, pre-Islamic and nomadic roots – although others are religious, glorifying the Prophet and divine laws.

When the Arabs were driven out of Spain, which they had known as al-Andalus, the different musical schools were dispersed across Morocco. The school of Valencia was re-established in Fes, that of Granada in Toua and Chefchaouen. Today, the most famous **orchestras** are those of **Fes** (led by **Mohammed Briouel**), **Rabat** (led by **Haj Mohamed Toud**) and **Tetouan**. Many fans of Andalous music mourn the passing of the "golden age" in the 1970s and 1980s, when a trio of much lamented masters – **Abdelkrim Rais**, **Abdesadak Chekara** and **Moulay Ahmed Loukili** – led the Fes, Tetouan and Rabat orchestras.

A typical Andalous orchestra uses the following instruments: *rabab* (fiddle), *oud* (lute), *kamenjah* (violin-style instrument played vertically on the knee), *kanun* (zither), *darabouka* (metal or pottery goblet drums), and *taarija* (tambourine). Each orchestra has featured unusual instruments from time to time. Clarinets, flutes, banjos and pianos have all been used with varying degrees of success.

Milhûn

Milhûn is a semi-classical form of sung poetry. Musically it has many links with Andalous music, having adopted the same modes as *al-âla* orchestras, and, like them, it uses string instruments and percussion, though the result can be quite wild and danceable. Unlike Andalous music, which has always been the province of an educated elite, *milhûn* was originally the poetic expression of artisans and traders. Indeed, many of the great *milhûn* singers of the twentieth century began their lives as cobblers, tanners, bakers or doughnut sellers. The greatest *milhûn* composer was **Al-Thami Lamdaghri**, who died in 1856.

The *milhûn* suite comprises two parts: the *taqsim* (overture) and the *qassida* (sung poems). The *taqsim* is played on the *oud* or violin in free rhythm, and introduces the mode in which the piece is set. The *qassida* is divided into three parts: *al-aqsâm*, verses sung solo; *al-harba*, refrains sung by the chorus; and *al-drîdka*, a chorus where the rhythm gathers speed and eventually announces the end of the piece. The words of the *qassida* can be taken from anywhere – folk poetry, mystical poems or nonsense lines used for rhythm.

A **milhûn orchestra** generally consists of *oud*, *kamenjah*, *swisen* (a small, high-pitched folk lute related to the *gimbri*), the *hadjouj* (a bass version of the *swisen*), *taarija*, *darabouka* and *handqa* (small brass cymbals), plus a number of **singers**. The most renowned *milhûn* singer of recent times was **Hadj Lhocine Toulali**, who dominated the vibrant *milhûn* scene in the city of Meknes for many decades before his death in 1999. Contemporary singers of note include **Abdelkrim and Saïd Guennoun** of Fes, **Haj Husseïn** and **Abdallah Ramdani** of Meknes, **Muhammad Berrahal** and **Muhammad Bensaïd** of Salé, and the brothers **Mohammed and Ahmed Amenzou** from Marrakesh. In the past ten or so years, some female singers have become stars, including Touria Hadraoui (who is also a novelist) and Sanaa Marahati, whom many consider the future of *milhûn*.

Gharnati

Gharnati, the third music of Arab–Andalucian tradition, derives from the Arabic name of the Andalucian city of Granada. It is mainly played in Algeria, but Rabat, and Oujda are centres for it in Morocco. As with *al-âla*, it is arranged in suites or *nuba*, of which there are twelve complete and four unfinished suites. The *gharnati* orchestra consists of plucked and bowed instruments together with percussion: the usual *ouds* and *kamenjahs* supplemented by the addition of banjo, mandolin and Algerian lute or *kwîtra*.

Brotherhoods and Trance music

Among the **Sufi brotherhoods**, music is seen as a means of getting closer to Allah by reaching a trance-like state of mystical ecstasy. In a private nocturnal ceremony called the *hadra*, Sufis may attain this by chanting the name of Allah or dancing in a ring holding hands. The songs and music are irregular in rhythm, and quicken to an abrupt end. Some brotherhoods play for alms in households that want to gain the favour of their patron saint.

The best known Moroccan brotherhood is the **Gnaoua** – whose members are descendants of slaves from across the Sahara. They claim spiritual descent from **Sidi Bilal**, an Ethiopian who was the Prophet's first *muezzin*. Gnaoua ceremonies are often held to placate spirits, good and evil, who are inhabiting a person or place. They are often called in cases of mental disturbance or to help treat someone stung by a scorpion. These rites have their origins in sub-Saharan Africa, and African influence is evident in the music. The main instrument, the *ginbri* or *sentir*, is a long-necked lute almost identical to instruments from West Africa. The other characteristic sound of Gnaoua music is the *garagab*, a pair of metal castanets. Each Gnaoua troupe is lead by a *ma'alem*, or "master", who plays the *ginbri* and sings the lead vocal parts. The ceremonial part of the proceedings is usually led by a female *mogadema*, or "medium", who is mistress of the arcane spiritual knowledge and huge gallery of saints and spirits, both good and evil, that underpin and influence Gnaoui ritual. In recent decades Gnaoua music has been blended with jazz, rock, funk, hip hop and even drum n' bass. Essaouira holds an annual festival dedicated to Gnaoua music (see p.337).

Jilala are another brotherhood – the devotees of **Moulay Abdelkader Jilal**. Their music is perhaps even more hypnotic and mysterious than that of the Gnaoua and sometimes seems to come from a different plane of existence. The plaintive cycling flute (*qsbah*) and mesmeric beats of the *bendir* (frame drums) carry you forward unconsciously. While in a trance, Jilala devotees can withstand the touch of burning coals or the deep slashes of a Moroccan dagger, afterwards showing no injury or pain.

Other Sufi brotherhoods still practising their own brand of psychic-musical healing in various parts of Morocco include the **Hamadja**, followers of Sidi Ben Ali Hamduj and Sidi Ahmed Dghughi, two saints who lived at the end of the eighteenth century, and the **Aissaoua** from Meknes, who venerate the sixteenth century holy man Sidi Mohamed Ben Aïssa. The boundaries between these different brotherhoods are often quite blurred, and they tend to hold a common veneration for many saints and spirits, prominent amongst whom is the fiendish female *djinn* Aisha Kandisha.

Chaabi – Morocco's pop music

Chaabi simply means "popular" music – which covers a huge mix of styles, just as it does in the west. More or less since the advent of radio, the whole Arab world has listened to **Egyptian popular songs**. The tradition is epitomized by Umm Kulthum (Oum Khalsoum) and Mohammed Abdalwahab. but Morocco has added names of its own to the tradition, in particular **Houcine Slaoui** (in the 1940s), and in the following decades, **Ahmed Bidaoui**, **Abdelhadi Belkhayat** and **Abdelwahab Doukkali**. These stars tended to record in Cairo or Beirut, and their music – and language – is essentially Egyptian. The most recent star in this vein is the singer **Samira Saïd**, who is hugely popular around the Arab world, and has recorded with *raï* singer Cheb Khaled.

Al'aïta

The oldest of Morocco's own *chaabi* styles is **al'aïta**, the music of the Arabic-speaking rural populations of Morocco's Atlantic coast. It is performed at private and public celebrations, as well as in concert, and is usually sung in Darija (Moroccan colloquial Arabic). Its songs tell of love, loss, lust and the realities of daily life. They begin with a *lafrash*, a slow instrumental prelude (usually played on the violin), then move into free rhythm verses before shifting gear for the finale or *leseb*, which is often twice the speed of the song and forms a background for syncopated clapping, shouting and dancing. An al'aïta ensemble usually consists of a male or female vocalist, a violinist, and several percussionists and backing singers, though some groups add a *lotar*. Stars over the years have included the singers **Bouchaïb el Bidaoui** and **Fatna bent Lhoucine**, and the (literally) six-fingered violinist, **Abdelaziz Staati**. In the 1990s, an electric style of al'aïta developed, adding keyboards, electric guitars and drum machines. This is still very popular and is the music you most often hear blasting out of stalls in Casablanca or Rabat. Top artists include **Orchestre Jedouane**, **Orchestre Senhaji**, **Khalid Bennani** and **Moustapha Bourgogne**.

Chaabi groups

During the 1970s, a more sophisticated Moroccan *chaabi* began to emerge, using *hadjuj* (bass *ginbri*), lute and *bendir* percussion, along with bouzoukis and electric guitars, to combine Berber music with elements of Arab *milhûn*, Sufi and Gnaoua ritual music, western rock and reggae. More recently, rap has had a huge influence. The songs were often political, carrying messages that got their authors into trouble with the authorities – even jailed. The leading lights in this movement were **Nass el Ghiwane**, **Jil Jilala** and **Lemchaheb**. The music was hugely influential in the development of **raï music** in neighbouring Algeria, where *raï* singers like Khaled, Cheb Mami, Chaba Fadela and Chaba Sahraoui emerged in the 1980s.

In the 1980s, another wave of *chaabi* groups emerged, based in Marrakesh and employing Gnaoua rhythms. One of the most successful of these has been **Muluk El Hwa** (Demon of Love), a group of Berbers who used to play in Marrakesh's Djemaa El Fna. By far the most popular of the Berber *chaabi* singers, however, is singer **Najat Aatabou**, whose sensational debut, *J'en ai marre* (I am sick of it), sold 450,000 copies – many of them in France. Each of her subsequent recordings have sold more than half-a-million copies, and she is now a huge star throughout the Maghreb and can fill large venues in Europe. By contrast, in the 1990s, a much more hedonistic and poppy breed of *chaabi* artist came to the fore, to whom good times are as important as social or political commentary. Pre-eminent amongst this younger generation of popsters is the singer and violinist **Mustapha Bourgogne**.

Fusion and imported genres

Morocco is an ideal starting point for all kinds of fusion experiments. From the 1960s on, such disparate figures as Brian Jones, Ornette Coleman, Jimi Hendrix, Robin Williamson, John Renbourn and Pharaoh Sanders have been attracted by its rhythms, and in recent decades collaborations have come thick and fast. One of the earliest attempts to combine Moroccan music with European electronic sounds was made by the German group **Dissidenten** in the 1980s. Since then all manner of Moroccan sounds have been successfully blended with reggae, funk, hip-hop, house and drum n' bass by groups like **Gnawa Diffusion** and **Gnawa N'joum Experience**

Folk instruments

The most common **stringed instrument** is the **ginbri**, an African lute whose soundbox is covered in front by a piece of hide. The rounded, fretless stem has two or three strings. The body of the smaller treble *ginbri* is pear-shaped, that of the bass *ginbri* (*hadjuj* or *sentir*) rectangular. The Gnaoui often put a resonator at the end of the stem to produce the buzz typical of Black African music. The **lotar** is another type of lute, used by Chleuh Berbers. It has a circular body, also closed with a piece of skin, and three or four strings which are plucked with a plectrum. The classic Arab lute, the **oud**, is used in classical orchestras and the traditional Arab orchestras known as *takhts*. Its pear-shaped body is covered by a piece of wood with two or three rosette-shaped openings. It has a short, fretless stem and six strings, five double and one single. The most popular stringed instruments played with a bow are the **kamanjeh** and the **rabab**. The former is an Iranian violin which was adopted by the Arabs. Its present Moroccan character owes a lot to the Western violin, though it is held vertically, supported on the knees. The *rabab* is a spike fiddle, rather like a viol. The bottom half of its long, curved body is covered in hide, the top in wood with a rosette-shaped opening. It has two strings. The Chleuh Berbers use an archaic single-stringed *rabab* with a square stem and soundbox covered entirely in skin. Lastly, there is the **kanum**, a trapezoidal Arab zither with over seventy strings, grouped in threes and plucked with plectra attached to the fingernails. It is used almost exclusively in classical music.

Rapid hand-clapping and the clashes of bells and cymbals are only part of the vast repertoire of Moroccan **percussion**. Like most Moroccan drums the **darbuka** is made of clay, shaped into a cylinder swelling out slightly at the top. The single skin is beaten with both hands. It is used in both folk and classical music. The **taarija**, a smaller version of the *darbuka*, is held in one hand and beaten with the other. Then there are treble and bass **tan-tan** bongos, and the Moorish **guedra**, a large drum which rests on the ground. There is also a round wooden drum with skins on both sides called a **tabl**, which is beaten with a stick on one side and by hand on the other. This is used only in folk music. As for **tambourines**, the ever-popular **bendir** is round and wooden, 40 or 50cm across, with two strings stretched under its single skin to produce a buzzing sound. The **tar** is smaller, with two rings of metal discs round the frame and no strings under its skin. The **duff** is a double-sided tambourine, often square in shape, which has to be supported so that it can be beaten with both hands. Only two percussion instruments are made of metal: **karkabat**, also known as *krakesh* or *karakab*, double castanets used by the Gnaoui, and the **nakous**, a small cymbal played with two rods.

The **Arab flute**, known by different tribes as the *nai*, *talawat*, *nira* or *gasba*, is made of a straight piece of cane open at both ends, with no mouthpiece and between five and seven holes, one at the back. It requires a great deal of skill to play it properly, by blowing at a slight angle. The **ghaita** or *rhaita*, a type of oboe popular under various names throughout the Muslim world, is a conical pipe made of hardwood, ending in a bell often made of metal. Its double-reeded mouthpiece is encircled by a broad ring on which the player rests his lips in order to produce the circular breathing needed to obtain a continuous note. It has between seven and nine holes, one at the back. The **aghanin** is a double clarinet, identical to the Arab *arghoul*. It consists of two parallel pipes of wood or cane, each with a single-reed mouthpiece, five holes and a horn at the end for amplification.

from France, **Gnawa Impulse** from Germany, and **MoMo** from London. UK-based Moroccan-born producer **U-cef** has also been a pioneer in this field, while in Belgium the madcap Flemish globetrotters **Think Of One** have recorded enjoyable, accessible and authentic Moroccan music with a number of Moroccan musicians, notably the Marrakesh-based female trio, **Bnet Houaryet**.

Bill Laswell has been involved in production work with the group **Aisha Kandisha's Jarring Effects** (or AKJE), who mix Moroccan trance sounds with rock, hip-hop and techno. They released an amazing debut CD, *Buya*, in 1991 on the Swiss Barbarity label, and followed up with a techno-driven, Laswell production, *Shabeesation*. They are only known on a subterranean level in Morocco and are yet to perform or release a cassette at home. Their name refers to a female spirit, whose very mention is taboo, and their lyrics question Moroccan social and religious norms.

Some other Moroccan fusionistas of note are: the long-haired rocker **Houssaine Kili**, who is based in Germany; blues fanatic **Majid Bekkas;** the accomplished and outward-looking **Nass Marrakech**, who seem to be able to mix all manner of sounds in their Gnaoui-influenced pot; and the blind *oud* player **Hassan Erraji**, now living in Wales.

Hip-hop is immensely popular in Morocco, as throughout Africa. The homegrown scene is still largely underground, though the most popular crews – **H-Kayne** from Meknes and **Fnaïre** from Marrakesh – have some national visibility. Hipsters in Casablanca, Rabat and Agadir have also become fond of **House, R&B and funk**, and the desert near Ouarzazate has hosted massive raves. **Heavy metal** is also burgeoning, but in 2003 the authorities imprisoned members of the heavy metal bands **Nekros**, **Infected Brain** and **Reborn**, along with five of their fans, on charges of moral depravity and playing "anti-Islamic" music.

Moroccan raï

Raï – the word means "opinion", "outlook" or "point of view" – originated in the western Algerian region around the port of Oran. It has traditional roots in Bedouin music, with its distinctive refrain (*ha-ya-raï*), but as a modern phenomenon has more in common with Western music. The backing is now solidly electric, with rhythm guitars, synthesizers and usually a rock drum kit as well as traditional drums. Its lyrics reflect highly contemporary concerns – cars, sex, sometimes alcohol – which have created some friction with the authorities.

Moroccans have taken easily to the music, especially in the northeastern part of the country around the towns of Oujda and Al Hoceima, an area that shares the same cultural roots as the province of Oran over the border in Algeria, where *raï* was born. Home-grown *raï* stars include **Cheb Khader, Cheb Mimoun** and the superb **Cheb Djellal**, a pop-*raï* legend from Oujda whose recordings are well worth seeking out. **Sawt El Atlas** have also made huge strides with a poppy *raï*-flavoured sound and have sold handsome amounts of CDs in their adopted home of France. *Raï* influence can also be heard in the sound of folk artists like **Rachid Briha** and **Hamid M'Rabati**, from the Oujda region.

Discography

Most record stores in Britain or the US with a decent World Music section should yield at least a few discs of ethnic, folk and Andalous music, or fusion with European groups. In Morocco itself, cassettes are still dominant.

Compilations

Various *Morocco: Crossroads of Time* (Ellipsis Arts, US). An excellent introduction to Moroccan music that comes with a well-designed and informative book. The disc includes everything from ambient sounds in the Fes Medina, to powerful Jilala and Gnaoua music, andalous, *rwai*, Berber, and some good contemporary pop from Nouamane Lahlou.

Various *The Rough Guide to the Music of Morocco* (World Music Network, UK). This Rough Guide's release focuses on contemporary Moroccan sounds, featuring selections from the Amenzou Ensemble, Nass El Ghiwane, Nass Marrakech, Jil Jilala, Mustapha Bourgogne, Bnet Marrakech and U-cef. It is backed up by fulsome liner notes.

Various *Anthologie de la Musique Marocaine* (Ministère de la Culture, Morocco). These four boxed sets (with a total of 31 CDs) cover most bases in Moroccan folk and traditional music. All include liner notes in French and Arabic and can be purchased at the Ministry of Culture in Rabat.

Classical/Andalous

Ensemble Amenzou *Le malhûn à Marrakech* (Institut du Monde Arabe, France). The Amenzou brothers belong to a revered dynasty of *milhûn* singers and their energetic, youthful approach to the genre is much admired.

El Hadj Houcine Toulali *Le malhûn de Meknes* (Institut du Monde Arabe, France). A fine live recording of the great *milhûn* master on top form.

Ihsan Rmiki *Al-Samâa: Ecstatic Spiritual Audition* (Institut du Monde Arabe, France). Rmiki is the new voice of andalous music – and this is a moving set, her voice leading a six-person ensemble.

Orchestre Moulay Ahmed Loukili de Rabat *Nuba Al-'Ushshâq* (Inédit, France). This expensive six-CD box is not for the casual – but quite an experience, finely presented with informative notes.

Ustad Massano Tazi *Musique Classique Andalouse de Fes* (Ocora, France). Again, beautifully recorded and presented. Includes Nuba Hijaz Al-Kabir and Nuba Istihilal.

Various *Maroc: Anthologie d'Al-Melhûn* (Maison des Cultures du Monde, France). A three-CD set containing performances from many of Morocco's finest *milhûn* singers. An excellent introduction.

Berber music

Compagnies musicales du Tafilalet *The Call of the Oasis* (Institut du Monde Arabe, France). Sublime recordings from the edge of the Sahara, showcasing four groups recorded live at a festival in Erfoud.

Hmaoui Abd El-Hamid *La Flûte de l'Atlas* (Arion, France). Hypnotic and haunting flute-like ney, backed by percussion, *oud* and zither.

Les Imazighen *Chants du Moyen-Atlas* (Institut du Monde Arabe, France). A fantastic live recording of musicians from the Middle Atlas, full of power and extravagant emotion.

Muluk el Hwa *Xara Al-Andalus* (Erde Records, Germany). A collaboration between this acoustic Berber band and the Spanish group Al Tall, fusing medieval Valencian music and Arabic poetry from Andalucía.

Gnaoua and trance

Les Aissawa de Fes *Trance Ritual* (L'Institut du Monde Arabe, France). Entrancing and intricate music from the Aissawa brotherhood of Fes.

Gnawa Njoum Experience (Night and Day, France) One the most successful fusions of trad Gnaoua with modern day electronica. Sounds especially majestic in a club setting.

Maleem Mahmoud Ghania with Pharaoh Sanders *The Trance of the Seven Colours* (Axiom/Island, US) Gnaoua-jazz crossover, featuring the great sax player from Coltrane's band.

The Master Musicians of Jajouka *Apocalypse Across the Sky* (Axiom, UK). The power and clarity of these remarkable performers stands out on this Bill Laswell production.

Various *Gnawa Night – Music of the Marrakesh Spirit Masters* (Axiom, UK). Gnaoua music at its evocative best, again recorded by Bill Laswell.

Various *Moroccan Trance Music* (Sub Rosa, Belgium). Not for the faint-hearted, this is intense Gnaoua and Jilala music, combined on the disc with some of Paul Bowles' personal recordings.

Chaabi

Najat Aatabou *The Voice of the Atlas* (GlobeStyle, UK). A superb collection of some of Najat's best-loved songs, including "Shouffi Rhirou" which has been covered brilliantly by the 3Mustaphas3.

Bnet Marrakech *Chama'a* (L'empreinte Digitale, France). A legendary women's group from Houara in their favoured unstoppable freight-train mode. Powerful to say the least.

Jil Jilala *Chama'a* (Blue Silver, France). A classic early recording of the seminal *chaabi* rockers, which was only available on cassette until very recently. The title track "Chama'a" ("candle") is an old *milhûn* song which is given a very moody and edgy modern makeover.

Nass el Ghiwane *Maroc: Chants d'Espoir* (Créon Music, France). Many recordings by the "Rolling Stones of North Africa" are marred by atrocious sound quality. This set however captures them razor sharp and passionate and it includes their moving nine-minute long tribute to victims of the Sabra and Chatila massacres in Lebanon.

Contemporary and fusion

Aisha Kandisha's Jarring Effects *El Buya* (Barbarity, Switzerland). An intoxicating mix of Moroccan melodies and traditional string instruments with scratching reverb and rushes of industrial noise.

Yosefa Dahari *Yosefa* (Worldly Dance, UK). Just what the label says: dance music with English and Maghrebi songs. A bit of an exotica product but one with promise.

Houssaine Kili *Mountain to Mohammed* (Tropical Music, France). How Morrocan music sounds when reworked by an inveterate Neil Young fan... some great contemporary Maghrebi rock.

Nass Marrakech *Bouderbala* (World Village, USA). A curious mix of styles on a vaguely gnaoui foundation, with some excellent songs and innovative arrangements.

Sephardic music

Moroccan Jews, many of whom have now emigrated to Israel, left an important legacy in the north of the country, where their songs and ballads continued to be sung in Ladino, the medieval Spanish spoken at the time of their expulsion from Spain five centuries ago. Apart from the narrative ballads, these were mainly songs of courtly love, as well as lullabies and biblical songs, usually accompanied on a tar. Rounder Records released a two-CD set of Paul Bowles' rousing recordings of Moroccan Jewish liturgy, which transport you into the heart of what was once a vibrant subculture but is now, sadly, almost extinct in Morocco.

Moroccan Jewry also produced a great classical Arabic singer, Samy el Maghribi, who was born in Safi in 1922. Inspired by the Algerian singer Say el Hilali, he was one of the most appreciated Arabic singers of the 1950s. In 1960 he moved to Canada and in later years devoted himself to a liturgical repertoire. Moroccan Sephardic traditions and music continue to thrive in Israel, the best known names including Albert Bouhadanna and Rabat-born Emil Zrihan, whose music mixes Arab and Andalucian influences with the Hebrew liturgy.

Juan Peña Lebrijano and the Orquesta Andalusi de Tanger *Encuentros* (GlobeStyle, UK). A stunning cross-cultural blend that combines the passion of flamenco with the beauty and grace of andalous music.

MoMo *The Birth Of Dar* (Apartment 22, UK). House-flavoured Moroccan madness with a heavy dance beat. *Dar* means "house" in Arabic…you get the picture.

Sawt El Atlas *Donia* (Small/Sony Music, France). Unapologetically pop and *raï*-flavoured tunes from one of the most popular contemporary Moroccan groups in France.

Think of One *Marrakech Emballages Ensemble* (De Beek, Belgium). This remarkable Belgian band collaborated with a Marrakesh-based group, Bnet Houaryet, to produce one of the most accessible and authentic Moroccan crossover albums.

U-cef *Halalium* (Apartment 22, UK). A Moroccan producer based in London who fuses the roughneck sounds of the English capital with traditional *chaabi* and Gnaoua, often to wondrous effect.

Jewish Moroccan music

Samy el Maghribi (Club du Disque Arabe, France) A collection of old recordings by this legendary Jewish musician whose pride of place in the annals of Moroccan music proves what a big influence Jews once had on urban music.

Various *Sacred music of the Moroccan Jews* (Rounder Select, USA). Haunting recordings from 1959 of Jewish liturgies from Essaouira and Meknes made by Paul Bowles.

Books

There is a wealth of books about Morocco, set in Morocco, or by Moroccans, and you won't regret having one or two along on a trip. The main internet bookstores – **Amazon** in particular (try both US and UK sites) – are likely to yield the highest returns on the more esoteric recommendations below, while **abebooks.com** is good for those out of print (o/p in our listings). You might also want to try the UK-based **Maghreb Bookshop**, 45 Burton St, London WC1 (Ⓣ020/7388 1840, Ⓦwww.maghrebbookshop.com), which supplies current, out-of-print and rare books on all aspects of North Africa, and will ship worldwide.

General and travel

Edmondo de Amicis *Morocco: Its People and Places* (1882). Intrepid journeying through Morocco in an era when few Europeans travelled beyond Tangier or the coast. Illustrated with copious line drawings.

Paul Bowles *Points in Time, Their Heads Are Green*. Novelist, poet and composer Paul Bowles (1910–99) lived in Tangier for half a century and, more or less single-handedly, brought translations of local writers to Western attention (see p.606). These two books of his own are superb. *Points* is a series of tales and short pieces inspired by episodes and sources from earliest times to the present day. *Heads* includes a couple of travel essays on Morocco and a terrific piece on the psychology of desert travel.

Elias Canetti *The Voices of Marrakesh*. A small, compelling volume of impressions of Marrakesh in the last years of French rule, by the Nobel prize-winning author. The atmosphere of many pieces still holds

R.B. Cunninghame Graham *Mogreb-El-Acksa: A Journey in Morocco* (1898). Fin-de-siècle adventuring and anecdotes, the most interesting of which is an enforced stay in a caidal kasbah in the High Atlas (Graham's host did not understand the motive of "curiosity").

Nina Epton *Saints and Sorcerers* (1958, o/p). A very readable – and inquiring – travelogue, concentrating on folk customs and religious sects and confraternities in the 1950s.

Walter Harris *Morocco That Was*. Harris, *Times* correspondent in Tangier from the 1890s until his death in 1933, saw the country at probably the strangest ever stage in its history – the last years of "Old Morocco" in its feudal isolation and the first of French occupation. *Morocco That Was*, first published in 1921, is a masterpiece – alternately sharp, melodramatic and very funny. It incorporates, to some extent, the anecdotes in his earlier *Land of an African Sultan* (1889, o/p) and *Tafilet* (1895, o/p).

Orin Hargraves *Culture Shock! Morocco*. Hargraves worked in Morocco in the 1980s as a Peace Corps volunteer and this valuable paperback, revised in 2007, is a distillation of his experience, supported by an impressive range of research and, clearly, a lot of conversations throughout the country. He offers perceptive accounts of almost every aspect of contemporary Moroccan life, along with a good overview of history and religion, and an instructive section of dos and don'ts.

John Hopkins *Tangier Journals 1962–79* (1997). Highly entertaining journals of Tangier life – and travels across Morocco – from an American novelist, resident in Tangier during the Beat years. Paul and Jane Bowles and William Burroughs all figure large in the diary entries.

Peter Mayne *A Year in Marrakesh*. Mayne went to Marrakesh in the early 1950s, found a house in an ordinary district of the Medina, and tried to live like a Moroccan. He couldn't, but wrote an unusually perceptive account explaining why.

Budgett Meakin *The Land of the Moors* (1900), *The Moors: A Comprehensive Description* (1902, o/p). These wonderful encyclopedic volumes were the first really detailed books on Morocco and Moroccan life. Many of Meakin's "Comprehensive Descriptions" remain accurate and the sheer breadth of his knowledge – from "Berber Feuds" to "Specimen Recipes" and musical notations of "Calls to Prayer" – is fascinating in itself.

Barnaby Rogerson (ed.) *Marrakech Through Writers' Eyes* . A feast of an anthology, ranging from the earliest accounts, through eighteenth- and nineteenth-century explorers and envoys, to contemporary writers such as Esther Freud and Juan Goytisolo.

Antoine de Saint-Exupéry *Wind, Sand and Stars and Southern Mail*. Accounts by the French aviator (and author of the children's classic, *The Little Prince*) of his postal flights down to West Africa, by way of Cap Juby in the then Spanish Sahara. Stacy Shiff's biography, *Saint-Exupéry* is, if anything, even more gripping, taking the story through to Saint-Exupéry's disappearance flying for the Free French in 1944.

Tahir Shah *The Caliph's House*. This is a terrific read, good for anyone's holiday: a funny, eccentric and insightful look at Casablanca, and Morocco as a whole, through the narrative of buying and restoring a house in the city.

Jeffrey Tayler *Valley of the Casbahs*. Tayler set out, in 2001, on a journey to trace the Drâa valley from source to sea, on foot and by camel. His chief objective was to try to meet and understand the "Ruhhal" – the remaining desert nomads. The journey – one of the most compelling of modern accounts – left him by turns appalled and inspired.

Gordon West *By Bus to the Sahara* (1932, Black Swan, UK; o/p). This fascinating travelogue, reprinted in the 1990s but again out of print, describes a journey from Tangier to Rissani, as undertaken by the author and his wife, an amateur artist, coyly referred to as "the spirit". As a touristic insight into colonial Morocco, it is unique.

Edith Wharton *In Morocco* (1920). Wharton dedicated her book of travels in Morocco to General Lyautey, resident general of the Protectorate, whose modernizing efforts she greatly admired. By no means a classic, it is nonetheless worth reading for glimpses of harem life in the early years of the twentieth century.

History

J.M. Abun-Nasr *History of the Maghreb in the Islamic Period*. Morocco in the wider context of North Africa by a distinguished Arab historian.

Barnaby Rogerson *A Traveller's History of North Africa*. A good, up-to-date, general history, authoritative but very readable, covering not just Morocco, but also Tunisia, Algeria and Libya, which Rogerson sees as a kind of island, isolated by sea and desert, and thus set apart from Europe and sub-Saharan Africa.

E.V. Bovill *The Golden Trade of the Moors*. An account of the historic trans-Saharan caravan trade, and especially the routes between Morocco and Mali, and the influences of those countries on each other.

Moshe Gershovich *French Military Rule in Morocco: Colonialism and its Consequences*. A detailed but not overly academic study of the French colonial period. The reputation of General Lyautey, still seen in France as the embodiment of "enlightened colonialism", is severely reassessed.

Marvine Howe *Morocco: The Islamist Awakening and Other Challenges*. A former *New York Times* correspondent who had known the country since the 1950s, returns to live there in 1999. Her return coincides with the new king, Mohammed VI, and the rise of Islamic radicalism in the Arab world. She takes the story through to 2005.

Gavin Maxwell *Lords of the Atlas*. Drawing heavily on Walter Harris's accounts of the Moorish court (see p.601), this is the story of the Glaoui family – literally the "Lords" of the High Atlas, where they exercised almost complete control from the turn of the nineteenth century right through to Moroccan independence in 1956. Not an attractive tale but a compelling one, and superbly told. Originally published in 1966, it was republished in a superbly illustrated edition in 2000.

Giles Milton *White Gold – The Extraordinary Story of Thomas Pellow and North Africa's One Million European Slaves*. Milton tells a story as well as any popular historian – and this is quite a tale. Pellow was captured by Barbary pirates in 1715, aged eleven, and spent the next 23 years in Morocco, converting to Islam and becoming a commander in Sultan Moulay Ismail's slave army. Milton postulates that Pellow was one of a million Europeans enslaved in North Africa – a figure much higher than other historians have suggested.

C.R. Pennell *Morocco from Empire to Independence*. This is the first general history of modern Morocco. It covers the major strands of power but also the social and cultural life of ordinary Moroccans and is strong on the country's pressing contemporary concerns of poverty, drought, and worsening agricultural land.

Douglas Porch *The Conquest of Morocco*. Accessible and fascinating account of the extraordinary manoeuvrings and characters in Morocco at the turn of the twentieth century.

Susan Raven *Rome in Africa*. A well-illustrated survey of Roman (and Carthaginian) North Africa.

David Woolman *Rebels in the Rif* (o/p). An academic but fascinating study of the Riffian war in the 1920s and of the tribes' uprising against the Moroccan government in 1956.

Anthropology

Michael Brett and Elizabeth Fentress *The Berbers*. An overview of the Berber peoples of Morocco, Algeria and beyond, ranging through anthropology, history and literature.

Elizabeth Fernea *A Street in Marrakech*. A nicely written account of a woman anthropologist's study of and experiences in Marrakesh in the 1980s.

David Hart *Tribe and Society in Rural Morocco*. A collection of essays, dating from 1985 to 2000, around the themes of tribalism and Berber identity in Morocco. More accessible than it sounds, with titles such as *Scratch a Moroccan, Find a Berber*.

David A. McMurray *In and Out of Morocco*. McMurray is an American who based himself in Nador to study migrants and smugglers in this frontier boomtown. He unearths some fascinating material.

Fatima Mernissi *Doing Daily Battle: Interviews with Moroccan Women*. Eleven women – carpet weavers, rural and factory workers, teachers – talk about all aspects of their lives, from work and housing to marriage. A fascinating insight into a normally very private world.

Malika Oufkir and Michele Fitoussi *Stolen Lives: Twenty Years in a Desert Jail*. Bestselling account by the daughter of a general who was executed for his role in a 1973 coup attempt. As a result, she and her family were imprisoned for the next fifteen years.

Islam

The Koran (translated by Arthur J. Arberry, Oxford University Press; translated by J.M Rodwell, o/p but online at ⓦwww.gutenberg.org/etext/2800). The word of God as proclaimed by Mohammed is notoriously untranslatable. Arberry's version attempts to preserve its poetic beauty and retains the traditional arrangement of suras (according to their length). Rodwell's 1861 translation is a little dated, but provides analytical footnotes, and was originally arranged, as far as possible, in the order in which the suras were composed, making it easier to follow the development of ideas; unfortunately most modern editions of Rodwell's translation revert to the traditional order.

S.H. Nasr *Ideas and Realities of Islam*. A good general introduction.

Barnaby Rogerson *The Prophet Muhammad – A Biography* and *The Heirs to the Prophet*. Rogerson's gripping, modern biography of the Prophet could hardly be more timely. He captures a real sense of Mohammed's time and his struggles, as well as his historical and spiritual significance. The "sequel" carries the story forward to the split in Islam between Sunni and Shia.

Art, architecture and crafts

In addition to the recommendations below, a number of large, glossy books on Moroccan jewellery, gardens, paintings, manuscripts, carpets and buildings, usually with French texts, are to be found in most of the larger bookshops in Morocco.

Salma Damluji *Zillij: the Art of Moroccan Ceramics*. An expensive but beautifully illustrated study of the art of ceramic mosaic-work.

Lisl and Landt Dennis *Living in Morocco*. An entrancing picture study of Moroccan craft and domestic design, both traditional and modern.

James F. Jereb *Arts and Crafts of Morocco* (o/p). A fine introduction, with over 150 colour photographs.

Lisa Lovatt-Smith *Moroccan Interiors*. A coffee-table tome aimed at the interior design market, but goes beyond that in its coverage of traditional crafts, and traditional and modern architecture, with lots of gorgeous colour photographs.

Andre Paccard *Traditional Islamic Craft in Moroccan Architecture* (2 vols). Expensive coffee-table book written by an architect much favoured by King Hassan. The text is none too engaging but it is massively illustrated and – uniquely – includes photographs of Moroccan Royal Palaces currently in use.

Brook Pickering et al *Moroccan Carpets*. Edited by a New York collector and dealer, this is the best book on Moroccan carpets – a l arge format, fully illustrated guide, showing examples region by region.

Herbert Ypma *Morocco Modern*. A superbly illustrated book that traces the origins of the great artisan traditions of Morocco (weavers, woodworkers, potters, zellij-makers) and looks at the way contemporary designers and architects reinterpret these influences to create surprisingly modern work.

Photographs

Ann and Yann Arthus-Bertrand *Morocco Seen From The Air*. Be amazed at Moroccan cities, valleys, kasbahs, carpet souks captured from the air in this stunning, large-format book.

Hugues Demeude, Jacques Bravo, Xavier Richer *Morocco*. A magnificent assembly of photographs, published in 1998, and hard to beat (in quality and price) if you want a photo book to browse before or after a trip.

Abderrahman Slaoui *The Orientalist Poster* (Slaoui Foundation, Marrakesh). A fascinating selection from the Marrakesh Museum, depicting travel to and throughout Morocco in the early twentieth century.

Jean-Marc Tingaud and Tahar Ben Jelloun *Medinas: Morocco's Hidden Cities*. Wonderful photos of the mansions and palaces of Fes, Marrakesh and other cities, whose existence you could hardly imagine from the street outside. Tingaud's photos are accompanied by poems from the Moroccan novelist Ben Jelloun.

Food

Zette Guinaudeau *Traditional Moroccan Cooking: Recipes from Fez*. Madame Guinaudeau lived in Fes for over thirty years and first published her recipes in French in 1964. Now translated into English, they redress the imbalance of Robert Carrier's focus on Marrakesh cuisine.

Anissa Helou *Street Café Morocco*. This sumptuous book is the best of the many recent Moroccan cookery guides. It combines good recipe writing with colourful background – and stunning photography – on the food (from street snacks to haute cuisine) and its origins.

Paula Wolfert *Couscous and Other Good Food from Morocco*. This is a new edition of a book originally published in the 1960s, which at the time was groundbreaking in its emphasis on ordinary, rural cooking. Its recipes work and there's a nice line in anthropological background.

Moroccan fiction/biography

Translations by Paul Bowles

By far the largest (and finest) body of Moroccan fiction published in English is the translations by the American writer Paul Bowles, who lived in Tangier from the 1940s until his death in 1999, and also translated the first part of Mohammed Choukri's autobiography (see below). The short stories share a common fixation with intrigue and unexpected narrative twists, and are often punctuated by episodes of violence. None have particular characterization, though this hardly seems relevant as they have such a strong, vigorous narrative style – brilliantly matched by Bowles' sharp, economic language.

Driss Ben Hamed Charhadi *A Life Full of Holes*. Bowles' first Moroccan translation – in 1964 – a direct narrative of street life in Tangier. It was published under a pseudonym, the author being Larbi Layachi who, two decades later, published *Yesterday and Today*, a kind of sequel, describing in semi-fictionalized (and not very sympathetic) form his time with Paul and Jane Bowles.

Mohammed Mrabet *Love with a Few Hairs; The Boy Who Set the Fire & Other Stories; The Lemon; M'Hashish; The Chest; Marriage With Papers; The Big Mirror, Harmless Poisons, Blameless Sins; The Beach Café and The Voice; Look and Move On: An Autobiography*. Mohammed Mrabet's stories – *The Beach Café* is perhaps his best – are often *kif*-inspired, and this gives them a slightly paranoid quality, as Mrabet himself explained: "Give me twenty or thirty pipes… and an empty room can fill up with wonderful things, or terrible things. And the stories come from these things."

Other translations

Abdelkader Benali *Wedding by the Sea*. Moroccan magic realism, and an impressive debut novel by a Moroccan-born author living in the Netherlands since childhood. The story is about a young man who returns (from Holland) to his seaside village in Morocco for his sister's wedding, and during the festivities finds the bridegroom has made off to the local brothel. Sweet revenge lies in store from his sister.

Mahi Binebine *Welcome to Paradise*. Binebine grew up in Morocco, lived in America and has now settled in France, where he has become a significant novelist. This is his first book to be published in English and it is utterly engaging: a tale of life in the poorest areas of contemporary Morocco and the motivations that drive the country's boat people (and migrants from West Africa) to hand over all their savings to a trafficker to cross the Straits of Gibraltar and take their chances as illegals in Europe. Superbly translated and hugely evocative.

Mohamed Choukri *For Bread Alone* and *Streetwise*. Choukri's two-part autobiography (the first volume translated by Paul Bowles, the second by Ed Emery) ranks among the best works of contemporary Arabic literature. Born in the Rif, he moved with his family to Tangier at a time of great famine, spending his childhood in abject poverty. During his adolescence he worked for a time for a French family. He then returned to Tangier, where he experienced the violence of the 1952 independence riots. Throughout his adversities, two things shine through: Choukri's determination to use literacy to surmount his desperate circumstances; and his compassion for the normally despised human beings who share this life of "the lowest of the low".

Driss Chraibi *Heirs to the Past* (Heinemann, UK & US; o/p). A benchmark novel, written in French, this takes the crisis of Moroccans' post-colonial identity as its theme; it is semi-autobiographical as the author-narrator (who has lived in France since the war) returns to Morocco for the funeral of his father. A number of other Chraibi novels are also available in translation.

Fatima Mernissi *Dreams of Trespass: Tales of a Harem Girlhood*. Part fairy tale, part feminist manifesto, a mix of biographical narrative, stories and fantasies by a renowned Moroccan sociologist (author of *Doing Daily Battle*; see p.604), who was born in a Fes harem in 1940.

Tahar Ben Jelloun *The Sand Child* and *Corruption*. The best of around a dozen books by Ben Jelloun that have been translated into English. *The Sand Child*, which won the prestigious Prix Goncourt, is the tale of a girl brought up in southern Morocco as a boy in order to thwart Morocco's inheritance laws. *Corruption*, as its title suggests, explores the endemic corruption in contemporary Morocco, through the story of Mourad, the last honest man in the country, who attempts to stay clear of brown envelopes in Casablanca and Tangier.

Brick Ousaïd *Mountains Forgotten by God*. Autobiographical narrative of an Atlas Berber family, which gives an impressive sense of the harshness of mountain life. As the author describes it, it is "not an exercise in literary style [but] a cry from the bottom of my heart, of despair and revolt".

Foreign fiction set in Morocco

Once again, the late Paul Bowles is the outstanding figure in American and European fiction set in Morocco, so no apologies for splitting this section into "Bowles" and "Others". Though the "Others" do include a couple of gems.

Paul Bowles

NOVELS: *The Sheltering Sky*; *Let It Come Down*; *The Spider's House*.

STORIES: *Collected Stories of Paul Bowles 1939–76* gathers together work from numerous editions, as does the more selective *Collected Stories*. Post-1976 collections include *Midnight Mass* and *Unwelcome Words*.

Bowles is the most interesting and the most prolific foreign writer using North African themes, and many of his stories are similar in vein to those of Mohammed Mrabet (see opposite), employing the same sparse forms, bizarre twists and interjections of violence. The novels are something different, exploring both Morocco and the ways in which Westerners react to it. If you read nothing else on the country, at least get hold of *The Spider's House* – one of the best political novels ever written, its backdrop the traditional daily life of Fes, its theme the conflicts and transformation at the last stages of the French occupation of the country.

The best of the biographies and memoirs of Bowles and his literary friends and acquaintances in Tangier are:

Michelle Green *The Dream at the End of the World: Paul Bowles and the Literary Renegades of Tangier.* A strong narrative, compulsively peopled: the best read if you're looking for one book on Tangier literary life.

Paul Bowles *Without Stopping.* Bowles' autobiography is of interest for its Moroccan episodes (though William Burroughs wryly dubbed it "Without Telling"), as is his *Two Years Beside the Strait* (published in US as *Days: A Tangier Journal, 1987–89*).

Other fiction

William Burroughs *Naked Lunch.* Iconic Beat novel written in a Tangier hotel room in 1954–57, and published in France in 1959, though its brazen obscenity prevented publication in the US until 1962 and in the UK until 1964. The book is a confused series of nightmarish sex-and-drugs-obsessed tableaux dreamed up by Burroughs while withdrawing from a heroin habit. It isn't especially about Morocco, but Tangier features as "Interzone", and is undoubtedly the place to read it.

Aldo Busi *Sodomies in Eleven Point.* A (highly) picaresque tour of Morocco by the Italian novelist.

Elisa Chimenti *Tales and Legends of Morocco.* Travelling in the 1930s and 1940s with her father, personal physician to Sultan Moulay Hassan, Chimenti learned many of these simple, fable-like tales from Berber tribesmen whose guest she was.

Rafael Chirbes *Mimoun.* Compelling tale of a Spanish teacher, based south of Fes, adrift amid sexual adventures and bizarre local life and antagonisms.

Esther Freud *Hideous Kinky.* You've seen the film? Well read the book – it's even better. An English hippy takes her two daughters to Marrakesh, where they live simply, as locals. The narrative – funny, sad, and full of informed insights – is narrated by the 5-year-old.

Brion Gysin *The Process.* Beat novel by ex-Tangier resident and friend of Paul Bowles and William Burroughs. Fun, if a little caught in its zany 1960s epoch.

John Haylock *Body of Contention.* An enjoyable romp set amid the expat community of Tangier in the months following Independence in 1957.

John Hopkins *All I Wanted Was Company.* Another Tangier novel – this time a gossipy tale about an American and his lovers, one of whom disappears to the Sahara.

Jane Kramer *Honor to the Bride Like the Pigeon that Guards its Grain Under the Clove Tree* (1970, Farrar, Straus & Giroux, US; o/p). Fictional narrative based on the true story of a Berber woman's kidnap in Meknes.

Amin Malouf *Leo the African*; published in the US as *Leo Africanus.* Superb historical novel, re-creating the life of Leo Africanus, the fifteenth-century Moorish geographer, in Granada and Fes and on later travels.

Umberto Pasti *Age of Flowers.* An Italian novel, once again set in Tangier, with a decadent scene of writers and artists counterposed with the Islamicists taking control of the city.

Moroccan street names

Moroccan streets are often named after well-known historical figures, events and dates. Transliteration from Arabic into the Roman alphabet means that there are often many variations of the same name.

Abdelkrim El Kattabi Leader of the 1921–27 Rif war against the Spanish (see p.144).
Al Jamia Al Arabi The Arab League, founded in Egypt in 1945.
Allal Ben Abdallah House-painter from Guercif shot down in 1953 after driving an open-topped car into a royal procession and attacking France's puppet sultan Ben Arfa with a kitchen knife.
Al Massira Al Khadra/La Marche Verte The Green March of November 1975 to occupy the Western Sahara (see p.552).
Bir Anzarane Town in the Western Sahara and site of fierce 1979 battle between Morocco and the Polisario.
El Farabi Islamic philosopher (870–950) from Farab in Uzbekistan who tried to harmonize Greek philosophy with Islamic thinking.
El Houria Freedom.
El Mansour Eddahbi Saadian sultan 1578–1603 (see p.571).
F.A.R. (Forces Armées Royales) The armed forces.
Ferhat Hachad Tunisian trade union leader and Arab nationalist murdered in 1952 by extremist French settlers.
Hassan Ii King 1975–99.
Ibn Batouta Fourteenth-century Tanjawi traveller who visited China and India as well as most of the Islamic world.
Ibn Khaldoun Tunisian historian (1332–1406), who first proposed a cyclical view of history.
Ibn Rochd One of Islam's greatest philosophers (1126–98), also known as Averroes, who was based in Marrakesh and doctor to Yacoub el Mansour.
Ibn Toumert/Mehdi Ibn Toumert Founder of the Almohads (see p.408).
Ibn Zaidoun Eleventh-century Andalucian poet.
Istiqlal Independence; also the name of Morocco's first political party (see p.576).
Mohammed Ben Abdallah/ Sidi Mohammed Ben Abdallah Grandson of Moulay Ismail, sultan 1757–90.
Mohammed V Sultan and subsequently king 1927–53 and 1955–61 (see p.576).
Mohammed Vi King since 1999.
Mohammed Zerktouni Armed resistance leader, accused of killing twenty people in a 1953 bomb attack on Casablanca's central market, who took cyanide to avoid giving information under torture.
Mokhtar Soussi Poet and intellectual who inspired the nationalist movement during the French occupation.
Moulay Abdallah/Prince Moulay Abdallah Younger son of Mohammed V, brother of Hassan II.
Moulay El Cherif/Moulay Rachid First Alaouite sultan, ruled 1666–72 (see p.572).
Moulay Hassan/Hassan I Sultan 1873–94 (see 573).
Moulay Idriss Moulay Idriss I (788–91) or Moulay Idriss II (804–28), Morocco's first Arab rulers (see p.568).
Moulay Ismail Second Alaouite sultan (1672–1727) (see p.572).
Moulay Youssef French-appointed sultan (1912–27), brother of Moulay Hafid, father of Mohammed V and great-grandfather of Mohammed VI.

Moussa Ibn Noussar General who consolidated the Arab conquest of Morocco in the eighth century (see p.567).
Oqba Ibn Nafi Arab general who brought Islam to Morocco (see p.567).
Oued El Makhazine Site of the Battle of the Three Kings (see p.571).
Salah Eddine El Ayoubi Kurdish-born Islamic leader, known in English as Saladin, who ruled Egypt and Syria 1171–93, and recaptured Jerusalem from the Crusaders in 1187.
Tarik Ibn Ziad Berber chieftain who led the 711 Islamic invasion of Spain and gave his name to Gibraltar – Djebel (mount) Tarik.
Yacoub El Mansour Third Almohad sultan (1184–99) (see p.569).
Youssef Ibn Tachfine First Almoravid sultan (1062–1106) (see p.569).

Dates

January 11, 1944 The Istiqlal party issued a manifesto demanding independence.
February 29, 1960 The Agadir earthquake (see p.485).
March 2, 1956 French recognition of Moroccan independence.
August 16, 1953 Anti-French riots in Casablanca, Rabat, Marrakesh and Oujda.
August 20, 1953 Mohammed V was deposed by the French and exiled on the eve of Aïd el Kebir.
November 6, 1975 The Green March (see p.552).
November 16, 1955 Mohammed V's return from exile.
November 18, 1927 Mohammed V's accession to the throne.
November 18, 1955 Officially considered independence day (though full independence was achieved the following year).

Language

Language

Moroccan Arabic

Few people who come to Morocco learn to speak any Arabic, let alone anything of the country's three Berber languages, but you'll be treated very differently if you make even a small effort to master basic phrases.

If you can speak French, you'll be able to get by almost anywhere. Spanish is also useful, especially among older people in the former Spanish colonial zones around Tetouan and the Rif, and in Ifni, Tarfaya and the Western Sahara. People who have significant dealings with tourists will know some English, but that is still a small minority.

Moroccan Arabic

Moroccan Arabic, the country's official language, is substantially different from classical Arabic, or from the modern Arabic spoken in Egypt or the Gulf. If you speak any form of Arabic, however, you should be able to make yourself understood. Egyptian Arabic, in particular, is familiar to most Moroccans from TV soaps.

Pronunciation

There are no silent letters – you pronounce everything that's written including double vowels. Letters and syllables **in bold** should be stressed.

Here are some keys to follow:

kh	like the "ch" in Scottish lo**ch**
gh	like the French "r" (a slight gargling sound)
ai	as in "**eye**"
ay	as in "s**ay**"
ou/oua	w/wa (Essaouria is pronounced Essa-weera)
q	like "k" but further back in throat
j	like "s" in plea**s**ure

Arabic and French glossary

English	**Arabic**	French

Basics and everyday phrases

yes	**eyeh**, **na**am	oui
no	la	non
I	ena	moi
you (m/f)	enta/entee	vous
he	**hoo**wa	lui

she	**hee**ya	elle
we	**neh**noo	nous
they	hoom	ils/elles
(very) good	mez**yen** (b**zef**)	(très) bon
big	ke**beer**	grand
small	se**gheer**	petit
old	ke**deem**	vieux
new	je**deed**	nouveau
a little	**shwee**ya	un peu
a lot	b**zef**	beaucoup
open	mah**lul**	ouvert
closed	mas**dud**	fermé
hello/how's it going?	le **bes**?	ça va?
good morning	s**bah** l'**kheer**	bonjour
good evening	m**sa** l'**kheer**	bon soir
good night	**lei**la sa**ee**da	bonne nuit
goodbye	bise**lama**	au revoir
who...?	shkoon...?	qui...?
when...?	**im**ta...?	quand...?
why...?	a**lash**...?	pourquoi...?
how...?	ki**fesh**...?	comment...?
which/what...?	shnoo...?	quel...?
is there...?	kayn...?	est-ce qu'il y a...?
do you have...?	**an**dak...?/kayn...	avez-vous...?
please	**a**f**a**k/min**fad**lak *to a man* or **af**ik/min**fad**lik *to a woman*	s'il vous plaît
thank you	**shuk**ran	merci
ok/agreed	**wa**kha	d'accord
that's enough/that's all	**sa**fee	ça suffit
excuse me	is**mah**lee	excusez-moi
sorry/ I'm very sorry	is**mah**lee/ana **a**sif	pardon/je suis désolé
let's go	**nim**sheeyoo	on y va
go away	**im**shee	va t'en
I (m/f) don't understand	mafahemsh/mafahmash	je ne comprends pas
do you (m/f) speak English?	takelem/ta**kel**mna ing**lee**si?	parlez-vous anglais?

Directions

where's...?	fayn...?	où est...?
the airport	el ma**tar**	l'aeroport
the train station	ma**hat**tat el tren	la gare de train
bus station	ma**hat**tat el car	la gare routière
the bank	el bank	le banque
the hospital	el mos**tash**fa	l'hôpital
near/far (from here)	qu**rayab**/ba**eed** (min **hun**a)	près/loin (d'ici)
left	li**seer**	à gauche
right	li**meen**	à droit

straight ahead	**nee**shan	tout droit
here	hi**na**	ici
there	hi**nak**	là

Accommodation

hotel	**fun**duq	hôtel
do you have a room?	kayn beet?	avez-vous une chambre?
two beds	jooj **tlik**	deux lits
one big bed	**wa**had **tlik** ke**bir**	un grand lit
shower	doosh	douche
hot water	maa s**khoo**na	eau chaud
can I see?	**Mum**kin a**shoo**fha?	je peux le voir?
key	sa**rut**	clé

Shopping

I (don't) want...	**e**na (mish) b**gheet...**	je (ne) veux (pas)...
how much (money)?	sha**hal** (flooss)?	combien (d'argent)?
(that's) expensive	(**ha**da) **gha**lee	(c'est) cher

Numbers

0	٠	sifr	zéro
1	١	**wa**had	un
2	٢	jooj	deux
3	٣	**tla**ta	trois
4	٤	**ar**baa	quatre
5	٥	**kham**sa	cinq
6	٦	**sit**ta	six
7	٧	**seb**aa	sept
8	٨	te**man**ya	huit
9	٩	**tis**aoud	neuf
10	١٠	**ash**ra	dix
11	١١	ha**dash**ar	onze
12	١٢	et**nash**ar	douze
13	١٣	tala**tash**ar	treize
14	١٤	arba**tash**ar	quatorze
15	١٥	khams**tash**ar	quinze
16	١٦	sit**tash**ar	seize
17	١٨	seba**tash**ar	dix-sept
18	١٨	taman**tash**ar	dix-huit
19	١٩	tisa**tash**ar	dix-neuf
20	٢٠	ash**reen**	vingt
21	٢١	**wa**had wa ash**reen**	vingt-et-un
22	٢٢	jooj wa ash**reen**	vingt-deux
30	٣٠	tala**teen**	trente
40	٤٠	arba**een**	quarante

50	٥٠	kham**seen**	cinqante
60	٦٠	sit**teen**	soixante
70	٧٠	saba**een**	soixante-dix
80	٨٠	tama**neen**	quatre vingts
90	٩٠	tisa**een**	quatre-vingt-dix
100	١٠٠	mia	cent
121	١٢١	mia wa **wa**had wa ash**reen**	cent vingt-et-un
200	٢٠٠	mia**teen**	deux cents
300	٣٠٠	**tol**ta mia	trois cents
1000	١٠٠٠	alf	mille
a half		nuss	demi
a quarter		**rob**a	quart

Days and times

Monday	na**har** el it **neen**	lundi
Tuesday	na**har** et te**lat**	mardi
Wednesday	na**har** el **ar**baa	mercredi
Thursday	na**har** el khe**mis**	jeudi
Friday	na**har** el je**ma**a	vendredi
Saturday	na**har** es sabt	samedi
Sunday	na**har** el had	dimanche
yesterday	im**ba**rih	hier
today	el yoom	aujourd'hui
tomorrow	**ghe**da	demain
what time is it?	sha**hal** fisa'a?	quelle heure est-il?
one o'clock	sa'a **wah**da	une heure
2.15	jooj wa **ro**ba	deux heures et quart
3.30	**tla**ta wa nuss	trois heures et demi
4.45	**ar**baa ila **ro**ba	quatre heures moins quart

Food and drink

Basics

restaurant	**mat**aam	restaurant
breakfast	if**tar**	petit déjeuner
egg	beyd	ouef
butter	**zib**da	beurre
jam	marma**lad**	confiture
cheese	**jib**na	fromage
yoghurt	**ra**yeb	yaourt
salad	sa**la**ta	salade
olives	zi**toun**	olives
oil	zit	huile
bread	khobz	pain
salt	**mel**ha	sel

pepper	ha**roor**	piment
without	bi**lesh**	sans
sugar	**suk**kar	sucre
the bill	el hi**saab**	l'addition
fork	for**shaat**	fourchette
knife	mooss	couteau
spoon	malka	cuillère
plate	tab**seel**	assiete
glass	**kess**	verre
What do you have …	**Ash**noo **kane**…	Qu'est ce que vous avez…
…to eat?	…f'l-**mak**la?	…pour manger?
…to drink?	…f'l-mucha**r**oubat?	…pour boire?
What is this?	Shnoo **had**a?	Qu'est ce que c'est?
I (m/f) am a vegetarian	**a**na na**ba**ti/naba**ti**ya wa la a**ku**lu lehoum **wa**la hout	Je suis vegetarien/ vegetarienne
This is not what I asked for!	**He**dee **mesh**ee **hee**a **li tlubt**!	Ceci n'est pas ce que j'ai demandé
The bill, please.	El hi**saab**, min**fad**lik	L'addition s'il vous plaît
Please write it down.	Minfadlik, k**'tib'h**	Est-ce que vous pouvez l'écrite s'il vous plaît?

Meat, poultry and fish

meat	**la**hem	viande
beef	**baq**ri	boeuf
chicken	djaj	poulet
lamb	**hou**li	mouton
liver	**kib**da	foie
pigeon	**ham**am	pigeon
fish	hout	poisson
prawns	**qam**bri	crevettes

Vegetables

vegetables	khadra**wat**	légumes
artichoke	qoq	artichaut
aubergine	badin**jan**	aubergine
beans	**loo**bia	haricots
onions	**ba**sal	oignons
potatoes	ba**ta**ta	patates
tomatoes	ma**tee**sha	tomates

Fruits and nuts

almonds	looz	amandes
apple	tu**fah**	pomme
banana	ba**nan**	banane
dates	tmer	dattes
figs	ker**mooss**	figues

grapes	**ai**nab	raisins
lemon	li**moon**	limon
melon	bat**tikh**	melon
orange	li**moon**	orange
pomegranate	roo**man**	granade
prickly pear (cactus fruit)	hen**di**ya	figues de Barbarie
strawberry	fr**ow**la	fraise
watermelon	del**lah**	pastèque

Beverages

water	maa	de l'eau
mineral water	Sidi Ali/Sidi Harazem (brand names)	eau minérale
ice	je**lee**di	glace
ice cream	glace	glace
milk	ha**leeb**	lait
coffee	**qah**wa	café
coffee with a little milk	nuss nuss	café cassé
coffee with plenty of milk	qahwa bi ha**leeb**	café au lait/café crème
tea (with mint/with wormwood)	**a**tay (bi **na**na/ bi **shee**ba)	thé (à la menthe/ à l'absinthe)
juice	a**seer**	jus
beer	**bir**ra	bière
wine	sha**rab**	vin
almond milk	a**seer** looz	jus d'amande
apple milkshake	a**seer** tu**fah**	jus de pomme
banana milkshake	a**seer** ba**nan**	jus des bananes
orange juice	a**seer** li**moon**	jus d'orange
mixed fruit milkshake		jus panaché

Common dishes and foods

bisara	thick pea soup, usually served with olive oil and cumin
chakchouka	a vegetable stew not unlike ratatouille, though sometimes containing meat or eggs
couscous aux sept legumes	seven-vegetable couscous (sometimes vegetarian, though often made with meat stock)
harira	bean soup, usually also containing pasta and meat
kefta	minced meat (usually lamb)
loobia	bean stew
mechoui	roast lamb
merguez	small, spicy dark red sausages – typically lamb, though sometimes of beef – usually grilled over charcoal
pastilla	sweet pigeon or chicken pie with cinnamon and filo pastry; a speciality of Fes
(pommes) frites	French fries
salade Marocaine	salad of tomato and cucumber, finely chopped

tajine	a Moroccan casserole cooked over charcoal in a thick ceramic bowl (which is what the word really refers to) with a conical lid	**tajine aux olives et citron**	tajine of chicken with olive and preserved lemon
		tanjia	a Marrakshi speciality, jugged beef – the term in fact refers to the jug

Breads and pastries

briouats/ doits de Fatima	sweet filo pastry with a savoury filling, a bit like a miniature pastilla	**m'hencha**	almond-filled pastry coils, often covered in honey or syrup
briouats au miel	sweet filo pastry envelopes filed with nuts and honey	**millefeuille**	custard slice
cornes de gazelles (Fr.)/ kab l-ghazl (Ar.)	marzipan-filled, banana-shaped pastry horns	**msammen**	flat griddle bread made from dough sprinkled with oil, rolled out and folded over several times, rather like an Indian paratha
harsha	flat, leavened griddle bread with a gritty crust, served at cafés for breakast		

Berber words and phrases in Tashelhaït

There are three Berber languages, which encompass roughly geographical areas. They are known by several names, of which these are the most common:
Tarfit, Riffi – The Rif mountains (Northern Morocco)
Tamazight, Zaian – The Middle and High Atlas (Central Morocco)
Tashelhaït, **Soussi**, **Chleuh** – The Anti-Atlas and Souss Valley (southern Morocco)
As the most popular Berber areas for visitors are the High Atlas and South, the following is a very brief guide to **Tashelhaït words and phrases**.

Basics

Yes, no	Eyeh, Oho	**Tomorrow**	Sbah
Thank you, please	Barakalaufik	**Yesterday**	Eegdam
Good	Eefulkee/Eeshwa	**Excuse me**	Semhee
Bad	Khaib	**Berbers**	Shleuh
Today	Ghasad		

Greetings and farewells (All Arabic greetings understood)

Hello (response – la bes)	La bes darik (man) La bes darim (woman)
How are you?	Meneek antgeet? (response – la bes lmamdulah)
See you later	Akrawes dah inshallah
Goodbye	Akayaoon Arbee
Say hello to your family	Sellum flfamilenik

Directions and names on maps

Where is…?	Mani heela…?
…the road to…	…aghares s…
…the village…	…doowar…
…the river…	…aseet…
…the mountain…	…adrar…
…the pass…	…tizee…
…your house	…teegimeenik
Is it far/close?	Ees yagoog/eeqareb?
Straight	Neeshan
To the right/left	Fofaseenik/fozelmad
Where are you going?	Manee treet? (s.) Manee drem? (pl.)
I want to go to…	Reeh… (literally, "I want")

On survey maps you'll find these names:

Mountain	Adrar, Djebel
River	Assif, Oued
Pass (of)	Tizi (n.)
Shepherd's hut	Azib
Hill, small mountain	Aourir
Ravine	Talat
Rock	Azrou

("n" between words indicates the possessive, "of")

Buying and numbers

1	yen
2	seen
3	krad
4	koz
5	smoos
6	sddes
7	sa
8	tem
9	tza
10	mrawet
11	yen d mrawet
12	seen d mrawet
20	Ashreent
21	Ashreent d yen d mrawet
22	Ashreent d seen d mrawet
30	Ashreent d mrawet
40	Snet id ashreent
50	Snet id ashreent d mrawet
100	Smoost id ashreent/ meeya
How much is it?	Minshk aysker?
No good	oor eefulkee
Too expensive	Eeghula bzef
Come down a little (in price)	Nuqs emeek
Give me…	Feeyee…
I want …	Reeh…
Big/Small	Mqorn/Eemzee
A lot/little	Bzef/eemeek
Do you have…?	Ees daroon…?
Is there…?	Ees eela…?
…food	…teeremt
…a mule	…aserdon
…a place to sleep	…kra lblast mahengwen
…water	…amen

Imperatives you may hear

Sit	Gawer, Skoos	Here	Rede (when handing something to someone)
Drink	Soo		
Eat	Shta		

Arabic/Berber phrasebooks & learning materials

Arabic phrasebooks and dictionaries

Moroccan Arabic Phrasebook (Lonely Planet, Australia). The most functional English–Moroccan Arabic phrasebook.
Richard S. Harrell, Harvey Sobelman and Thomas Fox, *A Dictionary of Moroccan Arabic* (Georgetown UP). Two-way Arabic-English dictionary.

Arabic coursebooks

Ernest T. Abdel Massih, *An Introduction to Moroccan Arabic; Advanced Moroccan Arabic* (Michigan UP). Text-books with tapes, but now out of print.

Richard S. Harrell, Mohammed Abu Talib and William Carroll, *Basic Course in Moroccan Arabic* (Georgetown UP). Eleven CDs and a textbook.

Berber coursebooks

Ernest T. Abdel Massih, *A Course in Spoken Tamazight* (Michigan UP). A course-book with seven cassettes, out of print but can be found at a price. The same author's *A Reference Grammar of Tamazight* provides back-up.

Arabic lessons in Morocco

ALIF in Fes (see p.233), and the American Language Centre in Casablanca (ⓣ0522 277765, ⓦcasablanca.aca.org.ma).

Glossary

Adhan the call to prayer

Agadir fortified granary, where grain, dates, gunpowder and other valuables were kept safe during times of inter-clan conflict

Agdal garden or park containing a pool

Aguelmane lake

Aïn spring

Aït tribe (literally, "sons of")

Alaouite ruling Moroccan dynasty from the seventeenth century to the present king, Mohammed VI

Almohad the greatest of the medieval dynasties, ruled Morocco (and much of Spain) from c.1147 until the rise to power of the Merenids c.1224

Almoravids dynasty that preceded the Almohads, from c.1060 to c.1147

Amazigh Berber

Andalous Muslim Spain (a territory that centred on modern Andalucía)

Arabesque geometrical decoration or calligraphy

Assif river (often seasonal) in Berber

Bab gate or door

Babouches slippers

Baladiya town hall or local council

Bali old

Baraka sanctity or blessing, obtained through saints or *marabouts*

Barbary European term for North Africa in the sixteenth to nineteenth centuries

Beni tribe (literally, "sons of")

Berbers original inhabitants of Morocco and their descendants, particularly those whose first language is Berber (though most Moroccans claim to be at least partly Berber)

Bildi country-style (of the bled)

Bled countryside, or, literally "land"; **Bled es Makhzen** – governed lands; **Bled es Siba** – land outside government control

Borj fort

Caid district administrator; **Cadi** is an Islamic judge

Chleuh Tashelhaït-speaking Atlas and Souss Valley Berbers

Col mountain pass (French)

Dar house or palace; **Dar el Makhzen**, royal palace

Darj W Ktaf literally "cheek and shoulder", an Almohad architectural motif resembling a fleur-de-lis (see the *Architecture* colour section)

Daya, **Deyet** lake

Djebel mountain peak or ridge; a **Djebali** is someone from the mountains; the **Djebala** are the main tribe of the Western Rif

Djedid new

Djellaba wool or cotton hooded outer garment

Djemaa, **Jamaa** mosque, or Friday (the main day of worship)

Djinn nature spirits (genies)

Erg sand dune

Fakir Koranic schoolteacher or lawyer, or just an educated man

Fantasia display of horsemanship performed at larger festivals or moussems

Fassi inhabitant of Fes

Filali alternative name for the Alaouite dynasty – from the southern Tafilalt region

Firdaous Paradise

Fondouk inn and storehouse, known as a caravanserai in the eastern part of the Arab world

Gandoura man's cotton garment (male equivalent of a kaftan); also known as a *fokia*

Gharb coastal plain between Larache and Kenitra

Gnaoua itinerant musician belonging to a brotherhood of West African origin (the name is from the same root as "Guinea")

Habbous religious foundation or bequest of property for religious charities

Hadj pilgrimage to Mecca

Hammada stony desert of the sub-Sahara

Hammam Turkish-style steam bath

Harka "burning" raid undertaken by sultans in order to raise taxes and assert authority

Idrissid first Arab dynasty of Morocco – named after its founder, Moulay Idriss

Imam prayer leader and elder of mosque

Istiqlal nationalist party founded during the struggle for independence

Jedid, Jdid, Djedid new

Jebel, Jbel, Djebel mountain

Joutia flea market

Kasbah palace centre and/or fortress of an Arab town; also used to mean a walled residential quarter around the Medina (eg Fes), or the citadel (eg Tangier and in Tunisia), or the whole Medina (eg Algiers). In the south of Morocco, it is a feudal family castle – and it's the root of the Spanish *alcazar*

Khettara underground irrigation canal

Kedim old

Kif marijuana, cannabis

Koubba dome; small *marabout* tomb

Ksar, Ksour (pl.) village or tribal stronghold in the south

Lalla "madam", also a saint

Litham veil

Maghreb "West" in Arabic, used for Morocco and the North African countries

Maison D'hôte guesthouse, usually upmarket

Makhzen government

Marabout holy man, and by extension his place of burial. These tombs, usually whitewashed domes, play an important (and heterodox) role in the religion of country areas

Mechouar assembly place, court of judgment

Medersa student residence and, in part, a teaching annexe, for the old mosque universities

Medina literally, "city", now used for the original Arab part of any Moroccan town

Mellah Jewish quarter

Merenids dynasty from eastern plains who ruled from the thirteenth to fifteenth century

Mihrab niche indicating the direction of Mecca (and for prayer)

Minaret tower attached to a mosque, used for call to prayer

Minbar the pulpit, usually placed next to the mihrab, from which the imam delivers his sermon at the midday Friday service in the mosque

Minzah pavilion in a (usually palace) garden

Moulay descendant of the Prophet Mohammed, a claim and title adopted by most Moroccan sultans

Mouloud festival and birthday of the Prophet

Moussem pilgrimage festival

Msalla prayer area

Muezzin, Mueddin singer who calls the faithful to prayer

Nazarene, Nsrani Christian, or, more loosely, a European

Oued (wadi in its anglicized form) river, but particularly a seasonal river or creek

Pisé mud and rubble building material

Piste unsurfaced road or track

Protectorate period of French and Spanish colonial occupation (1912– 56)

Qahwa coffee or café

Qahouaji café *patron*

Ramadan month of fasting (see p.50)

Ras source or head

Ras el Ma water source

Riad patio garden, and by extension a house built around a patio garden; now also used to signify an upmarket guesthouse

Ribat monastic fortress

Romi urban, sophisticated – the opposite of *bildi* (see opposite)

Saadian southern dynasty from Drâa Valley, who ruled Morocco during the fifteenth century

Sebgha lake or lagoon

Sebsi pipe for smoking *kif*

Seguia irrigation canal

Sheikh leader of religious brotherhood

Shereef descendant of the Prophet

Sidi, **Si** respectful title used for any man, like "Sir" or "Mister", also a saint

Souk market, or market quarter

Sufi religious mystic; philosophy behind most of the religious brotherhoods

Tabia mud building material, as *pisé*

Tighremt similar to an agadir – fortified Berber home and storage place

Touareg nomadic Berber tribesmen of the disputed Western Sahara, fancifully known as "Blue Men" because of the blue dye of their cloaks (which gives a slight tinge to their skin)

Tizi mountain pass

UMA (Union du Maghreb Arabe) regional association whose members are Morocco, Algeria, Tunisia, Libya and Mauritania

Wattasid fifteenth-century dynasty who replaced their cousins, the Merenids

Zaouia sanctuary established around a *marabout* tomb; seminary-type base for religious brotherhood

Zellij geometrical mosaic tilework

Small print and

Index

A Rough Guide to Rough Guides

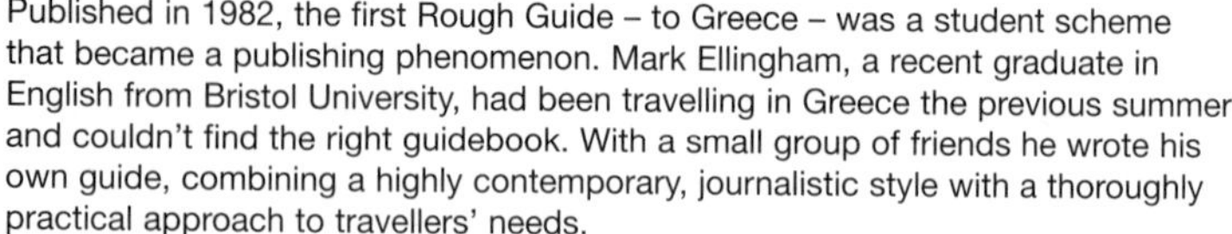

Published in 1982, the first Rough Guide – to Greece – was a student scheme that became a publishing phenomenon. Mark Ellingham, a recent graduate in English from Bristol University, had been travelling in Greece the previous summer and couldn't find the right guidebook. With a small group of friends he wrote his own guide, combining a highly contemporary, journalistic style with a thoroughly practical approach to travellers' needs.

The immediate success of the book spawned a series that rapidly covered dozens of destinations. And, in addition to impecunious backpackers, Rough Guides soon acquired a much broader and older readership that relished the guides' wit and inquisitiveness as much as their enthusiastic, critical approach and value-for-money ethos.

These days, Rough Guides include recommendations from shoestring to luxury and cover more than 200 destinations around the globe, including almost every country in the Americas and Europe, more than half of Africa and most of Asia and Australasia. Our ever-growing team of authors and photographers is spread all over the world, particularly in Europe, the US and Australia.

In the early 1990s, Rough Guides branched out of travel, with the publication of Rough Guides to World Music, Classical Music and the Internet. All three have become benchmark titles in their fields, spearheading the publication of a wide range of books under the Rough Guide name.

Including the travel series, Rough Guides now number more than 350 titles, covering: phrasebooks, waterproof maps, music guides from Opera to Heavy Metal, reference works as diverse as Conspiracy Theories and Shakespeare, and popular culture books from iPods to Poker. Rough Guides also produce a series of more than 120 World Music CDs in partnership with World Music Network.

Visit www.roughguides.com to see our latest publications.

Rough Guide travel images are available for commercial licensing at www.roughguidespictures.com

Rough Guide credits

Text editor: Róisín Cameron, Keith Drew & Emma Gibbs
Layout: Anita Singh
Cartography: Richard Marchi
Picture editor: Sarah Cummins
Production: Rebecca Short
Proofreader: Helen Castell
Cover design: Chloë Roberts, Dan May
Photographer: Suzanne Porter
Editorial: Lara Kavanagh, Andy Turner, Edward Aves, Alice Park, Lucy White, Jo Kirby, James Smart, Natasha Foges, James Rice, Emma Traynor, Kathryn Lane, Monica Woods, Mani Ramaswamy, Harry Wilson, Lucy Cowie, Alison Roberts, Joe Staines, Peter Buckley, Matthew Milton, Tracy Hopkins, Ruth Tidball; **Delhi** Madhavi Singh, Karen D'Souza, Lubna Shaheen
Design & Pictures: **London** Scott Stickland, Dan May, Diana Jarvis, Mark Thomas, Nicole Newman, Emily Taylor; **Delhi** Umesh Aggarwal, Ajay Verma, Jessica Subramanian, Ankur Guha, Pradeep Thapliyal, Sachin Tanwar, Nikhil Agarwal, Sachin Gupta
Production: Liz Cherry
Cartography: **London** Katie Lloyd-Jones, Ed Wright; **Delhi** Rajesh Chhibber, Ashutosh Bharti, Rajesh Mishra, Animesh Pathak, Jasbir Sandhu, Karobi Gogoi, Alakananda Bhattacharya, Swati Handoo, Deshpal Dabas
Online: **London** Faye Hellon, Jeanette Angell, Fergus Day, Justine Bright, Clare Bryson, Aine Fearon, Adrian Low, Ezgi Celebi; **Delhi** Amit Verma, Rahul Kumar, Narender Kumar, Ravi Yadav, Debojit Borah, Rakesh Kumar, Ganesh Sharma, Shisir Basumatari
Marketing & Publicity: **London** Liz Statham, Louise Maher, Jess Carter, Vanessa Godden, Vivienne Watton, Anna Paynton, Rachel Sprackett, Laura Vipond; **New York** Katy Ball, Judi Powers; **Delhi** Ragini Govind
Reference Director: Andrew Lockett
Operations Assistant: Becky Doyle
Operations Manager: Helen Atkinson
Publishing Director (Travel): Clare Currie
Commercial Manager: Gino Magnotta
Managing Director: John Duhigg

Publishing information

This ninth edition published April 2010 by
Rough Guides Ltd,
80 Strand, London WC2R 0RL
14 Local Shopping Centre, Panchsheel Park, New Delhi 110017, India
Distributed by the Penguin Group
Penguin Books Ltd,
80 Strand, London WC2R 0RL
Penguin Group (USA)
375 Hudson Street, NY 10014, USA
Penguin Group (Australia)
250 Camberwell Road, Camberwell, Victoria 3124, Australia
Penguin Group (Canada)
195 Harry Walker Parkway N, Newmarket, ON, L3Y 7B3 Canada
Penguin Group (NZ)
67 Apollo Drive, Mairangi Bay, Auckland 1310, New Zealand
Cover concept by Peter Dyer.
Typeset in Bembo and Helvetica to an original design by Henry Iles.
Printed in Singapore

648pp includes index
A catalogue record for this book is available from the British Library
ISBN: 978-1-84836-477-6

5 7 9 8 6 4

Help us update

We've gone to a lot of effort to ensure that the ninth edition of **The Rough Guide to Morocco** is accurate and up-to-date. However, things change – places get "discovered", opening hours are notoriously fickle, restaurants and rooms raise prices or lower standards. If you feel we've got it wrong or left something out, we'd like to know, and if you can remember the address, the price, the hours, the phone number, so much the better.

Please send your comments with the subject line "**Rough Guide Morocco Update**" to ⓔmail@roughguides.com. We'll credit all contributions and send a copy of the next edition (or any other Rough Guide if you prefer) for the very best emails.

Have your questions answered and tell others about your trip at ⓦwww.roughguides.com

Acknowledgements

Daniel Jacobs would like to thank: Abdellah Akiyat (Délégation de Tourisme, Agadir); Karen Jones (SPANA); Houssine Laroussi; Alison Macdonald (*Tea House*, Essaouira); James McConnachie; Hmad Ouardarass (Tafraout Adventure); Mohammed Ouhammou Sahnoun; Mohammed at the *Hôtel Tioute*, Taroudant; and Mohammed, Hassan and Fatima at the *Hôtel Aday* in Marrakesh.

Kate Hawkings would like to thank: Nancy and Daoud in M'Hamid for insight and music; Allal the Mad Nomad for introductions and gossip; Farid at *Hôtel Tombuctou* in Tinerhir for hospitality and guidance, the brothers at *Les Amis* in Tamtatoucht for lunch and jokes, Youness at Gouffre du Friouato for steadying my nerves, King Mohammed's policemen for unfailing courtesy, Mohammed at Oujda airport for putting me up, Deirdre and Phil Hardwick for bailing me out and John Stokes for having me in stitches.

Daniel Lund would like to thank: Abdelghani Znati, Aziz Elkhaldi, Felicity Meerloo and Christina Lund.

Readers' letters

Thanks to all the readers who have taken the time to write in with comments and suggestions (and apologies if we've inadvertently omitted or misspelt anyone's name):

John Adams, Juliette Amielle, John Averill, Rose Balfour, Joe Bevan, Susan Bienen Johnson, Rachel Blech, Rozalinda Buyong, Jim and Margie Campbell, Sophia Cheema, Sung Chik, Serena Chong, Alan Curragh, Suzi Davies-Lane, Peter de Groot, Louise Derham, D. Dixon, Lisa Dobinson, Dietmar Dzieyk, Gareth Edwards, Angelos Evangelidis, Felix Flicker, Helen Fry, Peter Golding, Grace Ho, Matt Hopkinson, Greg Horner, John Houde, Jeff and Lola, Ruth John, Eddie Joseph, Hollie Kearns, Anna King, Martin Kraus, Eddy le Couvreur, Jayne Lee, Valérie Lehouck and Toon Spanhove, Rodney Lord, Amy MacNaughton, Chris Martin, Eamon McCafferty, A. Murray Wells, Clara Night, Pierre Pampide, Fabio Pesaresi, Jan Piebe, Guy Poirier, Norman Provor, Tariq Rafiq, Mrs H. Rees, Archie Sample, Judy Scheible, Julia Schulz, Mike Scott, Carola Scupham, Mary and John Sergeant, Joy Skipper, Robert Smith, Mike Souter, Richard Spencer, Jane Stark, Graham Symonds, Valerie Thoen and Marc Droessaert, Jim Tomb, Tine Twittmann, Suzanne Valade, Ankie van Oosten, Nienke Verkuyl, Sheena Wellesley, James Wilson, Andreas Zieger.

Photo credits

All photos © Rough Guides except the following:

Introduction

Camels on the beach, Morocco © Neil Emmerson/Robert Harding

Boy in doorway, Chefchaouen © Peter Rayner/Axiom

Beach, Tangier © Alvaro Leiva/Photolibrary

Things not to miss

02 Flamingos in the Laayoune area © Bruno Morandi/Photolibrary

05 Tizi n'Tichka Pass, High Atlas © Chris Caldicott/Axiom

06 Essaouria © Lars Thuli/Photolibrary

12 Chefchaouen © Ethel Davies/Robert Harding

16 Tangier Medina © J D Dallet/Photolibrary

17 Skiing at Oukaimeden ski resort © Christian Kober/Photolibrary

19 Imilchil Wedding Festival © Du Boisberranger Jean/Photolibrary

20 Tin Mal Mosque © John & Lisa Merrill/Getty

21 Trekkers, Siroua Massif © David C Poole/Robert Harding

23 Riad Al Moussika, Marrakech © Mark Thomas/Axiom

24 Asilah © Bruno Morandi/Photolibrary

25 Ruins of Glaoui Kasbah at Telouet © Lee Frost/Robert Harding

27 Ouzoud waterfall © Bruno Morandi/Robert Harding

28 Barbary ape © Eye Ubiquitous/Robert Harding

Moroccan architecture colour section

Courtyard in Riad Al Moussika, Marrakesh © Mark Thomas/Axiom

Carved cedarwood, Ben Youssef Medersa © Dan Jacobs

Painted ceiling, Bahi Palace © Dan Jacobs

Bab Makina, Fortress © PCL/Alamy

Crafts and souvenirs colour section

Shopping in the Medina, Marrakesh © Timothy Allen/Axiom

Black and whites

p.80 Chefchaouen © Miguel Carminati/Photolibrary

p.101 Tangier Kasbah © Jacques Bravo/Photolibrary

p.110 Gallery in Asilah © Nicolas Thibaut/Photolibrary

p.126 Tetouan © Xavier Richer/Photolibrary

p.140 Empty road in the Rif Mountains © Bjanka Kadic/Alamy

p.150 Al Hoceima © Alvaro Leiva/Photolibrary

p.158 Melilla © Herv Gyssels/Photolibrary

p.254 Atlas street scene © Roland T Frank/Photolibrary

p.384 Oukaimeden ski resort © Hughes Herv/Photolibrary

p.399 Toubkal region © Bernard Van Dierendonck/Photolibrary

p.540 Tarfaya © Frederic Soreau/Photolibrary

p.549 Artisans Centre, Laayoune © Worldwide picture library/Alamy

Index

Map entries are in colour.

A

B

C

G

H

I

J

K

L

M

N

O

P

R

S

T

U

V

W

X

Y

Z

Map symbols

maps are listed in the full index using coloured text

International boundary
Chapter divisions boundary
Motorway
Main road
Minor road
Pedestrianized road
Piste (unpaved road)
Steps
Footpath
Trek
4-wheel drive
Railway
River
Ferry route
Wall
Dune
Rocks
Mountain range
Peak
Gorge
Refuge hut
Mountain pass
Cave
Waterfall
Oasis
Bridge
Fort/fortress
Lighthouse
Tower
Ruins
Ksar
Battle site

Picturesque village
Tomb
Point of interest
Viewpoint
Church (regional maps)
Synagogue
Mosque
Campsite
Gardens/fountain
Swimming pool
Restaurant
Accommodation
Arch
Gate
Airport
Bus/taxi stop
Parking
Hospital
Tourist office
Post office
Internet access
Building
Church (town maps)
Mosque
Market
Stadium
Park
Christian cemetery
Jewish cemetery
Muslim cemetery
Beach
Saltpan